Neuropsychology of Malingering Casebook

American Academy of Clinical Neuropsychology/Psychology Press Continuing Education Series

Series Editors: Joel E. Morgan and Jerry J. Sweet

AACN/Psychology Press Continuing Education Series publishes authored and edited volumes containing a blend of cutting-edge primary research and practical/professional material for clinicians, researchers, and students of clinical neuropsychology and clinical psychology.

Each volume is written or edited by leading scholars in the field and is specifically designed to assist readers in advancing their relevant research or professional activities in clinical neuropsychology. Volumes in this series have been selected by the series editors because they provide one or more of the following: overview of a core or emerging area of concern to clinical neuropsychologists; in-depth examination of a specific area of research or practice in clinical neuropsychology; update of a neglected or controversial clinical application; information pertaining to relevance of a new inter-disciplinary discovery/technique to neuropsychological function; or current ethical matters and other professional considerations in the application of new knowledge or methods to the understanding of neuropsychological functions.

AACN Online System

Any licensed psychologist who reads one of the books in the AACN/Psychology Press series will be able to earn CE credits by reading designated books and completing an online quiz.

To Receive Online Credit

- Read one of the CE-designated books in its entirety
- Access the CE quiz online at the AACN website (**www.theaacn.org**)
- Register for the specific book for which you wish to receive CE credit, and
- Complete all questions on the quiz.

The estimated time to read the book and complete the related quiz is determined by the length of each book, which also determines the number of possible credits.

The cost of CE credits is noted on the AACN website, and is reduced for AACN members and affiliates. Credit will be awarded to individuals scoring 80% or higher on the quiz. Participants will receive an immediate confirmation of credits earned by email.

CE Accreditation Statement

AACN is approved by the American Psychological Association to sponsor continuing education for psychologists. AACN maintains responsibility for this program and its content.

For more information on new and forthcoming titles in the Series and for instructions on how to take the accompanying online CE tests, please visit **www.theaacn.org** or **www.psypress.com/AACN**

Neuropsychology of Malingering Casebook

Edited by
Joel E. Morgan & Jerry J. Sweet

American Academy of
Clinical Neuropsychology

Psychology Press
Taylor & Francis Group
NEW YORK AND HOVE

Published in 2009
by Psychology Press
270 Madison Avenue
New York, NY 10016
www.psypress.com

Published in Great Britain
by Psychology Press
27 Church Road
Hove, East Sussex BN3 2FA

Psychology Press is an imprint of the Taylor & Francis Group, an Informa business

Typeset by RefineCatch Limited, Bungay, Suffolk, UK
Printed and bound by Sheridan Books, Inc. in the USA on acid-free paper

10 9 8 7 6 5 4 3 2 1

Library of Congress Cataloging in Publication Data
A catalog record for this book is available from the Library of Congress.

ISBN: 978–1–84169–478–8 (hbk)

We dedicate this casebook to our loving and supportive families and especially to our deceased and living parents, whose positive influences have continued.

Contents

About the editors

Joel E. Morgan has been active in professional neuropsychology for over 20 years as teacher, clinician, and journal editor. He is board certified by the American Board of Clinical Neuropsychology of ABPP and currently serves as an oral examiner. Dr. Morgan is active in professional affairs having served on the BOD of the American Academy of Clinical Neuropsychology and Division 40 of APA where he is currently a representative to APA Council. He maintains an active private practice in addition to his editorial, board, and other professional activities.

Jerry J. Sweet is Director of the Neuropsychology Service, Head of the Psychology Division, and Vice Chair of the Psychiatry & Behavioral Sciences Department at Evanston Northwestern Healthcare, Evanston, IL. He is Professor in the Department of Psychiatry and Behavioral Sciences of the Feinberg School of Medicine of Northwestern University, and is board certified in clinical neuropsychology and clinical psychology by the American Board of Professional Psychology. He edited the textbook *Forensic Neuropsychology: Fundamentals and Practice*, co-authored *Psychological Assessment in Medical Settings* and co-edited *Handbook of Clinical Psychology in Medical Settings*, and he is Co-Editor of *The Clinical Neuropsychologist.* Dr. Sweet is Past President of the American Academy of Clinical Neuropsychology.

List of contributors

Lidia Artiola i Fortuny, Ph.D., ABPP-CN, Independent Practice, Tucson, AZ, USA

Bradley N. Axelrod, Ph.D., John D. Dingell Department of Veterans Affairs Medical Center, Detroit, MI, and Independent Practice, Ann Arbor, MI, USA

W. John Baker, Ph.D., ABPN, Psychological Systems, Inc., Royal Oak, MI, USA

Heather G. Belanger, Ph.D., ABPP-CN, James A. Haley Veterans Hospital; University of South Florida Department of Psychology; and Defense and Veterans Brain Injury Center, Tampa, FL, USA

Scott D. Bender, Ph.D., University of Virginia Department of Psychiatric Medicine, Neurocognitive Assessment Laboratory, Charlottesville, VA, USA

Maria A. Bergman, Ph.D., Evanston Northwestern Healthcare, Evanston, IL, USA

David T. R. Berry, Ph.D., Department of Psychology, University of Kentucky, Lexington, KY, USA

Kevin J. Bianchini, Ph.D., ABPN, Department of Psychology, University of New Orleans, New Orleans, LA and Jefferson Neurobehavioral Group, Metairie, LA, USA

Laurence M. Binder, Ph.D., ABPP-CN, Beaverton, OR, USA

Kyle Boone, Ph.D., ABPP-CN, Harbor-UCLA Medical Center and Los Angeles Biomedical Institute, Los Angeles, CA, USA

David S. Bush, Ph.D., ABPP-CN, ABPN, Independent Practice, Palm Beach Gardens, FL, USA

Shane S. Bush, Ph.D., ABPP, ABPN, Long Island Neuropsychology, P.C., Lake Ronkonkoma, NY, USA

Donald J. Connor, Ph.D., Ph.D., Cleo Roberts Center for Clinical Research, Sun Health Research Institute, Sun City, AZ, USA

Henry G. Conroe, M.D., Social Security Medical Disability Regional Medical Advisor, Chicago, IL, USA

Mark D. DeBofsky, JD, Daley, DeBofsky & Bryant, Chicago, IL, USA

John DeLuca, Ph.D., ABPP-RP, University of Medicine and Dentistry of New Jersey—New Jersey Medical School, Newark; and Kessler Medical Rehabilitation Research and Education Corporation, West Orange, NJ, USA

Robert L. Denney, Psy.D., ABPP-CN, FP, ABPN, U.S. Medical Center for Federal Prisoners; and The School of Professional Psychology at Forest Institute, Springfield, MO, USA

Lloyd Flaro, Ed.D., Private Practice, Edmonton, Alberta, Canada

Richard I. Frederick, Ph.D., ABPP-FP, U.S. Medical Center for Federal Prisoners, Springfield, MO, USA

Mary Fuller, M.Ed., Disability Claim Consulting Services, Portland, ME, USA

Roger O. Gervais, Ph.D., Independent Practice, Edmonton, Alberta, Canada

Robert P. Granacher, Jr., M.D., M.B.A., University of Kentucky College of Medicine; Lexington Forensic Neuropsychiatry, Lexington, KY, USA

Jeff Green, Ph.D., Disability Management Services, Springfield, MA, USA

Paul Green, Ph.D., Private Practice, Edmonton, Alberta, Canada

Manfred F. Greiffenstein, Ph.D., ABPP-CN, Psychological Systems, Inc., Royal Oak, MI, USA

Kevin W. Greve, Ph.D., ABPP-CN, Department of Psychology, University of New Orleans, New Orleans, LA and Jefferson Neurobehavioral Group, Metairie, LA, USA

Jason Hassenstab, M.A., Department of Psychology, Fordham University, New York, NY, USA

Robert L. Heilbronner, Ph.D., ABPP-CN, Chicago Neuropsychology Group, IL, USA

Grant L. Iverson, Ph.D., Department of Psychiatry, University of British Columbia, Vancouver, BC, Canada

Joseph Krakora, J.D., Office of the Public Defender, State of New Jersey, Trenton, NJ, USA

Glenn J. Larrabee, Ph.D., ABPP-CN, Independent Practice, Sarasota, FL, USA

Paul R. Lees-Haley, Ph.D., ABPP-FP, Independent Practice, Huntsville, AL, USA

Julie K. Lynch, Ph.D., Albany Neuropsychological Associates, Albany, NY, USA

Quintino R. Mano, M.S., Department of Psychology, University of Wisconsin-Milwaukee, WI, USA

Robert L. Mapou, Ph.D., ABPP-CN, Independent Practice, Silver Spring, MD, USA

Robert J. McCaffrey, Ph.D., ABPN, University at Albany, State University of New York and Albany Neuropsychological Associates, Albany, NY, USA

Jacqueline Mesnik, M.A., New York University School of Medicine, New York, NY, USA

Scott R. Millis, Ph.D., ABPP (CN, CL, RP), CStat, Department of Physical Medicine and Rehabilitation, Wayne State University School of Medicine, Detroit, MI, USA

Wiley Mittenberg, Ph.D., ABPP-CN, Nova Southeastern University, Ft. Lauderdale, FL, USA

Darci Morgan, Ph.D., University of Oklahoma Health Science Center, Oklahoma City, OK, USA

Joel E. Morgan, Ph.D., ABPP-CN, Independent Practice, Madison, NJ, USA

Nathaniel W. Nelson, Ph.D., ABPP-CN, Department of Psychology, Minneapolis VA Medical Center; Department of Psychiatry, University of Minnesota, Minneapolis, MN, USA

David C. Osmon, Ph.D., ABPP-CN, Department of Psychology, University of Wisconsin-Milwaukee, WI, USA

Chris Paniak, Ph.D., Glenrose Rehabilitation Hospital, University of Alberta, and Independent Practice, Edmonton, Alberta, Canada

Neil Pliskin, Ph.D., ABPP-CN, University of Illinois College of Medicine, Chicago, IL, USA

Richard Rogers, Ph.D., ABPP, University of North Texas, Denton, TX, USA

John E. Sargent, M.S., CRC, Independent Practice, 500 Market Street, 1G, Portsmouth, NH, USA

James D. Seward, Ph.D., ABPP-CN, Independent Practice, Phoenix, AZ, USA

Elisabeth M. S. Sherman, Ph.D., Neurosciences Program, Alberta Children's Hospital; and Paediatrics and Clinical Neurosciences, Faculty of Medicine, University of Calgary, Calgary, AB, Canada

Daniel J. Slick, Ph.D., R. Psych, Neurosciences Program, Alberta Children's Hospital; and Paediatrics and Clinical Neurosciences, Faculty of Medicine, University of Calgary, Calgary, AB, Canada

Jerry J. Sweet, Ph.D., ABPP-CN, CL, Evanston Northwestern Healthcare, Evanston, IL and Feinberg School of Medicine, Northwestern University, Chicago, IL, USA

J. Sherrod Taylor, J.D., Institute on Social Exclusion, Adler School of Professional Psychology, Chicago, IL, USA

Wilfred G. van Gorp, Ph.D., ABPP-CN, Department of Psychiatry, Columbia University College of Physicians & Surgeons, New York, NY, USA

Rodney D. Vanderploeg, Ph.D., ABPP-CN, James A. Haley Veterans Hospital; University of South Florida Department of Psychiatry and Behavioral Medicine, and Department of Psychology; and Defense and Veterans Brain Injury Center, Tampa, FL, USA

James Youngjohn, Ph.D., ABPP-CN, Independent Practice, Scottsdale, AZ, USA

Foreword

Robert K. Heaton

The science of neuropsychology constantly transforms its clinical practice, by increasing the clinician's available knowledge, as well as the complexity of his/her decision making. Compared with just a few decades ago, the clinical neuropsychologist today has access to much more information about the biological bases and behavioral manifestations of most neuropsychiatric disorders. We also have many more tests, better normative standards, and more solid scientific bases for interpreting test results to answer clinical questions. In addition, our science has challenged us by identifying important limitations in our clinical activities.

One of the most vexing and yet fascinating challenges to the validity of clinical neuropsychological assessments is the topic of the current volume: the problem of insufficient effort and response bias on testing. Beginning in the late 1970s, research demonstrated the embarrassing truth that clinicians were not good at distinguishing between poor test performances caused by brain dysfunction versus inadequate effort or even frank malingering. Subsequent studies provided evidence that insufficient effort is quite commonly encountered in certain forensic populations. This is particularly true in patients undergoing litigation-related and disability determinations, which constitute a sizeable proportion of many clinical neuropsychological practices. After the problem of insufficient effort was identified, a very large and rapidly growing body of research has provided methods for detection and classification of such cases (see the more than 1000 citations in the Appendices of this volume!).

Clearly, this huge body of research represents considerable progress in the development and validation of new methods for detecting insufficient effort and response bias. As a result, standards of neuropsychological practice have evolved to the point where multiple approaches to determining insufficient effort should be included in neuropsychological assessments, especially when there is a known, external incentive for the patient to perform poorly on the testing.

Having all this new information and being armed with an explosion of new methods to identify insufficient effort is good, but such advances also place considerable new demands on clinician decision making. For example, how many detection methods should be used, and which ones are most appropriate for the case at hand? Which normative standards or cut-points should be used on measures that are specifically designed for effort assessment, and what do they mean? Given the claimant's history and differential diagnoses, which patterns of test results should be considered suspicious (or worse than expected) on a single exam or across multiple exams? How should inconsistent evidence on effort indicators be interpreted? What level of evidence should be required to classify an examinee as a malingerer? How does one establish conscious intent to fabricate abnormal results (part of the "malingerer" definition), and how does one evaluate possible motivations based upon external incentives versus psychological factors (to adopt the sick role)? What are the ethical issues involved in using, or not using, the "malingerer" label?

These are not easy questions. They require considerable clinical judgment in addition to familiarity with a rapidly expanding body of literature. Also, it clearly helps to have experience with this decision-making process in actual cases of suspected insufficient effort and response bias. The

Neuropsychology of Malingering Casebook is an invaluable reference work and teaching tool for all of these purposes.

The experts who have contributed to this volume are responsible for much of the existing research in this complex area, and share with the reader a wealth of clinical experience about seemingly every type of clinical condition and testing situation in which one is likely to encounter problems with response validity. In the *Casebook*'s forty-five chapters the reader will find careful reviews of: (1) the most up-to-date assessment methods and proposed methods for classifying different types of questionable effort and response bias; (2) the relevant literature concerning clinical conditions frequently associated with concerns about effort (e.g., persisting cognitive complaints associated with whiplash or mild traumatic brain injury, mold toxicity, fibromyalgia, or chronic fatigue syndrome); and (3) legal and ethical issues involved in neuropsychological assessments that occur within the context of civil litigation, adjudication of disability claims, and criminal prosecution and defense. The authors then use their case material to illustrate different ways in which problems with effort and response bias may be manifested, and share their analyses and conclusions about the relevant history, medical findings, test data, and patient reports.

Importantly, the *Casebook* authors are not always in "lock step" with their approaches to classifying or labeling problematic effort on neuropsychological testing. For example, the reader will note differences in the experts' willingness to attach the "malingering" label, and in their views regarding the adequacy of simply concluding that the test results are invalid due to the examinee's inability or unwillingness to put forth adequate effort. On the other hand, all of the presentations are thoughtful and well reasoned. Thus, when (typically subtle) differences of opinion are encountered, this adds to the rich texture of the book as a whole and encourages the reader to think more deeply about the merits of the different approaches.

Ultimately, of course, each clinician must choose his or her own approaches to the problem of response validity and the complex diagnosis of malingering. The *Casebook* will enhance that process for experienced and novice clinicians alike: It is an outstanding reference work and a good read.

Robert K. Heaton, Ph.D., ABPP-CN

Preface

The genesis of this textbook was hundreds of conversations between the editors and numerous neuropsychology colleagues whose experience and wise perspective in forensic matters we value. These dialogues often included interesting case material pertaining to the topic of malingering, the likes of which had not been described in the relevant professional literature. We knew that practicing clinical neuropsychologists commonly face evaluating individuals within a forensic context and therefore must address the inevitable questions regarding the possible presence of malingering. With seemingly abundant instructive case experiences from our expert forensic colleagues, we reasoned that if clinical neuropsychologists had access to a comprehensive collection of malingering examples it would facilitate informed and well-considered opinions on this inescapable topic.

The authors of the contributed chapters contained in this textbook are presenting vivid depictions of actual case experiences, which, of necessity, have been altered in parts that could have otherwise revealed the identities of the litigants, claimants, attorneys, or judges involved. Moreover, some of the cases described are actually an amalgam of more than one malingerer, fashioned into a prototypical or exemplary case, which is intended to depict multiple dimensions and characteristics of malingering presentations, and in so doing provide the reader with a richer educational experience. The editors also intended to present cases in which overlapping diagnoses or more challenging scenarios were present as well as the authors' analysis of their cases as they arrived at their diagnostic conclusions.

To date, there has been no comparably sized collection of malingering cases relevant to clinical neuropsychology published.

Acknowledgments

We greatly appreciate the trust of the many colleagues who have shared their experiences and wisdom with us. We want to thank our Psychology Press publisher, Paul Dukes, for his generous support and encouragement in the long journey of this textbook. We also want to thank the initial publisher representative, Martin Scrivener, of Swets & Zeitlinger, who supported the preliminary ideas for this text.

Clearly, the ability of any editor to gather together a sizeable collection of cases relevant to malingering and clinical neuropsychology stems entirely from many years of scientific research by literally hundreds of neuropsychologists and neuropsychologists in training. It is this now very sizeable, some would say enormous, body of research that enabled the development and application in practice of procedures and techniques that ultimately allows probabilistic statements to be made regarding the likelihood of an individual having demonstrated neuropsychological malingering. The names of these researchers are too numerous to list, but are in fact well represented in the lengthy Appendices placed at the back of this volume as a resource to readers. This list originated with the second editor during the development of a prior text *Forensic Neuropsychology: Fundamentals and Practice*, and represents an ongoing attempt to maintain a comprehensive collection of literature citations relevant to forensic neuropsychology. In addition to those individuals whose names appear at the beginning of the Appendices, we especially thank Daniel Condit for his extensive assistance in finalizing the Appendices and Jacqueline Mesnik for her editorial assistance.

Finally, and most importantly, we thank the numerous contributors to this volume, all of whom took valuable time from their very busy professional lives to share their perspective on unique and interesting case material for this complex forensic topic.

SECTION I

FOUNDATIONS OF MALINGERING IN NEUROPSYCHOLOGY

All clinical neuropsychologists and clinical psychologists who gather formal test data during the course of an assessment are reliant on those data being valid. Otherwise, accurate conclusions founded on test interpretation are precluded. A secondary gain context (i.e., a context in which abnormal test performances can benefit the examinee in some tangible manner, rather than improved health, which is the goal of clinical evaluations) is known to promote invalid and inaccurate performance on formal psychological and neuropsychological tests. Consequently, there may be no more important matter to address when evaluating a claimant or litigant (i.e., a civil *plaintiff* or a criminal *defendant*) than the issue of malingering, and the broader issues of response bias versus response validity and sufficient effort versus insufficient effort. Understanding the complexity of the context within which questions of malingering arise is an important first step which can lead to a more ready grasp of the reasons why questions regarding response validity and malingering are so frequently asked of forensic experts. The three chapters within this section provide fundamental information regarding the context of the evaluation, the common occurrence of invalid responding in a forensic context, and the statistical issues that underlie decision making, all of which will allow a greater appreciation of the numerous case examples that follow in subsequent sections of the book.

Neuropsychology and the law: Malingering assessment in perspective

1

Jerry J. Sweet

Forensic neuropsychology, the application of clinical neuropsychological knowledge to forensic activities (i.e., litigation, administrative proceedings, consultations to attorneys and courts, disability determination), is neither a new nor an unfamiliar practice area for most clinical neuropsychologists. In fact, a number of professional practice surveys have demonstrated that involvement in forensic activities is relatively commonplace and that attorneys are a relatively frequent source of referrals for practicing neuropsychologists (e.g., Sweet, Moberg, & Suchy, 2000; Sweet, Nelson, & Moberg, 2006). Moreover, the relevant scientific peer-reviewed literature pertaining to forensic neuropsychology has grown dramatically since 1990. The strong evidence of this fact was documented by Sweet, King, Malina, Bergman, and Simmons (2002), who catalogued the entire peer-reviewed contents of the three most popular clinical neuropsychology journals from 1990 through 2000. During this period of time, articles pertaining to forensic practice increased from 4% in 1990 to 14% in 2000. The total number of published articles that addressed forensic practice during this interval was 139. Most relevant to the present casebook, 120 (86%) of these articles were in part or in whole focused on the topic of malingering. Sweet et al. in the same study also examined the content of conference presentations in published abstracts from national meetings that were contained in the same three clinical neuropsychology journals from 1990 through 2000. Forensic presentations at national meetings accounted for 1% of the program content in 1990 and 10% in 2000. As was the case with the forensic articles, the majority of forensic presentations at conferences addressed malingering. Specifically, of 337 forensic presentations, 242 (72%) addressed malingering.

It seems clear then that the topic of malingering during forensic neuropsychological assessments is of keen interest within the specialty of clinical neuropsychology. Where did this growing interest come from, and why has so much of the interest in forensic practice focused on malingering? The answers to these questions provide an important background for the appreciation of the contents of this book. Though these answers could fill an entire volume, we will be brief.

REASONS FOR THE GROWTH OF FORENSIC NEUROPSYCHOLOGY

To be certain, there are inherent differences between the fields of law and healthcare. Among the salient differences, ideally, when mainstream healthcare professionals engage in clinical practice they do so based on scientific evidence related to the disorder being assessed and treated, as well as scientific evidence related to the assessment and treatment techniques involved. In general, the American legal system operates on rules that are intended to engender fair decision making when it comes to understanding and enforcing the laws that societal governance has created. Science is not a natural part of the equation in the American legal system. Yet, because science underlies, or at least should underlie, the testimony of healthcare witnesses who contribute information to the legal system, an evolution has occurred across time to allow consideration of scientific inquiry and scientific knowledge in the courtroom (cf. Faigman & Monahan, 2005; Foster & Huber, 1999). In fact, the evolution of the evidentiary standards in the American legal system reflects an increasing desire to force expert witnesses to rely on scientific knowledge, which, as noted above, fits very well with the scientist-practitioner mindset of clinical neuropsychologists.

In recently reviewing the current status of forensic neuropsychology, Sweet, Ecklund-Johnson, and Malina (2008) noted that the historical predominance of the scientist-practitioner model within the broader field of clinical psychology likely provides a major explanation for the growth in interest of the American legal system in the expert opinions of clinical neuropsychologists. In a general sense, as Sweet (1999) stated:

> Among the "relevant by-products of a scientist-practitioner approach are: familiarity with disciplined scrutiny (i.e., peer review), clinical procedures emphasizing data-based decision-making (i.e., accountability), and comfort with hypothesis-testing (i.e., objective differential diagnosis)."
>
> (p. xviii)

In a more specific sense, the fundamental reason relates to the legal concept of an expert's *bases of opinions*. Clinical neuropsychology is a field in which scientific research, regarding the clinical disorders of interest and the assessment procedures used to identify or rule out associated neuropsychological dysfunction, is paramount in the decision making of practitioners. Ideally, a clinical neuropsychologist minimizes the use of intuition, "gut feelings," and a vague sense of knowing, in favor of drawing conclusions based upon empirical data, which is itself able to be compared to published peer-reviewed data from individuals whose clinical conditions are well documented. In short, impressions give way to facts, which in both clinical and forensic contexts are viewed as acceptable, and even desirable, bases of opinions.

A separate reason for the impressive growth of forensic neuropsychology pertains to the issue of *relevance*. Though the practice areas of psychiatry, neurology, and neuropsychology often overlap in terms of the types of clinical conditions of interest, and therefore the patients we see in clinical practice, neuropsychology's purview is relatively unique. That is, the detailed and intensive study of cognition, behavior, and emotion by way of formal testing procedures is rather uniquely the activity of a clinical neuropsychologist. To be certain, psychiatrists and neurologists have interests in cognition, behavior, and emotion, but they do not approach these dimensions of human experience in the same manner or with the same emphasis. Though neuropsychological tests have variable generalizability to daily life, and the results of some can be difficult to generalize, the results of psychiatric interviewing and neurological examination, brain scans, and electrical recordings of the brain may have little to no generalizability to the daily life of the individual who was examined. As a result of decades of clinical neuropsychological research and practice, our colleagues in psychiatry and neurology have come to defer to neuropsychologists when it comes to detailed questions pertaining to possible changes in cognition and emotion or the implications in day-to-day living activities that are associated with such known changes in their patients. In the same manner, the legal system has come to realize that it is within the purview of clinical neuropsychologists to objectify and explain possible disorders of cognition, behavior, and emotion. That is, the rather unique purview of the specialty of clinical neuropsychology is relevant to frequent decisions that must be made regarding questions of damages and questions of accountability for behavior within the civil and criminal components, respectively, of the American legal system. Fundamentally, basic routine clinical tasks of practicing neuropsychologists, inclusive of the entire age range of adults and children (cf. Wills & Sweet, 2006), are highly relevant to administrative and legal decision makers in forensic settings.

REASONS FOR THE FOCUS ON MALINGERING BY FORENSIC NEUROPSYCHOLOGISTS

In 1964, U.S. Supreme Court Justice Potter Stewart provided an often-quoted definition in the years-long and complex attempts by court systems to define that which is obscene, as in what constitutes pornography. He stated in part, "I shall not today attempt further to define the kinds of material I understand to be embraced . . . [b]ut I know it when I see it" (*Jacobellis v. Ohio*, 1964). For many years, clinical psychologists and clinical neuropsychologists alike presumed that they, like Justice Stewart, would surely "know it when I see it." However, that view was forever shattered in the late 1980s by a series of empirical studies that showed clinicians were no better than chance at identifying feigned neuropsychological test data (e.g., Faust, Hart, & Guilmette, 1988; Faust, Hart, Guilmette, & Arkes, 1988). From this point forward, numerous clinical neuropsychologists took it upon themselves to remedy an unfortunate state of affairs, which was that relevant empirical research was nearly nonexistent; clinicians of that era had relied on impressionistic judgments, rather than investigating actuarial means or developing special methods to detect neuropsychological malingering. To be sure, clinical neuropsychologists even at that point in the 1980s already knew that in order to be useful, neuropsychological data needed to be valid. However, the presumption that we somehow impressionistically *knew* when it was not valid was inaccurate.

The literature addressing neuropsychological malingering, and related topics such as symptom reporting response bias and insufficient effort on cognitive tasks, has increased dramatically, beginning in the early 1990s (cf. the extensive bibliography in Appendices A–E of this text). As a result, it soon became clear that, minimally, in order to be effective when evaluating individuals in a forensic context, practitioners in clinical neuropsychology needed to appreciate at least two straightforward, simple facts, which in retrospect now seem blatantly obvious and can be considered truisms. These are: (1) evaluations conducted for forensic purposes are differentially vulnerable to forces that produce invalid test results, and (2) a proactive approach to detecting invalid responding in forensic evaluations, whether caused by response bias in the over-reporting or fraudulent reporting of symptoms on psychological inventories or via insufficient effort on cognitive tasks, is challenging and complex, requiring at minimum a great deal of advance thought and planning.

Addressing the first obvious fact above, a commonality across forensic settings is the potential for *secondary gain*. That is, individuals involved in civil and criminal legal proceedings, as well as disability determinations and educational due process hearings, can gain some form of external reward by assuming an illness or injury role. Secondary gain contexts such as these can be powerful motivators in determining behavior, which can undermine the validity of formal assessments intended to identify true illness or injury. Since the 1990s, numerous clinical researchers have provided convincing evidence of the substantial impact of secondary gain, in the form of *differential prevalence* and *known groups* research designs (Rogers, 1997). For example, using the former type, studies of individuals with a documented condition can be compared to those who claim the condition within a context of secondary gain. Gervais, Russell, Green, Allen, Ferrari, and Pieschl (2001) demonstrated that 96% of individuals diagnosed with fibromyalgia and 100% of individuals diagnosed with rheumatoid arthritis in a clinical setting, with no identifiable secondary gain potential, passed simple cognitive effort measures. However, only 56% of individuals diagnosed with fibromyalgia who were seeking disability status, a context within which secondary gain potential exists, passed simple cognitive effort measures. Keeping in mind that the effort measures employed by these authors had been shown in separate studies to be passed by patients with well-documented brain dysfunction from a variety of neurological conditions, and that a condition such as fibromyalgia, characterized by diffuse musculoskeletal aches, pains, and tenderness, has no known or plausible brain mechanism that would cause disabling cognitive dysfunction, this study offers strong evidence of the power of a secondary gain context on measures relied upon by neuropsychologists. Similarly, a meta-analytic review by Iverson (2005) demonstrated that the neuropsychological test results of mild traumatic brain injury (TBI) outside of a litigation context are indistinguishable from normal, non-brain injury test results. Yet, within a context of litigation, neuropsychological test results after mild TBI are often measured as more extreme psychometrically than those of well-documented severe TBI, because of invalid performances and malingering (e.g., Greiffenstein & Baker, 2006). From a different perspective, the power of external incentive was shown by Flaro, Green, and Robertson (2007), who demonstrated that effort test failure was 23 times higher in mild TBI claimants than in litigants who were seeking parental custody of their own children. The power of external incentives is indeed great, and can in some instances push behavior in opposing directions, as is the case with a potential financial award for impairment versus potential child custody for being intact!

Numerous additional studies of this type have been performed and, to be certain, the effect of a secondary gain context is not limited to cognitive measures. The powerful impact of a secondary gain context is also evident on psychological measures, such as the MMPI–2 (e.g., Nelson, Sweet, & Heilbronner, 2007; Youngjohn, Davis, & Wolf, 1997).

Relating to the second of what I have labeled as two obvious facts, the need for proactive assessment of response bias and insufficient effort because of the potential for malingering in forensic cases has been well known and established for years (cf. Nies & Sweet, 1994). In fact, failure to proactively assess for possible malingering in a forensic case is now considered below the standard of acceptable practice, as noted in the following quote that closed a review of the subject in 1999:

> We can no longer take comfort in the belief, now shown to be false, that we will simply know when malingering is evident, without addressing the issue deliberately and prospectively. We would also do well to rethink the "throw-away" statement, often found at the end of the behavioral observations section of formal reports, that we were once taught by our mentors to make (i.e., "Present findings are a valid indication of the patient's functioning"). Such a statement should now be reconstructed to indicate the limitations of mere observation of overt behavior that appeared or did not appear to indicate that sufficient effort was invested on tasks presented to the patient. Gross observations of behavior as a means of determining presence or absence of malingering are no longer acceptable as sole criteria for ruling out insufficient effort. Without prospective consideration of strategies to detect or rule out malingering, we are left to ponder the philosopher Teuber's admonition, "Absence of evidence is not the same as evidence of absence."
>
> (Sweet, 1999, p. 278)

In fact, it is not just individual investigators who have asserted this standard. The forensic practice expectation is now the official position of the National Academy of Neuropsychology (Bush et al., 2005).

Differential diagnosis in a clinical context normally involves considering the alternative diagnostic hypotheses that appear relevant to the history, presentation of symptoms, and objective test findings of a patient as one rules out or rules in (i.e., confirms) various clinical conditions. The complex nature of the differential diagnosis of malingering in a forensic context is represented in the repeated guidance from serious forensic researchers and experts that multiple methods and strategies are needed (e.g., Bender & Rogers, 2004; Larrabee, Greiffenstein, Greve, & Bianchini, 2007; Slick, Sherman, & Iverson, 1999; see Appendix F for article reprint). Again, such recommendations are not new; they have been made and remade for many years (cf. Nies & Sweet, 1994; Rogers, Harrell, & Liff, 1993; Youngjohn, Lees-Haley, & Binder, 1999; Youngjohn, Spector, & Mapou, 1998), underscoring the complex nature of the differential diagnosis of malingering.

WHAT CAN BE ACCOMPLISHED BY ANALYZING COMPLEX FORENSIC CASES

What then, with the hundreds of empirical peer-reviewed research studies on the subject, can analysis of individual forensic cases provide? The answer is simple. The hundreds of published studies relevant to response bias, insufficient effort, and other aspects of behavior that may represent malingering produce snapshots of the *average* neuropsychological malingerer. For the most part, group studies do not reveal the range of individual presentations seen when evaluating an individual forensic case or the possible evolution of this presentation across time. At times, individual cases demonstrate unique or rare presentations of malingering which appear quite different from the stereotypical or average malingerer. Moreover, the instances in which a degree of response invalidity is present or selectively part of a comprehensive assessment is not illustrated and yet is informative in a case study as a means of demonstrating when a conclusion of malingering would not be appropriate. The present editors concluded that case study presentations would indeed be informative and instructive regarding the complex differential diagnostic process related to malingering.

As examples, consider three brief vignettes of personal injury litigation. First, consider a young non-dramatic presentation of symptoms subsequent to a well-documented severe TBI in a young adult who demonstrates spasticity of both upper limbs that is well documented as caused by the TBI. Early on in the two-day assessment process, she demonstrates very substantial failure on a single effort test. Second, consider a middle-aged man with a well-documented severe TBI whose first of three neuropsychological evaluations (only the first pertained to litigation) demonstrated an early effort test failure at a below-chance level. Third, consider a clinically referred middle-aged woman whose minor "fender bender" three months earlier does not appear to have caused any initial brain injury. The prospect of litigation could be on the horizon, but is not yet apparent. Failure on multiple effort measures and test validity indicators is grossly apparent, and the overall level of very impaired performances is not at all credible. Which of these three cases will end up being labeled malingerers? All three? None? One or two? We will return to these three cases in greater detail as we bring closure to this text in the final chapter. Until then, there is much to consider among the informative introductory chapters and the subsequent fascinating cases contributed by our many experts in forensic neuropsychology.

REFERENCES

Bender, S., & Rogers, R. (2004). Detection of neurocognitive feigning: Development of a multi-strategy assessment. *Archives of Clinical Neuropsychology*, *19*, 49–60.

Bush, S. S., Ruff, R. M., Tröster, A. I., Barth, J. T., Koffler, S. P. Pliskin, N. H., Reynolds, C. R., & Silver, C. H. (2005). Symptom validity assessment: Practice issues and medical necessity NAN policy and planning committee. *Archives of Clinical Neuropsychology*, *20*, 419–426.

Faigman, D., & Monahan, J. (2005). Psychological evidence at the dawn of the law's scientific age. *Annual Review of Psychology*, *56*, 631–659.

Faust, D., Hart, K., & Guilmette, T. J. (1988). Pediatric malingering: The capacity of children to fake believable deficits on neuropsychological testing. *Journal of Consulting and Clinical Psychology*, *56*, 578–582.

Faust, D., Hart, K., Guilmette, T. J., & Arkes, H. R. (1988). Neuropsychologists' capacity to detect adolescent malingerers. *Professional Psychology: Research and Practice*, *19*, 508–515.

Flaro, L., Green, P., & Robertson, E. (2007). Word Memory Test failure 23 times higher in mild brain injury than parents seeking custody: The power of external incentives. *Brain Injury*, *21*, 373–383.

Foster, K., & Huber, P. (1999). *Judging science: Scientific knowledge and the federal courts.* Cambridge, MA: MIT Press.

Gervais, R., Russell, A., Green, P., Allen, L., Ferrari, R., & Pieschl, S. (2001). Effort testing in fibromyalgia patients with disability incentives. *Journal of Rheumatology, 28,* 1892–1899.

Greiffenstein, M. F., & Baker, W. J. (2006). Miller was (mostly) right: Head injury severity inversely related to simulation. *Legal and Criminal Psychology, 11,* 131–145.

Iverson, G. L. (2005). Outcome from mild traumatic brain injury. *Current Opinion in Psychiatry, 18,* 301–317.

Jacobellis v. Ohio, 378 U.S. 184, 197 (1964).

Larrabee, G., Greiffenstein, M., Greve, K., & Bianchini, K. (2007). Refining diagnostic criteria for malingering. In G. Larrabee (Ed.) *Assessment of malingered neuropsychological deficits.* New York: Oxford University Press.

Nelson, N., Sweet, J., Berry, D., Bryant, F., & Granacher, R. (2007). Response validity in forensic neuropsychology: Exploratory factor analytic evidence of distinct cognitive and psychological constructs. *Journal of the International Neuropsychological Society, 13,* 440–449.

Nelson, N., Sweet, J., & Heilbronner, R. (2007). Examination of the new MMPI–2 Response Bias Scale (Gervais): Relationship with MMPI–2 validity scales. *Journal of Clinical and Experimental Neuropsychology, 29,* 67–72.

Nies, K., & Sweet, J. J. (1994). Neuropsychological assessment and malingering: A critical review of past and present strategies. *Archives of Clinical Neuropsychology, 9,* 501–552.

Rogers, R. (1997). Researching dissimulation. In R. Rogers (Ed.) *Clinical assessment of malingering and deception* (pp. 398–426). New York: Guilford Press.

Rogers, R., Harrell, E., & Liff, C. (1993). Feigning neuropsychological impairment: A critical review of methodological and clinical considerations. *Clinical Psychology Review, 13,* 255–274.

Slick, D. J., Sherman, E. M. S., & Iverson, G. L. (1999). Diagnostic criteria for malingered neurocognitive dysfunction: Proposed standards for clinical practice and research. *The Clinical Neuropsychologist, 13,* 545–561.

Sweet, J. J. (Ed.) (1999). *Forensic neuropsychology: Fundamentals and practice.* Lisse, Netherlands: Swets & Zeitlinger.

Sweet, J. J. (1999). Malingering: Differential diagnosis. In J. J. Sweet (Ed.) *Forensic neuropsychology: Fundamentals and practice.* Lisse, Netherlands: Swets & Zeitlinger. (Reprinted in I. Schultz & D. Brady (Eds.) (2003). *Psychological injuries at trial.* Chicago, IL: American Bar Association.)

Sweet, J., Ecklund-Johnson, E., & Malina, A. (2008). Overview of forensic neuropsychology. In J. Morgan & J. Ricker (Eds.) *Textbook of clinical neuropsychology.* New York: Taylor & Francis.

Sweet, J., King, J., Malina, A., Bergman, M., & Simmons, A. (2002). Documenting the prominence of forensic neuropsychology at national meetings and in relevant professional journals from 1990–2000. *The Clinical Neuropsychologist, 16,* 481–494.

Sweet, J., Moberg, P., & Suchy, Y. (2000). Ten-year follow-up survey of clinical neuropsychologists. Part II: Private practice and economics. *The Clinical Neuropsychologist, 14,* 479–495.

Sweet, J., Nelson, N., & Moberg, P. (2006). The TCN/AACN "Salary Survey": Professional practices, beliefs, and incomes of U.S. neuropsychologists. *The Clinical Neuropsychologist, 20,* 325–364.

Wills, K., & Sweet, J. (2006). Neuropsychological considerations in forensic child assessment. In S. Sparta & G. Koocher (Eds.). *Forensic mental health assessment of children and adolescents.* New York: Guilford.

Youngjohn, J., Davis, D., & Wolf, I. (1997). Head injury and the MMPI–2: Paradoxical severity effects and the influence of litigation. *Psychological Assessment, 9,* 177–184.

Youngjohn, J. R., Lees-Haley, P. R., & Binder, L. M. (1999). Comment: Warning malingerers produces more sophisticated malingering. *Archives of Clinical Neuropsychology, 14,* 511–515.

Youngjohn, J. R., Spector, J., & Mapou, R. L. (1998). Failure to assess motivation, need to consider psychiatric disturbance, and absence of objectively verified physical pathology: Some common pitfalls in the practice of forensic neuropsychology. *The Clinical Neuropsychologist, 12,* 233–236.

Why questions regarding effort and malingering are always raised in forensic neuropsychological evaluations

2

Wilfred G. van Gorp and Jason Hassenstab

The accurate interpretation of neuropsychological tests in a non-forensic context typically relies upon a presumption that the examinee is trying his or her best, and has put forth full effort in the examination, much as a student taking other tests, such as an SAT or LSAT examination would have done. However, in contrast to the LSAT where a positive outcome (e.g., admission to law school) usually results from good effort, in a forensic context there may be a reward for putting forth less effort and, therefore, appearing more impaired than is truly the case (e.g., "secondary gain"). In these circumstances, the presumption of "best effort" can and should be routinely questioned. Situations in which secondary gain may occur include avoiding legal sanctions or punishment (e.g., appearing incompetent to stand trial, unable to assist in one's defense, appearing mentally retarded to avoid the death penalty) or achieving monetary rewards for being impaired cognitively or emotionally (e.g., receiving monetary disability benefits, greater financial award in a civil tort action, etc.).

Historically, psychologists and neuropsychologists administered tests, such as intelligence tests, and merely reported and interpreted their results. As neuropsychologists became more familiar with—and utilized within—the legal system, the development of methods to assess level of effort or credible performance began to increase. Because an individual's true (conscious) motivation to perform poorly can rarely be directly known or assessed, we utilize the terms "level of effort" or "non-credible performance" to describe poor effort, though "malingering" is appropriate in certain circumstances as well (e.g., see Sweet, 1999; specific references to "malingering," its definition, and presentation can be found elsewhere in this volume).

One of the first widely used methods of assessing response style relied on specialized scales from the Minnesota Multiphasic Personality Inventory (MMPI; Hathaway & McKinley, 1943). The need for the MMPI to include measures of response style was apparent from its inception (Meehl & Hathaway, 1946). Meehl and Hathaway focused upon three strategies to assess defensiveness ("faking good") and non-credible performance ("faking bad"): inconsistent responses, socially desirable but unrealistic and infrequently endorsed items, and items sensitive to impression management through empirical studies (Greene, 1995).

The measurement of inconsistent responses in the second iteration of the MMPI, the MMPI–2 (Butcher, Dahlstrom, Graham, Tellegen, & Kaemmer, 1989), relies on providing the patient with the opportunity to distort responses by giving answers inconsistently either to pairs of similarly phrased items or to item pairs phrased in opposite valence. The scales are the Variable Response

Inconsistency scale (VRIN) and the True Response Inconsistency scale (TRIN). A high number of inconsistent responses would suggest that the patient did not attend to the items appropriately, either because of unwillingness or an inability to do so (Greene, 1995).

The measurement of socially desirable but unrealistic and infrequently endorsed items was considered by Meehl and Hathaway (1946) as an opportunity to measure a patient's willingness to structure their responses so that they may appear more favorable. Similar to the MMPI, the MMPI–2 items on the Lie (L) scale were based on earlier work of Hartshorne and May (1928) and were designed to measure behaviors that were socially desirable but rarely true in the common population. A patient with a high score on the L scale would be considered as responding in a manner that suggested a moral superiority or an overly rigid, moralistic stance. As an additional strategy, an infrequency (F) scale was developed to provide the opportunity for the patient to endorse items that were rarely endorsed by the majority of the original normative sample. A patient who endorses a large number of items from the F scale would be considered to be responding in a manner that was atypical and is most likely making an attempt to appear more emotionally distressed than might realistically be the case. The MMPI–2 extended this strategy with the addition of the Back Infrequency scale (F_B), which consists of items that were rarely endorsed in the last 300 items of the test (Greene, 1995).

The third strategy adopted by Meehl and Hathaway (1946) consisted of using an empirical procedure to differentiate between individuals who responded appropriately and individuals instructed to malinger. The first empirical scale to receive wide attention was the Gough Dissimulation Scale (Ds; Gough, 1954). This scale significantly differentiated a group of neurotic patients from groups of college students and professional psychologists who were asked to simulate neurotic responding on the MMPI. On the MMPI–2, a widely used empirical procedure is the Gough Dissimulation Index, a method carried over from the original MMPI. The Gough Dissimulation Index, also referred to as the F–K Index, is an attempt to provide a measure of defensive or malingered responses based on the relationship between the F and Correction (K) validity scales. In its original use on the MMPI, Gough (1950) suggested that the difference between the raw score on the F scale and the raw score on the K scale provides an estimate of where an individual lies on the spectrum of accuracy of item endorsement.

More recently, the Fake Bad Scale (FBS) has been developed (Lees-Haley, English, & Glenn, 1991) and research has offered at least some validation for its use (Nelson, Sweet, & Demakis, 2006) though others question its accuracy (Butcher, Arbisi, Atlis, & McNulty, 2003). It has been shown that feigning or exaggeration of emotional symptoms can occur apart from feigning of cognitive symptoms (Nelson, Sweet, Berry, Bryant, & Granacher, 2007). The MMPI–2 validity scales, including the FBS, have generally been validated to detect exaggeration (or minimization) of emotional symptoms, and in fact, the University of Minnesota Press recently added the FBS to their scoring and output for the MMPI–2, further substantiating its scientific validity.

Another scale—the Response Bias Scale (RBS; Gervais, 2005)—has recently been developed to detect feigned or exaggerated *cognitive* (versus emotional) symptoms. A validation study concluded that the RBS consistently outperformed existing MMPI–2 validity scales in detecting cognitive symptom complaints in medicolegal evaluations (Gervais, Ben-Porath, Wygant, & Green, 2007). However, in a recent study (Nelson, Sweet, Berry, Bryant, & Granacher, 2007), the RBS was found to be most associated with MMPI–2 scales measuring the over-reporting of neurotic type symptoms, implying that it might measure this construct as well, perhaps measuring the construct of "symptom validity" overall (Nelson, Sweet, & Heilbronner, 2007).

In the 1970s, methods of "symptom validity testing" began to appear in the literature (e.g., Pankratz, Fausti, & Peed, 1975). Symptom validity tests were generally simple tests using the Binomial Theorem wherein the test taker is given two choices, one of which is correct. In these tests, the question became: Did the test taker perform statistically below chance, thereby producing non-credible performance? However, many test takers became sophisticated and were aware that performance well below 50% correct (i.e., chance) would appear non-credible; as a result, the assessment of motivation had to become more sophisticated. It did, and tests were soon developed based upon the "ceiling effect"—that is, tests that almost everyone, including brain-damaged patients, would do well on except those exerting poor effort because the test appeared difficult to the naïve test taker. An example of this type of test is the Rey Fifteen Item Test (FIT), which was developed many years ago (Rey, 1941), but only in more recent history has appeared consistently in the literature on malingering. The Rey FIT superficially appears difficult but is for most persons actually quite easy. Some of the "ceiling effect" methods, however, have come under scrutiny because for some persons (e.g., with severe mental illness or dementia) they are not easy, and persons in some of these clinical groups have been shown to "fail" them (Schretlen, Brandt, Krafft, & van Gorp, 1991).

Additional measures of non-credible performance combine the binomial theorem plus ceiling effect tests and add other methods of analysis such as looking at consistency of responding within intervals across a range of items of varying difficulty, thereby adding to the sophistication of the test. An example of this type of test is the Validity Indicator Profile (VIP; Frederick, 1997).

We will now examine various settings in which non-credible performance may exist and how they illustrate the importance of assessing effort in these settings.

SECONDARY GAIN

There are a number of settings in which symptom amplification may be expected to occur. One of the most common situations for a neuropsychologist in this context is the independent neuro-psychological evaluation in which the neuropsychologist has been asked by a third party to evaluate an individual seeking financial recovery or other benefits. The examinee in this context may feign or exaggerate cognitive impairment or emotional distress in order to receive disability benefits, veteran's benefits, worker's compensation, or tort damages for alleged psychological injuries (Mills & Lipian, 2005). The criminal forensic context also forms a frequent setting for feigning of symptoms, such as a competency evaluation or when the court must determine sentencing. Test takers may introduce symptoms in order to avoid criminal responsibility by feigning insanity at the time of the crime or they may feign psychopathology or cognitive impairment sufficient to appear incompetent to stand trial or to attenuate financial penalties and sentencing.

The distinction between non-conscious and conscious reasons for suboptimal effort is difficult and often impossible to determine. Clinicians have traditionally attempted to define non-conscious simulation as a phenomenon analogous to a somatoform disorder, whereas conscious or deliberate simulation is considered a factitious disorder or outright malingering. The utility of this distinction has been controversial since Miller (1961) argued that any attempt to distinguish the two would fail due to its inability to be effectively scrutinized with acceptable experimental methods. Absent performance that is statistically below chance or procedures involving surveillance in which he/she is shown doing something he/she professes they are unable to do may lead to a reasoned belief of non-credible performance due to conscious intent, yet this is not a provable construct. (Of course, the same is true for many clinical situations, such as somatoform disorder, in which the distinction between conscious versus non-conscious factors is incapable of being proven).

History of secondary gain

The history of secondary gain can be traced as far back as the ancient Greeks. Ulysses, in an attempt to escape duty in the Trojan War, is said to have feigned insanity by yoking a bull and horse together and plowing the seashore, sowing salt instead of grain. His deception was believed to be revealed when Palamedes placed the infant son of the King of Ithaca in the path of the plow. When Ulysses diverted the plow to avoid the infant, this was considered proof that he was indeed sane (Larson, Haney, & Keeler, 1932). Jones and Llewellyn (1917) cite an account presumably from the Middle Ages which described how a young villager, hoping to exchange punishment for convalescence, was exposed while simulating a particularly violent epileptic fit. After overhearing a surgeon insist upon an infallible cure via immediate castration, the villager jumped up and without hesitation begged forgiveness.

During the industrial revolution, the increasing danger of the workplace resulted in an increase in work-related injuries. The responsibility for covering work-related injury costs began to shift from the employee to the employer. Thus began the birth of workers' compensation programs (Lande, 2005). As the feasibility of seeking financial compensation for personal injury increased, so did the popularity of feigning illness or injury. In the early days of the US railroads, railway workers and passengers often presented for workmen's compensation or personal injury with a vague cluster of symptoms known collectively as "railway spine" (Cohen, 1996).

PREVALENCE OF FEIGNING IN NEUROPSYCHOLOGICAL ASSESSMENTS

Malingering is highly prevalent in certain populations including military personnel, the criminal population, and in litigious Western societies more generally. Malingering is also more common in men from youth through middle age (Mills & Lipian, 2005). The frequency estimates of symptom exaggeration in neuropsychological assessment vary considerably depending on the type of illness or injury and context of the assessment, and whether the setting is treatment related or a forensic context. Estimates of base rates of malingering in assessment settings vary considerably but can be reasonably expected to occur in approximately 15% across settings (Rosenfeld, Sands, & van Gorp, 2000). In the forensic context, where issues of secondary gain are more prominent, a large survey of clinicians' practices revealed that 29% of personal injury, 30% of disability, 19% of criminal, and 8% of medical cases involved probable malingering and symptom exaggeration (Mittenberg, Patton, Canyock, & Condit, 2002). Larrabee (2003) found a slightly higher rate, identifying base rates of malingering in forensic context at an overall rate of 40% across 11 studies. As Mittenberg et al. (2002) noted, the presence of a substantial external incentive increased the rate of probable malingering from 8% in medical cases to over 30% in cases that are potentially compensable. In the case of mild head trauma, a meta-analytic study has shown that 95% of patients exhibit no significant cognitive impairment within three months or more following the injury (Binder, Rohling, & Larrabee, 1997). Mittenberg et al. (2002) point out that if this statistic is accurate, only 5% of mild head trauma cases exhibit persistent cognitive impairment and therefore the base rate of malingering in this population is likely a significant underestimate.

Several studies have shown that secondary gain significantly influences test performance. The British neurologist Henry Miller published a landmark report of 50 individuals who were reportedly unfit to return to work following head injuries of varying degrees of severity (Miller, 1961; Miller & Carlidge, 1972). Miller found an inverse relationship between severity of injury and severity of disability. In addition, a sample-wide non-response to therapy was observed until compensation issues were resolved, and 48 of the 50 individuals were able to return to work after the completion of their settlements. The dose-dependent relationship between injury and disability has received little attention in published literature; however, some studies reporting dose-dependent inconsistencies in various symptom profiles provide inferential support (Albers & Berent, 2000; Pliskin et al, 1998; Greiffenstein and Baker, 2001; Paniak et al., 2002). To date, only one known study has directly examined the dose-dependent relationship between injury severity and disability severity. In an archival study of compensation seekers with a wide range of CNS injury severity, Greiffenstein and Baker (2006) found that whiplash and minor head injury litigants produced "striking inverse linear trends" between injury severity and disability severity. In addition, more invalid results on tests of cognitive and motor functioning were seen in less severely injured litigants than in brain-injured litigants with severe injuries.

The use of specifically tailored tests of effort sheds more light on the prevalence of non-credible performance in forensic contexts. Multiple studies utilizing the "significantly less than chance" methodology to identify malingerers have found that mere involvement in compensation seeking can significantly impact test performance. Using a forced-choice symptom validity format, Binder and Willis (1991) found that a group of mild head trauma patients who were seeking financial compensation performed significantly worse than a group of patients with well-documented brain dysfunction who were not seeking financial compensation. In a larger study, Binder (1993) found similar results and concluded that one-third of mild head trauma patients who were seeking financial compensation in this study evidenced extremely poor performance when compared to patients with well-documented brain dysfunction. Overall, Binder (1993) and Binder and Willis (1991) found that patients with severe brain damage performed at least as well as, or better than, mild head trauma patients in this context. Several additional studies have confirmed these findings. Youngjohn, Burrows, and Erdal (1995) found that nearly half of 55 consecutive patients with persisting post-concussive syndrome who were seeking or receiving financial compensation performed extremely poorly on a forced-choice procedure, with only 28% performing as well as verified brain-injured patients not involved in financial compensation. Further, Guilmette, Whelihan, Sparadeo, and Buongiorno (1994) evaluated 50 Social Security disability applicants and found that approximately 20% of the test results were considered invalid due to extremely poor performance on forced-choice procedures, and an additional 20% were of questionable validity. Taken together, these studies suggest that a financial incentive may predict test performance regardless of the presence or absence of brain damage (Haines & Norris, 1995).

Insurance fraud

Prevalence and cost estimates of insurance fraud vary greatly depending upon the source. Reports from the insurance industry indicate that approximately 10% of Americans would commit insurance fraud if they knew they could get away with it (Accenture Ltd., 2003). Approximately one-third of Americans reported a willingness to exaggerate their symptoms in order to stay off work and receive worker's compensation (Insurance Research Council, 1999). In contrast, labor advocacy groups report much lower estimates, arguing that the large estimated losses by insurance companies are used to justify increases in premiums and that most of the cost associated with worker's compensation fraud are attributable to dishonest billing practices by employers and practitioners (Labor Research Association, 1998).

MECHANISMS OF FEIGNING

Role assumption and threat of courtroom scrutiny

In addition to secondary gain, there are other factors specific to effort in forensic neuropsychological evaluations that are less common in traditional clinical evaluations. One such factor is brought forth via the inherent relationship between the attorney and the litigant (examinee), which we will refer to as role assumption. It is customary that prior to seeking a forensic evaluation the evaluee and attorney have discussed in some detail the person's symptoms and their impact upon his or her daily functioning. In discussing these symptoms, particular attention is likely to be paid to certain symptoms, which the attorney may (even unintentionally) emphasize in an effort to ensure the best possible outcome for their case, thereby reinforcing this type of reporting or emphasis. In addition, during the course of multiple assessments in a compensation claim, an individual acquires a notion of the behavior that is expected of him based on the content of the questions and responses from examiners (Rawling & Brooks, 1990). Collectively, this process formulates a narrative outlining the litigant's symptom profile as it relates to the legal matter. Thus the litigant, consciously or not, begins to associate with the role in the narrative and may attempt to fulfill or "act out" this role in the most complete way possible. Moreover, Walsh (1985) suggests that in cases of multiple assessments, longitudinal analysis of symptoms may reveal alterations in the emphasis given to particular symptoms as well as the introduction of novel symptoms. This process is not unlike the concept of demand characteristics in behavioral research first described by Orne (1962). If research participants can be motivated to perform in a certain way when issues of secondary gain are less salient, then it seems likely that examinees in a forensic context, where the outcome of the evaluation may lead to significant monetary and other rewards, are more susceptible to role assumption of this nature.

Role assumption becomes extremely relevant when the injured party's (i.e., plaintiff) attorney is present during the evaluation. The examinee then is facing enhanced expectations and may be more inclined to perform in a manner consistent with the role formulated with his or her attorney, even in a non-conscious attempt to "please" the attorney. Role assumption is not only linked to the examinee's own attorneys and experts, but may come about during an assessment by the opposing side. In the adversarial system, the examinee's claims of impairment will be evaluated thoroughly and attempts will be made to discredit these claims. This can be perceived by the examinee as an attack on his/her credibility that may evoke a range of responses including an attempt to validate the presence and severity of impairment. In effect, the examinee may attempt to "prove" how disabled he/she is by accurately, but selectively, reporting their symptoms and associated impairment (Rogers & Payne, 2006).

Due diligence by the examinee

One way to determine non-credible performance is to analyze scores from tests of effort, but another way is to examine whether scores make "neuropsychological sense." There are occasions in which test takers perform normally on tests of effort indicating valid responding, but their scores on traditional tests of neuropsychological functioning are implausibly impaired—that is, they are inconsistent with the injury or objective levels of daily functioning. It could be that these test takers may have specific knowledge of aspects of the testing methods, such as the names of tests of effort. When these are encountered, the person exerts full effort, in contrast to performance on other tests. As Rogers (1997) notes, individuals who are intent upon manipulating their performance may prepare for the evaluation beforehand by becoming familiar with symptom profiles and test materials. In addition, the test taker may glean information from contacts with their attorneys, psychologists, or physicians who may quite unintentionally provide information that may augment the test taker's ability to feign impairment (Youngjohn, Lees-Haley, & Binder, 1999). But where do they acquire this information?

Perhaps the biggest source of information with respect to tests of effort is the Internet. Examinees can access considerable information about virtually any disorder, and more importantly, can access information regarding test materials and procedures used in a neuropsychological evaluation including tests of effort (Bauer & McCaffrey, 2006). Ruiz, Drake, Glass, Marcotte, and van Gorp (2002) instructed five test naïve individuals to search the Internet for information that would assist them in simulating depression in an independent psychological evaluation. The authors report that—in 2002—approximately 2–5% of the websites identified posed a "direct threat to the security of psychological tests and evaluations" (p. 296). The percent is assuredly higher now. Certain websites were identified that provided names of tests commonly used in psychological evaluations and their purposes, including tests of effort. Other websites posted several stimuli from popular tests such as the Dementia Rating Scale, the Rorschach Inkblot Test, and the MMPI–2. Still others provided detailed information on the purpose of the independent medical evaluation and suggestions for potential test takers on how to feign impairment in order to obtain disability benefits. One of us (WvG) once encountered an elderly woman who had for years been declared by the Court incompetent to manage her own finances. When asked to undergo a neuropsychological evaluation as part of her challenge to this issue, the woman indicated she knew which tests would be administered because she had read many of the neuropsychologist's articles and saw what tests he used in his studies. "How did you do that?" she was asked. "I hired a college student to find your articles and he did," she replied. If a person who had been found legally incompetent by the Court performed this due diligence, what about an examinee with thousands (even hundreds of thousands or millions) of dollars at stake, largely related to the evaluation?

DETECTING DISTORTION USING STANDARD TESTS

When the neuropsychologist suspects malingering despite valid performance on effort tests, there are several methods available to detect poor effort using clinical measures.

Wechsler Adult Intelligence Scale

The Digit Span subtest of the Wechsler intelligence scale has shown promise in detection of poor effort for two primary reasons: extremely low scores are rare even among patients with severe neurological impairments including Alzheimer's disease, and persons feigning impairment may misperceive the test as a test of memory rather than an attention test and therefore perform much more poorly (Iverson & Tulsky, 2003).

Mittenberg, Theroux-Fichera, Zielinksi, and Heilbronner (1995) used the difference between the age-corrected scaled scores on the Vocabulary subtest and the Digit Span subtest of the WAIS–R in order to identify simulated malingerers. Large differences between Digit Span and Vocabulary were relatively uncommon in the WAIS–R normative sample as well as in non-litigating patients with brain injuries, but simulated malingerers exhibited large differences. Subsequent validation studies have confirmed the potential utility of this method in the WAIS–III in studies using simulated and non-simulated malingerers (Greve, Bianchini, Mathias, Houston, & Crouch, 2003; Mittenberg, Theroux, Aguila-Puentes, Bianchini, Greve, & Rayls, 2001); however, others have urged caution in its use as a measure of effort (Axelrod, Fichtenberg, Millis, & Wertheimer, 2006).

Methods using discriminant analysis have utilized a design similar to Heaton, Smith, Lehman, and Vogt (1978), wherein subtest age-corrected scaled scores are entered into a stepwise discriminant function to predict group membership (malingerer vs. non-malingerer). Out of this research, Greiffenstein, Baker, and Gola (1994) developed the Reliable Digit Span (RDS) using the WAIS–R Digit Span subtest. RDS is the sum of the longest string of digits repeated over two trials without error under both forward and backward conditions. Different cutoff scores have shown varying rates of specificity and sensitivity, with more recent findings of good to excellent specificity with moderate sensitivity using a cutoff score of less than or equal to seven (Babikian, Boone, Lu, & Arnold, 2006; Etherton, Bianchini, Greve, & Heinly, 2005).

Wechsler Memory Scale

Use of the Wechsler Memory Scale (WMS) for the detection of malingering has focused on pattern analysis and qualitative analysis of error types. Pattern analysis has identified simulated malingerers through discriminant analysis of WMS–R index scores. Simulated malingerers produced lower Attention/Concentration index scores relative to the General Memory index, while subjects with verified brain injury produced opposite results (Mittenberg, Azrin, Millsaps, & Heilbronner, 1993). Rawling and Brooks (1990) developed the Simulation Index, a method of objectively analyzing qualitative errors on the WMS such as confabulations on Logical Memory or addition of excessive or unrelated features to the Visual Reproduction subtest. Results indicated an excellent classification score among suspected malingerers. However, Milanovich, Axelrod, and Millis (1996) failed to replicate these results using the Simulation Index–Revised.

California Verbal Learning Test–II

The Critical Item Analysis (CIA) and Forced-Choice Recognition (FCR) measures added in the second iteration of the California Verbal Learning Test (CVLT–II; Delis, Kramer, Kaplan, & Omer, 2000) have recently received attention as potentially useful measures of effort. FCR is administered approximately ten minutes after the Recognition trial. Words are read in pairs and the test taker is asked to select the word in the pair that was from the original word list. In the original normative sample, over 90% of participants achieved perfect scores (16/16), and no participants achieved scores less than 87.5% correct (14/16; Delis et al., 2000, p. 54). CIA rests on the assumption that items recalled on more difficult recall and recognition trials should also be recalled on easier forced-choice recognition trials. CIA Recall compares recall of an item on any trial with recognition of the same item during the FCR trial. CIA Recognition compares responses of the yes/no recognition trial to the responses of the FCR trial. In the original normative sample, items remembered on the more difficult recall and yes/no recognition trials were also recalled on the easier FCR trial in 90% or more of participants. A recent study using a forensic sample found moderate sensitivity and high specificity rates using a FCR cutoff score of 14/16 (Root, Robbins, Chang, & van Gorp, 2006). The authors also reported low sensitivity but high specificity for both the CIA Recall and CIA Recognition. Overall, the low to moderate sensitivity of the FCR and CIA indices err on the side of caution in that they are more likely to miss a substantial portion of test takers with suboptimal effort, yet the low false-positive rate augurs well for the identification of suboptimal effort in test takers with scores below the suggested cutoff values.

SUMMARY AND GUIDELINES FOR IMPLEMENTATION

Non-credible performance on neuropsychological tests may be far more common than was historically assumed. Coming from a tradition of academic and intellectual assessment, psychologists have generally presumed good motivation on the part of test takers, an assumption that began to wane as neuropsychologists increasingly engaged in forensic or medicolegal practice. Today, many assessment tools exist for the neuropsychologist, and these will be explored in this book. We provide several suggestions for implementing assessment of non-credible effort when there is potential reward or gain (tangible or not) for non-credible performance.

1. As a matter of routine practice, include formal measures of motivation anytime secondary gain

is possible, whether hired by plaintiff or defense. Emphasize the broadness of the secondary gain concept, as it is not always financial (avoidance of incarceration, parental approval).

2. Always use multiple measures of effort. Use both emotional and cognitive measures of effort.

3. Always consider base rates of malingering; see above for a summary of numbers. Use of the base rate in your clinical practice will increase your diagnostic accuracy overall.

4. Always use tests with good psychometric properties, especially good sensitivity and specificity. It is essential to choose tests that emphasize low false-positive rates. Use tests with a strong empirical foundation and that can be supported by research in court testimony.

5. Consider "real world behavior/demands" versus performance on neuropsychological tests. Independent living and functioning demands an array of instrumental behaviors and activities that require multiple aspects of at least a minimal level of cognitive functioning. It has been established that persons feigning cognitive impairment or those malingering tend to "aim too low"—that is, they often present with such low performance on tests that the results are non-credible (van Gorp et al., 1999). A person who obtains scores in the impaired range (at or below the second percentile) on a test of verbal and/or spatial memory, and yet arrives unaccompanied or unassisted to the office, takes an independent lunch break, returns unassisted, and finds her or his way back to the examination room, is engaging in behaviors that are inconsistent with the memory scores. Every clinician must attempt to relate known functioning in the real world with the results on the neuropsychological examination as further indicia of credible versus non-credible performance.

6. Inconsistencies between documented information in medical records versus self-report should also be considered and attempts made to reconcile or discredit. Caution, of course, must be exercised as information in medical records is not always correct; however, observations recorded at the time are often more valid than recollection or retrospective report several years later. An inconsistency, for instance, in which the ambulance and emergency room records state "no loss of consciousness" and an examinee's report three years later in the context of litigation states definite loss of consciousness requires an attempt to reconcile. Although some persons who are dazed or confused at the time of injury may misreport a loss of consciousness, the same misreporting can occur due to a revisionist historian.

7. Incontrovertible signs of feigning, and here we may appropriately say "malingering," must be acknowledged when they are present. Performance significantly below chance (statistically correcting for multiple trials which would otherwise result in a Type I error) on a symptom validity test may constitute one clear sign of intentional fabrication or exaggeration of symptoms. Some (e.g., Slick et al., 1999) have even suggested that this is one of the few indicators of conscious malingering in which the *wrong* answer is intentionally chosen. The other incontrovertible sign is video or audio (or personal witness) surveillance in which the "injured" party is observed or recorded engaging in some activity that he or she claims is not possible. One of the authors (WvG) once evaluated a plaintiff who claimed he could not do two things at once and even held a paper over and above the line of print being read because of the "distraction" by lines of print above and below the target line to read. This same person was—in the same timeframe—recorded on video surveillance driving while appearing to effortlessly talk on a cellular telephone. When confronted, the plaintiff was unable to reconcile the test behavior with the recorded behavior in surveillance.

As can be seen, the detection of feigning of cognitive or emotional symptoms is a complex and challenging process. Caution must be exercised in determining or concluding that feigning is (or may be) present, as the stakes are high if the clinician is wrong. The examinee may lose his/her disability benefits, award in a civil judgment, etc. Incorporation of these recommendations will assist the clinician in conducting an assessment in which distortion or feigning may affect interpretation or accuracy of the results. As examinees become more sophisticated test takers, the challenge now is for clinicians to become more sophisticated assessors. When confidence can be established that the test results are indeed accurate in representing an examinee's level of functioning, both the clinician and the examinee are placed in a better light.

REFERENCES

Accenture Ltd. (2003). One-fourth of Americans say it's acceptable to defraud insurance companies. Retrieved February 2007 from http://accenture.tekgroup.com/article_print.cfm?article_id=3970

Albers, J. W., & Berent, S. (2000). Controversies in neurotoxicology: Current status. *Neurology Clinics*, *18*(3), 741–764.

Axelrod, B., Fichtenberg, N., Millis, S., & Wertheimer, J. (2006). Detecting incomplete effort with Digit Span from the Wechsler Adult Intelligence Scale–Third Edition. *The Clinical Neuropsychologist*, *20*, 513–523.

Babikian, T., Boone, K. B., Lu, P., & Arnold, G. (2006). Sensitivity and specificity of various digit span scores in the detection of suspect effort. *The Clinical Neuropsychologist*, *20*(1), 145–159.

Bauer, L., & McCaffrey, R.J. (2006). Coverage of the Test of Memory Malingering, Victoria Symptom Validity Test, and Word Memory Test on the Internet: Is test security threatened? *Archives of Clinical Neuropsychology*, *21*, 121–126.

Binder, L. M. (1993). Assessment of malingering after mild head trauma with the Portland Digit Recognition Test. *Journal of Clinical and Experimental Neuropsychology*, *15*, 170–182.

Binder, L. M., Rohling, M. L., & Larrabee, G. J. (1997). A review of mild head trauma. Part I: Meta-analytic review of neuropsychological studies. *Journal of Clinical and Experimental Neuropsychology*, *19*(3), 421–31.

Binder, L. M., & Willis, S. C. (1991). Assessment of motivation after financially compensable minor head trauma. *Psychological Assessment: A Journal of Consulting and Clinical Psychology*, *3*, 175–181.

Butcher, J. N., Arbisi, P. A., Atlis, M. M., & McNulty, J. L. (2003). The construct validity of the Lees-Haley Fake Bad Scale. Does this scale measure somatic malingering and feigned emotional distress? *Archives of Clinical Neuropsychology*, *18*, 473–485.

Butcher, J. N., Dahlstrom, W. G., Graham, J. R., Tellegen, A., & Kaemmer, B. (1989). *MMPI–2: Manual for administration and scoring*. Minneapolis: University of Minnesota Press.

Cohen, M. L. (1996). The derailment of railway spine: A timely lesson for post-traumatic fibromyalgia syndrome. *Pain Reviews*, *3*, 181–202.

Delis, D. C., Kramer, J. H., Kaplan, E., & Ober, B. A. (2000). *California Verbal Learning Test–2nd ed.* San Antonio, TX: The Psychological Corporation.

Etherton, J. L., Bianchini, K. J., Greve, K. W., & Heinly, M. T. (2005). Sensitivity and specificity of reliable digit span in malingered pain-related disability. *Assessment*, *12*(2), 130–36.

Frederick, R. (1997). *The Validity Indicator Profile manual*. Minneapolis: NCS Pearson.

Gervais, R. (2005, April). *Development of an empirically derived response bias scale for the MMPI–2*. Paper presented at the Annual MMPI–2 Symposium and Workshops, Ft. Lauderdale, FL, USA.

Gervais, R. O., Ben-Porath, Y. S., Wygant, D. B., & Green, P. (2007). Development and validation of a Response Bias Scale for the MMPI–2. *Assessment*, *14*(2), 196–208.

Gough, H. G. (1950). The F minus K dissimulation index for the MMPI. *Journal of Consulting Psychology*, *14*, 408–413.

Gough, H. G. (1954). Some common misconceptions about neuroticism. *Journal of Consulting Psychology*, *18*, 287–292.

Greene, P. (1995). Assessment of malingering and defensiveness by multiscale personality inventories. In R. Rogers (Ed.) *Clinical Assessment of Malingering and Deception–2nd ed.* (pp. 169–206). New York: Guilford Press.

Greiffenstein, M. F., & Baker, W. J. (2001). Comparison of premorbid and postinjury MMPI–2 profiles in late postconcussion claimants. *The Clinical Neuropsychologist*, *15*(2), 162–170.

Greiffenstein, M. F., & Baker, W. J. (2006). Miller was (mostly) right: Head injury severity inversely related to simulation. *Legal and Criminological Psychology*, *11*, 131–145.

Greiffenstein, M. F., Baker, W. J., & Gola, T. (1994). Validation of malingered amnesia measures with a large clinical sample. *Psychological Assessment*, 6, 218–224.

Greve, K. W., Bianchini, K. J., Mathias, C. W., Houston, R. J., & Crouch J. A. (2003). Detecting malingered performance on the Wechsler Adult Intelligence Scale: Validation of Mittenberg's approach in traumatic brain injury. *Archives of Clinical Neuropsychology*, 18(3), 245–260.

Guilmette, T. J., Whelihan, W., Sparadeo, F. R., & Buongiorno, G. (1994). Detecting simulated memory impairment: Comparison of the Rey 15-item Test and the Hiscock Forced-Choice Procedure. *Clinical Neuropsychologist*, 8, 283–294.

Haines, M. E., & Norris, M. P. (1995). Detecting the malingering of cognitive deficits: An update. *Neuropsychology Review*, 5, 125–148.

Hartshorne, H., & May, M. A. (1928). *Studies in deceit*. New York: Macmillan.

Hathaway, S. R., & McKinley, J. C. (1943). *The Minnesota Multiphasic Personality Inventory*. Minneapolis, MN: University of Minnesota Press.

Heaton, R. K., Smith, H. H. Jr., Lehman, R. A., & Vogt, A. J. (1978). Prospects for faking believable deficits on neuropsychological testing. *Journal of Consulting and Clinical Psychology*, 46, 892–900.

Insurance Research Council (1999). One in three Americans say it's acceptable to inflate insurance claims, but public acceptance of insurance fraud is declining. Retrieved February 2007 from http://www.ircweb.org/news/200307242.htm

Iverson, G. L., & Tulsky, D. S. (2003). Detecting malingering on the WAIS–III: Unusual digit span performance patterns in the normal population and in clinical groups. *Archives of Clinical Neuropsychology*, 18, 1–9.

Jones, A. B., & Llewellyn, L. J. (1917). *Malingering or the simulation of disease*. London: Heinemann.

Labor Research Association (1998). Workers compensation fraud: The real story. Retrieved from http://www.laborresearch.org/ind_temps/work_comp_fraud._rpt.html

Lande, R. G. (2005). Disability syndrome. *Journal of Psychiatry and Law*, 33, 491–506.

Larrabee, G. J. (2003). Detection of malingering using atypical performance patterns on neuropsychological tests. *The Clinical Neuropsychologist*, 17, 410–425.

Larson, J., Haney, G. W., & Keeler, L. (1932). *Lying and its detection: A study of deception and deception tests*. Chicago: University of Chicago Press.

Lees-Haley, P. R., English, L. T., & Glenn, W. J. (1991). A fake bad scale on the MMPI–2 for personal injury claimants. *Psychological Reports*, 68, 203–210.

Meehl, P. E., & Hathaway, S. R. (1946). The K factor as a suppressor variable in the MMPI. *Journal of Applied Psychology*, 30, 525–564.

Milanovich, J. R., Axelrod, B. N., & Millis, S. R. (1996). Validation of the Simulation Index-Revised with a mixed clinical population. *Archives of Clinical Neuropsychology*, 11, 53–59.

Miller, H. (1961). Accident neurosis. *British Medical Journal*, 5231, 992–998.

Miller, H., & Carlidge, N. (1972). Simulation and malingering after injuries to the brain and spinal cord. *Lancet*, 1, 580–585.

Mills, M. J., & Lipian, M. S. (2005). Malingering. In B. J. Sadock & V. A. Sadock (Eds.). *Kaplan and Sadock's Comprehensive textbook of psychiatry*, 8th ed. Philadelphia: Lippincott Williams & Wilkins.

Mittenberg, W., Azrin, R., Millsaps, C., & Heilbronner, R. (1993). Identification of malingered head injury on the Wechsler Memory Scale-Revised. *Psychological Assessment*, 5, 34–40.

Mittenberg, W., Patton, C., Canyock, E. M., & Condit, D. C. (2002). Base rates of malingering and symptom exaggeration. *Journal of Clinical and Experimental Neuropsychology*, 24, 1094–1102.

Mittenberg, W., Theroux, S., Aguila-Puentes, G., Bianchini, K., Greve, K., & Rayls, K. (2001). Identification of malingered head injury on the Wechsler adult intelligence scale–3rd edition. *The Clinical Neuropsychologist*, 15(4), 440–445.

Mittenberg. W., Theroux-Fichera, S., Zielinski, R. F., & Heilbronner, R. L. (1995). Identification of malingered head injury of the Wechsler Adult Intelligence Scale–Revised. *Professional Psychology: Research and Practice*, 26, 491–498.

Nelson, N. W., Sweet, J. J., Berry, D. T. R., Bryant, F. B., & Granacher, R. P. (2007). Response validity in forensic neuropsychology: Exploratory factor analytic evidence of distinct cognitive and psychological constructs. *Journal of the International Neuropsychological Society*, 13, 440–449.

Nelson, N. W., Sweet, J. J., & Demakis, G. J. (2006). Meta-analysis of the MMPI–2 Fake Bad Scale: Utility in forensic practice. *The Clinical Neuropsychologist*, 20, 39–58.

Nelson, N. W., Sweet, J. J., & Heilbronner, R. L. (2007). Examination of the new MMPI–2 Response Bias Scale (Gervais): relationship with MMPI–2 validity scales. *Journal of Clinical and Experimental Neuropsychology*, *29*(1), 67–72.

Orne, M. T. (1962). On the social psychology of the psychological experiment: With particular reference to demand characteristics and their implications. *American Psychologist,* *17*, 776–783.

Paniak, C., Reynolds, S., Toller-Lobe, G., Melnyk, A., Nagy, J., & Schmidt, D. (2002). A longitudinal study of the relationship between financial compensation and symptoms after treated mild traumatic brain injury. *Journal of Clinical and Experimental Neuropsychology*, *24*(2), 187–193.

Pankratz, L., Fausti, A., & Peed, S. (1975). A forced-choice technique to evaluate deafness in the hysterical or malingering patient. *Journal of Consulting and Clinical Psychology*, *43*(3), 421–422.

Pliskin, N. H., Capelli-Schellpfeffer, M., Law, R. T., Malina, A. C., Kelley, K. M., & Lee, R. C. (1998). Neuropsychological symptom presentation after electrical injury. *Journal of Trauma*, *44*(4), 709–715.

Rawling, P., & Brooks, N. (1990). Simulation index: A method for detecting factitious errors on the WAIS–R and WMS. *Neuropsychology*, *4*, 223–228.

Rey, A. (1941). Psychological examination of traumatic encephalopathy. *Archives de Psychologie*, *28*, 286–340 (sections translated by Corwin, J. & Bylsma, F. W. *The Clinical Neuropsychologist*, *7*, 4–9).

Rogers, R. (1997). *Clinical assessment of malingering and deception*. New York: Guilford Press.

Rogers, R., & Payne, J. W. (2006). Damages and rewards: assessment of malingered disorders in compensation cases. *Behavioral Sciences and the Law*, *24*(5), 645–58.

Root, J. C., Robbins, R. N., Chang, L., & van Gorp, W. (2006). Detection of inadequate effort on the California Verbal Learning Test: Forced choice recognition and critical item analysis. *Journal of the International Neuropsychological Society*, *12*, 688–696.

Rosenfeld, B., Sands, S., & van Gorp, W. (2000). Have we forgotten the base rate problem? Methodological issues in the detection of distortion. *Archives of Clinical Neuropsychology*, *15*, 349–359.

Ruiz, M. A., Drake, E. B., Glass, A., Marcotte, D., & van Gorp, W. G. (2002), Trying to beat the system: Misuse of the internet to assist in avoiding the detection of psychological symptom dissimulation. *Professional Psychology: Research and Practice*, *33*, 294–299.

Schretlen, D., Brandt, J., Krafft, L., & van Gorp, W. G. (1991). Some caveats in using the Rey 15-item memory test to detect malingered amnesia. *Psychological Assessment: A Journal of Consulting and Clinical Psychology*, *3*, 667–672.

Slick, D. J., Sherman, E. M. S., & Iverson, G. L. (1999). Diagnostic criteria for malingered neurocognitive dysfunction: Proposed standards for clinical practice and research. *The Clinical Neuropsychologist*, *13*, 545–561.

Sweet, J. (1999). Malingering: Differential diagnosis. In J. Sweet (Ed.), *Forensic neuropsychology: Fundamentals and practice*. Lisse, Netherlands: Swets & Zeitlinger.

van Gorp, W. G., Humphrey, L. A., Kalechstein, A., Brumm, V. L., McMullen, W. G., Stoddard, M., & Pachana, N. A. (1999). How well do standard neuropsychological tests identify malingering? A preliminary analysis. *Journal of Clinical and Experimental Neuropsychology*, *21*(2), 245–250.

Walsh, K. W. (1985). *Understanding brain damage: A primer of neuropsychological evaluation*. Edinburgh: Churchill Livingstone.

Youngjohn, J. R., Burrows, L., & Erdal, K. (1995). Brain damage or compensation neurosis? The controversial post-concussion syndrome. *Clinical Neuropsychologist*, *9*, 112–123.

Youngjohn, J. R., Lees-Haley, P. R., & Binder, L. M. (1999). Comment: Warning malingerers produces more sophisticated malingering. *Archives of Clinical Neuropsychology*, *12*(3), 511–515.

What clinicians really need to know about symptom exaggeration, insufficient effort, and malingering: Statistical and measurement matters

3

Scott R. Millis

Detection is, or ought to be, an exact science, and should be treated in the same cold and unemotional manner. You have attempted to tinge it with romanticism, which produces much the same effect as if you worked a love-story or an elopement into the fifth proposition of Euclid.
Sir Arthur Conan Doyle (1859–1930)
The Sign of Four, 1890

JUDGMENT UNDER UNCERTAINTY

Contrary to popular mythology, neuropsychologists do more than administer tests. When evaluating patients, neuropsychologists rarely have at their disposal a single "gold standard" test that clinches the diagnosis—whether it is brain dysfunction or malingering. In addition to the neuropsychological test results, the clinician is inundated with a plethora of information (e.g., the patient's history, physical examination findings, laboratory results, and neuroimaging data). The dilemma is what to do with all of these data. Clinical judgment figures keenly in managing and interpreting this information as part of the diagnostic process. But how accurate are the clinical judgments of most neuropsychologists? This chapter will not attempt to answer this question directly, but will focus instead on: (1) discussing the limitations of clinical judgment, (2) the absolute need to use explicit quantitative methods in the diagnostic process, and (3) potential remedies and their limitations.

Certain assumptions are necessary. First, assessment of effort should be part of the overall diagnostic process and should involve more than giving a "malingering test." Second, the consequences of erroneously labeling someone as "brain damaged" can be as egregious as labeling them as malingering. Third, the assessment of effort should be part of every neuropsychological examination, whether litigation or external incentive are present or not. The meaning of insufficient or suboptimal effort will differ across diagnostic groups but, nonetheless, potentially impacts the validity of the cognitive data. The findings from a study of the performance of persons with schizophrenia on an effort test, the Word Memory Test (WMT), are particularly sobering: 72% failed the WMT (Gorissen, Sanz, & Schmand, 2005). Additional studies will be needed to better understand the implications of this finding, but it raises the issue of whether the entire literature on cognitive deficits in schizophrenia will need to be reconsidered. Fourth, whether we are dealing with an effort test or standard neuropsychological test, the roles of test sensitivity, specificity, and disorder prevalence on diagnostic accuracy are the same.

FLIES IN THE OINTMENT

It is difficult to imagine not using clinical judgment in making diagnoses. Humans often make inferences about the presence of a disorder in the context of limited information and time—and will depend on heuristics, i.e., mental shortcuts. Gigerenzer and Goldstein (1996) have shown how a certain family of heuristics, based on one-reason decision making, can be fast and accurate. Yet, human reasoning can be hampered by heuristics and biases. Elstein (1999) states, "Heuristics are mental shortcuts commonly used in decision making that can lead to faulty reasoning or conclusions; biases are faulty beliefs that affect decision making" (p. 791). Common errors that clinicians make include:

- *Overreliance on salient sata*. Clinicians tend to overestimate the prevalence of salient or unusual conditions (Wedding & Faust, 1989). The frequency of rare diagnostic conditions is more likely to be overestimated than common or routine disorders.
- *Representativeness*. When evaluating a new patient, clinicians will generally compare the patient's symptom pattern with those of several other diagnostic categories in an attempt to find the best fit (Elstein & Schwartz, 2002). However, the various disorders may have widely differing prevalence rates. This "base-rate neglect" often leads to diagnostic errors (Elstein, 1999).
- *Failure to account for covariation*. Left to their own devices, it is difficult for clinicians to accurately determine the nature of the relationship among variables, including various tests, symptoms, and disorders (Wedding & Faust, 1989). For example, headaches and forgetfulness may be associated with a mild head injury but these symptoms are also very common in the general population. Put another way, clinicians may fail to appreciate the difference between the symptoms that are highly sensitive to a wide variety of conditions and symptoms that are highly specific to a single disorder.
- *Conservatism*. Clinicians tend to evaluate data in a sequential fashion but generally fail to revise their diagnostic probabilities accordingly. This bias has been termed "conservatism" (Edwards, 1968). Complicating matters even further are various degrees of dependency or covariation among tests and other diagnostic indicators. The practical impact of this covariation is that some tests will provide minimal incremental diagnostic evidence because of high correlations with other indicators.
- *Confirmatory bias*. Clinicians may unwittingly seek information that confirms a favored diagnosis while ignoring data that are supportive of competing diagnoses. This bias is also known as "pseudodiagnosticity" (Kern & Doherty, 1982).
- *Anchoring and adjustment*. Clinicians have different initial diagnostic anchors, starting points, or "prior probabilities." For example, some clinicians might estimate the prevalence of malingering in litigated mild head injury cases to be 75% while others would estimate it to be 5%. Even when given the same data, the final or "posterior probabilities" might be quite discrepant owing to the power of the initial anchor (Tversky & Kahneman, 1974).

- *Processing configural data.* Clinicians have difficulty with optimally weighting and combining diagnostic information and rely, instead, on simplified decision strategies that may reject or misuse relevant information (Slovic & Lichtenstein, 1971).

Potential remedies

Meehl (1993) argued that, "It is absurd, as well as arrogant, to pretend that acquiring a PhD somehow immunizes me from errors of sampling, perception, recording, retention, retrieval, and inference to which the human mind is suspect" (p. 728). To that end, there are a number of remedial steps that clinicians can take.

- *"A man's gotta know his limits."* It is essential that the clinician develop more than a passing familiarity of the literature regarding limitations of human reasoning and clinical judgment. In addition to the references already cited, the reader is also referred to Plous (1993).
- *List alternative diagnoses* (Garb & Lutz, 2001; Garb & Schramke, 1996).
- *List disconfirmatory data for favored diagnosis* (Garb & Lutz, 2001; Garb & Schramke, 1996).
- *Make use of base-rate or prevalence information.* In a later section of this chapter, readers will be shown how to make explicit use of base-rate data for diagnostic decision making. At this juncture, clinicians are cautioned about becoming enamored with diagnosing esoteric or rare disorders (i.e., "When you hear hoof beats, think horses, not zebras"). There are many sources on which to base prevalence estimates for disorders (e.g., clinical experience, regional or national prevalence statistics, practice databases, studies devoted specifically to determining prevalence rates) and studies in which diagnostic tests were developed to detect specific disorders (Straus, Richardson, Glasziou, & Haynes, 2005).
- *Be aware of statistical artifact.* No test is without measurement error. Moreover, there tends to be a great deal of neuropsychological variability even among persons without neurological disorders. For example, in a normative database developed by Heaton and associates (2004), only 13.2% of the normal adult sample had *no* impaired neuropsychological test scores. The group median was three abnormal scores (of a possible 25). It is often an unchallenged assumption that it is not only reasonable but also necessary to integrate *all* test data into an orderly and meaningful pattern (Faust, 2003). This assumption is not only erroneous but may also present an impossible task in the face of measurement error. As Faust (2003) notes:

  > The great emphasis on synthetic and integrative thinking may lead us to miss instances in which it is as, or more, helpful to decompose decision tasks into component parts . . . Holistic pattern matching is sometimes an excellent strategy, with facial recognition providing a good example. At other times, contrasting strategies work as well or better.
  >
  > (p. 438)

- *When available, use statistical decision rules.* In a subsequent section of this chapter, readers will be shown how to use statistically-derived classification formulas to assist in diagnostic decision making. Meehl (1954) was among the first to alert psychologists to the superiority of statistical prediction compared to clinical judgment. Little has changed in this regard over the last 46 years. In a meta-analysis of 136 studies on health and human behavior, Grove, Zald, Lebow, Snitz, and Nelson (2000) found that statistical prediction techniques were about 10% more accurate than clinical predictions. Statistical prediction significantly outperformed clinical prediction in 33% to 47% of the studies; clinical prediction was more accurate in 6% to 16% of the cases. The superiority of statistical prediction was consistent regardless of type of judgment or judge, judges' amount of experience, or type of data.
- *When available, use multivariable statistical decision rules.* As will be discussed in a later section of this chapter, statistically-derived multivariable classification formulas can assist the clinician

to empirically identify tests that are the most diagnostically efficacious while finding optimal weighting and combination algorithms for those tests.

USING TESTS TO REFINE DIAGNOSTIC HYPOTHESES

Neuropsychologists will use patient history, physical examination findings, laboratory results, neuroimaging data, and psychosocial variables to develop diagnostic hypotheses. Nonetheless, significant uncertainty will likely remain. Standard neuropsychological tests along with symptom validity or "effort" measures can be used to refine diagnostic hypotheses. As Kassirer and Kopelman (1991) observe:

> Testing is used in the process of hypothesis refinement to help formulate a working diagnostic hypothesis, defined previously as one that is sufficiently unambiguous to set the stage for making decisions about further invasive testing, treatment, or judgments about prognosis.
>
> (p. 17)

However, not all tests are created equal. First, basic psychometric qualities such as reliability and unidimensionality may be quite variable, or even unknown, across tests. Second, a test's diagnostic sensitivity and specificity may be variable across disorders. It is incumbent upon neuropsychologists to know how their standard tests *operate* diagnostically in the disorders they commonly encounter. An ongoing critical review of studies of diagnostic accuracy will assist clinicians in gaining that knowledge. Common methodological flaws in diagnostic studies include:

- *Spectrum bias.* For example, this bias can occur when only severely cognitively impaired patients are included in the sample. When compared to a normal sample, virtually any cognitive measure will be discriminating.
- *Selection bias.* Patients are selected in a manner that will systematically influence the outcome of the study. For example, selection bias is present in mild head injury studies when patients are selected based on the subjective symptom endorsement.
- *A failure to replicate on an independent sample.*

Potential remedies

- *Use the Standards for Reporting of Diagnostic Accuracy (STARD) guidelines.* There are many additional threats to the internal and external validity of studies dealing with the diagnostic accuracy of tests. In 1999, the Cochrane Diagnostic and Screening Test Methods Working Group discussed the poor quality and substandard reporting of many diagnostic test evaluations (Bossuyt et al., 2003). The Working Group then developed the STARD initiative. The STARD checklist for the reporting of studies of diagnostic accuracy appears in Table 3.1. Neuropsychologists can easily apply the STARD guidelines to evaluate diagnostic studies of standard neuropsychological and effort measures.
- *Defining the reference standard.* The reference standard, according to STARD, is "the best available method for establishing the presence or absence of the condition of interest. The reference standard can be a single method, or a combination of methods, to establish the presence of the target condition" (Bossuyt et al., 2003, p. 575). Defining the reference sample in diagnostic studies of malingering tests can be challenging because there is no universally accepted "gold standard" for malingering. Persons engaged in malingering during litigation

TABLE 3.1   Standards for Reporting of Diagnostic Accuracy (STARD) Checklist for reporting of studies of diagnostic accuracy. First Official Version, January 2003

SECTION AND TOPIC	ITEM	
Title, Abstract & Keywords	1	Identify the article as a study of diagnostic accuracy (recommend MeSH heading "sensitivity and specificity").
Introduction	2	State the research questions or study aims, such as estimating diagnostic accuracy or comparing accuracy between tests or across participant groups.
Methods *Participants*	3	Describe the study population: the inclusion and exclusion criteria, setting and location where the data were collected.
	4	Describe participant recruitment: Was recruitment based on presenting symptoms, results from previous tests, or the fact that the participants had received the index tests or the reference standard?
	5	Describe participant sampling: Was the study population a consecutive series of patients defined by selection criteria in items 3 and 4? If not, specify how patients were further selected.
	6	Describe data collection: Was data collection planned before the index test and reference standards were performed (prospective study) or after (retrospective study)?
Test methods	7	Describe the reference standard and its rationale
	8	Describe technical specifications of material and methods involved including how and when measurements were taken, and/or cite references for index tests and reference standard, or both.
	9	Describe definition of and rationale for the units, cutoffs, or categories of the results of the index tests and the reference standard.
	10	Describe the number, training, and expertise of the persons executing and reading the index test and the reference standard.
	11	Were the readers of the index tests and reference standard blind (masked) to the results of the other test? Describe any other clinical information available to the readers.
Statistical methods	12	Describe methods for calculating measures of diagnostic accuracy or making comparisons, and the statistical methods used to quantify uncertainty (e.g., 95% confidence intervals).
	13	Describe methods for calculating test reproducibility, if done.
Results *Participants*	14	Report when study was done, including beginning and ending dates of recruitment.
	15	Report clinical and demographic characteristics of the study population (e.g., age, sex, spectrum of presenting symptoms, comorbidity, current treatments, and recruitment center).
	16	Report how many participants satisfying the criteria for inclusion did or did not undergo the index tests or the reference standard or both; describe why participants failed to receive either test (a flow diagram is strongly recommended).
Test results	17	Report time interval from the index tests to the reference standard, and any treatment administered between.
	18	Report distribution of severity of disease (define criteria) in those with the target condition and other diagnoses in participants without the target condition.
	19	Report a cross-tabulation of the results of the index tests (including indeterminate and missing results) by the results of the reference standard; for continuous results, report the distribution of the test results by the results of the reference standard.

(Continued...)

TABLE 3.1   (Continued)

SECTION AND TOPIC	ITEM	
	20	Report any adverse events from performing the index tests or the reference standard.
Estimates	21	Report estimates of diagnostic accuracy and measures of statistical uncertainty (e.g., 95% confidence intervals)
	22	Report how indeterminate results, missing responses, and outliers of the index tests were handled.
	23	Report estimates of variability of diagnostic accuracy between readers, centers, or subgroups of participants, if done.
	24	Report estimates of test reproducibility, if done.
Discussion	25	Discuss the clinical applicability of the study findings.

generally loathe admitting that they are doing so. In addition, malingering is not associated with a virus or bacteria that can be detected with current laboratory tests, and its neuroimaging correlates are unknown. However, this lack of a diagnostic gold standard is actually rather common in medicine and epidemiology, and not limited to neuropsychology. Joseph, Gyorkos, and Coupal (1995) note, "In fact, one may argue that this is virtually always the situation, since few tests are considered to be 100% accurate" (p. 262). Slick, Sherman, and Iverson (1999) adapted an approach used in defining the reference standard in Alzheimer's disease and applied it to malingering. Recognizing that there are various levels of diagnostic certainty, they proposed separate criteria for *definite, probable*, and *possible* malingered neurocognitive disorder. Multiple sources and types of data are used in the criteria: (A) presence of a substantial external incentive, (B) evidence from neuropsychological testing, (C) evidence from self-report, and (D) behaviors meeting necessary criteria from groups B or C that are not fully accounted for by psychiatric, neurological, or developmental factors. These criteria can be of great assistance to investigators in explicitly defining the reference standard for diagnostic studies of effort tests. However, whether investigators use the Slick et al. (1999) criteria, readers are encouraged to carefully examine how the reference standard was defined in each study.

PUTTING A TEST TO WORK

Whether it is detecting brain dysfunction or malingering, the fundamental diagnostic question that every clinician wants to answer is, "Given a positive test result or score, what is the probability that the patient has the disorder or condition?" Unfortunately, this is a deceptively complicated question. One is tempted to conclude that there is a high probability that the examinee has a disorder (e.g., brain dysfunction or malingering) if she has a positive test result. Unfortunately, such reasoning is often erroneous. The clinician needs to combine the positive test result with several other pieces of information in order to answer this question, as will be explained in the next subsection. This is best accomplished through the use of explicit quantitative algorithms.

Potential remedies

For the sake of simplicity, we will focus on working with a single test result, while acknowledging that neuropsychologists deal with dozens of test results. Handling multiple test results will be addressed in the next section. To put a positive test result into proper context, we need to consider several indices of diagnostic accuracy, e.g., sensitivity and specificity, likelihood ratios, and the area under a receiver operating characteristic (ROC) curve. Let's begin with a simple table describing the relationship between a diagnostic test (e.g., the mythical Millis Effort Test) and a diagnosis (e.g., malingered neurocognitive disorder based on the Slick et al. criteria). The results for the 340 participants enrolled in this hypothetical study are shown in Table 3.2. From these results, one can generate measures of accuracy of the Millis Effort Test in detecting malingering.

1. Sensitivity is the proportion of persons in the malingering group who obtain a positive score on the effort test (i.e., fail the test). That calculation goes:

   a/ (a + c) = 200/216 = 0.93, or 93%

2. Specificity is the proportion of persons in the traumatic brain injury group who obtain a negative score on the effort test (e.g., pass the effort test). That calculation goes:

   d/ (b + d) = 100/124 = 0.81, or 81%

It should be pointed out that positive predictive value (PPV or posterior probability) and prevalence were not calculated from data in the table because this was a case-control study. That is, "cases" were gathered, namely, patients meeting the Slick et al. criteria for malingered neurocognitive disorder. Controls with unequivocal evidence of traumatic brain injury were then matched to cases. If PPV is to be accurately estimated from a case-control study, the prevalence of the disorder of interest must be a reasonable estimate in the population. In this contrived example, prevalence of malingering was 64%, which may or may not be an accurate reflection of malingering prevalence in forensic neuropsychology practice, but probably not for an inpatient rehabilitation hospital setting. For that reason, I strongly discourage the presentation of a single estimate of PPV, but recommend that investigators present a range of PPVs based on different prevalence rates.

TABLE 3.2   Diagnostic efficiency statistics for hypothetical test

			MALINGERED NEUROCOGNITIVE DISORDER		
			PRESENT	ABSENT	
Diagnostic Test Result (Effort Test)	Positive		0.93 **200** a	0.19 **24** b	**224** a+b
	Negative		c **16** 0.07	d **100** 0.81	c+d **116**
			a+c **216**	b+d **124**	a+b+c+d **340**

[TP/(TP + FN)]	Sensitivity	93%
[TN/(TN + FP)]	Specificity	81%
[Sensitivity/(1 − Specificity)]	Likelihood Ratio +	4.8
[(1 − Sensitivity)/Specificity]	Likelihood Ratio −	0.1

Next, we need to combine the sensitivity and specificity estimates into a single summary index. This can be done with the likelihood ratio (Straus et al., 2005):

LR = Sensitivity / (1 – Specificity)

Every test result has its own likelihood ratio. The likelihood ratio is the percentage of people with the disorder who have a positive test (i.e., true positives) divided by the percentage of people without the disorder who have a positive test result (i.e., false positives). In other words, it tells us how many times more (or less) likely persons with the disorder are to have a positive test result than persons without the disorder. A likelihood ratio greater than 1 indicates that the test result is associated with the presence of the disorder of interest. A likelihood ratio of less than 1 is associated with the absence of the disorder (Straus et al., 2005).

The likelihood ratio is then multiplied by the pre-test odds (i.e., base-rate odds) to obtain the post-test odds and converted algebraically back to a probability, which provides the answer to our original question, i.e., "Given a positive test result or score, what is the probability that the patient has the disorder or condition?" (Figure 3.1).

As an example, let's suppose that a 30-year-old man presents six months status post-traumatic brain injury with an initial Glasgow Coma Scale score of 5 and cranial CT within 48 hours of injury showing midline shift of 5.5 mm. When evaluated, the patient was not involved in litigation, but was receiving disability insurance coverage through his employer. Given this history, it would not be surprising if this patient continued to show evidence of cognitive sequelae associated with his injury. Hence, the prior probability (or base rate) of impaired performance on neuropsychological measures would be high (e.g., 75%).

1. To convert a probability to pre-test odds, the calculation goes,

    Odds = Probability / (1 – Probability) = 0.75 / (1 – 0.75) = 3.0

The patient was given the Halstead-Reitan Battery and obtained an Average Impairment Rating (AIR) T score of 39, based on the revised Heaton norms (Heaton et al., 2004). The AIR has a sensitivity of 0.77 and a specificity of 0.86, when using a T-score cutoff of less than 40 to define impairment, so we can calculate a likelihood ratio as follows:

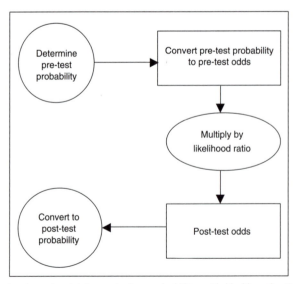

FIG. 3.1 Flowchart showing how to obtain posterior probability with likelihood ratio and base rate.

2. LR = Sensitivity / (1 – Specificity) = 0.77 / (1 – 0.86) = 5.5
3. Combining the pre-test odds with the LR from the AIR, the post-test odds, the calculation goes,

> Post-test odds = (3.0)(5.5) = 16.5

4. Converting post-test odds to a post-test probability, the calculation goes,

> Probability = Odds / (1 + Odds) = 16.5 / (1 + 16.5) = 0.94, or 94%

In other words, there is strong support that this patient is showing evidence of cognitive impairment. Likelihood ratios from 2 to 5 yield small increases in the post-test probability, from 5 to 10 moderate increases, and above 10 large increases (Grimes & Schulz, 2005). A nomogram (Figure 3.2) can facilitate clinical use of likelihood ratios by simplifying the calculation of the post-test probabilities. A ruler is placed on the estimated pre-test probability of the disorder (left column) and aligned with the test's likelihood ratio (middle column); the post-test probability (right column) can then be read from this line. For example, assume that the pre-test probability (or base rate) of the disorder is 10% and that a positive test result has a likelihood ratio of 10. Placing a ruler on a pre-test probability of 10 and intercepting the likelihood ratio column at 10 yields a post-test probability of about 50%, which is a relatively large shift in diagnostic probability.

Numerous issues arise when using this approach to weigh diagnostic evidence:

1. Use of likelihood ratios to refine clinical judgment is based on the assumption that reasonably accurate estimates of prior probabilities of the target disorder are available. It can be argued

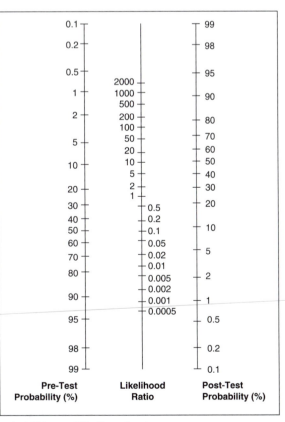

FIG. 3.2 Nomogram for probabilities and likelihood ratios.

that any system of diagnosis, whether explicitly quantitative or not, makes use of prevalence rates, whether or not the clinician realizes it. The accuracy of all diagnostic decisions depends on the estimates or assumptions that one makes about prevalence rates. When clinicians do not explicitly consider a disorder's prior probability, they implicitly assume that the prevalence is 50%. This is often not the case. Consequently, the diagnostic value of the test result may be inflated. This quantitative system advocated in this chapter simply forces the clinician to be explicit about the assumptions underlying the decision-making process.

2. The illustrative example used in this section involved a single cutoff score for didactic purposes. *However, neuropsychologists are encouraged not to rely on a single, fixed diagnostic cutoff score for any test.* The diagnostic decision-making process occurs in different contexts. Hence, the relative costs of false-positive and false-negative errors will not be constant across situations. Raising or lowering a test's cutoff score will increase or decrease the test's sensitivity and specificity in an inverse fashion. In other words, when sensitivity is increased, specificity decreases. To assist clinicians in this decision-making process, journal editors and test publishers are strongly encouraged to provide a broad range of cutoff scores with their likelihood ratios.

3. Related to the preceding point, diagnosis can be refined by considering the fact that high sensitivity and high specificity serve different purposes in the diagnostic process. When a test cutoff score has a *very high sensitivity*, a *negative test result rules out* the diagnosis. Conversely, when a test cutoff has *a very high specificity, a positive test result rules in* the diagnosis. In other words: **SnOut** (when a test has high **Sen**sitivity, a **N**egative result rules **OUT** the disorder) and **SpPin** (when a test has high **Sp**ecificity, a **P**ositive result rules **IN** the disorder) (Straus et al., 2005). When clinicians have access to a full range of cutoff scores and associated sensitivities and specificities for diagnostic tests, this type of sensitivity analysis is facilitated.

4. Although extremely useful in diagnostic decision making, the likelihood ratio does have limitations when used as a single measure of diagnostic accuracy. As its name suggests, it is a ratio of two random variables and, thus, it is difficult to estimate its standard error and sampling distribution (Zhou, Obuchowski, & McClish, 2002). This limitation poses a difficulty particularly when we want to compare two or more diagnostic tests statistically, i.e., to determine whether one test is superior to the other. The likelihood ratio is still important in defining the optimal decision thresholds but needs to be supplemented. A useful summary statistic in this regard is the area under the receiver operating characteristic (ROC) curve, or AUC. The ROC curve is a plot of a test's sensitivity (plotted on the y-axis) versus its false-positive rate (i.e., 1 − specificity) plotted on its x-axis. Each point on the graph is generated by a different cutoff score on the test. Each point can be connected, a curve can be generated, and the area of the curve can be estimated parametrically (via maximum likelihood estimation) or nonparametrically (via the trapezoidal rule). Data from Millis and Volinsky (2001) were used to generate an ROC curve to evaluate Recognition Hits from the California Verbal Learning Test (CVLT) to detect suboptimal effort (Figure 3.3). All ROC curve analyses in this chapter were calculated using Stata Release 9 (StataCorp, 2005).

5. *Interpreting AUC.* The ROC curve area has several interpretations (Zhou et al., 2002): (1) the average value of sensitivity for all possible values of specificity, (2) the average value of specificity for all possible values of sensitivity, and (3) the probability that a randomly selected patient with the disorder has a test result indicating greater suspicion than that of a randomly selected patient without the disorder. For example, Figure 3.3 indicates that a randomly selected individual from the litigation group had a lower Recognition Hits score than that from a randomly chosen person from the traumatic brain injury (TBI) group 87% of the time. CVLT Recognition Hits provides excellent discrimination in this sample (i.e., differentiating litigants from persons with TBI). Hosmer and Lemeshow (2000) offer some guidelines for interpreting the magnitude of AUC:

a.   AUC = 0.50: No discrimination
b.   0.70 – 0.80: Acceptable discrimination
c.   0.80 – 0.90: Excellent discrimination
d.   ⩾0.90: Outstanding discrimination

6.   *Comparing ROC curves.* Returning again to the data from Millis et al. (2001), ROC curves from Recognition Hits and Long Delay Free Recall (LDFR) were fitted and compared (Figure 3.4).

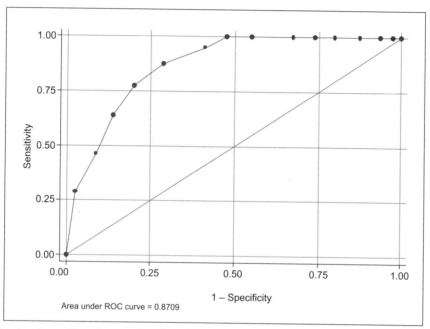

FIG. 3.3   Receiver Operating Characteristic (ROC) curve for CVLT Recognition Hits.

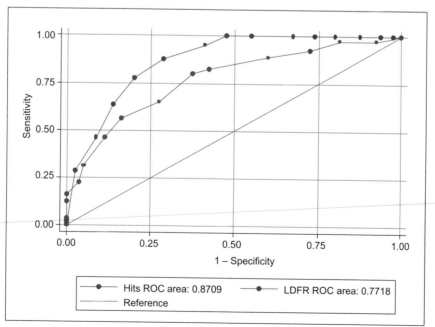

FIG. 3.4   Comparison of ROC curves for Recognition Hits and Long Delay Free Recall.

AUCs were 0.87 for Hits and 0.77 for LDFR. The difference between the curves was statistically significant, χ^2 (1) = 7.54, p = 0.006, which suggested that Recognition Hits was superior to LDFR in detecting suboptimal effort.

7. Journal editors and test publishers are encouraged to provide ROC curve statistics along with sensitivity, specificity, and LR parameter estimates.

PUTTING MANY TESTS TO WORK

As discussed earlier in this chapter, neuropsychologists typically deal with dozens of test scores. We now consider the multivariable context of combining the results from multiple effort measures. The same statistical and measurement issues apply to combining multiple standard neuropsychological tests, but additional complications are introduced that require a major digression. The neuro-psychologist faces a number of difficult questions with respect to dealing with results from multiple effort measures. Are they redundant or does each test provide incrementally useful information? Should the clinician be more confident in diagnosing malingered neurocognitive disorder if the examinee fails five effort measures rather than one? Should all effort measures be given equal weighting?

Potential remedies when relying on multiple measures

*   *Statistical independence*. If the tests are statistically independent, one could simply use the first test's posterior probability for the next test's prior probability and then use it in combination with the second test's likelihood ratio to obtain its posterior probability, and so on. However, it is highly unlikely that effort tests are uncorrelated with each other and, thus, the independence rule cannot be used to combine test results.
*   *Discriminant function analysis*. Multivariable composites to differentiate groups can be derived if samples of participants have been given the same set of tests. Discriminant function analysis (DFA) has been used for decades in the social sciences to derive optimal combinations of variables to differentiate groups. However, DFA has strong statistical assumptions that are rarely met in clinical samples (e.g., multivariate normality and homogeneous variance-covariance matrices). In addition, interpreting the DFA can be difficult because there is no consensus regarding whether one should use the discriminant weights (standardized coefficients) or dis-criminant loadings (structure correlations). Moreover, DFA has no inferential tests for the individual predictor variables to determine which are statistically reliable in differentiating the groups. Currently, there is little justification for using DFA to derive multivariable composites in the two-group situation. Logistic regression is superior.
*   *Logistic regression*. Logistic regression does not have the restrictive assumptions of DFA and is the standard method of choice in developing multivariable composites to differentiate two groups. Interpretation of the relative importance of individual predictor variables is straight-forward in logistic regression. The logistic regression function can also be used to calculate the probability that an individual belongs to one of the groups in the following manner. Analogous to ordinary least squares (OLS) multiple regression for continuous dependent variables, coef-ficients are derived for each predictor variable (or covariate) in logistic regression. Rather than using OLS to fit the model and derive the coefficients, logistic regression uses the method of maximum likelihood to iteratively fit the model. Once a model is derived, a linear composite known as the *logit* (also known as the *logged odds* or *linear predictor*) is calculated by multiplying each predictor variable's raw score by its respective coefficient (e.g., $\beta_1 x_1 + \beta_2 x_1$) and a constant

is added. The logit is exponentiated in the following manner to yield the probability that an individual belongs to one of two groups, based on the raw scores entered into this formula, where e is the mathematical constant e and is the base of the natural logarithm. Its value to the sixth decimal digit is $e = 2.718281$.

$$Probability = \frac{e^{a+\beta_1 x_1+\beta_2 x_2}}{1 + e^{a+\beta_1 x_1+\beta_2 x_2}}$$

Worked example. To illustrate with one predictor model ($\beta = 2.69$ and $\alpha = -14.79$), let's say that an examinee gets a raw score of 5 on the test. The model has been scaled such that higher probabilities are associated with an increased likelihood of malingering. The calculation goes,

$$Probability = \frac{e^{-14.79+(2.69)(5)}}{1 + e^{-14.79+(2.69)(5)}} = \frac{e^{-1.34}}{1 + e^{-1.34}} = \frac{0.2618}{1.2618} = 0.21$$

Discussion of worked example

In this hypothetical case, there is a relatively low probability that this individual was showing poor effort, i.e., probability was 21%. The clinical usefulness of the logistic regression model becomes immediately obvious: it frees us from rigid "all or nothing" thinking, diagnostically speaking. Rather than yielding dichotomous categories of examinee performance, the model produces a range of probabilities. A probability of malingering of 51% may be quite different from a probability of 91%. In addition, clinicians have the option of raising or lowering the probability threshold given the diagnostic context and the relative costs of making false positive versus false negative errors.

•   *Advantages and disadvantages of the multivariable model.* Multivariable effort composites may be more resistant to coaching, especially when based on standard neuropsychological tests. For example, people can be taught to readily identify digit recognition symptom validity tests but may have greater difficulty spotting validity multivariable indicators derived from the California Verbal Learning Test. If malingering is a complex set of behaviors, multivariable composites will likely measure the behaviors more adequately than single tests. In addition to the capacity to produce probability statements, the logistic regression can assist in determining which tests (or variables) produce incremental power in differentiating groups and estimate optimal weights for the tests. The downside is that one needs to have sufficiently large samples to fit the models, generally 10 to 20 persons per variable. In the case of binary logistic regression, this estimate is based on the sample size of the smaller of the two groups—not the total sample (Harrell, 2001). Another challenge is that the statistical technology has advanced far beyond clinical research and data collection. At this time, neuropsychologists have relatively few cross-validated multivariable composites to detect malingering or poor effort, with the exception of those derived from the California Verbal Learning Test (Ashendorf, O'Bryant, & McCaffrey, 2003; Coleman, Rapport, Millis, Ricker, & Farchione, 1998; Demakis, 2004; Millis, Putnam, Adams, & Ricker, 1995; Slick, Iverson, & Green, 2000; Sweet et al., 2000). Much work remains to be done in terms of coordinated multicenter data collection efforts to derive new multivariable effort formulas. The continued proliferation of stand-alone effort tests seems shortsighted. In the meantime, neuropsychologists will need to rely on primarily single tests and indices to assess effort. Although multivariable composites would seem to have advantages over univariate effort measures, it remains an empirical question. That is, it is entirely possible that a single effort measure could be as good or superior to multivariable composites in detecting poor effort.

ADDRESSING THE ULTIMATE QUESTION: CAUSATION

Up to this point, the focus of this chapter has been on the roles of clinical judgment and tests in diagnostic decision making. Following closely on the heels of diagnosis is the question of causation. If neuropsychological impairment is found, what is the likely cause? Although tests and likelihood ratios may be of some assistance, they alone will not be sufficient in answering this question. Sir Austin Bradford Hill proposed a set of criteria (Table 3.3) designed to establish an argument of causation related to toxins, which can be applied to causation more generally (Grimes & Schulz, 2002). Of the criteria, temporal sequence and experimental evidence provide the strongest support for cause-effect relations. However, experimental evidence in the form of randomized controlled trials is rare in the diagnostic arena. On the other hand, data on dose-response relationships, strength of association, and consistency of association are often available and can provide "intermediate" support for causation. For example, there is a dose-response relationship in traumatic brain injury (i.e., the greater the severity, the greater the degree of cognitive impairment; Rohling, Meyers, & Millis, 2003).

TABLE 3.3   Hill criteria for causation

CRITERIA	QUESTION	COMMENT
Temporal Sequence	Did the event, accident, or exposure precede the outcome?	If A is causing B, then A should necessarily occur prior to B. Recall bias may preclude accurate recollection of historical data. Longer intervals make interpretation more difficult. Outcome may be multidetermined.
Strength of the Association	How strong is the effect?	If A causes B, A and B can be shown to be associated with each other. This is a necessary but not sufficient condition for establishing causation.
Coherence with Existing Knowledge	Is the postulated causal relationship consistent with what is already known about the condition or disorder?	A new discovery will not have a track record. Others could have been consistently wrong.
Specificity of Association	Does the event, injury, or exposure result in only one outcome?	Multiple disorders produce the same symptoms. Or a single disorder can produce many symptoms.
Dose-Response Relationship or Biological Gradient	Does a higher exposure result in more of the outcome? Or is increased injury severity associated with greater impairment?	May be difficult to observe in all disorders.
Biological Plausibility	Does the association make neuropsychological, biological, and/or physiological sense?	Assumes that our current scientific model is correct and complete.
Consistency of Association	Is the association consistent with all of the available evidence?	If A causes B, then evidence supporting this relationship will be found consistently.
Analogous Evidence	Is the association similar to others?	If some condition similar to A causes an outcome similar to B, then this is evidence that A causes B.
Experimental Evidence	Has a randomized controlled trial been performed?	It is not always possible to conduct controlled trials.

Specificity is a weak criterion. Certainly, if a specific association can be found, e.g., rabies virus, this does provide support for causality, but a lack of specificity would not argue against causation in other contexts. Biological plausibility is also a weak criterion because our state of knowledge often lags. For example, Pasteur's germ theory was considered to be "ridiculous fiction" by some members in medical academia in the later 1800s (Mayer, 2004). Analogous evidence is often misleading. Because thalidomide can cause birth defects, it has been argued by analogy that Bendectin could also cause birth defects. However, decades of research and litigation found otherwise and led to the landmark *Daubert* ruling regarding the use of scientific evidence in federal courts (Foster & Hiber, 1999).

For illustration, Hill's criteria are applied to the following question, "Can an uncomplicated mild traumatic brain injury (mTBI) cause chronic and disabling neuropsychological impairment?" The majority of studies examining patients within hours or days following mTBI have *consistently* found significant *associations* between the injury event and cognitive difficulties; however the evidence for persistent and disabling impairment is lacking (Binder, 1997; Dikmen, Machamer, & Temkin, 2001; Dikmen, McLean, & Temkin, 1986; Dikmen, McLean, Temkin, & Wyler, 1986). The *specificity* criterion might be partially met because deficits in speed of information processing, attention, and memory appear to be common following mTBI; however, these cognitive impairments are often associated with a variety of disorders other than mTBI. In terms of *temporal sequence* and *experimental evidence*, there is the sport concussion literature, which suggests that mTBI is associated with transient cognitive impairment (McCrea et al., 2003). By *analogy*, there may be similarities between concussions sustained by athletes and mTBI sustained by persons in motor vehicle accidents. As noted earlier, there is a dose-response relationship in TBI (Dikmen, Machamer, Temkin, & McLean, 1990; Rohling et al., 2003) with greater cognitive impairment associated with longer period of coma. In terms of *biological plausibility*, there is evidence that a neurometabolic cascade is implicated in the cognitive deficits associated with mTBI (Giza & Hovda, 2001). In terms of *coherence* with what is known, there is general consensus that mTBI causes transient cognitive impairment. Taking the evidence from all of these criteria, there is sufficient evidence to support a causal link between transient neuropsychological impairment and mTBI.

EPILOGUE

Almost two decades ago, Chuck Matthews (1990) voiced concerns about what he characterized as the "malignant bloom nourished by the head injury industry" and neuropsychology's role in it, which, he predicted, "will end badly" (p. 333). At that time, there was a proliferation of for-profit head injury rehabilitation facilities that employed large numbers of neuropsychologists. Growth seemed unlimited. Whether fueled by naïveté, greed, or both, this was also a time when every head injury, regardless of severity or plausibility, seemed to get the label of permanent brain damage, typically buttressed by neuropsychological "data." But this irrational exuberance could not go on forever. Although many rehabilitation facilities provided much-needed treatment for their clients, some of these centers were nothing more than head injury charm schools that were designed to benefit treatment providers, plaintiff attorneys, and, occasionally, the litigating patient. Eventually, Medicare fraud, insurance audits, tort reform, and changes in insurance coverage caused a shakeout in the industry. During this period of change, the pendulum was also beginning to swing in the other direction in terms of how clinicians understood mild head injury and its natural course of recovery. Good experimental design was largely responsible for the conceptual shift, but effort measures alerted neuropsychologists to other diagnostic possibilities. Early in its inception, clinical neuropsychology's seminal contribution to science was the demonstration of the association between brain dysfunction and performance on behavioral tests. When its later development is viewed retrospectively, neuropsychology's finding that "effort matters" is likely to be judged as of equal importance. Some would also argue that this latter development helped to prevent events from ending badly for neuropsychology.

REFERENCES

Ashendorf, L., O'Bryant, S. E., & McCaffrey, R. J. (2003). Specificity of malingering detection strategies in older adults using the CVLT and WCST. *The Clinical Neuropsychologist, 17*(2), 255–262.

Binder, L. M. (1997). A review of mild head trauma. Part II: Clinical implications. *Journal of Clinical and Experimental Neuropsychology, 19*(3), 432–457.

Bossuyt, P. M., Reitsma, J. B., Bruns, D. E., Gatsonis, C. A., Glasziou, P. P., Irwig, L. M., et al. (2003). Towards complete and accurate reporting of studies of diagnostic accuracy: the STARD initiative. *Clinical Radiology, 58*(8), 575–580.

Coleman, R. D., Rapport, L. J., Millis, S. R., Ricker, J. H., & Farchione, T. J. (1998). Effects of coaching on detection of malingering on the California Verbal Learning Test. *Journal of Clinical and Experimental Neuropsychology, 20*(2), 201–210.

Demakis, G. J. (2004). Application of clinically-derived malingering cutoffs on the California Verbal Learning Test and the Wechsler Adult Intelligence Test-Revised to an analog malingering study. *Applied Neuropsychology, 11*(4), 222–228.

Dikmen, S., Machamer, J., & Temkin, N. (2001). Mild head injury: facts and artifacts. *Journal of Clinical and Experimental Neuropsychology, 23*(6), 729–738.

Dikmen, S., Machamer, J., Temkin, N., & McLean, A. (1990). Neuropsychological recovery in patients with moderate to severe head injury: 2 year follow-up. *Journal of Clinical and Experimental Neuropsychology, 12*(4), 507–519.

Dikmen, S., McLean, A., & Temkin, N. (1986). Neuropsychological and psychosocial consequences of minor head injury. *Journal of Neurology, Neurosurgery and Psychiatry, 49*(11), 1227–1232.

Dikmen, S., McLean, A., Jr., Temkin, N. R., & Wyler, A. R. (1986). Neuropsychologic outcome at one-month postinjury. *Archives of Physical Medicine and Rehabilitation, 67*(8), 507–513.

Edwards, W. (1968). Conservatism in human information processing. In B. Kleinmutz (Ed.), *Formal representation of human judgment* (pp. 17–52). New York: Wiley.

Elstein, A. (1999). Heuristics and biases: Selected errors in clinical reasoning. *Academic Medicine, 74*(7), 791–794.

Elstein, A., & Schwartz, A. (2002). Clinical problem solving and diagnostic decision making: Selective review of the cognitive literature. *British Medical Journal, 324*, 729–732.

Faust, D. (2003). Holistic thinking is not the whole story. *Assessment, 10*(4), 428–441.

Foster, K., & Hiber, P. (1999). *Judging science: Scientific knowledge and the federal courts.* Cambridge, MA: MIT Press.

Garb, H. N., & Lutz, C. (2001). Cognitive complexity and the validity of clinicians' judgments. *Assessment, 8*(1), 111–115.

Garb, H. N., & Schramke, C. J. (1996). Judgement research and neuropsychological assessment: a narrative review and meta-analyses. *Psychological Bulletin, 120*(1), 140–153.

Gigerenzer, G., & Goldstein, D. G. (1996). Reasoning the fast and frugal way: models of bounded rationality. *Psychological Review, 103*(4), 650–669.

Giza, C. C., & Hovda, D. A. (2001). The neurometabolic cascade of concussion. *Journal of Athletic Training, 36*(3), 228–235.

Gorissen, M., Sanz, J. C., & Schmand, B. (2005). Effort and cognition in schizophrenia patients. *Schizophrenia Research, 78*(2–3), 199–208.

Grimes, D. A., & Schulz, K. F. (2002). Bias and causal associations in observational research. *Lancet, 359*(9302), 248–252.

Grimes, D. A., & Schulz, K. F. (2005). Refining clinical diagnosis with likelihood ratios. *Lancet, 365*(9469), 1500–1505.

Grove, W. M., Zald, D. H., Lebow, B. S., Snitz, B. E., & Nelson, C. (2000). Clinical versus mechanical prediction: a meta-analysis. *Psychological Assessment, 12*(1), 19–30.

Harrell, F. (2001). *Regression modeling strategies: With applications to linear models, logistic regression, and survival analysis*. New York: Springer-Verlag.

Heaton, R., Miller, S., Taylor, M., & Grant, I. (2004). *Revised comprehensive norms for an expanded Halstead-Reitan Battery: Demographically adjusted neuropsychological norms for African-American and Caucasian adults*. Lutz, FL: Psychological Assessment Resources, Inc.

Hosmer, D., & Lemeshow, S. (2000). *Applied logistic regression*, 2nd ed. New York: Wiley Interscience.

Joseph, L., Gyorkos, T. W., & Coupal, L. (1995). Bayesian estimation of disease prevalence and the parameters of diagnostic tests in the absence of a gold standard. *American Journal of Epidemiology, 141*(3), 263–272.

Kassirer, J., & Koppelman, R. (1991). *Learning clinical reasoning*. Philadelphia: Lippincott, Williams, & Wilkins.

Kern, L., & Doherty, M. (1982). "Pseudodiagnosticity" in an idealized medical problem-solving environment. *Journal of Medical Education, 57*, 100–104.

Matthews, C. (1990). They asked for a speech. *The Clinical Neuropsychologist, 4*, 327–336.

Mayer, D. (2004). *Essential evidence-based medicine*. New York: Cambridge University Press.

McCrea, M., Guskiewicz, K. M., Marshall, S. W., Barr, W., Randolph, C., Cantu, R. C., et al. (2003). Acute effects and recovery time following concussion in collegiate football players: the NCAA Concussion Study. *JAMA, 290*(19), 2556–2563.

Meehl, P. (1954). *Clinical versus statistical prediction: A theoretical analysis and review of the evidence*. Minneapolis: University of Minnesota Press.

Meehl, P. (1993). Philosophy of science: Help or hindrance. *Psychological Reports, 72*, 707–733.

Millis, S. R., Putnam, S., Adams, K., & Ricker, J. (1995). The California Verbal Learning Test in the detection of incomplete effort in neuropsychological evaluation. *Psychological Assessment, 7*, 463–471.

Millis, S. R., Rosenthal, M., Novack, T. A., Sherer, M., Nick, T. G., Kreutzer, J. S., et al. (2001). Long-term neuropsychological outcome after traumatic brain injury. *Journal of Head Trauma Rehabilitation, 16*(4), 343–355.

Millis, S. R., & Volinsky, C. T. (2001). Assessment of response bias in mild head injury: Beyond malingering tests. *Journal of Clinical and Experimental Neuropsychology, 23*(6), 809–828.

Plous, S. (1993). *The psychology of judgment and decision making*. New York: McGraw-Hill.

Rohling, M. L., Meyers, J. E., & Millis, S. R. (2003). Neuropsychological impairment following traumatic brain injury: a dose-response analysis. *The Clinical Neuropsychologist, 17*(3), 289–302.

Slick, D. J., Iverson, G. L., & Green, P. (2000). California Verbal Learning Test indicators of suboptimal performance in a sample of head-injury litigants. *Journal of Clinical and Experimental Neuropsychology, 22*(5), 569–579.

Slick, D. J., Sherman, E. M., & Iverson, G. L. (1999). Diagnostic criteria for malingered neurocognitive dysfunction: Proposed standards for clinical practice and research. *The Clinical Neuropsychologist, 13*(4), 545–561.

Slovic, P., & Lichtenstein, S. C. (1971). Comparison of Bayesian and regression approaches to the study of information processing in judgment. *Organization Behavior and Human Performance, 6*, 649–744.

StataCorp. (2005). Stata statistical software: Release 9. College Station, TX: StataCorp LP.

Straus, S., Richardson, W., Glasziou, P., & Haynes, R. (2005). *Evidence-based medicine: How to practice and teach EBM*, 3rd ed. New York: Elsevier Churchill Livingstone.

Sweet, J. J., Wolfe, P., Sattlberger, E., Numan, B., Rosenfeld, J. P., Clingerman, S., et al. (2000). Further investigation of traumatic brain injury versus insufficient effort with the California Verbal Learning Test. *Archives of Clinical Neuropsychology, 15*(2), 105–113.

Tversky, A., & Kahneman, D. (1974). Judgment under uncertainty: Heuristics and biases. *Science, 185*, 1124–1131.

Wedding, D., & Faust, D. (1989). Clinical judgment and decision making in neuropsychology. *Archives of Clinical Neuropsychology, 4*, 233–265.

Zhou, X., Obuchowski, N., & McClish, D. (2002). *Statistical methods in diagnostic medicine*. New York: Wiley InterScience.

SECTION II

CIVIL LITIGATION

The majority of forensic work that involves clinical neuropsychologists relates to litigation that is under consideration in the body of law that is referred to as civil law or civil procedure. This body of law generally pertains to redressing or remedying a wrong that has been committed by one person against another. The remedy is often compensation in the form of money. A fundamental tenet is that the wrongdoer compensates the victim to a degree that makes good the wrong that was inflicted. Conceptually, this may be easy to understand, but in application there are obvious difficulties in determining liability (i.e., whether a wrong was truly committed by the person blamed) and in measuring damages (i.e., the degree to which harm was inflicted and the persistence of the harmful effects). Clinical neuropsychologists are most commonly involved in the assessment of possible damages, and only rarely would be involved in determining the more fundamental issue of liability. Valid measurement of possible damages is required, as is the use of an objective means of judging that abnormalities found are a result of the event at issue in the litigation, rather than premorbid (e.g., pre-existing and possibly longstanding) or caused by transient factors that have negatively influenced or confounded the claimant's or litigant's performances. The 28 chapters within this section provide numerous expert perspectives on the complex differential diagnostic problems that can arise in civil litigation, as well as the methods and reasoning that clinical neuropsychologists can use to increase the probability of an accurate conclusion.

Traumatic Brain Injury in Adults

Alleged and actual traumatic brain injuries represent the most frequent focus in forensic cases for which clinical neuropsychologists serve as expert witnesses. Because of this fact, much of the related forensic literature pertains to civil litigants with claims of traumatic brain injury. Though much of an attorney's energy on a case involving possible traumatic brain injury often seems focused on the question of whether an initial brain injury occurred, experienced clinical neuropsychologists know that an answer in the affirmative often sheds little to no light on the nature and severity of later complaints and performances on neuropsychological testing, which may occur years later. The seven chapters in this subsection elucidate the numerous aspects of forensic cases alleging traumatic brain injury that in misrepresenting genuine injury portray non-credible evidence, some of which reflect malingering. The reader will note that the first chapter may appear misplaced, as this subsection is found within a larger section dedicated to "litigation." However, the military context of the first chapter involves the equivalent of injury occurring on the job, which involves worker's compensation law. In the military, the secondary gain context of possible "service connection," by virtue of potentially receiving financial payments that continue after discharge from active duty, is comparable to civilian worker's compensation benefits.

Multifactorial contributions to questionable effort and test performance within a military context

Rodney D. Vanderploeg and Heather G. Belanger

Throughout this book the point is made that in psychological evaluations of various types, a determination of the validity of the data is essential. While reliability refers to the consistency of test scores, validity is the extent to which tests assess what they were designed to measure. In the situation of a neuropsychological evaluation, the validity of neuropsychological tests is compromised whenever variables other than the cognitive function and/or brain ability under investigation influence test performance. In neuropsychological assessment, the goal typically is to determine the best possible performance of the examinee's brain-based functions. For that neuropsychological assessment to be valid, it must accurately reflect the cognitive abilities and/or brain function presumed to be assessed by the tests administered. Thus, in neuropsychological assessment, test validity is compromised when performance is anything less than the client is capable of achieving under optimal testing conditions.

An obvious but important point is that one cannot perform better than one's functional capacity, yet test performance does not always reflect this capacity. A consequence of this fact is that a neuropsychologist can trust or believe intact performances, but must question poor performances—does the poor performance reflect impaired brain functioning, or are other factors responsible for the impaired score? Answering this question is a crucial step in validity determination and data interpretation.

EVALUATION CONTEXT

Neuropsychological evaluations take place in a context in which there are at least four important elements: (1) the measurement procedure, that is, the tests that are used, (2) the patient being evaluated, (3) the relationship between the evaluator and the patient, and (4) the context in which that relationship is taking place (e.g., clinical [indemnity insurance plans versus managed care versus cash-out-of-pocket], forensic, disability benefits, etc.). Validity concerns are relevant to each of these four elements, each of which will be briefly discussed.

Measurement procedures

There are no perfect tests and there are no pure tests. If three tests of verbal memory are administered, any patient will perform somewhat differently on each. Test performance will never be perfectly correlated across measures, and the difference in performance across the tests can simply reflect the psychometric error or normative differences associated with the various measures. Similarly, no test of verbal memory is a pure test of verbal memory. That is, impairment in other ability domains, such as hearing, attention, or language, can adversely affect performance on a verbal memory measure. When these other factors influence performance, the validity of the verbal memory instrument is compromised. Such psychometric measurement error is inevitable and limits the ability of neuropsychologists to validly interpret test results. Fortunately, limits to measurement reliability and validity, and test normative differences, are usually known from prior research and can be taken into account during test interpretation.

Patient variables

Validity assessment becomes particularly important whenever full cooperation and honest effort from the patient may be compromised. Although questions about malingering are often the focus of attention, particularly in compensation-seeking contexts, other behaviors can similarly compromise cooperation and effort, and consequently affect the validity of the evaluation. Patient-based validity effects can be divided into three areas: (1) presumed unconscious processes, such as carelessness, fatigue, reluctance to guess if not absolutely certain, passive-aggressive behavior, psychological conversion symptoms, somatization, unconscious acting out, and normal defensiveness, (2) conscious processes, such as angry resistance to assessment, "couldn't care less" attitude (i.e., the patient does not take the evaluation seriously and does not do his or her best), symptom exaggeration, or malingering, and (3) comorbid medical or mental health conditions. A skilled clinician can minimize the adverse effects of some of these factors; however, when there are multiple causative factors, ferreting out the correct interpretation for confusing or inconsistent findings remains as much art as science. Also, it is important to note that compromised validity may be due to more than one of these factors. For example, it is possible for a patient to both malinger and experience fatigue within the same evaluation, both of which may contribute to the production of invalid data.

Assessment relationship

The assessment relationship is a largely overlooked area in terms of its influence on validity. Establishing an effective working relationship with the client is crucial to a successful testing session. This is commonly referred to as "developing rapport." Under ideal conditions the assessment is a mutual endeavor in which both neuropsychologist and client are working cooperatively on the task of trying to better understand the behavior, cognitive strengths and problems, and coping abilities of the examinee. There is little point of engaging in testing if clients refuse to actively and fully participate. If the neuropsychologist proceeds with the evaluation under those conditions, the results will be of questionable validity and the brain-behavioral capabilities of the client will remain obscure. Under these conditions, the best that can be done is to draw conclusions about what cognitive domains are intact (i.e., those in which the patient performs normally).

Context in which the evaluation takes place

In this chapter, we will be discussing issues and presenting a case occurring as part of a clinically-based evaluation within the Department of Veterans Affairs, Veterans Health Administration (VHA). There is a separate administrative section of the VA, the Veterans Benefit Administration (VBA), which may require psychological or neuropsychological evaluations as part of the disability, vocational, educational, or other benefits determination.

VHA is essentially a managed healthcare system with eligible veteran enrollees entitled to necessary and appropriate healthcare. There may be financial charges for some services to the patient or to a secondary healthcare insurance company, depending upon the entitled benefits of the patient in question, which in turn depend upon a variety of factors, including whether or not a condition is considered "service connected," the financial resources of the veteran, the active duty versus veteran status of the patient, the era in which the military veteran served, etc. In addition, once a veteran is determined to be eligible and enrolled in the VHA system, this patient's healthcare is essentially the responsibility of the VHA for the rest of his/her life, as long as such healthcare is desired and requested.

In the current Operation Enduring Freedom/Operation Iraqi Freedom (OEF/OIF) "War on Terror" environment, individuals who were recently deployed in either OEF or OIF are entitled to VHA healthcare evaluation and treatment, particularly for any conditions that are likely to be service related. The two most common such conditions are posttraumatic stress disorder (PTSD) and traumatic brain injury (TBI). Indeed, TBI has been identified as the "signature injury" of the Iraq war. Injury from explosions (i.e., improvised explosive devises, landmines, rocket-propelled grenades, and other causes of blasts) is the most common cause of evacuation from OEF/OIF theater. A recent study found that 88% of military personnel treated at a medical unit in Iraq had been injured by improvised explosive devices or mortar (Murray et al., 2005). The potential neuropsychological implications of such widespread exposure to blast are still uncertain. However, the Defense and Veterans Brain Injury Center (DVBIC) has reported that 59% of an "at risk" group of injured soldiers returning from Afghanistan or Iraq suffered at least a mild TBI while in combat (Okie, 2005; Warden et al., 2005).

Recognizing the higher incidence of possible TBI and PTSD in veterans returning from OEF/OIF deployment, the VHA implemented both PTSD and TBI Clinical Reminder protocols that have been incorporated into its computerized medical record system. For example, the TBI Clinical Reminder must be completed by any provider within the VHA system of care who first encounters that patient, whether it is a primary care physician, a mental health professional, or a dentist. The TBI Clinical Reminder, which is completed only if the veteran served in Iraq or Afghanistan after September 11, 2001, and has not already been treated for TBI, consists of four questions:

1. During any of your OIF/OEF deployment(s), did you experience any of the following events? (Check all that apply: blast or explosion, vehicular accident or crash, fragment or bullet wound above the shoulders, fall).
2. Did you have any of these symptoms IMMEDIATELY afterwards? (Check all that apply: losing consciousness/"knocked out"; being dazed, confused, or "seeing stars"; not remembering the event; concussion; or head injury).
3. Did any of the following problems begin or get worse afterwards? (Check all that apply: memory problems or lapses; balance problems or dizziness; sensitivity to bright light; irritability; headaches; sleep problems).
4. In the past week, have you had any of the above symptoms? (Check all that apply: memory problems or lapses; balance problems or dizziness; sensitivity to bright light; irritability; headaches; sleep problems).

A veteran must respond affirmatively to all four questions to produce a positive screen. Positive screens automatically generate a consult to a TBI specialist or clinic. This specialist/clinic has one week to initiate contact with the patient for a more detailed follow-up evaluation. This TBI Clinical Reminder system began operations in April 2007.

The establishment of these PTSD and TBI Clinical Reminders reflects two responses to prevailing political pressures which are numerous and powerful. Given the denigration experienced by many returning Vietnam era veterans, there currently is a very strong desire to "do the right thing" for the OEF/OIF war-injured veteran. Also, if there is *any* indication of exposure to or injury from blasts, or having sustained even a mild TBI, there is political pressure to assume that current symptoms and complaints are valid and related to those deployment events. In that context, even if there is evidence for symptom exaggeration or overt malingering, there is pressure to base treatment decisions on patient preference in order to enhance customer satisfaction and avoid "bad press." Finally, even if the entire healthcare team believes that current symptoms are not related to a historic traumatic event, such as a mild TBI or other combat experience, the VHA system of care is nevertheless bound to work with the patient and his/her family to minimize subjective distress and symptoms, regardless of etiology (i.e., exaggeration, malingering, somatization, conversion, or other mental health condition). As such, this practice environment is unique.

THE CASE OF SERGEANT M.

Background injury information

This 41-year-old African-American patient was a US-activated Army Reserve Sergeant (Sgt.). He was injured in a motor vehicle rollover associated with an IED blast in Iraq in August 2007 about 20 days prior to the current neuropsychological evaluation. As is typical in most of these combat-related events, no medical records are available from medics at the site. Also, unless there is an extensive period of coma, Glasgow Coma Scores, length of loss or alternation of consciousness, and duration of post-event confusion are not obtained nor recorded in medical records. From the information provided by the patient, he apparently experienced several minutes of unconsciousness but was told he had given a "thumbs up" at the accident site, and he recalls the helicopter evacuation. Sgt. M. was transferred to Landstuhl Regional Medical Center (LRMC) the day after the injury. Head CT scan was normal. He was then transferred to Walter Reed Army Medical Center (WRAMC) seven days later. A TBI consultant at WRAMC evaluated Sgt. M. and reported findings of "decreased short term memory, decreased ability for calculations, and decreased concentration." Also at WRAMC, a speech therapy evaluation noted a "moderate cognitive-communicative disorder." However, an MRI of the brain nine days after the injury was normal. Physical and occupational therapists were consulted for strengthening, balance, safety, and back pain. Sgt. M. was noted to have cervical and lower back pain, and intermittent episodes of upper extremity tingling. Based on the patient's self-reported loss of consciousness and clinical presentation of somewhat impaired performance on memory and concentration measures, WRAMC diagnosed Sgt. M. with a mild to moderate TBI and recommended cognitive and brain injury rehabilitation.

Sgt. M. was sent to our VA medical center for further assessment and rehabilitation 19 days post-injury. A speech evaluation shortly after admission noted mild impairments in memory and verbal reasoning. Additional medical findings included degenerative joint disease and spondyloarthropathy with mid-spinal stenosis at C6-7 and disk bulges at L4-5 and L5-S1 that might be impinging on nerve roots. A mild right sensorineural hearing loss was also noted.

Current subjective complaints

Upon arrival at the Tampa VA Sgt. M. identified his major concern as his "anxiety attacks" that he reported were intermittent since the IED blast. He also described problems with memory and word-finding since the blast, back pain, headaches, hearing loss, blurry vision, difficulty sleeping, feelings of "emptiness," not wanting to be around other people, feeling "jumpy," and feelings of wariness and watchfulness. He described his main cognitive difficulties as forgetfulness and trouble concentrating. He also reported a decrease in his sense of smell and stated that his food tasted bland.

Education, psychosocial, vocational, and medical background

Sgt. M. was raised in a chaotic and abusive environment. He was raised with a physically abusive stepmother, often saw violence in his neighborhood, and saw multiple members of his own family being seriously injured or killed.

He reports attaining a high school education and graduating with a "C" average. He reports a history of learning disabilities in reading and spelling, both diagnosed and treated as a child. He reported receiving tutoring in reading and spelling in elementary school.

Sgt. M. has been married twice. Before being deployed to Iraq in March 2007, he had been living with his current wife and children in base housing. He and his wife have been married for the past 12 years but have been together for 15 years. He has a 21-year-old son from his first marriage. Sgt. M. reports a supportive relationship with his wife and their children.

Sgt. M. is currently on active duty in the Army Reserves (E-5) and works as a combat engineer. He was in the Army from 1985 to 1991 and joined the reserves thereafter. He was activated as Army Reserves in April 2006 and deployed to Iraq in March of 2007. In the past, he has worked as a truck driver, security guard, and postal worker.

Past medical history is generally unremarkable, except his history of learning disabilities and a three-year period in the early 1990s during which he drank very heavily. He reportedly stopped heavy drinking in 1993 and stopped drinking altogether in 1999. He smokes about six cigarettes a day.

Past disability-related complaints/activities

A review of remote VHA medical records revealed that Sgt. M. presented to a VA in the Midwestern United States about a year after his discharge from Active Duty status (nine years prior to the current evaluation). At that time he reported that he had been deployed to the Persian Gulf and served in Saudi Arabia and Kuwait and now was experiencing what he felt were Gulf War-related problems. He reported multiple medical complaints including headaches, bleeding gums, excessive fatigue, skin rashes, joint pain, stomach pain, difficulty breathing, increased anger, social isolation, and sleep disturbance. He was seen by a social worker, who provided information regarding Gulf War illnesses and information on how to file a Gulf War claim. Regardless of what Sgt. M. may have done to follow up with this, current medical and benefits records reveal no service-related disability determination or income.

Assessment findings

Initial screening evaluation

Sgt. M. was seen by both authors on consecutive occasions. The first author saw him 23 days after his injury and three days after his admission to our VA brain injury rehabilitation program. At that time a clinical interview was conducted and some brief screening procedures—WAIS–III Digit Span, Rey-Osterrieth Complex Figure drawing, and the Trail Making Test—were administered (Table 4.1).

TABLE 4.1   Results of WAIS–III Digit Span, Rey-Osterrieth Complex Figure drawing, and the Trail Making Test

TEST	SCORE	SCORE	PERCENTILE	DESCRIPTION
Validity				
MSVT	Immed. Recall	80	n.a.	Failed
	Delayed Recall	70	n.a.	Failed
	Consistency	70	n.a.	Failed
	Paired Assoc.	50	n.a.	Failed
	Free Recall	60	n.a.	Failed
Rey 15 + Recogn.	Rey 15 + Recogn.	8/30	Failed	Failed
CVLT–II	Hits	12 Raw	1	Failed
	Discriminability	72% Raw	2	Failed
	Forced Choice	16/16 Raw	Average	Intact
WAIS–III	Reliable Digit Span	9 Raw	Intact	Intact
Premorbid	WTAR	9 Raw	5	Borderline
	Demographic-based FSIQ	94 FSIQ	34	Average
Cognitive				
WAIS–III	Digit Span	9 ACSS	37	Average
	Forward Span	6 Raw	21	Low Average
	Backward Span	4 Raw	13	Low Average
	Information	5 ACSS	5	Borderline
	Block Design	9 ACSS	37	Average
	Digit Symbol	5 ACSS	5	Borderline
CVLT–II	Trial 1	5 Raw	16	Low Average
	Trial 2	8 Raw	32	Average
	Trial 3	7 Raw	7	Borderline
	Trial 4	11 Raw	32	Average
	Trial 5	13 Raw	50	Average
	Total 1–5	44 Raw	32	Average
	Trial B	6 Raw	50	Average
	SDFR	10 Raw	32	Average
	SDCR	9 Raw	16	Low Average
	LDFR	8 Raw	16	Low Average
	LDCR	7 Raw	7	Borderline
	Hits	12 Raw	1	Impaired
	False Positives	6 Raw	16	Low Average
	– List B	3 Raw	n.a.	n.a.
	– Prototypic	3 Raw	n.a.	n.a.
	Discriminability	72% Raw	2	Impaired
	Forced Choice	16 Raw	Intact	Average
BVMT–R	Trial 1	7 Raw	62	Average
	Trial 2	7 Raw	16	Low Average
	Trial 3	8 Raw	12	Low Average
	Total 1–3	22 Raw	24	Low Average

	Learning	1 Raw	< 1	Impaired
	Delayed Recall	5 Raw	1	Impaired
	Recog. Hits	4 Raw	4	Impaired
	Discriminability	4 Raw	4	Impaired
DKEFS	Letter Fluency	32 Raw	25	Average
	Semantic Fluency	29 Raw	9	Low Average
Rey-Osterrieth	Drawing Copy	36 Raw	> 16	Average
TRAILS	Trails A	33 seconds	25	Average
	Trails B	72 seconds	45	Average
WCST-64	Total Errors	15 Raw	27	Average
	Persever. Respon.	5 Raw	39	Average
	Persever. Errors	5 Raw	39	Average
	Categories	3 Raw	> 16	Average
Psychological				
PCL	Total Score	62 Raw	n.a.	PTSD
NSI	Total Score	67 Raw	n.a.	n.a.

Sgt. M. presented as alert and fully oriented, with fluent and articulate speech. He provided a detailed, logical, and coherent history that was consistent with the medical records. Concentration difficulties were noted during conversation and during some cognitive tasks. At one point he appeared to "zone out" for about five seconds and needed to be reoriented to the task. Despite this, performance on the initial cognitive measures was within normal limits with scores ranging from the 25th to the 45th percentile.

However, what was of greater concern at that time were his psychological and pain symptoms. He walked slowly using a cane and complained of back pain. He described his mood as "empty" and reported "feeling like he was missing something." His affect was flat and depressed, and he reported being quite tearful. The only time he smiled was when he talked about his young daughter. When questioned about psychological symptoms in an open-ended manner, he reported multiple symptoms of PTSD including anxiety, sadness, feelings of emptiness, nightmares, difficulty falling and staying asleep, social withdrawal, and over-arousal including difficulty concentrating and being on guard and hypervigilant. As with many other cases treated in our setting, the traumas are multiple—the event causing the injury itself (if there are memories of it or its immediate aftermath, as there were in this case), multiple other combat and deployment-related traumatic events, and (in this case) pre-military traumas.

Follow-up, more comprehensive evaluation

The second author saw him three days later over a two-day period. Results of all tests are presented in Table 4.1.

Premorbid estimation. One interpretive complexity of this case is the determination of his premorbid level of functioning against which to compare current test performance. Sgt. M. reportedly had a history of learning disabilities in reading and spelling. His performance on the WTAR was poor (5th percentile), a finding that could be consistent with the reported learning disability. In addition, Sgt. M. performed poorly on the WAIS–III Information subtest (5th percentile), a finding that again could be related to childhood academic problems. In contrast, his demographic-based predicted IQ score (Vanderploeg & Schinka, 1995) was 94 (34th percentile) and his WAIS–III Block Design performance was consistent with this (37th percentile), as were other neuropsychologically sensitive but less academically related test scores (e.g., Trail Making Test and WCST-64). Based on these findings, we predicted expected level of functioning to be in the mid to low end of the average range, with the exception of tasks which were academic-like or highly correlated with academic reading and spelling abilities.

Validity concerns.   A second interpretive complexity of this case is performance validity. Results of symptom validity tests (SVTs) are shown in Table 4.1. Sgt. M.'s performance was variable and inconsistent across examiners and across time.

On the initial screening evaluation, Sgt. M. demonstrated intact performance on Digit Span (Scale score of 9), Reliable Digit Span (score of 9) (Greiffenstein, Baker, & Gola, 1994; Greiffenstein, Gola, & Baker, 1995; Meyers & Volbrecht, 1998), Trail Making Test, and Rey-Osterrieth Complex Figure drawing. However, he appeared to "zone out" several times and had several episodes of losing his train of thought in conversation.

During the second examination several days later, Sgt. M. failed the Medical Symptom Validity Test (MSVT) as well as the Rey 15-Item Test with Recognition (Boone, Salazar, Lu, Warner-Chacon, & Razani, 2002). In addition, although performing poorly and at least questionably failing the validity checks on CVLT–II Recognition Hits and Discriminability (Sweet et al., 2000), he correctly chose 16/16 items on forced choice. Taken together, these findings were interpreted as reflecting variable effort or engagement, at least on memory measures.

Neuropsychological test performance pattern.   In general, despite Sgt. M's performance on the symptom validity measures, his cognitive test performance was intact. His speech was fluent, conversational comprehension intact, letter-based verbal fluency average, and semantic-based fluency low average. Visuospatial abilities were average on both the WAIS–III Block Design and his drawing of the Rey-Osterrieth Complex Figure. Similarly, executive abilities were intact on the Trail Making Test, WCST-64, letter-based verbal fluency, and working memory (Digit Span). The only executive measure that was performed poorly was WAIS–III Digit Symbol (5th percentile). However, given his intact performance on the Trail Making Test and his slightly better performance on Trails B than Trails A, his lower Digit Symbol score was interpretively seen as an anomaly, not as a cognitive impairment.

Memory abilities were reported as a problematic area by Sgt. M., specifically in the context of mostly psychological, pain, and somatic complaints and concerns. However, on formal evaluation, Sgt. M. failed several memory-related symptom validity measures. On the CVLT–II Sgt. M.'s performance was unusual. He had a variable learning rate (5, 8, 7, 11, and 13) but clearly demon-strated intact learning across trials, a finding consistent with intact new learning and consolidation. List B recall was average and slightly better than List A Trial 1. Short delay free recall was also average. However, his performance dropped on delayed recall, and on both short and delayed recall his cued recall was worse than his free recall. The latter finding may be related to his history of verbally-based learning disability, i.e., difficulty taking advantage of semantic cues. Finally, delayed recognition recall and discriminability were impaired, although forced choice was perfect. It is important to note that CVLT–II forced choice is generally considered a weak measure of valid effort. Overall this pattern was seen as reflecting intact verbal learning, recall, and retention, but variable effort or engagement in the task. Given his overall above average "rate" of learning and average acquisition total (Total trials 1–5), this variable effort was not seen as deliberate or conscious.

Sgt. M. performed even more poorly on a visual memory measure, the BVMT–R, than he did on the CVLT–II. Again, overall acquisition was generally within expected limits (Low Average range). However, delayed recall and recognition testing performance were poor, similar to his CVLT–II Recognition Hits performance.

PTSD findings.   A third interpretive complexity in this case was psychological and mental health factors. The PTSD Symptom Checklist (PCL) was administered and Sgt. M.'s total symptom score was 62. Raw scores over 50 are generally indicative of and consistent with PTSD. On follow-up interview Sgt. M. reported a history of deployment first in Desert Storm and more recently in OIF where he was injured in the IED blast and MVA. He reported exposure to frequent traumatic experiences in Desert Storm, such as seeing dead bodies, being shot at, shooting at others, and seeing bombs go off in the vicinity. In OIF he experienced IED blasts, mortars, being shot at, shooting at others, and seeing dead bodies. Currently Sgt. M. reported feeling afraid and helpless. He reported intrusive thoughts, nightmares, feeling upset with his physical reactions to traumatic reminders (e.g., seeing bricks on the street, Muslim-appearing people, smells, night time, wires, and loud noises), avoidance of thinking or talking about his OIF experience, avoidance of social activities, loss of interest in activities, feeling distant from others, feeling unable to have loving feelings toward his wife, difficulty sleeping, irritability, difficulty concentrating, hypervigilance, and a startle response.

Clearly there are diagnostic limitations when one relies on measures such as the PCL that do not have inherent validity scales. However, as explained earlier, the VHA philosophy is to be responsive to veterans' symptoms and complaints regardless of etiology. Also, unique to conducting assessments in an inpatient setting is the opportunity to monitor and observe patients 24 hours a day, seven days a week—equivalent to video monitoring. Sgt. M's clinical presentation was always consistent with psychological distress. His affect was consistently flat and depressed, and he was noted to be tearful in multiple settings. Concentration problems and psychomotor slowing were noted consistently on the ward and in therapy sessions. He tended to isolate and withdraw to his room, even from his family who was staying in a Fisher House on the grounds of the VAMC.

Clinical interpretive conclusions

Conclusions from the initial screening evaluation were reported as:

> Sgt. M. presents with significant mental health symptoms and concerns including significant PTSD symptoms. . . . Concentration difficulties were noted during conversation; at one point Sgt. M. appeared to "zone out" for about 5 seconds and needed to be reoriented to the task. Despite this, his performance on the initial screening cognitive measures was within normal limits on tasks of processing speed, working memory, and visuospatial functioning.
>
> Sgt. M. expressed interest in talking with the rehabilitation psychologist about his symptoms and feelings.

The results of the somewhat more extensive neuropsychological follow-up evaluation resulted in the following interpretive conclusion:

> Findings are difficult to interpret given the inconsistent engagement by Sgt. M. during the evaluation. There were inconsistencies in memory testing (e.g., recognition worse than free recall, worse performance on easier measures) that don't make neuropsychological sense and suggest that the patient had varying degrees of engagement in the tasks. This was also true behaviorally, as the patient would on occasion "space out." Nonetheless, his memory system does appear to be intact. Intact performance was also found in the areas of speech and language, visuospatial ability, basic attention, and executive functions.
>
> Sgt. M. is reporting significant symptoms of PTSD that require attention. A much clearer picture of his cognitive status can be obtained when his psychological symptoms are under better control. Also, Sgt. M. reports significant pain and sleep deficiency which may adversely affect cognitive performance.

ANALYSIS OF THE CASE OF SGT. M.

This case illustrates the difficulty sometimes inherent in using "symptom validity" or "effort" measures. Sgt. M. "failed" the more commonly accepted symptom validity procedures that were administered—MSVT, Rey 15-Item Test with Recognition, CVLT–II Recognition Hits, and CVLT–II Discriminability. Based on that, together with his history of having applied for VA disability following his Desert Storm deployment, we suspect that some neuropsychologists would conclude that Sgt. M. was malingering, particularly if the evaluation was part of the disability compensation process. Consistent with possible malingering or at least invalid effort, Sgt. M.'s cognitive performance was inconsistent across examiners and evaluation days, and his performance on formal memory testing was inconsistent with neurologically-based memory difficulties. For example, on the CVLT–II, his learning curve was variable and unusual, his recognition hits normative performance was far worse than free recall, and his raw cued recall was worse than raw free recall. Similarly, on the BVMT–R, his learning curve was flat, and his recognition performance was worse than expected given his initial acquisition performance.

Sgt. M's qualitative effort varied throughout the evaluation, seemingly in response to his degree of discomfort, general attitude, and/or emotional distress on any given day. It is important to remember that Sgt. M. returned from Iraq less than one month prior to this evaluation. He was spending significant time with his family for the first time since returning home and, therefore, just beginning the process of readjusting to stateside and family life. His high endorsement of PCS symptoms may reflect neurologic sequelae due to concussion, his high level of distress, or some combination of factors.

If we were to conclude that Sgt. M. was "malingering" based on failed symptom validity measures, we would be misrepresenting his largely intact cognitive performance, and we would not arrive at any useful treatment recommendations. Instead, if we view his inconsistent degree of engagement during the evaluation as symptomatic and characteristic of his current level of psychological distress, as well as his ambivalent feelings and attitudes about returning from Iraq, we are better able to develop rapport while providing necessary education on concussion, explain results in a manner more likely to induce behavior change, and triage future service provision. In a clinical, non-compensation evaluation context, the question is not, "Did this individual sustain a concussion that likely is at least in part responsible for his symptoms?" but rather, "What is his current optimal performance level from a cognitive and psychological standpoint and what services does he need given this level of functioning?" Given our data, it is clear that he is able to perform cognitively within normal limits. However, he is unlikely to do so as his attention fluctuates based on other factors (psychological distress, pain, sleep) and based on his degree of engagement and effort. The focus of treatment at this point should therefore be on these other factors, rather than on his head injury per se.

Our interpretive understanding of this case is that Sgt. M. is an individual with a pre-existing verbal learning disability in the areas of reading and spelling. This adversely affected his performance on measures related to reading, as well as on more academically-based cognitive tasks. In addition, we saw him as having significant psychological distress and symptomology at the time of evaluation. We believed he met DSM–IV diagnostic criteria for Acute Stress Disorder (on its way to becoming PTSD), as well as a major depressive episode and chronic pain. We understood and interpreted his concentration problems as secondary to these psychological conditions and post-deployment adjustment, and we understood his variable engagement in test procedures, "failed" performance on some of the symptom validity procedures, and variable cognitive test performance as related to these various factors.

Following a short rehabilitation stay, during which the above evaluation was part of a comprehensive interdisciplinary assessment, Sgt. M. was discharged, but set up in a PTSD treatment program, provided with additional mental health services, and provided with ongoing case management. Sgt. M. may well have some ongoing cognitive impairments given his still relatively acute status—about one month post mild TBI. Therefore, if cognitive symptoms remain after six to nine months and after his psychological symptoms are under better control, a neuropsychological reevaluation would be considered. However, in the interim our recommendations were PTSD and mental health treatment, and continued reassurance and education regarding expected recovery of postconcussive symptoms (Mittenberg, Canyock, Condit, & Patton, 2001; Mittenberg, Tremont, Zielinski, Fichera, & Rayls, 1996; Mittenberg, Zielinski, & Fichera, 1993).

DISCUSSION

This type of case is not at all unusual in the OIF/OEF returning military personnel, particularly those presenting to the VHA for medical services and responding positively on the TBI Clinical Reminder. Virtually all such patients have symptoms of anxiety, depression, PTSD, chronic pain, and/or insomnia. Most of them also have some variable and inconsistent performance across a spectrum of cognitive tests, and many have complicated histories and pre-existing conditions, such as academic problems or learning disabilities, behavioral problems, alcohol or drug abuse or dependence, or psychologically traumatic backgrounds. They may also be preparing for the medical boarding process in the military or they may be faced with the possibility of re-deployment. Many of these patients "fail" one or more indicators of cognitive or psychological symptom validity.

There is a multiplicity of factors that must be considered when determining the cause of poor test performances, and malingering is certainly one of those. In such patients, performance is often inconsistent. Some observations and test performances will suggest invalidity, while other observations and test performances will suggest valid effort and results. These cases are diagnostic challenges and at times result in an evaluation report that simply documents the inconsistencies and states that no clear interpretation of neuropsychological deficits is possible. However, often in these cases documentation of intact performance in some neuropsychological domains is possible.

Finally, it is essential to consider the overall context and political realities in which evaluation of these patients is taking place. The VHA system of care is obligated to work with these patients and their families to meet their legitimate healthcare needs and treat or help minimize subjective distress and symptoms, regardless of etiology (i.e., exaggeration, malingering, somatization, conversion, PTSD, other mental health conditions, various medical conditions, or more likely, a combination of these). Therefore, unlike within a forensic context, the relationship with the patient continues beyond the evaluation. While this does not make symptom validity any less important with regard to the evaluation, it is primarily used for case conceptualization for future treatment and recommendations rather than as a diagnostic label for the purpose of legal proceedings.

REFERENCES

Boone, K. B., Salazar, X., Lu, P., Warner-Chacon, K., & Razani, J. (2002). The Rey 15-Item Recognition Trail: A technique to enhance sensitivity of the Rey 15-Item Memorization Test. *Journal of Clinical and Experimental Neuropsychology, 24*, 561–573.

Greiffenstein, M. F., Baker, W. J., & Gola, T. (1994). Validation of malingered amnesia measure with a large clinical sample. *Psychological Assessment, 6*, 218–224.

Greiffenstein, M. F., Gola, T., & Baker, W. J. (1995). MMPI–2 validity scales versus domain-specific measures in the detection of factitious traumatic brain injury. *The Clinical Neuropsychologist, 9*, 230–240.

Meyers, J. E., & Volbrecht, M. (1998). Validity of reliable digit span for detection of malingering. *Assessment, 5*, 303–307.

Mittenberg, W., Canyock, E. M., Condit, D., & Patton, C. (2001). Treatment of post-concussion syndrome following mild head injury. *Journal of Clinical and Experimental Neuropsychology, 23*, 829–836.

Mittenberg, W., Tremont, G., Zielinski, R. E., Fichera, S., & Rayls, K. R. (1996). Cognitive-behavioral prevention of postconcussion syndrome. *Archives of Clinical Neuropsychology, 11*, 139–145.

Mittenberg, W., Zielinski, R. E., & Fichera, S. (1993). Recovery from mild head injury: A treatment manual for patients. *Psychotherapy in Private Practice*, *12*, 37–52.

Murray, C. K., Reynolds, J. C., Schroeder, J. M., Harrison, M. B., Evans, O. M., & Hospenthal, D. R. (2005). Spectrum of care provided at an echelon II medical unit during Operation Iraqi Freedom. *Military Medicine*, *170*, 516–520.

Okie, S. (2005). Traumatic brain injury in the war zone. *New England Journal of Medicine*, *352*, 2043–2047.

Sweet, J. J., Wolfe, P., Wattlberger, E., Numan, B., Rosenfeld, J. P., Clingerman, S., et al. (2000). Further investigation of traumatic brain injury versus insufficient effort with the California Verbal Learning Test. *Archives of Clinical Neuropsychology*, *15*, 105–113.

Vanderploeg, R. D., & Schinka, J. A. (1995). Predicting WAIS–R IQ premorbid ability: Combining subtest performance and demographic variable predictors. *Archives of Clinical Neuropsychology*, *10*, 225–239.

Warden, D. L., Ryan, L. M., Helmick, K. M., Schwab, K., French, L. M., Lu, W., Lux, W. E., Ecklund, J., & Ling, G. (2005). War neurotrauma: The Defense and Veterans Brain Injury Center (DVBIC) experience at Walter Reed Army Medical Center (WRAMC) (abstract). *Journal of Neurotrauma*, *22*, 1178.

Mild traumatic brain injury, depression, or malingered neurocognitive dysfunction: Change in zeitgeist, change in diagnosis

5

Glenn J. Larrabee

The following case study is unique in that I had the opportunity to evaluate this worker's compensation claimant twice: initially in 1987, prior to the veritable explosion of research on malingering, and again in 1996. In the intervening nine years, the seminal publications by Hiscock and Hiscock (1989) and Binder (1990, 1993) established forced choice methodology for the evaluation of malingering. Moreover, the decade of 1990 to 2000 resulted in a ten-fold increase in publications on forensic neuropsychology, with most of these papers focusing on evaluation of malingering (Sweet, King, Malina, Bergman, & Simmons, 2002). As the data will show, the diagnosis changed from the first evaluation to the second, largely as a result of a change in zeitgeist in neuropsychological assessment consequent to advances in research on malingering.

Case A was initially referred by the attorney for the worker's compensation insurance carrier for evaluation of possible traumatic brain injury following a slip and fall in October of 1983. He was a 43-year-old, right-handed Caucasian truck driver with eight years of education. He had undergone three prior neuropsychological evaluations. On the first examination, in July of 1984, conducted by another psychologist nearly one year post-trauma, he reported a blow to his head in the fall, but no loss of consciousness. He also reported sustaining a broken left wrist, left arm, broken ribs, and a damaged kidney (the broken wrist alone was documented as "possible" in the day of injury emergency room records; head trauma was not mentioned, nor was there any indication of other fractures or internal injuries). Neuropsychological testing yielded scores consistent with his educational and occupational attainment, with Wechsler Adult Intelligence Scale (WAIS) Verbal IQ of 98, Performance IQ of 114, Full Scale IQ of 105, and Wechsler Memory Scale (WMS) Memory Quotient of 94, and no other evidence of neuropsychological impairment on the Tactual Performance Test, Seashore Rhythm Test, or Multilingual Aphasia Examination. Mr. A. was described as performing poorly on the Trail Making Test and Speech Sounds Perception, with slowed Finger Tapping. Note that the actual raw data were unavailable for review. The MMPI was described as reflecting a mild to moderate conversion reaction with significant hypochondriacal preoccupation. The psychologist concluded that the neuropsychological evaluation showed some "soft signs" of possible brain damage; however, the results were viewed as far from conclusive. This examiner noted that the deviations from the norm could also be explained on the basis of tension and anxiety, as well as conversion features. The psychologist's working diagnostic impression was Postconcussion Syndrome with headaches, some dizziness, and mild depression.

The second neuropsychological evaluation was conducted in February and March of 1985, approximately 1½ years post injury, by a different psychologist. At the time of this examination, Mr. A. continued to complain of headache, but had new complaints of numbness in the left hand and arm, severe pain at the cranial-neck juncture, severe right arm pain, and right arm weakness. Test procedures included the Wechsler Adult Intelligence Scale–Revised (WAIS–R) and the Luria-Nebraska Neuropsychological Battery (LNNB). He obtained a Verbal IQ of 98, Performance IQ of 98, and Full Scale IQ of 98. The psychologist made note of the 16-point decline in Performance IQ relative to the first examination. He commented that although these tasks were sensitive to emotional factors such as depression, they were also susceptible to neurological damage, and since Mr. A.'s emotional status had improved compared to earlier evaluation, one had to be concerned about the possibility of neurological injury (note: the psychologist apparently was unaware that the natural course following most traumatic brain injuries is improvement over time rather than decline, unless complications develop such as normal pressure hydrocephalus). The LNNB Critical T-score level was 59.93. All LNNB subtests fell below this level (note that lower scores on the LNNB indicate better performance), including Motor (T = 33), Rhythm (T = 35), Tactile (T = 46), Visual (T = 31), Receptive Speech (T = 31), Expressive Speech (T = 44), Pathognomonic (T = 40), Left Hemisphere (T = 40), Right Hemisphere (T = 39), Writing (T = 52), Reading (T = 42), Arithmetic (T = 50), Memory (T = 53), and Intellectual Processes (T = 42). The psychologist commented that the afore-mentioned LNNB test results did not provide clear-cut evidence of neurological impairment, but he felt that item analysis affirmed a variety of difficulties, including verbally-described spatial rela-tionships, left hand tactile discrimination problems, difficulties with visual-verbal association memory, auditory memory, memory for complex auditory information when there is an intervening task, and verbal memory losses. The psychologist also interpreted these results as representative of impaired performance on skills governed by the right temporal lobe. He recommended neuro-logical evaluation to rule out spinal cord injury, cerebellar abnormalities, and cortical dysfunction; psychotherapy for emotional distress and family support; and development of vocational training plans.

Later testing with the MMPI by the same psychologist yielded a Welsh code of 1* 3" 924' 7-560/ FL/K. The psychologist interpreted the profile as showing signs of cerebral dysfunction and post-traumatic syndrome.

A third neuropsychological evaluation was conducted in August of 1986, nearly three years post-trauma, and over one year since the second evaluation, by a third psychologist. In addition to the complaints made to the second psychologist, he had a new complaint of visual disturbance, with the experience that he was trying to look through "white milk." He also emphasized memory problems, stating, "Today is my yesterday before today is over."

On this examination, Verbal IQ was 84, Performance IQ was 68, and Full Scale IQ was 76. Digit Span was a scaled score of 6. Memory testing scores were described as extremely poor. The psych-ologist noted that only rarely would such a pattern be obtained in someone whose central nervous system impairment could not be documented by neurological tests and examination. The psycholo-gist also commented that the performances were extremely impaired in relation to testing in 1984 and 1985, and this was an extremely rare finding since recovery from head injury is known to occur up to and beyond two years post injury, and Mr. A.'s recovery curve was exactly opposite to that of the vast majority of brain-injured individuals (note my comment above regarding the interpretation of deteriorated scores by the second psychologist). The psychologist also observed that Mr. A. performed poorly on tasks that are typically completed successfully by persons with moderate brain impairment, but often are done quite poorly by those who are presenting themselves as physically impaired when they are not. Personality testing was described as consistent with earlier test results (1984, 1985) in demonstrating somatization disorder. The psychologist concluded that the pattern of

Mr. A.'s test results was not suggestive of neuropsychological impairment that would be associated with any head injury. The clinical interview and personality testing suggested that Mr. A. was not malingering, but that Mr. A. did believe he was impaired. It was concluded that he had a somato-form pain disorder, and could benefit from a pain management program, and possible chemotherapy for depression.

Review of records from his initial evaluation in the emergency room showed a diagnosis of possible navicular fracture in the left wrist, with no mention of head injury, broken ribs, broken forearm, or kidney trauma (all information that later became part of the medical records, based on history provided by Mr. A. to subsequent physicians who did not have the benefit of review of his initial medical records). On follow-up evaluation nine days post-trauma, Mr. A. denied loss of consciousness, and there was no documentation that he even struck his head. EEG and CT scan of the brain in 1984 were both normal.

Mr. A. underwent two psychiatric evaluations. The first, in July of 1986, concluded that he suffered from Post-Traumatic Stress Disorder, with a rule out diagnosis of Postconcussion Syndrome. The second psychiatrist examined Mr. A. in October of 1986, and noted that although he could not be positive this was malingering, this possibility deserved further investigation.

Mr. A. also underwent pain rehabilitation for a two-month period in 1986. The neurologist in charge of his program noted several inconsistencies, including only showing severe memory problems when he was being formally tested or observed, and not on other occasions. Despite claims of remote memory loss, he was the best Trivial Pursuit player on the unit!

RESULTS OF 1987 EXAMINATION

On my first direct examination of Mr. A. in February and March of 1987, his behavior was marked by extreme psychomotor retardation with depressed facies and apparent great difficulty in concentration and formulation of thought processes. He required 7.5 hours to complete a "valid" MMPI. Repeated checking on his progress during the MMPI showed him to be apparently working on the task, but at an extremely slow pace. Due to his pronounced psychomotor slowing, limited examination was completed over three separate days. Upon completion of the examination, he walked up to the transportation vehicle in the parking lot, unaware he was being observed, but persisting in severely motorically retarded behavior with extremely slow gait. When he got in the car he sat, apparently talking to the driver but without any type of animation, taking on the appearance of a "wooden soldier." He was able to recall, with much display of effort, the original history of injury, recounting the same details of the accident as he had provided on his earlier examinations. Symptom complaints included seeing air bubbles and streaks in his vision, headaches, poor memory, and arm pain.

On the Benton Multilingual Aphasia Examination, he performed at the 32nd percentile for Visual Naming, but at the 3rd percentile for Controlled Oral Word Association (COWA). It was noted that his performance on COWA was significantly reduced compared to testing conducted three years earlier.

His Finger Tapping averaged 41.6 taps with the dominant right hand (8th percentile) and 38 taps with the left (14th percentile). Grip Strength averaged 50.5 kg with the right hand (34th percentile) and 20 kg with the left (< 1st percentile). He complained of pain in the left elbow during Grip Strength testing and that his hand felt numb and cold, but when I touched this hand, it was warm to the touch. His times on the Grooved Pegboard were 1 minute 52 seconds with the right hand (1st percentile) and 2 minutes 23 seconds with the left hand (< 1st percentile). On the Benton Tactile Form Perception Test, he correctly identified 4 of 5 designs with the right hand, and 3 of 5 with the left (testing was terminated at 5 trials for each hand due to extremely long average time per item; 55.4 seconds with the right hand, and 104.2 seconds with the left).

Despite gross impairments in attention, processing speed, and, as will be shown, verbal and visual learning and memory, he was normally oriented to time (correctly providing the month, year, and day of the week, with his only errors due to misstating the date by one day, and the time of day by 55 minutes). Speed of automatic mental processes was very impaired on the Wechsler Memory Scale Mental Control Subtest (he took 79 seconds to count from 20 to 1, 99 seconds to recite the alphabet, and 3 minutes 33 seconds to count from 1 to 40 in threes, making one error in the process). Trail Making A was performed in 1 minute 45 seconds (< 1st percentile) and Trail Making B was performed in 5 minutes and 46 seconds (< 1st percentile).

On the California Verbal Learning Test, his recall scores over the five learning trials were 2, 2, 1, 2, and 0. He recalled two words from Tuesday, but no words at short delay recall for the Monday list, and he did not provide any Monday items on cued recall. Due to his apparent severe impairment and expressed distress during testing, delayed recall, cued recall, and recognition were not conducted. On the Verbal Selective Reminding Test, the administration was terminated after six trials. He never once entered any words into long-term storage, with free recall values of 0, 2, 1, 2, 2, and 1 over the first six trials. He had 0 words on cued recall; and at the initiation of multiple choice recognition, he commented, "If I don't know the words on the list, how am I to know?" Delayed recall testing was deferred. On the Continuous Visual Memory Test, administration was terminated after the 52nd stimulus due to his apparent distress, repeated comments of "I don't know," and refusal to guess. On the Presidents Test, free recall was 3 of the last 6 Presidents (18th percentile), but sequencing of cards imprinted with their names in order of office was very impaired with a Spearman rho of 0.08 (< 1st percentile). He named only 4 of 6 photographs of the last 6 Presidents. The Photo Sequencing task was deferred.

The complete WAIS–R was not administered due to time constraints. Information was an age scaled score of 6 (he knew the capital of Italy, but did not know how many weeks were in a year). Digit Span was an age scaled score of 3 (he only responded correctly on 1 of 2 trials for the 3 forward sequence; 2 of 2 trials correct for the 2 reverse sequence; and 1 of 2 correct for the 3 reverse sequence). On Similarities, his age scaled score was 7 (he could not answer correctly how a boat and automobile were alike, but could give a 2 point response for poem and statue). He had age scaled scores of 4 for Block Design and 3 for Digit Symbol. These performances were grossly deteriorated from his performances on testing completed three years earlier.

On the Beck Depression Inventory, he scored 23 (moderate depression). On the MMPI, his scaled scores were L = 60, F = 55, K = 46, Hs = 85, D = 108, Hy = 80, Pd = 74, Mf = 67, Pa = 80, Pt = 85, Sc = 84, Ma = 50, and Si = 68.

Following this examination, I diagnosed him with depression of psychotic proportions, with pronounced psychomotor retardation. I pointed out that there was no evidence that his problems were due to brain injury, based on several factors including the initial ER report, which did not document loss of consciousness or the confusion and disorientation characteristic of post-traumatic amnesia. Moreover, the normal WAIS IQ, WMS MQ, and Tactual Performance Test scores when examined by the first psychologist in 1984 contradicted the presence of any neurologic dysfunction, as did his normal performance on the LNNB when examined by the second psychologist in 1985. I opined that he had an apparent conversion reaction (based on testing from the first and third examinations), with decompensation into a psychotic depression, in part due to iatrogenic factors (psychologist #2 misdiagnosing brain damage and treating him for brain damage).

RESULTS OF 1996 EXAMINATION

Mr. A. was referred by the carrier for reevaluation in 1996, regarding his current diagnosis, treatment recommendations, and need for attendant care. Since the time of my first examination, Mr. A. had been receiving Worker's Compensation Disability, plus supplemental compensation for attendant care.

Subsequent to my first examination, Mr. A. had left Florida and moved to another state, where he lived with a relative who served as an attendant. Curiously, despite prior history of severe memory dysfunction and current complaints of same by Mr. A. and his caretaker, he was able to drive himself to the caretaker's home in another state located over 500 miles from Florida.

Since my initial evaluation, Mr. A. had received inpatient and outpatient treatment, which was terminated in December of 1987 due to his expressed frustration that he was not getting any better. He also underwent additional psychiatric evaluation at a premier university medical center located in the state where he had moved within the year prior to my reevaluation of him. He was accompanied by his relative/caretaker to this psychiatric examination and both the caretaker and Mr. A. reported significant memory problems; for example, the caretaker had to place a note on Mr. A.'s bedroom door on a daily basis so that Mr. A. knew where he was. The psychiatrists conducting this evaluation did not obtain any evidence for neurovegetative symptoms suggestive of depression, hypomania, or frontal disinhibition. On direct examination, they noted poor eye contact and psychomotor retardation, but psychomotor speed was observed to be normal when Mr. A. was not aware he was being observed. The diagnostic impression was factitious disorder with the need to rule out possible malingering (note: factitious disorder would be precluded by the presence of an external incentive, such as worker's compensation, and Mr. A. had been referred for psychiatric evaluation by the insurance carrier). The psychiatrists found no neurological etiology for his symptoms, either clinically or on prior neuroimaging, and cognitive testing was noted to be inconsistent with any known organic amnestic syndrome.

On current examination, Mr. A.'s caretaker reported that Mr. A. spent most of his time around home, occasionally accompanying the caretaker on errands. Mr. A. still drove a car, but only if the caretaker was certain Mr. A. was familiar with where he was supposed to go. Mr. A. had to be reminded to take his medication. The caretaker also reported Mr. A. had lost his senses of smell and taste. In this regard, Mr. A. denied weight loss or change in appetite on the Beck Depression Inventory, and did not appear to be different in body mass compared to my recollection of his appearance in 1987.

On direct interview, Mr. A. denied memory for events subsequent to the accident in 1983. He reported he remembered he had an accident, which to him seemed to have happened yesterday, stating, "It seemed like yesterday was 1983." He knew the current year was 1996 because his caretaker had informed him of this the day of the evaluation.

On reevaluation, the psychomotor retardation I observed on earlier examination in 1987 was not as pronounced; for example, the MMPI took 4 hours on reexamination, as opposed to 7.5 hours on earlier examination. Despite memory complaints and extremely poor memory test performance, he remembered his way back and forth to the restroom located outside the office, as well as remembered to hang up the restroom key upon his return. He was also able to relate the names of the restaurants where he had lunch on each day of the evaluation.

In my reevaluation report, I specifically commented on the multiple professional publications that had appeared since my earlier examination of Mr. A., providing new technology for evaluation of motivation and malingering. Forced choice testing was explained in my reevaluation report, and a variety of these procedures were administered to Mr. A. He was extremely resistant to forced choice procedures, stating that he did not like to guess and did not want to guess or be forced to guess. On a couple of occasions, he had to be instructed that he could not consistently pick one side, or alternate his selections; rather, he truly had to guess.

On the Rey 15-Item Test, Mr. A. reproduced 10 of the 15 items, in the range of preserved motivation. On the Portland Digit Recognition Test (PDRT) he had an Easy Score of 22 out of 36, and a Hard Score of 22 out of 36. Given his complaints of anosmia, a 20-item forced choice odor identification task was devised, involving licorice, orange, vanilla, lemon, and peppermint food flavors. In the right nostril, he correctly identified only 4 out of 20, significantly worse than chance at $p < .01$. In the left nostril, he identified 11 of 20, a chance level of performance. The combined left and right identification of 15 out of 40 correct had a probability of 0.08.

Given his complaint of not remembering information since 1983, a 21-item forced-choice test was constructed for information he should have known since this year. Out of 21 items for which he denied any recollection, 8 responses were correct in forced-choice identification, $p < .19$. Mr. A. appeared quite surprised when I informed him he had been married following the accident. When presented with his wife's name and a foil, he chose the foil. Of the six items directly related to personal history (e.g., marriage), only one response was correct.

On the Warrington Recognition Memory Test (RMT) he correctly identified 22 of 50 words ($p < .24$), 19 of 50 Faces ($p < .06$), and his combined Words and Faces score of 41 of 100 was significantly worse-than-chance ($p < .05$).

In this reevaluation, I noted that the above performances raised serious questions about the validity of his complaints and performance. I also alerted the referral source to atypical patterns of performance that Mr. A. demonstrated on clinical measures of motor function and on the WAIS–R.

On this second examination, Mr. A. performed significantly better on COWA than on my previous examination, scoring at the 37th percentile on reevaluation. He produced 17 additional words compared to the earlier testing.

On retesting, right hand Finger Tapping averaged 33.8 taps (2nd percentile) with left hand averaging 35.2 taps (12th percentile), both performances lower than on prior examination. Grip Strength averaged 29 kg with the right hand (2nd percentile) and 22 kg with the left hand (< 1st percentile), both performances lower than baseline. On the Purdue Pegboard (not administered previously) he placed 10.5 pegs with the right hand (4th percentile), 11.5 pegs with the left (14th percentile), and 8.5 pairs of pegs for bimanual placement (6th percentile) averaged over two trials per hand. Last, on the Grooved Pegboard, he required 101 seconds with the right hand, and 95 seconds with the left, both times *faster* than on testing conducted nine years earlier. Thus, he slowed on Finger Tapping, and weakened on Grip Strength, but sped up on the Grooved Pegboard, compared to testing conducted nine years earlier.

On reexamination, Temporal Orientation was severely impaired. He misstated the month by two months, the date by 27 days, and the day of the week by three days. He correctly identified the year and estimated time of day within 17 minutes. This performance is significantly worse than his Temporal Orientation nine years earlier. Despite worsening Temporal Orientation, WMS Mental Control improved. He made two errors in counting 20 to 1 (errorless before), but was much quicker at 8 seconds (79 seconds previously). He was able to recite the alphabet in 13 seconds (99 seconds earlier), and counted from 1 to 40 in threes in 31 seconds (3 minutes and 33 seconds, with one error, on earlier testing). Trail Making A required 70 seconds (105 seconds previously), whereas Trail Making B required 2 minutes 22 seconds (5 minutes 46 seconds nine years earlier). On the Auditory Verbal Learning Test (AVLT) he recalled 19 words over the five learning trials. List B recall was 3 words. He recalled 2 List A words at short delay, with 0 at long delay recall. On the CVLT administered nine years earlier, he never recalled more than 2 words on any trial, recalled 7 words over all five trials, and recalled no words on Trial 5. On retesting, his AVLT Recognition score was 2 of 15 (below the cutoff and in the range consistent with malingering; see Binder, Villanueva, Howieson, & Moore, 1993). On a forced choice task that I constructed using the AVLT words and 15 foils, he got 6 of 15 correct, a chance level of performance. As noted earlier, his Warrington Recognition Memory Test Word total was 22 (below the cutoff published by Millis, 1992, and in the range consistent with malingering). His Warrington Words and Faces combined score of 41 out of 100 was significantly worse-than-chance at $p < .05$. Continuous Recognition Memory Total Correct was far below the 1st percentile, with 0 of 8 at 30 minute delayed recognition. On the Continuous Visual Memory Test, his Total Correct score was below the 2nd percentile, and 30 minute delayed recognition score was 0 of 7. He had a WAIS–R VIQ of 84, PIQ of 88, and FIQ of 85 (note these scores are 14, 26, and 20 points lower, respectively, than his WAIS IQ scores 12 years earlier during his first neuropsychological evaluation). His Wide Range Achievement Test-3 Arithmetic standard score was 92 (30th percentile). He had a score of 9 on the Beck Depression Inventory. On the MMPI–2 his only elevation was on Scale 2 (T = 66).

Following reexamination, I concluded that there continued to be no evidence for a neurologic basis to his symptomatic complaints. I did not see any evidence for the psychotic depression I felt was evident in 1987, nor did I see evidence for a somatoform disorder. I opined that his performances on symptom validity testing, memory testing, and other cognitive and sensorimotor functions were most similar to those produced by persons attempting to feign or malinger brain dysfunction. Last, I stated that it would be difficult to argue for attendant care for someone who was able to handle the basic activities of daily living and continue to drive an automobile safely.

Table 5.1 presents select test data from his five separate neuropsychological evaluations and allows comparison of performance over time. Note that the first two examinations in 1984 and 1985 demonstrate essentially normal intellectual and memory functions, which can be contrasted with significantly lower performance on memory and intellectual tasks over the last three examinations, conducted in 1986, 1987, and 1996.

After my reevaluation report was received, the carrier resolved the case. I was never deposed, nor was there any court appearance.

TABLE 5.1   Select test data for Case A, by year of examination[a]

TEST SCORE[b]	1984	1985	1986	1987	1996
VIQ	98	98	84	–	84
PIQ	114	98	68	–	88
FIQ	105	98	76	–	85
WMS MQ	94	–	"very poor"	–	–
LNNB Mem T	–	53	–	–	–
CVLT 1–5	–	–	–	7	–
AVLT 1–5	–	–	–	–	19
Temp Orient	–	–	–	2 error pts	28 error pts
Mental Cont	–	–	–	0 points	4 points
Trails A	–	–	–	105"	70"
Trails B	–	–	–	346"	142"
COWA	–	–	–	9 words	26 words
Tap R/L	–	–	–	46.6/38	33.8/35.2
Grip R/L	–	–	–	50.5/20	29/22
GPB R/L	–	–	–	112"/143"	101"/95"
FBS	–	–	–	27	12
Beck	–	–	–	23	9
Rel Digits	–	–	–	2	7

[a] All scores are raw scores, except for VIQ, PIQ, FIQ, WMS MQ, and LNNB Mem T.
[b] VIQ = Verbal IQ, PIQ = Performance IQ, FIQ = Full Scale IQ for WAIS (1984 examination) and WAIS–R (1985, 1986, 1997 examinations); WMS MQ = Wechsler Memory Scale Memory Quotient; LNNB Mem T = Luria-Nebraska Neuropsychological Battery Memory T score; CVLT 1–5 = California Verbal Learning Test Trial 1–5 Total; AVLT 1–5 = Rey Auditory Verbal Learning Test Trial 1–5 Total; Temp Orient = Benton Temporal Orientation Test; Mental Cont = Wechsler Memory Scale Mental Control subtest; Trails A = Trail Making Test part A; Trails B = Trail Making Test part B; COWA = Benton Controlled Oral Word Association Test; Tap R/L = Finger Tapping test right/left; Grip R/L = Grip Strength right/left; GPB = Grooved Pegboard test right/left; FBS = MMPI–2 Lees-Haley Fake Bad Scale; Beck = Beck Depression Inventory; Rel Digits = Reliable Digit Span.

DISCUSSION

The most unique feature of this case was my opportunity to examine Mr. A. nine years after my first examination of him. I distinctly recall being shocked when I reviewed my 1987 examination in 1996, prior to conducting the reevaluation. What a difference nine years made! In 1987, I was reluctant to insist that an apparently massively depressed Mr. A. "guess" on recognition memory testing. When I insisted he do this during the reevaluation, Mr. A. became quite angry. When I persisted in my demands, he did "guess"; however, he "guessed" significantly worse than chance.

My 1987 examination of Mr. A. occurred prior to the seminal publications by Hiscock and Hiscock (1989) and Binder (1990, 1993) establishing forced-choice methodology for the evaluation of malingering. As noted in the introduction to this chapter, the ensuing decade of 1990 to 2000 witnessed a ten-fold increase in publications on forensic neuropsychology, with the majority of these papers focusing on evaluation of malingering (Sweet et al., 2002).

Not only did my reexamination of Mr. A. benefit from the advances in malingering assessment as of 1996, but additional research since 1996 allowed a reanalysis of my 1987 data in 2005. In 1987, Mr. A. had a Reliable Digit Span of 2, which falls substantially below the cutoff of 7 or less for identification of malingering (Greiffenstein, Baker, & Gola, 1994). Also in 1987, Mr. A. obtained a Lees-Haley Fake Bad Scale (Lees-Haley, English, & Glenn, 1991) of 27, a value that falls substantially beyond cutoffs of 21 (Ross, Millis, Krukowski, Putnam, & Adams, 2004) or 22 (Larrabee, 2003b) for discrimination of probable or definite malingerers from moderate and severe traumatic brain injury. The combination of poor Reliable Digit Span and elevated Lees-Haley Fake Bad Scale at the levels produced by Mr. A. in 1987 was not associated with any false positives in discriminating litigants with either definite or probable malingered neurocognitive dysfunction (Slick, Sherman, & Iverson, 1999) from patients with moderate or severe traumatic brain injury, psychiatric, or other neurologic conditions (Larrabee, 2003a).

Mr. A.'s performance on my 1987 and 1996 examinations can also be considered relative to the diagnostic criteria for malingered neurocognitive dysfunction (MND) that have been proposed by Slick, Sherman, and Iverson (1999). These criteria take a multiple data source approach to diagnosis of malingering, and allow a gradation of certainty about MND ranging from possible, to probable, to definite. Diagnosis of MND requires the presence of a substantial external incentive (Criterion A), evidence from psychological testing (B criteria) and/or evidence from self-report (C criteria), and the requirement that the criteria from B and C cannot be fully accounted for by psychiatric, neurological, or developmental factors (Criterion D). B criteria include: definite negative response bias (B1) manifested by below chance performance ($p < .05$) on one or more forced-choice tests; probable response bias (B2) manifested by performance on one or more well-validated psychometric tests or indices consistent with feigning; discrepancy between test data and known patterns of brain functioning (B3; e.g., average memory test performance in the context of impaired performance on measures of attention); discrepancy between test data and observed behavior (B4; e.g., failing memory tests but showing evidence of normal memory in recalling his history during examination); discrepancy between test data and reliable collateral reports (B5; e.g., patient handles finances but is unable to do simple math problems); and discrepancy between test data and documented background history (B6; e.g., improbably poor performance on two or more standardized tests within one domain of cognitive function that is inconsistent with documented neurological or psychiatric history, such as memory test performance similar to that produced by patients with over one month of coma in a patient who did not lose consciousness). C criteria for evidence from self-report include: self-reported history is discrepant with documented history (C1; e.g., exaggerated severity of physical injury discrepant with actual records); self-reported symptoms are discrepant with known patterns of brain functioning (C2; e.g., claims of loss of autobiographical information after mild traumatic brain injury without loss of consciousness); self-reported symptoms are discrepant with behavioral observations (C3; e.g., claimed severe memory impairment but able to demonstrate normal memory functioning in everyday tasks); self-reported symptoms are discrepant with information obtained from collateral informants (C4; e.g., patient report of severe memory impairment and behavior consistent with this when seen in the clinic, with evidence of minimal memory impairment in the home); and evidence of exaggerated or fabricated psychological dysfunction (C5; e.g., well-validated validity scales on self-report measures of psychological adjustment such as the MMPI–2 are strongly suggestive of exaggerated or fabricated distress or dysfunction).

According to the Slick et al. criteria, Definite MND occurs in the context of a substantial external incentive (A), with evidence of significantly worse-than-chance performance (B1) that cannot be fully explained by Psychiatric, Neurological or Developmental factors. Probable MND occurs in the context of a substantial external incentive (A), with evidence of two or more of B2–B6 criteria, or one of B2–B6 criteria and one of C1–C5 criteria, that cannot be fully explained by Psychiatric, Neurological or Developmental factors.

The Slick et al. diagnostic criteria can be applied to the 1987 and 1996 examination findings for Mr. A. In 1987, Mr. A. was already receiving worker's compensation (Criterion A). He showed evidence of B2 (Reliable Digit Span of 2), B3 (normal Temporal Orientation despite gross impairments in attention and memory at the level consistent with dementia; gross deterioration in test performance compared to evidence of normal memory and intelligence testing within the first year post-trauma; better performance on more difficult compared to easier items on WAIS–R Information and Similarities subtests), B6 (grossly impaired test performance in the context of a history of no loss of consciousness), C1 (reports of serious orthopedic and internal injuries discrepant from the actual medical records), and C5 (Lees-Haley Fake Bad Scale of 27). Although one might question if he met Criterion D, due to an apparent severe depression, behavioral inconsistencies were noted in the pain management program that he went through within the year prior to my 1987 examination. Moreover, records subsequent to my 1987 examination showed that he declined to continue in psychiatric treatment that same year, due to his perception of no progress, yet he was subsequently able to drive alone to his relative's home, over 500 miles away. This reanalysis of Mr. A. using the Slick et al. criteria shows that he met the criteria for Probable MND in 1987.

In 1996, Mr. A. was still receiving worker's compensation, as well as supplemental payment for attendant care (Criterion A). Mr. A. now met Criterion B1 (significantly worse-than-chance performance on Warrington Recognition Memory Test combined score for Words and Faces, and on odor identification in the right nostril), as well as B2 (below objective cutoff on Warrington Recognition Memory Test for Words; AVLT Recognition of 2 of 15 words), B4 (grossly impaired memory performance with ability to go to the restroom by himself and remember to hang up the key upon return; also able to accurately report the name of the restaurant where he ate lunch each day, confirmed with his caretaker), and B6 (performance at levels of severe impairment inconsistent with absence of loss of consciousness, and inconsistent with earlier levels of normal memory and intelligence test performance in 1984). C criteria included C2 (claims of remote memory loss with ability to remember the accident; "yesterday is like it was 1983") and C3 (complaints of severe memory impairment but able to go to the restroom by himself and recall where he ate lunch on both days of examination). Given his essentially normal MMPI–2 in 1996, there was no basis whatsoever for concern over psychiatric factors that could entirely explain his clinical presentation. In 1996, Mr. A. clearly met the Slick et al. diagnostic criteria for Definite MND.

Furthermore, consider that Mr. A. showed evidence consistent with Probable Malingered Neurocognitive Dysfunction in 1987, even based on the limited data collected. Since Mr. A.'s performance improved on several measures in 1996 relative to 1987 (e.g., Controlled Oral Word Association, WMS Mental Control, WAIS–R Digit Span, Grooved Pegboard), it is reasonable to assume that had forced-choice testing been administered in 1987, Mr. A. would have produced significantly worse-than-chance performance in 1987. Consequently, Mr. A. would likely have shown evidence for Definite Malingered Neurocognitive Dysfunction had forced-choice symptom validity testing been conducted in 1987.

In closing, this unique case demonstrates a change in diagnosis due to advances in malingering research. Other cases of malingering evaluated prior to the proliferation of malingering research in the 1990s may well have been misdiagnosed as having legitimate psychiatric disorders, such as conversion reaction or depression.

ACKNOWLEDGMENTS

Portions of this work were presented at the 33rd Annual Meeting of the International Neuropsychological Society, St. Louis, Missouri, February, 2005. I acknowledge the assistance of Bridgette Rees, B.S., and Stefanie L. Bronson, B.A., B.M., in the preparation of this manuscript.

REFERENCES

Binder, L. M. (1990). Malingering following minor head trauma. *The Clinical Neuropsychologist, 4*, 25–36.

Binder, L. M. (1993). Assessment of malingering after mild head trauma with the Portland Digit Recognition Test. *Journal of Clinical and Experimental Neuropsychology, 15*, 170–182.

Binder, L. M., Villanueva, M. R., Howieson, D., & Moore, R. T. (1993). The Rey AVLT recognition memory task measures motivational impairment after mild head trauma. *Archives of Clinical Neuropsychology, 8*, 137–147.

Greiffenstein, M. F., Baker, W. J., & Gola, T. (1994). Validation of malingered amnesia measures with a large clinical sample. *Psychological Assessment, 6*, 218–224.

Hiscock, M., & Hiscock, C. K. (1989). Refining the forced-choice method for the detection of malingering. *Journal of Clinical and Experimental Neuropsychology, 11*, 967–974.

Larrabee, G. J. (2003a). Detection of malingering using atypical performance patterns on standard neuropsychological tests. *The Clinical Neuropsychologist, 17*, 410–425.

Larrabee, G. J. (2003b). Detection of symptom exaggeration with the MMPI-2 in litigants with malingered neurocognitive dysfunction. *The Clinical Neuropsychologist, 17*, 54–68.

Lees-Haley, P. R., English, L. T., & Glenn, W. J. (1991). A fake bad scale for the MMPI-2 for personal injury claimants. *Psychological Reports, 68*, 203–210.

Millis, S. R. (1992). The Recognition Memory Test in the detection of malingered and exaggerated memory deficits. *The Clinical Neuropsychologist, 6*, 406–414.

Ross, S. R., Millis, S. R., Krukowski, R. A., Putnam, S. H., & Adams, K. M. (2004). Detecting probable malingering on the MMPI-2: An examination of the Fake-Bad Scale in mild head injury. *Journal of Clinical and Experimental Neuropsychology, 26*, 115–124.

Slick, D. J., Sherman, E. M. S., & Iverson, G. L. (1999). Diagnostic criteria for malingered neurocognitive dysfunction: Proposed standards for clinical practice and research. *The Clinical Neuropsychologist, 13*, 545–561.

Sweet, J. J., King, J. H., Malina, A. C., Bergman, M. A., & Simmons, A. (2002). Documenting the prominence of forensic neuropsychology at national meetings and in relevant professional journals from 1990 to 2000. *The Clinical Neuropsychologist, 16*, 481–494.

Factitious or fictitious brain injury? An adventure in applying the DSM–IV

6

Manfred F. Greiffenstein

This case was chosen because it exemplifies the conceptual and practical problems in the DSM–IV diagnosis of medically unexplained presentations. By either design or oversight, the DSM–IV approach to atypical somatic or cognitive presentations ignores the multilevel nature of behavior causation and disability consequences (Cunnien, 1997). My purpose is to describe the difficulties in DSM–IV differential diagnosis and offer practical guidelines for resolving them.

I altered nonessential biographical and situational details in order to maintain plaintiff's anonymity. These alterations had no bearing on ultimate conclusions. There was no alteration of test scores, symptom reports, accident details, event sequences, or medical documentation. The "big picture" was intact.

LEGAL BACKGROUND AND INJURY HISTORY

Legal backdrop

Mrs. B. is a 43-year-old, high school educated, right handed, married female and part-time stock clerk. I saw her in June 2003 for an independent neuropsychological examination at the request of a defense attorney. Mrs. B. sought compensation for neurologic and psychological injuries that she blamed on a two-car accident in June 2001. Mrs. B. initiated a first party lawsuit for payment of benefits under Michigan's No Fault law, including payments to her family for replacement services; she also brought a third party lawsuit seeking money damages from the at-fault driver. The retaining attorney represented the third party defendant, and he requested I examine Mrs. B. for any psychological and neuropsychological damages incurred as the result of a June 2001 rear-end collision. He also asked whether secondary gain played any role in understanding the presentation. Financially, Mrs. B. was receiving partial wage loss and payment for ongoing individual psychotherapy; she felt this was insufficient.

Injury characteristics

Injury severity staging was quantitatively and qualitatively based on review of both the earliest records and Mrs. B.'s current self-report. ER records suggested generally unimpressive, but ambiguous, injury characteristics from a neurocognitive standpoint. Mrs. B. was the belted and restrained driver of a car rear-ended in June 2001. ER records documented that Mrs. B. served as her own historian. She denied memory loss for accident details, and reported only "some concentration problems" to the attending physician. The initial neurological examination was negative, the head appeared atraumatic with no report of blunt trauma from any witness, brief mental status testing showed a Glasgow Coma Scale of 15/15, and serial nursing notes also documented unremarkable mental status. Mrs. B. was discharged home with a diagnosis of cervical strain (whiplash). No head injury instruction sheet was provided or radiographic studies ordered.

My interview data in June 2003 further supported the evolving hypothesis of absent or negligible neurological injury. Mrs. B. recalled both her mental state at the time of the incident (e.g., "I wondered whether I would be pushed into the car in front") and her immediate reactions (getting out of car, refusing ambulance, calling family members). She preferred family members to come to the scene of the accident and take her to the hospital, raising a tentative hypothesis of dependency tactics. A time-intensity profile of the subsequent clinical course was also not consistent with the natural history of a mild closed head injury. Both records and self-report showed complaints abruptly waxing and waning but steadily multiplying over time, with late appearing subjective cognitive impairment voiced months post-accident. The delayed cognitive complaints emerged at the same time Mrs. B. started giving conflicting injury histories: Two months postaccident she told her internist there were no symptoms or functional problems; she had returned to work fulltime. However, four days later, she told a neurologist about new onset of depression, forgetting episodes, and "brief loss of consciousness" associated with the accident. The neurologist did not contact the internist, took Mrs. B.'s word, relied on new history to diagnose brain damage, and referred her to a rehabilitation center in January 2002. She underwent months of multidisciplinary treatment, including group-based education in brain injury symptoms.

Pre-injury records

County mental health records provided extensive documentation of pre-accident psychosocial problems and deviant experiences. Highlights of these mental health records showed Mrs. B.:

- Alleged severe sexual abuse by family-of-origin members, beginning in childhood.
- Dropped contact with family when they denied her allegations.
- Reported "little memory" of her childhood. Her husband told a social worker the memory loss indicated repression of ritualistic sexual abuse.
- Underwent ten years of weekly individual and group psychotherapy for "adult survivors of sexual abuse."
- Received chart diagnoses dating back to 1989 of: multiple personality disorder; dissociative disorder; major depressive disorder; dysthymia; nightmares; and "abuse-related chronic post-traumatic stress disorder."
- Alleged periodic disability due to severe depression, lack of motivation, severe withdrawal, heightened startle response, psychogenic fugue, and amnesia.

Post-incident treatment records

All post-incident treatment records were available for inspection. The head and spine injury team at a local hospital conducted extensive assessments in January 2002 and recommended cognitive and other rehabilitation sessions 3–4 times a week; no validity testing was performed. Mrs. B. rarely showed up for speech pathologist, cognitive rehabilitation specialist, or occupational therapist appointments, and attendance at physical therapy was sporadic. She was discharged for poor attendance in April 2002. Subsequent records showed visits to multiple new doctors and treatment facilities over a two-year span; there was much commentary on poor attendance and frank noncompliance (e.g., many excuses why she would not take medications, despite insurer pre-approval). She voluntarily returned to the original rehabilitation program in June 2002 only to get a driver's evaluation from the occupational therapy; she explained that she disagreed with her doctor's advice not to drive and she had already returned to part-time work. She passed the driving test based on a normal Trailmaking Test (Part B) administered by an occupational therapist.

Post-accident evaluations

Two psychologists conducted neuropsychological testing after the accident but prior to my examination. The first psychologist saw Mrs. B. on referral from the neurologist in February 2002. This assessment was limited to interview, history, and the Wechsler Memory Scale–3 (WMS-3). The psychologist found diffusely poor WMS-3 scores ranging from −1.5 SD to −3 SD below age appropriate means. The psychologist accepted these scores at face value, interpreted them in absolute terms without reference to injury severity, and gave a formal diagnosis of "Amnestic disorder due to head trauma and PTSD." There was no symptom validity testing.

A licensed psychologist retained by the first party attorney conducted a neuropsychological examination in June 2002. In addition to a more comprehensive test battery, a number of validity tests were added, including an abbreviated Portland Digit Recognition Test (PDRT), the Test of Memory Malingering (TOMM), Reliable Digit Span (RDS), the MMPI–2 Fake Bad Scale (FBS), and the traditional MMPI "F-family." The score summary sheet showed the following:

- TOMM scores of 25/50, 30/50, and 32/50 (chance or near-chance levels)
- 27-item PDRT = 44% correct (chance level)
- RDS = 5 (below cutoff of 7)
- Rey Word List = 9 correct with 3 false positives
- MMPI–2 FBS = 95-T (raw score of 32)
- Extremely low scores on Symbol Digit Modalities Test (SDMT)(< −4.0 SD below mean)
- Grip strength weak (< 10 kg) but Lafayette Grooved Pegboard scores in customary range for age and gender.

This neuropsychologist noted that Mrs. B. produced *unremarkable scores* on the genuine memory tests such as the Wechsler Memory Scale–Revised (WMS–R; Logical Memory and Visual Reproduction scales) and the California Verbal Learning Test–2nd Edition (CVLT–2) delayed recall indices. He theorized that suggestibility and/or test order might be responsible for the atypical score pattern that clearly violated a difficulty hierarchy: poor performance on simple but good performance on difficult memory tests. He also addressed ecological validity, noting that the discrepancy between the normally paced speech during the interview contrasted with Mrs. B.'s extremely slow speech during the oral portion of the SDMT.

EXAMINATION RESULTS

History and mental status

Mrs. B. came to my interview two years post-accident (June 2003). She was accompanied by her husband, but she served as the main historian. Her physical appearance was that of a 5 foot 7 inch overweight female with adequate hygiene. Her affect was mildly apprehensive and dysphoric, and mood was anxious and tense. She was fluent, animated, talkative, and communicated in an organized but circumstantial manner. Similarly, speech content showed a strong somatic trend and strong illness conviction regarding neurological injury; she repeatedly emphasized how "closed head injury" explained her difficulties in living. Cognitively, she served as sole historian and spontaneously recalled many physical, neurological, and cognitive complaints. She also reported the circumstantial details surrounding minor forgetting episodes from the prior week. There were no obvious memory retrieval problems for post-accident events. For example, she recalled her medications as well as their strengths, dosages, and indications. However, she refused to take them and proceeded to provide me with a lengthy and numbing explanation of how each medication makes her "worse." No attentional lapses, psychomotor retardation, or distractibility were appreciated this visit either. Overall, her dramatic and imploring interpersonal style, combined with treatment resistance (both self-reported and in records), led me to conclude Mrs. B. was someone more interested in being believed than in being relieved.

Systems review further elicited atypical complaints relative to expectations of a traumatic brain injury. She rated remote memory as more grossly disturbed than recent memory since the accident, with memory gaps of many years' duration. She denied any memory of childhood and forgot most of her adolescence. Other atypical and unusual complaints included loss of semantic memory (reading, spelling), headaches triggered only by heat, fatigue without any diurnal pattern, loss of taste without loss of smell, and vague visual distortions such as "poor depth perception." My overall impression at the interview stage was multiple pseudoneurologic complaints unexplainable by the injury characteristics or any recognizable supratentorial disorder.

Present social status indicated part-time work as a clerk at a local parts store. She acknowledged struggling to balance the demands of work, mental health appointments, financial management, childcare and other household chores. Her husband spoke up and provided an insight into this family's division of labor: He refuses to work. Asked why, he explained that the men in his family have histories of back problems, for which they receive disability checks. He was certain he would get hurt in the future, so he refused to work outside or inside the home in order to preempt future injury. He also acknowledged he was the source of the ritualistic abuse theory predating the accident.

School records

Scholastic records showed Mrs. B. to have been a fair student, graduating with a 2.15 GPA and ranking 39th in a class of 53 at graduation in a rural school district. Her coursework was geared towards domestic arts and practical work skills. She generally performed poorer in the few core academic classes she took.

Laboratory data

A brain CT scan without contrast and cervical spine films were obtained on the date of incident. Both the brain scan and the complete cervical spine series were normal. A routine EEG was obtained three months later and read as normal. A brain MRI with and without contrast was later obtained because of later appearing complaints; this study also showed a normal appearing brain.

Test results

Neurocognitive and psychiatric symptom validity testing during my examination yielded many suspiciously poor scores:

- TOMM scores were 36, 41, and 42/50 (improved over earlier testing but still below cutoff of 45/50)
- Greiffenstein RDS was again a poor 5 (3 digits forward and 2 backwards).
- CVLT–2 forced-choice recognition hits (d'): $z = -2.5$
- Combined finger tapping: 50.4 taps (R = 26.8; L = 23.6)(improved over earlier)
- Rey Word Recognition = 11 with 2 false positives (improved).

Repeat neuropsychological testing showed a pattern of both improved and worse scores. The following list highlights substantial change scores. Scores are listed in chronological order:

- CVLT–2 Total Recall = 54 earlier vs. 43 presently (worse)
- CVLT–2 Short Delay = 13/16 vs. 10/16 (worse)
- CVLT–2 Long Delay = 13/16 vs. 8/16 (worse)
- SDMT 15 written and 23 oral vs. SDMT–W = 22 and SDMT–O = 30 (better)
- Luria 3-Step sum (R + L) = 17 vs. 7 (much worse)
- Trailmaking B = 138″ vs. 181″ (much slower)
- Trailmaking B also slower than when she took her driver's evaluation
- Booklet Category = 114 errors vs. 79 (better)
- WMS–R Visual Reproduction I & II = 31 & 21 vs. 19 & 15 (much worse).

There was no interval history of new brain insult, so the marked decline in memory scores was not explainable on the basis of genuine brain dysfunction. In fact, I received a pattern opposite to that of the initial IME examiner: relatively better performance on symptom validity tests, poorer performance on genuine memory tests. This pattern of change scores was grossly inconsistent with the natural history of a TBI or any other form of cerebral dysfunction for that matter.

The MMPI–2 was of doubtful validity. The Infrequency score was 96-T, and F–K was +7. Although not automatically diagnostic of malingering, these scores are consistent with symptom magnification. The MMPI–2 FBS of 26 (raw) is also above established cutoffs for exaggerated somatic and neurotic complaints (Greiffenstein, Fox, & Lees-Haley, 2007; Iverson, Henrichs, Barton, & Allen, 2002). VRIN and TRIN were within normal limits, meaning Mrs. B. likely approached the items in a careful and attentive manner. This observation rules out alternate hypotheses of severe disengagement or "confusion" as explanations for the elevated validity scales.

CASE ANALYSIS

Conceptual and empirical background

The detection of deceptive elements in clinical presentations requires a relevant knowledge base in which the case facts and test scores are placed. Since the time of Charcot in 1888 (Goetz, 2007), detection of simulation requires fundamental knowledge of and direct experience with genuine organic brain syndromes, including their defining neurobehavioral manifestations, and their evolution across time. Prospects for simulation are raised any time there is a large subjective distance between expectations of a given brain syndrome and the behavior (or test scores) of the individual patient (Greiffenstein, Baker, & Gola, 1994). Large discrepancies between symptom presentation and expectation can be termed unexplained medical syndromes (Binder & Campbell, 2004). In the case of Mrs. B., there are disseminating and magnifying complaints across time, a presentation inconsistent with expectations of mild closed head injury. The Diagnostic and Statistical Manual, fourth edition (DSM–IV; APA, 1994) offers numerous considerations when confronted with pseudomedical presentations and nonstereotypical response to time or treatment (Eisendrath, 1994; Goetz, 2007). The applicable DSM–IV diagnoses to consider include somatization disorder, somatoform disorder, and pain disorder with psychological features, factitious disorder (FD), and malingering (M). These diagnoses differ however in degree of intentionality, awareness of motive, and incentive type (Cunnien, 1997).

The most difficult differentiation, and the central issue of this case study, is between FD and M. These diagnoses overlap because both entail *voluntary* production of feigned medical syndromes. The DSM–IV requires a diagnosis of FD if the only apparent motive is desire for the sick role. In M, the motive can be any external incentive, except for social validation of the sick role. The conceptual deficiencies of DSM–IV criteria are next discussed.

The first conceptual deficiency of the DSM–IV is violation of first principles. A fundamental premise of psychology is that human behavior is the final product of a dynamic process. This means behavior is shaped by the net effect of multiple motivations and considerations. The costs and benefits of a given action are weighed both consciously and unconsciously before acting. Nevertheless, as pointed out by Cunnien (1997), the DSM–IV approach to atypical medical presentations ignores the multilevel nature of behavior and its consequences. This creates practical difficulties because the situation where claimants have multiple motives is not addressed. This is particularly problematic when patients are enmeshed in complex psychosocial settings while pursuing compensation. In litigated minor head injury for example, it is common to see psychologically disturbed patients promote brain injury symptoms to get a doctor's attention but later pursue compensation (Paniak et al., 2002). Compensation seekers with questionable neurological trauma are also willing to put themselves through unnecessary surgery (Harris, Mulford, Solomon, van Gelder, & Young, 2005) with poor functional outcome. But in the DSM–IV scheme, the presence of external incentive (money, avoidance of criminal penalty) negates the diagnosis of FD. Similarly, the diagnosis of M is negated if the patient dramatizes symptoms to get a physician's or psychologist's attention.

The second conceptual deficiency is inferential: How should clinicians reason about an unobservable mental state, such as conscious motivation to assume the sick role versus knowingly false production of symptoms? The task is daunting by DSM–IV standards. As stated by Cunnien (1997):

> The pitfalls of diagnosing factitious disorder are emerging: The clinician must determine *conscious* production of symptoms, based on *unconscious* motives, in an *uncooperative* patient.

(p. 25)

The third conceptual deficiency is lack of empirical support for DSM–IV categories. One body of literature suggests the DSM–IV distinction between FD and M may not be valid. For example, Rogers, Bagby, and Vincent (1994) were unable to differentiate FD from simulators on the basis of a structured interview. Eisendrath and McNiel (2002) described 20 patients meeting criteria for FD whose symptoms were manufactured in the context of litigation, while Kluft (1987) also noted substantial overlap in the presentations. A further consideration is base rates. FD in unambiguous form is rare even in large psychiatric samples, with prevalence rates in the 0.2–1% range (Carlson, 1984; Sutherland & Rodin, 1990), and the legal characteristics of these patients are rarely described or considered. Finally, the frequent comorbidity of FD, M, conversion disorder, and somatization disorder raises doubts about pseudomedical syndromes as genuine psychopathology. The DSM–IV itself contains side commentary that increases this doubt, such as the advice that M is "not uncommonly" part of somatization presentations (APA, 1994, p. 449), while conversion disorder in females often evolves into "the full picture of SD" (p. 455). In men, conversion disorder is often associated with antisocial personality (p. 455), but antisocial personality is partial grounds for considering M (p. 683).

What is known with certainty however is that FD is typically associated with severe Axis II psychopathology (Cunnien, 1997). Borderline, dependent, avoidant, and histrionic personality disorders involve coping skills so poor that the manufacture of medical illness allows social control in difficult circumstances, either to terminate a stressful situation or express unacceptable feelings. Some patients with FD go so far as to drug, poison, or mutilate themselves to mimic real medical disorders. Some may even drug or poison their children to get sympathy (often referred to as Munchausen's Syndrome by Proxy). The level of effort and planning that supports abnormal illness-affirming behavior may be termed level of enactment. In other words, intentionally injuring oneself or spending much time in a wheelchair with eventual development of disuse atrophy represent high levels of enactment of factitial behavior, but simply self-labeling as "closed head injury" without accompanying actions is a low level of enactment. Essentially, the question the clinician should pose is: "How aggressively does the patient pursue unneeded treatment or act out the sick role in daily affairs?"

Hence, to the extent that one believes in the clinical validity of FD, there are four forms of evidence that favor a diagnosis of FD: (1) a history of severe psychopathology suggestive of Axis II disorder, (2) primary gain outweighing secondary gain, especially outweighing compensation, (3) abnormal illness-affirming behavior, and (4) high level of enactment, e.g., self-injury. The next section details the steps I took in differentiating M from FD.

Differential diagnosis

Both FD and M require evidence for voluntary production of false impairments, so the first question is a global one: "What is the evidence for insufficient effort and/or exaggerated cognitive defect of voluntary origin?" The answer to this question has multiple components, and is best addressed by the three-pronged, convergent validation method proposed by Sweet (1996): (a) positive SVT scores, (b) atypical patterns on genuine neurocognitive tests, and (c) gross violations of ecological validity. The more atypical signs produced, the greater the confidence in conscious production. In this light, there was strong evidence for exaggerated cognitive defect in the form of implausible score patterns. The basis for this conclusion was as follows:

- Two sets of TOMM scores all < 45/50 (SVT positive)
- Two low RDS scores associated with high positive predictive power for implausible cognitive defect (SVT positive)
- Neurologically unexplained "declines" on CVLT–2 (atypical pattern)
- Neurologically unexplained slowing in psychomotor speed (atypical pattern)
- Earlier WMS-3 performance worse than a Korsakoff patient (atypical pattern)
- Retarded oral speed on SDMT but normal interview speech (ecological validity)
- Able to multitask in real life but very poor divided attention implied by Trailmaking B (ecological validity)
- Motor scores implying bilateral semi-paralysis but neurological examinations WNL (ecological validity).

The second question is "What confidence do I have in diagnosing an implausible neuropsychological presentation?" While Sweet (1996) provides the general contours of diagnostic reasoning, Slick,

Sherman, and Iverson (1999) provide polythetic guidelines for assigning confidence levels to effort ratings. A label of "definite malingering" requires finding below-chance responding on multiple-choice cognitive tests, which is not the case with Mrs. B. A conclusion of "probable malingering" requires less stringent but nonetheless compelling evidence for discrepancies between test scores and observed behavior (definitely present here), strong deviations from known patterns of brain dysfunction, and/or self-reported symptoms discrepant with alleged brain disorder. Mrs. B. did not score below chance on any multiple-choice test on any occasion; so "definite" malingering cannot be diagnosed. However, she showed large discrepancies between observed versus test behavior (e.g., normal speech but extremely slow oral speed on the SDMT), deviations from expected patterns (e.g., memory scores worse than a Korsakoff patient), and many pseudoneurologic complaints inconsistent with the alleged disorder (e.g., "depth perception off," remote memory loss, semantic problems, nonstereotypical treatment response).

The third question is "What incentives or disincentives motivate the patient/plaintiff to distort test scores?" This question is crucial for the differential diagnosis of primary versus secondary gain, i.e., FD versus M. This requires an analysis of the social context of the evaluation as well as inferences about mental states linked as logically as possible to external correlates of motive. A series of sub-questions may include, "Are strong external incentives present, absent, or minimal?" "Do incentives to remain ill outweigh incentives to return to a productive lifestyle? Are there positive and negative reinforcers that shape chronic complaints and belief in a brain injury?" An important question always raised in this stage is offered by Slick et al. (1999): Can the invalid results be explained by nonvolitional factors such as psychiatric, neurological, physical, or developmental disorders?

In this case, there was strong external incentive present: Mrs. B. initiated joint first and third party lawsuits to pursue (1) attendant care payments to her husband at a skilled nurse's hourly rate in perpetuity, (2) past wages, (3) future wages, and (4) vaguely defined noneconomic damages. I weighed such clear secondary gain against the primary gain incentive of seeking social interaction with medical staff. There was little evidence for persistent abnormal illness-affirming behavior. Instead, records indicated low treatment attendance and noncompliance. Lacking was any history of multiple ER visits, efforts to join any medical self-help organization, nor any evidence she was centering her identity on that of a brain-injured person. Level of enactment was very low: She did not self-mutilate or use drugs to mimic the signs and symptoms of a brain disorder. With regards to psychiatric factors potentially explaining the findings as advised by Slick et al. (1999), there was evidence for anxious and depressive features, but these were of insufficient severity to affect observable communication, movement, or daily function. These negative emotional factors also could not explain the implausibly poor test scores that characterized all cognitive testing.

Final conclusions

I diagnosed Mrs. B. with probable malingering. The evidence favoring this position included positive findings on symptom validity tests across many domains (motor, symptom report, and cognition), atypical test performances that waxed and waned, noncompliance with treatment, illogical progression of complaints inconsistent with the natural history of a head injury, and a medical-legal assessment context. A diagnosis of FD could not be supported as poor treatment compliance disproved a primary gain theory that she manufactured brain injury symptoms to get a physician's attention. Anxiety and depression were present to mild degree and could not explain the improbable performance patterns or the symptom course. There was only indirect evidence of an Axis II personality disorder diagnosis. This included a long premorbid psychiatric history and prior implausible claims for which there was no possible compensation (e.g., ritualistic sexual abuse by entire family of origin). Mrs. B.'s history showed she aggressively pursued many mental health services for years prior to the accident, availing herself of many self-help groups, social workers, psychologists, and psychiatrists to uncover memory for ritualistic abuse. Following the accident however, Mrs. B. pursued only diagnostic evaluations in search of a brain injury label; she dropped out of community mental health. Otherwise, she quickly dropped out of "brain injury" treatment or did not pursue it. For example, she did not return to the brain injury program until she needed a driver's evaluation. Hence, the level of enactment was limited to brief diagnostic evaluations in pursuit of a closed head injury label. A critical reader may point out that Mrs. B. was working, albeit part-time, and this would be inconsistent with malingering. But such a motivational analysis ignores the social context: Her husband refused to work, having self-imposed disability. Hence, Mrs. B. could not risk total loss of income while awaiting compensation through the court system. She needed income to support the family, and under her insurance policy wage replacement was limited to three years post-accident. This is a case where multiple layers of motivation required consideration.

HOW DID THE CASE END?

The third party matter (personal injury) went to trial in November 2005. I testified via videotaped deposition. The jury awarded a small amount for subjective pain, but did not order the defendant to pay any attendant care or future wages. Post-verdict polling of the jury elicited agreement there was no evidence for brain injury, but there was evidence for exaggerated cognitive defect. The jury engaged in their own ecological validity analysis, noting the incongruence between Mrs. B.'s bitter cognitive complaints and poor test scores versus the deft and organized manner with which she retrieved key papers while assisting her attorney during the trial. This is an important lesson for any neuropsychologist wishing to perform expert witness work: "Make it real" for juries by describing actual behavior of a plaintiff (brain injured or not) and stating the implications for cognition and brain function (abnormal or healthy). They also did not find any aggravation of pre-existing emotional problems; the jury appreciated that attendance at mental health sessions was less frequent after than before the incident.

In retrospect, I did not address the credibility of the somatic pain component because of my focus on the plausibility of cognitive and neurological presentations. Had I done so, I could have pointed out that Mrs. B. twice showed high scores on the Lees-Haley Fake Bad Scale (FBS: Greiffenstein, Baker, Gola, Donders, & Miller, 2002; Lees-Haley, English, & Glenn, 1991). Larrabee (1998, 2003) validated the FBS as a measure of exaggerated pain complaints. The work of Etherton, Bianchini, and Greve (2005, 2006) could also have informed about the reliability of subjective pain reports.

REFERENCES

American Psychiatric Association (1994). *Diagnostic and statistical manual of mental disorders*, 4th ed. Washington, DC: APA.

Binder, L. M., & Campbell, K. A. (2004). Medically unexplained symptoms and neuropsychological assessment. *Journal of Clinical and Experimental Neuropsychology, 26*(3), 369–392.

Carlson, R. J. (1984). Factitious psychiatric disorders: diagnostic and etiologic considerations. *Psychiatric Medicine, 2*(4), 383–388.

Cunnien, A. (1997). Psychiatric and medical syndromes associated with deception. In R. Rogers (Ed.), *Clinical assessment of malingering and deception*, 2nd ed. (pp. 23–46). New York: Guilford.

Eisendrath, S. J. (1994). Factitious physical disorders. *Western Journal of Medicine, 160*(2), 177–179.

Eisendrath, S. J., & McNiel, D. E. (2002). Factitious disorders in civil litigation: Twenty cases illustrating the spectrum of abnormal illness-affirming behavior. *Journal of the American Academy of Psychiatry and the Law*, *30*, 391–399.

Etherton, J. L., Bianchini, K. J., Ciota, M. A., & Greve, K. W. (2005). Reliable digit span is unaffected by laboratory-induced pain implications for clinical use. *Assessment*, *12*, 101–106.

Etherton, J. L., Bianchini, K. J., Heinly, M. T., & Greve, K. W. (2006). Pain, malingering, and performance on the WAIS–III Processing Speed Index. *Journal of Clinical and Experimental Neuropsychology*, *28*, 1218–1237.

Goetz, C.G. (2007). J. M. Charcot and simulated neurologic disease: Attitudes and diagnostic strategy. *Neurology*, *69*, 103–109.

Greiffenstein, M. F., Baker, W. J., & Gola, T. (1994). Validation of malingered amnesia measures with a large clinical sample. *Psychological Assessment*, *6*(3), 218–224.

Greiffenstein, M. F., Baker, W. J., Gola, T., Donders, J., & Miller, L. (2002). The Fake Bad Scale in atypical and severe closed head injury litigants. *Journal of Clinical Psychology*, *58*(12), 1591–1600.

Greiffenstein, M.F., Fox, D., & Lees-Haley, P.R. (2007). The Fake Bad Scale in the detection of non-credible brain injury claims. In K. Boone (Ed.), *Assessment of feigned neuropsychological impairment* (pp. 270–291). New York: Guilford.

Harris, I., Mulford, J., Solomon, M., van Gelder, J. M., & Young, J. (2005). Association between compensation status and outcome after surgery: A meta-analysis. *Journal of the American Medical Association*, *293*(13), 1644–1652.

Iverson, G. L., Henrichs, T. F., Barton, E. A., & Allen, S. (2002). Specificity of the MMPI–2 Fake Bad Scale as a marker for personal injury malingering. *Psychological Reports*, *90*(1), 131–136.

Kluft, R. P. (1987). The simulation and dissimulation of multiple personality disorder. *American Journal of Clinical Hypnosis*, *30*(2), 104–118.

Larrabee, G. (1998). Somatic malingering on the MMPI and MMPI–2 in personal injury litigants. *The Clinical Neuropsychologist*, *12*, 179–188.

Larrabee, G. J. (2003). Exaggerated pain report in litigants with malingered neurocognitive dysfunction. *Clinical Neuropsychology*, *17*(3), 395–401.

Lees-Haley, P. R., English, L. T., & Glenn, W. J. (1991). A Fake Bad Scale on the MMPI–2 for personal injury claimants. *Psychological Reports*, *68*(1), 203–210.

Paniak, C., Reynolds, S., Toller-Lobe, G., Melnyk, A., Nagy, J., & Schmidt, D. (2002). A longitudinal study of the relationship between financial compensation and symptoms after treated mild traumatic brain injury. *Journal of Clinical and Experimental Neuropsychology*, *24*(2), 187–193.

Rogers, R., Bagby, R. M., & Vincent, A. (1994). Factitious disorders with predominantly psychological signs and symptoms: A conundrum for forensic experts. *Journal of Psychiatry and Law*, *22*(1), 91–106.

Slick, D. J., Sherman, E. M. S., & Iverson, G. L. (1999). Diagnostic criteria for malingered neurocognitive dysfunction: Proposed standards for clinical practice and research. *Clinical Neuropsychologist*, *13*(4), 545–561.

Sutherland, A. J., & Rodin, G. M. (1990). Factitious disorders in a general hospital setting: Clinical features and a review of the literature. *Psychosomatics*, *31*(4), 392–399.

Sweet, J. J. (1996). Malingering: Differential diagnosis. In J. J. Sweet (Ed.), *Forensic neuropsychology: Fundamentals and practice* (pp. 255–286). Lisse, Netherlands: Swets & Zeitlinger.

Mild traumatic brain injury in civil litigation

7

Wiley Mittenberg and Darci Morgan

The most frequent neuropsychological referral is for assessment of the potential cognitive and emotional consequences of head trauma (Rabin, Barr, & Burton, 2005). The injury scenario typically involves a motor vehicle accident, fall, or blow to the head with a blunt object (Levin, Benton, & Grossman, 1982). The majority of such injuries are mild (Sosin, Sniezek, & Thurman, 1996). Their neuropsychological consequences may become the subject of civil litigation in the context of personal injury, disability insurance, or worker's compensation claims. Appropriate examination involves review of medical records, neuropsychological testing, and a clinical interview regardless of the mechanism of trauma, severity of head injury, or type of subsequent civil litigation. The case described here therefore typifies a neuropsychological case that would be seen in the context of civil litigation, although this case was selected to illustrate the examination process more clearly than the modal referral might, particularly pertaining to the question of malingering.

The authors received a telephone call from a personal injury defense firm inquiring if we were willing to perform an Independent Medical Examination (IME) in the context of a personal injury lawsuit. The attorney contacted us because another firm for whom we had previously performed neuropsychological IMEs in disability and personal injury cases had recommended us. Recommendation by another attorney is the most frequent method used to locate an expert, although other methods include referral from another doctor, attendance at a presentation given by the expert, listing in a directory of experts, advertisements, and expert referral services (Essig, Mittenberg, Petersen, Strauman, & Cooper, 2001).

The attorney briefly described the case as involving head trauma sustained in a low speed motor vehicle accident five years ago. Ms. C., a 40-year-old legal assistant, had suffered no loss of consciousness, had walked home, and was not hospitalized after the accident. Ms. C. reported head impact on the driver's side window and rear view mirror, and next recalled being home and opening the front door. Eventually she was found to have a normal brain MRI. Subsequent neuropsychological examination had apparently shown *severe* cognitive and emotional impairment. The attorney solicited a second opinion.

On the basis of the information provided it was possible to determine that the injury was most likely mild, since it was characterized by less than 30 minutes of coma. Ms. C.'s ability to recall events within 24 hours of the injury suggested that the period of posttraumatic amnesia was less than a day, which also indicates mild trauma (American Congress of Rehabilitation Medicine, 1993). The fact that Ms. C. had been able to walk home indicated that the Glasgow Coma Scale Score at the scene was greater than 13, which is consistent with the subsequently normal brain MRI in suggesting mild head trauma. Mild head trauma does not typically produce cognitive or emotional impairment that persists beyond three months (Binder, Rohling, & Larrabee, 1997; Mittenberg & Strauman, 2000; Schretlen & Shapiro, 2003). The reportedly severe impairment on neuropsychological examination in this case was therefore *unlikely* to have been caused by the accident. The most frequently observed sign that symptoms are intentionally produced is a severity of apparent impairment that is inconsistent with the claimed condition (Mittenberg, Patton, Canyock, & Condit, 2002). A potential alternative explanation might be that the symptoms are caused by an independent pre- or co-existing neurological or psychiatric disorder. The attorney was apprised of this information by way of a preliminary opinion, medical records were requested, and a compulsory examination was scheduled. Assessment of the probability of malingering in civil litigation begins at the time of referral. A differential diagnosis involving malingering is typically an explicit referral question (Essig et al., 2001), but is implicit in every case involving potential financial compensation for injuries. The prevalence of malingering or symptom exaggeration in civil litigation cases is approximately 30%, and about 40% in those that involve a mild head trauma claim (Mittenberg et al., 2002).

RECORD REVIEW

An accident report indicated that Ms. C. was the driver of a vehicle that was struck on the passenger side by another vehicle that was backing out of a driveway. An ambulance was not summoned. Ms. C. presented for orthopedic examination four days after the accident with complaints of headache and pain in the back and neck. Impression was cervical/lumbar strain, treated with Lodine, Flexeril, and physical therapy. Referral was made for a neurological examination and MRI. Ms. C. began to complain of poor concentration and memory difficulty two months after the accident. These symptoms are consistent with postconcussion syndrome, which occurs in about 40% of mild head trauma cases (Mittenberg & Strauman, 2000). Results of the brain MRI were normal ten weeks post-injury. MRI of the spine was consistent with muscle spasm.

Neurological examination two weeks after the accident showed no cognitive deficits, and brain imaging was viewed as unnecessary by the neurologist. Ms. C. reported no loss of consciousness, was wearing a seatbelt, and went home after the collision. Impression was memory complaints and headache due to postconcussion syndrome. Neurologists typically treat the syndrome with antidepressant medication (Evans, Evans, & Sharp, 1994), and Elavil was prescribed in this instance. Ms. C. reported inability to return to work five months post-injury due to continued cognitive difficulties. Complaints included difficulty reading due to poor concentration, getting lost due to poor direction sense, and memory difficulties that led to resignation from employment as a legal assistant at a personal injury firm. These difficulties had also reportedly resulted in loss of eyeglasses, a cell phone, car keys, the ability to read music, and the ability to play the piano. It should be noted that even patients with profound amnestic disorder do not forget how to play or read music. Individuals who have *not* sustained head trauma frequently misplace personal possessions (Mittenberg, DiGiulio, Perrin, & Bass, 1992). An EEG was ordered that was subsequently normal, and neuropsychological testing was recommended. Ms. C. was viewed as having reached maximum medical improvement one year post-accident, and as having sustained a 15% permanent impairment due to postconcussion syndrome.

Neuropsychological examination by a psychologist six months after the accident showed "considerable evidence of cognitive disintegration" given Ms. C.'s premorbid level of function as estimated from reported educational level (Bachelor's degree). Diagnosis was postconcussion syndrome and posttraumatic stress disorder. Cognitive rehabilitation and biofeedback-assisted relaxation were recommended but not undertaken. Ms. C. obtained the following Index scores on the Wechsler Memory Scale–Revised: General Memory: 75, Attention/Concentration: 50, Delayed Recall: 75, Verbal Memory: 81, and Visual Memory: 75. It was possible to quantitatively compare the Index score pattern to the patterns reported for nonlitigating traumatic brain injury patients and malingerers in published studies. This pattern of obtained Indexes is *not* consistent with memory impairment caused by head trauma, but is similar to the pattern produced by neurologically normal persons who intentionally attempt to display memory impairment. It is not actually possible to remember more information than one can pay attention to initially. The 25-point discrepancy between the General Memory and Attention/Concentration Indexes corresponds to a 90% or greater probability that Ms. C. malingered memory impairment (Mittenberg, Azrin, Millsaps, & Heilbronner, 1993; Mittenberg, Puentes, Patton, Canyock, & Heilbronner, 2002). A majority of malingered cases are characterized by a pattern of cognitive test performance that is inconsistent with the claimed condition (Mittenberg et al., 2002). It should also be noted that Ms. C.'s memory indexes fall in the Borderline to Mentally Retarded range, and are thus not consistent with the minor nature of the head trauma sustained in this case.

Ms. C. apparently filed a claim for Social Security disability in addition to the personal injury lawsuit. A second neuropsychological examination was performed two years after the accident at the request of the Social Security Administration. A Registered Nurse who was not licensed to practice psychology performed this testing. Ethical concerns about qualifications to practice clinical neuropsychology are frequent in litigated cases (Grote, Lewin, Sweet, & van Gorp, 2000). The decision regarding how to proceed in such cases may not be straightforward. Concerns may be discussed directly with the expert, and if this fails to redress the problem a complaint may be reported to licensing authorities or professional organizations. Ethics complaints (justified or without basis) are not infrequently used as tactics to diminish the credibility of an opposing expert. However, the consequences of a formal complaint can be serious. The authors have seen cases in which other experts all sued each other for libel, resulting in substantial monetary settlements. An alternative view as expressed by James Watson (Nobel laureate for the discovery of DNA) is that society would benefit from less scientific ethics and more science. Novelist F. Scott Fitzgerald's observation that anyone over the age of 25 prefers forgiveness to judgment may also be pertinent, if not intuitively applicable in malingering diagnosis. We informed the referring attorney that the plaintiff's expert was not qualified. It was the attorney's considered opinion that this matter most profitably could be addressed in the context of the nurse's courtroom testimony, rather than by a formal complaint.

Ms. C. reported prescription of Aricept, Wellbutrin, Prozac, and Amerge for continued memory impairment, headache, and orthopedic pain. Educational history was reported to include a Bachelor's degree in Social Work. Test results are presented in Table 7.1. The magnitude of intellectual impairment is grossly inconsistent with the minor nature of the head trauma sustained (Demakis et al., 2001). It is possible to quantitatively compare the obtained subtest pattern to published patterns characteristic of malingerers and nonlitigant brain injury patients. The pattern of component IQ subtest scores is more similar to that produced by neurologically normal persons who attempt to appear intellectually impaired than to the pattern produced by head injury. There is a greater than 80% probability that Ms. C. malingered intellectual deficiency based on this pattern (Mittenberg, Fichera, Zielinski, & Heilbronner, 1995; Mittenberg, Theroux, Puentes, Bianchini, Greve, & Rayls, 2001).

Ms. C. also obtained 6 correct of 30 items on the Seashore Rhythm Test. This test requires a patient to indicate if each of 30 pairs of tonal sequences are the same or different. An individual that was completely unable to perform this test (e.g., due to deafness) would get about 50% of the questions correct by guessing, since each question has only two possible answers (correct or incorrect). Application of the Binomial Theorem indicates that there is a 99.9% chance that a patient who obtained a score of 6 (20% correct) knew the correct answers and gave incorrect answers. Alternatively, it is possible that the nurse administered this test improperly.

Apparently impaired performance was also demonstrated on tests of problem solving and upper extremity motor function. These impairments are inconsistent with the minor nature of the head trauma or orthopedic injury sustained, and in the context of other results are likely to have been intentional. For example, Ms. C.'s finger tapping scores were consistent with symptom embellishment (Arnold et al., 2005). However, the nurse interpreted these results as a valid indication of global cognitive disability, recommended restriction of activities, and provided 12 months of cognitive rehabilitation.

A videotaped deposition of Ms. C. was reviewed. Ms. C. testified to having completed a Master's degree in Law, which is not consistent with the Bachelor's degree-level education reported during prior examinations. Educational transcripts were obtained from the institutions that Ms. C. claimed

TABLE 7.1   Neuropsychological test scores 2 years after a mild head trauma

Wechsler Adult Intelligence Scale–3rd edition		
Full Scale IQ	65	extremely low
Verbal IQ	71	borderline
Performance IQ	63	extremely low
Verbal Comprehension	76	borderline
Perceptual Organization	69	extremely low
Working Memory	69	extremely low
Processing Speed	60	extremely low
Vocabulary	5	
Similarities	4	
Arithmetic	4	
Digit Span	4	
Information	8	
Comprehension	6	
Letter-Number Sequencing	7	
Picture Completion	3	
Digit-Symbol Coding	2	
Block Design	5	
Matrix Reasoning	6	
Picture Arrangement	4	
Symbol Search	2	
Halstead-Reitan Neuropsychological Battery		
Trail Making A	14T	impaired
Trail Making B	32T	impaired
Speech Perception (30/60)	19T	impaired
Seashore Rhythm (6/30)	19T	impaired
Tapping Dominant (19)	18T	impaired
Tapping Nondominant (18)	18T	impaired
Grooved Pegs Dominant	2T	impaired
Grooved Pegs Nondominant	10T	impaired
Dynamometer Dominant	16T	impaired
Dynamometer Nondominant	10T	impaired
Wisconsin Card Sorting Test		
Categories	1/6	impaired
Perseverative responses	39T	impaired

to have attended. These documented an Associate's degree with a C average, and 30 credits toward a B.A. Ms. C. had earned neither Bachelor's nor Master's degrees. Discrepancies between reported and actual educational level indicate a propensity for exaggeration, and occur with sufficient frequency in civil litigation to be worth reviewing (Greiffenstein, Baker, & Johnson-Greene, 2002; Johnson-Greene & Binder, 1995).

Medical records prior to the head trauma were reviewed. Ms. C. had been admitted to a hospital ten years before the motor vehicle accident due to a fall at work. Ms. C. reported possible loss of consciousness and headache related to this prior injury. Brain MRI and EEG had been normal at that time, and Ms. C. was discharged with a diagnosis of migraine headache which was treated with Elavil. Ms. C. had filed a worker's compensation claim. Results of an orthopedic examination related to this prior claim had suggested symptom magnification. Court documents indicated that the claim was settled and that Ms. C. had sustained no permanent impairment. Review of prior medical history may be pertinent because patients frequently reattribute pre-existing complaints to a subsequent head injury (Mittenberg et al., 1992). A documented history of malingering is atypical.

OUR NEUROPSYCHOLOGICAL EXAMINATION (PLAINTIFF'S THIRD)

On interview, Ms. C. was alert and oriented to person, place, and time. It should be noted that persons who have profound memory impairment are typically disoriented because memory for the passage of time is required in order to report the correct time of day, date, and day of the week. Spontaneous speech was fluent, coherent, and free of paraphasia or other signs of thought disorder. There was no observable evidence of delusions, hallucinations, or other psychotic symptoms. Affect was normal in range, intensity, and relatedness, with quality of mood appropriate to the circumstances of the examination. There was no observable evidence of depression. Eye contact was appropriate. Gross motor behavior was within normal limits, and without evidence of psychomotor retardation or agitation. Ms. C.'s ability to relate past events was not consistent with a mentally retarded level of memory function. Discrepancies among records, self-report, and observed behavior occur in a majority of malingered cases (Mittenberg et al., 2002).

Symptoms reportedly included memory problems, poor concentration, disorientation, migraine headaches, pain in the back, elbow, knee, and neck, blurry vision, depressed mood, poor frustration tolerance, and insomnia. Ms. C. reportedly started a fire while cooking as a result of forgetfulness, carried a cell phone when driving because of getting lost repeatedly, and had to carry a list in order to recall driving destinations. Ms. C. also complained of inability to read because of poor concentration and blurry vision, and frequent falls due to orthopedic pain that resulted in $17,000 of recent emergency room bills. Tearfulness, lack of emotional resilience, reduced appetite, and decreased libido were also reported.

Ms. C. reported difficulty recalling prescribed medications, but was able to state that these included Prozac, Wellbutrin, Elavil, Aricept, Wigraine, and Zyprexa. A primary care provider apparently prescribed these medications. Treatment also was said to include intermittent physical therapy for back and neck spasms.

Ms. C. claimed to have earned a B.A. in Law (which was false according to official transcripts from the reported university). Ms. C. had not worked as a legal assistant since the accident, but had reportedly attempted temporary work for five months as an administrative assistant. This patient claimed inability to continue this position because of headaches, falls, and poor concentration. The Social Security Administration had awarded benefits predicated on total disability due to the motor vehicle accident. Ms. C. had been married for many years, and had one grown child from a previous marriage. Ms. C. reported socializing at fund-raising events and in political advocacy contexts, and being politically active.

Test results appear in Table 7.2. Examination of the validity of Ms. C.'s complaints on the Portland Digit Recognition Test (Binder, 1993) showed intentional production of incorrect answers in order to demonstrate cognitive impairment that was not in fact present. The Portland appears to be a demanding test of concentration and verbal memory, but is actually insensitive to cognitive impairment. Ms. C. earned scores on each of three trials that were lower than those obtained by any patients with severe traumatic brain injury or depressive disorders. The test consists of a series of questions that each have two possible answers, one correct and one incorrect. Patients who do not know any of the answers would therefore score approximately 50% correct by guessing. Scores that are significantly lower than would be expected by chance (e.g., 36% correct) indicate that the individual knew the correct answer and intentionally answered incorrectly. This patient scored 36% correct on Trial 1, 28% correct on Trial 2, and 32% correct on the total test. Application of the Binomial Theorem indicates that these scores correspond to a 99.3%, 99.993%, and greater than 99.996% probability of malingering. Significantly lower than chance scores on symptom validity tests occur in approximately a third of malingered cases (Mittenberg et al., 2002). Evidence of

TABLE 7.2   Neuropsychological test scores 5 years after a mild head trauma

Test of Memory Malingering		
Trial 1	19/50	significant
Trial 2	22/50	significant
Retention	25/50	significant
Portland Digit Recognition Test		
Easy	13/36	significant
Hard	10/36	significant
Total	23/72	significant
Word Memory Test		
Immediate Recognition	42.5%	significant
Delayed Recognition	45.0%	significant
Consistency	77.5%	significant
Wechsler Test of Adult Reading Premorbid Estimates		
Full Scale IQ	108	average
Verbal IQ	108	average
Performance IQ	107	average
General Memory	109	average
Immediate Memory	107	average
Working Memory	104	average
Wechsler Adult Intelligence Scale–3rd edition		
Full Scale IQ	73	borderline
Verbal IQ	86	low average
Performance IQ	62	extremely low
Verbal Comprehension	98	average
Perceptual Organization	65	extremely low
Working Memory	71	borderline
Processing Speed	60	extremely low
Vocabulary	11	
Similarities	9	
Arithmetic	4	
Digit Span	5	
Information	9	
Comprehension	8	
Letter-Number Sequencing	7	
Picture Completion	3	
Digit-Symbol Coding	3	
Block Design	5	
Matrix Reasoning	4	
Picture Arrangement	4	
Symbol Search	1	
Wechsler Memory Scale–3rd edition		
General Memory	60	extremely low
Immediate Memory	69	extremely low
Working Memory	74	borderline
Auditory Immediate	86	low average
Visual Immediate	61	extremely low
Auditory Delayed	86	low average
Visual Delayed	53	extremely low
Auditory Recognition	55	extremely low
Logical Memory 1	7	
Faces 1	4	
Verbal Paired Associates 1	8	
Family Pictures 1	4	
Letter-Number Sequencing	7	
Spatial Span	3	
Logical Memory 2	8	

Faces 2					2	
Verbal Paired Associates 2					7	
Family Pictures 2					3	
Auditory Recognition					1	

Halstead-Reitan Neuropsychological Battery

Category Test		25T	impaired
Trail Making A		16T	impaired
Trail Making B		21T	impaired

Wide Range Achievement Test–3rd edition

Reading		90	average

Minnesota Multiphasic Personality Inventory–2nd edition

L	52		Hs	92		Pa	81
F	79		D	101		Pt	97
K	46		Hy	108		Sc	90
VRIN	61		Pd	89		Ma	74
TRIN	58F		Mf	40		Si	57
(FBS	31)						

malingering on a neuropsychological examination invalidates the examination, except for results that reflect normal functioning.

Extended examination of the veracity of Ms. C.'s cognitive complaints on the Test of Memory and Malingering (Tombaugh, 1996) also demonstrated performance characteristic of malingering. This measure appears to be a difficult test of visual memory, but is actually insensitive to memory impairment. Ms. C. earned scores that were lower than those observed in patients with severe traumatic brain injury, major depressive disorder, or dementias such as Alzheimer's disease. Each question on this test has two possible answers (correct or incorrect). Patients who cannot remember any of the items are therefore accurate about 50% of the time by chance. Ms. C. was 38% correct on Trial 1. The probability that she knew the correct answers but intentionally gave wrong answers is 95% on this test.

Assessment of the validity of Ms. C.'s claimed symptoms on the Word Memory Test (Green, 2003) resulted in scores that fell below malingering cutoffs on each of three measures. This test appears to be a difficult measure of verbal memory, but is actually insensitive to memory impairment. Ms. C.'s scores were significantly lower than those obtained by individuals that have suffered severe traumatic brain injury or major depression. Individuals with significant memory impairment due to head trauma typically obtain performance at a 90% accuracy level. Ms. C. earned accuracy scores of 45% or less.

On the Wechsler Adult Intelligence Scale, 3rd edition, Ms. C. obtained an IQ lower than that of 96% of the United States population. Intellectual impairment of this magnitude is not consistent with Ms. C.'s medical or social history. Performance consistent with mental retardation was obtained on measures of nonverbal intelligence and speed of thought process. The observed pattern of component abilities was similar to that of uninjured persons who are malingering intellectual impairment, and was not similar to the pattern seen in persons who have suffered concussion-related intellectual deficits. The obtained profile is associated with a greater than 99% probability that Ms. C. intentionally attempted to display deficiency of intellect that was not present (Mittenberg, Theroux, et al., 2001).

Assessment of memory function with the Wechsler Memory Scale, 3rd edition, showed apparent overall ability in the mentally retarded range. Memory impairment of this severity is markedly inconsistent with the minor nature of the head trauma sustained. Individuals with a similar magnitude of memory impairment are incompetent to manage daily affairs, and require 24-hour supervision and a legal guardian. Ms. C.'s ability to remember information that had been presented to her (Auditory Delayed Index) was apparently better than her ability to recognize the same information

(Auditory Recognition Index). This pattern characterizes intentional failure rather than actual memory disorder. Ms. C. was unable to identify events from a story she had heard that are correctly guessed by individuals that did not hear the story (Killgore & DellaPietra, 2000). This suggests intentional failure. When asked whether or not she had been previously shown each of a series of photographed faces (Faces 2), Ms. C. performed more poorly than individuals who are simply guessing. Application of the Binomial Theorem indicates that there is a 98.96% probability that Ms. C. knew the correct answers and intentionally gave incorrect answers on this test.

Performance on tests from the Halstead-Reitan battery was impaired at levels that are inconsistent with Ms. C.'s medical history, but consistent with embellishment of cognitive difficulty. Similar results on these measures were obtained on previous examinations.

Formal assessment of personality function on the MMPI–2 documented Ms. C.'s report of apparently physical symptoms that are unlikely to have a medical basis (Hy and Hs scales). Patients with similar profiles avoid responsibility by developing symptoms that do not fit the pattern of any known medical disorder. These symptoms are typically maintained by secondary gains. Ms. C. also reported severe depressive symptoms (D scale) that are inconsistent with the observed clinical presentation. In the context of previously described results, this profile suggests that Ms. C.'s reported physical symptoms and emotional distress are markedly exaggerated. Although this examination occurred prior to the currently available and extensive validity studies of the Lees-Haley Fake Bad Scale (Nelson, Sweet, & Demakis, 2006) Ms. C.'s score on this measure would have indicated malingered somatic complaints. Scores above validity scale cutoffs on objective personality tests occur in about a third of malingered cases (Mittenberg et al., 2002).

SUMMARY AND CONCLUSIONS

In summary, this 50-year-old legal assistant sustained mild head trauma five years prior to examination, when a vehicle that was backing out of a driveway collided with her car. Ms. C. sustained no loss of consciousness, walked home after the accident, and required no hospitalization. Subsequent neurological studies that included an MRI and an EEG were normal. Prior medical history was significant for symptom magnification related to a worker's compensation claim. Psychological testing six months and two years after the collision showed apparently mentally retarded levels of memory and intelligence that were due to intentional test failure. Ms. C. consistently claimed to have a Bachelor's degree, but did not. On examination five years after the accident, Ms. C. intentionally gave wrong answers, but knew the right answers, and displayed fabricated memory and intellectual difficulty across multiple independent objective measures. Ms. C. also reported physical symptoms that do not fit the pattern of any known medical disorder. There was no evidence in the medical record or the neuropsychological examination that Ms. C. had sustained *any* cognitive or emotional impairment as a consequence of the claimed mild trauma brain injury. A DSM–IV diagnosis of malingering was made. In terms of research diagnostic criteria, Ms. C. more than satisfied requirements for definite malingering (Slick, Sherman, & Iverson, 1999).

FINAL OUTCOME OF THE CASE

The results of the record review and examination were reported to the referring attorney by telephone shortly after testing was completed. The attorney indicated that our opinion confirmed his own suspicions about the case, and requested that a written report be prepared for submission to the court. Had the results been unfavorable to the defense, a written opinion would probably not have been requested. After the attorney read the report, he requested that we re-review the videotaped deposition for additional evidence of malingering so that he could use the tape as an exhibit during the trial. Review of the videotape revealed no additional useful information, but it was explained to the attorney that the examination results were compelling, incontrovertible, and unambiguous. Although it is unusual, no deposition was ever requested by the plaintiff's attorney. The case was eventually set for trial and a date for testimony was scheduled with the defense attorney's office. Trial dates are typically rescheduled several times, and after having scheduled testimony one can usually be certain only that testimony will not occur on that date. The trial was eventually cancelled and was to be reset at a future unspecified time, although the attorney's office failed to inform us that this had occurred.

The attorney called two years after the examination to inform us that he had hired a different neuropsychologist on a similar case, and parenthetically mentioned that our case had settled for $9000 without going to trial. Thus in the final analysis this case study demonstrates that technically competent work may not be appreciated by the occasional referrer, although it may make informative professional reading.

REFERENCES

American Congress of Rehabilitation Medicine (1993). Definition of mild traumatic brain injury. *Journal of Head Trauma Rehabilitation, 8,* 86–87.

Arnold, G. Boone, K., Brauer, L. P. Dean, A., Wen, J., Nitch, S., & McPherson, S. (2005). Sensitivity and specificity of finger tapping test scores for the detection of suspect effort. *Clinical Neuropsychologist, 19,* 105–120.

Binder, L. M. (1993). *Portland Digit Recognition Test Manual–2nd ed.* Beaverton, OR: Author.

Binder, L. M., Rohling, M. L., & Larrabee, G. J. (1997). A review of mild head trauma. Part 1: Meta-analytic review of neuropsychological studies. *Journal of Clinical and Experimental Neuropsychology, 19,* 421–431.

Demakis, G. J., Sweet, J. J., Sawyer, T. P., Moulthrop, M., Nies, K., & Clingerman, S. (2001). Discrepancy between predicted and obtained WAIS–R IQ scores discriminates between traumatic brain injury and insufficient effort. *Psychological Assessment, 13,* 240–248.

Essig, S. M., Mittenberg, W., Petersen, R. S., Strauman, S., & Cooper, J. T. (2001). Practices in forensic neuropsychology: Perspectives of neuropsychologists and trial attorneys. *Archives of Clinical Neuropsychology, 16,* 271–291.

Evans, R. W., Evans, R. I., & Sharp, M. J. (1994). The physician survey on the post-concussion and whiplash syndromes. *Headache, 34,* 268–274.

Green, P. (2003). *Green's Word Memory Test.* Edmonton, Canada: Green's Publishing.

Greiffenstein, M. F., Baker, W. J., & Johnson-Greene, D. (2002). Actual versus self-reported scholastic achievement of litigating postconcussion and severe closed head injury claimants. *Psychological Assessment, 14,* 202–208.

Grote, C, Lewin, J., Sweet, J., & van Gorp, W. (2000). Responses to perceived unethical practices in clinical neuropsychology: Ethical and legal considerations. *The Clinical Neuropsychologist, 14,* 119–134.

Johnson-Greene, D., & Binder, L. M. (1995). Evaluation of an efficient method for verifying higher educational credentials. *Archives of Clinical Neuropsychology, 10,* 251–253.

Killgore, W. D., & DellaPietra, L. (2000). Using the WMS–III to detect malingering: Empirical validation of the Rarely Missed Index (RMI). *Journal of Clinical and Experimental Neuropsychology, 22,* 761–771.

Levin, H. S., Benton, A. L., & Grossman, R. G. (1982). *Neurobehavioral consequences of closed head injury.* New York: Oxford University Press.

Mittenberg, W., Azrin, R., Millsaps, C., & Heilbronner, R. (1993). Identification of malingered head injury on the Wechsler Memory Scale–Revised. *Psychological Assessment, 5,* 34–40.

Mittenberg. W., Canyock, E. M., Condit, D., & Patton, C. (2001). Treatment of postconcussion syndrome following mild head injury. *Journal of Clinical and Experimental Neuropsychology, 23*, 829–836.

Mittenberg, W., DiGiulio, D. V., Perrin, S., & Bass, A. E. (1992). Symptoms following mild head injury: Expectation as aetiology. *Journal of Neurology, Neurosurgery and Psychiatry, 55*, 200–204.

Mittenberg, W., Fichera, S., Zielinski, R., & Heilbronner, R. (1995). Identification of malingered head injury on the Wechsler Adult Intelligence Scale–Revised. *Professional Psychology: Research and Practice, 26*, 491–498.

Mittenberg, W., Patton, C, Canyock, E. M., & Condit, D. (2002). Base rates of malingering and symptom exaggeration. *Journal of Clinical and Experimental Neuropsychology, 24*, 1094–1102.

Mittenberg, W., Puentes, G. A., Patton, C., Canyock, E. M., & Heilbronner, R. L. (2002). Neuropsychological profiling of symptom exaggeration and malingering. *Journal of Forensic Neuropsychology, 3*, 227–240.

Mittenberg, W., & Strauman, S. (2000). Diagnosis of mild head injury and the postconcussion syndrome. *Journal of Head Trauma Rehabilitation, 15, 783–791*.

Mittenberg, W., Theroux, S., Aguila-Puentes, G., Bianchini, K., Greve, K., & Rayls, K. R. (2001). Identification of malingered head injury on the Wechsler Adult Intelligence Scale–3rd edition. *The Clinical Neuropsychologist, 15*, 440–445.

Nelson, N. W., Sweet, J. J., & Demakis, G. J. (2006). Meta-Analysis of the MMPI–2 Fake Bad Scale: Utility in forensic practice. *The Clinical Neuropsychologist, 20*, 39–58.

Rabin, L. A., Barr, W. B., & Burton, L. A. (2005). Assessment practices of clinical neuropsychologists in the United States and Canada: A survey of INS, NAN, and APA Division 40 members. *Archives of Clinical Neuropsychology, 20*, 33–65.

Schretlen, D. J., & Shapiro, A. M. (2003). A quantitative review of the effects of traumatic brain injury on cognitive functioning. *International Review of Psychiatry, 15*, 341–349.

Slick, D. J., Sherman, E. M., & Iverson, G. L. (1999). Diagnostic criteria for malingered neurocognitive dysfunction: Proposed standards for clinical practice and research. *The Clinical Neuropsychologist, 13*, 545–561.

Sosin, D. M., Sniezek, J. E., & Thurman, D. J. (1996). Incidence of mild and moderate brain injury in the United States. *Brain Injury, 10*, 47–57.

Tombaugh, T. N. (1996). *The Test of Memory Malingering (TOMM)*. Toronto, Canada: Multi-Health Systems.

Malingering brain injury after whiplash trauma

Laurence M. Binder

Certain identifying details have been modified slightly to protect this man's identity. Mr. D. (not his real initial) was 62 when he was evaluated 40 months after a motor vehicle accident (MVA). His vehicle had been struck by another vehicle from the rear. The attorney referred him for independent neuropsychological examination for his insurer prior to binding arbitration regarding an underinsured motorist claim. Under Oregon law, monetary awards for underinsured motorist claims are reduced by the amount paid by the driver at fault, and he already had received a settlement from the insurer for the other driver.

PRE-MVA HISTORY

Records indicated that prior to 1982 Mr. D. worked in law enforcement successfully, rising to the rank of lieutenant in a large police department. In 1982, he went on leave for stress for unclear reasons and never returned to law enforcement work. An independent psychiatric evaluation in 1983 reported symptoms including memory loss, insomnia, rage, and depression. A treating psychiatrist diagnosed severe depression with psychotic features, with intellectual impairment so profound that a neurological referral was obtained in order to rule out a brain tumor. The neurologist found a tremor of likely emotional origin, interpreted an EEG as normal, and felt that depression explained the clinical presentation. The psychological testing in 1983 was summarized briefly in the psychiatric records; no psychological report was available. The Wechsler Full Scale IQ was 76 with severe memory deficits. Subsequently, a psychiatrist diagnosed alcohol abuse in remission, dementia, major depression, posttraumatic stress disorder, intermittent explosive disorder and mixed personality disorder and judged him to be at high risk for harming both himself and other persons. The psychiatrist reported that during the exam Mr. D. appeared markedly paranoid with wavering voice and poor eye contact. He had two psychiatric hospitalizations, but the hospital records were unavailable. Another examination in 1984 described him as cowering with contorted face, scratching himself, perseverating, and preoccupied with multiple concerns that the psychiatrist felt were out of proportion to the actual stressors. Mr. D. was rated as grossly disabled, incapable of both complex and repetitive work activities, and severely disabled in his ability to relate to his work peers and supervisors. The overall rating was severe to profound disability. He received a permanent disability from his employer for his psychiatric condition in the early 1980s, and he continued to receive disability benefits through the time of my independent neuropsychological evaluation. In addition, he was treated in the 1990s with Depakote for anger problems.

His medical history prior to the MVA included a possible mild myocardial infarction, intermittent back pain, and esophageal reflux disease.

MVA HISTORY

The reports of the emergency medical technicians showed no disturbance in Mr. D.'s level of consciousness. He complained of neck pain after his vehicle had been struck from the rear by another vehicle. He also reported dizziness and nausea briefly. He was communicative, alert, and fully oriented. In the emergency room Mr. D. complained of similar symptoms. The physician documented that he had not struck his head. Physical examination revealed full range of motion of the neck and no neurological deficit. The physician's diagnosis was cervical strain.

His primary provider examined him the day after the MVA and noted a whiplash (cervical hyperextension) injury. Reportedly, he had been leaning over to adjust his radio at the time of the impact and was not protected by the headrest. He complained of headache and neck pain, and a severe cervical strain was diagnosed.

Over the next several months Mr. D. was treated unsuccessfully for headache and cervical strain by his health maintenance organization (HMO). Six months after the MVA, he saw a neurologist who reviewed a cervical MRI that showed degenerative changes with no nerve root impingement, indicating that he was not a candidate for surgery of the cervical spine. His complaints of pain in the right arm led to nerve conduction studies that were consistent with both ulnar and median neuropathies, and an MRI of the shoulder was normal. No HMO provider ever expressed concern about a possible traumatic brain injury or ordered any diagnostic studies of the brain such as an MRI scan or neuropsychological evaluation.

Concurrent with his evaluation and treatment through his HMO, he was receiving a series of evaluations and treatment from a different set of healthcare providers. From the records it appeared that his HMO physicians were not aware of the other set of healthcare providers. In the first 14 months after the injury he received 34 chiropractic treatments.

An out of state psychologist saw Mr. D. two months after the MVA, but he did not prepare a report until almost three years had elapsed. One would infer from the addressee of the report that the case had been referred by an attorney. In contrast to the absence of neuropsychological complaints at the HMO, including to the neurologist who had evaluated his cervical problem, this psychologist reported that Mr. D. had problems with memory, word-finding, and confusion. His wife reported that there was progressive deterioration in his mental state; for example, he no longer was able to manage his rental properties. She also reported a personality change with withdrawal and emotional lability.

The psychologist provided limited psychometric data. Among the findings were an unspecified score described as normal on the Category Test, extreme slowness on Trail Making with times of 88 and 226 seconds on Parts A and B, respectively, and raw scores on Finger Tapping of 14 on the dominant right hand and 16 on the left hand. On the WAIS–R, Verbal IQ was 93, Performance IQ was 99, and Full Scale IQ was 94. On the Memory Assessment Scales his short-term memory was at the 25th percentile, but global memory was at the 1st percentile. The only motivational measure administered initially was the Rey 15-Item Test, and he obtained a passing score of 11 on this insensitive measure (Guilmette, Hart, Giuliano, & Leninger, 1994; Iverson & Binder, 2000; Lee, Loring, & Martin, 1992).

Almost two years after the MVA, the out of state psychologist administered the Portland Digit Recognition Test (PDRT; Binder, 1993, 2002). Mr. D. was correct on 41 of 72 items of this measure of motivation to remember. This score was above the cutoff with 100% specificity (no false positives in the validation sample of 120 examinees with well-documented brain dysfunction), but it was below the cutoffs with test specificity set at 99% (Binder & Kelly, 1996). The psychologist concluded that he was brain damaged as a result of the MVA. This psychologist reviewed none of the relevant records from the hospital emergency room on the date of injury or from the HMO.

Three years after the injury another out of state psychologist examined Mr. D. from primarily a vocational perspective at the request of Mr. D.'s attorney. On the Validity Indicator Profile, a measure of cognitive effort, the verbal test was invalid and the nonverbal test was valid. In the vocational interest testing, the psychologist described what he characterized as a "retirement profile" showing little interest in working. He was below the 50th percentile in all vocational interest areas. Despite the invalid effort test, this psychologist essentially agreed with the first psychologist regarding the diagnosis of traumatic brain injury, and he added a diagnosis of Dysthymic Disorder.

In the midst of many visits to his HMO for treatment of neck and right arm pain and five months before my neuropsychological exam, his HMO treated him for a hand laceration reportedly sustained while moving concrete blocks. This reported activity seemed inconsistent with his complaints of chronic pain.

Mr. D.'s sworn deposition testimony was inconsistent with the medical records from the early 1980s. Mr. D. testified that, despite the descriptions of his psychiatric status at that time and his disability award, he did not view himself as disabled at the end of his law enforcement career. He was unable to describe any specific stressors that led to this disability, and he denied having any problem performing his law enforcement job. He denied ever experiencing a memory problem prior to his MVA. He claimed that his symptoms from the MVA prevented him from working. Subsequent to receiving his law enforcement disability and prior to the MVA, Mr. D. was employed managing his rental properties and as a self-employed heavy equipment operator. He testified that prior to the MVA he had contracted to perform a quarter million dollar job operating heavy equipment, and the MVA prevented him from fulfilling his contract. This testimony explained his large claim for loss of earnings.

INDEPENDENT NEUROPSYCHOLOGICAL EVALUATION

In my independent neuropsychological evaluation of Mr. D. the interview was significant for his exquisitely detailed recollection of the MVA. No retrograde or anterograde amnesia was evident from the interview, an observation not consistent with the phenomenon of concussion. He claimed complete disability for gainful employment. He said he could not use his dominant right arm for tasks such as operating power tools. He also complained of a constant headache and forgetfulness. Medications included amitriptyline at bedtime, hydrocodone for pain, and cyclobenzaprine for muscle spasm.

Regarding his mental health history of two decades earlier, he was vague. He acknowledged some treatment, including two psychiatric hospitalizations. Contradicting the records, he stated that he was ordered into treatment by his employer, and he did not understand why treatment had been mandated. He reported no memory of having been treated for anger problems in the 1990s.

Social history included a childhood that he labeled as "hell." His father repeatedly abused his mother, eventually shot his mother with a pistol, and subsequently served a prison sentence. The examinee had some unspecified behavior problems as a youth, left high school before obtaining a diploma, and enlisted in the military. He reported serving four years in the military without participating in any combat and receiving an honorable discharge. He then obtained a regular high school diploma and later a Bachelor's degree. Mr. D.'s first marriage ended in divorce. At the time of the exam he had been married 20 years to his second wife. He had two biological children and three stepchildren.

His mental status exam was significant only for minor speech hesitancy. He arrived unaccompanied, having driven over 50 miles alone to the office. He was neatly dressed and groomed. There were no observations or symptoms suggestive of psychosis. He was affable, and at the conclusion of the exam he said the whole experience had been a pleasure.

Testing with the Portland Digit Recognition Test (PDRT; see Table 8.1) provided clear-cut

TABLE 8.1 Neuropsychological scores from the independent exam, 40 months post-MVA, age 62, male, 16 years of education, right hand dominant

Portland Digit Recognition Test	
Easy correct	16/36
Hard correct	5/36
WAIS–III IQ, Index, and Scaled Scores	
Verbal IQ	100
Performance IQ	106
Full Scale IQ	103
Verbal Comprehension	98
Perceptual Organization	111
Working Memory	102
Processing Speed	76
Vocabulary	9
Similarities	10
Arithmetic	11
Digit Span	9
Information	10
Comprehension	12
Letter-Number Sequencing	11
Picture Completion	11
Digit Symbol-Coding	5
Block Design	12
Matrix Reasoning	13
Picture Arrangement	14
Symbol Search	6
Trail Making Part A	75 sec (1st percentile)
Trail Making Part B	176 sec (5th percentile)
WMS–III Logical Memory I	7 (scaled score)
WMS–III Logical Memory II	10 (scaled score)
Rey Auditory Verbal Learning	
Trials 1–5 Total	44 (30th–39th percentile)
Short Delayed Free Recall	9 (37th percentile, approximately)
Long Delayed Free Recall	9 (50th percentile, approximately)
Recognition Correct	14/15 (within normal limits)
Recognition False Positives	2 (within normal limits)
Brief Visuospatial Memory Test–Revised	
Total Recall	10th percentile
Delayed Recall	14th percentile
Recognition Raw Score	3/6 true positives, 0 false positives
Recognition Discrimination	3rd–5th percentile
Wisconsin Card Sorting Test	
Categories	4 (> 16th percentile)
Errors	42 (18th percentile)
Perseverative Responses	35 (13th percentile)
Grip Strength	
Right	8 kilograms (below 1st percentile)
Left	29 kilograms (50th percentile)
Finger Tapping	
Right	31 (1st percentile)
Left	45 (47th percentile)

Grooved Pegboard	
Right	73 sec (50th percentile)
Left	70 sec (86th percentile)
MMPI–2	
L	56
F	61
K	41
S	48
Hs	70
D	64
Hy	71
Pd	42
Mf	30
Pa	37
Pt	39
Sc	49
Ma	47
Si	56

evidence that Mr. D. deliberately provided wrong answers. He was correct on only 21 of 72 items on this forced-choice test, a score well below the cutoff of 39 correct. He was correct on 16 of 36 of the easy items and five of 36 of the hard items. The z approximation of the binomial theorem was significant at the 0.0004 level, indicating that if he had guessed on each item, there was less than one chance in 2500 that he would have been unlucky enough to guess correctly on only 21 of the 72 PDRT items. No other motivational tests were necessary after obtaining a markedly positive, statistically significantly worse than chance result with the PDRT.

Other tests shown in Table 8.1 revealed some results that were unusually severe for a man who drove safely 50 miles to this exam. On Trail Making, his times were unusually slow, especially on Part A. His pattern of motor performances was more consistent with poor effort than brain injury, with normal times on Grooved Pegboard, including a faster than average time with his nondominant left hand, moderate slowing on finger tapping with the right hand, and severe grip strength abnormality on the right. After genuine traumatic brain injury the expected motor test pattern involves greater impairment on tapping than on grip strength and more impairment on the Grooved Pegboard than on tapping (Greiffenstein, Baker, & Gola, 1996). The examinee displayed the opposite of this expected pattern. Furthermore, his grip strength seemed quite inconsistent with moving concrete blocks a few months before, and his finger tapping speed, although moderately abnormal on the right, was dramatically improved compared with the first neuropsychological evaluation when his scores were 14 on the right and 16 on the left. In contrast to his poor PDRT performance, measures of verbal memory including WAIS–III Working Memory, the Rey AVLT, and WMS–III Logical Memory were within one standard deviation of the mean. Visual memory scores were abnormal. Except for Processing Speed, his WAIS–III index scores were normal. The MMPI–2 profile was mildly somatoform with elevations on Scales Hs and Hy. Although valid and relatively benign, it was not inconsistent with a diagnosis of malingering. Often, there is discordance between the results of the MMPI–2 validity scores and effort testing.

Under Oregon law, expert reports in arbitration are submitted as evidence to the panel of arbitrators prior to the hearing. Unlike jury trials in some states in which reports are not admitted into evidence, the arbitrators may rely on the report in the absence of any testimony by the author. Hence, it is useful in a case to be decided by arbitrators to write a scientifically persuasive report. My report was strongly worded, explicitly labeling Mr. D. a malingerer. I discussed the nature of the injury and my reasoning that he had not suffered any concussion or mild traumatic brain injury. I noted the incongruence between the HMO records, which contained no concerns about brain injury or postconcussive syndrome, and the reports of the two psychologist experts for the plaintiff. The inconsistency between the total disability award for reasons of mental illness after his law enforcement career and his subsequent occupational success in managing real-estate rental property and operating heavy equipment was described. I explained in detail the rationale of two alternative forced-choice testings, the forced-choice nature of the PDRT, and the validation data obtained from 120 patients with well-documented brain dysfunction. The testing of statistical significance was explained in lay terms by stating that such a result was likely to occur through guessing less than one out of 2500 times, rather than reporting the significance in terms of the p level of 0.0004.

Mr. D. scored normally on many neuropsychological tests, despite the markedly positive result on the PDRT. It is clear that he exaggerated more on some tests than on others. For example, his verbal memory and Grooved Pegboard performances were more normal than his scores on Trail Making and the PDRT. His selective exaggeration of deficits can be explained as a strategic decision to attempt to avoid detection. A study of multiple measures of effort with normal subjects instructed to simulate poor effort showed that the average subject exaggerated on less than half the measures (Orey, Cragar, & Berry, 2000).

LEGAL OUTCOME AND DISCUSSION

Some plaintiff attorneys argue that unusual results are obtained in independent exams because of a hostile environment that intimidates the examinee. While this argument could not possibly explain similar findings, it sometimes is made, nevertheless. In this case this argument was not, to my knowledge, made by Mr. D.'s lawyer, perhaps because my report quoted Mr. D.'s comment that my exam had been a pleasure.

Mr. D. had no history of head injury or concussion. The MVA caused a cervical strain, and it may have caused median and ulnar neuropathy to his dominant right arm, although these conditions could have been related to the physically demanding work that he often performed. There was no report of loss of consciousness, and his detailed recollections seemed to rule out retrograde or anterograde amnesia. He was motivated to provide a detailed description of the MVA, because it clearly was caused by the other party. The lack of any memory gap is an observation that argues against any concussion. At his HMO, he made no complaints suggesting concussion, postconcussion syndrome, or brain injury. His HMO neurologist was not concerned about the possibility of a brain injury, and she focused on his neck and right arm complaints. Consistent with this lack of concern about a brain injury, a brain scan never was obtained. Only when he went outside his HMO to the first psychologist was there concern about brain injury. This examining psychologist, having concluded that there was brain dysfunction without reviewing any medical records, failed to refer him for a dementia workup to rule out an alternative cause of cognitive dysfunction, and it appears this psychologist was unconcerned about his low PDRT score. The second examining psychologist ignored his own Validity Indicator Profile data showing invalid responding on the verbal subtest. My neuropsychological exam showed unequivocal evidence of deliberately providing wrong answers to PDRT items with 21 of 72 correct. Combined with the medical record, the PDRT result was diagnostic of malingering. Some other test results and observations were consistent with a diagnosis of malingering, but they were not pathognomonic of malingering. These data included his upper extremity abnormality on grip strength compared with his normal Grooved Pegboard score and his reported carrying of concrete blocks, and the slowing on Trail Making in contrast with his ability to drive distances safely. His old psychiatric history of symptoms that were judged, at the time, to be consistent with severe mental illness was followed by total disability from law enforcement. While receiving a total disability pension, he pursued successful careers in real-estate investing and heavy equipment operation. He may have been malingering in the 1980s. Clearly, his total disability award nearly 20 years before the MVA was inconsistent with his subsequent occupational success.

The independent neuropsychological exam was consistent with malingering with a score significantly below the chance level on the PDRT. There are many other well-validated measures of suboptimal effort that could have been administered to this man, but no single result could be more persuasive to arbitrators than a score on a forced-choice test that is significantly worse than chance. Such a result is very easy to explain as the product of a deliberate attempt to provide wrong answers and thereby appear to be impaired. Neuropsychologists agree that a forced choice result significantly worse than chance greatly increases their willingness to make a diagnosis of malingering (Trueblood & Binder, 1997). One can speculate that he might have failed many other motivational tests. However, had he failed other tests by scoring below the cutoffs, but above the level of chance, perhaps the data would not have been so persuasive to the arbitrators. I believe that the mild nature of the accident, the lack of head injury and loss of consciousness, the complete lack of evidence of brain injury aside from the report and testimony of the plaintiff's psychologist, and the testimony of the biomechanical expert also contributed to the arbitration panel's decision to not make any award for alleged brain injury.

The scientific literature does not support the notion that typical whiplash injuries associated with cervical hyperextension cause brain injury in adults. A meta-analysis revealed an association between chronic whiplash and cognitive deficits, but the authors conceded that the origin of the cognitive deficits could not be determined (Kessels, Aleman, Verhagen, & van Luijtelaar, 2000), and cognitive deficits can be explained by chronic pain (Hart, Martelli, & Zasler, 2000). Large studies in Lithuania, a country in which financial incentives for prolonged symptomatology after MVAs do not exist, showed no association between whiplash injuries and chronic pain or headaches (Obelieniene et al., 1998; Obelieniene, Schrader, Bovim, Miseviciene, & Sand, 1999). Alexander (1998, p. 337) stated there was "no credible mechanism for clinically meaningful DAI (diffuse axonal injury) in pure whiplash in awake humans who do not report loss of consciousness or amnesia beyond that psychologically appropriate for the acutely stressful time immediately around the accident and injury." Some professionals view whiplash as one of several syndromes in which the symptoms greatly outweigh the objective findings that might show tissue pathology (Barsky & Borus, 1999).

The PDRT, one of several well-validated measures of effort, was useful in this case. In my exam, it yielded below chance results after merely generating a score below the cutoff in the plaintiff's first neuropsychological exam. In a series of cases of alleged mild traumatic brain injury associated with financial incentives for the injuries, one sixth performed significantly worse than chance on the PDRT (Binder, 1993). There are no reports in the literature of the frequency of significantly below chance results with other forced-choice tests in clinical samples. Malingerers, it was said in an anonymous turn of phrase, are "blinder than the blind and lamer than the lame." This unsophisticated malingerer was more forgetful on the PDRT than people with true brain dysfunction.

It is of interest to speculate why the first examining psychologist was willing to testify that the man was brain damaged from the accident, the only expert to so testify. This psychologist was not well trained or board certified in neuropsychology in a meaningful way, although he had purchased a credential from a vanity board that sells board certification without requiring that candidates pass a proficiency exam. The PDRT score in the first exam was low; however, it was above the cutoff score with 100% specificity. In addition, the medical records that reported no concussion or complaints consistent with postconcussion syndrome were not reviewed. It is difficult to understand the faulty thought process that initially led to the incorrect diagnosis of traumatic brain injury. More puzzling is why my subsequent report was not persuasive to plaintiff's expert, unless he concluded that the plaintiff faked bad in my exam but also was truly brain damaged. The testimony of the plaintiff's psychologist did not address my PDRT data or my reasoning.

The plaintiff psychologist's failure to refer Mr. D. for a dementia workup to rule out an alternative neurological explanation for the alleged cognitive deficits after his initial evaluation was not consistent with sound neuropsychological practice. If a neuropsychologist concludes that cognitive functioning is abnormal, then the patient must be evaluated by a physician for the purpose of ruling out a treatable cause for the cognitive problems. Mr. D. was never evaluated by any of his physicians for the alleged cognitive problem.

At the arbitration hearing there was testimony from a fact witness that contradicted Mr. D.'s testimony that, had he not been injured, he would have earned a quarter million dollars from a heavy equipment-contracting job. This witness alleged that the contract was fraudulent and written after the accident. A biomechanical engineer hired by the defense testified that the rear-end collision was not of sufficient force and speed to cause brain injury.

The arbitrators provided what the attorneys considered a verdict in favor of the insurer by awarding Mr. D. less than $15,000. The award was reduced by the unknown amount already paid by the at-fault driver's insurer. The arbitrators rejected the claim of brain injury. This verdict was far less than the hundreds of thousands of dollars Mr. D. had demanded from the insurer. Out of this arbitration award, the plaintiff had to pay expert witness and other arbitration hearing expenses and his lawyer.

REFERENCES

Alexander, M. P. (1998). In the pursuit of proof of brain damage after whiplash injury. *Neurology*, *51*, 336–340.

Barsky, A. J., & Borus, J. F. (1999). Functional somatic syndromes. *Annals of Internal Medicine*, *130*, 910–921.

Binder, L. M. (1993). Assessment of malingering after mild head trauma with the Portland Digit Recognition Test. *Journal of Clinical and Experimental Neuropsychology*, *15*, 170–182.

Binder, L. M. (2002) The Portland Digit Recognition Test: A review of validation data and clinical use. *Journal of Forensic Neuropsychology*, *2*, 27–41.

Binder, L. M., & Kelly, M. P. (1996). Portland Digit Recognition Test performance by brain dysfunction patients without financial incentives. *Assessment*, *3*, 403–409.

Greiffenstein, M. F., Baker, W. J., & Gola, T. (1996). Motor dysfunction profiles in traumatic brain injury and postconcussion syndrome. *Journal of the International Neuropsychological Society*, *2*, 477–485.

Guilmette, T. J., Hart, K. J., Giuliano, A. J., & Leininger, B. E. (1994). Detecting simulated memory impairment: Comparison of the Rey Fifteen-Item Test and the Hiscock Forced-Choice Procedure. *The Clinical Neuropsychologist*, *8*, 283–294.

Hart, R. P., Martelli, M. F., & Zasler, N. D. (2000). Chronic pain and neuropsychological functioning. *Neuropsychology Review*, *20*, 131–149.

Iverson, G. L., & Binder, L. M. (2000). Detecting exaggeration and malingering in neuropsychological assessment. *Journal of Head Trauma Rehabilitation*, *15*, 829–858.

Kessels, R. P. C., Aleman, A., Verhagen, W. I. M., & van Luijtelaar, E. L. J. M. (2000). Cognitive functioning after whiplash injury: A meta-analysis. *Journal of the International Neuropsychological Society*, *6*, 271–278.

Lee, G. P., Loring, D. W., & Martin, R. C. (1992). Rey's 15-Item visual memory test for the detection of malingering: Normative observations on patients with neurological disorders. *Psychological Assessment*, *4*, 43–46.

Obelieniene, D., Bovim, G., Schrader, H., Surkiene, D., Mickeviaiene, D., Miseviaiene, I., & Sand T. (1998). Headache after whiplash: A historical cohort study outside the medico-legal context. *Cephalalgia*, *18*, 559–564.

Obelieniene, D., Schrader, H. Bovim, G., Miseviciene, I., & Sand, T. (1999). Pain after whiplash: A prospective controlled inception cohort study. *Journal of Neurology, Neurosurgery, and Psychiatry*, *66*, 279–283.

Orey, S. A., Cragar, D. E., & Berry, D. T. R. (2000). The effects of two motivational manipulations on the neuropsychological performance of mildly head-injured college students. *Archives of Clinical Neuropsychology*, *15*, 335–348.

Trueblood, W., & Binder, L. M. (1997). Psychologists' accuracy in identifying neuropsychological test protocols of clinical malingerers. *Archives of Clinical Neuropsychology*, *12*, 13–27.

Brain trauma, psychiatric disturbance, premorbid factors, and malingering

9

W. John Baker

A forensic neuropsychological evaluation can differ from a clinical evaluation in many ways. One of the most important differences lies in the ability to gather and analyze additional records. Unlike the clinician, a forensic examiner may have access to prior medical, academic, and employment records that allows for an informed opinion regarding premorbid status. Prior psychiatric and psychological evaluations and treatment records allow the forensic examiner to establish an accurate baseline against which evaluation data can be compared. It is not uncommon for individuals being evaluated in both clinical and forensic settings to provide inaccurate or incomplete histories. The forensic examiner has the advantage of gaining access to historical data leading to a more accurate and comprehensive evaluation. This case was selected because of the competing and overlapping analyses and the considerable impact of subsequently reviewed records.

LEGAL BACKGROUND AND INJURY HISTORY

Ms. E. was referred for evaluation by an attorney defending a personal injury lawsuit arising out of an automobile accident. The defendant in the case was actually her sister who had been the driver of the vehicle in which Ms. E. was a passenger. Chief among the damage claims was a traumatic brain injury (TBI). Ms. E. was the unrestrained right rear seat passenger in a vehicle that was driven by her sister, who was visiting from out of state. Ms. E. was evaluated two years post injury and claimed a multitude of physical, emotional, and cognitive damages. Based on her doctors' diagnoses and the report of a neuropsychologist in her home state, the defense attorney requested a professional opinion as to the nature and extent of the effects of the alleged TBI. According to Ms. E., the driver of her car (sister) pulled out in front of an oncoming vehicle, causing the collision. Ms. E. was thrown from the vehicle. Because the driver of her vehicle was deemed at fault, Ms. E.'s only course of action was against her sister.

Ms. E. is a 51-year-old, 9th grade educated, left-hand dominant, married woman. Born in Virginia and raised by her parents, Ms. E. was the sixth of ten children. She denied any developmental, childhood, or adolescent abnormalities. Prior medical history was significant for multiple ailments, including prior diagnoses of fibromyalgia, hypertension, diabetes, and cardiovascular disease. She was reportedly disabled since age 27; disability was attributed to pain problems, which resulted in not having worked in over 20 years. She had six cardiac stents and multiple surgeries for left knee problems. Ms. E. also reported a history of psychiatric treatment and hospitalizations, having been diagnosed with depression over 30 years ago. Though she denied ever being suicidal, she had been hospitalized on at least ten occasions, the last time being many years before. According to

Ms. E., she had dropped out of school in the 10th grade because of responsibilities at home. Grades were described as "good." According to Ms. E., when the oldest child in the family was married, the next in line assumed the responsibilities of caring for the remaining children as well as completing the household chores. Thus, she dropped out of school when her older sibling married and moved from home. Ms. E. was married a short time later, at the age of 16. She reportedly earned her GED later in life.

Ms. E. denied any memory of the accident. She stated that her last recall was of stopping at an intersection near where the accident occurred. She had some memory of her emergency room treatment, and she recalled being taken by helicopter to another hospital. Her memory was reportedly fairly continuous within two to three days. She was in the ICU for two days and discharged after six days. Ms. E. gave a history of a subdural hematoma (SDH) and cerebral edema. The history provided was consistent with TBI, likely of a moderate degree, based on an estimated posttraumatic amnesia (PTA) of greater than 24 hours and less than seven days. The additional complications of SDH and edema reported suggested the potential for secondary injury.

Inasmuch as it is preferential to review records at the time of the evaluation, when the appointment was scheduled the attorney's office was instructed to forward all available records prior to the date of the appointment. Unfortunately, though the records had been requested by subpoena, they were very slow in coming. Ms. E. was examined without the benefit of her medical records. As is not uncommon, this was an independent medical evaluation (IME) that had to be scheduled before the cutoff date for discovery. Just as records ordered before the end of discovery can be reviewed later, so can an evaluation be amended post discovery. Not unlike the conditions of a clinical evaluation, the examiner was left to accept the history provided by the examinee. Though the test data were to be interpreted within this context, as will be seen below, the subsequent review of pre- and post-injury records significantly altered the analysis and conclusions.

Ms. E. complained of memory problems, balance problems, irritability, and difficulty with basic activities, such as dressing herself. Her reported need for help dressing was intermittent. When rushed or pressured she had more difficulty thinking. She stated that her "mind goes blank" when under pressure. There were also complaints of remote memory loss. Ms. E. described not being able to remember how to tie her shoes and on occasion she could not recall how to sit in the bathtub. She also reported conflicts with her sister; because of the lawsuit, they were no longer speaking. Further questioning resulted in acknowledgment of even more symptoms. Ms. E. indicated that her memory problems were getting worse. She was having more difficulty paying attention. She acknowledged depression and onset insomnia. Ms. E. complained additionally of headaches, dizziness, neck and shoulder pain, poor vision, hearing loss, decreased reading, spelling and writing skills, and the loss of most of her childhood memories.

At the time of interview, Ms. E. provided a detailed history of her medical care following the accident. She was first seen in the ER of a local hospital and transferred via Life Flight to a large university hospital, where she remained for six days. After her discharge, Ms. E. was seen for outpatient rehabilitation therapies for five weeks. She then returned home and continued her usual medical care with the doctors she was seeing before the accident. In addition to her primary care physician, she was seen by specialists in orthopedic surgery, gastroenterology, vascular surgery, cardiology, and psychiatry. She was referred to a neurologist for follow-up care of her TBI. She had undergone neuropsychological evaluation in the rehab hospital. As indicated above, at the time of the evaluation and initial report, no records were available.

EXAMINATION RESULTS

Ms. E. was accompanied to the evaluation by her husband. The testing was completed over two days. Ms. E. presented with normal mental status. She was alert and oriented, with normal speech and thought patterns. Ms. E. completed the history forms without assistance and provided a detailed and organized history. She became tearful when discussing her symptoms and when talking of the conflict with her sister. Complaints of arm pain resulted in the need for many breaks, and discontinuation of the Tactual Performance Test (TPT). Though she performed most tests when instructed, encouragement was frequently required, and the testing assistant described Ms. E.'s attitude as indifferent and untroubled.

TABLE 9.1   Neuropsychological symptom validity testing

TOMM retention	38
Portland Digit Recognition	50%
Reliable Digit Span	3
Rey's Word Recognition	5
CVLT–II Y/N recognition	9 correct and 8 wrong
CVLT–II FC recognition	11 correct and 5 wrong

TABLE 9.2   Psychiatric symptom validity on the MMPI–2

F–K	5
F	82T
FBS raw score	30
Obvious–Subtle	220
TRIN	65True
F (p)	90T
Validity Index (Meyers, Millis, & Volkert, 2002)	8

TABLE 9.3   Neuropsychological data

WAIS–III	FSIQ = 65	VIQ = 64	PIQ = 71	WTAR = 72
WRAT–3	Reading = 70	Spelling = 59	Arithmetic 56	
Category	115 errors	SSPT = 18 errors	SRT = 15 errors	
WMSR	LM I = 16	LMII = 6	VR I = 18	VR II = 7
CVLT–II	Total = 23	I = 4	V = 6	SDFR = 4 LDFR = 5 LDCR = 4
WCST	4 categories	48 errors	44 perseverative errors	4 premature shifts
Trails		A = 54″	B = 300″	
Grip		(D) = 24.5 kg	(nD) = 20 kg	
Finger Tapping		(D) = 31.8	(nD) = 18	
Grooved Pegboard		(D) = 92″	(nD) = 150″	
SPS (errors)		Tactile (D) = 12	(nD) = 11	
		Auditory (D) = 7	(nD) = 5	
		Visual (D) = 8	(nD) = 11	

INITIAL ANALYSIS

Symptom validity testing (SVT) was positive for poor effort and possible malingering. Ms. E.'s TOMM score was below the cutoff of 45 (Tombaugh, 1996). Her reliable digit score of 3 was not only indicative of poor effort, but also very unusual. Ms. E. failed to correctly repeat 2-digits forward on both trials, but she was able to correctly repeat 3-digits on both trials (forward = 0, backward = 3). Her forced-choice digit recognition score of 50% was consistent with random responding. Taken together, the SVT findings are most consistent with poor effort and suggesting that the neuropsychological profile was likely an underestimate Ms. E.'s true abilities.

Intellectual status was measured in the impaired range, consistent with academic achievement scores. On the surface, this would suggest some pre-existing cognitive limitations, though symptom validity testing (SVT) implicates poor cooperation. Memory testing was more consistent with intellectual limitations than specific memory impairment. Long Delay Free Recall (LDFR) on the CVLT–II was nearly equal to Trial V. Recognition testing was extremely poor. Though Ms. E. was able to correctly identify 9 words in a yes/no recognition format, she also identified 8 words that were not on the list. Her adjusted hits score of 1 is implausibly poor and gives serious doubt to the validity of her CVLT–II findings. Ms. E.'s performance on the HRB measures was generally consistent with a picture of limited intellectual development. Her very poor score on the Speech Sounds Perception Test (SSPT) is not surprising given her deficient spelling skills on the Wide Range Achievement Test–3rd Edition (WRAT–3). Ms. E.'s score of 15 errors on the Seashore Rhythm Test (SRT) is essentially at chance. Studies by Millis, Putnam, and Adams (1996) and Trueblood and Schmidt (1993) suggest that Ms. E.'s scores on SSPT and SRT are more consistent with response bias than TBI.

Motor and sensory testing revealed mixed findings. The finger tapping and pegboard results were lateralized, with greater impairment found in right hand (nondominant) speed. Sensory perceptual screening was nonlateralized, though profoundly impaired (27 total errors on each side). Though the motor findings suggest greater involvement of the left hemisphere, the sensory findings are more consistent with poor effort or symptom promotion (Binder & Willis, 1991; Trueblood & Schmidt, 1993).

The MMPI–2 was of very questionable validity. The Gough score (F–K) of 5 is below the older traditional cutoffs (Graham, 1990; Greene, 1988), but consistent with exaggeration based on more recent studies with personal injury claimants (Berry et al., 1995; Lees-Haley, 1991, 1992). The validity index (Meyers, Millis, & Volkert, 2002) of 8 is classified as probable malingering. Her FBS score of 30 (raw) is well beyond established cutoff scores (Lees-Haley, English, & Glenn, 1991) and consistent with exaggeration of somatic symptoms (Larrabee, 2003). Mild elevation was found on F(p) at 90-T, consistent with exaggeration of psychiatric symptoms (Arbisi & Ben-Porath, 1998). The extremely high Obvious–Subtle score of 220 is indicative of over-reporting of psychiatric symptoms. Though the MMPI–2 profile is reflective of symptom promotion and an accurate analysis is not possible, this, in and of itself, does not rule out actual psychiatric disturbance. Subjective reports are consistent with depression and the effects of stress (e.g., irritability, insomnia).

Based on the history provided and the data generated by this evaluation, a number of impressions can be formulated. The history given by Ms. E. is certainly consistent with brain trauma likely to result in neuropsychological impairment. Both neuropsychological and psychological symptom validity testing indicate that impression management has impacted the results. Background is equivocal for pre-existing cognitive deficits. She dropped out of school, but gave a reasonable explanation and claimed good grades. IQ scores and achievement testing suggest longstanding deficits, inconsistent with claims of good grades and GED. Ms. E.'s psychiatric history and current complaints are relevant, as well. She has a history of depression, and interpersonal conflicts have developed as a result of litigation. She reported increasing cognitive symptoms and symptoms of depression, irritability, and insomnia. Thus, by history and subjective report, Ms. E. presents a picture of post-TBI impairment. However, objective data are more consistent with poor effort and symptom promotion. The self-reported history does not allow for exclusion of impairment due to TBI. Further, while there are reasons to suspect pre-existing limitations, the absence of supporting documentation renders little to justify such an interpretation. Whether the poor IQ and achievement results are due to poor effort or developmental limitations is an open question. This is a case in which both pre-accident and post-accident medical records are necessary to clarify the many possible interpretations. A preliminary report noted the possibility of cognitive impairment due to TBI, as well as possible longstanding deficiencies and evidence of poor effort. A final analysis was withheld pending review of records.

POST-EVALUATION REVIEW OF RECORDS

In addition to accident-related records, prior medical and psychiatric records, as well as records from the Social Security Administration, were reviewed.

Post-trauma records

Ambulance records indicated that Ms. E. was unconscious at the scene. The first ER records indicate that she regained consciousness prior to arrival at the hospital. The emergency room physician recorded a Glasgow Coma Scale (GCS) of 15 and described Ms. E. as alert and oriented. A computerized tomography (CT) scan of the brain revealed a right parietotemporal epidural hematoma with no mass effect. She was transferred to the university hospital, where records included a second CT scan of the brain confirming the epidural hemorrhage. Again, her GCS was 15. Nursing notes indicate no change in consciousness throughout her hospital stay. Serial CT scans documented resolution of the hemorrhage. She was cleared neurologically and scheduled for discharge two days after the accident, but complaints of dizziness and pain delayed her discharge for another two days. Though reference to neuropsychological testing was found in the hospital records, no reports or data were located. Her treating physiatrist classified Ms. E.'s TBI as mild and indicated that her condition was complicated by psychiatric overlay and likely premorbid cognitive problems. The acute care medical records differ significantly from the oral history. There was no subdural hematoma and there was no evidence of edema. The records indicate that Ms. E. was alert and fully oriented throughout her hospital stay. This is not consistent with her report of 2–3 day amnesia. A review of medication records did not indicate sedation as a possible explanation for reported amnesia. The labeling of Ms. E.'s TBI as mild is significant. The implication is that her physicians did *not* see the injury as complicated or indicative of serious pathology.

Outpatient rehabilitation records indicate that Ms. E. was seen for vestibular therapy, occupational therapy, and a brief course of speech and language therapy. She was discharged after having achieved *all* of her treatment goals.

Her speech pathologist reported mild memory problems that were *resolved* by the end of treatment. She was described as independent when discharged. No further treatment was recommended. Her occupational therapist reported functional independence and no need for assistive devices at the time of discharge from therapy. Ms. E. was followed by a physiatrist at the hospital for treatment of what he termed "postconcussive syndrome." Ms. E. was seen by an oral surgeon for TMJ-related symptoms. She reported a long history of bilateral TMJ clicking, bruxism, and headaches.

Following her return to home, Ms. E. continued her routine medical care. Her psychiatrist described the accident as "an unfortunate episode" and cited Ms. E.'s concern over suing her sister. He noted that Ms. E. had difficulty recalling whether her sister ran a red light or whether she had stopped. The conflict over relative support for her suit versus support for her sister was seen as significant. The psychiatrist's chart notes suggest that Ms. E. did have better recall of events surrounding the accident than she was now admitting. Whether these discrepancies are due to the natural fading of memory, resolution of the conflict with family, or litigation promotion is unclear. However, what is clear is that her PTA was far shorter than indicated in her oral history, and at one time Ms. E. could provide a more detailed history of events at the time of her accident.

Prior medical records

Ms. E.'s primary medical care records dated to 1984. The earliest records included diagnoses of irritable bowel syndrome (IBS), acute and chronic anxiety, thyroid cancer, diabetes, and chronic low back pain. A report from 1991 included diagnoses of major affective disorder, passive-aggressive, and histrionic personality. She was described as suicidal and sent to a psychiatrist. Ms. E.'s pre-accident medical records documented her ongoing care for the following conditions: osteoarthritis, lumbosacral sprain, lumbago, fibromyalgia, peptic ulcer disease, abdominal pain, IBS, hypertension, diabetes, chronic pain syndrome, chronic left knee pain, dizziness, anxiety, depression, and addiction to narcotic medications resulting from long-term treatment of her chronic pain. The picture of a chronically ill individual with a multitude of problems became clear. At the time of the evaluation, Ms. E. minimized her prior medical problems, citing only heart disease, fibromyalgia, hypertension, diabetes, and depression. In reviewing these old medical records, one comes to realize that Ms. E. had been quite ill most of her life and that her doctors had struggled to help her, with little success.

Prior neurology records

Ms. E.'s medical records also included neurology consultations and related hospitalizations, none of which were reported at the time of her neuropsychological evaluation. In 1998, she was hospitalized and seen by a neurologist who diagnosed a cerebral vascular accident (CVA). A CT scan of the brain revealed a left temporal stroke. One year later a CT scan revealed loss of volume, ventricle enlargement, and atrophy consistent with chronic changes due to the effects of the CVA. Ms. E. was hospitalized in 1999 with complaints of persistent and severe head pain. This time a CT scan of the brain was interpreted as positive for bilateral small hygromas in the frontal lobes and ventricular changes. Comparison to prior CT scans revealed significant changes. Another CT scan revealed a small old infarct in the periventricular white matter of the left frontal lobe. An MRI of the brain in early 2000 revealed chronic bifrontal subdural hematomas. By June of 2000 the hematomas had resolved, though atrophic changes were noted. These records demonstrate longstanding neurologic abnormalities, the nature of which probably resulted in neuropsychological deficits.

Prior psychiatric records

Ms. E.'s psychiatric records begin with a hospitalization in 1979. Her diagnoses were "depression and severe anxiety." Ms. E. was hospitalized for a month. The records also noted severe marital stress and family conflict. Subsequent psychiatric hospitalizations consistently noted depressive symptoms. Additional diagnoses included Borderline Personality Disorder, Panic Disorder, and possible Bipolar Disorder. The records documented continual outpatient psychiatric care. Over the years a number of antidepressants and anxiolytics were prescribed. These psychiatric records are largely consistent with the oral history. It does appear that Ms. E. tended to minimize her psychiatric past. She denied suicidal thoughts. She denied prior marital and/or family discord. Pre-accident psychological testing was found in the psychiatric records. Ms. E. was seen for psychological testing during her psychiatric hospitalizations. She was first tested in 1979. The test scores reported were VIQ = 71, PIQ = 81, and FSIQ = 74. She was tested next in May of 2000. Interestingly, at that time Ms. E. gave a history of having had two strokes, one in 1996 and one in 1999. The only test scores given were VIQ = 78, PIQ = 85, and FSIQ = 81. These records are consistent with longstanding cognitive limitations. The scores are significantly better than those obtained recently. The records from the Social Security Administration indicated that Ms. E. first applied for disability in 1980. Though she was initially denied benefits, in 1983 she was awarded Social Security Disability (SSD). Ms. E. had undergone IQ testing in 1980 and achieved an FSIQ of 71. The Social Security Administration cited "severe mental impairment and psychiatric disturbance due to severe depression and an inadequate dependent personality disorder." The final determination report documented many and lengthy psychiatric hospitalizations and Ms. E.'s inability to obtain and maintain employment.

FINAL CASE ANALYSIS

As noted earlier, initial neuropsychological findings, interpreted without the benefit of relevant records, left open a number of explanations. The oral history suggested significant injury characteristics. Symptom promotion and possible malingering were evident in the test data. Some findings suggested the possibility of pre-existing cognitive limitations. Lastly, psychiatric symptoms were implicated. Subsequent review of post-trauma records indicates that Ms. E. suffered a rather mild brain injury with minimal LOC and PTA. In spite of a small epidural hematoma, she was neurologically cleared in a day and diagnosed with a concussion. Her hospitalization was lengthened due to complaints of dizziness, which required further workup.

Conceptual formulation

Symptom validity testing was most consistent with malingering. This is supported by Ms. E.'s report of remote memory loss and her misleading history. She did not report prior neurological treatment. She denied prior neurologic conditions including two strokes and prior CT scans. She minimized her psychiatric history. Ms. E. denied prior interpersonal conflicts and claimed that her family relationships were close until this litigation began to separate her from her sister. She reported good grades and denied any prior learning problems. When these factors are added to the picture, an image of symptom promotion consistent with malingering emerges.

Premorbid factors account for much of the test data. Prior intellectual testing established borderline IQ scores as far back as 1979. Though her IQ scores had varied, Ms. E. never tested in the normal range. Deficient intellectual development is obvious. Her psychiatric history was far more disturbed than Ms. E. was willing to admit. During the evaluation, she presented her past psychiatric hospitalizations in a rather benign manner. She reported periods of depression without suicidal thoughts or other symptoms. Ms. E. indicated that her doctor admitted her to the hospital because of stress and depression. In reviewing her records, one finds a very troubled past. While depression was diagnosed, this was only one of a variety of other disorders, including various personality disorders. A history of interpersonal conflicts was noted at various times in the records. Ms. E. acknowledged being disabled but gave her fibromyalgia as a basis for receiving SSD. In fact, her disability was due to psychiatric disturbance and intellectual limitations. The pre-accident medical records indicate chronic and unrelenting pain complaints consistent with Ms. E.'s current complaints. Though she reported that these problems were exacerbated by her accident, Ms. E.'s doctors did not alter their treatment and their records did not reflect any significant change in symptoms or diagnoses. Lastly, neurological disease was evident many years before the accident. Ms. E. had at least two cerebral vascular accidents and prior head injuries, all of which she denied at the time of evaluation. Her earlier CT scans revealed prior subdural fluid collections (hematoma and hygroma) on separate occasions.

When the recent neuropsychological profile is considered within the context of pre-accident medical records, the results are not beyond reasonable expectations (Greiffenstein & Baker, 2003; Larrabee, 2000). Though some decline is noted in IQ scores, given her intervening strokes, this is not unexpected. Considering Ms. E.'s longstanding psychiatric disturbance, her clinical presentation and symptomatic complaints are not surprising. Given her report of increasing symptoms, psychiatric disturbance and personality factors are considered more causative (Dikmen, Machamer, & Temkin, 1993). Objective personality testing was most consistent with malingering (Berry et al., 1995; Greiffenstein, Baker, Gola, Donders, & Miller, 2002; Meyers, Millis, & Volkert, 2002). A review of the post-accident records is less supportive. These documents suggest a rather mild injury, in that her consciousness cleared rapidly and her epidural hematoma was rather small and resolved quickly. The relative contributions of premorbid and injury factors favor an interpretation consistent with pre-accident status. Combined with reports of remote memory loss, a misleading history, and symptom validity testing, malingering is a definite likelihood (Greiffenstein, Baker, & Gola, 1994; Slick, Sherman, & Iverson, 1999).

The post-trauma medical records indicate that Ms. E.'s TBI was relatively mild. Her GCS was 15 early on, and she remained neurologically stable. Her neurologist cleared her for discharge two days after injury. These facts would suggest a good prognosis with return to pre-accident status. Her epidural bleed was minimal and without signs of effacement or mass effect. Two years post injury, Ms. E. was still complaining of multiple symptoms, most of which were out of proportion to the severity of the injury, let alone long past the expected course of recovery (Binder, 1997; Dikmen, Machamer, Winn, & Temkin, 1995; Levin et al., 1987).

This case was chosen because it demonstrates the importance of medical records in an independent evaluation. Without the records, the oral history and neuropsychological test data could easily lead to an interpretation of significant brain injury and subsequent cognitive impairment. The importance of symptom validity testing is also evident. Without SVT, the neuropsychological profile was consistent with the oral history. The initial evaluation was conducted under conditions essentially identical to most clinical neuropsychological assessments. The individual was seen by referral, and the history was consistent with brain trauma suggesting the likelihood of residual impairment. Without SVT, one could have easily concluded that Ms. E. had sustained a severe brain injury leaving her impaired more than two years post incident.

Another important aspect of this case is the simultaneous presence of multiple etiologies. There is clear evidence of premorbid neurologic disease. Ms. E. has limited intellectual development and education. She has had two strokes and prior brain injuries with positive neurodiagnostic findings. With regard to the recent accident, there is no doubt that Ms. E. sustained a TBI. Her SVT results provide clear evidence of poor effort and, when combined with history and symptom complaints, malingering is evident. These are not competing or mutually exclusive conditions. Individuals can promote and exaggerate genuine symptoms for secondary purposes. The DSM–IV (American Psychiatric Association, 1994) allows for exaggerated symptoms in defining malingering. Symptoms can be exaggerated for different purposes, and a determination of malingering requires so-called secondary gain. In other words, Ms. E. is assumed to be motivated by her lawsuit. The differential diagnostic consideration here is factitious disorder versus malingering. Both conditions include the production or exaggeration of symptoms. The difference is one of intention or motivation (Sweet, 1999). There is evidence supporting factitious disorder. Ms. E. could be exaggerating her symptoms to manipulate family members and justify her lawsuit against her sister. However, even if this is a component, the weight of evidence supports a diagnosis of malingering. Family dynamics cannot explain the inaccurate history, particularly the omission of prior brain injuries and other neurologic conditions. Ms. E. clearly controlled and manipulated information in favor of her litigation. While I have no doubt that all of the identifiable factors (premorbid IQ, neurologic disease, premorbid psychiatric illness, and family conflicts) contributed to Ms. E.'s condition, her desire to appear brain damaged and her intentional poor performances were most prominent. This conclusion is based on the inaccurate pre- and post-accident histories, pseudoneurologic symptoms (remote memory loss, etc.), exaggerated disability, and SVT failure.

HOW DID THE CASE END?

My deposition was taken shortly after the addendum was completed. Both lawyers had received a copy of my report. Though they both had copies of all the documents that I had reviewed, I got the distinct impression that neither attorney had reviewed the records in much detail. It should be noted that the records from this case filled two very large boxes. The deposition took many hours and as the pre-accident records were discussed the defense attorney became more and more interested. The plaintiff attorney, on the other hand, reacted with displeasure and angst. The defense emphasized the absence of neurological abnormalities beyond the epidural bleed and the presence of significant premorbid pathology. The defense attorney also focused on the positive SVT findings. The plaintiff attorney could not get beyond the two CVAs and prior IQ testing, though he did try to minimize these factors, while emphasizing that his client suffered a hematoma. The plaintiff attorney became locked in a battle over the SVT results. He never accepted the fact that someone with a brain injury can also malinger. Throughout the deposition, he constantly challenged my opinions with evidence of brain injury. He saw the issue as dichotomous. This is not uncommon. In 20 years, only twice has an attorney asked me if positive SVT findings mean that the plaintiff does not have a brain injury. Because of their lack of training in psychological constructs, statistics, psychometrics, and related areas, attorneys may fail to appreciate that human behavior is rarely dichotomous or mutually exclusive. They often think that if the patient is malingering, he is faking and nothing is wrong. Conversely, the plaintiff attorney who believes his client is injured cannot reconcile the opinion that the client is malingering. In the end, after many hours of deposition testimony, the plaintiff attorney seemed to place less emphasis on the issue of cognitive impairment due to the brain injury. Instead, he emphasized Ms. E.'s depression and the impact that her injuries had on her already fragile emotional condition.

Prior to going to trial, this case went to mediation. The mediation panel was comprised of three attorneys, one who practices primarily in the area of personal injury defense, one who represents primarily plaintiffs, and a third attorney who is believed to be neutral. Each attorney presented his case to the panel. The massive amount of pre-accident records documenting a multitude of pre-existing and related medical conditions was overwhelming. In spite of his best efforts, the plaintiff attorney was unable to impress the mediation panel. The case was judged to be of minimal value. Shortly after mediation, the case was settled for $25,000. When the panel members were interviewed later, each one pointed to the pre-accident neurologic findings and the fact that none of the professionals treating Ms. E. was informed of these facts.

REFERENCES

American Psychiatric Association (1994). *Diagnostic and statistical manual of mental disorders*, 4th ed. Washington, DC: APA.

Arbisi, P. A., & Ben-Porath, Y. S. (1997). Characteristics of the MMPI–2 F(p) scale as a function of diagnosis in an inpatient sample of veterans. *Psychological Assessment*, 9, 102–105.

Berry, D. T. R., Wetter, M. W., Baer, R. A., Youngjohn, J. R., Gass, C. S., Lamb, D. G., Franzen, M. D., & MacInnes, W. D. (1995). Overreporting of closed-head injury symptoms on the MMPI–2. *Psychological Assessment, 7*, 517–523.

Binder, L. M. (1997). A review of mild head trauma, Part II: Clinical implications. *Journal of Clinical and Experimental Neuropsychology, 19*, 432–457.

Binder, L. M., & Willis, S. (1991). Assessment of motivation after financially compensable minor head trauma. *Psychological Assessment: A Journal of Consulting and Clinical Psychology, 3*, 175–181.

Dikmen, S. S., Machamer, J. E., & Temkin, N. R. (1993). Psychosocial outcome in patients with moderate to severe head injury: 2-year follow-up. *Brain Injury, 7*, 113–124.

Dikmen, S. S., Machamer, J. E., Winn, R., & Temkin, N. R. (1995). Neuropsychological outcome at 1-year post head injury. *Neuropsychology, 9*, 80–90.

Graham, J. (1990). *MMPI–2 Assessing personality and psychopathology*, 2nd ed. (pp. 46–48). New York: Oxford.

Greene, R. L. (1988). The relative efficacy of F–K and the obvious and subtle scales to detect over-reporting of psychopathology on the MMPI. *Journal of Clinical Psychology, 44*, 152–159.

Greiffenstein, M. F., & Baker, W. J. (2003). Premorbid clues? Preinjury scholastic performance and present neuropsychological functioning in late postconcussion syndrome. *The Clinical Neuropsychologist, 17*, 561–573.

Greiffenstein, M. F., Baker, W. J., & Gola, T. (1994). Validation of malingered amnesia measures with a large clinical sample. *Psychological Assessment, 6*, 218–224.

Greiffenstein, M. F., Baker, W. J., Gola, T., Donders, J., & Miller, L. (2002). The Fake Bad Scale in atypical and severe closed head injury litigants. *Journal of Clinical Psychology, 58*, 1591–1600.

Larrabee, G. (2000). Association between IQ and neuropsychological test performance: Commentary on Tremont, Hoffman, Scott, and Adams, 1998. *The Clinical Neuropsychologist, 14*, 139–145.

Larrabee, G. (2003). Exaggerated pain report in litigants with malingered neurocognitive dysfunction. *The Clinical Neuropsychologist, 17*, 395–401.

Lees-Haley, P. (1991). MMPI–2 F and F–K scores of personal injury malingerers in vocational neuro-psychological and emotional distress claims. *American Journal of Forensic Psychology, 9*, 5–14.

Lees-Haley, P. (1992). Efficacy of MMPI–2 validity scales and MCMI–II modifier scales for detecting spurious PTSD claims: F, F–K, Fake Bad Scale, Ego Strength, Subtle-Obvious Subscales, Dis, and DEB. *Journal of Clinical Psychology, 48*, 681–688.

Lees-Haley, P., English, L.T., & Glenn, W. J. A fake bad scale on the MMPI–2 for personal injury claimants. *The Clinical Neuropsychologist, 68*, 203–210.

Levin, H. S., Mattis, S., Ruff, R., Eisenberg, H. M., Marshall, L. F., Tabaddor, K., High, W. M., & Frankowski, R. F. (1987). Neurobehavioral outcome following minor head injury: A three-center study. *Journal of Neurosurgery, 66*, 234–243.

Meyers, J. E, Millis, S. R., & Volkert, K. (2002). A validity index for the MMPI–2. *Archives of Clinical Neuropsychology, 17*, 157–169.

Millis, S. R., Putnam, S. H., & Adams, K. M. (1996) Speech-sounds Perception Test and Seashore Rhythm Test as validity indicators in the neuropsychological evaluation of mild head injury [abstract]. *Archives of Clinical Neuropsychology, 11*, 425.

Slick, D. J., Sherman, E. M. S., & Iverson, G. L. (1999). Diagnostic criteria for malingered neurocognitive dysfunction: Proposed standards for clinical practice and research. *The Clinical Neuropsychologist, 13*, 545–561.

Sweet, J. J. (1999). Malingering: Differential diagnosis. In J. J. Sweet (Ed.), *Forensic neuropsychology: Fundamentals and practice* (pp. 255–286). Lisse, Netherlands: Swets & Zeitlinger.

Tombaugh, T. N. (1996). *Test of Memory Malingering (TOMM)*. North Tonawanda, New York: Multi-Health Systems Inc.

Trueblood, W., & Schmidt, M. (1993). Malingering and other validity considerations in the neuropsychological evaluation of mild head injury. *Journal of Clinical and Experimental Neuropsychology, 15*, 578–590.

Moderate to severe traumatic brain injury: Probable malingering . . . and then not

10

Chris Paniak

In contrast to malingering after mild and/or questionable traumatic brain injury, very little has been published about malingering after moderate to severe (M–S) traumatic brain injury (TBI). This might be due to a supposed lower incidence of malingering after M–S TBI than mild TBI (e.g., Binder & Rohling, 1996; Demakis, Sweet, Sawyer, Moulthrop, Nies, & Clingerman, 2001; Green & Iverson, 2001; Green, Iverson, & Allen, 1999), or possibly a reluctance to accuse someone who has been seriously injured of such behavior.

The published literature dealing specifically with malingering after M–S TBI largely consists of a few recently published case studies (e.g., Bianchini, Greve, & Love, 2003; Boone & Lu, 2003). Boone and Lu (2003) reported on two severe TBI survivors who performed poorly on symptom validity testing, put forth non-credible performances on neuropsychological tests, produced personality inventory results of questionable validity, and showed marked inconsistency in test performances across assessments or marked inconsistency between test scores and activities of daily living (documented by videotape). Bianchini et al. (2003) reported on three M–S TBI survivors who met Slick, Sherman, and Iverson's (1999) criteria for a diagnosis of "Definite Malingered Neurocognitive Dysfunction." That is, they had an external incentive, performed significantly ($p < .05$) below chance on one or more forced-choice cognitive tests, and the latter performance was not fully accounted for by psychiatric, neurologic, or developmental factors. These cases of malingered neurocognitive dysfunction serve to warn the clinician that the same healthy skepticism and symptom validity testing that is necessary in mildly or questionably injured cases needs to be applied to more seriously injured cases.

The present case deals with a situation of "Probable Malingered Neurocognitive Dysfunction" (Slick et al., 1999), where, for example, symptom validity testing scores are not significantly below chance. In addition, it deals with an individual from a foreign country, who is not a native English speaker, and who has little or no formal education. Despite the obvious difficulties that such factors present for neuropsychological assessment, the case illustrates that similar logic to that used in the previously published cases can be applied to draw reasonable conclusions in somewhat more challenging circumstances. The present case also illustrates how a person with M–S TBI can likely be malingering, while at the same time having almost irrefutable evidence of at least some persisting problems from a M–S TBI. Genuine neurological dysfunction and malingered neuropsychological dysfunction may therefore co-exist.

Finally, and serendipitously, the individual in question in this chapter appeared for a later assessment that had not been anticipated when the chapter was originally completed. At the final assessment, incentives were present for him to *not* malinger. This provided a rare opportunity to further evaluate the conclusion that he had probably been malingering when he was seen for prior assessments, when incentives to malinger *were* present. In order to preserve the original presentation of this chapter, and to prevent the changing of it with the benefit of hindsight, an addendum was added at the end (see below), outlining the results and interpretations from the final assessment, and a column of results from the final assessment was added to Table 10.5.

THE CASE OF MR. F.

Mr. F. was born in a South American country and from a young age lived the life of a "street child," receiving little or no formal education. When he was older, he found various labor jobs to support himself. He also was involved in periodic fraud and "scams" to support himself as a child and as an adult. He acknowledged that lying and cheating were accepted ways of life for him, which he and other street people he knew used to make money. He was often lonely and his mood suffered to the point that he seriously considered suicide on more than one occasion. He had not seen his family since he was a child, but he did later make contact with some relatives by mail. Most of his family died in a lengthy "drug war" in his homeland when he was an adult, which greatly saddened him.

As an adult Mr. F. was accepted into Canada as a refugee, more than a decade before the incident that caused his brain injury. He took some English as a Second Language (ESL) classes and learned how to speak and read English at a basic level. He obtained a job working as a janitor for a school board five years before his accident. Employee evaluations indicated that he did his job very well and that he had almost perfect attendance at work. However, he was quite socially isolated outside of work and very shortly before the accident he started to miss consecutive days at work, for the first time. This was reportedly because he started to drink heavily after learning that one of the few remaining members of his immediate family died.

The fall that caused his brain injury occurred early one evening, after Mr. F. had been out drinking all afternoon with some co-workers when he had a day off from work. Exactly what happened to cause him to fall onto the pavement and strike his head was unclear. There was some question of whether Mr. F. was responsible for his fall or whether someone else had pushed him, possibly from a moving car. On examination by emergency medical personnel at the injury scene, he was aggressive, combative, and refused to answer questions. He had a cut on his scalp and was bleeding from it. His Glasgow Coma Scale (GCS) score was 11/15. The effect of alcohol may well have contributed to this score, given that his blood alcohol level was 74 mmol/L approximately one hour after the injury. (The legal limit for driving, known as .08 in this jurisdiction, is 17.4 mmol/L.)

A CT scan of the head performed soon after hospital admission showed a basal skull fracture, and an acute hemorrhage within the left temporal-parietal region that measured $3 \times 4.5 \times 2$ cm. There was surrounding edema and significant mass effect, with compression of the left lateral ventricle and shift of the midline structures approximately 6 mm to the right. A focal hyperdensity in the right frontal lobe at the gray-white junction was said to likely represent an axonal shear type of injury. His GCS in the Emergency Ward was 14/15 and he kept saying that he was drunk, and wanted to be left alone so that he could go to sleep. He was prescribed an anticonvulsant medication and was monitored in the hospital for several weeks. He did not have any neurosurgery and his GCS remained 14/15 (because of confused speech) until 14 days post-injury, when his Galveston Orientation and Amnesia Test (GOAT) score also reached the normal range. He was very weepy during his hospitalization, especially during the latter weeks of his stay. At times, he indicated that he was concerned about supporting himself after he was discharged from hospital. Loneliness was also an expressed concern, and at other times he was unable to explain why he was so emotional and prone to crying.

Hospital social workers arranged for some government support payments after Mr. F. was discharged to his home. He managed to cope reasonably well living on his own and attempted a part-time, modified return to his janitorial job approximately five months post-injury. However, once he was on the job, his supervisor apparently demanded that he work regular hours and perform regular duties. He reported that he could not cope with such duties, because of fatigue, balance, and dizziness problems. His family physician then told him not to work until he had recovered further. As it turned out, he never returned to competitive employment and soon after leaving his job he started to receive a permanent government disability pension. He attended a community-based brain injury support program on an intermittent basis ever since his brain injury, and he was monitored by a psychiatrist who intermittently prescribed an antidepressant, an anxiolytic, and other medication.

Community-based neuropsychological assessment 1.5 years post-injury

This assessment was conducted as part of follow-up care with the community-based support program when Mr. F. was 37 years old. At that assessment, he reported during the interview that he had attempted suicide a few months previously, but that he called 911 and was taken to the hospital. He was discharged from the hospital on psychotropic medication and with visits to a clinical social worker, but he spent most of his time at home alone.

During the neuropsychological assessment at 1.5 years post-injury, the patient was 39 years old and spoke English with a thick accent. The assessment was done without the assistance of a translator. Mr. F. spontaneously spoke of his difficult childhood and was teary-eyed on more than one occasion, such as when he said that he doubted his condition (i.e., brain injury) would improve in the future. It was believed that the patient's limited English and emotional distress may have affected the assessment results. No symptom validity testing was done, and for normative purposes he was considered to have no formal education. He was right handed. Test scores and the psychologist's interpretations of them are presented in Table 10.1.

Because Mr. F. obtained so many below average scores, those that were said to be within the average range, or "normal," are typed in bold face. They were the percent delayed recall (i.e., savings) scores on the Wechsler Memory Scale–Revised (WMS–R; Wechsler, 1987) Logical Memory and Visual Reproduction subtests, the delayed recall trial score from the Rey Auditory Verbal Learning Test (RAVLT; Lezak, 1995), left-hand finger tapping, and the delayed recognition trial score on the Continuous Visual Memory Test (CVMT; Trahan & Larrabee, 1988). Despite being labeled "above average," the CVMT "hits" score was not considered a normal score because the patient responded that essentially all of the test stimuli on this recognition test were items that he had seen before, which also led to a very high false-positive score (so called "yea-saying").

The report concluded that although the fact that English was his second language may have accounted for some of the low scores, the patient's brain injury probably added significantly to his problems. It was said that he seemed to be unemployable and would probably remain so for the foreseeable future. Disability benefits were recommended on a permanent basis. These conclusions and recommendations appeared to be made on the basis of the patient's ongoing psychiatric problems and neuropsychological test findings, the latter emphasizing tasks with relatively few linguistic demands (e.g., Symbol Digit Modalities Test, WAIS–R Digit Symbol subtest, and the Test of Nonverbal Intelligence).

Neuropsychological assessment commissioned by the defense at 8 years post-injury

The insurance company defending the individual who Mr. F. was suing hired a neuropsychologist to assess Mr. F., with the assistance of a translator, at approximately 8 years post-injury, when Mr. F.

TABLE 10.1   Test scores at 1.5 years post-injury

TEST	SCORES	PSYCHOLOGIST'S INTERPRETATION OR GRADE EQUIVALENT SCORE
Wechsler Adult Intelligence Scale–Revised		
Digit Span age scaled score	5	Mildly impaired
Digit Symbol age scaled score	5	Mildly impaired
Symbol Digit Modalities Test		
Written trial	19	Severely impaired
Oral trial	41	Mildly impaired
Continuous Visual Memory Test		
Hits	41	Above average
False alarms	34	Severely impaired
Total score	61	Severely impaired
Delayed recognition	**4**	**Average**
Wechsler Memory Scale–Revised		
Logical Memory I raw score	10	Moderately impaired
Logical Memory II raw score	8	Mildly impaired
Percent recall (II/I)	**80%**	**Average**
Visual Reproduction I raw score	8	Severely impaired
Visual Reproduction II raw score	6	Severely impaired
Percent recall (II/I)	**75%**	**Average**
Rey Auditory Verbal Learning Test		
Trial one raw score	4	Mildly impaired
Trial two raw score	6	Mildly impaired
Trial three raw score	7	Moderately impaired
Trial four raw score	9	Mildly impaired
Trial five raw score	10	Mildly impaired
List B raw score	3	Mildly impaired
Short delay free recall raw score	8	Mildly impaired
Long delay free recall raw score	**10**	**Average**
Seashore Rhythm Test raw score	*14*	*Moderately impaired (chance level)*
Woodcock Johnson Revised Tests of Achievement		
Letter-Word Identification raw score	23	Grade 1.6
Passage Comprehension raw score	8	Grade 1.4
Calculation raw score	18	Grade 4.3
Test of Nonverbal Intelligence		
TONI Quotient	65	Moderately impaired
Finger Tapping		
Right hand raw score	34.6	Moderately impaired
Left hand raw score	**40.2**	**Average**
Grooved Pegboard Test		
Right hand raw score (seconds)	76″	Mildly impaired
Left hand raw score (seconds)	87″	Mildly impaired
Grip Strength		
Right hand raw score (kg)	36.8	Mildly impaired
Left hand raw score (kg)	36.5	Mildly impaired
Klove-Reitan Sensory Perceptual Examination		
Finger Agnosia right hand errors	4	Mildly impaired
Finger Agnosia left hand errors	0	Normal
Graphesthesia right hand errors	13	Severely impaired
Graphesthesia left hand errors	6	Mildly to moderately impaired

Note: Performances considered likely to be non-credible are italicized, and those considered average or "normal" by the psychologist who did the assessment are in bold face.

was 45 years old. It should be noted that the translator appeared to be used only when the patient was having problems understanding questions or test instructions in English. It did not appear that test stimuli (e.g., on verbal memory or language testing) were translated from English into Mr. F.'s native language. The only medication that Mr. F. was taking at that time was an antidepressant. He reported no retrograde amnesia for the incident that caused his injury (he said he was pushed out of a moving car and recalls hitting the pavement), but he reported one month of posttraumatic amnesia. The patient's reliability as a historian was questioned, in part because he reported consuming only one serving of alcohol per week prior to his brain injury and two servings on the day of his injury. Mr. F. complained of a variety of problems including chronic headaches, fatigue, olfactory hallucinations, sleep problems, a wide range of cognitive problems, and irritability, anxiety, depression, and suicidal thoughts. Test results and interpretations are presented in Table 10.2, and average or normal results, based on that neuropsychologist's interpretation, are again typed in bold face.

The neuropsychologist stated that because Mr. F. exhibited very poor effort on two measures designed to evaluate response bias (i.e., the Computerized Assessment of Response Bias and the 15-item test), the test findings did not reflect his ultimate capabilities, or best effort, and could not be used to delineate the sequelae of his brain injury. Similarly, measures to evaluate psychological maladjustment (e.g., the Symptom Checklist 90–Revised) were thought to be excessively elevated in some respects and the neuropsychologist reserved judgment as to the patient's true emotional state.

A functional capacity evaluation was recommended in order to evaluate the patient's ability to do his old job, as physical issues and fatigue were thought to be more likely limiting factors than any cognitive problems would be, in doing Mr. F.'s relatively physically-demanding former job. While the neuropsychologist acknowledged that there was no doubt that Mr. F. had a brain injury, she concluded that Mr. F. had emotional problems prior to the injury and thus the brain injury was not entirely responsible for Mr. F.'s current emotional problems. She also doubted that with lengthy posttraumatic amnesia and the extremely high blood alcohol level at the time of the injury Mr. F. would have no retrograde amnesia and could remember all events leading up to, and including, his injury. It was thought that Mr. F. made this up so that he could place the blame for his injury on someone other than himself.

Neuropsychological assessment commissioned by the defense at 12 years post-injury

The insurance company defending the individual who Mr. F. was suing hired the same neuropsychologist to assess Mr. F., with the assistance of a translator, at approximately 12 years post-injury, when he was 49 years old. It should be noted that the translator again appeared to be used only when the patient was having problems understanding questions or test instructions in English. As at the previous assessment, it did not appear that test stimuli (e.g., on verbal memory or language testing) were translated from English into the patient's native language. Mr. F. was taking an anxiolytic medication and an anticonvulsant medication. A recent EEG had shown grade II dysrhythmia in the left frontal-temporal region. The record was interpreted as abnormal by the neurologist who read the EEG, and the EEG tracing was felt to demonstrate frequent slowing in the left frontal-temporal region that was moderate in degree, though with no frank epileptic activity.

Mr. F. indicated that he had *virtually every* physical, cognitive, and emotional problem that was queried. Some of the more notable ones were a completely absent sense of taste, olfactory hallucinations, and recent suicidal ideation and suicide attempts. A treating social worker's notes were reviewed, and these indicated that persons who knew Mr. F. both before and after the accident had reported that he had seemingly made a full cognitive recovery, though his personality had changed. Specifically, he was said to have become more emotionally labile and almost paranoid at times. He had also been hospitalized for psychiatric reasons on more than one occasion since the injury,

TABLE 10.2 Test scores at 8 years post-injury

TEST	SCORES	PSYCHOLOGIST'S INTERPRETATION
Computerized Assessment of Response Bias		
Block 1 percent correct	*66%*	
Block 2 percent correct	*67%*	
Block 3 percent correct	*72%*	
Total percent correct	*68%*	*Very poor effort*
15-item test, number correct	*6/15*	*Very poor effort*
Wechsler Memory Scale–3rd edition		
Logical Memory I age scaled score	3	Severely impaired
Logical Memory II age scaled score	2	Severely impaired
Spatial Span forward age scaled score	*3*	*Severely impaired*
Spatial Span forward age scaled score	*3*	*Severely impaired*
Figure learning, points per trial	0.8	Moderately impaired
Figure learning, percent loss	**25**	**Normal**
Seashore Rhythm Test raw score	*14*	*Severely impaired (also at chance level)*
Wisconsin Card Sorting Test		
Categories achieved, raw score	4	Mildly impaired
Perseverative responses, raw score	32	Mildly impaired
Losses of set, raw score	3	Mildly impaired
Raven's Standard Progressive Matrices		
Raw score	**21/60**	**Normal for Mr. F.**
Color Trails Test 1 time in seconds	82	Moderately impaired
Color Trails Test 2 time in seconds	232	Severely impaired
Peabody Picture Vocabulary Test–3rd edition		
Standard score	40	Severely impaired
Finger Tapping		
Right hand raw score	**37**	**Normal**
Left hand raw score	**35**	**Normal**
Grooved Pegboard Test		
Right hand raw score (seconds)	**86**	**Normal**
Left hand raw score (seconds)	111	Moderately impaired
Grip Strength		
Right hand raw score (kg)	**44**	**Normal**
Left hand raw score (kg)	**44**	**Normal**
Symptom Checklist–90 Revised	*Excessively elevated in some respects*	
Somatization raw score/normal T-score	1.25/69	
Obsessive Compulsive raw score/normal T-score	1.50/70	
Interpersonal Sensitivity raw score/normal T-score	0.89/66	
Depression raw score/normal T-score	*2.54/99*	
Anxiety raw score/normal T-score	*2.40/99*	
Hostility raw score/normal T-score	0.83/63	
Phobic Anxiety raw score/normal T-score	1.43/77	
Paranoid Ideation raw score/normal T-score	1.17/66	
Psychoticism raw score/normal T-score	*1.50/99*	
Global Severity Index raw score/normal T-score	*1.68/99*	
Positive Symptom Total raw score/normal T-score	61/75	
Positive Symptom Distress Index raw score/normal T-score	2.48/72	

Note: Performances considered likely to be non-credible are italicized, and those considered average or "normal" by the psychologist who did the assessment are in bold face.

usually around Christmastime when he felt very lonely. The neuropsychologist opined that while Mr. F. had significant emotional problems before the brain injury, the brain injury likely exacerbated them. However, she also indicated that Mr. F. had ongoing serious concerns about his remaining family in South America and that these likely contributed to his current emotional problems. Test results and interpretations are presented in Table 10.3.

The neuropsychologist indicated that because Mr. F. exhibited very poor effort on three measures designed to evaluate response bias (i.e., CARB, Portland Digit Recognition Test, and

TABLE 10.3 Test scores at 12 years post-injury

TEST	SCORES	PSYCHOLOGIST'S INTERPRETATION
Computerized Assessment of Response Bias		
Block 1 percent correct	62%	
Block 2 percent correct	51%	
Block 3 percent correct	45%	
Total percent correct	53%	*Very poor effort*
Portland Digit Recognition Test		
Total "Easy"	17/36	
Total "Hard"	19/36	
Grand Total	36/72	*Chance level*
15-item test, number correct	3/15	*Very poor effort*
Wechsler Adult Intelligence Scale–3rd edition		
Digit Span age scaled score	3	*Severely impaired*
Digit Symbol age scaled score	3	*Severely impaired*
California Verbal Learning Test		
Trial one raw score	1	
Trial two raw score	3	
Trial three raw score	5	
Trial four raw score	3	
Trial five raw score	4	
Total trials 1–5, T-score	5	*Severely impaired*
List B raw score	0	
Short delay free recall raw score	2	
Long delay free recall raw score	2	
Figure learning, points per trial	1.0	Moderately impaired
Figure learning, percent loss	**20**	**Normal**
Wechsler Memory Scale–3rd edition		
Spatial Span forward age scaled score	3	*Moderately impaired*
Spatial Span backwards age scaled score	3	*Moderately impaired*
Seashore Rhythm Test raw score	18	Mildly impaired
Wisconsin Card Sorting Test		
Categories, raw score	1	No interpretation
Perseverative responses, raw score	18	No interpretation
Losses of set, raw score	8	No interpretation
Raven's Standard Progressive Matrices, raw score	15/60	Severely impaired
Color Trails Test 1 time in seconds	**71**	**Normal**
Color Trails Test 2 time in seconds	**139**	**Normal**
Peabody Picture Vocabulary Test–3rd edition		
Standard score	<40	Significant weakness
Woodcock Johnson–3rd edition Picture Vocabulary		
Standard score	68	Significant weakness
Finger Tapping		
Right hand raw score	36	Mildly impaired
Left hand raw score	34	Mildly impaired

(Continued . . .)

TABLE 10.3   (Continued)

TEST	SCORES	PSYCHOLOGIST'S INTERPRETATION
Grooved Pegboard Test		
Right hand raw score (seconds)	**74**	**Normal**
Left hand raw score (seconds)	89	Mildly impaired
Grip Strength		
Right hand raw score (kg)	**41**	**Normal**
Left hand raw score (kg)	**39**	**Normal**
Symptom Checklist–90 Revised		*Over-reporting*
Somatization raw score/normal T-score		*2.58/99*
Obsessive Compulsive raw score/normal T-score		*2.80/99*
Interpersonal Sensitivity raw score/normal T-score		*2.56/99*
Depression raw score/normal T-score		*3.46/99*
Anxiety raw score/normal T-score		*3.20/99*
Hostility raw score/normal T-score		*1.33/70*
Phobic Anxiety raw score/normal T-score		*3.57/99*
Paranoid Ideation raw score/normal T-score		*1.83/79*
Psychoticism raw score/normal T-score		*1.50/72*
Global Severity Index raw score/normal T-score		*2.64/99*
Positive Symptom Total raw score/normal T-score		*75/99*
Positive Symptom Distress Index raw score/normal T-score		*3.17/99*

Note: Performances considered likely to be non-credible are italicized, and those considered average or "normal" by the psychologist who did the assessment are in bold face.

15-item test), she could not reliably evaluate any neuropsychological deficits across her two assessments of Mr. F. Similarly, the extent of emotional distress reported on the Symptom Checklist 90–Revised was thought to go far beyond what was probably currently true, based on what was observed on interview, reported on interview by the patient, and observed during testing.

A functional capacity evaluation was again recommended in order to evaluate the patient's ability to do his old job, as physical issues and fatigue were thought more likely to be limiting factors than were any cognitive problems in doing Mr. F.'s relatively physically demanding former job. While the neuropsychologist acknowledged that there was no doubt that Mr. F. had a brain injury, she also concluded that Mr. F. had emotional problems *prior* to the injury and thus the brain injury was not entirely responsible for Mr. F.'s current emotional problems. She also doubted that with lengthy posttraumatic amnesia and the extremely high blood alcohol level at the time of the injury Mr. F. would have no retrograde amnesia and could remember all events leading up to and including his injury. It was thought that Mr. F. made this up so that he could place the blame for his injury on someone other than himself.

The report concluded that malingering could not be ruled out as a possible basis for the assessment findings and that one could not establish any disability based on the neuropsychological test findings. Disablement that was evident since the injury was thought to be primarily emotional in nature and not necessarily fully related to the sequelae of the injury.

Neuropsychological assessment commissioned by the plaintiff's lawyer 13 years post-injury

I assessed Mr. F. when he was 50 years old, at the request of his lawyer, approximately a year after the second assessment that was commissioned by the defense was completed. I noted that approximately two years prior to my assessment, a neurologist had diagnosed the patient as having had two seizures. This diagnosis appeared to be based on relatively solid evidence, including one witnessed seizure in a hospital where he had been taken minutes after a first seizure, and incontinence that was evident after the seizures. The neurologist who diagnosed the seizures prescribed an anticonvulsant medication. Social work records indicated that the patient had been quite depressed around the same time, as he had been forced to move to a different apartment, and a close relative with whom he had ongoing contact had died in his home country. Prozac was no longer controlling his mood very well, and he spent many hours of the day wandering aimlessly around city streets. He had been briefly hospitalized because of his emotional problems and a psychiatrist had diagnosed him with organic mood disorder and prominent emotionality secondary to severe head injury. At the time of his assessment with me, he was living on his own and was involved in the same community-based support program with which he had been involved since shortly after his injury. He was also doing some volunteer work, which essentially involved helping at a day care center.

The interview and assessment were conducted with the assistance of a translator. Mr. F. told me that he had consumed two or three beers on the day of injury. When I confronted him about this, given his extremely high blood alcohol reading in hospital soon after the injury, he then told me that he could not specifically recall how many drinks he had prior to the injury. However, he insisted that he recalled being pushed from a moving car by the person he was suing, as well as landing on the pavement and striking his head, before "going blank" and not recalling anything for a few weeks. He said that he did not miss work or drink heavily shortly before his injury and, if he did miss some work, it may have been due to a cold or the flu. He denied having any stress from family-related issues in his home country for many years, which was also in contrast to available documentation from his social worker. He told me that he could function in English in a group therapy situation, but had more problems in a one-to-one setting, which was the opposite of what his social worker's notes indicated. He did not like to be alone in his small apartment, and this was why he wandered the streets so much. He stated that he had financial problems and was upset that his personal injury litigation had been going on for so long, but that he could live on what he received from his disability pension. He was taking antidepressant and anticonvulsant medications. Because he spoke in broken English, the translator was used for most of the communication I had with him. In addition, most test instructions and some test stimuli (i.e., the California Verbal Learning Test–2nd edition and the Minnesota Multiphasic Personality Inventory–2nd edition) were translated into his native language by the translator.

It was notable that Mr. F. claimed to have never seen a certain member of my support staff before, despite her statement to me that she had known him from seeing him in a different context since shortly before his brain injury. She was shocked when he told her that he did not know who she was when he came for the present assessment and saw her working in a clerical capacity for me. She indicated that although they were not close friends, they had acknowledged each other's presence by saying "Hello," or a similar greeting, and sometimes making social "small talk" when they saw each other a few times per year. Test results are presented in Table 10.4.

Because Mr. F. did so poorly on the symptom validity testing, I interpreted scores that were within a standard deviation of the mean as being "normal" and considered the rest of the test scores likely to be of uncertain validity and did not interpret them. I also considered qualitative information in coming to my conclusion that Mr. F. was not putting forth a good effort at my testing. For example, despite showing that he could do mathematics at a grade 4.3 level at the assessment 1.5 years post-injury on the 15-item test, he wrote out the second row of that test at the present assessment to be "2 1 3" (a "Ganser-like" response), despite getting the top row correct. A gross inconsistency was noted on his Woodcock-Johnson Calculation subtest performance between assessments conducted 1.5 years post-injury versus the current assessment. Specifically, at the former assessment, he clearly demonstrated that he knew how to add, subtract, and multiply, attaining correct responses on 18 of 19 such test items not involving fractions or decimals. However, at the present assessment, he *added* on all of the 21 test items that he answered, obviously disregarding the signs for all non-addition problems.

I used a "best performance" approach to pull together test scores that were considered "normal"

TABLE 10.4   Test scores at 13 years post-injury

TEST	SCORES	PSYCHOLOGIST'S INTERPRETATION OR GRADE EQUIVALENT SCORE
Computerized Assessment of Response Bias		
Block 1 percent correct	64%	
Block 2 percent correct	56%	
Block 3 percent correct	56%	
Total percent correct	58%	Very poor effort
Test of Memory Malingering		
Trial 1	30/50	
Trial 2	30/50	
Retention Trial	29/50	Very poor effort
15-item test, number correct	7/15	Questionable effort
Wechsler Adult Intelligence Scale–3rd edition		
Digit Span age scaled score	3	
Picture Completion age scaled score	2	
Block Design age scaled score	4	
Matrix Reasoning age scaled score	4	
Picture Arrangement age scaled score	5	
Symbol Search age scaled score	1	
Digit Symbol age scaled score	3	
Perceptual Organizational index score	62	
Processing Speed index score	60	
Performance IQ	60	
California Verbal Learning Test–II (*N.B.* translated test instructions and test stimuli)		
Trial one raw score	4	
Trial two raw score	8	
Trial three raw score	8	
Trial four raw score	8	
Trial five raw score	7	
Total trials 1–5, T-score	**41**	**Normal**
List B raw score	0	
Short delay free recall raw score	**8**	**Normal**
Long delay free recall raw score	6	
Woodcock Johnson–3rd edition Tests of Academic Achievement		
Letter-Word Identification raw score	36	Grade 2.4
Passage Comprehension raw score	11	Grade 1.1
Calculation raw score	7	*Grade 1.8*
Spelling	14	Grade K.7
Oral Comprehension	0	*Grade < K.0*
Wechsler Memory Scale–3rd edition		
Spatial Span forward age scaled score	3	
Spatial Span backwards age scaled score	3	
Wechsler Memory Scale–Revised		
Logical Memory I raw score	11	
Logical Memory II raw score	9	
Percent recall (II/I)	**81%**	**Normal**
Visual Reproduction I raw score	10	
Visual Reproduction II raw score	3	
Percent recall (II/I)	30%	
Rey Auditory Verbal Learning Test		
Trial one raw score	5	
Trial two raw score	5	
Trial three raw score	7	

Trial four raw score	9	
Trial five raw score	9	
List B raw score	2	
Short delay free recall raw score	**7**	**Normal**
Long delay free recall raw score	*0*	
Symbol Digit Modalities Test, written raw score	17	
Symbol Digit Modalities Test, oral raw score	23	
Test of Nonverbal Intelligence–2 percentile rank	5	
Tactual Performance Test		
Dominant hand blocks	5	
Time	> 10′	
Non-dominant hand blocks	10	
Time	**8′**	**Normal**
Both hands blocks	10	
Time	**7.75′**	**Normal**
Memory score	*0*	
Localization score	0	
Rey Complex Figure Test		
Copy raw score	*4.5/36*	
Immediate recall raw score	2.5/36	
Delayed recall raw score	0.5/36	
Minnesota Multiphasic Personality Inventory–2 (fully translated); T-scores (Invalid protocol because of TRIN score)		
L	52	
F	92	
K	33	
VRIN	69	
TRIN	79	
Fb	145	
FBS	29	
HS	84	
D	87	
Hy	76	
Pd	69	
Mf	50	
Pa	86	
Pt	94	
Sc	94	
Ma	65	
Si	77	

Note: Performances considered likely to be non-credible are italicized, and those considered average or "normal" by the psychologist who did the assessment are in bold face.

from one or more of the four assessments that had been done over the years (see Table 10.5 for a summary of scores from those assessments). Based on this, I concluded that the patient was probably not suffering from significant and pervasive impairments in cognitive and motor functions as a result of his brain injury and that it was impossible to quantify with confidence any deficits that he might have as the result of his injury. While second language, cultural, and other factors "muddied the waters" of test score interpretation, per se, I concluded that the qualitative evidence (e.g., from my staff member and the patient's social worker's notes) and the quantitative evidence from the various assessments raised serious concerns about the veracity of Mr. F.'s self-reported plethora of problems and his often very low test scores. For example, according to notes from his social worker, he was living on his own, paying his bills, and functioning independently in a city in which he did not fluently speak the predominant language. This suggests that his adaptive capacity was much

TABLE 10.5   Summary of all test scores

TEST SCORES AT ASSESSMENT NUMBER	I	II	III	IV	V
Wechsler Adult Intelligence Scale–Revised					
Digit Span age scaled score	5				
Digit Symbol age scaled score	5				
Wechsler Adult Intelligence Scale–3rd edition					
Digit Span age scaled score			*3*	*3*	*5*
Digit Symbol age scaled score			*3*	*3*	*4*
Picture Completion age scaled score				*2*	*3*
Block Design age scaled score				*4*	*3*
Matrix Reasoning age scaled score				*4*	*4*
Picture Arrangement age scaled score				*5*	*6*
Symbol Search age scaled score				*1*	*4*
Perceptual Organizational index score				*62*	*62*
Processing Speed index score				*60*	*69*
Performance IQ				*60*	*63*
Finger Tapping					
Right hand raw score	34.6	**37**	36		
Left hand raw score	**40.2**	**35**	34		
Grooved Pegboard Test					
Right hand raw score (seconds)	76	**86**	**74**		
Left hand raw score (seconds)	87	111	89		
Grip Strength					
Right hand raw score (kg)	36.8	**44**	**41**		
Left hand raw score (kg)	36.5	**44**	**39**		
Symbol Digit Modalities Test					
Written trial	19			17	26
Oral trial	41			*23*	37
Continuous Visual Memory Test					
Hits	41				38
False alarms	34				28
Total score	61				64
Delayed recognition	**4**				**4**
Seashore Rhythm Test raw score	*14*	*14*	18		
Rey Auditory Verbal Learning Test					
Trial one raw score	4			5	3
Trial two raw score	6			5	5
Trial three raw score	7			7	8
Trial four raw score	9			9	6
Trial five raw score	10			9	6
List B raw score	3			2	2
Short delay free recall raw score	8			**7**	6
Long delay free recall raw score	**10**			*0*	5
Woodcock Johnson Revised Tests of Achievement					
Letter-Word Identification grade score	1.6				
Passage Comprehension grade score	1.4				
Calculation grade score	4.3				
Woodcock Johnson–3rd Edition Tests of Achievement					
Letter-Word Identification grade score				2.4	1.8
Passage Comprehension grade score				1.1	1.1
Calculation grade score				*1.8*	2.0
Spelling				K.7	K.7
Oral Comprehension				*< K.0*	< K.0
Test of Nonverbal Intelligence					
Quotient	65				

Test of Nonverbal Intelligence–2 Quotient				75	63
Reitan-Klove Sensory Perceptual Examination					
Finger Agnosia right hand errors	4				
Finger Agnosia left hand errors	0				
Graphesthesia right hand errors	13				
Graphesthesia left hand errors	6				
Wechsler Memory Scale–Revised					
Logical Memory I raw score	10			11	3
Logical Memory II raw score	8			9	1
Percent recall (II/I)	**80%**			**81%**	33%
Visual Reproduction I raw score	8			10	17
Visual Reproduction II raw score	6			3	0
Percent recall (II/I)	75%			30%	0%
Wechsler Memory Scale–3rd edition					
Logical Memory I age scaled score		*3*			
Logical Memory II age scaled score		*2*			
Spatial Span forward age scaled score		*3*	*3*	*3*	*6*
Spatial Span forward age scaled score		*3*	*3*	*3*	*6*
Computerized Assessment of Response Bias					
Block 1 percent correct		*67%*	*62%*	64%	**96%**
Block 2 percent correct		*68%*	*51%*	56%	**100%**
Block 3 percent correct		*72%*	*46%*	56%	
Total percent correct		*69%*	*53%*	59%	
15-item test, number correct		*6/15*	*3/15*	*7/15*	*8/15*
Figure learning, points per trial		0.8	1.0		
Figure learning, percent loss		**25**	**20**		
Wisconsin Card Sorting Test					
Categories achieved, raw score		4	*1*		
Perseverative responses, raw score		32	*18*		
Losses of set, raw score		3	*8*		
Raven's Standard Progressive Matrices, raw score		**21/60**	15/60		
Color Trails Test 1 time in seconds		82	**71**		
Color Trails Test 2 time in seconds		*232*	**139**		
Peabody Picture Vocabulary Test–3rd edition					
Standard score		40	<40		
Symptom Checklist–90 Revised					
Somatization normal T-score		69	99		
Obsessive Compulsive normal T-score		70	99		
Interpersonal Sensitivity normal T-score		66	99		
Depression normal T-score		99	99		
Anxiety normal T-score		99	99		
Hostility normal T-score		63	70		
Phobic Anxiety normal T-score		77	99		
Paranoid Ideation normal T-score		66	79		
Psychoticism normal T-score		99	*72*		
Global Severity Index normal T-score		99	99		
Positive Symptom Total normal T-score		75	99		
Positive Symptom Distress Index, normal T-score		72	99		
Portland Digit Recognition Test					
Total "Easy"			17/36		
Total "Hard"			19/36		
Grand Total			*36/72*		

(Continued . . .)

TABLE 10.5   (Continued)

TEST SCORES AT ASSESSMENT NUMBER	I	II	III	IV	V
California Verbal Learning Test (Translated at assessments IV & V only)					
Trial 1, raw score			1	4	7
Trial 2, raw score			3	8	7
Trial 3, raw score			5	8	10
Trial 4, raw score			3	8	9
Trial 5, raw score			4	7	9
Total trials 1–5, T-score			5	**41**	**48**
List B raw score			0	0	3
Short delay free recall raw score			2	**8**	**9**
Long delay free recall raw score			2	6	**11**
Test of Memory Malingering					
Trial 1 (score out of 50)				*30*	44
Trial 2 (score out of 50)				*30*	**50**
Retention Trial				*29*	
Tactual Performance Test					
Dominant hand blocks				5	**10**
Time				*>10′*	**6.6′**
Non-dominant hand blocks				**10**	**10**
Time				**8′**	**4.6′**
Both hands blocks				**10**	**10**
Time				**7.75′**	**3.1′**
Memory score				0	3
Localization score				0	0
Rey Complex Figure Test					
Copy raw score (out of 36)				*4.5*	11
Immediate recall raw score (out of 36)				2.5	3.5
Delayed recall raw score (out of 36)				0.5	2.5
Minnesota Multiphasic Personality Inventory–2 (fully translated); T-scores (Invalid protocol because of TRIN score)					
L				52	
F				92	
K				33	
VRIN				69	
TRIN				79	
Fb				145	
FBS				29	
HS				84	
D				87	
Hy				76	
Pd				69	
Mf				50	
Pa				86	
Pt				94	
Sc				94	
Ma				65	
Si				77	
Personality Assessment Inventory–2 (fully translated); T-scores					
ICN					52
INF					51
NIM					47
PIM					64

SOM	44
ANX	50
ARD	39
DEP	45
MAN	45
PAR	52
SCZ	42
BOR	39
ANT	51
ALC	47
DRG	48
AGG	48
SUI	49
STR	59
NON	45
RXR	61
DOM	60
WRM	60

Note: Performances considered likely to be non-credible are italicized, and those considered average or "normal" by the psychologist who did the assessment are in bold face. The latter explains why interpretation of scores across assessments is not always consistent.

better than that implied by many of his test scores, including his symptom validity test results (e.g., see Tombaugh, 1996).

On the other hand, I said that there was some solid evidence that he was suffering from ongoing problems from his brain injury, including the abnormal EEG results in the general region of his brain where he initially sustained a large intracerebral hemorrhage, and a diagnosis of a seizure disorder. He also appeared to be functioning quite well for several years before his brain injury, holding a job and performing well at it, albeit with some attendance and drinking problems right before his brain injury. In contrast, he could not do his job when he returned to it a few months after his injury. Although his credibility in many areas was questionable, it seems likely that he probably did return to work too soon after a very significant brain injury and that his difficulties coping on the job may well have been credible. In addition, Mr. F.'s emotional adjustment problems appeared to be substantially worse after his brain injury. Although the reasons for this may have not been restricted to his brain injury, it appeared to both the defense neuropsychologist and me that direct and/or indirect effects from the injury likely made Mr. F.'s emotional functioning worse.

Regardless, Slick et al.'s (1999) criteria for *probable* malingering of neurocognitive dysfunction (MND) appeared to be met. The criteria for *definite* MND were not met because Mr. F. did not perform significantly (i.e., $p < .05$) below chance on one or more forced-choice measures of cognitive function. Probable MND "is indicated by the presence of evidence strongly suggesting volitional exaggeration or fabrication of cognitive dysfunction and the absence of plausible alternative explanations" (Slick et al., 1999, p. 552). There are specific additional criteria. The first one is that there has to be the presence of a substantial external incentive; in Mr. F.'s case, it is the monetary settlement from his lawsuit.

The second criterion for probable MND is that there have to be two or more types of evidence from neuropsychological testing, excluding below chance ($p < .05$) performance on one or more forced-choice measures of cognitive function. In Mr. F.'s case, this requirement was partially fulfilled by "performance on one or more well-validated psychometric tests or indices designed to measure exaggeration or fabrication of cognitive deficits that is consistent with feigning" (Slick et al., 1999, p. 553). In Mr. F.'s case, at my assessment of him, these performances were on the TOMM and the CARB. The other type of evidence that led to fulfillment of the second criterion was a "discrepancy between test data and known patterns of brain function." In Mr. F.'s case, for example, he clearly demonstrated that he knew how to add, subtract, and multiply, by attaining 18 out of 19 such test items correct on the Woodcock Johnson–Revised Calculation subtest at his first assessment. However, at my assessment of him, he *added* for all of the 21 test items that he answered on the Woodcock Johnson–3rd edition Calculation subtest, obviously disregarding the signs for all non-addition problems, which he had previously shown that he noticed and understood.

The other way to fulfill the second criterion for probable MND is to have "one type of evidence from neuropsychological testing, excluding definite negative response bias, and one or more types of evidence from self-report" (Slick et al., 1999, p. 552). In Mr. F.'s case, the neuropsychological test performances are outlined in the preceding paragraph. The evidence from self-report for Mr. F. is the fourth of five possible behaviors listed by Slick et al., namely, "Self-reported symptoms are discrepant with information obtained from collateral informants" (p. 554). In Mr. F.'s case, this was incidentally found when he pretended not to know one of my support staff members when he came for his assessment with me. This was despite her reporting that they knew each other in a different context, and periodically spoke to each other, for over 10 years leading up to the assessment, including before his brain injury. Their contacts included one shortly before the assessment, and she was incredulous that he could claim that he had never seen her before and did not know her.

The third Slick et al. criterion for probable MND is that the behaviors described above that are evidence of malingering are not fully accounted for by psychiatric, neurological, or developmental factors. In Mr. F.'s case, one would be hard pressed to ascribe his malingering behaviors to such factors.

The Slick et al. criteria are considerably more detailed than are the DSM–IV guidelines for diagnosing malingering. This may be because the DSM–IV does not consider malingering to be a mental disorder, but "a condition that may be the focus of clinical attention," and it generally provides much more specific guidelines for diagnosing mental disorders than "other conditions" such as malingering. In any case, the DSM–IV indicates, "The essential feature of Malingering is the intentional production of false or grossly exaggerated physical or psychological symptoms, motivated by external incentives" (American Psychiatric Association, p. 739). In Mr. F.'s case, there can be little doubt that he was at least at some times grossly exaggerating psychological symptoms (e.g., memory problems on symptom validity tests). However, to give him very generous benefit of the doubt, we cannot be sure that he was "intentionally" producing such symptoms in the absence of significantly below chance symptom validity test performance, though his seemingly deliberate lying about not knowing my staff member likely qualifies as "intentional." We cannot be certain that he was necessarily motivated by external incentives, though, in the absence of methods that can definitely identify motives for behavior, this would seem to be a very likely reason. The DSM–IV guidelines for evaluating Malingering are older than those of Slick et al., and it is hoped that a more detailed operational definition of Malingering will be included in the next revision of the DSM.

In any case, the DSM–IV states that Malingering should be strongly suspected if any combination of four conditions is present. At least two of these four may have applied in Mr. F.'s case. The first was that he was referred by an attorney for evaluation, which in itself is a weak criterion. The second was that he showed a lack of cooperation during the diagnostic evaluation (e.g., see his performance on symptom validity tests) and in complying with the prescribed treatment regimen (e.g., he often failed to take medication that he was prescribed).

However, it might be argued that his lack of compliance with medication treatment was not evidence of malingering. For example, at times he may have not taken it because he did not want to do so or because he did not like some side effects, rather than that he was malingering the problems (e.g., faking emotional distress and seizures), for which he was receiving medication. If this is true, he more clearly meets diagnostic criteria for Slick et al.'s probable MND than DSM–IV's guidelines for Malingering.

Final adjudication of Mr. F.

A judicial dispute resolution meeting was held shortly after my report was submitted. This meeting involved each side presenting their case to a judge without the formalities involved in a court trial, including no witnesses being called. The judge then considers the evidence and later informs the parties how much money the case would likely be worth if it went to court. The judge in this case considered that the case would likely settle for approximately $250,000 (Canadian).

It should be noted that in Canada, even if malingering is an issue, legal precedent has been set that directs the plaintiff should be compensated for any "real" injuries that he has suffered. In this case, it was obvious that Mr. F. had suffered a moderate to severe brain injury and subsequently developed a seizure disorder. The opposing parties agreed to the judge's suggested settlement amount.

A public trustee was appointed, and he gave Mr. F. a monthly allowance from his settlement to take care of day-to-day bills (e.g., rent, food, and recreation). He also helped Mr. F. with major investment issues. All parties agreed that a guardian was not necessary, indicating that Mr. F. was thought to be capable of looking after all issues not controlled by the public trustee (e.g., deciding where to live, with whom to consort, what to buy with his monthly allowance, healthcare decisions, etc.). The decision that Mr. F. did not need a guardian was based on input from others who knew him well. These included his lawyers, physicians, rehabilitation professionals, and his treating social worker. This decision was inconsistent with his very poor symptom validity scores and his many very low cognitive scores at his assessments. It provides further evidence that he was likely malingering at least some neurocognitive dysfunction on neuropsychological assessment.

On the other hand, this case also illustrates that real neurological impairment can co-exist with malingering of neuropsychological impairment. For example, it will be recalled that Mr. F. had significant EEG abnormalities in the same general region that he had his initial large intracerebral hematoma, and he developed a seizure disorder. An important lesson to be taken from this case, then, is that the clinician needs to view each case with an open mind and realize that significant neurological impairment and malingering of neuropsychological dysfunction are not mutually exclusive.

ADDENDUM

I most recently assessed Mr. F. approximately three years after my prior assessment with him, at the request of the public trustee and Mr. F.'s current lawyer. Mr. F. was dissatisfied that he did not have ultimate control over all of his settlement and disability pension monies even though the public trustee gave him a monthly allowance to live on, which he spent as he saw fit. His major complaint was that he was not allowed to spend large sums of money from his settlement without prior approval from the trustee, and he was also not pleased that the public trustee charged a fee every time there was a transaction. A judge ordered that another assessment had to be done to help determine if Mr. F. was now capable of handling all of his own financial affairs, and to help determine if all trusteeship control could thus be discontinued.

The interview and assessment were conducted with the assistance of the same translator who had assisted at my prior assessment of Mr. F., and almost all of the same tests were re-administered. In contrast to his self-reports at prior assessments, Mr. F. insisted that there was nothing wrong with him beyond his longstanding problems with reading and writing in all languages, due to his lack of education, and English as a second language issues. In contrast to the assessments at 1.5 and 12 years post-injury, when he brought up recent suicide attempts that he had made, at the present assessment he denied any recent suicide attempts even though there was hospital documentation of two of them.

Despite obvious incentives to do as well as he could at the present assessment, so that trusteeship could be discontinued, his behavior during the testing did not appear to be consistently cooperative. He seemed to resent having to do the testing, and he repeatedly said that he did not know how to do many tasks because he did not know English very well. This was despite extensive interpretive assistance from the translator, and despite the fact that English language proficiency was not required for many tests, beyond understanding the test instructions, for which translation was provided.

Although there were concerns about his cooperativeness with the testing, Slick et al.'s (1999) criteria for probable MND were no longer met. Following are the key findings in this regard that were different from the prior assessment: First, there was no longer "performance on one or more well-validated psychometric tests or indices designed to measure exaggeration or fabrication of cognitive deficits that is consistent with feigning" (Slick et al., 1999, p. 553). Specifically, Mr. F.'s scores on the CARB and the TOMM were much improved, were within the acceptable ranges, and were perfect on one of two trials from each measure (see the assessment number V column in Table 10.5 for test results). Second, the previously cited example of self-reported symptoms being discrepant from information obtained from a collateral informant was no longer in evidence. Specifically, Mr. F. greeted the member of my support staff who he said he had not known at the prior assessment (despite having known her for many years), and now indicated that "of course" he knew her. Thus, he was no longer pretending that his memory in daily life was very bad.

Despite the aforementioned much improved and now normal symptom validity test results, Mr. F.'s scores on the neuropsychological testing were neither uniformly improved nor "normal." This is not surprising, given his moderate to severe traumatic brain injury, possible cultural difference issues, English as a second language issues (despite translation), and seeming lack of consistent cooperation with the testing, as noted above. However, there were substantially improved performances on some tests, such as the Tactual Performance Test and the Symbol Digit Modalities Test.

Ironically, Mr. F. was now sometimes not being truthful in the opposite direction compared to how he was presenting at prior assessments. Specifically, he was being very *defensive* about personal shortcomings, rather than fabricating or exaggerating them. For example, as noted above, he denied having attempted suicide in recent years, despite there being hospital admissions and documentation of it. In addition, the Personality Assessment Inventory (PAI) interpretive report indicated, in part, that "some denial or defensiveness is likely to be responsible for the generally trouble-free picture that he is reporting" which is consistent with his highest PAI T-score being on the Positive Impression Management (PIM) scale (see bottom of Table 10.5). This is in striking contrast to SCL-90-R results, for example, from the assessments conducted for the defense, cited above, where there was strong evidence that he was over-reporting emotional problems.

Although malingering is traditionally defined in terms of gross exaggeration or fabrication of problems, it should be considered that gross minimization or complete denial of virtually all problems can be just as misleading and potentially harmful. For example, in the case of Mr. F., a lack of knowledge of the extent of his emotional problems, including repeated suicide attempts, could have misled an unknowing neuropsychologist into overestimating his ability to function in a consistently adaptive fashion in daily life.

The results from this final, unexpected assessment do not change the conclusions made previously in this chapter. However, the results of this final assessment do allow some additional conclusions to be drawn. Two of the more obvious ones are as follows. First, an individual with no formal education, who is functionally illiterate in all languages, who only has a limited grasp of oral English, and who has had a moderate to severe traumatic brain injury can perform very well on measures such as the CARB and TOMM if he is motivated to do so. The second conclusion is that such an individual can attempt to mislead in opposite directions on successive assessments if he is motivated to do so.

REFERENCES

Allen, L. M., Conder, R. L., Green, P., & Cox, D. R. (1999). *Computerized assessment of response bias.* Durham, NC: CogniSyst, Inc.

American Psychiatric Association (2000). *Diagnostic and statistical manual of mental disorders*, 4th ed., text revision. Washington, DC: APA.

Bianchini, K. J., Greve, K. W., & Love, J. M. (2003). Definite malingered neurocognitive dysfunction in moderate/severe traumatic brain injury. *The Clinical Neuropsychologist, 17*, 574–580.

Binder, L. M. (2002). The Portland Digit Recognition Test: A review of validation data and clinical use. *Journal of Forensic Neuropsychology, 2*, 27–42.

Binder, L. M., & Rohling, M. L. (1996). Money matters: A meta-analytic review of the effects of financial incentives on recovery after closed-head injury. *American Journal of Psychiatry, 153*, 7–10.

Boone, K. B., & Lu, P. (2003). Noncredible cognitive performance in the context of severe brain injury. *The Clinical Neuropsychologist, 17*, 244–254.

Brown, L., Sherbenou, R. J., & Johnsen, S. (1982). *Test of Nonverbal Intelligence.* Austin, TX: PRO–ED.

Brown, L., Sherbenou, R. J., & Johnsen, S. K. (1990). *Test of Nonverbal Intelligence–2nd ed.* Austin, TX: PRO–ED.

Butcher, J. N., Dahlstrom, W. G., Graham, J. R., Tellegen, A., & Kaemmer, B. (1989). *Minnesota Multiphasic Personality Inventory (MMPI-2): Manual for administration and scoring.* Minneapolis: University of Minnesota Press.

Delis, D. C. (2000). *California Verbal Learning Test: Adult Version–2nd ed.* San Antonio, TX: The Psychological Corporation.

Delis, D. C., Kramer, J. H., Kaplan, E., & Ober, B. A. (1987). *California Verbal Learning Test: Adult Version.* San Antonio, TX: The Psychological Corporation.

Demakis, G. J., Sweet, J. J., Sawyer, T. P. Moulthrop, M., Nies, K., & Clingerman, S. (2001). Discrepancy between predicted and obtained WAIS–R IQ scores discriminates between truamatic brain injury and insufficient effort. *Psychological Assessment, 13*, 240–248.

Derogatis, L. R. (1983). *Symptom Checklist*–90 Revised. Towson, MD: Clinical Psychometric Research.

Dunn, L. M., & Dunn, L. M. (1997). *Peabody Picture Vocabulary Test–3rd ed.* Circle Pines, MN: American Guidance Service.

Green, P., & Iverson, G. L. (2001). Validation of the computerized assessment of response bias in litigating patients with head injuries. *The Clinical Neuropsychologist, 15*, 492–497.

Green, P., Iverson, G. L., & Allen, L. (1999). Detecting malingering in head injury litigation with the Word Memory Test. *Brain Injury, 13*, 813–819.

Heaton, R. K. (1981). *Wisconsin Card Sorting Test manual.* Odessa, FL: Psychological Assessment Resources, Inc.

Heaton, R. K., Grant, I., & Matthews, C. G. (1991). *Comprehensive norms for an expanded Halstead-Reitan Battery: Demographic corrections, research findings, and clinical applications.* Odessa, FL: Psychological Assessment Resources, Inc.

Lezak, M. D. (1995). *Neuropsychological assessment–3rd ed.* New York: Oxford University Press.

Meyers, J. E., & Meyers, K. R. (1995). *Rey Complex Figure Tests and Recognition Trial.* Odessa, FL: Psychological Assessment Resources, Inc.

Raven, J. C. (no date). *Raven's Progressive Matrices.* Examination kit. Lost Angeles: Western Psychological Services.

Reitan, R. M., & Wolfson, D. (1985). *The Halstead-Reitan Neuropsychological Test Battery: Theory and clinical interpretation.* Tucson, AZ: Neuropsychology Press.

Slick, D. J., Sherman, E. M. S., & Iverson, G. L. (1999). Diagnostic criteria for malingered neurocognitive dysfunction: Proposed standards for clinical research and practice. *The Clinical Neuropsychologist, 13*, 545–561.

Smith, A. S. (1973). *Symbol Digit Modalities Test*. Los Angeles: Western Psychological Services.

Tombaugh, T. N. (1996). *Test of Memory Malingering*. Toronto: Multi-Health Systems, Inc.

Trahan, D. E., & Larrabee, G. J. (1988). *Continuous Visual Memory Test*. Odessa, FL: Psychological Assessment Resources, Inc.

Wechsler, D. (1981). *Wechsler Adult Intelligence Scale–Revised*. Cleveland, OH: The Psychological Corporation.

Wechsler, D. (1987). *Wechsler Memory Scale–Revised*. San Antonio: The Psychological Corporation.

Wechsler, D. (1997). *Wechsler Memory Scale–III*. San Antonio: The Psychological Corporation.

Woodcock, R. W., & Johnson, M. B. (1989). *Woodcock Johnson Revised Tests of Achievement*. Allen, TX: DLM Teaching Resources.

Woodcock, R. W., McGrew, K. S., & Mather, N. (2001). *Woodcock Johnson III Tests of Achievement*. Itasca, IL: Riverside Publishing.

Psychiatric and Medical Disorders

The number of psychiatric and medical disorders that could become the subject of either formal litigation or involve some other secondary gain context, such as disability determination, is essentially the number of disorders known to exist. Though we cannot consider the universe of these many conditions, this section consists of nine chapters involving disorders that a forensic expert might expect to encounter. Importantly, these chapters include examples of specific presentations of genuine clinical disorders that can occur concurrently with specific presentations that are feigned. This is known to occur, as depicted in this section, in a manner that distinguishes physical disorder from emotional disorder. Clearly, an entire presentation of symptoms need not be wholly legitimate or wholly malingered.

Definite malingering or probable malingering: Multidimensional symptom exaggeration in a case of depression

11

Joel E. Morgan and Roger O. Gervais

Some cases are more challenging than others, even for the experienced forensic neuropsychologist. This chapter deals with those that present with a varied mix of cognitive and emotional symptoms of a (seemingly) severe nature. The reader of this volume will recognize that the diagnosis of malingering or the presence of exaggerated complaints and/or cognitive "impairment" along with *genuine* neurocognitive deficits and/or psychopathology are not mutually exclusive; they may co-exist. While some cases reported are fairly straightforward, in that they easily fulfill the criteria outlined in Slick, Sherman, and Iverson (1999) for unequivocal *definite malingered neurocognitive dysfunction*, others are somewhat less clear and require greater analysis and clinical judgment. This appears to be especially true in cases more appropriate for the *probable* and *possible* malingering categories and/or when the clinician believes that genuine cognitive deficits and/or actual psychopathology are present in a context of secondary gain (SG) behavior. Cases in which evidence of malingering exists, along with the presence of clinically determined actual psychopathology or cognitive dysfunction, sometimes become especially challenging; clinicians often wonder whether the diagnosis of "malingering" can and should be made when such circumstances exist. That is, can someone be both genuinely impaired/psychologically disturbed *and* a malingerer?

Cases in which "disease-deficit incompatibility" and/or "inconsistency with injury severity" (Larrabee, 1990, 2007) are not grossly evident to the examiner may suggest that the clinical presentation is plausible, given an appropriate history or medical record. This challenge can be expressed by the question, "how much of what I am seeing in this examinee is *real* (i.e., not exaggerated or feigned)?" The intellectually honest practitioner will not want to misattribute genuine psychopathology/impairment to exaggeration or dissimulation, but will always strive to know "which is which" or "how much of one and how much of the other is present," insofar as science and skill will allow.

In an effort to aid the forensic neuropsychologist with these and other such diagnostic challenges, research into the psychometrics of effort continues at a rapid pace (Sweet, Malina, & Ecklund-Johnson, 2006) and many new scales and tests have been developed, expanding our knowledge and theory of symptom validity and measures of non-credible effort (Boone & Lu, 2007; Millis, this volume, chapter 3). Other experts believe that the situation could be improved by re-defining the Slick et al. diagnostic criteria for the diagnosis of malingering (Larrabee, Greiffenstein, Greve, &

Bianchini, 2007). However, as the reader of this chapter will see, careful case analysis utilizing our current state-of-the-art definitions of malingering—following Slick et al.—can go a long way in resolving diagnostic decisions.

Developments in the detection of exaggerated complaints of emotional distress and psycho-pathology have largely centered on the MMPI–2, the most widely used and respected of personality inventory instruments (Archer, Buffington-Vollum, Vauter Stredny, & Handel, 2006; Pope, Butcher, & Seelen, 2000). Though certainly not a "new" scale, the FBS (Fake Bad Scale; Lees-Haley, English, & Glenn, 1991) of the MMPI–2 was recently incorporated into the Pearson scoring system, giving it incremental credibility in forensic contexts. Although there already was a large body of scientific evidence supporting its use as a measure of exaggerated somatic and emotional distress (Greve & Bianchini, 2004; Larrabee, 1998, 2003; Nelson, Sweet, & Demakis, 2006), the Pearson *imprimatur* is likely to result in even more expanded use among forensic clinicians.

Research and clinical data have suggested that examinees may selectively malinger, with perhaps feigned or exaggerated neurocognitive deficits, but normal or non-exaggerated emotional/personality test profiles, or vice versa (Nelson, Sweet, Berry, Bryant, & Granacher, 2007). Similarly, examinees in a secondary gain evaluation context may malinger more generally across domains. In an effort to relate MMPI–2 response patterns to the possible presence of cognitive response bias, Gervais, Ben-Porath, Wygant, and Green (2007) developed the RBS (Response Bias Scale) and found that it consistently outperformed more traditional validity scales (e.g., F) in its ability to predict the presence of cognitive response bias on cognitive SVTs (e.g., WMT, TOMM, among others). Support for use of the RBS in forensic contexts was recently documented by Wygant et al. (2006, May) and Nelson, Sweet, and Heilbronner (2007), suggesting that the RBS and FBS may "represent a similar construct of symptom validity" (p. 67). This would suggest that the MMPI–2, an instrument long respected for its window into personality and emotional factors, might also provide important information about *cognitive* test-taking attitudes and behavior, surely of importance to the forensic neuropsychologist.

Depression is among the most common of psychological disorders (American Psychiatric Association, 2000). Exaggerated or feigned symptoms of depression are common in forensic examinations (Mittenberg, Patton, Canyock, & Condit, 2002; Steffan, Clopton, & Morgan, 2003). Recognizing that efforts to detect feigned or exaggerated depression are an important enterprise, Steffan et al. (2003) developed the Malingered Depression Scale of the MMPI–2 (Md). Although in their initial study, promising results were achieved in discriminating depressed patients from simulators with the Md scale (Steffan et al., 2003), a recent study by Sweet, Malina, and Ecklund-Johnson (2006) found the Md to show little relationship to indices of cognitive malingering or secondary gain status. Researchers agree that the Md may be promising, however, and that further research in forensic contexts is clearly warranted.

Even with the development of these newer validity scales, "traditional" MMPI–2 validity indices such as "F" (infrequency) and F_B (F "back" referring to the F items in the second half of the test) continue to be important. F and F_B are measures of test-taking approach including deviant response styles, "faking bad," and exaggerated psychopathology (Graham, 2006; Hathaway & McKinley, 1951), while the Dissimulation Index (Ds/Ds-r; Gough, 1954) measures exaggerated neurotic complaints. The F_P scale (Infrequency Psychopathology; Arbisi & Ben-Porath, 1995) was developed to detect exaggerated severe psychopathology.

With these indices of exaggerated symptom complaints in mind, the following case presentation is offered for your consideration as representative of one of the more challenging diagnostic cases among those seen in a busy forensic neuropsychological practice. It is an actual case from the first author's practice. The utility of the measures presented here in detecting poor effort, with the ultimate aim of proper and accurate diagnosis, will be discussed. It is also important to state what may be obvious to readers, that no single test or measure, no matter how powerful or sensitive (i.e., how large its effect size), is sufficient by itself to diagnose malingering, a neurocognitive/brain abnormality, or an emotional disorder (Millis & Volinsky, 2001). Accurate diagnosis in cases where genuine dysfunction or psychopathology are present or suspected, along with negative response bias in a secondary gain context, are sometimes more challenging than they may at first appear.

THE CASE OF MS. G.

This 47-year-old Caucasian female was referred for neuropsychological/psychological evaluation by her insurance company to ascertain the nature and extent of her purported disability as a result of major depression. She was a college graduate and worked as an accountant and auditor for a corporation. There was no history of previous academic or psychiatric problems. She claimed the presence of cognitive problems in the form of impaired concentration and deficient memory; she described word retrieval difficulties and severe apathy, indifference, and fatigue and said she was unable to do very much at all. She reported having spent the bulk of her days in bed since the onset of her depression, mostly sleeping and crying. She reported that her husband and teenage children performed most of the household duties.

Ms. G. reportedly became depressed approximately one year earlier, after one of her children made "false accusations of abuse" and that triggered a cascade of emotional and social problems. At about the same time, or slightly before, she experienced increased stress at work as new audit managers came in and accounting regulations changed, bringing greater scrutiny on the part of management. She also reported longstanding marital difficulties. She reported suffering a "stroke" several years ago, but there was no mention of this in her medical record. Similarly, she said she also had a "TIA" but her medical record had no mention of this either. One hospitalization for "suicidal attempt" by ingesting medication was reported, approximately one year prior to the IME. On interview during this exam, she said she purposely took an overdose of pain medication, originally prescribed to her for back pain, in a suicide attempt: "I had enough, I wanted to die." But according to the medical record, she told ER personnel that she took an "accidental, unintended overdose," because she had a lot of back pain, wasn't getting sufficient relief, and "lost track of how much" she had taken. Experienced clinicians know that descriptions of suicidal behavior can evolve over time.

On interview, she presented with a flat affect. She showed psychomotor retardation and moved slowly. Questions were answered slowly with an uncomfortable latency between question and answer, and she had a downward gaze between questions. Speech was somewhat sparse and not spontaneous but she responded generally appropriately. She admitted to suicidal ideation ("I think about suicide all the time," she said), denied having a plan or any intent, and complained of racing thoughts and auditory hallucinations which she could not specify.

Test results

Cognitive symptom validity testing

Results of symptom validity tests (SVTs) are shown in Table 11.1. On the Test of Memory Malingering (TOMM; Tombaugh, 1996) the examinee correctly recognized 29 of 50 stimuli on Trial 1 and 32 of 50 on Trial 2 for a clearly invalid performance; 45 or more correct on Trial 2 is the accepted cutoff. There were numerous items correctly identified on Trial 1 that were not recognized on Trial 2, a counterintuitive finding. Trial 1 performance was nearly at chance value.

She had an overall "questionable" profile on the Victoria Symptom Validity Test (VSVT; Slick, Hopp, Strauss, & Thompson, 1997) with 27/48 correct. Her easy items correct score was 20/24 (valid); hard items correct score was 7/24 (invalid and significantly below chance). Missing any of the easy items was a rarity in the normative sample. She had a Reliable Digit Span (RDS; Greiffenstein,

Baker, & Gola, 1994) of 6, which has been associated with 100% probability of intentionally poor effort (Etherton, Bianchini, Greve, & Heinly, 2005).

Emotional/personality validity indicators

Traditional MMPI–2 validity scales are shown in Table 11.2 and resulted in the following T scores: VRIN 50; TRIN 58F; F 120; F_B 120; F_P 57; FBS 111 (raw 39); L 71; K 54; S 58. Additional scales revealed an RBS of 120 (raw 25), Ds-r of 84 (raw 20) (Dissimulation Scale–Revised; Gough, 1954), and an Md of 27. It is noteworthy that some of these validity scales were elevated to the highest levels possible, with some exceeding or approaching the highest scores obtained during the scale's development (i.e., Md and RBS; Stefan et al., 2003; Gervais et al., 2007), and others among the highest obtained in practice (i.e., FBS; Greiffenstein, Fox, & Lees-Haley, 2007; Lees-Haley et al., 1991).

Cognitive test results

The insurance carrier requested a reduced battery of neuropsychological tests, focusing instead on symptom validity and psychiatric diagnostic issues. Results of cognitive testing are shown in Table 11.3. On the WAIS-III she obtained an FSIQ of 88 with a VIQ of 90 and a PIQ of 87; WMI was 88, PSI was 84. These scores are clearly well below expectations considering her educational and vocational history.

There were numerous psychometric and qualitative examples of decreased effort on the WAIS–III. She had a Reliable Digit Span of 6 (RDS; Greifenstein, Baker, & Gola, 1994), associated with poor effort (Etherton, Bianchini, Greve, & Heinly, 2005). She had numerous "near miss" answers on the Arithmetic Test, for example $3.50 for $3.60 (#10), .20 for .30 (#12), $500 for $600 (#15) and others, reflective of Ganser-like symptoms (Dike, Baronoski, & Griffith, 2005; Merckelbach, Peters, Jelicic, Brands, & Smeets, 2006). She recognized only the first two items on Picture Completion where she earned a Scaled Score of 4. She earned a Scaled Score of 5 on Comprehension. This was no doubt well below her estimated ability, considering her education and vocational history. She was slow on Digit-Symbol-Coding, earning a Scaled Score of 5.

TABLE 11.1   Cognitive symptom validity test results

TOMM	Trial 1	29/50	Invalid
	Trial 2	32/50	Invalid
VSVT	Easy	20/24	Valid
	Hard	7/24	Invalid
	Total	27/48	Questionable
RDS	Total	6	Invalid

TABLE 11.2   MMPI–2 validity scale results

MMPI–2 VALIDITY SCALES	RAW SCORE	T SCORE	RANGE
VRIN	5	50	Average
TRIN	8	58(F)	Average
F	28	120	Most Extreme
F_B	21	120	Most Extreme
F_P	2	57	Average
FBS	39	111	Extreme
L	8	71	Significant

TABLE 11.3   Cognitive test results

		STANDARD SCORE	PERCENTILE	DESCRIPTION
WAIS–III	Verbal IQ	90	25	Average
	Performance IQ	87	19	Low Average
	Full Scale	88	21	Low Average
	Verbal Comprehension	98	45	
	Perceptual Organization	86	18	
	Working Memory	88	21	
	Processing Speed	84	14	
	Vocabulary	11	63	
	Similarities	7	16	
	Arithmetic	10	50	
	Digit Span	6	9	
	Information	11	63	
	Comprehension	5	5	
	Letter-Number Sequencing	8	25	
	Picture Completion	4	2	
	Digit-Symbol Coding	5	5	
	Block Design	8	25	
	Matrix Reasoning	11	63	
	Picture Arrangement	13	84	
	Symbol Search	9	37	
WMS	Logical Memory I		16	
	Logical Memory II		10	

On Logical Memory, she went from the 16th percentile after initial exposure (LMI) to the 10th percentile after the delay (LMII) and demonstrated a loss of half the memory elements she had originally remembered. She manifested a good deal of halting and long pauses during memory testing.

Emotional/personality test results

Table 11.3 shows the MMPI–2 clinical scales. These results were invalidated by numerous extreme elevations on validity scales and could not be interpreted clinically. Extreme elevations on validity scales artificially inflate clinical scales, thus rendering them clinically meaningless (Graham, 2006; Greene, 2000). Nonetheless, it is instructive to note the patient's performance on clinical scales. Her Welsh Code of 86 271**34 was reflective of T scores of 115 (Sc), 114 (Pa), 105 (D), 105 (Pt), 103, (Hs), 99 (Hy) and 94 (Pd). Her mean clinical scale elevation was 91.7, which is the fourth highest in the second author's clinical data set of 1187 cases, corresponding to a percentile rank of 99.7. If these scores had been valid, this would suggest a person who was perhaps psychotic, in acute distress, with marked paranoid ideation, severe anxiety, serious depression, and somatic complaints. Her elevation on Pd suggested anger and/or antisocial behaviors and trends.

Analysis of the restructured clinical scales suggested demoralization (RCd 83), somatic complaints (RC1 97), low positive emotions (RC2 100), ideas of persecution (RC6 88), dysfunctional negative emotions (RC7 75), and aberrant experiences (RC8 92) (T scores in parentheses). The normal score of 44 on RC4 suggests that the elevated Pd (94) was more a function of demoralization and feelings of alienation and anger than an acknowledgment of antisocial behaviors and tendencies. The mean RC scale profile elevation of 72.9 was at the 93rd percentile in the second author's clinical data set. At face value, assuming her validity scales had been valid, these scores would suggest a possible psychotic depression. This was, in fact, the clinical impression, i.e., that there was some level of depression, likely with mild psychotic features. But in cases where there is apparent scale inflation secondary to wildly invalid MMPI–2 validity scales, it is not possible to scientifically determine just how depressed and/or psychotic one might actually be from a psychometric perspective.

DISCUSSION

The examinee had convergent evidence of a clearly exaggerated response set on the MMPI–2 with extreme elevations on a variety of validity scales, well into the invalid range. This is consistent with gross symptom magnification in many emotional/psychiatric symptom domains. She reported exaggerated psychotic symptoms (F, F_B), exaggerated symptoms of neurosis (Ds-r), exaggerated physical complaints and suffering (FBS), and exaggerated complaints of depression (Md). She had a striking response bias associated with poor effort on cognitive effort tests (RBS), as well as actual poor performance on the TOMM and the VSVT, consistent with exaggerated cognitive complaints. With six validity scales of the MMPI–2 and two cognitive effort tests indicative of exaggerated complaints and poor effort, the patient had a grossly invalid assessment profile.

Interestingly, the patient did not exaggerate on F_P (infrequency psychopathology), perhaps suggesting that although she reports numerous symptoms, she does not see herself as severely psychiatric or "crazy." Similarly, her modest elevation on L (lie) suggests a self-presentation resembling that of a virtuous person, in a context of someone with serious psychopathology and tremendous suffering.

This case illustrates considerable consistency in exaggerated self-reports of emotional distress across numerous validity scales of the MMPI–2. Similarly, this patient also exerted insufficient effort on two separate cognitive symptom validity tests, consistent with exaggerated cognitive complaints and non-credible effort. Since there were so many indices of invalid performance it was not possible to interpret the clinical scales of the MMPI–2. Yet, the first author believed this person to be experiencing some psychological distress, primarily in the form of depression, but it was unclear precisely how much actual distress was present as a result of invalid psychometric testing and an obvious response bias. This case also illustrates that genuine psychopathology may co-exist with an exaggerated profile; they are not mutually exclusive. Of course, the determination on the first author's part that this claimant did have some genuine psychopathology was a clinical judgment, and others might disagree. In that vein, she manifested a rather consistent level of flattened affect, persistent psychomotor retardation, and her mood and behavior were consistently typical of depression. Work-related distress, coupled with family stress of a legal and social nature, appeared to provide legitimacy from her history to the possibility of a real depressive reaction.

The reader may wonder how common it is that an examinee has such striking concurrent elevations on so many MMPI–2 validity scales. This is an empirical question that as yet cannot be answered. But examining other chapters in this volume may provide tentative answers. Particularly interesting in the present case was the finding that both newer MMPI–2 scales (FBS, Md, RBS) and more established scales (F, F_B, Ds-r) were consistently reflective of response bias.

The examinee reported an exorbitant number of complaints of physiological suffering and disability, that which the FBS measures (Greiffenstein, Fox, & Lees-Haley, 2007). Her FBS raw score of 39 on the 43-item scale is among the highest reported. Indeed, this score is the third highest in the second author's clinical data set (N = 1187), with only two cases obtaining scores of 40. Scores above 30 have a 99–100% probability of indicating "promotion of suffering" (Greiffenstein et al., 2007). This case is representative of the findings of a meta-analytic study supporting the utility of the FBS in forensic practice (Nelson, Sweet, & Demakis, 2006) as a measure of non-credible somatic and cognitive complaints.

Although a recent analysis of the Malingered Depression scale (Md) suggested that it may have limited utility in forensic neuropsychological applications largely as a result of its low relationship to other validity indicators (Sweet, Malina, & Ecklund-Johnson, 2006), the authors noted that in cases where individuals had very high scores on other MMPI–2 validity scales, F or the combination of F, F_B, FBS (the "F family") and effort indicators, the Md surpassed cutoffs. These cases were what the authors termed "the grossest feigning of depressive symptoms" (p. 549). This seems to be the case with the current examinee who manifested high scores on multiple validity scales and who evidenced poor effort on cognitive symptom validity tests. Despite Sweet et al.'s (2006) concern about the utility of the Md, as this case illustrates, it may be incrementally useful in selected presentations where exaggerated depression is a concern. However, the usefulness of the Md in identifying exaggerated depression in the absence of other indices of invalidity and response bias remains to be studied.

One of the more interesting and encouraging findings of this case concerns the recently developed RBS (Gervais et al., 2007), an empirically derived validity scale. The RBS was developed on the basis of determining differential item endorsement by examinees that failed or passed cognitive symptom validity tests. The patient's extremely high raw score of 25, with corresponding T score of 120, is the highest score reported to date and is associated with a 100% probability of cognitive symptom validity test failure, which is exactly what occurred. Of note is the fact that although the RBS was developed using the Word Memory Test (WMT; Green, 2003), the Computerized Assessment of Response Bias (CARB; Allen, Conder, Green, & Cox, 1997), and the Test of Memory Malingering (TOMM; Tombaugh, 1996), this examinee failed an independent SVT, the VSVT, as well as the TOMM. The WMT was not administered in this case. This is consistent with the development objectives and validation of the RBS, which suggest that the scale is sensitive to the overall construct concerned with reduced cognitive effort. As was determined in a recent study, the RBS in this case likely correlated highly with the FBS, both scales apparently tapping into this broader construct of symptom validity/response bias (Nelson et al., 2006). Gervais, Ben-Porath, Wygant, and Green (2008) found that the RBS was a more sensitive predictor of exaggerated memory complaints than the MMPI–2 F-family validity scales and the FBS. This suggests that the RBS is specifically tapping into the cognitive effort and memory dysfunction dimension of the symptom validity/response bias construct. Thus, while Ms. G. reported various memory complaints, these could not be considered credible, nor her cognitive test scores valid in view of the marked response bias across multiple measures. The grossly elevated RBS score provided further confirmation of her non-credible cognitive symptom reports and cognitive test performance.

So what is diagnostically "challenging" about this case with multiple indices of response bias in an SG context? Isn't the patient a definite malingerer? It seems very obvious. The answer, of course, depends on how you define malingering. At first glance, it would seem fairly simple to call this person a Definite Malingerer, what with *six* MMPI–2 validity scales and two cognitive SVTs grossly invalid. But a more careful analysis of these data may suggest otherwise.

Analysis of these data using the criteria for a diagnosis of Malingered Neurocognitive Dysfunction (MND) by Slick, Sherman, and Iverson (1999) follows. She clearly meets Criterion A of the Slick et al. (1999) criteria—there is the presence of a substantial external incentive—which was an insurance IME for disability income.

For Criterion B, the issue may be more equivocal. There are two ways of looking at Criterion B1 in this case. One way of looking at B1 is that she did not exactly meet this criterion because she did not score below chance values on SVTs, neither the TOMM nor the VSVT *as a whole* (27/48 correct). She scored below chance on only the difficult trials of the VSVT (7/24) and her overall VSVT was "questionable" in terms of validity. Assuming that one uses the "overall" VSVT as the major measure of this test, then she fails to meet Criterion B1. In that case, she would not be considered a definite malingerer.

However, since she also had an RDS below cutoff, she does meet Criterion B2, on the basis of her cognitive SVTs (below cutoff but not at or below chance values), and B3, on the basis of her RDS. She also clearly meets Criterion C5 with evidence of exaggerated psychological dysfunction on the MMPI–2. She meets Criterion D in that, while the examiner judged some genuine psychopathology to be present, it was certainly not of sufficient magnitude as to fully account for groups B and C criteria. In this scenario, the most appropriate label would appear to be that of probable malingered neurocognitive dysfunction, despite convergence of numerous indicators of response bias on testing.

Is this the most appropriate way to interpret the VSVT, using the *overall* classification? Grote, Kooker, Garron, Nyenhuis, Smith, and Mattingly (2000) found that the easy items are insensitive to reduced effort and reported that the difficult items provided greater sensitivity. Non-compensation-seeking subjects earned VSVT difficult items scores of 21 or higher at a rate 2.61 times higher than that of compensation-seeking patients (93.3%/35.8%). They suggested that the most appropriate classification measure for the VSVT is not the overall score that combines the easy and difficult items, but is the difficult items score, following the "90% rule," i.e., 21 or greater on difficult items. In essence, combining the easy and difficult items, as in the overall score, reduces the sensitivity of the instrument. In a similar vein, a recent study also advocates use of the VSVT difficult items rather than the easy items or the overall score, noting that the easy items are failed by only the most blatant malingerers (Frazier, Youngstrom, Naugle, Haggerty, & Busch, 2007). Since our patient had a difficult items score on the VSVT of 7/24, well below chance value, her performance on SVTs is considered to have met Criterion B1. She therefore meets criteria for a diagnosis of *definite malingered neurocognitive dysfunction*.

How about the presence of malingered psychopathology? In the *Diagnostic and Statistical Manual of Mental Disorders–text revision* (DSM–IV–TR; APA, 2000), a diagnosis of malingering (V65.2) is made with the presence of "intentional production of false or grossly exaggerated physical or psychological symptoms, motivated by external incentives" (p. 739). In this case it is clear that grossly exaggerated psychological symptoms are present, as consistently manifested by the very high scores on MMPI–2 validity scales. These abnormal validity indicators all converge to reveal grossly exaggerated psychological complaints, well beyond expectations in consideration of her reported psychosocial stressors and the performance of known groups. She meets a DSM–IV–TR diagnosis of malingering, V65.2.

In this particular case, multiple diagnoses are appropriate and not mutually exclusive. These include the Axis I diagnoses of "Depressive Disorder, Not Otherwise Specified," "Definite Malingered Neurocognitive Dysfunction," and "Malingering" (psychopathology). Consistent with the grossest performance on MMPI–2 validity scales and below chance performance on cognitive effort tests, the most appropriate cognitive diagnosis was definite malingered neurocognitive dysfunction.

This case is instructive in that it illustrates the convergent evidence of exaggeration and definite response bias across multiple cognitive and emotional measures, providing unequivocal evidence of malingered cognitive and emotional distress. Importantly, actual psychopathology may co-exist with malingering or severe exaggeration. The convergent invalid results noted on various MMPI–2 validity scales illustrate their utility in clinical forensic contexts. The reader is advised to analyze test data carefully, following the criteria proposed by Slick et al. (1999), and to utilize current research that provides considerable interpretive assistance.

REFERENCES

Allen, L., Conder, R. L., Green, P., & Cox, D. R. (1997). *CARB' 97 Manual for the Computerized Assessment of Response Bias*. Durham, NC: CogniSyst, Inc.

American Psychiatric Association (APA) (2000). *Diagnostic and statistical manual of mental disorders*, 4th ed., text revision. Washington, DC: APA.

Arbisi, P. A., & Ben-Porath, Y. S. (1995). An MMPI–2 infrequent response scale for use with psychopathological populations: The Infrequency-Psychopathology Scale, "F(p)." *Psychological Assessment, 7*, 424–431.

Archer, R. P., Buffington-Vollum, J. K., Vauter Stredny, R., & Handel, R. W. (2006). A survey of psychological test use patterns among forensic psychologists. *Journal of Personality Assessment, 87*, 84–94.

Boone, K. B., & Lu, P. H. (2007). Non-forced-choice effort measures. In G. J. Larrabee (Ed.), *Assessment of malingered neuropsychological deficits*. New York: Oxford.

Dike, C. C., Baronoski, M., & Griffith, E. E. (2005). Pathological lying revisited. *Journal of the American Academy of Psychiatry and the Law, 33*, 342–349.

Etherton, J. L., Bianchini, K. J., Greve, K. W., & Heinly, M. T. (2005). Sensitivity and specificity of reliable digit span in malingered pain-related disability. *Assessment, 12*, 130–136.

Frazier, T. W., Youngstrom, E. A., Naugle, R. I., Haggerty, K. A., & Busch, R. M. (2007). The latent structure of cognitive symptom exaggeration on the Victoria symptom validity test. *Archives of Clinical Neuropsychology, 22*, 197–211.

Gervais, R. O., Ben-Porath, Y. S., Wygant, D. B., & Green, P. (2007). Development and validation of a response bias scale (RBS) for the MMPI–2. *Assessment, 14*, 196–208.

Gervais, R. O., Ben-Porath, Y. S., Wygant, D. B., & Green, P. (2008). Differential sensitivity of the Response Bias Scale (RBS) and MMPI–2 validity scales to memory complaints. *The Clinical Neuropsychologist*, DOI: 10.1080/13854040701756930.

Gough, H. G (1954). Some common misconceptions about neuroticism. *Journal of Consulting Psychology, 18*, 287–292.

Graham, J. R. (2006). *MMPI–2 Assessing personality and psychopathology*, 4th ed. New York: Oxford.

Green, P. (2003). *Green's Word Memory Test*. Green's Publishing Inc., Edmonton, Canada.

Greene, R. (2000). *The MMPI–2/MMPI: An interpretive manual*, 2nd ed. New York: Grune & Stratton.

Greiffenstein, M. F., Baker, W. J., & Gola, T. (1994). Validation of malingered amnesia measures with a large clinical sample. *Psychological Assessment, 6*, 218–224.

Greiffenstein, M., Fox, D., & Lees-Haley, P. R. (2007). The MMPI–2 Fake Bad Scale in the detection of noncredible brain injury claims. In K. Boone (Ed.), *Detection of noncredible cognitive performance*. New York: Guilford Press.

Greve, K. W., & Bianchini, K. J. (2004). Setting empirical cutoffs on psychometric indicators of negative response bias: a methodological commentary with recommendations. *Archives of Clinical Neuropsychology, 19*, 533–541.

Grote, C. L., Kooker, E. K., Garron, D. C., Nyenhuis, D. L., Smith, C. A., & Mattingly, M. L. (2000). Performance of compensation seeking and non-compensation seeking samples on the Victoria symptom validity test: cross validation and extension of a Standardization study. *Journal of Clinical and Experimental Neuropsychology, 22*, 709–719.

Hathaway, S. R., & McKinley, J. C. (1951). *MMPI manual*. New York: Psychological Corporation.

Larrabee, G. J. (1990). Cautions in the use of neuropsychological evaluations in legal settings. *Neuropsychology, 4*, 239–247.

Larrabee, G. J. (1998). Somatic malingering on the MMPI and MMPI–2 in personal injury litigants. *The Clinical Neuropsychologist, 12*, 179–188.

Larrabee, G. J. (2003). Exaggerated pain report in litigants with malingered neurocognitive dysfunction. *The Clinical Neuropsychologist, 17*(3), 395–401.

Larrabee, G. J. (2007). Identification of malingering by pattern analysis on neuropsychological tests. In G. J. Larrabee (Ed.), *Assessment of malingered neuropsychological deficits*. New York: Oxford.

Larrabee, G. J., Greiffenstein, M. F., Greve, K. W., & Bianchini, K. (2007). Refining diagnostic criteria for malingering. In G. J. Larrabee (Ed.), *Assessment of malingered neuropsychological deficits*. New York: Oxford.

Lees-Haley, P. R., English, L. T., & Glenn, W. J. (1991). A fake bad scale on the MMPI–2 for personal injury claimants. *Psychological Reports, 68*, 208–210.

Merckelbach, H., Peters, M., Jelicic, M., Brands, I., & Smeets, T. (2006). Detecting malingering of Ganser-like symptoms with tests: a case study. *Psychiatry and Clinical Neurosciences, 60*, 636–638.

Millis, S. R., & Volinsky, C. T. (2001). Assessment of response bias in mild head injury: beyond malingering tests. *Journal of Clinical and Experimental Neuropsychology, 23*(6), 809–828.

Mittenberg, W., Patton, C., Canyock, E. M., & Condit, D. (2002). Base rates of malingering and symptom exaggeration. *Journal of Clinical and Experimental Neuropsychology, 24*, 1094–1102.

Nelson, N. W., Sweet, J. J., Berry, D. T. R., Bryant, F. B., & Granacher, R. P. (2007). Response validity in forensic neuropsychology: Exploratory factor analytic evidence of distinct cognitive and psychological constructs. *Journal of the International Neuropsychological Society, 13*, 440–449.

Nelson, N. W., Sweet, J. J., & Demakis, G. J. (2006). Meta-Analysis of the MMPI–2 Fake Bad Scale: Utility in forensic practice. *The Clinical Neuropsychologist, 20*, 39–58.

Nelson, N. W., Sweet, J. J., & Heilbronner, R. L. (2007). Examination of the new MMPI–2 response bias scale (Gervais): relationship with MMPI–2 validity scales. *Journal of Clinical and Experimental Neuropsychology, 29*, 67–72.

Pope, K., Butcher, J., & Seelen, J. (2000). *The MMPI, MMPI–2, & MMPI–A in court*, 2nd ed. Washington D.C.: American Psychological Evaluation.

Slick, D. J., Hopp, G., Strauss E., & Thompson, G. B. (1997). *Victoria Symptom Validity Test: Professional manual*. Odessa, FL: Psychological Assessment Resources.

Slick, D. J., Sherman, E. M., & Iverson, G. L. (1999). Diagnostic criteria for malingered neurocognitive dysfunction: Proposed standards for clinical practice and research. *The Clinical Neuropsychologist, 13*, 545–561.

Stefan, J. S., Clopton, J. R., & Morgan, R. D. (2003). An MMPI–2 scale to detect malingered depression (Md scale). *Assessment, 10*, 382–392.

Sweet, J. J., Malina, A., & Ecklund-Johnson, E. (2006). Application of the new MMPI–2 malingered depression scale to individuals undergoing neuropsychological evaluation: Relative lack of relationship to secondary gain and failure on validity indices. *The Clinical Neuropsychologist, 20*, 541–551.

Tombaugh, T. N. (1996). *The Test of Memory Malingering (TOMM)*. Toronto, Canada: Multi-Health Systems.

Wygant, D. B., Ben-Porath, Y. S., Gervais, R. O., Sellbom, M., Stafford, K. P., Freeman, D. B., & Heilbronner, R. L. (2006, May). *Further validation of the Response Bias Scale (RBS)*. Paper presented at the 41st Annual Symposium of Recent Developments of the MMPI–2/MMPI–A, Minneapolis, MN.

Questioning common assumptions about depression

12

Paul Green

In psychology, psychiatry, and general medicine there are certain beliefs about depression that have become so widely accepted that they have rarely been questioned. One of them is that depression causes cognitive impairment or, at least, that the two are very strongly correlated with each other. Cognitive deficits, typically impaired memory and concentration, are assumed to coincide with the onset of depression and to resolve as the depression remits. Such cognitive deficits are listed as diagnostic criteria for depression in the psychiatric diagnostic manual, DSM–IV (Frances, Pincus, First, & DSM–IV task force, 1994). However, no distinction is made in DSM–IV between subjective cognitive complaints and objective memory deficits, as if the two were equivalent, when they are not. The reader of DSM–IV would be led to assume that a person in a major depressive episode (1) would complain of impaired memory (subjective impairment), (2) would show deficits on memory tests (objective impairment), and (3) would have impairment of memory in day-to-day life. Finally, (4) the more severe the depression, the greater the objective memory deficits we might expect on objective testing. In this chapter, it will be argued that assumptions (1) to (4) above are usually false. To illustrate how certain general principles apply in clinical practice, the case of a depressed woman making a Worker's Compensation Board (WCB) claim for cognitive impairment and depression after a motor vehicle accident will be presented.

DEPRESSION MYTHOLOGY

A common myth about depression is that it involves objective neuropsychological impairment, which was not already present prior to the depression. Veiel (1997) pointed out that the neuro-psychological impairment in many groups of depressed patients was as great as or greater than that found in patients with severe traumatic brain injuries (p. 600, paragraph 3). In the discussion section, Veiel (1997) highlighted the degree of apparent deficits in depressed patients with reference to the severely brain-injured patients of Dikmen, Machamer, Winn, and Temkin (1995). He stated that, although it might look like "a freak result," the depressed patients in one study obtained a mean score of 90 seconds on Trail Making B, comparable to the mean score of 87 seconds from Dikmen's patients with loss of consciousness of one to six days from traumatic brain injury. All the other studies of depressed patients reported even higher mean Trail Making B scores! How should we interpret such scores in depressed patients?

If we were to treat the group data from the latter depressed patients as being valid (i.e., indicative only of genuine cognitive impairment in depressed patients making their best effort), we might conclude that depression is typically associated with measurable cognitive deficits, greater than those found in patients with severe brain injuries. Before we do that, it is necessary to consider an alternative explanation, which to the writer's knowledge has never previously been considered in any published study of depression and cognition: that the mean scores in groups of depressed patients might have been artificially suppressed by incomplete effort and/or by deliberate symptom exaggeration.

The impact of poor effort on testing is certainly large enough to create spurious findings, if effort is not measured and controlled. In 904 consecutive patients of mixed diagnosis studied by Green, Rohling, Lees-Haley, and Allen (2001), a lack of full effort had a much greater effect than severe brain injury or neurological diseases in suppressing scores across a large neuropsychological test battery. Effort measured by the Word Memory Test (WMT; Green, 2003; Green, Allen, & Astner, 1996; Green & Astner, 1995) explained approximately 50% of the variance in a composite score from a total of 43 different neuropsychological test scores, in patients of various diagnoses, including cases of major depression. In comparison, education and age had very minor effects, respectively explaining only 11% and 4% of the neuropsychological test score variance. Similarly, in an independent study of epileptic and psychogenic non-epileptic seizure (PNES) patients it was found that 50% of the variance in scores from a neuropsychological test battery was explained by effort on the WMT (Drane, Williamson, Stroup, Holmes, Jung, Koerner, Chaytor, Wilensky, & Miller, 2006). The latter authors concluded that effort is a more important determinant of test scores than the person's diagnosis. That striking conclusion came from a study at the University of Washington epilepsy surgery center, in which failure of the WMT effort subtests was present in more than half of the cases of "psychogenic non-epileptic seizures," with very few failures in actual epileptic patients who were due for surgery and had been taken off their anti-seizure medication.

Patients in the Green et al. (2001) study with the mildest head injuries, who passed the effort tests, scored very close to the normal mean on the test battery. Yet, the mild head injury cases that failed the WMT effort tests scored almost 1.5 standard deviations below the normal mean on the same neuropsychological battery. This was three times lower than the group with the most severe brain injuries. Cases with a Glasgow Coma Scale score of 3 to 8, making a good effort, scored only half a standard deviation below the normal mean on the battery. *Thus, poor effort had a much greater overall effect in suppressing neuropsychological test scores than severe brain injury.* When present, poor effort seriously distorted and biased the test data, making it seem as if some cases of mild head injury actually had far more severe impairment than the most severely brain injured patients. Such paradoxical and nonsensical results will be quite familiar to clinicians who assess cases of mild head injury involved in compensation claims.

In the outpatient group of Green et al. (2001) previously diagnosed with major depression by physicians, being treated for depression, and sent for an independent assessment for insurance purposes, 28% of cases failed the effort testing. This was higher than the 16% failure rate in the group with neurological diseases and also higher than the 18% failure rate in those with the most severe traumatic brain injuries. In the 72% of patients with major depression who passed the WMT effort tests, the average score of as many as 43 neuropsychological tests was only 0.03 standard deviations below the normal mean. That is, the depressed outpatients with good effort performed like normal volunteers on a comprehensive battery of neuropsychological tests. Yet, in the 28% of cases of major depression who failed the effort tests, the mean score on neuropsychological tests was 1.45 standard deviations below the normal mean. *Hence, in depressed outpatients, poor effort suppressed test scores three times more than severe brain injuries.* Whether this was a reflection of an absence of good effort or deliberate exaggeration of cognitive deficits to achieve an external goal (e.g., financial compensation), the net result is the same. As a result of poor effort, the neuropsychological test scores in the depressed patients failing the WMT effort tests were invalid and considerably underestimated their actual abilities.

If effort suppresses test scores more than severe brain injury and if 28% of depressed patients fail effort testing, the mean test scores in a group with major depression would drop relative to a group of patients who all made a full effort. Poor effort in a third of cases would make it seem that the mean performance for the whole group of depressed patients was impaired relative to healthy adults, but that conclusion might be invalid. Rohling, Green, Allen, and Iverson (2002) removed those who failed WMT effort testing and studied a wide range of test scores in those who were making a full effort on testing. The battery included many of the most widely used tests, such as Trail Making, the Category Test, tests of word and design fluency, verbal and visual memory, and manual tests. In the presumed good effort cases, there was no difference between those with the most symptoms of depression versus those with the least symptoms on any neuropsychological test. What might have been expected did not happen. Depression had no effect on neuropsychological test scores. This is contrary to what most professionals would have expected.[1]

Against the documented and extremely large effects of effort on test scores, we may consider the frequent suggestion in the literature that depression is associated with at least mild cognitive deficits. For example, Neu, Bajbouj, Schilling, Godemann, Berman, and Schlattmann (2005) reported that, at the onset of a depressive episode, patients performed significantly worse than controls on all cognitive tests used. They also found that cognitive impairment was unrelated to MRI signal hyper-intensities in the brain. As with most past studies, no information is provided about the effort being made by the depressed patients. It is possible that poor effort could explain the apparent cognitive weaknesses in the depressed patients compared with controls. It is also possible that, if the con-founding effects of widely varying effort had been removed, correlates of the MRI abnormalities might have been found. It is possible that cognitive weaknesses do exist in some cases of major depression, but, until effort tests are used in studies of depression, we simply do not know whether actual cognitive impairment is linked with depression or whether poor effort artificially suppresses test scores in subgroups of depressed patients, skewing the overall mean scores.

EMPIRICAL TESTING OF ASSUMPTIONS

The patients in the latter studies of Green et al. (2001) and Rohling et al. (2002) were drawn from the private practice of the present writer. That cohort of patients has now grown to 1357 outpatients tested for more than one day each. Nearly all patients in this series were assessed in the context of a WCB claim, medical disability claim, or motor vehicle accident injury claim. This large database allows us to test several common assumptions about depression in outpatients with a compensation/disability incentive. Whether or not the findings generalize to other samples will need to be tested separately, although it seems unlikely that the findings to be presented are unique to this sample.

1. One hypothesis is that the people with more symptoms of depression will have more self-reported memory problems. As we shall see, this is true.
2. Another is that self-reported memory complaints will correlate significantly with objective memory test scores. This is false.
3. A third is that we might expect more severe depression to be linked with greater memory impairment on objective tests but, as we shall see, this is false.
4. Finally, it might be assumed that memory complaints are generally greater in those with well-established organic brain damage than in those with depression and no verified neurological disease. False again.

---

[1] This study was awarded the Nelson Butters Award by the National Academy of Neuropsychology in 2003 (Rohling, Green, Allen, & Iverson, 2002).

To test the above hypotheses, we can use the Beck Depression Inventory (BDI) as a yardstick for self-reported depressive symptoms. However, the same phenomena are found if we substitute the MMPI–2 depression scale or the depression scale of the SCL–90–R. Similarly, it makes little difference which memory test we choose, but we will focus on the California Verbal Learning Test (CVLT; Delis, Kramer, Kaplan, & Ober, 1987) as a well-known objective measure of verbal memory and, in particular, short delayed free recall of a 16-word list (SD Free Recall). As a measure of self-reported memory complaints, we may use the mean verbal memory problems (VMP) subtest of the Memory Complaints Inventory (MCI) for Windows, a 58-item computerized questionnaire, on which the person rates various aspects of their own memory (MCI; Green, 2004; Green & Allen, 1997).

The correlations between scores on the latter instruments were as follows:

1. For self-rated depressive symptoms on the BDI versus subjective verbal memory complaints on the MCI, there was a highly significant positive correlation ($r = 0.45$, BDI versus VMP, $n = 954$), supporting Hypothesis 1 above.
2. Objective memory test scores versus subjective verbal memory complaints revealed a very small and clinically insignificant negative correlation ($r = -0.1$, SD Free Recall versus VMP, $n = 930$), which does not support Hypothesis 2 above.
3. Self-rated depressive symptoms versus objective memory scores produced a statistically non-significant correlation ($r = -0.05$, BDI versus SD Free Recall, $n = 1,093$), which does not support Hypothesis 3 above.

Thus, people with depression complain of considerably more memory problems than those without depression. However, their memory complaints reveal almost nothing about their actual memory, as shown by memory test scores. Also, depression is not linked with impaired memory on neuropsychological tests, consistent with the findings of Rohling et al. (2002). Controlling for effort just strengthens the above conclusions. The mean effort score on the WMT [(IR+DR+consistency)/3] correlated at 0.5 with SD Free Recall (i.e., effort affects memory test scores). Mean effort correlated at −0.24 with the BDI score and at −0.32 with VMP (verbal memory problems; i.e., those with the highest self-rated depression also have the highest self-rated memory problems). If we examine only cases making a good effort, as judged by passing the WMT effort subtests, the correlation between SD Free Recall and VMP is non-significant ($r = 0.02$; against Hypothesis 2), and BDI does not correlate significantly with SD Free Recall ($r = 0.08$; against Hypothesis 3). However, the correlation between BDI and VMP remains at $r = 0.45$, in support of Hypothesis 1. Even in those making a full effort on testing, therefore, the only significant result is that self-rated depression is quite strongly correlated with self-rated memory complaints. In some cases, self-reported memory problems are symptoms of depression.

Very similar conclusions were drawn from the database of Dr. Roger Gervais, who provided data from 1942 clinical cases of many different diagnoses, including orthopedic injuries, anxiety based disorders, depression, and chronic pain. Among those passing the WMT there were 394 cases that had also taken the BDI, the MCI, and the CVLT. In these cases, there were no significant correlations between objective memory test scores (SD Free Recall) and either self-rated depression (BDI, $r = -0.01$) or verbal memory complaints (VMP, $r = -0.05$). Yet BDI correlated at 0.47 with VMP. Once again, self-rated depression correlated with self-reported memory problems, in support of Hypothesis 1. But, objectively, there was no relationship between depression and memory test scores, failing to support Hypotheses 2 and 3 above.

The final hypothesis (4) is that, in cases passing effort testing with the WMT, those with depression will have fewer memory complaints than those with severe brain injury or neurological disease. In fact, the mean memory complaints scores on eight out of nine MCI subscales were significantly higher in 68 patients with a primary diagnosis of major depression than in 77 neurological patients with disabling brain diseases, such as strokes and tumors. The depressed patients also had more memory complaints than 83 cases of severe brain injury with posttraumatic amnesia of more than one day. This was found on eight out of nine self-rating scales (for example, verbal memory problems, inability to work because of impaired memory, pain interferes with memory and impairment of remote memory). Thus, Hypothesis 4 is not supported. The only scale which did not differ between groups was the one measuring complaints of amnesia for antisocial behavior (e.g., I hit someone and don't remember doing it). Scores on the latter scale are typically very low in most diagnoses. Amnesia for antisocial behavior tends to be endorsed mainly by substance abusers and people denying responsibility for criminal acts.

The rates of effort test failure in cases of major depression were similar to the failure rates found in all other diagnostic groups tested. In the Gervais database, the failure rate on the WMT effort subtests in 48 cases with major depression was 30%, compared with an overall failure rate of 30% in the whole sample. Similarly, in the database of Green, the WMT failure rate in 126 patients with a primary diagnosis of major depression was 33%, compared with an overall failure rate of 31% in the whole sample of 1307 cases given the computerized WMT. Most were already receiving disability benefits. The presumed incentive in those failing WMT effort tests was to maintain disability benefits.

CLINICAL IMPLICATIONS

As scientists, neuropsychologists believe that evidence-based approaches are likely to be of greater benefit in the long term than untested clinical assumptions. What studies tell us about the relationships between depression, subjective cognitive complaints, objective cognitive impairment, and the effects of poor effort will influence how we interpret self-reports and behavior of the patients whom we assess. A clinician who believes that depression is linked with severe cognitive impairment on objective testing will interpret impaired test scores in a depressed patient differently than a clinician who assumes that major depression has no effect on test scores. A clinician who uses effort tests will often draw quite different conclusions than one who does not use effort tests.

Like any approach based on analysis of data, the above theoretical arguments are impersonal. They are like the facts of anatomy, which is a cold clinical discipline, although it is vital for understanding medical treatments applied to people. When applying our knowledge clinically, we must remain objective but at the same time treat patients with empathy, concern, and respect. As clinicians, we face an intellectual and an emotional challenge when we encounter invalid neuropsychological test results due to poor effort or symptom exaggeration. We face a breakdown in the expected cooperation between the patient and ourselves as psychologists. Does that mean that we dismiss all the concerns the person presents to us? If a person's self-reported cognitive complaints are not accompanied by valid evidence of deficits, does that mean that we take no account of the complaints? If the person scores at worse than chance levels, we have to dismiss the neuropsychological test data as invalid, but do we then also dismiss other information, or all the information about the client? Do we consider *everything* about the client potentially contaminated? One way in which we may handle invalid test results as part of a clinical assessment can be illustrated by consideration of an actual clinical case in which these issues were prominent.

THE CASE OF MS. H.

At the age of 42 years, Ms. H. had been involved in a motor vehicle accident in the course of her work. She believed that she had struck her head, and she felt that this must be responsible for her current "severe cognitive difficulties." In the accident, Ms. H. was driving and slid into the rear end of another vehicle. There was no evidence of loss of consciousness or posttraumatic amnesia. There was no brain abnormality on CT brain scan and no neurological signs were reported in the emergency room notes, where her Glasgow Coma Scale was recorded as 15 an hour after the accident. Given such details, we would not expect to find any permanent neuropsychological deficits (Dikmen et al., 1995; Iverson, 2005; Mittenberg & Roberts, 2008; Rohling, Meyers, & Millis, 2003). The Workers' Compensation Board referred Ms. H. for a neuropsychological assessment, 18 months after the accident, to determine if there was any objective evidence of neuropsychological impairment.

Ms. H. complained of numerous memory problems, which she thought were a result of brain injury and which she claimed were preventing her from working. She said that, before the accident, she was "competent to remember things and handle her own affairs but, for the past 18 months, she had just watched television and hung around the house." Ms. H. reported that, in the past, she had undergone back surgery, a stapled stomach for weight loss, and a tummy tuck. She was already being treated with Oxycontin for pain before the accident, but she said that her pain had increased after the accident. She had cancer of the sinuses, which was in remission after treatment ten years earlier, and she had elevated testosterone. Ms. H. was not working because of her symptoms.

At the time of her accident, she had been employed for eight months as a youth worker in a group home dealing with troubled teenagers. She had been married for about ten years to an alcoholic man who was unfaithful. He allegedly started a fire in the back yard while drunk, causing serious burns to her daughter. Ms. H. left her husband and remained single until an Internet meeting with a 45-year-old never-previously-married man, who lived a thousand miles away. They shared fundamentalist Christian beliefs and had both been lay preachers, but neither were practicing their religion any longer. They were hastily married, but the marriage was barely consummated in the two years they had been living together. Mr. H said that he had never engaged in sexual intercourse before the marriage "because of my religious beliefs." It emerged that Mr. H had his own serious sexual and emotional problems, which greatly affected his relationship with his wife.

Mr. H said that his wife seemed to be "physically wiped out as a result of the accident and subsequent depression." He said: "Now she's a different person. I can't depend on her for financial matters or housework. We make agreements on how to spend money, and she goes off and spends on other things. She forgets things we've agreed on. I have to carry the burden for the family." On the other hand, he had not worked at all since they had been married. Mr. H said that his wife's depression was affecting her physical health. She complained of headaches, neck and shoulder pain, knee pain, and a general lack of energy. She was grinding her teeth at night. He felt that Ms. H. was defensive because "She might not be as smart as she'd like to be" and was not as smart as he was.

In the course of an interview lasting almost three hours, it emerged that Ms. H. was severely depressed. She said: "I've got no desire for anything. I'm lucky to get myself out of bed. I've never been this absolutely useless. Since the accident, I'm good for nothing." She broke down during the interview, expressing a great deal of emotional distress and suffering. Her husband was unruffled and admitted that he could not empathize with his wife, despite her obviously distressed and very sad state. In front of his wife, Mr. H said with a deadpan face and neutral voice tone that he believed that she had become depressed "through her own wrong decisions." That was why he had stopped her from taking the antidepressants prescribed by her family doctor. When Ms. H. said that she felt that she was not a good wife, her husband said, matter-of-factly and callously, "I agree. She is not a good wife."

Although she was sobbing and obviously very distressed, at no point did he offer her any consolation, support, sympathy, or guidance. Mr. H repeatedly contradicted and criticized his wife. He told her that he could never relate to her feelings and could not understand her current sadness. When he said anything, it was invariably self-justifying and pointedly critical of his wife. Mr. H admitted that he had a problem communicating and empathizing with other people. Ms. H. said that the only thing that they used to have in common was their religious beliefs, but now neither of them was practicing those beliefs, and they had nothing in common. Near the end of the interview, she told him directly with much feeling: "You must leave me, so that I can heal."

In short, Ms. H. was presenting as a woman with severe depression, with feelings of worthlessness and hopelessness, lack of motivation, tearfulness, loss of drive, and a marriage in crisis. Another chapter might be written about her possible Axis II personality disorder, but she was severely depressed. Her husband did not think she had suffered a brain injury in the accident and said, "It is her choices that made her this way" (probably not intending to imply her choice of living with him). I tried to persuade Mr. H to allow his wife to take antidepressant medication and go for psychological treatment. These treatment recommendations were included in my report to the referral source (WCB), as such referrals typically involve requests for treatment recommendations. Superficially, Mr. H agreed, but he remained openly critical of antidepressant medication, and he still denied his wife's need for any form of treatment.

Dr. K, a psychiatrist, stated that Ms. H. had presented herself as "a very depressed lady." He stated, "I think Ms. H. has had a very hard life. She has been a single parent. She has had an unsatisfactory marriage. She has been disappointed in her ambition, and she has lost two babies in the past. I would think she is a woman who was depressed before the accident, but fought this off by becoming very overactive, altruistic and, although she denies it, self-denying. I think she puts other people first." He recommended psychiatric treatment but did not think that her depression was accident related.

Tests used

Test scores were not presented in the clinical report, but they are shown in Tables 12.1–12.3.

Table 12.1 shows beyond any reasonable doubt that Ms. H. was not making sufficient effort to produce valid data. Her scores were extremely low on very easy tasks.

Table 12.2 shows that she was choosing to do poorly, especially on memory tests, corresponding with her self-report of major memory problems, the only exception being Warrington's RMT for Faces.

Table 12.3 shows that, on average, her scores were about half a standard deviation below the normative comparison groups. This is disproportionate to the severity of her head injury. Those in this sample with severe brain injuries scored about half a standard deviation below the normal mean, when averaged across many neuropsychological test scores (Green, Rohling, Lees-Haley, & Allen, 2001; Rohling, Meyers, & Millis, 2003). Note that her mean Z-score across all the memory

TABLE 12.1   Ms. H. failed most tests containing effort measures

TEST	SUBTEST	MS. H.	DEMENTIA PATIENTS, AGE 78	EFFORT (PASS/FAIL)
Word Memory Test	Immediate Recognition	40%	71%	Fail (Below chance)
	Delayed Recognition	60%	65%	Fail
	Multiple Choice	40%	27%	Fail
	Paired Associates	30%	22%	Fail
Computerized Test of Response Bias	Total Score	43%	–	Fail (Below chance)
California Verbal Learning Test	Recognition Hits	4/16	–	Fail (Below chance)
Digit Span	Reliable Digit Span (RDS)	6	–	Fail

Note: RDS was first described by Greiffenstein, Baker, and Gola (1994).

TABLE 12.2 Ms. H.'s scores on selected memory tests

TEST	SUBTEST	MS. H.	DEMENTIA PATIENTS, AGE 78	PERCENTILE	Z-SCORE
California Verbal Learning Test	Short Delay Recall	6	–	1%ile	–2.3
	Long Delay Recall	6		2%ile	–2.0
Warrington (RMT)	Faces	48	–	91%ile	1.3
Rey Complex Figure Test	Copy	–	–	16%ile	–0.1
	Immediate Recall	–	–	3%ile	–1.9
Word Memory Test	Free Recall	20% correct	10.4% correct	1%ile	–2.3
	Delayed Free Recall	15% correct	–	1%ile	–2.3
MEAN OF MEMORY TESTS					**–1.4**

Note: WMT and Warrington RMT–Faces percentiles are based on 640 outpatients passing WMT effort subtests and with mean scores above 8 on CVLT short and long delayed free recall.

TABLE 12.3 Ms. H.'s scores on other neuropsychological tests

TEST	SUBTEST	SCORE	PERCENTILE	Z-SCORE
Multidimensional Aptitude Battery	Verbal IQ	94	34%ile	–0.4
	Performance IQ	81	10%ile	–1.3
	Full Scale IQ	87	19%ile	–0.9
Wide Range Achievement Test–3	Reading	–	55%ile	0.13
	Arithmetic	–	18%ile	–0.9
Wechsler Memory Scale Revised	Digit Span forward	–	16%ile	–1.0
	Digit Span back	–	3%ile	–1.9
Trail Making Test (TMT)	A	22 secs.	71%ile	0.6
	B	46 secs.	85%ile	1.0
Alberta Smell Test	Right nostril	3/10	3%ile	–1.9
	Left nostril	3/10	7%ile	–1.5
Category Test	Total errors	45 errors	48%ile	–0.05
Gorham's Proverb Interpretation	–	–	35%ile	–0.4
Grip Strength (GS) Right (preferred)	–	25.5 kg	31%ile	–0.5
Grip Strength (GS) Left	–	20.5 kg	18%ile	–0.9
Grooved Pegboard (GP) Right	–	66 secs.	54%ile	0.1
Grooved Pegboard (GP) Left	–	70 secs.	43%ile	–0.2
Emotional Perception Test (EPT)	–	12 errors	68%ile	0.5
MEAN OF ALL TESTS	–	–	30%ile	**–0.52**

Note: TMT, EPT, GS, and GP percentiles based on 297 women outpatients passing Word Memory Test effort subtests and with mean scores above 8 on California Verbal Learning Test short and long delayed free recall.

tests (other than the effort tests) was –1.4 (Table 12.2), which is even lower than her performance across the non-memory neuropsychological tests (–0.5). Such results suggest a heightened tendency to exaggerate difficulties on tests that appear to measure memory.

Even children with a verbal intelligence below 70 scored above 90% correct on the WMT Immediate Recognition subtest (Windows program; Green, 2003), but Ms. H. scored only 40% correct. Note that Ms. H. also scored far lower than 78-year-old patients with dementia on the extremely easy WMT Immediate and Delayed Recognition subtests (Table 12.1). Yet, inconsistently, she scored higher than the dementia patients on the more difficult subtests (Multiple Choice, Paired

Associates, and Free Recall). This is precisely the same pattern found in simulators, who are asked to simulate memory impairment in experimental studies (e.g., Green, 2003). It is the same pattern, on average, produced by large numbers of cases which fail WMT when tested clinically, as part of a compensation or disability insurance claim. WMT failure is invariably not explainable by low ability, but it is explainable based on an external incentive to appear impaired, usually to obtain disability payments (Flaro, Green, & Robertson, in press).

Self-rating scales used

Larrabee (2003) reported elevations in symptom exaggerators on the Minnesota Multiphasic Personality Inventory–2 (MMPI–2) scales 1, 2, 3, 7, and 8. Ms. H. had elevated scores on seven MMPI–2 clinical scales, including scales 1 (T 69), 2 (T 96), 3 (T 92), 4 (T 79), 6 (T 70), 7 (T 83), and 8 (T 85), with validity scales of T 52 on L, T 68 on F, and T 50 on K. A tendency toward being manipulative might be inferred from the high scale 4 score. On the FBS scale (Lees-Haley, English, & Glenn, 1991) Ms. H. scored 26, which is consistent with an 87% probability of poor effort (Greiffenstein, Baker, Axelrod, Peck, & Gervais, 2004), assuming a 50% base rate for poor effort. The original experimental MMPI–2 Response Bias Scale (RBS; Gervais, Ben-Porath, Wygant, & Green, 2007) consisted of 41 items from the MMPI–2, which best predicted WMT failure in over 1200 outpatients. On the RBS, Ms. H. scored 21, implying an 85% probability of failure on WMT.

Ms. H.'s mean score on the Memory Complaints Inventory (MCI) was 50%, which is considerably higher than the mean of 28% (SD = 16) for patients with severe brain injuries who passed the WMT. Her score was higher than the mean of 32% (SD = 16) in depressed patients passing WMT and higher than the mean of 42% (SD = 18) from depressed patients who failed the WMT. Ms. H. obtained the following elevated scores on the Symptom Checklist–90–R: somatization (71), obsessive-compulsive (71), depression (75), interpersonal sensitivity (71), hostility (73), and psychoticism (77). Her score on the Beck Depression Inventory (BDI) was very high at 39.

The section below contains an abbreviated version of sections of the actual clinical report, with identifying information removed or altered. The section concerning effort test results is reported just as it appeared in the original clinical report, to illustrate one approach to describing effort test data and their implications, while protecting test security.

EXCERPTS FROM CLINICAL REPORT

Interpretation

When people are severely depressed, their mood can distort the way they think and affect the decisions they make. I had a great deal of sympathy with Ms. H., who was obviously suffering from depression and needed help. Unfortunately, when she was given tests of the amount of effort she was applying to testing, it was very clear that Ms. H. was not making a full effort. This cannot be explained simply on the basis of depression because depression, in itself, does not cause a person to fail such tests.

On an extremely simple verbal memory test, on which adults with mental retardation scored an average of 96%, her score was only 60% (Flaro, Green, & Robertson, in press). On this test, Ms. H. was performing far worse than patients with severe brain injuries or brain tumors, worse than young children with disabling clinical conditions, and worse than inpatients with advanced dementia. It was quite clear from these results that Ms. H. was not putting forth sufficient effort to produce valid test results. On another test, she scored significantly worse than chance (i.e., deliberately picking wrong answers). If a person were responding in a purely random way, they would have to take the test a hundred times before they obtained one score as low as that obtained by Ms. H.

On a third test that contained measures of memory and effort, it looked as if she had severe memory impairment. However, her effort was clearly unsatisfactory. Again, she produced a score that was significantly worse than would be obtained by chance alone. Therefore, it is very likely that her other test results, especially memory test scores, considerably underestimated her actual capabilities. They will be reported, however, for the sake of completeness.

On intelligence testing, Ms. H. scored only in the low average range, and this is probably an underestimate of her actual abilities. Basic reading was found to be average, and mathematical abilities were low average. On a test involving learning a list of 16 words, Ms. H.'s initial learning was in the extremely low range, and her memory was in the impaired range. However, on a built-in measure of effort (recognition hits), she scored worse than the mean chance score. In other words, it is very likely that she knew the correct answers and was choosing the incorrect answers. On one visual memory test (WRMT Faces), her score was superior, but on another visual memory test, her score was impaired (RCFT).

According to the criteria of Slick, Sherman, and Iverson (1999), she would be described as malingering neurocognitive dysfunction (MND). That is, she was deliberately failing cognitive tests in the context of a financial claim, and her complaints were disproportionate to the accident details. The neuropsychological test results produced by Ms. H. cannot be regarded as valid or reliable.

Results within the normal range were observed on several tests, but even these test scores likely underestimate her actual capabilities. Explaining the meanings of proverbs (Gorham's Proverbs) was at the lower end of the average range; complex problem solving (Category Test) was also at the lower end of the average range; judgment of emotion in tone of voice was average, consistent with her choice of occupation; on a test involving visual search and alternating mental set, which is sensitive to recently acquired impairment (Trail Making B), her score was above average; manipulation of small pegs with either hand alone was average on both hands; grip strength was average on the right hand and low average on the left hand. On a test of short-term auditory attention and working memory, Ms. H.'s score was in the impaired range, but this result is of doubtful validity. Sense of smell is very vulnerable to severe brain injury. Ms. H.'s ability to identify odors presented separately to each nostril was at a borderline level on both nostrils, but these scores are also of questionable validity, owing to poor effort.

On the Beck Depression Inventory, Ms. H. obtained a score suggesting a very severe degree of depression. She reported symptoms of depression on the SCL–90–R symptom checklist, in addition to feelings of hostility, somatic concern, cognitive difficulties, interpersonal problems, and even possible psychotic symptoms, although she did not display psychotic symptoms on interviewing. She endorsed the idea that something was wrong with her mind.

On a memory complaints inventory, she reported numerous memory problems, including being unable to work because of impaired memory. Such high levels of memory complaints are typical for people who are depressed (but they are also found in people who are grossly exaggerating symptoms). It is important to make a distinction between subjective memory complaints versus objective memory impairment. Depression involves a large amount of subjective memory complaints, but, if effort is good, it is typically found that the person's cognitive abilities, including memory, are objectively no different than they were prior to their depression.

On the MMPI–2 personality profile, Ms. H. obtained elevated scores on scales measuring symptoms of depression and anxiety (2 and 7). This was considered to be an accurate reflection of her current state based on clinical observations. She obtained an elevated score on a scale measuring somatoform concerns (3), meaning that she was inclined to express physical complaints when under psychological stress. She also obtained an elevated score on a scale measuring feelings of distrust towards others (6) and a high score on a scale measuring a tendency to be manipulative (4). Her scores on two MMPI–2 scales sensitive to symptom exaggeration (FBS and RBS) both indicated symptom exaggeration.

Summary and conclusions

Ms. H. was found to be severely depressed, based on her behavior and self-reports. She presented her depression as being a direct result of her motor vehicle accident injuries, causing some increase in pre-existing back pain and marked cognitive complaints. She had been treated for pain previously and stated that her pain had increased since the accident. She was primarily complaining of severe cognitive difficulties, which was why she would be unable to work. Most importantly, however, Ms. H. was reporting many symptoms of depression, including feeling that she was a failure as a wife and mother, loss of drive, a pervasive sense of hopelessness, and despair. She expressed these emotions during the interview.

It was striking that her husband found himself apparently completely incapable of empathizing with his wife. He admitted that he had no ability to comprehend his wife's feelings or to sympathize with her. He said that he always tried to be logical and analytical, rather than emotional. It was very notable that, whereas his wife was sobbing and expressing genuine severe emotional distress and suffering, he was unable to offer her any solace or sympathy. On the contrary, Mr. H criticized her openly and blamed her for being depressed, saying that her depression was because of the decisions that she had made. Mr. H appeared to be incapable of establishing an emotional relationship with his new wife. Their relationship was in ruins. Ms. H. openly told him in my presence that, in order for her to heal, he must leave and go back to California. I recommended to Ms. H. that she should take the antidepressant medication that had been prescribed for her. [End of quote from clinical report]

DISCUSSION

In the context of a WCB claim, Ms. H. attributed her depression and subjective cognitive complaints to a brain injury, when there was actually no objective evidence to support the claim. It is likely that Ms. H. believed that she had cognitive impairment because self-rated memory complaints are highly correlated with self-reported symptoms of depression. On the other hand, depression, in itself, could not explain her severely lowered test scores on the neuropsychological battery (Rohling et al., 2002). According to the analyses earlier in this chapter, we would not expect impaired neuropsychological test results just because a patient is depressed. In fact, now that we know that effort can have a greater effect on test scores than severe brain injury, poor effort is the first thing to rule out if impairment is observed (Green et al., 2001).

Ms. H. produced some impaired scores on testing but they were assumed to be invalid because of her very poor effort test scores. She produced worse than chance scores on some tests, and she was not being honest when she flatly denied making anything less than a full effort on testing. Some of her scores on the CARB and WMT were considerably worse than expected from people suffering a severe brain injury and worse than people with advanced dementia. Her low scores were a function of poor effort and not depression (Rohling et al., 2002).

In failing the WMT, CARB, and CVLT Recognition Hits, she was scoring far lower than people with severe brain injuries. Ms. H. was malingering cognitive impairment (i.e., faking impairment, presumably to obtain money from WCB). It was very likely that she was also exaggerating her symptoms in general, including her depressive symptoms. Her self-reports were not reliable because she said that she was making a full effort, and it was apparent that she was not doing so. Independently of her symptom self-reporting, there was other information to consider, including her past history, her current marital crisis, and her behavior and emotional expressions in the interview. Based on the latter considerations, Ms. H. was judged to have valid problems, and it was felt that she was suffering psychologically. However, it would have been doing her and the referral source a disservice, and it would have been factually incorrect, if we had concluded that her impaired test scores reflected a disabling brain injury.

A benevolent interpretation of Ms. H.'s behavior during the assessment would be that her malingering of neurocognitive dysfunction resulted from poor judgment in a woman who was genuinely severely depressed. There was motivation to exaggerate her deficits on testing. She feared losing her Workers' Compensation Board benefits and knew that she would probably have few other benefits if they ended. Speculations about why she failed effort tests, however, are not essential to the conclusion that her test results were invalid and did not reflect her actual capabilities.

The detailed interview led to the identification of other non-injury factors, which were probably largely responsible for her depression, including heredity, a past abusive marriage, pre-existing pain, and serious incompatibility with her current husband. In a woman with cluster B personality features, there was evidence of major depression in the middle of a situational crisis. Her husband's bizarre belief that she had caused her own depression and his lack of empathy led him to deny her antidepressants, prescribed by her physician. Recommendations for individual psychological support, marital counseling, and antidepressants were made. Despite Ms. H.'s worse than chance scores and malingered cognitive deficits, she did continue to receive financial and therapeutic support from WCB for a limited time, but she was not classified as a case of brain injury. The main consequence of Ms. H.'s failure on effort tests was that the neuropsychological test results were laid aside as being unreliable. They were not interpreted as representing valid evidence of brain injury. Other clinical facts were gathered and interpreted independently of the neuropsychological test data but with the knowledge that she was distorting her symptom presentation. Apart from her self-reported cognitive complaints and her neuropsychological test scores, the validity of which was in doubt, there was no objective evidence to suggest brain injury as the cause of her problems. An important finding in this case is that genuine psychopathology may co-exist with malingering; they are not mutually exclusive (also see Morgan & Gervais, this volume, chapter 11).

REFERENCES

Delis, D. C., Kramer, J. H., Kaplan, E., & Ober, B. (1987). *The California Verbal Learning Test, Research Edition*. New York: The Psychological Corporation.

Dikmen, S. S., Machamer, J. E., Winn, H. R., & Temkin, N. R. (1995). Neuropsychological outcome at one year post head injury. *Neuropsychology*, 9, 80–90.

Drane, D., Williamson, D. J., Stroup E. S., Holmes, M. D., Jung, M., Koerner, E., Chaytor, N., Wilensky, A. J., & Miller, J. W. (2006). Cognitive impairment is not equal in patients with epileptic and psychogenic nonepileptic seizures. *Epilepsia*, 47(11), 1879–86.

Flaro, L., Green, P., & Robertson, E. (2007). Word Memory Test failure 23 times higher in mild brain injury than parents seeking custody: The power of external incentives. *Brain Injury*, 21(4), 373–383.

Frances, A., Pincus, H. A., First, M. B., & the DSM–IV task force (1994). *Diagnostic and statistical manual of mental disorders*. Washington, DC: American Psychiatric Association.

Gervais, R., Ben-Porath, Y., Wygant, J., & Green, P. (2007). Development and validation of the Response Bias Scale (RBS) for the MMPI–2. *Assessment*, 14, 196–208.

Green, P. (2003). *Green's Word Memory Test for Windows: User's manual*. Edmonton, Canada: Green's Publishing.

Green, P. (2004). *Memory Complaints Inventory for Windows*. Edmonton, Canada: Green's Publishing.

Green, P., & Allen, L. (1997). *Memory Complaints Inventory (DOS version)*, Durham, NC: CogniSyst.

Green, P., Allen, L., & Astner, K. (1996). *Manual for the Computerized Word Memory Test*. Durham, NC: Cognisyst.

Green. P., & Astner, K. (1995). *Manual for the Oral Word Memory Test*. Durham, NC: CogniSyst.

Green, P., Rohling, M. L., Lees-Haley, P. R., & Allen L. M. (2001). Effort has a greater effect on test scores than severe brain injury in compensation claimants. *Brain Injury*, *15*(12), 1045–1060.

Greiffenstein, M., Baker, J., Axelrod B., Peck, E. & Gervais, R. (2004). The Fake Bad Scale and MMPI–2 F-Family in detection of implausible psychological trauma claims. *The Clinical Neuropsychologist*, *18*(4), 573–590.

Greiffenstein, M., Baker, W. J., & Gola, T. (1994). Validation of malingered amnesia measures with a large clinical sample. *Psychological Assessment*, *6*(3), 218–224.

Iverson, G. (2005). Outcomes from mild traumatic brain injury. *Current Opinions in Psychiatry*, *18*, 301–317.

Larrabee, G. J. (2003). Exaggerated MMPI–2 symptom report in personal injury litigants with malingered neurocognitive deficit. *Archives of Clinical Neuropsychology*, *18*, 673–686.

Lees-Haley, P. R., English, L. T., & Glenn, W. J. (1991). A fake-bad scale for the MMPI–2 for personal injury claimants. *Psychological Reports*, *68*, 203–210.

Mittenberg, W., & Roberts, D. M. (2008). Mild traumatic brain injury and postconcussion syndrome. In J. E. Morgan & J. H. Ricker (Eds.). *Textbook of clinical neuropsychology*. New York: Taylor & Francis.

Neu, P., Bajbouj, M., Schilling, A., Godemann, F., Berman, R. M., & Schlattmann, P. (2005). Cognitive function over the treatment course of depression in middle-aged patients: correlation with brain MRI signal hyperintensities. *Journal of Psychiatric Research*, *39*(2), 129–35.

Rohling, M. L., Green, P., Allen, L. M., & Iverson, G. L. (2002). Depressive symptoms and neurocognitive test scores in patients passing symptom validity tests. *Archives of Clinical Neuropsychology*, *17*(3), 205–222.

Rohling, M. L., Meyers, J. E., & Millis, S. R. (2003). Neuropsychological impairment following traumatic brain injury: A dose response analysis. *The Clinical Neuropsychologist*, *17*(3), 289–302.

Slick, D., Sherman, E., & Iverson, G. (1999). Diagnostic criteria for malingered neurocognitive dysfunction: Proposed standards for clinical practice and research. *The Clinical Neuropsychologist*, *13*(4), 545–561.

Veiel, H. (1997). A preliminary profile of neuropsychological deficits associated with major depression. *Journal of Clinical and Experimental Neuropsychology*, *19*(4), 587–603.

Feigning mental disorders with concomitant cognitive deficits

13

Richard Rogers and Scott D. Bender

CONCEPTUAL ISSUES

Forensic evaluations must systematically evaluate the accuracy and completeness of the clinical data. Response styles, such as malingering, may grossly distort the clinical presentation and purported impairment. This chapter examines the complex interplay of malingered depression and feigned cognitive impairment in a disability referral.

Rogers (1997) underscored the importance of aligning detection strategies with broad domains of malingering. This chapter focuses on two domains (mental disorders and cognitive impairment), with the third domain (medical complaints) being beyond its scope. According to Rogers and Vitacco (2002), persons feigning a mental disorder must grapple with several related decisions: (1) which symptoms to create, (2) the progression of symptoms over time, (3) the purported impairment arising from these symptoms, and (4) their insight and awareness of these symptoms. In sharp contrast, persons feigning a cognitive impairment face a comparatively simpler task. Instead of creating a believable mental disorder, they must appear to put forth an apparent effort while failing at one or more cognitive skills. These "effortful failures" must be plausible, taking into account the complexity of the cognitive tasks. Differences in malingered presentations (i.e., elaborate fabrications of symptoms vs. effortful failures on cognitive tasks) require very different detection strategies. For instance, a detection strategy relying on bogus symptoms is ineffective at detecting effortful failures.

Detection strategies

Rogers and Bender (2003) identified eight detection strategies for feigned mental disorders. *Rare symptoms* rely on symptoms that occur very infrequently among genuine patients. *Improbable symptoms* are more extreme than rare symptoms because of their total implausibility. *Symptom combinations* capitalize on unusual pairs of symptoms that hardly ever occur together. *Indiscriminant symptom endorsement* relies on the blanket endorsement of symptoms by some malingerers. *Symptom severity* identifies feigners by the type and proportion of symptoms reported to be "extreme" or "unbearable." *Obvious versus subtle symptoms* distinguishes feigners by their overendorsement of blatant symptoms (e.g., suicidal thoughts) in contrast to less-identifiable symptoms (e.g., early morning awakening). *Erroneous stereotypes* take advantage of common misconceptions about mental disorders to identify malingerers. *Reported versus observed symptoms* examine marked discrepancies between the patient's account and clinical observations; the characteristic pattern for malingerers is a markedly more impaired account than noted in clinical observations.

Detection strategies for feigned cognitive impairment are fundamentally different from those used with malingered mental disorders. Rogers and Bender (2003) identified two domains of detection strategies: excessive impairment and unexpected patterns. These domains will be evaluated separately.

Within the domain of excessive impairment, three strategies emerge: (1) floor effect, (2) symptom validity testing (SVT), and (3) forced-choice testing (FCT). *Floor effect* capitalizes on items that are too easy to be failed, even by cognitively impaired persons. This strategy, widely used both in measures of feigned cognitive impairment and in some standard measures of neurocognitive function, can be moderately effective at identifying likely dissimulation but is vulnerable to coaching. *Symptom validity testing* (SVT) uses improbable failure rate. SVT is typically tested in a two-choice format in which feigning is detected by failure significantly below chance. Estimated in terms of probability, SVT can provide compelling evidence of feigned cognitive impairment in extreme cases of poor performance. For example, the consulting psychologist may conclude that there is a 98% probability that an individual with no short-term memory whatsoever would achieve such a low score. In contrast, *Forced-choice testing* (FCT) examines group differences on feigning measures between genuine patients and malingerers. Sometimes referred to as "empirical floor," the idea is to select a cut score on a neuropsychological measure below which very few genuinely impaired clients will score. The FCT must be exhaustively evaluated across a full range of neuropsychological impairments, taking into account comorbid conditions, such as Axis I disorders, and medical conditions. Bianchini, Mathias, and Greve (2001) provide an excellent overview of neuropsychological measures with utility estimates for SVT (below chance performance) and FCT (below empirical ground). From our perspective, FCT results should not be used in forensic practice. Unlike SVT and other detection strategies, FCT is based solely on unexpectedly poor results. As such, it is incumbent on clinicians to rule out systematically cognitive impairments (e.g., learning disabilities and intellectual deficits), comorbid disorders, and medical conditions.

The second domain, unexpected patterns, is represented by six cognitively-based detection strategies. *Performance curve* examines the patient's level of success with test items of increasing difficulty. Genuine patients typically produce a characteristic curve that often decreases sharply with more difficult items; malingerers often do not take into account item difficulty and produce much flatter curves. *Magnitude of error* examines the extent to which a response is incorrect. Combinations of near misses and/or gross errors can strongly suggest feigning. Recent research by Bender and Rogers (2004) suggests that this strategy may be highly effective at identifying feigned cognitive impairment. *Violation of learning principles* capitalizes on established rules regarding knowledge acquisition. One learning principle is that free recall is more difficult than recognition; blatant violations of this principle are indicative of feigning. *Consistency across comparable items* assesses the possibility of feigning by examining uncharacteristic variability. This strategy is not generally recommended because of the challenges in establishing truly comparable items. *Atypical presentation* examines whether the pattern of test scores or reported impairments is consistent with other patients with similar histories. For instance, it is unusual for appreciable cognitive dysfunction to persist beyond 30 days in cases of concussion or mild brain injury (Binder, Rohling, & Larrabee, 1997). Therefore, an individual presenting for testing three to four months post-injury with no positive findings on brain MRI, a Glasgow Coma Scale score of >13, very brief or no loss of consciousness, but significant impairments on neuropsychological testing likely has a non-neurogenic etiology of his or her deficits.[1] This detection strategy must be used judiciously because many genuine patients evidence uncharacteristic patterns of performance on neuropsychological measures.

---

[1] Of course, the effects of genuine mental disorders on cognitive test scores must be considered in these cases as well.

In summary, the malingering of mental disorders and cognitive impairment are best conceptualized as distinct domains that have domain-specific detection strategies. In the next section, we examine complicated cases that may implicate both domains.

Complex cases

Many malingerers appear relatively unsophisticated in their efforts at feigning, producing improbable symptoms and concomitant impairment. Often the easiest to recognize are those one-dimensional malingerers that adopt the "kitchen sink" approach, indiscriminantly fabricating symptoms and concomitant impairments. In contrast, other malingerers may present a more complex approach involving both disorders and impairments, which may span the domains of mental disorders and cognitive impairments. Two common variants are outlined:

1. *Genuine disorder with feigned cognitive impairment*: With this variant, malingerers have genuine disorders that they describe with little or no embellishment. Instead, they focus on the concomitant impairments, grossly exaggerating the effects of their disorders. As a notable example, a male dentist on full disability described plausibly his mild anxiety symptoms. However, he claimed that this anxiety diminished his concentration and capacity to think clearly about dental procedures. While the anxiety is likely true, the purported impairment in cognitive abilities is strongly questioned.
2. *Feigned disorder with feigned cognitive impairment*: With this variant, malingerers fabricate or grossly exaggerate both the disorders and the resulting impairments. Some malingerers will feign a mood disorder, such as depression, and will also falsify their concomitant impairment. Malingerers may bridge several domains when the simulated disorder "results" in feigned cognitive impairment.

The following case study exemplifies the latter version with both feigned disorder and impairment. The purpose of the disability evaluation was to ascertain whether Mr. I. was genuinely impaired and could no longer function as a senior systems analyst. Issues of medical complaints and intermittent pain were not addressed in this consultation. However, medical opinions, based on extensive surveillance, found his normal level of physical activity was highly inconsistent with his reported impairments.

THE CASE OF MR. I.

Mr. I., a 55-year-old European American, was involved in a motor vehicle accident in May of 1993 from which he had lower back pain and soreness. These symptoms gradually worsened over the next three years, leading to reports of limited physical activity and severe intermittent pain. In 1997, Mr. I. went on total disability from his work as a senior systems analyst. He is currently receiving $6000 per month in disability payments.

The motor vehicle accident involved Mr. I. being rear-ended while sitting in commuter traffic on a Chicago highway. The inattentive driver of the other vehicle apparently hit Mr. I.'s car while traveling at a relatively slow speed (less than 20 miles per hour). Mr. I. did not lose consciousness, and no brain CT scans were performed. He received emergency services and was subsequently released from the hospital on the following day.

Mr. I. had successfully completed his college degree with a major in business (3.20 average on a four-point scale) from the University of Kansas. He had moved quickly from computer programming to executive positions. After 20 years, he was an executive vice president for a computer company. He left this firm to form his own consulting firm, which was highly successful. At the time of his accident, Mr. I. had recently sold his successful consulting firm and was working for a competitor as a senior systems analyst.

The psychological component of the disability claim was Mr. I.'s severe depression and concomitant anxiety disorder that compromised his ability to be gainfully employed. The neuropsychological component of his claim involved complaints of marked problems with his attention, concentration, and memory functions.

Previous neuropsychological evaluation

Mr. I. had requested his own neuropsychological evaluation presumably to assist with treatment and strengthen his disability claim. Occurring eight years after the accident, his evaluation was conducted by Dr. D.D. on four separate days *spanning a three-month period*. According to Dr. D.D., this unusual span was due to Mr. I.'s reported distress and capacity to focus for sustained periods.

Mr. I.'s presenting problems were surveyed via an unpublished Psychological Symptom Checklist on which he endorsed most symptoms as occurring frequently. While this level of endorsement is suggestive of *indiscriminant symptom endorsement*, we found no malingering research on the Psychological Symptom Checklist. On the unpublished Neurocognitive Symptom Checklist, Mr. I. reported that the following symptoms occurred frequently: decreased attention, concentration, memory, naming, word-finding problems, slowed thinking, difficulty with decision making and problem solving, reversing letters and numbers, confusion, and losing his train of thought. In general, symptom checklists do not include any validated indicators of malingering or other response styles. Our searches of PsycInfo did not reveal any research on either checklist, including their diagnostic validity and vulnerability to response styles.

Dr. D.D. administered portions of the WAIS–R and examined the results using the 1991 *Comprehensive Norms for an Expanded Halstead-Reitan Battery and Supplement* (Heaton, Grant, & Matthews, 1991) (Table 13.1).

Upon inspection of the scaled scores alone, it appears that the patient's scores were generally worse on Performance subtests of the WAIS–R. However, after making demographic corrections for sex, age, and education, T scores reveal that his verbal scores are markedly impaired, while performance-based skills are less impaired. This pattern is highly unusual in patients with true brain injury, as crystallized abilities (i.e., largely verbal abilities as assessed by the WAIS–R) are less susceptible to these injuries than are fluid abilities, such as nonverbal reasoning. Mr. I.'s scores reflect an *atypical presentation*. His Vocabulary subtest score, the single most brain-injury resistant subtest on the WAIS–R, is the *lowest* in the profile (again, when corrected for age, sex, and education).

TABLE 13.1   WAIS–R results interpreted

SUBTEST	T SCORE	ADJUSTED SCALED SCORE
Information	28	8
Digit Span	27	6
Longest Digits Forward		5 (raw)
Longest Digits Backward		3 (raw)
Vocabulary	25	7
Comprehension	28	7
Picture Completion	34	6
Block Design	32	5
Digit Symbol	34	4

In contrast, one of the most sensitive subtests to brain injury, Digit Symbol, is his *highest* score from the WAIS–R. As further evidence of an *atypical presentation*, some researchers (Millis et al., 1998; Mittenberg et al., 1995) have reported that a Vocabulary/Digit Span split (with Digit Span being the lower score) of two scaled scores *is atypical* for genuine patients.[2] Similarly, Mr. I.'s Reliable Digits Span (RDS) score[3] was 8, a score that has been shown to have good sensitivity (82%), but poor specificity (54%) when used in malingering detection (Greiffenstein, Baker, & Gola, 1994).

Mr. I. was also administered five tests from the Halstead-Reitan battery (Table 13.2).

Dr. D.D.'s report did not address Mr. I.'s questionable performance on the Tactual Performance Test (TPT). As a *violation of a learning principle*, it is quite unusual for an individual to recall just 4 blocks (T score = 31), but then correctly recall the locations of 3 of the 4 blocks (T score = 48). Moreover, the Location score from the TPT is purported to be one of the most sensitive measures of cerebral dysfunction in the Halstead-Reitan battery, yet this score is the highest (i.e., least impaired) in Mr. I.'s profile.

Mr. I.'s T scores from motor testing (Hand Dynamometer; Grooved Pegboard) suggest profound deficits in grip strength, dexterity, and coordination, such that his ability to dress and feed himself, drive, and shave would likely be seriously affected. These findings are markedly inconsistent with Mr. I.'s reported functioning. He describes himself engaging a normal range of activities, albeit with less enjoyment because of his putative depression.

Because of his apparent memory problems, subtests of the WMS–III were also administered (Table 13.3).

Auditory Recognition–Delayed was well below expectations. While he retained 100% of the information presented during the VPA task (a performance that places him at approximately the 75th percentile) and 63% on LM (25th percentile), his Recognition memory score for the same stimuli falls around the 5th percentile. This pattern reveals a likely *violation of learning principles*: Both in healthy individuals and in most patients, recognition memory is facilitated by cuing and is an easier task than a free recall task; as such it should not yield a poorer performance.

Dr. D.D. concluded that Mr. I. warranted the diagnoses of Cognitive Disorder, Not Otherwise Specified, and Adjustment Disorder with Mixed Anxiety and Depressed Mood. Despite these diagnoses, she reported elsewhere that Mr. I. had "severe depression with suicidal ideation."

TABLE 13.2 Summary of T scores and adjusted scaled scores

TEST	T SCORE	ADJUSTED SCALED SCORE
Category Test	25	2
Trail-Making Test–A (sec)	24	3
Trail-Making Test–B (sec)	23	3
Tactual Performance Test (min/block)	30	4
Tactual Performance Test (Memory)	31	5
Tactual Performance Test (Location)	48	9
Hand Dynamometer (dominant)	33	8
Hand Dynamometer (nondominant)	34	8
Grooved Pegboard (dominant)	19	2
Grooved Pegboard (nondominant)	23	2

[2] Cautious interpretation is warranted as this technique has not yielded particularly robust classification rates (e.g., 71–79%).
[3] RDS = sum of the longest string of digits repeated without error over two trials under both forward and backward conditions.

TABLE 13.3 Raw and scaled scores for subtests of the WMS–III

SUBTEST	RAW SCORE	SCALED SCORE
Logical Memory I	26	6
Verbal Paired Associates I	11	7
Logical Memory II	12	7
Verbal Paired Associates II	4	8
Auditory Recognition–Delayed	43	5

Without providing the basis of her determinations, she also concluded Mr. I. was not malingering and had put forth good effort. Regarding his disability, Dr. D.D. determined that Mr. I. was totally disabled from both his depressed mood and cognitive impairment.

Current evaluation

The first author conducted a psychological evaluation as part of an Independent Medical Examination. Mr. I. had been on full disability for the eight years preceding the evaluation. The referral issues involved Mr. I.'s current diagnoses, impairment, and response style (e.g., malingering). Neuropsychological assessment was beyond his expertise and would be subsequently performed by a separate consultant. Key methods and findings are summarized in the subsequent sections.

Observations

Mr. I. was coherent, logical, and relevant in his speech. His rate of speech appeared slightly slowed but not to the extent that interactions were strained. His command and use of language were commensurate with his college education. No signs of formal thought disorder (e.g., derailment, neologisms, or impaired understanding) were observed. No psychotic content was noted in his verbalizations. He attended well to instructions and was able to recall earlier interactions without any difficulty.

On both evaluation times, Mr. I. expressed both verbally and through facial expressions that he was experiencing physical discomfort and pain. When walking in my presence, he walked slowly with small uneven steps and apparent discomfort (i.e., antalgic gait). A staff person with no knowledge of the case observed a marked disparity between his walking in my presence and his rapid, apparently unimpeded pacing when outside on a smoking break. In the latter case, no signs of distress were observed.

Mr. I. expressed little emotion during his assessment. During the first consultation, he expressed sadness and mild frustration at his current circumstances. His mood was unremarkable in the second consultation. Moreover, he did not appear depressed during either consultation.

In addition to clinical observations, the Cognitive Capacity Screening Examination (CCSE; Jacobs, Bernhard, Delgado, & Strain, 1977) was administered to assess his mental status; his overall score (20) is minimally above the impaired range. The question arises about whether Mr. I. was putting forth good effort. He evidenced very good short-term memory throughout structured interviews, but failed at a simple task of remembering a three-digit number after a very brief delay (5–10 seconds). His response was very atypical: "5–7–3" was reported as "9–7–2." On serial-sevens, his pattern of responses was also very atypical. He was correct on the first two responses, incorrect on the next four responses, and correct on the last two responses.

Standardized assessment of malingering

An important consideration in disability evaluations is whether the client is distorting his or her presentation of symptoms and impairment. The possibility of malingering must be considered separately for the domains of mental disorders and cognitive problems (e.g., memory and concentration).

For mental disorders, the Personality Assessment Inventory (PAI; Morey, 1991) includes several indices for the evaluation of inconsistent or feigned responses. Mr. I. evidenced some inconsistencies on items of similar content (Inconsistency Scale = 70T), which may arise from carelessness, confusion, or deliberate attempts to distort. The low score on the Infrequency Scale (raw = 1; 44T) would suggest that carelessness and confusion are unlikely explanations. Mr. I. also has a moderate clinical elevation on the Negative Impression Scale (70T), a scale for the assessment of feigning. However, elevations of this magnitude are occasionally observed among genuine patients. On the Malingering Index, Mr. I.'s score of 2 is in the indeterminate range.

The PAI clinical profile should be considered with considerable caution. While no clear-cut evidence of feigning was established, the elevation on NIM coupled with the extreme clinical elevations (Somatization = 95T; Depression = 94T; Suicidal Ideation = 97T) raise the distinct possibility of exaggeration.

The Structured Interview of Reported Symptoms (SIRS; Rogers, Bagby, & Dickens, 1992) is a well-validated measure of feigned mental disorders that has a very high positive predictive power. Mr. I. had four scales in the probable feigning range: Blatant Symptoms (11), Subtle Symptoms (21), Selectivity of Symptoms (20), and Severity of Symptoms (12). The profile indicates a very high probability (95%) of feigning. A prominent feature of the profile is Mr. I.'s indiscriminant claims of unbearable symptoms (e.g., strange smells and pronouncing difficult words).

The PDRT (Binder & Willis, 1991) is a deceptively easy, forced-choice test of digit recognition that has received substantial empirical support relative to other tests of feigned cognitive impairment. Genuine patients with cognitive disorders typically score at 39 or above (or better than 54% correct). Mr. I. had an extremely poor performance with a score of 24 (or 33% correct). Based on the detection strategy of symptom validity testing (SVT), a person with *no* memory of the stimuli should score at chance (i.e., 50%, or 36 of 72 trials) or close to chance (30–42). A PDRT score of 24 indicates a very high probability (> 99%) that Mr. I. is *deliberately* missing correct responses in an effort to feign his cognitive impairment.

The Test of Memory Malingering (TOMM; Tombaugh, 1997) has also received empirical support as a measure of cognitive feigning and was administered to Mr. I. Intact performance on the TOMM (a test of concentration and nonverbal memory) can easily be achieved by patients with a range of severe cognitive problems. Therefore, its primary detection strategy is the *floor effect*. With 50 items per trial, genuine patients are expected to score at least 90% correct for the 2nd trial and retention phase. Scores below the 90th percentile likely indicate feigning. Mr. I.'s scores of 25 (50%) and 23 (46%) respectively are extremely low and below the lowest reported scores for severely impaired patients. This pattern of slightly worse scores with an additional trial is potentially a violation of a learning principle. Focusing on his percent correct, these data are strongly indicative of feigning.

In summary, strong and consistent clinical data from standardized measures indicate that Mr. I. is malingering (V65.2) both his reported mental disorders and cognitive impairment. In addition, clinical observations suggest that the genuineness of Mr. I.'s reported pain deserves further examination.

Other clinical data relevant to malingering

Patients sometimes warrant the diagnosis of a genuine disorder in addition to malingering. The current data do not support this conclusion. In focusing on depression, the reported symptoms do not appear to be genuine. With respect to apparent depression and suicidal ideation, Mr. I. reported ongoing thoughts and plans. During the second consultation, however, his account was improbable. While describing himself as very depressed and suicidal, he disclosed that he had met an old love interest and reportedly wanted to pursue a sexual affair before killing himself. This investment in a romantic relationship outside his current marriage appears incompatible with severe depression, social withdrawal, and suicidality. Moreover, his accounts of fatigue and markedly diminished concentration are clearly inconsistent with his observed functioning during extended consultations, each exceeding four hours.

ANALYSIS AND CONCLUSIONS

Disability evaluations are greatly complicated when the apparent injuries bridge multiple healthcare specialties. Mr. I.'s case involved both medical (pain, neurological and orthopedic) and psychological (clinical and neuropsychological) specialists. These specialists focus on their respective areas of expertise. Unexpected or anomalous findings are often referred to other specialists. As a result, cases such as Mr. I. can generate volumes of medical records without a systematic appraisal of malingering or other response styles.

Mr. I. secured the services of Dr. D.D. at the behest of his attorney to document his continued disability. From our perspective, this endeavor does *not* suggest any increased likelihood that Mr. I. is attempting to malinger or defraud the insurance company; legitimate patients may be justifiably concerned about their disability status. As a self-referral, we surmise that Dr. D.D. did not fully appreciate her role in the disability process. Her involvement appears more consistent with a treating clinician than a consulting or forensic psychologist. Professionally, psychologists must clarify their roles at the onset of evaluations and whether forensic issues will be addressed.

Regarding the issue of malingering, Dr. D.D. appeared to accept at face value the client's reported distress and the genuineness of his impairment. She did not use any standardized methods to evaluate malingering and other response styles. Presumably, she did not closely examine the pattern of Mr. I.'s test results for evidence of possible malingering. Moreover, Dr. D.D. did not provide any data to support her conclusions about the client's best effort and lack of malingering. We submit that all psychological and neuropsychological evaluations involving disability claims should systematically address the possibility of malingering (Rogers & Payne, 2006; Slick, Tan, Strauss, & Hultsch, 2004). To clarify professional roles, many clinicians avoid self-referrals in disability cases and instead request that the claimant's attorney generate the referral.

Mr. I. claimed that he was unable to function in any work-related capacity as a result of his depression, impaired cognitive abilities, and pain. This consultation systematically addressed two domains of possible malingering: feigned depression and feigned cognitive abilities.

The possibility of feigned depression was assessed by standardized measures supplemented by clinical interviews and records. The PAI results indicated that feigning should be thoroughly investigated. The strongest evidence of feigning was found on the SIRS, a well-validated measure for feigned mental disorders with a very low false-positive rate. Mr. I.'s performance clearly exceeds the criterion for feigning with four primary scales in the "probable-feigning" range. During the clinical interviews, Mr. I. described his hopelessness and likely suicide. Incompatible with this description, he later expressed a desire to rekindle an old relationship and pursue a romantic liaison. In this consultation, the SIRS was effective at establishing the feigned mental disorders, whereas the clinical interviews assisted in ruling out the possibility of a genuine depression.

The possibility of feigned cognitive impairment was also addressed by standardized measures of malingering that were based on empirically validated detection strategies. The failure on *symptom validity testing* (SVT) provides the strongest evidence (99% likelihood) of feigned cognitive impairment. The failure on the TOMM's *floor effect* strategy provides strong corroborative evidence of feigned abilities regarding concentration and short-term memory.

Inspection of cognitive testing reveals other data indicative of feigning. However, neuropsychologists should not rely solely on these findings. Although based on validated detection strategies, they lack the precision of standardized measures, such as the PDRT and the TOMM. In this consultation, test findings included *floor effect* and *magnitude of error*: For example, Mr. I. "failed" to recall a very simple sequence of three digits and was grossly incorrect in his response; this blatant failure on an extremely simple task is evidence of possible feigning based on both *floor effect* and *magnitude of error* strategies. On neuropsychological testing, clear evidence of *violation of a learning principle* was observed (see TPT and WMS–III). Again, these findings should be viewed as ancillary to the standardized measures of malingering.

The current consultation did not completely rule out the possibility of genuine cognitive impairment. One possibility is the controversial Persisting Postconcussion Syndrome (PPCS; see Alexander, 1995; Gouvier, Uddo-Crane, & Brown, 1988; Satz et al., 1999). However, the ample evidence of feigning in this case essentially rules out this possibility. As illustrated in the case of Mr. I., it is critically important that clinical psychologists do not overstep their expertise with respect to neuropsychological assessment. Collaborative efforts between psychologists and neuropsychologists can often capitalize on their respective strengths in terms of both diagnostic issues and response styles.

The possibility of feigned medical disorders is clearly beyond the scope of this chapter. In this case study, surveillance tapes and clinical observations yielded information that was incompatible with Mr. I.'s medical complaints. These marked discrepancies are noted for the benefit of future medical evaluations. In most cases, however, psychologists lack the necessary medical background or knowledge of empirically validated detection strategies to draw expert conclusions regarding malingered medical presentations.

This case study illustrates the complex presentations found with many disability and forensic evaluations. Neuropsychologists not only must have a sound knowledge base of neurobehavioral syndromes like TBI, but also must be skilled at the application of detection strategies for separate domains of feigned mental disorders and feigned cognitive impairment. Each domain requires specialized knowledge of specific detection strategies and standardized measures. Especially with complex cases, neuropsychologists must critically evaluate the applicability of specific detection strategies, based on the client's background and clinical presentation.

REFERENCES

Alexander, M. P. (1995). Mild traumatic brain injury: Pathophysiology, natural history, and clinical management. *Neurology*, *45*, 1253–1260.

Bender, S. D., & Rogers, R. (2004). Detection of cognitive feigning: Development of a multi-strategy assessment. *Archives of Clinical Neuropsychology*, *19*, 49–60.

Bianchini, K. J., Mathias, C. W., & Greve, K. W. (2001). Symptom validity testing: A critical review. *The Clinical Neuropsychologist*, *15*, 19–45.

Binder, L. M., Rohling, M. L., & Larrabee, G. J. (1997). A review of mild head trauma: Part I. Meta-analysis review of neuropsychological studies. *Journal of Clinical and Experimental Neuropsychology*, *19*, 421–431.

Binder, L. M., & Willis, S. C. (1991). Assessment of motivation after financially compensable minor head trauma. *Psychological Assessment: A Journal of Consulting and Clinical Psychology*, *3*, 175–181.

Gouvier, W. D., Uddo-Crane, M., & Brown, L. M. (1988). Base rates of postconcussional symptoms. *Archives of Clinical Neuropsychology*, *3*, 273–278.

Greiffenstein, M. F., Baker, W. J., & Gola, T. (1994). Validation of malingered amnesia measures with a large clinical sample. *Psychological Assessment*, *6*, 218–224.

Heaton, R., Grant, I., & Matthews, C. (1991). *Comprehensive norms for an expanded Halstead-Reitan battery: Demographic corrections, research findings, and clinical applications.* Tampa: Psychological Assessment Resources, Inc.

Jacobs, J. W., Bernhard, M. R., Delgado, A., & Strain, J. J. (1977). Screening for organic mental syndromes in the medically ill. *Annals of Internal Medicine, 107,* 481–485.

Millis, S. R., Ross, S. R., & Ricker, J. H. (1998). Detection of incomplete effort on the Wechsler Adult Intelligence Scale-Revised: A cross-validation. *Journal of Clinical and Experimental Neuropsychology. 20*(2), 167–173.

Mittenberg, W., Theroux-Fichera, S., Zielinski, R., & Heilbronner, R. (1995). Identification of malingered head injury on the Wechslker Adult Intelligence Scale–Revised. *Professional Psychology: Research and Practice, 26*(5), 491–498.

Morey, L. C. (1991). *Personality Assessment Inventory: Professional manual.* Tampa: Psychological Assessment Resources, Inc.

Rogers, R. (Ed.) (1997). *Clinical assessment of malingering and deception,* 2nd ed. New York: Guilford.

Rogers, R., Bagby, R. M., & Dickens, S. E. (1992). *Structured Interview of Reported Symptoms (SIRS) and professional manual.* Odessa, FL: Psychological Assessment Resources, Inc.

Rogers, R., & Bender, S. D. (2003). Evaluation of malingering and deception. In A. M. Goldstein (Ed.), *Comprehensive handbook of psychology: Forensic psychology* (Vol. 11, pp. 109–129). New York: Wiley.

Rogers, R., & Payne, J. W. (2006). Damages and rewards: Assessment of malingered disorders in compensation cases. *Behavioral Sciences and the Law, 24,* 645–658.

Rogers, R., & Vitacco, M. J. (2002). Forensic assessment of malingering and related response styles. In B. Van Dorsten (Ed.), *Forensic psychology: From classroom to courtroom* (pp. 83–104). Boston: Kluwer Academic/ Plenum Publishers.

Satz, P., Alfano, P., Light, R., Morgenstern, H., Zaucha, K, Asarnow, R., & Newton, S. (1999). Persistent post-concussive syndrome: A proposed methodology and literature review to determine effects, if any, of mild head injury or other bodily injury. *Journal of Experimental and Clinical Neuropsychology, 21*(5), 620–628.

Slick, D., Tan, J., Strauss, E., & Hultsch, D. (2004). Detecting malingering: a survey of experts' practices. *Archives of Clinical Neuropsychology, 19,* 465–473.

Tombaugh, T. N. (1997). Test of Memory Malingering. Toronto: Normative data from cognitively intact and cognitively impaired individuals. *Psychological Assessment, 9,* 260–268.

Posttraumatic stress disorder and neuropsychological malingering: A complicated scenario

14

Jerry J. Sweet

Malingering of posttraumatic stress disorder (PTSD) has become a growing concern in healthcare settings, related in part to the fact that PTSD claims are increasing in number, and estimates of symptom exaggeration and malingering in these cases indicate an increasing loss of societal resources to fraud (Taylor, Frueh, & Asmundson, 2007). Questions regarding the possible presence of PTSD arise with some regularity in personal injury and worker's compensation cases. As such, numerous treatises have appeared in the relevant literature regarding the importance of carefully considering the logical difficulties in establishing the degree of evidence necessary for forensic assessment of stress claims, including differential diagnosis involving PTSD (e.g., Hall & Hall, 2006; Sparr & Pitman, 1999).

In some instances, the primary focus of the claimed injury is PTSD, whereas in other instances, PTSD may be alleged as one of a number of acquired conditions. The present case represents the latter situation, in which claims of traumatic brain injury (TBI) and PTSD, along with additional injury claims, were made in the context of a work-related accident. In the course of analyzing this case, we will consider the input and test data of three psychologists (two of whom consider themselves neuropsychologists), all of whom rendered more than one opinion across time as additional data was gathered. Also, we will consider extensive information from medical records and the opinions of numerous physicians.

The possibility of the co-existence of PTSD and TBI is entertained relatively frequently in litigated cases and is, in fact, a controversial topic. There are two fundamental reasons for the controversy, both of which appear grounded in common sense. That is, on the one hand the most serious accidents and assaults, which may carry higher risk of subsequent PTSD, *may* cause a serious TBI accompanied by a very significant disruption of consciousness, which causes an *inability* to encode events into memory storage. Without actual memory of the violent events of injury, it has been thought that PTSD, a condition within which unwanted and repetitive recollection of the trauma is a fundamental component, is not a likely outcome. Conversely, at the much milder end of TBI severity, where there is a much better chance of actual recall of at least some events of injury and a strong expectation that, barring complications, the neuropsychological dysfunction will resolve, one also has a lesser chance of having suffered the kind of violent triggering event that carries with it a higher risk of subsequent PTSD.

But *resolution of controversial topics is seldom accomplished through common sense reasoning.*

Instead, we need to consider empirical evidence. Therefore, we will begin by briefly reviewing some of the relevant literature related to the controversy of co-existing PTSD and TBI.

CAN PTSD CO-EXIST WITH TBI?

This question is more complex than one might first think. After all, if encoding of memories for a traumatic event is required in order for PTSD to occur, then PTSD should not be possible with brain injury severe enough to substantially disrupt encoding at the time of the traumatic event. However, when Turnbull, Campbell, and Swann (2001) examined a large series of emergency department cases to determine the influence of having no trauma memory on subsequent PTSD symptoms, the results were not what would be expected based on the presumption that traumatic memories are required for PTSD to develop. Though TBI no-memory patients had fewer PTSD symptoms than TBI patients with memory of the TBI-related accident, the no-memory patients had significantly more symptoms than a no-trauma group. To be sure, there can be difficulty separating symptoms of an anxiety disorder, such as acute stress disorder and PTSD, from symptoms associated with TBI because of considerable overlap of symptoms associated with each (Bryant, 2001). Nevertheless, the greater number of symptoms when trauma memory was absent forces one to reconsider the original presumption that memory is essential.

Though noting methodological weaknesses of the majority of studies addressing the question, based on review of relevant published studies, Bryant (2001) concluded that it was possible for patients suffering TBI to also experience PTSD as a result of the same accident-related injury. Bryant also concluded that post-trauma symptoms may be: decreased in individuals with no memory for the actual trauma, subject to memory reconstruction by the victim and therefore influenced by inaccurate memories, influenced by pain, and along with additional post-trauma stressors serve to reduce coping ability after TBI.

In keeping with the conclusion that PTSD can occur, but presents differently as a result of co-occurring TBI, Williams, Evans, Needham, and Wilson (2002) found that dysexecutive disorder in moderate to severe TBI survivors appeared to reduce PTSD symptoms due to lack of awareness. These authors also concluded that external causality of the trauma was a major factor associated with PTSD symptoms.

Feinstein, Hershkop, Ouchterlony, Jardine, and McCullagh (2002) also examined the presence of PTSD in TBI patients whose memory of traumatic events was disrupted. These authors found that even individuals with more than one week of posttraumatic amnesia (PTA) later exhibited PTSD-type symptoms. Patient groups having less than one hour of PTA versus more than one hour of PTA showed different levels of symptoms, with the more severely injured group showing significantly fewer symptoms.

In summary, clinical research investigators have shown that PTSD symptoms, which admittedly are not all unique to the diagnosis of PTSD, can occur in patients who have suffered TBI, even though the TBI survivor is amnestic for the event. However, the frequency with which the issue is raised during litigation appears to *far exceed* the actual rate of occurrence among non-litigants. It is important to keep in mind that the PTSD symptoms have been found to be less severe in individuals whose traumatic memories have been disrupted by TBI, which makes severity of symptom reporting one means of distinguishing malingered from genuine PTSD.

THE INFLUENCE OF FORENSIC CONTEXT TO INJURY OUTCOME AND PTSD CLAIMS

Rates of PTSD occurrence in response to traumatic events that are outside of civil litigation need to be considered in order to truly appreciate the presence of symptoms occurring in a context of civil litigation. Delahanty et al. (1997) found that a subset of motor vehicle accident victims demonstrated criteria for PTSD diagnosis soon after the accident, but only those whose accidents were caused by others showed later symptoms. Those who were responsible for their own injuries had comparable injury severity, yet initially the percentages meeting PTSD criteria were 19 for self-responsible and 29 for other-responsible accident victims. At six months post-accident, those who had caused their own accidents showed a PTSD frequency that was no different from a non-accident control group.

From a different perspective, though it might be *common sense* to believe that it would be *normal* and expected to develop PTSD after a serious traumatic event, the actual rates of PTSD show a wide range and often show that a minority of individuals develop PTSD. For example, a review of a number of published studies found that the lifetime rates of PTSD after physical assault are in the range of 23–39% (Acierno, Kilpatrick, & Resnick, 1999). From a different perspective, epidemiologic studies have shown that the lifetime prevalence of exposure to traumatic events is considered to be 50–60%, yet the lifetime prevalence of PTSD is considered to be 5–10% (Ozer, Best, Lipsey, & Weiss, 2003).

Decades of research have explored the question of what may cause one individual to develop PTSD when other individuals exposed to the same traumatic event do not develop it. Based on a review of research addressing the development, course, and behavioral expression of PTSD, Schnurr and Vielhauer (1999) found that personality is linked to the development of PTSD after trauma exposure, and separately Miller (2003) reported that the broad-band personality trait of "negative emotionality" is the primary personality risk factor. Reviews of large epidemiological studies have shown an impressive range of variables that are associated with different relative risks (either greater or lesser) of developing PTSD after traumatic stress, including such variables as education, income, gender, region of country, etc. (Kessler, Sonnega, Bromet, Hughes, Nelson, & Breslau, 1999). Similarly, based on meta-analytic review of published PTSD studies, even without considering the effects of litigation, Brewin, Andrews, and Valentine (2000) reported notable heterogeneity of variables that predicted the occurrence of PTSD in trauma survivors. A separate meta-analysis by Ozer, Best, Lipsey, and Weiss (2003) also found a range of predictors, with "prior adjustment" and family history of psychopathology showing small effect sizes, perceived social support showing small to moderate effect size, and peri-traumatic dissociation showing a moderate effect size. However, using a substantially different methodology, that of calculating odds ratios related to pre-existing risk factors for PTSD in the large database of The National Comorbidity Survey, Kessler et al. (1999) reported that presence and type of pre-existing psychiatric diagnoses (e.g., mood disorder, anxiety disorder, substance use disorder) were in fact associated with much higher risk of PTSD after exposure to a traumatic event.

According to Rosen (2004), documented cases of individuals falsely claiming post-trauma injuries occurred over 100 years ago. Rosen documents the confounding effect of litigation in the PTSD literature itself, showing that abnormally high PTSD rates have occurred in some studies within the context of litigated cases. In this regard, Rosen's observations place litigated PTSD in the same perspective as litigated closed head injury and litigated pain (e.g., Binder & Rohling, 1996; Larrabee, 2003).

As Koch, O'Neill, and Douglas (2005) have noted in discussing limitations of forensic assessment of PTSD litigants, the diagnosis of PTSD often relies upon self-report, which in a forensic context requires that methods of assessing response bias and validity are relied upon. For example,

Frueh, Elhai, Gold, Monnier, Magruder, Keane, and Arana (2003) reported that disability compensation-seeking veterans evaluated for PTSD reported greater symptoms of psychopathology than veterans not seeking compensation, despite the fact that the frequency of meeting diagnostic criteria was comparable in both groups. Guriel and Fremouw (2003) have offered a variety of motivations for malingering of PTSD, which within a context of civil litigation include external financial incentives.

COGNITIVE DYSFUNCTION ASSOCIATED WITH PTSD

Clinical neuropsychologists have for years studied a variety of psychiatric disorders, such as obsessive-compulsive disorder, depression, and schizophrenia (cf. review by Sweet & Westergaard, 1997), in which a neurological substrate was reasonably well identified or suspected. In this manner, PTSD has also been studied, with the intent of determining whether brain changes occur in individuals suffering from the condition.

Findings from relevant studies further complicate the already complex differential diagnosis of PTSD, especially subsequent to events that can be simultaneously physically *and* psychologically traumatic. In fact, a separate controversy has emerged concerning the possibility that PTSD alone without associated TBI can be associated with neurocognitive dysfunction, in the same manner that schizophrenia has been found to demonstrate neurocognitive dysfunction in the absence of independent acquired brain dysfunction. Chief contributor to the controversy surrounding cognitive dysfunction associated with PTSD has been the reported findings of abnormalities of the hippocampus among individuals with PTSD (cf., Sapolsky, 2001). However, carefully controlled study of monozygotic twins has since found that smaller hippocampal volume is a *pre-trauma* risk factor to developing PTSD if exposed to a serious traumatic event, rather than a result of having acquired PTSD (Gilbertson, Shenton, Ciszewski, Kasai, Lasko, Orr, & Pitman, 2002; Sapolsky, 2002). Such findings, along with the results of two independent separate reviews of the relevant neuropsychological literature (Danckwerts & Leathem, 2003; Horner & Hamner, 2002), suggest that a causative link between PTSD and cognitive dysfunction cannot be assumed. In fact, these two literature reviews concluded that there were numerous alternative hypotheses and methodological problems in published studies of neuropsychological dysfunction in PTSD patients, which have ultimately obscured the clarity of conclusions in this line of inquiry at present.

THE COMPLEX CASE OF MR. X.

Mr. X. was working as he walked across a parking lot and was struck by a vehicle. Five years later, litigation had progressed to the point that the defendants were retaining experts when I was asked to consult on the case. Record review led to an independent evaluation. The details and prior sequence of healthcare and litigation-related events of this particular case turned out to be multifaceted and very interesting. The narrative that follows places the salient events of this case in chronological order.

After a history of normal progress in early education, Mr. X. was receiving poor grades in high school at the time that he decided to drop out before completing eleventh grade and join the military. He scored reasonably well on military exams, qualifying for maintenance training, which he left once he realized it did not suit him well. Moving to an armored combat unit, he became a driver, gunner, and eventually a track commander in an armored personnel carrier (APC). He also earned a general equivalency diploma while in the military. Serving his country in time of war, Mr. X.'s APC struck a mine on three separate occasions and was involved in multiple battles. During his four years of service, Mr. X. received three Purple Hearts related to combat injuries. Many years of psychiatric treatment for posttraumatic stress disorder (PTSD) were provided to Mr. X. through the Veteran's Administration healthcare system. This treatment was ongoing and in place at the time of his work-related accident.

Subsequent to military service, Mr. X. completed a lengthy apprenticeship and became a skilled construction worker, and eventually a foreman. After years of work in shipyards and oil refineries, Mr. X. became a truck driver, which was his vocation at the time he was struck by the motor vehicle.

Medical records document a variety of physical injuries on the day Mr. X. was struck by a motor vehicle. Though the ambulance record notes "possible head injury," seemingly because of the nature of the pedestrian versus motor vehicle accident, there was no affirmative evidence of initial brain injury. Specifically, no loss of consciousness was noted by any medical personnel at the scene; Mr. X. denied loss of consciousness; the emergency department records noted that the possibility of head injury was considered, but that it was thought unlikely and that all neurological markers (e.g., Glasgow Coma Scale) were normal. These important accident injury details explain why a neurologist was not consulted at any point during the nearly two-month hospitalization that followed. Hospital records documented very serious injury to his leg, as well as dental, shoulder, and superficial facial injuries. Numerous surgical procedures occurred, with the majority of these pertaining to the bones and skin of the leg. Upon discharge from the hospital, Mr. X. was still unable to walk, and his arm was in a sling. Persistent pain was reported in multiple sites of Mr. X.'s body.

The first neurology consultation occurred months after the accident on an outpatient basis, related to the primary complaint of tinnitus. The neurologist noted that Mr. X.'s *lack of confidence* in his own ability seemed to be the most salient aspect of brief mental status testing. Nevertheless, for reasons that were unclear, and perhaps related to complaints by Mr. X. and his significant other regarding post-accident memory and personality change, the neurologist concluded that cognitive and memory difficulties were present. The neurologist also noted in a subsequent office visit that he expected these problems would improve over time. A later extensive evaluation by a different neurologist disagreed with the first neurologist, indicating that there was no evidence of post-concussion syndrome and instead there was positive evidence during physical examination of *lack of cooperation*.

Eight months after the accident, Mr. X. was referred to a clinical neuropsychologist for evaluation. Oddly, this psychologist documented loss of consciousness for "less than 30 minutes," which of course includes 0—the number of minutes reflecting every prior treater's opinion. The conclusions of this psychologist were that there was no evidence of postconcussion syndrome and that neuropsychological functions were all intact. Etiology of concentration and memory complaints was described as pain and loss of life structure secondary to other non-central nervous system injuries.

Two years after the accident, Mr. X. underwent a second evaluation by a clinical psychologist. This evaluation contained few tests of ability and included measures more commonly used by vocational counselors, such as the Wonderlic Personnel Inventory and Myers-Briggs Type Inventory. These facts made an interesting context therefore for the very surprising usage of the diagnosis of "Dementia due to Head Trauma" for Mr. X.

Several years after the work-related accident, the VA healthcare system increased Mr. X.'s PTSD status from "30% disabling" to "70% disabling." The written assessment of VA personnel at the time referred *only* to war-time events, *not* the civilian accident.

Neuropsychological evaluation as defense expert five years post-accident

As noted above, extensive medical records contained persistent post-accident complaints that along with inconsistent opinions by healthcare professionals in the ensuing years had kept alive a claim of persistent brain injury. These ongoing assertions by the plaintiff and his attorney in the context of ongoing worker's compensation litigation were viewed as requiring an independent evaluation. Thus, Mr. X. and his significant other were interviewed and Mr. X. underwent extensive formal testing.

Though it should have been obvious to the psychologists who carried out the prior evaluations that the circumstances of the accident would lead to litigation, no effort measures had been administered previously. In keeping with the now longstanding expectation that effort measures should be administered and validity indicators should be assessed in forensic evaluations, we did so. The results of effort measures and common ability test validity indicators can be seen in Table 14.1. The Minnesota Multiphasic Personality Inventory–2nd Edition (MMPI–2) was also given, though due to time constraints only 370 items were completed, thus precluding use of some of the validity scales, such as the Fake Bad Scale (FBS). However, it is possible to estimate an FBS score from the results of the first 370 MMPI–2 items (Nelson, Parsons, Grote, Smith, & Sisung, 2006). Estimated FBS in this instance was 27, well above accepted cutoffs. The F (Infrequency) scale was a T score of 101, which is clearly invalid. The Detailed Assessment of Posttraumatic Stress (DAPS) was also administered, the validity scales of which were well within normal limits.

Comparison of findings with earlier findings

Many of the measures administered in our independent evaluation, Mr. X.'s third evaluation, had not been administered in the two previous psychological evaluations. The majority of scores from measures administered previously to Mr. X. are not available. In reality, most measures administered in the second evaluation, by a psychologist with alleged expertise in vocational assessment, were not clinical measures and can shed no light on the presence or absence of either neuropsychological or psychological conditions. Some of the measures contained in the three evaluations are relevant to neuropsychological assessment, and among those, Table 14.2 shows the available data. Despite much missing data from the prior evaluations, some of the scores available show dramatically different results across time, in a direction that defies a neurological explanation. For example, among the WAIS–III findings, Full Scale IQ decreased 17 points, with the higher score being the one much closer in time to the accident at issue in the lawsuit. Reliable Digit Span, which was within normal limits initially, was twice within the range considered clearly unreliable in the third evaluation. Similarly, responses to general information questions and matrix reasoning tasks were much lower in the third evaluation when compared to the first. The same decrease from initially average to unrealistically low third evaluation performance occurred on WMS–III tasks involving simple mental control (i.e., the ability to direct attention while carrying out mental tasks that involve over-learned information) and immediate and delayed memory for story information.

Analysis of the case of Mr. X.

Medical records were clear in documenting significant physical trauma to Mr. X. at the time that he was struck as a pedestrian by the motor vehicle. However, examination of the relevant records makes it very clear that there were no obvious signs of brain dysfunction at the time of the injury. The "possible head injury" noted in ambulance records appears seemingly because of the nature of the accident (i.e., pedestrian versus motor vehicle), rather than because of any affirming evidence of head injury. There was no injury to the head externally, and it was not apparent to witnesses at the scene that any loss of consciousness had occurred. Emergency department entries note the low probability of brain trauma. Hence, there was no neurological care in either of Mr. X.'s first two post-accident hospitalizations, both of which were necessitated by leg injuries. Months later, an outpatient neurologist saw Mr. X. for tinnitus. Interview and neurological examination at that time

TABLE 14.1   Results and interpretations of effort test and common ability test validity indicators administered to Mr. X.

TEST	SCORE	INTERPRETATION
Letter Memory Test		
Total Correct	= 33%	Threshold surpassed
Victoria Symptom Validity Test		
"Easy" Correct	= 6/24	Below chance (deliberate)
"Easy" Response Latency	= 9.84 seconds	Threshold surpassed
"Difficult" Correct	= 4/24	Below chance (deliberate)
"Difficult" Response Latency	= 11.25 seconds	Threshold surpassed
Word Memory Test		
Immediate Recall	= 70%	Threshold surpassed
Delayed Recall	= 30%	Threshold surpassed
Consistency	= 45%	Threshold surpassed
Reliable Digit Span		
First administration	= 4	Threshold surpassed
Second administration	= 6	Threshold surpassed
California Verbal Learning Test		
Total of Learning Trials	= 10	Threshold surpassed
Long Delay Cued Recall	= 0	Threshold surpassed
Recognition Hits (Yes/No)	= 6	Threshold surpassed
Discriminability	= 41	Threshold surpassed
Wisconsin Card Sorting Test		
Bernard Formula[1]	= 6.36	Predicted group membership-malingerer
Suhr and Boyer Formula[2]	= 3.16	Above 80% probability of malingering
King et al. Formula[3]	= 1.45	Above 80% probability of malingering
Discrepancy of Predicted IQ[4] from Measured IQ		
Barona	= 29	Unrealistically poor
OPIE–3 (4 subtest)	= 14	Unrealistically poor
OPIE–3 (2 subtest)	= 17	Unrealistically poor
OPIE–3 Verbal	= 20	Unrealistically poor
OPIE–3 Performance	= 17	Unrealistically poor
OPIE–3 Matrix Reasoning	= 18	Unrealistically poor
Finger Tapping		
Dominant Hand	= 8.4	Threshold surpassed
Nondominant Hand	= 7.0	Threshold surpassed
Grip Strength		
Dominant Hand	= 14 kg	Unrealistically poor
Nondominant Hand	= 4 kg	Unrealistically poor
Grooved Pegboard		
Dominant Hand	= 256 sec	Unrealistically poor
Nondominant Hand	= 300 sec	Unrealistically poor

Note: "Threshold surpassed" means that the value is below established cutoffs identified in empirical studies in peer-reviewed literature of well-documented traumatic brain injury more severe than the improbable mild injury at issue in this case. "Unrealistically poor" is a conclusion based on known values for severe traumatic brain injury in peer-reviewed literature.

[1] Discriminant function: Bernard, McGrath, and Houston (1996).
[2] Logistic regression: Suhr and Boyer (1999).
[3] Logistic regression: King, Sweet, Sherer, Curtiss, and Vanderploeg (2002).
[4] Predicted IQ methods:
    Barona prediction: Barona, Reynolds, and Chastain (1984).
    OPIE–3 predictions: Schoenberg, Scott, Duff, and Adams (2002).

TABLE 14.2 Available results from measures administered to Mr. X.

MEASURE	8 MONTHS POST-ACCIDENT	1 YEAR POST-ACCIDENT	5 YEARS POST-ACCIDENT
WAIS–III	*Index or Raw (SS)*	*Index or Raw (SS)*	*Index or Raw (SS)*
VIQ	84		69
PIQ	92		77
FSIQ	87	IQ estimated 75	70
Verbal Comp			80
Percept Organ			84
Working Mem			57
Process Speed			69
Vocab	(7)		29 (6)
Similarities	(7)		18 (8)
Arithmetic			6 (3)
Digit Span	(9)		8 (4)
Digits Forward			
Digits Backwrd			
Information	(9)		8 (5)
Comprehension	(6)		(8)
L–N Sequence			2 (2)
Pic Completion			15 (6)
Digit Symbol			25 (3)
Block Design	(10)		33 (9)
Matrix Reason	(11)		8 (7)
Symbol Search	(7)		15 (5)
WMS–III	*Index or Raw (SS)*	*Index or Raw (SS)*	*Index or Raw (SS)*
Auditory Imm			56
Auditory Delay			55
Aud Recogn			55
Working Mem			57
Info/Orient (raw)	"intact"		5
Digit Span (SS)			6 (3)
Digits Fwd (span)			
Digits Bk (span)			
Mental Control	(8)		12 (4)
LM I	(7)		4 (1)
LM II	(9)		0 (1)
LM %Ret (SS)			0 (1)
LM Recog (of 30)			6
VR I			
VR II			
VR % Retent (SS)			
VR Recog			
VR Copy			
Spatial Span Fwd			
Spatial Span Bkd			
Aud. Del. Rec.			
Single Trial L			
Learning Slp			
Retention			
Retrieval			
CVLT	*Standard Form–Raw (Z)*	*Standard Form–Raw (Z)*	*Standard Form–Raw (Z)*
Trial 1			2 (–3)
Trial 2			3
Trial 3			2
Trial 4			1
Trial 5			2

Total 1–5	10 (T = 0)
Trial B	2 (–3)
Short Free	0 (–5)
Short Cued	0 (–5)
Long Free	0 (–4)
Long Cued	0 (–5)
Rec. Hits	6 (–5)
Rec. FP	16 (5)
FC Rec./16	n/a
Discrimination	41 (–5)
Repetition	0 (–1)
Intrusion	3
Semantic Clust	1 (–1)

WCST	Raw (%ile)	Raw (%ile)	Raw (%ile)
# Categories			0
Total Errors			87 (26)
Persev Resp.			57 (31)
Fail Maint Set			0

Category Test	Range		(T)
	"Average"		(46)

Trail Making	Seconds (T)	Seconds (T)	Seconds (T)
Part A			210 (19)
Part B			302 (20)

Gordon Dx	Raw	Raw	Raw
Vigilance (Com)			7 correct, 19 commissions
Distract (Com)			Discontinued

Stroop	Raw (T)	Raw (T)	Raw (T)
Word			46 (< 20)
Color			38 (22)
C–W			25 (30)

MAE	Raw (%ile)	Raw (%ile)	Raw (%ile)
Naming			44 (7)
COWA			15 (1)

Animals	Raw (Z)	Raw (Z)	Raw (Z)
Fluency			4 (–2.97)

Ruff	Raw (T)	Raw (T)	Raw (T)
Unique Designs			64 (34.9–36)
Error Ratio			.0854 (54)

Finger Tappng	Mean Raw (T)	Mean Raw (T)	Mean Raw (T)
DH			8.4 (10)
NDH			7 (9)

Dynamometer	Mean Raw (T)	Mean Raw (T)	Mean Raw (T)
DH	"normal"		14 (2)
NDH			4 (0)

Grooved Pegs	Mean sec (SS)	Mean Raw (T)	Mean Raw (T)
DH	"normal"		256 (12)
NDH			300 (13)

Wide Range Achievement Test–3rd Ed.	Standard Score (Grade Level)	Standard Score (Grade Level)	Standard Score (Grade Level)
Reading		88 (High Sc.)	82 (Eighth Gr.)
Spelling		55 (Second Gr.)	76 (Sixth Gr.)
Arithmetic		60 (Third Gr.)	66 (Fourth Gr.)

MMPI–2 (370 items only)	T	T	T

(Continued . . .)

TABLE 14.2   (Continued)

MEASURE	8 MONTHS POST-Accident	1 YEAR POST-ACCIDENT	5 YEARS POST-ACCIDENT
L			61
F			101
FBS estimate (raw)			(27)
K			41
Hs			79
D			98
Hy			76
Pd			82
Mf			44
Pa			90
Pt			98
Sc			110
Ma			51
Si			82
OVERALL CONCLUSION AT TIME OF EVALUATION	Normal, not even postconcussion symptoms	Dementia due to head trauma	No initial brain injury; now gross cognitive malingering

found that Mr. X. perceived memory and attention problems, which were not evident to the neurologist. With encouragement from the neurologist, Mr. X. was able to carry out "bedside mental status testing" normally, though he initially resisted doing so. Subsequent evaluation by a second neurologist found a great deal of conscious lack of cooperation on physical examination and no symptoms of postconcussion syndrome. However, both physicians appeared to accept, on self-report of Mr. X. alone without review of records, that an initial concussion had occurred. Both indicated prognosis was good.

The initial evaluation of Mr. X. by a neuropsychologist occurred eight months post-accident and resulted in an interpretation of "normal central nervous system function" without evidence of even subjective (i.e., patient reported) postconcussion symptoms. Specifically, among the numerous possible postconcussion symptoms that had not been endorsed by Mr. X., the neuropsychologist noted that tinnitus had not been reported. Even within this initial evaluation, Mr. X.'s performances were described as showing dramatic internal inconsistencies, which were viewed as caused by either situational or psychological variables.

The second evaluation by a psychologist with a vocational assessment background was almost entirely irrelevant to the issues of the case, which were in fact diagnostic issues related to the possibility that brain injury had been caused and persisted and the possibility that the pre-existing psychological condition of combat-related PTSD had been worsened by the accident. No clinical neuropsychological measures or clinical psychological measures were administered. Yet, the vocational psychologist had been the first healthcare professional to diagnose "dementia due to head trauma." This is an excellent example of a clinician assuming in *post hoc ergo propter hoc* fashion without supporting evidence that an historical event had caused the complaints of an examinee and with no other evidence to support or refute the hypothesis, simply concluding a presumptive diagnosis.

Interestingly, neither of the first two evaluations by psychologists concluded that posttraumatic stress disorder was present. In fact, neither of their reports even made reference to the litigant's well-documented psychiatric history, and neither used a detailed personality test that would have addressed mood and affective symptoms presented by Mr. X.

The results of our evaluation of Mr. X., which was his third, but the first comprehensive neuropsychological evaluation, were remarkably clear on a number of points. First, results were absolutely riddled with evidence of insufficient effort and unrealistically poor performances, a subset of which was grossly at odds with the first evaluation that had occurred much closer in time to the accident at issue in the litigation. Though the plaintiff's attorney had placed greatest emphasis on brain injury, the mere possibility, in fact low probability, of an initial very mild, uncomplicated brain injury became a non-issue given the results of our evaluation. That is, though it is unlikely, even if a very mild, uncomplicated brain injury had occurred, there is no possibility that the presentation on our testing five years later could reflect an initial injury of this type. First, injuries of that type are not known to have persistent cognitive sequelae. Second, our evaluation indicated deliberate, pronounced, and pervasive insufficient effort, which within a secondary gain context, such as a lawsuit, should be viewed as malingering.

But what of the possibility that combat-related PTSD had been worsened by the accident? Interestingly, at the request of lawyers involved with the lawsuit, the VA psychiatrist who had treated Mr. X. for years tendered an affidavit in which she stated that no worsening of his condition related to the civil injury was apparent to her. Recall that the VA had increased Mr. X.'s service-connected disability status after the accident. According to the VA psychiatrist, the increased disability status had not been in response to the civil accident.

However, Mr. X. had suffered a devastating injury to his leg, one that nearly caused him to have his leg amputated and one that left his leg very scarred and disfigured. Given these facts, and the fact that pre-existing PTSD increases the probability that subsequent major stressors will cause anxiety disorder, I rendered the opinion that it was possible that Mr. X.'s PTSD had worsened as a result of the civil accident. To me, there was no means of ruling out that possibility and it seemed entirely plausible. I also opined that there was no means available to distinguish "old" versus "new" PTSD in this instance, as we had no pre-accident test data. However, to be clear, the presence of PTSD, even worsened, would not have resulted in a malingering presentation on cognitive testing and effort measures.

Court outcomes can defy the reasoning of experts

Prior to the presentation at court of all the opinions of treaters and retained experts, the defense lawyer obtained the deposition testimony of the first psychologist who evaluated Mr. X. This psychologist had concluded that there was no evidence of brain injury, but instead evidence of situational or psychological factors. When shown the subsequent test data from the third evaluation, this first psychologist, who was in the role of a treater, not a retained expert, nevertheless amended his opinions and agreed with my much later opinion as a retained expert that Mr. X. was malingering. It seemed then that there was going to be very little evidence affirming the claim of persistent brain injury and much that would confirm that this portion of the case was in fact malingered. After all, it was not a close call, but rather one that could be made, proverbially speaking, "a mile away."

Much later I heard back from the defense attorney that the particular jurisdiction in which this case was tried was well known among defense firms as one that, facts of individual cases notwithstanding, often ruled in favor of plaintiffs. This was, as they say, "news to me," but it was also information that would not have made a difference had it been shared earlier, in that as a retained expert such information is not relevant to opinions rendered. The defense attorney went on to say that, in fact, a large award had been given to Mr. X. for "brain injury" . . . an appeal was likely.

Years have now passed, and as this text was going into production I contacted the defense attorney to determine if there had been an outcome to the appeal process. With names redacted, a portion of the attorney's e-mail response summarizing the initial and subsequent court proceedings appears below:

> The trial court found that Mr. X. was totally disabled from a mental and physical standpoint as the result of his work injuries. The defendants (our client in this case) appealed on the basis that the

review panel made numerous legal errors. The appellate court agreed. Then, the plaintiff appealed to the State Court of Appeals. The Court of Appeals agreed that the case should be remanded to the trial court to consider important facts concerning the plaintiff's prior neuropsychological care not previously considered. The trial court got the case back and "considered" the history of care issues presented and made the same rulings, that Mr. X. was totally disabled from a mental and physical standpoint as the result of his work injuries. We, the defendants, once again appealed on the way back up. The "Review Panel" of the State Worker's Compensation Court affirmed the trial court's decision as to Mr. X.'s disability. The defendants appealed this decision back to the State Court of Appeals and that is where we stand. Hopefully, we may get the issues resolved by mediation.

As can be seen from this summary, an accurate appreciation of complex neuropsychological issues, data, and interpretations can be difficult for courts. With unexpected legal rulings making the headlines with some regularity, sometimes in sensational fashion, the idea that neuropsychological reality should equal court outcomes would be naïve. All that experts can, and should, do is accurately and objectively inform the court.

LIMITATIONS OF PTSD TESTING

It is important within forensic contexts that experts who render opinions appreciate the rather substantial limitations of diagnosing PTSD. Diagnostic criteria for many psychiatric diagnoses are often considered by clinicians to have been met based solely on self-report. Yet, an experienced clinician will note the unreliability of symptoms presented by the same patient when seen across time and also when presented to different clinicians. It is also well known that some common symptoms of a condition may not be specific to that condition. For example, patients experiencing depression or chronic pain will endorse symptoms that could be misconstrued as representing concussion, even though no concussion has been experienced (Gunstad & Suhr, 2001; Iverson & McCracken, 1997; Smith-Seemiller et al., 2003). Moreover, it is well known that emotional states, such as anxiety and depression, can increase the subjective reporting of memory symptoms, which are then not supported by objective memory assessment (e.g., Derouesné et al., 1999; Otto et al. 1994; Schagen et al., 1999).

Perhaps more important, a forensic context, such as litigation, provides a context for additional unreliability of self-report, which has been demonstrated amply in studies of self-report on widely used personality tests, such as the MMPI–2 (e.g., Nelson, Sweet, & Demakis, 2006). This effect on self-report has been found even for the reporting of basic historical facts, such as prior health history (Gunstad & Suhr, 2001; Lees-Haley et al., 1997) and prior academic function (Greiffenstein, Baker, & Johnson-Greene, 2002). Thus, forensic experts must have a means of establishing the validity of self-reported symptoms that may be used to establish or rule out PTSD.

Some assessment instruments in clinical use do not have validity scales and acceptable psychometric properties that can be used to help identify or rule out response bias and non-credible self report. Such instruments are basically nothing more than symptom checklists. For example, Lees-Haley, Price, Williams, and Betz (2001) noted that the Impact of Events Scale, essentially a symptom checklist, will frequently misrepresent low-level anxiety symptoms as PTSD, to the point that college students feeling distressed at watching a television program may appear to have greater PTSD symptomatology than airplane crash survivors. Similarly, Shapinsky, Rapport, Henderson, and Axelrod (2005) found that some PTSD scales are overly sensitive to "nontraumatic stressors such as everyday distress and trait characteristics." Differently, manuals of relevant instruments with validity scales and known psychometric properties, such as the Trauma Symptom Inventory (Briere, 1995), may posit a cutoff for invalid responding in *clinical samples* that is at odds with research on PTSD *claimants* (e.g., Edens, Otto, & Dwyer, 1998). Moreover, not all validity scales in an instrument can be relied upon by neuropsychologists as equivalent in forensic applications. In this regard, for example, MMPI–2 traditional validity scales are at times not useful (cf. Crawford, Greene, Dupart, Bongar, & Childs, 2006; Nelson et al., 2006).

Clearly, there is reason to be circumspect and cautious when rendering diagnostic conclusions regarding conditions such as PTSD within a forensic context. The review paper by Guriel and Fremouw (2003) of methods used to identify or rule out malingering among PTSD claimants is instructive in this regard. Based on a critical review of limitations in available diagnostic methods, Guriel and Fremouw conclude: "Currently, there is no method or single instrument that is universally recognized as being the best tool to detect malingering in PTSD claimants."

RECOMMENDATIONS FOR PTSD ASSESSMENTS

PTSD assessments have limits that should be noted in forensic reports and to triers of fact. A symptom checklist approach is unacceptable as "psychometric" proof of PTSD. At least some measures chosen for a PTSD forensic assessment must have validity indicators and allow for a psychometric appraisal of self-reported symptoms. Typically, this would include at least one widely used personality measure with well-established validity scales (e.g., MMPI–2, Personality Assessment Inventory) and at least one PTSD measure with validity scales (e.g., Detailed Assessment of Posttraumatic Stress, Trauma Symptom Inventory). With instruments such as the MMPI–2, clinicians should recognize the limitations of relying solely upon traditional validity indicators, inasmuch as doing so will result in an inability to detect a substantial number of cases of response bias, and numerous additional validity scales are available and in widespread use. Finally, when measures with validity indicators (e.g., MMPI–2, DAPS, PAI, TSI) show evidence of response bias, results of related measures that do not have validity indicators (e.g., Beck Depression Inventory, Beck Anxiety Inventory, Clinician-Assisted PTSD Scale) should *not* be relied upon.

In closing, the consideration of the co-existence of PTSD and TBI deserves particular scrutiny when the alleged traumatic incident involves *mild* TBI. Greiffenstein and Baker (2008) summarized their empirical study of this topic, as follows:

> The more complex the post-traumatic presentation after mild neurological injury, the stronger the association with response bias. Late-appearing dual diagnosis is a litigation phenomenon so intertwined with secondary gain as to be a byproduct of it.

(p. 565)

REFERENCES

Acierno, R., Killpatrick, D., & Resnick, H. (1999). Posttraumatic stress disorder in adults relative to criminal victimization: Prevalence, risk factors, and comorbidity. In P. Saigh & J. D. Bremner (Eds.) *Posttraumatic stress disorder: A comprehensive text.* Boston: Allyn & Bacon.

Barona, A., Reynolds, R., & Chastain, R. (1984). A demographically based index of premorbid intelligence for the WAIS–R. *Journal of Clinical Psychology, 52,* 885–887.

Bernard, L. C., McGrath, M. J., & Houston, W. (1996). The differential effects of simulating malingering, closed head injury, and other CNS pathology on the Wisconsin Card Sorting Test: Support for the "pattern of performance" hypothesis. *Archives of Clinical Neuropsychology, 11,* 231–245.

Binder, L. M., & Rohling, M. L. (1996). Money matters: A meta-analytic review of the effects of financial incentives on recovery after closed-head injury. *American Journal of Psychiatry, 153,* 7–10.

Brewin, C., Andrews, B., & Valentine, J. (2000). Meta-analysis of risk factors for posttraumatic stress disorder in trauma-exposed adults. *Journal of Consulting and Clinical Psychology, 68*, 748–766.

Briere, J. (1995). *Trauma Symptom Inventory professional manual.* Lutz, FL: Psychological Assessment Resources.

Bryant, R., (2001). Posttraumatic stress disorder and traumatic brain injury: Can they co-exist? *Clinical Psychology Review, 21*, 931–948.

Crawford, E., Greene, R. L., Dupart, T., Bongar, B., & Childs, H. (2006). MMPI–2 assessment of malingered emotional distress related to a workplace injury: A mixed group validation. *Journal of Personality Assessment, 86*, 217–221.

Danckwerts, A., & Leathem, J. (2003). Questioning the link between PTSD and cognitive dysfunction. *Neuropsychology Review, 13*, 221–235.

Delahanty, D., Herberman, H., Craig, K., Hayward, M., Fullerton, C., Ursano, R., & Baum, A. (1997). Acute and chronic distress and posttraumatic stress disorder as a function of responsibility for serious motor vehicle accidents. *Journal of Consulting and Clinical Psychology, 65*, 560–567.

Derouesné, C., Lacomblez, L., Thibault, S., & LePoncin, M. (1999). Memory complaints in young and elderly subjects. *International Journal of Geriatric Psychiatry, 14*, 291–301.

Edens, J., Otto, R., & Dwyer, T. (1998). Susceptibility of the Trauma Symptom Inventory to malingering. *Journal of Personality Assessment, 71*, 379–92.

Feinstein, A., Hershkop, S., Ouchterlony, D., Jardine, A., & McCullagh, S. (2002). Posttraumatic amnesia and recall of a traumatic event following traumatic brain injury. *Journal of Neuropsychiatry and Clinical Neurosciences, 14*, 25–30.

Frueh, C., Elhai, J., Gold, P., Monnier, J., Magruder, K., Keane, T., & Arana, G. (2003). Disability compensation seeking among veterans evaluated for posttraumatic stress disorder. *Psychiatric Services, 54*, 84–91.

Gilbertson, M., Shenton, M., Ciszewski, A., Kasai, K., Lasko, N., Orr, S., & Pitman, R. (2002). Smaller hippocampal volume predicts pathologic vulnerability to psychological trauma. *Nature Neuroscience, 5*, 1242–1247.

Greiffenstein, M. F., & Baker, W. J. (2008). Validity testing in dually diagnosed post-traumatic stress disorder and mild closed head injury. *The Clinical Neuropsychologist, 22*, 565–582.

Greiffenstein, M. F., Baker, W. J., & Johnson-Greene, D. (2002). Actual versus self-reported scholastic achievement of litigating postconcussion and severe closed head injury claimants. *Psychological Assessment, 14*, 202–208.

Gunstad, J., & Suhr, J. A. (2001). "Expectation as Etiology" versus "The Good Old Days": Postconcussion syndrome symptom reporting in athletes, headache sufferers, and depressed individuals. *Journal of the International Neuropsychological Society, 7*, 323–333.

Guriel, J., & Fremouw, W. (2003). Assessing malingered posttraumatic stress disorder: A critical review. *Clinical Psychology Review, 23*, 881–904.

Hall, R., & Hall, R. (2006). Malingering of PTSD: Forensic and diagnostic considerations, characteristics of malingerers and clinical presentations. *General Hospital Psychiatry, 28*, 525–535.

Horner, M., & Hamner, M. (2002). Neurocognitive functioning in posttraumatic stress disorder. *Neuropsychology Review, 12*, 15–30.

Iverson, G., & McCracken, L. (1997). "Postconcussive" symptoms in persons with chronic pain. *Brain Injury, 11*, 783–790.

Kessler, R., Sonnega, A., Bromet, E., Hughes, M., Nelson, C., & Breslau, N. (1999). Epidemiological risk factors for trauma and PTSD. In R. Yehuda (Ed.) *Risk factors of posttraumatic stress disorder.* Washington, DC: American Psychiatric Press.

King, J., Sweet, J., Sherer, M., Curtiss, G., & Vanderploeg, R. (2002). Validity Indicators within the Wisconsin Card Sorting Test: Application of new and previously researched multivariate procedures in multiple traumatic brain injury samples. *The Clinical Neuropsychologist, 16*, 506–523.

Koch, W., O'Neill, M., & Douglas, K. (2005). Empirical limits for the forensic assessment of PTSD litigants. *Law and Human Behavior, 29*, 121–149.

Larrabee, G. J. (2003). Exaggerated pain report in litigants with malingered neurocognitive dysfunction. *The Clinical Neuropsychologist, 17*, 395–401.

Lees-Haley, P. R., Price, J. R., Williams, C. W., & Betz, B. P. (2001). Use of the Impact of Events Scale in the assessment of emotional distress and PTSD may produce misleading results. *Journal of Forensic Neuropsychology, 2*, 45–52.

Lees-Haley, P., Williams, C., Zasler, N., Marguilies, S., English, L., & Stevens, K. (1997). Response bias in plaintiffs' histories. *Brain Injury*, *11*, 791–799.

Miller, M. (2003). Personality and the etiology and expression of PTSD: A three-factor model perspective. *Clinical Psychology: Science and Practice*, *10*, 373–393.

Nelson, N. W., Parsons, T. D., Grote, C. L., Smith, C. A., & Sisung, J. (2006). The MMPI–2 Fake Bad Scale: Concordance and specificity of true and estimated scores. *Journal of Clinical and Experimental Neuropsychology*, *28*, 1–12.

Nelson, N., Sweet, J., & Demakis, G. (2006). Meta-Analysis of the MMPI–2 Fake Bad Scale: Utility in Forensic Practice. *The Clinical Neuropsychologist*, *20*, 39–58.

Otto, M. W., Bruder, G. E., Maurizio, F., Delis, D. C., et al. (1994). Norms for depressed patients for the California Verbal Learning Test: Associations with depression severity and self-report of cognitive difficulties. *Archives of Clinical Neuropsychology*, *9*, 81–88.

Ozer, E., Best, S., Lipsey, T., & Weiss, D. (2003). Predictors of posttraumatic stress disorder and symptoms in adults: A meta-analysis. *Psychological Bulletin*, *129*, 52–73.

Rosen, G. M. (2004). Litigation and reported rates of posttraumatic stress disorder. *Personality and Individual Differences*, *36*, 1291–1294.

Sapolsky, R. M. (2001). Atrophy of the hippocampus in posttraumatic stress disorder: How and when? *Hippocampus*, *11*, 90–91.

Sapolsky, R. M. (2002). Chicken, eggs, and hippocampal atrophy. *Nature Neuroscience*, *5*, 1111–1113.

Schagen, S., van Dam, F., Muller, M., Boogerd, W., Lindeboom, J., & Bruning, P. (1999). Cognitive deficits after postoperative adjuvant chemotherapy for breast carcinoma. *Cancer*, *85*, 640–650.

Schnurr, P., & Vielhauer, M. (1999). Personality as a risk factor for PTSD. In R. Yehuda (Ed.) *Risk factors of posttraumatic stress disorder*. Washington, DC: American Psychiatric Press.

Schoenberg, M., Scott, J., Duff, K., & Adams, R. (2002). Estimation of WAIS–III intelligence from combined performance and demographic variables: Development of the OPIE–3. *The Clinical Neuropsychologist*, *16*, 426–438.

Shapinsky, A. C., Rapport, L. J., Henderson, M. J., & Axelrod, B. N. (2005). Civilian PTSD scales: Relationships with trait characteristics and everyday distress. *Assessment*, *12*, 220–230.

Smith-Seemiller, L., Fow, N., Kant, R., & Franzen, M. (2003). Presence of post-concussion syndrome symptoms in patients with chronic pain vs mild traumatic brain injury. *Brain Injury*, *17*, 199–206.

Sparr, L., & Pitman, R. (1999). Forensic assessment of traumatized adults. In P. Saigh & J. D. Bremner (Eds.) *Posttraumatic stress disorder: A comprehensive text*. Boston: Allyn & Bacon.

Suhr, J. A., & Boyer, D. (1999). Use of the Wisconsin Card Sorting Test in the detection of malingering in student simulator and patient samples. *Journal of Clinical and Experimental Neuropsychology*, *21*, 701–708.

Sweet, J., & Westergaard, C. (1997). Evaluation of psychopathology in neuropsychological assessment. In G. Goldstein & T. Incagnoli (Eds.) *Contemporary approaches in neuropsychological assessment*. New York: Plenum.

Taylor, S., Frueh, B. C., & Asmundson, G. (2007). Detection and management of malingering in people presenting for treatment of posttraumatic stress disorder: Methods, obstacles, and recommendations. *Journal of Anxiety Disorders*, *21*, 22–41.

Turnbull, S., Campbell, E., & Swann, I. (2001). Post-traumatic stress disorder symptoms following a head injury: Does amnesia for the event influence the development of symptoms? *Brain Injury*, *15*, 775–785.

Williams, W. H., Evans, J., Needham, P., & Wilson, B. (2002). Neurological, cognitive, and attributional predictors of posttraumatic stress symptoms after traumatic brain injury. *Journal of Traumatic Stress*, *15*, 397–400.

Feigning of psychiatric symptoms in the context of documented severe head injury and preserved motivation on neuropsychological testing

15

David T. R. Berry and Robert P. Granacher, Jr.

Concern regarding the motivation and effort of forensic neuropsychological evaluees first became prominent in the 1980s when cases of patients claiming devastating impairment from apparently trivial or questionable head injuries began to appear with increasing frequency in the referral streams of neuropsychologists (Binder & Willis, 1991; Hiscock & Hiscock, 1989). Since that time, a number of objective procedures for evaluating the effort put forth by such evaluees have been validated (Bianchini, Mathias, & Greve, 2001; Vickery, Berry, Inman, Harris, & Orey, 2001). Similar to recommendations made for the examination of compensation-seeking psychological evaluees (Berry, Baer, Rinaldo, & Wetter, 2002), most sources in the area suggest that all forensic neuropsychological examinees should receive at least one, and preferably several, well-validated objective tests of motivation and effort (Reynolds, 1998; Sweet, 1999). Although these tests are invaluable in forensic neuropsychological examinations, a number of complex issues regarding detection of malingering arise in this setting. Among these are:

1. Some forensic evaluees have probably been "coached" prior to their forensic evaluations regarding motivational tests to assist them in avoiding detection of feigning.
2. Patients with documented severe TBIs may also fabricate or exaggerate neuropsychological deficits.
3. There can be different presentations of feigning within a forensic neuropsychological evaluation, including malingered neurocognitive deficit, exaggeration or fabrication of psychological symptoms, and feigning of somatic problems.

Following an overview of these concerns, the case study presented in this chapter raises possible or probable elements of these issues, highlighting the need to screen for *multiple* types of feigning in *all* compensation-seeking neuropsychological examinees.

Unease has been growing in recent years regarding "coaching" of plaintiffs to avoid detection on published procedures for identifying feigning on psychological and neuropsychological tests (Victor & Abeles, 2004). Youngjohn (1995) documented coaching regarding a motivational test in a report in which an attorney in a legal proceeding for a plaintiff who had undergone forensic neuropsychological evaluation admitted providing detailed information to his client. Wetter and Corrigan (1995) surveyed attorneys and law students and found that the majority felt it was their ethical obligation to inform clients about validity indices used in forensic psychological examinations. Lees-Haley (1997) suggested that coaching on malingering detection instruments might be pervasive in many settings. Allen and Green (2001) reported a steady decline in failure rates on the Computerized Assessment of Response Bias (CARB) administered to forensic evaluees over a six-year period, suggesting dissemination of information on the instrument. Ruiz, Drake, Glass, Marcotte, and van Gorp (2002) searched the Internet to determine instances of on-line information with the potential to compromise the validity of malingering detection instruments and found that up to 5% of sites offered information on psychological testing that posed a "direct threat to test security" (p. 294). In a letter to test users, Multi-Health Systems, Inc., publisher of the Test of Memory Malingering (TOMM), suggested that the test's acronym should be hidden from test takers because of concern that evaluees had searched the Internet for information about how to avoid detection on commonly used tests such as the TOMM (Multi-Health Systems, Inc.; letter to TOMM Users, January 8, 2003). Despite the difficulty of gathering objective data on the phenomenon of coaching, it appears that the validity of widely used motivational tests may be eroded through diffusion of knowledge of the procedures. One response to this concern has been the development of additional validated malingering tests so that the number of available procedures might undermine the coaching capacity of unscrupulous individuals (Vagnini, Sollman, Berry, Granacher, Clark, Burton, O'Brien, Bacon, & Saier, 2006).

Another complex issue in forensic neuropsychological assessment has been the recognition that even patients with well-documented brain injuries and resulting disability may exaggerate or fabricate additional deficits. Palmer, Boone, Allman, and Castro (1995) first drew attention to this phenomenon with a case report of a neuropsychological evaluee who had clear neuroimaging evidence of multiple, bilateral infarcts and was subsequently found to be exaggerating or fabricating deficits on cognitive testing. Later, Boone and Lu (2003) reported two cases of litigating TBI patients with clear objective evidence for severe brain injury who fell below recommended cutoff scores on multiple motivational tests, provided non-credible performances on standard neuropsychological tests, and elevated multiple fake bad scales on the MMPI–2. Iverson (2003) documented statistically significantly below chance accuracy on the Recognition Memory Test in a stroke patient. Bianchini, Greve, and Love (2003) described three cases of objectively documented moderate to severe TBI who scored statistically significantly below chance on the Portland Digit Recognition Test or the Test of Memory Malingering. The last two publications are particularly compelling; scores on forced-choice testing that fall statistically significantly below chance clearly document a *deliberate* attempt to present as cognitively impaired. This body of evidence suggests that assessment of possible feigning should be carried out even in forensic cases with unquestionable documentation of brain dysfunction (Bianchini et al., 2003).

Recognition that malingering during forensic evaluations may take many forms has gradually grown in recent years. Feigning of psychiatric symptoms has long been a concern in a variety of settings, particularly in the military during wartime. The MMPI, one of the first standardized instruments for the assessment of psychopathology, included two validity indices for the identification of feigning (F and $F–K$), and others were subsequently developed (Ds). Because the MMPI was typically included in neuropsychological assessments, there was early interest in determining whether neurocognitive malingering could be identified using the MMPI validity scales. Heaton, Smith, Lehman, and Vogt (1978) reported that the MMPI F scale was the best indicator of analog feigning in forensic neuropsychological examinations. However, Villanueva and Binder (1993) found that MMPI–2 F scale scores were only moderately correlated with scores on the Portland Digit

Recognition Test ($r = -.38$) in compensation-seeking mild head injury patients who had undergone forensic neuropsychological examination. Millis, Putnam, and Adams (1995) reported on results from compensation-seeking mild head injury patients undergoing forensic evaluation. They noted that concordance between unequivocal evidence of neuropsychological feigning and MMPI–2 validity scales was modest, with the exception of the *FBS* scale (see below). Greiffenstein, Gola, and Baker (1995) presented data from compensation-seeking head-injured evaluees who received motivational testing and the MMPI–2. They noted that the MMPI–2 *F* and *F–K* scales did not differ significantly between compensation-seeking probable malingerers and genuine head-injury patients from a private practice. Further, factor analysis of MMPI–2 validity scales and motivational indices from these samples identified two distinct dimensions characterized as feigned emotional problems and feigned neurobehavioral deficits. MMPI–2 validity indices loaded on the emotional feigning but not the neurobehavioral feigning factor. Greiffenstein et al. concluded that real-world TBI malingerers tended to feign neurobehavioral deficits like amnesia rather than emotional problems. Berry and Butcher (1998) presented case reports of three mildly head-injured patients who underwent forensic neuropsychological evaluation and received motivational testing as well as the MMPI–2 and the Structured Interview of Reported Symptoms (SIRS: Rogers, Bagby, & Dickens, 1992; see below for description). One of these cases failed motivational testing, had significantly elevated MMPI–2 validity scales, and failed the SIRS, suggesting feigning of both neurocognitive and psychiatric problems. The second case failed motivational testing but did not elevate MMPI–2 validity scales, suggesting only feigning of neurocognitive deficit. The final case passed motivational testing but elevated MMPI–2 validity scales and failed the SIRS, suggesting only feigning of psychiatric symptoms. Overall, this evidence suggests that screening for both psychiatric and neurocognitive feigning should be undertaken for all forensic neuropsychological evaluees.

A third type of feigning, somatic malingering, has been identified relatively recently. Larrabee (1998) pointed out that, in neuropsychological settings, somatic complaints such as pain, paresthesias, malaise, etc. are common and not well captured by MMPI–2 *F* and *Fb* scales, which are particularly sensitive to feigned psychotic symptoms. Thus, traditional MMPI–2 validity scales might be insensitive to feigned somatic symptoms. Larrabee (1998) showed, in a sample of compensation-seeking head-injured evaluees who failed motivational testing and obtained elevated MMPI–2 scales *Hs* and *Hy*, that the Lees-Haley Fake Bad Scale (*FBS*: Lees-Haley, English, & Glenn, 1991) was most sensitive to somatic feigning, whereas *F*, *Fb*, and *F(p)* were insensitive to this condition. Similarly, Boone and Lu (1999) presented evidence for somatic malingering during forensic neuropsychological examinations, which was not adequately identified by the traditional MMPI–2 validity scales but was detected by *FBS*. Additionally, Lanyon (2001) factor analyzed results from 101 forensic psychological evaluees who received the MMPI–2 as well as several other indicators of misrepresentation. He reported the presence of three distinct factors, including one characterized by exaggeration of physical health problems. Lanyon (2003) developed validity scales for the Psychological Screening Inventory and the Multidimensional Health Profile for the detection of feigned health problems, and showed that they were sensitive to somatic feigning by analog and suspected clinical malingerers. Overall, there appears to be growing evidence for the existence of a third major type of feigning in forensic neuropsychological examinations, involving exaggeration and/or fabrication of health problems. A growing body of work supports the utility of the *FBS* scale for identifying somatic feigning in forensic cases (Dearth, Berry, Vickery, Vagnini, Baser, Orey, & Cragar, 2005; Greiffenstein, Baker, Gola, Donders, & Miller, 2002; Larrabee, 1998; Larrabee, 2003; Ross, Millis, Krukowski, Putnam, & Adams, 2004; Vagnini et al., 2006). Although some negative findings have appeared (Butcher, Arbisi, Atlis, & McNulty, 2003; Elhai, Gold, Frueh, & Gold, 2000), a recent meta-analysis strongly supports the ability of the *FBS* scale to identify somatic feigning in forensic cases (Nelson, Sweet, & Demakis, 2006).

Overall, the available evidence reviewed above suggests that all forensic neuropsychological evaluees, even those with documented brain pathology, should be screened for multiple types of feigning, including malingered neurocognitive, psychiatric, and somatic symptoms. Additionally, examiners should remain alert for possible coaching of forensic evaluees. The present case of Mr. K. raises components of all these issues, and demonstrates that feigners may have surprising (to clinicians) ideas about appropriate symptoms to fake.

THE CASE OF MR. K.

Background

Mr. K. was examined by one of the authors at the request of his attorney. The referral question was whether there was neuropsychiatric impairment secondary to a motor vehicle accident. At the time of this evaluation Mr. K. was a 24-year-old white, single, left-handed male who prior to his accident earned a living constructing agricultural buildings. Approximately 2 years prior to the examination, Mr. K. was riding an all terrain vehicle (ATV) near his home when he lost control in a ditch and was thrown into the path of a vehicle traveling on a nearby road. The EMS report indicated that he was not wearing a protective helmet, but initially he was fully oriented and then he gradually became confused and combative. Upon arrival at a local hospital, Mr. K. was observed to be confused and combative, and eventually he lost consciousness. Significant lacerations of his scalp and other sites were noted. He required intubation due to pneumothorax and was diagnosed with rib and ankle fractures as well. Following medical stabilization, he was evacuated by air to a university hospital. CT scan of the head indicated a large left subarachnoid hemorrhage. He required a 24-day hospitalization complicated by infection and difficulty being weaned from a respirator. He eventually improved enough to be transferred to a rehabilitation facility where he was noted to be very impulsive, uncooperative with his non-weight-bearing status, and to have significant language and memory dysfunction. Mr. K. was ultimately discharged to a relative's care. At the time of this neuropsychiatric evaluation, his mother reported that he was more irritable since his accident as well as disinhibited with prominent coprolalia. He reportedly had attempted to return to construction work but was unsuccessful secondary to memory and concentration problems.

Following the ATV accident, he required three admissions to a state psychiatric hospital and two admissions to a private psychiatric facility within a 5-week interval. All admissions were due to outlandish social behavior and disinhibited verbal aggression. His behavior improved marginally following prescriptions of divalproex 1500 mg/day, lithium carbonate 1350 mg/day and escitalopram 20 mg/day.

Premorbid history

Mr. K.'s family medical history was unremarkable. Mr. K. was reportedly a normal term baby who met early developmental milestones at the usual times. Although his history was negative for sexual abuse, substance problems, legal difficulties, etc., he had trouble in grade school learning to read, was diagnosed with ADHD and treated with stimulant medications and counseling. A WISC–R administered at age 8 revealed VIQ of 106, PIQ of 93, and FSIQ of 100. He eventually graduated from high school, but he required special education classes. As previously noted, Mr. K. subsequently supported himself as a construction worker.

Neuropsychiatric evaluation

Mr. K. was referred for neuropsychiatric examination by his attorney and was evaluated 24 months after his accident. Following the method outlined by Granacher (2003), Mr. K. received a neuropsychiatric evaluation including mental status examination, neurological examination, neuroimaging, neuropsychological assessment, and psychological testing. His mental status examination was remarkable for mild confusion and significant difficulty communicating including disjointed conversation, tangential tendencies, and probable paraphasic signs, e.g., "There is no wick on my bomb." He complained of depression, nervousness, stress, panic, and difficulties with concentration, memory and thinking. Observed affect was constricted although delusions and hallucinations were denied. Neurological examination was remarkable only for anosmia; otherwise cranial nerve, motor, sensory, cerebellar, and gait/station findings were within normal limits. MRI of the brain was performed and interpreted as within normal limits. Positron Emission Tomography was also undertaken and revealed mild hypometabolism of the left medial temporal lobe.

Neuropsychological examination

Behavioral observations from neuropsychological testing were of some interest. Mr. K. took an early "smoking break" and failed to return. Ultimately, he had to be retrieved by his mother, who had accompanied him to the evaluation. He was noted to have obvious difficulty processing spoken language, particularly when test instructions were complex. Repetition and rephrasing were frequently required to orient him to tasks. He initiated no conversation and tended to respond to questions with very few words and little elaboration. Although more typically bored and unengaged, at times Mr. K. became angry when he had difficulty with a test, occasionally throwing down his pencil upon completing written tasks. On Part B of the Trail-Making Test, he became obviously annoyed and stated that he felt like "breaking something." Mr. K.'s behavior was also noteworthy for a nearly complete absence of social graces. Overall, Mr. K. presented as unenthusiastic and at times irritated about the testing although subjectively appearing to exert adequate effort.

Mr. K. was administered three motivational tests to assess effort during his evaluation. On the Victoria Symptom Validity Test he scored 94% correct (Slick, Hopp, Strauss, & Thompson, 1997). Scores were 100% correct for both the Test of Memory Malingering (Tombaugh, 1997) and the Letter Memory Test (Inman, Vickery, Berry, Lamb, Edwards, & Smith, 1998). Additionally, the Reliable Digit Span score (Greiffenstein, Gola, & Baker, 1995) from the WAIS–III was 8. As all these performances were above recommended cutoff scores, it was felt that he was adequately motivated during cognitive testing and that his test results were likely a reasonable representation of his neuropsychological status.

Results from neuropsychological testing were converted to T scores using the Heaton, Grant, and Mathews (1991) norms wherever possible in order to correct for age, education, and sex. For tests lacking coverage by Heaton et al. (1991), raw scores were converted to standard scores as indicated in the particular test manuals. Mr. K.'s neuropsychological findings are presented in Table 15.1. Using a conservative impairment threshold of a percentile ranking < 5, Mr. K. had impaired scores on a test of attention, multiple tests of language, a test of complex motor speed, right-sided sensation and perception, and a test of alternating responses. Given his history of left-sided subarachnoid hemorrhage, adequate performance on motivational testing, and current functional neuroimaging pointing to left-sided hypometabolism, these results were interpreted as consistent with brain dysfunction secondary to TBI, with greater involvement of the left hemisphere. He was diagnosed with Dementia due to TBI as well as Expressive Language Disorder due to TBI.

TABLE 15.1   Selected neuropsychological test results from Mr. K.

TEST/INDEX		STANDARD SCORE/PERCENTILE RANK
Ruff 2 & 7 Total Speed		37/10 PR
Total Accuracy		51/55 PR
Brief Test of Attention		< 2 PR*
Boston Naming		19/< 1 PR*
Controlled Oral Word Association		33/5 PR*
Wide Range Achievement Test Reading		58/< 1 PR*
Wechsler Adult Intelligence Scale–3rd ed.		
	FSIQ	81/10 PR
	VCI	80/9 PR
	POI	93/32 PR
	WMI	82/12 PR
	PSI	76/5 PR*
Wechsler Memory Scale–3rd ed.		
	Imm. Mem.	78/7 PR
	Gen. Mem.	86/18 PR
Reitan-Klove Sensory Perceptual Examination		
	Total R. Errors	30/3 PR*
	Total L. Errors	34/6 PR
Finger Oscillation Test		
	R. Hand	39/14 PR
	L. Hand	36/6 PR
Grooved Pegboard Test		
	R. Hand	24/1 PR*
	L. Hand	29/2 PR*
Grip Strength Test		
	R. Hand	44/27 PR
	L. Hand	38/13 PR
Trail-Making Test		
	Form A	39/14 PR
	Form B	27/1 PR*
Wisconsin Card Sorting Test		
	Total Errors	44/27 PR
	Persev. Responses	49/45 PR

Note: * = clearly impaired score (< 5th percentile).

Psychological testing

Because of his poor reading level as seen in Table 15.1, Mr. K. was administered the tape-recorded version of the Minnesota Multiphasic Personality Inventory–2nd edition in order to evaluate his self-reported psychological problems. His validity scale results were as follows (all in T scores):

VRIN	TRIN	L	K	S	F	Fb	Fp
46	72 (T)	56	30	38	113	120	77

His *VRIN* and *TRIN* scores suggest adequate attention and consistent responding to test questions, albeit with some tendency to "yea-saying" as indicated by the *TRIN* score. Results from these two scales are particularly important given Mr. K.'s observed language problems, as they suggest it is unlikely that he responded randomly or did not understand test questions sufficiently to answer consistently. Mr. K.'s "fake good" validity scale results (*L, K,* and *S*) were all in the acceptable range, suggesting that he did not minimize or deny the presence of psychological problems. In contrast, most of Mr. K.'s "fake bad" validity scale results were highly elevated, particularly *F* (113T) and *Fb*

(120T). In combination with acceptable scores on the two consistency measures (*VRIN* and *TRIN*), these results strongly suggest the presence of exaggeration or possibly fabrication of psychological problems (Graham, 2000). However, because these MMPI–2 validity scales are not thought to be sufficiently accurate to identify the presence of feigned symptom reports on their own (Berry et al., 2002), the Structured Interview of Reported Symptoms (Rogers, Bagby, & Dickens, 1992) was administered. This procedure has been well validated for detection of feigned psychiatric symptoms, and has a very high specificity rate which results in high positive predictive power in most base rate environments. Raw scores from each of the eight primary scales on the SIRS are classified into one of four ranges (Honest, Indeterminate, Probable Feigning, and Definite Feigning), based on extensive data provided by the test's authors. Mr. K.'s SIRS results indicated that three of his primary scales were elevated into the *Probable Feigning* range, a result that, according to the interpretive guide presented in the manual for the test, is characteristic of individuals who are feigning a mental disorder, and is rarely seen in clients responding truthfully. Taken together, results from the MMPI–2 and the SIRS indicate that Mr. K. was exaggerating and/or fabricating psychiatric complaints, and that his self-reports of psychological symptoms could not be taken as an accurate reflection of his psychological status.

Mr. K.'s MMPI–2 results were also scored for the *FBS* scale. His raw score on this scale was 27, which falls above the cutoff score suggested by Larrabee (2003) for identification of somatic feigning. This result suggests that some of Mr. K.'s complaints regarding somatic symptoms may have been exaggerated or possibly fabricated.

COMMENT

Mr. K.'s neuropsychiatric examination results suggested that he exerted adequate effort on neuropsychological testing. His observed deficits were quite consistent with his initial injury severity and localization indicators, as well as his current functional neuroimaging results. Taken together, the available evidence strongly suggested that Mr. K. was experiencing significant neuropsychological impairment as a result of his TBI. Although it is at least theoretically possible that Mr. K. was "coached" to avoid detection by the motivational tests administered to him, at least two points weigh against this possibility. First, the LMT, one of the three motivational tests used, was not widely known at the time of Mr. K.'s evaluation and had only recently been instituted as part of the motivational battery used in this neuropsychiatric practice. Second, in addition to "passing" the three specialized motivational tests, Mr. K. also performed adequately on the Reliable Digit Span procedure, which is derived from the "embedded" Digit Span subtest of the WAIS–III, and is also probably less well-known than the VSVT and TOMM as a measure of cognitive effort.

Despite this strong evidence for adequate effort on neuropsychological testing and the presence of converging lines of evidence suggesting genuine brain dysfunction secondary to his TBI, Mr. K. appeared to have feigned psychiatric symptoms on the MMPI–2. Although it is possible that Mr. K.'s dysphasic symptoms and disinhibited behavior contributed to his elevated infrequency scales on the MMPI–2, his results on the two consistency indices from this test (*VRIN* and *TRIN*) suggested that he processed item content sufficiently well to respond consistently across the rather lengthy MMPI–2. Additionally, Mr. K.'s probable feigning on the MMPI–2 was confirmed by his performance on the SIRS, which was consistent with false psychiatric symptom reports. It is worth noting here that if routine examination of the veracity of psychological complaints via the MMPI–2 validity scales had not been undertaken with follow-up using the SIRS, the presence of this type of feigning by Mr. K. would probably have gone undetected.

The possibility of somatic feigning was also raised by Mr. K.'s results from the *FBS* scale. Although the SIRS has not been validated for detection of this type of feigning, it is possible that

Mr. K.'s exaggeration or fabrication of physical symptoms may have contributed to his failure of this instrument.

Why did Mr. K. feign psychiatric symptoms? This strategy certainly did not appear to be in his best interest, as he presented with rather compelling evidence for genuine brain dysfunction secondary to his TBI. From the standpoint of obtaining justifiable compensation for his injury, exaggerating and/or fabricating psychopathology could only muddy the waters and open him to vulnerability to a defense attorney's arguments. It is possible that Mr. K. felt that he might obtain additional compensation for the presence of a psychiatric disorder as a result of his TBI. On the other hand, inability to understand fully the medical-legal issues in his examination may have played a role even though *VRIN* was not elevated. He had obvious impairment of complex language comprehension. More importantly, his ability to suppress inappropriate social responses was evident. This raises the possibility of ventromedial prefrontal cortex injury not detected by PET or MRI imaging affecting psychological performance (Granacher & Fozdar, 2007).

These data, as presented, were placed into his court record by deposition. Cross-examination by the defendant did not challenge the direct testimony by one of the authors. The defense focused upon liability issues and elicited on cross-examination that absence of a protective helmet likely contributed to Mr. K.'s injuries. The case settled out of court to Mr. K.'s favor the day before a jury trial was to have begun.

In the end, it is impossible to determine exactly why Mr. K. appeared to be feigning psychiatric symptoms. However, it is clear that, even in a case with unquestioned, genuine TBI as well as documented adequate effort on cognitive testing and apparently bona fide neuropsychological deficits, forensic evaluees may, for whatever reasons, choose to exaggerate and/or fabricate psychiatric symptoms. Taken together with other evidence reviewed above, this example strongly suggests that all forensic neuropsychological examinations should include screening for feigned psychiatric symptoms. If a clinician does not check for the presence of this type of feigning, it is unlikely to be detected.

REFERENCES

Allen, L. M., & Green, P. (2001). Declining CARB failure rates over 6 years of testing: What's wrong with this picture? *Archives of Clinical Neuropsychology, 16*, 846.

Berry, D. T. R., Baer, R. A., Rinaldo, J. C., & Wetter, M. W. (2002). Assessment of malingering. In J. N. Butcher (Ed.), *Clinical personality assessment: Practical approaches*, 2nd ed. (pp. 269–302). London: Oxford University Press.

Berry, D. T. R., & Butcher, J. N. (1998). Detection of feigning of head injury symptoms on the MMPI–2. In C. Reynolds (Ed.) *Detection of malingering during head injury litigation* (pp. 209–238). New York: Plenum Press.

Bianchini, K. J., Greve, K. W., & Love, J. M. (2003). Definite malingered neurocognitive dysfunction in moderate/severe traumatic brain injury. *The Clinical Neuropsychologist, 17*, 574–580.

Bianchini, K. J., Mathias, C. W., & Greve, K. W. (2001). Symptom validity testing: A critical review. *The Clinical Neuropsychologist, 15*, 19–45.

Binder, L., & Willis, S. (1991). Assessment of motivation after financially compensable minor head trauma. *Psychological Assessment, 3*, 175–181.

Boone, K. B., & Lu, P. H. (1999). Impact of somatoform symptomatology on credibility of cognitive performance. *The Clinical Neuropsychologist, 13*, 414–419.

Boone, K. B., & Lu, P. (2003). Noncredible cognitive performance in the context of severe brain injury. *The Clinical Neuropsychologist, 17*, 244–254.

Butcher, J. N., Arbisi, P. A., Atlis, M. M., & McNulty, J. L. (2003). The construct validity of the Lees-Haley Fake Bad Scale (FBS): Does this scale measure somatic malingering and feigned emotional distress? *Archives of Clinical Neuropsychology, 18*, 473–485.

Butcher, J. N., Dahlstrom, W. G., Graham, J. R., Tellegen, A., & Kaemmer, B. (1989). *Manual for administration and scoring of the Minnesota Multiphasic Personality Inventory–2nd ed.* Minneapolis: University of Minnesota Press.

Dearth, C. D., Berry, D. T. R., Vickery, C. D., Vagnini, V. L., Baser, R. E., Orey, S. A., & Cragar, D. E. (2005). Detection of feigned head injury symptoms on the MMPI–2 in head injured patients and community controls. *Archives of Clinical Neuropsychology, 20,* 95–110.

Elhai, J. D., Gold, P. B., Frueh, B. C., & Gold, S. N. (2000). Cross-validation of the MMPI–2 in detecting malingered Posttraumatic Stress Disorder. *Journal of Personality Assessment, 75,* 449–463.

Graham, J. R. (2000). *MMPI–2: Assessing personality and psychopathology–3rd ed.* New York: Oxford Press.

Granacher, R. P. (2003). *Traumatic brain injury: Methods for clinical and forensic neuropsychiatric assessment.* New York: CRC Press.

Granacher, R. P., & Fozdar, M. (2007). Personal injury litigation and acquired psychopathy. In A. Felthous & H. Sass (Eds.) *International handbook of psychopathic disorders and the law.* New York: John Wiley & Sons.

Greiffenstein, M. F., Baker, W. J., Gola, T., Donders, J., & Miller, L. (2002). The Fake Bad Scale in atypical and severe closed head injury litigants. *Journal of Clinical Psychology, 58,* 1591–1600.

Greiffenstein, M. F., Gola, T., & Baker, W. J. (1995). MMPI–2 validity scales versus domain specific measures in the detection of factitious traumatic brain injury. *The Clinical Neuropsychologist, 9,* 230–240.

Heaton, R. K., Grant, I., & Matthews, C. G. (1991). *Comprehensive norms for an expanded Halstead-Reitan battery: Demographic corrections, research findings, and clinical applications.* Odessa, FL: Psychological Assessment Resources.

Heaton, R. K., Smith, H. H., Lehman, R. A., & Vogt, A. J. (1978). Prospects for feigning believable deficits on neuropsychological testing. *Journal of Consulting and Clinical Psychology, 46,* 892–900.

Hiscock, M., & Hiscock, C. K. (1989). Refining the forced-choice method for the detection of malingering. *Journal of Clinical and Experimental Neuropsychology, 11,* 967–974.

Inman, T. H., Vickery, C. D., Berry, D. T. R., Lamb, D. G., Edwards, C. L., & Smith, G. T. (1998). Development and initial validation of a new procedure for evaluating adequacy of effort given during neuropsychological testing: The Letter Memory Test. *Psychological Assessment, 10,* 128–139.

Iverson, G. L. (2003). Detecting malingering in civil forensic evaluations. In A. M. Horton & L. C. Hartlage (Eds.) *Handbook of forensic neuropsychology* (pp. 137–177). New York: Springer Publishing Company.

Lanyon, R. I. (2001). Multimodal assessment of self-serving misrepresentation during personal injury evaluation. *American Journal of Forensic Psychology, 19,* 5–14.

Lanyon, R. I. (2003). Assessing the misrepresentation of health problems. *Journal of Personality Assessment, 81,* 1–10.

Larrabee, G. J. (1998). Somatic malingering on the MMPI and MMPI–2 in personal injury litigants. *The Clinical Neuropsychologist, 12,* 179–188.

Larrabee, G. J. (2003). Detection of symptom exaggeration with the MMPI–2 in litigants with malingered neurocognitive deficit. *The Clinical Neuropsychologist, 17,* 54–68.

Lees-Haley, P. R. (1997). Attorneys influence expert evidence in forensic psychological and neuropsychological cases. *Assessment, 4,* 321–324.

Lees-Haley, P. R., English, L. T., & Glenn, W. J. (1991). A fake bad scale on the MMPI–2 for personal injury claimants. *Psychological Reports, 68,* 203–210.

Millis, S. R., Putnam, S., & Adams, K. (1995). *Neuropsychological malingering and the MMPI–2: Old and new indicators.* Presented at the 30th Annual Symposium on Recent Developments in the Use of the MMPI, MMPI–2 & MMPI–A, St. Peterburg Beach, FL.

Nelson, N. W., Sweet, J. J., & Demakis, G. J. (2006). Meta-analysis of the MMPI–2 Fake Bad Scale: Utility in forensic settings. *The Clinical Neuropsychologist, 20,* 39–58.

Palmer, B. W., Boone, K. B., Allman, L., & Castro, D. B. (1995). Co-occurrence of brain lesions and cognitive deficit exaggeration. *The Clinical Neuropsychologist, 9,* 68–83.

Reynolds, C. R. (Ed.) (1998). *Detection of malingering during head injury litigation.* New York: Plenum Press.

Rogers, R., Bagby, R. M., & Dickens, S. (1992). *Structured Interview of Reported Symptoms: Professional manual.* Odessa, FL: Psychological Assessment Resources.

Ross, S. R., Millis, S. R., Krukowski, R. A., Putnam, S. H., & Adams, K. M. (2004). Detecting incomplete effort on the MMPI–2: An examination of the Fake Bad Scale in mild head injury. *Journal of Clinical and Experimental Neuropsychology, 26,* 115–124.

Ruiz, M. A., Drake, E. B., Glass, A., Marcotte, D., & van Gorp, W. G. (2002). Trying to beat the system: Misuse of the Internet to assist in avoiding the detection of psychological symptom dissimulation. *Professional Psychology: Research and Practice, 33,* 294–299.

Slick, D. J., Hopp, G., Strauss, E., & Thompson, G. B. (1997). *Victoria Symptom Validity Test version 1.0 professional manual.* Odessa, FL: Psychological Assessment Resources.

Sweet, J. J. (Ed.) (1999). *Forensic neuropsychology: Fundamentals and practice.* Exton, PA: Swets & Zeitlinger Publishers.

Tombaugh, T. N. (1997). The Test of Memory Malingering (TOMM): Normative data from cognitively intact and cognitively impaired individuals. *Psychological Assessment, 9,* 260–268.

Vagnini, V. L., Sollman, M. J., Berry, D. T. R., Granacher, R. P., Clark, J. A., Burton, R., O'Brien, M., Bacon, E., & Saier, J. (2006). Known-groups cross-validation of the Letter Memory Test in a compensation-seeking mixed neurologic sample. *The Clinical Neuropsychologist, 289–305.*

Vickery, C. D., Berry, D. T. R., Dearth, C. S., Vagnini, V. L., Baser, R. E., Cragar, D. E., & Orey, S. A. (2004). Head injury and the ability to feign neuropsychological deficits. *Archives of Clinical Neuropsychology, 19,* 37–48.

Vickery, C. D., Berry, D. T. R., Inman, T. H., Harris, M. J., & Orey, S. A. (2001). Detection of inadequate effort on neuropsychological testing: A meta-analytic review of selected procedures. *Archives of Clinical Neuropsychology, 16,* 45–73.

Victor, T. L., & Abeles, N. (2004). Coaching clients to take psychological and neuropsychological tests: A clash of ethical obligations. *Professional Psychology: Research and Practice, 35,* 373–379.

Villanueva, M., & Binder, L. (1993). *Association between MMPI-2 indices and the Portland Digit Recognition Test.* Presented at the 21st Annual International Neuropsychological Society Meeting, Galveston, TX.

Wechsler, D. (1981). *The Wechsler Adult Intelligence Test–Revised manual.* New York: Psychological Corporation.

Wechsler, D. (1997). *The WAIS–III/WMS–III: Technical manual.* San Antonio, TX: The Psychological Corporation.

Wetter, M. W., & Corrigan, S. K. (1995). Providing information to clients about psychological tests: A survey of attorneys' and law students' attitudes. *Professional Psychology: Research and Practice, 26,* 474–477.

Youngjohn, J. R. (1995). Confirmed attorney coaching prior to neuropsychological evaluation. *Assessment, 2,* 279–283.

Fabrication of psychiatric symptoms: Somatoform and psychotic disorders

16

Bradley N. Axelrod

Neuropsychologists involved in settings in which the presence or absence of cognitive impairment is assessed can easily get lost in the forced dichotomy of "is this individual malingering or brain injured?" However, as trained clinical psychologists and neuropsychologists, we must also consider other potential etiologies in the differential. This includes whether a primary psychiatric condition might be present, or whether there might be some combination of neurologic, psychiatric, and/or motivational issues simultaneously at play.

When assessing malingered *brain* injury, unusual responses and patterns of responding are noted. Uncommon performance on memory tests, such as performing worse than chance on a forced-choice test, alerts the neuropsychologist to the potential of *malingered* cognitive findings. Likewise, some examinees present with atypical responses in the context of a suspected psychiatric presentation. The scrutiny by the neuropsychologist for potentially malingered conditions should be as detailed and careful for *psychiatric* presentations as it is for *neurologic* disorders.

WHEN ARE EXAGGERATED OR MANUFACTURED SYMPTOMS NOT MALINGERING?

The *Diagnostic and Statistical Manual of Mental Disorders*—Fourth Edition Text Revision (DSM–IV–TR) is the compendium of psychiatric diagnoses. Malingering is defined by the DSM–IV–TR as the "intentional production of false or grossly exaggerated . . . symptoms." Importantly, the intent behind the falsification of these symptoms is initiated by a specific "external incentive." Examples of incentives include avoiding work, military service, and criminal prosecution. Other motivators include financial gain for the individual (e.g., a litigated civil case) or being prescribed medications. The DSM–IV–TR goes on to consider malingering when an evaluation is conducted in a medical legal context, when discrepancies are noted between objective findings and subjective report, and when cooperation is poor. The *International Classification of Diseases*, 10th Revision, Clinical Modification (ICD–10 CM), offers the same diagnosis, defining malingering as simulation of symptoms with the intent to deceive to obtain a specific goal.

A diagnostic entity that falls close to malingering is that of *factitious disorder*. In that condition, there is likewise "intentional production or feigning of physical or psychological signs or symptoms" (DSM–IV–TR, p. 517). As with malingering, a factitious disorder obtains when neither a medical condition nor a psychiatric condition is diagnosed. However, rather than seeking a specific tangible enticement, the purpose is "to assume the sick role" when other external incentives are not present. This presentation occurs in individuals who receive psychological satisfaction by being cared for by others. Their fabrication, exaggeration, and creation of symptoms are all done to receive that attention from medical professionals.

The distinction between malingering and factitious disorders seems to rest on one primary component. Namely, the crux of the diagnosis is whether the motivation for intentionally fabricating pathology is generated by an external incentive or by a psychological need to be medically treated. Professionally, I am reluctant to report malingering when factitious disorder cannot be definitively ruled out. It is the very rare patient—and something that has only occurred twice in my experience—who steps outside of the assessment and asks the question "is my performance bad enough to be considered brain injured?" However, there is external information that allows greater weight to be emphasized toward malingering and away from a factitious disorder. For example, when an individual gains no social attention, recurring trips to medical professionals, or special treatment by others by appearing ill, it is less likely that a diagnosis of factitious disorder obtains.

Regardless of the motivation of the individual being examined, a patient can offer an inaccurate and invalid presentation. It is the responsibility of the neuropsychologist to be mindful of the potential for exaggerated or fabricated responses, in the same way that the clinician must consider psychiatric diagnoses as being responsible for, or at least influencing, an individual's presentation.

ANALYSIS OF A NEUROPSYCHOLOGICAL EVALUATION

Neuropsychologists base their conclusions of an examinee on data external to the testing situation, as well as material from within the confines of the session. More specifically, external data can come from existing medical records that predated the incident that is seen as responsible for the changes in functioning as well as records that are subsequent to the event. In the best of circumstances, these records will also include: (1) academic (including grades and standardized test scores) and employment records; (2) psychological, neuropsychological, psychiatric, and neurologic evaluations; (3) records from the ambulance run sheet and the emergency room at the hospital where treatment was initially obtained; and (4) police reports of the incident. The information obtained from original sources, when possible, obviously reveals more accurate information than that obtained from the individual's recollections. Recall of such information (e.g., the time of loss of consciousness, grades in school) can be compromised by attempts at being intentionally misleading or by merely recalling inaccurately.

Material extracted from the neuropsychological evaluation proper includes: (1) background information, as presented subjectively from the examinee about the incident as well as academic, medical, and employment data; (2) behavior during the interview and assessment; and (3) test results from performance on the neuropsychological measures. To dissect the information even further, test results are not limited exclusively to the scores obtained via standardized scoring of the responses. In addition, the content of the material, pattern of scores, consistency across tests with the evaluation, and consistency of test scores across multiple evaluations over time all must be considered when reviewing the findings of a neuropsychological assessment.

It is the complexity and interactions of all these different types of information that allow the neuropsychologist to generate hypotheses and make conclusions regarding an individual's neurocognitive or psychological state. For example, patterns of performance, based on academic history, severity of an injury, report of current symptoms, consistency across tasks, and stability over time, are all examples of material that can be evaluated in an assessment protocol. The information should coincide in an individual case to point to a specific incident or series of events that parsimoniously explain the overall presentation of the person being evaluated.

When background information, behavioral presentation, and test results fail to merge into a single pattern, neuropsychologists investigate further to generate a reasonable hypothesis that would explain the disparity among the findings. When these pieces of information not only fail to converge into a single solution, but actually contradict each other, then the accuracy of the data is brought into question.

I view the role of the neuropsychologist as that of describing an examinee's cognitive and psychological status in order to reach diagnostic conclusions. Failure to obtain valid information offers nothing beyond a finding of "inaccurate presentation." I will readily inform examinees that test results indicate poor motivation or effort. As this behavior is seemingly in the control of the individual, so would be the cessation of such inaccurate performance, if it were an intentional act.

The two following cases are of individuals who presented with significant psychiatric symptoms following motor vehicle accidents. However, both produced findings that were indicative of factitious disorder or malingering, rather than psychiatric symptoms.

CASE 1: A PAIN IN THE NECK

Review of the critical incident

At the time of the motor vehicle accident, Ms. L. was a 53-year-old white female who was the driver of a Ford Taurus. She was wearing her seatbelt at the time of the accident and was reportedly waiting at a traffic light for the signal to turn green. As she waited, she was rear ended by another vehicle that approached the intersection. Ms. L. reportedly struck her head against the dashboard or steering wheel. She did not lose consciousness.

After she drove her vehicle home, Ms. L. was driven by a friend to the emergency department of the local hospital. She reported experiencing a "significant headache" at that time. She also expressed some discomfort in her neck, as well as pain on the left side of her face and head. Records from the emergency room indicate that she was alert and oriented. Her Glasgow Coma Scale score was within normal limits. Ms. L. was given x-rays and underwent a physical examination; both were unremarkable. She was discharged to home three hours later, with a diagnosis of cervical pain. Her friend then drove Ms. L. home.

Following her discharge from the emergency room, Ms. L. continued to experience neck pain. She also reported having a continuous headache that did not abate. By five months after the accident, she had acquired blurred vision. She reported left facial pain, left elbow pain, diminished bilateral grip strength, and pressure behind her ears. Right neck and shoulder pain radiated down her right arm. Carpal tunnel syndrome was diagnosed six months after the motor vehicle accident (MVA). Cognitively, she reported feeling disoriented. She claimed no memory of the accident or her emergency room visit following the collision. One month later, or seven months after the accident, her blurred vision abated and was reportedly replaced with double vision.

Ms. L. had sought evaluation by different orthopedic surgeons after the motor vehicle accident. Approximately 18 months after the accident, a third orthopedic surgeon evaluated Ms. L. She reported that the surgeon observed "all kinds of ruptured discs in the cervical region." He performed a C5–C6 disc fusion, followed by four weeks of physical therapy conducted three times weekly. The treatment did not improve her subjective report of pain. Prior to the surgical intervention, Ms. L. participated in group psychotherapy for individuals with chronic pain. According to the progress notes, the psychologist noted "resistance to treatment." She attended begrudgingly and did not contribute to the group during the sessions.

Background information

Ms. L. completed 12 years of education, obtaining her high school diploma from a school in a rural farming community. She then obtained a beautician certification and worked as a hair stylist for five years. Afterward, she worked on the assembly line at a nearby factory for 25 years.

Prior medical history was significant for breast cancer with a mastectomy. Socially, she was married twice and had three adult children who lived nearby. She was still with her second husband, having been married for more than 10 years. Her husband was unemployed at the time of Ms. L.'s accident, having been placed on Worker's Compensation from injuries to his back and knees.

Prior neuropsychological evaluation

Background

Seven months after the MVA, and 14 months prior to my evaluation of Ms. L., she was referred for a neuropsychological evaluation. According to that report, she was referred by a nurse case manager "to provide a comprehension [sic] assessment" of her cognitive and emotional status. She had already been diagnosed with carpal tunnel syndrome but had not yet undergone cervical disc fusion. In providing information about the MVA, Ms. L. denied a loss of consciousness and reported full recall of the event and her subsequent ride to the hospital.

Ms. L. reported minimal cognitive difficulties at the first assessment, although she admitted to being more forgetful than she had been previously. She reported being most concerned about her physical ailments. In addressing her emotional symptoms, Ms. L. reported heightened anxiety since the MVA, especially when she was required to drive. She reported having nightmares relating to the accident for two months, but those abated.

Upon arrival to her first neuropsychological evaluation Ms. L. wore a cervical collar and wrist braces. She spoke in a conversational manner, with speech that was "spontaneous and fluent." She was "cooperative and friendly" and remained compliant over the course of the evaluation. Although generally motivated to perform the tasks, she appeared discouraged when she experienced failed performance.

Test results

Ms. L. participated in a thorough neuropsychological evaluation (see Table 16.1), including measures of intellectual functioning, achievement, memory, executive functioning, and motor skills. Measures of motivation were employed, as was an assessment of her emotional status.

On the Wechsler Adult Intelligence Scale–III, Ms. L. obtained a Full Scale IQ in the high end of the low average range (FSIQ = 88), with higher performance (PIQ = 93) skills relative to verbal (VIQ = 85) abilities. Her Verbal Comprehension (VCI = 90) and Perceptual Organization (POI = 95) indexes were superior to her Working Memory skills (WMI = 77). In fact, her worst performance was on Digit Span (Age Scaled Score = 5), in which she was able to repeat as many as five digits forward and three digits backward.

On measures of achievement, Ms. L. demonstrated average sight reading skills, with math skills that fell in the low end of the average range. Low average performance was noted on tasks of reading comprehension, and vocabulary.

TABLE 16.1   Test results for Ms. L.

	PRIOR EVALUATION (7 MONTHS POST-EVENT)	AUTHOR'S EVALUATION (22 MONTHS POST-EVENT)
Age	53 years	55 years
Intellectual Functioning Wechsler Adult Intelligence Scale–Revised		
FSIQ	88	
VIQ	85	56
PIQ	93	
Information	8	2
Digit Span	5	2
Vocabulary	8	1
Arithmetic	7	1
Comprehension	8	2
Similarities	9	1
Picture Completion	10	
Picture Arrangement	8	
Block Design	9	
Object Assembly	8	
Digit Symbol	10	
Memory (Standard Scores) Wechsler Memory–Revised		
Immediate	85	<50
Delayed	80	
Executive Functioning (T scores) Trail Making Test		
TMT-A	30	
TMT-B	33	
Booklet Category Test	42	
Word Generation (COWAT) 37 (23 words)	< 20 (0 words)	
Motor Tests (T scores)		
Finger tapping–dominant	40	
Finger tapping–nondominant	40	

Note: Blank spaces indicate that the test was unable to be given.

Memory testing, based on the Wechsler Memory Scale–Revised, reportedly fell in the low average range. Her performance remained in the low average range following the 30-minute delay.

Assessment of executive functioning measures found low average performances on a verbal fluency test (SS = 81) and the Booklet Category Test (SS = 88). In contrast, she demonstrated mildly impaired (SS = 75) performance on Trail Making Test B.

Ms. L. refused to participate in any motor tasks that involved her left hand. For her right (dominant) hand, she demonstrated low average performance on tasks of motor speed and finger dexterity.

On the MMPI–2, Ms. L. had a validity configuration "associated with individuals who are attempting to avoid or deny unacceptable feelings, impulses, and problems." The psychologist described a naïve, simplistic, and concrete view of the world. Her clinical scale elevation, a 1-3-2 profile, was described in the report as a "conversion profile typically seen in those who endorse somatic discomfort rather than demonstrate emotional feelings directly." The profile demonstrated "limited awareness in how her behavior avoids emotional expression" and a "significant degree of denial of emotional distress." The neuropsychologist offered that there was "a significant psychogenic component to her neck and head pain."

Conclusion of first evaluation

The neuropsychologist summarized the findings pointing to the subjective complaints of increasing forgetfulness and orthopedic pain. Cognitive results were presented as generally falling in the Low Average range, considered below premorbid estimations. Her affective state was reportedly indicative of "distress and depression, as well as repression and denial." Diagnoses of Pain Disorder and Cognitive Disorder secondary to traumatic brain injury were offered.

Subsequent neuropsychological evaluation

My evaluation of Ms. L. occurred 14 months after the first one, two years and two months after the MVA. As evident in Table 16.1, the most striking aspect of the subsequent evaluation was the lack of standardized test data obtained from Ms. L. Contrasting with the initial evaluation, she was unable to perform tests she had previously completed successfully. Despite the minimal information obtained, sufficient material was gleaned from the assessment to reach the conclusion that Ms. L.'s presentation was an intentional fabrication of symptoms. The results of this primarily qualitative evaluation are noteworthy because of the amount of qualitative information that was obtained from this evaluation, which served to be little more than an extended clinical interview.

Background and behavioral presentation

The purpose of the evaluation was to evaluate the necessity for Ms. L. to obtain cognitive rehabilitation, as the psychologist treating her for chronic pain believed that it was indicated. Ms. L. was 55 years old when seen for the second evaluation. She arrived 20 minutes early for her appointment, brought to the evaluation by her husband. She was an overweight woman who walked with the assistance of a four-prong cane. She walked slowly and demonstrated difficulty maneuvering in the office. For example, when preparing to sit, she first approached the chair and then stopped while facing the seat. She then slowly turned around, first moving one foot about 30 degrees, and then the other foot by 30 degrees to meet it. After turning in this step-by-step manner, she then lowered herself slowly into the chair.

In terms of her presentation for the second evaluation, Ms. L. kept her eyes closed throughout much of the clinical interview and face-to-face testing. She communicated that she had a severe headache and that keeping her eyes closed provided relief. Ms. L. refused to perform any tasks requiring visual processing. She kept her eyes closed and shook her head "no" when asked to look at a visual stimulus.

In contrast to the fluent speech described in the behavioral observations of the first neuropsychology report, Ms. L. presented with degraded syntax in her speech. Her speech often presented as telegraphic phrases. In addition, she failed to maintain appropriate tense (as in present and past tense) within the same sentence when speaking. For example, she stated, "I was hit from behind and my car goes over" when providing information about the accident. She spoke very slowly and in a monotone.

Mental status

In contrast to her self-report from the prior evaluation, Ms. L. stated that she did not recall whether she lost consciousness. Also, she was unsure how she arrived at the hospital, offering that she might have been driven in an ambulance. She denied any memory of her emergency room care at the hospital. Ms. L.'s memory for personal information aside from that related to the accident itself was equally poor. She reported not knowing if she obtained any healthcare since the accident and stated that all she knew was that she had surgery once. She accurately provided her birth date, but stated that she did not know her age. Consistent with her unusual speaking style, she stated that her birth date was "45 in 25 in May" in describing the date of May 25, 1945.

Ms. L. was unable to accurately provide the date. She correctly reported the year, but was off by one month and refused to guess as to the numerical date. She claimed that the day was Tuesday at 11:00 AM, when in fact it was Saturday at 8:45 AM. Ms. L. did not recall the name of the current president, claiming that the last president she could recall was Kennedy. Incidentally, she had been in her late teens when Kennedy was president.

The following verbal exchange occurred when Ms. L. was asked about her current symptoms. The conversation demonstrates her disrupted language, as well as her reportedly impaired knowledge of personal and relevant information:

Doctor: What is different now for you in comparison to before the accident?
Ms. L.: I hurt. My body hurt.
Doctor: Where do you hurt?
Ms. L.: Hurt. Pain.
Doctor: I need to understand what hurts you and how it hurts.
Ms. L.: Bad. Pain bad.
Doctor: Do you have a headache?
Ms. L.: Bad hurt.
Doctor: Does it hurt right now?
Ms. L.: Pain. Head pain. Hurt pain.
Doctor: Did you take medication for your pain today?
Ms. L.: Maybe. I no know.

What is striking about this sample of dialogue is the apparent inability of Ms. L. to generate either full sentences or grammatically understandable phrases. In addition, the content of the conversation was typical of her inability to provide coherent information, a marked difference from the first assessment.

Test findings

The results from the Verbal subtests of the WAIS–R revealed a score in the Extremely Low range (VIQ = 52), significantly lower than the VIQ of 85 obtained 14 months earlier. Aside from the decline in overall scores, the specific content from the WAIS–R items offers additional material. Ms. L. successfully repeated three digits forward and two digits backward, but was unable to generate longer responses. Her scaled score of 2 is clearly more deficient than the 5 obtained during the first evaluation. On the Information subtest, Ms. L. offered that the colors of the American flag are "Red, blue, and white," there are 51 weeks in the year, and Louis Armstrong was a famous clarinet player. She incorrectly offered that Labor Day was in April or June. Some responses on this subtest are striking in the near-miss quality of the answers. For example, individuals who are simply mentally deficient will err that the number of weeks in a year is 48. Computing four weeks per months and 12 months per year generates this error. An answer of 51 is an error that rarely occurs. Likewise, the common incorrect response for the month in which Labor Day occurs is typically May, as individuals confuse that with Memorial Day. A guess of April or June is illogical and also rare. Similarly, although technically correct, the Ganser response of the colors of the flag being "red, blue, and white" and not "red, white, and blue" is also indicative of an atypical response. (Ganser's Syndrome is a factitious disorder, characterized by mimicking behavior assumed typical of a psychosis, although responses to questions are incorrect and nonsensical. However, the answers are usually so close to the actual response that it is clear that the query was understood.)

Comprehension subtest responses offer additional evidence of incorrect illogical responses. When presented with the item regarding washing clothes, Ms. L. replied, "heavy week . . . every week washing . . . spots washing." The explanation for cooking foods was "not hard cooking." Follow-up questioning did not clarify these responses. Finally, when asked the routine question regarding an emergency at the movies, Ms. L. stated, "I no go to movie." When the item was repeated, she stated, "Okay. Maybe I go movie." On Vocabulary, when asked to define the word "penny," she stated "brown means 'thank you' " and failed to explain further her response.

Formal memory testing was not performed, as Ms. L. generated recall output that was below testable limits. Consequently, paired associate learning was attempted. She again demonstrated an inability to perform any of the word pairs. Next, she was told only two pairs of words (east-west and gold-silver). When given the first word (east), she was to respond with the second word (west). Despite reading the word pairs 10 times, and providing the correct answers each time, Ms. L. responded either by repeating the word presented or by saying "I can't think" and "I no know." The "pair" of one-two was then presented. After the examiner stated "one" Ms. L. responded by saying "no number."

Quantitative test findings

An ad hoc forced-choice symptom validity test was performed in an attempt to see how Ms. L. would respond when recognition memory was limited to two options. In this assessment, she watched the examiner place an object in one of his hands and place both hands on the desk. She was to count to five aloud and then tell him in which hand the item was. She complained that she was unable to count aloud, so the examiner counted aloud for her. Of the 20 trials, Ms. L. correctly identified the hand in which the object was held four times. This response rate of 20% falls at a level that is statistically worse than chance ($z = 2.68$, $p < .01$). Such a result can only be accomplished when an individual knows the correct response and intentionally offers the incorrect one.

Performance on the MMPI–2

Ms. L. was given directions to complete the MMPI–2. For each item, she stared ahead for 45 to 60 seconds and then asked that the question be read aloud. After five items, the MMPI–2 questions were consistently read aloud. After completing item 27 of the 567 items, Ms. L. stood up and stated, "No. No question. It hurt. No more." She then swayed side to side and appeared to be losing her balance. After a few sways, she fell straight backwards, collapsing onto the couch that she had been standing in front of. The evaluation was then discontinued.

Conclusions

There were a number of specific findings that pointed to the likelihood of incomplete effort. They included:

1. Telegraphic speech in an individual who had fluent speech seven months post-injury and who had no subsequent neuropsychiatric illness.
2. Poor autobiographical memory for events that even preceded the accident.
3. Rarely occurring incorrect responses and Ganser-type (near miss) incorrect responses.
4. Inability to learn paired associates, even when the pair of words is over-learned and obvious, such as "one-two."
5. Performance on a forced-choice test that was statistically worse than chance.
6. An overall drop in performance on all cognitive measures in comparison to another neuro-psychological evaluation that had been performed post-ictus.

If Ms. L. indeed sustained a cognitively altering brain injury from the accident, her cognitive functioning had dramatically deteriorated from 7 months post-injury to 22 months post-injury. Such decompensation is *not* indicative of a traumatic brain injury, which improves rather than worsens over time. Although it is possible that she had a Pain Disorder at the time of my evaluation of Ms. L., her implausible presentation obscured my ability to evaluate accurately her emotional status.

CASE 2: "BONNIE IS IN MY EYE!"

Review of the critical incident

Ms. M. was 38 years old at the time of her motor vehicle accident. She was the driver of a sedan with manual transmission, traveling on a four-lane highway. She was not wearing a seatbelt. According to the police report, she lost control of her car, went into a spin, and struck a guardrail. Ms. M.'s family insisted that her car struck a large pothole. As a result of the incident, the two tires on the driver's side blew out, causing her to lose control of the vehicle. She was thrown inside the car, striking her face on the gearshift. The impact on the gearshift dislodged her right eye. By the time the ambulance arrived, the EMS technicians noted that on the Glasgow Coma Scale she obtained full credit for Verbal Responses and Motor responses. However, her injured eye prevented them from evaluating that portion of the GCS. The EMS report indicates that her GCS was 11 of 11.

Ms. M. was taken by ambulance to a nearby trauma hospital. In the emergency room, she presented with a GCS of 15 of 15. Despite her injured right eye, she reportedly read the information presented by the triage nurse, and completed some of the required forms. She was admitted to the hospital for 10 days. Treatment included repair of right shoulder dislocation and treatment of numbness in her shoulders, arms, and legs. She initially experienced arm and leg paralysis, but that abated over the course of her hospitalization. Ms. M. was also treated for numerous lacerations resulting from glass shards that struck her during the single-car collision.

The most significant treatment was obviously related to the replacement of Ms. M.'s eye. She was given an eye transplant from a woman, named Bonnie, who was killed in a motor vehicle accident two days after Ms. M.'s MVA. Aside from the surgeries for immediate implantation, Ms. M. underwent a number of subsequent surgeries. These additional treatments were to correct ingrown eyelashes around the replacement eye that continued to become infected, causing significant pain and discomfort for Ms. M.

Following discharge from the hospital for acute care, Ms. M. was referred for outpatient treatment at a freestanding rehabilitation clinic. In the preliminary rehabilitation evaluation, Ms. M. was oriented to person, place, and time. She demonstrated mild memory impairment, recalling only one of three words after a brief delay on a Mental Status Examination. The physician noted that Ms. M.'s speech was "clear and appropriate" during the evaluation conducted approximately one month post-injury. In discussing Ms. M.'s emotional state, the physiatrist noted that Ms. M. was often tearful during the interview. She expressed concern and distress about her appearance with the new eye. She was noted to have a low frustration tolerance during the clinical interview, crying easily and bemoaning how she "must look to others" who know her.

The physiatrist referred Ms. M. for psychological and psychiatric evaluations. She was subsequently evaluated by a physical medicine and rehabilitation clinic. Treatment over the subsequent two and a half years included physical, occupational, and speech therapies. Physical therapy addressed improving the range of motion in her right arm because of her shoulder dislocation. It also focused on improving and maintaining her balance when ascending and descending stairs. Physical therapy began five times weekly, but was reduced to twice weekly after six months.

Occupational therapy reportedly addressed daily living skills, such as cooking and household care, initially three times weekly and subsequently twice weekly. She attended speech therapy three times weekly to improve what was reported as stuttered speech. Protracted treatment such as that observed for Ms. M. is considered excessive by these three disciplines, as that long-term treatment typically does not document continued improvement over shorter-term treatment.

Background information

Ms. M. obtained a high school diploma in a large metropolitan city. She reported obtaining specialized training to be a registered nurse, a vocation in which she was employed for 20 years. At the time of my assessment with her, she had been employed in the inpatient medical units of a local hospital. Her medical history was previously unremarkable. She denied any hospitalizations, medical treatments, or prescription medications prior to the motor vehicle accident. She denied the use of alcohol or recreational drugs.

Prior mental health assessments and treatment

Ms. M. was referred for a psychiatric evaluation soon after seeing her physiatrist a few weeks after hospital discharge. However, she refused to follow through for over one year. At that time, 18 months prior to my evaluation, Ms. M. obtained a psychiatric evaluation. The psychiatrist noted that she had suicidal thoughts, but no specific plan. She also presented with a labile mood and depressed affect. Medication was recommended, but Ms. M. refused to return for treatment.

A neuropsychological evaluation was performed one year post-injury. Although a copy of the report was not available to me for review, the physiatrist summarized the results in one of her progress notes. The neuropsychological evaluation was noteworthy, according to the physiatrist, in that "it contained several inconsistencies." The evaluation reportedly recommended psychotherapy for Ms. M. to address ongoing depression and lability.

Mental health treatment was finally initiated six months later, approximately one year prior to my evaluation of Ms. M. She began both individual and family psychotherapy. Progress notes from the psychologist indicated that Ms. M. believed that she was under the influence of her eye donor, Bonnie. She stated that Bonnie was responsible for her feelings of depression and also for her intermittent suicidal thoughts. The psychologist offered the working diagnosis of Major Depression with psychotic features. He soon thereafter deemed her unable to tend to her own personal needs and requested that she be provided 24-hour attendant care.

An independent psychiatric evaluation performed shortly before her neuropsychological assessment with me found Ms. M. "emotionally and behaviorally agitated." The evaluation recommended, which she refused, that Ms. M. pursue inpatient hospitalization or an outpatient day treatment center to address her "Major Depression with psychotic features, Posttraumatic Stress Disorder, and Cognitive Disorder secondary to concussion." Interestingly, the treating physiatrist had followed Ms. M. for two and a half years. Although the psychiatrist noted that Ms. M. had concern regarding her appearance, anxiety, and depression, the dire psychiatric presentation she displayed to the psychologist and psychiatrist was not described by the physiatrist.

Subsequent neuropsychological evaluation

The request for my evaluation of Ms. M. came from her automobile insurance company. The claims representative noted that two of Ms. M.'s treating physicians considered neuropsychological evaluation important to better understand her deficits. The neuropsychological evaluation was conducted two and a half years after the accident. Ms. M. was 40 years old.

Background

Ms. M. arrived promptly for her appointment accompanied by her husband. They were brought to the office via a transportation service. Ms. M. wore a black patch covering her right eye. As they walked into the office, Ms. M. held onto her husband's arm as he navigated her into the room. He helped her find a place to sit by moving her directly in front of the chair, gently pushing her so the backs of her legs touched the seat, and then assisted her into a seated position on the chair.

Although informed the day before the evaluation that they should plan on a six to eight hour evaluation, they brought no food or medications. Upon arrival, Mr. D. reported that neither he nor his wife had eaten breakfast that morning, and they had not brought food with them either. Mr. D. asked how his wife was to have food given the circumstances. When it was suggested that he walk to a nearby store, Ms. M. quickly shouted that he was not to leave her alone at any point during the day. In fact, Ms. M. requested that her husband remain present during the clinical interview, screaming that she "could not make it" if he were to leave the building. She even refused to move into the testing room, pleading with her husband to allow her to be evaluated in the waiting room.

Language

Language comprehension was presented as being compromised by Ms. M. She appeared to have difficulty understanding questions pertaining to personal information. She also often repeated questions asked of her twice. Then, on the third occasion, she substituted the word "I" for "you" in an exaggerated fashion. For example, she was asked, "Where have you worked?" Ms. M. responded by saying, "Where have you worked . . . where have you worked . . . where have I worked?" Then she would look confused and state, "I don't know." Interestingly, she also mouthed the examiner's question at the same time that the examiner was speaking.

When asked what her last memory was before the accident, Ms. M. brightened and stated with enthusiasm that she was "working on 'before' and 'after' in speech therapy," as she had previously been getting them confused.

Ms. M.'s speech was often halting and slow. In contrast to her slow and halting speech, she presented with normal articulation, volume, and prosody. She stuttered on a few occasions. However, rather than stuttering on phonemes such as "d" and "t," she stuttered on the letter "s." She responded to most questions with brief answers, or by saying that she did not know the answer or understand the query.

During the interview, Ms. M. stated that she did not recall any of her history. She requested that her husband answer the questions. When doing so, Ms. M. stared into space and appeared disconnected from the interview. In fact, when asked if the information was correct, she continued staring without responding. After her name was called a number of times, and no response was observed, she was touched lightly on her arm by her husband. At that time, she slowly traveled her gaze to the interviewer. Interestingly, her speech went from halting and slow during the evaluation to being rapid and fluid afterward. In contrast to what appeared to be significant verbal comprehension difficulty during the interview and evaluation, her language expression and comprehension improved dramatically after the assessment was terminated. *While waiting for their ride outside of the office suite, Mr. D. spoke rapidly to Ms. M. She responded fluently, without requiring repetition or clarification of his comments.*

Behavioral presentation

Ms. M. demonstrated little difficulty understanding task instructions during the evaluation. This presentation, never requiring clarification, contrasted with her behavior during the clinical interview. At times, directions were as long as four or five sentences (e.g., verbal fluency; logical memory from the Wechsler Memory Scale). She appropriately followed the directions. On occasion, she raised her voice at the examiner, stating that the tasks were too difficult. On three occasions, she stood to leave the evaluation. Because of her apparent low frustration tolerance, a shortened assessment battery was conducted.

Mental status

Ms. M. was fully oriented to person, location, date, and time. She accurately provided her age at the time of the evaluation, as well as the month and date of her birthday. However, she stated that she did not know in what year she was born. Typically, individuals with cognitive compromise will recall their birth date, but may not be able to accurately provide the current year or their age. Another unusual error observed was when Ms. M. was asked about current political leaders. She stated that Laura Bush was the current president and that Hilary Clinton preceded her.

Qualitative test findings

Ms. M. performed tests of sight-reading, in which she was requested to read words aloud with as correct pronunciation as possible. She pronounced the word AISLE as "Alice" and the word "DEPOT" as "dee-boe." This presentation is considered abnormal for two reasons. First, as reading skills are not affected by the effects of a concussion, the presentation would suggest that Ms. M.'s premorbid reading skills were severely impaired. Second of all, the quality of the mispronouncing of the words was not consistent with that typically seen in individuals with poor reading skills. For example, on DEPOT, rather than "dee-boe," the poor reader would say "dee-pot" and, on AISLE, "eye-slee."

On the Wide Range Achievement Test–III, she performed in the severely impaired range, at the Second Grade level, on reading, spelling, and math tasks. Again, these results are atypical, as these skills are also unaffected by concussion. Second, the qualitative errors observed were not of the quality of errors typically seen, even in lesser-educated individuals. For example, the word CLIFF was pronounced "cloff" while the word GRUNT was read as "runt." In spelling, the letter F was written as a "7." The words WILL, TRAIN, and SHOUT were written as "well," "tran," and "shut," respectively. She was unable to add two-digit numbers (51+27 = "718") or perform division (15/5 = "4"). As noted with the first case presented in this chapter, the examinee generated near miss and inconceivable errors during her evaluation.

Ms. M. demonstrated an inability to consistently repeat digits forward or backward. She obtained a scaled score of 1. Her longest consecutive string, in which both trials were passed, was that of repeated three digits forward. She was unable to repeat two digits backward, even after four different sets of examples were provided. Performance this poor is below the total Reliable Digit Span score of 8 (Greiffenstein, Gola, & Baker, 1994) and the age scaled score of 7 (Axelrod, Fichtenberg, Millis, & Wertheimer, 2006), below which individuals who sustained moderate to severe brain injuries do not perform.

Verbal fluency was not only severely impaired, generating less than five words in one minute for each trial, but her responses included numerous perseverations as well as neologisms. She included the word "fute" as a type of vegetable or fruit.

Quantitative test findings

Ms. M.'s specific test results are contained in Table 16.2. As performed with Ms. L. (above), a forced-choice memory task was employed to assess Ms. M.'s recognition memory. On the verbal subtest of the Warrington Recognition Memory Test, the examinee is first asked to read 50 words, one at a time. Following this, they are given a list of word pairs and requested to identify which of the words in the pair was seen previously. Guessing on a forced-choice test should result in performance around the 50% accuracy level. The average performance on this test in the nonpatient sample is

TABLE 16.2   Test results for Ms. M.

Premorbid Intellectual Functioning	
North American Adult Reading Test	75
Academic Achievement	
Wide Range Achievement Test–3 (WRAT–3)	
Reading	56
Spelling	52
Math	50
Memory (Standard Scores)	
Wechsler Memory–Revised	
Immediate	< 50
Delayed	< 50
Warrington Recognition Memory Test	
Words	< 50 (24% correct)
Executive Functioning (T scores)	
Word Generation	
COWAT	< 20 (0 words)
Animals and Fruits/Vegetables	< 20 (10 words)

approximately 94% correct. As far as Ms. M.'s performance is concerned, she accurately identified 12 of the 50 items, a response rate of 24% correct. This response rate, using binomial distribution theory, is statistically worse than chance ($z = 3.68$, $p < .0001$). Such a result can only be accomplished when an individual knows the correct response and intentionally offers the incorrect one.

When performing the visual analogue of this test, viewing photos of White males one at a time, Ms. M. stated that she could not perform the test. She stated that she could not discriminate the images "because they all White men . . . they all look like White men."

Emotional functioning

When Ms. M. was requested to provide information about current symptoms, she began crying. She loudly stated, "Bonnie is making me cry! Bonnie is still in my eye and making me do things that I don't want to do!" During the evaluation she stated that Bonnie was making her perform poorly. On a few occasions, she stated that Bonnie was "trying to take over [her] mind."

Ms. M. claimed that she was experiencing nervousness, concentration difficulties, fatigue, impatience, disorganization, irritability, and lack of enjoyment. Interestingly, she stated that her depression, anhedonia, irritability, disorganization, and memory difficulties were all worsening in severity. When seen 30 months post-accident, she reported that those symptoms were all increasing in intensity, a finding inconsistent with the sequelae of a traumatic brain injury. Instead, psychiatric or motivational causes of her symptoms seemed indicated.

Conclusions

The qualitative and quantitative features of Ms. M.'s profile that point to compromised effort are seen in the following:

1. Difficulties that were observed intermittently (e.g., fluency of speech, language comprehension) over the course of the evaluation and depending on the other person present.
2. Behaviors and symptoms inconsistent with sequelae of traumatic brain injury, particularly in an individual who had minimal loss of consciousness.

(a) Intact orientation and age, with no recall of birth year
(b) Poor digit repetition
(c) Reported worsening of symptoms over time.

3. Rarely occurring incorrect responses.
4. Performance on a forced-choice test that was statistically worse than chance.

Regarding Ms. M.'s presentation, it is clear that diminished effort was intentionally produced. It appears that her presentation might have been to gain attention from others (i.e., Factitious Disorder) or for specific financial gain (i.e., Malingering). Although she might have had a psychotic depression, her failure to fully cooperate and her inability to present a truthful depiction of her current symptoms prevented me from obtaining an accurate assessment of her neuropsychological status.

SUMMARY AND FINAL CONCLUSIONS

The lack of a parsimonious clinical solution to explain these two individuals' presentations is of importance to the practicing clinician. As was seen in the analysis of the reported personal histories of these examinees, immediate behavior following the accidents, available medical records, behavioral presentations during the assessment, and neuropsychological test performance, the only viable explanation was that performance was suboptimal. Additional support for diminished effort is seen in the first individual whose test scores are not only profoundly deficient when taken in isolation but are also clearly demonstrated to represent a decline from a different neuropsychological evaluation that took place after the accident.

Both of the women presented in this chapter performed worse than chance and demonstrated qualitative errors that are inconsistent with normal functioning. The performance was also inconsistent with known neurocognitive conditions. A diagnosis of malingering would apply if the intentions of these women were clear, namely seeking a specific external incentive, such as money. However, it is also possible that the exaggeration of cognitive difficulties might have been used to gain sympathy and help from medical professionals. Although less likely because of the quality of their presentation, other potential conditions might be responsible for additional diagnoses in the differential. For example, somatoform or psychotic conditions might apply for these two women. The need to find a precise and accurate diagnosis is certainly desirable on the part of a clinician. And yet, when an examinee provides answers and patterns of performance that indicate an intentional manufacturing of symptoms, the speculation as to why they might be performing poorly intentionally becomes less important.

The clinical cases presented in this chapter were selected for two reasons. These cases depicted individuals who appeared to have significant psychiatric symptoms in addition to their cognitive deficits. Second, both examinees failed to complete a thorough formal neuropsychological evaluation. Importantly, the behavioral information extracted during the assessment served to be as useful as would have a complete neuropsychological evaluation. The qualitative material obtained provided sufficient evidence that the veracity of these patients' reports was doubtful. Statistical analyses of test performance are not necessary in all cases to determine fabricated cognitive deficits.

Finally, the two cases presented above demonstrate that exaggerated symptoms presented by individuals with a factitious disorder or malingering can be of a psychiatric nature, as well as cognitive. It is the responsibility of the neuropsychologist to tease out this information in an individual referred for assessment. Neuropsychologists can offer much information to neurologists and psychiatrists by capitalizing on our knowledge of mental health, psychiatric symptoms, neurological sequelae, behavior, and common errors.

REFERENCES

Axelrod, B. N., Fichtenberg, N. L, Millis, S. R., & Wertheimer, J. (2006). Detecting incomplete effort with Wechsler Adult Intelligence Scale–3rd edition Digit Span Subtest. *The Clinical Neuropsychologist, 20,* 513–523.

Butcher, J. N., Dahlstrom, W.G., Graham, J. R., Tellegen, A., & Kaemmer, B. (1989). *Minnesota Multiphasic Personality Inventory (MMPI–2).* Minneapolis: University of Minnesota Press.

Greiffenstein, M. F., Baker, W. J., & Gola, T. (1994). Validation of malingered amnesia measures with a large clinical sample. *Psychological Assessment, 6,* 218–224.

Greve, K. W. & Bianchini, K. J. (2004). Setting empirical cut-offs on psychometric indicators of negative response bias: a methodological commentary with recommendations. *Archives of Clinical Neuropsychology, 19,* 533–541.

Iverson, G. L., & Franzen, M. D. (1996). Using multiple objective measures to detect simulated malingering. *Journal of Clinical and Experimental Neuropsychology, 18,* 38–51.

Johnson-Greene, D., Dehring, M., Adams, K. M., Miller, T., Arora, S., Beylin A., & Brandon, R. (1997). Accuracy of self-reported educational attainment among diverse patient populations: A preliminary investigation. *Archives of Clinical Neuropsychology, 12,* 635–643.

Larrabee, G. J. (2003a). Detection of malingering using atypical performance patterns on standard neuropsychological test. *The Clinical Neuropsychologist, 17,* 410–425.

Larrabee, G. J. (2003b). Exaggerated pain report in litigans with malingered neurocognitive dysfunction. *The Clinical Neuropsychologist, 17,* 395–401.

Millis, S. R. (1992). The Recognition Memory Test in the detection of malingered and exaggerated memory deficit. *The Clinical Neuropsychologist, 6,* 406–414.

Teasdale, G., & Jennett, B. (1974). Assessment of coma and impaired consciousness. *Lancet, II,* 81–84.

The Psychological Corporation. (1997a). *WAIS–III: Administration and scoring manual.* San Antonio, TX: Harcourt Brace.

The Psychological Corporation. (1997b). *WAIS–III/WMS–III technical manual.* San Antonio, TX: Harcourt Brace.

Warrington, E. K. (1984). *Recognition Memory Test: Manual.* Berkshire, UK: NFER–Nelson.

Wechsler, D. (1981). *Wechsler Adult Intelligence Scale–Revised.* New York: The Psychological Corporation.

Wechsler, D. (1987). *Wechsler Memory Scale–Revised.* San Antonio, TX: The Psychological Corporation.

Wilkinson, G. S. (1993). *Wide Range Achievement Test–3rd ed.* Wilmington, DE: Wide Range.

Malingering of psychiatric disorders in neuropsychological evaluations: Divergence of cognitive effort measures and psychological test validity indicators

17

Nathaniel W. Nelson and Jerry J. Sweet

Commensurate with neuropsychologists' increasing forensic interests and increasing involvement in forensic activities in recent years, clinical researchers have explored with greater vigor effective methods of identifying patients' fraudulent objective test performances (Sweet, King, Malina, Bergman, & Simmons, 2002). Validity testing of alleged psychological symptoms has been in place for decades within the Minnesota Multiphasic Personality Inventory (MMPI: Hathaway & McKinley, 1943; MMPI–2: Butcher, Dahlstrom, Graham, Tellegen, & Kaemmer, 1989), and development of novel MMPI–2 validity scales in recent years (e.g., Back Infrequency, *Fb*: Butcher et al., 1989; Fake Bad Scale, *FBS*: Lees-Haley, English, & Glenn, 1991; Infrequency Psychopathology Scale, *Fp*: Arbisi & Ben-Porath, 1995) has improved the ability to evaluate psychological symptom exaggeration. Furthermore, although by comparison the application of cognitive effort measures is a relatively new phenomenon, great strides have been made recently through use of forced-choice methodology (e.g., the Word Memory Test, *WMT*: Green, Allen, & Astner, 1996; Victoria Symptom Validity Test, *VSVT*: Slick, Hopp, & Strauss, 1995; Test of Memory Malingering, *TOMM*: Tombaugh, 1996) and application of cognitive effort indicators derived from standard neuropsychological ability measures. As a result, neuropsychologists have a larger array of symptom validity tests to choose from than ever before (Bianchini, Mathias, & Greve, 2001).

In spite of the progress that has been made in the assessment of psychological and cognitive symptom exaggeration, it should not be assumed that cognitive symptom exaggeration represents the same or even a similar construct as psychological symptom exaggeration. In our experience, some neuropsychologists naively convey a strong conviction that elevations on MMPI–2 validity scales should predict insufficient cognitive effort, and vice versa. Though the parsimony of such an assumption may be appealing, there is not consistent empirical foundation to support it.

A small body of recent literature has reported relationships among cognitive effort measures and MMPI–2 validity scales. Overall, sample sizes have been modest, and findings have been equivocal, with some authors reporting substantial relationships among cognitive effort measures and psychological validity tests in compensation-seeking samples (Greiffenstein, Baker, Gola, Donders, & Miller, 2002; Greve, Bianchini, Love, Brennan, & Heinly, in press; Larrabee, 2003a; Slick, Hopp, Strauss, & Spellacy, 1996), and others reporting variable or nonsignificant relationships (Greiffenstein, Baker, & Gola, 1994; Larrabee, 2003b; Nelson, Sweet, Berry, Bryant, & Granacher, 2007; Sweet, Nelson, & Heilbronner, 2005).

Greve et al. (in press) examined whether varying probabilities of cognitive malingering were associated with increasing MMPI–2 validity scale elevations in a sample of traumatic brain injury (TBI) participants and non-litigating patients with a variety of clinical conditions. TBI participants were categorized according to the Slick, Sherman, and Iverson (1999) criteria for malingered neuro-cognitive dysfunction (MND), and classification accuracies were obtained for the MMPI–2 validity scales at varying cutoff scores. Groups with no external incentive and with incentive only (i.e., without evidence of cognitive malingering) performed similarly on MMPI–2 validity scales, while groups with statistically-likely, probable, and definite probabilities of cognitive malingering performed similarly across MMPI–2 validity scales. Overall, the authors found that "the degree to which the Slick et al. criteria were met was correlated with the frequency of positive MMPI–2 findings" (p. 18), supporting the notion of simultaneous presentation of cognitive and psychological malingering in TBI individuals with secondary gain.

Larrabee (2003a) observed correlational relationships in individuals with definite MND (Slick et al., 1999), moderate-severe closed-head injuries, and a group with less than chance performance on the Portland Digit Recognition Test (*PDRT*; Binder & Kelly, 1996), a widely used forced-choice measure of cognitive effort. The *PDRT* correlated minimally with MMPI–2 scales *F*, *Fb*, and *Fp*, and correlated significantly only with the *FBS*. In a sample of individuals with probable MND, Larrabee (2003b) found that the *PDRT* and Rey-15 item test (Rey, 1964) correlated minimally with the *FBS*.

Slick et al. (1996) reported a number of correlations among the various indices of the *VSVT* and select validity scales from the MMPI–2. They found the *VSVT* to correlate minimally with *O–S* and *Fp*, and found moderate correlations between the *VSVT* and *F* and *F–K* scales, and the *FBS*. They suggested that the moderate *VSVT*/MMPI–2 validity correlations supported the convergent validity of the *VSVT*.

Greiffenstein et al. (2002) compared a group of head-injured litigants with "atypical" symptom clusters with severely head-injured litigants. In the atypical group, the *FBS* correlated significantly (*p* < .005) with the *PDRT*, the Rey-15 item test, and the Rey Word List (Rey, 1941, in Lezak, 1983). In contrast, the *FBS* did not correlate significantly with any of these cognitive effort measures in the severely head-injured group. In a previous study, Greiffenstein, Gola, and Baker (1995) conducted a factor analytic examination of various MMPI–2 validity scales and cognitive effort measures in a sample of brain-injured individuals with evidence of probable malingering and patients with severe brain injury. Findings suggested that cognitive effort measures and MMPI–2 validity scales loaded on two distinct factors. These findings were suggestive of two separate malingering factors, "one reflective of feigned emotional problems and the other reflective of feigned neurobehavioral deficits" (p. 236).

Consistent with the findings of Greiffenstein, Gola, and Baker (1995), Sweet et al. (2005) found relatively little correspondence among individual MMPI–2 validity scales and individual cognitive effort measures in a sample of more than 150 individuals with secondary gain. In more than 130 correlations observed between cognitive effort measures and MMPI–2 validity scales, the over-whelming majority (98%) was statistically non-significant (*p* > .01). The authors concluded that correspondence between cognitive effort measures and MMPI–2 validity scales was weak enough to suggest that one could not predict the other; both types (i.e., cognitive and psychological validity measures) were necessary to evaluate the validity of patients' neuropsychological performances. In a more recent exploratory factor analysis (Nelson, Sweet, Berry, Bryant, & Granacher, 2007), findings suggested a complex relationship among psychological and cognitive response validity variables: Cognitive effort loaded independently from factors associated with over-reporting of psychological symptoms in general, though validity scales whose content reflected over-reporting of somatic/neurotic symptoms (e.g., *FBS*) showed some relationship with cognitive effort relative to over-reporting of psychotic symptoms (e.g., *F*, *Fp*, *F–K*).

Given the limitations and inconsistencies found in the current literature, it would be imprudent for neuropsychologists to assume that individual patients will consistently demonstrate valid or invalid cognitive and psychological test responses concurrently. To illustrate the potential divergence of cognitive and psychological malingering within the forensic setting, the present chapter juxtaposes two patients referred for independent neuropsychological examination in relation to alleged cognitive symptoms subsequent to a mild head injury (Ms. N.) and a coronary artery bypass grafting (CABG) surgery (Mr. O.). Although test performances were interpreted as potentially malingered in both cases, the quality of cognitive versus psychological symptom exaggerations and invalid response styles was distinctly different. The contrasting nature of these patients' exaggeration of symptoms exemplifies the importance of providing multiple sources (i.e., cognitive *and* psychological) of validity testing to patients with identifiable forms of secondary gain.

THE CASE OF MS. N.

Background

Ms. N., a 44-year-old, widowed, Latina woman, was referred for independent neuropsychological examination in relation to a mild head injury she sustained approximately six months prior to evaluation. On interview, Ms. N. reported that she had been struck by a 55-pound drum while at work. She recalled details of the event quite well and denied a loss of consciousness (later record review indicated that she had reported a brief loss of consciousness during a previous evaluation). The drum struck the left side of the posterior head, and she fell to her knees. She was not sure of the height from which the drum had fallen. After the injury, she experienced pain in her nose (with nosebleed) and ringing in the ears. A co-worker helped her regain a standing position, and an ambulance was called. She was taken to a local emergency room, but was not admitted. X-ray of the nose revealed that it was broken. She experienced pain and swelling of the knees. Eventually, she consulted a plastic surgeon regarding her nose, but did not undergo surgery. She continued to perceive her nose as looking "a little" different. On current evaluation, though, no outward sign of abnormality was visible.

In the weeks and months following the injury, Ms. N. was treated by her primary care physician for whiplash, a stiff neck, and back pain. She underwent six weeks of physical therapy, which alleviated her pain. She experienced frequent headaches, initially accompanied by emesis, photophobia, and sonophobia. She received injections for these symptoms, and they subsided after a few weeks. Headaches improved to the point that she experienced two or three "bad" headaches a month at the time of evaluation. These headaches did not interfere with her function. The headaches were described as originating from her nose and around the eyebrows. In the morning, she occasionally experienced temporary swelling in the upper nose or underneath the eye, but reportedly her physician was not concerned about these symptoms. She also experienced urinary leakage (with unclear etiology) and constipation (of unknown etiology) that continued at times.

In addition, certain sounds or motions triggered unwanted, intrusive thoughts pertaining to the accident. She continued to experience these symptoms daily at the time of evaluation, but they had decreased somewhat over time. She continued to have occasional nightmares of objects coming at her. The nightmares decreased over time (two or three nightmares in the month prior to evaluation), and she was usually able to get back to sleep. She "forced" herself to go back to the area of the plant where the incident occurred, and was able to do so.

In terms of cognition, Ms. N. experienced memory difficulties since the injury. In the days immediately after the accident she was "wandering" around her house being very distractible. She forgot doctors' appointments and misplaced items (e.g., she lost her keys temporarily). She continued to experience distractibility (e.g., left the water on; left clothes in the washer without moving them to the dryer; left the gas stove on; "burned up" and "overflowed" pans on the stove). She denied *any* improvement in these symptoms over time.

In terms of mood, Ms. N. experienced feelings of depression following the injury. However, she believed these symptoms were improving over time. She cried less than she had previously. At the time of evaluation, she obtained 12 hours of sleep overall (at night plus daytime nap), but did not feel rested upon awakening. Previously, she typically slept 8 hours each night. Appetite was diminished; she had lost 10 pounds since the time of the injury. She denied suicidal ideation.

Health history prior to her injury was unremarkable. She denied any other history of accidents or injuries. Ms. N. denied any history of depression or related treatments prior to the injury. She typically drank alcohol only socially, but had not consumed alcohol since being prescribed medications. She did not use tobacco or illicit substances. She continued to see a physician for medications and occasional follow-up visits. She was prescribed an antidepressant for two months for depressive symptoms and perceived this to be somewhat helpful.

Ms. N. grew up in orphanages in the Los Angeles area. She reported physical abuse at the hands of the guardians at the orphanage. She was adopted at age 11, but was not close with her adoptive family. Ms. N. left home at age 17 to live with an aunt because she did not get along with her adoptive mother. She graduated from high school and obtained secretarial training. Ms. N. worked in customer service (secretary, receptionist) for a retail company for three years prior to the injury. She returned to work two months after the injury, but headaches interfered with work-related responsibilities, and she discontinued work after a week. She resumed work part-time (10 hours weekly) after another two months in a position with fewer responsibilities relative to her previous position.

Ms. N. was tested over two sessions. During the initial interview, she stood up to demonstrate how her injury had occurred and what parts of the body had been struck. Prior to the initial testing session, she indicated that she was not feeling well, and that she was not planning to complete Part 2 of the testing session (as previously arranged) on the next day. She agreed to complete the second session a week later. Of note, Ms. N. presented with marked lability during the initial session. At times she expressed anger (e.g., when told that testing would last for most of the afternoon, when told she would need to move her car out of a restricted zone); at other times she expressed sadness and tearfulness over poor task performances; and at still other times she appeared content to complete the tasks at hand. During testing, it seemed apparent that her mood influenced her approach to tasks and her ability to complete them successfully. For instance, when asked questions pertaining to history/literature, she expressed irritation over her inability to provide correct answers, and effort seemed to decline on subsequent items (e.g., "see, I just can't even think of it"; "I'm drawing a complete blank"). On a task involving the immediate recall of previously administered symbols, she became extremely agitated and tearful, and stated, "I can't remember them, I'm sorry, I'm just so frustrated"). At the end of the first day of testing, Ms. N. was frustrated over test performances and began to cry and sob because her brain was "empty."

Prior to the second day of testing, Ms. N. apologized repeatedly for being 80 minutes late and stated that it was due to congested traffic. Mood was very different compared to the prior testing day. Mood was euthymic and affect was bright. During a break, Ms. N. called her employer to indicate that she would not be able to work that day (which, apparently, she had not arranged prior to evaluation). Based on observation alone, Ms. N. appeared to put forth a concerted effort on each of the presented tasks. She was very cooperative and seemed content to complete each of the tasks at hand.

Review of relevant records confirmed that Ms. N. sustained a broken nose in relation to the head injury. A CT of the brain was unremarkable. A neurological examination conducted shortly after the accident indicated that Ms. N. presented with anxiety and crying spells. A physical therapy report indicated that Ms. N. had reported a loss of consciousness of a few seconds. A letter from a neurologist written nearly three months after the injury indicated that Ms. N. had difficulty with balance and coordination. Sleep was variable in relation to severe headaches. She experienced periods of depression, anxiety, and anger. Cognitively, she was viewed as functioning very well.

Test results

Table 17.1 juxtaposes Ms. N.'s performances on a number of cognitive and psychological validity measures with those of Mr. O., and Table 17.2 presents neuropsychological and psychological performances of Ms. N. in relation to the case of Mr. O.

Three measures known to be sensitive to insufficient cognitive effort were well within normal limits. Intellectual functioning was within the average range with similar verbal and nonverbal abilities. Performances on measures of attention/concentration, cognitive efficiency, language functioning, learning and memory, visual-spatial functioning, select measures of executive functioning, and select measures of motor functioning were within expected limits. Poor performances on select cognitive tasks (e.g., rapid addition of digits; a single measure of concept formation) were consistently related to Ms. N.'s emotional reactivity.

On an extended inventory of personality functioning, a number of validity scales were *extremely* elevated. The *Fp* scale was elevated to a degree suggesting an endorsement of psychological symptoms that are rarely experienced, even among persons with severe mental illnesses (e.g., psychosis requiring inpatient hospitalization). As Ms. N. had not reported the experience of psychotic symptoms recently, this elevation was strongly suggestive of an exaggerated response style. *FBS was elevated to an unprecedented degree, in that no patient seen in our office and no study we could identify in the literature had ever shown an elevation this high.* This particular elevation appears to leave little question that with regard to overendorsement of bodily/somatic symptoms, it is almost certain that Ms. N. intentionally exaggerated her symptoms.

In light of this exaggerated response set, the clinical profile could not be interpreted as an accurate representation of Ms. N.'s current personality functioning. Multiple clinical scales were elevated to a degree that typically would not be observed among individuals with even the most serious of mental illnesses (e.g., severe depression, anxiety disorders, psychotic disorders) or physical maladies. In particular, Ms. N. endorsed such severe bodily, depressive, anxious, and psychotic symptoms that these should be presumed to reflect an invalid response style.

Ms. N. also completed two measures pertaining to the experience of posttraumatic stress, the format of which included validity scales. Validity scales on both of these measures were extremely elevated, suggesting that Ms. N. exaggerated the extent to which she experiences traumatic symptoms; Ms. N. responded affirmatively to the experience of traumatic symptoms that are rarely, if ever, experienced among even the most traumatized of individuals. Multiple clinical scales on these measures were also significantly elevated, and were interpreted to reflect an invalid response style. It should be noted that on one of these measures, she attributed the experience of traumatic symptoms to the head injury.

Ms. N. also completed four face-valid measures of emotional and psychological functioning that do not contain validity scales, and in this instance were viewed as most likely invalid. On these measures, she endorsed severe symptoms of depression, anxiety, hopelessness, and posttraumatic stress. As Ms. N. rated these symptoms (i.e., depression, anxiety, hopelessness, posttraumatic stress) at a level that far exceeded what is typical among clinically depressed, anxious, and traumatized cohorts, it is very likely that she exaggerated the experience of these symptoms.

TABLE 17.1   Validity performances for Ms. N. (invalid psychological performances) and Mr. O. (invalid cognitive effort performances)

MEASURE SUBTEST	MS. N. PERFORMANCE	MR. O. PERFORMANCE
VSVT[1]		
Easy Correct	24	23
Hard Correct	24	10*
Total Correct	48	33*
Easy Lat. (s)	1.08	2.94
Hard Lat. (s)	1.41	4.87*
Total Lat. (s)	1.25	3.90*
WMT[2]		
% Immediate Recall	100.0	70.0*
% Delayed Recall	97.5	47.5*
% Consistency	97.5	57.5*
TOMM[3]		
Trial 1 Correct	50	n/a
Trial 2 Correct	50	n/a
Retention	50	n/a
Rey-15[4]		
Rows	n/a	3
Recall	n/a	12
Digit Span		
Reliable[5] Time 1	8	8
Reliable[5] Time 2	9	9
ACSS[6] Time 1	7	9
ACSS[6] Time 2	8	n/a
Grip Strength		
DH Mean performance[7]	20	13.5*
MMPI-2		
L	T62	T56
F	T96*	T48
K	T46	T66
VRIN	T54	T38
TRIN	T58	T50
Fb	T97*	T42
Fp	T57	T48
S	T51	T55
F-K	Raw 4	Raw 19
FBS (Raw Score)	Raw 41*	Raw 18
Ds (Raw Score)	Raw 29	Raw 4
Md (Raw Score)	Raw 24	Raw 8

* Invalid Performance.

Notes: [1]Slick et al. (1995); [2]Green et al. (1996); [3]Tombaugh (1996); [4]Rey (1964); [5]Greiffenstein, Baker, & Gola (1994); [6]ACSS = Age-corrected scaled score, Iverson & Franzen (1994); [7]Inconsistent with real-life presentation (e.g., firm dominant handshake).

TABLE 17.2 Neuropsychological and psychological profiles of Ms. N. (invalid psychological performances) and Mr. O. (invalid cognitive effort performances)

MS. N. FUNCTIONAL DOMAIN MEASURE(S) SUBTEST	SCORE RAW	(STANDARD)	MR. O. FUNCTIONAL DOMAIN MEASURE(S) SUBTEST	SCORE RAW	(STANDARD)
General Intelligence			*General Intelligence*		
WAIS–III		*(Index/ACSS)*	*WAIS–R*		*(Index/ACSS)*
FSIQ		(91)	FSIQ		(95)
VIQ		(91)	VIQ		(96)
PIQ		(95)	PIQ		(92)
Vocabulary	47	(10)	Vocabulary	54	(12)
Similarities	22	(9)	Similarities	15	(9)
Arithmetic	13	(9)	Arithmetic	11	(10)
Digit Span	13	(7)	Digit Span	13	(9)
Information	12	(7)	Information	17	(9)
Comprehension	21	(9)	Comprehension	20	(10)
Picture Completion	10	(5)	Picture Completion	10	(7)
Digit Symbol	87	(13)	Digit Symbol	41	(9)
Block Design	29	(8)	Block Design	19	(9)
Matrix Reasoning	19	(13)	Object Assembly	28	(10)
Picture Arrangement	10	(8)	Picture Arrangement	12	(11)
Symbol Search	34	(12)			
Shipley		*(T)*	*Shipley*		*(T)*
Vocabulary	33	(55)	Vocabulary	32	(57)
Abstraction	28	(60)	Abstraction	14	(50)
Attention/ Concentration			*Attention/ Concentration*		
PASAT		*(Z)*	*PASAT*		*(Z)*
2.4 s	100%	(.90)	2.4 s	56%	(−1.10)
2.0 s	68%	(−.62)	2.0 s	50%	(−.69)
1.6 s	28%	(−2.21)	1.6 s	54%	(−.05)
1.2 s	36%	(−1.12)	1.2 s	36%	(.39)
Gordon Diagnostic			*Behavioral Inattention Test*		(WNL)
Vigilance	44	(WNL)			
Distractibility	45	(WNL)			
Cognitive Efficiency			*Cognitive Efficiency*		
Trail Making Test		*(T)*	*Trail Making Test*		*(T)*
Part A	26	(51)	Part A	31	(53)
Part B	53	(57)	Part B	53	(57)
Stroop		*(T)*	*Stroop*		*(T)*
Color Naming	126	(58–60)	Color Naming	110	(50–52)
Word Naming	86	(54)	Word Naming	65	(40)
Color/Word Naming	47	(52)	Color/Word Naming	51	(56)
Language			*Language*		
MAE		*(%ile)*	*MAE*		*(%ile)*
Visual Naming	60	(87)	Visual Naming	60	(87)
COWA	44	(69)	COWA	21	(3)
Animal Fluency	19	(41)	Animal Fluency	22	(66)
Executive Functioning			*Executive Functioning*		
Booklet Category		*(T)*	*Booklet Category*		*(T)*
Total Errors	116	(24)	Total Errors	82	(41)
WCST		*(%ile)*	*WCST*		*(%ile)*
Categories Completed	6	(> 16)	Categories Completed	2	(6–10)
Total Errors	14	(66)	Total Errors	75	(3)

(Continued . . .)

TABLE 17.2   (Continued)

MS. N. FUNCTIONAL DOMAIN MEASURE(S) SUBTEST	SCORE RAW	(STANDARD)	MR. O. FUNCTIONAL DOMAIN MEASURE(S) SUBTEST	SCORE RAW	(STANDARD)
Pers Responses	4	(79)	Pers Responses	67	(2)
Fail to Maintain Set	0	(> 16)	Fail to Maintain Set	0	(> 16)
Ruff Figural Fluency		(T)	*Ruff Figural Fluency*		(T)
Unique Designs	94	(50.3)	Unique Designs	79	(51)
Error Ratio	0.18	(58.2)	Error Ratio	0.21	(59)
Learning and Memory			*Learning and Memory*		
WMS–III		(Index/%ile)	WMS–R		(%ile)
Auditory Immediate		(99)			
Auditory Delayed		(99)			
Auditory Recognition		(95)			
Working Memory		(88)			
Information/Orient	14		Information/Orient	14	(84)
Mental Control	33	(91)	Mental Control	6	(82)
Logical Memory I	39	(50)	Logical Memory I	11	(5)
Logical Memory II	25	(63)	Logical Memory II	13	(24)
Logical Memory %Ret	93	(91)	Logical Memory %Ret	118	
Logical Memory Rec	24		Logical Memory Rec	15	
Verbal Pairs I	19	(50)	Verbal Pairs I	11	(< 1)
Verbal Pairs II	5	(37)	Verbal Pairs II	6	(23)
Visual Reprod I	66	(5)	Visual Reprod I	29	(48)
Visual Reprod II	52	(37)	Visual Reprod II	23	(33)
Visual Reprod %Ret	79	(63)	Visual Reprod %Ret	79	
CVLT–II		(Z/T)	*CVLT*		(Z/T)
Trial 1	7	(0.00)	Trial 1	6	(0.0)
Trial 2	8	(−0.5)	Trial 2	6	
Trial 3	10	(−0.5)	Trial 3	8	
Trial 4	9	(−1.50)	Trial 4	9	
Learning and Memory			*Learning and Memory*		
CVLT–II		(Z/T)	CVLT		(Z/T)
Trial 5	13	(0.00)	Trial 5	8	(−2.00)
Trials 1–5	47	(T = 47)	Trials 1–5	37	(T = 34)
Trial B	4	(−1.00)	Trial B	6	(0.00)
Short Free Recall	11	(0.00)	Short Free Recall	7	(−1.00)
Short Cued Recall	12	(0.00)	Short Cued Recall	7	(−2.00)
Long Free Recall	12	(0.00)	Long Free Recall	7	(−1.00)
Long Cued Recall	13	(0.05)	Long Cued Recall	7	(−2.00)
Recognition Hits	13	(−1.00)	Recognition Hits	14	(0.00)
Recognition FP	1	(−0.50)	Recognition FP	1	(0.00)
Discriminability	2.7	(−0.50)	Discriminability	93	(0.00)
Repetitions	8	(0.50)	Repetitions	12	(3.00)
Forced-choice Rec	16	(WNL)			
Visual Spatial		(ACSS)	*Visual Spatial*		(T)
WMS–III VR Copy	100	(12)	Spatial Relations	2	(58)
Motor Functioning			*Sensory & Motor Functioning*		
Behavioral Dyscontrol		(Z)	*Behavioral Dyscontrol*		(Z)
Total Score	16	(0.82)	Total Score	13	(−0.05)
Motor Functioning		(T)	*Sensory & Motor Functioning*		(T)
Finger Tapping DH	31.5	(30)	Finger Tapping DH	8.4	(11)
Finger Tapping NDH	37.8	(46)	Finger Tapping NDH	39.6	(39)

Grip Strength DH	20	(36)	Grip Strength DH	13.5	(4)
Grip Strength NDH	22	(42)	Grip Strength NDH	57	(67)
Grooved Pegboard DH	55	(64)	Grooved Pegboard DH	107	(33)
Grooved Pegboard NDH	77	(43)	Grooved Pegboard NDH	80	(52)
			TPT DH	2.5	(30)
			TPT NDH	0.66	(51)
			TPT Both hands	0.31	(54)
			TPT Total	0.82	(42)
			Sensory Perceptual Exam		
			Hand (R)	0	
			Hand (L)	0	
			R Hand/L Face (R)	0	
			R Hand/L Face (L)	1	
			L Hand/R Face (R)	0	
			L Hand/R Face (L)	0	
			Finger Identify (R)	0	
			Finger Identify (L)	1	
			Finger/Num. Write (R)	8	
			Finger/Num. Write (L)	2	
			Sensory & Motor Functioning Sensory Perceptual Exam		
			Auditory (R)	1	
			Auditory (L)	0	
			Visual (R)	0	
			Visual (L)	0	
Personality Functioning			*Personality Functioning*		
MMPI–2		(T)	*MMPI–2*		(T)
L		(62)	L		(56)
F		(96)	F		(48)
K		(46)	K		(66)
Hs		(105)	Hs		(79)
D		(105)	D		(76)
Hy		(115)	Hy		(76)
Pd		(68)	Pd		(54)
Mf		(55)	Mf		(38)
Pa		(81)	Pa		(57)
Pt		(105)	Pt		(72)
Sc		(105)	Sc		(72)
Ma		(49)	Ma		(69)
Si		(78)	Si		(38)
Emotional Functioning			*Emotional Functioning*		
BDI–II	55		*BDI–II*	17	
BHS	18		*BHS*	2	
BAI	51		*BAI*	27	
Psychological Functioning					
Det Ass Traumatic Stress		(T)			
PB		(< 36)			
NB		(> 100)			
RTE		(49)			
PDST		(73)			
PDIS		(90)			

(Continued . . .)

TABLE 17.2   (Continued)

Ms. N.			Mr. O.		
FUNCTIONAL DOMAIN MEASURE(S) SUBTEST	*SCORE RAW*	*(STANDARD)*	*FUNCTIONAL DOMAIN MEASURE(S) SUBTEST*	*SCORE RAW*	*(STANDARD)*
RE		(> 100)			
AV		(97)			
AR		(> 100)			
PTS-T		(> 100)			
IMP		(> 100)			
T-DIS		(> 100)			
SUB		(47)			
SUI		(47)			
Trauma Symptom Inventory		(T)			
ATR		(84)			
Psychological Functioning Trauma Symptom Inventory					
ATR		(84)			
RL		(46)			
INC		(< 35)			
AA		(> 81)			
D		(68)			
AI		(> 80)			
IE		(77)			
DA		(68)			
DIS		(87)			
ISR		(74)			
TRB		(60)			
Penn Trauma Inventory	59				

Summary and conclusions

Overall, the cognitive profile was interpreted to be within normal limits. Ms. N.'s performances on cognitive measures did not corroborate subjective complaints of cognitive difficulty and did not support the notion that Ms. N.'s mild head injury resulted in cognitive dysfunction. In fact, Ms. N. showed a number of particular strengths (e.g., cognitive efficiency/processing speed; select abilities on measures of abstraction/concept formation) that transcended an average level of intellectual functioning. Poor performances on select cognitive tasks (e.g., incidental recall of symbols; rapid addition of digits; a single measure of concept formation) were consistently related to Ms. N.'s emotional reactivity, and were not interpreted to reflect cognitive dysfunction.

Psychologically, results of objective personality testing and other self-report emotional inventories were consistently invalid and representative of an exaggerated response style. Thus, no diagnosis from a psychological perspective could be confidently provided. Though no such conclusions could be made based upon objective data, her presentation was strongly suggestive of significant psychological involvement (e.g., she presented with marked lability and histrionic behavior throughout the first testing session) that likely contributed to her subjective reporting of cognitive difficulties. Ms. N.'s injury may have exacerbated an already extant psychological vulnerability. Her tumultuous childhood and the likely tenuous psychological foundation that resulted was a considerable risk factor for poor adaptive response to a physical injury, which could have served to catalyze some of her psychological symptoms. Nevertheless, whether Ms. N.'s symptoms of head-aches, anxiety, and sleep difficulties of which she complained were directly related to her head injury was unclear vis-à-vis her obviously invalid response style on self-report personality and emotional state measures.

Given her variable emotional presentation over two testing sessions and her history, pharmaco-logical treatment of her symptoms, as well as brief psychotherapy (once a week for 3–4 months), were strongly recommended. Recommended goals for psychotherapy included attainment of a greater self-awareness of how her emotions contributed to disorganization in day-to-day living, increased stress management skills, an awareness of the fact that her cognitive abilities would in no way preclude a return to full-time work, and a timeline for rapid return to full-time work.

Per review of medical records and Ms. N.'s description of the incident, it was clear that she sustained a mild *head* injury. It was not clear that she sustained a mild traumatic *brain* injury in that she reported being knocked to her knees, which would not have occurred if she had experienced loss of consciousness. If this information was inaccurate, and she lost consciousness, it was for a *very* brief period of time; posttraumatic amnesia was not evident at all. *If* she sustained a mild traumatic brain injury, resultant cognitive symptoms would be expected to resolve within the first few months following the injury. As it had been approximately six months between the time of injury and evaluation, and she did not exhibit cognitive impairment on objective neuropsychological testing, disability status from a neuropsychological perspective was not indicated. Cognitively, test results suggested that Ms. N. should be able to return to work without restrictions.

THE CASE OF MR. O.

Background

Mr. O., a 48-year-old, right-handed, Caucasian gentleman, was referred for neuropsychological evaluation in the context of a work-related disability claim subsequent to a coronary artery bypass grafting (CABG) surgery conducted approximately seven months prior to evaluation. At the time of evaluation, he complained of chest pain (at the site of surgical incision), right-sided weakness and associated coordination difficulties, memory difficulties, fatigue, and anxiety. These symptoms allegedly impeded the ability to perform work-related responsibilities as a traveling salesperson.

On interview, Mr. O. reported that he had suffered a stroke following the CABG surgery. The stroke resulted in initial paralysis of the right side of the body. He claimed that his heart had "rejected the operation," and that he was in a "stupor" (e.g., difficulty recognizing family members; difficulty communicating) after the surgery. At discharge, he had difficulties sleeping for fear that he would die in his sleep. He was prescribed Valium and sleeping pills that alleviated this problem. He experienced constant "severe" pain at the site of the surgery, radiating to the shoulder blade, which was worsening over the last seven months. His pain occasionally became "tight," and his blood pressure increased by 20 to 30 points during times of stress, particularly while at work. As a result of the reported stroke, Mr. O. described having had difficulty walking in a straight line, and a tendency to drift to the right. His right arm (from shoulder to fingertips) felt numb and uncoordinated; coordination became worse when he was tired.

In terms of cognition, Mr. O. experienced memory problems since the time of surgery (e.g., going "blank" during conversations; failing to recall directions to his home; forgetting keys, wallet, and cellular phone). Memory difficulties were worse each day, and information would completely "vanish" if he did not write it down.

In terms of mood, Mr. O. experienced feelings of insecurity and worry regarding his physical health. He denied symptoms of depression, though he was "not the same person" as he had been prior to the surgery.

Mr. O. was raised in a midwestern city. He completed 12 years of education, and denied any history of learning difficulties or special education. He worked as a salesman for nearly 23 years and continued to work in this capacity at the time of evaluation. Prior to surgery, Mr. O. had been working 8–10 hours daily, and he returned to work two months after surgery (only 1 to 2 hours daily). Co-workers observed changes in his ability to work (e.g., slower, less confident), and he reported a diminished ability to argue or negotiate with customers.

Family medical history was significant for maternal (mother, grandparents, three aunts, uncle) and paternal (grandfather, uncle) heart disease and resultant deaths; also, his brother died of a heart attack in middle age. Prior to Mr. O.'s surgery and subsequent stroke, personal medical history was unremarkable. At the time of evaluation, he was prescribed Zocor, Cardizem, and Valium.

Behaviorally, in contrast to a complaint of upper extremity weakness, Mr. O did not demonstrate any obvious difficulties in movement of the hands, and there was no obvious upper extremity weakness. *In fact, Mr. O. presented with a strong right-handed handshake.* Affect was serious and mood was mildly anxious. Relationship to the examiner was deferential (e.g., he frequently responded to requests with "Yes, doctor"). Thought process was digressive, and Mr. O. required occasional redirection to complete tasks. He was grandiose, dramatic, and occasionally bragged about previous accomplishments. Thought content was marked by a significant preoccupation and concern about his physical limitations and symptoms. These included self-perceived difficulties in ambulation, right-sided clumsiness/weakness, and chest pain. On one occasion, Mr. O. requested the examiner to palpate his chest so that he may feel his "tightness." Complaints such as these persisted throughout the evaluation, and it is likely that Mr. O. would have spent even more time expressing his complaints without the examiner's prompts to continue testing. During testing, the patient occasionally stated he was unable to complete presented tasks, claming that his mind was "jumbled." On these occasions, he would discontinue the task and request that the next task be presented. With encouragement, however, Mr. O. completed the tasks. In light of these events, test-taking style was deemed to be variable, and it was evident on observation that he did not put forth a concerted effort at all times.

Review of available records confirmed a history of CABG surgery, which, apart from some post-operative right upper extremity weakness, Mr. O. tolerated well. The etiology of the upper extremity weakness was unclear and was attributed to either peripheral nerve damage or stroke. The weakness improved in time, and no recommendations for further assessment or treatment were made. Cardiac status was stable upon discharge. A follow-up medical visit three weeks post-surgery indicated no major post-surgical complications or neurological deficits. Sleep difficulties were reported, for which Mr. O. was prescribed Ambien and Valium. A second follow-up visit more than two months post-surgery was unremarkable, and Mr. O. was said to be doing well with no complaints. A medical report written nearly five months post-surgery indicated an uneventful post-operative course. It was suggested that Mr. O. could have returned to light work on a full-time basis three months after the surgery, which is customary of persons undergoing bypass surgery. A neurological consult note written nearly six months post-surgery noted a history of stroke within the middle cerebral artery distribution, depression, and anxiety. All strength ratings obtained during neurological examination were within normal limits. Sensation in the arms and legs was normal, as was coordination. The neurologist concluded that Mr. O. was disabled in relation to anxiety and depression. A neurological review conducted more than six months post-operatively indicated Mr. O.'s presentation was *not* consistent with a stroke of the middle cerebral artery, but was consistent with neuropraxia of the right arm secondary to prolonged blood pressure cuffing during surgery.

Mr. O. underwent neuropsychological evaluation at six months post-surgery. At that evaluation,

Mr. O. reported he had suffered two strokes, one before and another after the surgery. He also reported left-sided motor strength and sensation. All of the Luria-Nebraska Neuropsychological Inventory scales were within normal limits, with the exception of the Memory scale, which was within the pathological range. It was concluded that Mr. O. had normal overall intellectual ability, but showed memory difficulties, bradyphrenia, decreased two-point threshold bilaterally, and decreased motor speed/coordination in the bilateral upper extremities, but more in the right than left. (Comparison of these test results with those of the present neuropsychological examination was not possible as the previous neuropsychologist was unwilling to provide copies of the test data.)

Test results

Table 17.1 compares Mr. O.'s cognitive and psychological validity performances with those of Ms. N. Table 17.2 presents Mr. O.'s neuropsychological and psychological performances compared to those of Ms. N. Overall intellectual ability was within the average range with relatively commensurate verbal and nonverbal intellectual abilities. Performances on measures of cognitive efficiency, simple attention, nonverbal fluency and memory, naming, academic skills, and some measures of executive problem solving were within expected limits. Performances on measures of verbal learning and recall, phonemic fluency, and select measures of problem-solving/complex attention were impaired. Motor testing indicated significant right-hand impairment in strength, fine motor dexterity, finger-tapping speed, and motor sequencing/programming. Left-hand performances were essentially normal, though finger-tapping speed was somewhat slow. A similar pattern was observed for sensory functioning, as there were many right-handed errors in finger-number identification. *Results of cognitive effort testing were consistent with probable insufficient effort on two of three cognitive effort measures administered.*

Validity scales from an extended personality inventory were within normal limits. Clinical scale elevations were consistent with significant anxiety attributable to excessive concerns over somatic symptoms. Insight to the relationship between physical symptoms and psychological distress was interpreted to be poor. Results of face-valid measures of emotional functioning were consistent with mild to moderate symptoms of depression, and severe symptoms of anxiety.

Summary and conclusions

Results of effort testing were suggestive of probable insufficient effort on two of three cognitive effort measures administered. Further, right-hand performances on motor tasks were at times excessively impaired, and at a level that is not typically observed even among patients with documented left-hemispheric strokes. The validity of the latter performance was brought into question considering that Mr. O. presented with a strong, right-handed handshake, as well as the fact that previous neurological reports were suggestive of normal (or nearly normal) grip strength. Mr. O. also expressed limited effort on observation, and requested that he might discontinue certain tasks and move on to others.

Overall, effort testing results, review of records, and behavioral observations suggested that Mr. O. did not exert full effort during testing, and the cognitive test results were interpreted to be an inadequate representation of his cognitive ability. While it was possible that Mr. O.'s insufficient cognitive effort could represent malingering, it seemed more likely related to psychological issues surrounding his cardiac status and his perception of cognitive and motor disabilities. Although the large body of literature regarding the cognitive effects of CABG has suggested (excluding very serious stroke) subtle to mild cognitive deficits that may be more pronounced immediately after surgery (e.g., Selnes & Guy, 2005), current invalid cognitive effort performances precluded conclusions regarding the extent to which Mr. O.'s subjective cognitive complaints may have been the result of this procedure. Regarding the possibility that Mr. O. may have had a stroke following surgery, review of records was not definitive in this regard (e.g., absence of CT or MRI scans; weakness was more likely related to peripheral factors). Even if he had a stroke following surgery, performances on motor measures would not be expected to worsen over time, and they would not be as impaired as they had been on testing.

Results of personality and emotional testing were indicative of significant symptoms of anxiety, largely in relation to concerns over health. Concerns that he might have a heart attack were reasonable considering his familial history of multiple heart failures and the stressful nature of his work. As the course and duration of these symptoms were unclear, a diagnosis of Anxiety Disorder NOS (300.00) was warranted.

In sum, although no conclusion could be made regarding cognitive status (in light of invalid performances), it was concluded that Mr. O. would not be able to return to previous employment on a full-time basis in relation to significant symptoms of anxiety. Anxiety and health-related concerns were likely to affect motivation, stamina, and productivity. Return to full-time work seemed attainable with appropriate psychological management of emotional symptoms, and considering that cognitive abilities were generally intact (despite poor cognitive effort).

GENERAL DISCUSSION

The present case study compares two compensation-seeking patients with disparate forms of invalid cognitive effort performances and psychological response styles. In the case of Ms. N., performances on three of the most frequently employed forced-choice measures of cognitive effort (i.e., *WMT*, *VSVT*, *TOMM*) were suggestive of adequate effort. With the exception of a single cognitive validity indicator derived from the Booklet Category Test that was suggestive of insufficient effort (and observably related to emotional reactivity), all other cognitive effort measures and indicators were well within normal limits. The good effort she showed on these measures was presumed to have accounted for her largely intact cognitive performances.

At the same time, Ms. N. consistently over-reported psychological symptoms across all measures of personality, emotional, and psychological functioning. Three MMPI–2 validity scales were elevated beyond suggested cutoffs (i.e., *F*, *Fb*, *FBS*). In consideration of her highly inflated *F* and *Fb* scores, it seems clear that she affirmed rarely endorsed psychological items. But more dramatic than these elevations was her *FBS* performance. Previously employed *FBS* cutoffs have ranged from greater than 20 (Lees-Haley et al., 1991) to greater than 27 (Greiffenstein, Baker, Axelrod, Peck, & Gervais, 2004), and most clinicians would agree that any *FBS* score greater than 30 is clearly indicative of exaggeration of somatic symptoms (Larrabee, 2003a). Ms. N.'s *FBS* score was 41 of 43, a score that leaves no doubt that she exaggerated somatic symptoms. MMPI–2 clinical scale elevations suggested an endorsement of symptoms that transcend even the most psychologically disturbed of individuals. Of the ten MMPI–2 clinical scales, five (*Hs*, *D*, *Hy*, *Pt*, *Sc*) were elevated at or above a T score of 105.

Consistent with the notion that Ms. N. endorsed significantly greater psychopathology than severely impaired clinical samples, the Beck Depression Inventory–II (BDI–II; Beck, Steer, & Brown, 1996), Beck Anxiety Inventory (BAI; Beck & Steer, 1990), and Beck Hopelessness Scale (BHS; Beck & Steer, 1988) raw scores were much higher than what is typical even among the most severely depressed, anxious, and hopeless of individuals. According to their respective professional manuals, BDI-II performance was 2.18 standard deviations beyond the mean score for patients with recurrent episodes of major depression, BAI performance was 1.65 standard deviations above the mean score for patients with severe anxiety in the form of panic disorder, and BHS performance was 1.43 standard deviations above the mean score obtained in suicide attempters. Emotional symptoms of this severity are atypical of the usual course following a mild head injury, especially six months post-injury.

Ms. N. also appears to have exaggerated symptoms of posttraumatic stress. Validity scales from the Detailed Assessment of Posttraumatic Stress (DAPS; Briere, 2001) and the Traumatic Stress Inventory (TSI; Briere, 1995) were suggestive of atypical responding and negative response bias. Clinical scales on these measures were also elevated at levels at and beyond those observed in severely traumatized cohorts. According to Hammarberg (1992), Ms. N.'s performance on the Penn Trauma Inventory was elevated at a level consistent with a Vietnam combat veteran with bona fide symptoms of PTSD undergoing inpatient treatment. That Ms. N. experienced "PTSD" symptoms in relation to the mild head injury seemed ludicrous considering the very mild nature of her injury.

In short, Ms. N. did not discriminate when exaggerating psychological and emotional symptoms. Rather, she endorsed a broad range of symptoms (e.g., depression, anxiety, trauma) that she attributed to her mild head injury. Her profile was clearly indicative of suspect psychological presentation, despite excellent overall cognitive effort. Ms. N. sustained a mild traumatic *head* injury, and it is unclear that she sustained a *brain* injury at all (e.g., minimal, if any, loss of consciousness; no evidence of brain injury on imaging; minimal, if any, posttraumatic amnesia). The course, duration, and nature of her symptoms were clearly not consistent with those that are usually observed in mild head injury.

Present cognitive test results in the case of Ms. N. were not indicative of any cognitive impairment. This is not surprising considering that mild head injury is rarely associated with long-term objective evidence of neuropsychological impairment (Dikmen, Machamaer, Winn, & Temkin, 1995; Frencham, Fox, & Maybery, 2005). What, then, might have accounted for her complaints six months following the injury? One possibility relates to Ms. N.'s involvement in seeking financial compensation for present subjective complaints. Compensation-seeking status per se can be significantly associated with an increased incidence and severity of complaints (Paniak, Reynolds, Toller-Lobe, Melnyk, Nagy, & Schmidt, 2002). Paniak et al. observed a group of 50 individuals with history of mild traumatic brain injury (MTBI) who were not compensation seeking (CS) with 18 MTBI compensation seekers. Results indicated that at various times following the MTBI, the CS group reported nearly one standard deviation more symptoms and a higher severity of symptoms post-injury (i.e., on intake, 3 months, and 12 months afterward) than MTBI patients who were not CS. These findings highlight the potential negative effect that an external incentive may have on one's overall functioning. In other words, a context of secondary gain may have contributed to some of Ms. N.'s subjective complaints.

Another possible source of Ms. N.'s complaints may have related to emotional premorbid risk factors. Ruff, Camenzuli, and Mueller (1996) explored the negative impact that MTBI may have on persons with pre-existing psychological traits in the way of functional outcome. They refer to the small subgroup with persisting symptoms as the "miserable minority" since it includes the small proportion of MTBI patients with persisting complaints post-injury. It seemed that Ms. N. had premorbid risk factors (e.g., tumultuous childhood) that contributed *partially* toward a negative post-injury outcome. However, while some MTBI patients seem to fulfill this "diathesis-stress hypothesis" whereby a mild head injury serves to catalyze premorbid risk factors with a resultant negative outcome (Wood, 2004), Ms. N. presented with extreme psychological symptoms (to the point of invalidity) that could not be *fully* attributed to either the risk factors, the mild head injury, or the interaction between the two.

In contrast to Ms. N., Mr. O.'s performances on multiple cognitive symptom validity tests and indicators were clearly suggestive of suspect cognitive effort. Performances on the *VSVT* and *WMT* were at near-chance levels and obviously within the range of insufficient effort. Response latencies on the *VSVT* were of an extended duration, and also suggestive of possible malingering. Interestingly, Mr. O. presented with a very firm grip with his dominant hand on initial interview, but demonstrated very impaired grip strength. It is also of interest to note that despite his poor cognitive effort performances, the large proportion of Mr. O.'s cognitive ability performances were within normal limits. This is in keeping with what has been observed previously in post-CABG surgery patients; although patients undergoing CABG surgery may exhibit mild short-term cognitive impairments, a return of function is usually observed one month subsequent to surgery (Browndyke, Moser, Cohen, O'Brien, Algina, et al., 2002).

Psychologically, validity indicators from the MMPI–2 were within normal limits. Although Mr. O. was involved in a workers' compensation claim and not a personal injury claim, it is noteworthy that clinical scale elevations (especially *Hs*, *D*, *Hy*) were consistent with those that are typically observed in personal injury plaintiffs (Lees-Haley, 1997). On both the MMPI–2 and the BAI, Mr. O. endorsed significant symptoms of anxiety that were likely associated with health concerns, symptoms that were perhaps understandable considering his personal and familial history of heart problems. Overall, Mr. O.'s neuropsychological profile was the converse of Ms. N.'s profile: he showed insufficient cognitive effort with valid psychological presentation of anxious symptoms.

The question remains, were Ms. N. and Mr. O. in fact malingering? In the case of Ms. N., absence of poor performance on cognitive effort measures precluded her from further consideration regarding malingering under the Slick et al. (1999) criteria. However, there can be little question that she intentionally exaggerated psychological symptoms considering that multiple validity and clinical scales on psychological measures (i.e., MMPI–2, TSI–A, DAPS, Penn Trauma Inventory, BHS, BDI, BAI) were strikingly and consistently invalid. It is noteworthy that Ms. N. endorsed unusual psychological symptoms on multiple "rare symptom" scales. A T score of 96 on the MMPI–2 *F* scale is well within the "exaggerated" range according to Butcher (1998), and within the range of exaggerated psychopathology according to Greene (2000). On the Atypical Response Scale from the TSI, Ms. N.'s T score of 84 matches an endorsement of "statistically unusual" symptoms according to recommended cutoffs by Briere (1995), and is well above a suggested cutoff of T-61 for endorsement of unusual symptoms recommended by Edens, Otto, and Dwyer (1998). As noted, an *FBS* score of 41 of 43 is tremendously higher than a cutoff of 30, a score that is usually regarded as almost certain exaggeration of somatic symptoms. In consideration of these invalid performances, and the inflated elevations on multiple standard clinical scales, there can be little question that Ms. N. was malingering psychological symptoms. As suggested by the DSM–IV, malingering should be suspected when there is: (1) an identifiable form of external incentive, and (2) evidence of intentional production of symptoms. Monetary external incentives were clearly identifiable for Ms. N., and it seems that her consistent over-reporting of psychological symptoms across multiple measures was highly likely to have been endorsed in an intentional manner. Satisfaction of both of these conditions made malingering of psychological symptoms the more likely explanation as opposed to the differential alternatives (e.g., Factitious Disorder, Somatoform Disorder).

Whereas Ms. N. did not exhibit evidence of neurocognitive malingering (i.e., cognitive effort measures were within normal limits), rendering the Slick et al. criteria irrelevant to her, Mr. O.'s cognitive effort performances were applicable under the Slick et al. criteria. He clearly presented with an identifiable form of external incentive, satisfying the first necessary criterion. He showed a "probable" level of response bias on the *VSVT* and the *WMT*, and further showed a discrepancy between "real-life" behavior with a firm hand grip on interview with impaired grip strength on testing, which taken together satisfy the second criterion. Finally, the last condition for a diagnosis of malingering under the Slick et al. criteria states that invalid performances cannot be fully accounted for by psychological, neurological, or developmental factors. Although Mr. O. presented with what was deemed to be a legitimate anxiety disorder, his symptoms of anxiety could not fully account for his poor cognitive effort. Thus, Mr. O. met criteria for probable MND.

When insufficient effort and/or negative response bias are present, it is sometimes difficult to arrive at a diagnosis of "malingering" as present diagnostic schemes require the clinician to judge whether symptoms were feigned or exaggerated *intentionally*. This difficulty is related to the fact that "intention" is not among the constructs that neuropsychological measures were originally intended to measure. As Boone, Lu, Back, King, Lee et al. (2002) have observed, "The term 'malingering' refers to intention (i.e., deliberate conscious symptom fabrication for an external goal), when in fact we can only observe and measure behavior, not intent" (p. 640). Still, clinicians can arrive at various *probabilities* of intentional feigning of symptoms according to individual test performances. In the case of cognitive malingering, the level of confidence the clinician has in evaluating intentionally feigned or exaggerated cognitive symptoms is inversely proportional to performance on forced-choice effort measures (i.e., confidence increases as scores approach statistically less than chance performances). In the case of psychological malingering, the level of confidence the clinician has in evaluating intentionally feigned or exaggerated psychological symptoms is directly proportional to performance on objective psychological validity scales (i.e., confidence increases as validity scores are increasingly invalid). In the cases of both cognitive and psychological malingering, the clinician's confidence in evaluating intention is directly proportional to the number of consistently exaggerated performances observed (i.e., confidence increases with multiple invalid performances). Regardless of the clinician's level of confidence that an individual may be feigning or exaggerating symptoms, alternative labels to "malingering" may be more accurate in describing overall presentations of symptoms. Boone et al. prefer the phrase "suspect effort" to describe invalid performances or exaggeration of symptoms. Other descriptions of exaggeration may also be considered (e.g., "suboptimal effort," "insufficient effort").

CONCLUSION

The current neuropsychological literature has by no means reached a consensus regarding the construct(s) of cognitive versus psychological symptom validity. Indeed, there is reason to believe that feigned cognitive impairment may represent a distinct construct from feigned psychological impairment (Greiffenstein et al., 1995; Nelson et al., 2007; Sweet et al., 2005). As Greiffenstein et al. (2002, p. 1599) state, "malingering in one domain does not automatically imply malingering in another domain." Although Slick et al. (1996) suggested that the moderate correlations they observed among MMPI–2 validity scales and the *VSVT* indices lent support for the latter measure's construct validity, they also acknowledged that these correlations were, after all, only moderate in magnitude. They state that the moderate magnitudes were, "not surprising, because the tests differ considerably in task (self-report vs. actual performance), and domain (memory vs. psychological adjustment)" (p. 920). In light of the disparate forms of symptom exaggeration observed in Ms. N. and Mr. O., it is clear that exaggeration of neuropsychological symptoms (cognitive, psychological, or otherwise) can be an extremely complex and difficult phenomenon to assess. Therefore, in keeping with the recommendations of others (Arnett, Hammeke, & Schwartz, 1995; Boone, Lu, Sherman, Palmer, Back, Shamieh, et al., 2000; Meyers & Volbrecht, 1999; Nelson, Boone, Dueck, Wagener, Lu, & Grills, 2003; Rosenfeld, Sands, & van Gorp, 2000), we would highly recommend that clinicians employ multiple forms of measures in multiple domains of functioning when evaluating symptom exaggeration, as this will lead to increased accuracy in effort assessment.

A comprehensive neuropsychological evaluation should entail not only multiple measures of effort and validity assessment, but also a full battery of ability tests as well, regardless of the individual patient's initial effort performances. Although we consider the cases of Ms. N. and Mr. O. to be relatively "clean" examples of psychological versus cognitive exaggeration, respectively, there were times when ability performances were also suspect in both patients. For instance, Ms. N. showed suspect performance on the Booklet Category Test, and Mr. O. showed suspect performance on some measures of motor functioning. Valuable information regarding both of their symptom validity and overall abilities would have been lost had not a full evaluation been conducted.

REFERENCES

Arbisi, P. A., & Ben-Porath, Y. S. (1995). An MMPI–2 infrequent response scale for use with psychopathological populations: The infrequency psychopathology scale, F(p). *Psychological Assessment, 7*, 424–431.

Arnett, P. A., Hammeke, T. A., & Schwartz, L. (1995). Quantitative and qualitative performance on Rey's 15-item test in neurological patients and dissimulators. *The Clinical Neuropsychologist, 9*, 17–26.

Beck, A. T., & Steer, R. A. (1988). *Beck Hopelessness Scale manual.* San Antonio: The Psychological Corporation.

Beck, A. T., & Steer, R. A. (1990). *Beck Anxiety Inventory manual.* San Antonio: The Psychological Corporation.

Beck, A. T., Steer, R. A., & Brown, G. K. (1996). *Beck Depression Inventory–2nd ed. Manual.* San Antonio: The Psychological Corporation.

Bianchini, K. J., Mathias, C. W., & Greve, K. W. (2001). Symptom validity testing: A critical review. *The Clinical Neuropsychologist, 15*, 19–45.

Binder, L. M., & Kelly, M. P. (1996). Portland Digit Recognition test performance by brain dysfunction patients without financial incentives. *Assessment, 3*, 403–409.

Boone, K. B., Lu, P., Back, C., King, C., Lee, A., Philpott, L., Shamieh, E., & Warner-Chacon, K. (2002). Sensitivity and specificity of the Rey Dot Counting Test in patients with suspect effort and various clinical samples. *Archives of Clinical Neuropsychology, 17*, 625–642.

Boone, K. B., Lu, P. Sherman, D., Palmer, B., Back, C., Shamieh, E., Warner-Chacon, K., & Berman, N. G. (2000). Validation of a new technique to detect malingering of cognitive symptoms: The b Test. *Archives of Clinical Neuropsychology, 15*, 227–241.

Briere, J. (1995). *Trauma Symptom Inventory Professional Manual.* Lutz: Psychological Assessment Resources, Inc.

Briere, J. (2001). *Detailed Assessment of Posttraumatic Stress Professional Manual.* Odessa: Psychological Assessment Resources, Inc.

Browndyke, J. N., Moser, D. J., Cohen, R. A., O'Brien, D. J., Algina, J. J., Haynes, W. G., Staples, E. D., Alexander, J., Davies, L. K., & Bauer, R. M. (2002). Acute neuropsychological functioning following cardiosurgical interventions associated with the production of intraoperative cerebral microemboli. *The Clinical Neuropsychologist, 16*, 463–471.

Butcher, J. N. (1998). *Users guide for the Minnesota Report: Reports for forensic settings.* Minneapolis, MN: National Computer Systems.

Butcher, J. N, Dahlstrom, W. G., Graham, J. R., Tellegen, A., & Kaemmer, B. (1989). *Manual for the administration and scoring of the MMPI–2.* Minneapolis: University of Minnesota Press.

Dikmen, S. S., Machamer, J. E., Winn, H. R., & Temkin, N R. (1995). Neuropsychological outcome at 1-year post head injury. *Neuropsychology, 9*, 80–90.

Edens, J. F., Otto, R. K., & Dwyer, T. J. (1998). Susceptibility of the Trauma Symptom Inventory to malingering. *Journal of Personality Assessment, 71*, 379–392.

Frencham, K. A. R., Fox, A. M., & Maybery, M. T. (2005). Neuropsychological studies of mild traumatic brain injury: A meta-analytic review of research since 1995. *Journal of Clinical and Experimental Neuropsychology, 27*, 334–351.

Green, P., Allen, L. M., & Astner, K. (1996). *The Word Memory Test: A user's guide to the oral and computer-administered forms,* US version 1.1. Durham, NC: CogniSyst.

Greene, R. (2000). *The MMPI–2/MMPI: An interpretive manual,* 2nd ed. New York: Grune & Stratton.

Greiffenstein, M. F., Baker, W. J., & Gola, T. (1994). Validation of malingered amnesia measures with a large clinical sample. *Psychological Assessment, 6*, 218–224.

Greiffenstein, M. F., Baker, W. J., Axelrod, B., Peck, E. A., & Gervais, R. (2004). The fake bad scale and MMPI–2 F-family in detection of implausible psychological trauma claims. *The Clinical Neuropsychologist, 18*, 573–590.

Greiffenstein, M. F., Baker, W. J., Gola, T., Donders, J., & Miller, L. (2002). The fake bad scale in atypical and severe closed head injury litigants. *Journal of Clinical Psychology, 58*, 1591–1600.

Greiffenstein, M. F., Gola, T., & Baker, W. J. (1995). MMPI–2 validity scales versus domain specific measures in detection of factitious traumatic brain injury. *The Clinical Neuropsychologist, 9*, 230–240.

Greve, K. W., Bianchini, K. J., Love, J. M., Brennan, A., & Heinly, M. T. (in press). Sensitivity and specificity of MMPI–2 validity scales and indicators to malingered neurocognitive dysfunction in traumatic brain injury. *The Clinical Neuropsychologist.*

Hammarberg, M. (1992). Penn Inventory for Posttraumatic Stress Disorder: Psychometric properties. *Psychological Assessment, 4,* 67–76.

Hathaway, S. R., & McKinley, J. C. (1943). *Minnesota Multiphasic Personality Inventory.* Minneapolis: University of Minnesota Press.

Larrabee, G. J. (2003a). Detection of symptom exaggeration with the MMPI–2 in litigants with malingered neurocognitive dysfunction. *The Clinical Neuropsychologist, 17,* 54–68.

Larrabee, G. J. (2003b). Exaggerated pain report in litigants with malingered neurocognitive dysfunction. *The Clinical Neuropsychologist, 17,* 395–401.

Lees-Haley, P. R. (1997). MMPI–2 base rates for 492 personal injury plaintiffs: Implications and challenges for forensic assessment. *Journal of Clinical Psychology, 53,* 745–755.

Lees-Haley, P. R., English, L. T., & Glenn, W. J. (1991). A fake bad scale on the MMPI–2 for personal injury claimants. *Psychological Reports, 68,* 208–210.

Lezak, M. D. (1983). *Neuropsychological assessment–2nd ed.* New York: Oxford University Press.

Meyers, J. E., & Volbrecht, M. (1999). Detection of malingerers using the Rey complex figure and recognition trial. *Applied Neuropsychology, 6,* 201–207.

Nelson, N. W., Boone, K. B., Dueck, A., Wagener, L., Lu, P., & Grills, C. (2003). Relationships between eight measures of suspect effort. *The Clinical Neuropsychologist, 17,* 263–272.

Nelson, N. W., Sweet, J. J., Berry, D. T. R., Bryant, F. B., & Granacher, R. P. (2007). Response validity in forensic neuropsychology: Exploratory factor analytic evidence of distinct cognitive and psychological constructs. *Journal of the International Neuropsychological Society, 13,* 440–449.

Paniak, C., Reynolds, S., Toller-Lobe, G., Melnyk, A., Nagy, J., & Schmidt, D. (2002). A longitudinal study of the relationship between financial compensation and symptoms after treated mild traumatic brain injury. *Journal of Clinical and Experimental Neuropsychology, 24,* 187–193.

Rey, A. (1964). *L'examen clinique en psychologie.* Paris: Presses Universitaires de France.

Rosenfeld, B., Sands, S. A., & van Gorp, W. G. (2000). Have we forgotten the base rate problem? Methodological issues in the detection of distortion. *Archives of Clinical Neuropsychology, 15,* 349–359.

Ruff, R. M., Camenzuli, L, & Mueller, J. (1996). Miserable minority: Emotional risk factors that influence the outcome of a mild traumatic brain injury. *Brain Injury, 10,* 551–565.

Selnes, O A., & Guy, M. M. (2005). Neurocognitive complications after coronary artery bypass surgery. *Annals of Neurology, 57,* 615–621.

Slick, D. J., Hopp, G. A., & Strauss, E. H. (1995). *The Victoria Symptom Validity Test.* Odessa, FL: PAR.

Slick, D. J., Hopp, G., Strauss, E., & Spellacy, F. J. (1996). Victoria Symptom Validity Test: Efficiency for detecting feigned memory impairments and relationship to neuropsychological tests and MMPI–2 validity scales. *Journal of Clinical and Experimental Neuropsychology, 18,* 911–922.

Slick, D. J., Sherman, E. M. S., & Iverson, G. L. (1999). Diagnostic criteria for malingered neurocognitive dysfunction: Proposed standards for clinical practice and research. *The Clinical Neuropsychologist, 13,* 545–561.

Sweet, J. J., King, J. H., Malina, A. C., Bergman, M. A., & Simmons, A. (2002). Documenting the prominence of forensic neuropsychology at national meetings and in relevant professional journals from 1990 to 2000. *The Clinical Neuropsychologist, 16,* 481–494.

Sweet, J. J., Nelson, N. W., & Heilbronner, R. L. (2005, June). *Relative lack of correspondence of individual MMPI–2 validity scales with individual measures of cognitive effort.* Presented at the annual meeting of the American Academy of Clinical Neuropsychology. Minneapolis, MN.

Tombaugh, T. N. (1996). *Test of Memory Malingering.* Toronto, Ont: MultiHealth Systems.

Wood, R. L. L. (2004). Understanding the "miserable minority": A diathesis-stress paradigm for post-concussional syndrome. *Brain Injury, 18,* 1135–1153.

Factitious disorder in civil litigation

Lidia Artiola i Fortuny

Mental disorders are health conditions characterized by alterations in cognition, mood, or behavior associated with subjective distress and/or impaired functioning. In clinical practice, the assumption is that these abnormalities are largely out of the person's control and that the person does not desire them. Factitious disorder (FD) is a psychiatric condition in which a person acts as if he or she has a physical or mental illness when, in reality, the person has consciously and deliberately created the symptoms. The name factitious comes from the Latin word for "made up" or "fabricated." Medical and psychological practitioners assume that when an individual seeks assistance for a physical or mental condition the motivation is the desire to get better as soon as possible. Practitioners also assume that the history given by their patient is generally accurate. Repeated presentation to the doctor's office is frequently taken to mean that the patient is: very motivated to improve, physically or mentally vulnerable and therefore taking a long time to improve, or very focused on the illness. Doctors are not trained to suspect that an individual may be creating symptoms or even the illness in a willful manner. According to Elwyn and Ahmed (2007), individuals with FD are among the most challenging and troublesome for busy clinicians. These authors state that FD patients violate three key unwritten rules: (1) patients provide a reasonably honest history; (2) symptoms result from accident, injury, or chance; and (3) patients want to recover and cooperate with treatment toward that end. The individual with FD violates this unspoken doctor/patient contract by seeking to remain in the sick role as a primary goal (Eisendrath & McNiel, 2004).

People with factitious disorders deliberately create or exaggerate symptoms of an illness in a variety of ways: they may give an inaccurate or even totally fabricated history; they may lie about symptoms or fake them; they may deliberately injure themselves in order to bring on symptoms; or they may deliberately contaminate diagnostic tests in order to manipulate the results. The primary motivation for these behaviors appears to be a need to be perceived as ill or injured, thus obtaining the sympathy and attention from health practitioners and family members that individuals with legitimate medical conditions get. In their quest to obtain the attention they crave, individuals with FD become avid consumers of medical resources. They require multiple office visits and willingly, and even eagerly, undergo lengthy and unnecessary tests and invasive procedures or surgeries at a high cost to the medical system. The individual with FD may create the signs or symptoms using a fictitious history, by simulating symptoms, or by producing actual disease states (Eisendrath, 1984). Eisendrath and McNiel (2004) noted that individuals with factitious physical disorder have a strong tendency toward self-injurious behavior that may eventually result in death. They presented a series of 20 patients, 4 (20%) of whom died as a direct result of FD.

The *Diagnostic and Statistical Manual of Mental Disorders, Fourth Edition, Text Revision* (DSM–IV–TR) requires that the following three criteria be met for the diagnosis of FD: (1) intentional production or feigning of physical or psychological signs or symptoms; (2) the motivation for the behavior is to assume the sick role; and (3) absence of external incentives for the behavior (e.g., economic gain, avoiding legal or other responsibility). The DSM–IV–TR specifies three subtypes of FD: (1) patients with primarily physical signs and symptoms; (2) patients with primarily psychological signs and symptoms; (3) combined subtype. The first of these, factitious disorder with predominantly physical signs and symptoms, is the most familiar to medical professionals. Chronic FD of this type is often referred to as Munchausen syndrome. Many health professionals use the term Munchausen syndrome to describe all persons who intentionally feign or produce illness in order to assume the sick role. However, Munchausen syndrome is not included as a mental disorder in the World Health Organization's *International Statistical Classification of Diseases, 10th Revision* (ICD–10) or in the American Psychiatric Association's *Diagnostic and Statistical Manual of Mental Disorders, Fourth Edition, Text Revision* (DSM–IV–TR). In both systems, the official diagnosis in these cases is factitious disorder (FD) (F 68.1 in the ICD–10; 300.16 or 300.19 in the DSM–IV–TR).

In 1986, Bock and Overkamp made a recommendation for a sub-classification of factitious disease. They proposed three types: A, B, and C. Type B is described as follows and is particularly germane to the case presented in this chapter: self induced, mainly chronic illness; behavior adequate, highly compliant; often little emotion, contrasting with the sometimes severe illness; socially adapted; history remarkably blank with regard to psychosocial stress; several often long-lasting hospitalizations and many interventions; almost exclusively younger women from (para)-medical professions.

The underlying pathology of FD is poorly understood. Elwyn and Ahmed (2006) note case reports of abnormalities on MRIs of the brains of patients with chronic FD, suggesting that brain biology may play a role in some cases. Results of electroencephalographic studies have been non-specific. Some patients with FD have displayed abnormalities on psychological testing. Underlying personality disorders have been suspected.

The prevalence of factitious disorder worldwide is not known. In the United States, some experts think that FD is under-diagnosed because hospital personnel often fail to spot the deceptions that are symptomatic of the disorder. It is also unclear which subtypes of factitious disorders are most common. Observers in developed countries agree that the prevalence of factitious physical symptoms is much higher than the prevalence of factitious psychological symptoms. Elwyn and Ahmed (2006) reported that 10 of 1288 patients referred to a consultation service at a large teaching hospital in Toronto were diagnosed with FD (0.8%). The National Institute for Allergy and Infectious Disease reported that 9.3% of patients referred for fevers of unknown origin had factitious disorder. Fliege et al. (2007) estimated the one-year frequency at approximately 1.3%,[1] with the highest numbers estimated in dermatology and neurology.

The causes of FD are poorly understood. Elwyn and Ahmed (2006) cite underlying masochistic tendencies, a need to be the center of attention and to feel important, a need to assume a dependent status and receive nurturance, a need to ease feelings of worthlessness or vulnerability, and a need to feel superior to authority figures (e.g., the physician), that is, gratified by being able to deceive the physician. The same authors also mention the psychodynamic explanation that maintains that patients with FD often have a background of neglect or abandonment and are attempting to reenact unresolved early issues with parents.

FD must be distinguished from other clinical entities. Chief among these are hypochondriasis, the somatoform disorders, and, of course, malingering. The behavior of people with factitious disorders is viewed as an illness and thus differs from malingering or faking illness. The purpose of malingering is exclusively to obtain financial or other material gain (e.g., prescription medication) or to avoid normal responsibilities (e.g., work) or criminal prosecution. Malingerers may fabricate histories or symptoms, but they do not cause themselves to become ill. Malingering is not officially a mental disorder, although it can be the focus of attention in clinical or forensic settings.

In malingering, the goal is reached by obtaining a health professional's confirmation of an

[1] The authors surveyed over 100 physicians for frequency estimates of factitious disorder among their patients. They completed a questionnaire including the estimated one-year prevalence of factitious disorder among their patients. Frequency estimates averaged 1.3% (0.0001–15%). The number of patients treated correlated negatively with frequency estimates. Dermatologists and neurologists gave the highest estimations. One-third of the physicians rated themselves as insufficiently informed.

authentic illness or injury. The malingering individual tolerates the medical or psychological scrutiny necessary to achieve this goal with varying degrees of good cheer. Once the goal is achieved, malingerers do not continue to expose themselves to scrutiny. In contrast, persons with FD actively attempt to maintain the sick role and go to great lengths to undergo as much testing and treatment as possible.

The second major differential is the somatoform disorders. According to the DSM–IV–TR, the somatoform disorders represent a completely distinct category of psychiatric disorders and are distinguished from FD by the notion that patients with somatoform disorders do not deliberately exaggerate or feign illness; complaints in somatoform disorder are presumed to be the result of unconscious processes. In practice, however, it may be impossible to distinguish between somatoform disorders and FD in individuals who do not enact physical simulations or self-injury that might provide concrete evidence of intentional deception (Hamilton & Feldman, 2007).

Malingered neuropsychological deficits are encountered with some frequency in the forensic arena. Forensic settings provide strong incentives for distorting test results or interview data and simultaneously provide disincentives for returning to a productive lifestyle (Larrabee, 2005). Consequently, detection of malingering and deception has received a great deal of attention within forensic neuropsychology during the past two decades. While the focus of the studies has been on individuals claiming injury from relatively minor events (e.g., alleged mild head injury, alleged toxic exposure), the use of techniques to validate reported cognitive symptoms (i.e., symptom validity tests or SVTs) has become an integral part of the forensic examination regardless of severity of initial injury.

Until recently, it was assumed that faked illness was malingering *if* encountered in a forensic context, whereas in the absence of clear secondary gain it was FD. However, Eisendrath and McNiel (2004) reported on a series of cases of FD patients who were also in litigation. These authors noted that many FD patients want to be taken care of, and financial compensation may be considered part of this caretaking if someone is perceived as being at fault. These authors also noted that in the presence of litigation, the boundary between malingering and factitious disorder becomes blurred, as litigation creates an external or secondary gain in the form of a potential monetary award and validation by the authority of the court.

This chapter presents the case of an individual who was examined in the context of a medical malpractice lawsuit. The case is an example of the interface between the desire to be sick and the desire to obtain a reward or compensation, not necessarily monetary, through the legal system. From a forensic standpoint, this case underscores the importance of symptom validity testing and obtaining a complete set of current and past medical records. It also provides an example of an individual with legitimate neurological symptoms who had a clear need to appear even worse than her already significant condition.

BACKGROUND

Ms. P. was referred for independent neuropsychological evaluation by attorney CS, who was defending a physician in a medical malpractice suit. In his transmittal letter CS explained that the plaintiff was a European-born woman who had lived in the United States for the past 15 years. There was a question of whether the plaintiff should be examined in English or in her language of origin. According to attorney CS, the plaintiff claimed multiple cognitive and physical injuries that allegedly resulted in a significant level of disability. She was suing one of her surgeons for medical negligence. She had a complex medical history that had started approximately 30 years earlier following a minor bicycle accident.

Records available to this author at the time of the evaluation included only documents generated within the previous 10 years. Upon completion of the examination, it was this author's opinion that a great deal of important information that was diagnostically crucial was not being provided either by the plaintiff or by her mother. The referring attorney was asked to obtain a complete set of medical records all the way back to the time the plaintiff was 14 years old, if at all possible. This was eventually accomplished, although it took approximately 8 months because some of the records had to be obtained from clinics overseas and in three different states.

Record review

Ms. P.'s records indicated that her difficulties started 30 years earlier, when she was 14 years old. At that time, Ms. P. lived in a medium-sized city of a Western European country with her family. Ms. P. fell from her bicycle while playing with friends on the street. She evidently struck the right side of her head on the sidewalk and sustained abrasions of the right thigh. There was some question of very brief loss of consciousness, but this was not clear. She was admitted to the local hospital overnight. During the following few days, she apparently developed headaches and blurring and pressure behind the eyes. She was taken to the emergency room of the local hospital. Motor coordination was poor and gait was unsteady. She complained of "odd feelings" on the entire right side of her body. She described dissociative feelings and noted sensory disturbance persistent on the right hemibody including the face. CT scans and two EEGs were negative. The neurologist noted a mild right hemiparesis "which was of subtle nature and has been only intermittently noticed by the patient."

Three months after her injury she developed right frontal swelling of an intermittent nature. Eventually this became a firm swelling over the right forehead at the scalp line that was persistent. She was examined by a neurosurgeon who found no abnormality. Laminograms of the frontal sinuses were negative. She was admitted to the hospital for a course of antibiotic therapy in consideration of biopsy of the area. Laboratory tests were normal. She underwent elective surgery for removal of "cranial periosteum tumor" four months after the bicycle fall. She was discharged six days later, having improved from the surgery. However, she was readmitted three days after that because of recurrent swelling of the surgical area. She complained of dizziness, photophobia, and headache. She had continued administration of antistaphyloccocal antibiotics and anticoagulation. Five weeks after the surgery, she continued to present with swelling over the surgical area. The neurosurgeon voiced that her problem was "of a totally confusing nature." She was transferred to a major teaching hospital for further medical care.

At the teaching hospital, Ms. P. reported micropsia involving only the right eye. She described a bright linear visual phenomenon in the right visual field. She reported a change in her handwriting. She complained of severe, constant headache, photophobia, blurring of vision, unsteadiness of gait, and unusual bodily sensations. Examination of visual function by a professor of ophthalmology apparently indicated "papilledema and splinter hemorrhage of the right eye with venous engorgement." A biopsy of the right frontal swelling yielded some findings and provided some controversy. The impression was "connective tissue comparable with hypoplastic scar tissue or granulomatous inflammation with no definitive diagnosis."

Ms. P.'s neurological examination revealed multiple abnormalities including poor calculations, decreased visual acuity and micropsia in the right eye, slight blurring of the left disc, mild up-gaze difficulties, right facial sensory deficit, slight weakness of the right deltoid, left hemisensory deficit to pin prick including the face, right dysmetria, and a tendency to become unsteady in a backwards fashion. The neurosurgeon was of the opinion that it was difficult to come up with a single lesion to explain the neurological picture. He ordered numerous neurodiagnostic studies including a lumbar puncture, skull x-rays, and CT scans, all of which were read as normal. Review of histology from prior biopsy was thought to be consistent with "fibrosis without specific tumor or malignancy identified."

A brief psychological assessment at the same hospital estimated Ms. P.'s Full Scale IQ at 91 (average), a Performance IQ of 98 (average), and a Verbal IQ of 87 (low average). Results on memory tests "suggested impaired memory function." No raw data were available for inspection. Consistent with standard neuropsychological practice in the 1970s in Europe and in North America, no attempt was made at measuring effort. At the conclusion of the evaluation period, the professor of neurosurgery noted "possible psychiatric overlay may be contributing to the patient's symptom complex." His discharge diagnosis was "right frontal scalp mass, etiology undetermined." A hand-written note by a psychiatrist from the same institution who briefly saw the plaintiff during her hospital stay stated "the simple unifying diagnosis that fits all of above is hysteria." He suggested "tactful and thorough psychiatric evaluation to parents." This recommendation was not followed.

Over the next decade there were a number of continuing problems relating to the skull abnor-mality. Records from the local European hospital indicate that, starting with the above-mentioned elective removal of frontal skull mass four months after the fall, Ms. P. underwent *21 surgical interventions between her 15th and her 26th birthdays*. These interventions included, to mention only a few, excision of elevated scar tissue at margin on craniotomy plate, with no evidence of tumor material three months after the original surgery; bone excision and cranioplasty one year after that; removal of cranioplasty for staphylococcal infection six months after that; various replacements of cranioplasty and subsequent removals for multiple infection processes (organisms identified were primarily gram negative staphylococcus and flavobacterium), and numerous antibiotic treatments for infections. There was a last removal of infected cranioplasty 11 years after the original surgery, with subsequent cranioplasty three months later. On numerous occasions records indicate a degree of puzzlement on the neurosurgeon's part around Ms. P.'s symptoms and diagnosis of the skull abnormality. Pathology called it at various times proliferative fibromatosis, proliferative fibroma, low grade fibrosarcoma, osteomyelitic process, and skull tumor with metastasis.

A note by the neurosurgeon soon after the 10th surgical procedure indicated that Ms. P. had been an excellent student before her surgeries and continued to obtain high marks after the interventions. Eleven years later, another note by the same neurosurgeon (who had performed all the surgeries) indicated "I think Ms. P. has been causing her own injuries all along."

The medical history as it pertains to the plaintiff's head appears to remain essentially silent for approximately one decade. During that time, the plaintiff and her family moved to the East Coast of the United States. Records made available to this author approximately eight months after the neuropsychological examination, however, revealed that during those years, and while already in the United States, Ms. P. had undergone a hysterectomy and a cholecystectomy, both elective, both undertaken to alleviate pain, and both out of the state of her residence. Neither of these surgeries was preceded by a demonstration of pathology of any sort according to numerous invasive and non-invasive tests. Gynecological and gastroenterological records both document persistent complaints of pain with no improvement in spite of numerous conservative treatments. The records showed *92 visits to the gynecologist and 159 visits to the gastroenterologist during a period of about one decade.*

Approximately 10 years before the current evaluation, Ms. P. was examined by a maxillofacial surgeon, Dr. PG., for facial pain following an attempt to crack a walnut with her teeth. This event was succeeded by a long series of surgical interventions and other procedures that are summarized in the next paragraphs.

An MRI showed anterior dislocation of the left disc of the temporomandibular joint. She com-plained of pain. She was offered splints, but refused them. Notes indicated that she had also refused a night guard two years earlier when this was suggested by her dentist after she complained of jaw pain in the morning. She underwent arthrocentesis of the left temporal mandibular joint (TMJ). Three weeks later, she underwent right TMJ arthrocentesis. One year later she was still reporting TMJ pain bilaterally, and she underwent bilateral TMJ arthroplasties and reconstruction. Her left TMJ improved. However, she grew multiple bacteria on the right side and was treated with a variety of antibiotics. She was treated by Dr. PG. with frequent replacement of dressing and repacking. During the following 7 years, she underwent two incisions and widening of the opening of a draining fistula, five debridement procedures and reconstructions of the right area around the original surgery, and three debridements and excisions of scar tissue as well as reconstruction of right preauricular wound. She was monitored by three infectious disease physicians who, at one point or another, expressed puzzlement over the organisms that were cultured from Ms. P.'s poorly healing wounds and about her alleged poor tolerance of antibiotics and/or poor compliance with the prescribed antibiotic regimen. One of the infectious disease physicians, for example, noted a history of cultures positive for coagulase negative staphylococci sensitive to Cipro. He also noted severe allergies to vancomycin and Ancef. Another infectious disease specialist noted that Ms. P. had evidence of "a complicated soft tissue and bone infection of the head and neck due to multi-resistant bacteria."

Problems continued. She was examined by Dr. PG. 7 years after the original TMJ surgery with high fever and a severe swelling of the right face. She was treated with hyperbaric oxygen and Zithromax. A culture grew *Staphylococcus aureus* as well as yeast. She continued to be treated over the weeks and months with occasional periods of improvement followed by relapses. A laboratory report showed viridans streptococcus and *Xanthomonas maltophilia*. A few days later, Dr. PG. noted her parotid gland had suddenly blocked, and she had significant facial swelling. She had apparently lanced her parotid herself draining copious amounts of clear enzymatic fluid. In view of the persistently non-healing wound, she underwent right total parotidectomy and right facial nerve monitoring.

She continued to experience problems with self-reports of elevated temperature (103 degrees) for weeks after the surgery and supposedly continued treatment with a variety of antibiotics. Dr. PG. noted that Ms. P. had stopped taking the prescribed antibiotics without consulting him. She presented to the emergency room at a local hospital, with complaints of intermittent fevers during the previous 24 hours, although at the ER she was afebrile.

Ms. P. was hospitalized once again a few months later, this time with forehead edema and a question of infected cranioplasty, which was debrided. Notes by an infectious disease physician indicated the following possibilities to explain Ms. P.'s condition: (1) the result of salivary cutaneous fistula as well as non-healing temporal wound possibly secondary to infected cranioplasty with a resistant fastidious organism not yet cultured, versus (2) temporomandibular joint bony infection, versus (3) neurologic disorder, versus (4) malingering on the part of the patient. Ms. P. was discharged four days later with strict instructions to follow up with all involved physicians and to comply with the prescribed antibiotic regimen. Nevertheless, two months later she presented to neurosurgeon Dr. JM. with another cranioplasty infection. The organisms cultured were different from those cultured previously. Two weeks later she underwent exploratory craniotomy with removal of infected cranioplasty and evacuation of epidural empyema. There were complications during the following months. The cranioplasty became infected three times with unusual organisms, and the flap was finally removed. Dr. PG. noted she was upset and was not going to take any more antibiotics. She was examined by an infectious disease specialist for an infected remaining cranioplasty. The infectious disease physician cited evidence of growth of a number of organisms (e.g., non-*Candida albicans* yeast, *Lactobacillus*, and *Sphingobacterium spiritivorum*). He noted Ms. P.'s complaints of adverse reactions from the antibiotics.

Ms. P. remained without a bone flap for a period of more than 4 years during which time she experienced a number of mishaps. Approximately one year after the last cranioplasty, she reported to Dr. PG. that 3 weeks earlier she had fallen in the bathroom and hit her head. She said she did not realize she had a laceration in her scalp. The laceration did not heal. Dr. PG. also noted that Ms. P. was wrapping her head without medical advice. Records contain documents indicating continued difficulties with infectious processes of the cranioplasty scar along with continued treatment over the following months. She underwent incision and drainage as well as debridement and placement of a drain for infection of the same area.

Two months later, Ms. P. reported to Dr. PG. that she had hit her head while getting up from under a cabinet. She indicated she had been using water spickets in order to clean around her scalp wound. Apparently anaerobic *Pseudomonas* was cultured. Around that time Ms. P. reported fainting

spells, the origin of which was not clear. Two months later Dr. PG. noted a report from the micro-
biology department indicating a *Mycobacterium gilvum* infection. He was concerned about this and
referred her to an infectious disease physician. Three months later Ms. P. underwent a full thickness
skin graft from left postauricular area to right temporal area because the right temporal area was
not healing. A few days later she was examined by the infectious disease physician who noted chronic
draining sinus from parotid gland, history of cranioplasty infections, and *Mycobacterium gilvum*
isolation of unknown significance. Treatment with Cipro and minocycline was recommended. One
week later, the infectious disease physician noted the patient was reporting problems tolerating some
of the antibiotics. He discussed the multiple problems Ms. P. was experiencing with her medications
and stressed the importance of compliance to her. In his deposition, the same physician indicated
Ms. P. had only been taking half the recommended dose of antibiotics or had stopped taking some
of the medication altogether.

Two months later, Dr. PG. noted that Ms. P. had fallen that weekend and hit her head on the
cabinet in her garage. There was a puncture-like scalp wound that was debrided, irrigated, and
closed. Ms. P. indicated that cerebrospinal fluid had been draining from her wound. She was assessed
by neurosurgeon Dr. JM. He noted she was alert and awake with a Glasgow Coma Scale of 15.
Neurological examination was normal. A CT scan of the brain noted "status post extensive right-
sided craniotomy with removal of portions of the right frontal, parietal, and temporal bones . . .
there is a new focus of hemorrhage which is linear in configuration and obliquely oriented in the
right frontal lobe matter. There is also a small focus of air slightly more peripherally within the right
frontal lobe." The neurosurgeon expressed puzzlement over this and admitted her to the hospital
for observation. She began complaining of severe headaches. An MRI of the brain showed a 3 cm
enhancing lesion of the right frontal lobe. In addition there were "linear regions of decreased signal
intensity extending from the periphery of the surface of the frontal lobe to the deep periventricular
parenchyma and through the central region of decreased signal." The linear foci suggested to the
radiologist "prior instrumentation or penetrating injury." The neurosurgeon noted, "The area
seemed to track down from the area where the patient had her puncture-like laceration of the skin."
He felt the mass was most consistent with an abscess and that this "could represent an unusual
infection, such as fungus or mycobacterial infection."

Ms. P. underwent a right frontal temporal craniotomy with resection of brain abscess by a
neurosurgeon and drainage of a right carotid abscess by a maxillofacial surgeon. In his deposition,
the infectious disease physician indicated that Ms. P.'s abscess was "one of the most complicated
brain infections I have ever seen." Over the following months there were several consults. A consult
by an infectious disease physician noted, among other things, that Ms. P. reported being allergic to
multiple antibiotics, including cephalosporins and vancomycin, although no allergic reaction had
ever been observed by a health professional.

Ms. P. was followed by various physicians over the next few months to monitor her progress
from the surgeries. Inadequate healing was noted on several occasions over the following months,
and she had surgery for closure of her right cheek a few weeks later; she was treated with hyperbaric
oxygen. Two months later she underwent another procedure to close a flap dehiscence area in the
right temple.

One year after the abscess surgery, Ms. P. was found lying on the floor and nonresponsive. She
had another right scalp laceration. Studies demonstrated a right frontal interparenchymal hematoma. She underwent right-sided craniotomy for evacuation of large hematoma and reclosure of
cranioplasty. A radiology report on serial CT scans indicated "evacuation of the right frontal hematoma with air and hemorrhage in the operative area." The right frontal hematoma was thought to be
resolving when compared to a pre-abscess MRI. Encephalomalacic changes were present in the right
frontal lobe, with moderate mass effect and sufalcine herniation to the left. The ventricles were
mildly enlarged. Two weeks later, an EEG was read as "abnormal with diffuse slowing over the right
hemisphere, consistent with the medical history with no epileptiform abnormalities and no seizures."

A neurorehabilitation consult three weeks after her hospital admission found Ms. P. to have left-sided neglect, ataxia, dysphagia, communication deficits and possible cognitive deficits that were apparently difficult to assess, and deficits of activities of daily living and mobility. She was admitted for acute inpatient rehabilitation. A neurological consult concluded she had a left homonymous hemianopsia suppression related to her right parietal lobe injury. A neuropsychology consult concluded there was intact basic comprehension, difficulty with complex auditory comprehension, severe deficits in basic memory on testing, difficulties with expressive language and writing, and motor apraxia. A psychiatric consult was requested. She was noted to be depressed. Effexor was prescribed. Ms. P. was discharged home with family assistance. One month later Ms. P. reported a seizure (not witnessed by anyone) for which she was placed on Dilantin and Lamictal.

Ms. P. underwent outpatient neuropsychological examination three months after the surgery. At that time, full scale IQ was estimated at 84, with performance IQ of 93, and verbal IQ of 78. Arithmetic was poor. Initial learning of verbal and visual information was also poor. Speech was noted to have improved from previously more severely deficient levels. She was noted to have some expressive communicative abilities with persisting expressive aphasia and oral motor apraxia. Some difficulties with executive function tests were noted. She was also noted to be depressed. Five months later, Ms. P. underwent right frontoparietal occipital cranial vault reconstruction with split cranial bone graft. Her hospital course was uneventful. On the day of discharge, she was alert and oriented with oral apraxia. She was discharged home with her family.

She underwent a second neuropsychological evaluation one year later. The neuropsychologist noted a significant level of improvement relative to her previous testing. However Ms. P. continued to have significant impairment of expressive speech. Estimated IQ levels were at the "average" level (VIQ = 99; PIQ = 111; FSIQ = 105), which were thought to be significantly reduced from estimated premorbid abilities. Verbal memory difficulties, processing speed problems, difficulties with cognitive flexibility, complex problem solving, and fine motor coordination (dominant hand) results were felt to be consistent with prior testing, suggesting relative stability of cognitive deficits. No left neglect was observed. No symptom validity procedures were administered.

The records contain numerous documents from a neurology clinic where Ms. P. was being followed at the time of the current examination. Ms. P. was being treated for a seizure disorder. There are reports of a "long history of seizures going back to before her stroke and with intermittent episodes of loss of time with tongue bite." EEG reports continue to show right-sided slowing. The seizures have never been witnessed. She has reported having daily spells without loss of consciousness, described as sudden numbness of left arm and sometimes leg followed by tremor lasting seconds. She has also reported, "up to 4 per cluster and 2–3 clusters daily occurring most often while sleeping." Throughout the notes generated at the clinic, Ms. P. was noted to have "no speech difficulties," "no difficulty walking," "no tremors," and "normal station and gait."

A driver's evaluation three months before this author's evaluation of Ms. P. deemed her fit for driving with no restrictions. This driver's evaluation reached this author only two days before the scheduled trial.

Review of school records revealed a pattern of predominantly good to excellent grades. Similarly, employment records indicated uniformly good assessments.

NEUROPSYCHOLOGICAL EVALUATION

Presenting complaints

Ms. P. was asked to write a list of the problems she had been experiencing since her stroke. She wrote: "expressive aphasia; apraxia; memory; left hand strength decreased; choking; bumping into walls;

dyslexia; poor vision left eye; cognitive problems; poor night driving; unable to balance checkbook or do taxes; unable to do physical therapy; can't make complex decisions."

In response to an intake questionnaire in which specific questions are asked about different aspects of cognition, emotional status, and level of functioning, she had no attention or concentration complaints. She complained of forgetting what she reads or sees and needing to read material three times to understand it. She needed to make to-do lists. She was easily distracted, and her thinking was slow. She needed to rehearse everything before saying it. She was able to think faster than she could speak. She became very dysarthric after the stroke. Her semantic and syntactic knowledge are down. She had become presbyopic since her stroke. Her ability to taste changed; everything tasted bad. She lost weight. She reported decreased sensation in her left arm and leg. She had no pain complaints. Since she went on antidepressants, she had no problem sleeping. She denied sexual difficulties. She continued to have plans to return to work.

She was able to drive short distances. When asked about her seizure disorder vis-à-vis driving, she said that she had been told by an instructor and her neurologist that she could drive. She had no accidents or tickets at any time.

Ms. P. was asked to give her medical history. She was very focused on the physician she was suing. She tended to jump from one part of her medical history to another, and it was difficult to keep her focused on the chronology. At times she appeared to have a difficult time coming up with exact dates. Other times, she was able to give dates spontaneously with no difficulty whatsoever. She did not mention the abdominal surgeries she had a number of years previously, and she minimized the number of doctors' visits, surgeries, and medications she had been prescribed over the years. She gave the following information:

At 14 years of age she was injured when she fell from her bicycle. She had her bone flap removed because it created bone tumors in the right frontal, parietal, and temporal areas. It destroyed the mastoid area. She had more than 20 surgeries between the ages of 14 and 26.

At age 37 she had temporomandibular joint surgery after biting into a nut. She developed a seroma on the right jaw. There was an open hole on the right side of her face. Her skin grafts did not take. Nobody tested her for amylase that was leaking out of her wound until after a period of eight months. She was started on Robinul to decrease parotid fluids, but eventually she needed to have a parotidectomy. She had two cranioplasties that got infected. The doctors did not know why. Part of her skull was eventually removed (approximately one third) because of the infections. She did not have a bone flap for more than three years. She did not wear protective head-gear. Some time later she had a brain abscess. This caused her severe headaches. After they removed it, she remained confused for about two months. She needed nursing, and she needed to be close to her family. Six months later, she was found on the floor by a member of her family. She had had a stroke. After the stroke, she never had another headache. She tried seeing her doctors immediately when she had a very bad headache but was told that she could not be fitted in, therefore she had to go to the hospital Emergency Room instead. She volunteered that she is only suing the doctor because he did not pay sufficient attention to her headache complaints at the time of her abscess.

Background history

Ms. P. is a 44-year-old left-handed single woman born in Europe of British parents. She possesses native fluency in English and Spanish, having spent her early childhood in several Spanish-speaking countries. Her formal education from the age of 15 was exclusively in English. She has resided on the East Coast of the United States for the past 15 years. She denied experiencing difficulties at school as a child. None of her relatives had developmental learning disabilities. She completed 16 years of formal education: she has a four-year degree in physical therapy. After she graduated from physical therapy school, she applied to a number of medical schools but was not accepted.

Ms. P. reported that her work history was always outstanding. She was a physical therapist specializing in neurological patients for more than a decade. She stopped working approximately 10 years before the current examination for medical reasons.

Ms. P. lives independently in her own home near her parents' house. She needs help from her brother-in-law for complex business transactions, but otherwise takes care of all paperwork on her own. Before her stroke, she used to sculpt and ski in addition to working full time. She has never been married. She has no children. She supports herself through Social Security and medical disability benefits.

Ms. P.'s parents are alive and well. Her father is a retired international business consultant. Her mother is a retired teacher. She is the third of four girls. Ms. P. grew up with both her parents and her three sisters. She denied any history of abuse while growing up and called her childhood "wonderful." She denied a criminal history. She neither smokes nor drinks. She reported no history of excess alcohol consumption. She denied current or past recreational drug use of any sort. She flatly denied any history of psychological problems. She has never consulted a psychologist or psychiatrist for any reason. At the time of this evaluation Ms. P. was taking Dilantin and Keppra for seizures and Effexor for depression.

Interview with Ms. P.'s mother

Ms. P.'s mother described her daughter as fiercely independent and insisting on living alone, even during acute phases of her various medical problems. Until the brain abscess, Ms. P. bounced back immediately after all of her surgeries. She did very well in high school and was at the top of her physical therapy class even while going through various surgeries. Ms. P. started experiencing some bad headaches seven years ago that worsened over time. Her personality changed because of this. She experienced cognitive changes after her brain abscess. Her headaches disappeared after the stroke. She did not speak much for quite a while after her stroke. She was very dysphasic and dyspraxic, but she learned fast and experienced remarkable levels of recovery.

In response to a questionnaire regarding her daughter's memory, Ms. P.'s mother indicated that occasionally Ms. P. experiences forgetfulness. She has more serious problems in other areas such as losing her train of thought, remembering instructions, and doing calculations.

Ms. P.'s mother gave the impression of being a caring individual who provides a great deal of support to her daughter. She did not admit to any issues that may possibly have set the stage for her daughter's problems. She denied believing that her daughter experiences any psychiatric difficulties. Neither she not her husband believed it was appropriate for Ms. P. to be seen by a psychiatrist when this was suggested at the time of her first extensive neurological evaluation overseas.

Physical appearance

Ms. P. was in no acute distress and appeared about her stated chronological age. She is of shorter than average height at 5 feet and appeared underweight. She ambulated slowly, with a slight left limp. She had an obvious right frontal skull defect. She had an obvious left facial paralysis. Hygiene and dress were appropriate.

Behavioral observations

Ms. P. arrived on time the three days of the examination. She was accompanied by her mother. She was a pleasant, quiet woman who appeared generally familiar with the examination process. She made good eye contact with the examiner. Her speech was hypernasal and halting, with noticeable oromotor apraxia. The result of this was that it took her a long time to say what she wanted to say.

There were occasional word-finding difficulties. Her English was unaccented. Her oral Spanish was excellent, although she clearly favored English. She indicated she never became very literate in Spanish as she had primarily attended English schools when she lived overseas.

She was cooperative and generally able to give what appeared to be a coherent, if vague and choppy, personal history. She was able to describe her current deficits using technical medical terminology. She moved very slowly and this included writing. Completion of intake forms, demographic and other questionnaires took much longer than is customary. The result of this was that it took about three times longer than average to complete the examination, as latencies for both oral responses and written responses were extremely high.

Ms. P.'s mood was thought to be somewhat depressed and her range of affect was constricted. Ms. P. said she used to joke around a lot. Now nobody thinks she is funny. She flatly denied thoughts of suicide or of harming others.

During testing, Ms. P.'s level of cooperation appeared normal. She was quiet and volunteered little information. In retrospect, the psychomotor slowing may have been at least partially fabricated. She showed no other unusual behaviors. She had no difficulty whatsoever with instructions. She appeared to recognize some of the tests. She was able to sit for prolonged periods of time during interview and testing without any overt evidence of discomfort. She showed no signs of fatigue until the end of each day.

Procedures

Clinical Interview; Interview with the Plaintiff's Mother; Delis-Kaplan Executive Function System (Trail Making, Verbal Fluency, Design Fluency, Color-Word Interference); Wisconsin Card Sorting Test; Story Memory Test; Figure Memory Test; Rey-Osterrieth Complex Figure; California Verbal Learning Test–II; Wide Range Achievement Test–III (Arithmetic); Wechsler Test of Adult Reading (WTAR); Structured Inventory of Malingered Symptomatology (SIMS); Grip Strength; Finger Tapping; Word Memory Test. Interview and testing were conducted in English.

Neuropsychological results

Orientation

Ms. P. was well oriented to person, place, and circumstance. She was one day off in identifying the date. She was well informed on national current affairs and international news. However, she could not name the current President of the United States, though she was able to pick him correctly from a choice of four names, and she correctly identified his predecessor. She was able to recall correctly the specific dates of her three previous neuropsychological evaluations.

Cooperation

Ms. P. gave convincing evidence of poor or inconsistent best effort for success in cognitive tests. On the Word Memory Test (WMT), Ms. P.'s scores were as follows: immediate recognition = 57.5% (fail), delayed recognition = 72.5% (fail), consistency = 45.0% (fail), multiple choice = 50% ("warning"), paired associate recall = 35% ("warning"), free recall = 15.0% (fail). She gave evidence of response bias in the forced-choice recognition trial of the CVLT–II. Her Reliable Digit Span score was 5, and her Failure to Maintain Set score was 3, both also suggesting poor effort. Additionally, results were inconsistent with the fact that she is able to drive. Therefore, the results of the neuropsychological examination were deemed unreliable and not an accurate reflection of her true level of functioning (Table 18.1).

TABLE 18.1   Neuropsychological test scores

Name: Ms. P.
Year of Testing: 2006
Year of Birth: 1959
Age at Testing: 44 years

WAIS–III[1]

	IQ Equivalents of SS	Percentile
Verbal IQ	73	4
Performance IQ	88	18
Full Scale IQ	78	6

Delis-Kaplan Executive Function System[2]

	Raw Scores	Scaled Scores
Verbal Fluency	9	1
Category Fluency	14	1
Total Correct Responses	8	3
Total Switching Accuracy	7	5
Design Fluency		
Filled Dots	6	7
Empty Dots	5	6
Switching	3	6
Design Fluency Overall	19	6
Color Word Interference Test		
Color Naming	90	1
Word Reading	90	1
Inhibition	180	1
Inhibition/Switching	180	1
Trail Making Test		
Condition 1	53	1
Condition 2	58	4
Condition 3	104	1
Condition 4	154	3
Condition 5	39	9

		Z-scores
Boston Naming Test[3]	36	−6.9
Token Test[4]	40	24

Rey-Osterrieth Complex Figure[5]		Z-scores
Copy	19.5	−4.8
30′ Delayed Recall	5	−1.73

California Verbal Learning Test[6]		
Trial 1	4	−2
Trial 5	8	−2.5
Trials 1–5 Total	30	23 (T score)
Trial B	1	−2.5
Short Delay Free Recall	5	−3
Short Delay Cued Recall	4	−4
Long Delay Free Recall	6	−3
Long Delay Cued Recall	5	−3.5

Story Memory Test[7]		T-scores
Learning	2.88	29
Loss after 4-h delay (%loss)	52	27

(*Continued . . .*)

TABLE 18.1   (Continued)

Figure Memory Test[8]		
Learning	12	55
Loss after 4-h delay (% loss)	33.3	30
Finger Tapping Test[9]		
Right	53	66
Left	43	7
Grip Test[10]		
Right	22	39
Left	21	33
Wide Range Achievement Test–III[11]		*Grade Equivalent*
Arithmetic	33	5
Peabody Individual Achievement Test–R[12]		*Grade Equivalent*
Reading Comprehension subtest		6–9
Wechsler Test of Adult Reading		
Standard Score	107	
Demographics—Predicted Score	110	
Prediction Interval	90–130	
Word Memory Test[13]		
Immediate Recognition IR	57.5 FAIL	
Delayed Recognition DR	72.5 FAIL	
Consistency CNS	45 FAIL	
Multiple Choice MC	50 WARNING	
Paired Associates PA	35 WARNING	
Delay Free Recall DFR	15	
Long Delay Free Recall LDFR	10	

Notes: [1]Wechsler, 1997; [2]Delis et al., 2001; [3]Kaplan et al., 1983; [4]Benton & Hamsher, 1989; [5]Spreen & Strauss, 1991; [6]Delis et al., 2001; [7]Heaton et al., 1991; [8]Heaton et al., 1991; [9]Heaton et al., 1991; [10]Heaton et al., 1991; [11]Wilkinson, 1993; [12]Markwardt, 1989; [13]Green et al., 1996.

Psychological status

Ms. P. was administered the Structured Inventory of Malingered Symptomatology. This is a 75-item multiaxial, self-administered screening measure used for the detection of malingering across a variety of clinical and forensic settings. Ms. P.'s total score of 28 on the SIMS is 14 points above the recommended cutoff score for the identification of suspected malingering. She endorsed an unusual number of responses on the Neurologic Impairment Scale, the Affective Scale, the Low Intelligence Scale, and particularly also on the Amnesic Disorder Scale. This indicates that she is over-reporting her symptoms.

Given her reported reading difficulties and her extreme psychomotor slowing, Ms. P. was not administered an MMPI–2.

Impression

Ms. P. cooperated with the examination process inasmuch as she took the tests without complaining and responded to interview questions. During face-to-face contact with Ms. P. this author was somewhat alarmed by what appeared to be extreme slowing down, particularly in view that she reported driving. However, there were some clear neurological signs that cannot be faked, and there was also clear and significant neuroanatomical evidence of damage (per available records). Therefore, she was given the benefit of the doubt during the entire examination. She indicated she experienced great difficulty reading. Therefore, she was not administered the MMPI–2. Instead, she was only given the Structure Inventory of Malingering Symptomatology (SIMS). In retrospect, this author should have taken another day and administered the MMPI–2.

Test results gave convincing evidence that she did not always put forth full effort in completing the neuropsychological tests. Multiple symptom validity measures showed results that were significantly worse than those individuals with very severe neurological illness and were similar to results by individuals asked to feign illness. Research indicates that in individuals who are seeking compensation, effort has a greater effect on the test scores than even severe brain injury (Green et al., 2001). The neuropsychological results were unreliable for the purpose of identifying cognitive strengths and weaknesses. Results during the examination were not always consistent with results obtained during previous evaluations four and three years before the current evaluation. Examples of this were three different estimates of IQ, and a significantly fluctuating performance on the CVLT–II. Her results were also inconsistent with the fact that she lives independently and that she was deemed to be a safe and, indeed, excellent driver during a recent driver's evaluation on surface streets of a busy East Coast metropolis and on the interstate highway, resulting in her being given a green light to operate a vehicle without restrictions.

The above is not to say by any means that Ms. P. experiences no cognitive problems. She has significant and genuine neurological problems in keeping with objective anatomical evidence of brain damage. It is to say, however, that it is not possible to reliably distinguish between what may be genuine problems and what may simply be the result of poor motivation, lack of effort in completing the tasks, or, indeed, a desire to appear even more damaged than she is.

Test results reflected poor scores in areas of attention and concentration, memory, executive functioning, language, areas of praxis, and motor function. She also had poor results in tests of scholastic achievement. It was not possible to determine if any of the results were an accurate reflection of this patient's true level of cognitive functioning. If the scores (particularly those reflecting attention and concentration) were indeed representative of her true level of cognitive functioning, she would neither be able to drive (not even one or two miles) nor live on her own and take care of her own needs, as she appears to be able to do. The IQ estimates obtained overseas when she was 15 years old also appear very low, particularly in view of the fact that she went on to complete a physical therapy degree, and held a position of responsibility as the head of a large physical therapy department for a number of years. Her estimated premorbid IQ (WTAR) was 107, and this is likely to have been more accurate than the FSIQ of 91 estimated in the 1970s. She may not have put forth full effort into completing the tests even at the age of 14.

As far as her emotional status was concerned, it seemed at the time of the evaluation that a traditional self-report inventory would be too demanding on Ms. P.'s reported reading skills. However, results on a screening instrument, the SIMS, were well above the cutoff point used to identify suspected malingering. She endorsed numerous neurological and psychiatric symptoms. Hence, here again, Ms. P.'s credibility was significantly damaged. It is noted that in spite of over-endorsement of symptomatology in the SIMS, she flatly denied any psychological problems other than "some depression," and expressed the opinion that all her problems were physical in nature.

Ms. P. complained of cognitive problems (including language, memory, reading and writing), physical problems (including motor and visual), disability, and difficulty carrying out such activities as balancing a checkbook, making complex decisions, and doing yard work as a result of years of medical problems that culminated in significant neurological injury with accompanying symptomatology.

The examination yielded results that strongly point to (1) insufficient effort during test taking and (2) exaggeration of reported symptomatology. Both of the above can and frequently do co-exist with genuine neurological and/or psychiatric symptomatology. Involvement in litigation, by definition, means that secondary gain is involved. In other words, problems or symptoms can bring something positive or rewarding, leading some individuals to exaggerate existing symptoms. To some degree, this plaintiff's poor effort in test completion and exaggeration of symptomatology were thought to be related to her lawsuit.

In addition to the test results, evidence from available records was considered in attempting to understand this woman's plight and how she may have arrived at this point in her life. There has been an extraordinarily high number of surgical interventions, expressed puzzlement by treating physicians as to the possible nature of her problems, multiple infections with failure to heal in spite of multiple debridements and antibiotic treatments, reports of adverse reactions to multiple antibiotics, reports of unusual syncopal episodes, and culture of organisms rarely seen in patients. On a number of occasions over the years, there was mention of a possible psychiatric component. One physician even suggested hysteria as a possibility and recommended psychiatric evaluation. However, there was no evidence of psychiatric consult in the records in my possession. Ms. P.'s mother indicated that psychiatric illness was rejected as a possibility, as did Ms. P. herself. There also was frequent mention of lack of compliance, including failure to follow the prescribed medication regimen and interfering with wound care. Malingering was also mentioned as a possibility in the records.

Given the extreme nature of the medical history and having considered all possibilities, it was this author's opinion that Ms. P. had a factitious disorder. Ms. P. was a member of an allied medical profession and was well informed as to neurological and other illnesses. Ms. P.'s disorder probably manifested itself for 30 years and, as far as could be ascertained from most recent records, is ongoing. There were attempts to conceal many of the treatments received through minimization of medical history, frequent lack of compliance with prescribed regimens, multiple accidents, unwitnessed fevers, allergic reactions, and seizures, interference with wound care, multiple and unusual infections, and probable self-inflicted penetrating injuries. In other words, her illnesses, at least a significant number of them, had been self-inflicted and self-perpetuated. She seemed to accept easily numerous surgical procedures and invasive tests.

It was this author's impression that Ms. P. was very motivated to continue in her well-entrenched patient role. It was also this author's opinion that Ms. P.'s perceived lack of attention by the physician who had cared for her for a number of years was viewed as doubting her credibility. This led her to initiate legal action against that physician.[2] At the same time, through legal action, Ms. P. may also have been attempting to obtain "socially sanctioned and judicially certified approval" (Eisendrath & McNiel, 2004). The results of the evaluation, with evidence of poor effort and symptom exaggeration, reflected an attempt to appear worse than she is for the purposes of the litigation. However, during the lengthy interview, her focus appeared to be on punishing the person she perceived as not paying sufficient attention to her. She opted not to pursue legal action against the hospital, a choice that could not be explained by the defense attorney, given the hospital's "deeper pockets." This choice was interpreted as suggesting that it was attention and judicial validation, not monetary gain, that she craved most. In her zeal to obtain validation, she made every effort to appear more damaged than she was, thereby damaging her credibility and instigating a search for records that would ultimately reveal the extent of her true illness.

---

[2] Incidentally, over a period of seven years she had 312 face-to-face contacts with Dr. PG., 52 of which involved actual surgery or other invasive procedure. During that time the relationship had been harmonious until Ms. P. felt he did not pay enough attention to her.

CONCLUSION

Ms. P.'s trial took place in an East Coast court three months after completion of this author's report. Ms. P. was present in the courtroom throughout the trial and acted as her lawyer's assistant. While her facial paresis and her skull defect were very much in evidence, she was observed by witnesses, judge, and jury as she deftly went through three ring binders and found information to point to her attorney. She seemed quite able to read through pages and quickly point at specific lines.

This author gave her testimony as outlined above in the "Impression" section. The probability of a factitious disorder (Munchausen syndrome) was also raised by an infectious disease physician who testified in detail about her dramatic and confusing medical history, clear symptoms that were not predictable and that became more severe or changed once treatment began, frequent accidents (bumping her head), relapses following improvement, extensive knowledge of hospitals and medical terminology as well as familiarity with neurological illness (through her profession), interference with the healing of wounds, many surgical scars, appearance of new or additional symptoms following negative test results, presence of symptoms only when alone or not being observed, and apparent eagerness to have medical tests, operations, or other procedures. This physician also testified that the organisms cultured from Ms. P. "are not typically found in an immuno-compromised host or for that matter, in a normal host." Factitious disorder was also the diagnosis given by a neuroradiologist who opined that the linear foci and air visualized in the MRI around the time of the abscess (at which time Ms. P. had no bone flap) coincided with a scalp puncture and suggested self-inflicted injury with a needle-like instrument. Lastly, the now elderly surgeon who had performed the original cranial surgeries when Ms. P. was a teenager was flown in to testify from Europe. He remembered the case well and declared that there came a time after Ms. P. had a number of infected wounds and what appeared to be a contused scalp above the bone defect when he became convinced that Ms. P. had been causing her unusual problems all along. The jury found Ms. P. lacking in credibility and returned a defense verdict.

As has been mentioned in a previous section, there are a number of different theories regarding the origin of factitious disorders. Factitious disorders are treated primarily through psychotherapy. The investigation of the psychopathology of individuals with FD and their treatment can be difficult because most refuse psychiatric exploration and therapy. The therapeutic goal is to focus on changing the thinking and behavior of the individual with the disorder. Family therapy is sometimes helpful as well. Considerations of due diligence prompted this author to recommend urgent examination by a psychologist or psychiatrist with ample experience in the diagnosis and treatment of individuals with factitious disorders. The possibility of an underlying personality disorder was suggested. It was not possible to venture a most likely origin for Ms. P.'s long-lasting and self-destructive patterns of behavior. It was suggested, however, that Ms. P.'s chances of being assisted by therapy might increase once the litigation process had concluded.

Lastly, the reader may ask how it is possible that Ms. P. could undergo literally hundreds of medical visits, an inordinate number of surgical procedures, and experience numerous unusual infections and adverse reactions to antibiotics without "getting caught." The combination of two factors is thought to be at the root of this: (1) Health practitioners assume patients keep their end of the doctor/patient contract. Some may be reluctant to diagnose FD even if they suspect it. The reason behind this may be a measure of disbelief or fear of being accused of malpractice by an irate patient. (2) Health practitioners, particularly specialists, seldom have access to a complete set of patient records. In this case, the records became available only through sub-subpoena power. It was the bird's eye view of the medical history, coupled by the clear evidence of malingered test results, that allowed clarification of diagnosis in this case.

REFERENCES

American Psychiatric Association. (2000). *Diagnostic and statistical manual of mental disorders*, 4th ed., text revision. Washington, DC: APA.

Benton, A., Hamsher, K., & Sivan, A. (1993). *Multilingual aphasia examination, manual.* Odessa, FL: Psychological Assessment Resources, Inc.

Bock, K. D., & Overkamp, F. (1986). Factitious disease: Observations on 44 cases at a medical clinic and recommendations for a subclassification. *Klinische Wochenschrift 17*; *64*(4), 149–164.

Delis, D., Kaplan, E., & Kramer, J. H. (2001). *The Delis-Kaplan Executive Function System.* New York: Psychological Corporation.

Delis, D., Kramer, J. H., Kaplan, E., & Ober, B. (2000). *The California Verbal Learning Test–2nd ed.* New York: Psychological Corporation.

Eisendrath, S. (1984). Factitious illness: A clarification. *Psychosomatics, 25*, 110–117

Eisendrath, S. J., & McNiel, D. E. (2004). Factitious physical disorders, litigation, and mortality. *Psychosomatics, 45*, 350–353.

Elwyn, T. J., & Ahmed, I. (2006). Factitious disorder. Retrieved April 13, 2007 from http://www.emedicine.com/med/topic3125.htm

Fliege, H., Grimm, A., Eckhardt-Henn, A., Gieler, U., Martin, K., & Klapp, B. F. (2007). Frequency of ICD–10 factitious disorder: Survey of senior hospital consultants and physicians in private practice. *Psychosomatics, 48*, 60–64.

Green, P., Allen, L., & Astner, K. (1996). *The Word Memory Test: A users guide to the oral and computer-administered forms*, US version 1.1. Durham, NC: CogniSyst.

Green, P., Rohling, M. L., Lees-Haley, P. R., & Allen, L. M. (2001). Effort has a greater effect on test scores than severe brain injury in compensation claimants. *Brain Injury, 15*, 1045–1060.

Hamilton, J. C., & Feldman, M. D. (2006). Munchausen syndrome. Retrieved June 7, 2007 from http://www.emedicine.com/med/topic3543.htm

Heaton, R. K., Grant, I., & Matthews, C. G. (1991). *Comprehensive norms for an expanded Halstead-Reitan Battery.* Odessa, FL: Psychological Assessment Resources, Inc.

Kaplan, E., Goodglass, H., & Weintraub, S. (1983). *The Boston Naming Test–2nd ed.* Philadelphia: Lea & Febiger.

Larrabee, G. J. (2005). A scientific approach to forensic neuropsychology. In G. J. Larrabee (Ed.) *Forensic neuropsychology: A scientific approach.* New York: Oxford University Press.

Markwardt, J. (1989). *Peabody Individual Achievement Test–Revised, manual.* Circle Pines, MN: American Guidance Service (AGS).

Mitrushina, M., Boone, K. B., Razani, J., & D'Elia, L. F. (2005). *Handbook of normative data for neuropsychological assessment* (2nd ed.). New York: Oxford University Press.

Psychological Corporation. (2001). *WTAR: Wechsler Test of Adult Reading. Manual.* San Antonio, TX: Author.

Smith, G. P. (2003). *Structured inventory of malingered symptomatology.* Odessa, FL: Psychological Assessment Resources.

Spreen, O., & Strauss, E. (1991). *A compendium of neuropsychological tests: Administration, norms, and commentary.* New York: Oxford University Press.

Wechsler. D. (1997). *Wechsler Adult Intelligence Scale–III.* San Antonio, TX: The Psychological Corporation/Harcourt Brace & Company.

Wilkinson. G. S. (1993). *The Wide Range Achievement Test–III: Administration manual.* Wilmington, DE: Wide Range, Inc.

World Health Organization (1992). *International statistical classification of diseases and related health problem*, 10th rev. Geneva: World Health Organization.

Malingered dementia and feigned psychosis

19

Joel E. Morgan, Scott R. Millis, and Jacqueline Mesnik

The range and variety of behaviors exhibited by examinees in forensic contexts are enormous, spanning the full gamut from unremarkable behavior to all forms of psychopathology and illness behaviors. For both the novice and experienced forensic neuropsychologist, these various symptom presentations exhibited by claimants are a source of interest, curiosity, sometimes amazement, and even fascination. As well, sometimes examinee presentations are also a source of bewilderment, especially for the inexperienced forensic neuropsychologist.

The forensic neuropsychological examination seeks to unravel the claimant's symptoms and to elucidate the nature of myriad complaints often seen in medicolegal contexts. Some claimant presentations are blatantly absurd from the outset, making no sense diagnostically and following a course and symptom picture completely inconsistent with the well-documented medical, neurologic, or psychiatric literature. It is as if these claimants adopt symptoms that *they think* represent the disorder. Such examinees in forensic neuropsychological contexts have been referred to as "unsophisticated malingerers." These individuals might be contrasted with examinees that have some knowledge of the prominent symptom picture of an illness and are referred to as "sophisticated malingerers" (Morgan, in press). Some examinees interestingly present with a mixture of both characteristics and therefore could be referred to as "partially sophisticated malingerers."

That which also piques the curiosity of the clinician is provided by examinees that have a history of somatoform, conversion, or factitious illness, some of whom may show malingering behavior when seen in compensation-seeking contexts (Eisendrath & McNiel, 2002, 2004; also see Artiola i Fortuny, this volume, chapter 18). This phenomenon is becoming better documented and raises age-old, and heretofore unresolved, psychological questions concerning consciousness, intent, and awareness—issues that are beyond the scope of this chapter. Perhaps providing a degree of skepticism around the issue of the unconscious in this context is the fact that conversion symptoms have changed through the ages, as knowledge of illness and symptoms becomes more widespread (Shorter, 1993). Similarly, the reported association between antisocial personality disorder and conversion disorder in males (American Psychiatric Association, 2000; Bofelli & Guze, 1992) and its prevalence in military and criminal settings arguably also suggested a conscious component. Current scientific knowledge regarding insufficient effort, symptom exaggeration, and malingering might have given Freud some pause in simply attributing difficult-to-understand behavior to "unconscious processes."

Secondary gain refers to the presentation of illness or injury behavior that is not for the purpose of obtaining treatment, but in order to receive some other benefit. The concept of malingering clearly implies conscious intent to deceive for secondary gain purposes (Slick, Sherman, & Iverson, 1999) when an external incentive exists, as in financial compensation or the avoidance of prosecution and related benefits. Similarly, malingering's "behavioral cousin," *factitious disorder*, also inherently requires conscious intent. The difference diagnostically is that the secondary gain among factitious patients is restricted to taking on the sick role and receiving the benefits of medical and family attention and the possible gratification of dependency needs rather than tangible compensation that may accrue as a result (American Psychiatric Association, 2000).

In contrast to factitious disorders and malingering, symptoms associated with somatoform disorders are thought *not* to be intentionally produced or feigned (American Psychiatric Association, 2000). The DSM–IV lists a number of different somatoform disorders, including somatization disorder (formerly hysteria), pain disorder, conversion disorder, hypochondriasis, and others. Each of these diagnoses shares the central characteristic that symptoms, physical (somatic) in nature, are caused by psychological factors outside of the person's conscious awareness.

One fascinating manifestation of a probable somatization disorder is the phenomenon of Psychogenic Nonepileptic Seizures (PNES; Alper, 1994; Benbadis, 2006), formerly known as "pseudoseizures." PNES are paroxysmal episodes of presumed psychological origin that resemble epileptic episodes. They are typically diagnosed via 24-hour EEG monitoring and were previously often misdiagnosed as genuine seizures of neurological origin (Benbadis, 2006). Some patients with genuine epilepsy also manifest PNES. This comorbidity was previously thought to be relatively rare (Lesser, 1996), but is now recognized as more common (Benbadis & Hauser, 2000).

A long-term area of interest and research among behavioral scientists concerns the association between severe emotional stress or trauma experienced at a young age and the development of psychopathology later in life. Childhood sexual, physical, and/or emotional abuse has been associated with the subsequent development of many forms of psychopathology, placing the abused child at substantial risk for developing a variety of emotional disorders (Molnar, Buka, & Kessler, 2001). These include Borderline Personality Disorder (Zanarini, Yong, Frankenburg, Hennen, Reich, Marino, & Vujanovic, 2002) and other personality disorders (Grover, Carpenter, Price, Gagne, Mello, Mello, & Tyrka, 2007), chronic pain (Goldberg & Goldstein, 2000; Goldberg, Pachas, & Keith, 1999), Posttraumatic Stress Disorder (PTSD; Yehuda, Halligan, & Grossman, 2001), dissociative disorders (Ellason & Ross, 1997), anxiety disorders (Sareen, Cox, Afifi, de Graaf, Asmundson, Have, & Stein, 2005), pedophilia (Fagan, Wise, Schmidt, & Berlin, 2002), major depression (Reinherz, Pradis, Giaconia, Stashwick, & Fitzmaurice, 2003), and substance abuse (Molnar et al., 2001), among many others.

In addition, there is an expanding body of neurobiological research suggesting that the basis of this association between early traumatic experiences and the subsequent development of psychopathology lies in the nervous system. McEwen (1998, 1999) and colleagues (McEwen & Seeman, 2003) have substantial evidence suggesting that early disturbances in the hypothalamic-pituitary-adrenal (HPA) axis, as a consequence of environmental stress, leads to the later development of psychopathology. It is commonly believed that the HPA axis lies at the actual intersection between the central and autonomic nervous systems, connecting "mind and body." It has been hypothesized that early disruption of the HPA axis changes the way stressful, emotionally-valent events are processed, thus establishing a propensity to the possible development of abnormal behaviors, emotional perception, and experience. McEwen hypothesizes a critical period, a time window, at which point the organism is most vulnerable for such disruption. While much more needs to be learned about these putative relationships and their possible physiological basis, the conclusion that some individuals are prone to the development of psychiatric disorders on the basis of their *experiences* is not premature and is clearly warranted.

In this chapter we present the case of a woman whose symptom picture was complex and multifaceted. Her history was replete with many of the issues noted above. Although some of her symptoms could be seen as transparently fabricated, others were less obvious. As the reader will see, her history of numerous credible emotional stressors is likely to have been relevant with regard to an overall diagnostic formulation, evidence of malingering notwithstanding. Like several other cases in this volume, this one also exemplifies the fact that genuine psychopathology may, and often does, co-exist with an exaggerated or malingered presentation. This case provides an example of how to deal diagnostically with a multifaceted presentation of genuine and fabricated symptoms that is intended to be of use to the less experienced forensic examiner. In this regard, we hope to minimize bewilderment regarding the differential diagnosis by encouraging a scientifically sound, neuropsychological psychometric approach.

THE CASE OF MS. O.

Case synopsis

This 48-year-old, married female was referred for a disability evaluation by her insurance carrier. She allegedly developed an encephalopathy of unknown origin and subsequently she experienced "seizures" which were found to be nonepileptic in nature. More recently she alleged cognitive impairment and "Alzheimer's disease," and was being treated for that by a nurse practitioner. In a record review by a physician consultant for the insurance company, major depression was identified as the probable primary diagnosis. A comprehensive neuropsychological evaluation was requested to provide a comprehensive assessment of the claimant's cognitive, neurobehavioral, and psychological status and to "shed light on this complex, somewhat confusing clinical presentation."

Social history

This information was obtained during the clinical interview with the claimant and her husband. She presented for the exam accompanied by her husband of 30 years. She was a morbidly obese (reportedly weighing 325 lb, 5′ 4″ tall), Caucasian, right-handed woman, who appeared her stated age. She was casually dressed and appropriately groomed. When the claimant was unable to answer some questions, her husband was asked to provide the information. Ms. O. was born out of state and moved to the present state as a child. She reported that she was the oldest of four; she had two brothers and a sister. She stated that her mother died of pancreatic cancer and that her father was still living in his late seventies. Ms. O. described her father as an "abusive alcoholic." She reported that she had been emotionally, physically, and sexually abused throughout childhood. At that point in the interview her husband interjected that the claimant had told him of this childhood abuse "only recently." Other family medical history was positive for bipolar disorder in her youngest brother and Alzheimer's disease in her maternal grandmother.

Ms. O. reported that both of her children died in childhood, one of SIDS as an infant and the other at age 2 of a cerebral hemorrhage secondary to an arteriovenous malformation. She could not *remember* how she dealt with these experiences. Her husband simply shook his head.

When asked how much education she completed Ms. O. said, "I don't remember." Her husband said that she left school in the 12th grade and later earned a GED. At the time she left work on disability, Ms. O. had been a risk manager for a large bank, a job she held for 10 months. Prior to that, she worked for an insurance company for 17 years, also in risk management and related activities. She indicated that her last job required that she travel by automobile to many bank branches regularly, a task that she said she had no trouble doing, until she became ill.

Medical history

Past medical history was positive for hypertension, sleep apnea, and hyperlipidemia. Ms. O. denied any formal psychiatric treatment but said that she has probably been depressed her "whole life." At the time of the evaluation she was seeing a psychiatric nurse practitioner regularly. She was prescribed many medications: Ambien, Xanax XR, Inderal, Lipitor, Lisinopril, Namenda, Seroquel, Zoloft, and vitamins. Prior to taking Namenda, she had been prescribed Aricept.

History of present illness

According to the claimant and her husband, Ms. O.'s difficulties began approximately two years prior to this examination. The first manifestations of difficulty reportedly were problems finishing her work. She lost her job and became depressed. She began to forget her destination while driving the car. She reported these "spells" to her regular internist who referred her to a neurologist, as he thought her symptoms were possibly suggestive of a seizure disorder. Ms. O. had 24-hour EEG monitoring at a local hospital, which was interpreted as normal and consistent with the presence of several nonepileptic events (during her regular "spells"). A diagnosis of psychogenic nonepileptic seizures (PNES) was made. At the time of her hospitalization for the 24-hour EEG studies, Ms. O. underwent an evaluation by a second-year psychiatry resident who thought perhaps she was depressed, but could not rule out "early dementia." She was not seen by an attending psychiatrist.

After her discharge, she consulted with another neurologist who ordered a brain CT. The radiology report stated that the brain scan was "normal for her age group, with no signs of significant abnormality." This neurologist referred her to another psychiatrist who suggested that the claimant see a "psychodynamically-oriented therapist" and he gave her the names of several clinical psychologists and a psychiatrist-analyst. However, the claimant did not exactly follow that advice and somehow found her way to a psychiatric nurse practitioner. At that point, the claimant apparently had reported increased memory loss and word-finding difficulties. She told the nurse practitioner that she thought she had Alzheimer's but, "no one believes me that I have Alzheimer's." She told the nurse that she did not know her own age. In the nursing note, the nurse wrote, "she presents as a sweet, kind person who cannot remember words and is not oriented times three." On mental status exam she was "surely showing signs of some dementia." The nurse started her on Aricept. Nursing progress notes indicate the presence of "aphasia, agnosia and disturbances of executive functioning . . . significant memory impairment is present." Other progress notes from the nurse indicated that the claimant's husband was "researching stem-cell replacement for Alzheimer's patients in the UK."

Daily activities, symptoms, and complaints

The claimant reported problems with memory and word finding. Since Ms. O. could not perform *any* of the household chores, her husband said he performed these chores routinely. He added that his wife was not to be trusted to make any of the meals because she "forgets and leaves food on the stove to burn or catch fire." Before he leaves for work, he makes breakfast for both of them and leaves her lunch in the refrigerator. In her mental status exam, Ms. O. said that she was "profoundly sad." She said that her handwriting looks like that of a five-year-old. "If I have Alzheimer's," she said, "I'll kill myself."

She reported that she experienced hallucinations, primarily at night. "I see things and hear things," she said. "Logically I know they aren't real, but when I see them and hear them they feel real and scare me." Ms. O. reported that when she is with her dog it calms her and she no longer hears voices. She said, "Nighttime is viewed as ominous." Ms. O. claimed that she could no longer read because of an inability to retain any information.

During the interview Ms. O. presented with what appeared to be a normal range of affect. Although she had previously said that she was "profoundly sad," she denied feeling depressed or anxious. Ms. O. denied suicidal thoughts. Her husband waited in the waiting room while the technician began the testing. At that point, the husband said, "Doctor, please help my wife." After some of the first tests were administered the claimant spontaneously said, "I like this—being mentally challenged."

Test results

Cognitive symptom validity testing

Results of symptom validity tests (SVTs) are shown in Table 19.1. On the Test of Memory Malingering (TOMM; Tombaugh, 1996) the examinee correctly recognized 38 items of 50 on Trials 1 and 2.

TABLE 19.1   Cognitive symptom validity test results

TEST	RAW	CLASSIFICATION
TOMM		
Trial 1	38	Fail
Trial 2	38	Fail
RDS	7	At cutoff (Fail)
CVLT–II		
Forced-Choice Recog	15/16	4.7% with this score
Bayesian Modeling	See text	60% chance of poor effort

This was below the accepted cutoff of 45 on Trial 2. She had a Reliable Digit Span (RDS; Greiffenstein, Baker, & Gola, 1994) of 7, a score which is at the cutoff. Embedded validity indicators from the California Verbal Learning Test–2nd edition (CVLT–II; Delis, Kaplan, Kramer, & Ober, 2000) revealed a 60% chance of suspect effort based on a logistic regression formula derived from Bayesian model averaging (Millis, Wolfe, Larrabee, Hanks, Sweet, & Fichtenberg, 2007). Her forced choice recognition of 15/16 was consistent with only 4.7% of those in her age group, and below expectations. These cognitive symptom validity test results were consistent with incomplete effort.

Emotional/personality validity indicators

Table 19.2 shows the MMPI–2 validity scales (and the M–FAST). There were T score elevations on the MMPI–2 standard validity scales, the F-family (Greiffenstein, Fox, & Lees-Haley, 2007), including F (Infrequency) 99, F_B (F-Back) 105, F_P (Infrequency-Psychopathology) 81, and DS_R (Gough Dissimulation Scale–Revised) 82, suggestive of symptom exaggeration of severe psychopathology/psychosis (Graham, 2006). Her FBS of 77 (raw score 25) was consistent with exaggerated claims of non-psychotic, emotional, and somatic distress. However, given her history of emotional trauma and loss, it is possible that this history raises the threshold necessary to conclude that the FBS was reflective of symptom magnification (Greiffenstein, Fox, & Lees-Haley, 2007). Greiffenstein et al. (2007) suggest a cutoff of 29 and above in females with documented psychiatric histories. That she had not previously been diagnosed or treated raises a question regarding which is the appropriate FBS cut score for this case. She also demonstrated a significant elevation on the Infrequency-Posttraumatic Stress Disorder Scale of 92 (F_{PTSD}; Elhai, Ruggiero, Freuh, Beckham, & Gold, 2002), consistent with exaggeration of PTSD symptomatology.

The claimant was administered the Miller–Forensic Assessment of Symptoms Test (M–FAST; Miller, 2001). This instrument was developed as a screen for the detection of malingered mental illness. The test uses a structured interview format and comprises seven scales, including reported vs. observed (RO), extreme symptomatology (ES), rare combinations (RC), unusual hallucinations (UH), unusual symptom course (USC), negative image (NI), and suggestibility (S). The instrument has sound psychometric properties and validity in detecting malingered psychopathology (Guy, Kwartner, & Miller, 2006; Guy & Miller, 2004). The test was validated using known diagnostic groups and simulators. Research indicates that total M–FAST scores above 6 have a positive predictive power of 100%.[1] The claimant had a total M–FAST score of 8. This consisted of RO = 2; ES = 1; RC = 2; UH = 3; USC, NI, and S all 0. Her highest score was on the unusual symptoms scale where

---

[1] Average total M–FAST scores of documented, non-litigating patient groups: schizophrenia = 2.7; PTSD = 2.4; Bipolar = 2.7; Depression = 3.2. Average scores of simulators of these diagnostic entities: 11.4, 8.6, 10.2, and 8.8, respectively (Guy, Kwartner, & Miller, 2006).

she endorsed hearing voices telling her to do things (Q: "What things?"—A: "To go for a walk."). She endorsed experiencing things crawling on her when there is nothing there very often, and that she hears music "coming from nowhere." She endorsed rare combinations: when she can't fall asleep she often smells strange odors that aren't there and when she hears voices she develops fears of leaving the house. She said that whenever she is sitting in a chair she has to breathe deeply otherwise she gets sick. She also said that throughout the day she hears a loud radio playing, but there is no radio.

Validity analysis

Utilizing the Slick et al. (1999) criteria, *probable malingered neurocognitive dysfunction* (Probable MND) was the conclusion, based on the following analysis. Ms. O. clearly met Criterion A in that the nature of the examination context was a disability evaluation requested by her insurance company. For Criterion B, she met B2 in that a probable negative response bias was noted on the TOMM, RDS, and CVLT–II. She met Criterion C2 in that her cognitive symptoms, their course and pattern, were very unlike her claim that she had Alzheimer's dementia. Similarly, she met Criterion C3 in that although she reported cognitive symptoms, her behavior failed to reveal any credible cognitive problems. For Criterion D, although genuine psychiatric disturbance was thought to be present, it did not fully account for the behaviors observed in Criteria B and C, above. Likewise, a DSM–IV–TR diagnosis of probable malingering was also appropriate in view of her very exaggerated self-reported symptoms on the MMPI–2 and M–FAST findings.

It should be noted that although the claimant had a number of elevations on MMPI–2 validity

TABLE 19.2   Emotional/personality validity indicators

MMPI–2			
Scale	Raw	T Score	Classification
F	18	99	Exaggeration
F_B	16	105	Exaggeration
F_P	5	81	Exaggeration
FBS	25	77	Exaggeration
DS_R	19	82	Exaggeration
F_{PTSD}	9	92	Exaggeration
VRIN	8	62	Normal
TRIN	11	65T	Normal

M–FAST		
Scale	Raw	
RO	2	
ES	1	
RC	2	
UH	3	
USC	0	
NI	0	
S	0	
M–Fast Total	8	PPP* = 100%

* Positive Predictive Power

scales, following the stepwise analysis of Graham (2006, p. 51), the overall conclusion was that this was not a definite malingered MMPI–2 protocol. Certainly, however, there was no doubt about the presence of exaggerated psychopathology (F-family) and somatic/emotional distress (FBS). To determine the validity of a protocol, Graham first suggests checking the number of omitted items. If the CNS score is equal to or greater than 30, consider the protocol invalid and do not interpret. The claimant had fewer than 30 omitted items. Step 2 suggests checking the response inconsistency scales. If either VRIN or TRIN has a T score equal to or greater than 80, consider the protocol invalid and do not interpret. If both VRIN and TRIN are less than 80, proceed to the next step. The claimant's scores on VRIN and TRIN were below 80. Step 3 calls for checking the over-reporting scales, F and F_B. If both scales are less than 80 consider the protocol valid and interpret. If either F or F_B is equal to or greater than 80, symptom exaggeration is possible; continue to next step. The claimant had an F of 99 and F_B of 105. Finally, in Step 4 the F_P scale is checked. If it is equal to or greater than 100, malingering is probable and the protocol should not be interpreted. If F_P is between 80 and 99, malingering is possible and the protocol is interpreted with great caution; external information should be sought. If F_P is between 70 and 79, protocol validity is indeterminate and should be interpreted cautiously. If F_P is less than 70, consider the protocol valid and interpret. The claimant's F_P was 81. Thus, in the present case, malingering of psychopathology was possible.

Certainly, given the very many indices consistent with exaggeration of cognitive and emotional symptoms and complaints, there was convergent, unequivocal evidence of symptom promotion and exaggeration. Probable malingered psychopathology and probable MND were the final, empirically supported conclusions.

Cognitive test results[2]

Table 19.3 presents the cognitive test results. The findings from the neuropsychological examination were not consistent with a diagnosis of dementia. Despite evidence of insufficient effort on cognitive symptom validity tests, the claimant performed within normal limits on many neuropsychological tests. One could question though whether she was capable of producing even better performances and chose not to. On the WAIS–III the claimant earned a Full Scale IQ of 86 with a Verbal IQ of 91, and a Performance IQ of 86. Working Memory index was 80 and Processing Speed index was 69. She had particularly low scores on Arithmetic (SS 4), Coding (SS 4), and Symbol Search (SS 4), with average scores in vocabulary (SS 9), Similarities (SS 10), Information (SS 12), Comprehension (SS 10), Picture Arrangement (SS 9), and Matrix Reasoning (SS 11). Many of these scores, especially Matrix Reasoning, Vocabulary, and Similarities, appear too high, even in early Alzheimer's disease (DAT).

Testing of basic language skills resulted in average scores, again not at all consistent with the dysnomia seen in DAT. On the Boston Naming Test she had 57/60 correct (average for her age; T score 51). Word retrieval/fluency testing resulted in average scores for letter fluency (D-KEFS, SS 9) and category fluency (SS 8). DAT patients are often dysfluent. Moreover, the claimant did not make any paraphasic errors or circumlocutions, common in DAT.

Tests of motor and psychomotor ability were performed poorly. Scaled scores on Trail Making Parts A and B were 1 (T scores 11 and 21, respectively). On Finger Tapping, Ms. O. earned an age and education corrected SS of 6 (T 43) with her dominant (right) hand and of 7 (T 47) with her left hand, with raw mean taps of 39 and 38, respectively. Grooved Pegboard was worse, with SS of 4 and 3 for times of 115″ and 126″, dominant and non-dominant hand (T 22, 21) respectively.

Ms. O. performed tests of executive functioning without significant difficulty, with the exception of Trails, as noted above. Verbal-associative fluency was average. Auditory working memory (Auditory Consonant Trigrams) was normal and she earned a SS of 10 (average) on the Tower Test

---

[2] Where appropriate, norms were derived from Heaton, Miller, Taylor, and Grant (2004) for non-Wechsler tests and reported as T scores.

of the D-KEFS. Visuoperceptual skills were mixed with an average score on Benton's Facial Recognition, but impaired scores on the Complex Figure Copy, Judgment of Line Orientation, and low-average-to-average scores on WAIS–III Performance Tests.

Of course, most characteristic of DAT is significant memory impairment, even early in the course of the disease. The claimant earned a SS of 8 on Logical Memory I of the WMS-III and a SS of 9 on Logical Memory II. Impaired delayed recall in DAT is a hallmark feature of the disease, but the claimant's performance actually improved after a delay!

Examinee's performance on the CVLT–II Trials 1–5 Total corresponded to a T score of 46 (average, 33rd percentile). Short delay free and cued recall were average, with 9 and 13 words recalled, respectively. But long delay free and cued recall were borderline and low average respectively, with 7 and 9 words recalled. Incongruously, her performance on the delayed recognition trial was disproportionately impaired when compared to her performances on the more difficult free recall trials: she made 12 hits, consistent with performance about 2 standard deviations below average. She also committed four false-positive errors and her recognition discriminability was −1.5 standard deviations below average. Forced-choice recognition was 15/16, a score representing less than 5% of the scores in her age group. In summary, the claimant performed more poorly on the recognition parts of the test than expected and better on the recall parts, the reverse of what might be expected in dementia. Only on tests of nonverbal memory did she show a pattern more in keeping with DAT, where on WMS–III Family Pictures her score went from a SS of 7 on immediate recall to a SS of 5 on delayed.

Of course, with the claimant's performance on multiple cognitive symptom validity tests indicative of insufficient effort and exaggerated cognitive impairment, any impaired neuropsychological test scores in this case are suspect and are likely to be invalid. Any test scores in the unimpaired range could reflect the lower limit of the claimant's true abilities associated with those tests.

Emotional/personality test results

Table 19.4 shows the MMPI–2 clinical scales and restructured clinical scales. Although F, F_B, and F_P were elevated, the claimant's F_P T score did not exceed 100 and her VRIN and TRIN T scores were less than 80. As noted, her F-family T scores were in a range likely reflecting psychiatric symptom exaggeration. Given this overall MMPI–2 pattern, along with her performance on the M–FAST, the claimant's symptom presentation appeared to reflect some degree of symptom over-reporting or embellishment in the context of chronic and severe character pathology consistent with her history of emotional trauma and loss.

On the Restructured Clinical Scales (RCS), it is interesting to note that her RCd (Demoralization) is not terribly elevated compared to other standard clinical and RC scales, which suggests that the claimant was not reporting a high level of overall emotional distress and turmoil at the time of this evaluation. After taking into consideration the presence of symptom exaggeration, it appeared that the claimant might have had a chronic propensity to develop physical symptoms in response to interpersonal difficulties. Her interpersonal relationships may have been characterized as intense, conflictual, and unstable. She may have been prone to periodic bouts of depression.

DISCUSSION

To the authors, there are a number of features of this case that make it particularly interesting. We believe that this person had a clinical admixture of largely subclinical psychopathology, primarily in the form of character disorder and somatoform pathology. Although this was largely dormant during her marriage, ultimately a factitious disorder in response to her husband's caring nature, and

TABLE 19.3 Cognitive test results

WAIS–III	SS		RANGE
FSIQ	86		Low Average
VIQ	91		Average
PIQ	86		Low Average
WM	80		Low Average
PS	69		Impaired
VCI	101		Average
POI	84		Low Average
Vocabulary	9		Average
Similarities	10		Average
Arithmetic	4		Borderline
Digit Span	7		Low Average
Information	12		Average
Comprehension	10		Average
Letter–Number Seq	9		Average
Picture Completion	5		Borderline
Digit Symbol-Coding	4		Borderline
Block Design	6		Low Average
Matrix Reasoning	11		Average
Picture Arrangement	9		Average
Symbol Search	4		Borderline
Boston Naming Test	57/60	T 51	Normal
Letter Fluency (FAS)	35	SS 9	Average
Category Fluency (Animals)	17	SS 8	Average
Trail Making A	146"	T 11	Impaired
Trail Making B	283"	T 21	Impaired
Finger Tapping	R 39 – L 38	T 43, T 47	Average
Grooved Pegboard	R 115" – L 126"	T 22, T 21	Impaired
Auditory Consonant Trigrams	46/60	77%	Average
Tower (D-KEFS)		SS 10	Average
CVLT–II			
1–5	46	T 46	Average
Trial B	5	–0.5	Average
SDFR	9	–0.5	Average
SDCR	13	0.5	Average
LDFR	7	–1.5	Impaired
LDCR	9	–1.0	Low Average
Hits	12	–2	Impaired
False Positives	4	1	Low Average
Recog Discrim d[1]	1.8	–1.5	Impaired
Forced-Choice Recog	15/16	4.7% with	94.7% better

TABLE 19.4   Emotional/personality test results

MMPI–2 Scale	RAW	T SCORE
Hs	27	91
D	39	90
Hy	36	82
Pd	31	83
Mf	33	57
Pa	15	67
Pt	31	75
Ma	23	66
Si	40	64
RCd	15	67
RC1	18	82
RC2	9	70
RC3	9	58
RC4	14	80
RC6	5	73
RC7	17	74
RC8	15	95
RC9	13	53

later, probable malingered cognitive and psychiatric complaints in a disability context emerged. That which is possibly most obvious is the unusual nature of her cognitive complaints in light of the neuropsychological testing. As well, the initial presentation and course of her self-proclaimed (or presumed) dementia was equally absurd. It is apparent that although the claimant feigned some symptoms, memory loss was not among them, or was only subtly so. This is an obvious case of unsophisticated malingering, particularly since the symptom of memory loss is common knowledge in Alzheimer's disease even among the lay public. So, why did she not perform poorly on measures of actual memory ability, or at least to a more obvious extent, even though her effort test performance on procedures that only *appear* to require memory were failed? Apparently she was completely unable to discriminate "easy" from "difficult"!

Similarly, a cursory search on the Internet would have provided crucial knowledge concerning the language disturbance in DAT and "warned" her of the expected performance on tests of confrontation naming and fluency. But again, these scores were within normal limits. With relatively unimpaired scores on memory, language, and most other neuropsychological tests, she most likely did not have an actual cognitive disorder. However, because of her incomplete effort on cognitive symptom validity tests, rendering neuropsychological test results invalid, it was not possible to ascertain her genuine cognitive abilities.

Additionally, as a result of the possible invalid nature of her responses on emotional/personality tests, as well as apparent malingered psychopathology on the M–FAST, no psychometrically based inferences could be made as to whether or not the claimant did or did not have actual emotional disturbance, and, if present, how severe it might be. On that point, it is also interesting that she exhibited probable malingered psychopathology, again obviously not recognizing that such disturbances are not typically seen in DAT, at least not until very late in the disease progression. The plethora of her mixed complaint/symptom picture in light of her supposed disorder (DAT) would suggest a "shot gun" approach to symptom embellishment or fabrication in a completely presumptive way, which can be viewed as representative of unsophisticated malingering (Morgan, 2008). The claimant was clearly naïve.

What about her history? Assuming the information Ms. O. provided is true and also not fabricated, this woman endured many significant emotional stressors, some of which likely occurred in early life—physical, sexual, and emotional trauma. Her history of emotional and physical trauma and abuse, including the loss of her children, would predispose her to the development of genuine psychopathology. The extensive literature on early emotional trauma in such individuals is consistent with the development of emotional disturbance later in life. In a similar vein, she also manifested psychogenic non-epileptic seizures, a probable somatoform disorder of unconscious etiology, and common in individuals with histories of childhood abuse. Her apparent positive work history, at least until her recent "disability" and her overall adjustment—marital and social—clearly belied her purported early history of trauma. Contributory to her relatively adequate adjustment, no doubt, was the supportive nature of her relationship with her husband who gratified her strong dependency needs and provided stability and support.

Her relationship likely staved off the emergence of frank psychopathology throughout much of their marriage. When frank symptoms eventually emerged in the form of PNES, consistent with the presence of underlying unconscious conflicts and somatoform pathology, the additional support of her husband, stepping up to the plate as he did when she became "ill," was so reinforcing that factitious components emerged as well.

That her husband blindly and so willingly accepted his wife's "illness" and newfound dependency, suggests that their relationship likely fostered the conscious fabrication of her symptoms. Although the exact ordering of events is not completely clear in the history, it may be the case that the claimant began adopting symptoms well before disability initiatives began, consistent with a factitious disorder to begin with, which later evolved into probable malingering once the compensable context (disability) was entered, all layered over significant unconscious emotional conflicts and dormant somatoform pathology.

A number of weeks following the evaluation of this claimant, the first author received a letter from the claimant's husband. The gist of the letter was, "doctor, please help my wife . . . what's wrong with her?" It was obvious that the claimant's husband continued to believe that his wife was profoundly impaired.

CONCLUDING REMARKS

This individual presented with significant early childhood trauma and loss of her own children. She went on to seemingly manage to have a successful work history and maintain a marriage with a spouse who apparently gratified her dependency needs and provided support and stability. Based on the literature, one might predict that this person would have developed some type of emotional or psychiatric disorder earlier in life than she did. Based upon her history, it was not obvious that she had developed an extant psychiatric disorder prior to the emergence of her first "spells," which were apparently contemporaneous with the loss of her job. It is likely that her lost employment was a major stressor, exacerbating her dormant emotional issues and further weakening her marginal ability to cope with tenuous defenses. At first, this disturbance is likely to have been more consistent with somatoform pathology, largely out of awareness. Her "spells"—psychogenic seizures—represented primary somatoform pathology. In combination, however, with the obvious reinforcement provided by the extremely caring nature of her husband, factitious components probably also emerged. Once she entered the compensation context, however, Ms. O.'s apparent adoption of both cognitive impairment and psychosis was quite clear. Her efforts to be seen as having DAT were obviously reinforced by the well-meaning, but apparently ill-versed, nurse practitioner.

This case illustrates that malingering is not uncommon in a complex admixture of psychiatric comorbidities. Indeed, that many of these disorders are not totally distinct, either conceptually or behaviorally, provides the clinician with an opportunity to fine tune his/her diagnostic skills and understanding of nuances and the contextually specific nature of various forms of psychopathology. The skilled examiner will want to utilize the most scientifically validated procedures to achieve the most accurate diagnostic impression in all cases.

REFERENCES

Alper, K. (1994). Nonepileptic seizures. *Neurology Clinics*, *12*, 153–173.

American Psychiatric Association (APA) (2000). *Diagnostic and statistical manual of mental disorders*, 4th ed., text revision. Washington, DC: APA.

Benbadis, S. R. (2006). Psychogenic nonepileptic seizures. Available at http://www.emedicine.com

Benbadis, S. R., & Hauser, W. A. (2000). An estimate of the prevalence of psychogenic non-epileptic seizures. *Seizure*, *9*, 280–281.

Bofelli, T. J., & Guze, S. B. (1992). The simulation of neurologic disease. *Psychiatric Clinics of North America*, *15*, 301–310.

Delis, D. C., Kaplan, E., Kramer, J., & Ober, B. (2000). *California Verbal Learning Test–II*. San Antonio, Texas: The Psychological Corporation.

Eisendrath, S. J., & McNiel, D. E. (2002). Factitious disorders in civil litigation: 20 cases illustrating the spectrum of abnormal illness-affirming behavior. *Journal of the American Academy of Psychiatry and the Law*, *30*, 391–399.

Eisendrath, S. J., & McNiel, D. E. (2004). Factitious physical disorders, litigation and mortality. *Psychosomatics*, *45*, 350–353.

Elhai, J. D., Ruggiero, K. J., Frueh, B. C., Beckham, J. C., & Gold, P. B. (2002). The Infrequency Posttraumatic Stress Disorder Scale (Fptsd) for the MMPI–2: Development and initial validation with veterans presenting with combat-related PTSD. *Journal of Personality Assessment*, *79*, 531–549.

Ellason, J. W., & Ross, C. A. (1997). Two-year follow-up of inpatients with dissociative identity disorder. *American Journal of Psychiatry*, *154*, 832–839.

Fagan, P. J., Wise, T. N., Schmidt, C. W., & Berlin, F. S. (2002). Pedophilia. *Journal of the American Medical Association*, *288*, 2458–2465.

Goldberg, R., & Goldstein, R. (2000). A comparison of chronic pain patients and controls on traumatic events in childhood. *Disability and Rehabilitation*, *22*, 756–763.

Goldberg, R., Pachas, W., & Keith, D. (1999). Relationship between traumatic events in childhood and chronic pain. *Disability and Rehabilitation*, *21*, 23–30.

Graham, J. R. (2006). *MMPI–2 Assessing personality and psychopathology*, 4th ed. New York: Oxford.

Greiffenstein, M. F., Baker, W. J., & Gola, T. (1994). Validation of malingered amnesia measures with a large clinical sample. *Psychological Assessment*, *6*, 218–224.

Greiffenstein, M. F., Fox, D., & Lees-Haley, P. R. (2007). The MMPI–2 Fake Bad Scale in the detection of noncredible brain injury claims. In K. B. Boone (Ed.) *Assessment of feigned cognitive impairment: A neuropsychological perspective*. New York: Guilford.

Grover, K. E., Carpenter, L. L., Price, L. H., Gagne, G.G., Mello, A. F., Mello, M. F., & Tyrka, A. R. (2007). The relationship between childhood abuse and adult personality disorder symptoms. *Journal of Personality Disorders*, *21*, 442–447.

Guy, L. S., Kwartner, P. P., & Miller, H. A. (2006). Investigating the M–FAST: Psychometric properties and utility to detect diagnostic specific malingering. *Behavioral Sciences and the Law*, *24*, 687–702.

Guy, L. S., & Miller, H. A. (2004). Screening for malingered psychopathology in a correctional setting: utility of the M–FAST. *Criminal Justice and Behavior*, *31*, 695–716.

Heaton, R., Miller, S., Taylor, M. & Grant, I. (2004). Revised comprehensive norms for an expanded Halstead-Reitan Battery: Demographically adjusted neuropsychological norms for African-American and Caucasian adults. Lutz, FL: Psychological Assessment Resources, Inc.

Lesser, R. P. (1996). Psychogenic seizures. *Neurology*, *46*, 1499–1507.

McEwan, B. S. (1998). Stress, adaptation, and disease: allostasis and allostatic load. *Annals of the New York Academy of Science*, *840*, 33–44.

McEwan, B. S. (1999). Stress and the aging hippocampus. *Frontiers of Endocrinology*, *20*, 49–70.

McEwan, B. S., & Seeman, T. (2003). Stress and affect: applicability of the concepts of allostasis and allostatic load. In R. J. Davidson, K. R. Scherer, & H. H. Goldsmith (Eds.) *Handbook of affective sciences*. New York: Oxford.

Miller, H. A. (2001). *M–FAST: Miller Forensic Assessment of Symptoms Test and professional manual*. Oddessa, FL: Psychological Assessment Resources.

Millis, S., Wolfe, P., Larrabee, G., Hanks, R., Sweet, J., & Fichtenberg, N. (2007). The California verbal learning test-II in the detection of incomplete effort. *Journal of the International Neuropsychological Society, 13*(S1), 193–194.

Molnar, B. E., Buka, S. L., & Kessler, R. C. (2001). Child sexual abuse and subsequent psychopathology: Results from the National Comorbidity Survey. *American Journal of Public Health, 91,* 753–760.

Morgan, J. E. (2008). Noncredible competence: How to handle "newbies," "wannabes," and forensic "experts" who know better or should know better. In R. L. Heilbronner (Ed.), *Neuropsychology in the courtroom: Expert analysis of reports and testimony.* New York: Guilford.

Reinherz, R. A., Paradis, A. D., Giaconia, R. M., Stashwick, C. K., & Fitzmaurice, G. (2003). Childhood and adolescent predictors of major depression in the transition to adulthood. *American Journal of Psychiatry, 160,* 2141–2147.

Sareen, J., Cox, B. J., Afifi, T. O, de Graff, R., Asmundson, G. J. G., ten Have, M., & Stein, M. B. (2005). Anxiety disorders and risk for suicidal ideation and suicide attempts. *Archives of General Psychiatry, 62,* 1249–1257.

Shorter, E. (1993). *From paralysis to fatigue: A history of psychosomatic illness in the modern era.* New York: The Free Press/Simon & Schuster.

Slick, D. J., Sherman, E. M., & Iverson, G. L. (1999). Diagnostic criteria for malingered neurocognitive dysfunction: Proposed standards for clinical practice and research. *The Clinical Neuropsychologist, 13,* 545–561.

Tombaugh, T. N. (1996). *The Test of Memory Malingering (TOMM).* Toronto: Multi-Health Systems.

Yehuda, R., Halligan, S. H., & Grossman, R. (2001). Childhood trauma and risk for PTSD: Relationship to intergenerational effects of trauma, parental PTSD, and cortisol excretion. *Development and Psychopathology, 13,* 733–753.

Zanarini, M. C., Yong, L., Frankenburg, F. R., Hennen, J., Reich, D. B., Marino, M. F., & Vujanovic, A. A. (2002). Severity of reported childhood sexual abuse and its relationship to severity of borderline psychopathology and psychosocial impairment among borderline patients. *Journal of Nervous and Mental Disease, 190,* 381–387.

Difficult to Diagnose or Questionable Conditions

Illness behavior is especially interesting to forensic neuropsychologists because many claimants presenting for IMEs demonstrate behaviors allegedly associated with "unexplained illness." Unexplained illnesses are "disorders" with an as yet unidentified etiology or unknown pathology. Indeed, their acceptance as a genuine medical condition is far from universal. Prominent among such disorders are Chronic Fatigue Syndrome, Fibromyalgia, Mold Toxicity, and Multiple Chemical Sensitivity, among others. The controversial nature of the existence of these conditions is challenging and interesting to the forensic examiner, as are other legitimate disorders, such as HIV and Lyme Disease, that have a known physiological basis but also have controversial neuropsychological sequelae. The nine chapters that follow present cases that are instructive in terms of differential diagnosis, where somatoform psychopathology, malingering, and putatively genuine disease need to be teased apart.

Chronic fatigue syndrome and malingering

20

John DeLuca

While the assessment for malingering is a standard part of the neuropsychological evaluation in forensic cases, malingering is not limited to such cases. In one form or another, the assessment of suboptimal effort must be part of every neuropsychological evaluation. Other chapters in this book illustrate the breadth of conditions in which such assessment plays a crucial role in the accurate conceptualization of the patient's clinical status.

One clinical population in which suboptimal effort or malingering may be particularly prevalent is in the area known as "unexplained illnesses." Unexplained illness refers to those clusters of complaints for which there is little physiological basis or understanding for its symptom complex. These include Chronic Fatigue Syndrome (CFS), Fibromyalgia, Multiple Chemical Sensitivities, Irritable Bowel Syndrome, Sick Building Syndrome, Temporomandibular Disorder (TMD), Atypical Connective Tissue Disease after silicone breast implants, Mitral Valve Prolapse, Dental Amalgam Disease, and most recently Gulf War Illness (Aaron, Burke, & Buchwald, 2000; Binder & Campbell, 2004; DeLuca, Rogers, & Arango, in press; Wessely, Hotopf, & Sharp, 1998). While unexplained illness groups may be prone to poor motivation or malingering for a variety of reasons, it must also be recognized that research has shown that such behavior is not observed in the vast majority of these patients (Binder et al., 2001; Tiersky et al., 2001). By the nature of their work, there is an increased likelihood of clinical psychologists and neuropsychologists seeing individual patients who may display reduced effort or motivation during the examination. As such, clinical professionals must remain cognizant of this skewed sampling and resist the impression to generalize issues of poor motivation to the population as a whole, irrespective of which patient population is being evaluated. Further, individual beliefs regarding etiology should not become part of the objective clinical evaluation, since history has clearly shown that illnesses that were once considered unexplained medically (e.g., epilepsy, multiple sclerosis) were later shown to be legitimate medical conditions with central nervous system involvement.

CHRONIC FATIGUE SYNDROME

One illness that has been identified as unexplained is Chronic Fatigue Syndrome (CFS) (Aaron, Burke, & Buchwald, 2000; DeLuca, Rogers, & Arango, in press). CFS is characterized primarily by severe and debilitating fatigue, as well as infectious, rheumatological, and neuropsychiatric symptoms. CFS primarily afflicts middle-aged women with a female-to-male ratio of 2 or 3 to 1 (Torres-Harding & Jason, 2005). Individuals from a variety of socioeconomic and ethnic backgrounds develop CFS (Torres-Harding & Jason, 2005).

The Centers for Disease Control published the first case definition for CFS in 1988 (Holmes et al., 1988), which was subsequently revised in 1991 (Schluederberg et al., 1992) and again in 1994 (Fukuda et al., 1994). The symptom complex for a diagnosis of CFS is listed in Table 20.1. It is generally accepted that CFS is a heterogeneous disorder likely with multiple etiologies and that both physiological and psychological factors play a role to predispose an individual to develop, precipitate, and perpetuate the condition (Afari & Buchwald, 2003). The 1994 CFS definition calls for research to better understand the factors (e.g., psychiatric) that may be associated with this heterogeneity.

Prevalence estimates for CFS vary based on which case definition is utilized as well as the characteristics of the study sample. For example, using the 1994 criteria in a community-based sample in the US, Jason et al. (1999) reported prevalence rates of 0.4%, while a UK study reported the prevalence to be as high as 2.6% among primary care attendees (Wessely, Chalder, Hirsch, Wallace, & Wright, 1997). CFS has a substantial economic impact. Annual total lost productivity in the US is estimated to be $9.1 billion per year, with a 37% decline in household productivity and 54% reduction in labor force productivity among persons with CFS (Reynolds, Vernon, Bouchery, & Reeves, 2004). National productivity loss in CFS is comparable to losses from disease of the digestive, immune, and nervous systems, and skin disorders (Reynolds et al., 2004). Despite several reports (e.g., Bates et al., 1995; Natelson, Ellis, O'Braonain, DeLuca, & Tapp, 1995), no specific laboratory test abnormalities are associated with CFS. The primary reason that CFS has been identified as unexplained is that, at present, it remains a diagnosis by exclusion. That is, CFS is diagnosed after other known causes of fatigue have been ruled out and persons meet the current symptom complex for its diagnosis. Despite the known heterogeneity of the illness, many (if not most) clinical neuropsychologists treat CFS as a single categorical entity and often ascribe the lack of medical findings and high psychiatric manifestations of individual patients to the entire population. It would be more advisable for clinical neuropsychologists to challenge the potential diagnosis of CFS in such patients rather than to challenge its diagnostic viability. Readers interested in differential diagnosis between CFS and psychiatric illness are referred to DeLuca, Tiersky, and Natelson (2004).

Very few studies have investigated neuropsychological effort or malingering in CFS, and those few have produced mixed findings. One study found that some CFS subjects (30% vs. 17% of multiple sclerosis subjects) perform suboptimally on a measure of effort (van der Werf et al., 2000). Binder et al. (2001) examined veterans of the Persian Gulf War who met the definition for CFS using a forced-choice task modeled after the Portland Digit Recognition Test. None of the CFS subjects fell near the range associated with motivation to perform poorly. Busichio et al. (2004) administered the Test of Memory Malingering (TOMM: Tombaugh, 1996) to 34 subjects with CFS. None of the subjects' performance was indicative of malingering on the TOMM. Taken together, these data show that the vast majority of persons with CFS are not prone toward poor motivational performance or malingering.

THE CASE OF PATIENT R.

Ms. R. was a 44-year-old right-handed white female who was referred for a neuropsychological evaluation by her insurance company to determine the nature and extent of her disability related to CFS. She was applying for disability benefits due to her complaints of significant cognitive impairment, which she believed was due to a toxic exposure she sustained while working in the administrative offices of a large gas company. Ms. R. was under the care of a neurologist for her CFS and had extensive medical work-ups for her neurological problems, which were primarily complaints of vertigo and disequilibrium. The history was obtained from the patient and available medical records.

In February of 1988, she awoke one morning and reportedly could not get out of bed to stand up. She felt dizzy with vertigo. She saw several physicians, resulting in various suggestions for the

TABLE 20.1   CDC case definition for chronic fatigue syndrome. The 1994 definition requires major criteria plus four symptoms

	1994 CASE DEFINITION *(FUKUDA ET AL., 1994)*
Major Symptom Criteria	Unexplained persistent or relapsing fatigue that is of new or definite onset that results in a substantial reduction of previous levels of functioning for at least 6 months
Minor Symptom Criteria	Sore throat Tender lymph nodes Headaches of new type Myalgia Arthralgia Post-exertional fatigue Sleep disturbance Neuropsychological complaints

problem ranging from an inner ear infection to Eustachian tube dysfunction. An MRI of the brain in April 1988 was normal. At the end of April 1988, she was stricken with a flu-like illness with sore throat, "ulcers around my mouth," swollen glands, joint aches, chills, low-grade fever, nausea, vertigo, balance problems, and other symptoms. At this point in time, she was only able to work two days per week. Soon afterward, the patient was diagnosed with the Epstein-Barr virus. By the end of June 1988, she took a leave of absence from work and has not worked since. Subsequent medical work-ups ruled out multiple sclerosis, but she was reportedly diagnosed with "hyperparathyroidism." She saw several occupational medicine specialists, but apparently results were inconclusive or, as reported by the patient, not followed up. In 1990, she was evaluated at John's Hopkins and reportedly diagnosed with a "vestibular disorder" of unknown origin. She was diagnosed with CFS in March 1992.

The medical records document having several neurological evaluations since her initial symptoms, including: visual evoked potentials, somatosensory evoked potentials, an MRI of cervical and thoracic spine, as well as an MRI of brain in May 1988, and another MRI of brain in April 1989. The findings on all of these tests were within normal limits.

During the clinical interview, Ms. R. reported cognitive difficulty starting around March/April 1988, which reportedly "has gotten progressively worse." She complained of difficulties in memory, concentration, having a "short attention span," dyslexic-like letter reversals when she is tired, and left–right confusion. Prior to these difficulties, she reported herself as "sharp as a tack." Other difficulties included blurred and double vision, difficulties with balance and hearing. Ms. R. reported that if she closed her eyes while standing, she would fall backward. She also reported losing sensation in her feet and/or "pins and needles" in her extremities, below normal temperature, decreased sensitivity to hot and cold, particularly in her hands, and reported difficulty touching the "finger to the nose."

After my initial interview with the patient, I recommended that Ms. R. be examined by Dr. KH, a prominent physician in Environmental and Occupational Health, to assess whether her condition was consistent with a toxic exposure. In fact, the patient had already been evaluated by Dr. KH two years earlier. The report from Dr. KH (which was not part of the medical records I originally received) stated that her clinical condition had remained stable since she was last evaluated by him. However, it also indicated that she was now more definite that her condition stemmed from a toxic exposure in the workplace. Dr. KH reported that, "Our opinion still remains at this time that Mrs. R's symptoms are not likely to be explained by her occupational history and that there is inadequate evidence to postulate a chemical or otherwise toxic exposure to account for her illness."

The patient has been seeing a psychologist since 1987, with treatment reportedly centered originally on personal family issues. She also reportedly saw a psychologist for one month in the early 1970s following the death of her grandfather. The patient reported one episode of suicidal ideation in 1988, which she attributed to medication.

Ms. R. reportedly was born "small" ("4 pounds and something"), required incubation, and reportedly has an identical twin. She indicated that developmental milestones were achieved normally, reported no unusual childhood illnesses, nor presented a history suggestive of hyperactivity or learning disability.

Ms. R. indicated that she has a B.A. in liberal arts, specializing in English. She reportedly was an "A" student and a member of the "honor society." After school, she apparently worked at several different jobs including social work, and worked as an "automotive service writer" and an administrative specialist. She generally held her jobs from two to six years, reportedly leaving these jobs due either to job dissatisfaction or low pay. In her most recent job, she worked for a major gas company for approximately two years as an administrative specialist. She apparently never married, and described herself as a bit of a "hermit" socially.

Past medical history is significant for "minor concussion" in the late 1960s or early 1970s, for which she saw a neurologist, and which she reported resulted in headaches and blurred vision, requiring her to be out of work for one month. Other medical problems include infectious mononucleosis, "shingles," and "herpes simplex" while in college.

Behavioral observations

During the evaluation, the patient was alert and oriented ×3. She performed tasks very slowly and often had to be prompted to elicit an answer within requisite time limits. Thinking was goal directed and logical, without formal thought disorder. Ms. R. did not remember her birthday, her phone number, or her parents' phone number, and on another occasion did not remember her age. She spoke softly, but speech was clear, coherent, and prosodic. Language was fluent, grammatical, and without paraphasias. She presented as somewhat anxious, with a meek and self-effacing demeanor. She moved very slowly and deliberately. She did not acknowledge any symptoms of depression and was able to express appropriate affect. During testing, she was intermittently concerned and frustrated with her performance. She generally tolerated testing well, despite her overall poor performance.

Results of neuropsychological testing

Tests administered

Wechsler Adult Intelligence Scale–Revised (WAIS–R), Wechsler Memory Scale–Revised (WMS–R), Wisconsin Card Sorting Test, Rey-Osterrieth Complex Figure Test (ROCFT), Trail Making Test, Judgment of controlled Oral Word Association, Portland Digit Recognition Test (PDRT), Reitan-Klove Sensory Perceptual Exam, Rey Memorization of 15 Items, Beck Depression Inventory, State Anxiety Inventory, Personality Disorders Questionnaire–Revised, clinical interview.

Sensory-perceptual exam

Ms. R. had difficulty identifying information in her peripheral fields to confrontation visual field testing. The patient displayed unilateral errors on both the left (2 of 12 trials) and right (4 of 12) sides of her visual fields. Double simultaneous stimulation resulted in one and two errors on the left and right sides respectively. In the auditory domain, detection was intact to unilateral stimulation on the right, but she made two errors in four trials on the left side. Complete left ear extinction was observed during double simultaneous stimulation. Tactile stimulation on the Face-Hand test was detected accurately when presented unilaterally. However, with tactile double simultaneous stimulation, she showed intermittent errors on both sides, right greater than left. On tactile finger agnosia, she showed elevated errors bilaterally with six errors in 20 trials on the left and seven errors on the right hand. Testing for graphesthesia showed the same pattern of elevated bilateral errors.

The results of the standardized neuropsychological testing are presented in Table 20.2.

TABLE 20.2 Neuropsychological scores

		RAW	SS OR OTHER SCORE
CVLT	Trial 1–5	39	T = 17
	List A Trial 1	5	–2
	List A Trial 5	7	–5
	List B	6	–1
	SDFR	5	–4
	SDCR	4	–5
	LDFR	2	–5
	LDCR	4	–5
	Semantic Cluster	1.1	–2
	Serial Cluster	6.5	+3
	Slope	+0.6	–1
	Perseverations	4	0
	Free Recall Intrusions	0	–1
	Cued Recall Intrusions	2	+2
	Recognition Hits	6	–5
	Discriminability	77%	–3
	Response Bias	–0.82	–2
WMS–R	Verbal Memory	26	< 50 %ile
	Visual Memory	24	< 50 %ile
	Delayed Recall	13	< 50 %ile
	Attention/Concentration	28	< 50 %ile
	Digit Span forward	2	< 1st %ile
	Digit Span backward	4	9th %ile
	Visual Span forward	3	< 1st %ile
	Visual Span backward	2	7th %ile
	Logical Memory I	8	2nd %ile
	Logical Memory II	3	2nd %ile
	Visual Reproduction I	15	2nd %ile
	Visual Reproduction II	2	1st %ile
WAIS–R	VIQ	88	21st %ile
	PIQ	73	4th %ile
	FSIQ	80	9th %ile
WCST	Categories	6	> 16th %ile
	Perseverative Responses	24	8 %ile
JLOT	Adjusted correct	13	1.5 %ile
Trails A	Time to complete	59 sec	T = 22
Trails B	Time to complete	210 sec	T = 19 (2 errors)
ROCFT	Copy	69	12 (SS)
	Immediate recall	4	2 (SS)
	Delayed recall	2	2 (SS)
CFL	Adjusted correct	24	T = 20
PDQ–R	Total score	7	WNL
BDI	Total score	5	WNL
State Anxiety	State Form	25	WNL

WNL, within normal limits.
SS, standard score.

Attention and concentration

Ms. R. tested as severely impaired on tests of attention. She was not distracted and appeared to be making a great effort, although she performed very slowly. She obtained a WMS–R Attention/ Concentration Index score below the first percentile of individuals her age. In the auditory domain, simple attention and working memory, as measured by Digit Span forward and backward, were performed at the 1st and 9th percentile, respectively, for individuals her age.

In the visual domain, visual memory span forward and backward were performed at the 1st and 7th percentile, respectively, for individuals her age. On the Digit Symbol test of attention and psychomotor speed, Ms. R. performed at the 5th percentile. Similarly, Trails A and Trails B of the Trail Making Test were performed at less than the first percentile when corrected for age, gender, and education.

Intellectual operations and executive functions

On the WAIS–R, Ms. R. obtained a Full Scale IQ of 80 (prorated), classifying her overall intellectual ability in the low average range and performing at the 9th percentile of individuals her age. She obtained a Verbal IQ of 88 (low average, 21st percentile) and a Performance IQ of 73 (borderline, 4th percentile).

On the Verbal Scale, fund of knowledge was performed at the 25th percentile, while word knowledge and verbal abstract reasoning were at the 63rd percentile. Digit Span was performed at the 1st percentile, while the Arithmetic subtest was performed at the 9th percentile. On the Performance Scale, Object Assembly was performed at the 37th percentile, Block Design was at the 2nd percentile, and Picture Completion was performed below the 1st percentile.

On the Wisconsin Card Sorting Test, the patient displayed intact ability to form, maintain, and shift conceptual set, as well as the ability to incorporate feedback from her environment to solve the problem.

Memory functions

Verbal memory Overall, Ms. R. performed in the severely impaired range on measures of immediate and delayed recall and recognition memory. WMS–R Index scores for General Memory, Verbal Memory, and Delayed Recall were all below the 1st percentile for individuals her age. Immediate and delayed recall scores on the WMS–R Logical Memory subtest were both at the 2nd percentile. On a verbal list-learning task (CVLT), overall learning performance was at less than the 1st percentile, with a flat learning curve. No serial position effects were observed when recalling the word list. Recognition of the elements of the list was below the first percentile. Recognition memory was roughly equivalent to the items identified during recall trials.

Visual memory The Visual Memory Index Score from the WMS–R was below the 1st percentile of individuals her age. On Visual Reproduction, she performed at the 1st percentile on both the immediate and delayed recall trials on the test. Immediate and delayed recall of complex figural material (ROCFT) was also below the first percentile corrected for age. This severely impaired performance was obtained after Ms. R. copied the figure accurately, obtaining an above average score on the copy portion of the task (see below).

Language functions

Overall, linguistic functions were grossly within normal limits but not tested formally. Verbal fluency (Controlled Oral Word Association Test) was performed in the 1st percentile for individuals her age. As with other timed tests, her extremely slow performance penalized her on this test.

Visuospatial abilities

Visuospatial ability, as examined with the Judgment of Line Orientation Test, was performed in the 1.5th percentile, the severely defective range. As mentioned above, Block Design was also performed in the 2nd percentile for individuals her age. Yet, visuoconstructional ability on the ROCFT copy was above average and Object Assembly was in the average range.

Psychological measures

Ms. R. did not score in the depressed range on the Beck Depression Inventory (score of 5), nor did she score in the anxious range on the State-Trait Anxiety Inventory. On the Personality Disorders Questionnaire–Revised, an instrument designed to screen for formal personality disorders, the patient did not meet the criteria for any DSM–III–R personality disorder classifications.

Assessment of malingering

Certain patterns in Ms. R.'s performance, including CVLT recognition equivalent to recall performance, right side extinction in tactile and left side extinction in auditory domains on the sensory-perceptual exam, very poor recognition memory, severe impairment on very simple immediate memory (digit span), and behavioral observations such as poor memory for personal information, suggested invalid responding, insufficient effort, and, due to the secondary gain involved with receipt of disability benefits, the possibility of malingering (see Table 20.3). The patient was administered the Rey Memorization of 15 Items Test, and recalled only 3/15 items, well below expectations based on performance of brain-damaged populations and within the range of insufficient effort. On the PDRT, performance was below chance. Ms. R. was correct on only 12 out of 54 trials, which is highly significant ($p < .0001$) and by the Slick, Sherman, and Iverson (1999) criteria defines "definite malingering of neurocognitive dysfunction."

CONCLUSIONS AND RECOMMENDATIONS

The results of the evaluation yielded profoundly reduced cognitive performance across a broad spectrum of neuropsychological functions. However, given her performance on the indicators of effort, coupled with the clinical interview and history and the potential for secondary gain in the form of financial disability benefits, her pattern of performance was deemed more consistent with malingering than actual brain dysfunction. The subsequent report indicated that even if some level of toxic exposure in her previous workplace could be verified, her performance on the tests conducted in the neuropsychological evaluation were far below what would be observed with such

TABLE 20.3 Malingering data

PDRT	5-second trial	6 of 18 correct
	15-second trial	6 of 36 correct
Rey 15-Items	No. correct	3 of 15

exposure or even that observed in persons with CFS (Busichio et al., 2004; DeLuca, Christodoulou et al., 2004; DeLuca, et al., 1995, 1997). Rather, the evidence of malingering and the pattern of extreme difficulties were more suggestive of a need by Ms. R. for attention, medical recognition of her difficulties, and financial benefit. The report recommended continued psychotherapy with her psychologist, geared toward addressing the psychological difficulties that are likely contributing to her cognitive dysfunction, and to explore the complex interaction between emotional, personality, and any possible brain-based etiology. Unfortunately, the disposition of this patient after the evaluation remains unknown.

FINAL COMMENTS

As with any neuropsychological population, the possibility of suboptimal effort, factitious disorder, or frank malingering always exists and should be evaluated appropriately. The unexplained illnesses have been viewed as particularly susceptible toward reduced motivation and effort (Binder & Campbell, 2004). As such, sensitivity regarding the possibility of reduced effort or motivation during the evaluation is warranted. At the same time, generalizing suboptimal effort and motivation to the entire population is inconsistent with the research literature, at least for CFS (Binder et al., 2001; Busichio et al., 2004; van der Werf et al., 2000) and is not in the best interest of the patient. Although a case of malingering was presented in this chapter, the frequency of CFS cases in which there is no evidence of suboptimal effort or motivation is the norm. Thus, clinicians must make sure they keep abreast of the research literature in unexplained populations, and caution against an interpretation of reduced effort based primarily on the fact that the illness is medically unexplained. Absence of etiology is not evidence of poor effort or malingering. Neuropsychologists should embrace the clinical challenge offered by the unexplained illnesses and seize the opportunity to truly make a difference in an individual's life.

REFERENCES

Aaron, L. A., Burke, M. M., & Buchwald, D. (2000). Overlapping conditions among patients with chronic fatigue syndrome, fibromyalgia and temporomandibular disorder. *Archives of Internal Medicine, 160*, 221–227.

Afari, N., & Buchwald, D. (2003). Chronic fatigue syndrome: A review. *American Journal of Psychiatry, 160*, 221–236.

Bates, D. W., Buchwald, D., Lee, J., Kith, P., Doolittle, T., Ruthford, C., Churchill, W. H., Schur, P. H., Wener, M., Wyberga, D., Winkelman, J., & Komaroff, A. L. (1995). Clinical laboratory findings in patients with chronic fatigue syndrome. *Archives of Internal Medicine, 155*, 97–103.

Binder, L. M., & Campbell, K. A. (2004). Medically unexplained symptoms and neuropsychological assessment. *Journal of Clinical and Experimental Neuropsychology, 26*, 369–392.

Binder, L. M., Storzbach, D., Campbell, K. A., Rohlman, D. S., Anger, W. K., et al. (2001). Neurobehavioral deficits associated with chronic fatigue syndrome in veterans with Gulf War unexplained illness. *Journal of the International Neuropsychological Society, 7*, 835–839.

Busichio, K., Tiersky, L. A., DeLuca, J., & Natelson, B. H. (2004). Neuropsychological deficits inpatients with chronic fatigue syndrome. *Journal of the International Neuropsychological Society, 10*, 278–285.

DeLuca, J., Christodoulou, C., Diamond, B. J., Rosenstein, E. D., Kramer, N., & Natelson, B. H. (2004). Working memory deficits in chronic fatigue syndrome: Differentiating between speed and accuracy of information processing. *Journal of the International Neuropsychological Society, 10*, 101–109.

DeLuca, J., Johnson, S. K., Beldowicz, D., & Natelson, B. H. (1995). Neuropsychologic impairments in chronic fatigue syndrome, multiple sclerosis, and depression. *Journal of Neurology, Neurosurgery, and Psychiatry, 58*, 38–43.

DeLuca, J., Johnson, S. K., Ellis, S. P., & Natelson, B. H. (1997). Cognitive functioning is impaired in Chronic Fatigue Syndrome patients devoid of psychiatric disease. *Journal of Neurology, Neurosurgery, and Psychiatry, 62*, 151–155.

DeLuca, J., Rogers, H. L., & Arango, J. C. (in press). Fibromyalgia, chronic fatigue and related "neurasthenic" disorders. In G. Goldstein, T. Incagnoli, & A. E. Puente (Eds.), *New neurobehavioral disorders: Disorders of recent origin.* Mahwah, NJ: Lawrence Erlbaum Associates, Inc.

DeLuca, J., Tiersky, L., & Natelson, B. H. (2004). Chronic Fatigue Syndrome: Differential diagnosis with depression. In J. H. Ricker (Ed), *Differential diagnosis in adult neuropsychological assessment.* New York: Springer.

Fukuda, K., Straus, S., Hickie, I., Sharpe, M. C., Dobbins, J. G., Komaroff, A., & The International Chronic Fatigue Syndrome Study Group (1994). The chronic fatigue syndrome: A comprehensive approach to its definition and study. *Annals of Internal Medicine, 121*, 953–959.

Holmes, G. P., Kaplan, J. E., Gantz, N. M., Komaroff, A. L., Schonberger, L. B., Strauss, S. S., et al. (1988). Chronic fatigue syndrome: A working case definition. *Annals of Internal Medicine, 108*, 387–389.

Jason, L. A., Richman, J. A., Rademaker, A. W., Jordan, K. M., Plioplys, A. V., Taylor, R. R., McCready, W., Huang, C. F., & Plioplys, S. (1999). A community-based study of chronic fatigue syndrome. *Archives of Internal Medicine, 159*, 2129–2137.

Natelson, B. H., Ellis, S. P., O'Braonain, P. J., DeLuca, J., & Tapp, W. N. (1995). Frequency of deviant immunological test values in chronic fatigue syndrome. *Clinical and Diagnostic Laboratory Immunology, 2*, 238–240.

Reynolds, K. J., Vernon, S. D., Bouchery, E., & Reeves, W. C. (2004). The economic impact of chronic fatigue syndrome. *Cost effectiveness and resource allocation, 2*. Available at www.resource-allocation.com/content/2/1/4

Schluederberg, A., Straus, S. E., Peterson, P., Blumenthal, S., Komaroff, A., et al. (1992). Chronic fatigue syndrome: definition and medical outcome assessment. *Annals of Internal Medicine, 117*, 325–331.

Slick, D. J., Sherman, E. M. S., & Iverson, G. L. (1999). Diagnostic criteria for malingered neurocognitive dysfunction: Proposed standards for clinical practice and research. *The Clinical Neuropsychologist, 13*(4), 545–561.

Tiersky, L., A., DeLuca, J., Hill, N., Dhar, S. K., Johnson, S. K., Lange, G., Rappolt, G., & Natelson, B. H. (2001). Longitudinal assessment of neuropsychological functioning, psychiatric status, functional disability and employment status in chronic fatigue syndrome. *Applied Neuropsychology, 8*(1), 41–50.

Tombaugh, T. (1996). *Test of Memory Malingering.* USA, Canada: Multi-Health Systems, Inc.

Torres-Harding, S., & Jason, L. A. (2005). What is fatigue: History and epidemiology. In J. DeLuca (Ed.), *Fatigue as a window to the brain.* MA: MIT Press.

van der Werf, S. P., Prins, J. D., Jongen, P. J. H., van der Meer, J. W. M., & Bleijenberg, G. (2000). Abnormal neuropsychological findings are not necessarily a sign of cerebral impairment: A matched comparison between chronic fatigue syndrome and multiple sclerosis. *Neuropsychiatry, Neuropsychology and Behavioral Neurology, 13*, 199–203.

Wessely, S., Chalder, T., Hirsch, S., Wallace, P., & Wright, D. (1997). The prevalence and morbidity of chronic fatigue and chronic fatigue syndrome: A prospective primary care study. *American Journal of Public Health, 87*, 1449–1455.

Wessely, S., Hotopf, M., & Sharpe, M. (1998). *Chronic fatigue and its syndromes.* Oxford: Oxford University Press.

Lyme disease: Consideration of malingered disability

James Youngjohn

Lyme disease is one of the most common vector borne diseases in the United States (White et al., 1991). It is caused by a bacterial organism, the spirochete *Borrelia burgdorferi* (Burgdorfer et al., 1982), which is transmitted through the bite of an infected tick. Ticks must remain attached to their host for 12 to 48 hours for transmission to occur. Usually, after being bitten by the infected tick, most people develop a rash on their skin around the bite. Frequently it will have a bull's eye appearance with a red ring around a clear center, although it may vary in size, shape, and color. Within seven to ten days following the tick bite, people infected with Lyme disease will develop flu-like symptoms including fever, chills, swollen lymph nodes, headaches, fatigue, muscle aches, and joint pain. It is rare for the disease to be lethal. However, the organism has been shown to invade the central nervous system (*neuro-borreliosis*), joints, and other organs. Lyme disease is usually successfully treated with antibiotics, and most patients will have a full recovery following a single course of antibiotic therapy. A few patients can have symptoms of persisting infection and require additional antibiotic treatment.

It has been suggested that chronic Lyme disease infection might trigger an autoimmune response, although there is considerable controversy around this issue (Rowe, 2000). Specifically, the possibility that symptoms can persist following successful antibiotic treatment, with no objective evidence of ongoing infection, is a focus of debate. It has been proposed by some that this state of "chronic Lyme disease," defined as persisting symptoms in the absence of objective findings of infection, can cause a constellation of nonspecific symptoms, which include chronic fatigue, depression, and cognitive impairment (Westervelt & McCaffrey, 2002). These subjective complaints sometimes lead to disability compensation claims, due to an alleged inability to work.

The following case of purported chronic Lyme disease illustrates some of the controversies and issues involved, including the possibility of malingered partial disability. As is true throughout this casebook, important identifying information has been altered to prevent identification of the claimant.

CLINICAL INTERVIEW

The interview portion of the examination was audio taped. Audio taping the interview portion of forensic and/or medical-legal examinations is routinely performed in this office for risk management purposes. Audio taping interviews has eliminated or greatly reduced claims from disgruntled evaluees, typically with unfavorable outcomes from their evaluation, that they never said something to the evaluator, that the information from their interview was inaccurately reproduced, or that they were treated unprofessionally by the evaluator.

The claimant, Dr. S., was referred for independent neuropsychological examination by his disability insurance carrier. He was a 50-year-old clinical psychologist who claimed that he was ambidextrous, having been born left-handed, and having been forced to write with his right hand in Catholic school.

Dr. S. reported that he first became ill in 1995. He described the gradual onset of weakness, aching joints, swollen lymph nodes, and difficulty thinking clearly. He stated that his work became more difficult and his performance dropped due to difficulty concentrating, inability to remember things, and a need to rest frequently. He reported that he had always been very athletic, regularly working out, swimming, and running. However, beginning in the summer of 1995, he discovered that when he attempted to exercise, he would be unable to function the next day.

Dr. S. saw a rheumatologist and was worked up for a variety of medical conditions and autoimmune disorders. The hypothesis of Sjogren's syndrome was discussed, but the rheumatologist was ultimately perplexed by his problems.

Dr. S. changed doctors and began treating with a holistic naturopathic physician. This doctor diagnosed Lyme disease and confirmed the diagnosis with a positive blood test. Dr. S. stated that in addition, several immune function tests came back with positive results. None of these tests were carried out locally, but were sent to specialty labs out of state.

The doctor treated him with IV antibiotics for 90 days. He subsequently made the diagnosis of chronic fatigue immuno-deficiency syndrome (CFIDS). Dr. S. was given his diagnosis in the fall of 1996. Once given his diagnosis, Dr. S. decided he was no longer able to work and went on full-time disability. The naturopathic physician certified his disability, and Dr. S. continued treatment with that doctor through the time of this evaluation. He was treated with many homeopathic medicines and numerous nutritional supplements, including some that were injected, in addition to antibiotics.

Dr. S. remained on full-time disability for almost six months, until April of 1997. Then he switched to partial disability. At the time of this evaluation almost 10 years later, he was still receiving 80% of a half-time salary in disability benefits, in addition to a half-time salary from the university where he was on faculty. When he went out on disability, Dr. S. reportedly had to give up his clinical practice, teaching, and administrative duties. After returning to half-time employment, Dr. S. focused exclusively on research and writing. He reported publishing an average of two academic papers per year, as well as a textbook marketed to the general public. This book had been included with the materials that were provided to the evaluator for review by Dr. S.'s disability carrier.

Dr. S. claimed that since the onset of his condition, he continued to experience considerable aching in his joints, neck, back, shoulders, and knees. He reported suffering from considerable muscle tightness and soreness. In addition to the conditions noted above, he was also diagnosed with fibromyalgia. However, he stated that the greatest sources of disability were fatigue and cognitive problems, including difficulties concentrating and with memory.

Regarding social history, Dr. S. earned his bachelor's degree with a psychology major and then earned a Ph.D. in clinical psychology from the same university during the 1980s. After several years in the field, he returned to his alma mater to join the faculty. He eventually was promoted to the rank of associate professor. At the time of this evaluation, his 20-hour per week research job was funded through a private foundation grant. He earned $44,000 per year for the half-time job, plus $35,000 per year in disability benefits, less contingency fees for his attorney.

Dr. S. was single, although he had been in a monogamous relationship for a number of years. He never had children. He owned a home with his significant other and described a stable home life. He continued to drive an automobile, but claimed that he was unable to drive on freeways, for long distances, or at night. He was brought to my office for this evaluation by a limousine service.

Dr. S. denied the use of alcohol, tobacco, or illegal drugs. However, he took a number of prescription medications and numerous nutritional supplements and homeopathic remedies. He took Ambien to help him sleep and Soma for his muscle pain. He took Advil during the day for joint and muscle pain. Dr. S. reported taking 30 nutritional supplement pills per day. These included amino acid compounds, vitamins B, C, and E, calcium, and magnesium, among others. He stated that when he felt really bad he would go to his naturopathic physician for a vitamin B complex injection. He also had some gastrointestinal/digestive difficulties and took enzymes to aid his digestion.

Regarding past medical history, he described having been very healthy until the onset of his illness in 1995. He reported having been very athletic but was no longer able to participate because of his fatigue. He had been diagnosed with prostatitis, as well as with interstitial cystitis. Upon further questioning, Dr. S. stated that his prostatitis and interstitial cystitis involved an inflammation of the bladder, pelvic pain, and sensitivity.

Dr. S.'s mental health history was significant for psychotherapy in the 1980s dealing with issues surrounding the death of his father when he was a child. He entered psychotherapy again around 2000 after his mother passed away and his dog died. Dr. S. stated that he had unresolved emotional problems and conflicts regarding loss. He acknowledged having strong reactions to the loss of things and that following a loss he would develop more than a normal amount of depression and grief. Dr. S. quickly amended this answer, however, stating that he did not suffer from depression per se and that he did not suffer from clinical depression. Rather, he stated that his emotional reactions were merely fear and sadness, which he attributed to growing up without a father. He denied ever having been treated with psychotropic medication.

With respect to litigation history, Dr. S. stated that he retained an attorney two years before this evaluation to assist him in collecting disability benefits. He stated that he hired the lawyer after he was sent for an independent medical examination (IME) with a neurologist. He described that evaluation as a "nightmare" and "really awful," indicating that the doctor had treated him very badly. He claimed that he actually slapped him on the back and proclaimed him "healthy as a horse." Dr. S. stated that in his report, the IME neurologist indicated that he did not qualify for disability benefits. Following retention of an attorney, Dr. S.'s disability benefits continued uninterrupted.

MENTAL STATUS EXAMINATION

Upon examination, Dr. S. was alert and fully oriented. He presented as quiet, subdued, and depressed. When I asked him to describe his current emotional state, he stated that he had become more realistic about the things he could do and those that he could not do. He had transitioned from being someone who was very driven, accomplished, successful, and active, to someone who had to accept his limits and learn how to pace himself. He admitted that it was depressing to no longer be able to engage in the same activities that he did before his illness. He went on to describe himself as a mentally tough person and a hardy individual. These characteristics reportedly had helped him through some troubling times.

With respect to vegetative signs, Dr. S. stated that he had a hard time sleeping when he first became ill, but his sleep improved on Ambien. He described needing rest quite a bit during the day, although he tried not to nap. Appetite was described as normal, but he was no longer able to eat the same foods as previously, due to his gastrointestinal/digestion difficulties. He initially lost weight, then gained weight, and was now holding steady at an appropriate weight for him. Libido was described as somewhat decreased with advancing years, but still active.

Dr. S. denied any suicidal ideation or intent. He denied any homicidal ideation or intent. There was no evidence of delusions, hallucinations, or other signs of a formal thought disorder.

TEST RESULTS

Given the fact that Dr. S. was a clinical psychologist and had been trained to administer earlier versions of a number of the tests that we gave him, it was noted that there was a strong possibility that some of his scores were artificially inflated, secondary to his prior exposure to, training with, and knowledge of the various test items. This illustrates one of the relatively few instances of measurement error for overly high test results that might overestimate actual ability levels.

Dr. S. was also administered several formal instruments designed to measure his motivation and cooperation with the testing. He performed very well on one of them, the Dot Counting Test. He performed a bit more poorly on another one, the Portland Digit Recognition Test, although not so poorly as to conclusively demonstrate insufficient effort on neuropsychological tests. On the third motivation test, the Validity Indicator Profile (VIP; Frederick, Crosby, & Wynkoop, 2000), Dr. S. performed well on the verbal subtest, but performed quite poorly on the nonverbal subtest. He failed all six validity indicators on the nonverbal subtest and appeared to have responded essentially randomly throughout the majority of the test. His poor performance on the nonverbal subtest of the VIP suggested that the test scores reported above, particularly on nonverbal tests, might not accurately depict his true cognitive capabilities. Rather, he probably would have done better on the testing *if* he had tried harder.

TABLE 21.1   Test results for Dr. S.

Wechsler Adult Intelligence Scale–III

Full Scale IQ: 118
Verbal IQ: 127   Performance IQ: 105
Verbal Comprehension: 134   Perceptual Organization: 114
Working Memory Index: 106   Processing Speed: 99

Age-corrected Subtest Scaled Scores

Vocabulary	14	Picture Completion	18
Similarities	17	Digit Symbol-Coding	9
Arithmetic	13	Block Design	9
Digit Span	9	Matrix Reasoning	10
Information	16	Picture Arrangement	8
Comprehension	16	Symbol Search	11

Wechsler Memory Scale–III

Immediate Memory: 95   General (Delayed) Memory: 103
Auditory Immediate: 111   Delayed: 102 Delayed Recognition: 125
Visual Immediate: 78   Visual Delayed: 88
Working Memory: 96

Age-adjusted Subtest Scaled Scores

Logical Memory:	I: 13	II: 11
Faces:	I: 7	II: 9
Verbal Paired Associates:	I: 11	II: 10
Family Pictures:	I: 6	II: 7

Letter-Number Sequencing: 11
Spatial Span: 8

Benton Visual Retention Test	No. Correct: 6/No. of Errors: 7
Trail Making Test A	29"/0 Errors
Trail Making Test B	60"/0 Error
Finger Tapping Test	Right Hand: 52.4/Left Hand: 51
Dynamometer	Right Hand: 23.5 kg/Left Hand: 28.5 kg

(Continued . . .)

TABLE 21.1   (Continued)

| *Grooved Pegboard* | Right Hand: 70 seconds/Left Hand: 84 seconds |

Sensory Perceptual Examination
Tactile Errors: Right 0/Left 0/Both Right 0/Both Left 0
Visual Errors: Right 0/Left 0/Both Right 0/Both Left 0
Tactile Finger Recognition Errors: Right 0/Left 0
Finger Tip Number Writing Errors: Right 4/Left 4
Tactile Form Recognition: Right: 11″, 0 Errors/Left: 11″, 0 Errors

Dot Counting Test

Ungrouped			*Grouped*		
No. of Dots	Response	Time	No. of Dots	Response	Time
11	11	8″	12	12	3″
19	19	5″	20	20	1″
15	15	5″	16	16	2″
23	23	6″	24	24	4″
27	28	9″	28	28	4″
7	7	2″	8	8	1″

Portland Digit Recognition Test
5″ Delay   17 of 18 items correct
15″ Delay   12 of 18 items correct
30″ Delay   12 of 18 items correct

Validity Indicator Profile
Nonverbal Subtest: invalid
Verbal Subtest: valid

Dr. S.'s performances on tests of attention, concentration, and processing speed were consistently average relative to the general population of his age, although perhaps a bit low for a university psychology professor. For example, he had a WAIS–III Working Memory Index of 106, a WAIS–III Processing Speed Index of 99, and a WMS–III Working Memory Index of 96. His performances on both Trail Making A and Trail Making B were low normal relative to other men of his age with similarly advanced levels of education.

With regard to perceptual and motor skills, Dr. S.'s visual fields were full, and he did not extinguish double simultaneous visual or tactile stimulation. His tactile finger recognition and stereognosis were normal bilaterally, but he did commit multiple errors bilaterally during graphesthesia testing. His finger tapping speeds were superior bilaterally relative to other men of his age. His grip strength was weak on the right and average on the left. His hand coordination and manual dexterity, as measured by the Grooved Pegboard, fell at the bottom end of the normal range on the right and was borderline on the left.

With respect to memory and learning, Dr. S.'s performances overall would be considered average for the general population, but perhaps a bit low given his advanced education level. Memory test performance is summarized by his WMS–III Immediate Memory Index of 95 and his General (Delayed) Memory Index of 103. However, there was a significant split between his learning and memory for verbal information, which was average, as opposed to nonverbal information, which in some cases was much poorer. His drawings from memory of the geometric shapes from the Benton Visual Retention Test fell at the bottom end of the normal range relative to other men of his age with very advanced levels of education (Youngjohn, Larrabee, & Crook, 1993).

Regarding intelligence, Dr. S.'s WAIS–III Full Scale IQ of 118, if valid, suggested that he was functioning near the top of the above average intellectual range overall. This score may be artificially inflated, as Dr. S. was trained to administer the original WAIS.

Once again, there was a split between his performance on verbal cognitive abilities, which were consistently superior (Verbal IQ: 127; Verbal Comprehension Index: 134), as opposed to his non-verbal problem-solving abilities (Performance IQ: 105; Perceptual Organization Index: 114), which were merely average and above average, respectively.

Personality was measured with the MMPI–2 (Table 21.2). With respect to profile validity, a significant elevation was present on scale K, with a sub-clinical elevation on scale S. Dr. S.'s Lees-Haley Fake Bad Scale (FBS; Lees-Haley, English, & Glenn, 1991) score was elevated at 24, raising the possibility of physical and neurological symptom/disability exaggeration when seen in a litigation context. According to the traditional validity scale configuration, Dr. S. appeared to respond in a rather defensive, overcautious, and evasive manner. He seemed reluctant to disclose much about his personal adjustment and overly concerned with his social image. A low degree of "psychological mindedness" was suggested, which might be unexpected in a psychologist. Patients with this validity profile often are not willing to view their problems as psychological and have limited insight. In a medical setting, these patients seem to prefer to view their personal problems as physical.

Dr. S.'s basic clinical scale profile revealed a classic conversion V type configuration with significant elevations on scales 1 and 3. A significant, albeit modest, elevation was also noted on scale 8. There was a sub-clinical elevation on scale 6. Persons exhibiting this profile frequently exhibit chronic psychological maladjustment, with the possibility of somatic delusions. Anxiety, agitation, anger, and a general ineffectiveness in dealing with life are common descriptors of this profile. It tends to be a relatively stable and/or characterological profile configuration (Greiffenstein & Baker, 2001). Persons with this profile may have disturbed interpersonal relationships and tend to manipulate other people with claims of physical symptoms. Diagnostic considerations would include schizophrenia, a severe somatoform disorder, and, in a litigation context, malingering.

RECORD REVIEW

The records from Dr. S.'s treating holistic physician/naturopath were reviewed. These included numerous traditional and nontraditional laboratory study results. Early on in treatment, there was one weakly positive test for Lyme disease. Shortly thereafter was a borderline Lyme disease test result. Following that, some half a dozen Lyme disease studies were done, and all were negative. These were presumably obtained after the initiation of antibiotic therapy. Many other lab studies were conducted, and these appeared to have been almost entirely negative.

TABLE 21.2 MMPI–2 T scores

Validity Pattern

VRIN	TRIN	L	F	K	F(B)	S	FBS
42	58	47	44	67	46	64	24 (raw score)

Basic and Supplementary Scales

1	2	3	4	5	6	7	8	9	0	MAC-R	APS	AAS	PK	O-H
74	62	82	53	57	63	59	67	53	44	40	55	44	42	55

Content Scales

ANX	FRS	OBS	DEP	HEA	BIZ	ANG	CYN	ASP	TPA	LSE	SOD	FAM	WRK	TRT
43	35	44	42	64	39	42	35	36	45	40	46	42	48	35

The holistic/naturopathic doctor's clinical chart notes were also reviewed. During one of his earliest visits in January of 1996, Dr. S. told the doctor that he "teaches at the university as a psychologist. He wants to write fiction instead." Also indicated in this chart note were subjective complaints of memory loss. Throughout subsequent chart notes, the doctor made references to increased stress at work. In a later note, he indicated that he was "doing a lot of writing and it's going well. Making contacts in L.A. regarding writing." This particular chart note also included the statement "taking a screenwriting class." About a year and a half later, a chart note included the statement "high stress regarding work: new department head leads to depression." During this timeframe, the doctor's chart notes reveal that Dr. S. made numerous trips to California. Several years after treatment began there was a note that stated, "Stress regarding grant again. Looking for another job in California at either Stanford or in Hollywood."

Dr. S. underwent an IME examination with an infectious disease specialist in 1997, about a year after his Lyme disease treatment had begun. The doctor reviewed the studies that had been done to that point and conducted an examination of Dr. S. He indicated that his subjective condition had been unresponsive to two years of therapy and that he claimed to be unable to perform his occupation.

A second IME examination was performed in 1997 by a neurologist. This doctor's assessment was that "like most patients with chronic fatigue syndrome, his examination was unrevealing." He found evidence of good strength, which was discrepant with his complaints of weakness. He noted that he had not improved for quite some time, which was distinctly unusual in most illnesses. He did not feel that the laboratory studies supported his continuing complaints. He indicated that the diagnosis of chronic Lyme disease was a controversial condition. He indicated that he was receiving alternative medical care for illnesses lacking an objectively confirmed diagnosis.

An evaluation performed on behalf of the patient by a doctor identifying himself as a neuropsychologist was also reviewed. This doctor conducted a "neurotherapy evaluation using quantitative EEG (QEEG)." No formal neuropsychological testing appears to have been performed. The neuropsychologist indicated that the results of his QEEG were consistent with the cognitive difficulties that Dr. S. reported.

It should be noted that the QEEG is a controversial procedure. The American Academy of Neurology and The American Clinical Neurophysiology Society have offered formal positions on the use of the QEEG, stating that it remains an investigational procedure that carries a substantial risk of erroneous interpretations. Use of the QEEG in medical-legal contexts is discouraged. Their position is also that it is unacceptable for QEEG techniques to be used clinically by those who are not physicians (Nuwer, 1997).

SURVEILLANCE VIDEOTAPE

Surveillance videotape taken of Dr. S. on three consecutive days in 2002 and three more consecutive days in 2005 was reviewed. Dr. S. was observed to walk around in a free, easy, and unrestrained fashion. His behavior and movements on the videotape were discrepant from his behavior and movements during the evaluation. In the office, his movements seemed fatigued, listless, and effortful. On tape he was much peppier. He drove a sport utility vehicle, met friends for coffee and, remarkably, on every single day he was videotaped spending at least an hour at a physical fitness gym.

CONCLUSIONS AND OPINIONS

It was felt that Dr. S.'s neuropsychological test performances were quite variable. He tended to perform more poorly on measures involving nonverbal cognitive processes, but his very poor performance on the nonverbal subtest from the VIP suggested that these poor performances may have been due to motivational factors rather than genuine impairment.

His MMPI–2 personality profile revealed a classic conversion V type configuration. It was noted that despite the fact that Dr. S. was a clinical psychologist himself, his validity scale configuration suggested that he was not willing to view his problems as psychological and that he had a low degree of "psychological mindedness" with relatively poor insight. He instead appeared to prefer to view his personal problems as physical, rather than psychological. Indeed, the 3-1-8 basic scale configuration is sometimes associated with persons who develop somatic delusions. His elevated FBS score of 24 raises the possibility that he was exaggerating his symptomatic complaints and disability claims.

A review of the records failed to reveal much in the way of objective medical findings which would support his subjective complaints. It was noted that there were multiple indications of job dissatisfaction, which appeared to have been present at the very beginning of Dr. S.'s disability. This raised the obvious possibility that escaping a work environment that he found to be aversive and attempting to change careers to creative writing may have provided a source of secondary gain and played a significant role in his symptomatic complaints and disability.

The surveillance videotape demonstrated that Dr. S.'s behavior outside of a doctor's office was quite different from his behavior inside. His regular visits to the fitness center were most revealing in this person who claimed to be chronically fatigued and unable to exercise.

It was concluded that there was cogent evidence of a lack of motivation to return to his full-time occupation. Also demonstrated was the presence of clear secondary gain. It was felt that if Dr. S. were consciously aware of these factors, then the most appropriate diagnosis would be malingering. If he was not consciously aware of these factors, then it was felt that he might suffer from a somatoform disorder. In any event, it was concluded that the principal factor preventing Dr. S. from returning to his prior full-time occupation was personal choice. It was felt that there were no neuropsychological or psychological work restrictions.

RESOLUTION

The disability carrier provided the neuropsychological IME report to Dr. S.'s attorney. Shortly thereafter the disability carrier received a strongly worded 15-page letter from his attorney. That letter made a number of rather uncomplimentary references to the IME neuropsychologist. It stated that the neuropsychologist was nothing more than a hired gun for the insurance company and guilty of unethical and inappropriate behavior. That letter also referred to an earlier IME conducted by a neurologist, claiming that the physician's professional conduct during his examination was "horrifying" and that the insurance company had acted in bad faith when it contracted with both the physician and the neuropsychologist. The letter accused the neurologist of "berating" and "humiliating" Dr. S. The attorney's letter indicated that the neuropsychologist was a specialist in malingering and that the insurance company had contracted "a hired gun to shoot down claims from insureds whom he blithely labels malingerers." The attorney objected to the neuropsychologist's credentials, saying that he was not a physician who specialized in Dr. S.'s physical ailments, which the attorney specified as consisting of chronic fatigue syndrome, fibromyalgia, and a variety of autoimmune disorders. The attorney complained that Dr. S. was brought to the examination in a sport utility vehicle, which caused his severe physical distress and extreme anxiety.

The attorney referred to the neuropsychological interview of Dr. S. as "an interrogation." He indicated that the neuropsychologist was "extremely unfriendly" and "abruptly interrupted" him in the middle of responses in order to ask other questions or make "snide comments."

The attorney summarized that "the IME itself was a brutal experience." He stated that Dr. S. was "terrorized" by the evaluation process. He indicated that Dr. S. "was forced to submit to irrelevant, improper, unprofessional, and unethical questions and opinions. He was subjected in general to an experience that was no less horrifying than the first IME conducted by (the neurologist)."

The attorney concluded by stating "the after-effects of this ordeal" on Dr. S. included his being bedridden for more than two days after his neuropsychological evaluation. He subsequently developed additional symptoms, which demonstrated that his condition had been exacerbated by the examination, according to the attorney. He indicated that he had developed severe pelvic pain and interstitial cystitis. He underwent some anesthetic procedure to treat this condition and subsequently developed headaches. He apparently required intravenous fluids.

The insurance company requested that the IME neuropsychologist formally respond to these allegations in writing. Regarding being "a specialist on malingering," the neuropsychologist acknowledged publication of a number of papers in the peer reviewed literature and providing a number of invited presentations to various professional groups on this topic. However, it was noted that this was by no means the neuropsychologist's only area of specialization, and that he had published a majority of his papers on topics other than malingering.

With respect to the criticism that the neuropsychologist was not a physician specialized in the areas of chronic fatigue syndrome, fibromyalgia, and other purported autoimmune sicknesses, it was noted that he had previously commented on these topics in the professional literature (e.g., Youngjohn, Spector, & Mapou, 1998) and that he had examined hundreds of persons claiming these conditions.

Regarding the complaint that Dr. S. had developed severe physical distress from being transported in a limousine service SUV, it was noted that this seemed inconsistent with the fact that the surveillance videotape demonstrated that his own personal vehicle was an SUV, which he seemed to drive around with no problems.

With respect to the criticism that the neuropsychologist had been abusive and unprofessional with Dr. S., it was noted that Dr. S. and his attorney had leveled the same criticisms against the neurologist who had performed his previous IME. It was suggested that Dr. S. and his attorney might develop perceptions of abusiveness and unprofessionalism when in fact there is none present. The insurance company was referred to the audiotape of the interview portion of the independent neuropsychological examination to confirm the professionalism of the neuropsychologist and to evaluate the nature of his interactions with Dr. S.

After the IME neuropsychologist responded to the various criticisms leveled by Dr. S.'s attorney, there was no further contact or comment.

COMMENT

The allegations outlined above illustrate some of the risks and reactions inherent in conducting independent neuropsychological examinations. Neuropsychologists who offer unfavorable opinions regarding applicants' disability or injury claims must be prepared for attacks on their character and integrity, as well as for disagreements regarding the foundations of their conclusions. These patients often suffer from underlying personality disorders, which may alter their perception of events, their recollections of what was said, and their beliefs about how they were treated during the examination.

It should also not be surprising that a patient who chooses significantly more wrong than right answers on forced-choice symptom validity testing, or who is shown on surveillance video to perform activities that they say they are unable to do, might later prevaricate about what happened during their evaluation. Furthermore, plaintiff's attorneys may passionately advocate to win their cases using whatever means are available to them. Sometimes these strategies include *ad hominim* attacks against experts with unfavorable opinions.

Neuropsychologists who conduct independent or forensic evaluations are advised to conduct themselves with the highest levels of professionalism. They should strive to remain unbiased and objective. Evaluees should be treated humanely and courteously. Evaluations, data collection, records, and other materials reviewed should be thoroughly documented. The clinical and scientific foundations for one's conclusions should be clearly stated and the reasoning should be transparent.

Written informed consent should be obtained at the beginning of the evaluation. Informed consent should include a description of the nature and purpose of the evaluation, an outline of the possible risks and discomfort associated with the evaluation, the limits of confidentiality, and a statement indicating that the IME neuropsychologist's client is not the evaluee and that there is not a traditional doctor–patient relationship. Our informed consent statement also specifically advises evaluees to answer all interview and test questions honestly and encourages them to submit their best efforts for success on tests of ability. When these strategies fail, we have found that recording the interview, with the patient's consent, provides a powerful defense against many of these sorts of claims.

Both the American Academy of Clinical Neuropsychology and the National Academy of Neuropsychology have recently published formal position statements regarding these and related issues (Bush, NAN Policy, & Planning Committee, 2005; Sweet et al., 2003). These position papers provide welcome guidance to neuropsychologists considering conducting IMEs, as well as realistic warnings regarding some of the risks involved. For IME neuropsychologists who maintain the highest ethical standards and for those whose conduct conforms to their recommendations, these position papers perhaps provide an element of protection.

REFERENCES

Burgdorfer, W., Barbour, A. G., Hayes, S. F., Benach, J. L., Grunwalt, E., & Davis, J. P. (1982). Lyme disease: A tick borne spirochete? *Science, 216*, 1317–1319.

Bush, S. S., NAN Policy, & Planning Committee (2005). Independent and court-ordered forensic neuropsychological examinations: Official statement of the National Academy of Neuropsychology. *Archives of Clinical Neuropsychology, 20*, 997–1007.

Frederick, R. I., Crosby, R. D., & Wynkoop, T. F. (2000). Performance curve classification of invalid responding on the Validity Indicator Profile. *Archives of Clinical Neuropsychology, 15*, 281–300.

Greiffenstein, M. F., & Baker, W. J. (2001). Comparison of premorbid and postinjury MMPI–2 profiles in late postconcussion claimants. *The Clinical Neuropsychologist, 15*, 162–170.

Lees-Haley P. R., English L. T., & Glenn W. J. (1991). A Fake Bad Scale on the MMPI–2 for personal injury claimants. *Psychological Reports, 6*, 203–210.

Nuwer, M. (1997). Assessment of digital EEG, quantitative EEG, and EEG brain mapping: Report of the American Academy of Neurology and the American Clinical Neurophysiology Society. *Neurology, 49*, 277–292.

Rowe, P. M. (2000). Chronic Lyme disease: The debate goes on. *Lancet, 355*, 1436.

Sweet, J., Greiffenstein, M., Peck, T., Schmidt, M., & American Academy of Clinical Neuropsychology (2003). Official position of the American Academy of Clinical Neuropsychology on ethical complaints made against clinical neuropsychologists during adversarial proceedings. *The Clinical Neuropsychologist, 17*, 443–445.

Westervelt, H. J., & McCaffrey, R. J. (2002). Neuropsychological functioning in chronic Lyme disease. *Neuropsychological Review, 12,* 153–177.

White, D. J., Chang, H. G., Benach, J. L., Bosler, E. M., Meldrum, S. C., Means, R. G., et al. (1991). The geographical spread and temporal increase of the Lyme disease epidemic. *JAMA, 266,* 1230–1236.

Youngjohn, J. R., Larrabee, G. J., & Crook, T. H. (1993). New adult age- and education-correction norms for the Benton Visual Retention Test. *The Clinical Neuropsychologist, 7,* 155–160.

Youngjohn, J. R., Spector, J., & Mapou, R. L. (1998). Failure to assess motivation, the need to consider psychiatric disturbance, and the absence of objectively verified physical pathology: Some common pitfalls in the practice of forensic neuropsychology. *The Clinical Neuropsychologist, 12,* 233–236.

Fibromyalgia: Resignation, restitution, and response bias

22

Roger O. Gervais

Fibromyalgia is a chronic pain disorder of unknown etiology, affecting predominantly women, characterized by the presence of multiple tender points combined with widespread musculoskeletal pain. The prevalence of this disorder in international studies ranges from 0.5% to 5% in the general population and 2.0–3.3% of the general North American population (Gordon, 1999; Gran, 2003; Lindell, Bergman, Petersson, Jacobsson, & Herrstrom, 2000; Neumann & Buskila, 2003; White & Harth, 2001; Wolfe, Ross, Anderson, Russell, & Hebert, 1995; Yunus, 2002).

Up to 36% of fibromyalgia patients may become work disabled, accounting for 9% of all disability insurance payments in Canada (Gordon, 1999). Robinson et al. (2004) found that annual employer-paid medical benefits and disability costs were more than twice as high in fibromyalgia claimants as compared to general non-fibromyalgia beneficiaries ($5945 vs. $2486). Pain, fatigue, and weakness are the symptoms most frequently claimed to compromise patients' ability to work (White & Harth, 1999).

Fibromyalgia patients commonly report a variety of psychological symptoms, including depression, anxiety, and cognitive impairment (Kurtze & Svebak, 2001; Peres, Young, Kaup, Zukerman, & Silberstein, 2001; White, Nielsen, Harth, Ostbye, & Speechley, 2002). High lifetime and current prevalence of major depression, posttraumatic stress disorder and other psychiatric disorders, and psychological distress have been found in persons with fibromyalgia (Bennett, 1996; Cohen, Neumann, Haiman, Matar, Press, & Buskila, 2002; Epstein, Clauw, Klein, Kuck, Masur, & Waid, 1999; Roy-Byrne, Smith, Goldberg, Afari, & Buchwald, 2004; Sherman, Turk, & Okifuji, 2000). The disorder aggregates strongly in families and also co-aggregates with major mood disorder in families (Arnold et al., 2004). Fibromyalgia and related disorders, such as chronic fatigue and chronic widespread pain, have been associated with histories of victimization involving emotional, physical, or sexual abuse (Van Houdenhove et al., 2001). Other studies have found a link between somatization of emotional distress and chronic widespread pain, which is characteristic of fibromyalgia (McBeth, Macfarlane, Benjamin, & Silman, 2001; McBeth, Macfarlane, Hunt, & Silman, 2001).

Neuropsychological or psychological evaluation of fibromyalgia patients presenting with various cognitive, somatic, and emotional complaints may be requested as part of the disability assessment process. As with any disability evaluation for a condition that is defined largely by subjective symptom reports, the assessment process can be complicated by the presence of symptom exaggeration in some patients, particularly when litigation or the pursuit of financial benefits is involved.

Grace, Nielson, Hopkins, and Berg (1999) found that fibromyalgia patients performed more poorly on tests of memory and sustained auditory concentration than controls. The perceived memory deficits of the fibromyalgia patients were disproportionate to their objective deficits. Other studies have found that the presence of medicolegal incentives in chronic pain patients is associated with increased levels of reported memory impairment and exaggeration of disability (Kay & Morris-Jones, 1998; Schnurr & MacDonald, 1995). Rohling, Binder, and Langhinrichsen-Rohling (1995) concluded that compensation status is one factor influencing symptom presentation, accounting for 6% of the variance in the pain experience of chronic pain patients. Mailis et al. (2002) documented the prevalence of unexplainable nondermatomal somatosenory deficits in chronic pain patients in the context of compensation/litigation. Gervais, Russell, et al. (2001) found that disability incentives were associated with effort test failure in a clinical sample of fibromyalgia patients, with 35% of the patients on or claiming disability failing effort tests, compared to only 4% of the patients not involved in a disability claim. Other researchers have concluded that there is no association between fibromyalgia prevalence and compensation (White & Harth, 2001).

The present case study will illustrate the example of a disability claimant presenting with fibromyalgia, allegedly following a motor vehicle accident. The details of the case will be reviewed, followed by presentation and interpretation of the test data.

THE CASE OF MS. T.

Referral information

Ms. T., a 37-year-old teacher, was referred for a psychological assessment to assist in determining her eligibility for permanent disability pension benefits. She had left work 18 months before the present assessment due to chronic pain, fatigue, and cognitive difficulties, which she attributed to three motor vehicle accidents over a four-year span. The most recent of the accidents was two years prior to the present assessment. The primary diagnosis at the time of referral was that of fibromyalgia/chronic pain. Other diagnoses included major depression, generalized anxiety disorder, and posttraumatic myofascial pain. An opinion was sought regarding diagnostic conclusions, symptom validity, recommendations for treatment/management, and prognosis.

Background information

Personal history

Ms. T. is married, with two pre-teen children. Her husband is a tradesman with secure employment. However, despite her husband working at a second job, there are significant debts and financial stress. They would like to move into a larger home. The marital relationship was characterized as currently stable and supportive. "He looks after me. I couldn't ask for a better nurse." There was a history of previous martial discord attributed to an episode of post-partum depression 10 years earlier. Ms. T. initially denied any history of alcohol or drug abuse or other dysfunction in her marriage or in her family of origin. Later in the interview, she acknowledged childhood emotional and physical abuse from her mother. There was no report of previous physical, emotional, or sexual abuse from non-family members. There was no report of previous head injuries. Her history was positive for apparent seasonal depression. She denied any prior suicidal ideation or attempts, but admitted suicidal thoughts since the onset of her current problems.

Ms. T.'s educational attainment included Bachelor of Arts and Bachelor of Education degrees with high average academic standing. She denied any history of previous academic difficulties or learning disabilities. She had intended to eventually pursue further studies in psychology. Following completion of her Education degree, she had worked for a number of years as a substitute teacher.

She had applied for full-time teaching positions but was unsuccessful. She attributed her lack of success to the high level of competition from other applicants. Ultimately, ongoing symptoms led her to abandon plans of a teaching career.

Disability history

Ms. T. attributed her disability to the effects of three motor vehicle accidents. The first motor vehicle accident, six years earlier, occurred when Ms. T.'s vehicle was rear-ended while stopped in traffic, waiting to make a left turn. She was restrained by her seat belt, and there was no impact to her head or loss of consciousness. She struck her chest on the steering wheel. Damage to the vehicle was minimal. The accident was not attended by ambulance. Ms. T. was diagnosed with whiplash, myofascial pain, and a temporomandibular disorder. She reported some post-accident depression and apprehension when driving, but no cognitive difficulties. Ms. T. returned to work uneventfully.

The second motor vehicle accident occurred three years later when an oncoming vehicle turned left across Ms. T.'s path. Ms. T. was restrained by her seatbelt, and there were no airbags deployed. She struck her head on the headrest, but there was no loss of consciousness. Damage to the vehicle was minor. Emergency response personnel did not attend the accident scene. Ms. T. was aware of pain in the shoulders, upper back, neck and jaw. There was no lost time from work reported. Within a few weeks, however, Ms. T. began falling asleep in class and having episodes of vomiting, which caused her considerable embarrassment and which she felt would jeopardize her chances of securing full-time employment. The vomiting was fully investigated and was determined to be stress-induced.

Over the year following the second accident, Ms. T. began sleeping virtually around the clock; her vomiting persisted. Diagnoses of fibromyalgia and chronic fatigue syndrome were proposed. Upon the repeated advice of her physician, Ms. T. left teaching 15 months following the second motor vehicle accident, and applied for disability benefits. In her final months of work, she allegedly became aware of cognitive difficulties, especially problems with memory and forgetfulness. She denied any depression. Ms. T.'s application for disability was denied, and she was considering returning to teaching when she was involved in the third motor vehicle accident.

In the third motor vehicle accident, Ms. T. was riding as a passenger in a car driven by her husband when the vehicle was struck on the passenger side by a pick-up truck. Ms. T. was restrained by her seat belt, and the air bag deployed, bruising her chest. There was no impact to her head or loss of consciousness. The door of the car was pushed in and bruised her leg. The vehicle was a total loss. Ms. T. reported experiencing an acute emotional reaction following this accident. She cried for days and could not be calmed. She developed a fear of driving and felt that her life had fallen apart. She reported that her cognitive efficiency deteriorated further, and she stopped previously enjoyed activities such as reading. She made no further attempts to return to work.

At the time of assessment, Ms. T. reported that she was involved in litigation for the three motor vehicle accidents. Offers of settlement for the first accident had been received, but declined by Ms. T. Following the third accident, Ms. T. appealed the earlier denial of her application for disability benefits, leading to the present assessment.

Medical documentation

Ms. T.'s family physician noted that she suffers from a number of medical conditions, including chronic depression, chronic posttraumatic myofascial pain, and fibromyalgia. Her depression had been active for a number of years but was significantly worsened by a motor vehicle accident that left her with chronic myofascial pain. She was also quite fearful of driving because of her history of motor vehicle accidents. He concluded that Ms. T. had significant illnesses causing disability and daily symptoms.

A psychiatric assessment indicated that she was depressed but clearly uncomfortable being diagnosed as such. Family history of depression was documented. The impression was that of Major Depression, Generalized Anxiety Disorder, and Fibromyalgia. The psychiatrist also noted that the unresolved legal problems following the motor vehicle accidents complicated the clinical diagnosis and prognosis.

An orthopedic surgeon examined Ms. T. at the request of her lawyer two months following the second motor vehicle accident. Ms. T. demonstrated non-organic signs and inconsistencies which raised questions about the validity of her presentation. The surgeon also noted dependence on narcotic analgesics for pain control. He considered her to be significantly depressed and that her entire situation was colored by the depression.

Ms. T. underwent a sleep assessment, which noted that she reported a lifelong history of nightmares, dating back to age 3. On the history questionnaire, she reported a dysfunctional family of origin characterized by very significant physical and verbal abuse by her mother.

A second psychiatrist saw Ms. T. for treatment of her chronic fatigue/fibromyalgia symptoms and concluded that she had a somatoform disorder, a mood disorder, and dependent personality traits.

In a report to Ms. T.'s lawyer, a third psychiatrist concluded that Ms. T. was suffering from neuropsychiatric complications arising from chronic whiplash syndrome. These problems, including the depression, were considered to be largely iatrogenic in nature and caused in part by pain and disability as well as opiate addiction. He also critiqued the IME report of another psychiatrist, who found no evidence of anxiety, irritability, or other mental illness apart from fatigue and pain and concluded that Ms. T. was suffering from an Undifferentiated Somatoform Disorder.

The results of a functional capacity evaluation indicated that Ms. T.'s lifting maximums were considered *invalid*. Her perceived functional abilities ranked her well below the sedentary level. There was no evidence of competitive test performance, which indicated that maximum effort was not being put forth. Due to the apparent lack of full physical effort and significant pain behaviors, it was difficult to estimate Ms. T.'s true abilities and limitations.

EXAMINATION

Behavioral observations

The assessment was conducted over three days. Ms. T. presented as a fatigued-looking woman of 37 years, wearing a t-shirt and jogging pants and no make-up. Ms. T. wanted her husband present in the room with her during the assessment. When advised this was not possible, he remained in the waiting area for the three days of the assessment. Her affect was irritable, but otherwise she was in no emotional distress, apart from one episode of tearfulness near the end of the first day. She was reluctant to be photographed for identification purposes and only agreed to this when assured that the photo would remain on the file.

During testing Ms. T. often interrupted the examiner's instructions to complain about previous assessments she had undergone. She wrote detailed comments on many of the questionnaires and worked at an exceedingly slow pace. She generally declined breaks and remained seated at the desk for hours at a time. She ambulated slowly and stiffly. At one point, she dragged a large heavy armchair across the room with no apparent difficulty, preferring it to the regular office chair at the desk.

Ms. T.'s husband called on the morning of the second day of the assessment to indicate that he was having difficulty getting her out of bed. They eventually arrived at the office at 1:00 p.m. for her 9:00 a.m. appointment. On the third day of the assessment, Ms. T. again arrived late at 11:00 a.m. She required her husband's assistance to help her stand and walk.

I conducted a brief introductory interview with Ms. T. on the first day, to orient her to the assessment. The clinical interview was conducted for 3.5 hours on the afternoon of the third day of the assessment, as per my usual practice. This sequence allows me to review the assessment results in advance of the interview, which helps guide the enquiry and test diagnostic or interpretive hypotheses over the course of the interview.

Ms. T. was cooperative and forthcoming throughout the interview, and there was no indication of evasiveness. She intermittently closed her eyes as if tired, but there was no grogginess or fatigue noted in her voice. She seemed quite alert and articulate. There was no indication of any significant disruption in her cognitive processes. She sat relatively still in a standard office chair for the duration of the interview. There were no significant pain behaviors noted, and she relatively infrequently shifted her position. No breaks were requested during the interview. Review of Ms. T.'s psychosocial history, detailed accounts of each of the three motor vehicle collisions and their effects, treatment history, and symptom progression leading to her permanent disability claim contributed to the length of the interview.

Ms. T. called my office from a store in the late afternoon of the following day to advise that she had neglected to tell me of one aspect of her medical history, which she wished to have documented. Her voice at the time of this conversation was clear, alert, and articulate. There was no indication of any confusion, fatigue, or distress.

Reported symptoms

On her intake questionnaire, Ms. T. reported the following symptoms and concerns:

• Headaches	• Work
• Nausea, vomiting	• Lack of concentration
• Hearing loss	• Memory loss
• Poor appetite	• Organizing/planning
• Stomach pain	• Making decisions
• Vision loss/problems	• Stress
• Leg/arm pain	• Mood changes
• Bowel problems	• Self-control
• TMJ	• Fears
• Back pain	• Anxiety
• Tinnitus	• Shyness
• Sexual dysfunction	• Unhappiness
• Neck pain	• Depression
• Balance problems	• Loneliness
• Lack of taste	

At interview, Ms. T. provided a rather vague account of her symptoms. She described, "a strong aching pain everywhere," and that her symptoms were aggravated by overdoing any physical activity and not being able to rest when she needs to. She reported being unable to tolerate sitting, standing, or walking for more than five minutes. Short-term memory was described as impaired. She was no longer able to solve mental puzzles using logic because "my mind doesn't get into that level." Reading comprehension was described as poor. Mood was "in the toilet." She reported a fear of driving and "getting hit again," but no nightmares or intrusive recollections of the accidents.

Ms. T. indicated that her daily routine consists of spending the day in bed, either sleeping or watching television. Her mother comes over in the morning to see the children off to school and do the dishes. Ms. T. does minimal housework. She still has a driver's license and drives occasionally. She had no concerns with respect to fatigue or medications affecting her ability to drive.

Ms. T.'s medications at the time of assessment included Morphine SR (two per day), Celebrex 200 mg (two per day), Flexeril (two per day), fast acting Morphine when needed, Coumadin 7 mg, Neurontin, Gravol as needed, Rivotril 5 mg (a.m.), 2 mg (p.m.), Celexa 60 mg, and Wellbutrin 300 mg. She stated that these medications are not always effective and that she also derived benefit from massage therapy and acupuncture.

Test results

Ms. T. completed a battery of tests that included measures of cognitive functioning, symptom validity and effort, personality and emotional functioning, and self-reported symptoms. She scored below the cutoffs for biased responding on the Word Memory Test (WMT; Green, 2003; Green, Allen, & Astner, 1996) and the Test of Memory Malingering (TOMM; Tombaugh, 1996). She produced borderline scores on the Computerized Assessment of Response Bias (CARB; Allen, Conder, Green, & Cox, 1997). Reliable Digit Span (RDS; Greiffenstein, Baker, & Gola, 1994) was 7. In view of this performance, the test results and self-reports were considered to be of doubtful validity and appropriate caution was noted in the report.

In keeping with the effort test results, Ms. T.'s cognitive test results were significantly lower than would have been expected on the basis of her educational and demographic background. For example, her WAIS–R Verbal, Performance, and Full Scale IQs of 86, 81, and 83, respectively, were clearly inconsistent with her educational attainment consisting of two university degrees. Impaired scores were also noted on the CVLT and Story Recall Test. Details of the test results are presented in Table 22.1. Failed effort test scores are in bold. All scores are expressed as T scores, unless otherwise noted.

Interpretation

These excerpts are from my report on Ms. T., with identifying information altered or removed.

Summary and conclusions

In view of the response bias and suboptimal effort demonstrated by Ms. T. in this assessment, the cognitive test results are considered to be largely invalid. They quite likely represent her cognitive functioning as she wishes to portray it, rather than providing an objective and accurate reflection of her true functioning. Impaired scores were noted in a number of areas, including general intelligence and auditory memory, which is inconsistent with her actual educational and occupational achievement. In reality, she is probably capable of much stronger performance. These test results, therefore, cannot be used to support her claim of cognitive impairment and disability.

It should also be noted that, despite subjective complaints of cognitive impairment in persons

TABLE 22.1   Test results for Ms. T.

Computerized Assessment of Response Bias (CARB)	
Block 1	91.9%
Block 2	89.2%
Block 3	91.9%
Total Test	91.0%
Test of Memory Malingering (TOMM)	
Trial 1	30/50
Trial 2	**42/50**
Trial 3	**41/50**
Word Memory Test (WMT)	
Immediate Recognition	**72.5%**
Delayed Recognition	**67.5%**
Consistency	**60.0%**
Multiple Choice	35.0%
Paired Associates	35.0%
Free Recall	25.5%
Reliable Digit Span (RDS)	**7**
Wechsler Adult Intelligence Scale–Revised (WAIS–R)	Std./Scale Score
VIQ	86
PIQ	81
FSIQ	83
Information	8
Digit Span	6
Vocabulary	10
Arithmetic	7
Comprehension	7
Picture Completion	5
Picture Arrangement	6
Block Design	7
Object Assembly	7
Digit Symbol	5
Wide Range Achievement Test–3 (WRAT–3)	Std. Score
Reading	96
Spelling	94
Wisconsin Card Sorting Test (WCST)	Std. Score
Total Number of Errors (Standard Score)	87
Perseverative Responses	84
Perseverative Errors	85
Nonperseverative Errors	87
California Verbal Learning Test (CVLT)	Raw Score
List A Trials 1–5 Total (Raw, T = 20)	41
List A Trial 1	6
List A Trial 5	10
List B	4
Short Delay Free Recall	4
Short Delay Cued Recall	4
Long Delay Free Recall	6
Long Delay Cued Recall	8
Recognition Hits	11
Story Recall Test (SRT)	
Immediate Recall (–3.0 SD)	26/80
Emotional Perception Test (EPT)	14/45 errors

(Continued . . .)

TABLE 22.1   (Continued).

Alberta Smell Test (AST)	
Right nostril (borderline)	3/10
Left nostril (borderline)	3/10
Memory Complaints Inventory (MCI)	% of Max
General Memory Problems	82
Numeric Information Problems	42
Visuospatial Memory Problems	55
Verbal Memory Problems	95
Pain Interferes with Memory	92
Memory Interferes with Work	90
Impairment of Remote Memory	17
Amnesia for Complex Behaviour	52
Amnesia for Antisocial Behaviour	21
MCI Mean Score	61
Minnesota Multiphasic Personality Inventory–2 (MMPI–2)	T Score
VRIN	57
TRIN F	65
F	61
F_B	81
F_P	81
FBS (raw = 27)	82
L	71
K	56
S	60
RBS (raw = 15)	92
1 (non-K-corrected)	84 (78)
2	81
3	96
4 (non-K-corrected)	63 (60)
5	55
6	63
7 (non-K-corrected)	75 (64)
8 (non-K-corrected)	70 (62)
9 (non-K-corrected)	51 (49)
0	49
RCd	61
RC1	78
RC2	83
RC3	46
RC4	40
RC6	67
RC7	42
RC8	38
RC9	42
Beck Depression Inventory–II (BDI–II)	31
Beck Anxiety Inventory (BAI)	31
Pain Coping Inventory (PCI)	T Score
Pain Severity	62
Pain Continuity and Duration	61
Sleep Disturbance	60
Catastrophizing	53
Stress & Anxiety	41
Depression	51
Hostility	56
Paranoia & Alienation	56
Extreme Beliefs Frequency	49
Symptom Magnification Frequency	50

Multidimensional Pain Inventory (MPI)	T Score
Pain Severity	58
Interference	62
Life Control	32
Affective Distress	55
Support	60
Punishing Responses	44
Solicitous Responses	66
Distracting Responses	65
Household Chores	68
Outdoor Work	89
Activities Away From Home	42
Social Activities	47
General Activity Level	66
Stress Symptoms Checklist (SSCL)	
Posttraumatic Anxiety Symptoms (Pain pt. T score)	74
Pain and Impairment	73
Multifactor Health Inventory (MHI)	
Musculoskeletal System	Marked
Anxiety Cluster	Marked
Depression Cluster	Severe
Extreme Responses Physical Symptoms (Normal = 8)	24
Childhood Trauma Questionnaire (CTQ)	Percentile
Emotional Abuse (low to moderate)	73
Physical Abuse (moderate to severe)	93
Sexual Abuse (none or minimal)	70
Emotional Neglect (low to moderate)	60
Physical Neglect (none or minimal)	50

with chronic fatigue syndrome or fibromyalgia, there is little indication of objective cognitive dysfunction. Tiersky, Johnson, Lange, Natelson, and DeLuca (1997) undertook a comprehensive critical review of the scientific literature on neuropsychological functioning in chronic fatigue syndrome. They concluded that, despite the frequency and severity of complaints of cognitive impairment in these patients, there is little evidence to support a relationship between subjective cognitive complaints and objective neuropsychological findings. With respect to general intelligence, most patients fall into the average to high average range of intellectual ability and there is no evidence to suggest intellectual deterioration from pre-illness status.

The review of Ms. T.'s personality and pain questionnaires, combined with her illness history, strongly suggests that her presentation is the result of a number of influences. These include major depression, a somatoform disorder, and substantial reinforcement of illness behavior and dependant personality traits by her well-meaning and attentive family members. She also appears to have significant ongoing posttraumatic anxiety related to the third motor vehicle accident. Her condition also appears to be exacerbated by medication dependence. The medical reporting indicates that physical deconditioning is also contributing significantly to her presentation.

On the basis of this assessment, it is not possible to view Ms. T.'s condition as the result of a single cause-effect process. Rather, her condition is the culmination of a multifactorial process in which a number of influences, including psychosocial history factors, personality characteristics and vulnerabilities, injury, and other stressors within her personal and occupational life have interacted, leading to the production and maintenance of her symptoms. For example, she reported a history of physical abuse and family dysfunction in childhood. While this type of history does not invariably cause fibromyalgia or other chronic pain conditions, it can contribute to the development of maladaptive personality characteristics, a vulnerability to depression and anxiety, and the development of somatizing behavior.

Walling, O'Hara, and Reiter (1994) found that, among all early traumatic experiences, physical abuse in childhood was the best predictor of somatization disorder. Stuart and Noyes (1999) describe two models to explain the origin of somatization. In the first, adverse childhood experiences contribute to the development of somatizing behavior. They also note that exposure to trauma, such as physical or sexual abuse, may also predispose persons to respond to stress somatically. In the second model, somatizing behavior is viewed as a manifestation of maladaptive communication of distress and need for security and reassurance in response to environmental stress. This need results in persistent care-seeking behavior, which ultimately leads to rejection and hostility by family members or other caregivers, further exacerbating the person's care-demanding behavior. The authors explain that, rather than communicating a need for care or reassurance directly, somatizing patients frame their needs in terms of physical suffering. Inevitably, the caregivers become alienated and exit the relationship.

Hallberg and Carlsson (1998) review psychosocial vulnerability and maintaining forces relating to fibromyalgia. The authors identify four primary factors contributing to the psychosocial vulnerability in these patients: (1) Traumatic life history (early loss, responsibility early in life, social problems, powerlessness); (2) Overcompensatory perseverance (ambition, sociability, high personal standards and the need to be seen as capable and effective); (3) Pessimistic life view (loss of meaning in life and future prospects "life is over"); and (4) Unsatisfying work situation (low value job, strenuous job, personal dissatisfaction). In Ms. T.'s case, all four factors can be discerned. In regard to her work situation, it is also notable that she described her love and commitment toward the teaching profession, her high level of personal competence and success as a substitute teacher, yet was unable to secure a full-time teaching position. She now views her investment in education and her profession with bitterness and resentment.

Concerning Ms. T.'s rehabilitation, it is my opinion that at her young age, she should make every effort to avoid viewing herself as permanently disabled. Unfortunately, the cycle of psychosocial reinforcement of illness behavior has become exceedingly well entrenched with her husband, children, and mother, having assumed virtually all household responsibilities in the face of her overwhelming invalidism. This response to her illness behavior only serves to reinforce her disability and further undermine her self-esteem. Furthermore, this pattern of caregiving behavior is not sustainable indefinitely and will ultimately lead to growing frustration on the part of her family members. Indeed, this already appears to be happening as she indicated that her mother resents the burden of having to come every morning to get the children off to school. Similarly, I have concerns that her marital relationship will become increasingly strained under the demands of her chronic invalidism and may not survive. This would evidently have very unfortunate consequences for Ms. T. and her family. It is, therefore, essential that she make every effort to rehabilitate herself and resume a productive role within family and society. Finally, secondary gain issues associated with her pending litigations are probably also contributing to her perceived disability and should be resolved as soon as possible.

With respect to treatment/management recommendations, I would strongly recommend that every effort be made to mobilise and motivate Ms. T. to engage in a medically appropriate exercise program and participate in an interdisciplinary treatment program, such as described by Turk, Okifuji, Sinclair, and Starz (1998). Buckelew et al. (1998) also found that combined biofeedback/relaxation and exercise groups produced short- and long-term benefits for persons with fibromyalgia in the areas of self-efficacy, disease severity, and physical activity.

Finally, in drawing the above conclusions, I do not intend to diminish in any way the distress Ms. T. and her family are experiencing. Rather, I believe it is imperative that Ms. T. and her family make every effort to avoid viewing her as permanently disabled and encourage her to become more active and functional in her daily activities. This is essential to prevent her from falling into a cycle of increasing invalidism. Should she fail to reverse this cycle by gradually re-establishing a more productive and satisfying lifestyle, I fear that she will ultimately alienate her husband and family members and lose their support, which would have unfortunate consequences for everyone involved.

CASE ANALYSIS

The present assessment was requested to assist in evaluating Ms. T.'s claim for long-term disability benefits for chronic pain and cognitive impairment arising from fibromyalgia, which she attributed to the cumulative effects of three motor vehicle accidents. As in any assessment, the first step in the interpretation of the clinical data was to establish the reliability and validity of the data and the evaluee's presentation and self-report. In the case of Ms. T., the symptom validity tests clearly indicated the presence of suboptimal effort/response bias. While this did not imply that all of her test data and self-reports were unreliable, there were strong grounds to believe that she exerted insufficient effort to produce consistently valid results that could be used to evaluate her claims of cognitive impairment and other symptoms.

The effort tests utilized in this assessment have been shown to be insensitive to all but the most severe cognitive impairment (Green & Iverson, 2001; Green, Rohling, Lees-Haley, & Allen, 2001; Tombaugh, 1996). The WMT, in particular, has the benefit of extensive normative research documenting the performance of various diagnostic and research groups on the primary effort measures and the actual memory subtests. When utilizing the Green's Word Memory Test (2003) administration and scoring software, the evaluee's performance is automatically contrasted with the normative groups that provide three levels of "best fit" comparisons. The first level of comparison is with Immediate Recognition (IR), Delayed Recognition (DR), and Consistency (CNS), which together constitute the primary effort measures. The second level of contrast is with the two easier memory tests, Multiple Choice (MC) and Paired Associates (PA). The third comparison is with the most difficult of the memory tests, Free Recall (FR) and Long Delay Free Recall (LDFR). There are also options to select specific comparison groups to assist in the clinical interpretation.

As noted in Table 22.2, Ms. T.'s effort scores IR (72.5%), DR (67.5%), and CNS (60%) were virtually identical to the scores of a sample of sophisticated volunteer simulators (psychologists, physicians, and other professionals) who were asked to subtly fake cognitive impairment without being detected by the test (IR = 70.9%, DR = 67.2%, CNS = 63.5%). Other "best fit" comparisons included samples of patients with major depression and chronic pain syndrome who failed the WMT. The scores of two samples of patients, one with neurological diseases and impaired memory, and the other comprised of patients with moderate-severe traumatic brain injury, both making a good effort, are presented for further contrast and perspective. When one considers that these last two groups obtained effort scores equal or better than 95%, Ms. T.'s scores ranging from 60% to 72%, some 5 to 9 standard deviations below neurological or traumatic brain injury norms, are indisputably implausible and strongly suggest simulation of cognitive impairment.

After the first level of WMT interpretation, the contrasts involving the MC and PA subtests were examined. In keeping with Ms. T.'s poor performance on the effort measures, her scores on MC (35%) and PA (35%) were far weaker than those of the neurological (MC = 81%; PA = 78%) and brain injury groups (MC = 87%; PA = 80%). The "best fit" match generated by the scoring program was with a sample of 20 actual clinical patients asked to fake impairment without being detected by the test (MC = 39%; PA = 40%). Ms. T.'s scores in this dimension of the test were thus also implausible, generating a "warning" alert from the scoring program.

For the third level of interpretation, the comparisons involving the FR subtest were reviewed (Ms. T. was not administered LDFR). Her score of 25.5% on FR was closest to that of moderate-severe brain injury patients who failed the WMT (FR = 26.3%). The scores of a sample of fibromyalgia patients claiming disability who failed the WMT documented in Gervais, Russell et al. (2001) were also produced by the scoring program for contrast. It was interesting to note that Ms. T.'s memory test scores were not only lower than those of the disability-seeking fibromyalgia group, but her effort test scores were nearly identical. Thus, on the basis of a detailed examination of the data

TABLE 22.2   Best fit analysis of Ms. T.'s WMT Immediate Recognition, Delayed Recognition and Consistency scores

GREEN'S WORD MEMORY TEST

Patient: Ms. T.   Education: College Degree
Age: 37
Patient Scores

	IR	DR	CNS	MC	PA	FR	LDFR
Patient:	72.5	67.5	60	35	35	25.5	
	(Fail)	(Fail)	(Fail)	(Warning)	(Warning)		

Comparative Groups—Best Fit (IR, DR, AND CNS)

	IR	DR	CNS	MC	PA	FR	LDFR
Sophisticated Volunteer Simulators (Dr. Green) (N = 25)							
Mean:	70.9	67.2	63.5	46.8	48.2	35	
Standard Deviation:	12.6	16.5	12.4	17.9	19.9	19.2	
Patient Z-Score:	0.1	0	−0.3	−0.7	−0.7	−0.5	
Major Depression: fail WMT (Dr. Green) (N = 32)							
Mean:	67	69.9	67.2	53.7	49.5	33.6	30.6
Standard Deviation:	21.1	20.6	14.9	19.4	18.2	12.8	13
Patient Z-Score:	0.3	−0.1	−0.5	−1	−0.8	−0.6	
Major Depression: fail WMT (Dr. Gervais) (N = 10)							
Mean:	70.5	73.5	66.5	52	44.5	29.7	31.2
Standard Deviation:	16.9	15.8	12.9	18.2	19.6	15.6	18.8
Patient Z-Score:	0.1	−0.4	−0.5	−0.9	−0.5	−0.3	
Chronic Pain Syndrome: fail WMT (Dr. Green) (N = 75)							
Mean:	69.3	71.3	70	49.6	44.1	27.4	29.2
Standard Deviation:	16.6	17.7	13.5	20.8	19.7	12.3	12.9
Patient Z-Score:	0.2	−0.2	−0.7	−0.7	−0.5	−0.2	

derived from the WMT alone, there were strong grounds to question the validity of Ms. T.'s claimed cognitive impairment.

It could be argued, however, that chronic pain, depression, fatigue, and medication effects were responsible for Ms. T.'s effort test failure. Gervais, Green et al. (2001) examined this hypothesis and determined that it was unlikely that these factors would cause chronic pain patients to produce significantly lower scores on the effort tests than patients with severe traumatic brain injury or neurological disease. Rather, as concluded by Gervais, Russell et al. (2001), in a study of effort test performance in fibromyalgia patients, incomplete effort and response bias was associated with the presence of disability incentives and exaggeration of cognitive deficits. On the specific question of depression, Rohling, Green, Allen, and Iverson (2002) found that depression had no effect on objective neurocognitive functioning in patients who passed symptom validity tests.

Green, Rohling, Lees-Haley, and Allen (2001) reported that compensation claimants who failed the WMT scored 1.20 SD lower on the overall test battery mean (OTBM) compared to claimants who passed the WMT. Similarly, Gervais, Rohling, Green, and Ford (2004) found that non-head-injury disability claimants who failed the WMT and the TOMM scored −0.96 SD below the mean OTBM compared to claimants who passed both WMT and TOMM. Accordingly, Ms. T.'s WMT and TOMM failure in the present assessment predicted that her cognitive test scores would be lower than expected, and this indeed was the case.

Green (2007), in a study examining the influence of effort on a battery of commonly used neuropsychological tests, found that scores on most neuropsychological tests declined systematically with decreasing ranges of effort on the WMT. For example, in Ms. T.'s WMT–DR score range of

61% to 70%, the mean CVLT Short Delay Free Recall score was 7.4 (SD = 3.0) and the Long Delay Free Recall was 7.3 (SD = 3.3). Ms. T.'s short-delay and long-delay recall scores were within this range or lower at 4 and 6, respectively. An independent replication of the effect of effort on CVLT scores, drawn from a sample of cases from the author's practice (RG), found virtually identical results. Ms. T.'s Immediate Story Recall score of 26 was also consistent with the mean of 38.6 (SD = 8.9) predicted for her WMT–DR range, as were Verbal and Performance IQ. Tables 22.3 and 22.4 present the effect of effort on CVLT scores, with Ms. T.'s performance presented for contrast.

Clinically, it was also evident that Ms. T.'s test results were clearly incompatible with her educational and occupational history. Her WAIS–R Full-Scale IQ of 83 (1–2 SD below pre-disability expectations) was clearly inconsistent with her attainment of two undergraduate degrees. Similarly, her CVLT and story recall scores (SRT; Green & Allen, 1995), falling between 2 and 5 standard deviations below the normal means, were also implausible, especially considering that she denied ever sustaining a head injury, and there were no particular cognitive difficulties evident at the time of the clinical interview. Indeed, she was alert and articulate and lost her train of thought only once over the course of the 3.5-hour interview. In the final analysis, after weighing the clinical, demographic, and normative data as discussed above, Ms. T.'s poor performance on the cognitive tests was deemed to be a function of poor effort and symptom exaggeration. While it was possible to speculate on her reasons for this response bias, the primary conclusion was that the invalid and unreliable clinical data could not be used to substantiate her claims of cognitive impairment and disability.

The self-report symptom questionnaires also supported an interpretation of symptom exaggeration. Ms. T.'s completion of the Memory Complaints Inventory (MCI; Green, 2004b; Green & Allen, 1997) produced extreme scores on Verbal Memory Problems (95%), Pain Interferes with

TABLE 22.3   Mean California Verbal Learning Test Recall scores at each level of effort

WMT DR MEAN	N	CVLT SHORT DELAY FREE RECALL MEAN	CVLT SD FREE SD	CVLT LONG DELAY FREE RECALL MEAN	CVLT LD FREE SD
97.5%	745	**10.7**	3.2	**11.2**	3.2
88.1%	206	**8.3**	3.2	**8.9**	3.2
77.0%	105	**7.8**	3.5	**8.2**	3.4
67.1%	61	**7.4**	3.0	**7.3**	3.3
54.5%	50	**5.8**	2.9	**5.5**	3.1
41.1%	34	**4.4**	2.5	**3.3**	3.0

Note: Reproduced with permission from Green (2007). Ms. T.'s WMT DR = 67.5%, CVLT: Short Delay Free Recall = 4, Long Delay Free Recall = 6.

TABLE 22.4   Independent replication of the effect of effort on CVLT Scores in 678 cases tested by Dr. Roger Gervais: Scores on CVLT Short and Long Delayed Free Recall and Recognition Hits and on TOMM Trial 2

WMT DR MEAN	N	CVLT SD FREE MEAN	CVLT SD FREE SD	CVLT LD FREE MEAN	CVLT LD FREE SD	CVLT REC. HITS MEAN	CVLT REC. HITS SD	TOMM TRIAL 2 MEAN	TOMM TRIAL 2 SD
97.0%	365	**11.0**	3.0	**11.4**	3.1	**14.8**	1.6	**49.8**	.9
86.7%	128	**8.8**	3.4	**9.2**	3.2	**14.0**	2.0	**49.0**	2.5
75.7%	58	**8.9**	3.4	**8.7**	3.7	**13.5**	2.3	**46.5**	4.9
66.8%	46	**6.6**	2.8	**6.6**	2.8	**11.5**	3.7	**43.7**	8.0
55.4%	23	**6.6**	2.4	**6.3**	2.9	**11.6**	3.0	**38.8**	9.4
44.7%	13	**3.8**	2.5	**3.5**	2.7	**9.2**	4.4	**28.9**	10.9

SD = short delay, LD = long delay; Rec. Hits = Recognition Hits score. Reproduced with permission from Green (2007). Ms. T.'s WMT DR = 67.5%, CVLT: Short Delay Free Recall = 4, Long Delay Free Recall = 6.

Memory (92%), Memory Interferes with Work (90%), and General Memory Problems (82%). Her mean MCI score of 61% was elevated relative to the mean MCI score of 47% (SD = 17) observed in the sample of disability-seeking fibromyalgia patients documented in Gervais, Russell et al. (2001). Her total MCI score of 546 was greater than 1 standard deviation above the mean MCI total score of the High Depression group in the Rohling et al. (2002) study. It was also notable that she produced an extremely elevated score on Amnesia for Complex Behavior (52%), one of the three MCI scales that contain implausible memory problems.

Review of Ms. T.'s MMPI–2 profile revealed elevated F_B (T = 81) and F_P(T = 81), consistent with symptom exaggeration and possible malingering. Her Fake Bad Score (FBS; Lees-Haley, English, & Glenn, 1991) of 27 (T = 82) was also well within the range suggestive of symptom exaggeration as noted in numerous studies (Iverson & Binder, 2000; Larrabee, 2003a, 2003b, 2003c; Ross, Millis, Krukowski, Putnam, & Adams, 2004). She obtained a score of 15 (T = 92) on the Response Bias Scale (RBS; Gervais, Ben-Porath, Wygant, & Green, 2007), associated with a 64% probability of failing the WMT or the Medical Symptom Validity Test (MSVT; Green, 2004a). The elevated clinical scales 1 (non-K-corrected T = 78), 2 (T = 81), and 3 (T = 96) combined with RC1 (T = 78) and RC2 (T = 83) suggested depression and somatization, although demoralization (RCd) was within the normal range (T = 61).

There were also curious inconsistencies between Ms. T.'s MPI T scores. Whereas Interference (62) was above average, her Pain Severity (58) was high average and Outdoor Work (88), Household Chores (68), and General Activity Level (66) were well above average. Not only were these scores internally inconsistent, they were in contradiction to the account of her daily functioning and activities she provided in the interview. This also raised questions regarding the reliability and credibility of her presentation and claimed disability.

Despite Ms.T's effort test failure, invalid test results, and symptom exaggeration, I did not characterize her as malingering. To do so, I believe, would have served no useful purpose vis-à-vis the referral questions. The central conclusion was that her claims of cognitive impairment could not be objectively validated, and her reported pain and emotional symptoms were unreliable and could not be used to adjudicate her disability claim. The additional label of malingering was not essential to the ultimate management of the claim. There was, nonetheless, evidence of volitional symptom exaggeration, quite likely in the pursuit of an external incentive (disability benefits), as well as other psychosocial secondary gains. However, in the context of ongoing litigation for the three motor vehicle accidents, it was beyond the scope of the assessment to make a judgment on the specific motivations underlying her presentation. This, I felt, was the prerogative of the court.

Despite the evidence of symptom magnification and effort test failure, I concluded that Ms. T. was nonetheless suffering from depression, a somatoform disorder, posttraumatic anxiety, and medication dependence, occurring within the context of psychosocial reinforcement of illness and disability behavior and related secondary gains. I recommended implementation of a cognitive-behavioral rehabilitation program.

OUTCOME

I had no further involvement with Ms. T.'s claim following completion of the present assessment and, therefore, have no knowledge of the final outcome. A search of the relevant court judgment database produced a judgment from 2002, which decided the claim for the first motor vehicle accident (mid-1990s) could proceed to trial by jury. It is therefore reasonable to conclude that none of Ms. T.'s accident claims have settled at the time of this writing and her disability is ongoing.

REFERENCES

Allen, L. M., Conder, R. L., Green, P., & Cox, D. R. (1997). *CARB 97 Manual for the Computerized Assessment of Response Bias*. Durham: NC: CogniSyst.

Arnold, L. M., Hudson, J. I., Hess, E. V., Ware, A. E., Fritz, D. A., Auchenbach, M. B., Starck, L. O., & Keck, P. E. Jr. (2004). Family study of fibromyalgia. *Arthritis and Rheumatism*, *50*(3), 944–952.

Bennett, R. M. (1996). Fibromyalgia and the disability dilemma. *Arthritis and Rheumatism*, *39*(10), 1627–1634.

Buckelew, S. P., Conway, R., Parker, J., Deuser, W. E., Read, J., Witty, T. E., Hewett, J. E., Minor, M., Johnson, J. C., Van Male, L., McIntosh, M. J., Nigh, M., & Kay, D. R. (1998). Biofeedback/relaxation training and exercise interventions for fibromyalgia: A prospective trial. *Arthritis Care and Research*, *11*(3), 196–209.

Cohen, H., Neumann, L., Haiman, Y., Matar, M. A., Press, J., & Buskila, D. (2002). Prevalence of post-traumatic stress disorder in fibromyalgia patients: overlapping syndromes or post-traumatic fibromyalgia syndrome? *Seminars in Arthritis and Rheumatism*, *32*(1), 38–50.

Epstein, S. A., Clauw, D., Klein, D., Kuck, J., Masur, D., & Waid, R. (1999). Psychiatric disorders in patients with fibromyalgia: a multicenter investigation. *Psychosomatics*, *40*(1), 57–63.

Gervais, R. O., Ben-Porath, Y. S., Wygant, D. B., & Green, P. (2007). Development and validation of a Response Bias Scale (RBS) for the MMPI-2. *Assessment*, *14*, 196–208.

Gervais, R. O., Green P., Allen, L. M., & Iverson, G. L. (2001). Effects of coaching on symptom validity testing in chronic pain patients presenting for disability assessments. *Journal of Forensic Neuropsychology*, *2*, 1–19.

Gervais, R. O., Rohling, M. L., Green, P., & Ford, W. (2004). A comparison of WMT, CARB, and TOMM failure rates in non-head-injury disability claimants. *Archives of Clinical Neuropsychology*, *19*(4), 475–487.

Gervais, R. O., Russell, A. S., Green, P., Allen, L. M., Ferrari, R., & Pieschl, S. D. (2001). Effort testing in patients with fibromyalgia and disability incentives. *Journal of Rheumatology*, *28*, 1892–1899.

Gordon, D. A. (1999). Chronic widespread pain as a medico-legal issue. *Bailliere's Clinical Rheumatology*, *13*(3), 531–543.

Grace, G. M., Nielson, W. R., Hopkins, M., & Berg, M. A. (1999). Concentration and memory deficits in patients with Fibromyalgia Syndrome. *Journal of Clinical and Experimental Neuropsychology*, *21*(4), 477–487.

Gran, J. T. (2003). The epidemiology of chronic generalized musculoskeletal pain. Best Practice and Research. *Clinical Rheumatology*, *17*(4), 547–561.

Green, P. (2003). *Green's Word Memory Test for Windows—User's manual*. Edmonton: Green's Publishing.

Green, P. (2004a). *Green's Medical Symptom Validity Test (MSVT): User's manual*. Edmonton: Green's Publishing.

Green, P. (2004b). *Memory Complaints Inventory for Windows*. Edmonton: Green's Publishing.

Green, P. (2007). The pervasive influence of effort on neuropsychological tests. *Physical Medicine Rehabilitation Clinics of North America*, *18*(1), 43–68.

Green, P., & Allen, L. M. (1995). *CogniSyst Story Recall Test*. Durham, NC: CogniSyst.

Green, P., & Allen, L. (1997). *Memory Complaints Inventory*. Durham, NC: CogniSyst.

Green, P., Allen, L., & Astner, K. (1996). *The Word Memory Test: A user's guide to the oral and computer-administered forms, US Version 1.1*. Durham, NC: CogniSyst.

Green, P., & Iverson, G. (2001). Validation of the Computerized Assessment of Response Bias in litigating patients with head injuries. *The Clinical Neuropsychologist*, *15*(4), 492–497.

Green, P., Rohling, M., Lees-Haley, P., & Allen, M. (2001). Effort has a greater effect on test scores than severe brain injury in compensation claimants. *Brain Injury*, *15*(12), 1045–1060.

Greiffenstein, M. F., Baker, W. J., & Gola, T. (1994). Validation of malingered amnesia measures with a large clinical sample. *Psychological Assessment*, *6*, 218–224.

Hallberg, L. R., & Carlsson, S. G. (1998). Psychological vulnerability and maintaining forces related to fibromyalgia. *Scandinavian Journal of Caring Science*, *12*, 95–103.

Iverson, G. L., & Binder, L. M. (2000). Detecting exaggeration and malingering in neuropsychological assessment. *Journal of Head Trauma Rehabilitation*, *15*, 829–858.

Kay, N. R. M., & Morris-Jones, H. (1998). Pain clinic management of medico-legal litigants. *Injury*, *29*, 305–308.

Kurtze, N., & Svebak, S. (2001). Fatigue and patterns of pain in fibromyalgia: correlations with anxiety, depression and co-morbidity in a female county sample. *British Journal of Medical Psychology*, *74*(4), 523–37.

Larrabee, G. J. (2003a). Detection of symptom exaggeration with the MMPI–2 in litigants with malingered neurocognitive dysfunction. *The Clinical Neuropsychologist*, *17*, 54–68.

Larrabee, G. J. (2003b). Exaggerated MMPI–2 symptom report in personal injury litigants with malingered neurocognitive deficit. *Archives of Clinical Neuropsychology*, *18*, 673–686.

Larrabee, G. J. (2003c). Exaggerated pain report in litigants with malingered neurocognitive dysfunction. *The Clinical Neuropsychologist*, *17*, 395–401.

Lees-Haley, P. R., English L. T., & Glenn W. J. (1991). A Fake Bad Scale on the MMPI–2 for personal injury claimants. *Psychological Reports*, *68*, 203–210.

Lindell, L., Bergman, S., Petersson, I. F., Jacobsson, L. T., & Herrstrom, P. (2000). Prevalence of fibromyalgia and chronic widespread pain. *Scandinavian Journal of Primary Health Care*, *18*(3), 149–153.

Mailis, A., Papagapiou, M., Umana, M., Cohodarevic, T., Nowak, J., & Nicholson, K. (2002). Unexplainable nondermatomal somatosensory deficits in patients with chronic nonmalignant pain in the context of litigation/compensation: A role for involvement of central factors? *Journal of Rheumatology*, *28*(6), 1385–93.

McBeth, J., Macfarlane, G. J., Benjamin, S., & Silman, A. J. (2001). Features of somatization predict the onset of chronic widespread pain: results of a large population-based study. *Arthritis and Rheumatism*, *44*(4), 940–946.

McBeth, J., Macfarlane, G. J., Hunt, I. M., & Silman, A. J. (2001). Risk factors for persistent chronic widespread pain: a community-based study. *Rheumatology*, *40*(1), 95–101.

Neumann, L., & Buskila, D. (2003). Epidemiology of fibromyalgia. *Current Pain and Headache Reports*, *7*(5), 362–368.

Peres, M. F., Young, W. B., Kaup, A. O., Zukerman, E., & Silberstein, S. D. (2001). Fibromyalgia is common in patients with transformed migraine. *Neurology*, *57*(7), 1326–1328.

Robinson, R. L., Birnbaum, H. G., Morley, M. A., Sisitsky, T., Greenberg, P. E., & Claxton, A. J. (2004). Economic cost and epidemiological characteristics of patients with fibromyalgia claims. *Journal of Rheumatology*, *30*(6), 1318–1325.

Rohling, M. L., Binder, L. M., & Langhinrichsen-Rohling, J. (1995). A meta-analytic review of the association between financial compensation and the experience and treatment of chronic pain. *Health Psychology*, *14*, 537–547.

Rohling, M. L., Green, P., Allen, L. M., & Iverson, G. L. (2002). Depressive symptoms and neurocognitive test scores in patients passing symptom validity tests. *Archives of Clinical Neuropsychology*, *17*(3), 205–222.

Ross, S. R., Millis, S. R., Krukowski, R. A., Putnam, S. H., & Adams, K. M. (2004). Detecting probable malingering on the MMPI–2: An examination of the Fake Bad Scale in mild head injury. *Journal of Clinical and Experimental Neuropsychology*, *26*, 115–124.

Roy-Byrne, P., Smith, W. R., Goldberg, J., Afari, N., & Buchwald, D. (2004). Post-traumatic stress disorder among patients with chronic pain and chronic fatigue. *Psychological Medicine*, *34*(2), 363–368.

Schnurr, R., & MacDonald, M. (1995). Memory complaints in chronic pain. *Clinical Journal of Pain*, *11*, 101–111.

Sherman, J. J., Turk, D. C., & Okifuji, A. (2000). Prevalence and impact of post-traumatic stress disorder-like symptoms on patients with fibromyalgia syndrome. *Clinical Journal of Pain*, *16*(2), 127–134.

Stuart, S., & Noyes, R. (1999). Attachment and interpersonal communication in somatization. *Psychosomatics*, *40*(1), 34–43.

Tiersky, L. A., Johnson, S. K., Lange, G., Natelson, B. H., & DeLuca, J. (1997). Neuropsychology of Chronic Fatigue Syndrome: A critical review. *Journal of Clinical and Experimental Neuropsychology*, *19*, 560–586.

Tombaugh, T. N. (1996). *Test of Memory Malingering*. Toronto: Multi-Health Systems.

Turk, D.C., Okifuji, A., Sinclair, D., & Starz, D. (1998). Differential responses by psychosocial subgroups of fibromyalgia syndrome patients to an interdisciplinary treatment. *Arthritis Care and Research*, *1*(5), 397–404.

Van Houdenhove, B., Neerinckx, E., Lysens, R., Vertommen, H., Van Houdenhove, L., Onghena, P., Westhovens, R., & D'Hooghe, M. B. (2001). Victimization in chronic fatigue syndrome and fibromyalgia in tertiary care: A controlled study on prevalence and characteristics. *Psychosomatics*, *42*(1), 21–28.

Walling, M. K., O'Hara, M. W., & Reiter, R. C. (1994). Abuse history and chronic pain in women: II. A multivariate analysis of abuse and psychological morbidity. *Obstetrics and Gynecology*, *84*, 200–206.

White, K. P., & Harth, M. (1999). The occurrence and impact of generalized pain. *Bailliere's Clinical Rheumatology, 13*, 379–389.

White, K. P., & Harth, M. (2001). Classification, epidemiology, and natural history of fibromyalgia. *Current Pain and Headache Reports, 5*(4), 320–329.

White, K. P., Nielsen, W. R., Harth, M., Ostbye, T., & Speechley, M. (2002). Chronic widespread musculoskeletal pain with or without fibromyalgia: Psychological distress in a representative community sample. *Journal of Rheumatology, 29*(3), 588–594.

Wolfe, F., Ross, K., Anderson, J., Russell, I. J., & Hebert, L. (1995). The prevalence and characteristics of fibromyalgia in the general population. *Arthritis and Rheumatism, 38*, 19–28.

Yunus, M. B. (2002). Gender differences in fibromyalgia and other related syndromes. *Journal of Gender-Specific Medicine, 5*(2), 42–47.

Mold and the joy of malingering

23

Paul R. Lees-Haley

NEUROPSYCHOLOGICAL EVALUATION

Background information

This is the case of a female from South Carolina who complained of neuropsychological deficits and emotional distress symptoms due to toxic mold exposure in her apartment. The facts and data below have been altered to disguise identities. Any similarities of names or facts are unintentional and coincidental.

The referral came from an attorney who does primarily personal injury defense, which was her role in this case. The referral questions were to describe the nature and extent of neuropsychological and emotional distress injuries, if any, the cause of the injuries, and the expected outcome. Questions included whether the patient was disabled by exposure to mold spores or mycotoxins as alleged in this legal matter, and, if so, whether the disability was temporary or permanent. She also asked about alternative causation and pre-existing problems. Finally, the attorney asked for comments on the methodology and conclusions of the neuropsychologist retained by plaintiff counsel.

Ms. U. was examined on April 1, 2005 at my office. The evaluation began at 9:15 rather than 8 a.m. as planned because Ms. U. arrived late, saying she overslept. The evaluation was completed at 6:15 p.m. Note that this evaluation had been scheduled twice previously in South Carolina, but after my assistant and I traveled there two times to conduct the examination, and the patient no-showed both times, the court ordered her to come to my office in Los Angeles.

Ms. U. is a 45-year-old white female. Her only language is English.

The following history is as reported by the patient. My records review is contained in a separate report dated April 1, 2005.

Patient's description of causal events

Ms. U. reported that she was injured by "toxic mold exposure" in her apartment after a leak due to a tornado followed by a thunderstorm in July 2001. She did not see mold until a "few weeks later" and did not realize it was the cause of her problems until Dr. Moldcipher told her in January 2002. Realizing she was in imminent danger, she moved out of her apartment in May 2002, only sleeping there "a few times" in the ensuing couple of months when she had "fights with my boyfriend. But they weren't nothing serious ... they didn't bother me none" [sic]. She added that she also has experienced severe emotional distress due to the way her insurance company has handled her claim for damages. For example, the adjuster sometimes does not return her calls until the next day.

Her insurance company sent a remediation company to clean out the apartment, but one of Ms. U.'s attorney's experts discovered that they failed to remove some of the offending fungi hidden behind sheetrock in her bedroom.

Ms. U. was reluctant to provide details about the causation experience, saying her attorney had told her it was "irrelevant" and "not something to discuss with a psychiatrist" (referring to this neuropsychologist).

She was particularly distressed that her insurance company refused to sign a paper guaranteeing that she would never develop "chemical AIDS" or cancer at any point in the future. She emphasized that, "the certifiable fact that they wouldn't sign this guarantees proof positive of their guilt" [sic].

She first discovered that mold was "lethal" when she performed Internet searches on toxic mold at the suggestion of the paralegal at her lawyer's firm. Reading the scientific information posted on legal websites "was a real eye-opening experience, you know? Like, I had no idea. No idea" that mold "was like, it can kill you, you know? I mean, would you believe brain damage?" [sic]. Later Ms. U. said she first learned that mold was dangerous watching a television program. She did not recall which program. "But it don't matter none," she added, " 'cause everybody knows it. It's in USA Today."

When she moved out of her apartment she lived "in a hotel room for a year . . . then they got me my apartment, finally."

Complaints

Ms. U. told me that she has experienced emotional distress and neuropsychological complaints caused both by mold exposure and misconduct by her insurance company. Her cognitive complaints and emotional distress have both been worsening steadily since the initial insult. Her emotional distress is so severe that she cannot discuss it and has "flashbacks, like, daily, like, almost all the time." Asked how she experiences flashbacks, she asked for clarification of the question. When I explained that different people have different experiences, she asked me to give her "some choices" so she could "understand the question." Asked what she meant by "flashbacks" she equivocated and digressed and said, "It's hard to put into words." Asked several variations of "How would you define flashbacks?" she said "You're the psychologist" and "You're supposed to know that—why are you asking me?" and complained that it was "not the sort of question you should be asking . . . asking symptoms is like a deposition, you know?" but eventually said, "It's sort of like memories. It's hard to describe." She added that one example is sometimes she thinks about memories of visiting her grandmother when she was a child, and these memories are "like living it all over again . . . like it's happening to me again now."

She has difficulty comprehending things she reads, specifically including items she read without difficulty pre-injury, such as the Bible and newspapers.

Ms. U. said her memory was "terrible" and, without being asked, and without hearing the terms in this office, added, "My short-term memory is much worse than my long-term memory." She provided various examples of her excellent premorbid memory (e.g., for telephone numbers, grocery plans, names, work-related information, etc). "It was almost photogenic, you know what I mean?" [sic]. Asked if an example of her short-term memory versus long-term memory problem would be that she can clearly recall events that happened six months ago or one year ago but cannot recall events from one day ago, she affirmed that this is "exactly what I mean." (As noted above, her exposure is reported to have preceded this evaluation by three years.)

Aside from "flashbacks," when she reported emotional distress injuries she did not report specific symptoms or problems, such as depression or anxiety. When asked with leading questions, she reported that she has "terrible" and "extreme" depression and "unbelievable" anxiety. She defined/described her depression as "crying" and "feeling sad" and defined her anxiety as "the same. They're really the same to me."

Treatment history

Dr. Smith is Ms. U.'s family physician but she obtains treatment for her mold conditions "from a specialist" identified by her attorney because "regular docs don't really know how to treat you for mold, you know?" She said the "mold specialist" is Dr. Moldcipher, the neuropsychologist.

When asked for a complete list of all of the other psychological professionals she has seen, she said she sees a Licensed Professional Counselor (LPC) now for psychotherapy. She saw no psychological counselors until three weeks before this evaluation (three years after her mold exposure). The referral was at the suggestion of her attorney. The LPC's name is "something like Andrews or Anders." (I do not see a reference to these visits in the records.)

She took no medications on the day of this evaluation. She said she planned to take her antibiotics in the evening. She is uncertain whether the antibiotics are for mold-related injuries, adding that they "probably" are but again saying she is not sure. Otherwise she has taken no medications for mold-related injuries.

Other health history

Ms. U. said that the most emotionally distressing experience of her entire life has been "what [defendant]'s done to us." She said the second most emotionally distressing experience was "probably" when her grandmother died, because they were very close.

Ms. U. described her health prior to this injury as excellent. She denied any history of toxic exposure, brain injury, or loss of consciousness, except brain injury due to the mold exposure in this case.

She denied being in any treatment at present for any conditions unrelated to her toxic mold exposure.

She initially said she has never used street drugs or used prescription medication recreationally, later amending this to "maybe a little pot and stuff when I was real young . . . I'm not sure. Probably . . . it's been so long . . . everybody does it . . . just your normal stuff." She denied any history of alcoholism or excessive use of alcohol.

Later in the interview, despite the above history, when asked about references to drugs in her medical records, she told me she has used numerous street drugs and medications not prescribed by a physician at various points in her life, including "amphetamines . . . downers . . . acid . . . pot . . . crystal meth . . . ecstasy . . . cocaine . . . Percodans . . . valiums . . . you name it." Questions to determine frequency, duration, and possible dependence met with contradictory or equivocal answers or reports of lack of recall, giving a tentative impression of repeated use of several groups of substances with no one predominating for several years, at more than one point in her life. Apparently as if to qualify somewhat the quantity of drug consumption, she added that her brothers often stole her drugs from her.

After noting the alterations in the drug history, we discussed the references in her medical records to many years of alcohol abuse. At that point she revised her denial of any history of excessive use of alcohol, and reported alcohol abuse from her early teens until she quit. She reported that she drank "about a quart a day" of "white lightning" from approximately age 12 or 13 until about three years ago, explaining that this was the fault of her alcoholic older brothers. After concluding that this level of alcohol was more than she should be drinking, approximately three years ago she cut down to a fifth a day of "store-bought whiskey" for health reasons. Asked when she quit altogether, she said, "yesterday."

When asked if she has ever had any mental health treatment unrelated to this claim, Ms. U. first told me that she had never had any. Then when I asked her about the records showing two psychiatric hospitalizations, she said she had forgotten one and the other "don't count" because "it was just a misunderstanding." She completely recovered from those very temporary and "not really important" experiences. She denied any history of suicide attempts or suicidal ideation. When asked about the suicide attempt described in her medical records she explained that, "those was what they call gestures" [sic] and "nothing to worry about" and "besides, it ain't relevant. That's deposition stuff." She declined to explain what she meant by referring to plural suicide attempts when I only saw references to one in her medical records.

She initially denied any history of use of any medication for depression or anxiety or other psychological problems, but when asked about the references to Xanax, Librium, Valium, Prozac, BuSpar, Ativan, Anafranil, Halcion, and other medications in her records, she pointed out that these were "temporary" to help her "get by" some "little problems" that everyone has. She added that sometimes she did not fill the prescriptions and often she "just threw [the medications] down the toilet" instead of taking them, and sometimes her brothers took her medications "without permission."

She denied any family history (including her husbands) of mental health treatment. She denied any history of homicidal ideation.

Family, social, and developmental history

Ms. U. has been married four times. The first three marriages ended in divorce. Her most recent marriage has lasted four years, "and it's going great, except for the mold."

Her first two husbands were alcoholics. She has had no distressing interactions with any of her former husbands during the last five years. Ms. U.'s current husband is a 45-year-old unemployed retail clerk. She reported that her husband has no history of mental health treatment, except in connection with this case. Three weeks ago he began treatment with the same counselor she sees.

Her husband has never been arrested "for anything serious . . . maybe some fighting or something like that . . . I'm not sure . . . maybe . . . probably . . . some drinking and fighting, just guy stuff, nothing serious."

Ms. U. has five sons, one each by her first three husbands and two others whose paternity is not clear. All five sons are in good health. She gets along well with all five. She has not seen or talked to the three older sons for "a few years" but "we get along real good" when they get together.

She gave an extremely vague, digressive, and contradictory history concerning alcohol and drug use by her sons. Based on this fragmented history, apparently four of the five sons have used alcohol and/or drugs on numerous occasions. Apparently four of her sons have had some drug-related "run-ins with the law" leading two of them to spend time in prison. She expressed uncertainty but indicated that possibly two of them are in prison at present for "drug stuff" that apparently may include drug dealing. Again, her history on these points varied from clear but contradictory to vague, and cannot be presumed reliable.

Ms. U. resided for varying lengths of time with one or both of her parents, and with her grandparents, an uncle and aunt, and other relatives at various points from birth until she was 17, when she married her first husband. She was vague about the reasons for these relocations but in so many words indicated that her father had "problems with the law" and her mother "may have been a drunk, I really don't remember." She also reported that she had a happy, "normal" childhood with "no problems except what everybody has."

Although saying her mother "may have been a drunk," she denied that either parent was an alcoholic and denied ever being abused by either parent physically or emotionally. She denied any history of serious traumatic experiences in her childhood. She denied any history of sexual abuse or exposure to violence.

She told me there was no violence between members of her family of origin. Later in the interview she indicated that, "maybe . . . some of us got slapped around a little . . . nothing serious . . . just your normal stuff."

She stated that she has never been mistreated by an employer, supervisor, or coworker to the point of feeling upset about it.

She has been involved in three previous lawsuits but declined to discuss them, other than to acknowledge that two involved personal injury claims, and that she was the plaintiff in all three, not a defendant.

She admitted to having been arrested several times but did not recall how many and "anyway, it was not for nothing serious." She denied ever having been charged with a crime. Questions about possible convictions and questions about whether she had ever spent any time in jail or prison met with digressions, complaints that "that's deposition stuff" and delaying responses such as "ask me later" and "let's come back to that one."

She applied for Social Security disability benefits after her mold exposure, but the claim was denied because "my lawyer was a royal fuck-up. Any Mickey Mouse asshole could have won that."

She told me she has never been charged with driving under the influence of alcohol.

Educational history

Ms. U. completed 10 years of education. She said she dropped out of school in the 11th grade at age 17 when she married "to take care of my husband. He was young" and because "school was boring."

She told me she never failed a grade, was never held back for a year, never repeated a grade, and never skipped a grade. She said she was never suspended or expelled from school at any time in her school career. She was never in special education classes, and she denied any history of learning disabilities.

Occupational and related history

Ms. U. has worked as a waitress, a housekeeper, a "management assistant," and as an assembler and quality control assistant in an electronics manufacturing plant. She has worked in full-time or part-time employment since she was 18 except that she estimates that she was a homemaker for roughly 10 years in connection with child rearing.

At the time of her exposure, she was working as an assembler at XYZ Manufacturing, Inc.

She says she is totally disabled by toxic mold exposure. Her disability began approximately two years after her exposure, when she visited Dr. Moldcipher, who advised her that she was unable to continue full-time work due to her toxic mold symptoms. She variously explained that she had not realized she was disabled until she met the doctor, and so she had continued working through "sheer will power," was "faking it" at work, and she was being given "a helping hand" by her supervisor because he knew she had the complaints associated with this matter.

Initially she denied ever having been suspended from a job or fired. When asked if the records were in error concerning her dismissals from Company X and Company Y, she acknowledged that she has been fired twice by employers. Both times were due to unfair treatment by her employers. She was not responsible for the problems either time. Once she was fired "for standing up for my rights" when "none of the [other employees] would. They were chickenshits." The other time she was fired because her supervisor made erroneous records of her unexcused absenteeism and tardiness and these errors caused her to go over the company limit.

Description of patient at interview and mental status examination

Motor behavior

Ms. U. is right-handed. She moved with a normal gait on flat surfaces inside an office area. There was no evidence of hyperactivity or psychomotor retardation. Her energy level was within normal limits. Both gross and fine motor coordination were clinically within normal limits based on incidental observations of her movements around the office and handling materials such as snacks, soft drinks, and testing materials, with this exception: During the fine motor testing, her motor speed was inexplicably variable from moment to moment and total time was extremely slow.

Affect, mood, and demeanor

During the interview, Ms. U. appeared variably relaxed, worried, or annoyed, apparently partly in response to the topics at hand. During the testing, she appeared alert and watchful much of the time but toward the end of the day complained of boredom. Affect was appropriate to content. By self-report (with leading questions) she was experiencing depression and anxiety and a great deal of worry about her health due to her toxic mold exposure.

Attitude and interpersonal behavior

Ms. U. interacted in a variably friendly or bored but not discourteous manner during the interview and informal interactions surrounding the interview and testing. She thanked the examiner for taking an interest in her and for being courteous.

Speech

Expressive speech was fluent and clear in general, but she often contradicted herself or changed what she said (e.g., spontaneously following her statements with remarks like, "Oh, that's not what I mean" and "I take that back" and then producing a different answer to questions about her clinical history). There was no evidence of word-finding problems. There was no tangential or chaotic speech. There were no clear signs of thought disorder.

Speech comprehension was normal during the interview and incidental conversations before and after the testing, but she appeared utterly baffled by test instructions several times, even when the requested task was quite elementary. For example, she professed a lack of comprehension of the instructions to the Trail Making A task in which she was asked to connect numbers in order as quickly as possible.

When asked about her symptoms, she prefaced her answer by saying, "I want to warn you. I can't really talk about my problems . . . It's because of my post-trauma syndrome" [sic]. She then proceeded to discuss her symptoms and causal experiences with no sign of discomfort, other than indicating that certain topics were off limits based on her lawyer's advice.

She frequently declined to answer questions on the grounds that they were "irrelevant" or because "that's deposition stuff."

Thinking and perception

Ms. U. was alert and oriented × 3. There was no evidence of delusional activity. She denied any history of hallucinations.

Concentration and attention as observed clinically during the interview were grossly within normal limits. Although recognizing her self-reported level of alcohol consumption, she appeared sober and alert on the day of this evaluation.

Based on observations during the interview and related interactions, short-term memory and immediate memory were clinically normal. She readily recalled incidental observations on the day of the evaluation and the day before. Remote memory was within normal limits, clinically based on her ability to produce this history without assistance, except when advised that she would be asked a series of questions about her ability to remember information, and asked a series of questions beginning with "Are you able to remember. . . ." At that point, she commented that her memory is "terrible" for all sorts of information, including both short-term memory and long-term memory, although as noted above she also spontaneously reported that her short-term memory is "much worse" than her long-term memory. She interjected a report of steadily worsening memory deficits since the time of her injury. Her description of her short-term memory problem versus her long-term memory problem is not consistent with clinical expectations (see "Complaints" section above). Some illustrations of her purported memory lapses include an inability to recall her date of birth, her mother's maiden name, her mother's first name, the name of the dog she has had for 11 years, the names of the elementary school and high school she attended, or the name of the city in which she was born. She also reported forgetting her five sons' names at times but indicated that she was able to name them at the time of this evaluation.

She reported having no problems with seeing materials or hearing questions. She is not color blind. Ms. U. indicated that she put forth her best efforts in the testing and interview.

Tests administered and hypotheses based on test data

The following tests were administered:

Computerized Assessment of Response Bias (CARB)
Controlled Oral Word Association Test (COWAT)
Computerized Test of Attention and Memory (CTAM)
Grooved Pegboard Test (Pegs)
Minnesota Multiphasic Personality Inventory (MMPI–2)
Rey-Osterrieth Complex Figure Test (RCFT)
Stroop Color-Word Test (Comalli-Kaplan)
Test of Memory Malingering (TOMM)
Trail Making Test (TMT)
Wechsler Adult Intelligence Scale (WAIS–III)
Wechsler Memory Scale–III: Logical Memory (LM), Faces, Word Lists
Wide Range Achievement Test (WRAT–3)
Word Memory Test (WMT)

Validity tests

Ms. U.'s WMT profile was one associated with extreme exaggeration or response bias, including some below chance performance. There were indications of very poor effort on the CARB. Her performance on the TOMM was strongly indicative of poor effort and malingering. Her CTAM results provided further evidence of feigning. Her scores on the CTAM were well below chance, at a level found < 2% of the time from random answering. Her reliable digits score was in a range associated with malingering.

TABLE 23.1   Test data

Effort

TEST	VARIABLE	DATA	RESULT
CARB	CARB	Type	III
CTAM	CTAM Effort	Effort score	−6
TOMM	TOMM Trial 1	# correct	18
TOMM	TOMM Trial 2	# correct	20
WMT	WMT	Type	IV

Clinical

TEST	VARIABLE	STANDARD SCORE	APPROX PERCENTILE
COWA	FAS Fluency	67	1
Computerized Test of Attention & Memory	CTAM % Correct	39	1
Grooved Pegboard	Peg-Right	60	< 1
Grooved Pegboard	Peg-Left	56	< 1
Rey-Osterrieth Complex Figure Test (RCFT)	Immediate recall	93	30
RCFT	Recognition	60	1
RCFT	RCFT 30′ Recall	70	2
RCFT	RCFT % Retained	71	3
RCFT	RCFT Copy	67	1
Stroop (Comalli-Kaplan)	Stroop Word	47	< 1
Stroop (Comalli-Kaplan)	Stroop Color	60	< 1
Stroop (Comalli-Kaplan)	Stroop C-W	60	< 1
Trail Making Test	Trails A	27	< 1
Trail Making Test	Trails B	33	< 1
Wechsler Adult Intelligence Scale–III	VIQ	72	3
WAIS–III	PIQ	72	3
WAIS–III	FSIQ	71	3
WAIS–III	Verbal Compr	73	4
WAIS–III	Perc Org	72	3
WAIS–III	Working Mem	62	1
WAIS–III	Proc Speed	68	2
WAIS–III	Vocabulary	81	10
WAIS–III	Similarities	84	14
WAIS–III	Arithmetic	84	14
WAIS–III	Digit Span	70	2
WAIS–III	Information	70	2

(Continued . . .)

TABLE 23.1   (Continued)

Clinical

TEST	VARIABLE	DATA	RESULT
WAIS–III	Letter-Number Seq	74	4
WAIS–III	Picture Completion	71	3
WAIS–III	Digit Sym-Coding	76	5
WAIS–III	Block Design	84	14
WAIS–III	Matrix Reasoning	78	7
WAIS–III	Symbol Search	64	1
WMS–III	Log Mem I	66	1
WMS–III	Faces I	58	< 1
WMS–III	Log Mem II	70	2
WMS–III	Faces II	80	9
WMS–III	Log Mem %Ret	86	18
WMS–III	Faces–% retention	108	70
WMS–III	Word Lists I–1st	70	2
WMS–III	Word Lists I–Total	60	< 1
WMS–III	Word Lists II–Total	85	16
WMS–III	Word Lists II–% ret	91	27
WRAT–3	Reading	51	1
WRAT–3	Spelling	63	1
WRAT–3	Arithmetic	66	30

Minnesota Multiphasic Personality Inventory–2 (MMPI–2)

Validity—T scores (FBS, F-K = raw)

VRIN	TRIN	L	SD	K	F-K	F	FB	F-p	O-S	FBS	Dsr	ES
58	59	66	78	35	15	116	95	92	285	31	97	16

Clinical—T scores

HS	D	HY	PD	MF	PA	PT	SC	MA	SI
98	102	107	87	51	96	99	95	85	42

Attention/concentration

On Trails A and B and the Stroop Color, Word, Color-Word, and Interference measures, her scores were all at or below the 1st percentile. Her working memory score fell at the 1st percentile. Digit span was at the 2nd percentile.

Memory

On memory measures, Ms. U. produced scores ranging from Average to Extremely Low. The majority of her scores were lower than the mean score for the average mentally retarded examinee.

On two measures, her delayed memory performance exceeded her immediate recall. Her attention and concentration performance was far lower than her general memory testing.

Intelligence

Her Verbal, Performance, and Full Scale IQ all fell at the lower end of the Borderline range. Index scores and scaled scores ranged from the 1st to the 14th percentile.

Reasoning

On measures of conceptual thinking, Ms. U.'s performance was in the Borderline range.

Academic achievement

Ms. U. scored in the low end of the average range on the WRAT–3 Reading subtest. Spelling and Arithmetic scores were both at the 1st percentile.

Language

Measures of language functioning ranged from Low Average to Extremely Low.

Visual-motor

Visual-perceptual skill scores ranged from Extremely Low to Borderline and fine motor speed was Extremely Low.

Personality testing

As a precaution in view of her erratic complaints that included reading comprehension problems, Ms. U. was asked to read aloud the first 20 items of the MMPI–2, which she did accurately and with no evident difficulty. She was invited to ask for definitions of any words she did not understand, although advised that interpretation of each question was part of the test and therefore assistance could not be provided for interpretation. Her sole request was for a definition of the word "brood."

Although VRIN and TRIN were well within normal limits, FBS, F, F-K, Fb, Es, and Total Obvious minus Subtle were all extraordinarily elevated, and these along with the inconsistency between the extreme overall profile elevation and her observable behavior all point to malingering as the most plausible interpretation. The clinical scales cannot be meaningfully interpreted as measures of pathology. This is not to imply an absence of pathology in this examinee; rather, the point is that this particular set of data is not a valid measure of that pathology.

Diagnosis

Axis I	V65.2	Malingering
	303.90	Alcohol Dependence
	R/O 304.80	Polysubstance Dependence, by history, in remission
Axis II	R/O 301.9	Personality Disorder NOS
Axis III	Refer to appropriate specialists' reports	

Conclusions

The neuropsychological test results in this evaluation are uninterpretable, except as indications of some very minimal capabilities and as indications of lack of cooperation with the assessment. Valid neuropsychological evaluations require that the plaintiff put forth her best efforts. There is clear evidence that Ms. U. did not put forth her best efforts and that response bias explains the behavior better than neuropsychological deficits. For example, in order to score below chance on memory testing, she would have to remember information that she indicated not recalling. Her observable mental status stood in stark contrast to her test scores.

Ms. U.'s personality testing is similarly invalid. Her responses are associated with several possible explanations, only one of which applies to her. Overt disorganized psychosis, illiteracy or lack of comprehension of English, and incapacity related to concurrent influences, such as drugs, alcohol or illness, were all ruled out by a combination of observation and her denial of illness and concurrent substance use on the day of this evaluation. Consistency measures were well within normal limits, but measures such as F, F-K, Fb, Es, FBS, Total Obvious minus Subtle, the inconsistency between the extreme overall profile elevation, and her observable behavior all point to malingering.

Neuropsychological and psychological diagnoses rely in large part on subjective reports from the examinee, so the examinee's self-descriptions and history need to be complete and accurate. Based on her repeated self-contradictions during my interview and the contradictions from one examiner to the next documented in the records, she is an unreliable historian. Thus clinical diagnoses based solely on her self-reports are at best speculative. However, based on her self-report in the context of her history as documented in her medical records, it is entirely plausible to conclude that she has genuine and important psychological problems that merit professional attention. Attempts to attribute these problems to mold exposure is an unhelpful distraction in view of the present state of the art on the neuropsychology of mold exposure, along with the documentation and self-reports indicating the presence of these problems long before the mold exposure associated with this litigation.

Regarding the general causation question, the issue of possible neuropsychological effects of inhalation of mycotoxins or mold spores remains unknown. Dr. Moldcipher's conclusion that inhalation of spores and mycotoxins from *Stachybotrys atra* and aspergillus caused neuropsychological deficits and disability is post hoc conjecture and speculation. There is no basis in the scientific literature for asserting that inhalation of mold spores or mycotoxins in the residential, school, and office settings in which these cases arise causes neuropsychological impairment. These allegations are sheer speculation (for example, see Committee on Damp Spaces and Health, 2004; Fox, Greiffenstein, & Lees-Haley, 2005; Lees-Haley, 2003, 2004).

FINAL COMMENTS

How did this case end? Ironically, Ms. U. obtained a modestly large settlement. Based on a conversation later with one of the defense attorneys, the defendant's employees had made several errors, covered them up, and then lied about their errors during their depositions. The double irony is that the original errors were not egregious. Thus, if the defendant employees had admitted them and behaved responsibly, these errors would not have led to the same settlement, according to the defense attorney handling the case. She said that the consensus of speculation among the attorneys involved was that these errors were so minor that they probably would have had little impact on a jury verdict.

This was consistent with discussions the attorneys had with mock jurors. However, hiding the errors, changing documents, and lying in their depositions cast such a pall of suspicion over the people involved that the majority of participants in the mock trial in effect wondered, "If they did this, what else did they do?" and suspected the worst.

REFERENCES

Committee on Damp Spaces and Health, Board on Health Promotion and Disease Prevention, Institute of Medicine of the National Academies (2004). *Damp indoor spaces and health*. Washington, DC: National Academies Press.

Fox, D. D., Greiffenstein, M. F., & Lees-Haley, P. R. (2005). Commentary on "Cognitive impairment associated with toxigenic fungal exposure." *Applied Neuropsychology, 12*(3), 129–133.

Lees-Haley, P. R. (2003). Toxic mold and mycotoxins in neurotoxicity cases: Stachybotrys, Fusarium, Trichoderma, Aspergillus, Penicillium, Cladosporium, Alternaria, Trichothecenes. *Psychological Reports, 93*, 561–584).

Lees-Haley, P. R. (2004). Commentary on neuropsychological performance of patients following mold exposure. *Scientific Review of Mental Health Practice, 3*, 60–66.

Alleged mold toxicity

Lidia Artiola i Fortuny

Humans have shared the world with molds since the beginning of time. Molds are microscopic fungi found indoors and outdoors. Because molds are so ubiquitous, the chances are very high that we are exposed to them in a variety of environments. There are many species of molds, about 100,000 according to some experts (e.g., Terr, 2001). Of these, the Occupational Safety and Health Administration of the United States Department of Labor (OSHA) (2007) estimates that about 50 to l00 common indoor mold types have the potential for creating health problems. Physical reactions to certain types of molds are well known. Molds can cause respiratory illness, particularly in susceptible or immunosuppressed individuals. Airborne fungal allergens have been associated with allergic diseases, such as allergic rhinitis/conjunctivitis, allergic asthma, and hypersensitivity pneumonitis. Mycotoxins are natural products produced by fungi that evoke a toxic response when introduced in low concentration to higher vertebrates and other animals by a natural route. A position paper from the American College of Occupational and Environmental Medicine (ACOEM) (Bush et al., 2006) indicates that scientific evidence does not support the proposition that human health has been adversely affected by inhaled mycotoxins in the home, school, or office environment. Additionally, the contention that the presence of mycotoxins can give rise to a full array of nonspecific complaints is not consistent with what is known to occur (Bush et al., 2006). This position is also endorsed by the Institute of Medicine of the National Academies Committee on Damp Indoor Spaces and Health (2004). Additionally, there has not been sufficient research to support the notion that molds cause cognitive problems under conditions of adequate industrial hygiene in the workplace or in residences. In spite of the lack of scientifically plausible evidence that exposure to mold or mycotoxins causes measurable damage to the nervous system, in the United States there has been a veritable explosion of microbial tort litigation and a rush of claims of disability allegedly due to cognitive deficits caused by mold exposure. As has been pointed out by neuropsychologist Paul Lees-Haley: "In the context of litigation, speculative opinions are rendered in lieu of scientifically well-founded conclusions" (Lees-Haley, 2003, p. 561). The same author has warned of the dangers of hysterical claims and unfounded alarms by lawyers, doctors, and others that will have harmed many victims, if in reality it turns out that [the exposures] are neuropsychologically harmless. Lees-Haley has recommended that the effects of inhaling mycotoxins and mold spores should be explored through high-quality, well-controlled, scientific studies, rather than through speculation in adversarial settings (Lees-Haley, 2002). This view is shared by the ACOEM (Bush et al., 2006).

All these cautions notwithstanding, mold claims have become a cottage industry. Third-party suits abound. We are also seeing mold-related Worker's Compensation claims in the context of air quality concerns. Some lawyers now advertise themselves on the Internet as specializing in mold litigation.

The individual in this case presented a particularly egregious example of a baseless claim, probably made in order to detract attention from an ongoing fraud investigation. Not all individuals making claims of mold neurotoxicity give as florid and incredible a presentation as this particular claimant. This case serves as an example of the extreme claims that can be encountered in today's medical-legal arena.

The claimant alleged having sustained severe brain damage due to exposure to *Stachybotrys chartarum* on the workplace. By way of background, *Stachybotrys chartarum* (formerly known as *Stachybotrys atra*) is a greenish-black mold. It can grow on material with a high cellulose and low nitrogen content, such as fiberboard, gypsum board, paper, dust, and lint. Growth occurs when there is moisture from water damage, excessive humidity, water leaks, condensation, water infiltration, or flooding (Centers for Disease Control, 2007). Toxicologists note that exposure requires inhalation of mycotoxin-containing spores or fungal fragments in the breathable air. For example, satratoxin H can be found in a sample of material with heavy *Stachybotrys atra* growth, but *Stachybotrys* species are not easily aerosolized (Bush et al., 2006), hence, exposure via inhalation is improbable and, consequently, so is infection of the brain.

BACKGROUND

Ms. V. was a referral from an attorney specializing in Worker's Compensation claims. In his transmittal letter the attorney explained that Ms. V. was claiming total disability secondary to cognitive deficits due to mold-related toxic encephalopathy. Ms. V. claimed exposure to the mold *Stachybotrys chartarum* in her place of employment. This individual had been employed by a hospital in a low-level managerial capacity for the previous 10 years. Her office was located in the administration building, a distance from the laboratories or other areas where chemical or biological materials are handled. She had suddenly left her job six months earlier without an explanation. According to the referring attorney, Ms. V. was being investigated by her employer for suspicion of embezzlement of funds. On the day she walked out of her job, her superiors had sent her an e-mail summoning her to discuss the findings of the investigation. She never showed up for the meeting, gathered her belongings shortly after receiving the e-mail, and left the premises never to return. She proceeded to file a disability claim.

Ms. V.'s office was inspected by an independent environmental health company shortly after Ms. V. vacated it. No evidence of *Stachybotrys chartarum* was found beyond some isolated spores behind the baseboards. This was felt to be of no significance. According to the referral source, no other employee working in the same building as Ms. V. had reported any difficulties with mold or any other type of exposure at any point.

REVIEW OF RECORDS

In what the legal system refers to as *answers to interrogatories*, which is the formal means of exchanging key information between parties of a lawsuit, Ms. V. indicated that her injury occurred over the previous five years, with acute exposure occurring during a specific day about two years before the current assessment. Records indicated that the claimant saw Dr. AH, a physician specializing in toxicology, complaining that there had been a significant amount of water damage to the office area in which she worked. She indicated to Dr. AH that she smelled a musty odor two days earlier when she entered the building after she had been on vacation for a week. She said that during her absence there had been significant rains and water accumulation had apparently occurred in the building. Ms. V. also reported that in the past she had seen mold on the walls, but on that particular occasion there was an "extremely powerful" odor that she identified as being associated with moisture and molds. She reported that by noon she felt so ill that she had to leave work. Since her exposure on an almost daily basis, she had been experiencing headaches, numbness and tingling, lightheadedness and dizziness, tremulousness and shaking, confusion, feeling spacy, inability to concentrate, slurred words, difficulty finding words, low energy, fatigue of an unusually intense nature, itchy, watery eyes and nose, visual problems, ringing in the ears, rapid pulse, and palpitations. Insomnia and cessation of breathing [sic] during sleep were also reported. Coordination difficulties and dizziness when standing up after sitting occurred on a weekly basis. Nausea without vomiting was also reported. She insisted she had been in perfect health before the alleged exposure. Dr. AH felt that the claimant may have been exposed to toxicogenic molds and mycotoxins commonly associated with several different species of molds associated with structural water damage. There appeared to be no attempt at independent verification of alleged exposure or complaints. Dr. AH placed the claimant on medical leave, ordered a number of tests, including a quantitative electro-encephalogram (qEEG) and a complete neuropsychological examination, advised that an industrial hygienist should assess the severity of the problem, and recommended co-workers should not be permitted to enter offices potentially involved in the exposure.

Dr. AH saw the claimant again three weeks later. Once again, she presented with a large number of complaints, among others, inability to concentrate, memory problems, poor appetite, coughing, bloating, gas, cessation of breathing during sleep, headaches, nasal symptoms, fingertips turning white or blue, reflux of stomach acid, and nausea. Dr. AH thought that the claimant was signifi-cantly impaired with regard to remembering or following instructions, thinking clearly while read-ing, thinking clearly while doing simple arithmetic, writing or typing for more than an hour, interact-ing with people, and maintaining a regular work schedule. Additionally, he opined that she was "slightly impaired with regard to driving a car in heavy traffic, lifting 5–10 pounds with any fre-quency, or walking even short distances frequently." In a later office report, Dr. AH indicated that the claimant's situation was consistent with mycotoxicosis. Dr. AH's conclusions were based on "clinical impressions" and the results on a number of nonspecific immune-based tests.[1]

The claimant saw Dr. JO, a psychologist, two weeks later at Dr. AH's behest. Dr. JO's practice area is in the administration of quantitative encephalograms (qEEG) and neurotherapy.[2] Dr. JO's impression was that an analysis of Ms. V.'s qEEG was considered deviant and/or abnormal, with the frontal and frontal temporal areas of the cortex being the sites of greatest abnormalities. He recom-mended neurotherapy, and in fact Ms. V. underwent neurotherapy treatment using qEEG twice a week for a period of two years.

The claimant was examined by Dr. DT, a physician specializing in toxicology, during a fitness for duty evaluation. Dr. DT felt that the history indicated that the claimant "had progressive symptoms which had been going on for the past five years; although she has never sought medical treatment until they became acutely worse in spring of this year." Dr. DT was of the opinion that there was cognitive dysfunction of undetermined etiology and felt that the issue of toxicogenic molds needed to be further investigated. Dr. DT released the claimant to work with restrictions.

In June 2001, Dr. AH authored a letter to the claimant's employer making the recommendation that she return to work under Dr. DT's recommendations, which included that she not try to hold any supervisory position, adding the restriction that she was not to return to her normal workspace until testing at her place of work was completed for mold and mold spores.

Two weeks later, Dr. AH authored a letter to the claimant's employer. In that letter he indicated that he had discussed Ms. V.'s situation with Dr. JO, and that Dr. JO had indicated that Ms. V.'s abnormalities were "extremely severe," and that "the brain wave patterns he had found on quantita-tive electroencephalography were consistent with what you would expect to find in an 80-year-old

---

[1] "The practice of performing large numbers of nonspecific immune-based tests as an indication of mold exposure or mold-related illness is not evidence based and is to be discouraged" (Bush et al., 2006, p. 330).
[2] Neurotherapy, also known as neurofeedback and electroencephalographic (EEG) neurofeedback, is a form of behavior modification that uses EEG biofeedback technology to increase voluntary control over the amplitude and pattern of various brain wave frequencies. Proponents of this method claim that modifying brain wave patterns is effective against anxiety reactions, mood disorders, substance abuse, attention deficit disorders, and various other mental and emotional problems. However, it is not an empirically tested or proven treatment for behavior disorders (Lohr et al., 2001).

woman suffering significant dementia."[3] Further, he indicated that while progress was being made in neurotherapy, the claimant was "far from being ready to return to work." Dr. AH advised that Ms. V. should not return to work.

A few months later, the claimant was examined out-of-state by neuropsychologist Dr. RM, whose neuropsychological results were interpreted to show problems in verbal recall, Digit Symbol substitution, and reduced Information and Picture Completion. No symptom validity tests were administered. Dr. RM stated that "the diagnosis points to encephalopathy due to mold and myco-toxins causing brain impairment." No attempt was made at differential diagnosis. Examination of raw data provided by Dr. RM revealed scores within the normal range in all areas. It was not clear why Dr. RM interpreted the results as indicative of deficits of any sort.

In December 2001, Ms. V. was examined by three physicians during an independent group evaluation. The group's diagnostic impressions were as follows:

1. Multiple symptoms that allegedly were related to industrial airborne exposure, with no objective findings.
2. Clinical history suggestive of sleep apnea.
3. Systemic hypertension.

The group indicated that if further information were needed on the claimant regarding cognitive impairment and pulmonary impairment, formal neuropsychological testing and formal pulmonary function testing would be appropriate.

NEUROPSYCHOLOGICAL EVALUATION

Presenting complaints

According to the claimant, three years earlier she started having a number of problems with atten-tion and concentration, as well as memory. Additionally, she experienced difficulties with language, hearing, fatigue, and "pain everywhere for no apparent reason." She attributed her difficulties to exposure to a fungus, specifically *Stachybotrys chartarum*, while at work. The claimant had not returned to any sort of employment at the time of this evaluation.

The claimant was asked to make a list of the difficulties she had been experiencing since her alleged toxic exposure. She asked if she could avail herself of a list she had prepared beforehand. The list read as follows:

Automotor control dysfunction, character recognition problems, concentration problems, con-fusion, depression, dialing/typing efficiency problems, disorientation, internal clock dysfunction, irrational irritability, long and short term memory loss, mood swings, multitasking problems, numerical calculation ability loss, perception impairment, planning difficulties, spatial form and other visualization and recognition difficulty, speech and spelling impairment, word recognition/ finding problems, abdominal discomfort, nausea, coordination problems, diarrhea/constipation, dizziness, extremities going numb, debilitating fatigue, gas, headache, hearing deterioration, high blood pressure, insomnia, interior shakiness, jerking in sleep, joint discomfort, loss of motivation, muscle discomfort/sharp pains, muscle spasm/twitching, nervousness, numbness,

---

[3] There remains a lack of consensus about the clinical role of qEEG. The appropriate use of qEEG in both clinical settings and in medical-legal circumstances remains undetermined. Justification for use of qEEG in forensic evaluations of alleged mold neurotoxicity remains elusive.

palpitations, poor appetite, rapid pulse, reflex stomach acid, ringing/rushing in the ears, sleep apnea, sleeping while awake, snoring loudly, stomach/intestinal problems, unquenchable thirst, tingling, tremors/shaking, tunnel vision, migraine, visual deterioration/changes, weakness.

Ms. V. also endorsed multiple problems in response to intake, memory, and sleep questionnaires. She stressed that she previously had exceptional memory. When these problems started in the spring, she could not even talk or communicate, although there had been some improvement. She attributed this improvement to the fact that she is no longer exposed to the mold, and to the neurotherapy that she had been receiving from Dr. JO. She reported tunnel vision sporadically. Sometimes her vision "closes" down, and she "cannot see in the middle" but "can see around." Ms. V. was not certain whether she experienced changes in sense of smell, but described "funny smells" sometimes. More often, she noticed "unnatural smells." Ms. V. reported that for the longest time she ran into doors. She initially thought she was unable to open doors, like "turn knobs." Her fingers reportedly did not necessarily do what she wanted.

Ms. V. reported pain everywhere, for no reason. Sometimes "I experience pain on one spot at a time, like an electric shock or a needle, usually several times a day." Regarding her personality, Ms. V. indicated that she was not as outgoing as previously and became extremely embarrassed in public (she was unable to elaborate on what embarrassed her). Though formerly not irritable, now she becomes "real pissed, real fast" about anything. She also reported depression and frequent crying. Sexual difficulties were denied.

When asked what she did for entertainment, Ms. V. replied that she had been a basketball fan, but quit watching because "it irritates me, freaking out—too much to do with watching the game and someone talking to me." Soon after the exposure, she could not remember questions long enough to be able to come up with an answer. She also indicated, "automatic things disappear" and gave as an example that she even has walked into doors, having to think about "every single step" of how to do things. For example, taking showers is still not normal because "I have to pay attention or I forget what I haven't washed."

Regarding the alleged exposure, she indicated that for five years the ceiling in her office leaked every time it rained. She described the entire ceiling and west wall as having been saturated with water. "Mold grows on these things, toxic mold." "They said it was not there, and they finally found it." When asked who found it, she replied "the employer." Ms. V. reportedly always tried to get everything cleaned out and dried out. That day, when she returned from vacation, "I felt like I was having a stroke. I could not feel my heart, my temple, my ears, my fingers. I tried to call someone. I could not figure out how to do that. I could not figure out how to work a computer. I left. I drove home. I never returned. I do not remember driving home." The claimant indicated that she disposed of all the contents of her home, her and her husband's belongings. She said that she and her husband had to replace everything they owned, except for what was in storage. She indicated that she had someone "take off" the house, "destroy it," and they built another house. (This information was not true.)

When asked about the embezzlement investigation by her employer, Ms. V. denied knowing anything about it.

Ms. V. reported that she has attempted to return to work and that she has "tried mental and physical exercises." She could not give information on where she had attempted to obtain employment. However, her doctors had not released her to work.

Ms. V. reported taking several medications, but could not provide their names. She agreed to provide a list at a later time.

Significant-other interview

The claimant's husband of 20 years, Mr. V., was interviewed separately. He described his wife as having been an "incredibly intelligent" person. She had a hilarious sense of humor, she was very physically active, riding race bikes, climbing mountains, and training horses. She was able to "figure out anything." Mr. V. described his marriage with Ms. V. as "very good." He indicated that in early April 2001 his wife showed up at home before the end of the workday. She did not know why she had come home. She had a headache and ringing in the ears and went to bed. The next day Ms. V. was not feeling better and decided not to go to work. She thought she might have picked up a "bug." She complained of chest problems. Mr. V took his wife to Dr. AH. Dr. AH felt that perhaps she had been exposed to a mold (it is not clear why this conclusion was reached). Ms. V. became depressed three or four days after the alleged exposure. Mr. V said that it was "like my wife had had a stroke." By his description, she had nausea, muscle spasms, she was unable to complete sentences, her speech was slurred, and she could not remember anything. Ms. V. also experienced unusual physical symptoms: she stumbled, her speech was halting, she was unable to work on the computer, and she could not use the telephone or anything with numbers. Specifically, she could not remember how to run appliances or draw, symptoms that were ongoing at the time of the evaluation. She could not remember aspects of her past (e.g., her wedding, where they were married—although she did remember when he proposed to her). Recently, she did not recognize a longtime friend. According to Mr. V., his wife has improved since the first couple of months, particularly since she started going to Dr. JO for "brain retraining" twice a week. He has noticed that slowly her abilities are coming back. He also indicated that the claimant's mood depends on the day. She becomes frustrated very easily concerning not being able to do things she previously was able to do. During a normal day, the claimant arises between 1 a.m. and 5 a.m., goes to her office, and plays with the computer, "brain games and other games." She needs to be told when simple chores need to be done. Everything takes longer than normal. According to Mr. V., his wife "is paranoid about driving" and is attempting to train herself to drive again, but can only operate a motor vehicle within the confines of their property. Reportedly, Ms. V. tends to wander off when he takes her shopping.

Mr. V. also endorsed numerous problems with proactive, recent, and remote memory when he completed a questionnaire regarding Ms. V.'s memory.

Background history

Ms. V. is a 45-year-old, right-handed woman born in one of the Southern states. At the time of the evaluation, she had lived in the Southwest for 15 years. She denied ever experiencing difficulty learning to read, write, spell, or perform elementary math as a child. She reported having completed high school with an A average. She went to college "for years" but did not obtain a bachelor's degree. In the intake form, she indicated having attended a state university and another college during the 1970s. In her deposition, she indicated, "it seems I spent some time at a third college, but I couldn't find any records." Apparently, at the third school she had particular difficulty with agriculture, but "the teacher was wrong." No records on this woman's formal education were available. When evaluated, she reported she was supporting herself through investments and an inheritance. Although she had been employed in a variety of low-level managerial positions during the previous two decades, she appeared unable to name her employers.

The claimant was an only child raised in a middle class two-parent family. Her father was a real estate broker, and her mother was a homemaker. The claimant's parents were both college educated. She denied a history of abuse of any sort in the family of origin.

Ms. V. had been married for approximately 20 years. Her husband was unemployed. The couple had no children.

Family medical history appeared to be noncontributory. The claimant denied any significant past medical history. Medical records before the alleged injury were not available and, according to the referral source, efforts to obtain them had failed. Ms. V. indicated that she did not know she had high blood pressure until "this happened." A list of the medications she was taking at the time of the evaluation included Pulmicort 200 mg bid, and Accupril 10 mg once a day for hypertension.

Additionally, there was a list of *seven* nonprescription medical supplements and *ten* herbal detoxicants. She specifically denied ever having sustained a traumatic head injury. She also denied ever having received mental health treatment or hospitalization before that time. Use of tobacco products was denied. She admitted to having one alcoholic drink per week, and denied any past history of excessive alcohol consumption. Present and past use of recreational drugs was denied.

Physical appearance

Ms. V. presented as a well-looking woman of 5′ 8″ in height and appearing significantly obese at a reported 240 lb of weight. She ambulated normally, with no obvious postural disorder. Ms. V. was able to sit for long periods of time without apparent discomfort. Hygiene and dress were appropriate.

Behavioral observations

The claimant presented as a quiet woman who expressed herself in an unusual manner. Speech was remarkable for the fact that she frequently stopped in the middle of a sentence, apparently trying to come up with a specific name, coming up with near answers, or with a description of function (e.g., lawyer, the mold in question), and then, a number of minutes later, when we had moved on to a different subject, she frequently came out with the word spontaneously. She frequently used vague, imprecise language, but sentences were well formed. During the clinical interview, she took a long time to respond to each question. Responses were generally vague, frequently devoid of substance, and frequently bizarre.

Ms. V.'s mood was thought to be depressed and affect was constricted. She appeared to experience no difficulty filling out her demographic questionnaire, although she attempted to obtain her husband's assistance completing a memory questionnaire. Behavior toward both the examiner and the technical assistant was appropriate at all times. During interview, the claimant appeared guarded. There were a number of very bizarre responses to simple questions. For example, when asked about her occupation she indicated: "I was a nurse." But she said she did not remember what she did. When asked if she had a degree in nursing, she said, "I don't remember." "I used to take care of people."

Observations by the testing assistant were as follows: Ms. V. cooperated in that she showed no overt resistance to taking the tests. She experienced no difficulty whatsoever understanding instructions. She was sometimes very quick to say "I don't know" if she thought she was not able to answer. Ms. V. appeared to give up easily. This was especially true with tasks requiring mental juggling, math, or complex visual images. She appeared to have word-finding difficulties, there was some circumlocution, and she appeared to be slow in formulating verbal responses. Sometimes the content was vague, with frequent use of such terms as "stuff" or "thing." At the beginning of testing, her emotions seemed to be labile. She became tearful for no apparent reason. She expressed concern that we (this office) "won't find anything wrong and will report that I'm lying." She indicated, "There's a lot of things this company covers in issues related to my case and the damage being done to other people." She reported having seen four doctors meet together prior to testing and examining her, and that they talked amongst themselves "to decide what they had to do for the company attorneys." She indicated she used to be excellent at "putting things together" at "visualizing things and at spatial skills." She could "see things and put them together in my mind." Ms. V. appeared to have difficulty providing autobiographical memory (for example, how many years she went to college, where she lived, when and for how long).

She complained that she always has a headache. She took frequent short breaks during testing. She frequently interrupted the technician or interrupted herself while taking tests to ask questions, which may or may not have been relevant to the particular test or to testing in general.

During the first testing day, she took seven to eight breaks plus lunch. She also had one very long break (20 minutes) because she said she became confused by traffic and could not figure out how to get back across the street. On the second testing day, she took three breaks plus lunch. These breaks were 10 to 20 minutes long. At one point, during the second day, she was coughing. The technician offered cough drops and asked if she was catching a cold. She said, "no, it's because of the thing" (implying the exposure). Ms. V. indicated that she did not want her spelling test results released to anyone, not even her husband, because, "it's too embarrassing." She said, however, that it would be fine to release the final score and the report.

The claimant and her husband had prepared a "cheat sheet" that they keep for helping them fill out forms and keep track of information. She initially said we could keep it. On Day 2 of the examination, she wanted it back. She appeared upset when the technician indicated it was not in her possession (the technician usually keeps only testing materials with her, not the entire claimant file). The material was on the secretarial desk with the rest of the claimant's file. She did not want to leave the copy of the cheat sheet behind.

Procedures

Clinical interview; interview with the claimant's husband; Trail Making Tests (A and B); Symbol Digit Modalities Test; Stroop Color-Word Test; Controlled Oral Word Association Test; Thurstone Word Fluency Test; Rey-Osterrieth Figure (Copy, Delayed Recall); Wechsler Adult Intelligence Scale–III, Boston Naming Test, Paced Serial Addition Test, Story Memory Test; Figure Memory Test; Personality Assessment Inventory; Grip Strength; Finger Tapping; Dot Counting Test, Word Memory Test.

Orientation

The claimant was well oriented to person, time, place, and circumstance. She was aware of national news. Regarding international events, she said: "Terrorists. It's on their territory—they have the advantage." She correctly identified the current President, but identified Mr. Carter as his predecessor. She was able to draw the face of a clock, placing the hands at the appropriate requested time. Reproduction of the Necker cube showed good preservation of the three-dimensional element. Handwriting was well formed. Writing a simple sentence on dictation was educationally congruent. When completing office forms the claimant's responses and handwriting were consistent with a high school education or more.

Neuropsychological results

There were a number of indications that Ms. V.'s did not put forth consistent best efforts during testing. Specifically, she performed poorly on the two measures of motivation and cooperation that were administered. Her performance on the WMT was indicative of grossly suboptimal effort, and is associated with an attempt to appear more impaired than is truly the case. Additionally, Ms. V.'s pattern of performance on the Dot Counting Test has been associated in the literature with inadequate or inconsistent motivation or effort during neuropsychological testing: In all test items, the claimant took longer to count the grouped dots than the ungrouped dots. Unfortunately these results call into question the validity and representativeness of the rest of the test scores reported above. Other evidence of poor effort was present and included the following: near misses to simple questions, gross discrepancies from expected norms, inconsistency between reported and observed symptoms, avoidance, bizarre responses on standard tests, and discrepancies on test findings that measures similar cognitive ability (Table 24.1).

TABLE 24.1   Neuropsychological test scores

Name:	Ms. V.	
Year of testing:	2003	
Year of birth:	1968	
Age at testing:	45 years	

WAIS-III[1]

	IQ Equivalents of SS	T Score
Verbal IQ:	90	25
Performance IQ:	95	37
Full Scale IQ	91	27
Verbal Comprehension Index	100	50
Perceptual Organization	103	58
Working Memory	82	12
Processing Speed	68	2

Trail Making Test[2]		
Trail A	41	37
Trail B	138	29

Stroop Color-Word Test[3]			Percentile
Color-Word	40		<2

Thurstone Fluency Test[4]	38	40

Paced Auditory Serial Addition Test[5]		Z score
Presentation Rate 2.4″	26	−1.7
Presentation Rate 2.0″	22	−1.9
Presentation Rate 1.6″	19	−1.2
Presentation Rate 1.2″	10	−1.44

Symbol Digit Modalities Test[6]		
Written	25	−2.75
Oral	30	−3

Boston Naming Test[7]	36	−6.9	
			Percentile
Token Test[8]	40		24

Controlled Oral Word Association Test[9]	34	−0.6

Rey-Osterrieth Complex Figure[10]		
Copy	35	1
30′ Delayed Recall	18.5	0.3

California Verbal Learning Test[11]		
Trial 1	6	−1
Trial 5	14	1
Trials 1–5 Total	51	47
Trial B	4	−2
Short Delay Free Recall	5	−2
Short Delay Cued Recall	6	−3
Long Delay Free Recall	8	−1
Long Delay Cued Recall	8	−2

Story Memory Test[12]		T score
Learning	5.7	29
Loss after 4-h delay (%loss)	38.2	27

Figure Memory Test[13]

Learning	17	55
Loss after 4-h delay (%loss)	47.1	30

Finger Tapping Test[14]

Right	35.2	26
Left	29.4	21

Grip Test[15]

Right	63.7	67
Left	64.3	73

Wide Range Achievement Test–III[16]

		Percentile
Reading	27	2
Spelling	36	6
Arithmetic	34	9

Peabody Individual Achievement Test–R[17]

		Grade Equivalent
Reading Comprehension subtest	70	*Post High School*

Word Memory Test[18]

Immediate Recognition IR	37.5 FAIL
Delayed Recognition DR	32.5 FAIL
Consistency CNS	65 FAIL
Multiple Choice MC	25 WARNING
Paired Associates PA	35 WARNING
Free Recall DFR	20
Long Delay Free Recall LDFR	10

Dot Counting[19]

Grouped		*Percentile*
Card 1	3.2	0
Card 2	8	0
Card 3	6	0
Card 4	7.6	0
Card 5	10.7	0
Card 6	19	0
Ungrouped		
Card 1	3.7	50
Card 2	6.2	25
Card 3	10	0
Card 4	13	0–25
Card 5	13	25
Card 6	15	25

Notes: [1]Wechsler, 1997; [2]Heaton et al., 1991; [3]Golden, 1978; [4]Heaton et al., 1991; [5]Mitrushina et al., 2005; [6]Smith, 1973; [7]Kaplan et al., 1983; [8]Benton & Hamsher, 1989; [9]Gladsjo et al., 1999; [10]Spreen & Strauss, 1991; [11]Delis et al., 2000; [12]Heaton et al., 1991; [13]Heaton et al., 1991; [14]Heaton et al., 1991; [15]Heaton et al., 1991; [16]Wilkinson, 1993; [17]Markwardt, 1989; [18]Green et al., 1996; [19]Lezak, 1995.

Psychological status

Personality evaluation and screening for possible psychopathology were achieved through clinical interview and administration of the Personality Assessment Inventory (PAI). The PAI provides a number of validity indices that are designed to provide an assessment of factors that could distort the results of testing. The claimant endorsed items that present an unfavorable impression or represent particularly bizarre and unlikely symptoms. This result was indicative of exaggeration of complaints and problems. The pattern indicated a level of distortion that renders the test results uninterpretable.

Impression

Approximately three years following alleged chronic and acute exposure to the mold *Stachybotrys chartarum*, Ms. V. generated a neuropsychological profile that puts into question her credibility. Indeed, there is evidence that the claimant did not put forth maximum effort into completing the tests. She produced a number of results that do not constitute a clinically identifiable pattern in neuropsychology. Subjective complaints were exceptionally numerous, bizarre, and frequently implausible and not credible. There were claims of forgotten biographical information and claims of forgetting how to proceed in a number of activities of daily living (such as how to take a shower). Claims of significant disability arising from such implausible symptoms were not demonstrated.

Ms. V. showed some variability in tests of attention and concentration. Also, she performed worse than she had previously in very similar or identical tests. She performed extremely poorly in some tests of language, including naming, and also on some tests of scholastic ability. Such performances were much worse than expected given her linguistic competence in real life and her stated occupational achievement. Ms. V. generally performed well in tests of verbal memory, with some difficulty with long-term spontaneous recall but no evidence of a recognition disorder. Delayed visual memory was normal in one test and below expectation in another. More importantly, as mentioned in the previous paragraph, in tests designed to assess the validity of complaints, Ms. V.'s results indicate that level of effort was problematic.

The claimant's failure to show impairment outside the context of the evaluation (e.g., she was able to complete forms and clearly able to take care of her own personal needs independently), her guardedness, her vagueness, her reported remote memory failures, her performance changes on parallel testing, her worsening performance on tests successfully completed during the earlier alleged post-injury period, her neuropsychological results consistent with statistical rules for detecting malingering, her test scores outside of predicted confidence intervals, the inconsistency between her test behavior and known neurological syndromes, her clinical presentation, her very bizarre statements during interview and testing, and her failure to show improvement upon removal from the allegedly toxic environment are strongly indicative of deception. Inconsistencies between current and past test results are thought to reflect an attempt to manipulate the data. Also noted is the presence of serious professional issues immediately preceding the alleged acute exposure of April 2001 (stated in the attorney's transmittal letter).[4] Similarly, nobody else in the building had complaints that could be related to mold exposure. The conclusion was that the test results did not represent an accurate representation of Ms. V.'s true level of cognitive functioning. The results indicated, however, that the claimant was attempting to present herself as damaged or deficient. Given the strong evidence that Ms. V. portrayed herself unfavorably, exaggerated her symptomatology to an extreme degree, and put insufficient effort into completing the tests, the most likely diagnosis was Malingering (DSM–IV: v65.2).

A desire to exaggerate symptomatology may, and frequently does, co-exist with psychopathology and with genuine neuropsychological deficits. This can occur when the potential for secondary gain is significant. There was not enough information (through records or claimant's reports) to determine whether, in addition to malingering, there was also evidence of significant psychopathology. The recommendation was that if Ms. V.'s complaints persisted beyond the time of resolution of Worker's Compensation case, psychiatric assessment should be considered along with further neuropsychological investigation.

---

[4] Shortly after completing the report on this claimant, Ms. V. was indicted on charges of embezzlement.

CONCLUSION

Three months after this claimant was examined, this clinician testified at an industrial commission hearing. The testimony at hearing lasted approximately 45 minutes, during which time defense counsel asked for a detailed explanation of the opinion that the claimant was malingering. Her lawyer asked specific questions about his clinician's disagreement with other clinicians regarding his client's diagnosis. Testimony was given regarding other clinicians' failure to administer symptom validity tests, failure to consider the claimant's bizarre and essentially incredible clinical presentation, and failure to develop a differential diagnosis. The case was dismissed by the judge.

Appropriate diagnosis of mold-related illness (or other neurotoxicants) is based upon a clinical decision-making process that includes state of the art knowledge of the possible effects of potential neurotoxicants on cognition, behavior, and health. In this process, numerous interacting medical, psychiatric, and motivational factors must be considered. The evaluation requires the usual careful medical and personal history taking, administration of relevant measures of cognition, administration of symptom validity tests, and appropriate investigation of the mold-infested environment. The Centers for Disease Control (2007) acknowledge the need for taking precautions in mold-infested environments, but a link between mold exposure and cognitive deficits has not been established. A process of elimination of other possible sources of problems is required. In this case, the claimant's questionable test performance and clinical presentation essentially eliminated further perusal into possible etiologies of disease, at least in the confines of this forensic evaluation. Possible motivations behind this woman's desire to appear sick were considered. The possibility of co-existing psychopathology could not be categorically excluded. However, Ms. V.'s disingenuous clinical presentation, her lack of honesty about easily verifiable facts, the outlandish nature of some of her claimed losses, and her implausible reports of disability led to the conclusion that simple secondary gain and/or the desire to avoid facing criminal charges were the most plausible motivating factor(s). In fact, insofar as the central theme of malingering is that the person deliberately pretends to have an illness or disability in order to receive financial or other gain, or to avoid punishment or responsibility, Ms. V. embodies this definition.

Lastly, the egregious nature of this woman's presentation would not have been possible without the explicit or implicit complicity of some health and legal professionals. Examination of the records available suggests that a number of the clinicians who examined this woman "bypassed scientific evidence in favor of wholesale scare tactics is critical to the dissemination of toxic mold rhetoric" (Lees-Haley, 2003, p.14). As long as there are clinicians who choose to ignore scientific evidence and opt to use "scare tactics" to create or influence beliefs about disease states, real or imaginary, there will be individuals eager to embrace these beliefs. These beliefs can serve as an explanation or an excuse for their personal misery—and a justification for avoiding facing its root causes—or an excuse to obtain easy and undeserved compensation, or both. These beliefs can be associated with aggressive use and abuse of medical and psychological resources.

As of this writing, there is no scientific basis for claims of cognitive or emotional injuries by inhalation of mold-related products. Credible scientists are asking for well-controlled scientific studies to determine whether or not there are effects of mold exposure and mycotoxin inhalation. Such studies, not media sensationalism or propaganda from legal professionals eager to create victims or medical or psychological professionals who prefer to speculate on false beliefs, should guide the responsible examiner.

REFERENCES

Benton, A., & Hamsher, K. (1989). *Multilingual Aphasia Examination–2nd ed., Manual of instructions*. Iowa City, Iowa: AJA Associates.

Board of Health Promotion and Disease Prevention, Institute of Medicine of the National Academies (2004). *Damp indoor spaces and health*. Washington (DC): The National Academies Press.

Bush, R. K., Portnoy, J. M., Saxon, A., Terr, A. I., & Wood, R. A. (2006). The medical effects of mold exposure. *Journal of Allergy and Clinical Immunology, 117*, 326–333.

Centers for Disease Control (2007). Facts about toxic mold. Retrieved February 10, 2007 from http://www.cdc.gov/mold/stachy.htm#Q2

Delis, D., Kramer, J. H., Kaplan, E., & Ober, B. (2000). *The California Verbal Learning Test–2nd ed*. New York: Psychological Corporation.

Gladsjo, J. A., Miller, S. W., & Heaton. R. K. (1999). *Norms for letter and category fluency: Demographic corrections for age, education, and ethnicity*. Odessa, FL: Psychological Assessment Resources.

Golden, C. J. (1978). *Stroop Color and Word Test*. Chicago: Stoelting Company.

Green, P., Allen, L., & Astner, K. (1996). *The Word Memory Test: A users guide to the oral and computer-administered forms*, US version 1.1. Durham, NC: CogniSyst.

Heaton, R. K., Grant, I., & Matthews, C. G. (1991). *Comprehensive norms for an expanded Halstead-Reitan Battery*. Odessa, FL: Psychological Assessment Resources, Inc.

Kaplan, E., Goodglass, H., & Weintraub, S. (1983) *The Boston Naming Test–2nd ed*. Philadelphia: Lea & Febiger.

Lees-Haley, P. R. (2002). Mold toxicity: Validity, reliability, and baloney. *Quackwatch* Consumer Health Digest 02–53. Available online at http://www.quackwatch.com/search/webglimpse.cgi?ID=1&query=Lees-Haley

Lees-Haley, P. R. (2003). Toxic mold and mycotoxins in neurotoxicity cases: Stachybotrys, Fusarium, Trichoderma, Aspergillus, Penicillium, Cladosporium, Alternaria, Trichothecenes. *Psychological Reports, 93*, 561–584.

Lezak, M. D. (1995). *Neuropsychological assessment–3rd ed*. New York: Oxford University Press.

Lohr, J. M., Meunier, S. A., & Parker, L. M. (2001). Neurotherapy does not qualify as an empirically supported behavioral treatment for psychological disorders. *Behavior Therapist, 24*, 97–104.

Markwardt, J. (1989). *Peabody Individual Achievement Test–Revised, manual*. Circle Pines, MN: American Guidance Service (AGS).

Mitrushina, M., Boone, K. B., Razani, J., & D'Elia, L. F. (2005). *Handbook of normative data for neuropsychological assessment*, 2nd ed. New York: Oxford University Press.

Smith, A. (1973). *Symbol Digits Modality Test*. Los Angeles: Western Psychological Services.

Spreen, O., & Strauss, E. (1991). *A compendium of neuropsychological tests: Administration, norms, and commentary*. New York: Oxford University Press.

Terr, A. I. (2001). Stachybotrys: Relevance to human disease. *Annals of Allergy, Asthma, and Immunology, 87*, 57–63.

U.S. Department of Labor Occupational Safety & Health Administration (2007). Mold: Q and A. Retrieved February 28, 2007 from http://www.osha.gov/SLTC/molds/recognition.html

Wechsler, D. (1997). *Wechsler Adult Intelligence Scale–III*. San Antonio, TX: The Psychological Corporation/Harcourt Brace & Company.

Wilkinson, G. S. (1993). *The Wide Range Achievement Test: Administration manual*. Wilmington, DE: Wide Range, Inc.

Chronic pain as a context for malingering

25

Kevin J. Bianchini and Kevin W. Greve

A common source of physical disability attributed to work and other injuries is pain. Pain complaints result in millions of physician office visits per year (Woodwell & Cherry, 2004) and as many as 150 million days of lost work to the U.S. labor force (Guo, Tanaka, Cameron, Seligman, Behrens, & Ger, 1995; Guo, Tanaka, Halperin, & Cameron, 1999). Low back pain is one of the most debilitating, frequent, and costly health complaints. Of all major musculoskeletal complaints, low back pain is the symptom that is most related to poor health-related quality of life measures (Morken, Riise, Moen, Bergum, Hauge, Holien, et al., 2002).

Low back pain is also the most common musculoskeletal symptom (Picavet & Schouten, 2003), with the six-month incidence of clinically significant (disabling) low back pain at approximately 8% of the general adult population (George, 2002) and estimates of lifetime incidence range from 11 to 84% (Walker, 2000). Neck pain is another common condition in the industrialized world, often attributed to automotive accidents, with approximately half of motor vehicle accidents resulting in neck pain symptoms (Galasko, 1997, as cited in Dvir, Prushansky, & Peretz, 2001).

A significant portion of the cost of low back pain is accounted for by disability claims (Frymoyer & Cats-Baril, 1991). The high incidence of low back pain disability claims has had an "explosive socioeconomic impact" (Hazard, Reeves, & Fenwick, 1992, p. 1065), with estimates that it cost the equivalent of 1.7% of a gross national product of some western countries (van Tulder, Koes, & Bouter, 1995). Compensation status has been linked to outcome in surgery (Harris, Mulford, Solomon, van Gelder, & Young, 2005; Vaccaro, Ring, Scuderi, Cohen, & Garfin, 1997) and out-patient rehabilitation (Rainville, Sobel, Hartigan, & Wright, 1997) for back pain. Also, the return-to-work rates are lowest for back pain patients relative to all work-related injuries (Tate, 1992).

Much of the cost of neck injuries associated with automotive accidents may be generated by the incentive inherent in compensation systems. When one Canadian province instituted tort reform (i.e., changed to a no-fault automotive accident) the incidence of neck pain (whiplash) claims declined by 28% and the length of disability claimed declined by 200 days, despite an increase in the overall number of motor-vehicle accidents during the same period (Cassidy, Carroll, Cote, Berglund, & Nygren, 2003).

While the nature of the pathology and the magnitude of the resulting pain is often the primary medical focus, ultimately, the relevant practical question is *not* just "how much pain is this person experiencing," but "to what degree is this person disabled by their pain?" Thus, the *magnitude of pain-related disability* is a critical question for clinicians examining patients with pain (Bianchini, Greve, & Glynn, 2005). The disability guidelines of the American Medical Association (Cocchiarella & Andersson, 2001) quantify disability based on "objective findings of biological dysfunction" (p. 569) and clear causal links between the pathophysiology and observed signs and symptoms.

Unfortunately, objective physical findings do not fully explain the breadth and magnitude of disability seen in many patients with pain (Boden, Davis, Dina, Patronas, & Wiesel, 1990; Boden,

McCowin, Davis, Dina, Mark, & Wiesel, 1990). Therefore, examination of painful conditions and decisions/estimates of disability require substantial reliance upon subjective symptom report of pain and pain-related disability (Cocchiarella, Lord, Turk, & Robenson, 2001; Robinson, Bulcourf, Atchison, Berger, Lafayette-Lucy, Hirsch, et al., 2004). In their guidelines, the American Medical Association (AMA) anticipates the potential problems associated with subjective self-report of pain disability and warns that "examiners must be careful to provide ratings only for those who provide information that appears to be reasonable and accurate." Yet, how is the examiner to determine what information is "reasonable and accurate"?

Back and neck pain often occur in the context of a legally compensable event, such as a work-related injury or incident in which some other party is potentially liable. In fact, back pain is the most common reason for filing a worker's compensation claim (Guo et al., 1999). It is well understood that subjective complaints may be influenced by the potential for compensation. For example, Rohling, Binder, and Langhinrichsen-Rohling (1995) demonstrated that the presence and magnitude of compensation are related to increased reports of pain and decreased treatment efficacy. Moreover, with the addition of financial incentive, intentional exaggeration of subjective symptoms and physical limitations (i.e., malingering) becomes a significant problem.

Twenty percent of Americans believe that purposeful misrepresentation of claims in the compensation system is acceptable (Public Attitude Monitor, 1992, 1993). Covert video surveillance (Kay & Morris-Jones, 1998) demonstrated evidence of malingering in 20% of patients with incentive who were undergoing pain treatment. Reviews of the literature (e.g., Fishbain, Cutler, Rosomoff, & Rosomoff, 1999; Mittenberg, Patton, Canyock, & Condit, 2002) report base rates of malingering in pain ranging from 10% to approaching 40%. The relatively high rate of malingering creates the practical problem of diverting scarce resources in what may be one of the most under-served areas of healthcare. Patients who are malingering compete for these limited resources. Thus, it is important for clinicians to be able to identify malingering of pain-related symptoms and disability.

Complaints of pain are common in patients involved in disability claims, both as a primary symptom and as a secondary symptom in patients whose presenting problem is brain injury. Iverson and McCracken (1997) found that 42% of patients with chronic pain and no history of head injury endorsed at least one cognitive symptom and that by self-report alone 39% of their sample would have met criteria for postconcussion syndrome. Consistent with these findings, pain patients may also demonstrate deficits on cognitive testing (Eccleston, 1994; Kewman, Vaishampayan, Zald, & Han, 1991; Sjogren, Olsen, Thomsen, & Dalberg, 2000).

Chronic pain patients are typically more impaired on more complex attention-demanding tasks; however, tasks that require fewer attentional resources are relatively unaffected even when pain levels are high (Eccleston, 1994). In addition, other problems that may accompany pain (e.g., sleep disturbance, depression) have the potential to affect cognitive function (Brown, Glass, & Park, 2002; Cohen, Malloy, & Jenkins, 1998; Iezzi, Duckworth, Vuong, Archibald, & Klinck, 2004; Menefee, Cohen, Anderson, Doghramji, Frank, & Lee, 2000).

In addition to the clinical factors described above, the structure of disability awards may also influence the manifestation of cognitive symptoms (Bianchini et al., 2005). Specifically, one element in the valuation of damages involves loss of future wages. This is generally determined by calculating the difference between the pre-injury wage and the, presumably lower, post-injury wage, multiplied by the number of years the patient is expected to work after the injury. The lower the post-injury wage, the greater the award. Therefore, a patient who is physically able to work at medium or light demand levels (down from heavy demand) but is unable to work at all because of the cognitive or other psychological consequences of his injury will potentially garner a larger award settlement than if he were to return to work at the reduced demand level. The same logic applies to the issue of self-care because patients may demand awards to cover lost capacity for self-care, regardless of the domain of the disability. Thus, adding cognitive symptoms to the overall picture of disability can result in greater financial awards.

There is ample evidence of the influence of incentives on the cognitive complaints of patients with pain. Iverson, King, Scott, and Adams (2001) found that pain patients involved in worker's compensation claims and with no history of head injury reported more symptoms of cognitive disability than did patients with head injury but without the presence of financial incentive. Meyers and Diep (2000) have shown that chronic pain patients involved in disability litigation have much higher failure rates on symptom validity measures than do non-litigating pain patients or even non-litigating TBI patients, indicating likely intentional misrepresentation of their performance on tasks that appear to measure cognitive ability. Gervais, Green, Allen, and Iverson (2001) demonstrated that the poor performance on symptom validity tests of some chronic pain patients is under volitional control. Finally, other studies have clearly demonstrated the presence of cognitive malingering among chronic pain patients (Bianchini, Etherton, & Greve, 2004; Greve, Bianchini, & Ameduri, 2003; Larrabee, 2003).

Cognitive symptoms are (1) possible associated features of chronic pain syndromes and (2) valuable within the context of disability determination. Because subtle cognitive problems are reasonably expected in the context of chronic pain, it is important to understand the relationship between pain and cognitive impairment and to be able to discriminate genuine cognitive complaints from exaggerated cognitive complaints in this population. Neuropsychologists are particularly well-suited to addressing the question of cognition and malingering in pain, both because of their specialized training in cognition and the mechanisms underlying cognitive dysfunction and because of their experience with the broad array of cognitive assessment tools and instruments designed to detect intentional exaggeration of cognitive deficits.

Over the past 10 to 15 years, neuropsychology has made significant advances in the detection and diagnosis of malingering of cognitive impairment associated with alleged brain pathology (see, for example, Reynolds, 1998; Sweet, 1999). Numerous techniques for the detection of "response bias" have been developed and empirically validated (see, for example, Bianchini, Mathias, & Greve, 2001; Millis & Volinsky, 2001; Reynolds, 1998; Sweet, 1999). In 1999, Slick, Sherman, and Iverson proposed a systematic method for the diagnosis of cognitive malingering that serves as a framework for further empirical research and as a practical tool for the clinical diagnosis of malingering of cognitive deficits. More recently, Bianchini et al. (2005) adapted and expanded the Slick et al. criteria for use in patients with pain-related disability. Thus, the neuropsychologist potentially brings to the question of malingering in pain both a sophisticated conceptual framework and an extensive set of tools to detect malingering.

The presence of well-validated detection tools is important both for evidentiary reasons (e.g., *Daubert v. Merrell Dow Pharmaceuticals*, 1993) and from a clinical assessment standpoint. Regarding the latter, there are no published studies showing that clinicians can accurately determine whether or not someone is malingering based on interview and the adequacy of subjective judgments regarding malingering has been strongly questioned (Faust, 1995). Even the physical examination may not be able to accurately differentiate psychologically involved cases from those without psychological involvement (Grevitt, Pande, O'Dowd, & Webb, 1998). Waddell signs, which have been considered behavioral indicators of non-organic illness behavior and symptom magnification, have been sharply criticized (Fishbain, Cole, Cutler, et al., 2003). Contrary to the assertions of Bogduk (2004) that a diagnosis of malingering "can be refuted if a genuine source of pain can be established" (p. 409), the presence of objective physical findings does not ensure that a patient's report of their subjective limitations is valid. Persons with objectively demonstrated pathology can, and sometimes do, malinger (Bianchini, Greve, & Love, 2003; Greve et al., 2003; Iverson, 2003).

In this chapter, we present a patient who was formally diagnosed as malingering based in part on data from two neuropsychological evaluations and who nevertheless pursued and underwent a cervical discectomy and laminectomy despite being explicitly advised against surgery and told she did not have a problem for which surgery was indicated. This case demonstrates the process of diagnosing malingering in a pain patient and the complex interplay of psychological and social factors that may culminate in intentional exaggeration of pain-related disability. It also demonstrates how the misinterpretation of psychological data when interacting with surgeons and physicians can lead to problematic consequences. The following text will present the background of the case, describe the findings of both neuropsychological evaluations, and then contrast the conclusions of two neuropsychologists based on material from their reports, deposition testimony, and in the context of existing scientific literature.

CASE BACKGROUND

Ms. W., a 28-year-old woman, was involved in a motor vehicle accident in which she suffered an apparent blow to the head, as well as some physical trauma. In addition to medical evaluations, she underwent two neuropsychological evaluations, the first at the request of her attorney and the second by the first author at the request of the defense (hereafter referred to as Examination 2 by Neuropsychologist 2). Table 25.1 provides a chronology of important events in this case.

At the time of the accident, Ms. W. was a 27-year-old restrained driver of a car that was apparently struck on the passenger side by another car which ran a stop sign. The ambulance report documented no loss of consciousness and indicated that she was alert and oriented at the scene. There is indication that she had good recall of the events surrounding the accident. Records indicate that she *reported* being dazed. No Glasgow Coma Scale score was noted in either the ambulance or ER records. She also had acute complaints of neck, shoulder, and low back pain. X-rays of the left shoulder, cervical spine, and lumbar spine on the day of the accident were normal. She was released from the hospital within hours and was *not* given a concussion diagnosis at the time. Retrospective analysis of the acute injury characteristics indicates that at worst she may have suffered a very mild concussion and possibly suffered no brain trauma at all.

Ms. W.'s report of her accident history and symptoms changed over time. For example, in direct contrast to the early documentation, she later reported that she had lost consciousness in the accident. In follow-up evaluations she reported myriad, often progressing, symptoms which she attributed to the accident, including: blackouts, constant headaches, numbness on left side of body,

TABLE 25.1   Chronology of case events

MONTHS POST-INJURY	EVENT
–	Accident
3	Normal computed tomograph (CT) scan of the brain
10	Normal electroencephalogram
10	Normal magnetic resonance imaging (MRI) scan of the cervical spine
12	Evaluation by Neuropsychologist 1
15	Patient told by independent neurosurgeon that she was not a surgical candidate
24	Evaluation by Neuropsychologist 2
25	Cervical disc surgery
31	Deposition of Neuropsychologist 1
43	Deposition of treating neurosurgeon
43	Deposition of independently selected neurosurgeon
43	Deposition of defense retained neurosurgeon
44	Trial

lock jaw, cracking sound in jaw and neck, pain in neck and back, weakness in left leg, recent and remote memory problems, sleeping problems, and loss of balance. A list of her detailed symptoms reported during Examination 2 is provided in Table 25.2.

A CT scan of the head three months post-injury and an EEG 10 months post-injury were negative. Nine months post-injury she was seen in the emergency room with episodes of near syncope, and there is a mention in that medical evaluation of "possible malingering." An MRI of the cervical spine was done 10 months post-injury. The radiology report read: "No specific cervical findings are noted to correlate with the history of headaches and concussion syndrome. There is no mention of any specific cervical symptomology, such as neck pain or either radicular or myelo-pathic symptoms. There was a mild diffuse annular bulge in the posterior margin of the inter-vertebral discs at the C3–4 and C4–5 interspace levels, but there is no focal protrusion or focal herniation superimposed at these levels noted or at any other level."

NEUROPSYCHOLOGICAL EXAMINATION 1

Examination 1 was conducted 11 months post-injury. At that time Ms. W. reported a range of symptoms consistent with depression, anxiety attacks, constant pain, numbness and tingling in her left extremities, difficulty spelling simple words, and a number of additional cognitive problems including "impairments in memory, as well as difficulty concentrating, problems with speech and language, and impaired motor coordination." She also reported developing "a seizure disorder . . . involving grand mal seizures."

Included in the records from Examination 1 was a narrative written by the patient describing her perceptions of her past life and current situation. What follows are several passages from that narrative:

TABLE 25.2 Symptoms spontaneously reported by Ms. W. during the interview for the second evaluation

1. Blackouts—one per month now; seizures, she reported that the Dilantin helped her and she cannot remember the last time she had one. She has not had any this year and the last one was in November. She was enuretic during the blackouts/seizures.
2. Headaches that are constant. Headaches will be in a certain spot. When asked to rate the headaches on a pain rating scale of 0–10 with a "10" being the most severe amount of pain, she rates her headaches a "9.5."
3. Numbness on left side of face and whole left side of body.
4. "Lock jaw."
5. Clicking/cracking sound in her jaw and neck.
6. Pain in neck and back. She states that the pain in her neck is constant and rates this pain a "10" on the pain rating scale. She rates the pain in her back a "10" on the pain rating scale.
7. Sometimes loses strength in left leg.
8. Numbness in the thumb and forefinger of left hand. She is starting to get some feeling back in her thumb.
9. Hard time remembering things. She constantly has to go back and check. She forgets things all the time and will not be able to remember things in the past and recent events. With certain people, she will remember their faces but she cannot remember their names. Sometimes when she is supposed to pick up her mother, she will go to her grandmother's house because she forgot.
10. Sleeping problems. She states that she tosses and turns because of the pain and says that sometimes she cannot fall asleep. She averages about 4 hours of sleep per night and takes "cat naps" during the day.
12. Loses her balance and runs into walls and things. While walking down a hall, she will lose her balance and hit the wall.

Before [date of accident] I saw myself as a beautiful strong young graduate with high hopes on finally raising my daughter in a position that I saw fit for her and myself. Going into the field of Forensic Science was a dream that was rapidly coming true. I wanted everything in life to be with my daughter in a home of our own . . . After [date of accident] my life has totally changed. I get confused all the time as far as to the direction I want my life to go in. My daughter rides my ass. I should say drives me crazy. I sit in pain all the time looking for a quick way to end all the pain. Sometimes I don't feel comfortable with myself feeling like a waste of time and money has went into my education. My life is limited.

Examination 1 led to the following conclusions by Neuropsychologist 1:

Overall, Ms. W. demonstrates mild to moderate, diffuse cognitive deficits, consistent with her history of closed head injury due to motor vehicle accident in or around [date of accident], and consistent with her reported history of subsequent seizure disorder . . . Although Ms. W. should be able to manage her own basic self-care independently, she may have some difficulty with higher-level activities of daily living, such as financial management and planning . . . Vocational evaluation is also recommended, in order to determine the extent to which the patient's specific cognitive deficits may negatively impact her ability to obtain and maintain gainful employment.

At 15 months post-injury Ms. W. sought a neurosurgical opinion on her own, independent of both plaintiff and defense attorneys. This neurosurgeon confirmed the absence of cervical pathology and was also unable to document any objective findings to explain any of her myriad other symptoms. Specifically, he wrote, "I find no evidence of neurological injury to explain the host of complaints. There are no structural abnormalities within the cervical spine to explain her complaints . . . This was explained in detail to the patient. I explained that I was unable to identify a structural abnormality to explain her complaints . . . I recommended that she begin returning to work." Later this neurosurgeon testified, "It is my opinion that she did not have a brain injury."

Four months after this independent evaluation (19 months post-injury), the plaintiff attorney-referred neurosurgeon recommended surgery: "She is a candidate for an ACDF [anterior cervical fusion and discectomy] at C3–4 and C4–5." An oral surgeon who also assessed her 24 months post-injury reported that there was no objective evidence supporting complaints of temporomandibular joint dysfunction and found her report of neck and shoulder numbness "questionable." Twenty-five months post-injury the patient proceeded with discectomy and laminectomy at C3–4 and C4–5.

A third neurosurgeon hired by the defense later testified that the cervical fusion was unnecessary: "Neither the clinical picture nor the MRI of the cervical spine would justify the operation performed, which was a discectomy and fusion at C3–4 and C4–5. Notoriously, neither of these discs could have compressed or interfered with a nerve root capable of producing problems into the hand as the patient was clearly complaining of, and I have to conclude that the operation was not justified." The case subsequently went to a jury trial almost four years after the accident.

NEUROPSYCHOLOGICAL EXAMINATION 2

Ms. W. presented to the office unaccompanied. There was nothing especially unusual about her presentation. Her spontaneously reported symptoms are listed in Table 25.2. Exaggeration became apparent during the formal mental status examination and psychometric assessment. For example, she did not correctly answer orientation questions about her current location or day of the week. She could not follow multi-step commands. With the exception of brief periods of poor cooperation, her behavior during the examination was also fairly unremarkable. In short, there was not much remarkable about her clinical presentation. It was the testing results and the comparison of symptoms to the records that led to the malingering diagnosis.

Regarding the accident in question, Ms. W. reported having been injured in a motor vehicle accident two years prior to this evaluation. She provided considerable detail regarding her activities prior to being struck. She was able to report that her car was struck by a car that "came from out of nowhere and ran a stop sign and hit us." She reported that she was knocked unconscious but remembers the paramedics coming into the car. Then she remembers being in the hospital. She said she was in and out of consciousness during that time. She did not remember what happened in the hospital other than some tests were done and family was notified.

Regarding her pre-injury history, she reported nothing that would predict a worse than expected outcome (e.g., abuse, neglect, etc.). She denied any prior history of head injury with or without a loss of consciousness. She denied any prior history of blackout or seizures. She also denied any psychiatric history including having been prescribed any psychiatric medication. Her history was negative for stroke, diabetes, hypertension, and cardiac disease.

Ms. W. reported that she had graduated college and had just started a graduate program in business and public administration when the accident occurred. At the time of this evaluation she had not yet returned to school. She reported making the honor roll in college and was a scholarship recipient. She estimated that she had a "B" average. Actual transcripts demonstrated a cumulative GPA at graduation of 2.07, or a "C" average. Her worst subject was math. She denied any learning disabilities or need for special education. Socially, Ms. W. was living with her husband of three months, whom she met and married after the accident, and her six-year-old daughter.

Test results

Validity testing

On the Portland Digit Recognition Test, she correctly recognized 11 of 36 Easy items, 9 of 36 Hard items, and 20 of 72 Total items. All of these scores are significantly below chance and indicate that she intentionally performed poorly on the neuropsychological tests. On the TOMM she correctly recognized 23 of 50 on Trial 1, 31 of 50 on Trial 2, and 34 of 50 after delay. These scores are well below those reported for patients with objectively documented severe brain injury.

She performed similarly poorly on indicators derived from the WAIS–III. Ms. W. had a score of 5 on the Reliable Digit Span test and earned a score of 1.35 on the WAIS–III Mittenberg formula. These scores are worse than those seen in persons with comparable brain injuries and in chronic pain. In contrast, indicators derived from the CVLT were within normal limits. Her 105 errors on the Category Test occur in only about 2% of non-malingerers with comparable injury severity.

Ms. W. had an elevated MMPI Fake Bad Scale (FBS) (34 raw score). Both scores are in the range associated with intentional exaggeration of subjective symptoms. The F scale score (T = 75) is seen in 6% of non-malingering patients with comparable injuries and thus suggests exaggeration of psychological symptoms. The FBS score, particularly when combined with scores of 99 and 115 on Hs and Hy, respectively, suggests intentional exaggeration of physical symptoms.

In summary, examination of Ms. W.'s performance validity demonstrated psychometric evidence of exaggerated physical and psychological symptoms, as well as cognitive impairment. The below chance findings on the PDRT are definitive evidence that she did poorly on purpose. These findings mean that her current test results may not be an accurate reflection of her actual psychological status. A detailed summary of these findings with false-positive error rates and appropriate literature citations can be found in Table 25.3.

Cognitive testing

The results of the Wechsler Scales for both examinations are presented in Table 25.4 and, graphically, in Figure 25.1. Ms. W. performed in the borderline range of measured verbal intelligence and in

TABLE 25.3   Positive psychometric tests and indicators of malingering with associated false-positive error rates in traumatic brain injury

TEST/INDICATORS	#1	FP%	#2	FP%	SOURCE OF FP DATA
PDRT easy	20	0	11*	0	Greve & Bianchini, 2006
PDRT hard	15	0	9*	0	
PDRT total	35	0	20*	0	
TOMM 1	–	–	23	0	Greve, Bianchini, & Doane, 2006
TOMM 2	–	–	31	0	
TOMM Ret	–	–	34	0	
Mittenberg	0.78	0	1.35	0	Greve, Bianchini, Mathias, et al., 2003
RDS	6	7	5	0	Heinly et al., 2005
Digit Span	6	10	4	0	Heinly et al., 2005
Finger Tapping–Dom	28.6	0	31.1	0	Arnold et al., 2005
Finger Tapping–Nondom	33.4	wnl	refused[1]	–	
Booklet Category Test	–		105	2	Greve, Bianchini, & Roberson, 2007
MMPI F	75	6	72	6	Greve, Bianchini, Love, et al., 2006
MMPI Fb	74	10	50	–	
MMPI FBS	28	14	34	0	

F = Infrequency Scale; Fb = Infrequency (back) Scale; FBS = Fake Bad Scale; FP% = false-positive error rate and is based on performance of non-malingering mild TBI patients; MMPI = Minnesota Multiphasic Personality Inventory–2; PDRT = Portland Digit Recognition Test; RDS = Reliable Digit Span; TOMM = Test of Memory Malingering.
* Score is significantly below chance at alpha < 0.05.
Note: [1]Patient refused to do motor tests with dominant hand because of symptoms; note that she was able to do the task during the previous evaluation.

the average range of nonverbal intelligence. There were no meaningful differences between verbal and nonverbal IQ and Index scores. There was no meaningful scatter among the Verbal subtests. Among the Performance subtests, Digit Symbol Coding was a relative strength and Picture Completion was a relative weakness. Her verbal scores were substantially lower than would be expected given her premorbid functioning (college education, admitted to a graduate program). As can be seen in Table 25.4 and Figure 25.1, her verbal summary scores reflect a *decline* from previous testing.

Ms. W. performed in the moderately impaired range on motor tasks with the right (dominant) hand and refused with the left, claiming that her left thumb and index finger were numb. Note that a year earlier she had been able to do those tasks. She wore glasses and denied visual problems. Other than her report of numbness, there was no evidence of impaired sensory processing. Ms. W. was alert and grossly oriented during testing. She demonstrated that she was capable of normal processing speed. In contrast, her test scores suggested compromise of basic attentional functions, such as attentional span and focused attention and higher level working memory.

Interestingly, she performed in the severely impaired range on the Benton Facial Recognition Test, but showed no other evidence of impaired perception. Her Rey Figure was very carefully and accurately drawn. While the quality of her discourse was normal, formal testing of many language functions was in the severely impaired range. For example, she scored below the 3rd percentile on sentence repetition and earned a T score of 13 on the Boston Naming Test despite a Vocabulary

TABLE 25.4   Results of the Wechsler Scales with performance change across examinations

SUMMARY IQ/INDEX SCORE	EXAM 1	EXAM 2	CHANGE
Wechsler Adult Intelligence Scale–III			
Verbal IQ	88	76	−12
Performance IQ	84	90	+6
Full Scale IQ	85	80	−5
Verbal Comprehension	86	80	−6
Perceptual Organization	84	88	+4
Working Memory	82	71	−9
Processing Speed	88	106	+18
Wechsler Memory Scale–III			
Auditory Immediate	97	74	−23
Auditory Delayed	97	77	−20
Auditory Recognition Delayed	100	75	−25
Visual Immediate	84	75	−9
Visual Delayed	68	68	0
Immediate Memory	89	69	−20
General Memory	84	69	−15
Working Memory	74	66	−8

scaled score of 7 and a standard score of 98 on the Peabody Picture Vocabulary Test. Her reading was at the 6th grade level, and she was unable to execute multi-step commands.

Ms. W.'s WMS index scores ranged from the mid-60s to the upper 70s with a General Memory Index score of 69. Her California Verbal Learning Test performance was in the severely impaired range (4 to 5 standard deviation units below expectations on delayed recall and recognition). Despite very impaired performance in a number of domains, trouble following two-step commands, and a Category Test performance consistent with malingering, Ms. W. achieved six categories in 91 trials on the Wisconsin Card Sorting Test. None of the WCST scores were in the impaired range. Her WCST from Examination 1 was also within normal limits.

Personality testing

Ms. W. was administered the Minnesota Multiphasic Personality Inventory–2 (MMPI) during both examinations. The resulting profiles are presented in Figure 25.2. Despite evidence of exaggerated cognitive deficits and physical complaints, the MMPI–2 clinical scales were considered interpretable after traditional validity analysis. She had significant elevations on 8 of 10 clinical scales with the highest elevations on Scales 1, 2, and 3. This was interpreted to indicate high levels of anxiety, depression, and emotional lability. It was also noted that the profile indicated very high levels of somatic preoccupation and a pattern that is consistent with somatization or psychological involvement in physical complaints. This pattern of results, which was seen on the first evaluation as well, is a psychological contra-indication for spine surgery (Block, Gatchell, Deardoff, & Guyer, 2003; Block, Ohnmeiss, Guyer, Rashbaum, & Hochschuler, 2001; Epker & Block, 2001).

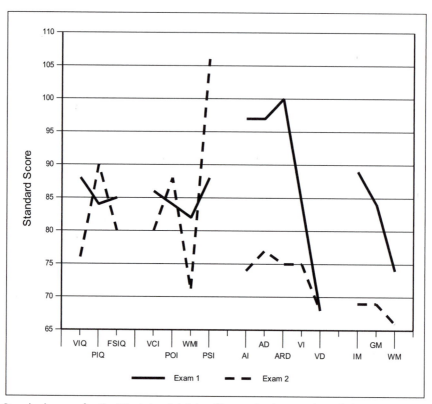

FIG. 25.1   Standard scores for the Wechsler Adult Intelligence Scale–III and Wechsler Memory Scale–III for the two examinations.

Note: AD = Auditory Delay Memory; AI = Auditory Immediate Memory; ARD = Auditory Recognition Delayed; FSIQ = Full Scale Intelligence Quotient; GM = General Memory; IM = Immediate Memory; PIQ = Performance Intelligence Quotient; POI = Perceptual Organization Index; PSI = Processing Speed Index; VCI = Verbal Comprehension Index; VD = Visual Delayed Memory; VI = Visual Immediate Memory; VIQ = Verbal Intelligence Quotient; WM = Working Memory; WMI = Working Memory Index.

Conclusions, recommendations

The report of Examination 2 concluded with the following paragraphs:

> Ms. W. is a 29-year-old woman with a history of a blow to the head during a motor vehicle accident 24 months ago. The records indicate that this patient was alert and oriented when she arrived in the emergency room. This indicates that she sustained at worst a concussion, which is typically characterized by some concentration and irritability problems for a period of about six months. Some patients have persistent problems for longer periods of time. However, global or focal neurocognitive impairments simply do not result from such injuries.
>
> A neuropsychological evaluation was administered to Ms. W. over the course of two days in our office. She shows impairments in nearly every area evaluated. That is, she has a pattern that would be suggestive of global neurocognitive impairment, which is not at all what would be expected, given the nature of this injury. Thus, the current evaluation findings did not result from the injury described in the medical records in this case.
>
> In the evaluation, effort measures were employed as part of a standard neuropsychological assessment for a medical legal context. Her effort tests show dramatic results; she performed both below expected norms for even severely neurologically impaired patients and significantly

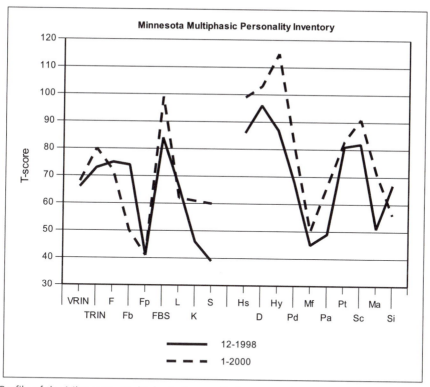

FIG. 25.2   Profile of the Minnesota Multiphasic Personality Inventory–2.

Note: D = Depression; F = Infrequency; Fb = Infrequency (back); Fp = Infrequency (psychopathology); Hs = Hypochondria-sis; Hy = Hysteria; K = Correction; L = Lie; Ma = Hypomania; Mf = Masculinity-Femininity; Pa = Paranoia; Pd = Psychopathic-Deviate; Pt = Psychasthenia; S = Superlative Self-Presentation; Sc = Schizophrenia; Si = Social Introversion; TRIN = True Response Inconsistency; VRIN = Variable Response Inconsistency.

below chance. This makes it quite clear that the patient was purposely producing incorrect responses in an effort to appear more impaired than is, in fact, the case.

In addition, this patient has had a previous neuropsychological evaluation; repeat neuro-psychological evaluations can sometimes be useful in evaluating brain injuries. When an evaluation is repeated, patterns of change can be examined. When the current results are compared with the results of [Neuropsychologist 1], Ms. W. shows a variety of substantial declines that would not be expected given the nature of this injury. Rather, it suggests that this patient purposefully produced incorrect responses to lower test scores but was not able to do so consistently.

The combination of the nature of her initial injury, the global nature of impairment in scores noted on the current evaluation, a substantial decline on some of the scores when the current evaluation is compared to [Neuropsychologist 1's], the dramatic positive malingering test results on the current evaluation, and the positive results on the malingering test adminis-tered by [Neuropsychologist 1] all lead to the diagnosis of malingering.

With this in mind, it is the opinion of this examiner that Ms. W. does not have any signifi-cant neurocognitive or psychological impairments and therefore she is capable of returning to any job for which she is qualified. It should be noted that since it is indicated in this examination that she is willing to purposely produce symptoms, this raises questions about other subjective complaints of symptoms, such as pain.

CASE INTEGRATION

The final conclusion of Neuropsychologist 2 is that Ms. W. met published criteria for a diagnosis of malingering. The following section summarizes the findings consistent with malingering in terms of the Slick, Sherman, and Iverson (1999) criteria for Malingered Neurocognitive Dysfunction (MND). These criteria reflect a systematic and fairly comprehensive method for organizing information from interview, testing, and records. The criteria of Bianchini et al. (2005) for Malingered Pain-Related Disability (MPRD) could also serve this purpose. In this case, however, the two sets of criteria overlap almost perfectly in their relevant particulars, so only the Slick et al. system will be used.

The Slick criteria are divided into four clusters: the first refers to the presence of incentive; the second to inconsistencies relative to neuropsychological testing (Criterion B, evidence from neuropsychological testing); the third to inconsistencies relative to self-report (Criterion C, evidence from self-report); and the fourth describes conditions under which a diagnosis of malingering would be ruled out even if the other criteria were met. See Table 25.5 for a summary of the criteria and the three levels of MND diagnosis.

Criterion A: Evidence of external incentive

The Slick et al. system requires that for a diagnosis of malingering, at least one "clearly identifiable and substantial incentive for exaggeration or fabrication" be present at the time of the evaluation (Criterion A). In the absence of such an incentive, one might still conclude on the basis of other criteria that intentional exaggeration or fabrication was present, but a diagnosis of malingering

TABLE 25.5 Summary of the Slick, Sherman, and Iverson (1999) criteria for Malingered Neurocognitive Dysfunction

A. Presence of substantial external incentive

B. Evidence from neuropsychological testing
1. Definite negative response bias.
2. Probable response bias.
3. Discrepancy between test data and known patterns of brain functioning.
4. Discrepancy between test data and observed behavior.
5. Discrepancy between test data and reliable collateral reports.
6. Discrepancy between test data and documented background history.

C. Evidence from self-report
1. Self-reported history is discrepant with documented history.
2. Self-reported symptoms are discrepant with known patterns of brain functioning.
3. Self-reported symptoms are discrepant with behavioral observations.
4. Self-reported symptoms are discrepant with information obtained from collateral informants.
5. Evidence from exaggerated or fabricated psychological dysfunction.

D. Behaviors meeting necessary criteria from groups B and C are not fully accounted for by Psychiatric, Neurological, or Developmental factors.

Definite	Meets Criterion A *AND* Criterion B1 *AND* Criterion D.
Probable	Meets Criterion A *AND* two or more B criteria (excluding B1); or, meets one B criterion (excluding B1) *AND* one or more C criteria. Meets Criterion D.
Possible	Meets Criterion A *AND* one or more C criteria *but NOT* Criterion D; or, meets all criteria for Definite or Probable *but DOES NOT* meet Criterion D.

would not be appropriate; a diagnosis of Factitious Disorder would be necessary. In any case, the current patient had a personal injury claim as motivation for misrepresentation of her psychological state and thus met Criterion A.

Criterion B: Evidence is derived from neuropsychological testing

Three forms of Criterion B evidence were present in this case. The most striking finding was significantly below chance performance on the PDRT which meet *Criterion B1*, evidence of "definite negative response bias." The interpretation of a significantly below-chance finding is well established in neuropsychology (Bianchini et al., 2001; Frederick & Speed, 2007; Reynolds, 1998). Specifically, a forced-choice test result that is significantly worse than 50% "is not a random or chance occurrence but represents a *purposive distortion* by the examinee" (italics added; Reynolds, 1998, p. 272). Thus it is considered definitive evidence of intent.

In this case, this patient also had positive *Criterion B2* evidence of "probable negative response bias," which refers to the fact that "performance on one or more *well-validated* psychometric tests or indices designed to measure exaggeration or fabrication of cognitive deficits is consistent with feigning" (Slick et al., 1999, p. 553). In particular, her performance on the TOMM was below published norms for even persons with objectively defined moderate-severe traumatic brain injury who gave good effort (Greve, Bianchini, Black, Heinly, Love & Swift, 2006; Tombaugh, 1996). Moreover, she was also positive on Reliable Digit Span (Heinly, Greve, Bianchini, Love, & Brennan, 2005) and Mittenberg's WAIS–III discriminant analysis formula (Greve, Bianchini, Mathias, et al., 2003; Mittenberg, Theroux, Aguila-Puentes, Bianchini, Greve, & Rayls, 2001; Mittenberg, Theroux-Fichera, Zielinski, & Heilbronner, 1995).

Criterion B3, the presence of a discrepancy between test data and known patterns of brain functioning, was also met. A core feature of the natural history of traumatic brain injury is improvement over time (Alexander, 1995; Dikmen, Machamer, Winn, & Temkin, 1995; Iverson, 2005). A decline in test score across evaluations would not be consistent with traumatic brain injury. The data from the two neuropsychological evaluations clearly demonstrates poorer performance on the second relative to the first in many but not all domains. The most notable area of decline was on memory testing. Thus, the two evaluations together demonstrate "a pattern of neuropsychological test performance that is markedly discrepant from currently accepted models of normal and abnormal CNS function" (Slick et al., 1999, p. 553). Moreover, during the interview for the second evaluation she reported remote memory disturbances, which would also meet this criterion.

It is possible she met *Criterion B4* in that the results of cognitive testing were arguably inconsistent with certain behavioral observations. First, her WMS–III index scores on the second evaluation ranged from 66 (Working Memory) to 77 (Auditory Delayed), yet she was able to drive to, and find, our office without assistance. Moreover, her performance on language-based tasks was consistently impaired on both evaluations, yet she was able to describe her problems and her history articulately. In addition, a written description of her circumstances provided to the first expert demonstrates intact writing ability.

Finally, she met *Criterion B6* by producing test results that were discrepant with the documented severity of her injury. The medical records clearly demonstrate that Ms. W. suffered at worst a mild concussion, and it is possible she suffered no brain injury at all. As a result, she should have shown no cognitive impairment on the first evaluation, which was conducted about one year post-injury. Nonetheless, she demonstrated grossly impaired performance (often in the moderately to severely impaired range) across a wide variety of tests on both evaluations. Again, this was most notable on memory testing, but was also evident on measures of language. Psychometrically, this is seen in her Digit Span scaled score and total errors on the Category Test.

Criterion C: Evidence from self-report

Criterion C1 refers to discrepancies between self-report and documented history. While this criterion encompasses denial of history, which could influence interpretation of test results (e.g., denying past neurological illness or injury or serious psychiatric illness), and over-stating academic or vocational achievement, in this case it was Ms. W.'s report of her experience of the accident that is inconsistent with records. Specifically, she stated that she was knocked unconscious and had only vague, spotty memories until she was in the hospital. She reported that even in the hospital she was "in and out of consciousness" and that she did not remember what happened in the hospital. In fact, she was alert and oriented at the scene and was able to describe to the EMTs how the accident occurred. She was transported to the ER at her request. She was similarly alert and oriented throughout her time in the ER. Comparison of the patient's report with the actual records indicates that she exaggerated the severity of her injury.

The final criterion met is *Criterion C5*, evidence of "exaggerated or fabricated psychological dysfunction." While her traditional validity scales (the F family) do not seem overly impressive as evidence of malingering, it is worth pointing out that an F score as low as 72 still only occurs in about 6% of non-malingering mild TBI patients (she scored 75 and 72, on the two evaluations, respectively). More impressive, however, are her FBS scores of 28 and 34. FBS scores in this range are only reported in patients with incentive and, even then, are relatively rare in non-malingering patients with incentive.

Criterion D describes conditions under which findings that are sufficient for an MND diagnosis would not be classified as malingering. Specifically, behaviors that meet the necessary criteria from B and C that can be *fully* accounted for by genuine psychiatric, developmental, or neurological disorders should not be labeled as malingering. This criterion makes it clear that malingering cannot be ruled out unless it can be reasonably demonstrated that positive B and/or C criteria are fully accounted for by psychological or neurological disturbance and are not at all motivated by any identifiable external incentives. There are no factors in this case that fully account for this patient's behavior. However, the argument can be made for the presence of somatization in this case. Moreover, her later behavior (i.e., pursuit of unnecessary surgery) suggests that she has features of Factitious Disorder, if not frank Factitious Disorder.

It has been argued that self-injurious behavior, as in Factitious Disorder, is not expected in malingering. Some (e.g., Fishbain, 2003) have argued that the unnecessary pursuit of, and submission to, unpleasant and/or potentially harmful invasive medical procedures cannot be accounted for by malingering and that the presence of Factitious Disorder may be sufficient to rule out malingering. However, this is an over-simplification of a very complex psychosocial process, and it is clear that some patients with Factitious Disorder or tendencies may also be motivated by external incentives, such that a diagnosis of malingering is also appropriate (Eisendrath, 1996).

Table 25.6 summarizes each of the Slick et al. criteria and whether or not each was met in the two evaluations. As can be seen, Ms. W. easily meets criteria for malingering, Definite MND in particular, on the basis of the results of the second evaluation. She also meets criteria for MND on the basis of findings from the first evaluation. However, the first expert did not make a diagnosis of malingering, despite the relevant details that have been afforded readers, and concluded that Ms. W. was experiencing at least moderate persisting cognitive impairment and psychological distress as a result of the injuries she sustained in the motor vehicle accident.

TABLE 25.6   Summary of the Slick, Sherman, and Iverson (1999) criteria for Malingered Neurocognitive Dysfunction as applied to Ms. W.

	Exam 1	Exam 2
A. Presence of substantial external incentive	Yes	Yes
B. Evidence from neuropsychological testing		
1. Definite negative response bias.	No	Yes
2. Probable response bias.	Yes	Yes
3. Discrepancy between test data and known patterns of brain functioning.	No	Yes
4. Discrepancy between test data and observed behavior.	Possible	Possible
5. Discrepancy between test data and reliable collateral reports.	No Data	No Data
6. Discrepancy between test data and documented background history.	Yes	Yes
C. Evidence from self-report		
1. Self-reported history is discrepant with documented history.	No Data	Yes
2. Self-reported symptoms are discrepant with known patterns of brain functioning.	No Data	No Data
3. Self-reported symptoms are discrepant with behavioral observations.	No Data	No Data
4. Self-reported symptoms are discrepant with information obtained from collateral informants.	No Data	No Data
5. Evidence from exaggerated or fabricated psychological dysfunction.	Yes	Yes
D. Behaviors meeting necessary criteria from groups B and C are not fully accounted for by Psychiatric, Neurological, or Developmental factors.	Yes	Yes

ANALYSIS

The preceding sections present the details of this case and the support for the diagnosis of malingering present in both neuropsychological evaluations. Despite very similar test findings, the two experts came to strikingly different conclusions. Neuropsychologist 1 concluded that Ms. W. had suffered significant and disabling cognitive and psychological injuries caused directly by the index motor vehicle accident. Neuropsychologist 2 concluded that Ms. W. was cognitively and emotionally intact and that her test findings reflect an intentional effort to appear impaired. If the two neuropsychologists are guided by the existing scientific literature, how can they come to such divergent conclusions?

The answer is that the expert opinion of Neuropsychologist 1 was not based on existing scientific literature but upon a subjective, idiosyncratic, and poorly informed understanding of several major issues that are relevant to this case. The following section illustrates this point based on passages from Neuropsychologist 1's own report and deposition testimony in the context of existing scientific literature. These points were selected because Neuropsychologist 1's opinions are so clearly out of step with well-established scientific neuropsychology.

Explicitly detailing these points is important because the approach to forensic neuropsychology they represent is not particularly uncommon and because failure to properly interpret findings can leave the door open to very risky and possibly unnecessary interventions. The end result in this case was not a year of unnecessary psychotherapy or six months of cognitive rehabilitation that often occurs, but unnecessary spinal surgery in a person who was clearly intentionally exaggerating and misrepresenting her symptoms and abilities.

Point 1

Neuropsychologist 1 minimizes the importance of the acute neurological characteristics of a head trauma in determining injury severity and instead relies on his test results for that determination. This result is the default assignment of causality to the index event; when any impaired score is observed, it is used as evidence of brain damage due to the index event, even when it is wildly divergent from expectations. The first deposition passage demonstrates how Neuropsychologist 1 discounted the findings documented in the Emergency Room records.

Q: On page 3, the first paragraph, you note that in the emergency room she was noted to be alert and oriented. Is that significant to you in trying to determine the significance of her head injury?

A: Certainly it mitigates against a worse head injury that she was awake and responsive at least at that point. Sometimes they miss a lot in the emergency rooms too. I noticed that they don't ask questions they should ask. They don't do any extensive mental status exam. They'll say, "Do you know who you are, where you are, that sort of thing, but that's about the extent of it. And so . . ."

Q: But if you assume that's accurate.

A: If I assume that's accurate, then that means that by that point she was—she might have still had deficits, been confused or whatever, but at least was responsive which means it's less likely to have been a moderate head injury as categorized by the time of injury certainly.

The following deposition passage illustrates that rather than using the initial characteristics of the injury as the comparison point as recommended by Stuss (1995) and by Alexander (1995) and later reiterated by Iverson (2005), he blends the concepts of initial neurological characteristics and subsequent sequelae.

Q: Aren't there some factors that you look at to decide whether to categorize someone's injury as mild, moderate or severe?

A: At the time of injury, again, confusion, loss of consciousness or possible loss of consciousness, whether there's a blow to the head or not, and how long it takes somebody to come out of their confusion, that sort of thing are things you look at.

Q: What did she have that you've considered sufficient to move her from the mild to moderate?

A: Well, again, the moderate comes from the fact that she's got moderate decline still a year later. I don't have any specifics that would move her from mild to moderate based on the information at the time of the injury. I don't have enough to go on to move her there as far as a mild injury. It had at least moderate deficits as a result. But I can say mild, at least a mild injury, maybe worse depending on how long she was out if she was unconscious.

Q: Based on what you've seen you think probably she had a mild head injury?

A: Yeah.

Q: But based on the testing you did a year later it had moderate consequences?

A: Yeah. At least a mild one with moderate consequences later on. The fact that those, even a year later were that striking. Plus the seizures as well, that's another ball game.

It is important to note that the acute medical records, which Neuropsychologist 1 referenced in his report and therefore to which he had access, not only do not refer to even questionable loss of consciousness, but note very clearly that Ms. W. was alert and oriented at the scene and that she, herself, requested to be transported to the hospital. In his report, Neuropsychologist 1 referenced an ER note and stated, "these records reflect a blow to the head against the windshield, and not that the patient was dazed by that impact." He did not acknowledge and may not have recognized that the ER record was simply Ms. W.'s subjective report and did not reflect the independent knowledge of a third party (such as an EMT). Moreover, while there are notes regarding abrasions and contusion on the patient's left side, there is no indication of any injury to the scalp or head other than complaints of pain. A diagnosis of concussion was never rendered.

Neuropsychologist 1's conclusion that Ms. W. suffered a moderate injury because she had moderate neuropsychological impairments on Examination 1 is in direct opposition to Alexander's (1995) point that "the severity of TBI must be defined by the acute injury characteristics and *not by the severity of symptoms at random points after trauma*" (p. 1253; italics added). Overall, the preceding excerpts illustrate how Neuropsychologist 1 discounts the relevance of the initial characteristics of the injury when discussing test results and functional impairments. That is, rather than commenting on the impressive disparity between the patient's test results and the nature of the original injury (what Larrabee [1990] refers to as biological indexing), he simply related the test findings, by default, to the index accident. From his deposition: "So there's got to be something to account for it. The only thing we have is a head injury to account for it."

Point 2

Neuropsychologist 1 relies on his anecdotal experience and subjective impression in his selection and interpretation of malingering tests. The following passages illustrate why he failed to at least suspect that the test findings were not an accurate representation of Ms. W.'s true capacity. In the first passage, Neuropsychologist 1 was asked to comment on points made by Neuropsychologist 2 that the severely impaired language scores documented on both evaluations were inconsistent with the severity of the injury and therefore had to be due to some other factor or factors. While this passage is also illustrative of his failure to properly index the severity of the injury, it is used here to begin to illustrate his non-empirical assessment of effort and malingering.

Q: *"Her scores on test of language functions range from normal to severely impaired."*
A: That's consistent with what I found.
Q: Did you get the same range here?
A: Right. I think they were.
Q: And his next line is *"Substantially impaired language would not be expected as a result of this injury."* Do you disagree with that?
A: Again, I don't know how long she was unconscious. I know we do have this and there's nothing else to account for it. So there's got to be something to account for it. The only thing we have is a head injury to account for it. This is not a developmental kind of pattern at all.
Q: I'm not meaning to speak for him, but as I interpret his report, he accounts for it—which he'll be deposed too—but, I think he's going to account for it by saying he doesn't think she was trying on the test.
A: I don't agree with that at all. Yeah. No, obviously she tried very hard on some things. And apparently tried to the point that she was pulling her hair out and crying and saying, what's wrong with me and that sort of thing. This was not a person who seemed to be just sort of sitting there saying I'm not going to give it an effort. I didn't have that feeling at any point.

Thus, the last two lines indicate that Neuropsychologist 1 was relying on his clinical judgment to conclude that Ms. W. was doing her best. Unfortunately, there are no published studies showing that clinicians can reliably determine whether someone is malingering or not based on clinical impressions. To the contrary, Ekman, O'Sullivan, and Frank (1999) demonstrated an average false-positive error rate of 40% when psychologists were asked to detect deception in video clips and opined that, "it is unlikely that judging deception from demeanor will ever be sufficiently accurate to be admissible in the courtroom" (p. 265).

It is also well understood that the results of psychological tests can be invalidated by biased responding and/or poor effort (Beetar & Williams, 1995; Heubrock & Petermann, 1998; Lees-Haley, 1989, 1990), but psychologists are also not very good at detecting malingered performance in their standard clinical tests without specific tests and indicators (Faust, Hart, & Guilmette, 1988; Heaton, Smith, Lehman, & Vogt, 1978). As a result, it is necessary to rely on special tests and clinical indicators.

In his report, Neuropsychologist 1 attempted to explain away a failed Portland Digit Recognition Test with scores of 20 "Easy," 15 "Hard," and 35 Total. This explanation appears to suggest that he just doesn't understand the research methodology supporting the PDRT. But as will be seen, he has selectively focused on only a single part of Binder's excellent validation of that test.

> On the Portland Digit Recognition Test, Ms. W. performed within normal limits on the first half of the test (the easy items), with a score of above 50%. As noted above, as testing continued, she appeared to fatigue significantly and began making more errors, performing slightly below the cut-off on the more difficult trials, with a score of 35. Nevertheless, it should be noted that approximately 1/3 of all patients with head injuries do score below the cut-off of 39 (i.e., variations do occur among patients).

It is likely that this "1/3" value reflects a misunderstanding of the original PDRT data of Binder and Willis (1991), which was derived from a differential prevalence research design. A differential prevalence malingering design (Rogers, 1997) examines test outcomes in a group of patients whose malingering status is not known. Mittenberg et al. (2002) and others (Ardolf, Denny, & Houston, 2007; Greve et al., 2006; Larrabee, 2005; Ord, Greve, Bianchini, & Curtis, 2007) reported base rates of malingering in differentiated patients with external incentive of between 30 and 40%. Binder and Willis (1991) found the PDRT failures in 33% (one third; a value later replicated by Bianchini, Mathias, Greve, Houston, & Crouch, 2001) of their undifferentiated compensation-seeking TBI patients. This number is consistent with the base rate of malingering in TBI.

When only non-malingering patients were examined using a known-groups design (Rogers, 1997), the significance of Ms. W.'s scores is clear. A score of 20 "Easy" was seen in only 1% of Binder and Kelly's (1996) moderate-severe TBI patients, patients who suffered much more significant and objectively defined brain trauma than Ms. W. Scores of 15 "Hard" and 35 Total were *never* observed in the Binder and Kelly (1996) sample. More recent research has demonstrated that the specificity of the PDRT in even moderate-severe brain injury is consistent with or better than that reported by Binder and Kelly (1996). Ms. W. may not have had any brain injury at all and certainly did not have one that could be objectively classified as moderate-severe. The false-positive error rate associated with her PDRT scores in mild TBI was *zero* for every PDRT score (Greve & Bianchini, 2006).

The empirical support for the validity of the PDRT as an effort test is both strong and consistent. Moreover, the scientific support for the conclusion that the PDRT reflects poor effort in this case is also strong. Nonetheless, Neuropsychologist 1 disregards this science and uses in its place his own subjective impressions:

Q: Are you saying that there was no indication, no suspicion of malingering from her on your test?

A: There was one test where she got so fatigued she couldn't do anything. There was one she did—she made no errors on.

Q: What page are you looking at?

A: I'm at the bottom of page 10: second to bottom and bottom paragraphs here. She had a perfect performance on two tests of effort. The other one which we tried to do at the end of the day—this is apparently when she left. This is why she left and came back. She was apparently wiped out. This is what happens sometimes during this test. We've quit using it since. Not only is it torture, it doesn't seem to be very valid. But, she did have trouble.

Q: Wait, wait. Why does it seem not to be very valid?

A: Because people who even are trying to do well sometimes don't. People who have every motivation to do well, every reason to do well, they're not in litigation, who stand to get money by doing well, for example, to get funding to go to college or whatever, still bomb on it sometimes. So, there's something wrong with the test and I don't like it.

Q: Do you have any authority you can cite to me on that?

A: I can probably find some stuff. It's really controversial. Can I . . . do you want me to look for some stuff?

Q: Please. I mean, I don't want you to make it a life research project, but if you can put your hands on it.

A: Yeah. I'll try to find some because it is—people are fighting over this test a lot now and it's . . .

Q: And that's the Portland Digit Recognition Test?

A: Yeah, that's right.

Q: Tell me how it works again.

A: It doesn't sound easy. It's not easy. That's the problem with the test. It's supposed to be easy and it's not. And that's why I don't like it anymore.

Q: How long did you use it before you discontinued using it?

A: Maybe on five or six cases. And it just became clearer and clearer that people who were really trying couldn't do it.

Q: You only used the test on five or six people?

A: Something like that. And I kept reading about it. And the more I read, the more I didn't like it. And the more people I used it on, I didn't like it. I don't know exactly how many total we did, but there was a period of time when we used it for a while and then we just said this is ridiculous, this is not a good test.

We have authored a review of symptom validity testing that included the PDRT (Bianchini, Mathias, & Greve, 2001), as well as three empirical papers on the PDRT (Bianchini et al., 2001; Doane, Greve, & Bianchini, 2005; Greve & Bianchini, 2006), and have never encountered any published papers that support any of the claims that Neuropsychologist 1 made regarding the PDRT beyond the assertion that the PDRT is not an enjoyable test. Although he may have been describing his own experiences with the test, it is not clear that this is what he is doing. Instead, he gives the incorrect impression that his experiences with the test reflect something in the neuropsychology literature.

Point 3

Neuropsychologist 1 does not appear to appreciate the significance of significantly below chance findings on a forced-choice symptom validity test. It is appropriate to consider alternative explanations for SVT findings. Neuropsychologist 1 seems to be doing this when he references the patient's fatigue during the PDRT and the unpleasantness of the test. However, there are certain SVT findings for which there is only one explanation: scores that are significantly below chance.

One of the advantages of forced-choice symptom validity tests is that their results can be referenced to the binomial distribution; therefore, the probability of achieving a particular score relative to chance or guessing can be determined (Bianchini et al., 2001). The interpretation of scores that are significantly below chance ($p < .05$) is well recognized in neuropsychology: A significantly below chance score reflects an intentional effort to get answers *wrong* (Frederick & Speed, 2007; Reynolds, 1998). Neuropsychologist 1's apparent failure to understand the implications of the below chance PDRT findings reported by Neuropsychologist 2 is demonstrated in the next passage.

Q: He [Neuropsychologist 2] refers to the Portland Digit Recognition test and that's one that you no longer give.

A: Right.

Q: . . . we've already talked about?

A: Right. I don't know how she did with him on that.

Q: He [Neuropsychologist 2] says: *"All three of these indices on this test are below chance indicating that this patient was purposely producing incorrect responses in order to appear more impaired than is, in fact, the case."* He made the point that by chance you'd get 50% of them right.

A: Yeah. And she got better than 50% of them right with me I know. I don't know with his. But she did better than chance. She just kept forgetting.

Q: According to his report he says, *"Out of 72 trials she made 20 correct responses; 11 easy and nine hard."*

A: Again, she did do better on the easy than the hard ones. That's something else you look at. Something he didn't address. But she did do well on something easier and do worse when it got harder.

Point 4

It appears that Neuropsychologist 1 recognized the issue of somatization in this case, though the implications of his own interpretations did not seem to influence his final opinions. He stated in the report: "This patient's MMPI–2 results suggest significant depression and anxiety, along with mild irritability. She noted a number of health concerns, with considerable preoccupation with her physical status. However, such preoccupation in no way negates real, documented medical problems."

Q: Is there a difference between malingering and the condition you talked about with Mr. [other attorney] earlier where someone is obsessing with the somatic disorder?

A: Yeah, there is.

Q: What's the difference?

A: Malingering means that somebody is deliberately aware that they don't have something wrong but trying to pretend they do. Somatizing means that they are totally caught up in their symptoms. They worry about that every little ache or pain could be due to some serious thing. It's an obsession with the problems. They convince themselves that there is a problem. There may really be one. They may convince themselves at times that there are things that aren't medically substantiable [sic] and, yet they may still believe, they still experience it. So, one is lying to other people. The other may be lying to oneself.

Q: So one is a conscious active effort on the part of the participant, i.e., the malingerer, to present a false front, correct?

A: Right.

Q: And the other person may unconsciously present a front that doesn't accurately reflect her abilities, correct?

A: Right.

Q: Doctor, you mentioned earlier with the somatic disorder discussion that there are certain personality factors that might predispose somebody to being excessively caught up in their symptoms. What personality factors are those?

A: Basically just a tendency to use physical problems as a defense mechanism. To focus on those rather than, in some cases, in place of, focusing on one's emotional distress or whatever. And people are predisposed to that.

Somatization refers to the way "certain patients use their physical symptoms as a way of dealing with, and communicating about, their emotional lives ... in this type of symptom magnification, physical symptoms may be easier to accept as causing current unhappiness and discontent than admitting that some psychological reason is contributing to it" (Gatchel, 2004, p. 204). In short, somatization reflects the expression of psychological problems manifested in physical symptoms and complaints, a tendency to complain of or develop physical symptoms and illness when under emotional stress, and it may be best viewed as a potentially maladaptive means of coping with stress in one's life. The MMPI, particularly Scales 1 (Hs) and 3 (Hy), is a powerful and well-validated method of detecting somatization (Friedman, Gleser, Smeltzer, Wakefield, & Schwartz, 1983; Marks & Seeman, 1963).

Even in the absence of malingering, the presence of somatization, as reflected in extreme elevations on Scales 1 and 3 in both examinations, has implications for the interpretation of this patient's somatic symptoms (pain, numbness, and "seizures"). Specifically, they likely reflect substantial psychological involvement in this patient's physical symptom presentation. The literature on spine surgery (Block et al., 2003; Block et al., 2001; Epker & Block, 2001; Linton, 2000) indicates that somatization is associated with an increased risk of poor outcome following spinal surgery, particularly if surgery is being considered solely or largely for symptom relief even in the context of a clear surgical pathology (Voorhies, Jiang, & Thomas, in press). Moreover, there is good evidence that somatization and related phenomena (e.g., pain catastrophizing) is a personality or coping style of longstanding that cannot be attributed to any specific event (Applegate, Keefe, Siegler, Bradley, McKee, & Cooper, 2005; Bigos, Battie, Spengler, Fisher, Fordyce, & Hansson, 1991; Linton, 2000; Schofferman, Anderson, Hines, Smith, & Keane, 1993; Schofferman, Anderson, Hines, Smith, & White, 1992).

In short, in this case, highlighting the somatization might have at least caused Ms. W.'s medical providers to reconsider their treatment options and hold off on the spinal surgery that was done only weeks after Examination 2. Recognizing and reporting this particular finding by Neuropsychologist 1 would have been an important contribution that the results of Examination 1 could have made to the ongoing care of this patient. The timing of the report of Examination 1 would have coincided with the independent neurosurgeon informing Ms. W. that she had no cervical pathology and was not a surgical candidate.

FINAL SUMMARY

There are important issues in this case that cross cognitive and physical symptom domains. The patient had improbably high levels of cognitive impairment and physical symptoms given the acute characteristics of the injury and the cervical spine MRI findings. In addition, her pain symptoms were not well explained by objective findings. She was claiming disabling cognitive and physical symptoms in the context of the lawsuit, and there was objective psychometric evidence of exaggeration of those symptoms.

The most definitive information that these discrepancies were a result of malingering was found in the cognitive symptom domain in the form of below chance findings on the PDRT. The finding of malingering in the cognitive symptom domain likely had significant implications for the assessment of the poorly explained physical symptoms, particularly in the context of high degrees of somatization/physical symptom exaggeration. The most negative result of her decision to malinger symptoms occurred in the physical domain in the form of an unnecessary cervical disc surgery intended to treat what were demonstrable exaggerated complaints.

This case demonstrates the active pursuit of medically unnecessary cervical surgery in a patient with definitive evidence of intentional symptom production and a diagnosis of malingering.

There are two psychiatric conditions characterized by intentional symptom production: Factitious Disorder and malingering. These two conditions differ in the underlying motivation for the symptom production. In Factitious Disorder, the symptoms are produced to meet some psychological need, such as interpersonal attention from the medical system, and the motivation is assumed to be unconscious. According to the Diagnostic and Statistical Manual (2000) criteria for Factitious Disorder, external incentive is absent. In contrast, in malingering the symptoms are produced to achieve some external or secondary gain, typically money, compensated time off work, and/or drugs.

Because malingering is intentional, it involves, by definition, a conscious choice to pursue the external goal. This fact has therefore provided some basis for the notion that this choice involves a rational calculation (i.e., secondary loss versus secondary gain). However, patients who malinger are subject to a variety of social and financial incentives and contingencies. They, like everyone, are also subject to the influence of largely unconscious intrapsychic needs and conflicts. The actions of the current patient call into question the assumption that the decision to malinger is made based on logic or a rational analysis. This case does not support Fishbain's (2003) contention that illogical choices rule out malingering as a diagnosis. Ultimately, malingering is a complex psychosocial phenomenon that should not be ruled in or ruled out on the basis of such simplistic clinical rules of thumb.

Patients with Factitious Disorder will intentionally engage in self-injurious behavior and seek out unnecessary medical treatment (Lande, 1996; Masterton, 1995; Paar, 1994; Wise & Ford, 1999). However, Factitious Disorder and malingering are not necessarily as distinct as DSM–IV seems to suggest. Eisendrath (1996) presented several cases in which the self-injurious behavior of patients with Factitious Disorder served as the basis of civil litigation. In these particular cases, the symptom production not only met the intrapsychic needs of the factitious patient but was also reinforced by the potential secondary gain associated with litigation. Similarly, Greve, Bianchini, and Ameduri (2003) reported a patient with a psychological profile consistent with Factitious Disorder who intentionally feigned sensory loss that she attributed to a work injury.

It is reasonable to assume that Factitious Disorder reflects greater psychopathology than that seen in most persons who choose to malinger. However, there is no reason to believe that patients with factitious tendencies or frank Factitious Disorder are any less subject to the influences of the potential secondary gain available in the medicolegal context than persons without the intrapsychic needs characteristic of Factitious Disorder. Moreover, the level of premorbid psychopathology in some patients who do malinger may approach that more characteristic of factitious patients, yet their behavior still reflects malingering. The current case demonstrates that some malingerers will engage in potentially self-injurious behavior and that malingering should not be ruled out simply on the basis that a person is seeking medically unnecessary treatment including surgery.

Appropriate early recognition of the malingering and psychopathology present in this case could have led to a rethinking of the surgery option. The MMPI revealed personality patterns which, even in the absence of malingering, would argue against a surgical intervention. However, given the magnitude of the malingering findings, the seriousness of the real, but pre-existing, underlying psychopathology did not become clear until this patient pursued cervical disc surgery after being told in no uncertain terms that there was not just an absence of surgical pathology, but no pathology in her cervical spine at all. The surgeon who did the surgery did it for symptom relief in a person whose symptoms were an unreliable (because of psychopathology, malingering, or both) reflection of her true physical status. Given the characteristics of this patient and other facts of the case, it is not at all certain that the psychological test findings from either evaluation would have had any influence on the ultimate surgery decision.

Ultimately the case was tried and went to the jury for a verdict. The jury returned an award that was substantially lower than requested by the plaintiff, an amount that was actually far less than the medical expenses in the case. The jury discounted brain injury and, considering the structure of their award, seemed to also conclude that the cervical disc surgery was unnecessary.

REFERENCES

Alexander, M. P. (1995). Mild traumatic brain injury: Pathophysiology, natural history, and clinical management. *Neurology*, *45*, 1253–1260.

American Psychiatric Association (2000). *Diagnostic and statistical manual of mental disorders*, 4th ed., text revised. Washington, DC: APA.

Applegate, K. L., Keefe, F. J., Siegler, I. C., Bradley, L. A., McKee, D. C., Cooper, K. S., & Riordan, P. (2005). Does personality at college entry predict number of reported pain conditions at mid-life? A longitudinal study. *Pain Medicine*, *6*(2), 92–97.

Ardolf, B. R., Denny, R. L., & Houston, C. M. (2007). Baserates of negative response bias and malingered neurocognitive dysfunction among criminal defendants referred for neuropsychological evaluation. *The Clinical Neuropsychologist*, *21*, 899–916.

Arnold, G., Boone, K. B., Lu, P., Dean, A., Wen, J., Nitch, S., & McPherson, S. (2005). Sensitivity and specificity of finger tapping test scores for the detection of suspect effort. *The Clinical Neuropsychologist*, *19*, 105–120.

Beetar, J. T., & Williams, J. M. (1995). Malingering response styles on the memory assessment scales and symptom validity tests. *Archives of Clinical Neuropsychology*, *10*(1), 57–72.

Bianchini, K. J., Etherton, J. L., & Greve, K. W. (2004). Diagnosing cognitive malingering in patients with work-related pain: Four cases. *Journal of Forensic Neuropsychology*, *4*, 65–85.

Bianchini, K. J., Greve, K. W., & Glynn, G. (2005). On the diagnosis of malingered pain-related disability: Lessons from cognitive malingering research. *The Spine Journal*, *5*, 404–417.

Bianchini, K. J., Greve, K. W., & Love, J. M. (2003). Definite malingered neurocognitive dysfunction in moderate/severe traumatic brain injury. *The Clinical Neuropsychologist*, *17*, 574–580.

Bianchini, K. J., Mathias, C. W., & Greve, K. W. (2001). Symptom validity testing: A critical review. *The Clinical Neuropsychologist*, *15*, 19–45.

Bianchini, K. J., Mathias, C. W., Greve, K. W, Houston, R. J., & Crouch, J. A. (2001). Classification accuracy of the Portland Digit Recognition Test in traumatic brain injury. *The Clinical Neuropsychologist*, *15*, 461–470.

Bigos, S. J., Battie, M. C., Spengler, D. M., Fisher, L. D., Fordyce, W. E., Hansson, T. H., Nachemson, A. L., & Wortley, M. D. (1991) A prospective study of work perceptions and psychosocial factors affecting the report of back injury. *Spine*, *16*(1), 1–6. Erratum in: *Spine*, *16*(6), 688.

Binder, L. M., & Kelly, M. P. (1996). Portland Digit Recognition Test performance by brain dysfunction patients without financial incentives. *Assessment*, *3*, 403–409.

Binder, L. M., & Willis, S. C. (1991). Assessment of motivation after financially compensable minor head trauma. *Psychological Assessment: Journal of Consulting and Clinical Psychology*, *3*, 175–181.

Block, A. R., Gatchel, R. J., Deardorff, W. W., & Guyer, R. D. (2003). *The psychology of spine surgery*. Washington, DC: American Psychiatric Association.

Block, A. R., Ohnmeiss, D. D., Guyer, R. D., Rashbaum, R. F., & Hochschuler, S. H. (2001). The use of presurgical psychological screening to predict the outcome of spine surgery. *The Spine Journal*, *1*(4), 274–282.

Boden, S. D., Davis, D. O., Dina, T. S., Patronas, N. J., & Wiesel, S. W. (1990). Abnormal magnetic-resonance scans of the lumbar spine in asymptomatic subjects: A prospective investigation. *Journal of Bone and Joint Surgery. American Volume*, *72*, 403–408.

Boden, S. D., McCowin, P. R., Davis, D. O., Dina, T. S., Mark, A. S., & Wiesel, S. (1990). Abnormal magnetic-resonance scans of the cervical spine in asymptomatic subjects. A prospective investigation. *Journal of Bone and Joint Surgery. American Volume*, *72*, 1178–1184.

Bogduk, N. (2004). Diagnostic blocks: a truth serum for malingering. *Clinical Journal of Pain*, *20*, 409–414.

Brown, S. C., Glass, J. M., & Park, D. C. (2002). The relationship of pain and depression to cognitive function in rheumatoid arthritis patients. *Pain*, *96*, 279–284.

Cassidy, J. D., Carroll, L., Cote, P., Berglund, A., & Nygren, A. (2003). Low back pain after traffic collisions: A population-based cohort study. *Spine*, *28*, 1002–1009.

Cocchiarella, L., & Andersson, G. (2001). *Guides to the evaluation of permanent impairment* (5th ed.). Chicago: AMA Press.

Cocchiarella, L., Lord, S. J., Turk, D. C., & Robenson, J. P. (2001). Guides to the evaluation of permanent impairment. In L. Cocchiarella & G. Andersson (Eds.), *Guides to the evaluation of permanent impairment* (5th ed.). Chicago: AMA Press.

Cohen, R. A., Malloy, P. F., & Jenkins, M. A. (1998). *Clinical neuropsychology: A pocket handbook for assessment*. Washington, DC: American Psychological Association.

Daubert v. Merrell Dow Pharmaceuticals, 113 S. Ct. 2786 (1993).

Dikmen, S. S., Machamer, J. E., Winn, H. R., & Temkin, N. R. (1995). Neuropsychological outcome at 1-year post head injury. *Neuropsychology*, *9*, 80–90.

Doane, B. M., Greve, K. W., & Bianchini, K. J. (2005). Agreement between the Abbreviated and Standard Portland Digit Recognition Test. *The Clinical Neuropsychologist*, *19*, 99–104.

Dvir, Z., Prushansky, T., & Peretz, C. (2001). Maximal versus feigned active cervical motion in healthy patients. *Spine*, *26*, 1680–1688.

Eccleston, C. (1994). Chronic pain and attention: A cognitive approach. *British Journal of Clinical Psychology*, *33*, 535–547.

Eisendrath, S. J. (1996) When Munchausen becomes malingering: Factitious disorders that penetrate the legal system. *Bulletin of the American Academy of Psychiatry and Law*, *24*(4), 471–481.

Ekman, P. O'Sullivan, M., & Frank, M. G. (1999). A few can catch a liar. *Psychological Science*, *10*, 263–266.

Epker, J., & Block, A. R. (2001). Presurgical psychological screening in back pain patients: A review. *Clinical Journal of Pain*, *17*(3), 200–5.

Faust, D. (1995). The detection of deception. *Neurologic Clinics*, *13*, 255–265.

Faust, D., Hart, K., & Guilmette, T. J. (1988). Pediatric malingering: The capacity of children to fake believable deficits on neuropsychological testing. *Journal of Consulting and Clinical Psychology*, *56*, 578–582.

Fishbain, D. A. (2003) Re: Secondary loss and pain-associated disability: theoretical overview and treatment implications. *Journal of Occupational Rehabilitation*, *13*, 197–198.

Fishbain, D. A., Cole, B., Cutler, R. B., Lewis, J., Rosomoff, H. L., & Rosomoff, R. S. (2003) A structured evidence-based review on the meaning of nonorganic physical signs: Waddell signs. *Pain Medicine*, *4*(2), 141–181.

Fishbain, D. A., Cutler, R., Rosomoff, H. L., & Rosomoff, R. S. (1999). Chronic pain disability exaggeration/malingering and submaximal effort research. *Clinical Journal of Pain*, *15*, 244–274.

Frederick, R. I., & Speed, F. M. (2007) On the interpretation of below-chance responding in forced-choice tests. *Assessment*, *14*(1), 3–11.

Friedman, A. F., Gleser, G. C., Smeltzer, D. J., Wakefield, J. A., & Schwartz, M. S. (1983). MMPI overlap item scales for differentiating psychotics, neurotics, and nonpsychiatric groups. *Journal of Consulting and Clinical Psychology*, *51*, 629–631.

Frymoyer, J. W., & Cats-Baril, W. L. (1991). An overview of the incidences and costs of low back pain. *Orthopedic Clinics of North America*, *22*(2), 263–271.

Gatchel, R. J. (2004). Comorbidity of chronic pain and mental health disorders: the biopsychosocial perspective. *The American Psychologist*, *59*, 795–805.

George, C. (2002). The six-month incidence of clinically significant low back pain in the Saskatchean adult population. *Spine*, *27*, 1778–1782.

Gervais, R. O., Green, P., Allen, L. M., & Iverson, G. L. (2001). Effects of coaching on symptom validity testing in chronic pain patients presenting for disability assessment. *Journal of Forensic Neuropsychology*, *2*, 1–19.

Greve, K. W., & Bianchini, K. J. (2006). Classification accuracy of the Portland Digit Recognition Test in Traumatic Brain Injury: Results of a known-groups analysis. *The Clinical Neuropsychologist*, *20*, 816—830.

Greve, K. W., Bianchini, K. J., & Ameduri, C. J. (2003). The use of a forced-choice test of tactile discrimination in the evaluation of functional sensory loss: A report of 3 cases. *Archives of Physical Medicine and Rehabilitation*, *84*(8), 1233–1236.

Greve, K. W., Bianchini, K. J., Black, F. W., Heinly, M. T., Love, J. M., Swift, D. A., & Megan Ciota, M. (2006). The prevalence of cognitive malingering in persons reporting exposure to occupational and environmental substances. *NeuroToxicology*, *27*, 940–950.

Greve, K. W., Bianchini, K. J., & Doane, B. M. (2006). Classification accuracy of the test of memory malingering in traumatic brain injury: Results of a known-groups analysis. *Journal of Clinical and Experimental Neuropsychology*, *28*(7), 1176–1190.

Greve, K. W., Bianchini, K. J., Love, J. M., Brennan, A., & Heinly, M. T. (2006). Sensitivity and specificity of MMPI–2 validity scales and indicators to malingered neurocognitive dysfunction in traumatic brain injury. *The Clinical Neuropsychologist*, *20*, 491–512.

Greve, K. W., Bianchini, K. J., Mathias, C. W., Houston, R. J., & Crouch, J. A. (2003). Detecting malingered performance on the Wechsler Adult Intelligence Scale: Validation of Mittenberg's approach in traumatic brain injury. *Archives of Clinical Neuropsychology*, *18*, 245–260.

Greve, K. W., Bianchini, K. J., & Roberson, T. (2007). The booklet category test and malingering in traumatic brain injury: Classification accuracy in known groups. *The Clinical Neuropsychologist, 21*, 318–337.

Grevitt, M., Pande, K., O'Dowd, J., & Webb, J. (1998). Do first impressions count? A comparison of subjective and psychologic assessment of spinal patients. *European Spine Journal, 7*, 218–223.

Guo, H. R., Tanaka, S., Cameron, L. L., Seligman, P. J., Behrens, V. J., Ger, J., et al. (1995). Back pain among workers in the United States: National estimates and workers at high risk. *American Journal of Industrial Medicine, 28*, 591–602.

Guo, H. R., Tanaka, S., Halperin, W E., & Cameron, L. L. (1999). Back pain prevalence in US industry and estimates of lost workdays. *American Journal of Public Health, 89*, 1029–1035.

Harris, I., Mulford, J., Solomon, M., van Gelder, J. M., & Young, J. (2005). Association between compensation status and outcome after surgery: A meta-analysis. *JAMA, 293*, 1644–1652.

Hazard, R. G., Reeves, V., & Fenwick J. W. (1992). Lifting capacity: Indices of subject effort. *Spine, 17*, 1065–1070.

Heaton, R. K., Smith, H. H., Jr., Lehman, R. A., & Vogt, A. T. (1978). Prospects for faking believable deficits on neuropsychological testing. *Journal of Consulting and Clinical Psychology, 46*, 892–900.

Heinly, M. T., Greve, K. W., Bianchini, K. J., Love, J. L., & Brennan, A. (2005). WAIS digit span-based indicators of malingered neurocognitive dysfunction: Classification accuracy in traumatic brain injury. *Assessment, 12*, 429–444.

Heubrock, D., & Petermann, F. (1998). Neuropsychological assessment of suspected malingering: Research results, evaluation techniques, and further directions of research and application. *European Journal of Psychological Assessment, 14*, 211–225.

Iezzi, T., Duckworth, M. P., Vuong, L. N., Archibald, Y. M., & Klinck, A. (2004). Predictors of neurocognitive performance in chronic pain patients. *International Journal of Behavioral Medicine, 11*, 56–61.

Iverson, G. L. (2003). Detecting malingering in civil forensic evaluations. In A. M. Horton & L. C. Hartlage (Eds.), *Handbook of Forensic Neuropsychology* (pp. 137–177). New York: Springer Publishing Company.

Iverson, G. L. (2005). Outcome from mild traumatic brain injury. *Current Opinion in Psychiatry, 18*, 301–317.

Iverson, G., King, R. J., Scott, J. G., & Adams, R. L. (2001). Cognitive complaints in litigating patients with head injuries or chronic pain. *Journal of Forensic Neuropsychology, 2*, 19–30.

Iverson, G. L., & McCracken, L. M. (1997). "Postconcussive" symptoms in persons with chronic pain. *Brain Injury, 11*, 783–790.

Kay, N. R., & Morris-Jones, H. (1998). Pain clinic management of medico-legal litigants. *Injury, 29*, 305–308.

Kewman, D. G., Vaishampayan, N., Zald, D., & Han, B. (1991). Cognitive impairment in musculoskeletal pain patients. *International Journal of Psychiatry in Medicine, 21*, 253–262.

Lande, R. G. (1996). Factitious disorders and the "professional patient". *Journal of the American Osteopathic Association, 96*, 468–472.

Larrabee, G. J. (1990). Cautions in the use of neuropsychological evaluation in legal settings. *Neuropsychology, 4*, 239–247.

Larrabee, G. J. (2003). Exaggerated pain report in litigants with malingered neurocognitive dysfunction. *The Clinical Neuropsychologist, 17*, 395–401.

Larrabee, G. J. (2005). Assessment of malingering. In G. J. Larrabee (Ed.), *Forensic neuropsychology*. New York: Oxford University Press.

Lees-Haley, P. R. (1989). Malingering traumatic mental disorder on the Beck Depression Inventory: Cancerphobia and toxic exposure. *Psychological Report, 65*, 623–626.

Lees-Haley, P. R. (1990). Malingering mental disorder on the Impact of Event Scale (IES): Toxic exposure and cancerphobia. *Journal of Traumatic Stress, 3*, 315–321.

Linton, S. J. (2000). A review of psychological risk factors in back and neck pain. *Spine, 25*, 1148–1156.

Marks, P. A., & Seeman, W. (1963). *The actuarial description of abnormal personality*. Baltimore: Williams & Wilkins.

Masterton, G. (1995). Factitious disorders and the surgeon. *British Journal of Surgery, 82*, 1588–1589.

Menefee, L. A., Cohen, M. J. M., Anderson, W. R., Doghramji, K., Frank, E. D., & Lee, H. (2000). Sleep disturbance and nonmalignant chronic pain: A comprehensive review of the literature. *Pain Medicine, 1*, 156–172.

Meyers, J. E., & Diep, A. (2000). Assessment of malingering in chronic pain patients using neuropsychological tests. *Applied Neuropsychology, 7*, 133–139.

Millis, S. R., & Volinsky, C. T. (2001). Assessment of response bias in mild head injury: Beyond malingering tests. *Journal of Clinical and Experimental Neuropsychology, 23*, 809–828.

Mittenberg, W., Patton, C., Canyock, E. M., & Condit, D. C. (2002). Baserates of malingering and symptom exaggeration. *Journal of Clinical and Experimental Neuropsychology*, 24, 1094–1102.

Mittenberg, W., Theroux, S., Aguila-Puentes, G., Bianchini, K., Greve, K., & Rayls, K. (2001). Identification of malingered head injury on the Wechsler Adult Intelligence Scale–3rd Edition. *The Clinical Neuropsychologist*, 15, 440–445.

Mittenberg, W., Theroux-Fichera, S., Zielinski, R. E., & Heilbronner, R. L. (1995). Identification of malingered head injury on the Wechsler Adult Intelligence Scale–Revised. *Professional Psychology: Research and Practice*, 26, 491–498.

Morken, T., Riise, T., Moen, B., Bergum, O., Hauge, S. H., Holien, S., Langedrag, A., Olson, H. O., Pedersen, S., Saue, I. L., Seljebo, G. M., & Thoppil, V. (2002). Frequent musculoskeletal symptoms and reduced health-related quality of life among industrial workers. *Occupational Medicine (London)*, 52(2), 91–98.

Ord, J., Greve, K. W., Bianchini, K. J., & Curtis, K. L. (February, 2007). *Prevalence of malingering in chronic pain: A comparison of two diagnostic systems*. A poster presented at the 35th Annual Meeting of the International Neuropsychological Society, Portland, Oregon.

Paar, G. H. (1994) Factitious disorders in the field of surgery. *Psychotherapy and Psychosomatics*, 62(1–2), 41–47.

Picavet, H. S. J., & Schouten, J. S. A. G. (2003). Musculoskeletal pain in the Netherlands: Prevalences, consequences and risk groups, the DMC3-study. *Pain*, 102, 167–178.

Public Attitude Monitor (1992). Survey. Oak Brook, IL: Insurance Research Council.

Public Attitude Monitor (1993). Survey. Oak Brook, IL: Insurance Research Council.

Rainville, J., Sobel, J. B., Hartigan, C., & Wright, A. (1997). The effect of compensation involvement on the reporting of pain and disability by patients referred for rehabilitation of chronic low back pain. *Spine*, 22, 2016–2024.

Reynolds, C. R. (1998) Common sense, clinicians, and actuarialism. In C. R. Reynolds (Ed.) *Detection of malingering during head injury litigation* (pp. 261–286). New York: Plenum.

Robinson, M. E., Bulcourf, B., Atchison, J. W, Berger, J., Lafayette-Lucy, A., Hirsh, A. T., et al. (2004). Compliance in pain rehabilitation: patient and provider perspectives. *Pain Medicine*, 5, 66–80.

Rogers, R. (1997). *Clinical assessment of malingering and deception*, 2nd ed. New York: Guilford Press.

Rohling, M. L., Binder, L. M., & Langhinrichsen-Rohling, J. (1995). Money matters: A meta-analytic review of the association between financial compensation and the experience and treatment of chronic pain. *Health Psychology*, 14, 537–547.

Schofferman, J., Anderson, D., Hines, R., Smith, G., & Keane, G. (1993). Childhood psychological trauma and chronic refractory low-back pain. *Clinical Journal of Pain*, 9(4), 260–265.

Schofferman, J., Anderson, D., Hines, R., Smith, G., & White, A. (1992) Childhood psychological trauma correlates with unsuccessful lumbar spine surgery. *Spine*, 17(6 Suppl), S138–144.

Sjogren, P., Olsen, A. K., Thomsen, A. B., & Dalberg, J. (2000). Neuropsychological performance in cancer patients: The role of oral opioids, pain and performance status. *Pain*, 86, 237–245.

Slick, D. J., Sherman, E. M. S., & Iverson, G. L. (1999) Diagnostic criteria for malingering cognitive dysfunction: Proposed standards for clinical practice and research. *Clinical Neuropsychology*, 13(4), 545–561.

Stuss, D. T. (1995). A sensible approach to mild traumatic brain injury. *Neurology*, 45, 1251–1252.

Sweet, J. J. (Ed.). (1999). *Forensic neuropsychology: Fundamentals and practice*. Lisse: Swets & Zeitlinger.

Tate, D. G. (1992). Worker's disability and return to work. *American Journal of Physical Medicine and Rehabilitation*, 71, 92–96.

Tombaugh, T. (1996). *Test of Memory Malingering manual*. New York: MultiHealth Systems.

Vaccaro, A. R., Ring, D., Scuderi, G., Cohen, D. S., & Garfin, S. R. (1997). Predictors of outcome in patients with chronic back pain and low-grade spondylolisthesis. *Spine*, 22, 2030–2034.

van Tulder, M. W., Koes, B. W., & Bouter, L. M. (1995). A cost-of-illness study of back pain in the Netherlands. *Pain*, 62, 233–240.

Voorhies, R. M., Jiang, X., & Thomas, N. (in press). Predicting outcome in the surgical treatment of lumbar radiculopathy using the Pain Drawing Score, McGill Short Form Pain Questionnaire, and risk factors including psychosocial issues and axial joint pain. *The Spine Journal*.

Walker, B. F. (2000). The prevalence of low back pain: a systematic review of the literature from 1966 to 1998. *Journal of Spinal Disorders*, 13, 205–217.

Wise, M. G., & Ford, C. V. (1999) Factitious disorders. *Primary Care*, 26, 315–326.

Woodwell, D. A., & Cherry, D. K. (2004). National Ambulatory Medical Care Survey: 2002 summary. *Advance Data*, 1–44.

Alleged carbon monoxide poisoning

26

David S. Bush

Carbon monoxide (CO) is a colorless, tasteless, odorless, non-irritating and commonly occurring substance. An individual exposed to potentially dangerous levels of CO is unlikely to detect its presence (US Environmental Protection Agency, 2000). CO is known to often be quite toxic, especially to organ systems that require high levels of oxygenization (i.e., the heart and brain) (e.g., Raub, Mathieu-Nolf, Hampson, & Thom, 2000). As CO enters the lungs, it is quickly absorbed into the bloodstream where it readily binds with hemoglobin (Hb) to form carboxyhemoglobin (COHb). Inasmuch as the affinity of CO for Hb is much (200 times) greater than that of oxygen (O_2), hypoxia can and often does result from the competitive displacement of life-sustaining levels of oxygen. The resultant disruption of oxygen delivery promotes cell injury and death and can set in motion a cascade of other pathophysiological events that place sensitive organs at risk. Factors that influence the toxicity of CO include length of exposure, concentration of the gas, respiratory processing, cardiac output, hematocrit, oxygen requirements of tissues, metabolic status, and preexisting disease (e.g., Raub & Benignus, 2002; Yudofsky & Hales, 1997).

Due to its high demands for oxygen and other blood products, the brain is especially vulnerable to injury via CO poisoning. The resultant patterns of brain injury depend on a number of factors. The clinical picture can include generalized findings of diffuse cortical atrophy as well as more specific or focal syndromes involving brain regions known to be uniquely susceptible to the effects of CO poisoning such as cerebral white matter, the globus pallidus, corpus collosum, hippocampus, and fornix (Gale, Hopkins, Weaver, Bigler, Booth, & Blatter, 1999; Kesler, Hopkins, Weaver, Blatter, Edge-Booth, & Bigler, 2001; Parkinson, Hopkins, Cleavinger, Weaver, Victoroff, Foley, & Bigler, 2002; Porter, Hopkins, Weaver, Bigler, & Blatter, 2002; Uchino, Hasuo, Shida, Matsumoto, Yasumori, & Masuda, 1994). Not surprisingly then, the neuropsychological symptom presentations are quite variable and can range from very minimal, relatively transient decrements on behavioral tasks to states of profound encephalopathy or even akinetic mutism, associated with very poor prognosis. Global cognitive impairment is uncommon, however. In the more severe cases, periods of coma and delirium are commonly followed by apathy, slowness, amnesia, and/or extrapyramidal features (e.g., Hartman, 1995; Lishman, 1998).

Representations of neuropsychological impairment due to CO poisoning are apt to present in a medical-legal context, as they are often based on alleged fact patterns that are ideally suited to compensable claims. First, CO poisoning frequently occurs by accident in industrial and domestic settings. Based on data compiled by the National Electronic Injury Surveillance System All Injury Program (NEISS-AIP) and 2001–2002 death certificate data from the National Vital Statistics System (NVSS), an analysis at the Centers for Disease Control and Prevention (CDC) found that there were approximately 15,200 persons with confirmed or possible non-fire-related CO exposure treated in emergency rooms in 2001–2003. During 2001–2002, there were 480 deaths on average, attributed to non-fire-related CO poisoning (CDC, 2005). Insufficient ventilation in work settings, defective equipment leading to incomplete combustion, and exposure to car or gasoline motor fumes in enclosed spaces are examples of potential accidental mechanisms of CO toxicity. Within the CDC analysis, furnaces and motor vehicles were the most common source of non-fatal, unintentional, non-fire-related CO exposure. Second, as noted above, an individual exposed to potentially danger-ous levels of CO may not detect its presence, a scenario made even more likely by the occurrence of unconsciousness in more severe cases. Third, although relatively rare and occurring only among severe cases, some individuals who suffer neurologic injury as a result of CO exposure exhibit patterns of delayed-onset neuropsychiatric sequelae or behavioral worsening following a latent interval or period of pseudo-recovery (e.g., Hartman, 1995; Lishman, 1998).

Many neuropsychologists reviewing the available literature on CO poisoning will notice certain parallels with the more established literature on traumatic brain injury (TBI) outcome. In particular, consistent with the neuropsychological effects of TBI, the literature on CO toxicity generally sug-gests a *dose-response* trend (i.e., greater levels of exposure are associated with higher levels of toxicity and a correspondingly increased likelihood of neurological injury). Furthermore, there appears to be some controversy and ambiguity concerning the potential for significant neurotoxicity at rela-tively low levels of exposure. This matter is made even more complicated by the fact that human beings produce endogenous CO, at levels that can run relatively high in tobacco smokers (Raub & Benignus, 2002). In one recent re-analysis of existing research, Raub and Benignus (2002) raised doubts about the association between low COHb levels (5–10%) and behavioral effects. Thus, it is often a technical challenge to differentiate between neuropsychological symptoms resulting from compensable claims of low level CO exposure versus other endogenous and exogenous factors. Of course, experienced neuropsychologists also understand that such distinctions are complicated by the potential biasing effects of financial incentives and are virtually impossible to resolve on the basis of self-report alone.

THE CASE OF MS. X.

Identifying data, reason for referral, and self-reported history

A 51-year-old, right-handed, married, Caucasian woman with 10 years of education and a GED was referred by defense counsel for a compulsory neuropsychological examination. Ms. X. presented with complaints of persistent changes in her cognitive and personality functioning following an alleged incident of work-related carbon monoxide poisoning, approximately six years prior. By the time of this referral, Ms. X. had already been determined to be permanently and totally disabled in a worker's compensation venue. She was under the care of a psychiatrist and neurologist and treated with antidepressants and an anxiolytic medication (Prozac 40 mg, Trazodone 40 mg, Xanax prn). She was now pursuing a claim for mental damages in the context of civil litigation. At the time of the alleged injury, Ms. X. was employed as a laborer in a fruit packing plant.

Ms. X. reported that she developed increasing symptoms of nausea, fatigue, and headache over the course of a week that she and several of her co-workers were based in a poorly ventilated cold storage area where she was exposed to the exhaust fumes of two gas-operated forklifts. By week's end, she reportedly drove home 20 miles but claimed to have no memory of stopping at her daugh-ter's house mid-way. She further claimed that she became "disoriented" later that evening. She felt acutely ill and barely able to walk or balance herself ("I knew I was in some kind of trouble . . . it was not me . . . I knew something just wasn't right . . . I felt very weak"). She was subsequently brought by family to a local emergency room where she was given oxygen and reportedly directed to not return to work in the cold storage area. Inasmuch as the employer denied her request to increase the ventilation in the area in question, she never resumed work. Ms. X. described herself as having extremely low tolerance for stimulation of all kinds (e.g., "I can't deal with people") and claimed she could no longer trust herself to operate potentially dangerous machinery.

Ms. X. did not know whether any of her former co-workers developed any long-term symptoms. She presented, however, with a wide range of various somatic and psychological complaints and symptoms. These included bilateral carpal tunnel syndrome (which she attributed to the alleged CO exposure), non-exertional chest pains, frequent urination, occasional urinary incontinence, heightened smell sensitivity, anxiety, depression, agoraphobia with panic symptoms, an inability to relax, rapid short-term forgetting, decreased appetite with weight loss, sleep disturbance, and reduced libido. Curiously, and in the absence of any supportive behavioral evidence, Ms. X. indicated that her short-term memory problem had gotten progressively worse over the years. While she claimed to not know the cause of her various problems, she felt inclined to attribute them to the alleged exposure because, "I'm not the person that I was" and "Whatever happened to me that day has changed my life."

Ms. X. denied use of alcohol and other recreational chemicals. She reported smoking six to seven cigarettes per day and *never* smoked more than one pack of cigarettes per day. There was no known history of learning or developmental problems. She denied having any pre-incident history of psychiatric problems or mental health treatment. She denied having any pre-incident history of neurological illness or injury. At age 15, she was involved in a motor vehicle accident in which she suffered a leg fracture but no head trauma. When asked if this was a serious accident, Ms. X. seemed to hesitate. She then went on to mention feeling "heartbroken" because her close friend was killed in this accident. She was not aware of any previous exposure to toxic substances. Interestingly, approximately six months prior to the alleged incident of CO exposure in the workplace, Ms. X. sustained a superficial gunshot wound in a freak accident, which "scared the hell out of us." She and her husband were asleep in their bed at home when a neighbor's shotgun discharged by accident. Buckshot penetrated their bedroom wall, resulting in a superficial leg wound. Residual signs and symptoms of Posttraumatic Stress Disorder (PTSD) related to this incident were denied, both immediately after the accidental shooting and at the time of the compulsory neuropsychological examination.

Information gleaned from the records review

As is often the case in forensic neuropsychology practice, a careful review of medical and other records revealed additional important history about Ms. X., as well as significant data that contradicted her self-report.

The Emergency Room record pertaining to the alleged CO exposure reflected complaints of headache, generalized weakness, and chest pains determined to be atypical for a cardiac condition. Cognitive symptoms and confusion, however, were specifically denied. There was no documentation of any history of disorientation, signs of neurologic deficit, or respiratory compromise. Her COHb level was 9.1%, though she was noted to be a smoker. (Normal ranges for COHb are 0–1.5% for non-smokers and 4–9% for smokers; Associated Regional and University Pathologists, Users Guide, 2004). It should be noted that Ms. X. was seen in the emergency room one day after she was last in the work environment, so it is possible that her COHb level had already dissipated from some higher level. She was treated with oxygen, given three days off from work, and told not to smoke. She was felt to have "carbon monoxide by history." She was given information about "the possibility of delayed neurologic sequelae" as well as the possibility of "subtle" neurologic damage due to "chronic exposure" to carbon monoxide. Additionally, she was advised to not smoke.

Approximately 10 days after the emergency room visit, Ms. X. was seen by a neurologist for complaints of headaches, nausea, blurry vision, and numbness involving her right face and elbow. There was no description of altered mentation or sign of cognitive impairment. The results of a brain MRI showed scattered non-specific foci of altered deep white matter signal intensity of undetermined etiology. While focal areas of demyelenation could not be ruled out, the distribution pattern was not typical for Multiple Sclerosis (MS), and the most likely etiology was small vessel disease due to ischemic changes. The results of a conventional EEG and "brain mapping" study were normal. Her headaches were attributed to a history of CO exposure and, later, in conjunction with her worker's compensation claim, a neurological examination led to a diagnostic impression of possible mild persistent neurological sequelae secondary to CO exposure. If present, however, this condition was described as not likely of disabling proportions.

Contrary to Ms. X.'s denial of past psychiatric problems and consultation with mental health professionals prior to the alleged work accident, her records included the report of a previous psychological evaluation. In fact, less than six months before the alleged incident of work-related exposure and only about one month after the accidental shooting, she sought treatment from a psychologist, characterizing herself as a "nervous wreck." At the time, she was smoking about one and a half packs of cigarettes per day, and she represented herself as struggling with various emotional and behavioral symptoms that are common among victims of recent traumas (i.e., nervousness/worry, irritability, feeling preoccupied that she or one of her family members could have been seriously injured, lingering feelings of vulnerability with fears of re-injury, uncontrollable thoughts about the shooting incident, hypersensitivity to loud noise, etc.). Standard intelligence and personality tests were administered, leading to a diagnosis of Major Depression secondary to the accidental shooting. Judging from the recommendation for the compensatory use of "data organization systems" "to help her retrieval memory mechanisms," it appears that her pre-exposure complaints likely included memory difficulty.

Among the records provided was the report of a detailed records review conducted by a physician specializing in emergency and occupational medicine, who had been retained as an expert in the worker's compensation matter. Basic principles of CO poisoning were summarized. It was noted that Ms. X.'s documented level of COHb in the emergency room one day after the alleged exposure (9.1%) was "common with heavy cigarette use." (This doctor did not know Ms. X.'s actual level of tobacco use.) On the assumption of an estimated half-life of 12 hours, it was likely that Ms. X.'s initial (24 hours prior) COHb level was in the vicinity of 36%. This assumption was judged improbable, however, because her major symptom was headache—a COHb level of 36% would be expected to produce serious neurologic impairment, inclusive of coma.

Moreover, the brain imaging findings were not characteristic of the typical pattern associated with CO poisoning (i.e., bilateral necrosis of the globus pallidus). Suggestions were made to recreate the work situation and investigate the health status of Ms. X.'s former co-workers as methods for empirically assessing the probable levels of CO exposure she actually sustained.

In medical-legal cases, it is not unusual for neuropsychologists to receive additional records after an examination has been completed and a report submitted. Often, these "late-arriving" records are highly relevant and may lend support to opinions already reached or lead to revisions of one's conclusions. In the case of Ms. X., additional materials were received following the completion of the compulsory neuropsychological examination and submission of the report. While these records did, indeed, include data relevant to a determination of the likelihood of a mental injury secondary to alleged CO exposure, the net impact of this additional information was to support opinions already formed.

The "late-arriving" records included the report of a previously undisclosed neuropsychological examination, conducted shortly before the compulsory neuropsychological examination (by the same clinical psychologist who evaluated Ms. X. after the accidental gun shot wound). Ms. X. told this psychologist that she had been highly prone to getting lost since the alleged exposure incident, which was information that was not mentioned during the compulsory exam. The psychologist opined that her test performance was effortful; there were no signs of "malingering and/or symptom exaggeration." However, the only measure of symptom validity or cognitive effort administered was the Rey 15-Item Visual Memory Test. Her (suspiciously low) score on this test (9/15) was neither documented nor discussed within the text of the report. On the basis of her neuropsychological test performance, the psychologist concluded "within a reasonable degree of psychological probability" that Ms. X. "demonstrated neuropsychological dysfunctioning and resultant emotional problems, more specifically related to her chemical exposure accident [sic]." There was no discussion or comparison of her pre-incident versus post-incident test performance, even though this same psychologist found her to have major depression due to the accidental shooting incident, and a comparison of her scores across a measure of psychometric intelligence did not support an inference of intellectual decline (see Table 26.2).

After the compulsory neuropsychological examination, Ms. X. was seen for a compulsory neurological examination, also on referral from defense counsel. The neurologist noted that her behavior was "quite unusual" during sensory-perceptual testing. While she had no problem hearing or feeling a vibratory tuning fork in the middle of her skull, she seemed to have no appreciation of vibratory sensation "anywhere from the neck down." Although she had preserved cold sensation in her hands and feet, she had no pinprick sensation anywhere, including her face. The neurologist concluded that, "The sensory examination cannot possibly be physiological or this woman would have been unable to tandem walk or have a negative Romberg." In all other respects, the neurological examination was normal. The conclusion was that there were no neurological problems secondary to CO exposure and no convincing evidence of any history of actual exposure.

Neuropsychological examination of Ms. X.

Behavior observations

Ms. X. presented as a plain-looking woman who looked somewhat older than her chronological age. There were no comportmental problems and no obvious features of memory difficulty or cognitive impairment. Over the course of a lengthy interview, questions did not have to be repeated, and she had no apparent difficulty learning her way around the office. Her affect and mood suggested underlying tension, anxiety, and worry, but she smiled easily and did not come across as clinically depressed. She evidenced a pattern of syntax and grammar that was consistent with her limited education and lower middle-class upbringing in the rural south ("Dr. Bush does people feel intimidated?"). There was no suggestion of aphasia or thought disorder. Standardized test procedures were followed, using a flexible battery approach. As will be seen, however, the test results were invalidated by unequivocal evidence of motivation to perform poorly, especially in the context of memory tasks.

Neuropsychological test performance

Table 26.1 presents Ms. X.'s test scores at the time of the compulsory neuropsychological examination. With the focus of the present chapter in mind, the data reflect several important trends. First, her scores across three well-known symptom-validity tests fell below recommended cutoffs known to reliably flag response bias. The symptom-validity tests used in the examination of Ms. X. were the Computerized Assessment of Response Bias (Allen, Conder, Green, & Cox, 1997), the Word Memory Test (Green, Allen, & Astner, 1996), and the Test of Memory Malingering (Tombaugh, 1996). These findings were strikingly consistent and established the unequivocal invalidity of the ability test data. The astute reader will note that this performance occurred against the background of a stable Low Average IQ that was statistically equivalent to her psychometric intelligence level prior to the alleged exposure incident. One especially salient feature of her effort test performance was her failure to exhibit any significant learning across Trials 1 and 2 of the TOMM, a finding that can only be accounted for on the basis of motivation to perform poorly in all but the most seriously impaired patient. Second, her memory test scores were grossly abnormal and clearly indicative of a non-neurological trend, especially for an individual who did not exhibit any "extra-test" signs of actual memory impairment. In particular, the reader's attention is called to the unusually high number (13) of false-positive errors on the recognition component of the Rey Auditory Verbal Learning Test

TABLE 26.1 Ms. X.'s test data: Compulsory neuropsychological examination, 2001

Cognitive Validity Tests

CARB Block 1:	83.8%	Block 2: 81.1%	Block 3: 78.4%	Total: 81%
WMT IR:	82.5%	DR: 80%	Cons1: 72.5%	Cons2: 45%
TOMM Trial 1:	30/50	Trial 2: 31/50	Retention Trial: 34/50	

Intelligence
WAIS–III VIQ: 88   PIQ: 84 FSIQ: 85   VCI: 86 POI: 86 WMI: 94   PSI: 76
   Voc: 6   Sim: 8   Arith: 9 DSpan: 9   Info: 8   Letter-Num Seq: 9
   PC: 9   Dig Symb-Coding: 7   BD: 8   MR: 6   SS: 4

Academic Achievement
WRAT–3 Reading: 86   Spelling: 74   Arithmetic: 81

Learning/Memory
BVRT: 3/10 correct   RMT-Words: 36/50, Faces: 32/50
RAVLT (raw scores): Trial 1: 5   Trial 2: 10   Trial 3: 11   Trial 4: 11   Trial 5: 14
   Total: 51
   List B: 2   Short Delay Recall: 10   Long Delay Recall: 10
   Recognition: 15/15   False Positives: 13
WMT: MC: 45%   PA: 50%   FR: 52.5%

Neuropsychological Tests	*Raw:*	*Heaton T:*	*Language:*
Trails A	33″	46	BNT: 52/60
Trails B–1st Administration	99″ (+3 errors)	41	
2nd Administration	110″ (+5 errors)	41	Letter Fluency–FAS (raw): 29
Tapping–D	40.4	43	
Tapping–ND	38	48	
Grooved Pegboard–D	84	32	
Grooved Pegboard–ND	101	30	
DVT-Time	462″	38	
DVT-Errors	12	39	
WCST Categories	4		
WCST-Perseverative Responses	14	55	

Affective Status/Personality
MMPI–2 (T scores): L = 57; F = 68; K = 46; TRIN = 58; VRIN = 54; FB = 101; FBS (raw) = 34; Hs = 95; D = 107;
Hy = 89; Pd = 58; Mf = 55; Pa = 74; Pt = 88; Sc = 87; Ma = 37; Si = 78.
PAI (T scores): ICN = 49; INF = 67; NIM = 73; PIM = 36; SOM = 73; ANX = 91; ARD = 66; DEP = 106; MAN = 48;
PAR = 43; SCZ = 9;1 BOR = 67; ANT = 41; ALC = 41; DRG = 44; AGG = 42; SUI = 82; STR = 57; NON = 53;
RXR = 40; DOM = 31; WRM = 37.
BAI (raw): 31

(AVLT) and scores on the Warrington Recognition Memory Test (RMT) that fell below documented average levels obtained by individuals who underwent temporal lobectomies for intractable epilepsy (Hermann, Connell, Barr, & Wyler, 1995; Millis & Dijkers, 1993; Naugle, Chelune, Schuster, Luders, & Comair, 1994). Third, performance on a repeat administration of the Trail Making Test, Part B was remarkable for unchanged time and increased errors (i.e., not only was there no practice effect, her performance was actually significantly worse). Fourth, relative to her grossly normal bilateral finger tapping speed, her moderately abnormal scores on the Grooved Pegboard test were suspiciously slow. Fifth, the Minnesota Multiphasic Personality Inventory–2 (MMPI–2) profile generated at the time of the compulsory examination was unusually high-ranging and suggestive of very extreme symptom endorsement relative to chronic pain and other medical groups (i.e., seven of the clinical scales were T ≥ 74; Larrabee, 2003a). Yet, despite her representation of severe memory impairment, Ms. X. was able to answer the MMPI–2 items in a consistent fashion (True Response Inconsistency, T = 58; Variable Response Inconsistency, T = 54). Additionally, the profile was characterized by very significant elevations on scales known to be associated with symptom exaggeration and response bias (F Back, T = 101; Fake Bad Scale = 34; Larrabee, 1998; Larabee 2003b). A similar response style characterized the Personality Assessment Inventory (PAI) profile, which reflected the endorsement of bizarre and highly atypical symptoms.

Inasmuch as the same psychologist evaluated Ms. X. both before and after the alleged exposure incident and concluded that she suffered a neuropsychological injury as a result of a "chemical exposure accident," a comparison of the test data generated by these two examinations is especially illuminating. These data are presented in Table 26.2. As can be seen, the WAIS–III PIQ and FSIQ

TABLE 26.2   Ms. X.'s test data: Outside examinations

	1995 (PRE-INCIDENT)	*2000 (POST-INCIDENT)*
Validity Tests		
Rey 15-Item Visual Memory	n/a	9/15 (raw)
Intelligence		
WAIS–III VIQ	90	84
PIQ	88	90
FSIQ	88	86
Info	7	7
Digit Span	10	9
Vocabulary	6	6
Arithmetic	8	7
Comprehension	8	7
Similarities	8	8
Picture Completion	8	12
Picture Arrangement	5	8
Block Design	7	9
Object Assembly	7	n/a
Matrix Reasoning	n/a	8
Digit Symbol	7	6
Academic Achievement		
WRAT–3 Reading	n/a	79
Spelling	n/a	76
Arithmetic	n/a	71

Memory Tests (only administered in 2000)
WMS–R General Memory Index: 82   Attention/Concentration Index: 78   Delayed Recall Index: 80
Verbal Memory Index: 79   Visual Memory Index: 93

Neuropsychological Tests (only administered in 2000)

	Raw	Heaton-T
Category Test	115	26
TPT–Total Time	0.54	47
Memory	4	31
Localization	0	34
Seashore Rhythm Test	15	29
Speech Perception Test	11	37
Finger Tapping-Dominant	33	36
Impairment Index	9	29
SDMT–Written	34	
Oral	48	

were statistically unchanged, an unlikely scenario in the context of an intervening neuropsychological injury. Similar inferences are drawn from a comparison of specific WAIS–III subtest scores (i.e., her post-incident scores on Picture Completion and Picture Arrangement were at least one standard deviation higher and her score on Digit Symbol-Coding was unchanged). While Ms. X. did poorly on a test of visual memory (BVRT) at the time of the compulsory neuropsychological examination (3/10 correct, see Table 26.1), she obtained an entirely normal Visual Memory Index score on the Wechsler Memory Scale–Revised (WMS–R) (93) just a few months prior (see Table 26.2). Due to technically poor copy, retroactive scoring of the pre-incident MMPI FBS could not be accomplished. Consistent with the finding at the time of the compulsory neuropsychological exam, however, retroactive scoring of the first post-incident MMPI–2 also yielded a significantly elevated FBS score (30).

Case analysis

Using contemporary evidence-based standards of practice, neuropsychologists have been advised to rely on multi-modal criteria for making inferences about malingering behavior (e.g, Iverson & Binder, 2000; Larrabee, 2005; Slick, Sherman, & Iverson, 1999; Sweet, 1999). Several aspects of this case were judged as supportive of probable malingering (Slick et al., 1999). Using the Slick et al. (1999) paradigm, this case was characterized by:

1. *Presence of a substantial external incentive.* As a result of her alleged neuropsychological injury, Ms. X. was found to be permanently and totally disabled in a worker's compensation venue. She was no longer required to work, and she presumably received some form of significant monetary compensation. At the time of the compulsory examination, she was involved in civil litigation where a finding of permanent disability due to brain damage would also presumably result in significant financial compensation.
2. *Two or more types of evidence from neuropsychological testing, excluding definite negative response bias.* Ms. X.'s scores across three symptom-validity tests fell below established cutoffs for response bias and average scores produced by diverse patient groups with objectively verified forms of severe mental impairment. Again, these scores occurred against a background of an essentially normal IQ score that was unchanged relative to her pre-incident intelligence level. Her ability test performance was characterized by a neuropsychologically implausible pattern of results on measures of recognition memory, visual memory (across two evaluations), and motor skills. Her MMPI–2 FBS score was consistent with extreme symptom exaggeration and grossly discrepant from what has been shown to usually occur among clinically referred brain-injured patients not involved in litigation (e.g., Greiffenstein, Baker, Gola, Donders, & Miller, 2002).
3. *Behavior not fully accounted for by psychiatric, neurological, or developmental factors.* Ms. X. had no known history of any developmental disorder, and there was no compelling objective evidence of any neurological illness or injury that could reasonably account for her neuropsychological test performance. Although she did appear to have a mood disorder, this condition was likely chronic and, according to her medical records, pre-dated the alleged exposure incident. Chronic mood disturbance could not fully account for several important findings and observations, which collectively implied a significant element of volitional goal-directed distortion. These findings and observations included (a) a claim of disorientation following the exposure incident that was not corroborated by the contemporaneous records, (b) misrepresentation of her prior mental health history, (c) representation of an improbable symptom course (i.e., progressive memory difficulty), (d) the likely presence of unreported pre-incident memory complaints, (e) atypical symptom reporting for the alleged fact pattern (e.g., carpal tunnel syndrome attributed to exposure, heightened smell sensitivity, urinary incontinence, etc.),

(f) documentation of a non-physiological sensory-perceptual examination, and (g) misrepresentation of her smoking history.

The behavioral features of probable malingering behavior outlined above were supported by the absence of any objective evidence of CO poisoning or significant risk factors for disabling neuropsychological impairment. Ms. X.'s measured level of COHb, approximately 24 hours after she was last in the workplace, was unremarkable for a tobacco smoker. Moreover, a psychologist documented a significant cigarette habit (one and a half packs per day) not long before the alleged exposure incident.

Within the text of the report submitted to the referral source, I concluded that, "There is no neuropsychological injury stemming from the alleged history of exposure and, in my opinion, she does not require any psychological or psychiatric treatment as a result of this incident." I pointed out that there was "unequivocal evidence of motivation to perform poorly" and cautioned against relying solely on her self-report and performance on effort-dependent tests for assessing possible injury effects. In deposition testimony, I expressed a similar opinion ("My opinion is that there is no evidence to justify an inference of acquired brain damage secondary to carbon monoxide exposure or any other condition.") When questioned about the meaning of the symptom validity test findings, I testified that:

> The relevant research shows that the symptom validity tests are performed at very high rates of accuracy, even by patients with objectively documented cases of brain damage . . . When an individual such as Ms. X., who doesn't have any objectively verified neurologic condition, obtains scores on these tests that are substantially below scores obtained from patients with obviously severe brain dysfunction, the most plausible explanation is that the person is either consciously and/or unconsciously motivated to appear impaired. And, in fact, that's exactly the finding in this case.

Of course, an inference of probable malingering behavior does not necessarily preclude the possible presence of acquired neuropsychological impairment due to a compensable mental injury or some other condition. In this case, however, there were multiple indicators of response bias and extreme symptom exaggeration against a background of a preexisting mood disorder and the absence of any convincing clinical evidence of a work-related neurological injury.

OUTCOME OF CASE

Ms. X.'s civil lawsuit was settled before going to trial. The defense lawyer informed me that the matter was resolved for a relatively small amount of money (i.e., an amount substantially less than what would ordinarily be expected for a case involving a compelling claim of permanently disabling brain damage). While many neuropsychologists may view the fact pattern of this case as being fairly transparent for strong elements of malingering behavior, the reader is reminded that Ms. X. had already been determined to be permanently and totally disabled in the worker's compensation venue before she was referred for examination. Of course, like many medical-legal cases that involve neuropsychological claims and inferences of malingering, it is likely that Ms. X.'s behavior was driven by multi-factorial influences (i.e., it is likely that her motivation was *over-determined* by a range of factors, especially economic and various psychosocial incentives). While speculation about her deeper dynamics exceeds the scope of the present chapter, her history certainly leads to questions about the potential effects of untreated PTSD, misattribution, and iatrogenesis related to the alleged work incident.

REFERENCES

Allen, L., Conder, R. L., Green, P., & Cox, D. R. (1997). *CARB' 97 Manual for the Computerized Assessment of Response Bias*. Durham, NC: CogniSyst.

Associated Regional & University Pathologists, Inc. (2004). *2004–2005 User's guide*. Salt Lake City: ARUP Laboratories.

CDC. (2005). Unintentional non-fire-related carbon monoxide exposures–United States, 2001–2003. *MMWR, 54*(2), 36–39.

Gale, S. D., Hopkins, R. O., Weaver, L. K., Bigler, E. D., Booth, E. J., & Blatter, D. D. (1999). MRI, quantitative MRI, SPECT, and neuropsychological findings following carbon monoxide poisoning. *Brain Injury, 13*, 229–243.

Green, P., Allen, L., & Astner, K. (1996). *Manual for the Computerized Word Memory Test*. Durham, NC: CogniSyst.

Greiffenstein, M. F., Baker, W. J., Gola, T., Donders, J., & Miller, L. (2002). The Fake Bad Scale in atypical and severe closed head injury litigants. *Journal of Clinical Psychology, 58*(12), 1591–1600.

Hartman, D. (1995). *Neuropsychological toxicology, identification and assessment of human neurotoxic syndromes*, 2nd ed. New York: Plenum Press.

Hermann, B. P., Connell, B., Barr, W. B., & Wyler, A. R. (1995). The Utility of the Warrington Recognition Memory Test for temporal lobe epilepsy: pre- and postoperative results. *Epilepsy, 8*, 139–145.

Iverson, G. L., & Binder, L. M. (2000). Detecting exaggeration and malingering in neuropsychological assessment. *Journal of Head Trauma Rehabilitation, 15*(2), 829–858.

Kesler, S. R., Hopkins, R. O., Weaver, L. K., Blatter, D. D., Edge-Booth, H., & Bigler, E. D. (2001). Verbal memory deficits associated with fornix atrophy in carbon monoxide poisoning. *Journal of the International Neuropsychological Society, 7*, 640–646.

Larrabee, G. J. (1998). Somatic malingering on the MMPI and MMPI–2 in personal injury litigants. *The Clinical Neuropsychologist, 12* (2), 179–188.

Larrabee, G. J. (2003a). Exaggerated MMPI–2 symptom report in personal injury litigants with malingered neurocognitive deficit. *Archives of Clinical Neuropsychology, 18*, 673–686.

Larrabee, G. J. (2003b). Detection of symptom exaggeration with the MMPI–2 in litigants with malingered neurocognitive dysfunction. *The Clinical Neuropsychologist, 17*(1), 54–68.

Larrabee, G. J. (2005). Assessment of malingering. In G. J. Larrabee (Ed.), *Forensic neuropsychology: A scientific approach* (pp. 115–158). New York: Oxford University Press.

Lishman, W. A. (1998). *Organic psychiatry, the psychological consequences of cerebral disorder*, 3rd ed. Oxford: Blackwell Science.

Millis, S. R. & Dijkers, M. (1993). Use of the Recognition Memory Test in traumatic brain injury: Preliminary findings. *Brain Injury, 7*, 53–58.

Naugle, R. I., Chelune, G. J., Schuster, J., Luders, H. O., & Comair, Y. (1994). Recognition memory for words and faces before and after temporal lobectomy. *Assessment, 1*(4), 373–381.

Parkinson, R. B., Hopkins, R. O., Cleavinger, H. B., Weaver, L. K., Victoroff, J., Foley, J. F., & Bigler, E. D. (2002). White matter hyperintensities and neuropsychological outcome following carbon monoxide poisoning. *Neurology, 58*, 1525–1532.

Porter, S. S., Hopkins, R. O., Weaver, L. K., Bigler, E. D., & Blatter, D. D. (2002). Corpus callosum atrophy and neuropsychological outcome following carbon monoxide poisoning. *Archives of Clinical Neuropsychology, 17*, 195–204.

Raub, J. A., & Benignus, V. A. (2002). Carbon monoxide and the nervous system. *Neuroscience and Biobehavioral Reviews, 26*, 925–940.

Raub, J.A., Mathieu-Nolf, M., Hampson, N.B., & Thom, S.R. (2000). Carbon monoxide poisoning—a public health perspective. *Toxicology, 145*, 1–14.

Slick, D. J., Sherman, E. M. S., & Iverson, G. L. (1999). Diagnostic criteria for malingered neurocognitive dysfunction: proposed standards for clinical practice and research. *The Clinical Neuropsychologist, 14*(4), 545–561.

Sweet, J. J. (1999). Malingering: differential diagnosis. In J. J. Sweet (Ed.). *Forensic neuropsychology, fundamentals and practice* (pp. 255–286). Lisse: Swets & Zeitlinger.

Tombaugh, T. (1996). *Test of Memory Malingering*. North Tonawanda, NY: Multi-Health System, Inc.

Uchino, A., Hasuo, K., Shida, K., Matsumoto, S., Yasumori, K., & Masuda, K. (1994). MRI of the brain in chronic carbon monoxide poisoning. *Neuroradiology, 36*, 399–401.

US Environmental Protection Agency (2000). Air quality criteria for carbon monoxide. EPA/600/P-99/001F, National Center for Environmental Assessment Research Triangle Park, NC.

Yudofsky, S. C., & Hales, R. E. (1997). *The American Psychiatric Press textbook of neuropsychiatry*. Washington, DC: American Psychiatric Press, Inc.

HIV disease, AIDS, and HIV-associated dementia in a secondary gain context

27

Robert L. Mapou

Individuals with acquired immunodeficiency syndrome (AIDS) can experience cognitive impairment. Both this, and the associated physical debilitation due to AIDS, can result in individuals applying for and receiving disability support. This may be through a private disability insurer, through the government, or a combination. When a private insurer is involved, there can be requests for disability evaluations, either at the time of application or after the individual has received payments for a number of years. Neuropsychological assessment, in particular, can be used as part of the disability evaluation to quantify the degree of cognitive impairment. However, as in any situation in which secondary gain is an issue, it is important to adequately assess effort and to determine whether the test results are valid.

In this chapter, I report the case of a man infected with the human immunodeficiency virus (HIV), whom I saw for neuropsychological evaluation. His disability insurer referred him, after many years of not working and receiving disability payments. Over the course of my assessment, questions arose regarding whether testing accurately reflected his self-reported problems and those reported by his physician. However, before reporting the case and my conclusions, I provide some background information on the neurobehavioral effects of HIV and AIDS.

A SUMMARY OF THE NEUROBEHAVIORAL ASPECTS OF HIV AND AIDS

In 1986, Navia and colleagues (Navia, Cho, Petito, & Price, 1986; Navia, Jordan, & Price, 1986) first described the clinical features of dementia associated with AIDS. They reported a constellation of symptoms in the cognitive, motor, and behavioral realms that fit best with those seen in subcortical dementias. Key findings included attentional difficulties, memory impairment, cognitive slowing, gait disturbance, weakness, lack of motor coordination, fine motor problems, social withdrawal, and apathy. Typically, individuals with AIDS-associated dementia progressed quickly to death. These difficulties also were distinct from those associated with brain-based opportunistic infections, such as toxoplasmosis, progressive multifocal leukoencephalopathy, cryptococcal meningitis, and lymphoma, although co-occurrence was common. The following year, Grant et al. (1987) reported the first findings of cognitive impairment in individuals infected with the human immunodeficiency virus (HIV), the cause of AIDS, who were otherwise medically asymptomatic. Although the study was considered controversial at first, research over the next 10 years ultimately established that cognitive and motor impairment occurred at all stages of HIV disease. However, there was a clear gradient of occurrence, with the least likelihood of impairment when individuals were HIV-seropositive (HIV+), but medically asymptomatic, and increasing likelihood of impairment as individuals progressed to medical symptoms and full-blown AIDS (Law & Mapou, 1997; Mapou & Law, 1994). This was demonstrated especially clearly in a study of a large cohort at the HIV Neurobehavioral Research Center (HNRC; Heaton et al., 1995). These authors found that impairment was mild when present at the asymptomatic stages and typically affected attention, information processing speed, and efficiency of learning. They noted that the profile fit with involvement of subcortical and frontal-striatal brain regions. In a critical review of 57 studies, the HNRC group also reported an impairment rate of 35% in otherwise medically asymptomatic HIV+ individuals (White, Heaton, Monsch, & the HNRC Group, 1995). They found that mode of infection and test battery size were both related to study outcomes. This appeared to answer the "Do they or don't they?" question characteristic of research studies in the late 1980s to mid-1990s examining impairment at the asymptomatic stages of HIV disease, as studies with short batteries tended not to report impairment, while studies using lengthy batteries did.

Research on the neuropsychological features of HIV disease and AIDS peaked in the mid-1990s, with a decrease in research over the past 10 years. Furthermore, instead of focusing on whether impairment does or does not occur at the early stages of disease, the emphasis of basic and applied neuropsychological research has shifted. For example, studies by Martin and colleagues, begun in the early 1990s, have focused on the detailed nature of impairment in attention, working memory, and executive functioning in HIV+ individuals (e.g., Bartok et al., 1997; Martin, Novak et al., 2004; Martin, Pitrak, Pursell, Mullane, & Novak, 1995; Martin, Pitrak et al., 2003; Martin, Pitrak, Robertson et al., 1995; Martin, Sullivan et al., 2001) and the positive effects of antiretroviral treatment on neuropsychological functioning (Martin, Pitrak, Novak, Pursell, & Mullane, 1999; Martin, Pitrak et al., 1998). In addition, this group has mainly studied women and substance abusers, as opposed to other research groups, which have mainly studied gay and bisexual men. Within a substance-abusing population, they have also examined the relationship among sensation seeking, executive functioning, and risk-taking behavior (Gonzalez et al., 2005). Studies at the HNRC have focused recently on the effects of HIV-associated impairment on everyday functioning. For example, using a battery of tests relevant to everyday functioning, including laboratory measures of shopping, cooking, financial management, medication management, and vocational abilities, and categorizing results of neuropsychological testing by domains, Heaton et al. (2004) found that those who were neuropsychologically impaired performed significantly more poorly on the functional measures. The domains of Abstraction/Executive Function, Learning, Attention/Working Memory, and Verbal abilities were the best predictors of failure on the functional tests. Finally, Hardy and Hinkin (2002) reviewed the literature on reaction time slowing in HIV+ individuals, a finding reported frequently in earlier research. Using Brinley plot analyses, a technique that they noted was similar to meta-analysis, they found that individuals with AIDS were, on average, 22% slower than uninfected control subjects. They concluded that HIV appeared "to modulate the mental chronometry of information processing in infected adults (p. 925)," although not every speed-related process was affected. Even more important, the authors summarized studies showing improvement in reaction time with standard antiretroviral treatment (one or two medications) and, in impaired individuals, with methylphenidate treatment. Finally, they reported preliminary data from their own studies that indicated that slower reaction time was associated with poorer adherence to highly active antiretroviral treatment (HAART; three or more medications).

For the most part, research has continued to support the conceptualization of HIV-associated impairment as rooted in the involvement of the frontal-subcortical systems of the brain (Woods & Grant, 2005). This has been bolstered by additional neuropathological studies. In their review, these authors also cited studies showing neuropsychological impairment was related to lower CD4 cell count and higher cerebrospinal fluid (CSF) viral load.

Examining more specific patterns of impairment, Lojek and Bornstein (2005) studied the neuropsychological performance of HIV-infected men from archived data. These were also individuals who were treated with earlier antiretroviral medications but not with HAART. The authors reported considerable diversity in the patterns of cognitive impairment and progression of impairment. One group was found to have psychomotor slowing as the main area of impairment, a second group showed impairment in learning and memory as dominant, and a third group showed various cognitive deficits. Although the authors concluded that results supported prior conceptualizations of HIV-associated impairment as frontal-subcortical in nature and fit with cognitive profiles reported by others, they also noted that there was not "a unitary neuropsychological profile" (p. 679) in their subjects.

Finally, Cysique, Maruff, and Brew (2006), in a meta-analysis of studies that had been completed prior to the use of HAART, confirmed a gradient of impairment across individuals with symptomatic HIV disease without AIDS, AIDS, and HIV-associated dementia (HAD). As in other studies, impairment was most prominent in attention, psychomotor speed, motor skills, and learning/memory. Although there was more widespread and severe impairment in those with HAD, impairment in learning and memory exceeded impairment in attention and processing speed, while naming and visuospatial skills were relatively preserved. Thus, the authors found both quantitative and qualitative differences among the groups. In addition, treatment with standard antiretroviral therapy had a beneficial effect on complex attention in those with symptomatic HIV disease but not in those with AIDS.

However, some researchers have begun to question whether the nature of HAD is changing, particularly given changes in treatment and the wide availability of HAART. In a review, McArthur (2004), who has researched the neurobehavioral aspects of HIV disease for many years, noted that although HIV/AIDS has become a more manageable chronic disease, this has not been without complications due to the effects of treatment and the long-term effects of HIV on the brain. He reported that following a drop in the incidence of HAD, the incidence started to increase in 2003, perhaps because more individuals were living longer with HIV disease. He cited a study that found the prevalence of both HAD and HIV-associated minor cognitive/motor disorder (MCMD) was 37% among those with advanced disease, even with HAART. He added that predictors of HAD included depression and impairment on measures of executive functioning and psychomotor speed. McArthur expressed concern about studies showing that with HAART the relationship of blood and CSF markers of viral load to neurological status is less clear. Although noting that neuropsychological and neurological improvements had been seen with HAART, he stated that improvement may prove to be slower than initially predicted. He added that the course of HAD since the introduction of HAART appeared to be more variable. McArthur hypothesized three phenotypes of HAD: (1) a subacute, but gradually progressive dementia in untreated individuals, (2) a chronic and active dementia in those with poor adherence or viral resistance to HAART, and (3) a chronic inactive dementia in those who respond well to HAART and may have had some neurological recovery. Very similar conclusions were reached by another longtime researcher (Brew, 2004). He noted changes not only in the time course of HAD, but in its cognitive features, citing neuropsychological and neuroimaging studies that have found more cortical involvement than reported in the past. He, too, believed that HAART had changed the features of HAD, because individuals were living longer, were potentially exposed to other conditions affecting the brain, and were showing less of a relationship between blood and CSF measures of viral load and clinical symptoms. Particularly striking was a report that found four of six individuals with HIV had suppressed viral load in CSF.

Suffice to say, in the evaluation of an individual with HIV disease or AIDS for whom cognitive impairment is a referral question, neuropsychological assessment is key. In support, Woods and

Grant (2005) pointed out the limitations of self-report of cognitive functioning. They noted that studies have frequently found discordance between objective and subjective measures of cognitive functioning. For this reason, they stressed the need for a comprehensive neuropsychological battery sensitive to the domains affected by HIV disease. In addition, they stressed the importance of measuring motivation level due to fatigue, malaise, psychiatric disturbance, or frank feigning of deficits, using standard symptom validity measures. They noted that this was especially important when individuals were applying for disability benefits.

THE CASE OF MR. Y.

Mr. Y., a 45-year-old man, had been diagnosed with HIV disease approximately eight years prior to my evaluation and had not worked since the year of his diagnosis, reportedly because of fatigue, nausea/vomiting, and memory problems. He was referred for neuropsychological evaluation at the request of his long-term disability insurer to obtain objective measures of his cognitive functioning and emotional status. He had been followed by only one physician since his diagnosis. Medical record review corroborated Mr. Y.'s reports that although he was HIV+, (1) he had never met criteria for diagnosis of AIDS, despite a listing of this diagnosis by his physician several times in the medical records, (2) he had never been hospitalized for an opportunistic infection or other AIDS-defining condition, and (3) his CD4 cell counts and viral loads had been in the normal range, based on the range of normality given in the laboratory reports. Records also showed no evidence that he had ever been evaluated by a neurologist or had ever completed any neurodiagnostic tests, despite memory complaints that dated to shortly after his diagnosis. Mr. Y. stated that he had been seen for a neuropsychological evaluation in the past, but could not recall anything about it; there was no evidence of such an evaluation in the medical records. His medications included Invarase, Viramune, and Norvir, standard components of HAART; Gemfibrozil for high cholesterol, a common side-effect of HAART; and Celexa for depression.

In terms of background, Mr. Y. completed high school and went on to college. In his third year of college, he became depressed and began to fail. He reported that he had been "hospitalized" in a clinic on the college campus for this. He ultimately returned to college and graduated the following year. Mr. Y. stated that he had always been very shy and that, over the years, he had had episodes of depression, some of which had been severe. Although he sought psychotherapy on one occasion, he did not find it helpful.

Mr. Y. went on to work in the business field. He reported that he had stopped working because it had been stressful and because his viral load was very high, noting that he was "forgetting everything" and that people at work were "starting to yell at me." He added that he was "messing up projects," that he could not remember where he was on projects, and that he kept doing things "over and over." He stated that he had been told that he should consider leaving his job because of his problems.

Mr. Y. reported seeing his family of origin monthly, with some ambivalence about contact with them. He had a partner and estimated that he and his partner had been together about 15 years, reporting a number of tensions in the relationship, including guilt over his having contracted HIV.

When asked about cognitive problems, Mr. Y. stated that he "sometimes" could not remember things, reporting that this included things that he had "seen a few minutes ago." However, he added that his memory problems were "not constant." He reported that his partner had told him that he did not follow through with tasks and that other people had made fun of him because of his memory problems. Mr. Y. reported that his partner had become upset when he had forgotten things and when he did not follow through on instructions posted on a home bulletin board. He reported having become very depressed about his memory problems, as well as about friends dying from AIDS. He avoided groups, because he was concerned that he would run into someone whom he did not remember. With more specific questions, Mr. Y. reported that he had problems paying attention and concentrating and that his speed of thinking was slower, whereas it "used to be so good." He was unsure whether he had any problems understanding what people said to him, but stated that he sometimes "blanked out." When asked about problems getting his own words out, he stated, "I don't like to" and, in the past year "I can't think," which did not entirely make sense. He was unsure of whether he was having any visual problems, commenting only that after going outside and coming back inside, it took him a while "to see anything." When asked about whether he had any difficulty solving problems on an everyday basis or figuring out how to do tasks, he stated, "I avoid solving problems."

When asked more about his mood, Mr. Y. responded, "I sleep a lot. I try not to think of things." He went on to state that he had frequent diarrhea at night and was very tired during the day because of this. He reported that he could enjoy himself "sometimes," and he watched television for fun. He felt guilty much of the time, adding that he always cried after visiting his family because of his guilt. Although he did not report changes in his appetite, he described a pattern of losing a lot of weight, then eating to gain it back. With regard to worries and obsessive thoughts, he stated that he frequently thought, "that I'm going to die a very ugly death." He indicated some thoughts of suicide, but no plan, commenting that he did not believe he could ever kill himself. In terms of hallucinations, he reported that he had heard phones ringing but that this had not occurred recently.

Mr. Y. did not report problems completing basic activities of daily living (grooming, dressing, toileting, showering) independently, but commented, "I make myself." His typical day began around 6 a.m., when he woke up with his partner but remained in bed. He drove his partner to the train station a little later, noting that upon returning home, he might or might not eat breakfast, depending on his appetite. He then went back to bed until around noon, after which he had lunch and watched television for several hours. He often took another nap around 2 or 3 p.m., typically until 5 or 5:30 p.m. His partner would call around 6 or 7 p.m., after which Mr. Y. went back to the train station to pick him up. After returning home, he made dinner with his partner, and they ate together. He watched television in the evening, before going to bed between 9 and 10:30 p.m. At the end of describing his day, Mr. Y. added that he took out his dog two or three times a day. In terms of recreational and social activities, Mr. Y. reported that friends sometimes came over on weekends or that he and his partner sometimes visited another couple, that he watched videos, and that he and his partner occasionally went out to eat nearby. Reading often caused him to be upset because of his memory problems, and he added, "I hate myself for that." Mr. Y. shopped with a list his partner compiled, but noted that his partner became very upset if he forgot something. He cooked some simple dishes, commenting that he cooked more than his partner, did laundry, and did housecleaning. Regarding finances, Mr. Y. stated that he had filed for personal bankruptcy in the past and was in debt.

Review of an interview with an investigator, a brief surveillance video, and a written summary of surveillance of Mr. Y. indicated that he left his home more frequently than he reported during my interview, was gone for longer periods of time, and appeared to be doing more than just taking his partner to and from the train and going to the store. He also was observed to lift items that were heavier than he recounted to the investigator.

Mr. Y. was evaluated in two sessions. He arrived on time for both sessions and did not report any problems finding the office. He was casually but neatly dressed and adequately groomed for both sessions. His affect was flat during the first day, punctuated with tearfulness, but brighter and with a wider range of expression on the second day. His verbalizations were logical and goal-directed. There were no signs of delusional thinking or hallucinations.

The first session was completed by the author. After reading and completing the Informed Consent form for our practice, Mr. Y. appeared to fall asleep in the waiting room. When awakened, he reported that he was tired. He walked independently. Upon entering my office, Mr. Y. told me that he had not caught my name, which had been given to him in the written materials and which I had given him orally a few minutes earlier. He appeared anxious and, when asked, told me he felt anxious. Shortly after sitting down, he appeared upset and on the verge of tears. He asked to change seats, because he said he was upset by seeing my poster of The Names Project AIDS Memorial Quilt on the wall. He apologized for becoming upset. He could not see the poster from the seat to which he moved. During our interview, his speech was hesitant. He seemed to have a hard time answering some questions about his problems, and he was sometimes difficult to follow. He made essentially no eye contact, looking out of the window while talking with me. A few minutes into the interview, when talking about his memory problems, he became tearful, stating that he felt guilty because "I've seen so many die." Yet, he said that he had talked to no one about his feelings, because "No one wants to hear." He was unsure about dates and about some key historical information, including his age and the number of years he and his partner had been together. He gave his age as 50. He could not recall what medications he was taking and gave me a list. Although he stated that he had copied the names from the bottles, several had been misspelled. He frequently asked for repetition of questions or test instructions. However, Mr. Y. did not get upset or frustrated when completing the neuro-psychological evaluation. During a break, one of our staff reported that Mr. Y. had asked whether we had a bathroom and appeared "spacey and out of it."

The second session, which was longer, was completed by a younger female psychometrist. Mr. Y.'s demeanor that day, which I observed as well, appeared different. He was friendly, made eye contact, and seemed comfortable with testing. He also did not appear to be tired or "spacey." Mr. Y. told the psychometrist that he was 45, often forgot his age, and had reminded himself the night before and that day that he was 45. Although he initially appeared alert, he made many comments about fatigue and about getting tired easily throughout the evaluation, particularly when cognitive effort was required. As on the previous day, he asked for repetition of instructions a number of times. During two measures of attention to verbal information, Mr. Y. rested his forehead on his arms, had his eyes closed, and appeared to need much effort to complete the tasks. On measures of fact knowledge and verbal reasoning, however, his answers came quickly and easily. The psychometrist wrote that Mr. Y. appeared to give "more effort on tasks he perceived as challenging, yet did not do well on them and often became overwhelmed." Mr. Y. approached me during a morning break and told me that he had made some erroneous responses on a computer-administered task the day before (the Word Memory Test). When told of the planned schedule by the psychometrist at 10:45 a.m., with plans for a lunch break at noon, he asked whether he could lie down during lunch. At 11 a.m., after two hours of seated testing, he was told he had to wait a few minutes for another examiner to finish with the computer, before doing the next test. He immediately said, "I need to sit down," and sat on a small child's chair in the hallway. He then explained that he was very tired, due to having not slept well the night before. He added that he had also been tired during testing the day before and was finding testing to be tiring and draining. Mr. Y. slept on the couch in the psychometrist's office almost 40 minutes during the lunch break. I saw him after this break, to complete an additional measure. I asked him about his errors the day before; he stated they were limited to only one section of the task and did not occur at other portions.

Test results

Test results are listed in Table 27.1. At the beginning of testing, Mr. Y. was warned that testing would include measures of his effort, that it was to his benefit to put in full effort, and that failure to put in full effort would be reported. However, the specific measures used to do this were not identified. While outwardly Mr. Y. appeared to put forth good effort, a number of test findings contradicted this. On the Word Memory Test (WMT), Mr. Y.'s scores much more closely resembled those of patients asked to fake impairment or volunteers asked to simulate impairment than those of (1) normal individuals doing their best, (2) patients with early or advanced dementia, and (3) neurological patients with documented memory impairment (Green, 2003). He also performed

TABLE 27.1   Mr. Y.: Neuropsychological data

Symptom Validity Measures
Word Memory Test
Immediate Recognition: 42.5% correct (Fail)
Delayed Recognition: 45% (Fail)
Consistency: 32.5% (Fail)
Multiple Choice: 20% (Warning)
Paired Associates: 30% (Warning)
Free Recall: 30%
Long Delay Free Recall: 27.5%

Test of Memory Malingering
Trial 1: 28/50
Trial 2: 33/50
Retention Trial: 30/50

Intellectual Skills
Wechsler Adult Intelligence Scale–3rd edition (WAIS–III)

Summary Measure	STD	%ile	T Score
Full Scale IQ	98	45	36*
Verbal IQ	101	53	38*
Performance IQ	92	30	35*
Verbal Comprehension Index	107	68	44*
Perceptual Organization Index	95	37	38*
Working Memory Index	90	25	33*
Processing Speed Index	91	27	38*

Subtest	AASS	%ile	T Score	Subtest	AASS	%ile	T Score
Vocabulary	11	63	44*	Picture Completion	7	16	34*
Similarities	12	75	48*	Digit Symbol-Coding	8	25	39*
Arithmetic	9	37	36*	Block Design	11	63	46*
Digit Span	7	16	33*	Matrix Reasoning	10	50	42*
Information	11	63	42*	Picture Arrangement	9	37	39*
Comprehension	12	75	48*	Symbol Search	9	37	41*
Letter-Number Seq.	9	37	41*				

Academic Skills
Woodcock-Johnson–III Tests of Achievement (WJ3ACH)

Summary Score/Subtest	STD	%ile
Academic Skills	106	65
Academic Fluency	91	28
Word Attack	93	32
Letter-Word Identification	102	55
Basic Reading Skills	98	44
Reading Fluency	87	20
Spelling	101	54
Writing Fluency	107	68
Math Fluency	95	38
Calculation	113	81
Math Calculation Skills	107	68

Alertness and Attention
Alertness—Awake and alert

Focused Attention/Processing Speed

Measure	AASS/STD	%ile	T Score
WAIS–III Digit Symbol-Coding	8	25	39*
WAIS–III Symbol Search	9	37	41*
WAIS–III Processing Speed Index	91	27	38*

Measure	Raw Score	T Score
Trail Making Test, Part A	50 seconds	29*
Trail Making Test, Part B	110 seconds	30*
Digit Vigilance Test–Time	284 seconds	50*
Digit Vigilance Test–Errors	6	35*

Sustained Attention

Test of Variables of Attention	Raw Score	STD
Reaction Time (milliseconds)	461	< 40
Variability (milliseconds)	186	< 40
Omission Errors (percent)	4.01	< 40
Commission Errors (percent)	5.59	76
ADHD Score	−18.77 (≤1.8 suggests ADHD)	

Span for Verbal Information

Measure	Raw Score	STD/AASS	%ile	Performance Level
WAIS–III Digit Span–Forwards	4–5 digits			Low average
WJRCOG Memory for Sentences		72	3	
WMS–III Logical Memory 1st Recall Total		3	1	

Mental Manipulation/Divided Attention (Working Memory)

Measure	Raw Score	AASS/STD	%ile	T Score	Performance Level
WAIS–III Digit Span–Backwards	4 digits				Low average
WAIS–III Arithmetic		9	37	36*	
WAIS–III Letter-Number Sequencing	4 items	9	37	41*	
WAIS–III Working Memory Index		90	25	33*	
WMS–III Mental Control		2	0.4		

Motor Skills

Gross Motor Strength	Raw Score	T Score
Strength of Grip–Dominant	22.5	12*
Strength of Grip–Nondominant	24.5 kg	24*

Fine Motor Speed	Raw Score	T Score
Finger Tapping–Dominant	44.6 taps	33*
Finger Tapping–Nondominant	44.8 taps	41*

Fine Motor Dexterity	Raw Score	T Score	Pegs Dropped
Grooved Pegboard–Dominant	86 seconds	33*	0
Grooved Pegboard–Nondominant	98 seconds	34*	0

Executive Functions, Problem-Solving Skills, and Reasoning Abilities
Flexibility of Thinking, Hypothesis Testing, and Use of Feedback
Wisconsin Card Sorting Test

Measure	Score	STD	%ile
Categories	1		2–5**
Total Errors	59	68**	2**
Perseverative Responses	23	80**	9**
Perseverative Errors	20	80**	9**
Non-perseverative Errors	39	61**	< 1**
Unique Errors	5		
Failure to Maintain Set	5		2–5**

Reasoning

Measure	AASS/STD	%ile	T Score
WAIS–III Similarities	12	75	48*
WAIS–III Comprehension	12	75	48*
WAIS–III Picture Completion	7	16	34*
WAIS–III Picture Arrangement	9	37	39*
WAIS–III Matrix Reasoning	10	50	42*

(Continued . . .)

TABLE 27.1   (Continued)

D-KEFS Twenty Questions Test	AASS	%ile
Initial Abstraction Score	16	98
Total Questions Asked	12	75
Total Weighted Achievement Score	14	91

Language Skills
Comprehension

Measure	AASS/STD	%ile	T Score
WAIS–III Vocabulary	11	63	44*
WJ3ACH Understanding Directions	92	29	
WJ3ACH Oral Comprehension	103	58	
WJ3ACH Listening Comprehension Cluster	97	43	

Production

Measure	Raw Score	T Score
Boston Naming Test–Spontaneous total	54/60	
Boston Naming Test–With semantic cuing	55/60	37*
Boston Naming Test–With all cuing	60/60	
COWAT–Letters F,A,S	29 words total	38*
COWAT–Animals	14 total	31*

Visuospatial Skills
Constructional Skills

Measure	Raw Score	AASS	%ile	T Score
ROCFT Copy	26.5/36	7	11–18	
WAIS–III Block Design		11	63	46*

Learning and Memory
Orientation

WMS–III Information and Orientation	10/14 correct	5th percentile

Verbal Learning and Memory

WMS–III Subtest Measure	Raw Score	AASS	%ile	T Score
Verbal Paired Associates I Recall Total		5	5	30*
Verbal Paired Associates I Learning Slope		7	16	
Verbal Paired Associates II Recall Total		5	5	30*
Verbal Paired Associates Retention	100%	12	75	
Logical Memory I Recall Total		2	<1	15*
Logical Memory I Learning Slope		9	37	
Logical Memory II Recall Total		3	1	20*
Logical Memory Percent Retention	40%	5	5	
Logical Memory I Thematic Recall Total		6	9	
Logical Memory II Thematic Recall Total		4	2	

WMS–III Index	STD	%ile	T Score
Auditory Immediate	62	1	18*
Auditory Delayed	64	1	20*
Auditory Recognition Delayed	55	0.1	14*

WMS–III Auditory Process Composites	%ile
Single-Trial Learning	1
Learning Slope	17
Retention	25
Retrieval	11

Visual Learning and Memory

WMS–III Subtest Measure	Raw Score	AASS	%ile	T Score
Faces I Recall Total		5	5	33*
Faces II Recall Total		4	2	28*
Faces Retention	109%	12	75	
Family Pictures I Recall Total		4	2	28*
Family Pictures II Recall Total		3	1	25*
Family Pictures Retention	86%	5	5	

WMS–III Index	STD	%ile	T Score
Visual Immediate	65	1	25*
Visual Delayed	59	0.3	20*

Measure	Raw Score	AASS	%ile
ROCFT Immediate Recall	10.5/36	7	11–18
ROCFT 20 Minute Recall	7.5/36	5	3–5
WAIS–III Digit Sym. Incidental Learning			
Pairing	3/9	10	
Free Recall	7/9	50	

Overall Memory

WMS–III Index	STD	%ile	T Score
Immediate Memory	55	0.1	15*
General Memory	52	0.1	12*

Personality and Emotional Functioning
Minnesota Multiphasic Personality Inventory–2

Scale	T Score	Scale	T Score
F	95	ANX	87
Fb	116	FRS	67
Fp	41	OBS	73
L	56	DEP	97
K	37	HEA	95
Hs	92	BIZ	77
D	93	ANG	53
Hy	89	CYN	51
Pd	74	ASP	40
Mf	66	TPA	38
Pa	105	LSE	96
Pt	100	SOD	89
Sc	108	FAM	71
Ma	47	WRK	87
Si	89	TRT	94

Key: STD: standard score; AASS: age-associated scaled score; %ile: percentile; COWAT: Controlled Oral Word Association Test; D-KEFS: Delis-Kaplan Executive Functioning System; normative data are based on age only, except as follows: *normative data include age, gender, education, and ethnicity; **normative data include age and education or education only; ROCFT: Rey-Osterrieth Complex Figure Test; WJRCOG: Woodcock-Johnson Revised Tests of Cognitive Ability; WMS–III: Wechsler Memory Scale–3rd edition.

relatively better on the harder free recall portions of the task than on the easier recognition portions, which is not consistent with neurologically based memory impairment. On the Test of Memory Malingering (TOMM), his scores on the three trials were all just slightly above chance and far below those of patients with documented cognitive impairment, including memory impairment, due to a variety of causes. His scores were most similar to those of individuals asked to simulate impairment and to those of patients with brain damage who were judged to be at risk of embellishing or exaggerating impairment (Tombaugh, 1996).

There were also inconsistencies within the neuropsychological test results that were not compatible with a neurological cause. On the three Wechsler Memory Scale–III (WMS–III) forced-choice recognition measures, his performances were near chance (50% correct), similar to his performance on the TOMM. In fact, his performances on all WMS–III subtests were at the level of a profoundly demented patient who would not be expected to live or function independently. His verbal recognition memory was worse than his verbal recall memory on the WMS–III, and, similar to his performance on the WMT, did not make sense from a neuropsychological standpoint. This was largely because he made rare responses in which he identified pairs of words as having been presented to him, when, in fact, they had not. The presented words were not similar in any way to the real word pairs, and patients with neurological impairment rarely make this type of error. All of these results can indicate insufficient effort (Glassmire et al., 2003; Langeluddecke & Lucas, 2003). His performance on a sustained attention task, the Test of Variables of Attention (TOVA), was far below that of most individuals with attentional disorders and in the range of someone who is virtually unable to pay attention. In fact, performances this poor have been linked to insufficient effort and questions of malingering (Henry, 2005; Leark, Dixon, Hoffman, & Huynh, 2002). In contrast, Mr. Y. had above average scores on a measure of written arithmetic and on a problem-solving task, which one would not expect in someone with HIV-associated dementia of the severity implied by the scores on the memory measures. Finally, despite a virtual inability to hold sentences or brief stories in mind and repeat them back immediately after hearing them, Mr. Y. performed at an average level on language comprehension tasks, which also required holding verbal information briefly in mind.

In summary, results from symptom validity measures and the noted inconsistencies strongly suggested that most neuropsychological test results were not valid indicators of Mr. Y.'s actual functioning. The results were very consistent with insufficient effort and could indicate exaggeration/ malingering of deficits. With that in mind, the following is a summary of the neuropsychological test results.

Mr. Y. obtained an estimated Verbal IQ of 112 on the American Version of the National Adult Reading Test. On a second single-word reading measure, the Letter-Word Identification subtest of the Woodcock-Johnson–III Tests of Achievement, Mr. Y. had a slightly lower score of 102. These scores suggested that Mr. Y.'s scores on other measures should have been at least average to above average, and his educational and vocational background suggested that his functioning, at least in the past, might have been higher than this. Furthermore, Mr. Y. made several errors on both reading tests that were unusual for someone with a college education and without a history of a reading disorder, suggesting that, even here, his effort may not have been optimal. Alternately, this might have indicated a pre-existing reading disorder. However, this possibility was not explored further. Consequently, these results were thought to provide a lower limit of Mr. Y.'s expected functioning.

As can be seen in Table 27.1, Mr. Y.'s subtest scores on the Wechsler Adult Intelligence Scale–Third Edition (WAIS–III) ranged from low average to slightly above average, resulting in IQ and Index scores that were in the average range. In comparison with scores of a demographically-similar group, his Verbal subtest scores and summary measures ranged from mildly/moderately impaired to average, with his weakest scores on subtests that tapped attention. His Performance subtest scores and summary measures ranged from mildly impaired to average. Mr. Y.'s academic skills fell in a similar range, although he did somewhat less well on timed measures of academic skills.

Mr. Y.'s performances on almost all measures of attention were impaired, although he had his strongest average scores on the WAIS–III Working Memory subtests and, to a lesser degree, Processing Speed subtests. He also worked at an expected speed on the Digit Vigilance Test. In addition to the errors on Digit Vigilance, all of which were omissions, he made two false-positive errors on Symbol Search and one self-corrected error on Trail Making A (started to go from 18 to 20, which was nearby). With one exception, his motor skills were impaired, with especially poor grip strength using his dominant right hand. The exception was a low average score on Finger Tapping with his nondominant hand.

In terms of executive functioning, problem-solving skills, and reasoning abilities, Mr. Y. was virtually unable to complete the Wisconsin Card Sorting Test. He could not use feedback effectively to determine the correct sorting category and, instead, he shifted back and forth between the two categories that were incorrect, sorted the cards in a way that did not match any of the categories, or else stuck with the same incorrect category, despite feedback. Although he was given some additional cuing during the task (e.g., "Continue to do it the same way"; "See if you can figure out why that one is right"), this did not help him. He also failed to maintain the response set five times, and, on three of these, did so after sorting the cards correctly *nine times* in a row. These are often signs of poor effort (Sweet & Nelson, 2007). His overall performance was severely to profoundly impaired, in comparison with a group of similar age and education. Yet, when asked at the end of the task what the sorting categories were, he easily and correctly stated all three. Mr. Y. used the organization well when copying the Rey-Osterrieth Complex Figure. Scores on reasoning measures were average to above average and consistent with expectations, except for Picture Completion and Picture Arrangement, which were mildly impaired. His scores on the D-KEFS Twenty Questions test were the highest on the evaluation, with elimination of half of the items on three of the four initial questions and subsequent questioning that was fairly systematic.

Regarding spoken language, Mr. Y.'s vocabulary was low average in comparison with demographically similar peers. His spoken language comprehension at the sentence level was low average to average, with a weaker performance on Understanding Directions, which placed more demands on attention than Oral Comprehension. His naming and timed word retrieval skills were mildly to moderately impaired, in comparison with demographically-similar peers, with the poorest performance on animal name generation. However, Mr. Y. named all five items that he missed on the Boston Naming Test, when given phonemic cues.

There were no indications of visuospatial perceptual impairment, although a semantic cue was given when Mr. Y. was initially unable to identify the tripod on the Boston Naming Test. However, his question, "Do artists use it?" indicated that this was not a gross misperception. His performances on visuospatial constructional tasks varied, with low average copy of the ROCFT, despite an organized approach, due to slight distortion or misplacement of a number of details. He performed better on Block Design, working somewhat slowly, but completing all but the hardest design correctly.

Mr. Y.'s performances on almost all measures of learning and memory were impaired, with impairment ranging from moderate to profound. The exceptions were (1) his ability to recall freely seven of the nine symbols from the Digit Symbol subtest, which was average, (2) his average improvement with repetition of the second Logical Memory Story, (3) his adequate retention of the four Verbal Paired Associates he learned, and (4) his recognition of two additional faces following the delay. The California Verbal Learning Test–Second Edition was not administered, due to lack of time and the belief that it would provide results similar to those on other memory measures.

Mr. Y.'s scores on the standard validity indices (F, Fb, Fp, L, K) of the MMPI–2 indicated that he endorsed an exceptionally large number of rare and unusual symptoms. This type of endorsement, most characteristic of individuals who are psychotic and unable to function independently, but which can also be seen in individuals who are profoundly demented or who have severe reading problems, was at odds with his reports, his clinical presentation, the surveillance video, and the medical records. Five of the ten Clinical Scales were at a T score of 90 or higher, and two were between a T score of 80 and 90, with the highest scores on those measuring severe psychopathology, including delusional thinking, hallucinations, paranoid thinking, and agitation. Again, this was inconsistent with Mr. Y.'s clinical presentation. Most of his scores on the Content Scales were similarly elevated, with the highest scores on scales sensitive to anxiety, depression, health problems, bizarre thinking, low self-esteem, and discomfort in social situations. He also had a high score on a scale that indicates low motivation to make changes in one's life through psychotherapy. Finally, Mr. Y.'s score of 36 on the Lees-Haley Fake Bad scale (FBS) is one that is associated with an exaggerated over-reporting style, as a score this high has not been found to occur in non-litigating individuals with several different types of disorders (Greiffenstein, Fox, & Lees-Haley, 2007). In fact, these authors concluded that an FBS score higher than 30 was associated with "near perfect confidence in finding symptom magnification."

In summary, results of my evaluation were of highly questionable validity and were not believed to be an accurate indicator of Mr. Y.'s level of functioning. As noted above, (1) Mr. Y.'s performances on symptom validity measures showed insufficient effort and were most consistent with an attempt to embellish, exaggerate, or wholly feign deficits, rendering the remainder of the evaluation highly suspect, (2) his deficits on testing far exceeded expectations, based on his everyday functioning, and (3) his responses to the MMPI–2 were inconsistent with his everyday functioning and also showed very substantial evidence of symptom embellishment.

CONCLUSIONS

Cognitive impairment can occur at any stage of HIV disease. However, the frequency of impairment increases at later stages of disease, when physical symptoms are prominent, and, especially when there is evidence of neurological compromise. In the case presented here, Mr. Y. had some physical symptoms of HIV disease (diarrhea and fatigue). However, there had never been an AIDS diagnosis and, with treatment, indices of immune system functioning were good. In addition, both fatigue and diarrhea are common side effects of HAART. In this case, although there were some findings on testing that were consistent with the neuropsychological effects of HIV disease, administration of symptom validity measures and the MMPI–2, combined with inconsistencies among test performances and inconsistencies between test results and reported everyday functioning led to a conclusion that results were not valid. Although Mr. Y. may, in fact, have been suffering from HIV-associated cognitive impairment, it was not possible to determine the presence of, or degree of, impairment from the test results. There were also strong indications of a psychiatric overlay, based on Mr. Y.'s presentation and history. Finally, there were many reasons for secondary gain, including his financial need.

To my knowledge, this is the first case report of probable symptom exaggeration/malingering in an individual diagnosed with HIV disease. However, in my practice I have seen two other HIV+ individuals whose performances on symptom validity measures and neuropsychological testing raised questions about symptom exaggeration and malingering. One was self-referred through his psychiatrist and was considering applying for long-term disability benefits. I advised him that his test results "for whatever reason" were not a valid indication of his skills and should not be used to try to support a disability claim. He asked me not to write a report and also did not provide consent for me to speak with his psychiatrist about the evaluation results. The second individual was referred through his long-term disability insurer. These three cases all illustrate the need to use symptom validity measures, even in individuals with a chronic and potentially life-threatening disease, when there is a context of secondary gain.

REFERENCES

Bartok, J. A., Martin, E. M., Pitrak, D. L., Novak, R. M., Pursell, K. J., Mullane, K. M., & Harrow, M. (1997). Working memory deficits in HIV-seropositive drug users. *Journal of the International Neuropsychological Society, 3*, 451–456.

Brew, B. J. (2004). Evidence for a change in AIDS dementia complex in the era of highly active antiretroviral therapy and the possibility of new forms of AIDS dementia complex. *AIDS, 18*(suppl 1), S75–S78.

Cysique, L. A. J., Maruff, P., & Brew, B. J. (2006). The neuropsychological profile of symptomatic AIDS and ADC patients in the pre-HAART era: A meta-analysis. *Journal of the International Neuropsychological Society, 12*, 368–380.

Glassmire, D. M., Bierley, R. A., Wisniewski, A. M., Greene, R. L., Kennedy, J. E., & Date, E. (2003). Using the WMS-III Faces subtest to detect malingered memory impairment. *Journal of Clinical and Experimental Neuropsychology, 25*, 465–481.

Gonzalez, R., Vassileva, J., Bechara, A., Grbesic, S., Sworowski, L., Novak, R. M., Nunnally, G., & Martin, E. M. (2005). The influence of executive functions, sensation seeking, and HIV serostatus on the risky sexual practices of substance-dependent individuals. *Journal of the International Neuropsychological Society, 11*, 121–131.

Grant, I., Atkinson, J. H., Hesselink, J. R., Kennedy, C. J., Richman, D. D., Spector, S. A., & McCutchan, J. A. (1987). Evidence for early central nervous system involvement in the acquired immunodeficiency syndrome (AIDS) and other human immunodeficiency virus (HIV) infections. *Annals of Internal Medicine, 107*, 828–836.

Green, P. (2003). *Green's Word Memory Test*. Edmonton, Alberta: Green's Publishing.

Greiffenstein, M., Fox, D., & Lees-Haley, P. R. (2007). The MMPI–2 Fake Bad Scale in the detection of noncredible brain injury claims. In K. Boone (Ed.), *Assessment of feigned cognitive impairment: A neuropsychological perspective* (pp. 270–291). New York: Guilford Press.

Hardy, D. J., & Hinkin, C. H. (2002). Reaction time performance in adults with HIV/AIDS. *Journal of Clinical and Experimental Neuropsychology, 24*, 912–929.

Heaton, R. K., Grant, I., Butters, N., White, D. A., Kirson, D., Atkinson, J. H., McCutchan, J. A., Taylor, M. J., Kelly, M. D., Ellis, R. D., Wolfson, T., Velin, R., Marcotte, T. D., Hesselink, J. R., Jernigan, T. L., Chandler, J., Wallace, M., Abramson, I., & the HNRC Group. (1995). The HNRC 500—Neuropsychology of HIV infection at different disease stages. *Journal of the International Neuropsychological Society, 1*, 231–251.

Heaton, R. K., Marcotte, T. D., Mindt, M. R., Sadek, J., Moore, D. J., Bentley, J., McCutchan, J. A., Reicks, C., Grant, I., & the HNRC Group. (2004). The impact of HIV-associated neuropsychological impairment on everyday functioning. *Journal of the International Neuropsychological Society, 10*, 317–331.

Henry, G. K. (2005). Probable malingering and performance on the Test of Variables of Attention. *The Clinical Neuropsychologist, 19*, 121–129.

Langeluddecke, P. M., & Lucas, S. K. (2003). Quantitative measures of memory malingering on the Wechsler Memory Scale-Third edition in mild head injury litigants. *Archives of Clinical Neuropsychology, 18*, 181–197.

Law, W. A., & Mapou, R. L. (1997). Neuropsychological findings in HIV-1 disease and AIDS. In A. M. Horton, D. W. Wedding, & J. Webster (Eds.), *The neuropsychology handbook*–2nd ed. (Vol. 2, pp. 367–308). New York: Springer Publishing Company.

Leark, R. A., Dixon, D., Hoffman, T., & Huynh, D. (2002). Fake bad test response bias effects on the Test of Variables of Attention. *Archives of Clinical Neuropsychology, 17*, 335–342.

Lojek, E., & Bornstein, R. A. (2005). The stability of neurocognitive patterns of HIV infected men: Classification considerations. *Journal of Clinical and Experimental Neuropsychology, 27*, 665–682.

Mapou, R. L., & Law, W. A. (1994). Neurobehavioral aspects of HIV disease and AIDS: An update. *Professional Psychology: Research and Practice, 25*, 132–140.

Martin, E. M., Novak, R. M., Fendrich, M., Vassileva, J., Gonzalez, R., Grbesic, S., Nunnally, G., & Sworowski, L. (2004). Stroop performance in drug users classified by HIV and hepatitis C virus serostatus. *Journal of the International Neuropsychological Society, 10*, 298–300.

Martin, E. M., Pitrak, D. L., Novak, R. M., Pursell, K. J., & Mullane, K. M. (1999). Reaction times are faster in HIV-seropositive patients on antiretroviral therapy: A preliminary report. *Journal of Clinical and Experimental Neuropsychology, 21*, 730–735.

Martin, E., Pitrak, D. L., Pursell, K. J., Andersen, B. R., Mullane, K. M., & Novak, R. M. (1998). Information processing and antiretroviral therapy in HIV-1 infection. *Journal of the International Neuropsychological Society, 4*, 329–335.

Martin, E. M., Pitrak, D. L., Pursell, K. J., Mullane, K. M., & Novak, R. M. (1995). Delayed recognition memory span in HIV-1 infection. *Journal of the International Neuropsychological Society, 1*, 575–580.

Martin, E. M., Pitrak, D. L., Rains, N., Grbesic, S., Pursell, K. J., Nunnally, G., & Bechara, A. (2003). Delayed nonmatch-to-sample performance in HIV-seropositive and HIV-seronegative polydrug abusers. *Neuropsychology, 17*, 283–288.

Martin, E. M., Pitrak, D. L., Robertson, L. C., Novak, R. M., Mullane, K. M., & Pursell, K. J. (1995). Global-local analysis in HIV-1 infection. *Neuropsychology*, *9*, 102–109.

Martin, E. M., Sullivan, T. S., Reed, R. A., Fletcher, T. A., Pitrak, D. L., Weddington, W., & Harrow, M. (2001). Auditory working memory in HIV-1 infection. *Journal of the International Neuropsychological Society*, *7*, 20–26.

McArthur, J. C. (2004). HIV dementia: an evolving disease. *Journal of Neuroimmunology*, *157*, 3–10.

Navia, B. A., Cho, E.-S., Petito, C. K., & Price, R. W. (1986). The AIDS dementia complex: II. Neuropathology. *Annals of Neurology*, *19*, 525–535.

Navia, B. A., Jordan, B. D., & Price, R. W. (1986). The AIDS dementia complex: I. Clinical features. *Annals of Neurology*, *19*, 517–524.

Sweet, J. J., & Nelson, N. M. (2007). Validity indicators within executive function measures: Use and limits in detection of malingering. In K. B. Boone (Ed.), *Assessment of feigned cognitive impairment: A neuropsychological perspective* (pp. 152–177). New York: Guilford.

Tombaugh, T. N. (1996). *Test of Memory Malingering*. North Tonawanda, NY: Multi-Health Systems.

White, D. A., Heaton, R. K., Monsch, A. U., & the HNRC Group (1995). Neuropsychological studies of asymptomatic human immunodeficiency virus-type-1 infected individuals. *Journal of the International Neuropsychological Society*, *1*, 304–315.

Woods, S. P., & Grant, I. (2005). Neuropsychology of HIV. In H. E. Gendelman, I. Grant, I. P. Everall, S. A. Lipton, & S. Swindells (Eds.), *The neurology of AIDS* (pp. 607–615). New York: Oxford University Press.

Electrical injury and malingered cognitive dysfunction

Neil Pliskin

CASE PRESENTATION

Accident history

Mr. Z. reported living in a house that became charged with electricity. The phone company was digging in the yard, and disconnected a wire, which turned out to be the house ground wire, and instead of standard electrical service, the patient's house was energized in excess of 240 volts. All appliances were destroyed. The paper filter inside the air conditioner caught on fire. When he went to take the filter out, he reported that he received an electric shock when he touched the air filter hosing with his right hand. He also stated that he felt "vibrations to [his] feet" from the surge protector. He did not receive emergency/medical services the day of the event.

Mr. Z. apparently sought medical attention for the first time four days later, when he presented to his local Emergency Room. He complained of discomfort on the right chest, under the right arm, and numbness of the left hand and arm. He also complained of back and side pain and left elbow pain and chest discomfort. Neurologic exam was normal, though he did note hyperthesia on the left hand. There were no signs of thermal injury and no obvious entry or exit wounds. His electrocardiogram indicated normal sinus rhythm. He was found to be hyperglycemic and was started on an oral hypoglycemic agent at that time. He had no prior history of underlying medical problems and did not have a physician at the time. He reported no history of psychiatric or emotional difficulties. Upon discharge his diagnoses included: (1) hyperglycemia; (2) left ulnar peripheral neuropathy; and (3) electric shock. He was not observed to have any difficulty understanding his discharge instructions, nor any signs of significant cognitive impairment at that time.

One week after the emergency room visit, Mr. Z. was evaluated by a neurologist. He reported to the neurologist that he had sustained a loss of consciousness of unknown duration in the electrical accident, which he had not reported initially. Indeed, ER records did not record any evidence of mental status abnormality. He also reported to the neurologist that he was experiencing tingling in the upper extremities bilaterally, the right side greater than the left. Mr. Z. also complained of dizziness, memory, and other cognitive problems. He felt mentally foggy and had sharp pains in his feet. He reported a history of prior disc displacement in his low back. The neurologist also noted that Mr. Z. had short-term memory problems upon examination. When seen by the neurologist one month later, he was described as having the same difficulties, along with attention and concentration problems, and "possibly an element of somatization."

Mr. Z. was subsequently followed by an internist who documented the presence of multiple physical (e.g., numbness and paresthesias in both upper extremities, shoulder and low back pain, headaches, decreased vision, dizziness) and cognitive (e.g., feeling "spacey," mentally slow, decreased vision, and poor memory "of his own phone number and zip code") complaints that did not improve over time. During the year after his alleged electrical injury, medical records indicate that Mr. Z. developed additional symptoms including bowel and bladder incontinence, vertigo (for which he began taking Antivert), and difficulty comprehending conversation. His internist described his speech as labored and "almost aphasic." All of these symptoms, including his bowel and bladder incontinence, were considered by the internist to be related to a central nervous system injury caused by his electrical shock.

Initial neuropsychological assessment (conducted by treating neuropsychologist)

Mr. Z.'s neurologist referred him to a local neuropsychologist for evaluation three months after the electrical incident. In addition to the above-described complaints, Mr. Z. reported to the neuropsychologist that he could no longer play bridge (i.e., couldn't keep the cards straight in his head) or work with simple computer programs that he routinely used prior to his electrical injury. He complained of difficulty with attention and concentration, a decline in short-term memory, retrograde and anterograde amnesia, and feeling very stressed.

Test results from this initial evaluation (i.e., Evaluation 1) are presented in Table 28.1, which contains all of the neuropsychological test scores from his three evaluations.

Performance on this initial evaluation was interpreted by the neuropsychologist as significant for decline in visual-spatial ability, and although auditory skills were diminished, they continued to be at a level significantly higher than visuospatial abilities. He further reported that Mr. Z. evidenced severely impaired memory and executive functions. The neuropsychologist concluded that Mr. Z. had experienced "extended and prolonged deficits" secondary to electrical trauma and was totally unable to function as a computer programmer. He was also diagnosed as having major depression as a result of his electrical injury.

The neuropsychologist then engaged Mr. Z. in psychotherapy, and he was seen several more times with his diagnosis remaining the same. Mr. Z. had additional reports of getting lost in the parking lot coming to the appointment, increased low back pain, and continued bowel and bladder incontinence. He reported difficulty with driving and specifically judging the speed of other vehicles, and difficulty keeping his checking account. He was diagnosed with an Adjustment Disorder with Mixed Emotional Features and "elements of Posttraumatic Stress Disorder" (he reported having flashbacks of the incident) in addition to his problems, which were attributed to his "electrocution" (which technically means death by electrical shock) injury. When seen again by the neuropsychologist one year after the incident, he recommended that Mr. Z. have attendant care because he could not safely live at home alone.

It is important to note that true malingering/effort tasks were not administered during Mr. Z.'s evaluation by this neuropsychologist. The neuropsychologist later acknowledged this in his deposition, although he stated that he "knew the patient very well," and "simply did not believe he was consciously malingering," although he also noted that "there was evidence of somatization, which might have affected overall performance."

Second neuropsychological evaluation (conducted by author as plaintiff's expert)

Mr. Z. was referred to me by his attorney and to the Chicago Electrical Trauma Program for an evaluation of his current medical, neurocognitive, and psychiatric status. By way of background, the Chicago Electrical Trauma Program is an interdisciplinary and multi-institutional program

TABLE 28.1 Comparison of neuropsychological test results across three evaluations

INTELLECTUAL/GLOBAL FUNCTIONING	EVAL 1 S/P 3 MONTHS		EVAL 2 S/P 21 MONTHS		EVAL 3 S/P 35 MONTHS	
	WAIS–R		WAIS–III			
VIQ	85		85 (84)		84	
PIQ	72				78	
FIQ	73				81	
Barona V	113.8 (± 11.8)		113.8			
P	110.1 (± 13.2)		110.1			
Memory						
CVLT						
Trial 1	Raw = 4		Raw = 5		Raw = 6	
Total (Trials 1–5)	Raw = 24		Raw = 29		Raw = 36	
List B	Raw = 4		Raw = 5		Raw = 4	
S Free	Raw = 2		Raw = 3		Raw = 5	
L Free	Raw = 0		Raw = 5		Raw = 6	
Hits	Raw = 4		Raw = 10		Raw = 11	
Disc	0.73 (.70)		0.82			
Problem Solving						
WCST						
# Categories			4	> 16%ile	1	2–5%ile
Perseverative Responses			9	55%ile	25	19%ile
Perseverative Errors			9	55%ile	21	21%ile
Failure to Maintain Set			5		3	
Language						
Verbal Fluency						
FAS/CFL	23	Z = −1.86	Raw = 10		19	Z = −1.75
Motor						
Grooved Pegboard						
Right			Discontinued		Discontinued	
Left			Discontinued		Discontinued	
Grip Strength						
Right					15	
Left			18.5 kg		32	

Note: S/P = status post.

comprising a team of clinicians, epidemiologists, biologists, and engineers working towards a better understanding, improved diagnosis, and treatment of electrical injuries. It was in my role as neuropsychologist for the Electrical Trauma Program that I came to evaluate Mr. Z. He was also evaluated by specialists in Plastic Surgery, Psychiatry, Physical Medicine, and Neurology, and underwent physical therapy evaluation, MRI, EMG, and laboratory studies.

Findings of the Electrical Trauma Program comprehensive evaluation are summarized as follows: Laboratory results were all within normal limits. Neurological consultation found Mr. Z. to be presenting "a very unusual and extensive set of complaints" and "a very unusual neurologic examination" which appeared "not to be physiologically based." Objective findings on the examination found no significant central nervous system pathology and an MRI of the brain was unremarkable. An EMG showed a probable bilateral mid-cervical radiculopathy. There was no evidence for a diffuse polyneuropathy. Physical Therapy Evaluation found numerous inconsistencies throughout his assessment. Psychiatric consultation found Mr. Z.'s presentation as difficult to understand. He denied symptoms of psychiatric disorders and complaints during this evaluation; he reportedly had received no psychiatric care, nor was he on any medication. Rather he focused on his physical and cognitive complaints. He did speak at length, though, about rather esoteric topics with ease, i.e., chaos theory, etc., which is puzzling in light of the fact he stated he was unable to do clear thinking. No psychiatric diagnoses were offered.

At the time of my neuropsychological evaluation, which was his second and was conducted 21 months after his electrical injury, Mr. Z. had complaints of pain "all over," especially in his right arm and leg, constant fatigue, numbness and tingling to upper right and left extremities and also to his head and neck. Mr. Z. complained of slowness of speech, and difficulty with his memory. He also reported low back pain, and constant burning in his lower extremities, headaches, tinnitus in his ears, dysphasia, and also bowel and bladder incontinence. Mr. Z. was taking Glyburide 5 mg daily at the time of evaluation.

Mr. Z. was able to provide details to multiple Electrical Trauma Program specialists about events occurring right up to the occurrence of the alleged shock, including recalling reaching for the plug, but not the shock itself. Following the alleged shock, he reported remembering being on the floor, on his back, looking at smoke on the ceiling, and related subsequent events, including opening the window to let the smoke out, interacting with the man from the phone company, going to his next door neighbor's house, and recalling interactions with his business associate and the electric company representatives the day following the alleged event.

Prior to the electrical accident, Mr. Z. was described by friends and co-workers as very physically active, biking seven miles a day, playing on a hockey team, and performing as a very valued computer programmer. Now he was described as staring off into space, falling asleep in conversations, confused, and having slurred speech and short-term memory problems. He was a "superb" mathematician but now is not able to do even simple math. He was further described as a highly intellectual person, and an excellent bridge player before the accident, who now just seems "stunned" and is unable to play bridge at any level.

At the time of evaluation, Mr. Z. was single and living alone. Prior to the accident he reported that he was a self-employed computer software developer. However, at the time of evaluation he stated he was residing with friends. He reported he did not smoke, drink alcohol, or use illicit drugs. Mr. Z. stated that he did some shopping last week but couldn't remember where he had left his groceries.

Notable behavioral observations

Mr. Z. was alert and fully oriented on the day of evaluation. He evidenced an unusual slowed and dysrhythmic speech with no evidence of paraphasias or other obvious word-finding abnormalities. His thought processes were coherent. The most noteworthy behavioral observation was that Mr. Z. performed nearly all tasks with his left hand (despite being right-handed) because of pain complaints in his right hand, which rested by his side most of the time. This limited some of the tests we were able to give Mr. Z. He was also very preoccupied with concerns regarding his physical health and its implications for his future to return to work. His affect was wide, ranging from jovial to uncontrollable sobbing. After the lunch break, he became less cooperative with testing procedures, refusing to guess on items he was unsure about and becoming tearful at other times, stating he knew he performed poorly, and that he would never get better and go back to work.

Test findings

Mr. Z. was administered tests designed to assess his level of effort and motivation during the neuropsychological evaluation process. He was administered the Victoria Symptom Validity Test in which he obtained only 32/48 correct responses (18/24 easy, 14/24 hard) indicating questionably valid effort. Mr. Z. was administered two other tests of effort throughout the day with similar findings. He demonstrated a below chance performance on the TOMM (Trial 1 12/50; Trial 2 16/50; Retention 9/50) and only obtained 7 of 15 items on the Rey-15 Item Test. His frequent "I don't know" responses were the hallmark of his below chance performance on these measures. Taken together these data suggested that Mr. Z. was not fully motivated and engaged during the testing process and generated less than adequate effort during the evaluation, which compromised my ability to validly assess his current neuropsychological status (Table 28.2).

Because of his inability or unwillingness to use his right upper extremity during the evaluation process, Mr. Z. was only administered tests that had a minimal timed motor component to them. He obtained a Verbal IQ of 85, placing him in the low average range of general intellectual functioning. By contrast, his estimated pre-injury Verbal IQ was average to high average (AMNART VIQ = 116) based on his knowledge of infrequent words and an estimation based on his sight-reading ability (WRAT–III reading SS = 107; 68th percentile) consistent with his educational and vocational background. In light of his invalid and below-chance performances on symptom validity testing, it is not

TABLE 28.2 Summary of Mr. Z.'s test results

Intellectual/Global Functioning		
WAIS–III IQ Scores		
VIQ	85	
VCI	100	
WMI	63	
WAIS–III Subtests		
Vocabulary	SS = 10	
Similarities	SS = 5	
Arithmetic	SS = 3	
Digit Span	SS = 4	
Information	SS = 15	
Comprehension	SS = 8	
Letter-Number Sequencing	SS = 5	
WRAT–3		
Reading	SS = 104	
AMNART	14 Errors	
Estimated VIQ	116	
Memory		
CVLT		
Trial 1	Raw = 5	Z = −1.0
Trail 2	Raw = 5	
Trial 3	Raw = 5	
Trial 4	Raw = 7	
Trial 5	Raw = 7	Z = −3.0
Total	Raw = 29	T = 18
List B	Raw = 5	Z = −1.0
S Free	Raw = 3	Z = −3.0
S Cued	Raw = 6	Z = −3.0
L Free	Raw = 5	Z = −2.0
L Cued	Raw = 5	Z = −3.0
Hits	Raw = 10	Z = −3.0
FP	Raw = 2	Z = 0
Disc	Raw = 82.0	Z = −2.0
WMS–III		
Logical Memory I	SS = 1	
Logical Memory II	SS = 4	
Logical Memory 2% Retention	SS = 11	
Visual Reproduction I	SS = 2	
Visual Reproduction II	SS = 3	
Visual Reproduction % Retention	SS = 2	
Visual Reproduction Discrimination	Raw = 5	

(Continued . . .)

TABLE 28.2   (Continued)

Attention	
Stroop Color Word Test	
Word	T = 20
Color	T = 20
C-W	T = 20
Interference	T = 54
Problem Solving	
WCST	
# Categories	4
% Errors	T = 48
% Preservative Responses	T = 53
% Preservative Errors	T = 53
% Conceptual Level Responses	T = 47
Motor	
Grip Strength	
Dominant (Right)	
Nondominant (Left)	T = 9
Symptom Validity	
TOMM	
Trial 1	Raw = 12
Trial 2	Raw = 16
Recognition Trial	Raw = 9
VSVT	
Easy	18/24
Difficult	14/24
Visual-Spatial	
RCF	
Copy	Raw = 11.5
Delay	Raw = 2.00
Personality	
BDI	Raw = 30 Severe

surprising that Mr. Z. demonstrated significantly impaired scores on tests of attention, learning and memory, and executive abilities. Marked anxiety, depression, and emotional lability were evident throughout the evaluation process.

Comment: Clinical experience has taught me that low effort on symptom validity tests does not necessarily indicate that someone is malingering, which is why I conservatively refer to cases such as these as "low effort" rather than " 'malingering" in my report, and I typically add a caveat like "poor performance on effort tests doesn't preclude the presence of cognitive impairment, just my ability to validly measure it." Indeed, his labile clinical presentation made me reluctant to rule out psychological adjustment difficulties as a potential influencing factor. I therefore concluded, "The presence of neurocognitive impairment cannot be validly identified at this time."

The Electrical Trauma Program multidisciplinary team was unable to render a diagnosis because different members of the team received conflicting information from Mr. Z. Multiple examinations done and shared in group discussions revealed repeated examples of inconsistencies and poor effort. An outpatient physical therapy program was recommended to address self-care, mobility, and strengthening issues because of upper extremity *disuse*. Also recommended was ongoing psychiatric intervention, and ultimately vocational counseling to develop a plan for work reentry. MRI of the cervical spine was recommended, and it was also advised that the patient would benefit from a swift resolution of the lawsuit.

Third neuropsychological evaluation (conducted by defense expert)

Mr. Z. was ordered by the court to undergo a videotaped independent neuropsychological evaluation by an expert hired by the defendant (The Power Company). At the time of this evaluation, 35 months after the incident, Mr. Z. was described as presenting with dramatic displays of pain behavior. He walked up the stairs to the second floor using both hands on the rail, as if climbing a rope. He complained of dizziness and tingling when upstairs. He displayed unusual speech that was high pitched, with variable articulation and rate. His speech impairment was variable throughout the three days of examination, on occasion appearing better when he was not focused on it, and on occasion worse when he was doing tasks such as the oral reading test on the Wide Range Achievement Test. Data from this neuropsychological examination that could be directly compared to previous evaluations are summarized in Table 28.1.

On the third examination, Mr. Z. failed the Rey 15-Item Test, Test of Memory Malingering, Warrington Recognition Memory Test, and PDRT-27, with all scores in the range of poor effort/ motivated performance deficit/malingering. He also showed performance patterns on standard neuropsychological tests indicative of poor effort/motivated performance deficit/malingering, including failure on the recognition trials of the California Verbal Learning Test–II, as well as scoring worse-than-chance on identification of recurring items on the CVMT. He showed definite symptom exaggeration on the Lees-Haley Fake Bad Scale on the MMPI–2, with a score of 36, exceeding the most conservative cutoff of 24 or higher. His elevated Lees-Haley Fake Bad Scale and extreme elevations on Scales 1 and 3 of the MMPI–2 significantly exceeded the conservative criteria for presence of somatic malingering. On current standard neuropsychological tests, he performed in the motivationally impaired range on the Benton Visual Form Discrimination Test, Finger Tapping, Reliable Digit Span, and Wisconsin Card Sorting Test failure to maintain set. According to this neuropsychologist, these above performances, along with his elevated Lees-Haley Fake Bad Scale, met criteria for definite/probable malingered neurocognitive deficit on 5 of 5 indicators.

The defense neuropsychologist concluded that Mr. Z. produced multiple indicators of symptom exaggeration, poor effort, and malingering on the current examination that were consistent with data obtained from both prior evaluations (including my own). As a result, Mr. Z.'s symptom history or other self-report indicators of injury severity were not considered to be informative in understanding this man's current presentation.

The feedback

After the evaluation was complete, I contacted the plaintiff's attorney directly to discuss with him the results of the evaluation. This, of course, was not a comfortable experience as the attorney had gone to considerable expense to send his client to Chicago for an evaluation. Indeed, when I indicated that my results and those of the team had raised serious questions about Mr. Z.'s motivation, effort, and clinical presentation, he reacted with shock and genuine surprise. He stated that he "just couldn't believe that he would be faking it during all the meetings he had with him," but at the end of the conversation summed it up by saying that as an attorney, "we take the cases as they are, warts and all." From that point on, the plaintiff's attorney forwarded to me numerous testimonials provided by Mr. Z.'s friends to attest to how different he was compared to prior to his injury as well as updated medical records. One of the most interesting was a note from the treating neuropsychologist who reported that the patient had no control of bowel or bladder and was wearing a diaper constantly. The possibility of moving to an assisted living facility was being raised.

CASE ANALYSIS

There was no evidence based upon review of medical records that Mr. Z. suffered an acute mental status alteration secondary to his alleged electrical injury. ER records did not report any evidence of mental status abnormality. The patient could recall events leading up to the alleged shock and events immediately following his point of regaining consciousness. He recalled events on the day of injury, both preceding and following the alleged injury, based on reports to multiple specialists and statements made in the patient's deposition. He also recalled events the day after the shock, when the electrical company representatives came to his home.

The house that Mr. Z. was in had its ground altered, which resulted in Mr. Z. apparently receiving an electrical shock. However, the electrical exposure related to the injury was difficult for the Electrical Trauma Program team to assess because the details of the circuit path were entirely unclear. This was considered a conceivable scenario, but the voltage drop and current experienced by Mr. Z. was considered to have been "quite small." No burn or contact wounds had been noted, and there was no documentation of cardiopulmonary arrest with resuscitation.

Despite the multisystemic nature, frequency, and intensity of his complaints, there was no objective evidence of abnormality on any diagnostic test given to Mr. Z. during the months following his electrical shock incident. Diagnostic studies included normal MRI of the brain without contrast, normal nerve conduction studies of the left extremities, essentially normal EMG/NCS of the left upper extremity, EMG of right upper extremity, and NCS of left lower extremity, and normal awake, drowsy, and light sleepy EEG. The lone exception was his initial neuropsychological evaluation, although it is important to note that symptom validity tests were not administered during Mr. Z.'s evaluation by this neuropsychologist.

The patient presented with unremitting cognitive, physical, and affective complaints. However, the multiple indicators of poor effort and motivated performance deficit noted on the last two evaluations suggest that the most likely explanation for his continuing complaints and problems on neuropsychological testing is motivated performance deficit and symptom exaggeration in the pursuit of secondary gain in the current litigation.

EPILOGUE

The deposition

I was eventually deposed in this matter (at the request of the defense in this case), and a request was made by defense attorneys for the deposition to take place in a room that had a VCR and TV monitor. At the point in the deposition where I was describing Mr. Z.'s unusual behavioral presentation during the evaluation in which he performed nearly all tasks with his left hand because of complaints of pain and weakness in his right hand, I was asked to view a surveillance video that showed Mr. Z. walking along the beach and throwing food to the seagulls with his right hand! I was asked if seeing that videotape was significant (it was), and if it had an impact on my opinions in this case (it did). This was one of the few times that I felt totally comfortable offering an opinion of definite malingering.

The verdict

Four years after the incident, a jury returned a verdict of $3 million against the Power Company arising out of the alleged electrical injury sustained by the plaintiff. On the Power Company's website, the following statement appeared in relation to this case: "If the verdict is not overturned, the plaintiff will also be entitled to recover attorney's fees. The Power Company intends to seek a new trial; however, if it is not successful in obtaining a new trial, the Power Company intends to pursue an appeal. The ultimate outcome of this matter cannot now be determined, but is not expected to have a material impact on the Power Company's financial statements."

Pediatric and Learning/Academic Disorders

For a time, neuropsychologists were of the opinion that children either did not, or would not, malinger on neuropsychological tests. The naïveté of this statement became clear in time, as forensic examiners began to encounter children who quite clearly malingered in secondary gain assessment contexts. Related, researchers demonstrated that effort measures could be used effectively with children to identify potential malingering. More expected is the teen or young adult who may feign cognitive impairment in order to receive special test-taking accommodations on standardized admissions tests. The three chapters in the next section expand the universality of the malingering phenomenon well beyond our earlier, naïve presumptions.

Using objective effort measures to detect noncredible cognitive test performance in children and adolescents

29

Lloyd Flaro and Kyle Boone

An increasing awareness of the fact that children and adolescents can fake neuropsychological impairments and exaggerate symptoms under a variety of conditions (e.g., civil and criminal litigation, securing disability benefits) has fostered in psychologists and neuropsychologists a growing desire to develop reliable methods for the detection of symptom exaggeration and faked psychological disturbance in this population (Faust, Hart, & Guilmette, 1988; Faust, Hart, Guilmette, & Arkes, 1988; McCann, 1998; Reitan & Wolfson, 1997; Rogers, 1997). Traditionally, clinical judgment was relied upon in the detection of invalid test scores, but empirical research has shown that clinical intuition is not accurate in identifying malingering or symptom exaggeration in children and adolescents (Faust, Hart, & Guilmette, 1988). More objective and valid methods for assessing effort levels and symptom exaggeration are needed to assess the veracity of symptom complaints and exaggerated psychological impairments in minors (Green & Flaro, 2003). In this chapter, we will present cases illustrating the use of such measures in the identification of noncredible symptoms in a child and an adolescent.

CASE 1 (FEIGNING TO EVADE CRIMINAL RESPONSIBILITY)

A.A. was a 16-year-old Caucasian male referred by the Justice Department to determine the possibility of underlying brain dysfunction as a cause for his aggressive and violent behaviors over the years. The defense lawyer wanted to establish whether or not previous history of mild head injuries from a number of fights could account for his current legal problems, which related to the vicious stabbing of another adolescent male. Data regarding his ability to stand trial and be tried in an adult court were also requested.

Information obtained from collateral sources (parents, Child Welfare, Justice Department) established a history of early onset Conduct Disorder behavioral characteristics (lying, stealing, fire setting, physical aggression and violence, and use of weapons). Available medical and psychiatric reports documented that A.A. demonstrated learning problems from an early age and was placed in a classroom for children with behavioral problems. Even though he was identified as having learning difficulties, school reports indicated that when he put in strong effort and controlled his moods, he achieved high marks in most subject areas. Many of the educator's remarks noted problems with poor effort and his inability to manage his anger. During these school years, A.A. was frequently suspended for a number of aggressive and antisocial acts including verbal and physical threats with weapons (e.g., knives, BB gun, and sticks). At home, the mother reported that A.A. had attempted to assault his younger brother by choking him. He also threatened to hurt his sisters by pointing knives at them. As a result of his early onset disruptive behavioral problems, his mother contacted Child Welfare services and requested his removal from the home when he was 6 years of age. He was placed in numerous foster homes but his stay in each one was short-lived because of his escalating behavioral problems and persistent violent acts. However, it was also observed that A.A. could be "charming" and control his anger for lengthy periods of time "when he wanted something."

At the age of 13, A.A. was charged with manslaughter and placed in a juvenile detention center where he spent two years. During this time, he was seen by a psychiatrist who diagnosed him with severe conduct disorder and severe anger management dysregulation. He was prescribed medication (Risperdal and Paxil) to control his violent outbursts and suspected depression, which he refused to take. During his stay at this treatment facility, a Secure Treatment Risk Report characterized A.A. as an adolescent youth with severe behavioral and antisocial problems who was making little progress in response to various treatment methods.

At 15, he was released from this detention center and placed under the care of the Child Welfare Department. He continued to refuse all medication for managing his explosive outbursts. With help from social services, he managed to avoid legal contact for several months. However, shortly after his sixteenth birthday, he viciously attacked a member of another gang, stabbing him multiple times. At his arrest, he showed no remorse or guilt for his actions and claimed that the victim had borrowed money from him and refused to repay it. A.A. was again placed in a juvenile detention center. In A.A.'s court appearance, the judge agreed with the defense lawyer that A.A.'s history of abuse and mild head injuries sustained from fights might suggest that underlying neuropsychological damage could be responsible for his current legal problems. A neuropsychological assessment was court ordered.

Test behavior and results

A.A. presented as "tough" and oppositional and affected a stance of bravado, hostility, and confrontation. He stated that he understood the reason for the evaluation, and commented, "I hope this assessment will reduce my sentence because of head injuries I received during numerous fights. My lawyer suggested that brain damage might explain my behavioral problems." While he was generally cooperative in the assessment, on many tasks he became extremely frustrated and agitated, and would essentially "give up."

On neuropsychological testing, A.A. scored within the severely impaired range in verbal and visual memory, executive functions, auditory comprehension, and in perception of emotion from vocal cues. In addition, performance on a continuous performance task was impaired and consistent with Attention Deficit Disorder. In contrast, overall IQ was average (WISC–III FSIQ = 94), although there was a 17-point discrepancy between Verbal and Performance IQs; VIQ was average (VIQ = 103) while PIQ was low average (PIQ = 86). Normal performances were observed in visual motor integration, visuoconstructive and visual perceptual skills, auditory discrimination, receptive and expressive language skills, spelling and reading recognition, math calculation ability, psychomotor speed, and manual dexterity, and there was no evidence of finger agnosia, dysgraphesthesia, or astereognosis.

However, performance on two tests assessing veracity of effort was abnormal. On the Computerized Assessment of Response Bias (CARB), A.A.'s individual trial scores were 91.7, 78.4, and 73, and his Total Score was 80.9; all scores were significantly lower than expected for his age. Similarly, his scores on the Word Memory Test (WMT) also reflected poor effort: Immediate Recognition (IR) = 82.5; Delayed Recognition (DR) = 85; Consistency (CNS) = 77.5; Multiple Choice (MC) = 85; Paired Associates (PA) = 95; and Delayed Free Recognition (DFR) = 40. In addition, A.A.'s response pattern on the WMT was highly inconsistent; specifically, he scored extremely well on a difficult memory subtest (PA), but poorly on an easier one (MC) and the effort measures (IR, DR, and CNS). The overall pattern of performance strongly suggested that A.A. was attempting to feign cognitive deficits and that obtained neuropsychological scores were an underestimate of true ability. Further, results of psychological testing revealed the presence of severe conduct disorder and emerging Cluster B traits (i.e., antisocial, narcissistic).

A.A. was subsequently provided with feedback regarding the results of his assessment. His response was to laugh and shrug his shoulders, commenting, "Oh, well." When asked why he had chosen to feign, he stated that he deliberately attempted to appear more cognitively impaired than was the case because his lawyer informed him that the presence of neuropsychological deficits would probably lighten his sentence. He provided this information in a matter-of-fact manner with no affect. When A.A.'s intellectual abilities were reported to the defense lawyer, he expressed surprise and indicated that IQ scores obtained in Grade 6 were above average to superior, quickly adding that he had just received A.A.'s early educational records and therefore had not been able to provide them at the time of the assessment.

It is informative to contrast A.A.'s performance on the two effort measures with those of a 14-year-old female, B.B., who was referred for a neuropsychological assessment due to obvious language deficits and ongoing behavioral problems including wide mood swings, temper tantrums, severely inappropriate behaviors, aggression, and externalizing behaviors, as well as possible executive dysfunction.

B.B. was found to have a WISC–III Full Scale IQ of 93, a Verbal IQ of 63, and a Performance IQ of 91 (28 point difference). More importantly, her Verbal Comprehension Index was 62, whereas her Perceptual Organization Index was 102 (a 40-point difference!). In addition, impaired neuropsychological results were noted on receptive vocabulary, expressive vocabulary, auditory verbal comprehension, verbal fluency, verbal memory, and verbal reasoning. Academic skills were equally impaired, especially with respect to language-based subject matter.

In contrast, B.B. obtained normal scores on all remaining neuropsychological tests, including visual motor integration, visual perceptual and visuoconstructive abilities, sensory perceptual functioning, motor abilities, visual memory, and executive skills.

Thus, test results revealed a clearly lateralized pattern suggesting significant left hemispheric dysfunction. B.B.'s focal language impairments might have been expected to compromise performance on verbal effort measures. However, in contrast to A.A., *B.B. achieved normal results on both the CARB and WMT.* On the former, B.B. was 100% accurate on all three trials. On the effort measures of the Word Memory Test, she obtained the following scores: IR = 97.5%; DR = 100%; CNS = 97.5%. On the memory measures of the WMT, she earned the following scores: MC = 100%; PA = 100%; Free Recall (FR) = 35%. (See Figures 29.1 and 29.2 for a comparison of both cases on the WMT.)

In addition, B.B. was given a newly published effort measure, the Memory and Concentration Test (MACT; Green, 2004). The MACT (now named MSVT (Medical Symptom Validity Test)) is structured in a similar manner to the WMT, but with only ten pairs of words. Her scores on the MACT also reflected credible performance and were as follows: IR = 95%; DR = 100%; CNS = 95%; PA = 100%; FR = 50%.

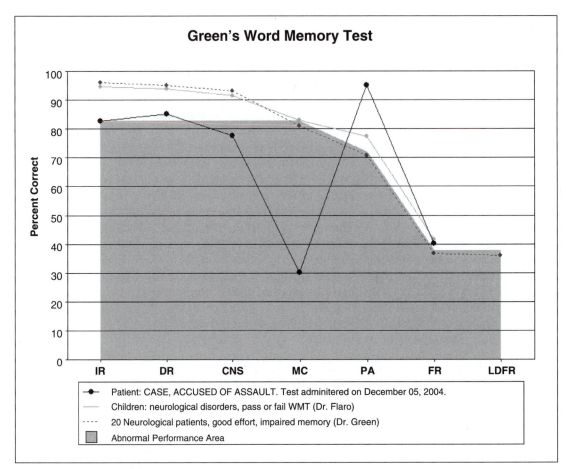

FIG. 29.1   A.A.'s performance on the WMT.

CASE 2 (FEIGNING IN THE CONTEXT OF PERSONAL INJURY LITIGATION)

C.C., a 9-year-old male, had been struck by a car three years prior to the current evaluation. He did not lose consciousness but was disoriented, with a Glasgow Coma Scale of 11. Head CT revealed a subarachnoid hemorrhage and right frontal lobe contusion. He remained hospitalized for 13 days and then was transferred to a rehabilitation facility for treatment of motor and cognitive deficits. Upon discharge 19 days later, his cognition was rated as within normal limits, although some weaknesses in visual discrimination and paper and pencil copying skills persisted.

On return to school, C.C. was placed in a resource classroom. Six months following the accident, the patient was noted to be 1 year delayed in reading and 1.5 years behind in math. However, these scores were essentially equivalent to scores documented four months prior to the accident (overall reading = 9th percentile; spelling = 23rd percentile; math = 9th percentile). Of interest, 1.5 years following the accident, C.C.'s academic test scores were consistently above average (math = 94th percentile; reading = 91st percentile; written language = 72nd percentile) and grades were average.

C.C.'s mother reported that following the head injury C.C. became easily angered and physic-

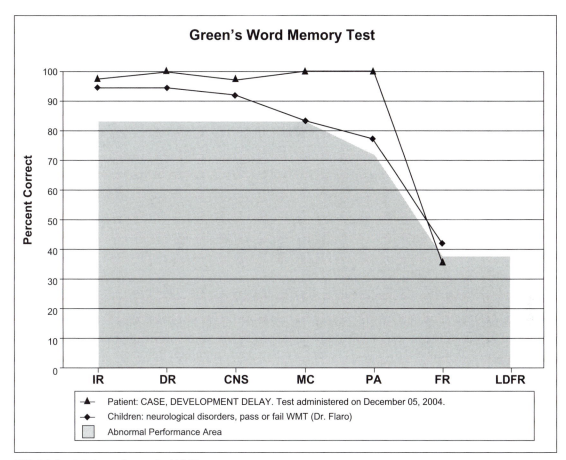

FIG. 29.2   B.B.'s results on the WMT.

ally violent, and he was also described as isolating himself from his friends. However, school records revealed that four months prior to the accident she had sought counseling for him due to overly aggressive behavior.

The family filed suit against the city in which the accident had occurred, claiming unsafe conditions. School records revealed that *the plaintiff attorney was also the child's step-father*. The child underwent neuropsychological evaluation at the request of defense counsel.

Test behavior and results

C.C.'s behavioral presentation was unremarkable, with the exception that he appeared subdued and speech output was sparse. Intellectual scores were within the extremely low/mentally retarded range (WISC–III VIQ = 60; PIQ = 63; FSIQ = 58), and scores on measures of processing speed, visual perceptual/spatial skills, verbal and visual memory, and motor function were all within the impaired range.

However, C.C. failed five of five effort measures. Specifically, he only reproduced four stimuli and committed two confabulations on the Rey 15-item test (cutoff < 9; Lezak, 1995), he recognized 10 words on the Rey Word Recognition Memory Test but produced 9 false-positive errors (> 6 false-positive errors = 100% specificity; Nitch, Boone, Wen, Arnold, & Warner-Chacon, 2006), he made five errors on the Dot Counting Test and his E score was 25 (cutoff ≥ 19; Boone, Lu, & Herzberg, 2002a), and he made 16 "d" commission errors on the first page of the b Test (cutoff ≥ 1 "d" error for all 15 pages; Boone, Lu, & Herzberg, 2002b). Additionally, he produced a *significantly below chance* performance on the Warrington Recognition Memory Test–Words (17/50). Further, his performance on Finger Tapping was noted to be noncredible; the number of taps executed within 10 seconds for the left hand was wildly variable and ranged from 10 to 41 across trials.

In this case, evidence of noncredible performance was observed not only from dedicated effort measures, but also from standard neuropsychological tests (e.g., Finger Tapping) and documentation of the marked discrepancy between performances on the current exam (i.e., all scores within the impaired range) versus academic achievement scores from 1.5 years post-accident (all > 90th percentile) and exit testing upon discharge from a rehabilitation program one month post-injury (all skills normal although some weaknesses in visual discrimination). Further information regarding this case can be found in Lu and Boone (2002).

DISCUSSION

The case of A.A. illustrates that adolescents can feign cognitive impairment in the context of evading criminal responsibility, while the case of C.C. reveals that even children as young as 9 can fabricate cognitive symptoms in the context of personal injury litigation. Suboptimal effort was identified in A.A. through use of the WMT and the CARB, while noncredible test performance was flagged in C.C. through the use of the Rey 15-item, Dot Counting, Rey Word Recognition, and b Tests, and significantly below chance performance on the Warrington Recognition Memory Test–Words. In addition, in the case of A.A., malingering was suggested by marked inconsistency in performance across memory measures and confirmed by his admission of malingering when confronted with the test results. The conclusion that C.C. was feigning was buttressed through observation of his implausible performance on finger tapping, as well as through comparison of his impaired scores on current testing with his superior scores documented on academic achievement testing in the school setting and his essentially normal cognitive scores upon discharge from rehabilitation treatment.

These cases illustrate that malingering of cognitive symptoms does occur in children and adolescents and that the same techniques used to identify suspect effort in adults may be appropriate for use in younger patients. The cases also add to the very limited literature on feigning of cognitive symptoms in children and adolescents. The only other study of which we are aware, published 25 years ago, involved a presentation of "pseudodementia" in a 10-year-old boy who was attempting to obtain compensation following a mild head injury without loss of consciousness (Adler, 1981). Additionally, some examples of feigning of psychiatric symptoms for external incentive (i.e., to obtain disability compensation, to remove oneself from an undesirable residence) have been reported in children aged 9 to 14 (Cassar, Hales, Longhurst, & Weiss; 1996; Greenfield, 1987; Roberts, 1997). When this behavior occurs at the direction of parents, it has been termed "malingering by proxy" (Cassar et al., 1996), which appears to have been operating in the case of C.C.

Faust and colleagues, in studies conducted nearly 20 years ago (Faust, Hart, & Guilmette, 1988a; Faust, Hart, Guilmette, & Arkes, 1988b), demonstrated that children and adolescents instructed to feign were able to convincingly malinger cognitive deficits and evade detection. However, at that time, effort measures were not routinely included in test batteries. In subsequent years, numerous effort tests and indices have been developed and validated in adult populations (cf., Vickery, Berry, Inman, Harris, & Orey, 2001), but, until recently, whether these techniques were appropriate for use in pediatric and adolescent populations has been unknown. Evidence that: (1) children over age 11 score comparably to adult control populations on such measures as the Dot Counting Test, 21-item Test, and an adaptation of the Rey 15-item test (Martin, Haut, Stainbrook, & Franzen, 1995); (2) that healthy children and adolescents (age 5 to 12) and patients (age 6 to 16) with various clinical disorders referred for neuropsychological assessment exhibit a < 2% false-positive rate on the TOMM (Constantinou & McCaffrey, 2003; Donders, 2005; Nagle, Everhart, Durham, McCammon, & Walker, 2006); (3) that children ≥ age 11 produce Word Memory Test (WMT) and Computerized Assessment of Response Bias (CARB) performances similar to adults (although younger children perform worse) (Courtney, Dinkins, Allen, & Kuroski (2003); (4) that children with at least a third grade reading level pass the WMT (Green & Flaro, 2003); and (5) that children, even of low intelligence, score at or near 100% on MACT effort subtests, and immediate and delayed recognition subtests, even if tested in a foreign language (Green, 2004), confirms excellent specificity of these measures in at least older children and adolescents.

In addition, recent simulation studies on children have suggested that some free-standing effort measures (e.g., TOMM; Constantinou & McCaffrey, 2003) as well as standard cognitive measures (Raven's Standard Progressive Matrices; McKinzey, Prieler, & Raven, 2003) can be highly accurate in detecting children instructed to feign. However, how well the results of simulation studies translate to detection of "real world" child malingerers is unknown. For example, Constantinou and McCaffrey (2003) reported that the Rey 15-item test was not useful in identifying child simulators, although it did provide evidence of feigning in our "real world" case of C.C.

Although the rate of fabrication of cognitive symptoms is likely to be much less common in children and adolescents as compared to adults, the cases presented here argue that effort indices should be routinely administered to minors in the context of medical-legal and criminal evaluations. Additional research is needed to determine which effort tests are most effective in this population, and whether the tests differ in sensitivity and specificity depending on such variables as age of the child or reading level.

REFERENCES

Adler, R. (1981). Pseudodementia or Ganser syndrome in a ten year old boy. *Australian and New Zealand Journal of Psychiatry*, *15*, 339–342.

Boone, K. B., Lu, P., & Herzberg, D. (2002a). *The Dot Counting Test*. Los Angeles: Western Psychological Services.

Boone, K. B., Lu, P., & Herzberg, D. (2002b). *The b Test*. Los Angeles: Western Psychological Services.

Cassar, J. R., Hales, E. S., Longhurst, J. G., & Weiss, G. S. (1996). Candisability benefits make children sicker? *Journal of the American Academy of Child and Adolescent Psychiatry*, *35*, 700–701.

Constantinou, M., & McCaffrey, R. J. (2003). Using the TOMM for evaluating children's effort to perform optimally on neuropsychological measures, *Child Neuropsychology*, *9*, 81–90.

Courtney, J. D., Dinkins, J. P., Allen, L. M., & Kuroski, K. (2003). Age related effects in children taking the Computerized Assessment of Response Bias and the Word Memory Test. *Child Neuropsychology*, *9*, 109–116.

Donders, J. (2005). Performance on the test of memory malingering in a mixed pediatric sample, *Child Neuropsychology*, *11*, 221–227.

Faust, D., Hart, K., & Guilmette, T. J. (1988). Pediatric Malingering: The capacity of children to fake believable deficits on neuropsychological testing. *Journal of Consulting and Clinical Psychology*, *56*, 578–582.

Faust, D., Hart, K., Guilmette, T. J., & Arkes, H. R. (1988). Neuropsychologists' capacity to detect adolescent malingerers. *Professional Psychology Research and Practice*, *19*, 508–515.

Green, P. (2004). *Green's Memory and Concentration Test (MACT): User's manual*. Edmonton: Green's Publishing Inc.

Green, P., & Flaro, L. (2003). Word Memory Test performance in children. *Child Neuropsychology: Journal of Normal and Abnormal Developments in Childhood and Adolescence*, *9*(3), 189–207.

Greenfield, D. (1987). Feigned psychosis in a 14-year-old girl. *Hospital and Community Psychiatry*, *38*, 73–75.

Lezak, M. D. (1995). *Neuropsychological assessment*, 3rd ed. New York: Oxford University Press.

Lu, P. H., & Boone, K. B. (2002). Suspect cognitive symptoms in a 9-year-old child: Malingering by proxy? *The Clinical Neuropsychologist, 16*, 90–96.

Martin, R. C., Haut, J. S., Stainbrook, T., & Franzen, M. D. (1995). Preliminary normative data for objective measures to detect malingered neuropsychological deficits in a population of adolescent patients, *Archives of Clinical Neuropsychology, 10*, 364–365.

McCaffrey, R. J., & Lynch, J. K. (1992). A methodological review of "Method Skeptic" reports. *Neuropsychology Review, 3*, 193–214.

McCann, J. T. (1998). *Malingering and deception in adolescents: Assessing credibility in clinical and forensic settings.* Washington, DC: American Psychological Association.

McKinzey, R. K., Prieler, J., & Raven, J. (2003). Detection of children's malingering on Raven's Standard Progressive Matrices, *British Journal of Clinical Psychology, 42*, 95–99.

Nagle, A. M., Everhart, D. E., Durham, T. W., McCammon, S. L., & Walker, M. (2006). Deception strategies in children: Examination of forced choice recognition and verbal learning and memory techniques. *Archives of Clinical Neuropsychology, 21*, 777–785.

Nitch, S., Boone, K. B., Wen, J., Arnold, G., & Warner-Chacon, K. (2006). The utility of the Rey Word Recognition Test in the detection of suspect effort, *The Clinical Neuropsychologist, 20*, 873–887.

Reitan, R. M., & Wolfson, D. (1997). *Detection of malingering and invalid test scores.* Tucson, AZ: Neuropsychology Press.

Roberts, M. D. (1997). Munchausen by proxy. *Journal of the American Academy of Child and Adolescent Psychiatry, 36*, 578–580.

Rogers, R. (1997). Current status of clinical methods. In R. Rogers (Ed.), *Clinical assessment of malingering and deception* (pp. 373–397). New York: Guilford Press.

Vickery, C. D., Berry, D. T., Inman, T. H., Harris, M. J., & Orey, S. A. (2001). Detection of inadequate effort on neuropsychological testing: A meta-analytic review of selected procedures. *Archives of Clinical Neuropsychology, 16*, 45–73.

Malingering following documented brain injury: Neuropsychological evaluation of children in a forensic setting

30

Robert J. McCaffrey and Julie K. Lynch

It is fairly typical for children or adolescents to show fluctuations in their level of engagement in testing during the neuropsychological evaluation. This may be due to a number of reasons, including boredom, disinterest, or fatigue, that develop after a lengthy period of cognitive testing. It is also the case that some children or adolescents show poor participation across the evaluation, perhaps due to their unwillingness to undergo evaluation, or due to behavioral issues. These potential obstacles to a valid neuropsychological evaluation in pediatric settings are well known. Perhaps less known is that children and adolescents can feign psychological and neuropsychological symptoms. While there are certainly situations with clear incentives for a child or adolescent to falsify symptoms (e.g., academic accommodations, monetary compensation, parental attention or approval), there has always been some doubt as to whether this young population would even conceive of engaging in this form of deception, as well as whether children have the skills necessary to intentionally engage in deceptive behavior. Regarding the latter, there is research that has shown that preschool age children are capable of intentionally deceiving an adult stranger and can do so in a manner that is difficult for the adult to detect. The deceptive behavior of the very young child is not complex, taking the form of unelaborated denials or acknowledgements to questions posed by the adult. After the age of six, however, children become capable of deception that is more elaborate. By adolescence, the ability to control emotional responses and facial expressions is well developed, and this allows for more skillful deceptive behavior (McCann, 1998; Oldershaw & Bagby, 1997).

In addition to having the capability for deceptive behavior, children have been found to use this skill to fabricate symptoms during medical, psychological, and neuropsychological examinations. The literature contains several case studies of children and adolescents who have engaged in dissimulation. As defined by Rogers (1997), dissimulation is the deliberate distortion or misrepresentation of one's psychological symptoms. Dissimulation refers to intentional exaggeration or falsification of symptoms as well as the intentional denial or minimization of symptoms, although it is more commonly used in reference to the former. In those situations in which there is exaggeration or feigning of symptoms, the motivation for dissimulation will vary. In malingering, dissimulation is motivated by some external factor, whether to obtain something positive (e.g., disability benefits, financial compensation in civil litigation, academic services or accommodations) or to avoid something negative (e.g., return to work, imprisonment). In Factitious Disorder, dissimulation is motivated by the psychological need to assume a sick role. Both Malingering and Factitious Disorder have been identified in children.

In many of the reports of feigned symptoms in children and adolescents, the influential role of the parents or family system in these conditions becomes very clear. The most obvious and perhaps extreme form of parental influence is found in Factitious Disorder by Proxy. Also known as Munchausen's Syndrome by Proxy, this is a psychological disorder that is characterized by a caregiver who falsely reports or produces psychological or medical symptoms in his/her child in order to fulfill the caregiver's psychological need to assume a sick role, although indirectly. The caregiver is typically female and usually the child's mother. There are case reports of parents reporting or inducing neurological symptoms in their children. Seizures are the most common symptom that is falsely reported by a parent, although there are cases in which parents have been found to have actually induced a seizure in the children by suffocation, medication, or by other means (Meadow, 1984; O'Shea, 2003). There is also a case report of a 4-year-old child who was trained by his mother to feign seizures. While in the hospital, the child would lie "unconscious" and tremble. At one point, the child feigned a paralyzed arm for two days following a feigned seizure. At school, he would fall off his chair, tremble, and flicker his eyes. He was prescribed medication for suspected seizures for a short time, but the fictitious nature of the seizure behavior became clear as he was able to be easily aroused from "unconsciousness" during these episodes by mentioning his favorite food, and had good recall of events that occurred during the episodes (Croft & Jervis, 1989). This case illustrates the point that the child proxy in Factitious Disorder by Proxy may become actively involved in maintaining the false illness. In some cases, the child may believe that he/she has an actual illness as described by the parent over the years.

Factitious Disorder can occur in children without a history of Factitious Disorder by Proxy. Libow (2000) reviewed the literature on factitious illnesses in children and specifically focused on cases in which the child consciously falsified medical symptoms without the involvement of a parent and without any obvious externally motivating factor. The primary motivation for feigning or intentionally producing symptoms appeared to be for the purpose of assuming a sick role. Children as young as age 8 were found to have induced physical symptoms sometimes through benign methods (e.g., warming a thermometer with a heating pad) and other times through medically risky actions. As examples, some had induced diabetic ketoacidosis with insulin manipulation, inserted foreign substances into their bladders to produce illness, and self-inflicted wounds. A few children had also endured invasive diagnostic procedures such as biopsies, gastrointestinal studies, and bone marrow aspirations. On average, it was 1.5 years before falsification of the illness was identified. Several children, particularly those younger than age 16, apparently admitted to falsely producing symptoms when confronted.

Malingering has also been identified in children, although this is typically at the instruction of an adult. The diagnostic phrase "Malingering by Proxy" has been used to refer to situations in which the child has fabricated symptoms at the direction of a parent. Cassar, Hales, Longhurst, and Weiss (1996) first used this terminology in their report of a case of a 13-year-old girl who was admitted to an inpatient unit for diagnostic evaluation following her mother's report of severe mood and behavioral problems. The psychiatric evaluation yielded no diagnosis, and it was later found that the child's mother was attempting to have her diagnosed with a psychiatric condition in order to qualify for psychiatric disability benefits. Stutts, Hickey, and Kasdan (2003) report another case of Malingering by Proxy that involved a 13-year-old who feigned inability to use his upper extremity for two years after sustaining a laceration from a glass window that fell from a concession stand on school property. The family pursued litigation with the school. X-rays and nerve conduction studies were normal; however, a hand surgeon identified a pre-existing condition that had surfaced as a result of the injury, and the child subsequently underwent surgery. Following the absence of improvement in his use of the arm following surgery, additional conditions were diagnosed by the surgeon and causally attributed to the injury at the school. Finally, video surveillance showing that the child had full use of his upper extremity revealed that his symptoms had been fabricated.

Malingering by Proxy has also been identified in the context of a neuropsychological evaluation. Lu and Boone (2002) report a case study of a 9-year-old child who had sustained a traumatic brain injury with a subarachnoid hemorrhage and a right frontal contusion when he was struck by a motor vehicle. He initially evidenced motor and cognitive deficits that improved within the first three weeks of injury with the exception of visuoconstructive difficulties. A neuropsychological evaluation was completed at least one year after the accident, at which time the family was pursuing litigation. The child's performance at the time of the evaluation showed global cognitive impairment. There were several indications, however, that the child's performance on the neuropsychological testing was not a valid indication of his cognitive functioning. His performance on the Warrington Recognition Memory Test was significantly below chance. On the Finger Tapping Test, his performance across trials was markedly variable, and his overall performance fell in the deficient range, which was discrepant from his within normal limits performance on this measure one month after injury. He showed a decline in copying skills relative to his performance on an initial neuropsychological evaluation shortly after the injury. In addition to atypical performance patterns on neuro-psychological testing, the child failed cognitive symptom validity testing using adult cutoff criteria for suboptimal effort (Rey Word Recognition Test, Rey Fifteen-Item Memorization Test, Dot Counting Test, Harbor-UCLA b Test). There were also inconsistencies between the neuro-psychological findings, intellectual test performance within the extremely low range, and his most recent academic records that indicated average grades and high average achievement test scores. Finally, his parents denied any history of academic problems predating the accident, which was not consistent with academic records that showed poor academic performance within a few months prior to injury. The records also described pre-injury behavioral problems.

This case study is informative on a number of issues. It provides evidence that children may manifest inadequate effort on neuropsychological testing with the intent to create a false picture of their neuropsychological status. The authors also described the 9-year-old as having provided a convincing description of his cognitive difficulties and interacting in a cooperative manner during the testing. This provides further evidence that children are capable of deception, and indicates that reliance on behavioral observations alone is insufficient for determining the validity of symptom reports and test performance. A final point elucidated by this case is that cognitive symptom validity testing has a role in the neuropsychological evaluation of children.

Thus, it appears that children have the skills necessary for deceptive behavior and that some children have been known to feign neuropsychological, psychological, and medical symptoms. Some adults, and particularly family members, readily influence children to knowingly or unknowingly feign symptoms. The child may collude with the parent in order to obtain parental love or recognition, or to satisfy dependency needs. The motivations for the parent to coach the child in producing symptoms are varied. The symptomatic child may serve to detour attention from marital problems and therefore play an essential role in maintaining the integrity of the family. In custody evaluations, symptom coaching may be one parent's attempt to malign the capability of the other parent to properly care for the child. The parent may be fulfilling psychological needs through their sick child, such as affirmation of their parenting by medical personnel or general attention from medical professionals (McCann, 1998). Another motivating factor for the parent to coach the child to produce symptoms is monetary gain, such as disability benefits or financial compensation associated with civil litigation.

We provide another case report of Malingering by Proxy of cognitive symptoms and neuro-psychological test performance for the purpose of financial gain.

THE CASE OF D.D.

An attorney who represented one of several defendants in this matter referred this case approximately three years following the accident. The 13-year-old child had been involved as a passenger in a high-speed motor vehicle accident. There were no fatalities; however, several individuals did sustain injuries. D.D. was the most severely injured. She was trapped in the vehicle for an extended period and required extraction with the Jaws of Life. Her Glasgow Coma Scale (GCS) score at the scene was 13, and she may have been unconscious briefly, but the exact duration was not contained in the records. She was transported via helicopter to a regional trauma center. At the Emergency Department, she was awake, alert, and following commands. Her GCS was 15. Neuroradiological studies revealed the presence of a right temporal contusion, right frontal epidural hematoma requiring evacuation, depressed skull fracture involving the frontal bone and orbital roof, and multiple orthopedic injuries. Her hospital course was notable only for complaints of headache and pain associated with the orthopedic injuries. There was no gross evidence of cognitive or behavioral deficiencies. Following a two-week hospitalization, she was discharged with recommendations for outpatient physical therapy for orthopedic injuries, and neuropsychological evaluation prior to returning to school.

D.D. remained home while recovering from orthopedic injuries and was provided a tutor in order to continue with her academic studies. She was seen for a speech and language therapy evaluation approximately two months after the accident. This evaluation documented a mild delay in receptive language skills, and the therapist recommended that she undergo a psychoeducational evaluation to assist with preparation for school re-entry. A psychoeducational evaluation was completed approximately two months later, the findings from which were deemed consistent with her performance on intellectual and achievement testing completed *before* the accident. The report indicated that prior to the accident D.D. had been referred to the Committee on Special Education for an evaluation based upon both her behavior issues and recent academic performance. Her teachers had apparently noted her to have difficulty with auditory comprehension, direction following, and writing skills. At that time, she was not eligible for any special services, but was described as showing characteristics of Attention-Deficit/Hyperactivity Disorder (ADHD) and a verbal learning disability. Following the accident, she was classified as Traumatically Brain Injured and provided with a consultant teacher and test accommodations. At school, D.D. had academic difficulties and her behavior was problematic in the classroom. She was described as hyperactive and somewhat oppositional. These academic and behavioral issues were similar in description to those reported pre-accident, but the problems were now attributed to the traumatic brain injury.

Plaintiff's counsel referred D.D. to a psychologist for a neuropsychological evaluation. The plaintiff's psychologist saw D.D. for neuropsychological evaluation 2.5 years after the accident. The evaluation documented severe deficits in verbal and nonverbal memory, receptive language, visuoperceptual skills, and attention. The results from behavioral rating scales were consistent with a diagnosis of ADHD. The Rey Fifteen-Item Memory Test was administered as a measure of effort, and D.D. performed well on this measure. The plaintiff's expert concluded that there was no evidence of dissimulation or deficient effort and that D.D. evidenced impairment in her cognitive and behavioral functioning as a direct result of the traumatic brain injury. The psychologist acknowledged the presence of pre-injury academic and behavioral issues but considered D.D.'s difficulties to be significantly worse after the accident.

Very shortly afterward, D.D. was seen for neuropsychological evaluation at the request of the defense attorney. During clinical interview, D.D.'s mother described her as having declined significantly in academic performance since the accident, as well as having experienced a rather drastic change in behavior. She described her daughter as impulsive and hyperactive. She also described D.D.'s memory and attention as very poor. In terms of pre-accident functioning, her mother stated that D.D. may have had occasional behavior problems and some difficulty with academics, but these problems were not significant. During the clinical interview and neuropsychological testing, D.D.'s behavior was very cooperative, polite, and respectful. There was no evidence of poor impulse control. She appeared to be engaged in the testing process.

D.D.'s performances on tests of symptom validity are summarized in Table 30.1.

TABLE 30.1   Summary of performance on symptom validity tests

SYMPTOM VALIDITY TESTS	D.D.'s PERFORMANCE	
Rey Fifteen-Item Test	13 of 15	
Test of Memory Malingering	Trial 1 = 28 Trial 2 = 29 Retention Trial = 40	
Word Memory Test	Immediate recognition: no. correct 20/40 Delayed recognition: 21/40 Consistency score: 22/40 Multiple choice recognition = 4/20 Paired associates = 4/20 Short delay free recall = 4/40 Long delay free recall = 4/40	IR %correct = 50% DR %correct = 52% % consistency = 55% MCR %correct = 20% PA %correct = 20% FR %correct = 10% FR %correct = 10%

D.D.'s Verbal IQ was 95 (average), Performance IQ was 83 (low average), and Full Scale IQ was 86 (low average). Verbal subtest scores ranged from 6 to 11, while Performance subtest scores ranged from 4 to 9.

D.D.'s performance on the Children's Memory Scale is shown in Table 30.2.

TABLE 30.2   Summary of performance on the Children's Memory Scale

INDEX SCORES	STANDARD SCORE	PERCENTILE RANK	QUALITATIVE DESCRIPTION
Visual Immediate	64	1	Extremely Low
Visual Delayed	62	1	Extremely Low
Verbal Immediate	66	1	Extremely Low
Verbal Delayed	56	0.2	Extremely Low
General Memory	50	< 0.1	Extremely Low
Attention/Concentration	76	5	Borderline
Learning	63	1	Extremely Low
Delayed Recognition	54	0.1	Extremely Low

D.D.'s performance on the Halstead-Reitan Neuropsychological Test Battery for Older Children (Reitan & Wolfson, 1992) using the neuropsychological deficits scale (NDS) score is summarized in Table 30.3. D.D.'s total NDS score of 48 is above the cutoff for the identification of brain dysfunction; however, in view of the findings across the symptom validity tests, extreme caution is necessary in the interpretation of any of the test findings from this examination. A subtest analysis of her performance on the HRNB-OC revealed that her performance on the Tactual Performance Test (TPT Total Time; as well as Memory and Localization from the domain of Immediate Memory and Recapitulation) were neuropsychological deficit scale scores of zero, which represents perfectly normal scores. In addition, D.D.'s performance on Part B of the Trail Making Test and the Category Test were also neuropsychological deficit scale scores of zero, which represents perfectly normal scores in the domain of Abstraction, Reasoning and Logical Analysis. These subtests are sometimes viewed as sensitive to brain dysfunction and yet they were perfectly normal. This was in contrast to D.D.'s performance on the Seashore Rhythm Test and Speech

TABLE 30.3   Summary of performance on the Halstead-Reitan Neuropsychological Battery for Older Children

LEVEL OF PERFORMANCE	D.D.'S PERFORMANCE	AVERAGE CONTROLS	AVERAGE BRAIN-DAMAGED	CUTOFF SCORE
Motor Functions	2	6.29	14.05	
Sensory-Perceptual Functions	18	5.15	10.77	
Visual-Spatial Skills	6	4.06	7.69	
Attention and Concentration	6	1.91	3.78	
Immediate Memory and Recapitulation	0	2.23	3.31	
Abstraction, Reasoning, Logical Analysis	1	2.63	6.03	
LEVEL OF PERFORMANCE TOTAL	**33**	**22.27**	**45.63**	**33/34**
Right-Left Differences				
Motor Functions	3	2.61	6.29	
Sensory-Perceptual Functions	6	3.09	5.28	
Both Motor and Sensory-Perceptual functions	1	1.09	2.17	
RIGHT-LEFT DIFFERENCES TOTAL	**10**	**6.79**	**13.74**	**9/10**
Dysphasia and Related Variables	**5**	**1.37**	**7.97**	**3/4**
TOTAL NEUROPSYCHOLOGICAL DEFICIT SCALE SCORE	*48*	*30.43*	*67.34*	*43/44*

Sound Perfection Test where her neuropsychological deficit scale scores of 3 were indicative of severe brain dysfunction in the domain of Alertness and Concentration. Given the time since her accident, D.D.'s poor performance on the Seashore Rhythm Test and Speech Sound Perception Test is inconsistent with her perfectly normal performance on tests in the domains of Abstraction, Reasoning and Logical Analysis, and Immediate Memory and Recapitulation. The memory findings from the HRNB-OC are also inconsistent with D.D.'s performance on the Children's Memory Scale. It would be highly unlikely to obtain perfectly normal scores in the domain of Immediate Memory and Recapitulation on the HRNB-OC given the extremely low performance on seven out of the eight index scores on the Children's Memory Scale. Within the Dysphasia and Related Variables, D.D.'s difficulties were with spelling and reading, which according to academic records, were long-standing educational skill deficits and contributed three of the five NDS score points.

In all, the findings from our evaluation did *not* support the presence of cognitive/neuropsychological deficits or behavioral problems that were a direct consequence of the motor vehicle accident. D.D.'s effort was judged as suboptimal, and there were several atypical findings on neuropsychological testing that were inconsistent with her injury and current functioning. There also appeared to be discrepancy between the report of D.D.'s prior functioning provided by her mother during the clinical interview, and that documented across educational and medical records. Our impression was that D.D.'s performance on this evaluation did not represent her "true" abilities.

CASE ANALYSIS

There are several important issues raised by interpretation of the evaluation conducted on behalf of plaintiff's counsel. First, D.D. performed above cutoff for suboptimal effort on the Rey Fifteen Item Test during our evaluation and that of the plaintiff's neuropsychologist. If we had administered only the Rey Fifteen-Item Test, we would have concluded that there was no objective evidence of deficient effort by D.D. on symptom validity testing. We did, however, administer two additional symptom validity tests that are more sensitive measures of effort than the Rey Fifteen-Item Test. D.D. performed poorly on these two tests. This highlights the importance of using multiple measures sensitive to an examinee's effort. Secondly, D.D. was reported as pleasant, polite, and cooperative during clinical interview and testing during both evaluations. Such behavioral observations alone are insufficient to determine the child's level of engagement and effort during formal testing. Lu and Boone (2002) reported a similar behavioral presentation of a child who failed symptom validity measures, despite his apparent engagement in the evaluation.

The child's mother acknowledged that she had some behavioral and academic problems prior to the injury but had described these problems as insignificant. Her daughter's current behavior and academic performance were described as markedly worse since the injury. Based upon this, the plaintiff's expert concluded that the child's hyperactive and impulsive behaviors were a direct result of the accident. An analysis of the child's educational and medical records indicated that not only were hyperactive and impulsive behaviors and academic problems present pre-accident, but she was described in the records as exhibiting strong indications of ADHD and a possible verbal learning disability. In fact, the child had been referred to the Committee on Special Education, in part, based upon the teachers' concerns regarding her disruptive behavior in class. Careful review of medical records provided further indication that D.D.'s behavioral issues prior to the accident were substantial and not dissimilar from current behavioral issues. An office note of D.D.'s primary care physician documented her mother's concern about her difficult behavior at home eight months before the accident. Further, in a neurosurgical office note two months after the accident, her mother reported that her behavior problems were no different from prior behavior.

This case also underscores the need to be up-to-date with the current clinical neuro-psychological literature. The use of objective measures of symptom validity is relatively new in the neuropsychological evaluation of children. There is a small but growing body of research on the use of several of these tests with children. Although the plaintiff's psychologist did administer the Rey Fifteen-Item Test during his evaluation, he was critical of us because of the use of "adult" measures of symptom validity testing with children. Yet, research on the use of these symptom validity measures had been published in peer-reviewed neuropsychological journals at the time that the neuropsychological evaluations were completed with D.D.

In brief summary of this research, there are three studies providing some empirical support for the use of the Word Memory Test with children (Courtney, Dinkins, Allen, & Kuraski, 2003; Green & Flaro, 2003; Palav, 2004) though further research is needed as there have been some inconsistent findings regarding the age at which the adult criteria for suboptimal effort is appropriate. Two of the studies found that the majority of children older than age 7 (Green & Flaro, 2003) or age 8 (Palav, 2004) pass the Word Memory Test using the adult criteria. A third study, however, has found a high failure rate using the adult criteria with children younger than age 11 (Courtney et al., 2003). The researchers reported a positive correlation between reading level and Word Memory Test performance but did not specify whether reading level was considered in the analysis of failure rates at different age levels. It is possible that the poor performance of children under age 11 was due to reading level. Green and Flaro (2003) identified a third-grade reading level as a prerequisite for the use of adult cutoff criteria for the Word Memory Test. There has been consistency among the findings across studies that the child's intellectual capacity is not related to performance. In addition, the studies have incorporated children with a variety of psychiatric and neurological diagnoses, and each have failed to identify diagnostic group as a significant factor in performance on the Word Memory Test. The clinical samples have included children with diagnoses of Attention-Deficit/Hyperactivity Disorder, learning disabilities, seizure disorder, Pervasive Developmental Disorder, Fragile X Syndrome, Fetal Alcohol Syndrome/Effects, Wilson's disease, meningitis, cerebral palsy, Asperger's Syndrome, mental retardation, head injury, Posttraumatic Stress Disorder, Bipolar Disorder, Tourette's Syndrome, and schizophrenia.

The Test of Memory Malingering (TOMM) has also been examined with pediatric samples (Constantinou & McCaffrey, 2003; Donders, 2005; Palav, 2004). The research with this measure has supported the use of the adult criteria for suboptimal effort with children as young as age 5 with a variety of diagnoses including Attention Deficit/Hyperactivity Disorder, learning disability, autism, Fetal Alcohol Syndrome, meningitis, seizure disorder, anoxic encephalopathy, Asperger's disorder, tumor, encephalitis, anxiety disorders, Oppositional Defiant Disorder, and traumatic brain injury. In Donders' study (2005), a child who was amnestic did fail the TOMM, and this was considered a false-positive error. The utility of the Rey Fifteen-Item Test has been examined in a sample of children (Constantinou & McCaffrey, 2003). This study found a significant positive correlation between performance and both age and education. Based upon their findings, the authors recommended use of this measure with children that are age 11 or older.

CONCLUSIONS

In final analysis, our case is of a child who had made an excellent recovery from traumatic brain injury with neuroradiological findings. Her performance on two of three symptom validity tests revealed that her level of effort was so poor as to raise serious doubts with regard to the validity of her performance on the remaining neuropsychological tests. On the TOMM, her performance was below the cutoff for identifying suboptimal effort, especially when children as young as age 5 perform with 100% accuracy on this measure (Constantinou & McCaffrey, 2003; Donders, 2005; Palav, 2004). In order to perform poorly on symptom validity testing, the individual must be able to determine what the correct answer should have been and then choose the wrong answer, thus creating the impression of "memory impairment." The cognitive abilities necessary to produce a poorer performance than that which one is actually capable of involve intact problem-solving abilities, planning abilities, and the ability to remember and execute the plan. The presence of these intact cognitive abilities in D.D. did not support the position that she was experiencing clinically significant cognitive or neuropsychological deficits. In addition, her ability to relate knowledge of prior testing situations, describe her current curriculum, and to discuss her favorite television episodes viewed recently are incompatible with the results of memory testing, which were in the "extremely low" range of performance. If the results for memory testing were valid, we would expect her to exhibit a generalized memory impairment that would be reflected in her functional living skills. This child was caring for her younger siblings at least once weekly for several hours while her mother was out. This would seem incompatible with the memory test findings.

Mother's disingenuous reporting of D.D.'s prior academic and behavioral history, the presence of identifiable secondary gains, ongoing litigation, implausible test scores, and failure on symptom validity testing strongly support intentionality on the part of both D.D. and her mother and are suggestive of a case of Malingering by Proxy. Importantly, this conclusion is based upon several pieces of converging evidence and not solely upon failed symptom validity testing. The determination that an individual is malingering "is a multi-method assessment that integrates data from unstructured interviews, psychological tests, and collateral sources" (Rogers, 1997, p. 325).

REFERENCES

Cassar, J. R., Hales, E. S., Longhurst, J. G., & Weiss, G. S. (1996). Can disability benefits make children sicker? *Journal of the American Academy of Child and Adolescent Psychiatry, 35*(6), 700–701.

Constantinou, M., & McCaffrey, R. J. (2003). Using the TOMM for evaluating children's effort to perform optimally on neuropsychological measures. *Child Neuropsychology, 9*(2), 81–90.

Courtney, J. C., Dinkins, J. P., Allen, L. M., & Kuroski, K. (2003). Age related effects in children taking the Computerized Assessment of Response Bias and Word Memory Test. *Child Neuropsychology, 9*(2), 109–116.

Croft, R. D., & Jervis, M. (1989). Munchausen's syndrome in a 4 year old. *Archives of Diseases in Childhood, 64,* 740–741.

Donders, J. (2005). Performance on the Test of Memory Malingering in a mixed pediatric sample. *Child Neuropsychology, 11,* 221–227.

Green, P., & Flaro, L. (2003). Word memory test performance in children. *Child Neuropsychology, 9*(3), 189–207.

Libow, J. (2000). Child and adolescent illness falsification. *Pediatrics, 105*(2), 336–342.

Lu, P. H., & Boone, K. B. (2002). Suspect cognitive symptoms in a 9-year-old child: Malingering by proxy? *The Clinical Neuropsychologist, 16*(1), 90–96.

McCann, J. T. (1998). *Malingering and deception in adolescents: Assessing credibility in clinical and forensic setting.* Washington, DC: American Psychological Association.

Meadow, R. (1984). Munchausen by proxy and brain damage. *Developmental Medicine and Child Neurology, 26,* 669–676.

Oldershaw, L., & Bagby, R. M. (1997). Children and deception. In R. Rogers (Ed.), *Clinical assessment of malingering and deception–2nd ed.* (pp. 153–166). New York: Guilford.

O'Shea, B. (2003). Factitious Disorder: the Baron's legacy. *International Journal of Psychiatry in Clinical Practice, 7,* 33–39.

Palav, A. (2004). Performance of children with neurodevelopmental disorders on neuropsychological effort tests. *Dissertation Abstracts International: Section B—The Sciences and Engineering, 64*(9B), 4629.

Reitan, R. M., & Wolfson, D. (1992) *Neuropsychological evaluation of older children.* Tucson, AZ: Neuropsychology Press.

Rogers, R. (1997). Introduction. In R. Rogers (Ed.), *Clinical assessment of malingering and deception–2nd ed.* (pp. 1–19). New York: Guilford.

Stutts, J. T., Hickey, S. E., & Kasdan, M. L. (2003). Malingering by proxy: A form of pediatric condition falsification. *Journal of Developmental and Behavioral Pediatrics, 24*(4), 276–280.

Malingered attention deficit hyperactivity disorder: Effort, depression, and dependence in the pursuit of academic accommodations

31

David C. Osmon and Quintino R. Mano

Neuropsychology has a long tradition in the study of learning disability (LD), starting in the late 19th and early 20th century with the study of psychic-blindness and congenital word-blindness (as cited in Lange, 1988) and continuing in the modern era of neuroscience with the ideas of Geschwind (1965) regarding visual perception and naming speed (Denckla & Rudel, 1976) and Galaburda, Rosen, and Sherman's (1989) discovery of a neuropathological substrate for learning problems. Such work encouraged others to explore the functional neuroanatomy of LD, including the detailing of corpus callosum and planum temporale abnormalities in dyslexia (e.g., Hynd, Hall, & Novey, 1995). Others pursued classification issues in relation to brain function lateralization (Obrzut, 1991), while still others extended the taxonomy of learning difficulties in new directions (Rourke, 1991; Weintraub & Mesulam, 1983) or explored the cognitive correlates of academic difficulties (Badian, 2001; Evans, Floyd, McGrew, & Laforgee, 2002; Wolf & Bowers, 1999).

Despite these theoretical developments, the technology of assessment has not kept pace, causing a gap between the conceptual understanding of LD and the clinical practice related to diagnosis of LD. For example, most neuropsychologists continue to use intelligence tests that evaluate the core phonological and orthographic deficits of dyslexia poorly and that fail to take full advantage of the dictates of the Cattell-Horn-Carroll model of intellectual factors (McGrew, 1997). Likewise, well-validated assessment instruments that fully explore the orthographic aspects of dyslexia (Hultquist, 1997) and the visual and executive aspects of math disorder (Geary, 1993; Strang, & Rourke, 1985) are lacking. However, perhaps the greatest current deficiency in LD assessment technology is an instrument demonstrated to detect malingering and poor effort.

Besides lacking effort instruments, there may even be an under-appreciation for the extent to which evaluations for LD occasions the occurrence of insufficient effort and malingering. Telling in this regard, we are aware of no studies to date that evaluate effort in LD. However, since beginning to use the Word Memory Test (Green, 2003) and an experimental effort test designed specifically for claims of dyslexia (Word Reading Test: Osmon, Plambeck, Klein, & Mano, 2006) in our university learning disorder clinic, we have found a 21% failure rate on effort testing. In fact, this figure may underestimate effort issues in LD because the only well-validated effort test used (i.e., Word Memory Test) was designed for traumatic brain injury, not LD, populations.

The academic and vocational benefits of an LD diagnosis provide the incentive for malingering and/or poor effort. Specifically, the Individuals with Disabilities Education Act (IDEA, 1997, PL 101–476) governs how primary and secondary schools respond to LD and guarantees an academic experience appropriate to each child's individual educational needs. Therefore, children with a diagnosis of LD have available a myriad of accommodations such as special classes, tutoring, and allowances on assignments and exams. More importantly, those with LD have come to expect an altered educational experience. Likewise, over the course of several evaluations and interventions throughout primary and secondary schooling, individuals diagnosed with LD learn about the nature of learning disability. Upon entry into college, often an option for those with LD (41% of those with disabilities in college report LD: U.S. Department of Education report entitled *Students with Disabilities in Postsecondary Education: A Profile of Preparation, Participation, and Outcomes*, available free: 1–877–4ED-Pubs), students are well aware of the availability of academic accommodations. The Americans with Disabilities Act (ADA, 1994, a federal legislative act: PL 101–336) covers learning disability after secondary school and is not an entitlement act like the IDEA (see Gordon & Keiser, 1998). Instead of entitling one to an adequate education, the ADA guarantees only that individuals cannot be discriminated against based upon their learning disability. As a result, it provides for accommodations such as extra time for exams, tutoring, taped books, and other reasonable alterations in the academic experience that serve to "level the playing field," in effect nullifying the disadvantages of the LD. The possibility of such benefits, among others (e.g., money for educational advantages from the Department of Vocational Rehabilitation), in the context of gaining something as important as a college degree can be sufficient to trigger insufficient effort on learning disability evaluations.

The necessity of detecting insufficient effort potentially gives neuropsychology its most unique and important contribution to the LD evaluation. Neuropsychology's well-developed effort test technology has been amply demonstrated with Green's (2003) finding that effort accounts for large amounts of variance in explaining test performance, even overwhelming the effect of brain damage at times. The varieties of response bias and validity indicators within personality tests to stand-alone symptom validity tests to validity indices developed for cognitive ability measures have allowed the detection of insufficient effort in traumatic brain injury and other forensic populations. Furthermore, detecting insufficient effort is more than finding poor performance on one symptom validity measure. Larrabee (2000) has shown, for example, that malingering can occur in a wide array of cognitive domains as represented by tests of visual perception (Visual Form Discrimination), motor functioning (Finger Tapping), memory/attention (Reliable Digit Span), problem solving (Wisconsin Card Sorting), and symptom exaggeration (MMPI–2 Fake Bad Scale). Furthermore, insufficient effort may be detected on one or another, but not necessarily each of these domains in any given individual, and most clinicians advocate using a wide array of effort measures spaced throughout the evaluation because of the likelihood of insufficient effort on only some instruments within the evaluation.

Despite the success of effort indices in forensic populations, existing effort measures have not been well studied in LD, and effort potentially manifests idiosyncratically based upon the person's knowledge of the disorder to be malingered (Lanyon, 1997). Based upon this conceptualization of effort, Osmon, Plambeck, Klein, and Mano (2006) developed the Word Reading Test, a measure of effort designed according to lay notions of deficits in dyslexia, including the tendency to confuse similar looking letters and homophones (e.g., b for d; there and their). Results of this study supported the need for disorder-specific effort measures, in that the Word Reading Test performed better at detecting LD simulators than traditional effort measures. However, an existing effort test (Word Memory Test: Green, 2003) also identified LD simulators reasonably well. Thus, well-validated memory-based effort measures can also be useful in LD, suggesting that a general effort effect may be operating in addition to a disorder-specific effort effect.

As a result of the apparent existence of insufficient effort in an LD population mentioned above and our experience with the Word Reading Test in a college LD clinic, we present the following case of insufficient effort, demonstrating that effort testing can sometimes serve to both assess validity of testing and contribute to case conceptualization.

CASE STUDY: MR. E.E.

Presenting problem

Mr. E.E. presented with complaints of attention difficulties that he first noticed in his junior year of high school when his grades started to slip. He believed attention problems were not noticeable until then because previously he rarely studied in school, noting that school was easy. During a semi-structured interview he reported seven of nine symptoms of inattention, including such items as daydreaming during lecture, being unable to find motivation to complete projects until the last minute, inability to focus on his studies unless he is alone in a quiet place, and being careless with details in math problems. Mr. E.E. denied most symptoms of hyperactivity/impulsivity, noting only that he has problems sitting still and that he sometimes talks to excess.

Mr. E.E. reported significant stress associated with his college goal of being admitted into the Architecture program. Gaining admittance is highly competitive because only the top students, based upon reducing the class to half each of the first three years of the program, are accepted into the program. Furthermore, the criteria are vague (i.e., idiosyncratic each year depending upon whom one is competing against), adding to the stress of performance. Mr. E.E. attributed the importance of gaining admittance and the stress attendant to this goal as the main reason he fell into a depression in the spring semester of his first year. He reported a two-month period during which he skipped classes and spent most of the day at home and much of the time in bed, with symptoms including hypersomnia, fatigue, guilt, and concentration difficulties. At the behest of his girlfriend, Mr. E.E. reported finally seeking treatment for his depression at the student health center. As part of this intervention, he was referred to the LD clinic for an evaluation of possible attention problems.

Educational history

Mr. E.E. reported excellent grades in primary, middle, and the first two years of high school without grade repeats or evaluation for learning difficulties or attention problems. He described academic pursuits as easy for him through his sophomore year in high school and admitted that he rarely studied. He reported that his grades dropped slightly in junior and senior years, but, because he still received average to above average grades and graduated with a 3.0 grade point average, he did not become too concerned. However, his performance declined immediately in college. For example, Mr. E.E. failed calculus twice and currently carries a less than 2.5 grade point average in the beginning of his second year compared to a 3.5 average through his sophomore year in high school. Mr. E.E. attributed this academic decline to being unable to study because of an inability to stay focused on his work. In addition, Mr. E.E. felt like he did not know how to study because he had never had to work hard in primary or secondary grades. As a result, college was described as a shock because the approach he used in high school was not effective, and he was confused about why his grades were so low and felt consternated about what to do to succeed. However, he did note that during summer school he received tutorial help while taking calculus for the third time and was able to pass with an A-grade. Close questioning revealed that Mr. E.E. had difficulty with the concepts of calculus and that attempts to study without a tutor always led to failure because he would get stuck conceptually, then become frustrated and give up. The tutor was able to explain the concepts allowing Mr. E.E. to feel success in his study sessions.

Psychosocial background

Mr. E.E. grew up in an intact family of four until he reached the eighth grade, at which time his parents divorced. He denied any effect of the divorce on his academic experience, noting that his grades remained the same after the divorce. His father and mother both have math and business backgrounds and have both worked as chief financial officers and had owned a business for a short time. Family environment appeared to support academic pursuits, with both parents having college degrees and his younger sister being an excellent student in high school. Likewise, Mr. E.E.'s parents pay for his education, and he works part-time on the weekends for about 16 hours a week for the purpose of obtaining spending money.

Mr. E.E. reported typical social development with an active extra-curricular experience in high school and a wide circle of friends. He was involved in a long-term relationship until recently, when he and his girlfriend decided to take a break from each other. Additionally, Mr. E.E. appeared to enjoy an adequate recreational lifestyle currently, playing sports and video games with friends.

Medical history

Medical history was largely non-contributory, with no report of birth history problems, no unusual childhood illness, no regular medication use, and no hospitalizations or surgeries. Additionally, Mr. E.E. reported only sparse use of alcohol and occasional use of marijuana and no history of legal difficulties. Mr. E.E. denied psychiatric history prior to seeking services for the episode of depression last academic year. His treatment consisted of a short course of psychotherapy without psychotropic medication. Although he reported the depression to remit within the first few sessions of therapy, close questioning revealed many residual depressive symptoms.

Behavioral observations

Evaluation behavior was remarkable for punctual appearance at all appointments, with a cooperative and slightly reticent demeanor and appropriate, but low-key, social skills. However, Mr. E.E. displayed frequent yet subtle signs of impatience, especially in the second evaluation. Mood was euthymic to slightly low with a normal range of appropriate but low amplitude affect that tended toward a neutral tone of expressed emotion with occasional displays of smoldering resentment. Mr. E.E. smiled infrequently and never laughed during the evaluation, relating in a sedate and serious manner. Speech was well articulated without instance of paraphasic error and was well formulated, with a fully informative running narrative that was organized at the paragraph level of discourse. He appeared to understand the purpose of the evaluation and was aware of frustrations with academic pursuits for the past 3–4 years that he believed were outside the range of normal experience. He had a cooperative test-taking attitude, with attentive on-task behavior and a normal to low frustration tolerance. Mr. E.E. had no difficulty understanding test instructions, although he had poor test-retest improvement on a measure of mental speed given at the beginning and ending of the longest test session. He took the usual two sessions to complete the first testing, finishing quickly (6.5 hours instead of the usual 7–8). Similarly, he completed the second testing quickly. On metacognitive ratings, Mr. E.E. tended to estimate both his performance relative to others and the number of his errors accurately and rated himself as expending generally above average to maximum effort on the tasks.

INITIAL TEST RESULTS AND DISCUSSION

Effort tests

Two symptom validity tests and two measures of personality with validity indices were administered. Since there are no well-validated effort measures for use with learning disability, interpretation of these indices should be conservative, although results are highly consistent with insufficient effort. For example, on an experimental measure of effort in LD (Word Reading Test), Mr. E.E. had five errors, a result found in no control subjects in the original simulation study (Osmon et al., 2006). In fact, no control subject had more than three errors. Even more convincing was Mr. E.E.'s performance on an accepted measure of effort (Word Memory Test). Figure 31.1 shows Mr. E.E.'s scores on five of the main measures from that test compared to control values (gray). A score of less than 90% on IR places Mr. E.E. in the suspicious range while his performance on DR, CNS, MC, and PA are well below even conservative cutoffs for insufficient effort and indicate definite effort issues in his performance. In addition to his cognitive test performance, Mr. E.E. showed a mild elevation of 61 on the Negative Impression Management scale and a large discrepancy between this score and the Positive Impression Management scale (42) on the Personality Assessment Inventory (PAI: Morey, 1991). Such results suggest that Mr. E.E. is presenting an overly symptomatic picture on the personality test. Therefore, the entire evaluation could be called into question; no score from the cognitive test battery can be confidently interpreted, and personality results should be interpreted with great caution.

Cognitive tests

Even though his results cannot be interpreted for diagnostic purposes, it is interesting to examine the level and pattern of performance on cognitive measures in relation to his concerns about attention

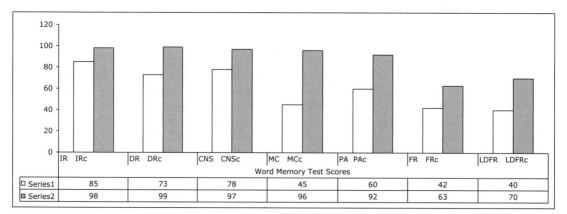

FIG. 31.1 Word Memory Test scores from the first evaluation with ingenuine performance on DR, CNS, MC, and PA scores but not IR. Clinical cutoffs for those scales are 82.5% for definite effort problems and 90% suspicious effort problems. Abbreviations: IR = immediate recall, DR = delayed recall, CNS = consistency, MC = multiple choice, PA = paired associate, FR = free recall, LDFR = long delayed free recall, c = control.

problems. In general, most of his results could be consistent with Attention Deficit/Hyperactivity Disorder (ADHD), and it is easy to see how a diagnosis could be made if effort tests were not administered. Specifically, his intellectual (Figure 31.2) and neuropsychological performances (Figures 31.3 and 31.4) generally fall in the average range, although variances in ability occur on measures associated with ADHD. Achievement measures are also average, both for age and grade level. More detailed discussion of results follows below.

Figure 31.2 shows that verbal and thinking abilities from the Woodcock-Johnson–III (WJ–III) are in the low part of the average range. Likewise, achievement scores are in the middle to upper part of the average range and confirm his report of math skills better than language skills. Thus, results would be consistent in arguing against a specific learning disability, such as reading or written expression disorder. Furthermore, there are indications of attention problems.

Attention problems are often associated with reduced cognitive efficiency and slowed processing

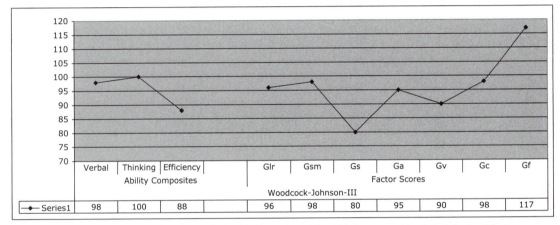

	Ability Composites				Factor Scores						
	Verbal	Thinking	Efficiency		Glr	Gsm	Gs	Ga	Gv	Gc	Gf
				Woodcock-Johnson-III							
Series1	98	100	88		96	98	80	95	90	98	117

FIG. 31.2 Composite scores for the Verbal, Thinking, Cognitive Efficiency, and basic intellectual factors are all in the broad range of average, although processing speed is a significant weakness. Abbreviations: Glr = long-term retrieval factor, Gsm = short-term memory factors, Gs = processing speed factor, Ga = auditory processes factor, Gv = visual processes factor, Gc = crystallized intelligence factor, Gf = fluid reasoning factor.

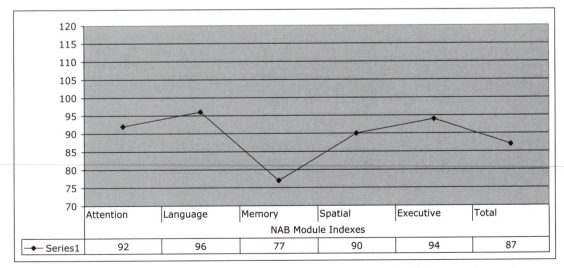

	Attention	Language	Memory	Spatial	Executive	Total
	NAB Module Indexes					
Series1	92	96	77	90	94	87

FIG. 31.3 Composite scores of the Neuropsychological Assessment Battery (NAB) show weaknesses in Memory and Spatial ability.

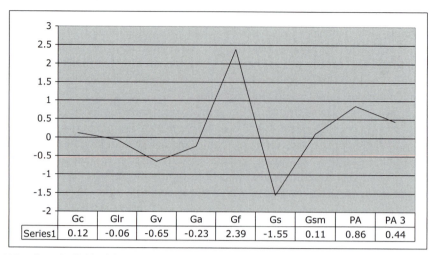

	Gc	Glr	Gv	Ga	Gf	Gs	Gsm	PA	PA 3
Series1	0.12	-0.06	-0.65	-0.23	2.39	-1.55	0.11	0.86	0.44

FIG. 31.4 WJ–III intra-individual discrepancy scores for factors at the bottom of the table showing the strength in fluid intelligence (Gf) and the weakness in processing speed (Gs). Abbreviations: Gc = crystallized intelligence factor, Glr = long-term retrieval factor, Gv = visual processes factor, Ga = auditory processes factor, Gf = fluid reasoning factor, Gs = processing speed factor, Gsm = short-term memory factor, PA = phonemic awareness cluster, PA3 = alternate phonemic awareness cluster.

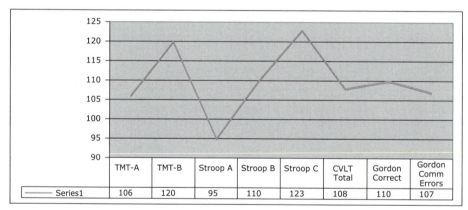

	TMT-A	TMT-B	Stroop A	Stroop B	Stroop C	CVLT Total	Gordon Correct	Gordon Comm Errors
Series1	106	120	95	110	123	108	110	107

FIG. 31.5 Neuropsychological scores from the second evaluation, indicating normal performance. Abbreviations: TMT-A = Trail Making Test, Part A; TMT-B = Trail Making Test, Part B; CVLT Total = California Verbal Learning Test Total Words Recalled score; Gordon Correct = total correct items on Vigilance test; Gordon Comm Errors = number of commission errors on Vigilance test.

speed, perhaps more so in the inattentive variety of ADHD (Barkley, Grodzinsky, & DuPaul, 1992; Holdnack, Moberg, Arnold et al., 1995). Such a pattern is true in our LD clinic, with ADHD-inattentive clients being about 10 IQ-score points below undiagnosed and LD-diagnosed clients on the processing speed factor (WJ–III Gs = 89, 100, 98 for each diagnosis, respectively) while being no different from undiagnosed clients on the overall IQ score (WJ–R BCA-Standard = 101 vs. 99, respectively). As is evident in Figure 31.2 and the discrepancy scores from the WJ–III in Figure 31.5, Mr. E.E. showed absolute weaknesses on both the WJ–III composite scores for cognitive efficiency and processing speed (Gs), with the intra-individual discrepancy index indicating Gs as being statistically worse than other abilities. While the overall Neuropsychological Assessment Battery (NAB) Attention Index was in the average range, two subtest scores were below average (Dots and Numbers, and Letters Part A Errors), and the ecologically valid subtest (Driving Scenes) was moderately impaired at the first percentile. It would generally not be too suspicious to see variability among different attention measures in ADHD. In this instance, his NAB Memory Index was mildly impaired, and the Spatial Index was below average, supporting the interpretation of cognitive difficulties that might accompany attention problems.

Despite the above analysis, the effort test performances override interpretation of cognitive test results, and a comparative analysis of test performances reveals the unlikelihood of the overall pattern of results for Attention Deficit/Hyperactivity Disorder (ADHD). First, memory performance on the NAB forced-choice task was inconsistent with overall memory performance. Despite average ability to learn a word list and retain it across delay, Mr. E.E. performed at the fourth percentile on the Long Delayed Forced-Choice Recognition task with two misses and one false alarm on a 12-word list. This impairment also occurred in the context of a 97% retention score at the long delayed interval. He also had a severely impaired performance on the Shape Learning Delayed Forced-Choice Recognition False Alarm score. Second, as mentioned above, inconsistent performance in attention might not be suspicious in ADHD; however Mr. E.E.'s inconsistent performance on the NAB Attention module is incongruous. Specifically, Mr. E.E. performed better on the harder than easier Numbers and Letter tasks. That is, he performed in the average to below average range on the three tasks where only one thing had to be completed (mark the target letters, count the target letters, or add the target numbers), while he performed in the above average range on the more difficult task where he had two things to complete (mark the target letters and add the numbers). Finally, his performance did not improve on the second trial of the Stroop Color Word Test (Golden, 1975), a low probability event in our LD clinic. For example, his score fell at the 2nd percentile according to norms generated from a prior LD clinic sample that included only 25 of 141 clients who did not improve their standard score on the second Stroop trial. Furthermore, of the 11 individuals diagnosed with ADHD-inattentive type in that sample, none performed worse on the second Stroop trial. In fact, 9 of the 11 clients with ADHD-inattentive type performed above the 50th percentile, indicating large improvement on the second trial, as if attention problems on the first trial were compensated on the second trial. Taken together, these performance inconsistencies support the impression of insufficient effort gleaned from the symptom validity tests.

Personality testing revealed no clear indication of malingering, and, while slight exaggeration of symptoms may have been present on one measure (PAI), results are interpretable. PAI results support Mr. E.E.'s complaints and recent history of depression accompanying the stress of poor performance in his Architecture major, showing elevations on anxiety, depression, and stress scales. Additionally, subscale analysis shows that cognitive, affective, and physical symptoms of depression, as well as physical symptoms of anxiety, are contributing to clinical scale elevations. A mildly elevated Borderline scale, with subclinical elevations on all subscales, reflects an individual who is "moody, sensitive, and having some uncertainty about life goals" (Morey, 1991, p. 17) and probably relates to Mr. E.E.'s concerns about gaining admittance to his major course of study. Subclinical elevation on the Schizophrenia scale resulted from a peak on the Thought Disorder subscale and likely reflects the items having to do with concentration problems. Thus, personality results indicate psychological issues that may be relevant to Mr. E.E.'s academic problems and subjective complaints of cognitive difficulty.

The NEO results showed a coefficient of profile agreement with Dependent Personality Disorder higher than 90% of normative subjects. Furthermore, Mr. E.E.'s score was very high on Agreeableness, indicating a humble, unassuming manner in which he is likely to give in to others too often and have difficulty expressing anger and being assertive. In relation to this, his score was very low on Conscientiousness, reflecting a tendency evident in his academic history to be inefficient, disorganized, and unreliable in his studies. He likely finds it difficult to control his impulses to achieve a well-planned and dutiful approach to his responsibilities.

RESULTS FROM THE SECOND ASSESSMENT

During the feedback session with Mr. E.E. after the first testing, his insufficient effort on symptom validity testing was offered in the context of several possible interpretations and outcomes that needed to be explored with his help. This approach allowed Mr. E.E. to frame his effort on testing in light of how he wanted to proceed. Three options were offered. First, the results of the evaluation could be dismissed simply as not helpful and testing could be sought elsewhere. Second, the results could be accepted as indicating that he deliberately failed the examination and does not have a disorder, making further testing unnecessary. Third, the results could mean that he just did not put forth his best effort on some parts of the examination. In that case, another LD evaluation could be completed to determine whether he actually has some ADA-covered learning difficulty and requires accommodations in the classroom. Not surprisingly, Mr. E.E. chose the latter option.

Mr. E.E. was given a different effort test (Victoria Symptom Validity Test) in the second evaluation and a valid performance was indicated according to the Total Correct score (45/48) and response time (2.42 average reaction time, halfway between mean of non-compensation and compensation group and much different than the 3.28 average for the Feigning group). However, a borderline score of 21/24 correct on the difficult items led again to some concern about Mr. E.E.'s effort.

A brief cognitive battery was given in the second evaluation because few indications of attention or other cognitive deficits were expected given results of the first evaluation. As evident in Figure 31.6, test scores confirmed this suspicion. All scores, including attention tests, were in the average to above average range. Additionally, the WAIS–R estimated score from the Shipley-Hartford was 111 and WRAT–3 scores were in the average to lower part of above average range, consistent with prior achievement scores.

In contrast to cognitive ability scores, personality testing showed significant difficulties without indication of malingering or exaggerated symptom reporting. Validity scale configuration suggested that Mr. E.E. reported symptoms that were largely consistent with a recent history of depression severe enough to withdraw from classes and intimates. Additionally, all validity indicators were

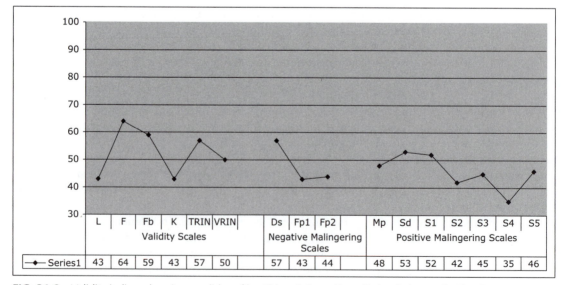

	L	F	Fb	K	TRIN	VRIN		Ds	Fp1	Fp2		Mp	Sd	S1	S2	S3	S4	S5
	Validity Scales							Negative Malingering Scales				Positive Malingering Scales						
—•— Series1	43	64	59	43	57	50		57	43	44		48	53	52	42	45	35	46

FIG. 31.6 Validity indices showing a valid profile. Abbreviations: Ds = dissimulation scale, Fp1 & 2 = psychopathology infrequency subscales, Sd = social desirability scale, S1–5 = superlative subscales.

within normal limits (see Figure 31.7, additionally FBS = 15). Therefore, the inverted V profile of the L, F, and K scales is interpreted as indicating distress and low self-efficacy.

Given a valid profile, Mr. E.E.'s code type (8/7) was indicative of serious psychological turmoil associated with his failing attempt to gain admittance to the Architecture program, a long-time goal and his singular interest as a career. Secondary scale elevations indicated subjective depression manifesting in physical functioning and being associated with mental dullness, malaise, and personality features. Personality features help to explain both his depression and his academic difficulties.

Mr. E.E.'s personality is reflected in the supplemental scales of Do, Es, A, MT and Re. Specifically, Mr. E.E. lacks both self-confidence and a belief in his ability to succeed, feeling anxious and pessimistic about his future. At the root of his anxious and pessimistic cognitions is a poor sense of self-efficacy and a less than conforming and responsible attitude. Such self-efficacy precludes an active coping style and promotes an alienated stance and may lead to a sense of futility and a need to seek external help as a way out of his academic difficulties.

SUMMARY

In summary, we have found effort testing to be an invaluable component of the test battery in the LD clinic, not only for its ability to validate the adequacy of a client's effort but also for its ability to guide case conceptualization. However, a simple dichotomous indictment of an evaluation as valid or invalid turning upon the performance on effort tests is inadequate. A configural analysis of effort results is necessary, wherein insufficient effort results are conditionally interpreted based upon all test battery results.

In the present case, for example, insufficient effort test performance had to be reconciled with generally good cognitive and achievement scores, making a simplistic interpretation of insufficient effort across the entire evaluation implausible. While it is possible that Mr. E.E.'s true abilities lie in the superior range of functioning and current cognitive test performance does reflect insufficient

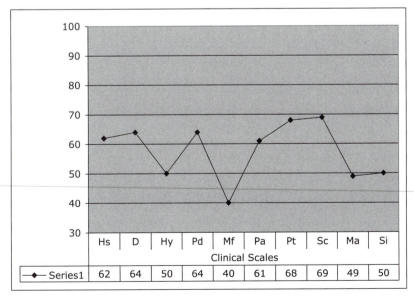

	Hs	D	Hy	Pd	Mf	Pa	Pt	Sc	Ma	Si
Series1	62	64	50	64	40	61	68	69	49	50

Clinical Scales

FIG. 31.7   MMPI–2 clinical scales showing mild elevations indicative of psychological turmoil without hesitancy to admit problems within the context of ruminativeness and low self-efficacy.

effort, this interpretation seems unlikely for three reasons. First, if Mr. E.E. were trying to "pull the wool over our eyes" and feign cognitive deficits, it is unlikely that some of the most mentally effortful tests in the battery (fluid intelligence) would be some of his best scores, being in the above average range. Second, if Mr. E.E. were attempting to portray attention deficit disorder, selective attention deficits would be expected, although Mr. E.E. performed roughly equivalently on attention-type versus other cognitive tests. Finally, malingerers tend to exaggerate cognitive deficits, but Mr. E.E.'s performances were all generally within the normal range. Lacking these performance patterns, the reason for Mr. E.E.'s insufficient effort and current complaints of attention problems was not immediately evident.

Using a configural analysis and accepting the validity of some of Mr. E.E.'s results, the conceptualization of this case turns on five data points: (1) insufficient effort on symptom validity tests, (2) normal performance on cognitive and achievement testing, (3) depression both by history and current personality test results, (4) characterological dependency and low self-efficacy, and (5) Mr. E.E.'s single-minded pursuit of an Architecture career.

A hard-line approach to effort test performance would argue that failure on the WMT in the first evaluation, and most likely the borderline VSVT performance in the second evaluation, is sufficient evidence to assume intent to deceive. This approach would ignore all other test results, even those with indicators of adequate validity, and conclude insufficient effort or potentially even diagnose malingering.

A less extreme interpretation would emphasize the importance of trying to reconcile the multiple indicators into a coherent picture. Thus, symptom validity measures strongly indicate insufficient effort while valid measures of personality strongly indicate residual symptoms of depression and characterological dependency and low self-efficacy. Finally, cognitive performance across both evaluations is largely consistent and suggestive of only mild cognitive inefficiency attributable to the effects of depression and uncharacteristic of the exaggerated deficits typical of malingerers. This approach would diagnose depression in the context of dependent personality disorder and recommend psychotherapy to examine Mr. E.E.'s goal of completing the Architecture program. Additionally, this approach would view his low effort and limited motivation as a misplaced and desperate cry for help. When viewed in the context of the results of the whole evaluation, his current help-seeking behavior reflects low self-efficacy and an inability to cope with the stress and demands of gaining acceptance into the Architecture program.

In the end, there is no solid scientific evidence that allows an unequivocal interpretation of the present case. Ultimately, clinical judgment must prevail in cases of this kind given current knowledge, and confidence in our diagnostic acumen should be modest. However, perhaps this case does make clear that effort is more accurately viewed as a dimensional construct, and personality style and psychological disorder like depression should be considered as potential moderators of the correlation between symptom validity test scores and the interpretation of insufficient effort in individual cases.

REFERENCES

Americans with Disabilities Act, 42 U.S.C. 12101 et seq. (1994).

Badian, N. A. (2001). Phonological and orthographic processing: Their roles in reading prediction. *Annals of Dyslexia, 51*, 179–202.

Barkley, R. A., Grodzinsky, G., & DuPaul, G. J. (1992). Frontal lobe functions in attention deficit disorder with and without hyperactivity: A review and research report. *Journal of Abnormal Child Psychology, 20*, 163–188.

Denckla, M. B., & Rudel, R. G. (1976). Rapid "automatized" naming (R.A.N.): Dyslexia differentiated from other learning disorders. *Neuropsychologia, 14,* 471–479.

Evans, J. J., Floyd, R. G., McGrew, K. S., & Laforgee, M. H. (2002). The relations between measures of Cattell-Horn-Carroll (CHC) cognitive abilities and reading achievement during childhood and adolescence. *School Psychology Review, 31,* 246–262.

Galaburda, A. M., Rosen, G. D., & Sherman, G. F. (1989). The neural origin of developmental dyslexia: Implications of medicine, neurology, and cognition. In A. M. Galaburda (Ed.), *From reading to neurons.* Cambridge, MA: The MIT Press.

Geary, D. C. (1993). Mathematical disabilities: Cognitive, neuropsychological and genetic components. *Psychological Bulletin, 114,* 345–352.

Geschwind, N. (1965). Disconnexion syndromes in animals and man. *Brain, 88,* 237–294, 585–644.

Golden, C. J. (1975). *The Stroop Color and Word Test: A manual for clinical and experimental uses.* Chicago: Stoelting Co.

Gordon, M., & Keiser, S. (1998). *Accommodations in higher education under the Americans with Disabilities Act (ADA): A no-nonsense guide for clinicians, educators, administrators, and lawyers.* New York: The Guildford Press.

Green, P. (2003). *Green's Word Memory Test: User's manual.* Edmonton, WA: Green's Publishing, Inc.

Holdnack, J. A., Moberg, P. J., Arnold, S. E., Gur, R., et al. (1995). Speed of processing and verbal learning deficits in adults diagnosed with attention deficit. *Neuropsychiatry, Neuropsychology, and Behavioral Neurology, 8,* 282–292.

Hultquist, A. M. (1997). Orthographic processing abilities of adolescents with dyslexia. *Annals of Dyslexia, 47,* 89–114.

Hynd, G. W., Hall, J., & Novey, E. S. (1995). Dyslexia and corpus callosum morphology. *Archives of Neurology, 52,* 32–38.

Individuals with Disabilities Education Act, Pub. L, 105–117, 111 Stat. 37 (1997) (codified at 20 U.S.C. 1499–1487).

Lange, J. (1988). Agnosia and apraxia. In J. W. Brown (Ed.), *Agnosia and apraxia: Seleted papers of Liepmann, Lange, and Potzl.* Hillsdale, NJ: Lawrence Erlbaum Associates.

Lanyon, R. (1997). Detecting deception: Current models and directions. *Clinical Psychology: Science and Practice, 4,* 377–387.

Larrabee, G. J. (2000). Forensic neuropsychological assessment. In R. D. Vanderploeg (Ed.), *Clinician's guide to neuropsychological assessment,* 2nd ed. Hillsdale, NJ: Lawrence Erlbaum Associates.

McGrew, K. S. (1997). Analysis of the major intelligence batteries according to a proposed comprehensive Gf-Gc framework. In D. P. Flanagan, J. L. Genshaft, & P. L. Harrison (Eds.), *Contemporary intellectual assessment: Theories, tests, and issues.* New York: The Guilford Press.

Morey, L. C. (1991). *The Personality Assessment Inventory: Professional manual.* Lutz, FL: Psychological Assessment Resources, Inc.

Obrzut, J. E. (1991). Hemispheric activation and arousal asymmetry in learning-disabled children. In J. E. Obrzut & G. W. Hynd (Eds.), *Neuropsychological foundations of learning disabilities.* New York: Academic Press, Inc.

Osmon, D. C., Plambeck, E. A., Klein, L., & Mano, Q. (2006). The Word Reading Test of effort in adult learning disability: A simulation study. *The Clinical Neuropsychologist, 20,* 315–324.

Rourke, B. P. (1991). *Neuropsychological validation of learning disability subtypes.* New York: Guilford Press.

Strang, J. D., & Rourke, B. P. (1985). Arithmetic disability subtypes: The neuropsychological significance of specific arithmetic impairment in childhood. In B. P. Rourke (Ed.), *Neuropsychology of learning disabilities: Essentials of subtype analysis.* New York: The Guilford Press.

Weintraub, S., & Mesulam, M. M. (1983). Developmental learning disabilities of the right hemisphere: Emotional, interpersonal, and cognitive components. *Archives of Neurology, 40,* 463–468.

Wolf, M., & Bowers, P. G., (1999). The double-deficit hypothesis for the developmental dyslexias. *Journal of Educational Psychology, 91,* 415–438.

SECTION III

CRIMINAL PROSECUTION

Though still not approximating the frequency of involvement in civil litigation, increasingly, clinical neuropsychologists are becoming involved as experts in criminal litigation. A quote found in *Black's Law Dictionary*, Seventh Edition (1999), attributed to William Geldert, provides a succinct description of the difference between civil law and criminal law:

> The difference between civil law . . . and criminal law turns on the difference between two different objects which the law seeks to pursue—redress and punishment. The object of civil law is the redress of wrongs by compelling compensation or restitution: the wrongdoer is not punished, he only suffers so much harm as is necessary to make good the wrong he has done. The person who has suffered gets a definite benefit from the law, or at least avoids a loss. On the other hand, in the case of crimes, the main object of the law is to punish the wrongdoer; to give him and others a strong inducement not to commit the same or similar crimes, to reform him if possible, and perhaps to satisfy the public sense that wrongdoing ought to meet with retribution.
>
> (p. 239)

There are numerous matters on which a clinical neuropsychologist might provide expert opinion in a criminal proceeding, but unlike the opinions given in civil proceedings, the focus is not on damages. Instead, the focus is on such matters as competency (e.g., to stand trial, to assist in one's own defense, among others), relief from the normal outcomes of conviction (e.g., guilty but insane leading to hospitalization, rather than prison), and mitigation of post-conviction sentencing (e.g., determination of mental retardation to avoid the death penalty). The four chapters in this section provide detailed examples of the issues specific to neuropsychological evaluation of criminal defendants that can be expected to arise. Readers will note that some presentations of malingering among criminal defendants resemble those of malingering civil plaintiffs, which makes sense in that exaggerated or feigned cognitive impairments can lead to favorable outcomes in both types of proceedings. However, as compared to civil proceedings, because exaggerated or feigned mental illness can lead to favorable outcomes, it is more likely that malingering of serious mental illness, especially psychotic disorders, will occur in criminal proceedings.

Competency to stand trial and the insanity defense

32

Joel E. Morgan

The practice of forensic neuropsychology is becoming more common in criminal settings. Neuropsychologists are more frequently being asked to examine individuals charged with a variety of crimes to determine their competency to stand trial and/or the determination of criminal responsibility. This has been, and still largely remains, the province of forensic psychiatrists, clinical psychologists, and forensic psychologists. But this is an area of practice that is beginning to be more common for neuropsychologists, particularly as attorneys and courts gain greater familiarity with our profession's development of theory and tests in the area of motivation and symptom validity and appreciate the work we can do. In fact, our proficiency with such techniques would seem to make us ideal professionals for such evaluations and clearly better suited than many whose assessment techniques are largely impressionistically based. There is little doubt that science wins out in court—all other things being equal. Because competency evaluations are so common, neuropsychologists who practice in the criminal/forensic setting need to be aware of the various presentations and guises which defendants may assume in order to project an image of incompetence and/or mental illness.

In every legal venue in the United States, a defendant accused of a criminal offense must be mentally fit to stand trial. The competency test is based upon *Dusky v. United States* (1960). In that seminal case, the United States Supreme Court set forth a definition of competency to stand trial that has come to be considered the standard in all federal courts and in most state jurisdictions in the United States. The Supreme Court stated that, "the test must be whether the defendant has sufficient present ability to consult with his attorney with a reasonable degree of rational understanding and a rational as well as factual understanding of the proceedings against him." In this definition, the defendant must have the capacity to understand the proceedings against him; that is, he or she must understand the criminal process. In that regard, the defendant must have knowledge and understanding of all of the participants who take part in the criminal process including the roles of the prosecutor, defense attorney, jury, and judge. Further, the rule indicates that the defendant must possess the ability to function within that process insofar as the ability to consult with his attorney in the preparation of a defense for his case. Although this ruling, as most laws written in the United States, has some vague language, this wording is typically interpreted as requiring that competency indicates that the defendant has the present ability to consult with his attorney and to understand the proceedings against him. This is quite unlike the definition of criminal responsibility, which requires that one focus on the state of mind of the defendant at the time the crime was committed. Thus, the difference between the test of competency and the test of criminal responsibility has to do with the present mind of the defendant. Inherent in this understanding of competency is the notion of the defendant's capacity to understand the proceedings against him and participate in the process. *Capacity* as opposed to *willingness* is important as it relates to the proceedings.

As will be illustrated by the case that follows in later sections of this chapter, sometimes defendants have the mental capacity to participate but decide for a variety of reasons against doing so. Thus, they are unwilling to participate even though they certainly could if they desire to do so. It is in the context of unwillingness to participate in legal proceedings when a defendant clearly has the mental abilities to do so that raises the specter of the possible presence of malingering. Recall that the working definition of malingering in neuropsychological contexts refers to the conscious presentation of oneself as having neuropsychological impairment. In that vein, the typical neuropsychological malingerer presents himself as having more severely reduced cognitive capacities than he actually does. In order to achieve this presentation, they purposefully perform poorly on neuropsychological tests. Typical neuropsychological patterns of malingered neuropsychological deficits include failure on symptom validity tests, implausible test scores in the form of unbelievable intra-test and inter-test scores, and/or implausible results vis-à-vis the nature of the purported injury or neurological disorder (Vitacco, Rogers, Gabel, & Munizza, 2006). Other important clues also include an implausible pattern of test results on the same tests given on multiple occasions and test results that are clearly discrepant with the known and well-established cognitive correlates of cerebral function (Mittenberg, Aguila-Puentes, Patton, Canyock, & Heilbronner, 2002).

The concept of mental capacity has been dealt with in various legal venues on both the federal and state level. Since the standard established by the Supreme Court concerning capacity was put forth, most states have established a definition of capacity that has been introduced in the rules of criminal procedures. Generally, most jurisdictions agree that the term *capacity* refers to a defendant's ability to (1) appreciate the allegations or charges against him; (2) appreciate the range and nature of possible penalties as they may apply which could be imposed in the proceedings against him; (3) understand the nature of the legal system and its adversarial process; (4) disclose to his attorney facts and information which are pertinent to the charges and proceedings; (5) be able to maintain appropriate courtroom behavior; and (6) testify in a relevant way (Melton, Petrila, Poythress, & Slobogin, 1997). These specific criteria fulfill the requirements established by Dusky. Ultimately, the issue regarding competency to stand trial has to do with the present level of functioning of the defendant and not his level of functioning during the crime. (In forensic settings an evaluation of the defendant's mental capacity at the time of the crime or a *mens rea* assessment has to do with the issue of criminal responsibility and not the issue of competency. This is the basis of the insanity defense: i.e., was the perpetrator mentally competent at the time of the crime; did he know right from wrong, etc.?) It is not necessarily relevant whether or not the defendant has or had a mental illness or a neuropsychological impairment. What matters is if that mental illness or neuropsychological impairment is severe enough to interfere with the defendant's capacity to stand trial as enumerated in the points above. The mere presence of mental illness or neurological disorder is insufficient, in and of itself, to warrant a ruling of incompetency to stand trial. Similarly, the presence of a mental disorder is insufficient by itself to establish "insanity."

Because of the very nature of the competency issue, competency is most typically raised by defense counsel in criminal settings. Once this issue is raised and granted by the court, a defense expert is typically retained by counsel to examine the defendant. If a report is served, it is entered into evidence and received by the court. At that point, most typically the prosecution will seek an independent examination of the defendant by requesting the court to grant an independent medical examination (IME) by prosecution's expert.

This is precisely the scenario that occurred when this writer was contacted by a United States attorney to see if I would be interested in examining a criminal defendant where a defense neuropsychologist expert had submitted a report declaring the defendant to be mentally incompetent to stand trial.

THE CASE OF F.F.

At the time of his arrest, Mr. F.F. was a 27-year-old, unmarried, Dominican male with no children. In mid-August of 2002, agents from the Drug Enforcement Administration began a surveillance of Mr. F.F. and several of his associates. During the course of the next several months, a number of different telephone conversations involving Mr. F.F. were recorded and transcribed. Meetings were arranged involving DEA undercover agents pretending to purchase narcotics from Mr. F.F. The undercover agents told the defendant that they wanted to buy heroin and asked how much he could supply. Mr. F.F. replied that his source could provide any amount of heroin or cocaine or actually any drug, for that matter, that they wanted. Mr. F.F. told the agents that the price for the heroin would be $74.00 per gram. When the agents complained, Mr. F.F. said that the price could be lower for the next purchase but for the first purchase this would have to be the price. Mr. F.F. said that his associates had an apartment in a surrounding town, which could be used to stash any of the narcotics and conduct transactions.

Mr. F.F. asked the agent how much heroin he wanted. He replied that he wanted 30 grams to start but would want to place a larger order later on. Mr. F.F. told him that his supplier would not be interested in such a small order and that he really required a purchase of at least 100 grams. The agent then asked if Mr. F.F. could obtain crack cocaine because he had a customer who was looking for a substantial amount of crack. Mr. F.F. responded that he also had a very good connection for crack, and he could "cook" powdered cocaine and convert it to crack himself if he wished.

The DEA investigation documented a series of such transactions leading up to the arrest of Mr. F.F. and two of his associates in September of 2002 after he was observed and photographed delivering approximately 500 grams of crack cocaine to the undercover agents. At the time of his arrest he received his Miranda warnings, and he waived his right to an attorney and agreed to cooperate with authorities and answer questions. He then gave a detailed post-arrest statement to the special agents interviewing him.

In that statement Mr. F.F. said that he had received a telephone call from the undercover agent who pressured him to obtain crack cocaine. Mr. F.F. told the agent that he could obtain the crack and then called his associate Mr. L.A. and told him that he needed about 500 grams of crack cocaine. Approximately 2½ hours later, Mr. L.A. brought 500 grams of cocaine to Mr. F.F.

Mr. F.F. and Mr. L.A. delivered 500 grams of crack cocaine to the two undercover agents in a meeting that had been arranged in a local park. As soon as the transfer took place between their hands, the agents identified themselves as officers of the law, showed them their badges, and read them their Miranda rights. Mr. F.F. and Mr. L.A. waived their Miranda rights, waived their rights to an attorney, and agreed to answer questions. Mr. F.F. gave a detailed post-arrest statement to the special agents. In that statement, he clearly articulated both the sequence of events leading up to the arrest and an accurate memory of the conversations he had had with the undercover agents pretending to be customers.

Further, transcriptions of telephone conversations between Mr. F.F. and his associates in both English and Spanish unquestionably indicate that Mr. F.F. was well versed in drug procurement, had been involved in previous distribution activities, made a sizable income from such sales, and had, heretofore, successfully avoided being detected.

Further, in these transcriptions of the telephone conversations that Mr. F.F. had with his associates, it was absolutely clear that Mr. F.F. had no difficulty with either English or Spanish and no difficulty with memory, concept formation, or simple arithmetic (at one point on one of the tapes Mr. F.F. and his supplier worked out a financial agreement whereby Mr. F.F. would keep 55% of the gross proceeds of the sale; he quickly figured 55% of the total amount and did it correctly). More than 20 pages of transcribed telephone conversation between Mr. F.F. and his associates were reviewed. There were no indications of any degree of mental impairment on the part of Mr. F.F. in those transcriptions.

The defendant's history

Mr. F.F. was born and raised in Santo Domingo, Dominican Republic until the age of 15 at which time he emigrated to the United States. He lived with his biological mother and three of five older siblings. His mother was employed as a machine operator. His father remained in Santo Domingo.

Records indicated that Mr. F.F.'s childhood acquisition of language skills was delayed and his school attendance in Santo Domingo was irregular during the two years prior to his coming to the United States. Although records are quite sketchy, one psychiatric evaluation report conducted when he was approximately 21 years old and living in the United States stated that he attended special education classes while in Santo Domingo; however, this could not be corroborated in an extensive review of the available records. Upon his arrival to the United States, he was placed in English as a Second Language classes (ESL). He was 15 years old at the time he attended the seventh grade, and he reportedly experienced difficulty with learning English. Records indicate that he dropped out of school in May of the seventh grade.

Hospital records from when the defendant was 15 years old were reviewed. Records indicate that he had fallen off of a bicycle when his bicycle hit a stone in the road. Mr. F.F. fell off of the bicycle and sustained a blow to his head; there was a minor scalp laceration. He was taken to the emergency room of a local hospital. His condition on arrival at the hospital was reported as alert, verbal, cooperative, in no acute distress. There was minor bleeding from a scalp laceration. A skull x-ray was performed at that time which was normal. A CT of the brain was also performed at that time revealing no pathology. Mr. F.F. had his scalp laceration closed with four stitches; he was given some analgesic medication and released the following morning. A report of an evaluation by a pediatric neurologist revealed a normal neurological exam with no focal or generalized deficits. At the time of his discharge, a mental status examination revealed him to have no cognitive deficits. His memory was intact; sensory and motor functions were intact; and there was no evidence of any neurological abnormality. Mr. F.F. was released to his mother's care with the instructions to take Tylenol as needed for headache. He returned to the hospital outpatient clinic eight days later to have his stitches removed, and at that time his examination was again found to be fully normal.

Several months after his bicycle accident, Mr. F.F. was referred to the school psychologist where a psychological evaluation was performed. The referral to the school psychologist indicated that Mr. F.F.'s school attendance was "irregular" and that he was repeatedly suspended for "acting out behavior." Psychological testing (see Table 32.1) at that time revealed a WISC–R Full Scale IQ of 74 with a VIQ of 75 and a PIQ of 77. These tests were performed approximately seven months after his bicycle accident.

With WISC scores in the borderline range, Mr. F.F. was classified as "perceptually impaired" and placed in special education classes. However, at the end of that school year, he dropped out.

Four years later Mr. F.F. filed for Supplemental Income Benefits for alleged disability due to "organic mental disorder." He had seen a psychiatrist three years earlier. He complained of having

TABLE 32.1   Results of psychological evaluation at 15 after "head injury"

	STANDARD SCORE	PERCENTILE
FSIQ	74	4.0
VIQ	75	4.5
PIQ	77	6.1

headaches and auditory hallucinations calling his name. The psychiatrist indicated that Mr. F.F. had blunted affect but "did not look particularly psychotic in his contact with reality." He was diagnosed with "organic personality syndrome, mental retardation moderate and brain contusion." The psychiatrist noted that Mr. F.F.'s global assessment of functioning was between 31 and 40. He was prescribed Imipramine and Mellaril. A psychiatrist indicated that Mr. F.F. continued to be at home, not involved in doing any activities in particular. The psychiatrist concluded that Mr. F.F. "is not able to engage in any social activity with other people for long times." He opined that Mr. F.F. would have difficulties in finding employment.

One year later, Mr. F.F. saw another psychiatrist for a social security disability evaluation. He arrived for the appointment accompanied by his mother because he was "allegedly unable to use transportation due to global memory loss." The psychiatrist noted that Mr. F.F. claimed that he could not remember the days of the week, the month, or the year and that he stated that he did not understand simple Spanish words such as the words "boat" and "house." The psychiatrist noted the "limited veracity of Mr. F.F.'s self-report," as well as "his selected reticence." The examining psychiatrist ultimately concluded that, "the claimant's ostensive display of gross impairment in all intellectual functions is contrived" and that "hallucinatory experiences that he reported also appear to be contrived." The examining psychiatrist also noted that Mr. F.F. displayed "fictitious memory problems, a contrived general impairment in intellectual ability and likely voluntary distortion in his reproductions of the Bender Figures." Psychiatric report concluded with "the claimant seems to have good enough concentration to persist in a relatively simple attempt to fake a gross intellectual impairment. This is not to say that he has good enough capacity to persist eight hours a day, five times a week in a responsible job, however."

One year later, Mr. F.F. was examined by a clinical psychologist working for the State Department of Labor, Division of Disability Determination. The psychologist noted that Mr. F.F. "scored below the minimum obtainable score of 55 for his age on the Ravens Progressive Matrices Test." The psychologist deferred a conclusive diagnosis but opined that, "it would appear that malingering is a definite possibility; however, this cannot be concluded definitively until attempts are made to review the records from the Organic Personality Syndrome hypothesis. If Mr. F.F., in fact, has had a significant head injury, then his symptoms including flat affect, inappropriate behavior, lack of responsiveness, and auditory hallucinations would be consistent with that Syndrome." Nevertheless, the psychologist concluded that Mr. F.F.'s level of functioning based on "what he says and his performance on the Ravens Progressive Matrices shows significant cognitive impairment placing him in the mild range of mental retardation. Whether this is malingering or not cannot be detailed without a review of medical records."

A year and a half later, Mr. F.F. saw another psychiatrist for the purpose of disability evaluation. The psychiatric examination diagnosed Mr. F.F. as having mental retardation-severe; schizophrenia-paranoid type; and grand mal seizure disorder. A psychiatrist stated, "since the time of the bicycle accident, he has had seizures and strangely enough has not been receiving any medication for them." The psychiatrist prescribed Risperdal. The psychiatrist observed that, "during the entire interview, Mr. F.F. sat mutely alongside his mother and only with great urging was I able to get him to give his first name." The psychiatrist noted, however, that Mr. F.F.'s mother indicated that, "at times he is much more verbal."

The records also contained a master treatment plan from a local outpatient mental health clinic. Mr. F.F. was diagnosed with having a Psychotic Disorder, NOS and a Seizure Disorder. Records indicate that after the diagnostic interview he did not come for scheduled appointments. In fact, throughout the extensive medical record, there were no treatment or progress notes whatsoever. Mr. F.F. had only seen mental health professionals when required to do so for purposes of examination for disability benefits.

After his arrest, Mr. F.F. did not cooperate with his public defender. The public defender brought in a licensed psychologist to examine Mr. F.F. for competency to stand trial. Plaintiff's expert concluded that Mr. F.F. suffered "significant cognitive deficits as a result of his 1989 head injury." The psychologist further noted that Mr. F.F. exhibited "a wavering level of alertness" and was "verbally withdrawn during the evaluation." The psychologist noted that "Mr. F.F.'s medical records appear to establish unequivocally that he sustained tangible organic deficits as a result of his head injury; however, I was unable to confirm this through objective testing at the time of this evaluation." In so doing, the plaintiff psychologist based her opinions and conclusions primarily upon Mr. F.F's prior medical records and "validation of his disability status by the social security administration."

Shortly thereafter, the prosecutor retained a rather high profile forensic psychiatrist to examine Mr. F.F. In an extensive review of the records and clinical interview, prosecution's forensic psychiatric expert concluded that, "to a reasonable degree of medical probability, Mr. F.F. suffers from a serious cognitive disorder as a result of a head injury some 15 years ago. Despite his cognitive limitations, however, his condition has not deteriorated, and he has demonstrated that he is able to function independently in the community. He was able to communicate adequately with others during the crime and the post-crime period. It is my opinion that Mr. F.F. is now malingering; that is, he is faking or exaggerating psychiatric symptoms in order to avoid going to trial."

After the prosecution psychiatric expert's report was filed, this author was contacted in order to "break the tie." In two independent examinations of Mr. F.F., two differing opinions regarding his competency to stand trial resulted. Prosecution's expert opined that Mr. F.F. was exaggerating or malingering symptoms of psychiatric illness in order to avoid trial. The defense expert, however, opined that, in fact, Mr. F.F. was severely mentally ill, organically brain damaged, and was, as a result, incompetent to stand trial. Defense expert's opinion was, in large part, based on the social security administration's decision to award Mr. F.F. monthly disability benefits several years prior. Defense expert's opinion was not based on objective test data but based much more on the review of the records which appeared to substantiate the presence of serious mental symptoms.

Against this backdrop of two different opinions regarding Mr. F.F.'s mental status and his ability to participate adequately in his own defense, i.e., his competency to stand trial, this author undertook an extensive examination of the records and the defendant.

NEUROPSYCHOLOGICAL EXAMINATION OF MR. F.F.

It should be noted that in no previous assessment of Mr. F.F. did any clinician administer symptom validity tests. Similarly, in no recent forensic assessment of Mr. F.F. did any examiner administer any neuropsychological or psychological tests; that is to say, the previous opinions rendered in this case from both defense and prosecution experts were based entirely upon an interview of Mr. F.F. and the voluminous records provided in the discovery materials from the attorneys.

The defense attorney who was an employee of the State Public Defender's Office, an assistant public defender, initially contacted me concerning this case. While I had never worked for her previously, I had done some work for the Public Defender's Office, and she became aware of me through those internal channels. It is unclear whether or not she realized that I do as much if not more work as a prosecutor's expert than I do for the defense. Nonetheless, after a rather lengthy telephone conversation concerning the case, she referred to the United States attorney, the federal prosecutor on the case. The U.S. attorney explained that I would be working directly for the court in this case rather than one side or the other and that my opinion would necessarily be the "tie breaker" in this case. He indicated that he would need to interview me extensively and review my CV before he would be comfortable accepting me inasmuch as I had been referred by the public defender's office. After a rather lengthy interview, discussion of my background and previous forensic work, and a review of my CV, the prosecutor called within a few days and said that he was, indeed, comfortable with my apparent neutrality and would refer me to the judge as an acceptable tie-breaking expert.

Having been approved by both defense counsel and the prosecutor, my credentials were accepted by the court and an examination date was set for Mr. F.F. to be seen by myself.

Inasmuch as Mr. F.F. at this point in time was now stating that he did not understand English (even though there were large amounts of taped transcriptions of conversations in English), I would need to have a Spanish translator with me. I was able to arrange to do so. In fact, this "Spanish translator" is a doctoral level psychologist who was a former postdoctoral fellow under my supervision. She was, therefore, not only a native Spanish speaker but trained as a neuropsychologist and clinical psychologist.

Arrangements were made to see Mr. F.F. at the correctional facility where he was being held on charges of possession and distribution of narcotics. These charges carried a sentence of a possible 15–20 years in prison. Mr. F.F. was seen on two occasions, and the administration of the procedures and interview required approximately 10½ hours.

A mental status examination was completed or should I say attempted, as Mr. F.F. was, at best, only marginally cooperative and at times frankly uncooperative. His answers to questions were mostly vague and avoidant wherein he stated quite frequently, "I don't know" or "I don't remember" to almost all questions. He was interviewed in Spanish though it was clear to both my assistant and myself that when English was spoken he understood it. With the privilege of previously reviewing documents in this case, it was easy to see that many of Mr. F.F.'s answers to questions were frankly wrong, and some were "near misses" consistent with a Ganser-like Syndrome. For instance, on interview he said that he was 35 years old and that he was single. He said that he didn't remember if he was ever married. He said that he didn't know his date of birth. In answer to the question "What is your date of birth?" he said that he only remembered "the number 6." The record, of course, indicated that Mr. F.F. was born on July 6th, but he stated, "I only remember the number 6." Experienced neuropsychologists will immediately know that one's date of birth is typically a very strong and robust memory, typically remembered by even moderately impaired patients, such as early Alzheimer's patients. Certainly extremely severe dementia or other generalized neurological or focal neurological disease may lead to such personal episodic memory loss, but it is rare.

When asked where he was born, Mr. F.F. said that he was born "here." The record clearly showed that he was born in the Dominican Republic. At that point in the interview, Mr. F.F. said, "I don't remember a lot of things." He said that his mother was still living and that he had seven brothers and sisters, but he said that he didn't know where they lived, and he couldn't remember their names or their ages. He remained alert and verbal insofar as attempting to answer questions throughout the examination process but quite clearly he was very guarded throughout the interview. He displayed a constricted affect. He said that he experienced auditory hallucinations, but these were reported as being quite implausible, such as "I hear the sand on the beach." When asked if that is exactly what he meant, he reiterated that he heard the sand on the beach and not the ocean. When asked exactly what the sand on the beach would sound like, he said he didn't know. Observations by this examiner at the time of the interview and throughout the testing did not reveal the appearance of Mr. F.F. responding to or being preoccupied with internal hallucinations. Other than these gross exaggerations and implausible symptoms, there was no hint of impaired reality testing.[1]

When asked about his educational background, Mr. F.F. said that he didn't remember attending school at all. Then a moment later he said, "Well, I think I remember a little bit." He said that the only thing he remembered was, "being yelled at in school by a teacher." Of course, the record indicates that he attended school until the seventh grade.

---

[1] In one previous examination for the Social Security Administration some time before his arrest, the masters level psychologist who had done the Social Security examination reported that Mr. F.F. stayed in the corner throughout most of the examination and appeared to be talking to someone else in the room. The examiner, however, indicated that he and Mr. F.F. were the only people in the room. The examiner opined that this was evidence of "severe psychosis and an obvious break with reality."

When asked about his medical history, he said that he did not remember anything. He said, "I hear voices," and again he reiterated that he hears "sand." When asked if he heard anything else, he said that sometimes he heard his name being called. He said that he didn't know if he had ever been in the hospital or if he had ever had any surgical procedures. He said he thinks he saw a psychologist or psychiatrist at the correctional facility, but he wasn't sure about that. He said he thinks he saw a psychiatrist "on the outside" but said that he was not sure about that either. He said he thought he had had a head injury riding a bicycle that "threw me." He said, "I suppose they took me to the hospital" but then said he wasn't really sure about that either. He said he didn't know if he had ever used drugs or alcohol but the record clearly indicates that he had an extensive substance abuse history.

When asked about his work history, he said that he did not remember if he ever worked; he said that he thought he lived with his mother, but he wasn't sure, and he thought he got his social security check but he wasn't really sure about that either. In fact, Mr. F.F. either didn't know much or wasn't sure about anything.

He was questioned about why he believed this interview was taking place—what my purposes were and who I was. He said he didn't know. When asked what kind of place we were in, he said it was a "jail." When asked why he was in jail, he said he didn't know that either but thought that perhaps he had been falsely arrested. He did not know if he had done anything wrong; he said that he had been in jail there perhaps a year or two.

Clearly, Mr. F.F. was an unreliable and essentially uncooperative historian during the interview. With regard to the actual facts as documented in the record, Mr. F.F. had come to the United States from Santo Domingo, Dominican Republic at the age of 14. Records indicated that he lived with his mother and three older siblings; his mother was employed as a factory worker.

Records further indicated that he had some difficulty acquiring language skills in childhood but had gone to school in regular classes in the Dominican Republic. After his emigration to the United States, he attended schools in a northeast community. A review of a Child Study Team report when he was 15 years old revealed a WISC-R IQ of 74 with a Verbal IQ of 75 and a Performance IQ of 77 (see Table 32.1). He was administered a Wide Range Achievement Test–Revised at that time also and had a Reading Score below the third percentile and an Arithmetic Score at the seventh percentile. This evaluation was performed some seven months after his alleged head injury, which other professionals had indicated left him with "organic brain damage."

School records also indicated that Mr. F.F. did generally quite poorly academically but this was thought by his teachers to be due to behavioral problems, as he was constantly talking in class, throwing spitballs, being sent to the principal's office, and never turned in homework assignments. His teachers felt that he was working well below his abilities, and several even went so far as to say that if he applied himself even just a little bit he could be getting at least average grades.

Excerpted from the neuropsychological report

The following paragraph is excerpted from my neuropsychological report concerning a summary of the review of the medical and school records:

> Medical history indicates that Mr. F.F., at the age of 15, fell off a bicycle and had a benign blow to the head. There were no neurological symptoms either at the time of the accident, in the hospital, or afterwards. If a loss of consciousness was present it was so brief as to be completely benign. On arrival at the hospital, he was awake, alert, and cooperative at the time of his admission to the ER. He was not combative, not in a delirious state, nor did he exhibit any frank neurological features of a generalized or focal nature. A skull x-ray obtained at the time was completely normal. A CT of his brain at the time was completely normal. He was kept in the hospital overnight for observation and for treatment of an orthopedic injury to his knee and a scalp laceration that required some stitches. There

is, therefore, no evidence whatsoever in the medical history to sustain the belief that Mr. F.F. incurred any resultant brain damage as a consequence of his bicycle accident. Other examiners' conclusions regarding the presence of a mental disorder, neuropsychiatric condition, mental retardation, organic personality syndrome, and the like relative to the bicycle fall, therefore, have absolutely no basis in the medical history and are wrong. If this type of injury actually causes brain damage, the vast majority of the public would look like Mr. F.F.—in short, the brain just does not work that way.

Neuropsychological test results

Table 32.2 contains all the scores from the neuropsychological evaluation of Mr. F.F. Several measures of symptom validity were administered. Results of the Test of Memory Malingering (TOMM; Tombaugh, 1996) revealed that on the first trial he correctly answered 26 of the 50 stimulus items, which is about at chance level, and on Trial 2 his performance worsened, correctly identifying only 21 of the 50 items. His Trial 2 performance was well below chance expectations and completely incongruous with the expected improvement on Trial 2. Excerpting from the report: "What this means is that even if he had his eyes closed and simply guessed, he would likely have done better." The only possible interpretation of these scores is that Mr. F.F. made a conscious, concerted effort to perform poorly on this test.

TABLE 32.2   Summary of effort evaluation

Test of Memory Malingering (Trial 1)	26/50	
Test of Memory Malingering (Trial 2)	21/50	Below Chance
Victoria Symptom Validity Test (Easy Items)	17/24	
Victoria Symptom Validity Test (Difficult Items)	2/24	Below Chance
Victoria Symptom Validity Test (Total)	19/48	Invalid

He was also administered the Victoria Symptom Validity Test, a computer administered test similar to the Portland Digit Recognition Test (Binder, 2002) following the Hiscock and Hiscock procedure. His performance on this test also fell into the invalid range. He correctly remembered 17 of the 24 "easy items" and two of the 24 "difficult items" for a total score that was 19 of 48 correct. "This score, again, falls well below the 50% cutoff—again revealing the presence of a conscious effort to feign memory impairment. Again, as in the TOMM, had Mr. F.F. had his eyes closed and simply guessed on the basis of chance and statistical probability alone, he would likely have done better. Again, as before, his below-chance performance again illustrates a conscious effort to feign memory loss. No other explanations make sense."

The Wechsler Adult Intelligence Scale, Third Edition, was administered entirely in Spanish. He obtained a Full Scale IQ of 54 with a Verbal IQ of 57 and a Performance IQ of 59 (see Table 32.3). These scores would place him within the moderately severe range of mental retardation. Mr. F.F.'s test performance was best characterized as one exhibiting vagueness, uncooperativeness, and significant inconsistencies throughout the range of subtests of the Wechsler Scales. His test scores

TABLE 32.3   Wechsler scores

	STANDARD SCORE	PERCENTILE
Full Scale IQ	54	0.1
Verbal IQ	57	0.1
Performance IQ	59	0.1

were clearly invalid. When Mr. F.F. completed a similar Wechsler Intelligence Scale (the WISC–R), he obtained IQ values that were some 20 points higher in all domains. These scores were achieved after Mr. F.F.'s alleged head injury—the head injury that according to some experts so disabled him. Since that time Mr. F.F. has had no significant medical history whatsoever, no additional head injuries, no neurological illness or disease, and no definitive psychiatric or neuropsychiatric diagnosis or treatment. There is no medical reason why his IQ should now have dropped so significantly in the absence of any contributory history.

On the Wechsler Scales, his intra-test variability was strikingly odd—correctly answering harder questions and missing easier ones in every subtest. For example, in the Vocabulary Subtest, he knew the definition of *yesterday* but he could not define *winter*. Similarly, on Picture Completion, he saw that the jogger had missing footprints (item number 12) but he missed most of the earlier items (testing of the limits procedures were utilized). On Digit Symbol Coding, his total score was 14; he made three errors. In other words, he completed the top row plus one extra after subtracting his errors. He was only able to correctly answer the first five items on the Arithmetic Subtest; yet, he was taped in conversation with his associate showing that he was able to quickly calculate 55%. Digit Span of three forward and two in reverse is remarkable for being so poor.

Performances on the Grooved Pegboard Test were also instructive. The test was administered on two occasions. On the first administration of the Grooved Pegboard he required 84 seconds to complete the task with his right, dominant hand. On the second administration, which was one week later, he now required 145 seconds with his right hand. There were no physical changes in Mr. F.F. during the time interval; again, these findings are clearly implausible and consistent with suboptimal effort.

His performance on the Benton Judgment of Line Orientation Test is also interesting. His pattern was consistent with correctly judging the most difficult angles but missing the most apparent and easy ones.

On the WRAT–3 Arithmetic Test he only attempted the first five items. He correctly answered 2 for the problem 1 + 1, but could not handle 5 − 1 where his answer was 5, and he thought that 2 + 7 was 14—obviously mistaking the "+" for a multiplication sign. In a simple addition problem, where he was required to add three two-place numbers, he missed the correct answer by 1. Yet, he went on to correctly answer a more difficult problem.

He was administered the WRAT–3 Reading Test in English and he, again, had a very strange performance where he, again, was unable to read easier words but was quite able to read more difficult words.

On the Wechsler Memory Scale, Third Edition, Logical Memory Subtest completely translated into Spanish by my assistant, Mr. F.F. had a total correct score of 2 for the first administration and 0 at the 30-minute delay.

Further, his incongruous performance on Trail Making was also interesting. He completed Trail Making Part A in 39 seconds without making any mistakes. However, on Part B, he required 3 minutes and 10 seconds to get himself from the beginning point to number 5 without having made any mistakes—again, a grossly implausible performance.

On the California Verbal Learning Test, Second Edition, Mr. F.F. recalled a total of 31 words over the first five trials for a T score of 27. Incongruously, he performed better on the long delay

TABLE 32.4   Results of neuropsychological evaluation

	RAW SCORE	PERCENTILE
WRAT	2	0.1
CVLT (Trial 5)	7	
CVLT (Recognition)	7/16	
CVLT (Forced Choice)	9/16	
Grooved Pegboard (Trial 1)	84 seconds	
Grooved Pegboard (Trial 2)	140 seconds	

free recall than he did on the short delay free recall (i.e., he recalled one on short delay and five on long delay). Similarly, on the delayed recognition trial, he had only seven correct hits and made 15 false-positive errors. On the forced-choice recognition trial, his total accuracy was 9 of 16—again, a grossly implausible performance.

Summary of neuropsychological test interpretation

As can be seen from the data in Table 32.4, Mr. F.F. exhibited insufficient effort on every test that he was administered. It seems quite clear from the results of the symptom validity tests that he made a conscious effort to perform poorly. This is the only reasonable explanation for well below chance performances, as were demonstrated by Mr. F.F. on both the TOMM and the Victoria Symptom Validity Test.

Several methods exist for the analysis of neuropsychological test scores in an effort to determine their validity. While, on the one hand, it is clear that his suboptimal performance on symptom validity tests raises suspicion, such performances do not necessarily invalidate entire profiles. This concept is currently a debatable issue in professional neuropsychology, and it is this author's opinion that some individuals may selectively malinger on various neuropsychological tests. It would, therefore, not necessarily raise suspicion in me if an examinee were to perform poorly on a symptom validity test but perform normally on a memory test. Selective suboptimal performance is not uncommon in forensic venues, and an examiner must carefully consider each test result.

That being said, in this particular case, it is clear that Mr. F.F. put forth suboptimal effort on every test that he was administered. This is obvious on the basis of an implausible pattern of correct versus wrong answers throughout the Wechsler Scales, wherein he correctly answered harder items and missed easier items on most every test. Similarly, his performance on the WRAT Arithmetic Test when juxtaposed against his ability to quickly calculate a percentage on the telephone with his crony can only be interpreted as a result of suboptimal motivation.

It is also clearly implausible that such discrepant performances would be demonstrated on the Grooved Pegboard Test within one week, with no change in physical or medical status. Such discrepancies make no sense whatsoever. In a similar vein, correctly judging the lines of more difficult angles and missing the angular judgments of easier stimuli also makes no sense. This is simply not the way brain–behavior relationships work.

It should be abundantly clear to the sophisticated reader that Mr. F.F. performed suboptimally on every test and every facet of the examination. Taken together, his neuropsychological test results with his uncooperativeness during the interview and the implausible symptom picture he presented, Mr. F.F. could be said to be an "unsophisticated malingerer."

One of the more alarming aspects of this case—at least to this writer—is the fact that mental health professionals who had previously evaluated Mr. F.F. failed to detect his very apparent malingering. From that prospective, this writer often wonders just how many people are collecting disability or insurance benefits who actually deserve none.

In the final analysis of this case, then, Mr. F.F. was found to be malingering both mental illness and neuropsychological impairment. His "head injury" sustained in a fall from a bicycle when he was 15 years old clearly served as a "historical opportunistic incident," which Mr. F.F. exploited to the maximum. That he so convincingly portrayed mental impairment to other examiners is quite remarkable given his obvious transparency to a seasoned neuropsychologist.

FINAL ADJUDICATION OF MR. F.F.

The report of neuropsychological evaluation was submitted to the court on a Tuesday morning at approximately 10:00 a.m., and I received a telephone call from the prosecutor's office shortly after the lunch hour. The prosecutor was calling to tell me that defense counsel had withdrawn her motion for a competency hearing on the basis of my report. The prosecutor thanked me for my work and indicated that they would be going to trial shortly. Shortly thereafter, I learned that Mr. F.F., in fact, began to cooperate with his counsel. Apparently, he had an amazing recovery of neuropsychological functions. Despite cooperation with his attorney, Mr. F.F. was convicted of all charges and sentenced to a minimum term of 15 years in the state prison.

One of the most important lessons of this case is that a clinical neuropsychologist should not necessarily accept the conclusions of other professionals pertaining to the mental condition of a criminal defendant. It is incumbent upon the ethical and well-trained professional to gather independent evidence in formulating his or her opinion of a case at hand. Whether or not physicians, psychologists, and other mental health professionals lack sophistication or training relevant to important issues or perhaps have erred due to not being careful and thorough, *it is prudent for the forensic neuropsychologist to not simply accept the work of others and instead to perform his or her own examination and own interpretation of all of the historical information and available test data.* This case and case analysis illustrate the fact that it is not rare or uncommon that transparent, unsophisticated malingerers can evade detection if not examined proactively and knowledgably. The goal is to always be on the side of science and, therefore, always on the side of truth, whatever it may be. In the memorable words of one distinguished supervisor of mine, "always tell the truth and let the chips fall where they may."

REFERENCES

Binder, L. M. (2002). The Portland Digit Recognition Test: A review of validation data and clinical use. *Journal of Forensic Neuropsychology*, 2, 27–41.

Dusky v. United States, 362 U.S. 402 (1960).

Melton, G. B., Petrila, J., Poythress, N. G., & Slobogin, C. (1997). *Psychological evaluations for the courts*, 2nd ed. New York: Guilford.

Mittenberg, W., Aguila-Puentes, G., Patton, C., Canyock, E. M., & Heilbronner, R. L. (2002). Neuropsychological profiling of symptom exaggeration and malingering. In J. Hom & R. L. Denney (Eds.) *Detection of response bias in forensic neuropsychology* (pp. 227–240). New York: Haworth Press.

Tombaugh, T. N. (1996). *The Test of Memory Malingering (TOMM)*. Toronto, Canada: Multi-Health Systems.

Vitacco, M. J., Rogers, R., Gabel, J., & Munizza, J. (2006). An evaluation of malingering screens with competency to stand trial patients: A known-groups comparison. *Law and Human Behavior*, 31, 249–260.

Evaluating competency to stand trial and sanity in the face of marked amnesia and claimed psychosis

33

Robert L. Denney

Practicing clinical neuropsychology in the criminal forensic setting is a unique endeavor (Denney & Wynkoop, 2000; Martell, 1992). The examiner must understand specific legal standards for a given jurisdiction and apply his or her understanding of a specific individual's neurocognitive strengths and weaknesses to those standards. It is also a unique setting because clinicians often see combinations of neuropathology and psychopathology not commonly seen with typical neuropsychological evaluations performed in hospital or community settings (e.g., psychopathy, violence, and extreme cluster B personality disorders). Lastly, all of this activity occurs in the context of the criminal adversarial venue, a situation ripe for symptom exaggeration and a situation that often requires specialized assessment methods. This case exemplifies each of these areas.

REFERRAL OF THE CASE

Mr. G.G. was a 52-year-old man charged with a variety of federal and state offenses, including cultivation of marijuana with intent to distribute, receipt and possession of stolen firearms, use of firearms in drug trafficking, possession of false identification documents, possession of child pornography, and child molestation. The U.S. District Court requested opinions regarding his competency to stand trial and his mental state at the time of the alleged offenses (i.e., sanity). The court placed the defendant in a secure forensic evaluation center for mental health evaluation. Midway through the 30-day evaluation, however, he was forwarded to the U.S. Medical Center in Springfield, Missouri, due to his apparent severe psychiatric and neurological condition.

INITIAL PRESENTATION

When Mr. G.G. arrived at the U.S. Medical Center, he was alert and in no acute distress. He arrived under suicide precautions because he had cut his left wrist in two locations while at the study center and required six sutures. He claimed no recollection of that self-mutilation. He said he did not know the day, date, or month but was able to report the accurate year. Reportedly, he did not know when he arrived at the facility, nor could he recall arriving at the institution. He also claimed not to know if he had experienced any kind of head injury recently. When asked about his childhood, he denied having any recollection of those events. He did not know where he grew up, whether or not he had brothers or sisters, and whether or not his parents were still alive. He said he could not recall anything about his life and could not state his last memory. Suicidal ideation and hallucinations were denied. Beyond the fact he was transferred emergently from a secure forensic study center we knew little because scant information came with him.

FORENSIC STUDY CENTER CONCLUSIONS

Although there was no summary or report from the other institution, a telephone call to the examiner assigned to Mr. G.G. revealed considerable information. He was able to complete a neuropsychological evaluation prior to cutting his left wrist. He was considered to have definite neuropsychological deficits, including severe memory disturbance. He was considered to have moderate to severe diffuse impairment, including dementia without significant depression. He had apparently indicated to the prior evaluators that he had numerous closed head injuries and at least one drowning episode with anoxia, as well as a history of alcohol abuse. He described a history of rage-generated blackouts since childhood. He described hearing "good and bad" voices since he was a child as well. He indicated that members of his family had a history of mental illness but never had any treatment. The prior neuropsychological report was acquired and provided these conclusions:

> Neurological Implications: Mr. G.G. obtained an Impairment Index of 1.0 and a General Neuropsychological Deficit score of 61, which placed at the upper level of the moderately impaired to severely impaired range. There was some evidence of some right hemisphere impairment, but most of the deficits were of a diffuse nature. He evidenced some pathognomonic signs, including dysnomia, central dysarthria, and constructional dyspraxia. These signs are significant indicators of brain damage and cannot be accounted for completely by his low IQ. It is likely that he will have extreme difficulty with tasks requiring memory and spatial orientation, such as conversations he has had, medication schedules, or finding his way in a new environment. Since he also has difficulty learning from information and environmental cues, he will have difficulty adapting to change in his environment.
>
> Psychological Implications: Mr. G.G. could best be managed behaviorally in a structured environment with supervision. His anxiety and lack of attention are likely to interfere with his ability to learn new information and apply it to new situations. Therefore, his ability to care for himself independently is in question as is his ability to understand and comprehend changes in his environment. He is likely to become anxious and confused, maybe even disoriented at times.
>
> Summary: This man is evidencing significant neuropsychological deficits, especially involving memory and sensory perceptual tasks, as well as cognitive flexibility and nonverbal abstracting and reasoning abilities. His deficits appear moderate to severe and are diffuse in nature. There is some slight evidence of right hemisphere dysfunction. However, there appear to be other factors, which may contribute to the patient's poor performance, such as psychosis or multiple personality disorder.

These conditions should be ruled out. However, there remains sufficient impairment that cannot be accounted for by these disorders and is suggestive of brain impairment.

It was recommended he receive brain imaging studies, as well as placement in a more structured and supervised environment. Neuropsychological test results from the prior evaluation are presented in Table 33.1. No measures sensitive to insufficient effort and malingering were administered, and the issue was not addressed in the neuropsychological report.

PERSONAL HISTORY

Information about Mr. G.G.'s background and history was obtained during individual clinical interviews. This was possible because his memory complaints differed at various times throughout the 45-day inpatient evaluation. There were times when he provided relatively detailed accounts of his background, details of which appeared consistent with information contained in investigative materials.

Mr. G.G. described being raised initially by his mother and father in a small rural town. His father worked on farms until his death from cancer when the defendant was a child. Reportedly, he could not recall how old he was when his father died. He described two older brothers. He said his mother disciplined the children by hitting them with belts and switches. His father was described as a harsh disciplinarian who would "beat the hell out of you." At about 10 years of age, he allegedly became the victim of ongoing sexual abuse at the hands of two teenage males in his neighborhood. He characterized the abuse as rape and indicated he was abused between two and four times per month for about six months to a year. Apparently, no one in his family was aware of this abuse, and he received no treatment. Significant academic problems were described, in part due to his family moving so frequently. He often missed the start of the academic years because his father's work was seasonal. He had trouble keeping pace with other students and obtained poor grades, and as a result he was retained in grades at least twice. He was not enrolled in special classes, but also noted none were available. He dropped out of school after completing seventh grade at almost 17 years of age.

Mr. G.G. reported having started working on farms at the age of 8 or 9 years. The work increased gradually until he was working full-time at 17. He eventually enlisted in the U.S. Army, where he reportedly remained for 20 years and attained the rank of sergeant, first class, prior to receiving an Honorable Discharge. He worked in military police and in motor pools, but most of his work was in food service. He completed a one-year tour of duty in Vietnam, where he was involved in food service operations in combat zones. After Vietnam, he was stationed in Japan and the U.S. His work history after discharge was sporadic because he was discontent working in food service industries. He reportedly married in 1967, but separated in 1990. He said he had no children.

Mr. G.G. denied a history of mental illness or treatment, although he was referred for "mental hygiene and character guidance" in the military. His father had been considered "delirious, crazy, or out of his head." Near the time of his death his father was considered "completely mad." Mr. G.G. reported numerous head injuries with loss of consciousness. He fell off a horse, fell off a train trestle, and was struck by a piece of farm equipment. He believed he was only unconscious for up to several minutes in any of these injuries. No mention was made of a near-drowning accident.

Mr. G.G. reported using alcohol heavily during his youth and while he was in the military. He often engaged in fistfights while drinking and received a broken nose in one instance. One of his supervisors in the military considered his drinking problematic. He denied ever receiving treatment. Prior to his arrest, he said he drank alcohol two to three times per week and became intoxicated once or twice a month. He used marijuana up to four times per month and denied other drug use. He

TABLE 33.1   Neuropsychological test results from previous study center

GENERAL NEUROPSYCHOLOGICAL DEFICIT SCALE (NDS)		Category Test	114 errors
Level of Performance	45	Errors on I & II	2
Pathognomonic Signs	6	Errors on VII	7
Patterns	0	Bolter Items Incorrect	6
Right/Left Differences	10	Easy Items Incorrect	7
Total G-NDS Score	61 (moderate)	Number Criteria Positive	5
Left NDS	9		
Right NDS	7	Tactual Performance Test	
		Dominant	12
Halstead Impairment Index	1.0	Non-dominant	10
		Both	10
Grip Strength		Total Time	32
Right 51 kg		Memory	2
Left 51 kg		Localization	0
Finger Tapping		Trail Making Test	
Dominant 37		Part A	274 seconds
Non-dominant 31		Part B	Discontinued
WECHSLER ADULT INTELLIGENCE SCALE–REVISED		Seashore Rhythm Test	16 correct
Verbal IQ 76			
Performance IQ 81		Speech Sounds Perception	N/A
Full Scale IQ 78		(did not have glasses)	

Verbal Scale Score		*Performance Scale Score*		Sensory Perceptual Exam Errors	
Information	4	Picture Completion	3	Tactile Right	1
Digit Span	6	Picture Arrangement	4	Tactile Left	0
Vocabulary	6	Block Design	7	Auditory Right	2
Arithmetic	5	Object Assembly	7	Auditory Left	4
Comprehension	3	Digit Symbol	3	Visual Right	0
Similarities	6			Visual Left	1

WECHSLER MEMORY SCALE–REVISED		Tactile Finger Recognition
Verbal Memory Index	66	Right 1
Visual Memory Index	81	Left 0
General Memory Index	61	
Attention/Concentration Index	71	Finger-Tip Number Writing
Delayed Recall Index	63	Right 3
		Left 3
		Tactile Form Recognition
		Right 14 seconds 0 errors
		Left 11 seconds 0 errors

stated this instance was his first arrest. He claimed that there were no family or close friends that we could call to gain a better understanding of his life and recent history.

THE ALLEGED OFFENSE

Investigative report of offense

According to the indictment and investigative reports, Mr. G.G. is alleged to have engaged in a variety of illegal behaviors which were somewhat interrelated. First, he was charged with the manufacture of greater than 50 marijuana plants in a barn on his property and that he possessed those plants with an intent to distribute them. He allegedly exchanged marijuana with minor females in return for sexual activity. Some of his sexual relationships were videotaped, and he was charged with possession of videotapes containing depictions of minors engaged in sexual conduct. He was charged with possession of a stolen shotgun and with carrying firearms in relation to drug trafficking crimes. Materials indicated he had false identification documents in six different names including driver's licenses, Social Security cards, and credit cards. Finally, documents alleged that he had forcible sexual contact with a 5-year-old girl, both in his home and in parks across the state border.

CURRENT EVALUATION RESULTS

Hospital observation findings

Very quickly after his arrival, Mr. G.G. began denying suicidal ideation, and we were able to progressively change his living arrangements from remaining in a locked room under camera observation to open population status, where he had access to other patients and defendants, as well as the cafeteria, recreation centers, chapel, and law library. His mental status varied considerably during the hospitalization. Upon admission, he claimed to be disoriented and to have virtually no memory for his entire life. About an hour later, however, a physician's assistant who conducted the physical examination interviewed him, and he was able to provide a reasonably detailed account of his past. During meetings and clinical interviews thereafter, he was alert and maintained good eye contact. No difficulties were noted in his ability to attend or concentrate. His mood appeared somewhat anxious, and he confirmed feelings of uneasiness. He repeatedly contended that he heard voices on an infrequent basis. Apart from his verbal reports, there was no evidence of psychotic thought processes noted. He never appeared to be responding to internal stimuli. His speech was clear, coherent, logical, and goal-oriented.

The physical examination revealed possible hypertension, and later laboratory results revealed elevated blood glucose levels. He was evaluated further and found to have glucose intolerance, which was successfully treated by diet. He underwent a neurological consultation, which included neurological examination, electroencephalogram (EEG), and computerized tomography (CT) scan of the brain. EEG and CT results were normal. The neurological examination results suggested mild peripheral neuropathy and "impaired intellect."

Current validity test results

Standard neuropsychological testing was not repeated because Mr. G.G. recently completed the testing at the previous study center. However, as there was no validity testing completed during that evaluation, and there was considerable suspicion regarding the veracity of Mr. G.G.'s complaints and presentation, he was administered a small battery of tests with the capability of detecting insufficient effort in neurocognitive domains and disingenuous claims in the psychiatric domain (Table 33.2).

Cognitive

On the Shipley Institute of Living Scale (Zachary, 1986) and the Test of Nonverbal Intelligence–2 (Brown, Sherbenou, & Johnsen, 1990), both screening measures of intelligence, Mr. G.G. obtained estimated IQ scores in the mentally deficient and borderline ranges, respectively. Such scores were

TABLE 33.2   Current neurocognitive and psychiatric testing results

Shipley Institute of Living Scale	WAIS–R IQ Estimate	61
Test of Nonverbal Intelligence–2	75	
Rey 15-Item Test:	2 Rows 6 Items	
Rey Auditory Verbal Learning Test	1st Trial recall	4
Rey Word Recognition Test	Correctly recalled	7
	Correctly rejected	14
	Total correct	21/25
Rey Dot Counting Test	Grouped Time	51.81
	Ungrouped Time	58.89
	Dots miscounted	21
Abbreviated Hiscock Digit Memory Test	Trial 1–5″	11	Correct
	Trial 2–10″	7	Correct
	Trial 3–15″	6	Correct
		Negative Slope	

Forced-Choice Test of Nonverbal Ability (precursor to the VIP nonverbal subtest)

Score	54	Consistency Ratio	0.556
Correlation	−0.2502	Slope*Consistency Ratio	−0.000866197

(Performance corresponds to Invalid/Irrelevant on VIP Nonverbal)

Forced-Choice Test of Verbal Ability (precursor to the VIP verbal subtest)

Score	29	Consistency Ratio	0.483
Correlation	−0.0664	Slope*Consistency Ratio	−0.000282718

(Performance corresponds to Invalid/Irrelevant on VIP verbal)

Wechsler Memory Scale–Revised

Logical Memory I	Raw score 9	Logical Memory II	Raw score 6
	Percentile 4th	Percentile 8th	
Forced-Choice Recognition	Raw score correct	21	
	Percentage correct	42	
	Z = −0.99	p = 0.16 (random range)	

Structured Interview of Reported Symptoms

RS	Definite Feigning Range
SC	Probable Feigning Range
IA	Honest Range
BL	Probable Feigning Range
SU	Probable Feigning Range
SEL	Probable Feigning Range
SEV	Definite Feigning Range
RO	Probable Feigning Range

Minnesota Multiphasic Personality Inventory–II

Cannot Say	0		Hs		T97
VRIN	3		D		T89
TRIN	10		Hy		T89
F	35	T120	Pd		T84
F(B)	30	T120	Mf	T64	
F(P)	10		Pa		T112
FBS	31		Pt		T109
L	3	T48	Sc		T120
K	8	T35	Ma	T69	
F-K	27		Si		T92

Subtle – Obvious Total T-score Diff: 320

inconsistent with both his work history and his behavioral presentation during this evaluation period. His vocabulary, pattern of speech, adaptive living skills, and social skills all suggested a higher level of intelligence than did the test results. His performance on both the Rey 15-Item Test (Frederick, 2002a; Rey, 1958) and Abbreviated Hiscock Digit Memory Test (Guilmette, Hart, Giuliano, & Leininger, 1994) were sufficiently poor to suggest he was suppressing his abilities. Extremely slow response times on the grouped portion of the Dot Counting Test in relation to his response latency on the ungrouped portion, with a great number of miscounts, also suggested suppression. On the Forced Choice Test of Verbal Ability and the Forced Choice Test of Nonverbal Ability (Frederick & Foster, 1991; precursors to the Validity Indicator Profile; Frederick, 2002b), Mr. G.G.'s performance did not decline as test items became more difficult. This pattern corresponds to an Invalid-Irrelevant finding on the VIP currently and suggested he was not putting forth appropriate effort during both portions of the test. These performances did not appear consistent with his general level of functioning during this hospitalization.

Psychiatric

On the Minnesota Multiphasic Personality Inventory–2 (Butcher, Graham, Dahlstrom, Tellegen, & Kaemmer, 1989), Mr. G.G. endorsed a large number of items indicative of a wide variety of severe psychopathology. The validity scales suggested extreme exaggeration of mental health difficulties. His F and FB were both T-120, and F-K was 27. Pa, Pt, and Sc were T-112, T-109, and T-120, respectively. Despite these severe elevations, his Variable Response Inconsistency scale (VRIN) score demonstrated he was organized enough in his thinking to consistently apply himself to these 567 items. His responses to clinical scales suggested a person who was grossly confused and disoriented, extremely anxious, and extremely paranoid. However, such traits were not noted in his behavioral presentation. Also revealing was the elevated F(p) of 10, indicating he endorsed a great number of highly atypical psychiatric manifestations. Such a performance suggested gross over-exaggeration. He also produced a Lees-Haley FBS raw score of 31, which suggested he was grossly over-endorsing somatic concerns as well (Larrabee, 2003a; Lees-Haley, 1992).

Mr. G.G. was administered the Structured Interview of Reported Symptoms (Rogers, Bagby, & Dickens, 1992). He elevated five scales to the *probable feigning* range and two scales to the *definite feigning* range. He reported symptoms that were qualitatively and quantitatively far more extreme than symptoms reported by individuals with genuine mental illnesses. Such results strongly suggested Mr. G.G. was exaggerating his condition.

CRITICAL REVIEW OF PRIOR TESTING RESULTS

Prior to arriving at our facility Mr. G.G. was administered the Halstead-Reitan Neuropsychological Test Battery (Reitan & Wolfson, 1993), including the Wechsler Adult Intelligence Scale–Revised (Wechsler, 1981) and the Wechsler Memory Scale–Revised (Wechsler, 1987) (see Table 33.1). The neuropsychologist, however, did not use measures designed to detect negative response bias. Nonetheless, it is possible to identify validity indicators inherent within that testing. The neuropsychologist attributed his neurocognitive dysfunction to repeated head injuries, and there are a number of indices developed to identify exaggerated data sets from legitimate closed head injury results. One point to keep in mind is that Mr. G.G. also reported significant psychiatric manifestations (including hallucinations), which hypothetically might make the results less reliable.

Mittenberg, Theroux, Zielinski, and Heilbronner (1995) developed two methods to help identify malingered head injury on the WAIS–R: Vocabulary-Digit Span and a discriminant function. Both were successfully cross-validated and applied to previously published data (Mittenberg,

Aguila-Puentes, Patton, Canyock, & Heilbronner (2002). Applying these indices to the data revealed no significant finding on Vocabulary-Digit Span (6 – 6 = 0), but a positive discriminant function result (0.5989). This result suggested Mr. G.G.'s pattern of WAIS–R scores was more similar to simulated malingerers than individuals with genuine head injuries. Reliable Digit Span is another potential malingering index within the WAIS–R (Greiffenstein, Baker, & Gola, 1994; Mathias, Greve, Bianchini, Houston, & Crouch, 2002). This index is the number of forward digits recalled for the best two-point response added to the number of backward digits recalled for the best two-point response. Scores less than 7 are more solidly indicative of atypical performance in head injury claims, but scores below 8 also raise suspicion. Mr. G.G. obtained an RDS of 7 on the WAIS–R and 9 on the WMS–R. This finding was at least suggestive of variable effort during the WAIS–R.

Indices have been developed to identify malingered performance on the WMS–R as well (Mittenberg, Azrin, Millsaps, & Heilbronner, 1993). These indices included a General Memory-Attention Concentration difference score and a discriminant function score. Mr. G.G.'s General Memory-Attention/Concentration difference score was not meaningful, but his discriminant function score of 0.19 suggested his WMS–R pattern of scores more closely resembled simulated malingerers than genuine head injury patients.

A similar discriminant function was developed for the Halstead-Reitan Battery (Heaton, Smith, Lehman, & Vogt, 1978; Mittenberg, Rotholc, Russell, & Heilbronner, 1996). This discriminant could not be used because the neuropsychologist did not administer the Speech Sounds Perception Test due to the fact Mr. G.G. did not have glasses. There are hidden indices within the HRB, however, that can occasionally shed light on test-taking effort. There are several measures within the Category Test (Sweet & King, 2002). His total score of 114 was positive, and he made two errors on subtest II, two exceedingly rare events (Forrest, Allen, & Goldstein, 2004). He incorrectly answered six of the Bolter Items and seven of the Easy Items. Lastly he made seven errors on subtest VII. Sweet and King (2002) recommend a positive sign of negative response bias if more than one of these indices were positive; Mr. G.G. was positive on all five. Lastly, one can sum the two means for Finger Tapping and identify poor effort for individuals claiming closed head injury when the scores fall too low (Larrabee 2003b). Mr. G.G.'s performance was just above the cutoff and within acceptable limits.

Overall, there appeared to be considerable evidence of invalidity in the neuropsychological test data received from the study center. Those findings suggested the neuropsychological test results did not reflect Mr. G.G.'s true neurocognitive ability. Given the overall context of the evaluation and presentation during our hospitalization, it appeared Mr. G.G.'s presentation was consistent in suggesting a disingenuous attempt to appear more cognitively and psychiatrically disabled than was truly the case.

CLINICAL FORMULATION

Mr. G.G.'s behavioral presentation and the results of his psychological testing, considered in conjunction with the psycholegal context in which he was evaluated, overwhelmingly suggested the presence of malingering. In other words, we believed he was feigning or grossly exaggerating symptoms of mental illness to achieve a specific goal. His behavioral presentation and his reports of abilities varied markedly, often within a short time span. They appeared to change based on who was observing him. For example, he claimed an inability to recall almost anything from his personal history when speaking to a psychologist, but was able to provide a detailed medical history for a physician's assistant later that afternoon. A variety of different types of psychological tests produced similar results. Positive results on two or more measures of neurocognitive response bias, in addition to indications from tests of self-report (MMPI–2 and SIRS), suggested not only probable malingered neurocognitive dysfunction but malingered psychosis as well (Slick, Sherman, & Iverson, 1999).

COMPETENCY TO STAND TRIAL

The presence of exaggerated neurocognitive deficits and psychosis does not eliminate the need to answer the question of competency to stand trial for an individual who has a mental disease or defect. However, Mr. G.G.'s history did not include a documented mental illness, other than his recent superficial attempt at self-harm. His presentation during the evaluation did not suggest a mental illness or defect existed. By definition then, in federal jurisdictions, he would be considered competent to stand trial because the statute requires a mental disease or defect (Title 18, U.S.C., § 4241). Even in such instances, we assess whether defendants are able to understand basic legal concepts and ask questions regarding their recollections of events leading up to the charges.

Competency interview

Mr. G.G. was aware that his current charges related to the cultivation or "manufacturing" of marijuana and that certain charges were related to weapons. He denied awareness of other charges and claimed that he had not seen any written material concerning those charges. He said that he was unaware of possible consequences should he be found guilty on any of the charges. Although he remembered learning about his charges during a conversation with his attorney, he stated that he could not remember his attorney's name, and that he had not spoken to his attorney since his admission to the U.S. Medical Center. He expressed doubts about his ability to trust any attorney, and stated that he anticipated problems cooperating with an attorney should he become angry. He stated, "When I get angry and mad, I lose it and I can't maintain stability." Mr. G.G. reported an inability to define the concept of attorney–client privilege. The concept was explained to him, and he appeared to understand it based on his responses. He accurately recalled that information during a meeting four days later.

Mr. G.G. was able to describe roles of various individuals who participate in a trial in simple, but accurate, terms. He understood that the prosecuting attorney sought a conviction in his case, and he viewed the prosecutor as working against him. He understood that the role of his defense attorney was to aid in his defense against the charges. He recognized that the judge controlled the courtroom, and that a jury consisted of 12 members. The purpose of the jury was explained to him, and he later recalled that information accurately in concluding the fact that jury decisions must be unanimous. He accurately described the pleas of guilty and not guilty, but stated that he had never heard of the plea *not guilty by reason of insanity*. He ventured, "If a person were insane, they'd be not guilty." The meanings and potential consequences of the pleas "not guilty by reason of insanity" and "no contest" were explained to him. He demonstrated an ability to learn that information. When asked about plans for handling his case, he stated that he had none. After a brief discussion of possible options, he stated that he would prefer to be found not competent to stand trial, but he had difficulty explaining his rationale for that preference.

Although Mr. G.G. appeared to have certain deficits in knowledge that might impact on his ability to stand trial, he did not appear to have any difficulty learning the necessary information. He appeared capable of understanding both the charges against him and the necessary information about the workings of the trial process. Finally, he appeared able to cooperate with an attorney. Should he choose to do so, he appeared capable of disclosing appropriate information, considering various courses of action, and making decisions following consultations with his attorney. His responses and presentation suggested he was competent to stand trial, but I still had questions about his claimed amnesia regarding activities constituting the alleged offense.

AMNESIA AND COMPETENCY TO STAND TRIAL

Claims of amnesia for criminal offenses are not unusual, although they mostly occur with charges of homicide (Schacter, 1986). Prevalence estimates range from 23% to 65% for homicide, 8% for non-homicide violent crimes and 0% among 47 non-violent crimes (Bradford & Smith, 1979; Guttmacher, 1955; Leitch, 1948; Parwatikar, Holcomb, & Menninger, 1985; Taylor & Kopelman, 1984). A claim of amnesia for the type of alleged crimes of Mr. G.G. appears to be a rare event. It also appears from the literature that most researchers have long believed a substantial number of amnestic claims for criminal events are feigned (Adatto, 1949; Bradford & Smith, 1979; Hopwood & Snell, 1933; Lynch & Bradford, 1980; O'Connell, 1960; Parwatikar et al., 1985; Power, 1977; Price & Terhune, 1919). Even so, defendants can experience a brain-based amnesia for an alleged crime due to drug and alcohol intoxication during an offense of relatively short duration or the occurrence of stroke or traumatic brain injury shortly after the criminal activity (Denney, 2005a; Melton, Petrila, Poythress, & Slobogin, 1997; *Wilson v. U.S.*, 1968; Wynkoop & Denney, 1999).

Amnesia for the crime does not necessarily make a person incompetent to stand trial, but it could do so in certain circumstances (Denney & Wynkoop, 2000). Defendants are expected to be able to assist in their defense by telling their attorneys important facts about those events. In the absence of this inside information, mounting an effective defense can be potentially daunting. The DC Circuit Court of Appeals addressed the issue in 1968 (*Wilson v. U.S.*), and most courts appear to follow a similar ruling. The courts look at other important issues, as well as memory, including how much the amnesia impairs the defendant's ability to consult with counsel, testify on his or her own behalf, or reconstruct the behaviors constituting the offense (Denney, 2005a).

Symptom validity testing for remote memory

To assess the veracity of his claimed amnesia, a two-alternative, forced-choice questionnaire was developed based on investigative information about details of his offense. This test was developed as outlined by Frederick, Carter, and Powel (1995) and Denney (1996). Thirty-five questions were developed from investigative materials (see Table 33.3 for examples). He was asked about recollection for each of the questions and reiterated he had no memory for any of those events. Mr. G.G. correctly answered two questions based on clear reasoning, which excluded one alternative. For example, he was asked to choose between a greenhouse or a barn located on his property, and responded, "It would have to be a barn because I don't have a greenhouse." Of the remaining 33 forced-choice questions, he answered only 7 correctly. Applying this score to the binomial theorem formula, as outlined by Denney, produced a Z-score of -3.14 and a one-tailed probability of $p = .0008$. In other words, the probability of such a poor performance occurring by chance alone for an individual with no memory for those events was *less than 1 in 1000*.

These below chance results indicated that Mr. G.G. actually had memory for those events that led up to the charges against him, but was intentionally choosing the wrong answer to appear mentally incompetent. These results combined with the other test results, and atypical clinical presentation, led to the conclusion of definite neurocognitive malingering, rather than probable neurocognitive malingering (Slick, Sherman, & Iverson, 1999). His performance on these questions also increased my confidence in the competency to stand trial opinion.

TABLE 33.3 Example forced-choice, two alternative questions developed to assess claims of amnesia. All names were altered for anonymity

1. Do you remember your attorney's name?
   David Johnson   or   Martin Kline
2. In addition to charges related to marijuana and weapons, do you remember another charge?
   Possession of false I.D.   or   Possession of explosives
3. How many false identification documents were you alleged to have had?
   Four   or   Six
   Do you remember any of the names that were alleged to be on the false documents?
4. John G. Hughes   or   Ron S. Enyeart
5. Wayne T. Bright   or   Steven Whiting
6. Do you remember when police came to you with a search warrant?
   December 8, 1996   or   December 23, 1996
7. Do you remember at approximately what time you were arrested?
   11:00 a.m.   or   3:30 p.m.
8. According to investigative materials, approximately how many marijuana plants did law enforcement officials claim they found during the search?
   Just under 50   or   Over 50
9. Were the plants allegedly found in a field or building?
   Field   or   Building

SANITY FORMULATION

Federal standard for sanity

In the federal jurisdiction, the statute reveals that to be found insane "at the time of the commission of the acts constituting the offense, the defendant, as a result of a severe mental disease or defect, was unable to appreciate the nature and quality or the wrongfulness of his acts" (Title 18, U.S.C., §17). This federal standard has been in place since shortly after Hinkley shot President Reagan in 1981 and has become the standard in a majority of states (Denney, 2005b). It is clearly apparent that the statute requires presence of mental disease or defect, and it does *not* contain a volitional component. It can be divided into three sections: appreciation of the nature of the acts, appreciation of the quality of the acts, and appreciation of the wrongfulness of the acts. Although there are differences of opinion on how, or whether or not, nature and quality are unique constructs, I agree with Shapiro's earlier writing (1984, 1991) which views them as different aids in the forensic analysis. Nature refers to the basic aspect of the act (e.g., Did the defendant realize the object was a gun?), and quality refers more to an understanding of the natural consequences of the act (e.g., shooting a gun at someone can harm them). For practical purposes, however, the majority of sanity evaluation opinions using this strictly "right/wrong" standard will be determined by the understanding of wrongfulness (Denney, 2005b). Nearly all but the most severely compromised individuals retain an understanding of the two more basic elements.

Mr. G.G.'s recollection of the offense

Mr. G.G. denied memory of any behaviors constituting the alleged offenses. Instead, he claimed he had mental health problems that had become progressively worse since the late 1980s. When asked about specific symptoms, he reported periods of time for which he had no memory. Reportedly, he often gets lost and loses things. He indicated these experiences were more common when he was angry, anxious, or depressed. Despite the apparent severity of these difficulties, he never sought treatment; rather, he "never really worried about it." He did not believe anyone else was aware of his condition.

Mr. G.G. also reported experiencing auditory hallucinations around the time of the alleged offenses. His descriptions of them were rather atypical. He described them as experiences similar to "coming out of a dream." He reiterated hearing both good voices and bad voices at the time. He also said that sometimes these experiences woke him from his sleep.

Opinion regarding sanity

It was my opinion that Mr. G.G. did not have a mental illness at the time of the commission of the alleged offenses. This opinion was based on several factors. His descriptions of memory loss were not consistent with observed behaviors, nor were they consistent with any common mental illness, psychological condition, or known neurocognitive disorder. Further, test data suggested a pattern of feigned psychological symptoms. Finally, the symptoms he reported, even if genuine, would not have meaningfully impacted his ability to understand the nature, quality, or wrongfulness of his behaviors.

There were significant indications that he understood the nature, quality, and wrongfulness of the alleged actions. First, it was noteworthy that the marijuana plants that he allegedly cultivated were concealed in a barn. Investigative materials indicated a rather elaborate set-up, which included irrigation and artificial lighting for the plants, as opposed to growing the plants outside (it was a part of the country where such plants would grow well outside). Such efforts to conceal the operation suggested an awareness of its criminal nature. According to the DEA Special Agent, Mr. G.G.'s video camera was also well concealed among other electronic components in his home, yet was positioned to record events in the room. The DEA agent surmised that Mr. G.G. was able to videotape sexual activities without the knowledge of the other party. The fact that the camera was concealed also suggested an acute awareness of the nature and quality of his actions. The contention that he was aware of the wrongfulness of his behaviors was further supported by the fact he was found to possess false identification documents, which could be used to conceal his true identity.

Finally, statements that Mr. G.G. made during an interview with the DEA agent indicated his awareness of the wrongfulness of his actions. According to a report following an interview with Mr. G.G., "When asked about having sex with children, Mr. G.G. stated that he had made a big mistake doing that, but the little girl on the video was asleep and never knew it happened." When the DEA agent further questioned Mr. G.G. about sex with children, he said he "had messed with that one little girl and the rest were grown." During that interview, Mr. G.G. also inquired about "what would happen to him." Such statements indicated an awareness of the wrongfulness of those actions and appropriate concern about potential consequences.

Based on the above information, it was my opinion that at the time of the commission of the acts constituting the alleged offense, Mr. G.G. did not suffer from a severe mental disease or defect, and he would have been able to appreciate the nature, quality, and wrongfulness of his acts.

CASE OUTCOME

I was never called to testify in this case, and I never heard anything else about the matter until, in preparation for this chapter, I contacted the Assistant U.S. Attorney involved on the case. The defense apparently could not find a mental health professional willing to opine regarding his mental status, and no mental health reports were offered by the defense. The judge found Mr. G.G. competent to proceed as a result of my report, and the defendant had a miraculous *recovery*. Mr. G.G. then fired his attorney. The defendant's wife (from whom he had been separated for several years) hired an excellent lawyer who knew the local law well. The defense then moved to suppress all evidence (federal as well as state) due to the fact that state law enforcement officials had seized items beyond the scope of the initial warrant. The initial warrant had been federal and for the purpose of identifying the marijuana production. Information acquired during a search after the DEA agent departed with the defendant in custody included the video camera and tapes documenting illegal sexual activity and child pornography.

The judge suppressed all the evidence of the search, even though the case law suggested the only evidence needing suppression was that seized by local law enforcement that was considered "over-broad." The defense then moved to dismiss the case against Mr. G.G., and the judge asked the government why this relief should not be granted, as the government could surely not win at trial with all the suppressed evidence. The Assistant U.S. Attorney told the defense lawyer and judge, "You can suppress the evidence, your Honor . . . but you can't suppress the people—I intend to call several victims to the stand to testify about the defendant's abuse and drug activities." The testimony of these individuals would address the time before the seizures and, therefore, was not subject to the court's suppression order. The defense then sought to enter a plea of guilty to the state charges and did so for a 10-year sentence. The federal charges were dropped. The defendant completed the state sentence and is now living outside the country.

This case exemplifies several important issues regarding providing neuropsychological services in forensic settings. Under the best of circumstances, neuropsychological evaluations are complicated endeavors. This case was diagnostically complicated due to the combination of neurocognitive and psychiatric concerns. It was also complicated by the need to understand how Mr. G.G.'s condition relates to multiple legal standards. The complexity increases exponentially over standard clinical practice given the various assumptions, roles, alliances, and methods inherent in forensic practice (Denney & Wynkoop, 2000; Goldstein, 2003; Greenberg & Shuman, 1997; Heilbrun, 2001). In relation to the complex diagnostic situation, the case demonstrates that competent clinical neuropsychologists can miss what turned out to be even the most extreme exaggeration if response bias, exaggeration, and malingering are not assessed systematically. Multiple measures designed to identify negative response bias were used in this evaluation, but even reviewing the embedded validity indices within standard neuropsychological tests should have raised some concerns about the veracity of Mr. G.G.'s condition. Lastly, the case demonstrates the use of a multi-method, multidimensional assessment for the detection of negative response bias, a method that research has found can increase sensitivity without decreasing specificity (Iverson & Binder, 2000; Larrabee, 2003a, 2003b; Meyers & Volbrecht, 2002; Nies & Sweet, 1994; Slick et al., 1999).

ACKNOWLEDGMENTS

Opinions expressed in this chapter are those of the author and do not necessarily represent the position of the Federal Bureau of Prisons or the U.S. Department of Justice. The author also acknowledges the assistance of Richart DeMier, Ph.D., ABPP, in the evaluation of this particular criminal defendant.

REFERENCES

Adatto, C. P. (1949). Observations on criminal patients during narcoanalysis. *Archives of Neurology and Psychiatry*, *62*, 82–92.

Bradford, J. W., & Smith, S. M. (1979). Amnesia and homicide: The Padola case and a study of thirty cases. *Bulletin of the American Academy of Psychiatry and Law*, *7*, 219–231.

Brown, L., Sherbenou, R. J., & Johnsen, S. K. (1990). *Test of Nonverbal Intelligence–2nd ed.* Austin, TX: Pro-Ed.

Butcher, J., Graham, J., Dahlstrom, W., Tellegen, A., & Kaemmer, B. (1989). *Minnesota Multiphasic Personality Inventory-2: Manual for administration and scoring*. Minneapolis, MN: University of Minnesota Press.

Denney, R. L. (1996). Symptom validity testing of remote memory in a criminal forensic setting. *Archives of Clinical Neuropsychology*, *11*, 589–603.

Denney, R. L. (2005a). Criminal forensic neuropsychology and assessment of competency. In G. J. Larrabee (Ed.), *Forensic neuropsychology: A scientific approach* (pp. 378–424). New York: Oxford University Press.

Denney, R. L. (2005b). Criminal responsibility and other criminal forensic issues. In G. J. Larrabee (Ed.), *Forensic neuropsychology: A scientific approach* (pp. 425–465). New York: Oxford University Press.

Denney, R. L., & Wynkoop. T. F. (2000). Clinical neuropsychology in the criminal forensic setting. *Journal of Head Trauma Rehabilitation*, *15*, 804–828.

Forrest, T. J., Allen, D. N., & Goldstein, G. (2004). Malingering indexes for the Halstead Category Test. *The Clinical Neuropsychologist*, *18*, 334–347.

Frederick, R. I. (2002a). A review of Rey's strategies for detecting malingered neuropsychological impairment. In J. Hom & R. L. Denney (Eds.), *Detection of response bias in forensic neuropsychology* (pp. 1–25). New York: Haworth.

Frederick, R. I. (2002b). *Validity indicator profile manual*, 2nd ed. Minnetonka, MN: NCS/Pearson Assessments.

Frederick, R. I., Carter, M., & Powel, J. (1995). Adapting symptom validity testing to evaluate suspicious complaints of amnesia in medicolegal evaluations. *Bulletin of the American Academy of Psychiatry and Law*, *23*, 227–233.

Frederick, R. I., & Foster, H. G. (1991). Multiple measures of malingering on a forced-choice test of cognitive ability. *Psychological Assessment*, *3*, 596–602.

Goldstein, A. M. (2003). Overview of forensic psychology. In I. B. Weiner (Series Ed.) & A. M. Goldstein (Vol. Ed.), *Handbook of psychology: Vol. 11. Forensic psychology* (pp. 3–20). Hoboken, NJ: Wiley.

Greenberg, S. A., & Shuman, D. W. (1997). Irreconcilable conflict between therapeutic and forensic roles. *Professional Psychology: Research and Practice*, *28*, 50–57.

Greiffenstein, M. F., Baker, W. J., & Gola, T. (1994). Validation of malingered amnesia measures with a large clinical sample. *Psychological Assessment*, *6*, 218–224.

Guilmette T. J., Hart, K. J., Giuliano, A. J., & Leininger, B. E. (1994). Detecting simulated memory impairment: Comparison of the Rey Fifteen-Item Test and the Hiscock Forced-Choice Procedure. *Clinical Neuropsychologist*, *8*, 283–294.

Guttmacher, M. S. (1955). *Psychiatry and the law*. New York: Grune & Stratton.

Heaton, R. K., Smith, H. H., Lehman, R. A., & Vogt, A. T. (1978). Prospects for faking believable deficits on neuropsychological testing. *Journal of Consulting and Clinical Psychology*, *46*, 892–900.

Heilbrun, K. (2001). *Principles of forensic mental health assessment*. New York: Kluwer Academic/Plenum Publishers.

Hopwood, J. S., & Snell, H. K. (1933). Amnesia in relation to crime. *Journal of Mental Science*, *79*, 27–41.

Iverson, G., & Binder, L. (2000). Detecting exaggeration and malingering in neuropsychological assessment. *Journal of Head Trauma Rehabilitation*, *15*, 829–858.

Larrabee, G. J. (2003a). Detection of symptom exaggeration with the MMPI–2 in litigants with malingered neurocognitive dysfunction. *The Clinical Neuropsychologist*, *17*, 54–68.

Larrabee, G. J. (2003b). Detection of malingering using atypical performance patterns on standard neuropsychological tests. *The Clinical Neuropsychologist*, *17*, 410–425.

Lees-Haley, P. R. (1992). Efficacy of MMPI–2 validity scales and MCMI-II modifier scales for detecting spurious PTSD claims: F, F–K, Fake Bad scale, Ego Strength, Subtle-Obvious subscales, DIS and DEB. *Journal of Clinical Psychology*, *48*, 681–689.

Leitch, A. (1948). Notes on amnesia in crime for the general practitioner. *Medical Press, 219,* 459–463.

Lynch, B. E., & Bradford, J. M. W. (1980). Amnesia: Its detection by psychophysiological measures. *Bulletin of the American Academy of Psychiatry and the Law, 8,* 288–297.

Martell, D. A. (1992). Forensic neuropsychology and the criminal law. *Law and Human Behavior, 16,* 313–336.

Mathias, C. W., Greve, K. W., Bianchini, K. J., Houston, R. J., & Crouch, J. A. (2002). Detecting malingered neurocognitive dysfunction using the reliable digit span in traumatic brain injury. *Assessment, 9,* 301–308.

Melton, G. B., Petrila, J., Poythress, N. G., & Slobogin, C. (1997). *Psychological Evaluations for the Courts,* 2nd ed. New York: Guilford.

Meyers, J. E., & Volbrecht, M. (2002). A validation of multiple malingering detection methods in a large clinical sample. *Archives of Clinical Neuropsychology, 18,* 261–276.

Mittenberg, W., Aguila-Puentes, G., Patton, C., Canyock, E. M., & Heilbronner, R. L. (2002). Neuropsychological profiling of symptom exaggeration and malingering. In J. Hom & R. L. Denney (Eds.) *Detection of response bias in forensic neuropsychology* (pp. 227–240). New York: Haworth Press.

Mittenberg, W., Azrin, R., Millsaps, C., & Heilbronner, R. (1993). Identification of malingered head injury on the Wechsler Memory Scale–Revised. *Psychological Assessment, 5,* 34–40.

Mittenberg, W., Rotholc, A., Russell, E., & Heilbronner, R. (1996). Identification of malingered head injury on the Halstead-Reitan Battery. *Archives of Clinical Neuropsychology, 11,* 271–281.

Mittenberg, W., Theroux, S., Zielinski, R. E., & Heilbronner, R. L. (1995). Identification of malingered head injury on the Wechsler Adult Intelligence Scale–Revised. *Professional Psychology: Research and Practice, 26,* 491–498.

Nies, K. J., & Sweet, J. J. (1994). Neuropsychological assessment and malingering: A critical review of past and present strategies. *Archives of Clinical Neuropsychology, 9,* 501–552.

O'Connell, B. A. (1960). Amnesia and homicide. *British Journal of Delinquency, 10,* 262–276.

Parwatikar, S. D., Holcomb, W. R., & Menninger, K. A., II. (1985). The detection of malingered amnesia in accused murderers. *Bulletin of the American Academy of Psychiatry and the Law, 13,* 97–103.

Power, D. J. (1977). Memory, identification and crime. *Medicine, Science, and the Law, 17,* 132–139.

Price, G. E., & Terhune, W. B. (1919). Feigned amnesia as a defense reaction. *Journal of the American Medical Association, 72,* 565–567.

Reitan, R. M., & Wolfson, D. (1993). *The Halstead-Reitan Neuropsychological Test Battery–2nd ed.* Tucson, AZ: Neuropsychology Press.

Rey, A. (1958). *L'examen clinique en psychologie* [The psychological examination]. Paris: Presses Universitaires de France.

Rogers, R., Bagby, R. M., & Dickens, S. E. (1992). *SIRS Structured Interview of Reported Symptoms: A professional manual.* Odessa, FL: Psychological Assessment Resources.

Schacter, D. L. (1986). Amnesia and crime: How much do we really know? *American Psychologist, 41,* 286–295.

Shapiro, D. L. (1984). *Psychological evaluation and expert testimony: A practical guide to forensic work.* New York: Van Nostrand Reinhold Co.

Shapiro, D. L. (1991). *Forensic psychological assessment: An integrative approach.* Boston, MA: Allyn & Bacon.

Slick, D. J., Sherman, E. M. S., & Iverson, G. L. (1999). Diagnostic criteria for malingered neurocognitive dysfunction: Proposed standards for clinical practice and research. *The Clinical Neuropsychologist, 13,* 545–561.

Sweet, J. J., & King, J. H. (2002). Category Test validity indicators: Overview and practice recommendations. In J. Hom & R. L. Denney (Eds.), *Detection of response bias in forensic neuropsychology* (pp. 241–274). New York: Haworth.

Taylor, P. J., & Kopelman, M. D. (1984). Amnesia for criminal offences. *Psychological Medicine, 14,* 581–588.

Wechsler, D. (1981). *Manual for the Wechsler Adult Intelligence Scale–Revised.* San Antonio, TX: Psychological Corporation.

Wechsler, D. (1987). *Manual for the Wechsler Memory Scale–Revised.* San Antonio, TX: Psychological Corporation.

Wilson v. U.S., 391 F.2d 460 (1968).

Wynkoop, T. F., & Denney, R. L. (1999). Exaggeration of neuropsychological deficit in competency to stand trial. *Journal of Forensic Neuropsychology, 1,* 29–53.

Zachary, R. A. (1986). *Shipley Institute of Living Scale–Revised manual.* Los Angeles, CA: Western Psychological Services.

The malingering incompetent defendant

34

Richard I. Frederick

Sometimes a defendant will be found incompetent who is not. While it is true that the defendant is technically "incompetent," because such designations reflect a legal status, in reality, this sort of defendant can pretend to be not competent and be declared incompetent in error.

There are many obvious reasons for malingering to be undetected at the initial evaluation. First, the amount of evidence of incompetency that needs to be demonstrated to result in a finding of "incompetent" is minimal. Generally, in light of the Supreme Court decision in *Cooper v. Oklahoma* (1996), most courts and jurisdictions have a preponderance standard, in which there simply needs to be more evidence that the defendant is incompetent than competent. Any deviations from this standard within a state are in the direction of protection for the defendant. Bobby Frank Cherry, ultimately convicted as one of the four Klansmen who bombed a church in Birmingham, Alabama, was initially found incompetent even though there was good evidence he was suppressing his true cognitive abilities and feigning memory problems. The Alabama competency standard at that time was "clear and convincing," which means that the prosecution had to demonstrate by "clear and convincing" evidence that the defendant was competent. After a period of inpatient hospitalization, the evidence presented by the hospital staff that he was faking was considered to surpass that standard. He was found competent and sent to trial.

Second, many prosecutors are quite willing to have defendants found incompetent. The percentage of cases in which patients are not helped by hospitalization, especially for individuals with psychosis, is generally low. Persons who are not restored to competency are likely to have had a bona fide mental health defense; hence the risk to prosecutors of failing to prosecute a malingerer is generally low. Consequently, when there is an evaluation by the defense that indicates incompetency, and the prosecutor does not suspect obvious faking, the finding may go unchallenged at a competency hearing, and given the legal standards described above, the finding of incompetency is rather routine. This case involves a defendant in which the defense evaluation went unchallenged.

Third, as in this case, in which the defense experts were well known and well regarded, there may be little benefit in a prosecution challenge, because the methodology of discovering malingering may often be no more than one professional stating, "He is faking," and another stating, "He is not." This defendant was feigning amnesia, continuing memory problems, and cognitive insufficiency. When I first met the defendant, I had an immediate and strong sense that he was faking. Had I immediately returned the defendant to court with a finding, "I'm sure he is faking," the court would have faced the prospect of determining which experts had more credibility. Given additionally that it would have been "one psychiatrist and one psychologist" (both with nationally recognized abilities) vs. "one psychologist" from rural Missouri, the outcome would not have been difficult to predict. What was needed was evidence to sustain a finding of malingering, and the period of hospitalization made it possible to develop that evidence. As in the Cherry case, the prosecution usually benefits from an increased opportunity for observation and documentation of everyday abilities when a person found to be incompetent is hospitalized. In this case, the evidence that the person was malingering was established by more than observation of daily behavior.

THE CASE OF MR. H.H.

Mr. H.H. was a 53-year-old divorced white male. He was charged with committing four bank robberies. There was good evidence that Mr. H.H. had committed the bank robberies. The evidence included fingerprints on the teller counters and the demand notes, eyewitness identification from bank employees, and his being in possession of some of the stolen money. A co-defendant was arrested, and he later told the prosecution (in making a plea) that Mr. H.H. was going to fake amnesia in order to avoid prosecution. Although no federal jurisdiction recognizes amnesia as a routine basis for incompetency, bona fide amnesia does potentially interfere with the defendant's capacity to assist attorney, primarily by impinging on the defendant's capacity to explain the behavior that is being prosecuted. Not only did Mr. H.H. claim total amnesia for the bank robberies, he claimed poor memory for most of his adult life.

Mr. H.H. had been incarcerated a number of times, with a 30-year period of criminal activity, including burglary, fraud, forgery, larceny, various drug possession charges, assault, and bond jumping. Mr. H.H. severely abused intoxicating drugs, particularly cocaine and alcohol, throughout his adulthood. About 15 years prior to his arrest for these bank robberies, Mr. H.H. had been living in a federal halfway house, completing a sentence for another crime. He was a heavy user of cocaine, and he was brought to the emergency room in cardiovascular arrest, apparently having gone into arrest after using cocaine intravenously. He was comatose and apparently suffered an episode in which his brain was deprived of oxygen. He was transferred to the U.S. Medical Center, and remained there for six months. Nursing and medical progress notes indicate that he was profoundly confused, speech impaired, and impaired in motor skills on admission. He demonstrated a steadily improving course over the next few months. He reported severe memory impairment for remote and recent events, but reported in a neurological evaluation four months after admission that his memory was improving. At that time, a neurological examination did not reveal any neuropathology. All neurological signs were normal. Follow-up CT scan was normal. The neurologist concluded: "His general demeanor and behavior suggested that maybe he is not as impaired in his mental faculties as he would have us believe." A consulting psychologist noted five months after admission: "Patient appears to have exhibited some improvement in intellectual functioning in the past three months."

After this anoxic event, Mr. H.H. continually called attention to his putative cognitive impairment to try to forestall prosecutions against him and to seek disability payments. These efforts received some moderate success. At the initial competency evaluation for this prosecution, the psychiatrist retained by the defense noted that previous radiographic and electroencephalographic tests conducted with Mr. H.H. after his drug overdose had been normal. Nevertheless, the psychiatrist cited poor performance on psychological tests and deficits demonstrated in clinical interview to conclude that Mr. H.H. had "severe impairments" that precluded competency to stand trial. In the concurrent evaluation, the psychologist concluded that Mr. H.H. manifested severe impairment on an intelligence test. He further concluded that there was no evidence of malingering on testing, because the "consistency of [his subnormal] scores makes the likelihood of malingering virtually impossible."

The test scores referred to included these three performances on the Wechsler scales:

1. Four months post-event FSIQ = 64; VIQ = 74; PIQ = 55
2. Three years post-event FSIQ = 68; VIQ = 77; PIQ = 60
3. Defense competency exam FSIQ = 65; VIQ = 75; PIQ = 59

The first two testings were with the WAIS–R; the third was with the WAIS–III. The psychologist concluded that his manifested impairments were real and reflected serious mental deficiency, including mild mental retardation and other organic brain disorders. Based on their belief that his impairments were real, they concluded that he was incompetent to stand trial. The claim was undisputed by the prosecution. The judge determined he was incompetent and committed him to the U.S. Medical Center for a four-month commitment.

Upon admission, Mr. H.H. immediately called attention to his claims of amnesia. He said he had "longstanding" memory problems. In my initial discussions with him, he demonstrated great interest in the potential outcomes of his admission here. When I told him that individuals found permanently incompetent were subject to review for the necessity of indefinite commitment, he was quite taken aback. It was obvious that he was able to retain information because his early involvement with a psychoeducational group devoted to teaching incompetent defendants about the courts was devoted to his initiating discussions about this potential indefinite commitment. He persistently insisted in the group that he could not be found competent because of his amnesia. Mr. H.H. demonstrated a good capacity to remember relevant information during his admission. He was allowed to go throughout this large and complex institution without escort. He never required assistance making his way to areas that offered programs he was interested in. He was never cited for failure to follow the rules. He ordered commissary items for his own use, which requires that he solicit funds from family members or friends outside the prison and manage his own commissary account.

In contrast to these obvious elements of a sound working memory, Mr. H.H. often presented in individual contacts with me in a feeble-minded manner, claiming not to remember my name, my position, his reason for being here, or what could happen to him. Consequently, our early interactions were replays of our initial discussion about his placement here. When asked to complete psychological testing, he also presented as mentally impaired. He was tested on a number of occasions throughout his four-month admission and always presented as if he did not recall having been tested before. As time went by, the dramatic nature of his presentation moderated, and he would often greet me by name as we passed in the hallways. Nevertheless, he persisted until the end of his admission in claims that he could recall practically nothing of the events of his adult life. He always claimed that he had no knowledge of the charges against him or any recall of participating in the alleged events. No problems were noted on neurological examination except the claim for lack of memory and the representation of limited intellectual functioning. The neurologist declined to pursue radiographic examinations.

The psychological testing by the defense psychologist included a Rey 15-Item Test (Rey) and a California Verbal Learning Test (CVLT). On the Rey, Mr. H.H. recalled 12 items in four rows. On the CVLT, he recalled two words from the first presentation of the list and four words from the fifth presentation of the list. The psychologist noted the Rey was evidence of compliance, and the CVLT performance was indicative of cognitive impairment.

At this facility, Mr. H.H. recalled 10 items on the Rey. He completed only one object in the figure line. He recalled three items on the first trial of the Rey Auditory Verbal Learning Test (AVLT) and recalled six items on the fifth trial.

These performances on the first and last trials of 15- or 16-word lists for memorization are certainly consistent with malingering and inconsistent with significant bona fide impairment (e.g., see Greiffenstein, Baker, & Gola, 1996). The performances on the Rey are noteworthy. Although this test is generally considered a poor indicator for malingering, unusual performances are worthy of reflection. It seems noteworthy that he could not complete the row of figures when he already had done so in a recent test. It is difficult to generate a plausible reason for his poorer second performance.

Mr. H.H. was administered the Shipley Institute of Living Scale (Shipley) and the Test of Nonverbal Intelligence–2nd edition (TONI–2; Brown, Sherbenou, & Johnsen, 1982). Both of these tests are substandard for the purpose of evaluating intellectual abilities, but they provide some useful information about how the defendant intends to represent his abilities. Furthermore, they provide some useful comparisons with the Validity Indicator Profile (VIP; Frederick, 1997, 2003), which has the same nonverbal items as the TONI–2 and has a word-choice subtest that is similar to the word-choice subtest of the Shipley.

On the Shipley, Mr. H.H.'s performance generated a WAIS–R estimate of 66, with a T score for the word-choice subtest of 27. On the TONI–2, he correctly completed all items rated at the "5–7 years old" range and only one item at the "8–9 years old" range. His WAIS–R estimate for performance was 69. These scores are consistent with the performances noted earlier. A review of records did not support the performance on the Shipley. For example, a Bureau of Prison's request to staff, written one-year post-anoxic event reads:

> To Dentist. Dear Sir, My impressions were taken over a month ago. My diet has been suffering and my gums are beginning to ache something terrible. Please see if I can be helped. Need my dental plates as soon as possible. I would appreciate it "very" much.

Of course, this sentence construction and appropriate spelling would seem to be well beyond the capacity of someone who routinely scores about 2 standard deviations below the mean on verbal ability tests.

The MMPI–2 was administered twice, by audiotape. (On no occasion of repeat testing was Mr. H.H. informed that a test was going to be repeated. He was simply presented with, "I'd like for you to do some testing." He never volunteered that he had already taken the test.) The score of primary interest on these tests was VRIN, a measure of the consistency of response. In the first testing, his VRIN was 11, which is considered "markedly inconsistent," but interpretable. |F – Fb| was equal to 1, which supports the conclusion that he understood the test items sufficiently to allow interpretation. (Clinical elevations on scales 7 and 2.) In the second testing, three months later, his VRIN was equal to 5, a much more confident finding that he understood the test items, and a contradiction to his performance on verbal subtests. (Clinical elevation on scales 7 and 4.)

The nonverbal subtest of the VIP was administered four times. The verbal subtest was administered three times.

The nonverbal subtest of the VIP comprises 100 items from forms A and B of the TONI–2 (Frederick & Crosby, 2000). The TONI–2 has 10 other items that are designed for individuals with very superior intelligence. TONI–2 test items have 4–6 answer choices to choose among; the VIP has only two answer choices to choose between. Mr. H.H. answered the five easiest items on the TONI–2 Form A correctly. Because Forms A and B have equivalent difficulty, we can safely assume, if the TONI–2 performance was valid, that he could solve the 10 easiest TONI–2 items and, hence, the 10 easiest items on the VIP nonverbal subtest. Out of the 90 remaining VIP items, we could expect him to answer about 50% correct, for a total score of about 55 (10 + 45). Mr. H.H. received a score of 51, which is not significantly different from 55. However, the VIP generates a performance curve, which shows the progression of performance as a function of item difficulty (Frederick, Crosby, & Wynkoop, 2000). The items on the VIP are administered randomly with respect to difficulty and the test taker is required to choose an answer for all items. Consequently, it is useful to view the progression of correct responses by difficulty. In Mr. H.H.'s case, it is evident that his performance was no different than guessing through the entire range of difficulty.

A review of Mr. H.H.'s responses shows that he answered 7 of the 10 easiest items correctly, which is consistent with the performance level expected for mild mental retardation (M = 7.7, SD = 2.1). In the VIP validation sample, the average number of total correct responses for individuals with mental retardation was 57 (M = 56.7, SD = 8.3). Therefore, if we are expected to believe this performance, we must consider that he really has mental retardation. Given the prospect that he appears to have completed four bank robberies with fairly good skill, given his other extensive criminal background, given his writing skills, and given his capacity for living effectively in the prison, this seems rather unlikely. The VIP nonverbal subtest was repeated in a couple of days. On this second administration of the test, his total score was 59. This score is not significantly different

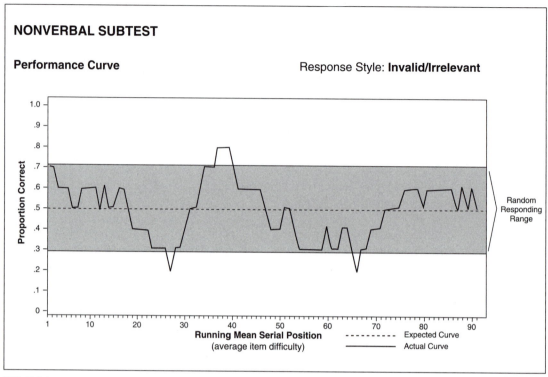

FIG. 34.1

from 55, either. But in this second test, he answered most of the easiest 30 items correctly. This is certainly substantially better than his first performance. The VIP classification for this performance was "Inconsistent." This classification has a typical interpretation of representing compromised effort, suggesting that he would have performed even better with greater cooperation.

The VIP nonverbal subtest was repeated a couple months later. This time, he scored only 45. Even though he was making some effort to answer the easiest items correctly, the classification of Inconsistent indicates that his effort was compromised, which is confirmed by a comparison with the second test.

The fourth nonverbal subtest was administered just prior to his return to court. His total score of 51, the "Irrelevant" classification, and the flat performance curve all contribute to a conclusion that he answered the test items without consideration of the content.

The first administration of the VIP verbal subtest was at the time of the first VIP nonverbal administration. The 78 items of the verbal VIP comprise a hierarchy of difficulty from very easy to extremely difficult. *The items have a word that means the same as two other words (one correct, one incorrect).* The items are presented randomly without respect to difficulty. On the first administration, Mr. H.H. earned a score of 57. The mean score for mentally retarded individuals in the validation sample was 46 (SD = 7). So, his score is about 2 standard deviations better than persons with mental retardation. The VIP estimates verbal ability range based on the number of correct responses and based on certain features of the performance curve. The VIP estimated his range of verbal ability to be at least low average to average, which is certainly a great deal higher than his performance on the Shipley (T score = 27), a test with comparable word choice tasks.

His performance curve reveals that he answered most of the 50 easiest words correctly. The classification of Valid/Compliant indicates that there is good evidence he intended to answer correctly and that he exerted sustained effort in order to answer correctly.

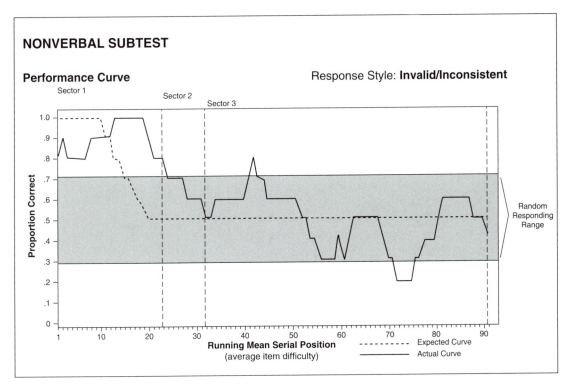

FIG. 34.2

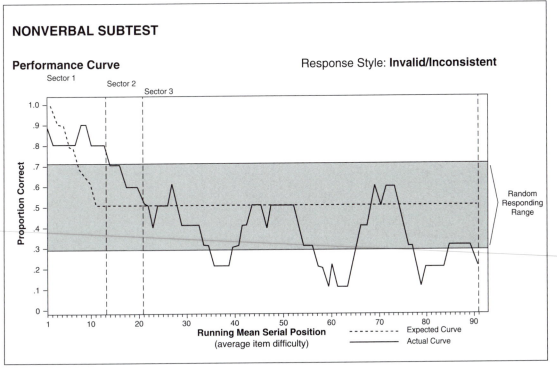

FIG. 34.3

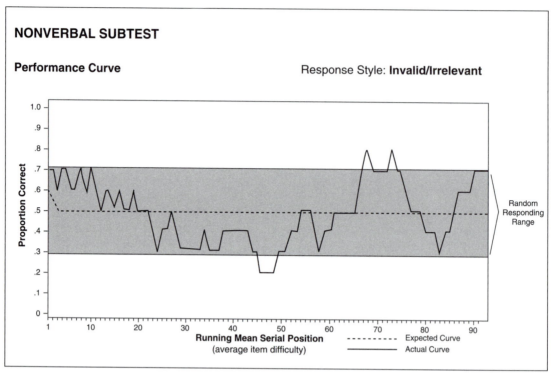

FIG. 34.4

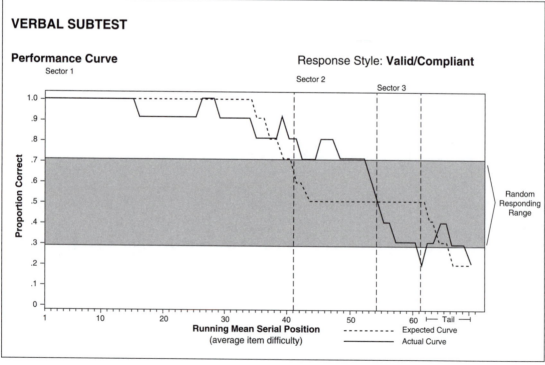

FIG. 34.5

The primary interpretation from the VIP to this point is that he attempts a variety of strategies when completing testing to the extent that testing should not be considered a valid means of concluding that his abilities are subnormal. As in the case of this verbal VIP performance, we can make conclusions that his verbal abilities are well above the level of persons with mental retardation and most likely greater than "borderline retarded." Furthermore, in comparison to the nonverbal VIP administered at the same time, we support our conclusion that it represents lack of intention to answer correctly, because it does not generally make sense that a person with no obvious brain injury would have near normal verbal abilities and be incapable of solving items that most young children could answer correctly. And, of course, his performances on two other nonverbal VIPs make that evident. If the performances had been switched, and he demonstrated near normal ability on the nonverbal subtest, but random responding on the verbal subtest, other explanations are possible and require exploration. Many defendants with normal intellectual capacity are undereducated and have poor reading skills.

The other two verbal VIP performances were classified as "Inconsistent," as he failed to exert the same effort he did on the first test. In the second administration, his total score was actually higher, but it is evident that he failed to sustain effort for the more difficult words.

An overview of testing to this point indicates that we cannot believe his representations of impairment in memory, verbal ability, or reasoning capacity. As just noted, this provides a good basis to reject testing as the method for primarily assessing abilities and focusing more on observable daily behavior and records of other activities. In the case of Mr. H.H., this included records of past criminal activities and reports of apparent excellent planning and execution of bank robbery in the instant offenses. Clinicians should tread carefully before heavily relying on alleged criminal activity to make estimations about ability, but with the uncooperative defendant, it may be useful to cite witness and police reports. In doing so, the clinician should overtly cite this as alleged information and allow the defense attorney the opportunity to dispute the alleged information as a basis for estimation.

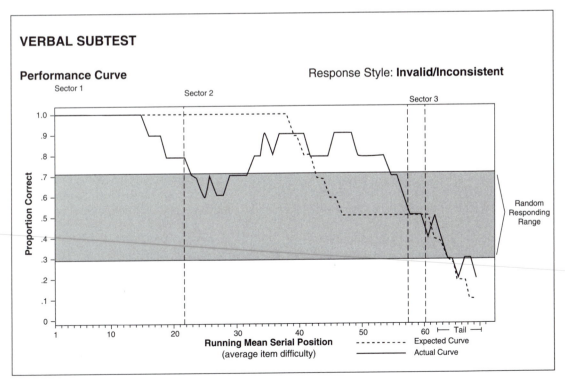

FIG. 34.6

Mr. H.H.'s primary basis for being found incompetent was amnesia. At this point in the assessment, I felt fairly confident that he had sufficient cognitive capacities to understand the nature and potential consequences of the prosecution against him. I also believed that he had no amnesia and could assist his attorney. I could demonstrate poor performance on memory tests as a basis for malingering and argue that this should make the court highly suspicious of claims of amnesia. However, this would have provided poor and disputable evidence. Given the willingness of Mr. H.H. to invest energy into malingering his presentation (as I saw it), I decided to directly assess his claims of amnesia through a process first reported in 1993 (Frederick & Carter, 1993) and published in 1995 (Frederick, Carter, & Powel, 1995). The procedure is based on the forced-choice paradigm championed by Pankratz (1979) and adapted to a variety of modalities, most commonly as a digit memory test. Denney (1996) and Frederick and Denney (1998) have published comments and cautions about this technique.

The procedure requires that the examiner identify a domain of information that the defendant claims to be unable to remember. In this case, Mr. H.H. claimed to be unable to recall the facts of the case (as laid out by the prosecution) and many biographical details. It is important to define what it is being investigated, because investigating whether the defendant recalls engaging in the crime is outside the purview of the forensic examiner. In this case, I developed 72 possible questions based on information he said he did not know when interviewed. For example, the first question was "You are alleged to have committed how many bank robberies?" Another question was "What is your phone number?"

Mr. H.H. was asked the questions and asked to answer them. If he said he could not or if he provided a wrong answer, he was presented with the correct answer and a plausible alternative. Positions of correct and incorrect choices were randomly assigned. Questions were ordered so that information from a prior question would not suggest the answer to a later question. Mr. H.H. gave the correct answer on nine occasions when asked the question (no alternatives presented). Those questions were discarded. On the remaining 63 questions, he either gave an incorrect answer or said he did not know the answer. On those occasions, he was directed to choose between the alternatives presented to him. For example, for the question, "How much money do the authorities say was taken from the bank?" he said he did not know and was presented with the choices: "Approximately $6000" or "Approximately $1400"? He chose the incorrect answer.

Out of the 63 items for which he claimed not to know the correct answer, he was given two alternatives, and he chose correctly between them 12 times. It is easy to compute a Z-score for this performance. The expected score is one-half the items presented, or 31.5. The score we use for comparison is 12.5, because we are obtaining a Z-score under the assumption that scores are continuous, and they are not. Increasing or decreasing the score one-half point *toward* the mean corrects for this lack of continuity (Siegel, 1956). The standard deviation for guessing for this number of items is given by the square root of Npq, where N is 63, the number of items, p is 0.5, the probability of correctly guessing the answer, and q is 0.5, the probability of incorrectly guessing the answer. Therefore, the Z-score for Mr. H.H.'s performance is −4.79. Using a two-tailed test, we are able to inform the court that this performance would be observed once for every 1.2 million times in which a person was truly guessing.

Because we obviously conclude that such performances are not the result of chance, I further concluded that Mr. H.H. had produced the score by intentionally answering incorrectly. Additionally, I assumed that he had not intentionally answered *all* the items incorrectly as a strategy to avoid appearing "too obvious." Anticipating a question by the defense to the effect, "Doctor, isn't it possible that he knows some answers but still has some amnesia?," I further informed the court that Mr. H.H. most likely knew the answers to at least 39 items (nearly 2/3 of the items). The correction for guessing in two-alternative tasks is "right minus wrong" (Cronbach, 1991). Here, we take the absolute value of (12 − 51) to get 39. We construe this to mean that under the circumstances in which he actually took a strategy to incorrectly answer *all* the questions that he knew the correct answer to and to guess on all others, he would incorrectly answer those 39 items. Out of the 24 questions he would not know, under these circumstances, the expected score for guessing would be 12, his score. It would not be difficult for the court to understand that he knew the answers to most of these items.

Having eliminated the last prospect for bona fide incompetency, I informed the court that Mr. H.H. was malingering and competent. Although defense counsel challenged my testimony for about 30 minutes, the two prior experts did not appear. Mr. H.H. was found competent to stand trial. After the hearing, he decided to make a plea.

REFERENCES

Brown, L., Sherbenou, R. J., & Johnsen, S. K. (1982). *Test of nonverbal intelligence: A language-free measure of cognitive ability*. Austin, TX: Pro-Ed.

Cooper v. Oklahoma, 517 U.S. 348 (1996).

Cronbach, L. J. (1990). *Essentials of psychological testing*, 5th ed. New York: HarperCollins.

Denney, R. L. (1996). Symptom validity testing of remote memory in a criminal forensic setting. *Archives of Clinical Neuropsychology, 11*, 589–603.

Frederick, R. I. (1997). *Validity Indicator Profile*. Minnetonka, MN: NCS Assessments.

Frederick, R. I. (2003). *Validity Indicator Profile*. Bloomington, MN: NCS Pearson, Inc.

Frederick, R. I., & Carter, M. (1993, August). *Detection of malingered amnesia in a competency evaluee*. Paper presented at the Annual Convention of the American Psychological Association, Toronto, Canada.

Frederick, R. I., Carter, M., & Powel, J. (1995). Adapting symptom validity testing to evaluate suspicious complaints of amnesia in medicolegal evaluations. *Bulletin of American Academy of Psychiatry and Law, 23*, 231–237.

Frederick, R. I., & Crosby, R. D. (2000). Development and validation of the Validity Indicator Profile, *Law and Human Behavior, 24*, 59–82.

Frederick, R. I., Crosby, R. D., & Wynkoop, T. F. (2000). Performance curve classification of invalid responding on the Validity Indicator Profile. *Archives of Clinical Neuropsychology, 15*, 281–300.

Frederick, R. I., & Denney, R. L. (1998). Minding your "p's" and "q's" when conducting forced-choice recognition tests. *The Clinical Neuropsychologist, 12*, 193–205.

Greiffenstein, M. F., Baker, W. J., & Gola, T. (1994). Validation of malingered amnesia measures with a large clinical sample. *Psychological Assessment, 6*, 218–224.

Pankratz, L. (1979). Symptom validity testing and symptom retraining: Procedures for the assessment and treatment of functional sensory deficits. *Journal of Consulting and Clinical Psychology, 47*, 409–410.

Siegel, S. (1956). *Nonparametric statistics for the behavioral sciences*. New York: McGraw-Hill.

Malingering, mental retardation, and the death penalty

35

Robert L. Heilbronner

This case is notable for a number of reasons, first because it seems to clearly elucidate the differences between an assessment of malingering of cognitive deficits versus psychiatric symptoms, a distinction that is especially important in criminal cases. Second, it is notable because it represents an unusual situation in which the neuropsychological test results actually helped to spare a defendant's life! This occurrence is rare in forensic settings, even less common than its infrequent occurrence in an acute neurosurgical context.

In March 2003, I presented a talk entitled, "The importance of neuropsychological evidence in capital cases" at the National Legal Aide and Defender Association (NLADA) "Life in the Balance" seminar in Memphis, Tennessee. The talk was fairly well attended, largely by mitigation specialists and public defenders who are on the front lines representing defendants who are facing the death penalty. At the evening reception, I met a social worker from a city in the northwestern part of the U.S. who said that she was involved in a murder case in which she suspected that the defendant may have "brain damage" from a history of head injuries and prominent substance abuse; he was also allegedly under the influence of hallucinogens at the time of the murders. She subsequently introduced me to Attorney S., the lead public defender on the case. He described the case in greater detail, handed me a copy of a newspaper article (see below) describing the murders, and requested that I forward a copy of my CV and fees to him upon my return to Chicago.

RECENT LEGAL DECISIONS REGARDING MENTAL RETARDATION AND THE DEATH PENALTY

Over the last decade, there has been a shift in public opinion regarding the execution of the mentally retarded: the majority of those surveyed did not favor execution of those with mental retardation (Cunningham & Goldstein, 2003). Two landmark U.S. cases reached differing majority opinions on this issue. In *Penry v. Lynbauch* (1989), the U.S. Supreme Court, in a 5 to 4 vote, reasoned that if defendants were "profoundly or severely retarded and wholly lacking the capacity to appreciate the wrongfulness of their actions," they would most likely avoid conviction using an insanity defense. At the time, there were no constitutional barriers to executing those with mental retardation, but the U.S. Supreme Court wrote: "The sentencing body must be allowed to consider mental retardation as a mitigating circumstance in making individual determination whether death is appropriate in a particular case."

In *Atkins v. Virginia* (2002), the U.S. Supreme Court reversed itself, forbidding execution of the mentally retarded, declaring it to be a violation of the Constitution. They acknowledged a "dramatic shift in state legislature landscape" since the initial *Penry* decision as 16 additional states (beyond the two when *Penry* was decided in 1989) enacted legislation prohibiting the execution of the mentally retarded. The Court reasoned: "Mentally retarded defendants . . . face a special risk of wrongful execution," raising questions of "reliability and fairness of capital proceedings . . . in such cases." States were given the task of establishing "ways to enforce the constitutional restriction upon its execution of sentences." In a dissenting opinion, a concern was expressed that the symptoms associated with mental retardation "can readily be feigned." Yet, the implications of *Atkins v. Virginia* are clear. Defendants in capital cases are likely to raise questions regarding sub-average intellectual functioning, requiring objective evaluations of their intellectual functioning. Post-conviction assessments will be required to assist the courts on ruling on the validity of claims of mental retardation for those on death rows awaiting execution.

FACTS OF THE CASE

An article from the local newspaper best describes the events that transpired and the charges against the defendant:

> On October 17, 2001, local police went to a home at 4300 Bay Ridge after the victims' relatives called, concerned that they hadn't been able to reach them. When the police arrived, they discovered the bodies of two boys, ages 8 and 13. They had suffered massive head injuries from a hammer, and the older one had also been stabbed multiple times. Their mother was found unconscious and so was Mr. I.I. Police said that he was lying in the hallway, foaming at the mouth after apparently downing various prescription medications. The victims' 2-year-old sister escaped injury, after having been placed in a nearby room. Police said that Mr. I.I. and his girlfriend had lived together for seven years but had split up over his alcohol and drug problems. Less than a week before the murders, Mr. I.I. was arrested after being accused of assaulting his girlfriend, and a court had ordered him to stay away from her. Mr. I.I.'s criminal history includes assault convictions and arrests on charges of driving under the influence and possessing crack cocaine. The girlfriend remains in the hospital in critical condition with head injuries. Mr. I.I. has been charged with two counts of Aggravated Murder in the First Degree and one count of Attempted Murder in the First Degree. The prosecution has not yet indicated whether or not they will seek the death penalty.

Upon my return to Chicago after the conference, I emailed Attorney S. a copy of my CV and fees. Three weeks later he emailed me to inform me that the judge had approved his request to have his client evaluated, and we set up a date for the evaluation. I made my airplane reservations, and flew out to the northwest a few weeks later with virtually all of the tests that I keep in my office inside a large piece of luggage. In fact, the baggage screeners were a bit concerned when they saw things like Purdue Pegs, a finger oscillation test, tape recorder, etc. After explaining to them what these instruments are used for and my reasons for traveling out west, they let me pass through (as long as I didn't bring any of the instruments in the cabin with me!). After arriving at my destination, I checked into a hotel near the county jail and read some materials that Attorney S. had provided for me.

PREVIOUS TESTING

A review of the records indicated that Mr. I.I. underwent a neuropsychological evaluation three years earlier in the context of a workers' compensation injury. He worked in construction and reportedly fell 10 feet from the roof of a building, landing on his back and sustaining a right hip contusion, laceration to the lower portion of his right leg, and an alleged concussion/mild traumatic brain injury. Initial Glasgow Coma Scale (GCS) score was 15, and he was noted to be fully alert and oriented in the hospital ER. A post-injury onset of impaired memory and other thinking difficulties were noted, but a history of premorbid learning disability, poor academic achievement, and post-injury depression were all felt to be relevant moderating variables that could affect his test performance. His treating physician diagnosed him with a chronic pain syndrome and moderate to severe depression. Mr. I.I. was off work for six months and received worker's compensation benefits until they were discontinued after three months. The evaluation was requested by the insurance carrier and done by a board-certified neuropsychologist.

Results of cognitive assessment were felt to reflect adequate effort, as measured by his scores on the Rey AVLT (Recognition = 15/16), The Rey 15-Item Test (14/15), and Test of Memory Malingering (TOMM: 44, 49, 50). Basic errors in spelling and arithmetic were noted and felt to be essentially consistent with his history of a long-standing learning disability. In fact, he did not even seem to know the alphabet; this affected his performance on tests like Trail Making B. He did not show any basic perceptual or motor impairment, but several errors on tests of complex attention and those requiring a high level of mental flexibility were noted. Memory was characterized by a normal learning curve and retention on auditory and visual tasks.

Results of personality assessment revealed an invalid MMPI–2 profile (F scale T = 119; FB T = 104). VRIN and TRIN were within normal limits, suggesting that Mr. I.I. probably deliberately over-endorsed pathological items, perhaps as a "cry for help" or an agenda to look bad for purposes of secondary gain. The clinical scale profile was not felt to be interpretable because of this response set. FBS, Fp, MDS, and other indices of effort were not calculated. In contrast to the MMPI–2, Mr. I.I.'s MCMI–II profile suggested only a moderate tendency toward self-depreciation and some over-reporting of pathology, but not to the point of invalidating the clinical scale profile. Yet, this may be secondary to the lack of an empirical validity indicator on this particular inventory. On Axis I, he produced elevated scores on both the Anxiety and Dysthymic Disorder scales. A single Axis II elevation was noted on a scale indicating long-term tendencies toward an inflated self-image and interpersonal exploitation.

It was the prior examining neuropsychologist's impression that Mr. I.I.'s injury history (e.g., the nature of his fall and his recollections, brief PTA) suggested that "he had a minor concussion with very mild cognitive impairment" that appeared to be slowly resolving. This occurred in the context of a history of academic weaknesses and some auditory-verbal processing difficulties consistent with his reported learning disability. With regard to motivational or attitudinal barriers, it was notable that Mr. I.I. was frustrated and angry with his employer. Mr. I.I. believed his employer was exploiting him by not providing the necessary compensation from the work-related accident. His anger was believed to be valid with no clear evidence that it was translating into a "disincentive to be well," although it may be complicating his depression and anxiety. Diagnoses included: Adjustment Disorder with Mixed Emotional Features, Psychological Factors affecting Physical Condition, and Personality Disorder NOS. An Axis V GAF of 65 was assigned. It was felt that Mr. I.I.'s Adjustment Disorder was "causally related to his industrial injury" and that he would require a combination of antidepressant medication and psychotherapy in order to promote his capacity to return to work.

On the day of the examination, I went to the jail at 7:30 a.m. to check in. I was met there by Attorney S. and Attorney C., another public defender who was not involved in the mitigation aspects of the case but was involved in the guilt and innocence phase. Interestingly, in this particular state, the defense is allowed to present a mitigation strategy outlining their approach should the prosecution decide to seek the death penalty. The prosecution reviews the defense's position and makes a determination whether or not to seek capital punishment based upon the particular factors identified by the defense. If the death penalty is not pursued, the attorney who was previously doing the mitigation work is removed from the case. The other attorney takes over and focuses on the guilt/innocence phase, although he/she may use the information obtained by the other attorney to assist in sentencing.

At the county jail, I was searched and "patted down" by a correctional officer and, once again, my luggage was searched for any illicit material, firearms, etc. I was accompanied to a cell just outside of the main atrium on the unit where murder defendants were housed. It was there that I first met Mr. I.I. He was sitting at a table with shackles on his wrists and ankles, wearing a bright orange jumpsuit, distinguishing him from the rest of the population who wore beige coveralls. I introduced myself, put my equipment down on the floor, and proceeded to begin the evaluation in my customary manner. As I pulled out my notepad, I noticed that Attorney C. was taking a seat next to Mr. I.I. I said, "What are you doing?" He replied, "I'm going to watch the evaluation." I replied, "No, you're not" and then proceeded to explain why that was not going to be possible, the effects it could have on the validity of the results, etc. Attorney S. seemed to understand and had no intention of staying. He deferred to my position and recommended to his colleague that he do the same, which he did reluctantly. Mr. I.I. did not seem at all disturbed by the fact that his attorneys would not be present, and nothing further was ever mentioned about this until later on when I met the attorneys for lunch.

INTERVIEW

I began the interview, after inquiring with the correctional officer whether the shackles could be removed from his hands; they were taken off without incident. Information related to Mr. I.I.'s crime, arrest, and incarceration was available in the other records and was not to be the focus of the interview. Rather, emphasis was directed toward information relevant to understanding his neuro-cognitive and neurobehavioral status, with primary emphasis on his academic, substance abuse, and medical history.

Mr. I.I. said that school was always difficult for him as a child. Math and reading were his poorest subjects and he had at least one year, perhaps more, of special education; he also said that he was held back in 6th Grade. He recalled that he completed the 8th Grade but believed that he left during his freshman year in high school (although some records indicate that he left during the 11th Grade). He said that he left school because he "got in too many fights. People were picking on me and calling me dumb." He recalled sitting in the back of class with other children who were also slow. When asked whether or not he was ever diagnosed as "mentally retarded," Mr. I.I. said "yea, they told my folks about it; lots of teachers didn't treat me well because of it. I don't like to talk about it."

Mr. I.I. was asked about his use/abuse of alcohol and recreational drugs. He said that he first began drinking beer when he was about 15 or 16 years old and had already left school and was working. He began to drink hard liquor in his early 20s but was always able to work during this time. Yet, he started getting into trouble and was arrested for breaking and entering at an airforce base. He said that he began to smoke marijuana when he was 14 or 15 years old. When asked how often he did it, he replied, "all the time . . . seven days a week." He said that he tried windowpane acid once and "saw pink elephants and stuff." He began using crack cocaine in his mid 20s: he started to use it because he was getting DWIs from drinking and the crack would reportedly sober him up. When asked how often he did it, he said that at first it was weekends only or when he wasn't working, but then it progressed to daily use/abuse. He would reportedly steal things in order to pay for his habit. He reported that there were periods of time in which he would become violent while high on crack. He served time in prison on several occasions secondary to violence, which he believes was caused by crack cocaine use. When he moved to the northwest in 1995, he was not doing drugs, but he started getting back into them shortly upon his return. Thereafter, he reportedly "cleaned up" when he met his girlfriend, and he stayed clean for over 7 years. He began using again in 2001 up until May of 2002 when he went into a substance abuse treatment program. He entered into treatment because his girlfriend threatened to leave him if he didn't seek treatment. He began abusing crack two weeks after he left the program and continued to do so up until his arrest and incarceration in January 2003.

Mr. I.I. reported a history of a number of head traumas. He recalled knocking heads with another boy when he was 7 or 8 years old; he recalled being unconscious for about one month (although this was not independently verified). He was hospitalized and had to miss school for an extended period of time. Mr. I.I. also lost his sense of taste for a "long time," but it eventually came back. His mother later told him that he "became more violent" following this event: he would pick-up sticks and hit other kids, throw bottles at them, talk back to teachers, and his school performance also suffered. Mr. I.I. said that he has been in a couple of car accidents. One time, he was "thrown from the car" and landed in a ditch where he was not discovered until a few hours later. He does not recall much from this incident, but remembers being hospitalized for a "long time." On another occasion when he was in his early 20s, Mr. I.I. was in a car accident where another car went on top of the roof of the car he was in. He reported being knocked out and taken to a trauma center. Mr. I.I. had fallen from a roof in 1997 and apparently sustained a concussion. He recalls experiencing blackouts and back pain because of this and was off work for over six months, then went back to light duty. He apparently received a Workers' Compensation settlement, which he recalled did not cover much more than medical bills.

After interviewing and examining Mr. I.I. for four hours in the morning, I took a break for lunch and met with the two attorneys. Prior to sitting down, Attorney S. handed me an envelope with a letter inside. The contents were as follows:

> I want to apologize for the confusion this morning involving my colleague on the issue of his insistence of staying during the testing of Mr. I.I. Personally, I felt that it was the right decision to have asked Attorney C. to leave the testing room. I also feel that neither myself nor Attorney C. should be present during any of your contacts with Mr. I.I. I place a great deal of confidence in all of the experts that I have hired on behalf of Mr. I.I. and I insist that there should not be any outside interference from myself or others in carrying out responsibilities that each expert has been hired to complete. My colleague, Attorney C., has a certain proclivity for wanting to exercise a great deal more control than I feel is either necessary or helpful at times, which, in turn, has created a need for me to remain constantly vigilant of any "overextending" of control on his part into my area (the mitigation) of the case. My mission is to obtain as much substantive evidence as I am able to collect to present the strongest mitigation package as possible. You have my support in whatever decision you make regarding the testing of Mr. I.I. Thank you, once again, for accepting this case and allowing us to use your services.

TESTS ADMINISTERED

An extensive battery of commonly used neuropsychological tests, personality assessment instruments, and symptom validity measures was administered to Mr. I.I. (see Table 35.1).

TABLE 35.1   Neuropsychological test results of Mr. I.I.

WAIS–III	IQ/Index	%ile	Verbal	SS	Performance/Visual	SS
FSIQ	73	4th	V	6	PC	6
VIQ	74	4th	S	7	DSy	5
PIQ	76	5th	A	3	BD	8
VCI	84	14th	DSp (5/3)	5	MR	7
POI	82	12th	I	8	PA	5
WMI	65	1st	C	5	SS	5
PSI	73	4th	L–N	5		

WTAR: FSIQ   demographic: 81   reading: 77

WRAT–3	SS	%ile	Grade
Reading	65	1st	4th
Spelling	57	5th	2nd
Arithmetic	51	8th	2nd

WMS–3	Index	%ile	Subtest	Raw	SS
Aud. Immed.	80	9th	LM1	31	8
Vis. I Immed.	109	73rd	LM2	17	9
Immed. Memory	93	32nd	Faces1	39	11
Aud. Delayed	89	28th	Faces2	42	13
Vis. Delayed	118	88th	VPA1	3	5
Aud. Recog.	95	37th	VPA2	3	7
Gen. Memory	101	58th	Fam. Pic.1	51	12
Working Memory	79	8th	Fam. Pic.2	50	13

CVLT–II	Raw score	Z score
List A Trial 1	3	−2.5
Trial 5	8	−1
Trials 1–5	39	T = 45
List B	5	−0.5
List A short-delay free recall	6	−1
short-delay cued	9	−0.5
long-delay free	8	−0.5
long-delay cued	11	0
Semantic cluster	−0.2	−0.5
Serial cluster	−0.4	−1.5
% primacy	13%	−2.5
% middle	51%	+1
% recency	36%	+1
Total Learning Trials 1–5	1.2	0
Consistency	74	−0.5
List B vs. Trial 1	86.7%	+2
SDFR vs. Trial 5	−25%	0
LDFR vs. SDFR	33.3%	0.5
Total Repetitions	12	1.5
Total Intrusions	15	2
Y/N Recognition	14	0
Response bias ("no")	0	−0.5
FC Recognition (%accuracy)	94	cum. % w/ better score = 94.7

BVMT–R	Raw	T score	%ile	REY FIGURE	Raw	T score
Trial 1	4	39	14	Copy		
Trial 2	4	26	1	Immediate	10.5	28
Trial 3	5	22	< 1	Delayed	11.5	30
Total	13	27	1	Recognition	19	40
Learning	1	35	7			

(Continued . . .)

TABLE 35.1   (Continued)

Delay	5	27	1		
% Retention	100		> 16		
Hits	6		> 16		
FP	0		> 16		
Disc.	6		> 16		
Resp. Bias	0.5		> 16		

WCST-128

# categories	4	(11–16%ile)	
trials for 1st	12	(> 16%ile)	
# errors	41	16	
PSV resp.	20	34	
PSV errors	18	30	
% Conceptual	47	16	
Failure to maintain set	1	(> 16%ile)	
Learning to Learn	−12.14	(6–10%ile)	

	Raw score	T score			
TMT A	43	56	BTA	Total	%ile
TMT B	91	59		9	62nd

	Raw score	T score		Raw score	Z score
FLUENCY			BNT	51	−1.46
Animals	21	64			
Letters	35	54			

	Raw score	%ile		Raw score	%ile
JLO	17	4	VFD	27	5

	Raw score	T score		Raw score	T score
TAPPING			PEGS		
Dom	44.8	42	Dom	76	44
Nondom	35.0	33	Nondom	100	32

TOMM Trial 1	41	REY 15 Recall	11/15	
Trial 2	50	Recog.	27/30	
Retention	50			

VIP	Verbal	Irrelevant Resp. Style
	Nonverbal	Inconsistent Resp. Style

M-FAST	RO = 1	*BDI–II* 39 (Severe Depression)	SCL-90	All T scores > 74
	ES = 3			All %ile > 98
	RC = 7			
	UH = 3			
	USC = 1			
	NI = 1			
	S = 0			
	Total = 16			

BEHAVIORAL OBSERVATIONS

Mr. I.I. was seated throughout most of the evaluation, but occasionally had to get up and stretch. He was dressed in prison garb and his hygiene appeared generally appropriate. On observation, there was no overt evidence of any disturbances in gait and/or other lower or upper extremity motor abnormalities. Mr. I.I. came across as someone with rather limited social and interpersonal skills, but he interacted appropriately throughout the interview and testing. On the other hand, he tended to perseverate around religious themes throughout the evaluation. It appeared as if he wanted to demonstrate how his life had changed since he was incarcerated, and he expressed an interest in helping others to see things from his new point of view. Throughout, he seemed sincere in his expressions, but he left the impression of perhaps being a bit too overly enthusiastic about this new approach to life; it also seemed to border on delusional in quality, with his belief that he could influence other inmates and their future. His affect appeared mildly depressed; in fact, he became somewhat teary when discussing the circumstances surrounding his incarceration. Mr. I.I.'s frustration tolerance was generally good throughout the evaluation, and he did not seem to get too upset when he made errors or had difficulty performing certain tasks. He did not give up or complain, and he persisted in the face of his apparent frustration. Receptive and expressive speech/language abilities were grossly intact, and there was no evidence of any hallucinations, delusions, or other forms of psychosis.

TEST RESULTS

Validity and test interpretation considerations

In order to assess level of effort, motivation, and potential response bias on cognitive testing, measures sensitive to malingering, erratic performance, and invalid response patterns were obtained. Mr. I.I. appeared to put forth adequate effort on all aspects of the cognitive testing. His performance on the forced-choice component of the CVLT–2 (16/16) was perfect, and his scores on the 15-Item Test (11/15 recall; 12/15 recognition) and the TOMM (41; 50; 50) were all within normal limits, reflecting no overt evidence of any attempt to malinger or feign deficits. In contrast, his scores on the VIP subtests were invalid (Verbal: irrelevant response style; Nonverbal: inconsistent response style). The pattern of his responses on this measure did *not* imply a malingered response style: it may simply represent his limited intellectual abilities, a random response style, and effects of fatigue or distraction. His score (46/100) on the Nonverbal subtest suggested that he probably responded without regard to item content, he was not sufficiently engaged in the test, or that he has such poor reasoning ability that the subtest could not validly assess his ability. His score (47/100) on the Verbal subtest suggested that he may have tried to do poorly on this test, but the results have to be understood in the context of his (limited) intellectual abilities. Based upon his scores on the VIP, "other ability tests that were administered concurrently should be interpreted with caution." He endorsed some strange/unusual experiences on one questionnaire (M-FAST) that were not consistent with his observed behavior. Additional discussion of the validity of his responses to the personality inventories will be addressed in the relevant section below.

Intellectual/academic functions

Mr. I.I. is presently functioning in the Extremely Low to Borderline Impaired range with a WAIS–III FSIQ of 73 (4th %ile). There was a 2-point discrepancy between his verbal skills (VIQ = 74; 4th %ile) and his nonverbal skills (PIQ = 76; 5th %ile), which is not considered statistically significant. His overall IQ is 8 points less than his predicted score based upon demographic factors (WTAR FSIQ = 81), and it falls almost 2 standard deviations below the population mean. Moreover, 96% of the people in the general population would score higher than he did on this measure. Given the standard error of measurement, there is a 95% degree of confidence that his true IQ score falls in the range of 69 and 78 and a 90% confidence that his score falls between 70 and 77. Thus, it is possible that Mr. I.I.'s IQ score could have fallen in the Extremely Low range. It is also important to note that his IQ score may have been elevated secondary to test practice effects, as he was previously tested with these same measures and demonstrated "cognitive-intellectual difficulties" and "long-standing problems with basic academic skills and learning" at that time.

Examination of the WAIS–III factor scores reveals Low Average scores in Verbal Comprehension (14th %ile) and Perceptual Organization (12th %ile). Working Memory (1st %ile) and Processing Speed (4th %ile) were in the Extremely Low and Borderline Impaired ranges, respectively. On the verbal subtests, Mr. I.I. obtained scores ranging from extremely low to average. His lowest score was on Arithmetic, a task requiring mental calculation skills, and his best score was on Information, a test measuring a fund of information. Low average scores were obtained on tasks measuring verbal abstract reasoning and vocabulary knowledge; borderline impaired scores were obtained on tasks requiring simple attention and digit recall, social judgment/conventionality, and working memory. On the performance tests, Mr. I.I. performed in the average range on a task measuring visual-spatial synthesis and analysis and in the low average range on measures requiring nonverbal reasoning skills and the capacity to distinguish essential from nonessential details. Borderline impaired scores were obtained on tasks requiring anticipation and planning in a social context, symbol search skills, and information processing speed.

On the WRAT–3, Mr. I.I.'s written arithmetic skills fell at the 2nd grade level (8th %ile): over 99% of the general population would do better on this task than he did. His spelling skills also fell at the 2nd grade level (5th %ile), and his reading skills were at the 4th grade level (1st %ile). Thus, all of these academic abilities are well below his obtained level of academic attainment (8th Grade). Further academic testing with the WIAT–II also supports the presence of significant difficulties in the academic realm characterized by impairments on tasks requiring Reading, Mathematics, Written and Oral Language, with grade equivalents ranging from the 1st to 5th percentile ranks and ranging from the 1st to 3rd grades. Because his current level of intellectual functioning is classified as Borderline Impaired (and not Average), the difficulties Mr. I.I. demonstrated on all of these tests cannot be classified as representing specific learning disabilities per se. But, clearly they represent rather longstanding weaknesses/inadequacies that are most likely a product of social and academic deprivation and/or limited intellectual functions.

Attention/concentration

Mr. I.I. exhibited variable performances on tasks measuring attention and concentration. Mental control abilities were mild to moderately impaired for simple (e.g., counting forwards, reciting the alphabet, etc.) and more complex tasks (e.g., reciting the months of the year backwards). Immediate memory for auditorally presented digits and on a visual analog of this test were both borderline impaired. Mr. I.I.'s performance on sequencing tasks (Color Trails; DK-EFS Trail Making) that require attention and concentration was good, except for a component that required cognitive flexibility. Auditory attention for numbers and letters (BTA) was moderately impaired. Vigilance and attention skills (DVT) were generally within normal limits, although Mr. I.I.'s total number of omission errors fell in the borderline impaired range, suggesting some carelessness and/or inattention to details.

Learning and memory

Mr. I.I.'s scores on tasks measuring learning and memory ranged from borderline impaired to above average. On the WMS–III, he obtained the following Index scores: Auditory Immediate = 80 (9th %ile); Visual Immediate = 109 (73rd %ile); Immediate Memory = 93 (32nd %ile); Auditory Delayed = 89 (28th %ile); Visual Delayed = 118 (88th %ile); Auditory Recognition Delayed = 95 (37th %ile); General Memory = 101 (58th %ile); and Working Memory = 79 (8th %ile). These scores are all higher than his current IQ and Index scores, suggesting that memory is not a primary problem for Mr. I.I. In fact, his WMS–III scores are better than expected based upon his current level of intellectual functioning. Results of the rest of the memory testing revealed a good performance on a task measuring verbal learning and memory (CVLT–2). In contrast, his visual memory skills (BVMT–R; RCF) were poorer. He had difficulty learning and recalling simple and complex figures but did well on the recognition portion of these tests, suggesting that there may be some subtle problems with retrieval skills.

Executive functions

Mr. I.I.'s verbal abstract reasoning skills (WAIS–III Similarities) and nonverbal abstract reasoning skills (WAIS–III Matrix Reasoning) both fell in the low average range. His performance on the WCST, a task that requires cognitive flexibility in response to changing rules, was generally good and there was little evidence of perseverative responding. But, he achieved less than the expected number of categories, and it took him longer than expected to complete the first category, which reflects some problems initially coming up with an appropriate solution to solve problems. His scores on DK-EFS subtests measuring conceptual reasoning, anticipation, and planning were generally commensurate with his current level of intellectual functioning. On the other hand, proverb interpretation was moderately impaired, most likely as a result of verbal, linguistic difficulties. Overall, results of tests of executive functions reflect some problems with reasoning, mental flexibility, and difficulty coming up with alternative solutions to problems when his initial ideas do not work.

Language functioning

Mr. I.I.'s conversational speech was generally unimpaired, and there was no evidence of any gross impairment in expressive or receptive speech/language abilities. Again, his general verbal intellectual abilities (WAIS–III VIQ = 4th %ile) and verbal comprehension skills (WAIS–III VCI = 14th %ile) are in the Borderline Impaired and Low Average ranges, respectively. Phonemic and semantic verbal fluency skills were both solidly within normal limits. Object naming abilities were borderline impaired, although cultural factors may have affected his score on this measure.

Other neuropsychological measures

Results of the rest of the testing revealed a moderately defective score on a task requiring visuospatial perception (JOLO) without a constructional component. A mildly defective score was obtained on VFD, another visuospatial task requiring discrimination among visual stimuli. Fine psychomotor speed was within normal limits for the dominant right hand and was borderline impaired for the left hand. Likewise, Mr. I.I.'s motor speed and dexterity was normal for the right hand and borderline impaired for the left hand.

Emotional functioning

Mr. I.I.'s score of 39 on the BDI–2 reflects the endorsement of symptoms of severe depression. He reported feeling sad much of the time, was hopeless about the future, had feelings of failure, worthlessness, guilt, and self-blame, felt as though he was being punished, and expressed a lot of self-hate. He also acknowledged that he gets restless and agitated, has difficulty making decisions and problems concentrating, and he reports a number of physical symptoms (e.g., fatigue, sleep difficulty, changes in appetite). His endorsement of these items is not particularly unusual for individuals who have been incarcerated and are awaiting trial. However, his responses to some of the items may reflect rather longstanding personality/emotional issues for him.

Mr. I.I. responded affirmatively to a large number of clinical symptoms on the SCL-90, which resulted in a profile that reflects an extremely high level of distress. However, his endorsement of a number of notable symptoms makes it difficult to interpret this profile, and it raises a concern about the validity of his complaints and/or the possibility that he may not have entirely understood the test items. For example, Mr. I.I.'s responses to the items of the M-FAST raise a concern about the validity of his psychological and emotional complaints. His total score of 16 suggests that he may be exaggerating psychiatric symptoms and complaints. He endorsed a number of extreme symptoms, rare combinations, and unusual experiences that suggest the possibility of malingered mental illness. He endorsed items such as: "I experience hallucinations that last continually for days;" "Whenever I see people who are not really there, they are always in black and white;" and "When I hear voices, my hands begin to sweat," and other items that do not make psychological or neuropsychological sense. Because of his elevated score on the M-FAST, it is difficult to ascertain the degree to which Mr. I.I. is actually experiencing symptoms of emotional distress or psychological turmoil. This is something that should be evaluated more extensively by a forensic psychiatrist/psychologist through the administration of other instruments designed to assess the reliability and validity of his emotional complaints.

Summary and conclusions

Results of the present evaluation provide objective evidence of impairments in a number of neurocognitive domains for Mr. I.I. The most prominent among them include a level of intellectual functioning that ranges from Extremely Low to Borderline Impaired. Given the standard error of measurement of the WAIS–III, the probability that Mr. I.I.'s true level of intellectual functioning is actually in the Extremely Low range is quite high. There were no academic records available for review, but it is my opinion that Mr. I.I.'s current level of intellectual functioning likely represents a lifelong pattern for him and was present before age 18. Moreover, there also appear to be limitations in adaptive functioning (e.g., social/interpersonal skills, functional academic skills), although this is something that was not formally assessed. (For criteria and definitions for mental retardation and mild mental retardation see notes[1].)

---

[1] American Association of Mental Retardation (2002) essential criteria for a diagnosis of mental retardation:
- Significantly subaverage intellectual functioning;
- Significant limitations in adaptive functioning (3 categories: conceptual, social, practical);
- Onset of these limitations prior to age 18.

Beyond his scores on the intellectual and academic measures, Mr. I.I. also demonstrated impairments on a number of tests that reflect brain-based disturbances in functioning. Primary among these include moderate to severe deficits on tasks measuring visual learning and memory, certain executive functions, auditory attention, visuospatial skills, and non-dominant hand motor speed and dexterity. It is difficult to ascertain the exact cause of these deficits, but they exist on tests that are reliable and valid measures of brain function and are not solely a product of subjective self-report or any psychological/emotional factors. Given Mr. I.I.'s history, the most likely factors would appear to be chronic crack cocaine use and the effects of multiple head traumas. Interestingly, both of these conditions have a predilection for the frontal lobes of the brain, the area responsible for higher-order thinking skills, like reasoning, organization and planning, the capacity to inhibit one's impulses, consider the consequences of actions, etc. Damage to this part of the brain can also result in problems with impulse control and increased aggression. The effects of psychoactive drugs, especially hallucinogens and psychostimulants, would likely exacerbate these deficit areas, thereby causing a person to be more susceptible to release inhibitions, increase impulsivity, exacerbate underlying personality disturbances, and distort perception and reality. When taken by someone with limited intellectual capacities and a history of psychosocial and environmental problems, such substances could cause these kinds of problems to emerge more prominently, thereby posing an even greater threat to one's capacity to exercise sound judgment, think of alternative solutions to problems, and inhibit aggressive impulses.

LEGAL PROCESS

Two weeks after my evaluation of Mr. I.I., a copy of the neuropsychological report was submitted to the Office of the District Attorney as part of the mitigation package. It wasn't until five weeks later that I learned of the outcome of a meeting between the public defenders and the prosecuting attorney. This was conveyed via a letter from Attorney S. It read:

> I had a meeting with the top prosecutor himself and his second in command a few days ago. They had read with great interest your report classifying Mr. I.I. with an IQ of 73 with the possibility that the score could fall below 70. I had also provided a legal analysis in the package on why they are still barred from seeking the death penalty in this case even though the state statute requires that an IQ of 70 or lower is required for a classification of mental retardation. They asked a lot of questions regarding your report and how my analysis applied to bar them from seeking the death penalty. It was a long meeting. I told them that I was extremely confident in your findings and that you had taken a very conservative approach in your interpretation of the data and in all of your evaluations as a neuropsychologist. Strangely, even offering that they may have their expert re-score the data, I did not get the feeling that they were interested in doing that. They were apparently convinced enough of the

American Psychiatric Association (1994) definition of mild mental retardation:

- Significantly subaverage intellectual functioning: an IQ of 70 or below;
- Concurrent deficits or impairments in present adaptive functioning in at least 2 of the following areas:
  - communication, self-care, home living, social/interpersonal skills, use of community resources, self-direction, functional academic skills, work, leisure, health, and safety;
- Onset of these limitations before age 18.

The DSM–IV notes that individuals with mild mental retardation are "often not distinguishable from children without mental retardation until a later age. By their late teens, they can acquire academic skills up to approximately the 6th grade level. During their adult years, they usually achieve social and vocational skills adequate for minimum self-support, but may need guidance, and assistance when under unusual social or economic stress. With appropriate supports, individuals with mild mental retardation can usually live in the community, either independently or in supervised settings."

strength of your findings that they decided they were not going to call them into question. I subsequently received a call from the assistant prosecutor earlier today informing me that they had decided to accept your findings and the application of my analysis to your findings and that they were NOT going to seek the death penalty against Mr. I.I. This was a HUGE victory for us at the office and everyone was ecstatic over the news. Doctor, I want to personally thank you for your time and commitment to our case. Mr. I.I. asked me to express his overwhelming gratitude to you. Thank you.

Now that the death penalty was removed from the case, the prosecution and defense began to prepare for the guilt and innocence phase of the trial. Attorney S. was no longer going to be involved. Rather, Attorney C. (the one who wanted to sit in on the evaluation) was to be the primary defense attorney. I did not anticipate that I would be needed for any further aspect of the trial nor would my evaluation serve much of a purpose in the guilt and innocence phase. However, my role became more prominent in the case once Attorney C. intimated to the prosecution that the defense would likely put forth the issue of diminished capacity, involuntary intoxication, or some combination of the two. As a result of this intent, the state requested that Mr. I.I. undergo an examination at the State forensic facility. This was for the purpose of assessing his mental state at the time of the offense and to look more closely at the issue of malingering, which is something that the prosecuting attorney felt explained Mr. I.I.'s mental condition at the time of the offense (i.e., why he maintained that he did not remember anything about the murders or events from the entire day, despite having previously given a statement contradicting that position).

Mr. I.I. underwent a forensic mental health evaluation 16 months after I had evaluated him. This was for the purpose of determining "whether he suffered from a mental disease or defect such that he suffered from 'diminished capacity' at the time of the alleged crime." Interestingly, Attorney C. and a defense forensic psychologist were both allowed to sit in and observe the examination. The examination consisted of an interview and testing over three days and a review of relevant records. In the report, the examiner pointed out several things from my examination of Mr. I.I., which they felt were relevant to their opinions. First, they acknowledged that Mr. I.I. demonstrated "some apparent impairments, such as a low reading level and difficulty with sustained attention" during their interview with him. They also wrote that Mr. I.I. had told me some things during my interview with him that he did not disclose to them, including hearing voices all his life, that he had started smoking "sherm" (pot laced with PCP) two weeks prior to the offense, and that when he was on sherm he felt like "being in hell fighting demons." He also provided considerable detail about the crime to me, which led the examiners to believe that his mental state was not so impaired as to meet the legal definition of insanity or diminished mental capacity.

As for the actual test results from my evaluation, the examiners noted that Mr. I.I.'s IQ was in the borderline to low average range and that "considering measurement error, there was a chance that his true level of intellectual functioning was in the range associated with mental retardation." They also highlighted my statements that Mr. I.I.'s "endorsement of a number of notable symptoms makes it difficult to interpret this profile, and raises a concern about the validity of his complaints/or the possibility that he may not have entirely understood the test items." His responses to the M-FAST also raised a concern for them about the validity of his psychological complaints. His total score of 16 suggested to them that he was exaggerating psychological symptoms, and his endorsement of a number of extreme symptoms, rare combinations, and unusual experiences suggested the possibility of "malingered mental illness."

Mental status examination of Mr. I.I. revealed that he demonstrated occasional mildly circumstantial responses to questions, but there was no evidence of delusions. He reported to the examiners that he had a continuous course of hearing voices, beginning in childhood, that he hears voices "all the time" and that they encourage him to do bad things. Mr. I.I. reported that he sometimes has formed visual hallucinations of people coming through the walls when he is hearing voices. Intellectual functioning was not formally assessed, but his use of language and level of academic attainment suggested sub-average intellectual ability. Memory was felt to be within normal limits, except for reported memory deficits regarding the murders. Judgment and insight were fair, but the examiners felt that Mr. I.I. was rather unsophisticated in his attempts to present himself as markedly impaired. As for the test data, the examiners wrote, "Mr. I.I. has several demographic variables that can commonly confound test results, such as low intellectual function, low level of academic attainment, history of brain injury, and an extensive substance abuse history. Test subjects sharing these characteristics are frequently excluded from test validation studies. Thus, any comparison between Mr. I.I. and the subjects in the samples used to validate the tests must be done with caution."

Mr. I.I. was administered the Structured Interview of Reported Symptomatology (SIRS) and The Competence Assessment for Standing Trial for Defendants with Mental Retardation (CAST-MR). His responses to the SIRS were felt to be consistent with the examiners' general observations, suggesting that he reports (1) an unusual breadth of symptoms, (2) an unusual number of symptom combinations, (3) an unusual number of blatant symptoms, and (4) he rates an unusual number of symptoms as severe or unbearable. The examiners noted that the questions from the SIRS are more face valid than instruments like the MMPI–2 and that, in theory, the SIRS would be more robust when a subject does not closely match the normative sample. Preliminary evidence suggests that the SIRS can discriminate between intellectually limited malingerers and honest responders; yet, its use with intellectually limited populations should only serve as a source of corroborative data rather than a diagnostic tool. On the first section of the CAST-MR, measuring knowledge of basic legal concepts, Mr. I.I. correctly answered only 3 of 25 questions. In the validation sample, subjects with mental retardation averaged over 19 correct responses. In fact, a person would be expected to get approximately 8 correct responses by chance alone. Thus, Mr. I.I.'s score was 2 standard deviations below the mean of the most impaired group in the validation study. On Section 2, Mr. I.I. correctly answered 10 of 15 questions, which is very near the mean for subjects who are mentally retarded. On Section 3, he obtained 1 of 10 possible points, which is significantly below the mean of subjects diagnosed with mental retardation, but this is difficult to interpret.

In the Clinical Formulation section of the report, the examiners state, "Mr. I.I. presents as a man with limited intellectual function, a concrete thinking style, and likely cognitive impairments. He self-reports a broad range of severe psychiatric symptoms and memory problems. It is our clinical opinion that he is not an accurate reporter of symptoms." Their opinion was based on (1) discrepancies between observed signs of mental illness and reported symptoms; (2) self-report of unlikely symptoms, (3) self-report of unlikely course of symptoms, (4) test performance that is significantly lower than would be predicted based on his level of intellectual function and academic attainment, (5) selective memory impairment for particular content (e.g., the crime), and (6) Mr. I.I.'s statement that he did not want to remember details of the crime or his history of violence as it could be used against him. Of the features commonly used to detect symptom over-reporting, the only data that were not strongly supportive were that (1) it does not appear that there were frank attempts to perform poorly on Dr. Heilbronner's neuropsychological testing, and (2) the evidence is mixed as to whether Mr. I.I. has developed coping strategies for his self-reported psychosis, as would be common in people with major mental illness. It does not appear that Mr. I.I. has a primary psychotic disorder. Given that he reports some use of hallucinogenic drugs around the time of the murders, it is possible that he may have experienced transient hallucinations and delirium. Yet, given his apparent over-reporting of symptoms, we are unable to assess whether these symptoms may have persisted into times when he was not either acutely intoxicated or experiencing withdrawal. There is clear evidence supporting a diagnosis of Antisocial Personality Disorder that dates back to adolescence. There also appears to be a relative lack of remorse, including minimization and rationalization of his prior and current offenses.

In terms of competency, the examiners noted, "there is some probability that Mr. I.I.'s IQ falls within the range associated with mental retardation." Yet, they contended that his scores were depressed by measures that would not be commonly used in court such as performing arithmetic, repeating sequences of digits, and rapidly transforming symbols and digits. On measures of acquired knowledge, verbal reasoning, fluid reasoning, and attention to detail, Mr. I.I.'s scores are on the margin of Borderline to Low Average. In the absence of other major functional limitations, most people in this range of ability would have sufficient intellectual ability to understand the justice system, understand their legal peril, and participate in their defense. It is also noteworthy that, while statistically speaking, there is some possibility that Mr. I.I.'s scores fall at the upper margin of the range associated with mental retardation, it is extremely unlikely that Mr. I.I. would meet the other major diagnostic criteria of demonstrating impairments in adaptive functioning. Indeed, he has participated in the competitive job market, has lived independently, has been married, and has successfully negotiated complex systems, such as probation. Thus, his overall level of functioning is not consistent with even mild Mental Retardation. In our interview, Mr. I.I. reported almost no knowledge of the criminal justice system, no knowledge of the charges against him, and no knowledge of the factual allegations. His scores on tests designed for subjects with mental retardation covering basic concepts of the justice system were below the bottom 5% of persons with Mental retardation on whom the test was normed. Thus, neither his self-report nor his test performance can be regarded as credible. The examiners felt that there was "no plausible explanation for his selective memory deficits for information that was encoded, and was retained over several months. Furthermore, the presence of multiple prior convictions suggests that the court and counsel have previously been satisfied that Mr. I.I. was competent in those instances, and there is no evidence that his level of competency has changed."

In their final section of the report, the examiners addressed the issue of premeditated intent. This requires an analysis of: (1) the presence of a mental illness; (2) analysis of what symptoms were likely present at the time of the offense; and (3) identification of the mental abilities impaired by the symptoms. Also, the analysis must address the probability and degree to which these impairments may have interfered with the ability to form the requisite mental state. Based upon all of the available data, it was the examiners' impression that Mr. I.I. suffered from polysubstance abuse and alcohol dependence. There was also evidence of transient psychosis as a result of the polysubstance abuse. Yet, there was little evidence to suggest a primary psychotic disorder or a severe mood disorder and little data to suggest that Mr. I.I. was experiencing symptoms that could negate the ability to premeditate or act intentionally. It is plausible that he may have been hearing voices at the time of the crimes as he reports, secondary to Alcohol or PCP intoxication. But, there is little data to suggest that he was incapable of the mental states of premeditation or intent. Indeed, the facts of the case required an ongoing sequence of purposeful activity: he armed himself with two different weapons, struck and stabbed people in two different rooms, and returned to strike one of the victims again. By his own report, Mr. I.I. placed the 2-year-old child in a different room so that she would not see him engaging in these acts. This suggests that the capacity for premeditated intentional conduct was preserved.

Upon receiving the forensic mental health report, Attorney C. contacted me to see if I could testify about Mr. I.I.s' diminished capacity. I told him that I was originally retained to assist in the mitigation aspects of the case and that my evaluation was not really adequate for addressing his mental state at the time the crimes were committed (a *mens rea* analysis). He said that he understood, but persisted in requesting that I assist him in the preparation of an affidavit documenting my opinion about Mr. I.I.'s mental state. I politely refused to prepare or sign such an affidavit, but indicated that I would be happy to testify about his history of substance abuse, head injury, neuropsychological impairments, etc. I felt that it would be better if the forensic psychiatrist who had been retained by the defense to address mental state at the time of the offense would testify about issues such as competency and diminished mental capacity. I did not hear from Attorney C. for several weeks until a phone call from his assistant, requesting that I make arrangements to fly out west so that I could testify at trial. I called back asking the assistant to clarify my role and the intended content of my testimony. She indicated to me that it would focus on the issue of Mental Retardation and the effects that various psychoactive substances (e.g., alcohol, PCP) may have on Mr. I.I.'s mental state at the time of the offense. I reiterated my concerns to her and said that I did not address these issues in my examination of Mr. I.I. Furthermore, I was not a toxicologist and could not opine about the role that alcohol or PCP may have played in the commission of the crime. She said that she would relay my concerns to Attorney C. and that I would hear back from him in the next day or two. I never received a phone call from Attorney C. It was not until after the trial had ended that I received an e-mail from Attorney C. informing me that Mr. I.I. had been found guilty of two counts of aggravated murder in the First Degree and one count of attempted murder in the First Degree and was sentenced to life without parole.

CONCLUDING THOUGHTS

As I stated at the outset of this chapter, it is extremely rare when the results of a neuropsychological evaluation can be of such importance as to spare someone's life. But, that is essentially what happened in this case. With a Full Scale IQ score at, or very close to meeting, the IQ criteria for mental retardation, Mr. I.I.'s attorneys were able to get the death penalty removed from his case despite the obvious fact that neither in terms of psychometric intelligence nor in social, adaptive functioning did he really meet the criteria for mental retardation! For the purposes of this book, this evaluation was also important in its demonstration that a person can put forth adequate effort on cognitive measures and associated measures of malingering, yet still exaggerate or malinger psychiatric symptoms. This type of profile is especially common in criminal cases. Indeed, defendants are usually opposed to any kind of indication that they may be mentally retarded or have some kind of brain damage. Thus, it is rare (but certainly not out of the question) when a criminal defendant malingers cognitive symptoms outside of a competency-assessment context. They are more likely to malinger psychiatric symptoms, especially when issues of insanity or diminished mental capacity are part of the defense. In Mr. I.I.'s case, the inconsistency between his recall of the crime as told to me versus his claim to the prosecution examiners that he did not remember anything about the event raised enough of a concern as to discredit his report. Ultimately, it was used as evidence against him and was an important factor in the judge's decision to find him guilty and sentence him to a life in prison without parole.

One other aspect about this case that is important to note is the issue of the neuropsychologist's commitment to staying within a defined boundary and not going beyond the test data. I was retained to assist in the mitigation aspects of the case and to examine whether or not there were any neuropsychological impairments as a result of a history of head trauma and/or substance abuse. I did not examine him with the intent to understand Mr. I.I.'s mental state at the time of the offense. My interview did not query him in great detail about the circumstances surrounding and leading up to the murders. Thus, I felt that I did not have sufficient basis to opine about whether or not there was diminished capacity, despite the defense attorney's attempts to bring me in as an expert witness. Mr. I.I.'s elevated scores on some of the inventories measuring psychiatric symptoms raised enough of a concern for me that I did not feel that I could assist the defense in their claims of diminished capacity. Whether or not this will limit the degree to which I receive cases from Attorney C. or other public defenders in this particular state is unknown. Yet, in this case, as in all other cases in which I serve as a consultant or expert, I am confident knowing that I did a comprehensive assessment, was attentive to the influence of multiple sources of bias, performed an adequate differential diagnosis, considered and ruled out the effects of malingering/exaggeration of cognitive as well as psychological deficits, and ultimately came to an opinion that would not be revised just to meet the demands of a well-intentioned attorney, no matter how committed he was to the pursuit of a successful outcome in his case.

REFERENCES

Atkins v. Virginia 260 Va. 375, 534 S.E. 2d 312, reversed and remanded (U.S. Supreme Court, No 00–8452, decided July 21, 2002).

Cunningham, M. D., & Goldstein, A. M. (2003). Sentencing determinations in death penalty cases. In A. M. Goldstein (Ed.). *Handbook of psychology: Vol. 11. Forensic psychology*. Hoboken, NJ: John Wiley & Sons.

Penry v. Lynaugh 492 U.S. 1 (1989).

SECTION IV

PERSPECTIVES OF LEGAL EXPERTS AND DISABILITY DECISION MAKERS

The focus of forensic experts, including clinical neuropsychologists, is on providing clear and accurate evidence for the consideration of individuals who will decide the matter at issue. In formal litigation involving civil plaintiffs and criminal defendants, the decision makers are the judge and jury, often referred to collectively as the triers-of-fact. In other less formal proceedings, such as disability determination and due process educational hearings, the decision makers may be case managers, arbitrators, or mediators. In many of these scenarios, attorneys are involved in presenting expert findings and attempting to frame these findings to the decision makers. This section provides the viewpoints of individuals who are part of the decision-making process, even if not the ultimate decision maker. Specifically, the six chapters in this section present the perspective of individuals involved in disability case management, legal representation of disability claimants, consultation to Social Security, legal representation of civil plaintiffs, and legal representation of criminal defendants. Issues related to assuring the validity of assessment information gathered by neuropsychology experts and the veracity of the claim or condition at the heart of the case vary in the eyes of these individuals, but at some level such issues are involved in all these perspectives.

Disability insurance case management: External consultant

36

Jeff Green

An independent medical evaluation (IME) is requested by the disability carrier to authenticate the level of function or dysfunction of an individual who contends disability. The report produced addresses the central question: Does the individual have the ability to conduct himself/herself in the occupation outlined?

A comprehensive evaluation will typically include the utilization of multiple data sources in conjunction with neurocognitive assessment, which meets the standards of a sound clinical forensic evaluation. Conclusions drawn from an evaluation are routinely supported by the use of empirically-based procedures and evidence-based decision rules where applicable.

A key role of the evaluator within the context of such an evaluation is to identify any sources of inconsistency that may exist, and, as much as possible, explain the reasons for those inconsistencies. Within the context of the evaluation, an independent evaluator will attempt to address and explain the inconsistencies that arise in the context of the assessment process and discuss whether the information presented as part of the evaluative process also contains inconsistencies. Findings, whenever possible, are then related to functional capacity with the explanation of function linked to the individual's work requirements at the time of claim. The evaluator is often asked to address the claimant's ability to engage in work activities within the context of functional abilities and limitations. Any issues of motivation, when found or observed, are then addressed in accordance with how those factors may impact an individual's ability to return to work.

Ultimately, the determination of disability does not rest with the evaluator, but with the insurance company as trier of fact. The facts are applied to the particulars of any given contract. Thus, the significance of a thorough and comprehensive evaluation, which clearly describes and articulates aspects of inconsistency across multiple data sources, is apparent. The hope of the carrier, as would be true of any consumer of service, is a work product that is thorough, well-reasoned, considers all possible facts presented, and clearly addresses all questions asked in a readable and understandable format.

A comprehensive assessment now, as was true when psychometric inquiry was in its formative stages, is considered a product of thorough review of all available information gathered to answer the questions posed. With this in mind, the more relevant information an evaluator has at his disposal, the greater the likelihood that an ultimate determination will be sound. Sources of information often included in an independent medical evaluation focusing on disability routinely include a comprehensive vocational history, work activity descriptions, personnel and/or work issues, license restrictions, malpractice actions, historical information pertaining to or impacting an alleged condition, medical records from all treating sources, observational information, and any other sources of data that are relevant to the questions being asked. This information, when incorporated with sound testing procedures and evidence-based interpretation, has a greater likelihood of facilitating an objective and impartial decision. Recommendations the evaluator may wish to make that may be determined helpful to arrive at a reasoned conclusion may need to be addressed and information obtained to allow for this eventuality. The writer will typically strive to provide the report to the carrier in a timely fashion.

Wall and Applebaum (1998) noted that information regarding the Insured's current income, disability benefit and policy terms, current symptoms and stressors, a description of the Insured's typical day before and after onset of disability, and future plans and prognosis is beneficial to provide as part of a comprehensive assessment. The authors contend that it is also helpful to learn how the Insured functioned prior to disability, what led up to a claim, and what may have changed to create incapacity. Treatment response and work return plans when available are also viewed as a means of assessing motivation. Wall and Applebaum (1998) suggest that data discrepancies provide an important means of assessing malingering as well.

Russell and Russell (2003) note the importance of background information in interpretation and conclusions. They believe that sources of data, test information, and situational or historic information need to be used in unison with appropriate testing techniques and protocols. They have expressed concern about "inadequate exploration of the patient's background information," which is operationally defined as insufficient provision or recapitulation of history.

The need for thorough history taking, review of all medical records, and assessment of prior occupational and situational factors in conjunction with appropriate assessment techniques is mitigated by the complexity of cases being evaluated. Disability claims are often complex and inherent is the possibility of motivational factors, due to the benefit derived from the disability policy. It is not uncommon for a neuropsychologist to be asked to assess the functional capacity of an individual who has been on disability claim for a protracted period of time. Even if direct gain may not have been a factor at the time of disability inception, the passage of time in conjunction with the factors present at the time of claim may now conspire to create financial incentive to malinger or exaggerate symptoms so as to remain on claim. The necessity of a comprehensive longitudinal history, including detailed medical history and a thorough psychiatric history, is imperative.

The requirements of a thorough, detailed history as part of a medical review and clinical interview should include: diagnosis, chronicity, history of psychiatric disturbance and/or psychotherapeutic treatment, history of substance use and abuse, and family history of psychiatric and/or substance use. Some evaluators choose to recapitulate medical records within their evaluation. While this demonstrates that the clinician has reviewed all available medical records, the review may fall short of the writer's intent if the material available is not adequately synthesized and/or if examination of inconsistencies, which are apparent from the review of the medical record, are not commented upon and integrated into a cohesive formulation of the particulars of the case.

Within the context of the clinical interview and assessment procedures, evidence-based procedures dictate the need whenever possible to assess not only the observed patterns of speech and behavior but also to conduct a thorough review of memory deficits and other symptoms as described by the claimant. The consistency of symptom complaints will typically involve examination across multiple data sources including the medical record, collateral contact, and available surveillance when complaints have been noted in the record. These same observations and endorsements are then compared to findings from psychometric inquiry, which then affords an objective measure of consistency.

A detailed clinical history and interview is a significant aid to clarify the patient's understanding of their current condition. This approach also includes self-reported constitutional symptoms along with a detailed history of cognitive complaints if they exist. Once this task is completed the clinician's work product strives to help the reader understand how these symptoms evolved over time, including onset patterns, symptom trends, and consistency with what is known about symptom expression. Additionally, it has been our observation that thorough neuropsychological evaluations include, whenever possible, a comprehensive educational and work history, as well as psychiatric history including a review of prior psychological or psychotherapeutic interventions.

It is difficult to assess functional capacity when there is an insufficient understanding of the occupational roles. Consequently, the more detailed the description of work activities and work responsibilities, the more likely an examiner will be able to extrapolate from objective test findings to real-life activity. Within the context of the clinical history, it is also helpful to assess current functioning by a description of activities of daily living, financial factors and/or other stressors, and current family life, as well as a description of how the individual symptoms affect the individual's social, sleep, and sexual functioning. These factors and the degree of consistency between self-report, medical documentation, collateral contacts, and psychometric assessment are then considered in response to insurance company questions and in the process of arriving at final conclusions.

A sound independent medical evaluation (IME) is only as useful as the information provided to the examiner prior to evaluation. A comprehensive packet of information including the information delineated previously is helpful for the evaluator to utilize as part of the evaluation process. Clinicians are encouraged to incorporate as much information as possible from a variety of resources to insure a thorough assessment. This approach works well in the assessment of a disability claimant. Insurance companies may be concerned that sending data that go beyond medical documentation may convey the appearance that the insurance company is attempting to "lead the evaluator." On the other hand, sending only some of the available data may curtail the evaluator's ability to fully understand the case, and may inadvertently give the impression of leading by limiting information and thereby limit the evaluator's ability to conduct a comprehensive evaluation. Fortunately, this concern has been lessened in the face of a more scientific approach. Disability carriers and those who litigate these cases have come to recognize that the best approach is to provide as much file information as possible for the evaluator's review and interpretation. Neuropsychologists often report that they prefer to receive all information available to make independent judgments about data potentially relevant to questions being posed. Neuropsychologists should not hesitate to request additional information in order to help them arrive at a more complete understanding of the case.

A referral by an insurance company typically can be expected to provide all pertinent information and the source records upon which this information is based. This information often includes, as indicated earlier, contract details outlining the type of policy and definition of occupation, as well as whether the policy is for total or partial incapacity. In addition, through an insurance company's normal claim assessment strategies, contributory factors to claims are routinely researched. These factors include but are not limited to financial, situational, and investigation of legal or malpractice difficulties relative to work where applicable. In addition, occupational/vocational histories obtained from the person claiming disability and/or confirmation of the same through employers or associates are requested by the insurance companies and provided when available. It is not unusual for an insurance company to generate observational information (surveillance) and independent financial appraisals conducted as a means of determining the possible presence of inconsistencies, misrepresentations, or distortions. This information is often provided to the independent evaluator when available as part of a forensic evaluation. Again it has been our experience that neuropsychologists will, in the conduct of their evaluations, utilize this information as part of their data gathering practice and incorporate their perceptions of the information into their findings.

A confounding factor seen in disability adjudication is the effect the treating clinician may have on reinforcing the sick role of the individual applying for benefit. This is often unwitting, but the result of endorsement to disability is to reinforce disability status, even when a truly disabling condition does not exist. The writer has seen a number of cases where a claimant's avoidance to return to work is maintained in the presence of solid evaluative information, which supports functional capacity as a result of the treater's acceptance of disability. Even in situations where a treating clinician has concurred with the findings of evaluation, the previous perception of disability has now created a situation where the claimant has come to see himself as impaired and often feels betrayed by the treating clinician who is now altering his/her position. An article written by Strasburger et al. (1997) summarizes the dilemma accurately. It is not that the treating clinician is in collusion with the patient to defraud, dissimulate, or exaggerate; rather, as pointed out by the authors, "the treating clinician is wholly dependent on his patient's self-reported experiences."

Unlike a treating clinician, a forensic evaluator has an obligation to consider multiple data sources in arriving at conclusions of functional limitation. Strasburger et al. (1997) also point out that an independent forensic, psychiatric, or psychological expert has an ethical obligation to the trier of fact to consider all reasonable hypotheses that may serve to explain the insured's complaint. They also acknowledge that an independent examination report benefits from inclusion of information independent of the subject's self-report through record reviews, forensic examination, and psychological testing. The literature supports the contention of the need for a more stringent assessment (Greenberg & Shuman, 1997). Clinicians who act as healthcare providers are often unavoidably drawn into advocacy roles vis-à-vis the patient's insurance coverage and benefits, as their identification with their patient predisposes them to becoming invested in their patient's welfare. The clinician then becomes part of the dilemma rather than a more objective appraiser of fact. Disability carriers frequently encounter circumstances in which the certifying clinician is not aware of the financial factors in the case and has limited or no understanding of the individual's job activities, career demands, or work performance issues outside of a cursory overview related to them piecemeal by their patient. Indeed, it is not unusual to note that concerns about resuming work are not at the forefront of the clinical work and may only be mentioned in passing. Work cessation is often purported to be a by-product of self-reported symptoms. Moreover this self-reported history may be accepted uncritically without further inquiry into other potential factors that may have contributed to work cessation. The multiple interpersonal and intrapersonal factors surrounding motivation toward work return get lost, and the focus of treatment oftentimes becomes a continued self-endorsement of symptom complaint without resolution. The longer a case persists without work return, the greater the likelihood that there will be no return, and the clinician becomes an unwitting and/or unknowing accomplice in the continued cycle of complaint and "disability."

The importance of the relationship between evaluator and clinician speaks to the benefit of collateral contact (phone consultation with the treating clinician or clinicians) as part of a thorough neuropsychological evaluation. If collateral contact is not accomplished in concert with thorough record review and clinical interview, potential data sources with respect to clinical treatment issues are potentially lost as an independent source of information. Sweet (1999) notes, "Malingering is a real world behavior, not just a behavior seen in the office." Collateral contact in this arena serves as an important component of evidence-based assessment. An added advantage to this consideration is that when clinicians certifying disability are afforded the professional respect to be brought into the process, the process may be seen as more collegial and objective.

A treating clinician, unless having a caseload disproportionately weighted with patients who seek compensation, is often unfamiliar with the rigors of forensic appraisal. Thus, clinicians primarily involved in patient care activities are likely to have a somewhat different worldview than clinicians specializing in disability assessment. This different worldview may also contribute to the clinician's reticence to become involved in the forensic process, even if it is seen as potentially helpful in clarifying issues. This reticence may be misinterpreted as resistance by the evaluator, and this may be countered if the evaluator serves to instruct about the process of requesting information by collateral contact, thereby establishing a working alliance designed to develop a better understanding of all the case factors. The author would contend that clinicians, who are more rigorous in their assessment of self-reported information in clinical practice, do not lose in the process of developing therapeutic alliance. This contention recognizes that a skilled clinician will be able to address inconsistent information while managing to maintain a therapeutic alliance. Many clinicians, especially those who are inexperienced, have fear that the pursuit of objectivity may threaten the alliance. This may also serve to create a defensive posture in the service of advocating for one's patient and inadvertently may act to reinforce the perception of the person requesting disability as impaired. In our observation, this dynamic is one that clinically astute forensic evaluators take into consideration when they approach treating clinicians.

Williams, Lees-Haley, and Dojanogly (1999) address this dilemma by examining the fundamental difference between those seeking compensation and those in treatment. After taking multiple factors into consideration, symptom rates were assessed, and it was observed that litigating patients reported almost twice as many symptoms as their nonlitigating counterparts. The author recommends that clinicians must, in addition to providing support and empathic understanding, also increase their efforts to objectively assess self-report.

There are cases where the evaluator asked to assess a case has also relied heavily on self-report and assumed the information reported was valid without comparing this information to outside sources including collateral resources, the historic record, and inconsistencies commented upon within the body of the same report. When this occurs, a forensic effort is compromised and becomes a simple repetition of patient complaint, without the benefit of a necessary critical analysis of all sources of information. Evaluations that rely largely on patient self-report are also typically remiss in utilizing a thorough test battery to assess all dimensions of complaint. They also tend to be evaluations where paradoxically the final conclusions are often overreached in the absence of supportive data. Frequently deficient work products have used insufficient and/or inadequate assessment techniques and methods as well.

Presuming that the insurance company is in receipt of a comprehensive report that is well reasoned, basing conclusion on a thorough analysis of all data and resulting inconsistencies of fact, but has not attempted collateral contact with the treating clinician, a problem may still remain. Since collateral contact is, in and of itself, another data point, it is helpful in developing a greater understanding of all the potential sources of inconsistency that may exist. It is also an opportunity to invite the clinician involved in treatment to provide valuable information about the treatment dyad, which can clarify the interplay between symptom expression and treatment. When apparent inconsistencies exist, the evaluator and clinician are in a position to address the potential reasons for discrepancy in a collegial manner. The lack of contact may impact and/or impair the capacity of such a report to aid in a resolution process. One potential impact is seen in the present illustration where contact was not initiated.

A recent case of an individual on claim for fibromyalgia who had remained in receipt of benefit for an extended period of time while engaging in activities inconsistent with her complaint of disability was evaluated both medically and neuropsychologically. Both evaluators conducted a thorough evaluation including the use of appropriate psychometric assessment strategies. A thorough review of records was completed and inconsistencies from those efforts were incorporated into the findings of the reports. The neuropsychologist and rheumatologist who acted as evaluators found evidence of secondary gain, and the results of neuropsychological assessment were consistent with malingered response. Unfortunately, both evaluators declined to contact the treating clinician as requested. The treater who had been previously contacted by insurance company consultants had expressed some concerns about his patient's presentation and indicated that he was in a clinically difficult position. He wished to provide service to his patient but was afraid that if he confronted the woman with his concerns she would flee and seek someone else to validate her claim. When presented with the results of the evaluation, the treater and, as expected, the patient and her attorney degraded the evaluation for lack of contact, thereby diminishing or detracting from the otherwise comprehensive work of the evaluation. While the case was amicably resolved, it may well have been able to be accomplished in a less confrontational style had the evaluators been more inclusive in their efforts to evaluate. Parenthetically, had the treating clinician been included, it may have allowed opportunity for therapeutic intervention in a case where motivation was an issue.

Independent evaluations are frequently transmitted to attending clinicians as a means of information sharing and an opportunity for discourse. There have been a number of cases in which the author has been involved where this process has either been helpful to effective resolution or a hindrance. Successful resolution benefits all parties involved, beyond the needs of the insurance company. When an IME is otherwise comprehensive but has not taken the opportunity to engage the attending clinician in discourse, opportunities for resolution and/or further clarification may be lost even when evidence of functional ability is overwhelming. As noted earlier, engaging the clinician in discourse allows the evaluator to develop an understanding of the clinician's position, how he or she arrived at that position, and what sources of information were used to do so. Such contact also affords the opportunity to reconcile potential differences attributed to the rigors of forensic evaluation versus clinical inference. In cases where the treating clinician is afforded an opportunity to share valuable insights and where that information is treated dispassionately and with respect, recognizing the differences in roles, more positive outcomes may be reached. Under these collaborative circumstances, the evaluator and the insurance company gain a greater understanding of the circumstances while the treater benefits from a heightened awareness of factors impinging on the patient's claim of difficulty. In addition, the patient/claimant potentially benefits from improved treatment or rehabilitative efforts aimed at improving function. Most importantly, as Morgan (this volume, chapter 32) entreats us, in what he refers to as the memorable words of one distinguished supervisor, "Always tell the truth and let the chips fall where they may." Morgan notes that the goal of the evaluator is to always be on the side of science and in so doing be on the side of truth. The evaluation is designed to be independent and objective and the ultimate goal is to arrive at the ground truth. To ignore or avoid including relevant data sources when available undermines the process.

Many, though not all, evaluations are requested to determine the functional capacity of the individual being assessed. The role of the evaluator is to assess response style and identify sources of discrepancy between self-report testing and real-life behavior. Objective sources of inconsistency are described using normative data where applicable (testing) and any observed or noted contradiction between self-report or complaints and clinical findings where encountered. Question of treatment compliance or inadequate treatment is also explained in the context of motivational factors that may impinge on functional capacity.

Similarly, the use of Symptom Validity Tests (SVTs) as an indicator of insufficient effort in objective evaluations is an accepted standard (Bush et al., 2005). The efficacy of their use has been well documented. They may serve to help explain inconsistencies and unexpected findings observed in performance testing (Rohling et al., 2002).

It has been our observation that evaluators who conduct thorough review of all records, and compare that information with self-report and observed behaviors for consistency, also conduct neuropsychological evaluation using strategies consistent with those suggested by Sweet (1999). These include: (1) tests of insufficient effort, (2) evaluation of insufficient effort on common measures with forced-choice format, and (3) examination of nonsensical or unique malingering responses or response patterns on other common measures. These recommendations are compatible with either a fixed or a flexible battery approach. An additional element of a sound neuropsychological evaluation is the evaluator's documentation of normative studies and research data, which supports the observations made. These same evaluations also routinely follow Sweet's recommendations to compare real-life data to test data and whether there are real-life losses that comport with the data juxtaposed to a self-serving description of loss. Neuropsychologists, in arriving at their conclusions, are also encouraged to address any limitations for neuropsychological results to predict real-life function.

Social and emotional reasons for poor motivation, or suboptimal or incomplete effort, are more comprehensively evaluated when multiple data sources are utilized. While financial incentive may not be determined to be the overriding factor in any given case, it is nevertheless a consideration to be addressed. Financial compensation may mean different things to different people, and it needs to be considered in the context of the evaluation. Some factors could include economic security and/or stability, retribution against an employer or group perceived as causing the problem, a desire to be taken care of, a sense of entitlement to benefit after a number of years of "paying one's dues" in a difficult or stressful work environment, and the opportunity to care for a family member who may be incapacitated.

Neuropsychological factors potentially impinging on suboptimal effort are identified in the field as decreased interest and effort due to a genuine brain dysfunction, stress, and/or preoccupation with the consequence of the evaluation itself (i.e., threatened loss of benefit), suboptimal performance resulting from a comorbid psychiatric condition, and the effect of medication as a possible interference to optimal performance. The interplay of factors that exist in disability cases therefore requires vigilance and attention to detail, further establishing the necessity of a comprehensive evaluation.

According to Sweet (1999), "There is little doubt that if the present rate of expansion continues, the malingering literature pertaining to clinical neuropsychology will provide new methods for detection on a regular basis." The promulgation of new assessment procedures, while helpful, does not, nor will likely in the foreseeable future, dispense with the need for thorough history taking, comprehensive record review, obtaining information from a collateral contact, and conducting a comprehensive clinical interview. All of these factors are taken into consideration before arriving at any opinion relative to issues of deception, which might be observed to impinge on functional capacity. Decision rules, cutoff scores, and adequate norming in a more secure environment, while helpful in protecting detection methods, do little to advance a comprehensive evaluation if the decisions arrived at are relied on solely by objective data collection in the absence of those elements outlined above.

A number of respected researchers in the field, Russell and Russell (2003), Sweet (1999), and Mittenberg et al. (2002), have either inferred or directly noted that the detection of deception requires a multimethod, multidimensional approach to determine the presence or absence of malingering. Parenthetically, this is consistent with recommendations to clinicians to utilize multimethod, multistrategy, multidimensional approaches to the diagnosis and application of treatment to patients in psychotherapy. Research continues to bear out that such strategies are the most efficacious in both treatment as well as assessment.

Binder and Rohling (1996) conducted a meta-analysis of cases presented on behalf of disability adjudication in several arenas including Workman's Compensation, Personal Injury litigation, and individual disability cases. They concluded that evaluators should be mindful of financial incentives as a factor in all these types of cases. Other studies of base rates for symptom exaggeration and/or malingering vary across sources from 10% in military studies where discharge is sought (Resnick, 1970) to 20% of people seeking disability claim for neurobehavioral impairment (Guilmette et al., 1994). A comprehensive survey of over 30,000 cases described across multiple research efforts demonstrated base rates of up to 30% that were categorized as malingering (Mittenberg et al., 2002). These findings reflect the need to rigorously assess the presentation of a claim for disability, to protect not only the assets of an insurance company but the personal reputation at stake for the individual on claim if such a diagnosis is made erroneously.

Binder and Rohling (1996) and Rohling et al. (1995) found that financial incentives are a factor associated with greater disability. Greenough and Fraser (1989) also demonstrated that the disability condition does not necessarily resolve with claim resolution, even if a disability is suspect. Consequently, it is imperative that the findings be well substantiated. Financial incentives aside, this demonstrates that an individual who perceives himself as disabled may continue to act comparably in the absence of benefit. As mentioned earlier, this points out that the inherent danger for clinicians attesting to disability is to become an unwitting, and sometimes reluctant, participant in the reinforcement of a disability role.

Questions designed by the insurers in their efforts to clarify uncertainties in cases are typically developed and asked in order to address the multifaceted issues facing disability insurers. Consequently, all results in the context of motivation need to rule out any contributory factor at play in the process of establishing a finding of malingering. The evaluator will consider: Is there a loss of home, family, or security? These factors are taken into account when arriving at a finding of malingering. They are relevant questions since it is unusual for someone who is feigning illness to have incurred such loss. If it is determined that the findings represent a malingered response style, it is imperative to differentiate whether the response is to the length of time on claim and resulting perception of self as disabled versus a distinct effort to feign illness as a means of obtaining gain. The benefit of clear diagnosis and explanation is useful when able to differentiate between symptom exaggerations versus frank malingering versus assuming the sick role. In addition to elucidating the definition of those terms in the process of report, the evaluation may also educate the disability carrier about how the circumstances impact the individual's present mindset with respect to work return, as well as identifying how it may impact eventual work return considerations.

Simply stated, cases presented for disability adjudication may be complicated by multiple factors, which can include but are not limited to financial gain and/or maintenance of income, career, and work stressors in conjunction with age and family factors, often in concert with health issues. While any one of the factors broadly outlined above may not be sufficient to create functional limitation they can, and often do, impact issues of gain. These factors must be adequately assessed in arriving at decisions of limitation through a careful multimodal evaluation process that leads to conservative evidence-based conclusions.

The insurance company's expectation of a sound independent medical evaluation is to authenticate the level of function contended by the individual on claim. Identification of deception and/or the diagnosis of malingering are secondary to the primary task. The evaluator's role within the context of such an evaluation is to clarify sources of inconsistency that may exist and explain the reasons for any observed inconsistency. It is imperative that a comprehensive evaluation includes the utilization of multiple data sources as outlined in this chapter, in addition to psychometric assessment employing multimethod procedures and utilizing normative data. Conclusions following examination are based on a logical and clear delineation of all available data and reliance on empirically-based procedures. Ultimately, explanation of the clinical findings should be directly related to functional capacity, with special attention paid to the individual's prior work duties and responsibilities. Functional capacity is thereby addressed from a framework of measured capacity, not diagnosis.

REFERENCES

Binder, L., & Rohling, M. (1996). Money matters: A meta-analytic review of the effects of financial incentives on recovery after closed head injury. *American Journal of Psychiatry, 153*(1), 7–10.

Bush, S. S., Ruff, R. M., Tröster, A. I., Barth, J. T., Koffler, S. P., Pliskin, N. H. et al. (2005). NAN position paper: Sympton validity assessment: Practice issues and medical necessity. *Archives of Clinical Neuropsychology, 20*, 419–426.

Greenberg, S., & Shuman, D. (1997). Irreconcilable conflict between therapeutic and forensic roles. *Professional Psychology Research and Practice, 28*, 50–57.

Greenough, M., & Fraser, R. (1989). The effects of compensation on recovery from a low back injury spine. *Journal of Rehabilitation Medicine 14*(9), 947–955.

Guilmette, T. J., Hart, K. J., & Giuliano, A. J. (1993). Malingering detection: The use of a forced choice method in identifying organic versus simulated memory impairment. *Clinical Neuropsychologist, 7*, 59–69.

Mittenberg, W., Patton, C., Canyock, E., & Condit, D. (2002). Base rate of malingering and symptom exaggeration. *Journal of Clinical and Experimental Neuropsychology, 24*(8), 1094–1102.

Resnick, P. (1984). The detection of malingered mental illness. *Behavioral Sciences and the Law, 2*, 21–38.

Rohling, M., Binder, L., & Langhinrichsen-Rohling, J. (1995). Money matters: A meta-analytic review of the association between financial compensation and the experience and treatment of chronic pain. *Health Psychology, 14*(6), 537–547.

Rohling, M. L.,Green, P., Allen, L. M., & Iverson, G. L. (2002). Depressive symptoms and neurocognitive test scores in patients passing symptom validity tests. *Archives of Clinical Neuropsychology, 17*, 205–222.

Russell, E. W., & Russell, S. L. K. (2003). Twenty ways and more of diagnosing brain damage when there is none. *Journal of Controversial Medical Claims, 10*(1), 1–14.

Strasburger, L. H., Gutheil, T. G., & Brodsky, A. (1997). I'm wearing two hats. *American Journal of Psychiatry, 154*.

Sweet, J. J. (1999). Malingering: Differential diagnosis. In J. J. Sweet (Ed.), *Forensic neuropsychology fundamentals and practice*, New York: Psychology Press.

Wall, B. W., & Applebaum, H. L. (1998). Disabled doctors: The insured's industry seeks a second opinion. *Journal of American Academy of Psychiatry and the Law*, *26*(1).

Williams, C., Lees-Haley, P., & Dojanogly, S. E. (1999). Clinical scrutiny of litigant's self-report. *Professional Psychology Research and Practice*, *30*(4), 361–367.

Disability insurance case management: Insurance company

John E. Sargent and Mary Fuller

Financial protection from an injury or illness that restricts a person's ability to work comes in a variety of forms. At the federal level, Social Security Disability Insurance provides money to individuals who are unable to engage in any substantial gainful activity by reason of any medically determinable physical or mental impairment (Social Security Administration, 2003). State-mandated workers' compensation insurance provides money to workers disabled while in the act of working. Group Disability Insurance is provided by employers for disabilities of short duration (STD). Generally STD coverage lasts up to six months. Many large employers also provide compensation for a disability that is long term (LTD). LTD benefits begin when STD benefits end.

Workers who are not covered by a corporate benefits package can purchase individual disability policies. These policies, available to professionals, small business owners, and business executives who seek additional income protection, can pay up to 80% of annual income from all sources, depending on the occupational risk classification. For a physician earning $250,000 annually, an individual policy may pay $16,666 per month to age 65 if the physician is unable to work in their regular occupation. This monthly payment, because it is not purchased through an employer-sponsored benefit plan, is tax-free.

In the 1970s and 1980s, individual disability policies were aggressively marketed to professionals, particularly physicians and attorneys, as these professionals were viewed as having a low risk for a long-term disability. The assumption made by actuaries, based on morbidity tables incorporating disability frequency and duration for specific occupations, was that a high-income professional who sustained a disabling injury or illness would be highly motivated to return to work and would do so. After all, it was motivation that produced the high income.

Policy provisions that would provide a monthly disability benefit for life could be purchased. In addition, to protect from the monthly benefit being eroded by inflation, a Cost of Living Adjustment (COLA) rider that increased the benefit by a percentage pegged to the Consumer Price Index (CPI) could also be purchased.

Perhaps the most attractive feature of these policies was the definition of disability. A professional could receive 80% of monthly earned income as long as they were unable to perform the material and substantial duties of their own or regular occupation. Regular occupation was defined as the work performed at the time of disability. For a surgeon, being disabled meant not being able to do surgery even though the surgeon could perform other occupations, even jobs in the field of medicine such as teaching or administration. Because of the quality-of-life guarantee that these policies provided, many were sold. Versions of these policies were also sold through professional associations.

For a time, the premiums generated by these policies were a boon for insurance companies. Money poured in and the competition for the professional market intensified. Then came the 1990s. Physicians were feeling diminished by the loss of independent clinical decision making and staggering malpractice insurance increases. The financial impact of managed care was also beginning to be felt. Physician concerns were well documented in the news media at the time, and these very same issues continue to make headlines today. The gilded path of medicine was no longer quite so bright, and many physicians were unhappy.

In the legal world, many attorneys were beginning to have second thoughts about the rewards of their profession. In 1996, *The Boston Globe Magazine* featured an article on job satisfaction among lawyers (Dahl, 1994). The article cited many reasons why lawyers were dissatisfied with their work. A study referenced in the article made by the California Bar Association found that 70% of the lawyers surveyed would choose a different career if they had a chance.

At the same time that job dissatisfaction among medical and legal professionals was increasing, demands on business executives were also increasing. The expectations from consumers and shareholders were increasing. Business operations needed to change fast in order to deal with increased competition in a global marketplace.

The skills that allowed business leaders to succeed in the past were no longer sufficient. The new formula for success was documented in two books published in the mid-1990s: *Managing at the Speed of Change* and *Managing in the Age of Change* (Connor, 1993; Ritvo, Litwin & Butler, 1995). The message in both books was this: if you work in big business and want to survive, you had better learn how to deal effectively with rapid change. For many, the change was chaotic and personally challenging; for some, it meant the loss of employment.

While changes were occurring with professionals and business executives in their respective work environments in the late 1980s and early 1990s, individual disability claims began to increase. In the mid-1990s, the trickle became a flood. An article published in *The Washington Post* chronicled the increase in disability claims by physicians (Hilzenrath, 1998). An executive at one insurance company indicated that the incidence of claims from doctors was twice the number expected from all occupations. Another disability insurer indicated that doctors' claims soared 60% in 1994. The article stated that declining morale was the underlying cause for the growth in disability claims from physicians.

Although physicians, particularly specialists, led the race to disability, increases also occurred for attorneys, stockbrokers, floor traders, and business executives. These professionals didn't suddenly experience more traumatic accidents, neurological disorders, or other progressive illnesses. The conditions that were driving up the incidence of disability claims were psychiatric conditions and consisted mostly of anxiety, substance abuse, and depression.

Data gathered by the Health Insurance Association of America from member companies in 1993 indicated that a significant proportion of total individual long-term disability claim dollars resulted from mental and nervous (M&N) disorders (Health Insurance Association of America, 1995). Individual long-term policies had the highest proportion of M&N claim dollars paid for substance abuse, and 65% of all individual long-term psychiatric cases had a diagnosis of anxiety.

Insurance companies made adjustments for the unanticipated increases in disability claims. Some companies simply exited the individual disability market. Others merged operations to gain the critical mass needed to manage the increasingly difficult and costly claims. Those that stayed in the business adjusted the policy language and removed the rich benefits.

Occupational risk classifications were adjusted particularly for the professional groups, such as physician specialists, based on the new disability experience. Two-year limitations on mental and nervous conditions were instituted. However, these changes would only affect the new generation of buyers. The benefits-rich policies that were on the books would remain there as long as the premiums were paid. Insurance companies had to find appropriate ways to manage claims in the new, dynamic economy.

Determining who is and is not eligible for disability benefits is a complex process. Unlike life insurance, where a death certificate generates a benefit, disability insurance claims require careful analysis to determine the actual occupation performed and if the person is truly unable to functionally perform the key work tasks.

The operative word is "function." Insurers don't protect an individual from economic downturns, poor business decisions, bankruptcy, mergers, layoffs, terminations, lawsuits, malpractice claims, or loss of license. Nor do they insure an individual's occupational desires or personal wants, or provide protection from work-related ennui.

Disability insurance is for income loss due to the inability to function in the defined occupation. The determination is ongoing and is not a one-time event. Function is not static; it changes over time. Insurers anticipate, in fact it is required in many of the policies now being sold, that a person receiving disability payments receive medical care that is appropriate for the condition. It is expected that function will improve. The claims examiner has to, therefore, periodically assess the claimant's functional status and determine whether appropriate treatment is being received.

Assessing psychiatric disability is particularly challenging for a claims examiner. In over 20 years of reviewing progress notes and functional capacity statements, what I have generally seen is the voice of the patient or client in psychological terms. Self-reported symptoms pass through the mental health clinician to the insurance company with a professional stamp of validity and a diagnosis. There is rarely objective evidence gathered outside of the clinician's office supporting loss of work function. The patient is viewed as honest and reliable, and there is little if any challenging of the patient's presentation of facts. What the client says is believed.

From a clinical perspective, the clinician should, indeed *must*, create a therapeutic alliance with the patient. Trust has to be established with the patient, and this is done through empathy, care, and concern. It is not done by challenging credibility or digging for truth. One can imagine a patient storming into a therapist's office demanding why disability benefits have been terminated. Months of therapeutic gains could be lost if a therapist and patient disagreed over disability issues. The therapist could also be the focus of a malpractice suit or an ethical violation if a patient felt they were misrepresented to an insurance company and thereby harmed.

Treating clinicians are protective of their relationship with their clients and have a professional and ethical obligation to act in their client's best interest. This is spelled out clearly in the Codes of Ethics for all types of therapists (e.g., American Mental Health Counselors Association, 2000; American Psychiatric Association, 2001; American Psychological Association, 2002). Within this context, it is much easier for a therapist to provide additional information to support disability than to provide additional information that would bring into question or refute the disability status.

It is difficult for clinicians to set aside their professional bias and evaluate their clients with the analytical rigor and cool objectivity of a forensic clinician. To do so would be antithetical to the therapist–client relationship. The best that a claims examiner can rely on from a treating therapist, particularly with a client with mild symptoms, is a presentation of self-reported symptoms. In a situation where the duration of a claim may result in millions of dollars in disability payments, this is not sufficient.

The problem is complicated further by the educational level and skill of the individual disability claimant. A claimant with a professional background who is intent on receiving disability benefits will undoubtedly have studied the policy in minute detail and be conversant at a clinical level with symptoms and reasons why they cannot function vocationally.

In disability insurance, the only tool that a claims examiner has in evaluating a disability claim is information. Information coming from the treating clinician may not have been substantiated with specific examples of impairment outside of the clinician's office. The claims examiner requires information beyond self-reported symptoms. The question then arises, where is an objective functional assessment of a claimant with a psychiatric diagnosis going to come from when the claimant appears headed for retirement?

Challenged by the need to be fiscally responsible, while honoring contracts with lucrative benefits that could not be recalled or changed due to a "guaranteed renewable" clause, insurance companies needed to change. Ironically, they turned to the medical community for a solution—case management.

Although heralded as a new idea by the insurance industry, the case management model has been around for a long time. First used in the early 1900s for communicable disease management, the concept was simple but powerful: Treatment outcomes are improved if the disease process is aggressively managed from beginning to end (Case Management Society of America, 1995). The case management approach expanded the focus from treatment in a doctor's office to education and prevention in the community by public health nurses. A system of disease management was born.

The first step insurance companies took in the case management direction was bringing expertise in-house. Vocational rehabilitation counselors were hired to help with identifying occupational duties and assist in return-to-work efforts. Nurses were brought in to evaluate medical conditions and treatment. Insurance companies then hired physicians and psychologists who moved from a centralized consulting service on the most complex medical cases to day-to-day involvement in all claims. Inadequate treatment and discussion of function was now addressed early in a peer-to-peer consultation with treatment providers.

Further refinements included moving claim examiners from generalists working on a variety of medical conditions to specialists working in units focusing on a single condition or group of related conditions. The psychiatric claim units were among the first specialized units, and claim examiners received training specific to psychiatric conditions. The insurance industry was again following the movement of medicine by becoming specialized and creating centers of expertise.

Claim meetings now had the look of a multidisciplinary treatment team in a comprehensive pain program or inpatient psychiatric facility. Instead of a medical chart, there was a claim file. In addition to the doctor, nurse, social worker, psychologist, and rehabilitation counselor, there was a claims examiner. The two teams shared the same goal: What can be done to improve outcome? Instead of a treatment plan, a file plan was created that outlined the steps necessary to maximize medical improvement, and, in the case of the insurance company, to manage the duration of disability payments.

Characteristics of the case management model in the insurance industry included:

*   Outcome driven
*   Early intervention
*   Bias for action
*   Quick and reliable communication
*   Solid information base
*   Effective use of experts and specialists
*   Team approach—collaborative
*   Use of multiple strategies concomitantly
*   Frequent monitoring, follow-up, and reassessment
*   Use of treatment guidelines

With an integrated case management model that brought expertise to the beginning of the claim, insurance companies were in a better position to identify those claims that were potentially problematic. Early signs of trouble included:

*   A statement by the clinician on the initial claim form that the claimant is permanently and totally disabled
*   The clinician pushing back the projected return-to-work date repeatedly
*   No modification in treatment despite the lack of progress
*   Ongoing supportive therapy without any clear treatment objectives
*   Morphing of a diagnosis from substance abuse to depression, or an Axis II diagnosis to an Axis I diagnosis
*   Closing or selling of the practice or business at the beginning of the disability claim or prior to the claim
*   Refusal to consider return-to-work assistance

- Refusal to be treated by a specialist
- Claim statement completed in the claimant's writing with the clinician's signature
- Initial claim form from an attorney
- Refusal to sign a consent for release of information form

In addition to hiring clinical staff, creating specialized units, and utilizing the case management model, the industry took other means to obtain information that would provide a complete picture of the claimant's personal and medical situation. The ability to see the claimant beyond the therapist's view and outside of the therapist's office was necessary.

Certified public accountants were hired to review financial statements and determine the financial strength of the practice or business. Insurance representatives, who have historically gathered information in the "field," visited the claimant, business or practice partners, and the treating clinician, and reviewed public documents for divorce proceedings and lawsuits. These information-gathering tools significantly broadened the vision of the claim examiner.

Surveillance, a standard tool of the insurance industry, was used with greater frequency and in some cases produced dramatic results. In one claim of note, the clinician reported that the claimant was so severely impaired that he would sometimes curl up in a fetal position in the corner of the therapist's office. This same individual was seen on a surveillance video socially animated and conversant with fellow members of his congregation outside of church. Clearly, the symptoms presented to the therapist were not the same as those exhibited outside of the therapist's office.

In many instances, the information obtained supports the disability. In a few instances, it dramatically demonstrates inconsistencies in reported symptoms and/or a clear financial need. Sometimes, the information is inconsistent and inconclusive and becomes a challenge for the claims examiner. The claims examiner suspects that the claimant is not disabled but does not have enough information to make a thorough and informed evaluation of work function.

In many long-term disability cases with a psychiatric diagnosis, an acute situation requiring professional intervention lasts longer than necessary. Symptoms that may once have been moderate are now mild or not evident. Function has been improved, but the client is comfortable in a new role and reluctant to go back to work. Situational factors, not necessarily related to the psychiatric condition, tend to gradually work their way into the claim picture.

Given the lucrative disability payments, without the hassles, frustrations, and work-related stresses, the choice to continue to remain "disabled" may not be a difficult one, particularly if the therapist is supportive. Does this situation rise to the level of malingering?

The DSM–IV defines malingering as "the intentional production of false or grossly exaggerated physical or psychological symptoms, motivated by external incentives such as avoiding military duty, avoiding work, obtaining financial compensation, evading criminal prosecution, or obtaining drugs" (American Psychiatric Association, 1994, p. 683). Certainly, the financial incentives are real, but are the symptoms false or grossly exaggerated? Is there a conscious plan to deceive?

Malingering in a criminal case is different than the usual presentation in a psychiatric disability case. In a criminal case, the defendant has a clear motivation to appear cognitively impaired or psychotic in order to avoid prosecution and a jail sentence. There may be a very limited history of medical treatment or impairment prior to the offense, but afterwards the offender may appear more psychotic than institutionalized schizophrenics or more cognitively impaired than severe traumatic brain injury victims.

The presentation of a well-educated and highly skilled professional with a diagnosis of generalized anxiety disorder or major depression is much more subtle. Symptom severity will have moved on a continuum from acute symptoms to milder symptoms. Function may have improved, but because the therapist may never have had a complete grasp of function in the first place it remains the same as originally reported or isn't discussed. The clinician continues to provide the initial diagnosis and a restatement of the presenting symptoms.

Diagnosis doesn't equal disability, because it doesn't address the functional level of the individual with the diagnosis. There are many people in the United States who have a diagnosis of depression, and many who remain undiagnosed who meet the diagnostic criteria for depression, yet are working.

The professional class of claimants receiving individual disability payments raises additional complications. Who wants a mild to moderately impaired surgeon or dentist as a treatment provider? Is it possible that the therapist may believe that they are protecting the public by supporting the disability of a healthcare provider? Perhaps the clinician simply wants the client to avoid the stresses of work in order to prevent relapse. Protection from a possible future disability is impossible for insurance companies to manage but is one issue that cannot be regarded lightly given the potential life and death exposure some healthcare providers encounter in their work.

Perhaps the last tool in the claimant's information-gathering tool bag is the Independent Medical Evaluation (IME). Insurance companies are very reluctant to use an IME because, of all of the tools in the claimant's tool bag, the IME is the dullest. An IME is viewed as a highly risky intervention and an act of claim desperation, because there is no guarantee that the evaluating clinician will competently measure function demonstratively. In a single IME, an individual disability insurance company may be putting millions of dollars at risk.

Often, the IME will split the difference between the treating clinician and insurance company finding that the level of impairment is not as severe as reported, but impairment still exists. In my professional experience working with psychiatric claims for over 20 years, I cannot recall a single instance in which an IME by a psychiatrist or psychologist rendered a diagnosis of malingering. Does this represent a problem with the definition of malingering, a problem with IME clinicians, a challenge in evaluating highly educated and skilled professionals, or unrealistic expectations by the insurance industry?

Perhaps it is time to sharpen the IME tool. In the *Guides to the Evaluation of Permanent Impairment*, published by the American Medical Association, the section on Mental and Behavioral Disorders States:

Three principles are central to assessing mental impairment:

1. Diagnosis is among the factors to be considered in assessing the severity and possible duration of the impairment, but it is by no means the sole criterion.
2. Motivation for improvement may be a key factor in the outcome of impairment.
3. A complete assessment requires a longitudinal history of the impairment, its treatment, and attempts at rehabilitation (American Medical Association, 1998, p. 227).

The first principle appropriately warns evaluating clinicians to look beyond the diagnosis for information to determine disability. The second raises the issue of motivation. This is a key issue that often doesn't get addressed in psychological assessments but is a critical component in the context of disability duration. How does a clinician assess a claimant's true motivation? Perhaps the answer lies in the third principle; motivation can be determined by a complete assessment of the impairment, treatment, and attempts at rehabilitation.

As indicated previously, on problematic, high benefit claims, insurance companies will generally have acquired detailed information regarding current employment, appointment records, past employment, driving history, personal finances, tax returns, credit history, current treatment history, past treatment history, family issues, social functioning, current stressors, and legal or licensing issues. This information is generally not seen or commented upon in an IME. Without this information, a complete understanding of the claimant is not known. How then can one determine the fraudulent from the genuine? And, how can an accurate Global Access of Functioning (GAF) rating be determined?

Perhaps the insurance companies are partially to blame. In efforts to schedule IMEs quickly and contain costs, intermediaries are sometimes used that may not focus questions clearly or provide sufficient background information. The evaluating clinician doesn't have enough information to obtain a broad picture of the claimant and must rely solely on the claimant's self-report and test data.

It is recommended that in difficult and contested cases, evaluating clinicians request and carefully review all of the information in the possession of the insurance company. In particular, inconsistencies in reported symptoms and level of function should be probed in a clinical interview. Too often, the evaluating psychologist relies solely on test data. For the sophisticated and skilled test taker, this is not sufficient.

It is also recommended that a complete test battery be performed that includes subtle and sensitive measures of validity. Professionals who desire disability benefits will not make the same kinds of mistakes that less sophisticated test takers will make. There will not be extreme or bizarre combinations of symptoms. They will not grossly exaggerate symptoms but will embellish symptoms just enough to look occupationally impaired. It may be difficult to assess motivation and effort on test-taking observations and test data alone.

A third recommendation involves the test battery. The psychologist should select tests that will effectively measure the functions in question. Generally, the problems that prevent a professional from working are cognitive functions including the ability to:

- focus concentration
- think clearly
- remember
- multitask
- problem-solve
- maintain attention
- synthesize information

What the insurance company wants is an objective and validated understanding of the claimant's ability to reason and think clearly, regardless of the diagnosis. Another crucial point is whether an attempt at exaggerating symptoms has occurred. It is ultimately the disability claim examiner's job to gather all pertinent information and make the determination regarding the claimant's ability to perform the occupation in question. While recognizing that pure objectivity and perfect truth will never be obtained, the claim examiner still has to make a reasoned decision regarding the claim.

Psychological testing, particularly neuropsychological testing, should be a critical component in determining disability where subtle exaggeration of symptoms is suspected. However, to be useful to the claim examiner, it has to be relevant to the functions in question and address the claimant's motivation in the context of life circumstances. How does the claimant functionally compare before the disability and after the disability? What has changed?

While the use of technicians for the administration of tests is common among many neuropsychologists, practitioners must remember that they alone are ultimately responsible for the validity of their data and interpretation of their findings. Thus, neuropsychologists must be confident that their findings can withstand the scrutiny of their peers within the context of IMEs and potential litigation.

A final recommendation regarding the evaluation is that clinicians should not delegate a portion to a technician or graduate student. The use of a technician or student will diminish the credibility of the report. If the stakes are high and the claim examiner relies upon the report to terminate the disability claim, it is possible that a lawsuit will result. If this is the case, another psychologist will carefully scrutinize the psychological IME for weakness. If one flaw is identified, the entire evaluation will be brought into question.

Additionally, IMEs should *not*:

- Make treatment recommendations unless specifically requested to do so
- Suggest that the insurance company settle the claim
- Criticize the treatment provider
- Contact the treatment provider, unless it is to request records

- Comment on claim handling
- Comment on the possibility for litigation

CASE HISTORY 1

The following case history has been altered to protect confidentiality and is a composite of actual cases encountered over the years.

The claimant was an attorney who claimed disability due to severe fatigue and malaise. The treating physician, a psychiatrist, made the diagnosis of Chronic Fatigue Syndrome (CFS). Treatment consisted of antidepressant medication and a mood stabilizer. Psychotherapy was provided by a clinical psychologist.

The claimant was a successful student in high school, college, and law school. She entered law school, as she was attracted to the legal process and the political process. She thought about eventually running for Congress. However, the claimant became disillusioned by the "power sources" and "the whole political process."

Following graduation from law school, the claimant joined a law firm in the capacity of litigation associate. Satisfactory performances were received up until her third year at which time a senior partner lost confidence in her, and she was advised that it would be in her best interest to secure employment elsewhere.

The claimant moved to be near her parents. She was again hired as a litigation associate but remained at the large firm only 15 months, explaining, "I hated it. It was very political; generally the people in power there were just not a nice group of human beings." She joined a relatively small law firm. She resigned in protest after the firm wanted to extend her application for partner another year.

She then joined two other lawyers in a small firm with the stipulation that she would be made a partner. Although she was made a partner, she began having physical symptoms such as malaise, memory loss, and headaches. She also reported particularly difficult litigation, "It was just really stressful. I would have anxiety attacks going into depositions." She sought treatment with a psychologist, who referred her to a psychiatrist, who ultimately made the diagnosis of CFS and advised her to take a medical leave.

A year after terminating the practice of law, she obtained employment as an instructor at a university. She reported that she "loves" teaching.

Correspondence from her treating psychiatrist stated: "Current psychiatric symptoms are mental confusion, forgetfulness, difficulty concentrating for moderate to long periods of time, lapses in short term memory and vocabulary, thoughts of hopelessness and overwhelming need to run away from unpleasant tasks or confrontations." These symptoms were viewed as secondary to CFS.

A field visit revealed the insured would never go back to work as a litigation attorney because she believed that she would quickly relapse. Personal choice over disability was raised.

Two IMEs, one by a psychiatrist and the other by an internist, both confirmed disability due to CFS based on the claimant's self-report. Surveillance was undertaken for three consecutive days. The claimant was seen actively engaged socially with appropriate affect, energy, and stamina, and with no acute distress or symptomatology.

A Forensic Psychiatric IME challenged the objective basis for CFS, but rendered a psychiatric diagnosis:

Axis I   A. Major Depressive Disorder, Single Episode, Mild, Chronic
        B. Undifferential Somatoform Disorder
Axis II Personality Disorder NOS

The forensic psychiatrist stated: "Given the time span of this claim and the claimant's invest-ment in her medical and psychiatric treatment, it is extremely doubtful that she will ever feel well enough or motivated enough to return to her previous vocation."

In light of the fact that the claimant was able to teach at the graduate level, she demonstrated significant functional ability. Does, "not feeling well" and being unmotivated amount to being unwell and disabled? A neuropsychological assessment would have been the tool of choice in this situation. It could have provided a clear diagnostic picture as well as a standardized assessment of cognitive functioning.

CASE HISTORY 2

The following case has been altered to protect confidentiality of the insured and encompasses general information from a composite of cases over a span of years.

The claimant is an individual employed in a professional occupation who is disabled from a psychiatric diagnosis of Posttraumatic Stress Syndrome as a result of both workplace issues and family-related trauma. Neither of the trauma sources were fully investigated by the insurance com-pany; however, medical records provided consistent reporting of the facts in significant enough detail to support the accuracy of the claimant's reports.

Treatment records reflected participation in weekly therapy as well as a variety of medication trials. In addition to establishing stability for the patient and alleviation of symptoms, the initial treatment plan included a goal of return-to-work in the occupation that had been the source of success and professional fulfillment for the insured. Treatment records reflected various attempts at graduated return-to-work with an initial focus on limited duties and hours. Despite an incremental approach to return-to-work, efforts were unsuccessful and resulted in the claimant experiencing increased symptoms and overall regression in function.

Although the workplace was one of the areas precipitating the onset of the trauma, there were no performance issues, licensure concerns, or financial difficulties associated with the claim. The insured's educational background and professional achievements were consistent with those of a highly motivated, highly intelligent person.

The recommendation of the treatment provider following more than a year of therapy was that the claimant not return to the prior occupation; in addition, the frequency of treatment was reduced based on the claimant having reached a plateau in the recovery process. Following the reduction in treatment, the insurance company began to challenge the severity of impairment and the determin-ation on the part of the treating physician that the claimant would never be able to return to her occupation.

The insurance company utilized initial medical investigative tools in order to obtain further understanding of the condition, including requests for a psychiatric assessment form from the treating psychiatrist, requests for additional records, and a call to the treating physician. Additional information pursued by the insurance company (as is often the case in psychiatric disability) was for specific, "objective" evidence obtained by the treating doctors in determining the diagnosis and treatment plan, as well as prognosis for recovery.

Neuropsychological testing had been obtained by the treatment provider and provided signifi-cant findings including the current level of intellectual performance of the insured compared to the normal or baseline level of performance. Testing included findings relative to areas of functioning including ability to pay attention, concentration, use of immediate recall, and the insured's coping skills. In addition, the provider noted information pertaining to the types of cognitive and emotional responses one would expect to see from the insured when placed in a variety of situations including those that were representative of the demands of the occupation in which the insured worked.

The report noted key functions essential to the performance of a professional's work with which the claimant was unable to deal, including sustained attention, concentration, ability to manipulate abstract concepts or to deal with complex instructions, and severe limitation in the ability to deal with details. The diagnosis of PTSD was based on the test results, as well as symptoms evidenced by the examiner, test responses, and information obtained throughout the medical records.

Additional treatment was recommended; however, the prognosis for return-to-work in the occupation was stated to be uncertain and clearly dependent upon the individual's ability to regain the level of functioning that existed prior to the onset of disability.

Although neuropsychological testing assisted in obtaining a more in-depth analysis of the various aspects of psychosocial functioning, it did not provide conclusive findings relative to a prognosis for recovery and return to work. As evidenced in this case, testing is not always definitive in this regard.

Although the final outcome was not clearly established through testing, the insurance company did obtain a much greater level of understanding regarding specific cognitive impairments as well as the type of triggers that contribute to or precipitate dysfunction. Neuropsychological testing also provided a framework for a more thorough vocational analysis and assessment of return-to-work potential within the insured's occupation.

The role of neuropsychological testing in this case study did not result in the elimination of an existing liability, nor did it provide a clear prognosis relative to recovery. Testing did, however, provide the insurance company with valid information in support of the claimant's disability, as well as information in support of the treating physician's uncertainty relative to the likelihood of a return-to-work.

REFERENCES

American Medical Association (1989). *Guides to the evaluation of permanent impairment*, 3rd ed. Chicago.
American Mental Health Counselors Association (2000). *Code of ethics*. Arlington, VA.
American Psychiatric Association (1994). *Diagnostic and statistical manual of mental disorders*, 4th ed. Washington, DC.
American Psychiatric Association (2001). *The principles of medical ethics*. Arlington, VA.
American Psychology Association (2002). *Ethical principles of psychologist and code of conduct*. Washington, DC.
Case Management Society of America (1995). *Standards of practice for case managers*. Little Rock, AR.
Connor, D. R. (1993). *Managing at the speed of change*. New York: Villard Books.
Dahl, D. (1994, April 14). The trouble with lawyers. *The Boston Globe Magazine*, 26–33.
Health Insurance Association of America (1995). *Disability claims for mental and nervous disorders*. Washington, DC.
Hilzenrath, D. S. (1998, February 16). How managed care is making doctors sick. *The Washington Post*, p. A1.
Ritvo, R. A., Litwin, A. H., & Butler, L. (Eds.) (1995). *Managing in the age of change*. New York: Irwin Professional Publishing.
Social Security Administration, Office of Disability Programs (2003). *Disability evaluation under social security*. SSA Publication, No. 64–039.

Disability benefits adjudication: Attorney representing disability claimants

38

Mark D. DeBofsky

Forensic neuropsychological testing is growing in importance in the adjudication of disability benefit claims. Although the majority of courts have ruled that claimants are not required to provide strictly "objective" evidence of disability (*Mitchell v. Eastman Kodak*, 1997), neuropsychological testing bolsters a disability claim and substantially increases the likelihood of benefit payments. Moreover, although the Social Security Administration does not differentiate between physical and mental disabilities, some self-funded disability plans refuse altogether to cover "mental" impairments, and most long-term disability insurers limit the length of time disability benefits may be paid to claimants suffering from "mental" disorders. Such distinctions have survived challenges under the Americans with Disabilities Act (2008) based on court rulings (*EEOC v. Aramark Corp.*, 2000; *EEOC v. Staten Island Savings Bank*, 2000; *Weyer v. Twentieth Century Fox*, 2000), finding that the ADA does not regulate the content of insurance policies. Thus, the principal means of challenging the applicability of such exclusions and limitations, which are usually applied only to functional mental impairments, is for the claimant to come forth with evidence of an organic impairment, the proof of which may be established or corroborated by neuropsychological testing.

A groundbreaking legal opinion on this issue in *Fitts v. Federal National Mortgage Association* (2007) is instructive. In *Fitts*, the plaintiff suffered from a bipolar disorder of such severity that she qualified for disability benefits. However, the disability insurer terminated payment of benefits after 24 months based on a policy provision limiting the payment of benefits for "mental and nervous" disorders to no more than two years' duration. The policy defined mental illness as a "mental, nervous or emotional disease[ ] or disorder[ ] of any type," a definition the court found unhelpful since it failed to clearly "specify whether a disability qualifies as a mental illness based on its causes, symptoms, forms of treatment, markers, or other aspects." The court found that classifying mental illnesses based on symptoms was unconvincing since many illnesses and conditions, such as brain damage from an accident, Alzheimer's disease, brain cancer, or a stroke, manifest psychological symptoms. The court also rejected the insurer's argument that its limitation applied, simply because bipolar disorder is listed in the *Diagnostic and Statistical Manual of Mental Disorders–IV* (1994). *Fitts* noted that the DSM–IV itself cautions against a strict distinction between physical and mental disorders:

> The term *mental disorder* unfortunately implies a distinction between "mental" disorders and "physical" disorders that is a reductionistic anachronism of mind/body dualism. A compelling literature documents that there is much "physical" in "mental" disorders and much "mental" in "physical"

disorders. The problem raised by the term "mental" disorders has been much clearer than its solution, and, unfortunately, the term persists in the title of DSM–IV because we have not found an appropriate substitute. Moreover, although this manual provides a classification of mental disorders, it must be admitted that no definition adequately specifies precise boundaries for the concept of "mental disorders."

Thus, the court ultimately precluded the insurer from utilizing the policy limit applicable to mental disorder. Nor is *Fitts* a unique court ruling. According to *Phillips v. Lincoln National Life Ins. Co.* (1992), an insurance policy containing limitations relating to mental illness that fails to define the meaning of "mental illness" is ambiguous. Therefore, under the rule of *contra proferentem*, a legal principle that construes an ambiguity in the insurance policy against the insurer that drafted the contract, the court ruled that mental disorders caused by organic trauma or disease could not be excluded from coverage due to ambiguity as to the policy's meaning of mental illness.

Likewise, in *Patterson v. Hughes Aircraft Co.* (1993), the court relied on psychological evidence to conclude, "the Plan does not make clear whether a disability qualifies as a 'mental disorder' when it results from a combination of physical and mental factors." Thus, [s]ince this ambiguity must also be resolved in [plaintiff's] favor, he is not within the limitation for mental disorders if his disability is caused in any part by headaches." Finally, *Lang v. Long Term Disability Plan of Sponsor Applied Remote Technology, Inc.* (1997) rejected an insurer's efforts to characterize as a mental disorder a claim of disability caused by fibromyalgia, a condition described in the case of *Sarchet v. Chater* (1996) as:

a common, but elusive and mysterious, disease, much like chronic fatigue syndrome, with which it shares a number of features. Its cause or causes are unknown, there is no cure, and, of greatest importance to disability law, its symptoms are entirely subjective. There are no laboratory tests for the presence or severity of fibromyalgia. The principal symptoms are "pain all over," fatigue, disturbed sleep, stiffness, and—the only symptom that discriminates between it and other diseases of a rheumatic character—multiple tender spots, more precisely 18 fixed locations on the body (and the rule of thumb is that the patient must have at least 11 of them to be diagnosed as having fibromyalgia) that when pressed firmly cause the patient to flinch.

The court applied the doctrine of *contra proferentem* to conclude, "the phrase 'mental disorder' does not include 'mental' conditions resulting from physical disorders."

What these cases highlight is the need for evidence to support a physiologic (i.e., biological) cause for claimed disabilities that arguably fall within disability policy exclusions and limitations. While some disorders may be demonstrable on an MRI or other radiological or electrophysiological tests, in the absence of positive findings on such tests, the most persuasive evidence is only obtainable from neuropsychological evaluations. This is because studies have proven the value of neuropsychological evaluations in documenting the functional status of the brain and the ability of such testing to either prove or disprove claims of brain injury or disorder. Thus, it becomes crucial for counsel representing disability claimants to present demonstrable proof that can either be clinically correlated with other evidence such as an MRI or EEG showing brain abnormalities or can independently demonstrate functional deficits.

However, while the issue of the underlying etiology of an impairment is important, the major value of neuropsychological testing in disability claim adjudications is that, unlike medical tests such as x-rays or MRI scans, or even blood tests, the data themselves directly establish functional limitations in areas such as memory, comprehension, information processing, language, and perception. The utility of such evidence is that it directly correlates to a claimant's ability to work. Therefore, both claimants and insurers have come to rely on such testing and evaluation as the gold standard in proving a claim of disability.

THE VALUE OF NEUROPSYCHOLOGICAL TESTING

Two recent court rulings conclusively demonstrate the value of neuropsychological testing. In *Smith v. Reliance Standard Life Ins. Co.* (2004), the plaintiff alleged disability due to chronic fatigue syndrome, a condition described in the medicolegal literature (Social Security Ruling 99–2p, 1999) as "a systemic disorder consisting of a complex of symptoms that may vary in incidence, duration, and severity. It is characterized in part by prolonged fatigue that lasts 6 months or more and results in substantial reduction in previous levels of occupational, educational, social, or personal activities." Because there are no known diagnostic laboratory tests for chronic fatigue syndrome, and since the insurer alleged it could not assess the insured's self-reports of fatigue, the disability determination turned on the severity of the claimant's claimed cognitive impairment associated with his physical condition. The plaintiff submitted a detailed neuropsychological evaluation, which the insurer had a psychiatrist review. The court determined that the psychiatrist completely overlooked many of the findings made by the neuropsychologist and offered no rebuttal at all to the following finding made by the neuropsychologist:

> Neuropsychological testing revealed a variety of cognitive deficits, inconsistencies or relative weaknesses most suggestive of executive dysfunction. Specifically, he demonstrated inconsistent sustained attention and concentration abilities. Alternating attention and logical sequencing abilities were in the borderline range. Speed of auditory information processing was inconsistent. Verbal fluency was mildly to moderately impaired and response inhibition was mildly impaired. In addition, he demonstrates several motor deficits suggestive of executive motor dysfunction. Executive dysfunction is common in individuals with the chronic fatigue immune deficiency syndrome diagnosis.

Because of such glaring deficiencies in the insurer's review and consideration of the neuropsychological evidence, which so convincingly demonstrated the insured's disability, the court ordered benefits to be paid.

Likewise, the court's analysis of the proof of the claimant's disability in *Hunter v. Federal Express Corp.* (2004) proved the value of neuropsychological testing. There, an employee of FedEx became disabled due to a stroke, which occurred shortly after the claimant gave birth. Although disability benefits were subsequently paid for a period of time, FedEx terminated benefit payments after concluding Ms. Hunter had sufficiently recovered to be able to work at an occupation. The court overruled that determination based in substantial part on a neuropsychological evaluation that correlated with an MRI of the brain showing the infarct. The court specifically relied on the neuropsychological test results, which demonstrated significant deficits in "visual perceptual and visuospatial reasoning," "difficulty judging relationships, reproducing them, reasoning in visuospatial terms and engaging in rapid visual scanning," "weak conceptual rule learning and difficulty with coordinated movements" and "reduced mental speed and flexibility." Ms. Hunter also demonstrated "reduced scores in both visuospatial and verbal memory," including "most notably . . . reduced retention for the material over time." Hence, based on the objective evidence of cognitive impairment, the court ordered benefits reinstated with interest and also found the insurer's actions "culpable" and awarded attorneys' fees.

From the foregoing discussion, it is evident that neuropsychological testing has proven its value in the forensic arena of disability evaluations and has been unquestionably accepted by the courts as a valuable tool in determining benefit eligibility.

NEUROPSYCHOLOGICAL ASSESSMENT

The utility of neuropsychological testing in disability evaluation is enhanced both by the quality and specificity of the test instruments utilized. A well-designed battery of neuropsychological tests affords near-conclusive proof in a disability case, while a poorly designed battery can often be harmful to the claimant's efforts to establish disability, as shown in the following examples.

Example 1

Mr. J.J. worked as a commodity trader until he suffered a series of transient ischemic attacks. Although Mr. J.J.'s claim for benefits was initially approved by his insurer, benefits were terminated after approximately one year of payment following the administration of a battery of neuropsychological tests, which included the Test of Malingered Memory, which was interpreted by the examiner to demonstrate malingering with respect to claimed memory impairments. A second examiner administered a different battery of tests, which included the following: the Wechsler Abbreviated Scale of Intelligence (WASI), portions of the Halstead-Reitan neuropsychological battery (Finger Tapping Test, Trail Making Tests A and B, Tactual Performance Test, Computer Category Test, Fingertip Number Writing Test, and Grip Strength Test) the Gordon Diagnostic System Model–III (GDS), which included the Adult Vigilance Test and Adult Distractibility Test, Memory Assessment Scales (MAS), the Stroop-Color Word Test, the Hooper Visual Organization Test, the Digit Vigilance Test, the Ruff Figural Fluency Test, FAS Letter and Category Fluency Test, Grooved Pegboard Test, Computerized Assessment of Response Bias (CARB), Word Memory Test (WMT), the Rotter Sentence Completion Test, and the Minnesota Multiphasic Personality Inventory (MMPI–2). One of the goals of the testing was to evaluate Mr. J.J. under conditions of distraction, since the environment of the commodity exchanges involves visual, oral, and even physical distractions occurring on a constant basis. The test results showed severe decompensation under conditions of distraction, and the claimant conclusively established the validity of the test results and an absence of malingering. Benefits were reinstated.

Example 2

Mr. K.K. was a practicing attorney whose professional career was focused on courtroom litigation. After experiencing a closed head injury in an automobile accident, Mr. K.K. complained of memory and cognitive deficits, withdrew from his practice, and submitted a claim for disability benefits. Although Mr. K.K.'s claim was supported by limited neuropsychological testing results and by the unequivocal opinion of the treating neurologist, a specialist in head injuries, the insurer refused to pay the claim because the initial battery of neuropsychological tests failed to include any validity testing to rule out malingering. The insurer demanded the claimant undergo a second round of testing which utilized the following tests: Wechsler Adult Intelligence Scale–III (WAIS–III), Wechsler Memory Scale–III (WMS–III), Shipley Institute of Living, Stroop Color-Word Test, Trail Making Test (Parts A and B), Gordon Diagnostic System (GDS), Test of Variables of Attention (TOVA), Paced Auditory Serial Addition Test (PASAT), Visual Naming and Controlled Oral Word Association subtests of the Multilingual Aphasia Examination, Animal Name Fluency, Ruff Figural Fluency, Wisconsin Card Sorting Test (WCST), Booklet Category Test, California Verbal Learning Test–II (CVLT–II), Tactual Performance Test (TPT), Sensory Perceptual Examination, Victoria Symptom Validity Test (VSVT), Test of Memory Malingering (TOMM), Word Memory Test (WMT), MicroCog (reaction timers 1 and 2), Finger Tapping, Grip Strength, Grooved Pegboard,

Behavioral Inattention Test (BIT), Beck Depression Inventory–II (BDI–II), Beck Hopelessness Scale (BHS), Beck Anxiety Inventory (BAI), Minnesota Multiphasic Personality Inventory–2 (MMPI–2), Spatial Relations, and the Behavioral Dyscontrol Scale (BDS). This battery included several formal tests of malingering, tests of executive decision making, tests of functioning under conditions of distractibility, as well as timed tests relating to memory and recall in order to evaluate Mr. K.K.'s abilities to work as a trial lawyer. Although the testing showed many of the claimant's abilities were preserved, he functioned poorly on tests that correlated to courtroom work. In particular, Mr. K.K. was unable to recall information quickly and process disparate facts and legal principles, as he would have to do in taking a deposition or conducting a trial. Because there was absolutely no evidence of a malingered performance on testing, benefits were paid.

Example 3

Like Example 2, the claimant, Mr. L.L., a business executive, alleged disability due to a closed head injury suffered in a car accident. He underwent a battery of neuropsychological tests that showed significant impairment in memory, concentration, and executive functioning. However, as was the case in the previous example, the examiner administered no testing that would validate the results and rule out malingering. When Mr. L.L. refused to undergo additional testing, the insurer determined the claimant was grossly exaggerating his impairment and benefits were denied.

Example 4

Mr. M.M. ceased working as a commodity trader due to severe depression, which he claimed prevented him from making timely and accurate decisions on the floor of the exchange where he worked. He was under the care of a psychiatrist who certified disability; however, the insurer refused to pay benefits claiming a lack of sufficient supporting evidence. Neuropsychological testing showed diminished capacity for processing information and decision making; and a highly experienced forensic psychiatrist conducted a probing forensic psychiatric examination that corroborated the test results. The neuropsychological test battery included several measures to detect malingering, which the claimant passed. However, despite the evidence presented, the insurer refused to pay benefits, and only had the claimant examined after suit was filed. Instead of retaining a neuropsychologist, however, the insurer hired a psychiatrist, who administered the Millon Clinical Multiaxial Inventory (MCMI) test and several malingering tests that are not part of the standard neuropsychological test battery. Despite test results showing the claimant was not malingering, the insurer's examiner nonetheless characterized the claimant as a malingerer and opined that his impairment was due to excessive consumption of alcohol. Needless to say, when the test results proved contrary to the examining doctor's opinion, the case was quickly settled.

Example 5

Mr. N.N., in his late fifties, worked as a physician in a highly stressful university hospital setting. He became severely depressed and applied for disability benefits, which were approved. After several years of benefit payment, based on a psychiatrist's suspicion that Mr. N.N. was suffering from dementia, he underwent several rounds of neuropsychological testing. Although one psychologist confirmed dementia, others did not. The insurer also demanded that Mr. N.N. undergo testing and a psychiatric evaluation. The insurer's psychiatrist confirmed there were clinical duties the insured could not perform due to psychiatric symptoms; however, the insurer's psychologist formulated an opinion that the MMPI test results supported malingering and that memory testing was also indicative of malingering. Further examination of the test results by Mr. N.N.'s consulting psychologist, however, contradicted the insurer's psychologist by pointing out that the claim of malingered memory was contrary to the manual developed by the author of the memory test; and the MMPI score was well below what most experts would consider the cutoff for a finding of malingering. The claim settled.

Example 6

Mr. O.O. was a business executive who suffered a stroke. An initial round of neuropsychological testing validated cognitive impairments due to the stroke; however, a second round of testing performed approximately one year later by the same psychologist suggested a malingered profile. The insurer demanded the psychologist's data, and its reviewing psychologist suggested the evidence of cognitive impairment due to a stroke was not persuasive, even though an MRI showed a lesion in the brain. Subsequent neuropsychological testing corroborated the finding of a malingered profile on psychological testing, even though other physical impairments appear to be of sufficient severity to qualify him for benefits.

Example 7

Mr. P.P. was a financial analyst in his early fifties, who began experiencing symptoms of severe memory loss as well as loss of bladder control and unexplained falls. His neurologist suspected either partial-complex seizures or early dementia, particularly since PET scan results showed abnormal brain activity. The insurer initially accepted that the claimant was disabled; however, the determination was based on finding that the claimant suffered from depression, since three rounds of neuropsychological testing failed to demonstrate a definitive cognitive abnormality. Consequently, benefits were terminated after two years of payment due to insurance policy provisions limiting the payment of disability benefits for depression to 24 months.

Discussion

These examples illustrate several different types of claims in which neuropsychological testing played a significant role in disability benefit disputes. What these examples also demonstrate is that neuropsychological testing, when properly performed, yields irrefutable objective proof of functional abnormalities supporting the payment of disability benefits. So long as the data are consistent and malingering can be ruled out, the insurer is left with no legitimate basis to deny benefit payments.

Our experience has shown us that many insurers employ highly qualified consultants experienced in reviewing neuropsychological test data. They focus on test results consistent with established criteria and are quick to seize on any data suggesting a malingered profile. Thus, it is crucial for the claimant to present validated test results that support the claimed disability and rule out any issues relating to secondary gain.

Further, to the extent the disability insurance policy is of the type that pays benefits if the claimant cannot perform the duties of his or her occupation, it is important for the neuropsychologist to select test instruments that come as close as possible to simulating the particular demands of the occupation. The first example, where testing of performance under conditions of distraction was crucial to success, is illustrative of this point. Likewise, the second example shows how test instruments focused on evaluating the occupational duties performed by the claimant were decisive in establishing an entitlement to benefits. However, no matter how well chosen the test instruments, the testing is worthless without rigorous testing of response bias or potential malingering in view of the risk of secondary gain as shown in the third example.

The fourth and fifth examples further demonstrate the significance of testing aimed at detecting malingering. The elimination of malingering as an explanation for abnormal neuropsychological test results provides powerful corroboration of the substantive findings, while detection of malingering clearly undermines those findings.

The remaining examples demonstrate how testing can be used to either validate physical findings of disability or to support a conclusion that an identifiable physiological cause is not the basis of a claimed disability. Hence, the final example illustrates that the test results were so contrary to what is seen in patients suffering from dementia that the initial theory was confidently ruled out. However, it is important to keep in mind the following common-sense observation made in a leading text on forensic neuropsychology (Sweet, 1999):

> Not all insufficient effort is malingering. There are multiple dimensions of insufficient effort; determination of insufficient effort as caused by malingering occurs within a real life context, not simply examination of test performances. Malingering can have variable degrees of intention, selectivity in presentation, variable degrees of exaggeration, and more than one strategy on the part of the malingerer or across malingerers. Moreover, malingering need not be an all or none concept; co-occurrence of malingering and brain dysfunction is possible although not commonplace.

Thus, the guiding principle is that each case presents unique facts and circumstances and must be evaluated from a multidimensional perspective utilizing the tools of both medicine and neuropsychology.

THE LIMITS OF NEUROPSYCHOLOGICAL ASSESSMENT IN VOCATIONAL ASSESSMENT

Although neuropsychological testing has tremendous value in disability evaluation, it is important to point out its limits, particularly if the results of testing are not clear-cut. The direct utility of neuropsychological test results in disability determination also depends on the nature of the disability claim: whether the claimant's disability is being evaluated from the perspective of an ability to perform a particular occupation or whether the definition of disability is more generalized, i.e., the inability to engage in any occupation. While neuropsychologists are highly qualified to furnish opinions on impairment, they are not vocational experts or lawyers; and it is important to keep in mind that the determination of "disability" is a legal construct, made up of both medical and vocational components. "Disability" is a term defined either by statute or by contract. For example, the Social Security Act (2008) defines "disability" as the "inability to engage in any substantial gainful activity." A typical insurance policy, on the other hand, might define "disability" as the "inability to engage in the material duties of your occupation." In order to answer the question of whether an individual meets either of those definitions, one has to analyze the medical (or neuropsychological) findings in relation to the specific physical and mental requirements of an occupation.

Unlike the private disability insurance sector, the Social Security Administration, in a policy statement, Ruling 85–15 (1985), has furnished far more detailed guidance on the evidence necessary to establish an inability to perform unskilled work:

> The basic mental demands of competitive, remunerative, unskilled work include the abilities (on a sustained basis) to understand, carry out, and remember simple instructions; to respond appropriately to supervision, coworkers, and usual work situations; and to deal with changes in a routine work

setting. A substantial loss of ability to meet any of these basic work-related activities would severely limit the potential occupational base. This, in turn, would justify a finding of disability because even favorable age, education, or work experience will not offset such a severely limited occupational base.

The Social Security guideline also notes:

> Stress and Mental Illness—Since mental illness is defined and characterized by maladaptive behavior, it is not unusual that the mentally impaired have difficulty accommodating to the demands of work and work-like settings. Determining whether these individuals will be able to adapt to the demands or "stress" of the workplace is often extremely difficult. This section is not intended to set out any presumptive limitations for disorders, but to emphasize the importance of thoroughness in evaluation on an individualized basis.
>
> Individuals with mental disorders often adopt a highly restricted and/or inflexible lifestyle within which they appear to function well. Good mental health services and care may enable chronic patients to function adequately in the community by lowering psychological pressures, by medication, and by support from services such as outpatient facilities, day-care programs, social work programs and similar assistance.
>
> The reaction to the demands of work (stress) is highly individualized, and mental illness is characterized by adverse responses to seemingly trivial circumstances. The mentally impaired may cease to function effectively when facing such demands as getting to work regularly, having their performance supervised, and remaining in the workplace for a full day. A person may become panicked and develop palpitations, shortness of breath, or feel faint while riding in an elevator; another may experience terror and begin to hallucinate when approached by a stranger asking a question. Thus, the mentally impaired may have difficulty meeting the requirements of even so-called "low-stress" jobs.
>
> Because response to the demands of work is highly individualized, the skill level of a position is not necessarily related to the difficulty an individual will have in meeting the demands of the job. A claimant's condition may make performance of an unskilled job as difficult as an objectively more demanding job. For example, a busboy need only clear dishes from tables. But an individual with a severe mental disorder may find unmanageable the demands of making sure that he removes all the dishes, does not drop them, and gets the table cleared promptly for the waiter or waitress. Similarly, an individual who cannot tolerate being supervised may not be able to work even in the absence of close supervision; the knowledge that one's work is being judged and evaluated, even when the supervision is remote or indirect, can be intolerable for some mentally impaired persons. Any impairment-related limitations created by an individual's response to demands of work, however, must be reflected in the RFC [residual functional capacity] assessment.

The Social Security guidelines therefore make it evident that neuropsychological evaluations can be of tremendous value in assessing disability. However, *Heinrich v. Prime Computer Long Term Disability Plan* (1996) points out:

> The physician, of course, is qualified to determine a claimant's physical condition, which the administrator may properly rely upon in reaching its own determination as to whether the claimant is disabled under the terms of the plan. But we know of no reason, nor do the defendants offer one, why a physician has any expertise in determining employment qualifications, which is a wholly separate question from physical condition.

Although written in the context of a physical disability claim, the quotation above is equally applicable to a mental disability claim and highlights the importance of a vocational analysis coupled with the neuropsychological evaluation. While neuropsychologists may have a basic understanding of what mental tasks an attorney, a physician, or a business executive must be capable of performing in order to engage in their occupational duties, from an evidentiary standpoint, courts question the competency of neuropsychologists to furnish vocational opinions, and separate opinions from individuals trained and experienced in vocational analysis may be required. Mild impairment in memory or cognitive abilities may have little or no effect on some individuals' ability to function in their jobs, whereas the same impairment may be catastrophic to a commodity trader, an emergency room physician, or a trial lawyer whose occupations require the ability to assemble, recall, and analyze large amounts of data in split-second timeframes. This perhaps explains why there is frequently so much disagreement in disability evaluation—while a neuropsychologist may opine that test results would preclude an individual from functioning in a particular occupation, an insurer's consulting neuropsychologist may draw just the opposite conclusion from the same data and determine that the impairments would not preclude functioning. Similarly, the insurer's own vocational expert may describe different functional demands than those understood by the neuropsychologist to be at issue. For that reason, in our experience, we frequently couple a neuropsychological evaluation with a vocational analysis.

The issue is perhaps easier to resolve with Social Security adjudications since entitlement to Social Security disability benefits requires an individual to be so profoundly impaired that all work would be precluded. In determining the question of disability, the Social Security Administration relies heavily on vocational assessments. Nonetheless, the utility of neuropsychological testing is that it directly answers the basic questions of whether an impairment interferes with a claimant's ability "(on a sustained basis) to understand, carry out, and remember simple instructions; to respond appropriately to supervision, coworkers, and usual work situations; and to deal with changes in a routine work setting." Each of these functions is capable of being tested, and the test results will yield valid data enabling the psychologist to offer meaningful opinions.

THE LEGAL LIMITS OF NEUROPSYCHOLOGICAL ASSESSMENT

In addition to the limitations of neuropsychological assessment in vocational determinations, various evidentiary requirements also affect the use of psychological testing in court. At the outset, the testing has to pass the reliability standards set forth by the Supreme Court in *Daubert v. Merrell Dow Pharmaceuticals* (1993), which requires, as a condition of admissibility of psychological testing, evidence that the test instrument in question has been validated by research, and has been subject to peer review and publication, and there is evidence establishing that the known or potential rates of error are minimal, and which also considers the general acceptance of the instrument. Although the Minnesota Multiphasic Personality Inventory (MMPI/MMPI–2) has been accepted as a valid test under the *Daubert* standard according to Pope, Butcher, and Seelen (2000), other test results showing cognitive abnormalities may not pass the evidentiary threshold because of the absence of sufficient research and publication in which the test has been validated. There is also a judicial suspicion of any instrument that purports to function as a detector of truth. For example, polygraph results have long been deemed inadmissible by courts due to doubts about the reliability of such testing. The Supreme Court noted in *United States v. Scheffer* (1998):

> To this day, the scientific community remains extremely polarized about the reliability of polygraph techniques. 1 D. Faigman, D. Kaye, M. Saks, & J. Sanders, Modern Scientific Evidence 565, n. + 14–2.0, and § 14–3.0 (1997); see also 1 P. Giannelli & E. Imwinkelried, Scientific Evidence § 8–2(C), pp. 225–227 (2d ed. 1993) (hereinafter Giannelli & Imwinkelried); 1 J. Strong, McCormick on Evidence § 206, p. 909 (4th ed. 1992) (hereinafter McCormick). Some studies have concluded that polygraph tests overall are accurate and reliable. See, e.g., S. Abrams, The Complete Polygraph Handbook 190–191 (1968) (reporting the overall accuracy rate from laboratory studies involving the common "control question technique" polygraph to be "in the range of 87 percent"). Others have found that polygraph tests assess truthfulness significantly less accurately—that scientific field studies suggest the accuracy

rate of the "control question technique" polygraph is "little better than could be obtained by the toss of a coin," that is, 50 percent. See Iacono & Lykken, The Scientific Status of Research on Polygraph Techniques: The Case Against Polygraph Tests, in 1 Modern Scientific Evidence, supra, § 14–5.3, p. 629 (hereinafter Iacono & Lykken).

Psychological testing has been subject to the same skepticism; and evidentiary issues remain about the admissibility of opinions relating to the subject of malingering.

The leading court ruling on the subject is the federal appellate ruling in *Nichols v. American National Ins. Co.* (1998), an employment discrimination case in which the plaintiff alleged she had been the victim of sexual harassment. In an effort to discredit the plaintiff's testimony, the employer introduced testimony from a psychiatrist who had examined Nichols and administered testing. The witness testified that the plaintiff exhibited "recall bias," and opined that her statements were affected by secondary gain and malingering, terms which were explained to mean that the plaintiff's psychological symptoms were motivated by financial gain and that symptoms were feigned or made up for the purpose of secondary gain. The trial court ruled the testimony was admissible, but the appellate tribunal found the trial court erred in allowing such testimony to be presented to the jury. The court ruled that expert testimony couldn't reach "conclusions within the jury's competence or within an exclusive function of the jury." The court then explained that the psychiatrist's testimony "sought to answer the very question at the heart of the jury's task—could Nichols be believed?" The danger of such testimony, according to the court, was that it could lead to the jury "substitut[ing] the expert's credibility assessment for its own common sense determination." In its briefing to the court, the employer argued that the testimony was not about the plaintiff as a witness, but about her psychological state. However, the court flatly rejected that argument, holding, "an expert should not offer an opinion about the truthfulness of witness testimony."

Subsequent to *Nichols*, a state appellate court in Missouri reaffirmed *Nichols'* conclusions in a case that coincidentally involved the same psychiatrist whose opinion had earlier been rejected. In *McGuire v. Seltsam* (2004), a personal injury suit, the court found testimony on the subject of malingering prejudicial and reversed a lower court's ruling since the testimony constituted an improper expert opinion on a witness's credibility.

However, the conclusions reached in *Nichols* and *McGuire* are by no means the universal state of the law in the United States. In *United States v. Kokoski* (1994), the court held that a criminal defendant's competency to stand trial was established by a forensic evaluation that included the administration of psychological tests demonstrating gross malingering. Indeed, the United States called a witness it characterized as a "malingering expert," who testified that the defendant was faking his symptoms. The testimony related solely to the issue of the defendant's competency to stand trial, however; it was not introduced as evidence of the defendant's guilt or innocence, and the *Kokoski* ruling cannot be taken as support for admission of malingering evidence in a jury's determination of guilt or innocence.

Testimony and opinions as to malingering on psychological testing are generally accepted, though, by administrative agencies such as the Social Security Administration in the course of evaluating a disability claim, according to the *Nichols* ruling. Opinions about malingering are also frequently allowed in state court proceedings; however, a recent news story in the *Lawyers Weekly USA* (2004) described how a plaintiff in a personal injury suit was able to overcome testimony charging her with malingering and received a sizable jury verdict compensating her for injuries. The article noted the plaintiff challenged the proffered testimony by having her consultant reexamine the underlying raw data, which supported a conclusion contrary to the examiner's finding (see Example 4 above for a similar situation). The plaintiff's consultant also offered an alternative explanation for short-term memory deficits that had been characterized as malingered—the findings could equally be explained as the consequence of traumatic brain injury. The test results were apparently quite close to the cutoff scores for a finding of malingering, and the conclusion drawn was, therefore, one of a degree of probability rather than clear certainty.

What this discussion illustrates is that while cognitive deficits may be convincingly demonstrated, opinions with respect to malingering remain controversial. It is possible that the controversy turns more on the use of the term "malingering" than on what the term represents, since characterization of a litigant's test results as showing malingering says "liar" to a jury, whereas the term clearly presents a different meaning to the psychologist. Certainly, there are situations where a psychologist's opinion as to malingering would be admissible although different terminology would probably be more appropriate. When neuropsychological test results support impairment, but there is an indication of a malingered performance, there is no reason to preclude the expert from testifying as to why the test results are invalid and cannot be used to support a claim of disability (see Example 3, above). There may also be situations in which experts dispute one another on the issue of the validity of test results (see Example 5, above). However, in the example given of the individual whose test results showed a malingered performance on neuropsychological testing (Example 6), such results should not be admissible solely to impugn the credibility of the remaining medical test results that demonstrate a disability separate and apart from any claim of cognitive impairment.

It becomes very tempting for insurers in disability benefit disputes to use the appellation "malingerer" as a synonym for prevaricator, yet it is well known that impairment may co-exist with malingering; and science has yet to develop an accurate lie-detector. Thus, the point made by the *Nichols* ruling is quite valid. Expert testimony that someone has been untruthful is extremely powerful evidence and may sway the jury from reaching its own independent conclusion on the issue. Certainly, it is appropriate for the lawyers to argue an inference of untruthfulness, but that is the role of the advocate, not the expert witness. The expert witness must be limited to opinions regarding the validity or invalidity of the test data and the reasons for their conclusions. Although *Nichols* involved employment discrimination rather than a claim for disability benefits, the court's conclusion as to the improper use of the label "malingerer" would no doubt also be applied to disability benefit claims. Thus, while an entitlement to disability benefits can be proven and challenged with psychological test results, the experts must be careful not to usurp either the role of the advocate or the court.

CONCLUSION

We have examined the utility and limits of neuropsychological testing in disability evaluation from the point of view of a claimant's representative. Clearly, as the examples given point out, neuropsychological testing possesses tremendous evidentiary value. In the first place, such testing demonstrates functional restrictions and limitations that can be correlated with work duties. Neuropsychological testing can also be utilized to differentiate between mental conditions that have an organic cause, such as dementia, and functional mental impairments, such as depression. Further, like all good science, built into neuropsychological testing are instruments that can be used to either validate or invalidate results relating to deficiencies found by other test instruments. The ability to validate thereby makes the evidence exceptionally persuasive in establishing the claimant's limitations by ruling out issues such as secondary gain and bias. Without such validation, the psychologist's opinions are subject to being challenged.

However, even well-validated testing has its limits. As we have seen, neuropsychologists are able to demonstrate impairments in memory, concentration, language, perception, and in other areas of functioning, but do not necessarily have the appropriate credentials to furnish an opinion as to "disability," a legal term that has both medical and vocational components. In many cases, therefore, a thorough neuropsychological evaluation should be coupled with an equally rigorous vocational evaluation.

In addition, there are evidentiary considerations that affect the admissibility of neuropsychological testing. The test instruments themselves have to be validated in order to meet the scientific requirements imposed by the courts. However, even where the validity of the test instruments can be scientifically proven, an opinion of "malingering" has a very powerful effect in the courtroom and cannot be used to characterize the claimant's credibility in general. On the other hand, an opinion of malingering tailored toward challenging the validity of a determination of impairment is entirely appropriate. In a close case, which many disability disputes are, there may be differing interpretations of data. Such cases should not be determined based on one side's expert vouching for the claimant's credibility while the other side gives the opposite opinion—neither opinion is appropriate in litigation. Instead, the opinions need to be refocused on validation of disability versus a challenge to the legitimacy of findings of cognitive impairment. By avoiding providing direct opinions upon the claimant's credibility, the merit of neuropsychological testing and the opinions that result as a basis for evaluating claims of disability is unsurpassed.

REFERENCES

Americans with Disabilities Act (2008). 42 U.S.C. §12117.

Daubert v. Merrell Dow Pharmaceuticals (1993). 509 U.S. 579.

Diagnostic and Statistical Manual of Mental Disorders–IV (1994). At xxi.

EEOC v. Aramark Corp. (2000) 208 F.3d 266, D.C. Cir.

EEOC v. Staten Island Savings Bank (2000). 207 F.3d 144, 2d Cir.

Fitts v. Federal National Mortgage Association (2007, May 7). No. 98–00617, 2007 U.S.Dist.LEXIS 33397, D.D.C.

Heinrich v. Prime Computer Long Term Disability Plan (1996). U.S.Dist.LEXIS 12564 *14–*15, N.D.Ill.

Hunter v. Federal Express Corp. (2004). U.S.Dist.LEXIS 13271, E.D.Pa.

Lang v. Long Term Disability Plan of Sponsor Applied Remote Technology, Inc. (1997). 125 F.3d 794, 799, 9th Cir.

Lawyers Weekly USA (2004, March 1). Plaintiff contests "malingering" test results to win verdict. LWUSA 167.

McGuire v. Seltsam (2004, March 28). 2004 Mo.App.LEXIS 328, Mo.Ct.App.

Mitchell v. Eastman Kodak (1997). 113 F.3d 433, 3d Cir.

Nichols v. American National Ins. Co. (1998). 154 F.3d 875, 883, 8th Cir.

Patterson v. Hughes Aircraft Co. (1993). 11 F.3d 948, 950, 9th Cir.

Phillips v. Lincoln National Life Insurance Company (1992). 978 F.2d 302, 7th Cir.

Pope, K., Butcher, J., & Seelen, J. (2000). *The MMPI, MMPI–2, and MMPI–A in court*, 2nd ed. Washington, DC: American Psychological Association.

Sarchet v. Chater (1996). 78 F.3d 305, 306–07, 7th Cir.

Smith v. Reliance Standard Life Ins. Co. (2004). 322 F.Supp.2d 1168, 1177, D.Colo.

Social Security Act (2008). 42 U.S.C. §423(d)(1)(A).

Social Security Ruling 85–15 (1985). 1985 SSR LEXIS 20 *11, *14–*16, C.E.

Social Security Ruling 99–2p (1999). C.E.

Sweet, J. (1999). Malingering: Differential Diagnosis. In J. Sweet (Ed.), *Forensic neuropsychology: Fundamentals and practice* (p. 277). Lisse, Netherlands: Swets & Zeitlinger.

United States v. Kokoski (1994). 865 F.Supp. 325, S.D.W.Va.

United States v. Scheffer (1998). 523 U.S. 303, 309–312.

Weyer v. Twentieth Century Fox Film Corp. (2000). 198 F.3d 1104, 9th Cir.

Social Security adjudication: Regional consultant

39

Henry G. Conroe

Social Security disability payments, administered by the Social Security Administration (SSA), are presently provided through two programs, Title II and Title XVI, to about 9 million people and their families. There are more than 2 million new applicants, both adults and children, yearly. Title II eligibility is determined by FICA contributions made when the individual worked, while Title XVI eligibility is based on financial need. The cash payments and associated health coverage are important resources for recipients with serious mental disorders.

After the individual applies in the local field office, their claim proceeds to the Disability Determination Services (DDS) at the state level. The case is then reviewed by a disability examiner and, in most instances, by a medical or psychological consultant after the medical and lay evidence has been developed. An initial decision is made regarding the presence or absence of disability. A percentage of the completed cases are sent to one of the ten regional offices for quality assurance review. Unfavorable decisions can be appealed for reconsideration by the state or for adjudication by an administrative law judge who is part of the SSA Office of Hearings and Appeals.

Two definitions are essential to understanding the program's approach to malingering. These are contained in the Social Security Administration's publication *Disability Evaluation under Social Security* (Social Security Administration, Office of Disability, January 2005), which is also known as the "Blue Book." First is the definition of disability (p. 2) as "the inability to engage in any substantial gainful activity (SGA) by reason of any medically determinable physical or mental impairment(s), which can be expected to result in death or which has lasted or can be expected to last for a continuous period of not less than 12 months." Second is the definition of a "medically determinable impairment" (p. 3) as "an impairment that results from anatomical, physiological, or psychological abnormalities, which can be shown by medically acceptable clinical and laboratory diagnostic techniques." This "impairment must be established by medical evidence consisting of signs, symptoms and laboratory findings—not only by the individual's statement of symptoms."

Based on my inquiries to the Office of the Inspector General and the Central Office of Disability Programs, statistics regarding the incidence of malingering in the Social Security program are not maintained. The reason cited is that the gathering of data on claimants does not encompass this entity as a diagnosis. This does not mean that the program is unaware of this problem. It has issued DI 23025.010H.1 as part of "Identifying Cases That are High Risk for FSF [Fraud or Similar Fault]." The following are excerpts from this section:

> "Certain impairments have been found to be particularly prevalent in FSF claims. Generally, these are impairments in which self-serving statements by an applicant may play a more important role in evaluating severity than in other conditions." Mental impairments, when associated with the following specific characteristics are considered to be "high risk for FSF":

(a) There is an allegation of mental retardation, with any of the following conditions:

- A history of semi-skilled/skilled work activity.
- Available school records show no history of special education.
- Early school/medical records are unavailable with no reasonable explanation or the records lack any indication of significant problems. The records do not necessarily have to show a diagnosis of mental retardation in order to indicate significant problems.
- Poor cooperation on psychological or intelligence tests, with no indication of another physical or mental impairment, including educational or linguistic limitations that could account for the behavior.
- Absent, unreliable, or conflicting information concerning activities of daily living (ADL).

(b) A mental impairment other than mental retardation is alleged, with any of the following conditions:

- There is no history of treatment, or only very recent outpatient treatment, and there is no valid reason or explanations as to why treatment has not been sought or has only started recently.
- There is a suspicious situation involving a third party providing information, e.g., a third party provides all answers to questions even when the claimant appears capable of doing so, or the third party frequently interrupts or contradicts the claimant.
- Highly unusual or bizarre claimant behavior is reported by the FO [field office] or at a CE [consultative examination], and does not appear to be related to a psychotic or other alleged mental disorder. It is important to consider the degree of consistency with other evidence in the file regarding the claimant's behavior.
- Absent, unreliable, or conflicting information concerning activities of daily living (ADL).

(c) "Allegations of severe mental problems first surface during an appeal or subsequent application process." A caution is provided regarding the need to "consider that claimants are sometimes reluctant to bring up mental illness or that individuals dealing with chronic illness/pain may begin to exhibit symptoms of depression."

The SSA in DI 23025.020 suggests development techniques in potentially fraudulent cases. The following are sources that are listed as potentially helpful sources in developing the claim:

- Evidence from medical sources not previously contacted, which are shown on reports already in file.
- Prescription records and other data on the frequency and type of medication received.
- Teachers' reports and school records to include grades and standardized test results.
- Employer reports.
- Records from State agencies responsible for driving licenses and automobile registration, and trade or similar licenses.
- Welfare records to include such information as recent training and education, allegations of health status, ADLs, family situations, readiness for employment, etc.
- Prison intake assessments and probation/parole officer reports.
- For immigrants: relevant records from the Immigration and Naturalization Service or from the country of origin.
- Input from sources knowledgeable about the claimant's activities of daily living and their "usual behavior and appearance." These contacts include social workers, welfare agency workers, foster care licensing/placement agencies, insurance companies involved in injuries relating to a vehicle or worksite injury, clergy, past employers, neighbors, teachers, or personnel from community-based organizations.
- Home visits by professional healthcare workers.
- An independent consultative examination after prior files and background information have been gathered. This accumulated evidence should be provided to the psychiatrist or psychologist

prior to the evaluation. The examiner is requested to "state whether the claimant's presentation is consistent with the alleged impairment(s), ADLs [activities of daily living], and medical history." The mental health professional is alerted, "to record anything unusual concerning third parties, e.g., a claimant may respond in a limited fashion but an interpreter provides an elaborate response."

- Caution is urged when obtaining information about functioning from the claimant's family or friends as "on occasion, family members have been found to exaggerate the claimant's limitations."

Another concept that the Social Security Administration uses in addressing malingering is the credibility of a claimant's statements about symptoms and the ensuing functional effects. As noted in an unpublished policy clarification paper titled "Credibility, Malingering and Psychological Testing" by Michael Kovar (2000), credibility focuses on the believability of statements by the individual while malingering focuses on the believability of symptoms described by the claimant and behavior exhibited by the individual. Social Security Ruling SSR 96-7p provides the following details regarding the assessment of credibility that apply to malingering:

- No symptom or combination of symptoms can be the basis for a finding of disability, no matter how genuine the individual's complaints may appear to be, unless there are medical signs and laboratory findings demonstrating the existence of a medically determinable physical or mental impairment(s) that could reasonably be expected to produce the symptoms.
- When the existence of a medically determinable physical or mental impairment(s) that could reasonably be expected to produce the symptoms has been established, the intensity, persistence, and functionally limiting effects of the symptoms must be evaluated to determine the extent to which the symptoms affect the individual's ability to do basic work activities. This requires the adjudicator to make a finding about the credibility of the individual's statements about the symptom(s) and its functional effects.
- Because symptoms, such as pain, sometimes suggest a greater severity of impairment than can be shown by objective medical evidence alone, the adjudicator must carefully consider the individual's statements about symptoms with the rest of the relevant evidence in the case record in reaching a conclusion about the credibility of the individual's statements if a disability determination decision that is fully favorable to the individual cannot be made solely on the basis of objective medical evidence.
- In determining the credibility of the individual's statements, the adjudicator must consider the entire case record, including the objective medical evidence, the individual's own statements about symptoms, statements and other information provided by treating or examining physicians or psychologists and other persons about the symptoms and how they affect the individual, and any other relevant evidence in the case record. An individual's statements about the intensity and persistence of pain or other symptoms or about the effect the symptoms have on his or her ability to work may not be disregarded solely because they are not substantiated by objective medical evidence.

The ruling warns that:

The credibility of the individual's statements cannot be based on an intangible or intuitive notion about an individual's credibility. The reasons for the credibility finding must be grounded in the evidence and articulated in the determination or decision. . . . Moreover, a finding that an individual's statements are not credible, or not wholly credible, is not in itself sufficient to establish that the individual is not disabled. All of the evidence in the case record, including the individual's statements, must be considered before a conclusion can be made about disability.

In addition to what has already been described earlier regarding identifying cases that are of high risk for FSF (Fraud or Similar Fault), SSR 96-7p emphasizes the consistency, "both internally and with other information in the case record" needed to establish the credibility of the individual's statements. The adjudicator is urged to consider the following factors:

- The degree to which the individual's statements are consistent with the medical signs and laboratory findings and other information provided by medical sources, including information about medical history and treatment.
- The consistency of the individual's own statements. The adjudicator must compare statements made by the individual in connection with his or her claim for disability benefits with statements he or she made under other circumstances.
- The consistency of the individual's statements with other information in the case record, including reports and observations by other persons concerning the individual's daily activities, behavior, and efforts to work.

As can be seen above, the Social Security Administration does not formally address the use of specific tests for malingering such as the Portland Digit Recognition Test, the Rey Word Recognition List, the Fifteen Item Memory Test and the validity scales of the MMPI–2. This does not mean that it is unaware of these tools. Because of the nature of the Social Security Disability process as described above, these tests are considered of limited usefulness in assessing malingering in the broader context of the program. Claims are not adjudicated solely on the basis of symptoms or behaviors, which is the form that malingered complaints and malingered responses take. Even if there is indication that the individual is not being truthful, the full evaluation process is carried out with reliance on information from sources such as records from treating physicians, treating psychologists or hospitals, the findings from the consultative examination, and the accounts of reliable third parties. With the use of this additional evidence, the lack of a claimant's veracity is viewed as not necessarily significantly hampering the evaluation of allegations and nevertheless reaching a balanced assessment.

For example, a claimant might allege having suffered a traumatic brain injury several years before, which currently impairs their ability to work because of poor memory and concentration. SSA would typically request documentation of the head trauma from a hospital and/or rehabilitation center to establish the credibility of the claimant's allegations and to assess the initial severity of the head trauma. Neuropsychological testing performed in the months following the incident when the deficits seem to have stabilized would allow the program to gauge both the resulting cognitive and emotional impairments and the degree of recovery that has occurred. At the point at which the claimant has applied for disability, which might be a considerable period after the initial brain injury, SSA needs to develop a longitudinal picture of whether the person's claims of cognitive and/or emotional impairment are consistent with the actual posttraumatic course. Reports from the early neuropsychological testing would be crucial in this assessment, as it would provide a foundation with which subsequent clinical and non-clinical data can be compared. For instance, if marked improvement was documented in the individual's memory, concentration, and attention by the neuropsychological testing, it is unlikely that significant deterioration in functioning would occur without an additional insult to the brain, such as substance abuse or another head injury, or the development of another condition, such as a mood disorder or psychosis. If the presence of these additional conditions cannot be established, the claimant's credibility might be brought into question.

To help resolve this question, SSA would request medical documentation from the claimant for the period between the initial head injury and the date of application for disability. If the person was not actively involved in a rehabilitation program or being followed by a mental health professional, the cognitive and emotional medical evidence from the intervening period might be sparse. SSA might then have to rely upon collateral information from family, friends, and employers about the person's day-to-day functioning in order to bridge the gap in data. If the claimant currently describes the inability to perform daily activities such as living independently, maintaining personal care, driving, cooking, providing child care, managing their household, interacting appropriately with others, paying bills, and pursuing hobbies, a search would be needed to find physical or psychological reasons for these deficits. If reliable third party information is not congruent with the person's account, then the claimant's credibility might be questioned. For instance, this might occur if the person was employed for a considerable period following the head injury in a job that required the use of higher-level abilities involving memory, concentration, attention, and judgment. If contact with the former employer elicited praise for the person's job performance, no indication of the use of special accommodations to help the individual with the demands of the work and no problems with supervisors and co-workers, and if the reason for the termination of employment was a non-disability factor, such as a layoff or the person seeking a higher paying position, then serious discrepancies would be apparent between the claimant's account of functional limitations and the information from an employer who has no vested interest in the disability decision.

If the picture remains unclear, then the program will do additional development to help resolve the question of credibility. This next step might include an independent medical evaluation of the claimant's current mental status and cognitive abilities. The usual psychological tests requested would be a Wechsler Memory Scale and possibly intelligence testing. Other specific neuropsychological tests, including tests of effort or malingering, are rarely ordered. As noted on pages 69 and 152 of the *Disability Evaluation under Social Security* or "Blue Book" (Social Security Administration, Office of Disability, January 2005), the validity of a formal psychological test result is to be addressed by the consulting psychologist by noting and resolving discrepancies between test results and the individual's behavior and daily activities. Neuropsychologists will recognize this method of noting invalid results as one that is recommended in their relevant literature.

When a neuropsychologist is the consultative exam panel member hired to perform the testing, expertise in evaluating response bias and test invalidity can be helpful in assessing the claimant's clinical course after the initial trauma and in evaluating the possibility of malingering. Additional neuropsychological input into the ultimate evaluation of the person's credibility might come at the state level (Disability Determination Services), the Regional Office level, and the Central Office level, where psychologists with experience in neuropsychology often play a central role in weighing the conflicts in evidence and helping to resolve the inconsistencies.

SUMMARY

In conclusion, through the use of the development of a medically determinable impairment and the concept of credibility, the Social Security Administration monitors the integrity of its disability program. Neuropsychological tests of malingering, which are part of the medical evidence from external sources, are considered as part of the review of a claimant who may be dissimulating; however, other than common measures such as the Wechsler tests, only rarely does the program order other specific neuropsychological tests or effort/malingering tests and use them as the basis of their determination that an individual is not being truthful. At this point in time, SSA makes only general observations regarding the validity of psychological testing, which is essentially that the psychologist should attempt to discern validity by noting and resolving "any discrepancies between formal test results and the individual's customary behavior and daily activities." Given the extent to which an extensive and relevant literature now exists regarding numerous methods of detecting invalid and biased responses, some of which are quite sophisticated in determining response bias and invalid performances, the use of these additional contributions in this area might be open for consideration by the program in the future.

ACKNOWLEDGMENTS

The author thanks Terrence Dunlop, Ph.D., Michael Kovar, Ph.D., Ms. Janice Parker, and Mr. Alan Pryka for their assistance in preparing this chapter. The content is based on personal work experience in the Social Security Disability Program as the regional medical advisor, and on communications with program personnel and my review of materials. The views expressed are those of the author and not necessarily those of the Social Security Administration.

REFERENCES

Kovar, M. (2000). *Credibility, malingering, and psychological testing*. Unpublished paper.

Social Security Administration, Office of Disability (2005, January) *Disability evaluation under social security*. Available at http://www.socialsecurity.gov/disability/professionals/bluebook/Entire-Publication1-2005.pdf

Personal injury court: Plaintiff attorney

J. Sherrod Taylor

The quest to develop procedures that reliably detect malingering in personal injury plaintiffs is equivalent to seeking the Holy Grail in neuropsychology. The results of this quest thus far, however, are mixed and controversial. Many neuropsychologists, buttressed by a plethora of published data, maintain that evidence demonstrating the presence or absence of malingering can be identified accurately. Consequently, plaintiff and defendant attorneys now present testimony about malingering during legal proceedings. On the other hand, some clinical and legal authorities remain unconvinced by this research. For example, in a seminal article, Friedland (1998) urged that science has not yet discovered the magic elixir for distilling truthfulness from malingering and concluded that it can be difficult, even insuperable, to detect malingering. Thus, as readers may suspect, clinicians and lawyers have varying views on whether testing possesses the capacity to uncover malingerers. Accordingly, this chapter explores these divergent viewpoints and offers neuropsychologists insight into the plaintiff's perspective on this subject.

The plaintiff's view of malingering will be examined here using principles enunciated in the emerging field of medical jurisprudence called "neurolaw." Neurolaw is chiefly concerned with the medicolegal ramifications of neurological injuries—especially traumatic brain injury (TBI) (Taylor, 1991; Taylor, Harp, & Elliott, 1991). Since its inception, health professionals have embraced neurolaw, and several journals have devoted entire issues to its principles, e.g., *NeuroRehabilitation, 16*(2) (2001); *Brain Injury Source, 4*(3) (2000). Additionally, a legal treatise dealing with neurolaw has been published (Taylor, 1997). As we delineate the plaintiff's perspective on malingering, we shall review various tenets of neurolaw, so neuropsychologists may learn how neurolaw interfaces with neuropsychology. For now it suffices to say that much, if not all, of the plaintiff's perspective on malingering rests upon principles of neurolaw.

This chapter addresses malingering in five ways. First, we shall discuss malingering generally so readers may secure an understanding of its role in personal injury lawsuits. Second, we shall describe the plaintiff's approach to evidence dealing with malingering. Third, we shall examine the defendant's approach to malingering evidence—albeit from the plaintiff's perspective—while recognizing that a further discussion is presented by a defense attorney elsewhere in this volume. Fourth, we shall consider a case study illustrating how evidence about malingering can shape the course of litigation. Finally, a modest proposal on how neuropsychologists may effectively navigate the troubled waters surrounding malingering will be offered. Since neuropsychologists often testify as witnesses during TBI cases, this chapter focuses on neurolitigation.

EVIDENCE CONCERNING MALINGERING

Evidence concerning the presence or absence of malingering possesses the capability to tip the scales of justice toward either the plaintiff's or the defendant's side during personal injury cases. Among litigated issues, malingering may be the most dominant because deciding whether the plaintiff is malingering or actually disabled is before the jury during every moment of civil trials (*United States Fidelity & Guaranty Co. v. McCarthy*, 1931). Malingering is an octopus whose tentacles grip virtually every aspect of personal injury actions. As we shall see, the far-reaching arms of malingering exert a powerful—sometimes crushing—influence not only on the compensation side of the litigation equation but on the liability side as well.

The power of testimony about malingering revolves around what may be called the "worthiness factor" that is ever-present in court proceedings. Since juries tend to award money damages to plaintiffs deemed "worthy" of such recoveries, plaintiff lawyers strive to prove that their clients are not malingerers. Because juries also tend to award no monetary relief, or only inadequate sums, to claimants deemed to be "unworthy," defense attorneys seek to show that plaintiffs either are malingerers or are possibly malingering. Many years ago, the Montana Supreme Court recognized the impact of malingering evidence when it observed that it was for the jury to determine whether the evidence touching the character and extent of plaintiff's illness was worthy of credit, and that the verdict was their answer to this inquiry: was she malingering or was she seriously injured? (*Kelley v. John R. Daily Co.*, 1919). Juries are especially sensitive to allegations of malingering because malingerers are thought to be trying to cheat the judicial system to obtain money to which they are not entitled. Juries fear that malingerers may be compensated for unfounded or manufactured injuries (*Southwire Co. v. George*, 1996). Juries inherently desire to make their verdicts in favor of parties that deserve them. For these reasons, both plaintiff and defense attorneys seek evidence concerning malingering from a variety of witnesses. Expert witnesses often have knowledge about the existence or non-existence of malingering that is beyond the ken of lay jurors. However, determining whether the plaintiff may be feigning injury through malingering is often difficult, and perhaps its very difficulty accounts for the readiness with which courts have encouraged experts to decide the question. Thus, it becomes important for plaintiff and defense lawyers to consult with experts early in litigation to determine whether malingering can be ruled out or ruled in through testing procedures.

PLAINTIFF'S APPROACH TO MALINGERING EVIDENCE

Plaintiff attorneys have developed a multifaceted approach to deal with malingering using the following techniques. First, they consider how evidence about malingering may impact upon whether they should accept or decline legal representation to claimants who seek their services. Second, after agreeing to serve as the plaintiff's lawyer, they often mold their cases in accordance with the tenets of neurolaw. Third, they strive to obtain evidence demonstrating that their clients are not malingering. Fourth, they work closely with neuropsychologists and other clinicians to identify examination procedures that may detect malingering, while keeping in mind the daunting nature of that task.

Accepting the personal injury case

Counsel know from experience that meritorious lawsuits possess three characteristics. These attributes combine to form what is often called the "three-legged stool" of successful litigation. The first leg of this stool embraces the factual circumstances surrounding the incident that precipitates the lawsuit. Those facts must indicate that the defendant is legally responsible—i.e., liable—for causing both the accident and the plaintiff's alleged injuries. If liability—e.g., fault or culpability on the part of the defendant—is absent, attorneys generally will decline to provide legal representation. Liability is a prerequisite for recovery of damages in civil actions. The second leg usually requires that the plaintiff's alleged injuries and damages be substantial. Minor injuries rarely lead juries to award the monetary compensation needed to support civil litigation. In the absence of permanent injuries, trial lawyers customarily will not pursue litigation because it is not cost-effective to do so. The third leg of the litigation stool consists of the actual ability to recover compensation that may be awarded. This means that funds to satisfy a court's judgment must exist. Plaintiffs are able to collect judgments when (1) defendants are well insured, (2) defendants have assets, and/or (3) plaintiffs possess some additional source of recovery—e.g., uninsured motorist insurance coverage in motor vehicle accident cases.

Using the three-legged stool method to analyze their cases, lawyers are able to determine whether potential litigation is likely to be successful. If any leg of this stool is missing, or in doubt, counsel usually decline representation. Basic economic factors tend to determine whether lawyers accept cases. These economic factors are paramount because litigation is a time-consuming and costly endeavor for attorneys. Litigation requires lawyers to spend many hours engaging in pre-trial activities—e.g., preparing and reviewing documents, taking depositions, organizing evidence, preparing witnesses for testimony, etc. More time is needed to prepare for and participate in court proceedings. The expenditure of attorney time, however, is not the only significant element of personal injury actions. Since many claimants cannot afford to pay the costs of litigation, plaintiff attorneys customarily advance case expenses from their own funds. Those expenses may be quite high. These advancements drain lawyers' own financial resources and may reduce the ability of attorneys to take on new clients during the pendency of already-accepted cases. The expenditure of time and funds becomes especially important when one considers that plaintiff lawyers provide representation pursuant to contingency fee contracts. Under those agreements, attorney fees and reimbursements for litigation costs are paid only upon successful resolution of the case. Unlike defense lawyers who receive hourly fees for their services, win or lose, plaintiff lawyers must win their cases to receive compensation for their work. Unlike defense attorneys, whose litigation expenses are paid by their clients or by those clients' insurers, plaintiff lawyers must win their cases to recover litigation costs. For these reasons, attorneys engage in litigation only on behalf of clients whose cases have merit. Thus, as a practical matter, lawyers lack incentives to represent persons who are likely to be found to be malingering because juries probably will not award substantial monetary compensation to those individuals.

Neurolaw

Modern neurolitigation derives from the field of jurisprudence known as "neurolaw." Neurolaw is a synthesis of medicine, rehabilitation, and law that deals with neurological injuries—especially traumatic brain injury (TBI) (Lemkuhl, 1993; Weed & Field, 1994). The central thesis of neurolaw proposes that the financial resources obtained through civil justice remedies contribute to improving quality of life for individuals with neurological injuries and their families by (1) funding rehabilitation programs, (2) replacing income lost due to injury, and (3) compensating for the physical pain and mental anguish commonly accompanying injury (Taylor, 1995). Neurolaw recognizes that successful plaintiff litigation depends heavily upon the quality and quantity of expert testimony—especially evidence proffered by neuropsychologists (Taylor, 1996). Neurolaw holds that mutual cooperation among concerned professionals enhances the probability of successful neurolitigation (Taylor, 1999). Consequently, plaintiff attorneys have developed and enjoyed positive relationships with neuropsychologists.

These relationships have proven advantageous to both the plaintiff's counsel and neuropsychologists. Although it is well known that physicians refer individuals for neuropsychological evaluations to assist in establishing and confirming diagnoses (Tremont, Westervelt, Javorsky, Podolanczuk, & Stern, 2002), it is perhaps less appreciated that lawyers make similar referrals for identical reasons. Indeed, a survey by Sweet, Moberg, and Suchy (2000) determined that attorneys are the number one referral source for private-practice neuropsychologists. Relationships between neuropsychologists and lawyers appear in a myriad of other contexts. For example, plaintiff lawyers, acting through their national organization, the Association of Trial Lawyers of America (ATLA), have joined members of the National Academy of Neuropsychology to survey practices in forensic neuropsychology (Essig, Mittenberg, Petersen, Strauman, & Cooper, 2001). Moreover, legal writers have worked with neuropsychologists to publish research that is of interest to the neuropsychological community (Taylor, 1999). Additionally, neurolawyers have teamed with members of a state psychological association to draft amendments to statutory laws in order to legislatively overrule an appellate court decision (*Chandler Exterminators, Inc. v. Morris*, 1992) that precluded neuropsychological testimony on the cause of brain injury (*Drake v. LaRue Construction Co.*, 1994; Taylor, 1999).

Sweet and Kuhlman (1995) observed that, in the burgeoning area of neurolaw, an increasing number of cases have been entering into litigation. Since expert testimony has the potential for affecting court decisions (Klee & Friedman, 2001), plaintiffs often tender evidence from neuropsychologists to prove the existence of serious injuries. Neuropsychologists recognize that common medical tests—e.g., CT scans, MRIs, PET scans, EEGs—may fail to identify brain damage, especially that associated with so-called mild traumatic brain injuries (MTBIs). Since neuropsychologists utilize test batteries that are useful in diagnosing brain injury, courts welcome testimony by these experts (Miller, 1992). Subtle neurological deficits, however, may be difficult to prove, and plaintiffs who have these impairments are regularly accused of being malingerers. Stern (1997) suggested that charges of malingering have become a major theme of many defense cases. Trial lawyers, therefore, have a keen interest in proving that their clients are not malingering (*Salas v. United States*, 1997).

Evidence showing that plaintiff is not malingering

When attorneys introduce evidence showing that the claimant is not malingering, the plaintiff's credibility may be enhanced, and that litigant may be found worthy of recovering a monetary award (*Mascenti v. Becker*, 2001). Courts generally find that evidence demonstrating that the claimant is not a malingerer is sufficient to support a plaintiff's award (*Wasiak v. Omaha Public Power District*, 1997). Sometimes, however, trial courts refuse to admit evidence reflecting that the plaintiff is not malingering. When that occurs, plaintiffs may have to resort to an appeal to gain access to this vital evidence. In *Means v. Gates* (2001), the trial court refused to admit testimony from plaintiff's neuropsychologist. On appeal, the plaintiff contended that the testimony was needed to rebut the defendant's implication that he was malingering. The appellate court agreed and ordered a new trial so that the jury could consider the neuropsychologist's testimony.

During trial, plaintiffs may employ at least three methods to demonstrate that they are not malingerers. First, they may introduce testimony from expert witnesses. The *Means* case illustrates that technique. Plaintiffs are not, however, confined to presenting such testimony through their own witnesses. Sometimes, they are successful in eliciting evidence from defense witnesses to show that they are not malingerers (*Sudduth v. State Dept. of Transp. & Dev.*, 1993). Second, plaintiffs themselves may offer testimony to demonstrate the absence of malingering. The power of the plaintiff's own testimony may be considerable. One court has observed: "The plaintiff knew whether he was hurt and whether he suffered, and, if entitled to credit, his knowledge would and ought to have outweighed the opinion of a 'whole college of physicians' " (*Southern Railway v. Tankersley*, 1908). Other courts have accepted that view (*A. C. Lawrence Leather Co. v. Loveday*, 1970). In most actions, plaintiffs should testify on their own behalf. When plaintiffs fail to testify, they may not prevail in the case. Third, plaintiffs may introduce the testimony of lay witnesses to prove that they are not malingering. One court, for example, noted that well-founded lay testimony indicated almost conclusively the sincerity of the plaintiff's complaints of pain and disability (*Shaw v. F. & C. Engineering Co.*, 1960). Thus, when defense experts opine that plaintiffs are malingerers, wise trial lawyers will present lay witness testimony to bolster plaintiffs' credibility. This practice has been recognized by appellate courts (*Terrebonne v. Goodman Manufacturing Corp.*, 1996) and by the principle of neuro-law providing that persuasive evidence presented by lay witnesses contributes heavily to successful neurolitigation (Taylor, 2001).

Detection of malingering

The increased role of neuropsychologists in the courtroom has led to an increased effort in the detection of possible malingering (O'Bryant, Duff, Fisher, & McCaffrey, 2004). Moreover, the advent of new and more sophisticated tests has led many authorities to conclude that malingering can be readily diagnosed. Some clinicians have determined that neuropsychological assessment offers a testable and refutable method for detecting the consequences of brain injury and for providing data regarding potential malingering (Bordini, Chaknis, Ekman-Turner, & Perna, 2002). One commentator suggests that an extensive review of the plaintiff's background and history, coupled with the results of neuropsychological testing, allows the examiner to detect malingering (Sbordone, 1991). The idea that health professionals may accurately identify malingering, however, is not new. About 50 years ago, one court declared that medical science had developed to the point where competent witnesses could detect bona fide illnesses and distinguish them from those conceived in fraud (*Moses v. R. H. Wright & Son, Inc.*, 1956). Plaintiff lawyers recognize that some clients do malinger, and they want to know which claimants are not legitimate before too much time and too many resources are invested in any case (Sweet, 2000). Counsel also want to identify malingerers to spare legitimately injured claimants from being tarred with the same brush (Miller, 2001). Many lawyers, however, are somewhat skeptical about whether any testing can detect malingering. Investigators who also question the ability of clinicians to identify malingerers have fueled these doubts.

Notwithstanding advances in testing designed to recognize exaggeration or fabrication of cognitive dysfunction, some researchers believe that diagnosing malingering remains difficult and idiosyncratic (Slick, Sherman, & Iverson, 1999). Methods of investigating malingering that are currently available are not perfect (Lovell & Franzen, 1994). Although the results of testing may lead to a suspicion of malingering, some authorities note that there is no clear way to detect fabrication or exaggeration (Puente & Gillespie, 1991). Thus, clinicians should not be convinced that they are capable of uncovering malingerers (Ruff, Wylie, & Tennant, 1993). Such people rarely admit that they have fabricated test results (Cullum, Heaton, & Grant, 1991). Vanderploeg and Curtiss (2000) assert that, unless individuals confess to malingering, neuropsychologists cannot really know whether invalid test performance is conscious and deliberate or a reflection of other factors. The American Medical Association's *Guides to the Evaluation of Permanent Impairment* (5th ed.) agrees that confirmation of malingering is extremely difficult and generally depends on surveillance. Since malingering is often suspected, but seldom proved, one commentator suggests that experts exercise caution and use "diagnostic humility" when presenting evidence about malingering (Bernad, 1994). Most plaintiff lawyers endorse that recommendation.

Neuropsychologists usually recognize the need for caution when they express opinions about malingering. Recently, four researchers conducted a survey that addressed the practices of neuropsychologists in handling compensation issues during litigation (Slick, Tan, Strauss, & Hultsch, 2004). Those investigators discovered that 41.7% of responding neuropsychologists rarely used the term "malingering" and 12.5% never used that term. Instead, more than 80% of respondents simply observed that test results were invalid, inconsistent with the severity of the injury, or were indicative of exaggeration. Regrettably, only 29.2% of respondents contacted the referring attorney to report their suspicions of malingering. Since plaintiff attorneys want to know whether clients may be malingering, more neuropsychologists should consider informing lawyers of this possibility. When attorneys receive such information, they can act promptly to either withdraw from the litigation or settle cases without going further.

Conflicts in the medical literature are not the only factors influencing the skepticism of many plaintiff lawyers about whether malingering can be diagnosed accurately. Counsel also fear that defendants may retain "hired gun" experts to inject malingering into cases without justification. Although plaintiff attorneys are the individuals most often accused of relying upon "hired gun" witnesses at trial, defense counsel may present dishonest experts during court proceedings. The threat of defendants employing such witnesses has been a source of concern to plaintiff lawyers for a long time and has become more apparent recently due to the prevalence of so-called independent medical examinations (IMEs). Rules of evidence permit defendants to have claimants examined by their own experts. Even though such experts are labeled "independent," they rarely possess that attribute. Instead, defendants retain clinicians who conduct IMEs, typically in an effort to obtain evidence that supports defendants' cases. The astounding testimony adduced during *Ladner v. Higgins* (1954) illustrates plaintiffs' concerns about some defense expert witnesses.

In the *Ladner* case, the defendant's expert, Dr. Herbert Randolph Unsworth, was asked: "Is it your conclusion that this man is a malingerer?" Dr. Unsworth responded: "I wouldn't be testifying if I didn't think so, unless I was on the other side, then it would be a post traumatic condition." Amazingly, this expert admitted that his testimony was based solely upon which side had retained his services. Interestingly, this same Dr. Unsworth had been the only expert who concluded that another plaintiff was malingering in a case tried over 20 years before the *Ladner* case. In that action, the court rejected Dr. Unsworth's testimony and found that the preponderance of the evidence was with the plaintiff (*Klein v. Medical Building Realty Co., Inc.*, 1933). Similarly, the *Ladner* court rejected Dr. Unsworth's opinion. Thus, if readers will pardon the pun, both the *Ladner* and the *Klein* courts determined that this expert's testimony was "un(s)worth(y)" of belief. All neuropsychologists should want courts and juries to believe their testimony. For this reason, Miller (2001) urges neuropsychologists, no matter which "side" of the case they are on, to serve the cause of justice as honestly and as competently as they can.

Neuropsychologists should also exercise caution in diagnosing malingering for other reasons as well. Current research reveals that some investigators are now expanding the scope of their testing to determine whether litigants claiming brain injury of any sort may be malingering. For example, Boone and Lu (2003) have recommended that tests to verify cognitive effort should be routinely given to all patients in litigation. Another study, examining three patients involved in litigation, presented evidence of an intentional effort to appear impaired in the context of documented moderate/ severe brain injury (Bianchini, Greve, & Love, 2003). Such studies foreshadow the possibility that defendants may soon try to allege that plaintiffs with major brain injuries are malingering. Those studies, however, come at a time when certain recognized tests are being questioned. Some clinicians, for example, have contended that the Fake Bad Scale (FBS) is a useful index of symptom magnification (Tsushima & Tsushima, 2001). Other experts have found that the FBS also correlates with documented abnormal neurological signs within the moderate/severe brain injury group (Greiffenstein, Baker, Gola, Donders, & Miller, 2002). Those evaluators note that use of the FBS as a symptom infrequency measure may have to be modified in more severely injured litigants because some FBS items may reflect true long-term outcome in severe cerebral dysfunction.

These are just a few examples of how current neuropsychological research is leading clinicians to reassess their ability to confirm malingering. They are, however, important exemplars—especially in a legal environment that is often controlled by the United States Supreme Court's decisions in *Daubert v. Merrell-Dow Pharmaceuticals, Inc.* (1993), *General Electric Co. v. Joiner* (1997), and *Kumho Tire Co. v. Carmichael* (1999). Those decisions, in part, deal with the validity of scientific tests as it relates to the admissibility of evidence derived from testing. Pursuant to those cases, neuropsychologists must be careful when they testify about the validity of the test instruments they employ during examinations. Stern (2001) aptly points out that neuropsychologists generally are required to demonstrate the same scientific validity of their methodology during their expert testimony as they usually do during presentations to professional colleagues at scientific meetings. Since Vanderploeg and Curtiss (2000) have observed that the area where neuropsychologists tend to have the most concern about test validity is malingering, exercising caution before making a diagnosis of malingering would seem to be in order. Caution is recommended even when the criteria in the venerable *Diagnostic and Statistical Manual of Mental Disorders* are employed.

Diagnostic and Statistical Manual of Mental Disorders

The *Diagnostic and Statistical Manual of Mental Disorders, Fourth Edition, Text Revision* (DSM–IV–TR) defines malingering as "the intentional production of false or grossly exaggerated physical or psychological symptoms, motivated by external incentives such as . . . obtaining financial compensation" (American Psychiatric Association, 2000, p. 739). This manual states that malingering should be strongly suspected if any combination of the following is noted: (1) medicolegal context of presentation (e.g., person is referred by an attorney to the clinician for examination); (2) marked discrepancy between the person's claimed stress or disability and the objective findings; (3) lack of cooperation during the diagnostic evaluation and in complying with the prescribed treatment regimen; and (4) the presence of Antisocial Personality Disorder. Many courts permit reference to the DSM during legal proceedings; some even take judicial notice of its contents (*Gough v. Metropolitan Life Insurance Co.*, 2003; *United States v. Cantu*, 1993; *United States v. O'Kennard*, 2004). However, since some commentators have observed that the DSM's diagnostic categories may be as much a reflection of the values and beliefs of its drafters as they are of scientific data (Cornwell, 1996), plaintiff lawyers sometimes doubt whether the factors listed in this manual concerning raising the suspicion of malingering are always appropriate.

Although plaintiff lawyers recognize that the DSM is useful in diagnosing certain injuries, many also believe that it prejudices psychologists and psychiatrists against their clients before any examinations occur. Even though the DSM requires "any combination" of the four factors listed above to exist before authorizing suspicion of malingering, it appears to many lawyers that some clinicians jump to the conclusion that a medicolegal context of presentation automatically suggests malingering. One well-respected researcher, however, has observed that, while many clinicians, insurance industry officials, and defense attorneys think that litigation is a chief cause of persistent symptoms in claimants that promptly resolve when the litigation is completed, most literature does not support that position (Evans, 2004). That same investigator noted that (1) litigants and nonlitigants have similar recovery rates; (2) most plaintiffs who have persistent symptoms at the time of settlement of their litigation are not cured by a verdict; and (3) available evidence does not support bias against patients just because they have pending litigation. Thus, while the first step toward making a clinical diagnosis is to think of it (Thibault, 1992), neuropsychologists should remain mindful of the old proverb saying that we usually see what we look for. If clinicians see a medicolegal presentation in an examinee, they may suspect malingering. Plaintiff lawyers believe that automatic reaction by clinical experts does not serve the ends of justice in most cases.

Defense attorneys customarily look for signs that plaintiff attorneys have referred clients for neuropsychological examination or have paid the neuropsychologist's bill. This is ironic because, as we have seen, Sweet, Moberg, and Suchy (2000) report that attorneys are the number one source of referral for private practice neuropsychologists. By urging that attorney referral is indicative of malingering, the DSM and members of the defense team infer that plaintiff lawyers may be trying to construct a case for an injury that does not exist, rather than seeking, like physicians who make similar referrals, to obtain or confirm legitimate diagnoses. Neuropsychologists and psychiatrists who use the DSM may be insulted by this implication. Additionally, the inference that attorney referral carries with it an unseemly connotation belies the fact that defense attorneys obtain neuropsychological evaluations of plaintiffs through referrals to so-called independent medical examiners. Thus, the question may be asked: Are defense lawyers seeking evidence of malingering when no such evidence actually exists?

Despite the predisposition of some clinicians to infer that a medicolegal presentation indicates malingering, courts generally do not adhere to that position. At least one jurisdiction—Louisiana

—has numerous appellate decisions that adamantly rebut such claims. For example, in *Bridges v. Brown Paper Mill Co.* (1946), the court wrote:

> This Court does not look upon plaintiffs claiming compensation as likely malingerers, but on the contrary, it has regarded them in the past, and will continue to regard them in the future, as honest and bona fide claimants of rights guaranteed them under the laws of this State, unless and until in specific cases the open, direct, and unequivocal charge of malingering shall be made and legally established.

Later, the Louisiana Court of Appeals observed that the principle that courts will stigmatize a claimant as a malingerer only upon positive and convincing evidence justifying such conclusion is so well embedded in that state's jurisprudence as to preclude the necessity for specific citations (*Williams v. Bituminous Casualty Corp.*, 1961).

Some clinical researchers have at least tacitly endorsed the views of the Louisiana courts. Morton (2004) observed that the mere fact of filing a claim should not be a criterion for supposedly dishonest behavior. Evidence from other medical disciplines shows that new data contradict the notion that litigation promotes malingering (Sapir & Gorup, 2001). Notwithstanding the DSM position, it should be clear that experts ought not to consider the existence of medicolegal claims to be per se evidence of malingering. Instead, before making a diagnosis of malingering, evaluators should carefully explore whether any signs of symptom magnification revealed on tests are related to anxiety disorder or some other psychological/psychiatric disorder (Patterson & White, 2004).

Single versus many tests

Although neuropsychologists possess an array of instruments designed to reveal malingering, some experts hinge their testimony on only one test. When a defense expert concludes, on the basis of a single test, that the plaintiff is a malingerer, appellate courts may scrutinize that expert's opinions—especially when the trial court has excluded rebuttal testimony by the plaintiff's expert. In *Classic Imports, Inc. v. Singleton* (1997), a neuropsychologist conducted extensive testing of the plaintiff over a five-year period and concluded that she suffered brain damage as a result of the accident. At trial, the defendant presented the testimony of a neurologist who opined that the plaintiff did not have significant brain injury. Using a low score on one of the plaintiff's neuropsychologist's tests, the neurologist concluded that the plaintiff was a malingerer. The plaintiff then sought to rebut that testimony through the testimony of a psychiatrist. The psychiatrist pointed to a number of tests administered by the plaintiff's neuropsychologist to determine whether the plaintiff was a malingerer. Those tests showed the plaintiff was not malingering. The trial court, however, refused to allow the plaintiff's psychiatrist to testify before the jury. The appellate court reversed, finding that, coming as it did near the end of the trial and being powerful in its content, the defense neurologist's testimony had to have had a significant impact on the jury. The court concluded that the rebuttal testimony of the plaintiff's psychiatrist should have been admitted. Despite the attempt of the expert in the *Classic Imports* case to use a single test to label the plaintiff as a malingerer, neuropsychologists usually acknowledge that the evaluation of response bias and malingering in cases of mild head injury should not rely on a single test (Millis & Volinsky, 2001). Lynch (2004) noted that several effort-level measures—including the Computerized Assessment of Response Bias (CARB), Portland Digit Recognition Test (PDRT), Test of Memory Malingering (TOMM), Validity Indicator Profile (VIP), Victoria Symptom Validity Test (VSVT), and Word Memory Test (WMT)—have withstood the scrutiny of cross-validation research. That researcher recommended that at least two of the above-listed tests be used for proper assessment of effort level.

DEFENDANT'S APPROACH TO MALINGERING EVIDENCE

Although the defense perspective on malingering evidence will be discussed elsewhere in this volume, a few words concerning the perceptions of plaintiff lawyers about defense views are now appropriate. Defense attorneys recognize that the charge of malingering taints virtually every plaintiff's case. When a jury believes that the plaintiff is a malingerer, it may refuse to award damages even when the defendant is clearly responsible for causing an accident. Charges of malingering, moreover, may raise the specter that the plaintiff actually staged the incident that led to the lawsuit and may result in the plaintiff losing the case outright (*Williamson v. Haynes Best Western*, 1997). Additionally, when a jury thinks that a plaintiff is malingering, it may award damages in an amount below what the plaintiff may have reasonably anticipated. The Alaska case *Glamann v. Kirk* (2001) illustrates that point. In this case, the defendant offered to settle for $50,000 before trial; the jury, however, awarded only $10,000. On appeal, the plaintiff argued that the trial court erred by admitting evidence of malingering. The appellate court rejected that argument, finding that the contention that the plaintiff was a malingerer was relevant not only to the plaintiff's credibility, but also to the more fundamental question of how much harm the defendant's negligence actually caused.

The word "malingering" is one of the most injurious words in the lexicon of damning. One court has observed that "malingering" is a "strong and ugly term" (*Sleek v. J.C. Penney Company, Inc.*, 1963). Defense attorneys know that raising the issue of malingering will permit them to demonize claimants in court. "Malingering" embodies connotations that bode ill for plaintiffs. Plaintiffs may be stigmatized by the charge of malingering (*Harrison v. Chicago Mills & Lumber Co.*, 1984). Plaintiffs may be "branded" as malingerers (*Corasio v. Imhoff Berg Silk Dyeing Co.*, 1937; *Ebarb v. Southern Industries Co.*, 1955). Like cattle ranchers, defense lawyers recognize that they may "own" those plaintiffs that they have "branded" at trial. Legal fact-finders often stereotype individuals accused of malingering as liars (*Ratto v. Secretary, Dept. of Health & Human Servs.*, 1993) or as loiterers, or undesirable/unsavory characters (*Iannelli v. Powers*, 1986; *Sears Roebuck and Co. v. Manuilov*, 2001). Such instances of guilt-by-association with other sorts of "unworthy" individuals can be quite deleterious to the plaintiff's case.

Although most courts do not allow witnesses to opine that a party or victim is lying or telling the truth, they do allow experts to testify about the presence or absence of malingering because that testimony is not considered a direct opinion on the issue of lying (*Rose v. Figgie International, Inc.*, 1997). In today's legal environment, in which many judges and jurors evince concerns about our allegedly "overly litigious" society, accusations of malingering can have a powerful impact upon the outcome of civil litigation. "Malingering" is a word of division and diversion. As a term of division, it (1) drives a wedge between juries and plaintiffs by denying that claimants are injured at all or as seriously as they contend (*Evans v. Wilson*, 1983), (2) separates juries from plaintiff lawyers by calling into question their motivations for filing lawsuits, and (3) decomposes the legitimacy of legal actions by suggesting that cases may be frivolous or even fraudulent. As a term of diversion, "malingering" affords defense attorneys opportunities to refocus lawsuits, by shifting emphasis away from defendants' blameworthiness and toward plaintiffs' unworthiness. Images of plaintiffs as malingerers are especially potent because they are borrowed from the ordinary reality of jurors —all of whom have known liars and slackers. For these reasons, defense attorneys succumb to the temptation to introduce evidence about plaintiffs' malingering whenever the chance to do so is presented.

CASE STUDY

The recent New Jersey case *Ostrowski v. Cape Transit Corp.* (2004) presents a "classic" example of how defendants attempt to destroy the personal injury cases of legitimate plaintiffs using charges of malingering. Since that court's opinion reviews many of the matters typically involved in traumatic brain injury litigation, we shall now examine this case closely.

Ostrowski was injured when his vehicle was hit in the rear by the defendants' bus. The plaintiff's witnesses testified that he sustained a permanent brain injury, resulting in his no longer being able to work and requiring him to need assistance in carrying out activities of daily life. The defendants conceded liability, and their witnesses testified (1) that the plaintiff suffered only a mild concussion, which did not cause any permanent consequences, and (2) that the plaintiff was able to work and enjoy his life in the same manner as before the accident. The case was tried before a jury solely on the issue of the plaintiff's damages. The only defense offered was that Ostrowski was a malingerer and that the cognitive damages he claimed were fraudulent.

Before the accident, one of the plaintiff's primary activities was playing saxophone in a band that marched in Philadelphia's New Year's Day Mummers Parade. Witnesses for the plaintiff testified that, prior to the incident, Ostrowski had been among the best musicians in the band and that, even though he had remained with the band since the accident, his skills had diminished, and he now played only a secondary role in the group. The defendants conducted videotaped surveillance of the plaintiff, designed to show that the plaintiff was still an active band member. The plaintiff sought to counter the surveillance evidence with testimony by band members, who compared video-tape footage of the plaintiff's performances before the incident with the footage collected by the defendants after the accident.

The plaintiff presented the testimony of four treating doctors who supported his brain injury claim and who concluded that the plaintiff's serious cognitive and emotional problems resulted from the accident and were permanent. The plaintiff's primary care physician stated that he had seen the plaintiff on numerous occasions since the accident. He found that the plaintiff had blurred vision, facial asymmetry, neurocognitive deficits, and depression as a result of the accident, and he sent the plaintiff to Magee Rehabilitation Center for treatment of the brain injury. A psychiatrist found that the plaintiff had serious deficits in short-term memory and judgment and concluded that Ostrowski should not drive a motor vehicle, could not work, and needed someone with him at all times. The psychiatrist also noted that, although the plaintiff's CT scans and MRIs did not reveal injury, these tests frequently do not detect brain injuries. A neuropsychologist determined that the plaintiff suffered from moderately severe postconcussion syndrome and was clinically depressed with evidence of a high level of anxiety about his future. The neuropsychologist further found that the plaintiff exhibited deficits in verbal and nonverbal memory, motor sequencing, visual-spatial reasoning, and complex problem solving. The neuropsychologist opined that those problems were permanent. A physiatrist at the Magee Rehabilitation Center testified that in the accident the plaintiff sustained traumatic brain injury to the left front part of his brain, resulting in physical weakness and impairment of coordination of the right side of his body. The physiatrist opined that the plaintiff should not drive and could not return to gainful employment. That physician also stated that the plaintiff should be supervised in any complex environment or situation. The plaintiff also tendered the testimony of ten lay witnesses to support his claims. The plaintiff and his wife, who sought compensation for the loss of her husband's consortium, also testified during the trial. Knowing before trial that the defendants intended to allege malingering, the plaintiff's attorney presented evidence demonstrating the plaintiff's character for truthfulness.

As anticipated, the defendants focused on the plaintiff's veracity by alleging that the plaintiff was faking his brain injury. The defendants tendered three medical experts in support of that contention. A neurologist, who viewed the surveillance videotapes, opined that the plaintiff's performance during the parades shown thereon was incompatible with the results of neuro-psychological tests performed by his doctors. On cross-examination, however, that neurologist admitted that, despite the discordance between the neuropsychological testing and what was depicted on the surveillance videotapes, he could not say that the plaintiff was absolutely normal or that the plaintiff did not have some deficits. The defendants' own neuropsychologist noted that some of the responses the plaintiff gave to questions posed during his examination were not very credible. That defense neuropsychologist opined that the plaintiff looked like an individual who was deliberately doing poorly and faking the results. The defendants' psychiatrist found no signs of cognitive dysfunction and no psychosis; he further opined that Ostrowski had completely recovered and that the psychiatric prognosis was "good." The defendants also presented evidence showing that the plaintiff had made false statements during his deposition when he contended that he had not continued to march in the band after the collision and that he had failed to disclose to his doctors that he had been treated for depression before the accident.

Following 13 days of trial, the jury awarded the plaintiff $94,828.50 for medical expenses, $2.2 million for other economic damages (e.g., lost earnings) and $1.1 million for pain, suffering, disability, and loss of enjoyment of life. The jury also awarded the plaintiff's wife $416,720 for loss of consortium. The trial court later denied the defendants' motion for a new trial, and the defendants appealed. On appeal, the defendants argued primarily that the trial court had committed harmful error by allowing numerous witnesses to testify about the plaintiff's character for truthfulness. In rejecting the defendants' arguments, the appellate court noted that, under the surrounding factual circumstances and the New Jersey Rules of Evidence, those opinions were admissible. Affirming the jury's verdict, the court found that the plaintiff had countered the defendants' evidence about malingering and stated that the jury had concluded that the plaintiff had suffered a serious brain injury in the accident.

The issues described in this case study arise often during neurolitigation. Plaintiffs who allege brain injury usually are injured in accidents caused by the defendants that they sue. Indeed, plaintiff attorneys have accepted employment in those cases because the criteria established by the afore-mentioned "three-legged stool" have been met before the filing of the case in court. When the facts and applicable law compel them to accept liability, defendants commonly are left only with defenses predicated upon malingering. By suggesting that plaintiffs are malingerers, defendants challenge plaintiffs' "worthiness" for recovering damages. Defense assaults based on charges of malingering frequently occur when plaintiffs claim brain injuries not discerned by traditional medical tests—i.e., when negative MRIs and CT scans are present. Moreover, it is not uncommon for defendants to employ expert witnesses to support their allegations of malingering and to use surveillance video-tapes in an effort to capture plaintiffs engaging in behavior that is inconsistent with injury. To counter these defense attacks, plaintiff attorneys usually proffer evidence from plaintiffs, significant others, lay witnesses, and a variety of healthcare experts.

CONCLUSION

When neuropsychologists agree to testify during neurolitigation, they accept a formidable responsibility. Their task includes making a careful and impartial assessment of plaintiffs to identify the presence or absence of genuine neuropsychological deficits. It may also involve attempting to expose any exaggeration of symptoms that may be present. Clinicians, however, should remain ever-cognizant of the potentially controversial nature of their testimony; and, they should stand ready to defend their clinical findings using objective and unbiased procedures. They should always express their opinions utilizing the caution required of all scientists who render evidence about the workings of the human mind. When they perform their duties in accordance with the law and within the bounds of their professional ethics, neuropsychologists furnish evidence that may be used to resolve personal injury cases. By straying beyond the realm of their expertise, neuropsychologists subject themselves and their testimony to the careful scrutiny of lawyers and appellate courts.

REFERENCES

A. C. Lawrence Leather Co. v. Loveday, 455 S.W. 2d 141 (Tenn. 1970).

American Medical Association (2001). *Guides to the evaluation of permanent impairment*, 5th ed. Chicago: AMA Press.

American Psychiatric Association (2000). *Diagnostic and statistical manual of mental disorders*, 4th ed., text revision. Washington, DC: American Psychiatric Association.

Bernad, P. G. (1994). *Closed-head injury: A clinical source book*. Charlottesville, VA: The Michie Company.

Bianchini, K. J., Greve, K. W., & Love, J. M. (2003). Definite malingered neurocognitive dysfunction in moderate/severe traumatic brain injury. *The Clinical Neuropsychologist*, 17(4), 574–580.

Boone, K. B., & Lu, P. (2003). Noncredible cognitive performance in the context of severe brain injury. *The Clinical Neuropsychologist*, 17(2), 244–254.

Bordini, E. J., Chaknis, M. M., Ekman-Turner, R. M., & Perna, R. B. (2002). Advances and issues in the diagnostic differential of malingering versus brain injury. *NeuroRehabilitation*, 17(2), 93–104.

Bridges v. Brown Paper Mill Co., 28 So.2d 76 (La. App. 1946).

Chandler Exterminators, Inc. v. Morris, 416 S.E.2d 277 (Ga. 1992).

Classic Imports, Inc. v. Singleton, 702 So.2d 1187 (La. App. 4 Cir. 1997).

Corasio v. Imhoff Silk Dyeing Co., 195 A.2d 620 (N.J. 1937).

Cornwell, J. K. (1996). Protection and treatment: The permissible civil detention of sexual predators. *Washington and Lee Law Review*, 53, 1293–1337.

Cullum, C. M., Heaton, R. K., & Grant, I. (1991). Psychogenic factors influencing neuropsychological performance: Somatoform disorders, factitious disorders, and malingering. In H. O. Doerr & A. S. Carlin (Eds.), *Forensic neuropsychology: Legal and scientific bases* (pp. 141–174). New York: Guilford.

Daubert v. Merrell-Dow Pharmaceuticals, Inc., 509 U.S. 579 (1993).

Drake v. LaRue Construction Co., 451 S.E.2d 792 (Ga. App. 1994).

Ebarb v. Southern Industries Co., 78 So.2d 553 (La. App. 1955).

Essig, S. M., Mittenberg, W., Petersen, R. S., Strauman, S., & Cooper, J. T. (2001). Practices in forensic neuropsychology: Perspectives of neuropsychologists and trial attorneys. *Archives of Clinical Neuropsychology*, 16(3), 271–291.

Evans, R. W. (2004). The postconcussion syndrome and whiplash injuries: A question and answer review for primary care physicians. *Primary Care*, 31(1), 1–17.

Evans v. Wilson, 650 So.2d 569 (Ark. 1983).

Friedland, S. I. (1998). Law, science and malingering. *Arizona State Law Journal*, 30, 337–395.

General Electric Co. v. Joiner, 522 U.S. 136 (1997).

Glamann v. Kirk, 29 P.3d 255 (Alaska 2001).

Gough v. Metropolitan Life Insurance Co., 2003 U.S. Dist. LEXIS 25252.

Greiffenstein, M. F., Baker, W. J., Gola, T., Donders, J., & Miller, L. (2002). The Fake Bad Scale in atypical and severe closed head injury litigants. *Journal of Clinical Psychology*, 58(12), 1591–1600.

Harrison v. Chicago Mill & Lumber Co., 446 So.2d 843 (La. App. 1984).

Iannelli v. Powers, 498 N.Y.S. 2d 377 (1986).

Kelley v. John R. Daily Co., 181 P. 326 (Mont. 1919).

Klee, C. H., & Friedman, H. J. (2001). Neurolitigation: A perspective on the elements of expert testimony for extending the *Daubert* challenge. *NeuroRehabilitation*, 16(2), 79–85.

Klein v. Medical Building Realty Co., Inc., 147 So. 122 (La. App. 1933).

Kumho Tire Co. v. Carmichael, 526 U.S. 137 (1999).

Ladner v. Higgins, 71 So.2d 242 (La. App. 1954).

Lemkuhl, L. D. (1993). *Brain injury glossary*. Houston: HDI Publishers.

Lovell, M. R., & Franzen, M. D. (1994). Neuropsychological assessment. In J. M. Silver, S. C. Yudofsky, & R. E. Hales (Eds.), *Neuropsychiatry of traumatic brain injury* (pp. 133–162). Washington: American Psychiatric Press.

Lynch, W. J. (2004). Determination of effort level, exaggeration, and malingering in neurocognitive assessment. *Journal of Head Trauma Rehabilitation, 19*(3), 277–283.

Mascenti v. Becker, 237 F.3d 1223 (10th Cir. 2001).

Means v. Gates, 558 S.E.2d 921 (S.C. Ct. App. 2001).

Miller, L. (1992). Neuropsychology, personality, and substance abuse in the head injury case. *International Journal of Law and Psychiatry, 15*(3), 303–316.

Miller, L. (2001). Not just malingering: Syndrome diagnosis in traumatic brain injury litigation. *NeuroRehabilitation 16*(2), 109–122.

Millis, S. R., & Volinsky, C. T. (2001). Assessment of response bias in mild head injury: Beyond malingering tests. *Journal of Clinical and Experimental Neuropsychology, 23*(6), 809–828.

Morton, W. E. (2004). Letter to the Editor. *Journal of Occupational and Environmental Medicine, 46*(3), 193–195.

Moses v. R. H. Wright & Son, Inc., 90 So.2d 330 (Fla. 1956).

O'Bryant, S. E., Duff, K., Fisher, J., & McCaffrey, R. J. (2004). Performance profiles and cut-off scores on the Memory Assessment Scales. *Archives of Clinical Neuropsychology, 19*(4), 489–496.

Ostrowski v. Cape Transit Corp., 853 A.2d 985, *Affirmed*, 868 A.2d 321 (2004).

Patterson, W., & White, R. F. (2004). Symptom magnification and neurocognitive dysfunction. *Journal of Occupational and Environmental Medicine, 46*(7), 608–610.

Puente, A. E., & Gillespie, Jr., J. B. (1991). Workers' compensation and clinical neuropsychological assessment. In J. Dywan, R. D. Kaplan, & F. J. Pirozzolo (Eds.), *Neuropsychology and the law* (pp. 39–63). New York: Springer-Verlag.

Ratto v. Secretary, Dept. of Health & Human Servs., 839 F. Supp. 1415 (USDC D. Or. 1993).

Rose v. Figgie International, Inc., 495 S.E.2d 77 (Ga. App. 1997).

Ruff, R.M., Wylie T., & Tennant, W. (1993). Malingering and malingering-like aspects of mild closed head injury. *Journal of Head Trauma Rehabilitation, 8*(3), 60–73.

Salas v. United States, 974 F.Supp. 202 (USDC W.D. N.Y. 1997).

Sapir, D. A., & Gorup, J. M. (2001). Radio frequency medial branch neurotomy in litigant and nonlitigant patients with whiplash: A prospective study. *Spine, 26*(12), E 268–273.

Sbordone, R. J. (1991). *Neuropsychology for the attorney*. Orlando, FL: Paul M. Deutsch Press.

Sears Roebuck and Co. v. Manuilov, 742 N.E.2d 453 (Ind. 2001).

Shaw v. F. & C. Engineering Co., 120 So. 2d 523 (La. App. 1960).

Sleek v. J. C. Penney Company, Inc., 324 F.2d 467 (3rd Cir. 1963).

Slick, D. J., Sherman, E. M. S., & Iverson, G. L. (1999). Diagnostic criteria for malingered neurocognitive dysfunction: Proposed standards for clinical practice and research. *The Clinical Neuropsychologist, 13*(4), 545–561.

Slick, D. J., Tan, T. E., Strauss, E. H., & Hultsch, D. F. (2004). Detecting malingering: A survey of experts' practices. *Archives of Clinical Neuropsychology, 19*(4), 465–473.

Southern Railway Co. v. Tankersley, 60 S.E. 297 (Ga. App. 1908).

Southwire Co. v. George, 470 S.E.2d 865 (Ga. 1996).

Stern, B. H. (1997). Anticipating defenses: A proactive approach to handling traumatic brain injury cases. *Trial Diplomacy Journal, 20*(4), 201–205.

Stern, B. H. (2001). Admissibility of neuropsychological testimony after *Daubert* and *Kumho*. *NeuroRehabilitation, 16*(2), 93–101.

Sudduth v. State Dept. of Transp. & Dev., 619 So. 2d 618 (La. Ct. App. 3 Cir. 1993).

Sweet, J. J. (2000). The role of neuropsychologists in brain injury litigation. *Brain Injury Source, 4*(2), 14–16.

Sweet, J. J., & Kuhlman, R. S. (1995). Evaluating malingering in brain injury claims: Genuine injury versus proven malingerer. *Trial Diplomacy Journal, 18*(1), 1–7.

Sweet, J., Moberg, P., & Suchy, Y. (2000). Ten-year follow-up survey of clinical neuropsychologists: Part II. Private practice and economics. *The Clinical Neuropsychologist, 14*(4), 479–795.

Taylor, J. S. (1991). Neurolawyers: Advocates for TBI and SCI survivors. *The Neurolaw Letter, 1*(2), 1.

Taylor, J. S. (1995). Neurolaw: Towards a new medical jurisprudence. *Brain Injury, 9*(7), 745–751.

Taylor, J. S. (1996). Neurorehabilitation and neurolaw. *NeuroRehabilitation, 7*(1), 3–14.

Taylor, J. S. (1997). *Neurolaw: Brain and spinal cord injuries*. New York: Clark Boardman Callaghan.

Taylor, J. S. (1999). The legal environment pertaining to clinical neuropsychology. In J. J. Sweet (Ed.), *Forensic neuropsychology: Fundamentals and practice* (pp. 421–442). Lisse, Netherlands: Swets & Zeitlinger.

Taylor, J. S. (2001). An overview of neurolaw for the clinician: What every potential witness should know. *NeuroRehabilitation, 16*(2), 69–77.

Taylor, J. S., Harp, J. A., & Elliott, T. (1991). Neuropsychologists and neurolawyers. *Neuropsychology, 5*(4), 293–305.

Terrebonne v. Goodman Manufacturing Corp., 687 So.2d 124 (La. Ct. App. 5 Cir. 1996).

Thibault, G. E. (1992). Clinical problem solving: Failure to resolve a diagnostic inconsistency. *New England Journal of Medicine, 327*(1), 36–39.

Tremont, G., Westervelt, H. J., Javorsky, D. J., Padolanczuk, A., & Stern, R. (2002). Referring physicians' perceptions of the neuropsychological evaluation: How are we doing? *The Clinical Neuropsychologist, 16*(4), 551–554.

Tsushima, W. T., & Tsushima, V. G. (2001). Comparison of the Fake Bad Scale and other MMPI–2 validity scales with personal injury litigants. *Assessment, 8*(2), 205–212.

United States v. Cantu, 12 F.3d 1506 (9th Cir. 1993).

United States v. O'Kennard, 2004 U.S. Dist. LEXIS 9546.

United States Fidelity & Guaranty Co. v. McCarthy, 50 F.2d 2 (8th Cir. 1931).

Vanderploeg, R. D., & Curtiss, G. (2000). Neuropsychological validity and malingering assessment. *Brain Injury Source, 4*(4), 14–16, 43–45.

Wasiak v. Omaha Public Power District, 568 N.W. 2d 229 (Neb. 1997).

Weed, R. O., & Field, T. F. (1994). *Rehabilitation Consultant's Handbook*, Rev. ed. Athens, GA: Elliott & Fitzpatrick.

Williams v. Bituminous Casualty Corp., 131 So. 2d 844 (La. App. 2d Cir. 1961).

Williamson v. Haynes Best Western, 688 So. 2d 1201 (La. App. 4 Cir. 1997).

Criminal court: Defense attorney

41

Joseph Krakora

A criminal defendant's history of mental illness has, for all practical purposes, become a double-edged sword for criminal defense attorneys. On one hand, psychiatric defenses, such as insanity and diminished capacity, are available in a limited number of cases, and mental illness may tend to mitigate punishment at sentencing. On the other hand, however, a criminal defendant's claim of mental illness can sometimes be used to portray him as antisocial, dangerous, and violent. It also sets up a possible characterization by prosecution experts as a *malingerer*—one who fakes or exaggerates psychiatric or cognitive symptoms in order to gain some type of benefit in the system. This label is particularly problematic for a defendant because it not only challenges the existence of the claimed mental illness itself, but it also interjects purposeful deceit on his part as well. In this chapter, I will focus on a recent client of mine charged in 2003 with two murders committed two months apart in separate counties. Mental health issues, including a claim by a prosecution expert that the defendant was a malingerer, played an integral role in the resolution of the cases.

On March 13, 2003, at approximately 11:00 p.m., Mr. Q.Q. was arrested in Essex County, New Jersey shortly after stabbing a woman to death in his apartment building. Mr. Q.Q. had attacked the victim for no apparent reason. He had no relationship with her other than living in the same building, and the crime did not involve robbery or sexual assault. He was taken into custody near the scene and questioned initially about the incident by Detective M.D. of the local Police Department and Investigator N.B. of the Essex County Prosecutor's Office. Between 3:15 a.m. and 4:15 a.m. on March 14, 2003, Mr. Q.Q. gave a four-page typed statement to the detectives confessing to the Essex County homicide. He provided no real explanation for why he stabbed the victim other than his assertion that "it was in my mind to stab her for like 4 days." He also said that he was about to choke another woman he had never seen before at the time police apprehended him.

According to the Detective, at the conclusion of the statement, Mr. Q.Q. then made a voluntary reference to the murder of a woman at a local mall in Middlesex County located about 15 miles away. There was, in fact, an unsolved murder at that mall committed on January 8, 2003. The victim was a woman who had apparently been abducted by her car, as she was about to enter the mall to do some shopping after work. She was strangled, and her body had been found the following morning in a nearby parking lot. Local authorities were contacted and, by approximately 6:30 a.m. that morning, Detective E.G. of the local Police Department and Investigator K.M. of the Middlesex County Prosecutor's Office arrived in Essex County to interview Mr. Q.Q. about the mall killing. They conducted a pre-interview that lasted until the taking of a formal taped statement that started at 9:00 a.m. and ended at 9:50 a.m. In that statement, Mr. Q.Q. confessed to the mall murder.

In essence, Mr. Q.Q. stated that he was in a van in the mall parking lot with two other persons whose names he claimed not to know. He said that he asked the victim, who was standing by her car, for the time. When she did not respond immediately, he became angry. He grabbed her, dragged her into the van and, ultimately, strangled her with a cord in the back of the van. He denied any participation in robbery (a necklace and rings were missing when the victim was found), and he denied any intention to sexually assault the victim during the incident. At some point, according to Mr. Q.Q., he got out of the van because he was afraid they would be stopped while driving around with a dead body in the back. As a result of the confession, Mr. Q.Q. was formally charged with the murder. The confession became the only evidence against him, and no other evidence, physical, forensic, or otherwise, linking him to the crime was ever developed in the case.

Mr. Q.Q. qualified for representation by the Public Defender's Office, and we undertook his defense in both cases. Initially, the Middlesex County Prosecutor's Office announced its intention to seek the death penalty in the mall case based on its allegation that the murder was committed during robbery. Another factor, in all likelihood, was the Prosecutor's knowledge that if Mr. Q.Q. were convicted of murder in Essex County, that conviction would be an additional basis under New Jersey law for seeking the death penalty in another county. It was obvious from the outset that Mr. Q.Q. had substantial psychiatric issues. We began an extensive investigation of our client's background as a means of exploring defenses to the charges and developing mitigating factors to be used in a potential death penalty phase. That investigation revealed as extensive a mental health history as I have seen in over 20 years of defending criminal cases, most of that time as a specialist in both capital and non-capital murder cases.

Mr. Q.Q. was 32 years old at the time of his arrest. Starting at age 17, he had almost continually been in and out of mental health institutions. We accumulated three large boxes of records reflecting his history of mental health treatment at numerous facilities throughout New Jersey. Our investigator prepared a 75-page chronology of Mr. Q.Q.'s social history, with over 60 pages of it devoted primarily to mental health treatment from age 17 to 32. At various points, he had been diagnosed with numerous types of mental disorders, including schizophrenia, schizoaffective disorder, depression, bipolar disorder, and various personality disorders. He often complained of hearing voices and of being both suicidal and homicidal. He was a chronic drug abuser, with a long history of polysubstance abuse. At times, mental health professionals also characterized him as a malingerer who was manipulative and deceptive. He also engaged in criminal and violent behavior resulting in a number of arrests and periods of incarceration. Even while in prison, he received psychiatric treatment on a number of occasions. He had been on various forms of psychiatric medication for almost all of his adult life.

Significantly, our review of Mr. Q.Q.'s psychiatric records revealed that he had on several occasions fabricated or exaggerated his prior criminal record when interviewed by mental health professionals. For example, in 2002, he reported to staff at two separate institutions that he had been incarcerated for killing a drug dealer. That was simply not true. He once made a claim that he had nine murders pending, which also was not true. As far back as 1989, medical records from another institution reflect that "there is a somewhat grandiose and boastful quality to the patient's statements about his destructive behavior, and his reports are not entirely consistent." Mr. Q.Q. is described as "invested in his self-identification as a powerful, destructive individual."

We retained Dr. R.H., a forensic psychiatrist, to perform an initial evaluation of our client shortly after his arrest. We had considerable information about the two cases but had not yet assembled the defendant's complete psychiatric history. Dr. R.H. met with Mr. Q.Q. on June 27, 2003 and prepared his first report shortly thereafter. Dr. R.H. diagnosed him as suffering from schizoaffective disorder, bipolar type and antisocial and narcissistic personality disorder with borderline traits. He also noted his cocaine abuse, attention deficit hyperactive disorder, history of conduct disorder, and a traumatic brain injury with secondary seizure disorder. Dr R.H. emphasized Mr. Q.Q.'s need for types of psychiatric treatment unavailable in a jail setting. He did not believe that our client was a malingerer.

Mr. Q.Q. never denied that he had committed the homicide in Essex County. Notwithstanding his history of mental illness, it was clear that an insanity or diminished capacity defense was not viable. He obviously intended to stab the victim, knew what he had done, and knew it was wrong. There was no indication that he was delusional or otherwise psychotic at the time. We therefore tried to use his history to negotiate a plea to a lesser offense and thus avoid a murder conviction that could be used against him in his capital case. About a year after our client's arrest, we were able to do so. The prosecutor offered him a plea to aggravated manslaughter with a 25-year sentence recommendation, and our client accepted the offer. The plea called for Mr. Q.Q. to serve 85% (or 22) of the 25 years without parole. He began to serve that sentence while the Middlesex County case was still pending.

In contrast to the homicide case, Mr. Q.Q. took a very different stance with respect to the mall case in Middlesex County. He claimed that he had falsely confessed to the crime. Beyond that, he related a version of the facts surrounding the interrogation session on March 14, 2003 that amounted to his claim that he had falsely confessed (or attempted to confess) to a number of murders that morning. In fact, he provided a detailed account in which he identified specific crimes, his discussions about them with the detectives, and his willingness to take responsibility for their commission. For example, he claimed to have confessed to the murder of a woman whose body was found behind a Restaurant P in Essex County. There was actually a reference to the crime in his confession to the Essex County homicide. We eventually learned that the detectives determined that Mr. Q.Q. was incarcerated when that crime was committed and therefore could not have committed it. We recognized almost immediately the potential relationship between false confession claims and mental illness and began to research false confession cases and the use of mental health experts to support such claims.

In this context, we asked Dr. R.H. to conduct a follow-up evaluation to specifically assess the defendant's false confession claim in the context of his previously diagnosed mental illnesses. After meeting with Mr. Q.Q. and reviewing all of the information available concerning the circumstances of the interrogation process, Dr. R.H. first determined that his diagnosis of schizoaffective disorder was not relevant to the false confession claim. He concluded that it did not appear to him that Mr. Q.Q. was symptomatic for that illness at the time of his arrest and interrogation. While acknowledging that schizoaffective disorder may interfere with one's judgment and insight, he nevertheless felt that it did not help to understand Mr. Q.Q.'s allegedly false confession.

The diagnosis of narcissistic and antisocial personality with borderline characteristics, on the other hand, took on a very important role in Dr. R.H.'s assessment. He concluded that Mr. Q.Q.'s narcissistic personality disorder, in particular, was critical to an understanding of why Mr. Q.Q. might confess to murders he did not commit notwithstanding the obvious ramifications of doing so. Such individuals have an inflated view of their importance, and need to feel powerful and engage in conduct designed to draw attention to them. Dr. R.H. opined that Mr. Q.Q.'s claim of having falsely confessed was consistent with his narcissistic personality disorder, given his rather grandiose description of how he controlled the interrogation process with his confessions. Significantly, he did not offer an opinion as to whether the confession was in fact false. Rather, we envisioned expert testimony designed to explain why someone with a particular mental disorder might do something as counterintuitive as confess to a crime he did not actually commit.

Mr. Q.Q. told Dr. R.H. that he attempted to confess to as many as eight different homicides. He claimed that police investigated some of his claims and found that at least on one occasion he was in jail at the time of the crime he claimed to commit. He claimed that the detectives showed him pictures of murder victims, and he took credit for their murders. He said that he felt he was helping them, and they gave him cigarettes and coffee in return. Dr. R.H. later testified in court that, consistent with his narcissistic personality disorder, Mr. Q.Q. felt important and in control. He felt empowered by his ability to help the detectives solve cases that they had otherwise been unable to solve.

Dr. R.H. finalized his report, and we turned it over to the prosecutor. The State then sought to have an evaluation by its own expert and moved to bar Dr. R.H.'s testimony on the grounds that it was inadmissible to support a claim of false confession. The State's argument was essentially that there is no scientific evidence that persons with narcissistic personality disorders are more likely to falsely confess than anyone else. New Jersey law at the time had no clear precedent on the issue. The only reported case ruled inadmissible was the testimony of social psychologists who offer generalized expert testimony on the effects of police interrogation methods. Consequently, the trial court decided to conduct a pre-trial hearing at which Dr. R.H. and members of law enforcement involved in the interrogation testified. At that hearing, Dr. R.H. elaborated on the opinions expressed in his report concerning the relationship between Mr. Q.Q.'s narcissistic personality disorder and the false confession claim. His opinions, of course, were based in part on the information related to him by our client during the clinical interview. Not surprisingly, the detectives involved contradicted much of what Mr. Q.Q. said about the interrogation process and the so-called false confessions. Dr. R.H. conceded that the weight to be given to his opinions was, to some extent, dependent upon the reliability of Mr. Q.Q.'s statements. Given Mr. Q.Q.'s history and the testimony of the various detectives, he had to acknowledge the possibility that Mr. Q.Q. was, at a minimum, exaggerating the extent to which he made false confessions that morning.

Although there were many discrepancies between Mr. Q.Q.'s version of the interrogation session and that of law enforcement, we were able to show some corroboration for our client's assertions. Essentially, the detectives uniformly denied that Mr. Q.Q. confessed to other crimes. At various points in their testimony at the pre-trial hearing, however, they conceded certain facts consistent with Mr. Q.Q.'s claims. The Detective admitted that Mr. Q.Q. discussed the murder of a woman found by Restaurant P and that it was later determined that Mr. Q.Q. was in jail in North Carolina at the time of the crime. He acknowledged that Mr. Q.Q. talked about the stabbing of a Puerto Rican man in or near a container used for trailers in a specific section of Essex County, but that they could not find such an attack. Finally, he admitted that the detectives had contacted law enforcement in City Y, North Carolina to ascertain if there were any unsolved crimes there.

The Detective and Investigator confirmed the discussion by Mr. Q.Q. of the Restaurant P murder. The Investigator specifically testified that he understood that the Essex County detectives were looking into whether Mr. Q.Q. could have committed that murder until they learned that he was incarcerated at the time. The Detective testified that Mr. Q.Q. brought up the murder of a drug dealer in City Z, New Jersey at one point. The Investigator told the court that at some point that morning the detective from her office in charge of "cold cases," Investigator M.S., was called to participate in the interrogation.

Finally, we elicited testimony from a former prosecutor who had been the director of the homicide unit in Essex County at the time of Mr. Q.Q.'s arrest. He recalled the case he had spoken to me about prior to the hearing. He said that Mr. Q.Q. was going to be charged with the Restaurant P murder until it was determined that he was incarcerated at the time the crime was committed. Although he characterized the comment as a "joke" when testifying in court, he acknowledged telling me that Mr. Q.Q. had been willing to close out all of the unsolved homicides in Essex County.

After the hearing, the trial judge ruled that Dr. R.H. would be permitted to testify subject to an important limitation. The court held that he would not be permitted to relate to the jury our client's statements concerning what happened during the interrogation—a limitation that would have prevented Dr. R.H. from explaining the basis of his testimony to the jury. The court's ruling left neither side satisfied, so interlocutory cross-appeals followed. We appealed the limitation imposed by the trial judge, and the State appealed from the decision permitting Dr. R.H. to testify in the first place. The Appellate Division granted leave to appeal and, ultimately, issued an opinion holding that Dr. R.H. would be permitted to testify without the limitation imposed by the trial judge.

In the meantime, the State's expert, Dr. L., a forensic psychologist, had conducted his evaluation of our client and his false confession claim. He conducted a clinical interview as well as administering a battery of psychological tests. He had access to all of Mr. Q.Q.'s medical and psychiatric records. He, like Dr. R.H., prepared a detailed report setting forth his expert opinions. In essence, notwithstanding Mr. Q.Q.'s history, he concluded that he suffered from no significant mental illness other than an intermittent explosive disorder. Rather, he characterized him as a malingerer with an antisocial personality disorder who was a violent and dangerous individual fitting the profile of a serial killer. He rejected Dr. R.H.'s assertion that Mr. Q.Q.'s personality disorder could be related in any fashion to a claim of false confession. In fact, he rejected the notion that he even suffered from a narcissistic personality disorder. He described him as a manipulative individual who truthfully confessed and then tried to avoid the consequences of that confession. He rejected everything that

Mr. Q.Q. told him that would have otherwise supported the opinions formed by Dr. R.H. and isolated several references in the voluminous records in which Mr. Q.Q. was described as manipulative and malingering.

After Mr. Q.Q. accepted the plea offer in Essex County, the Middlesex County Prosecutor's Office reconsidered its position and decided not to seek the death penalty. That decision was likely driven in part by the fact that our client was not convicted of murder in the other case and in part by the extent of his history of mental illness. Nevertheless, our client was still faced with the possibility of a life sentence in the case consecutive to the 25-year sentence he was already serving. His defense depended entirely on convincing a jury that he had, for whatever reason, falsely confessed to the crime. Dr. R.H.'s expert testimony was critical to that effort because it was only through that testimony that we would be able to portray our client as the kind of grandiose, narcissistic individual whose mental illness might help explain a false confession. His testimony would also allow us to get our client's version of the interrogation before the jury without subjecting him to cross-examination. On the other hand, we were confronted with the rebuttal testimony of Dr. L. who would paint a very different picture of our client for the jury if permitted to do so.

Consequently, issues pertaining to the scope of that rebuttal became paramount especially given Dr. L.'s opinion that the defendant was a manipulative malingerer. The first was the extent to which he would be permitted to testify to that opinion. He seemed to be applying that label to Mr. Q.Q. in the context of dismissing Dr. R.H.'s diagnosis of schizoaffective disorder. Because Dr. R.H. did not make any connection between the diagnosis of schizoaffective disorder and the false confession, we could argue that the malingering diagnosis was irrelevant. We believed that Dr. L. should only be permitted to testify that he disagreed with the diagnosis of narcissistic personality. Our problem was that there was no way to know exactly how the court would view such an argument, and the trial judge was not inclined to make such rulings in advance of the actual testimony of the experts before the jury. We knew that Dr. L. would testify that his assessment of Mr. Q.Q. as a malingerer was an integral part of his evaluation and essential to his determination of what, if any, mental disorders were properly diagnosed.

Similarly, Dr. L.'s emphasis in his report on the defendant's antisocial and criminal behavior certainly created another problem for us. We had no way of knowing the extent to which he would be permitted to testify about our client's history of violence and other criminal activity. He would certainly claim that it was necessary for him to do so in order to explain the basis of his opinion that the antisocial personality, rather than the narcissistic personality disorder, was the correct diagnosis.

Also looming as we approached trial was the related and also unresolved issue of the admissibility of evidence of the Essex County killing. The issue was inevitably going to arise both in the context of describing the interrogation process and in the course of Dr. L.'s expert testimony. As a general rule, so-called "other crimes" evidence is not admissible to prove that a defendant has a propensity to commit crimes or that he committed a particular one. Obviously, evidence that only two months after the mall murder the defendant committed another random killing had the potential, in and of itself, to totally prejudice the jury against our client. Although the trial court had given us a preliminary indication that it recognized the potential prejudice of the evidence and was inclined to preclude it, we had no guarantee as to the ultimate outcome of the issue during trial. There are recognized exceptions to the rule—one or more of which arguably applied in our case.

For example, we anticipated that our false confession claim could potentially lead to the admission of evidence of the "truthful" confession to the Essex County killing. Our case depended on our client's claim that he not only falsely confessed to the mall murder but also that he attempted to falsely confess to a number of other crimes. The prosecutor was certainly going to argue that he should be entitled to demonstrate to the jury that at least one of the so-called confessions was true, as evidenced by Mr. Q.Q.'s guilty plea in the Essex County case. In other words, there was a perfectly reasonable argument that the confession to the Essex County killing was an integral part of the interrogation process and highly relevant to an assessment of the false confession defense.

We also knew there would be an argument that the "truthful" confession was admissible because of the likelihood that Dr. L. would testify that he based his expert opinions at least in part on it. If permitted to do so, he was certainly going to express his view that the "truthful" confession undercut the claim of a false confession to the mall case. He was going to bolster that opinion by expressing his view that, consistent with the malingering label, Mr. Q.Q. fabricated or exaggerated the extent to which he actually gave false confessions to other murders during the interrogation session. In his report, he emphasized that there was no proof, other than Mr. Q.Q.'s word, that he had in fact attempted to falsely confess to other crimes. Although he ignored those facts elicited during the hearing corroborating Mr. Q.Q.'s claims, we knew he could argue that Mr. Q.Q. had lied about giving false confessions.

We will never know how these issues would have been resolved. As we neared the trial date, the Middlesex County Prosecutor's Office offered our client a plea to a 40-year sentence (to serve 85% before parole) to run concurrent to the 25-year sentence he was already serving. This meant that Mr. Q.Q. would serve approximately an additional 13 years for the mall murder. When we actually appeared in court for the trial date, the prosecutor agreed to reduce the offer to 38 years, meaning only an additional 11 years beyond that which our client was already going to serve. Mr. Q.Q. accepted the offer.

In the end, we will never know how the court would have ruled on the specific issues related to the malingering label and the scope of the rebuttal of the prosecutor's expert. And, of course, we will never know how a jury would have assessed the false confession claim in a case in which the defendant has a history of falsely claiming to have committed crimes, and there is literally no other evidence linking him to the crime. We do know that there was at least some truth to Mr. Q.Q.'s version of what happened in the interrogation process. It is not coincidence that the detective in charge of cold cases was called to speak to Mr. Q.Q. that morning. It is not a coincidence that an Assistant Prosecutor in the homicide unit at the time observed that Mr. Q.Q. was looking to take credit for the unsolved cases of Essex County. It is not a coincidence that the police investigated whether Mr. Q.Q. was in custody at the time a particular crime was committed. In the final analysis, however, the case is an excellent study in how a criminal defendant's mental illness can actually be both good and bad for his case, particularly when the malingering label is applied to him. This case also illustrates how important it is that the correct diagnosis be made in every case, regardless of which side retained the expert. Attorneys know full well that some experts' opinions may be formed on the basis of the side that has retained them. A false or incorrect label of "malingering" is as much an injustice as not making the call when it is actually present.

SECTION V

ETHICAL AND PROFESSIONAL ISSUES

The differential diagnosis process, including the consideration of malingering, involves ethical considerations. That is, the assignment or withholding of a diagnostic conclusion of malingering or any diagnosis could occur in such an inappropriate manner that questions of potential ethical violation might be raised. Particularly in adversarial proceedings, within which emotions often run high, the perception of unfair treatment by one side or the other can increase the likelihood of such concerns. This is an unfortunate reality that must be considered by clinical neuropsychologists who are involved in expert witness activities. As the common expression goes, *forewarned is forearmed*. This section contains two chapters. The first addresses ethical issues. The second addresses what one might do after determining that malingering is present, a topic largely neglected in the relevant literature.

Ethical issues in assigning (or withholding) a diagnosis of malingering

James D. Seward and Donald J. Connor

> *We seek the truth and will endure the consequences.*
> Charles Seymour

PROLOGUE

This chapter will explore the ethical issues involved in assigning or withholding a diagnosis of malingering, relying heavily on the guidance offered by the *Ethical Principles of Psychologists and Code of Conduct* (hereinafter referred to as the *Ethics Code*) (American Psychological Association [APA], 2002) and the *Specialty Guidelines for Forensic Psychologists* (hereinafter referred to as the *Guidelines*) (Committee on Ethical Guidelines for Forensic Psychologists, 1991).[1] We will discuss reasons why a neuropsychologist may choose not to diagnose an examinee with malingering, and will then explain why these reasons, although perhaps well intentioned, are not ethically justified.

INTRODUCTION

Distinct from other diagnostic procedures in the healthcare field (e.g., x-rays or laboratory studies), neuropsychological evaluation depends on the active participation of the examinee. A valid interpretation of the resultant scores is based on the assumption that the examinee was a willing partner in the process and put forth his or her best efforts. However, as will be discussed,

---

[1] At the time of writing, the *Guidelines* are being revised. Drafts can be viewed at www.ap-ls.org

a significant percentage of examinees do not do this, and instead deliberately perform poorly in a conscious, goal-directed attempt to influence the results in order to obtain some external benefit.

This deliberate distortion for gain is termed malingering. The following description of malingering is contained in American Psychiatric Association's *Diagnostic and Statistical Manual of Mental Disorders–Fourth Edition–Text Revision* (DSM–IV–TR) (2000):

> The essential feature of Malingering is the intentional production of false or grossly exaggerated physical or psychological problems, motivated by external incentives such as avoiding military duty, avoiding work, obtaining financial compensation, evading criminal prosecution, or obtaining drugs.
>
> (p. 739)

Today's malingerers are part of a long tradition.[2] Odysseus unsuccessfully tried to avoid military service in the Trojan War by feigning insanity, yoking an ox and an ass together and sowing his fields with salt instead of grain. His deception was unmasked when his infant son was placed in the path of the plow and Odysseus turned aside rather than harm him, thus demonstrating that he was in touch with reality (Bullfinch, 1978). In the Old Testament, David pretended to be mad to successfully escape from King Achish: "And he changed his behavior before them, and feigned himself mad in their hands, and scrabbled on the doors of the gate, and let his spittle fall down upon his beard" (1 Samuel 21:13 [King James Version]).

The actual frequency of modern day malingering is difficult to measure. (How many personal injury plaintiffs will volunteer, "Yeah, I lied to get a big settlement"?) However, it is clearly a problem with an enormous potential impact on society. A limited review of the literature reveals estimates for the frequency of "malingering-type" behavior in neuropsychological evaluations ranging from 8% to 76% among various diagnostic groups (Ardolf, Denney, & Houston, 2005; Chafetz & Abrahams, 2005; Larrabee, 2003; Mittenberg, Patton, Canyock, & Condit, 2002). Despite this, some psychologists may be unwilling to diagnosis malingering. We will explore some of the reasons for this, and examine the ethical issues related to giving or withholding a diagnosis of malingering.

SOURCES OF ETHICAL GUIDANCE

The practice of psychology in general, and forensic psychology in particular, is fraught with ethical pitfalls. To provide guidance, the American Psychological Association (APA) has formulated the *Ethics Code*. These guidelines are enforceable for members of APA and have also been incorporated into many State and Provincial licensure acts. However, even for psychologists who are not bound by the *Ethics Code*, it provides a reasonable touchstone for the ethical practice of psychology. The *Ethics Code* includes both *General Principles* (hereinafter referred to as *Principles*), which "are aspirational in nature," and *Ethical Standards* (hereinafter referred to as *Standards*), which are obligations.

For psychologists involved in forensic activities, the *Guidelines* performs a similar function, supplementing the *Ethics Code* by providing "more specific guidance to forensic psychologists in monitoring their professional conduct when acting in assistance to the courts, parties to legal proceedings, correctional and forensic mental health facilities, and legislative agencies" (p. 655). As cited throughout this chapter, both the *Ethics Code* and *Guidelines* can provide guidance germane to assigning or withholding a diagnosis of malingering.

---

[2] For a brief and entertaining history of malingering see Mendelson and Mendelson (2004).

REASONS WHY NEUROPSYCHOLOGISTS MAY WITHHOLD A DIAGNOSIS OF MALINGERING: GENERAL ISSUES

There are several reasons that neuropsychologists may give for withholding a diagnosis of malingering, or for not even investigating the possibility.

Diagnostic uncertainty

Writing in 1990, Erickson argued, "In medicine and psychiatry in general and neuropsychology in particular, the identification of the malingering patient rests on a chancy and undeveloped technology" (Pankratz & Erickson, 1990, p. 381). While this may have been true at the time, since 1990 the science of detecting malingered neuropsychological deficits has advanced considerably (cf. Hom & Denney, 2002; Larrabee, 2005a; Sweet, 1999). However, even following the use of a "scientific approach" as described by Larrabee (2005b) and others, the neuropsychologist may have suspicions of malingering but lack a full conviction. Further confusing this issue is the fact that forensic opinions are typically proffered "to a reasonable degree of medical/psychological/neuropsychological certainty," even though there is no consensus in the legal profession as to what level of certainty these terms imply (Lewin, 1998).

This issue may be addressed by communicating the level of certainty (or uncertainty) that the neuropsychologist has in the diagnosis of malingering. Slick et al. (1999) proposed a set of diagnostic criteria for *possible, probable*, and *definite* malingering of cognitive dysfunction. These include presence of a substantial external incentive (generally financial), evidence from neuropsychological testing (such as below-chance performance on forced-choice techniques), and evidence from self-report (such as a discrepancy between the examinee's symptoms and his or her observed level of functioning). These criteria provide useful guidelines, although some researchers have suggested that they are too conservative (Larrabee, 2005a). By using these or similar criteria, the neuropsychologist can communicate the level of diagnostic certainty while still making a diagnosis of malingering.

However, the DSM–IV–TR diagnosis of malingering requires not just the presence of "false or grossly exaggerated" symptoms but also an assertion that the patient is consciously doing this in order to obtain some material gain or benefit. This is necessary in order to distinguish malingering from other conditions characterized by the production of "false" symptoms such as Conversion Disorder, where the symptom or deficit is a consequence of "psychological factors" and "is not intentionally produced or feigned" (p. 495), or Factitious Disorder, where the signs or symptoms are intentionally produced but with the motivation "to assume the sick role" (p. 517) (American Psychiatric Association, 2000).

As noted by DeClue (2002), diagnosing feigned symptoms is not the same as diagnosing malingering:

> ... using the best assessment techniques, there is potential for evaluators to say with a specifiable level of certainty that a person is feigning (exaggerating or fabricating) psychopathology, but whether or not a person is malingering (deliberately distorting responses for external gain) requires interpretation on the *meaning* of the facts.
>
> (p. 725)

This attribution of motivation can add another level of diagnostic uncertainty, and the ability of mental health professionals to determine a patient's internal state and motivation has been questioned (for example, see Erickson in Pankratz & Erickson, 1990). However, in a rejoinder in that same article, Pankratz noted that mental health professionals frequently come to conclusions regarding the internal states of patients based upon their observable behavior, writing, "It would not be 'highly speculative' to infer the presence of misery and rumination inside the head of a patient with flat affect, psychomotor retardation, and disdain of previously interesting activities" (p. 387). More recently, Slick, Sherman, and Iverson (1999) wrote:

> Judgments about internal states are in fact necessary, if not crucial, for many clinical diagnoses. For example, hallucinations—a decidedly nontrivial clinical symptom—are like volition in that they are an internal event or state, the presence or absence of which can only be inferred from behavior.
>
> (p. 548)

Thus, the assignment of many psychological diagnoses typically requires some speculation on the part of the psychologist regarding internal states that are not directly observable. This can be aided by use of standardized instruments (e.g., the Minnesota Multiphasic Personality Inventory–2 [Butcher et al., 2001]) as well as adherence to a set of reproducible/reliable guidelines (e.g., DSM–IV–TR). Similarly, an ethical psychologist may ascribe a diagnosis of malingering within a level of certainty if a sufficient assessment is completed and the diagnostic criteria are met.

As in the procedure of ascribing any psychological diagnosis, implicit in assigning a diagnosis of malingering is the requirement to carefully consider other possible explanations for the examinee's presentation. This situation is illustrated in the following vignette:

> A 60-year-old patient is referred from her primary care physician for memory loss and "cognitive disorganization." She complains about not being able to track things anymore and that her memory is very bad. Upon testing she shows significant impairment in several domains, and notably incorrectly identified 80% of the tones on the Seashore Rhythm Test. On a forced-choice addition to the California Verbal Learning Test (CVLT), she incorrectly chose 11 of the 12 distractors. However, she was living independently and by report was functioning well in all routine activities of daily living. An MMPI–2 was consistent with depression, anxiety, and somatization. She was referred for treatment of a psychiatric condition at which time her donepezil was discontinued and treatment for an anxiety disorder was initiated. The examiner was unaware of any pending application for disability or other litigation at the time of the assessment.

Although an examinee may be manufacturing poor performance, this fact does not rule out the presence of comorbid disorders including mood disorders, delirium, anxiety, and psychosis that may be in addition to—or actually generating—the behavior. Malingering may also co-exist with genuine organic impairment (Bianchini, Greve, & Love, 2003). While there may be identifiable external gain to the examinee, other motivations and thus other diagnoses must also be considered. It is essential that the neuropsychologist adequately eliminate other possible explanations for the examinee's presentation prior to assigning a diagnosis of malingering.

> The appropriate approach is to treat malingering in the same manner as any other "disorder": as a diagnosis to be made after a comprehensive evaluation . . . A "reasonable doubt" strategy should always be applied about the probability that a patient is malingering.
>
> (Slick et al., 1999, p. 558)

Inadequate training

When one of the authors was in a well-regarded doctoral program in the mid-1980s, no classroom training was given in the detection of malingering, although it was a component of a predoctoral internship at a forensic hospital. Years later, the other author, also a graduate of a prestigious doctoral program, had his first exposure to the issue of malingering during his internship in a secured inpatient facility. While less true in the current training era, it remains possible that many psychologists and neuropsychologists (especially those who were trained a decade or more ago) lack adequate (or any) training in the detection of malingering.

Ignorance is not an excuse. Malingered neuropsychological symptoms are an ever-increasing topic at national meetings and in professional journals, providing sources of information from which neuropsychologists can gain expertise in the detection of malingering (Sweet, King, Malina, Bergman, & Simmons, 2002). Given the estimated prevalence of malingering cited later in this chapter, a consideration of symptom validity should be a part of any neuropsychological evaluation, especially those involving a forensic component (Bush et al., 2005). Lacking the expertise to do this would likely violate section (a) of *Standard 2.01 Boundaries of Competence*:

> Psychologists provide services, teach, and conduct research with populations and in areas only within the boundaries of their competence, based on their education, training, supervised experience, consultation, study, or professional experience.

Likewise, *Standard 2.03 Maintaining Competence* states, "Psychologists undertake ongoing efforts to develop and maintain their competence."

It is incumbent on all those who specialize in neuropsychology—and their training programs—to become well versed in the detection of effort and the diagnosis of malingering as part of their assessment of the validity of the test results.

Stigmatization

There may also be a reluctance to stigmatize the patient with a diagnosis of malingering. This may be especially true in a treating relationship (see below). When you call someone a malingerer, you are in essence saying that they are a fraud (at least in that situation), and this may have significant consequences in the patient's future. In particular, this diagnosis may be misused by others, such as to deny insurance claims, and may bias future treatment. Once entered into a medical record, the label may follow the patient, affecting diagnosis of future disease, treatment of medical conditions (e.g., prescription of narcotic pain medications), and access to unbiased legal counsel.

Fear of stigmatization does not justify ignoring the diagnosis of malingering any more than it would justify ignoring a diagnosis of Schizophrenia or Conversion Disorder, both of which could also be potentially stigmatizing. In the case where the neuropsychologist fears that his or her findings will be misused by others, he or she should take care to ensure that the bases of the findings are communicated appropriately and honestly and that the limitations of the interpretation are clearly stated.

Regarding the potentially stigmatizing implications of the term "malingering" itself, Slick, Sherman, and Iverson (1999) wrote:

> If psychologists collectively determine that the pejorative connotations associated with the term malingering preclude objective application in legal or other arenas, a new term could be coined, as happened when formal diagnostic labels such as *idiot* and *moron* were dropped from psychiatric nosology because of the pejorative colloquial connotations these terms acquired. However, this would probably be a short-term solution, as any new term brought in to replace malingering will likely become just as unpalatable.

(p. 558)

Social pressures

Neuropsychologists, similar to most people, like to be liked. This is especially true in a treatment situation, where one of the major satisfactions of the job is the opportunity to help others by relieving human suffering. This can result in significant social pressure for the neuropsychologist to refrain from giving a diagnosis of malingering. Some neuropsychologists may sidestep this issue completely by not assessing for malingering. However, as discussed later in this chapter, the discomfort experienced by the neuropsychologist does not outweigh the potential harm to both the patient and society that may be engendered by withholding a diagnosis of malingering.

Deceit

Some neuropsychologists may object to administering specific symptom validity tests, asserting that some of these tests are inherently deceitful. That is, for many tests to "work," the examinee must be explicitly or implicitly led to believe that an easy task is actually quite hard, and that the test is a valid measure of a cognitive ability (as opposed to symptom validity). Thus, the claim could be made that this practice may violate *Principle C: Integrity*, "Psychologists seek to promote accuracy, honesty and truthfulness in the science, teaching, and practice of psychology. In these activities, psychologists do not steal, cheat, or engage in fraud, subterfuge, or intentional misrepresentation of fact."

Gutierrez and Gur (1998) explored this issue with their university's Biomedical Ethics Center, and were "told that it may very well be ethical to deceive a patient who is suspected of malingering, but it must be done in a manner that affords the patient the opportunity to deny any deficit and perform well on any given test" (p. 101). While the examinee should be encouraged to provide a good and honest effort on the tests, examinees should not be warned that symptom validity assessment techniques will be used as this may enable the examinee to be more skillful at effectively feigning impairment (Youngjohn, Lees-Haley, & Binder, 1999). Thus, a statement that full cooperation and good effort is necessary for an accurate assessment—and requesting an overt agreement from the patient to provide both—is both ethically responsible and minimally informative to a potentially malingering examinee.

Personal beliefs

A unique ethical issue is raised by death penalty cases. The recent Supreme Court decision of *Atkins v. Virginia* (2002) barred the execution of mentally retarded individuals, providing a strong impetus to malinger (Brodsky & Galloway, 2003). In general, it is most likely that neuropsychologists involved in these cases would be acting in the role of the forensic expert (see below), with a clear-cut duty to make a diagnosis of malingering if appropriate. Forensic experts who are opposed to the death penalty should not become involved in these types of cases; Melton, Petrila, Poythress, and Slobogin (1997) wrote, ". . . mental health professionals should determine, before conducting an evaluation, whether their personal beliefs will make an objective assessment difficult" (p. 183). However, it is conceivable that a treating neuropsychologist could be involved in such a case, such as a psychologist working at a correctional facility. Regardless of their moral beliefs, psychologists are still ethically obligated to be truthful, and should clearly communicate any personal factors that may have affected their judgment.

"A victimless crime"?

Some may argue that the cost of giving a diagnosis of malingering to a patient (particularly when there is some uncertainty about this diagnosis) outweighs the benefits of diagnosing a relatively "victimless" crime. However, in addition to the personal consequences mentioned later in this chapter, this ignores the impact of this behavior on society.

Chafetz and Abrahams (2005) noted "evidence for malingering" in 76% of the adult claimants and 67% of the child claimants in a sample of individuals applying for Social Security Disability in Louisiana and that, "The estimated outlay for Social Security Disability insurance in 2004 was $80.3 billion." Thus, if their estimate of the frequency of malingering is accurate and generalizable to the entire United States, the cost of malingering for the already beleaguered Social Security Administration is billions of dollars annually.

Limiting their focus to civil litigation, Gouvier, Lees-Haley, and Hammer (2003) analyzed the financial cost of malingering in Louisiana. They extrapolated their estimates to the rest of the United States, writing:

> In closing, if the Louisiana statistics ($107.2 million annual direct statewide costs of malingering) are taken as typical or average for each of the 50 states, then needless medical claims, defense costs, and cash payouts to malingerers by negotiated settlements or courtroom awards represent a $5.36 billion a year industry in the United States. This is a conservative estimate as well, which does not take into account the costs to society of missed work and hiring replacement workers to make up for the absent malingerer in the work place.
>
> (p. 421)

Malingering in criminal cases also places a significant burden on society. Ardolf, Denney, and Houston (2005) noted that about 50% of a sample of criminal defendants gave indications of malingered neurocognitive dysfunction. Felons who successfully malinger incompetence to stand trial will have their criminal charges dropped, thus possibly avoiding lengthy incarcerations.[3] In addition to the intangible cost of allowing criminals to avoid sanction for their crimes, this can also give repetitive criminals opportunity to further victimize society with the accompanying significant costs. For example, Bartley (2000) estimated that the costs of a rape range from $6875 to $72,192 in 1980 to 1990 dollars, and the costs of a robbery from $2239 to $4094. Further, criminal defendants malingering mental illness can lead to protracted litigation increasing the cost and burden on our legal system.[4]

In the experience of one author, some inmates malinger mental illness to obtain psychiatric medications such as bupropion, quetiapine, or benzodiazepines, which have abuse potential and therefore black market value in a jail or prison. The cost of these medications is ultimately born by the taxpayer, and the demands on correctional medical resources may detract from meeting the needs of genuinely mentally ill inmates.

Thus, malingering has significant real costs to society that divert important resources from other areas. In acknowledgement of the prevalence and potential impact of malingering, a recent position paper by the National Academy of Neuropsychology on symptom validity assessment states in part, "the assessment of symptom validity is an essential part of a neuropsychological evaluation. The clinician should be prepared to justify a decision not to assess symptom validity as part of a neuropsychological evaluation" (Bush et al., 2005, p. 421).

---

[3] Technically, a finding of incompetence to stand trial (ITST) is only applicable to the defendant's mental state at the time of adjudication for the instant offense. However, in the experience of one of the authors once a defendant has been found ITST (rightly or wrongly) it is difficult from a practical standpoint for him to be found competent for future offenses. Thus, a class of offenders is created that is to an extent immune from future criminal prosecution.

[4] For example, reputed mob boss Vincent Gigante fought a seven-year court battle maintaining that he was incompetent to stand trial, prior to pleading guilty to obstruction of Justice in 2003 (Raab, 2005, December 20). This protracted dispute was undoubtedly very costly for all involved parties, and likely tied up a great deal of the court's time.

REASONS WHY NEUROPSYCHOLOGISTS MAY WITHHOLD A DIAGNOSIS OF MALINGERING: ISSUES RELATED TO SPECIFIC ROLES

Although the difference is not always clear-cut, "the two most common roles for a neuropsychologist are diagnostician/treater/advocate *or* impartial forensic evaluator/non-advocate" (Fisher, Johnson-Greene, & Barth, 2002, p. 4). *Standards 3.10 Informed Consent* and *9.03 Informed Consent in Assessments* mandate that the examinee be informed of the nature and purpose of the assessment, which would include the role in which the neuropsychologist is acting. Guidance is available regarding the specifics of informed consent for neuropsychological evaluations from the National Academy of Neuropsychology (Bush & NAN Policy and Planning Committee, 2005; Johnson-Greene & NAN Policy and Planning Committee, 2005).

Fisher, Johnson-Greene, and Barth (2002) provided an excellent discussion of the distinction between the treating and the forensic role, and interested readers are referred to their original work. For the purposes of discussing how these roles may influence making a diagnosis of malingering, we will provide a summary here.

The forensic expert

The "impartial forensic evaluator/non-advocate" or "forensic expert" is required to be an impartial seeker of truth. According to the *Guidelines VI-C*:

> As an expert conducting an evaluation, treatment, consultation, or scholarly/empirical investigation, the forensic psychologist maintains professional integrity by examining the issue at hand from all reasonable perspectives, actively seeking information that will differentially test plausible rival hypotheses.
>
> (p. 661)

Furthermore, *Guidelines VII-D* states:

> When testifying, forensic psychologists have an obligation to all parties to a legal proceeding to present their findings, conclusions, evidence, or other professional products in a fair manner . . . Forensic psychologists do not, by either commission or omission, participate in partisan attempts to avoid, deny, or subvert the presentation of evidence contrary to their position.
>
> (p. 664)

Per the above, for the forensic expert, the issue is relatively straightforward. If after performing a scientifically sound evaluation the expert believes that malingering may be present, then that expert is ethically bound to offer that opinion to the appropriate degree of diagnostic certainty.

However, although ethically unambiguous, forensic experts may open themselves to retaliation after diagnosing malingering. Forensic experts have been the target of licensing board and ethics committee complaints after diagnosing examinees with malingering in the course of forensic evaluations (e.g., Youngjohn, 1997; Youngjohn & Perrin, 1994). The American Academy of Clinical Neuropsychology (AACN, 2003) stated, "It appears that some of these complaints may be intended to weaken a particular expert's credibility and thereby strengthen either the plaintiff's present cases or future plaintiff's cases that will be seen by the same expert." The authors pointed out that this practice may violate the *Standard 1.07 Improper Complaints*: "Psychologists do not file or encourage the filing of ethics complaints that are made with reckless disregard for or willful ignorance of facts that would disprove the allegation." Regardless, working as a forensic psychologist requires maintaining a clear set of ethics despite the multiple challenges of that specialty which may sometimes be at odds with that of a "treating" psychologist.

The treating psychologist

The role of the diagnostician/treater/advocate or "treating doctor" differs significantly from that of the "forensic expert." The treating doctor is looking out for the patient's best interests, and thus this role is primarily one of advocacy. "When undertaking the treating role, the neuropsychologist should understand that he or she is serving as the consumer's advocate. Advocacy, by definition, requires a departure from impartiality" (Fisher, Johnson-Greene, & Barth, 2002, p. 4). This advocacy role is a source of potential conflicts for the issue of diagnosing malingering.

As illustrated by the vignette below, especially with the economic pressure engendered by managed care, the treating doctor may be tempted to not diagnose malingering to ensure the availability of treatment. This pressure may be especially strong if the patient is genuinely troubled, and the psychologist believes that ongoing contact would be helpful.

> A postdoctoral fellow in neuropsychology at an outpatient rehabilitation facility performs a follow-up evaluation of a patient enrolled in a multidisciplinary "mild head injury" program following an apparently minor motor vehicle accident. Although no formal tests of symptom validity are performed, the fellow is concerned that the patient's scores on neuropsychological tests have actually decreased, in spite of six months of cognitive remediation, individual, group and family psychotherapy, speech therapy, and occupational therapy. For example, the patient displayed a drop in his score on the Wechsler Adult Intelligence Scale–Third Edition (WAIS–III) Information subtest, revealing profound deficits in his fund of general knowledge that were not there before. He also did very poorly on the Digit Span subtests of both the WAIS–III and the Wechsler Memory Scale–Third Edition (WMS–III), again receiving worse scores than were previously noted. The patient is currently in litigation against the insurance company of the driver of the other vehicle.
>
> The fellow expresses her concerns to her supervisor at the facility and raises the possibility that the patient may be malingering. The supervisor advises that it would be unwise to raise that issue in the report in that it may jeopardize the patient's insurance funding, and thus the patient's access to care. The supervisor instead suggests that the patient is a genuinely troubled individual with a long history of emotional disturbance who would genuinely benefit from ongoing psychological treatment. When writing the report of this evaluation, the supervisor instructs the fellow to describe the patient as displaying an "emotional reaction" to the accident, and discourages any further investigation into malingering.

The practice of not diagnosing malingering (or of ignoring the possibility entirely) for "the benefit of the client" is unethical even in a treating relationship. Psychologists performing evaluations have an obligation to consider all possibilities that may realistically affect assessment results including poor effort or purposeful deception. According to the *Standard 9.06 Interpreting Assessment Results:*

> When interpreting assessment results, including automated interpretations, psychologists take into account the purpose of the assessment as well as the various test factors, test-taking abilities, and other characteristics of the person being assessed, such as situational, personal, linguistic, and cultural differences, that might affect psychologists' judgments or reduce the accuracy of their interpretations. They indicate any significant limitations of their interpretations.

Furthermore, as mentioned, *Principle C: Integrity* advises psychologists "to promote accuracy, honesty and truthfulness in the science, teaching, and practice of psychology" and to not engage in "intentional misrepresentation of fact."

There are instances in which not diagnosing malingering when appropriate may actually be physically harmful to the patient. For example, misdiagnosing a patient as having a medical condition (e.g., Attention-Deficit/Hyperactivity Disorder) may result in him or her being unnecessarily exposed to the possible side effects of medications, including the potential for addiction (e.g., Conti, 2004). This would violate *Standard 3.04 Avoiding Harm*; "Psychologists take reasonable steps to avoid harming their clients/patients, students, supervisees, research participants, organizational clients, and others with whom they work, and to minimize harm where it is foreseeable and avoidable." *Principle A: Beneficence and Nonmaleficence* is also applicable: "Psychologists strive to benefit those with whom they work and take care to do no harm." The argument can also be made that by diagnosing the presence of an illness or impairment where there is none, the neuropsychologist is restricting the patient's autonomy and freedom—be it freedom to pursue gainful employment, to plead one's case before a criminal court, or freedom to go through life without the label of brain injury. Again this is in keeping with *Principle A: Beneficence and Nonmaleficence*.

On a subtler note, there is a moral issue involved in enabling less-than-truthful behavior for the patient. Malingering, by definition, is faking for some personal gain. Is it good for the patient to be abetted in being deceitful? By not diagnosing malingering, the psychologist is reinforcing deception as an acceptable way of obtaining goals, thus impeding the examinee's moral development. At the risk of seeming moralistic, it is our opinion that as a professional the neuropsychologist should be an example of integrity. In support of this, Alexander (1980) proposed that physicians adopt a "truth in mending" act, writing:

> Perhaps we should state clearly that just as we will not lie to a patient and his family about his condition, we will not lie on the witness stand, to the patient's insurance company, nor to the Social Security Administration about his condition—that we understand and are concerned about his financial situation, but we cannot condone or take part in improving that condition through fraud, no matter how minor.
>
> (p. 1240)

For our part, informed consent should be obtained from the examinee for any clinical evaluation. Even when the evaluation is legally mandated or the examinee is incapable of giving informed consent, neuropsychologists should nonetheless inform the examinee of their role, the limits of confidentiality, and the reasons for the evaluation.

PRESENTATION OF RESULTS

Despite advances in detection and recognition of the validity of the diagnosis, many neuropsychologists are apparently uncomfortable using the term "malingering" even when they are strongly suspicious of it. Slick, Tan, Strauss, and Hultsch (2004) surveyed a small sample of "expert" neuropsychologists who frequently handled civil litigation cases. They found that while "virtually all" of the respondents made some statement in their reports when the findings indicated the possibility of malingering, the term "malingering" was generally not used. Instead, the experts "tended to state that the test results were invalid, inconsistent with the severity of the injury or indicative of exaggeration" (p. 470).

This practice can be viewed as disingenuous. Writing in regards to psychiatry, Simon (1970) asserted:

> If malingering is not fully characterized as such, it tends to confuse and contaminate the issue with respect to other cases where organic findings are equally lacking but motivations are different, such as psychoneurosis, especially hysteria. *A priori* elimination of malingering as a possible diagnosis in the

name of caution for the sake of protecting the psychiatrist is really unfair to the psychiatrist because it limits his precision in declaring himself, and it is also unfair to those patients whose diagnoses are accordingly muddled and made equivocal.

(p. 332)

Therefore, for all the reasons stated previously, we believe it is ethical to make the diagnosis of malingering when warranted by the results of the full assessment.

A word of caution, when diagnosing malingering in a report, care should be taken not to describe the test finding in such detail as to "educate" a report recipient on how to successfully malinger. Doing so may detract from the future ability of the test to detect symptom invalidity (e.g., DiCarlo, Gfeller, & Oliveri, 2000; Gorny, Merten, Henry, & Brockhaus, 2005; Suhr & Gunstad, 2000), and may violate *Standard 9.11 Maintaining Test Security*, which states, in part, "Psychologists make reasonable efforts to maintain the integrity and security of test materials and other assessment techniques consistent with law and contractual obligations, and in a manner that permits adherence to this Ethics Code." The National Academy of Neuropsychology provides guidelines on the proper release of sensitive test materials (National Academy of Neuropsychology, 2000, 2003).

Gouvier, Lees-Haley, and Hammer (2003) have also provided guidelines for reporting malingering and other invalid results without going into detail on the specific tests, writing, "It is suggested that the report author simply state that on several measures specifically designed to detect malingering, as well as on standard neuropsychological testing, the client's performance indicated malingering, response bias, or exaggeration" (p. 420). We simply add that the practitioner should assign whichever diagnosis the evidence supports.

A FINAL WORD

The readers are reminded that regardless of the examinee's presentation, the psychologist is obligated to treat all examinees with respect. Failure to do so would violate *Principle E: Respect for People's Rights and Dignity*, which states in part, "Psychologists respect the dignity and worth of all people." While there is a natural tendency to resent someone trying to deceive us—regardless of their motivation—the psychologist must maintain the standards of objectivity, professionalism, and ethics dictated by our profession and demanded by our field.

REFERENCES

Alexander, E. (1980). A "truth in mending" act. *JAMA, 243*, 1239–1240.

American Academy of Clinical Neuropsychology (2003). From the Academy: Official position of the American Academy of Clinical Neuropsychology on ethical complaints made against clinical neuropsychologists during adversarial proceedings. *The Clinical Neuropsychologist, 17*, 443–445.

American Psychiatric Association (2000). *Diagnostic and statistical manual of mental disorders*, 4th ed., text revision. Washington, DC: APA.

American Psychological Association (2002). Ethical Principles of Psychologists and Code of Conduct. *American Psychologist, 57*, 1060–1073.

Ardolf, B. R., Denney, R. L., & Houston, C. M. (2005, October). *Base rates of malingered neurocognitive dysfunction among criminals*. Poster session presented at the annual meeting of the National Academy of Neuropsychology, Tampa, FL.

Atkins v. Virginia, 260 Va. 375, 534 SE 2d 312 (2002).

Bartley, W. A. (2000). A valuation of specific crime rates. Doctoral dissertation, Vanderbilt University. *Dissertation Abstracts International, 61,* 1545.

Bianchini, K. J., Greve, K. W., & Love, J. M. (2003). Definite malingered neurocognitive dysfunction in moderate/severe traumatic brain injury. *The Clinical Neuropsychologist, 17,* 574–580.

Brodsky, S. L., & Galloway, V. A. (2003). Ethical and professional demands for forensic mental health professionals in the post-*Atkins* era. *Ethics and Behavior, 13,* 3–9.

Bullfinch, T. (1978). *Bullfinch's mythology.* New York: Avenel.

Bush, S. S., & NAN Policy and Planning Committee (2005). Independent and court-ordered forensic neuropsychological examinations: Official statement of the National Academy of Neuropsychology. *Archives of Clinical Neuropsychology, 20,* 997–1007.

Bush, S. S., Ruff, R. M., Tröster, A. I., Barth, J. T., Koffler, S. P., Pliskin, N. H., Reynolds, C. R., & Silver, C. H. (2005). Symptom validity assessment: Practice issues and medical necessity. NAN Policy & Planning Committee. *Archives of Clinical Neuropsychology, 20,* 419–426.

Butcher, J. N., Graham, J. R., Ben-Porath, Y. S., Tellegen, A., Dahlstrom, W. G., & Kaemmer, B. (2001). *Minnesota Multiphasic Personality Inventory-2 (MMPI-2): Manual for administration and scoring,* revised edition. Minneapolis: University of Minnesota Press.

Chafetz, M., & Abrahams, J. (2005, October). *Green's MACT helps identify internal predictors of effort in the Social Security Disability Exam.* Paper presented at the annual meeting of the National Academy of Neuropsychology, Tampa, FL.

Committee on Ethical Guidelines for Forensic Psychologists (1991). Specialty guidelines for forensic psychologists. *Law and Human Behavior, 15,* 655–665.

Conti, R. P. (2004). Malingered ADHD in adolescents diagnosed with conduct disorder: A brief note. *Psychological Reports, 94,* 987–988.

DeClue, G. (2002). Practitioner's corner: Feigning ≠ malingering: A case study. *Behavioral Sciences and the Law, 20,* 717–726.

DiCarlo, M. A., Gfeller, J. D., & Oliveri, M. V. (2000). Effects of coaching on detecting feigned cognitive impairment with the Category Test. *Archives of Clinical Neuropsychology, 15,* 399–413.

Fisher, J. M., Johnson-Greene, D., & Barth, J. T. (2002). Evaluation, diagnosis, and interventions in clinical neuropsychology in general and with special populations: An overview. In S. S. Bush & M. L. Drexler (Eds.), *Ethical issues in clinical neuropsychology* (pp. 3–22). Lisse, Netherlands: Swets & Zeitlinger.

Gorny, I., Merten, T., Henry, M., & Brockhaus, R. (2005, July). *Information, warning, coaching—How much do they need? An analogue study on feigned cognitive symptoms.* Poster session presented at the Joint Meeting of the International Neuropsychological Society, British Neuropsychological Society and Division of Neuropsychology of the British Psychological Society, Dublin, Ireland.

Gouvier, W. D., Lees-Haley, P. R., & Hammer, J. H. (2003). The neuropsychological examination in the detection of malingering in the forensic arena: Costs and benefits. In G. P. Prigatano & N. H. Pliskin (Eds.), *Clinical neuropsychology and cost outcome research: A beginning* (pp. 405–424). New York: Psychology Press.

Guttierrez, M., & Gur, R. C. (1998). Detection of malingering using forced-choice techniques. In C. R. Reynolds (Ed.), *Detection of malingering during head injury litigation* (pp. 81–104). New York: Plenum Press.

Hom, J., & Denney, R. L. (Eds.). (2002). *Detection of response bias in forensic neuropsychology.* New York: Haworth.

Johnson-Greene, D., & NAN Policy and Planning Committee. (2005). Informed consent in clinical neuropsychology practice: Official statement of the National Academy of Neuropsychology. *Archives of Clinical Neuropsychology, 20,* 335–340.

Larrabee, G. J. (2003). Detection of malingering using atypical performance patterns on standard neuropsychological tests. *The Clinical Neuropsychologist, 17,* 410–425.

Larrabee, G. J. (2005a). Assessment of malingering. In G. J. Larrabee (Ed.), *Forensic neuropsychology: A scientific approach* (pp. 115–158). New York: Oxford University Press.

Larrabee, G. J. (2005b). *Forensic neuropsychology: A scientific approach* (pp. 3–28). New York: Oxford University Press.

Lewin, J. L. (1998). The genesis and evolution of legal uncertainty about "reasonable medical certainty." *Maryland Law Review, 57,* 380–504.

Melton, G. B., Petrila, J., Poythress, N. G., & Slobogin, C. (1997). *Psychological evaluations for the courts,* 2nd ed. New York: Guilford.

Mendelson, G., & Mendelson, D. (2004). Malingering pain in the medicolegal context. *Clinical Journal of Pain*, *20*, 423–432.

Mittenberg, W., Patton, C., Canyock, E. M., & Condit, D. C. (2002). Base rates of malingering and symptom exaggeration. *Journal of Clinical and Experimental Neuropsychology*, *24*, 1094–1102.

National Academy of Neuropsychology (2000). Test security: Official position statement of the National Academy of Neuropsychology. *Archives of Clinical Neuropsychology*, *15*, 383–386.

National Academy of Neuropsychology (2003). *Test security: An update*. Retrieved March 4, 2006, from http://www.nanonline.org/paio/security_update.shtm

Pankratz, L., & Erickson, R. C. (1990). Two views of malingering. *The Clinical Neuropsychologist*, *4*, 379–389.

Raab, S. (2005, December 20). Vincent Gigante, mob boss who feigned incompetence to avoid jail dies at 77. *New York Times*, p. A29.

Simon, J. L. (1970). The psychiatrist's role in personal injury adjudication. *Diseases of the Nervous System, 31*, 329–332.

Slick, D. J., Sherman, E. M. S., & Iverson, G. L. (1999). Diagnostic criteria for malingered neurocognitive dysfunction: Proposed standards for clinical practice and research. *The Clinical Neuropsychologist*, *13*, 545–561.

Slick, D. J., Tan, J. E., Strauss, E. H., & Hultsch, D. F. (2004). Detecting malingering: a survey of expert's practices. *Archives of Clinical Neuropsychology*, *19*, 465–473.

Suhr, J. A., & Gunstad, J. (2000). The effects of coaching on the sensitivity and specificity of malingering measures. *Archives of Clinical Neuropsychology*, *15*, 415–424.

Sweet, J. J. (1999). Malingering: Differential diagnosis. In J. J. Sweet (Ed.), *Forensic neuropsychology: Fundamentals and practice* (pp. 255–286). Lisse, Netherlands: Swets & Zeitlinger.

Sweet, J. J., King, J. H., Malina, A. C., Bergman, M. A., & Simmons, A. (2002). Documenting the prominence of forensic neuropsychology at national meetings and in relevant professional journals from 1990 to 2000. *The Clinical Neuropsychologist*, *16*, 481–494.

Youngjohn, J. R. (1997). Nine consecutive board complaints from Arizona Psychologists. *Arizona Psychologist*, *17*, 6–8.

Youngjohn, J. R., Lees-Haley, P. R., & Binder, L. M. (1999). Comment: Warning malingerers produces more sophisticated malingering. *Archives of Clinical Neuropsychology*, *14*, 511–515.

Youngjohn, J. R., & Perrin, G. (1994). Board actions: Independent psychological examinations. *Arizona Psychologist, 14*, 6–7.

What to do after making a determination of malingering

Shane S. Bush

Every neuropsychological evaluation requires a determination regarding the validity of the data obtained. The confidence that can be placed in such determinations is dependent upon the nature of the data and the context in which they were obtained. Although, in clinical contexts, decisions of whether to use symptom validity measures or symptom validity indicators embedded within or derived from neurocognitive measures remains at the discretion of the examiner, psychometric assessment of response validity is clearly superior to an examiner's subjective opinion when making an informed judgment about the validity of neuropsychological data (Faust, Hart, Guilmette, & Arkes, 1988). Furthermore, neuropsychologists must administer symptom validity tests and perform relevant procedures to aid in the determination of the validity of data obtained during the evaluation when (1) the potential for secondary gain increases the incentive for dissimulation and (2) the examiner becomes suspicious of insufficient effort or inaccurate or incomplete reporting (Bush et al., 2005). The need to assess symptom validity with appropriate quantitative methods applies to examinees ranging in age from childhood through older adult (Ashendorf, O'Bryant, & McCaffrey, 2003; Faust, Hart, & Guilmette, 1988; Lu & Boone, 2002), as well as to those with well-documented neurological impairment (Bianchini, Greve, & Love, 2003).

Although determining that an examinee has dissimulated can sometimes be obvious, making such determinations can often be quite challenging. Psychological and neuropsychological researchers have generated a considerable amount of information in recent years to assist practitioners in their determinations of symptom validity. Symptom validity tests (SVTs), embedded indicators, and other strategies for assessing symptom validity have been developed and applied clinically. However, the use of techniques for assessing symptom validity currently seems to exceed professional consensus on the meaning and use of the results (Sharland & Gfeller, 2007). That is, with the exception of extreme cases (and even then sometimes) neuropsychologists may not always agree on the interpretation of measures of symptom validity (e.g., valid, invalid, or some point in between).

Noncredible and inconsistent performance and responding are the cardinal features suggestive of dissimulation (Boone & Lu, 2003; Slick, Sherman, & Iverson, 1999). Examinees who perform in a manner that is markedly inconsistent with (i.e., poorer than) usual performances by individuals with similar, or more severe, neurological injury or illness raise suspicion of dissimulation. The greater the inconsistency or the more evidence of noncredible responding that exists, the greater the degree of confidence that the examiner can place in conclusions regarding the examinee's honesty and effort. Despite the proliferation of symptom validity research and the emergence of proposed guidelines for diagnosing neurocognitive malingering (e.g., Slick, Sherman, & Iverson,

1999), universally accepted criteria for making determinations regarding symptom validity do not yet exist.

In addition to challenges that may be encountered when making determinations about the validity of neuropsychological data, the meaning that is attributed to invalid data may be subject to disagreement among neuropsychologists. For example, questions such as whether malingering can always be inferred from invalid performance on neuropsychological or symptom validity tests in the context of litigation generate considerable debate among practitioners. There are a number of reasons why an examinee may produce invalid neuropsychological data (Iverson, 2003; Sweet, 1999), with malingering being one possibility.

As with the challenges that emerge in the assessment of response validity and the meaning attributed to invalid data, neuropsychologists may face considerable difficulty in deciding how to report a finding of dissimulation and how to conclude the matter with the examinee and the referral source or retaining party. For example, when invalid test performance is evident during an evaluation, should the examiner confront the examinee? Should the examiner complete the test battery or discontinue test administration? The potential advantages and disadvantages of each course of action must be considered in advance.

Reactions to accusations of invalid performance by examinees may range from acknowledgement that, for any of a variety of reasons, full effort to perform in an accurate and optimal manner was lacking, to emotionally charged statements that the examinee has done his or her best. Reactions from referral sources or retaining parties also may vary considerably depending on the purpose of the evaluation. Although neuropsychologists are not all of the same opinion regarding how to proceed when it is apparent that invalid data has been produced, it is clear that a plan to address this possibility must be in place prior to beginning the evaluation. The purpose of this chapter is to illustrate the importance of anticipating findings of dissimulation and potential ways of handling the matter with the examinee and the referral source should dissimulation occur.

CASE ILLUSTRATION

Identifying information

Mr. S.S. was a 42-year-old married man who, according to his self-report and a consultation report from his neurologist (Dr. B.), began experiencing numerous physical, cognitive, and emotional problems following a motor vehicle accident. The accident occurred nine months prior to his neuropsychological intake appointment. Mr. S.S. was referred by his neurologist to clarify cognitive strengths and weaknesses and emotional adjustment, and to provide rehabilitative and psychotherapeutic services as needed. He was seen for the neuropsychological evaluation in an independent practice setting.

Behavioral observations

Mr. S.S. presented for his appointment by himself and was a few minutes late, having forgotten the address of the office building. He was appropriately dressed and groomed. He ambulated without gait disturbance or apparent difficulty, and movement of his upper extremities was free of gross impairment. Receptive language was functional for interview questions. Conversational speech was fluent. He was fully oriented. His thoughts were clear and goal-directed. Affect was euthymic. Social pragmatics (greeting, eye contact, etc.) were appropriate.

Informed consent

The session began with the informed consent process. The purpose and nature of the evaluation were discussed, with Mr. S.S. indicating understanding and agreement. In order to provide specific information regarding limits to confidentiality, the neuropsychologist inquired about litigation. Mr. S.S. acknowledged that he was a plaintiff in a personal injury suit related to the accident of nine months before, and he denied additional litigation history. Mr. S.S. was informed of the potential limits to confidentiality resulting from his litigation status. He was informed that, at a minimum, Dr. B. and the no-fault insurance company would require copies of the neuropsychological report. In addition, attorneys for both sides would likely require copies of neuropsychological records, and the potential existed that the information could end up, through court transcripts, in the public domain. Mr. S.S. was also informed that accurate interpretation of the evaluation results was dependent upon him putting forth his best effort on all tests and responding honestly to questions about himself; he was informed that his effort and truthfulness would be assessed. Following review of all relevant information, the informed consent process concluded with Mr. S.S. providing his consent to the evaluation.

Clinical interview

Mr. S.S. reported that his accident occurred when he was sitting at a stoplight in his pick-up truck and he was rear-ended by an SUV traveling at highway speed. A toolbox flew through the back window of his truck and struck him on the back of his head. His face struck the windshield, resulting in a large laceration. He experienced a loss of consciousness of a few minutes. His last memory before the accident was driving down the road. His first memory following the accident was thinking "my head's wet. I messed up my face." He reported having continuous memories from that point on. He felt "dazed" and had a severe headache. He was taken by helicopter to a local trauma center. He was treated and was discharged home the following day.

He followed up with his primary care physician (PCP) later in the week, and then began chiropractic treatments. Mr. S.S. reported that he continued to experience headaches and problems with attention, memory, and processing speed. In addition, he reported experiencing weakness on the left side of his body. Five months after his accident, his PCP referred him to Dr. B., who diagnosed Mr. S.S. with persistent postconcussion syndrome and recommended neuroimaging studies.

Mr. S.S. reported that the neuroimaging studies revealed two ACoA aneurysms, which required a right frontal craniotomy for clipping. He further stated that MRIs detected a brain stem tumor, which his doctors considered "inoperable but slow growing." Mr. S.S. paused as the neuropsychologist finished writing down this information. He then asked, "You don't have to report those things, do you?"

The neuropsychologist replied, "Yes. They are an important part of your medical history."

Mr. S.S.: "But they're not related to my accident."

Neuropsychologist: "No, but they're probably contributing to the problems with attention and memory and to the other neurological symptoms that you've been experiencing."

Mr. S.S.: "But my problems started after the accident, way before the aneurysms and the tumor."

Neuropsychologist: "Even though you didn't know about the aneurysms and the tumor, they were probably there. And, even if they didn't contribute to the symptoms that you experienced right after the accident, the fact that you underwent surgery . . ."

Mr. S.S.: "After the surgery, everything was the same as it was before the surgery. Nothing got worse."

Neuropsychologist: "In any event, these things are a significant part of your medical history and cannot be left out of my report."

Mr. S.S.: "Dr. B. knows about all of this, and he agreed not to put any of it in his reports. Call him and talk to him about it."

At this point, the neuropsychologist was aware that the case was more complicated than most clinical referrals. Mr. S.S. appeared to be more concerned about his lawsuit than he was about better understanding and addressing his reported cognitive and emotional problems. Mr. S.S. was willing to omit, and possibly misrepresent or fabricate, important information in order to achieve his financial goals, and he was willing to ask others to do the same. This alone was a clear-cut case of malingering. There was no need to infer the patient's motives from evaluation data. The only concern at that point was how to best handle the situation. In addition to concerns about Mr. S.S., the possibility existed that taking a higher ethical ground than the neurologist had reportedly taken could negatively impact the neuropsychologist's relationship with the referring neurologist.

Mr. S.S. says, "Let's forget I ever said anything about the aneurysms and the surgery and the tumor. I'll come in again, and we can start over."

Neuropsychologist: "I can't do that."

Mr. S.S.: "Why not? It's just ethics."

Neuropsychologist smiles, "As fate would have it, you happen to be sitting across from someone who takes ethics pretty seriously."

Mr. S.S.: "O.K. Then I don't want you to tell anyone I was ever here. I want to take back what I said about you talking to Dr. B. or to other people or sending your report."

CONSIDERATIONS

This was the first time that the neuropsychologist had ever had an examinee rescind consent to release neuropsychological information or findings to the referring party. A number of thoughts and possibilities ran through the neuropsychologist's mind, including the following:

1. Should I just tell Mr. S.S. that I could not help him and send him back to his neurologist?
2. Should I give Mr. S.S. the names of other local neuropsychologists? If not, could I be accused of abandoning him? If I do give him the names, he will certainly withhold important medical history from them, and I do not have authorization to call and warn them. Some of the lateralizing symptoms are likely to be detected and will be confusing to a neuropsychologist who lacks the complete medical history. Have I simply made Mr. S.S. a better malingerer?
3. How am I going to get paid for this session? No-fault insurance rules require a copy of my notes or reports, and Mr. S.S. won't authorize me to send them. I can't really chalk up the loss of the fee to "pro bono" since it was not done "for good." How do you say "lost income by default" in Latin?
4. What am I going to say to Dr. B. when he wants to know my findings?
5. How will Dr. B. react when he realizes that I would not engage in the same unethical behavior in which he seems to engage? Can I even trust that what Mr. S.S. said about Dr. B. is true? Knowing Dr. B., it would not surprise me; however, I know that Mr. S.S. cannot be trusted.

The neuropsychologist considered his professional and ethical responsibilities, acutely aware of the need to resolve the dilemma promptly. His thoughts were along the following lines: I have a responsibility to Mr. S.S. to give him some direction (Ethical Standard A, Beneficence and Nonmaleficence; American Psychological Association, 2002). Despite my personal feelings toward him (dare I say "countertransference"?), I cannot just send him away without offering any suggestions. On the other hand, referring him to another neuropsychologist would be of no clinical value to Mr. S.S. because, without providing accurate medical history, the conclusions of the neuropsychologist would be inaccurate, and any recommendations provided would be inappropriate. I can share that fact with Mr. S.S., and, to the extent that he is concerned about his neuropsychological functioning at all, he may benefit from hearing it. In addition, unnecessary allocation of neuropsychological and financial resources to evaluate Mr. S.S. would be inconsistent with appropriate use of those resources (General Principle D, Justice). Ultimately, I concluded I must refer him back to his neurologist to re-examine his options.

I have a responsibility to the referring party, Dr. B., to inform him, at a minimum, that the patient was seen for an initial session, but would not be undergoing neuropsychological testing. Dr. B. was going to want to know why. How would I respond to that question? I did not want to tell him that I refused to selectively omit significant aspects of medical history, as, according to Mr. S.S., Dr. B. apparently had no problem doing this.

Actual case resolution

I determined that I should attempt to preserve Mr. S.S.'s consent to release at least minimal information to Dr. B. Therefore, I explained to Mr. S.S. that Dr. B. would want to know the status of the evaluation, including why the evaluation was not performed. Mr. S.S. responded that *he* would tell Dr. B. I, however, persisted, stating I preferred to have the ability to discuss the matter with Dr. B., for the potential benefit of Mr. S.S. After a relatively lengthy pause, Mr. S.S. agreed. I then drafted a modified informed consent form, outlining the parameters as agreed upon by Mr. S.S., within which I could discuss the case. Mr. S.S. signed the new consent form, waited while the original consent form was shredded, and left the office. I then called Dr. B.

CASE MODIFICATIONS

For purposes of elaboration and illustration, the following sections present alternative ways of resolving this case example. These modifications are intended to strengthen the reader's knowledge of potential malingering situations and the various pitfalls that may ensue. The issue to be considered is whether to continue the evaluation in the face of failed SVTs or other unequivocal evidence of dissimulation, malingering, or prevarication.

Case modification 1

Suppose that, in the above scenario, the idealistic outcome did not occur. Suppose that I, having been taken by surprise and feeling considerable pressure to complete the evaluation, agreed to proceed with the evaluation. Imagine that the administration of the WAIS–III was begun. During the initial subtests, Mr. S.S. answered with "I don't know" to numerous items, and considerable prompting for a "guess" resulted in unusual responses. For example, to the Picture Completion item that consists of a water pitcher and glass, he responded that the aspect missing was "a goal post." In addition to frequently responding with "I don't know" and producing unusual responses, he at times responded incorrectly to easier items while responding correctly to more difficult items. For these reasons, completion of the WAIS–III would be put on hold while I administered a symptom validity test, in this case the TOMM.

Mr. S.S. may have then proceeded to achieve the following scores on the TOMM: 21, 29, and 11. At that point, I might have stopped the evaluation. It was evident that Mr. S.S.'s test performance was invalid. I might then consider how to handle the situation.

Considerations for modification 1

I considered the following two options and the related issues. First, should I inform Mr. S.S. that it is clear that he is not trying his best, as he agreed to do during the informed consent process? Some colleagues have indicated that once examinees are confronted and are informed that they are only doing themselves a disservice, they perform in a valid manner from that point on. However, other practitioners do not confront or inform examinees when insufficient effort is evident.

Second, should I complete the evaluation? Colleagues may disagree as to what to do with invalid test performance. Some practitioners argue that neuropsychological evaluations need not be stopped. They argue that performance on a SVT only indicates that invalid performance was generated on that specific test and that such findings cannot necessarily be generalized to other measures or to the evaluation results as a whole. They argue that absence of evidence (i.e., absence of invalid performance on all measures) is not evidence of absence (i.e., absence of appropriate effort across tests). They also argue that obtaining a minimum level of neurocognitive ability can be important and justify (to payers, referral sources/retaining parties, and peer reviewers) completion of the test battery. Although the results of the evaluation will be invalid for the purposes for which the evaluation was initiated, at least a minimum level of neurocognitive ability can be established, especially when normal (average or better) test results are obtained, as occurs when examinees selectively malinger. Such information may be of value to someone at some point in the future.

With regard to the above options and issues, I considered that SVTs, in addition to indices of effort derived from neurocognitive tests, are used to provide psychometric evidence of examinee effort, and that such information is used to establish confidence in the examinee and in the validity of the neurocognitive test results produced by the examinee. I then considered that the purpose of the evaluation was to provide a clinical diagnosis and recommendations for treatment; the purpose was not to establish a minimum level of neurocognitive ability based on invalid test results. Thus, there was no need to administer additional tests.

I also considered informing Mr. S.S. that his poor effort had been detected and that, as such, the test results would be of no clinical (or forensic) value to him. However, I believed that I risked simply making Mr. S.S. a better malingerer and that, despite improved performance on SVTs and perhaps neurocognitive measures, the test results ultimately may still not reflect Mr. S.S.'s potential. Thus, I did not believe that I could be confident in the test results if I discussed the matter with Mr. S.S. and completed the test administration.

Case resolution for modification 1

I informed Mr. S.S. that it was clear that the test results did not reflect Mr. S.S.'s optimal performance, which was necessary for accurate interpretation of the evaluation results and which he had agreed to provide during the informed consent process. I further stated that the evaluation would be discontinued and that Dr. B. would be informed of the outcome.

Mr. S.S. acknowledged his attempt to mislead me, stating that he just wanted the insurance company, his family, and his doctors to know that he really had been injured in the motor vehicle accident and was suffering as a result. With tearful affect, he promised to try his best if he could begin the evaluation again. Although touched by Mr. S.S.'s display of emotion and his apparent genuineness, I nevertheless maintained the position that Mr. S.S. could not continue the evaluation. Instead, I offered to provide Mr. S.S. with the names of other neuropsychologists in the area who may be willing to conduct the evaluation.

It was at that point that Mr. S.S. informed me that he wanted to withdraw his consent to have information about the session released to anyone. Unsure of how to handle the situation, I wanted to stall for more time in order to determine an acceptable course of action. I thought that Mr. S.S.

would only agree to a request for more time if he believed the delay was in his own interest. Thus, I asked Mr. S.S. if he would reschedule for the next day so that I could think things through, with the possibility that the evaluation may be continued. Although I had no intention of continuing the evaluation, I believed that my deception of Mr. S.S. was justified in order to discover and pursue the most appropriate course of action. Mr. S.S. agreed to meet the following day, but maintained that I could not release information about the case to anyone.

After Mr. S.S. left, I reviewed professional guidelines and consulted with colleagues. Based on the information obtained, I determined that the best course of action would be to attempt to negotiate a modified consent to discuss the matter with the referral source (Dr. B.), as had been done in the original scenario. This time, however, Mr. S.S. was angry about having had to return without the benefit of further testing, and he refused my request. As uncomfortable as the situation was for me, I was legally and ethically bound to not disclose information about the session to anyone.[1]

Case modification 2

Suppose that, in the above scenario, Mr. S.S. performed fairly well on the WAIS–III. No "red flags" were raised to alert me to the likelihood of dissimulation. Suppose that, consistent with my usual protocol, I administered the TOMM following completion of the WAIS–III, and suppose that Mr. S.S.'s scores were 50, 50, and 50. However, following completion of the TOMM, Mr. S.S. stated, "I always liked that one." I queried, "What do you mean?" Mr. S.S. explained, "A couple years ago I saw an ad in the paper and volunteered for a study over at the University. They taught us how to take these tests and fake like we had a brain injury without getting caught. Who'd have thought that I'd actually get a brain injury and need to take these tests for real someday? Pretty ironic, isn't it?"

I was dumbfounded, and my face registered the shock. Mr. S.S. followed up, "But don't worry Doc. I wouldn't try to trick *you*. Even if I wanted to, I know that you'd catch me. And besides, I want to get the help that I need. No, Doc, I'm being straight with you; I'm trying my best."

Considerations for modification 2

I was well aware that malingering research involves a variety of methodologies, which together have improved the ability of neuropsychologists to understand and detect examinee dissimulation. I further understood that one research method involves coaching research participants to malinger. My reading of recent professional literature (e.g., Powell, Gfeller, Hendricks, & Sharland, 2004) revealed that coaching in the context of malingering research typically takes one of two forms: symptom-coaching or test-coaching. Of the two forms, test-coaching may be particularly problematic for neuropsychology and the public. Test-coached participants are asked to feign cognitive impairment on neuropsychological tests and are taught test-taking strategies to help them avoid detection. Mr. S.S. had apparently been a test-coached research participant.

Confronting the dilemma of what to do with an examinee who admits to having been instructed (in this case non-maliciously) how to malinger neurocognitive deficits, I struggled with my options. I first considered that I had no psychometric evidence that Mr. S.S. was attempting to feign or exaggerate cognitive impairment. However, despite the lack of psychometric evidence, Mr. S.S.'s incentive to dissimulate and his earlier attempt to have me collude with him (and perhaps Dr. B.) to cover up important aspects of his medical history, combined with Mr. S.S.'s acknowledged sophistication with malingering neurocognitive test performance, left me questioning the value of

---

[1] Should the neuropsychologist be subpoenaed or otherwise legally instructed to disclose to the court information about the session, such requirements may preempt his responsibility to maintain privilege and/or confidentiality. Seeking personal legal counsel and/or explaining the dilemma to the court would be advisable under such circumstances.

completing the test administration. If test administration were to be completed, what degree of confidence could be placed in the results? Conversely, should Mr. S.S. be penalized for having been a neuropsychological research participant? Having never anticipated such an occurrence, I had no idea what to do. I felt pressured to make a quick decision when Mr. S.S. stated, "Doc, you O.K.? I'm ready to continue."

Case resolution for modification 2

Despite the pressure to proceed, I knew that I needed more time and input from colleagues. I informed Mr. S.S. that I had never been in such a situation, was not sure what to do, and would need to consult with a colleague. Mr. S.S. countered that he had done nothing wrong, did not want to postpone the evaluation, would rescind his consent for me to release information, and would consider filing an ethics complaint if the evaluation were not completed at that time, as originally agreed to by both of us. Aware that I was close to responding to the pressure and intimidation tactics in an inappropriately defensive manner, I suggested that we take a brief break. Following the break, I informed Mr. S.S. that I wanted to consult with a colleague to insure that the evaluation was conducted appropriately, for the benefit of Mr. S.S. He agreed to postpone completion of the evaluation, but he reiterated that if the evaluation were prematurely discontinued, he would follow through with the ethics complaint.

Following the session, I contacted several respected colleagues to discuss the matter. The colleagues agreed that, although it was unfortunate that the examinee had been a test-coached research participant, such participation should not automatically disqualify a person from receiving a complete neuropsychological evaluation. The colleagues emphasized that any reservations regarding symptom validity should, as always, be reported. They further suggested that other indicators of symptom validity, such as those embedded within or based upon neurocognitive tests, be carefully considered.

The possible need to discuss these issues with the referral source was also examined. I concluded that because the evaluation was performed for clinical purposes, any limitations of his conclusions could, appropriately, be described in the written report. In contrast, had I been retained by an attorney to perform a forensic neuropsychological evaluation, it may have been appropriate to contact the retaining attorney to determine if the limitations that would need to be placed on the conclusions would alter the attorney's decision to pursue the evaluation.

I met Mr. S.S. for the second session and informed him that it was appropriate to complete the evaluation as originally intended. Test administration was completed, and I indicated in my written report and in verbal feedback all relevant factors pertaining to my conclusions.

CONCLUSION AND RECOMMENDATIONS

Interpretation of neurocognitive and psychological test data requires that a determination first be made regarding the validity of the data obtained. As a result, the assessment of examinee characteristics that may threaten the validity of the test results or evaluation conclusions is an essential component of the neuropsychological evaluation. In fact, the assessment of response validity, as a component of a medically necessary neuropsychological evaluation, has been described as "medically necessary" (Bush et al., 2005).

In addition to the *assessment* of response validity, implementation of an appropriate course of *action* once invalid responding or performance has been detected is equally vital. Determining what steps to take following detection of invalid performance is best done in advance. The informed consent process provides neuropsychologists with the opportunity to clarify, at the outset of the evaluation, expectations and responsibilities, both for themselves and for examinees.[2] Although examinee consent indicates agreement with the purposes and procedures of the evaluation, examinees in clinical settings are free to rescind their consent, and neuropsychologists should be prepared to negotiate this challenge if it occurs. In contrast to the current case and its modifications, examinees in some forensic contexts are not afforded the same rights regarding consent. Neuropsychologists must be aware of the consent requirements for the contexts in which they practice.

The following recommendations are offered to assist the neuropsychological examiner when considering courses of action to take when invalid or incomplete effort or responding is suspected or clearly evident:

1. Plan ahead. Attempt to anticipate where in the informed consent[2] or evaluation process challenges may lay. Determine beforehand how such challenges will be handled. Have a plan for what to do if examinee consent is rescinded or if invalid performance is suspected or established.
2. Do not succumb to pressure or threats. Do not allow examinees or retaining parties to convince you to do something that you know or suspect is inappropriate. Take your time, being sure to gather adequate information from all relevant sources. Review professional guidelines and jurisdictional laws, and consult with colleagues.
3. Openness to input may be valuable during decision making. Open communication with the examinee or retaining party may help to clarify misunderstandings and establish a course of action that satisfies the goals of the evaluation. Consultation with colleagues may help to clarify ambiguous situations and result in the selection of good courses of action.
4. Inquire about prior exposure to psychological and neuropsychological tests. Such exposure may occur in a variety of contexts or from a variety of sources, including prior evaluations, research participation, the Internet, and attorneys. Consideration of prior exposure to psychological and neuropsychological measures may be important when selecting tests and interpreting test results.
5. When conducting an evaluation subsequent to one in which poor performance on SVTs was obtained, carefully consider the use of the same SVTs that were used in the previous evaluation. The examinee, having previously been exposed to the SVTs, may have exploited that experience between evaluations by researching the measures or by having another party coach them on how to "pass" the tests. Of course, if other psychometrically adequate measures are unavailable, the examiner may have little choice but to use the same measures, documenting any concerns about the validity of the results.
6. When *clear* evidence of invalid responding has been detected, carefully weigh the merits of continuing versus discontinuing the remainder of the planned evaluation. The context and goals of the evaluation are important considerations when determining the course of action. It should be noted that some neuropsychologists routinely complete the entire evaluation in situations in which unequivocal evidence of noncredible performance, suboptimal effort, or frank malingering was identified early in the examination process.

---

[2] It is acknowledged that in some evaluation contexts, such as some forensic contexts, examinee consent is not required. However, even in such contexts, neuropsychologists will benefit from determining in advance how to negotiate examinee lack of assent to engage in the evaluation.

REFERENCES

Amerian Psychological Association (2002). Ethical principles of psychologists and code of conduct. *American Psychologist, 57*(12), 1060–1073.

Ashendorf, L., O'Bryant, S. E., & McCaffrey, R. J. (2003). Specificity of malingering detection strategies in older adults using the CVLT and WCST. *The Clinical Neuropsychologist, 17*(2), 255–262.

Bianchini, K. J., Greve, K. W., & Love, J. M. (2003). Definite malingered neurocognitive dysfunction in moderate/severe brain injury. *The Clinical Neuropsychologist, 17*(4), 574–580.

Bush, S., Ruff, R., Tröster, A., Barth, J., Koffler, S., Pliskin, N., Reynolds, C., & Silver, C. (2005). Symptom validity assessment: Practice issues and medical necessity. Official position of the National Academy of Neuropsychology. *Archives of Clinical Neuropsychology, 20*, 419–426.

Boone, K. B., & Lu, P. (2003). Noncredible cognitive performance in the context of severe brain injury. *The Clinical Neuropsychologist, 17*(2), 244–254.

Faust, D., Hart, K., & Guilmette, T. J. (1988). Pediatric malingering: The capacity of children to fake believable deficits on neuropsychological testing. *Journal of Consulting and Clinical Psychology, 56*, 578–582.

Faust, D., Hart, K., Guilmette, T. J., & Arkes, H. R. (1988). Neuropsychologists' capacity to detect adolescent malingerers. *Professional Psychology: Research and Practice, 19*, 508–515.

Iverson, G. L. (2003). Detecting malingering in civil forensic evaluations. In A. M. Horton, Jr. & L. C. Hartlage (Eds.), *Handbook of forensic neuropsychology* (pp. 137–177). New York: Springer Publishing Company.

Lu, P. H., & Boone, K. B. (2002). Suspect cognitive symptoms in a 9-year-old child: Malingering by proxy? *The Clinical Neuropsychologist, 16*(1), 90–96.

Powell, M. R., Gfeller, J. D., Hendricks, B. L., & Sharland, M. (2004). Detecting symptom- and test-coached simulators with the Test of Memory Malingering. *Archives of Clinical Neuropsychology, 19*(5), 693–702.

Sharland, M. J., & Gfeller, J. D. (2007). A survey of neuropsychologists' beliefs and practices with respect to the assessment of effort. *Archives of Clinical Neuropsychology, 22*, 213–223.

Slick, D. J., Sherman, E. M. S., & Iverson, G. L. (1999). Diagnostic criteria for malingered neurocognitive dysfunction: Proposed standards for clinical practice and research. *The Clinical Neuropsychologist, 13*, 545–561.

Sweet, J. J. (1999). Malingering: Differential diagnosis. In J. J. Sweet (Ed.), *Forensic neuropsychology: Fundamentals and practice* (pp. 255–285). Lisse, Netherlands: Swets & Zeitlinger.

SECTION VI

CURRENT STATUS AND FUTURE DIRECTIONS

Identifying malingering with an acceptable degree of confidence is difficult enough when one is proactively looking for it, largely because of a clear secondary gain context. When the strong possibility of malingering presents itself in an unexpected circumstance, without any identifiable high risk factor associated with a case, the issues surrounding the differential diagnosis can take on a new and instructive perspective. The first of two chapters in this section illustrates such a situation. The second chapter approaches the topic of neuropsychological malingering from the vantage point that, because there is so much relevant peer-reviewed literature on the topic and also because of seemingly omnipresent formal presentations and informal conversations among forensic experts at national meetings, there *should* be some issues and some knowledge base on which most experienced clinical neuropsychologists can achieve consensus. From this approach, in the final chapter of this book, the Editors summarize what is currently known about malingering and what clinical neuropsychologists would like to know in the future.

Complexities of the differential diagnosis of malingering: Arguments for the use of effort tests with patients

Maria A. Bergman and Jerry J. Sweet

The purpose of this chapter is to highlight the topic of response validity as one that transcends forensic evaluations, such as personal injury, medical malpractice, disability determination, and worker's compensation. Adequate effort on the part of an examinee is a necessary underpinning of *all* neuropsychological evaluations, not just forensic evaluations that are known to have a higher risk of insufficient effort. Differently, we know from the head injury literature (e.g., Bianchini, Greve, & Love, 2003; Boone & Lu, 2003) and personal experience that even individuals with genuine injury may demonstrate insufficient effort or exaggerate their physical or cognitive problems even though genuine illness or injury exists. Phenomenologically, it seems that this behavior may occur among persons who do not believe that they will get their legitimate needs met by their healthcare providers and thus exaggerate their problems and answer questions in a manner that creates an impression of a greater severity of neurological disorder. Other non-injury factors, such as attention and sympathy from significant others and avoidance of responsibility—in the absence of a forensic context—may also contribute to compromised effort among persons with valid neurocognitive deficits.

This chapter will present a neuropsychological case example with no apparent forensic context. The test results of this case vignette demonstrate how a patient with a valid neurological disorder might perceive, presumably inaccurately, that exaggerated cognitive deficits are needed to assure that treatment services would be made available. We will continue in the next section with a brief review of examples of compromised effort on neuropsychological tests in non-litigating medical patients. Because most readers are not likely to be familiar with the rare genetics disorder that is the condition of interest in the central case discussion, we will thereafter give a description of the very rare degenerative genetically-confirmed neurological condition that this patient had, and briefly talk about its cause, illness progression, and consequences. In the next section, we will discuss the interesting clinical presentation of Ms. R.R., a non-litigant, who nevertheless blatantly exaggerated her neurocognitive symptoms. Finally, we will conclude with a brief discussion of diagnostic dilemmas and the complexities of making accurate diagnoses that inherently require a high degree of reliance on self-report and voluntary behaviors.

INSUFFICIENT EFFORT IN THE CONTEXT OF VARIOUS DOCUMENTED MEDICAL CONDITIONS

Effort is important fundamentally to *all* neuropsychological evaluations, not just those that are forensic in nature. The reality is that effort is much more consistently adequate or "within normal limits" in non-forensic contexts, a fact which is well documented in the relevant literature. For example, a review by Allen, Iverson, and Green (2002), the supplement to the professional users' manuals of the Word Memory Test (WMT) and Computerized Assessment of Response Bias (CARB), describes effort test results of 40 patients with documented neurological diseases, specifically brain tumor, ruptured aneurysm, stroke, and multiple sclerosis. The average performance of these neurological patients was 97.2% correct on the CARB. Gervais, Russell, Green, Allen, Ferrari, and Pieschl (2001) found that 100% of all fibromyalgia and rheumatoid arthritis patients who were not seeking compensation of any kind passed the effort threshold of the CARB.

Similarly, Woods, Conover, Weinborn, Rippeth, Brill, Heaton, Grant, and the HIV Neuro-behavioral Research Center Group (2003) demonstrated that of individuals diagnosed with HIV-associated neurocognitive disorders, 95% attained perfect scores (i.e., 100% correct) on a 36-item version of the Hiscock Multi-Digit Memory Test and a total of 97.5% of the patients scored at or above the 90% correct level. Grote, Kooker, Garron, Nyenhuis, Smith, and Mattingly (2000) found that consecutive patients with intractable epilepsy, all of whom suffered uncontrolled seizures to the extent that all were candidates for temporal lobectomy, had no problem demonstrating adequate effort on the Victoria Symptom Validity Test (VSVT), with 93.3% scoring above or approximately at the 90% correct level. Tombaugh (1997) demonstrated that the Test of Memory Malingering (TOMM) was easily accomplished by samples of non-litigating patients with dementia (i.e., etiologies including Alzheimer's, cerebrovascular, "frontal," and "other"), aphasia (i.e., fluent, nonfluent, global, mixed, and "other"), and cognitive impairment (i.e., etiologies including Parkinson's disease, multiple sclerosis, stroke, substance abuse, Huntington's disease, carbon monoxide poisoning, colloid cyst resection, learning disability, and others), and traumatic brain injury. Trial 2 performances averaged 97% correct responding or greater in all groups, except the dementia group, which demonstrated an average score of 92% correct.

Taking assessment of effort a step farther, Flaro, Green, and Allen (2000) demonstrated that a sample of *children* with learning disability, conduct disorder, fetal alcohol syndrome, or other disorders had little difficulty completing the CARB at normal *adult* effort levels. In fact, 92% surpassed the typical adult effort threshold. Constantinou and McCaffrey (2003) also reported that elementary and middle school children showed normal effort on an adult effort test, the TOMM. These authors found that among children whose average age was 8.4 years old, only two of 61 (approximately 3%) were below the normal adult effort threshold, with the overall sample showing a mean accuracy score of 99% correct responding on Trial 2. Even these two young children, ages 6 and 9, were normal on the subsequent retention trial of the TOMM!

Perhaps even more impressive is the series of cases of patients with *profound* memory impairment who demonstrated near perfect performances on the VSVT (Slick, Tan, Strauss, Mateer, Harnadek, & Sherman, 2003). These six patients had various serious medical disorders, including anterior communicating artery aneurysm, Korsakoff's disease, pulmonary edema with secondary anoxic brain injury, and epilepsy from different etiologies. Three of these six patients with resulting profound memory impairments had *perfect* performances on the VSVT, one demonstrated 95.8% accuracy, and the remaining two had 91.7% accuracy. Clearly, effort can be distinguished from memory; memory impairment does not lead to abnormal performance on formal testing of effort.

Examples, such as those described above, from the large literature on use of effort tests with medical patients demonstrate clearly that when outside of a forensic context, such patients are quite able to perform well above thresholds of insufficient effort. Yet, among medical patients, for whom there is no obvious external reward, insufficient effort can occur, even if infrequently. For example, Binder, Kindermann, Heaton, and Salinsky (1998) reported that among 30 non-epileptic seizure (NES) patients, one (representing 3.3%) was significantly below chance on the Portland Digit Recognition Test, and two additional patients were above a chance level but nevertheless below thresholds that identify motivational impairment. Patients diagnosed with NES are often described as more psychopathological than those demonstrating well-documented epileptic seizures, which allows authors such as Binder and colleagues to speculate that NES patients as a group may not have the psychological resources to maintain their motivation. After all, the diagnosis of NES can be made in patients with no demonstrable neurological disorder. What would it mean if, within the context of a well-documented and potentially devastating neurological condition that has no forensic implications, a neuropsychological evaluation revealed undeniable evidence of insufficient effort?

MACHADO-JOSEPH DISEASE

Machado-Joseph disease (MJD) (also called spinocerebellar ataxia type 3 [SCA3]) (Gordon, Joffe, Vainstein, & Gadoth, 2003) is an autosomal dominant, inherited movement disorder of primarily adult onset (Lima, Mayer, Coutinho, & Abade, 1998; Twist et al., 1994). Ataxia refers to incoordination of voluntary movement. The term autosomal dominant means that if one of your parents has MJD, you have a 50% chance of also developing the disease. MJD involves abnormal repetition of the letters "CAG" within the MJD1 gene in chromosome 14q32.1 (Kawaguchi et al., 1994) leading to ataxin-3, a protein that causes cell death (Fujigasaki et al., 2000; Koeppen, 1998; Takiyama et al., 1993; Twist, et al., 1995).

MJD primarily affects the motor system (McKusick, 1990), and the disease causes cerebellar ataxia, progressive weakening and wasting of the muscles (particularly the arms and legs), dysphagia (swallowing difficulties), speech difficulties, diplopia (double vision), dystonia (involuntary muscle contractions of the body, often in the legs, arms, neck, and face), progressive external ophthalmoplegia (a rare progressive eye disease that leads to loss of extraocular muscle function), hearing loss, urinary dysfunction, and/or twitching of the tongue or face (Barbeau et al., 1984; Coutinho & Sequeiros, 1981; Higgins et al., 1996).

MJD was first reported in the 1970s (Nakano, Dawson, & Spence, 1972). The name MJD comes from the two Portuguese-American families who immigrated to the United States in the late 1890s (Lima, Mayer, Coutinho, & Abade, 1998). The disease originated in families of the Azore Islands off the coast of Portugal (Gaspar et al., 1996; Lima, Mayer, Coutinho, & Abade, 1998). Currently, it is unclear how many persons are affected by MJD. Among the general population, it is considered a very rare disease. Prevalence is the highest in the world on the island of Flores, where 1 in 103 persons is affected with the disease, and 1 in 21 individuals is at risk for MJD (Lima, Mayer et al., 1998). Within the U.S., the condition is quite rare, with the exception of individuals with Portuguese-Azorean ancestry who reside primarily within one region of the country. The U.S. Department of Health and Human Services (2001) estimated the prevalence of MJD within this ethnic group in the New England region to be approximately 1 in 4000 people.

MJD can be divided into three different types, although some researchers argue that four subtypes may exist, based on clinical presentation and age of onset (Tuite, Rogaeva, St. George-Hyslop, & Lang, 1995). The U.S. Department of Health and Human Services (2001) reported that early onset of MJD has been associated with a more severe prognosis. Specifically, Type I has the most rapid course and begins between the adolescent years to 30 years of age (Sequeiros & Coutinho, 1993; U.S. Department of Health and Human Services, 2001). Type I MJD is characterized by extrapyramidal and pyramidal features, such as dystonia, athetosis (constant involuntary snake-like twisting movement of the arms, hands, feet, toes), and spasticity (involuntary increase in muscle tone) (Ikeda et al., 2001; Shinotoh et al., 1997). Type II MJD is most often seen during the individual's second to fifth decade, and clinical symptoms are most often cerebellar in nature (U.S. Department of Health and Human Services, 2001); this subtype is the most common form of MJD, and it has an intermediate progression (Rosenberg, 1991; van Schaik et al., 1997). Average age for disease onset has been estimated from 35 (van Schaik et al., 1997) to 40 years (Maciel et al., 2001). Type III MJD has the slowest progression and occurs late in life from the fifth to seventh decade; cramps, numbness, and muscle atrophy (wasting of muscle tissue) is usually associated with this phenotype (Barbeau et al., 1984). Finally, Type IV MJD is a very rare subtype that involves sensory loss, ataxia, and muscle atrophy (Tuite et al., 1995). MJD and seven other disorders (e.g., Huntington's disease, Friedreich's ataxia) currently make up the polyglutamine or CAG repeat diseases (Rüb et al., 2002).

Neuropathologically, MJD causes gliosis (i.e., overgrowth of glial cells in the brain and/or spinal cord that may occur after injury or disease) and neuronal loss in the pons (Shinotoh et al., 1997; Yoshizawa, Watanabe, Furusho, & Shoji, 2003) and the cerebellum, specifically in the dentate nuclei (Rosenberg, 1992; Schols et al., 1995). Atrophy of the frontal and temporal lobes (Imon et al., 1998), the anterior horn cells, and spinocerebellar tracts, as well as demyelination in the spinal cord, are also common characteristics (Kanai et al., 2003; Schols et al., 1995; Sequeiros & Coutinho, 1993; Sudarsky, Corwin, & Dawson, 1992). Neuronal loss may also occur in the subthalamic nuclei, substantia niagra, and the peripheral nerves (Rosenberg, 1992; Sudarsky, & Coutinho, 1995). Yoshizawa, Nakamagoe, Ueno, Furusho, and Shoji (2004) recently reported that one of the most vulnerable systems of the brain to MJD is the vestibular system.

There is currently no cure for MJD, and treatment, such as medications and assistive technology, can only ease some of the symptoms (U.S. Department of Health and Human Services, 2001). The impact of a neurodegenerative disorder like MJD can be seen in multiple domains of life, such as work, health, family functioning, and functional independence. A diagnosis of MJD may result in loss of healthcare insurance and sometimes even job discrimination and/or termination and can give rise to legal challenges. Consequently, many persons who are diagnosed with MJD suffer social, economic, and/or psychological hardship.

In addition to physical problems, individuals who suffer from MJD may develop emotional and/ or cognitive dysfunction (Higgins et al., 1996; Zawacki, Grace, Friedman, & Sudarsky, 2002). Zawacki et al. (2002) noted that executive functioning (e.g., goal-directed behaviors, such as planning, reasoning, hypothesis testing) impairments seem to be especially prominent. Visual attention deficits with reduced cognitive processing abilities of complex visual information and ability to shift attention are also common (Maruff et al., 1996). Persons with MJD may further experience neuropsychological impairments in areas of visual memory (Berent et al., 1990; Radvany et al., 1993). Some investigators have reported delirium in the middle to end stage of the disease (Fukutani et al., 1993; Ishikawa et al., 2002). Still, relatively little research has been conducted on the effects of MJD on neuropsychological functioning.

Some authors have argued that MJD does not lead to intellectual deterioration (e.g., Goldberg-Stern, D'jaldetti, Melamed, & Gadoth, 1994). However, this has been a controversial area, as a number of investigators who utilized more extensive neuropsychological testing have noted that spinocerebellar ataxias or olivopontocerebellar atrophies (SCA/OPCA), a group of very similar autosomal disorders, may lead to severe cognitive impairments and dementia (Berent et al., 1990; Critchley, & Greenfield, 1948; Cummings, & Benson, 1983; Geschwind, Perlman, Figueroa, Treiman, & Pulst, 1997; Shelhaas, van de Warrenburg, Hageman, Ippel, van Hout, & Kremer, 2003).

THE CASE OF MS. R.R.

The present case study was conducted several years ago at an urban public hospital and reports findings from a comprehensive neuropsychological evaluation performed on a woman, Ms. R.R., with MJD. As noted above, this is a very rare hereditary disorder that causes ataxia and *may* also lead to cognitive decline, specifically executive dysfunction and dementia (Maruff et al., 1996). The patient's disorder was DNA verified. A comprehensive neuropsychological battery of tests was administered to Ms. R.R. Results of the evaluation revealed that the patient was impaired on all but one measure administered. The neuropsychological test results, in conjunction with the medical history, could be viewed as consistent with a neurocognitive disorder. However, Ms. R.R.'s test performances on many measures indicated insufficient effort. Still, this patient had no obvious external reward, other than receiving treatment, which then by definition excludes a diagnosis of malingering.

Behavior and observations during interview and testing

Ms. R.R. arrived at the testing session accompanied by her husband, who was interviewed separately to corroborate information. Ms. R.R. was friendly and cooperative throughout testing. Rapport was easily established. Ms. R.R. was a very attractive, petite woman who appeared much younger than her chronological age. She was casually dressed, appropriately groomed, and wore reading eyeglasses. She seemed to be an accurate historian but reported that she started to have increased memory problems approximately five years ago. Complaints included reduced ability to think clearly, short- and long-term memory complaints, bilateral leg weakness and pain, reduced hearing in her right ear, severe tension-type headaches above her eyes, increased balance and gait problems, frequent urination, diplopia, and dysarthria (uncoordinated, slow speech).

During the testing session, Ms. R.R. became increasingly more tired and requested two rest breaks. Gross motor behavior/gait seemed impaired. According to Ms. R.R., she started to experience increased difficulties with walking and an unsteady gait approximately eight years prior to the testing. She reported that she often, at this point in her life, needed a walker for ambulation. Ms. R.R. was alert and oriented to person, place, and time, and she demonstrated very good eye contact with the examiner. Her speech was intelligible, yet slowed. Some word-finding difficulties were noted at times. There was no evidence of delusional symptoms, auditory/visual hallucinations, or other psychotic process. Ms. R.R.'s affect was stable and appropriate to speech content. Though mood appeared non-distressed during the interview and was reported as "fine," at times, when discussing her medical condition, Ms. R.R. became tearful. Balance problems had caused a specific worry about possibly falling. However, in terms of self-described emotional status, she denied feeling anxious, nervous, or depressed. Ms. R.R. denied suicidal ideation, having a plan, intent, or history of suicide attempts.

Ms. R.R.'s background information from interview

At the time of her evaluation, Ms. R.R. was a 58-year-old, right-handed, married Caucasian woman with 13 years of education. She had been born and raised in the southwestern United States. No concerns were reported regarding Ms. R.R.'s developmental history. Ms. R.R. was referred for a neuropsychological evaluation by her neurologist to assess current neurocognitive functioning and to assist in differential diagnosis and treatment planning.

Ms. R.R. had been diagnosed with MJD and osteoporosis by her physician and neurologist.

Detailed genetic testing had been used to confirm the MJD diagnosis. No brain imaging or electro-physiological data were available at the time of the evaluation. Ms. R.R.'s self-reported mental health history was unremarkable. Family psychiatric history was also unremarkable. Family medical history was significant for MJD and Type II diabetes mellitus (DM), MJD on the father's side and DM on her mother's side of the family. Ms. R.R.'s father reportedly was diagnosed late in life with MJD, and one of her two siblings was also affected by the disease.

Ms. R.R. graduated from high school and indicated that her grades were average, "typically Bs and Cs." She was in regular classes, and after graduating from high school she completed one year of college. She had been married for over 30 years and had two daughters (18 and 15 years old). One daughter lived at home with Ms. R.R. and her husband at the time of the evaluation. Neither one of Ms. R.R.'s two daughters wanted to get genetic testing to rule out MJD. Ms. R.R. was not working at the time she was evaluated and was receiving disability income for her medical condition. For most of her life she worked full-time as a secretary. According to Ms. R.R., she was unable to perform any type of competitive work for approximately two years prior to the current evaluation due to increased thinking, memory, and gait problems. She also reported that increased fatigue had contributed to her disabling condition. Ms. R.R. did not drive a car or handle her own finances at the time of the evaluation, and her husband had assumed primary caregiver responsibilities, such as daily decision making and housekeeping duties. She reported a significant decline in her functional status since the onset of MJD and had experienced reduced appetite and sex drive for the past two years. She also reported that she constantly feels "drained and tired" even though she sleeps 11 or more hours each night. Medication regimen included Extra Strength Excedrin, Fosamax, and daily multivitamins. Ms. R.R. denied any prior or current tobacco, alcohol, or illicit drug use.

Neuropsychological evaluation

The evaluation began with review of available records (i.e., background and illness referral forms) and a clinical interview.

The following neuropsychological tests were administered to Ms. R.R.: Wechsler Adult Intelligence Scale–Third Edition (WAIS–III), selected subtests; Wechsler Memory Scale–Third Edition (WMS–III), selected subtests; Test of Memory Malingering (TOMM); Phonemic Fluency Test (FAS); Verbal and Nonverbal Cancellation Test; Symbol Digit Modalities Test (SDMT, written and oral); Reitan-Indiana Aphasia Screening Test; Boston Naming Test (BNT); Rey Auditory Verbal Learning Test (RAVLT); Finger Tapping Test; Grooved Pegboard Test; Grip Strength Test; Trail Making Test, Parts A and B (TMT); Line Bisection Test; Hooper Visual Organization Test (HVOT); Draw-a-Clock Test; Brief Construction Praxis Screening; Burns Depression Checklist (BDC); and Burns Anxiety Inventory (BAI). Results are presented in Table 44.1.

At the outset of the evaluation, there were no expectations that formal effort measures would be needed. However, after Ms. R.R. had completed the first two measures (i.e., the Trail Making Test, Parts A and B, and selected subtests of the WAIS–III), during which she displayed unrealistically, extremely poor performance, it became apparent that her effort needed to be assessed. For example, Ms. R.R.'s performance on the WAIS–III Information subtest was interesting as she made numerous near misses. Also, she knew the answers to some of the more difficult questions, but missed several easy ones (e.g., she stated that there are 10 months and 54 weeks in a year). Ms. R.R. had not previously undergone any psychological or neuropsychological assessment. As is routine in clinical examinations, prior to test administration, Ms. R.R. was instructed to always try to do her very best on each individual test. Still, she worked very slowly and took a very long time before responding to each question. In response to these types of unexpected behaviors, the TOMM (Tombaugh, 1996) was administered to formally assess effort.

The TOMM is a forced-choice recognition test in which the examinee is asked to recognize a simple line drawing from two choices. Ms. R.R. answered only 15 of the 50 items correctly on the first trial and, equally unexpectedly, her test performance *worsened* on Trial 2, on which she was only able to get 11 items correct. Finally, Ms. R.R.'s performance declined even more on the delayed task, on which she recognized only 7 of the 50 items. These results obviously are significantly worse than expected and because they are also significantly below chance can only be consistent with *deliberate* insufficient effort. As Tombaugh (1996) notes, "scores below 18 are unlikely to occur by chance" (p. 19). In fact, such extremely low scores on the TOMM should lead one to question the validity of other test scores within this evaluation.

TABLE 44.1   Neuropsychological test scores for Ms. R.R.

DOMAIN/TEST	SCORE	RANGE
Effort		
Test of Memory Malingering (TOMM)		
Trial 1	15	Below Chance
Trial 2	11	Below Chance
Retention	7	Below Chance
Intelligence		
Wechsler Adult Intelligence Scale–3rd ed. (WAIS–III)		
Prorated Verbal IQ	64	Mentally Deficient
Prorated Performance IQ	69	Mentally Deficient
Prorated Full IQ	63	Mildly Mentally Retarded
Attention/Concentration		
Verbal & Nonverbal Cancellation Test		
Verbal Target Search	6 errors in 2'42"	Severely Impaired
Nonverbal Target Search	20 errors in 2'49"	Severely Impaired
Symbol Digit Modalities Test (SDMT)		
Written Task	10	Severely Impaired
Oral Task	9	Severely Impaired
Language		
Reitan-Indiana Aphasia Screening Test	(see text)	Severely Impaired
Boston Naming Test (BNT)	24 of 60	Severely Impaired
Phonemic Fluency Test (FAS), Total Raw	6 of 64 >	Severely Impaired
Learning and Memory		
Wechsler Memory Scale–3rd ed. (WMS–III)		
Logical Memory I	2nd percentile	Mod-Sev Impaired
Logical Memory II	2nd percentile	Mod-Sev Impaired
Family Pictures I	2nd percentile	Mod-Sev Impaired
Family Pictures II	1st percentile	Severely Impaired
Rey Auditory Verbal Learning Test (RAVLT)		
Trial I	4 of 15	Mod-Sev Impaired
Trial II	6 of 15	Mod-Sev Impaired
Trial III	6 of 15	Mod-Sev Impaired
Trial IV	6 of 15	Mod-Sev Impaired
Trial V	7 of 15	Mod-Sev Impaired
Rey Auditory Verbal Learning Test (RAVLT)		
Total Trials 1–5	29 of 75	Moderately Impaired
Delayed Recall	3 of 15	Mod-Sev Impaired
Recognition	4 of 15	Mod-Sev Impaired
Motor		
Finger Tapping Test (Mean Taps)		
Dominant Hand	15 average taps	Severely Impaired
Non-Dominant Hand	14 average taps	Severely Impaired
Grooved Pegboard Test (Seconds)		
Dominant Hand	233"	Severely Impaired
Non-Dominant Hand	226"	Severely Impaired

(Continued . . .)

TABLE 44.1   (Continued)

DOMAIN/TEST	SCORE	RANGE
Grip Strength Test (kilograms)		
Dominant Hand	8 kg	Mod-Sev Impaired
Non-Dominant Hand	5 kg	Mod-Sev Impaired
Executive		
Trail Making Test, Seconds		
Part A	93″	Mod-Sev Impaired
Part B	Discontinued at 300″	Severely Impaired
Visuospatial/Visuoconstruction		
Line Bisection Test	Mild displacement of responses	Within Normal Limits
HVOT, Age & Education-Adjusted Score	9	Severely Impaired
Draw-a-Clock	(see text)	Moderately Impaired
Command Drawing	(see text)	Moderately Impaired
Three-Dimensional Cross Copy	(see text)	Severely Impaired
Five-Point Star Copy	(see text)	Moderately Impaired
Emotional Indices		
Burns Depression Checklist (BDC)		
Overall Score	15	Borderline Depr Sxs
Burns Anxiety Inventory (BAI)		
Overall Score	41	Severe Anxiety

Note: COWA = Controlled Oral Word Association Test (FAS); HVOT = Hooper Visual Orientation Test; Mod = moderately; Mod-Sev = moderately to severely; Depr = Depressive; Sxs = Symptoms.

Overall results revealed that she was impaired on all but one measure (i.e., a screening for visual attention/neglect). Partial administration of the Wechsler Adult Intelligence Scale, Third Edition (WAIS–III), a commonly used test for intellectual ability, resulted in a prorated Verbal IQ of 64, a prorated Performance IQ of 69, and a prorated Full IQ score of 63. Test data from her intelligence testing placed Ms. R.R. within the mildly mentally retarded range of overall intellectual ability, with a significant amount of intra-subtest scatter. Neurocognitive functioning was in the severely impaired range for all domains assessed.

Ms. R.R.'s performance on the Verbal and Nonverbal Cancellation Test, a measure of visual attention, revealed 6 errors in 162 seconds for the verbal target search, and 20 errors in 169 seconds for the nonverbal target search. This pattern of attention suggested severely impaired complex attention for the patient's age. Ms. R.R.'s approach to the task was unremarkable, and she performed top to bottom and left-to-right searches.

The Symbol Digit Modalities Test (SDMT), a multi-factor assessment of attention that also involves a written response, revealed scores of 10 and 9 for written and oral conditions, respectively. Both scores were within the severely impaired range.

The Wechsler Memory Scale–Third Edition (WMS–III), an instrument which assesses several domains of general memory and which is highly correlated with the WAIS–III, was partially administered. Results revealed moderate to severe impairment in immediate recall for verbal, paragraph-level presented information (Logical Memory I = 2nd percentile) and moderate to severe impairment for 30-minute delayed recall (Logical Memory II = 2nd percentile). Memory for visual and nonverbal information was in the moderately to severely impaired range for immediate recall (Family Pictures I = 2nd percentile) and within the severely impaired range for a 30-minute delayed recall (Family Pictures II < 1st percentile).

The Rey Auditory Verbal Learning Test (RAVLT), a supraspan list-learning task, was also administered. The task involves 15 common nouns read aloud to the examinee for five consecutive trials, with immediate recall after each trial. A moderately to severely impaired learning curve (Trial I = 4, Trial V = 7) was noted. Ms. R.R. also demonstrated moderately to severely impaired 30-minute delayed recall, as she only recalled three words. Recognition, which is known to be useful in identifying insufficient effort, was only four words.

Fine motor speed, as measured by finger tapping, was in the severely impaired range bilaterally for both the dominant (RH = 15.4 mean taps) and non-dominant hand (LH = 14.2 mean taps). On a test of fine motor dexterity, as measured by speed of insertion of grooved pegs into matching shaped holes, Ms. R.R. scored in the severely impaired range, using both her dominant and non-dominant hand (RH = 233 seconds; LH = 226 seconds). Grip strength was in the moderately to severely impaired range for both the right and left hand (RH = 8 kg; LH = 5 kg). At these low performance levels, daily functioning would be greatly compromised.

A gross screening for aphasic disturbance, the Reitan-Indiana Aphasia Screening Examination, was in the severely impaired range, with numerous errors noted in naming, spelling, visuoconstruction, conceptualization, articulation, and calculation. For example, she was unable to draw very simple line drawings. Performance on the Phonemic Fluency Test (FAS) revealed a total score of only six words. The Boston Naming Test (BNT), a measure of confrontation picture naming, was in the severely impaired range at 24 words. Ms. R.R. often stated that she "did not know" the answer to many of the pictures.

The Trail Making Test, Part A and B, were attempted. Trails A was completed in 93 seconds, indicating moderate to severe impairment. An attempt was made to administer Trails B, but the test was discontinued after five minutes, indicating severely impaired performance, with numerous set-shifting errors.

Ms. R.R.'s performance on a screening for neglect, the Line Bisection Test, was within normal limits; however, some unexpected mild displacement of responses was noted to the right attentional space. A visuospatial measure, the Hooper Visual Organization Test, was administered and revealed an age and education-corrected score of 9, which was in the severely impaired range. Ms. R.R.'s performance on this task was interesting, in that she made numerous errors on many of the very easy items, including the first item. The Draw-a-Clock Test, a screening measure of multiple cognitive functions, such as semantic memory, constructional praxis, inattention, and planning abilities, was in the moderately impaired range for drawing a clock on command. The hand in the upper right quadrant pointed incorrectly, and there were errors in the position and sequence of the numbers, particularly in the left quadrant. Copy of a three-dimensional cross showed a three-armed design without three-dimensional perspective. Ms. R.R.'s five-point star was rotated, extremely distorted, and largely without symmetry.

Ms. R.R. completed two self-report inventories pertaining to depression and anxiety. Her responses to the Burns Depression Checklist (BDC), a paper-and-pencil self-report measure of depression, were consistent with borderline to mild depression (score of 15). The Burns Anxiety Inventory (BAI), a similar self-report anxiety inventory, revealed a score of 41 suggesting severe anxiety. Interestingly, behavioral observation had not suggested either depression or anxiety. When asked about this discrepancy, Ms. R.R. indicated to the examiner that her high score on the BAI and her elevated score on the BDC reflected her physical symptoms, rather than depression or anxiety. Ms. R.R. also insisted that neither anxiety nor depressive symptoms were contributing to her current disability.

The entire assessment took place at a publicly funded hospital, where the intake interview, all of the neuropsychological testing, as well as the feedback to the patient took place on the same day. Due to time constraints, no personality tests, such as the Minnesota Multiphasic Personality Inventory–2 (MMPI–II), were administered during this evaluation.

Ms. R.R.'s test performance on many neuropsychological measures, including assessment for memory symptom amplification (i.e., well below chance TOMM scores), is highly suggestive of selective suboptimal effort, in that she seemed to amplify her real problems, with the end result being that she appeared much more impaired on formal testing than clinical presentation and reported daily functioning. In this circumstance, which is not associated with any type of forensic context, the term "malingering" does not appear to make sense. Interestingly, the label "factitious disorder," which is normally appropriate and applied to individuals who consciously present feigned illness symptoms to assume a sick role, at first blush appears not to be a good fit. After all, patients with factitious disorder most commonly are healthy and feign their entire condition, whereas this patient had a well-recognized disorder with clear medical documentation of physical effects of that injury. Yet, we have to consider that the public hospital at which she was seeking services had no exclusionary criteria; treatment was available to all. Therefore, the feigned cognitive impairment in this particular patient is presumptively related to meeting psychological needs, even though it was obvious to the staff that this patient had a definite, well-documented serious medical condition. Without understanding the situation from the patient's perspective (i.e., what additional psychological needs were being met by feigning cognitive impairment), and even though not at all a common scenario for a truly ill individual, the applicable diagnosis of feigned cognitive impairment in this instance is factitious disorder.

Ms. R.R. was found to have several strengths, including insight into her medical status and good social support from both family and close friends. Specific recommendations were made to the patient, her husband, and the referral source to aid in her treatment planning.

SUMMARY

Insufficient effort demonstrated by sophisticated and well-educated patients (i.e., in regard to their medical condition) may be difficult to detect, especially when there is both central and peripheral nervous system impairment present. At times, however, patients perform so inconsistently and poorly that their test performances are simply implausible, such as in this case.

Findings from the case vignette described in this chapter suggest that a person with genuine illness or injury who may or may not have valid neurocognitive disorders could think that her clinical neuropsychologist will not be able to fully appreciate her perceived deficits. Subsequently, such a person may purposely exaggerate her deficits in the apparent hope that the healthcare provider will validate her physical and/or cognitive impairments. That is, this case example provides support for the fact that insufficient effort can occur, even if much less frequently, as a real-life phenomenon during routine neuropsychological evaluations in a clinical context, and not just in criminal and civil forensic settings. These types of behaviors may arise when a patient does not trust that the "system" will meet his/her legitimate needs. Such individuals may therefore enhance various physical and/or cognitive symptoms even though they are receiving treatment services.

Neuropsychological tests and symptom validity tests (SVTs) not only greatly aid in detecting insufficient effort during criminal and civil litigation but on occasion can also aid in identifying insufficient effort during routine clinical (i.e., non-forensic) neuropsychological evaluations. We realize that because of the current American healthcare economic environment, in which there are numerous time-based pressures on clinicians, the routine use of effort measures with clinical referrals may not be possible. However, clinical neuropsychologists are encouraged, when possible, to consider using effort measures in non-forensic evaluations.

The present case illustrates how important it can be to evaluate the possibility of feigning and exaggeration of cognitive symptoms even when the patient has been diagnosed with a genuine neurocognitive condition. Of course, even extreme insufficient effort, such as in this case, does not equal "malingering," as Ms. R.R. did not appear to have the type of external motivation for her behavior that is required for use of this term. By definition, significantly below chance insufficient effort is purposeful, but because it apparently was to obtain treatment (even though treatment was free to all), we cannot call it malingering. Ms. R.R.'s feigning in the absence of external reward is instead considered Factitious Disorder, though in this instance it appeared to be situation-specific in that, other than accepting assistance from her husband, she did not appear to be assuming a sick role in her daily life. Instead, she grossly exaggerated her neurocognitive symptoms during the neuropsychological evaluation. Ms. R.R. did not meet diagnostic criteria for a somatization disorder, as she indeed has a well-documented physical disease. Ms. R.R. denied being clinically depressed and did not appear persistently depressed during the evaluation, so a diagnosis of a mood disorder would not be appropriate. Even if she had been depressed, we know that most common comorbid psychiatric conditions do not produce blatantly exaggerated physical and/or cognitive symptoms (e.g., see Rees, Tombaugh, & Boulay, 2001, showing negligible effects of major depression on effort among psychiatric inpatients).

Numerous neuropsychologists have written about their experiences with individuals who have put forth insufficient effort. For example, Hiscock and Hiscock (1989) presented an interesting case study of a 45-year-old man receiving worker's compensation, with well-documented head injury and seemingly genuine symptoms who claimed for several years that he was suffering from such severe memory problems that he was unable to perform any type of competitive work. An effort measure was, however, able to detect significantly below chance effort and the fact that the man was consciously exaggerating his symptoms. This scenario is well known to experienced clinicians who see *litigants* or *claimants*, such as in the instance of this worker's compensation case. Much less familiar, however, is the *reverse* situation, perhaps best exemplified in a published case study involving a series of evaluations by physicians. Thimineur, Kaliszewski, and Sood (2000) reported a case study in which a woman's genuine medical condition was previously undiscovered by six physicians in separate evaluations, four of which were carried out at the request of the worker's compensation carrier. The prior evaluations had concluded that the woman was malingering back pain after a fall. Reportedly, the woman was later correctly diagnosed when it was found that she had a brain tumor compressing her brainstem that was believed to account for her symptoms. The article notes that physicians do not have valid criteria to determine malingering of chronic pain. It seems very possible that the validity scales of psychological tests and effort testing would have been useful in ruling out "malingering" if they had demonstrated valid responding, and thereby would have helped point medical personnel toward more serious medical investigations, rather than toward "malingering" as was thought by the physicians who had previously consulted on the case.

Effort testing can be helpful in ruling out some medical conditions as the cause of unexplained symptoms in medical patients. A case reported by Pankratz, Binder, and Wilcox (1987) provides another example of how difficult it can be to identify deception in a patient with a documented medical history of neurological disorder. These authors described the medical case of a male patient who reported memory and concentration problems, numbness all over his body, headaches, and neck and lower back pain. The patient's medical history was significant for abnormal EMG findings and viral encephalitis. His test data revealed impairments in the areas of visuoconstruction skills, concept formation abilities, and cognitive flexibility; all other test results fell within the average range. Pankratz and his colleagues were able to identify consciously compromised effort relevant to the patient's self-reported sensory deficits by demonstrating that the patient identified lateralized touch to the hands at *well below chance levels*.

Neuropsychological evaluations that include effort measures are more likely to offer insight into questionable test results and provide patients, families, and referring physicians with more accurate diagnoses and recommendations. Our case study, as well as others we have briefly reviewed, suggests that, when possible, clinical neuropsychologists should actively look for excessive inconsistencies and unrealistic performances in their *patients'* (not just *litigants'* and *claimants'*) behaviors and test responses and should compare their test data to the patients' real-life behavior in order to make more accurate diagnoses. In this regard, we have instruments and techniques available to us that provide information that is otherwise unavailable to the physicians at whose referral we conduct consultations.

REFERENCES

Allen, L. M., Iverson, G. L., & Green, P. (2002). Computerized assessment of response bias in forensic neuropsychology. *Journal of Forensic Neuropsychology*, *3*(1–2), 205–225.

Barbeau, A., Roy, M., Cunha, L., de Vincente, A. N., Rosenberg, R. N., Nyhan, W. L., MacLeod, P. L., Chazot, G., Langston, L. B., & Dawson, D. M. (1984). The natural history of Machado-Joseph disease: An analysis of 138 personally examined cases. *Canadian Journal of Neurological Sciences*, *11*(4), 510–525.

Berent, S., Giordani, B., Gilman, S., Junck, L., Lehtinen, S., Markel, D. S., Boivin, M., Kluin, K. J., Parks, R., & Koeppe, R. A. (1990). Neuropsychological changes in olivopontocerebellar atrophy. *Archives of Neurology*, *47*, 997–1001.

Bianchini, K. J., Greve, K. W., & Love, J. M. (2003). Definite malingered neurocognitive dysfunction in moderate/severe traumatic brain injury. *The Clinical Neuropsychologist*, *17*(4), 574–580.

Binder, L. M., Kindermann, S. S., Heaton, R. K., & Salinsky, M. C. (1998). Neuropsychologic impairment in patients with non-epileptic seizures. *Archives of Clinical Neuropsychology*, *13*(6), 513–522.

Boone, K. B., & Lu, P. (2003). Noncredible cognitive performance in the context of severe brain injury. *The Clinical Neuropsychologist*, *17*(2), 244–254.

Constantinou, M., & McCaffrey, R. J. (2003). Using the TOMM for evaluating children's effort to perform optimally on neurological measures. *Child Neuropsychology*, *9*(2), 81–90.

Coutinho, P., & Sequeiros, J. (1981). Aspects clinique et pathologique de la maladie de Machado-Joseph. *Journal de Genetique Humaine*, *29*(3), 203–209.

Critchley, M., & Greenfield, J. C. (1948). Olivo-ponto-cerebellar atrophy. *Brain*, *71*, 343–364.

Cummings, J. L., & Benson, D. F. (1983). *Dementia: A clinical approach*. Stoneham, MA: Butterworths.

Flaro, L., Green, P., & Allen, L. (2000). Symptom validity test results with children: CARB and WMT (abstract). *Archives of Clinical Neuropsychology*, *15*, 840.

Fujigasaki, H., Uchihara, T., Koyano, S., Iwabuchi, K., Yagishita, S., Makifuchi, T., Nakamura, A., Ishida, K., Toru, S., Hirai, S., Ishikawa, K., Tanabe, T., & Mizusawa, H. (2000). Ataxin-3 is translocated into the nucleus for the formation of intranuclear inclusions in normal and Machado-Joseph disease brains. *Experimental Neurology*, *165*(2), 248–256.

Fukutani, Y., Katsukawa, K., Matsubara, R., Kobayashi, K., Nakamura, I., & Yamaguchi, N. (1993). Delirium associated with Joseph disease. *Journal of Neurology, Neurosurgery and Psychiatry*, *56*(11), 1207–1212.

Gaspar, C., Lopes-Cendes, I., DeStafano, A.L., Maciel, P., Silveira, I., Coutinho, P., MacLeod, P., Sequeiros, J., Farrer, L. A., & Rouleau, G.A. (1996). Linkage disequilibrium analysis in Machado-Joseph disease patients of different ethnic origins. *Human Genetics*, *98*(5), 620–624.

Gervais, R., Russell, A., Green, P., Allen, L., Ferrari, R., & Pieschl, S. (2001). Effort testing in patients with fibromyalgia and disability incentives. *Journal of Rheumatology*, *28*, 1892–1899.

Geschwind, D. H., Perlman, S., Figueroa, C. P., Treiman, L. J., & Pulst, S. M. (1997). The prevalence and wide clinical spectrum of the spinocerebellar ataxia type 2 trinucleotide repeat in patients with autosomal dominant cerebellar ataxia. *American Journal of Human Genetics*, *60*(4), 842–850.

Goldberg-Stern, H., D'jaldetti, R., Melamed, E., & Gadoth, N. (1994). Machado-Joseph (Azorean) disease in a Yeminite Jewish family in Israel. *Neurology*, *44*(7), 1298–1301.

Gordon, C. R., Joffe, V., Vainstein, G., & Gadoth, N. (2003). Vestibulo-ocular arreflexia in families with spinocerebellar ataxia type 3 (Machado-Joseph disease). *Journal of Neurology, Neurosurgery, and Psychiatry*, *74*(10), 1403–1406.

Grote, C. L., Kooker, E. K., Garron, D. C., Nyenhuis, D. L., Smith, C. A., & Mattingly, M. L. (2000). Performance of compensation seeking and non-compensation seeking samples on the Victoria Symptom Validity Test: Cross-validation and extension of a standardization study. *Journal of Clinical and Experimental Neuropsychology*, *22*, 709–719.

Higgins, J. J., Nee, L. E., Vasconcelos, O., Ide, S. E., Lavedan, C., Goldfarb, L. G., & Polymeropoulos, M. H. (1996). Mutations in American families with spinocerebellar ataxia (SCA) type 3: SCA3 is allelic to Machado-Joseph disease. *Neurology*, *46*(1), 208–213.

Hiscock, M., & Hiscock, C. K. (1989). Refining the forced-choice method for the detection of malingering. *Journal of Clinical and Experimental Neuropsychology*, *11*, 967–974.

Ikeda, K., Kubota, S., Isashiki, Y., Eiraku, N., Osame, M., & Nakagawa, M. (2001). Machado-Joseph disease with retinal degeneration and dementia. *Acta Neurologica Scandinavica*, *104*(6), 402–405.

Imon, Y., Katayama, S., Kawakami, H., Murata, Y., Oka, M., & Nakamura, S. (1998). A necropsied case of Machado-Joseph disease with a hyperintensive signal of transverse pontine fibres on long TR sequences of magnetic resonance images. *Journal of Neurology, Neurosurgery, and Psychiatry*, *64*(1), 140–141.

Ishikawa, A., Yamada, M., Makino, K., Aida, I., Idezuka, J., Ikeuchi, T., Soma, Y., Takahashi, H., & Tsuji, S. (2002). Dementia and delirium in 4 patients with Machado-Joseph disease. *Archives of Neurology*, *59*(11), 1804–1808.

Kanai, K., Kuwabara, S., Arai, K., Sung, J.Y., Ogawara, K., & Hattori, T. (2003). Muscle cramp in Machado-Joseph disease: Altered motor axonal excitability properties and mexiletine treatment. *Brain*, *126*(4), 965–973.

Kawaguchi, Y., Okamoto, T., Taniwaki, M., Aizawa, M., Inoue, M., Katayama, S., Kawakami, H., Nakamura, S., Nishimura, M., & Akiguchi, I. (1994). CAG expansions in a novel gene for Machado-Joseph disease at chromosome 14q32.1. *Nature Genetics*, *8*(3), 221–228.

Koeppen, A. H. (1998). The hereditary ataxias. *Journal of Neuropathology and Experimental Neurology*, *57*(6), 531–543.

Lima, M., Coutinho, P., Abade, A. Vasconcelos, J., & Mayer, F. (1998). Causes of death in Machado-Joseph disease: A case control study in the Azores (Portugal). *Archives of Neurology*, *55*(10), 1341–1344.

Lima, M., Mayer, F. M., Coutinho, P., & Abade, A. (1998). Origins of a mutation: Population genetics of Machado-Joseph disease in the Azores (Portugal). *Human Biology*, *70*(6), 1011–1023.

Maciel, P., Costa, M., Ferro, A., Rousseau, M., Santos, C., Gaspar, C., Barros, J., Rouleau, G., Coutinho, P., & Sequeiros, J. (2001). Improvement in the molecular diagnosis of Machado-Joseph disease. *Archives of Neurology*, *58*(11), 1821–1827.

Maruff, P., Tyler, P., Burt, T., Currie, B., Burns, C., & Currie, J. (1996). Cognitive deficits in Machado-Joseph disease. *Annals of Neurology*, *40*(3), 421–427.

McKusick, V. A. (1990). Mendelian inheritance in man. *Catalogs of autosomal dominant, autosomal recessive and X-linked phenotypes*, 9th ed. Baltimore: The Johns Hopkins University Press.

Nakano, K. K., Dawson, D. M., & Spence, A. (1972). Machado disease: A hereditary ataxia in Portuguese emigrants to Massachusetts. *Neurology*, *22*(1), 49–55.

Pankratz, L., Binder, L. M., & Wilcox, L. M. (1987). Evaluation of an exaggerated somatosensory deficit with symptom validity testing. *Archives of Neurology*, *44*(8), 798.

Radvany, J., Camargo, C. H., Costa, Z. M., Fonseca, N. C., & Nascimento, E. D. (1993). Machado-Joseph disease of Azorean ancestry in Brazil: The Catarina kindred. Neurological, neuroimaging, psychiatric and neuropsychological findings in the largest known family, the "Catarina" kindred. *Arquivos de Neuro-Psiquiatria*, *51*(1), 21–30.

Rees, L., Tombaugh, T., & Boulay, L. (2001). Depression and the Test of Memory Malingering. *Archives of Clinical Neuropsychology*, *16*, 501–506.

Rosenberg, R. N. (1991). Joseph disease: An autosomal dominant motor system degeneration. In de Jong (Ed.), *Handbook of clinical neurology–revised series. Hereditary neuropathies and spinocerebellar atrophies*, *16* (pp. 467–479). New York, NY: Elsevier.

Rosenberg, R. N. (1992). Machado-Joseph disease: An autosomal dominant motor system degeneration. *Movement Disorders*, *7*(3), 193–203.

Rüb, U., de Vos, R. A. I., Schultz, C., Brunt, E. R., Paulson, H., & Braak, H. (2002). Spinocerebellar ataxia type 3 (Machado-Joseph disease): Severe destruction of the lateral reticular nucleus. *Brain*, *125*(9), 2115–2124.

Schelhaas, H. J., van de Warrenburg, B. P., Hageman, G., Ippel, E. E., van Hout, M., & Kremer, B. (2003). Cognitive impairment in SCA-19. *Acta Neurologica Belgica*, *103*(4), 199–205.

Schols, L., Amoiridis, G., Langkafel, M., Buttner, T., Przuntek, H., Riess, O., Vieira-Saecker, A.M.M., & Epplen, J. T. (1995). Machado-Joseph disease mutations as the genetic basis of most spinocerebellar ataxias in Germany. *Journal of Neurology, Neurosurgery, and Psychiatry*, *59*(4), 449–450.

Sequeiros, J., & Coutinho, P. (1993). Epidemiology and clinical aspects of Machado-Joseph disease. In A. Harding & T. Deufel (Eds.). *Inherited ataxias: Advances in neurology*, *61* (pp. 139–153). New York: Raven Press.

Shinotoh, H., Thiessen, B., Snow, B. J., Hashimoto, S., MacLeod, P., Silveira, I., Rouleau, G. A., Schulzer, M., & Calne, D. B. (1997). Fluorodopa and raclopride PET analysis of patients with Machado-Joseph disease. *Neurology*, *49*(4), 1133–1136.

Slick, D. J., Tan, J. E., Strauss, E., Mateer, C. A., Harnadek, M., & Sherman, E. M. S. (2003). Victoria Symptom Validity Test scores of patients with profound memory impairment: Nonlitigant case studies. *The Clinical Neuropsychologist, 17*(3), 390–394.

Sudarsky, L., Corwin, L., & Dawson, D. M. (1992). Machado-Joseph disease in New England: Clinical description and distinction from the olivopontocerebellar atrophies. *Movement Disorders, 7*(3), 204–208.

Sudarsky, L., & Coutinho, P. (1995). Machado-Joseph disease. *Clinical Neuroscience, 3*(1), 17–22.

Takiyama, Y., Nishizawa, M., Tanaka, H., Kawashima, S., Sakamoto, H., Karube, Y., Shimazaki, H., Soutome, M., Endo, K., & Ohta, S. (1993). The gene for Machado-Joseph disease maps to human chromosome 14q. *Nature Genetics, 4*(3), 300–304.

Thimineur, M., Kaliszewski, T., & Sood, P. (2000). Malingering and symptom magnification: A case report illustrating the limitations of clinical judgment. *Connecticut Medicine, 64*(7), 399–401.

Tombaugh, T. N. (1996). *TOMM: Test of Memory Malingering.* Toronto, Canada: Multi-Health Systems, Inc.

Tombaugh, T. N. (1997). The Test of Memory Malingering (TOMM): Normative data from cognitively intact and cognitively impaired individuals. *Psychological Assessment, 9*(3), 260–268.

Tuite, P. J., Rogaeva, E. A., St. George-Hyslop, P. H., & Lang, A. E. (1995). Dopa-responsive parkinsonism phenotype of Machado-Joseph disease: Confirmation of 14q CAG expansion. *Annals of Neurology, 38*(4), 684–687.

Twist, E. C., Casaubon, L. K., Ruttledge, M. H., Rao, V. S., MacLeod, P. M., Randvany, J., Zhao, Z., Rosenberg, R. N., Farrer, L. A., & Rouleau, G. A. (1995). Machado Joseph disease maps to the same region of chromosome 14 as the spinocerebellar ataxia type 3 locus. *Journal of Medical Genetics, 32*(1), 25–31.

Twist, E. C., Farrer, L. A., MacLeod, P. M., Radvany, J., Chamberlain, S., Rosenberg, R. N., & Rouleau, G. A. (1994). Machado-Joseph disease is not an allele of the spinocerebellar ataxia 2 locus. *Human Genetics, 93*(3), 335–338.

U.S. Department of Health and Human Services (2001). *Machado-Joseph Disease.* Bethesda, Maryland: National Institute of Neurological Disorders and Stroke.

Van Schaik, I. N., Jobsis, G. J., Vermeulen, M., Keizers, H., Bolhuis, P. A., & de Visser, M. (1997). Machado-Joseph disease presenting as severe asymmetric proximal neuropathy. *Journal of Neurology, Neurosurgery, and Psychiatry, 63*(4), 534–536.

Woods, S. P., Conover, E., Weinborn, M., Rippeth, J., Brill, R., Heaton, R. Grant, I., & HIV Neurobehavioral Research Center Group (2003). Base rate of Hiscock Digit Memory Test failure in HIV-associated neurocognitive disorders. *The Clinical Neuropsychologist, 17*, 383–389.

Yoshizawa, T., Nakamagoe, K., Ueno, T., Furusho, K., & Shoji, S. (2004). Early vestibular dysfunction in Machado-Joseph disease detected by caloric test. *Journal of the Neurological Sciences, 221*(1–2), 109–111.

Yoshizawa, T., Watanabe, M., Furusho, K., & Shoji, S. (2003). Magnetic resonance imaging demonstrates differential atrophy of pontine base and tegmentum in Machado-Joseph disease. *Journal of the Neurological Sciences, 215*(1–2), 45–50.

Zawacki, T. M., Grace, J., Friedman, J. H., & Sudarsky, L. (2002). Executive and emotional dysfunction in Machado-Joseph disease. *Movement Disorders, 17*(5), 1004–1010.

What we currently know about malingering "to a reasonable degree of neuropsychological certainty" vs. what we would like to know in the future

Jerry J. Sweet and Joel E. Morgan

WHAT WE CURRENTLY KNOW

Within clinical neuropsychology, surveys have demonstrated that approximately four of five practitioners eventually come into contact with forensic cases (Sweet, Nelson, & Moberg, 2006). These forensic assessments can occur within the context of assessing civil or criminal litigants, disability claimants, or students seeking educational accommodations, and represent a non-trivial average of 4.5 hours per week and an average 14.3% of a neuropsychologist's practice. For some, forensic neuropsychology practice has become a major or even full-time professional activity. Though it may be arguable from a somewhat cynical perspective that this demand for forensic consultations involving neuropsychologists simply reflects the well-known litigious environment of the United States, the demand for neuropsychology expertise appears greater than for other psychology specialists (e.g., clinical health psychologists) and greater than for a number of related medical specialties (e.g., physiatry, psychiatry, neurology, neurosurgery).

Why would that be the case? Likely, there are multiple reasons. First, the specialty area of clinical neuropsychology concerns itself with *behavior*, whether psychologically-based or related to brain dysfunction. It is, in fact, the behavioral implications of accidents, injuries, disabilities, and medical conditions that greatly interest triers-of-fact in litigated cases as well as adjudicators and decision makers of disability and educational entitlement cases. The image of a lesion in the brain establishes only whether a structural brain change has occurred and may indicate nothing about change in behavior. Some brain lesions have little or no behavioral consequences, whereas others have measurable and at times devastating consequences. A neurological examination can identify fundamental changes in physical response to a lesion but often has little relationship or predictive value assessing day-to-day functioning. Though the interventions developed by physicians in physiatry, psychiatry, and neurology are integral and important to individuals suffering from brain-based conditions, and psychiatry's interventions can also be integral and important to individuals suffering from psychologically-based conditions, the objective assessment techniques of these specialties are relatively fundamental with regard to the implications of the conditions of the individuals most often the subject of treatment. The scientist-practitioner history of clinical neuropsychology is quite different from that of its closest medical specialty peer groups, and has uniquely involved quantification of brain and psychological disorders. It is this quantification that has fostered the enormous interest of lawyers and adjudicators. But that is far from the whole story.

As has been made clear within the preceding chapters of this text, forensic cases are evaluated in a context involving a potential external gain not associated with the customary goal of seeking treatment for a health condition. A forensic context is therefore a secondary gain context, which the scientific literature has demonstrated carries with it a high risk of invalid responding on psychological and neuropsychological measures, due to response bias, insufficient effort, and even frank malingering (e.g., Ardolf, Denney, & Houston, 2007; Mittenberg, Patton, Canyock, & Condit, 2002). Related to this context, there is a universal need to discriminate malingerers from individuals suffering from genuine disorders. To be clear, "universal" is meant literally here, as even a subset of individuals with well-documented injury has also been shown to engage in frank malingering on occasion (Bianchini, Greve, & Love, 2003; Boone & Lu, 2003). Hence, the degree of interest in developing and improving methods of malingering detection and heuristics that might assist in the differential diagnosis has been acute. In fact, the interest has been so strong among neuropsychology's scientist-practitioners that substantial portions of the scientific presentations at the major annual neuropsychology conferences and the pages of the most popular peer-reviewed neuropsychology journals have been devoted to the subject matter of forensic neuropsychology, with the vast majority of these presentations and articles addressing detection methods related to malingering (Sweet, King, Malina, Bergman, & Simmons, 2002).

Therein lies the second and critical reason why the opinions of clinical neuropsychologists are sought in such great numbers. No medical specialty has even 5% of the size of neuropsychology's scientific literature that has addressed essential questions in forensic practice, and in particular has developed methods of identifying invalid responding, insufficient effort, and malingering. This obvious fact can be illustrated quite easily by a quick perusal of Appendices A through E of this book. From a different perspective, a real-life example is instructive. In 2006, one of this text's co-editors (Sweet) was invited to put together a multidisciplinary panel on the topic of malingering for a multidisciplinary audience of psychiatrists, neuropsychologists, and neurologists. It was very easy to identify neuropsychologists with expertise in forensic practice, who had researched and published on malingering, to invite to join the panel. Indeed, there was an abundance of such experts from which to choose. It was more difficult to identify a psychiatrist, as a computerized literature search identified only two names that suggested national recognition and prominence on the topic of malingering. When they turned out to be unavailable, personal contacts with forensic experts around the country turned up only one well-qualified individual. Though there are undoubtedly additional well-qualified and very capable forensic psychiatrists in the United States and Canada, apparently very few can claim national prominence on the topic of malingering detection. With regard to neurology, the search was even more difficult. Computerized literature searches failed to yield a single neurologist who had been the first author of a peer-reviewed empirical publication on the subject matter of malingering. Even more problematic, apart from those who had published on the topic, personal contacts also failed to identify a neurologist who had developed a reputation as an expert on malingering. Again, there are very experienced and competent clinical neurologists with expertise in providing forensic opinions, but it seems clear that neurology's evolution has not included an emphasis on malingering detection or relevant empirical investigation. To bring closure to the anecdote on the multidisciplinary panel on malingering, the healthcare and non-healthcare experts recruited proved to be an exceptionally good group, and the goals of the presentation were met. Interestingly, the forensic psychiatrist gave a very good presentation, in which he acknowledged relying heavily on the malingering detection methods of a local neuropsychologist with whom he very frequently collaborated when evaluating litigants and claimants. Part of his message to the audience was that psychiatry had not developed its own relevant methodology, and it was clear to the psychiatrist (as it has been clear to forensic neuropsychologists) that interviewing alone is not a sufficient approach.

Those readers who are skeptical of our general point on the empirical literature and detection method expertise of other specialties on the subject of malingering and related topics have only to perform their own literature searches in specialties such as physiatry, psychiatry, and neurology. Doing so will demonstrate quickly and without very much effort at all that neuropsychology's literature pertaining to malingering dwarfs that of related medical specialties, and in fact continues to grow at an astonishing pace. The reality is that *opinions* are sought to settle adversarial questions pertaining to genuine injury from all manner of specialists, but what is really sought are *objective bases* of opinions from relevant experts, of the types provided by quantified measures of behavior, ability, psychological states, response bias, invalidity, and insufficient effort. The history of clinical neuropsychology has brought about unique types of quantified measurements that can inform those who must adjudicate civil and criminal cases and provide due process for disability claimants and those seeking entitlements.

Does this mean that a capable clinical neuropsychologist using all the current methods available can always make a reliable and definite conclusion regarding malingering? No, definitely not. As with all types of assessment in any well-established field, there is no perfect diagnostic tool that will always ensure the correct diagnostic conclusion with every individual who is assessed. All healthcare specialties strive to develop better and more accurate diagnostic tools. Such is the case with forensic methods used by clinical neuropsychologists. As well, this volume illustrates that the complexity of litigants' presentations sometimes taxes the current limits of our science in its theoretical/nosological sense and in terms of psychometrics.

The numerous forensic experts whose chapters comprise this text have shared with readers their very interesting cases. In doing so, numerous elements of current thinking on the subject of the neuropsychology of malingering have been delineated. For example, it has been made clear that the majority of effort tests currently in widespread use by clinical neuropsychologists are not commonly known to be affected by factors such as pain (e.g., Etherton, Bianchini, Ciota, & Greve, 2005; Gervais, Russell, Green, Allen, Ferrari, & Pieschl, 2001; Iverson, Le Page, Koehler, Shojania, & Badii, 2007) and depression (e.g., Ashendorf, Constantinou, & McCaffrey, 2004; Rees, Tombaugh, & Boulay, 2001; Yanez, Fremouw, Tennant, Strunk, & Coker, 2006). Such information is critical to accurate diagnosis with forensic cases because of the large proportion of litigants and claimants who complain of depression and pain. Moreover, though over-represented in civil litigation and in the effort and malingering literature, it should now be clear that it is not just head-injury litigants who are at risk of demonstrating insufficient effort and potential malingering. Those who engage in neuropsychological malingering can do so with or without well-documented disorders of all types; this problem is not confined to those with a history of head injury. The scientifically-based tests and procedures that neuropsychologists have developed for these diagnostic purposes have also led to requests for disability evaluation by insurers for a plethora of neurologic and psychiatric disorders (e.g., PTSD, depression, psychosis, among others).

CONCLUSIONS ON THREE VIGNETTES; MORE OF "WHAT WE KNOW"

We closed Chapter 1 of this volume with three brief personal injury litigation vignettes, and now return to our views of those cases as part of "what we currently know about malingering." The first case was that of a young adult litigant who had experienced a well-documented severe TBI. This individual demonstrated spasticity of both upper limbs that was also well documented in the records as having been caused by the TBI. At the outset of the formal testing, which is a day-and-a-half assessment process, this individual demonstrated very substantial failure on a single effort test, though not below chance. Throughout the remainder of the day-and-a-half comprehensive evaluation, there were no subsequent indications of problems on additional effort tests, embedded validity indicators, or validity scales of a respected personality test. In other words, this individual demonstrated what all experienced forensic experts have seen in their practices—validity of test responses can vary tremendously within an evaluation. This explains, as does the next case, (1) why we do not prematurely stop the evaluation if an effort test is failed and (2) why we continue to examine effort and response bias throughout the entire exam, even if effort was good in the beginning of the evaluation. This individual was not labeled a malingerer. Instead, mention was made of an initial effort problem, which did not recur during the remainder of the 12-hour evaluation, and the report focused on what were viewed as the legitimate residua of the injury. Thus, "what we currently know" is that effort may vary across the length of an exam and the totality of the data set that addresses effort needs to be considered. This case settled before trial.

The second case was that of a middle-aged male litigant with a well-documented severe TBI, whose first of three neuropsychological evaluations demonstrated an early effort test failure at a below-chance level. As with the first case, the remainder of the comprehensive evaluation did not contain *any* indications of response invalidity. In fact, despite the obvious presence of prominent depressive symptoms, this man's test performances indicated less residual cognitive impairment than often associated with the severity of the injury and the nature of the subsequent complications that were well documented in the medical records. Again in this case, we did not conclude malingering, and instead noted that an initial apparently deliberate effort problem occurred in isolation. Interestingly, the remainder of the effort tests, embedded validity indicators, and personality validity scales were "squeaky clean," which again allowed the report to focus on legitimate residua of the injury, with test findings appearing to be highly correlated with information in medical records. This case also settled before trial. A unique angle of this case was that two subsequent neuropsychological evaluations occurred after the litigation related. These latter two evaluations related to the financial settlement award. Over the next few years, the plaintiff became increasingly upset that he had been forced to give legal control of the money awarded over to his wife. The plaintiff's attorney sent him back to the *defense* expert for the subsequent evaluations. Though the context had changed, the comprehensive retesting results were quite consistent across time. This latter fact reflects a separate point regarding what "we know"; in the absence of a progressive disorder, legitimate disorders should produce reasonably consistent neuropsychological test results across time, regardless of the context (litigation, competency for financial management—"guardianship," etc.) of the evaluation. When a secondary gain context has a significant effect, response invalidity is likely present.

The third case was a clinically referred middle-aged woman whose minor "fender bender" three months earlier had not appeared to have caused *any* initial brain injury. The prospect of litigation was presumed to be on the horizon, but was not acknowledged. Failure on multiple effort measures and test validity indicators was gross and included below-chance performances on multiple measures. The overall level of very impaired performances on ability tests was not at all credible and self-report validity scales indicated gross over-reporting. The report concluded that none of the test results could be relied upon, and that the individual had deliberately engaged in insufficient effort and over-reporting of symptoms. The "M" word could not be used in the initial report, as a secondary gain context of litigation had not yet been acknowledged. Whereas at the later deposition the conclusion of malingering was made, with the explanation that the only criteria missing at the time of the evaluation had subsequently been supplied by virtue of the litigation-related deposition. An important point to consider when evaluating any "patient" referred by a clinician is whether the circumstances associated with possible neuropsychological dysfunction are likely to involve a forensic context, as the contingencies of the impending forensic involvement may already be operating. Even if they are not, the detailed questioning regarding response validity that is certain to occur in a later deposition will require that the appropriate data was gathered at the time of the evaluation.

In the event that it matters to readers in analyzing the above information, the evaluations described in cases one and two were initiated by a defense attorney. In these two evaluations the ultimate conclusions clearly were more favorable for the plaintiff, only because there had been numerous means of establishing that despite isolated initial effort failure, the remaining responses were *valid*. A final point then regarding what "we know" is that methods of identifying invalid responding on ability and self-report measures are not simply a means of identifying individuals who are exaggerating or completely feigning their problems. Additionally, they are a means of identifying individuals who have legitimate problems by ruling out alternative explanations for their abnormal test results. As such, they are a necessary and essential part of the differential diagnosis of a litigant or claimant.

WHAT WE WOULD LIKE TO KNOW IN THE FUTURE

A clinical neuropsychologist who is knowledgeable with regard to the relevant literature and assessment methods can reliably identify invalid responding (e.g., response bias on tests of psychological states or insufficient effort on tests of ability) as distinct from responses that may reflect genuine conditions of brain dysfunction or a psychological disorder. However, the distinction between invalid responding and malingering requires indication of conscious intent, which is understandably a more difficult distinction. After all, even the best neuropsychologist cannot, as is said colloquially, *read* another person's mind. There has been and continues to be much discussion among experts in forensic neuropsychology regarding what constitutes an indication of conscious intent.

Numerous authors have opined that the differential diagnosis of malingering requires consideration and integration of multiple methods and multiple types of relevant information (e.g., Nies & Sweet, 1994). In some ways, this is no different to the approach used with other difficult differential diagnoses, such as those involving "excessive symptomatology" (Delis & Wetter, 2007) as in somatoform disorders (see Morgan & Gervais, this volume, chapter 11), or unexplained illness such as chronic fatigue syndrome or multiple chemical sensitivity (McCaffrey & Yantz, 2007). In fact, it has become common to formulate strategies involving difficult differential diagnosis in a probabilistic manner. With regard to neuropsychological malingering, Slick, Sherman, and Iverson (1999; see Appendix F for article reprint), using the general approach of having multiple methods and types of relevant information, developed criteria for *possible, probable*, and *definite* malingering. These criteria, often referred to in a shorthand manner as "the Slick criteria," have had a very positive impact and are now commonly used by researchers investigating malingering and are increasingly used by practitioners. However, as with all diagnostic systems, these criteria are not perfect. For example, numerous authors in our current text and many more in the relevant peer-reviewed literature have opined that below chance performance should signal conscious intent to deceive and be viewed as very strong evidence of malingering. The Slick criteria in part state that definite malingering is "indicated by the presence of clear and compelling evidence of volitional exaggeration or fabrication of cognitive dysfunction and the absence of plausible alternative explanations." Associated criteria include "definite negative response bias, which is defined singularly as below chance performance that would not be fully explained by psychiatric, neurological, or developmental factors." The obvious problem to experienced forensic experts, which is also borne out in the literature (e.g., Sweet, 1999), is that an individual can be proven by other means to be definitely malingering, without having below chance performance on a forced-choice test. Consider the malingerer who on formal neuropsychological testing shows numerous highly improbable performances that are wholly inconsistent with the claimed injury and the known effects of actual brain injury or neuropathology, and in whom there is an abundance of instances of normal functioning well-documented by history and perhaps even shown on videotape to be completely at odds with statements made by the civil litigant and test behaviors shown during the neuropsychological evaluation. If this person met criteria for insufficient effort on forced-choice tests, but effort was not so reduced as to have resulted in below chance performances, would we not still classify the person as a malingerer? It would seem that below chance performance is one agreed-upon operational definition of conscious intent, but not entirely sufficient, in that malingering can be present even when below chance performance is not present. This determination is probably easiest in cases when the putative brain injury or neuropathology is a well-documented phenomenon (e.g., TBI) and most difficult in the so-called "unexplained illnesses" (e.g., chronic fatigue syndrome) or in cases where genuine disability/injury is present, but is exaggerated or over-reported. What we would like to know or discover in future then is—a greater number of means of reliably identifying *definite* neuropsychological malingering.

But certainly that is not all we want to know. It should be obvious that we also want to know when there is a high probability of malingering, even if it cannot be determined definitively. After all, the common threshold in courts for any expert witness determination is *not* narrowly framed, as in the question, "Doctor, is it your opinion within a reasonable degree of neuropsychological certainty that Mr. X. is definitely a malingerer?" Instead, the threshold is conveyed broadly in such questions as, "Doctor, is it your opinion within a reasonable degree of neuropsychological certainty that Mr. X. is more probably than not a malingerer?" In fact, it is not nearly as common for an expert witness, if being objective, to have the type of information on which to base an opinion that would allow a "definite" or completely certain conclusion.

Differential diagnosis can become more challenging in some cases in which probable, rather than definite, malingering exists, especially in the presence of genuine psychopathology or neuropathology. As was made clear in a number of chapters in this volume, individuals with real psychiatric or neurological disorders may exaggerate or embellish their symptoms, sometimes to the level of malingering, or to a level consistent with possible or probable malingering. Some "patients" present with noncredible symptoms in a purely medical/clinical (i.e., non-compensation seeking) setting who are best characterized as a Factitious Disorder. Of course, as illustrated by several chapters in this volume, they may "convert" to being malingerers, if they, for reasons such as disability seeking, enter a secondary gain context. Another interesting twist on such presentations is the examinee who performs normally on effort tests but who nonetheless reports excessive symptoms and behaves in a manner "as if" he/she had a serious cognitive problem. This phenomenon, recently conceptualized as a "Cogniform Disorder" (Delis & Wetter, 2007) and "Neuropsychological Hypochondriasis" (Boone, in press), obviously requires closer scientific scrutiny, greater clarification and elucidation, and greater scientific vetting. There is a clear need for neuropsychologist expert witnesses to know more about this conceptually important topic.

When two or more forensic experts congregate, which happens multiple times at any major professional meeting of clinical neuropsychologists, the conversation often turns to anecdotes of interesting forensic cases. These are often the unusual cases of noncredible presentations of litigants and claimants. Among these, the occasional interesting case involving a differential diagnosis of genuine somatoform disorder versus malingering enters the discussion. What we have learned about this differential is that our psychometric instruments may be particularly helpful, in consideration of a detailed history, in making such diagnostic determinations. In this vein, somatoform disorders are distinguished by history, traditional profiles on personality instruments (MMPI/MMPI–2), and successful performance on emotional validity indices, whereas cognitive malingering, often associated with a context of noncredible history, is characterized by the presence of positive Slick et al. (1999) criteria. However, the differential diagnosis of somatoform disorder and malingering is an area that clinical neuropsychologists would like to know more about in the future.

Having their conceptual origins in the notion of hysteria, somatoform disorders are primarily thought to be out of conscious awareness (i.e., "unconscious") (Lamberty, 2008). Somatoform patients may be said to have a false belief in their illness, while malingerers, at least as traditionally conceptualized, are thought to know the truth regarding their health and yet misrepresent it. One point stressed throughout a number of chapters of this casebook is that sometimes these differing entities can co-exist within the same examinee; these behaviors and disorders need not be mutually exclusive. When claimants and litigants present with *equivocal* evidence of malingering, but with unequivocal and clear evidence of insufficient effort in a compensation-seeking context, there is a greater diagnostic challenge. An important tool in these diagnostic issues is the Fake Bad Scale (FBS) of the MMPI–2 (Lees-Haley, English, & Glenn, 1991). A large body of literature now exists underscoring the validity of the FBS in detecting exaggerated physical and emotional complaints (Greiffenstein, Fox, & Lees-Haley, 2007; Nelson, Sweet, & Demakis, 2006). In fact, Pearson Assessments has recently incorporated this scale into its computerized scoring of the MMPI–2, lending further credibility to its use. Of importance, data exists indicating the relative infrequency of an elevated FBS in non-compensation-seeking patients, particularly those without premorbid psychiatric histories (Greiffenstein et al., 2007), aiding differential diagnostic concerns among somatically presenting examinees. Yet, the fact remains that a minority of non-litigants who do not have a psychiatric history have an elevated FBS. Thus, precisely what to make of this finding requires further investigation. Experienced examiners will know, however, that true conversion disorders may exist, giving rise to odd symptom presentations and endorsements.

Differentiation of more common, straightforward psychiatric disorders (e.g., depression, anxiety, psychosis) versus malingering is not difficult or controversial. For example, consider the research evidence that indicates major depressive disorder can be distinguished reliably and relatively straightforwardly from feigned major depression (Bagby, Marshall, & Bacchiochi, 2005), even when the simulators are mental health experts. Sometimes claimant presentations are so out of line with what is known about a psychiatric condition as to make the differential diagnosis immediately obvious (see Morgan, Millis, & Mesnik, this volume, chapter 19).

Cognitive effort testing does not show insufficient effort among non-litigants with genuine major depressive disorder. Thus, claimants who exaggerate or feign cognitive impairment secondary to depression in compensation-seeking contexts are less diagnostically challenging than they might seem at first glance (Rohling, Green, Allen, & Iverson, 2002).

One recent addition to the arsenal of MMPI–2 scales in differential diagnosis of cognitive complaints is the Response Bias Scale (RBS; Gervais, Ben-Porath, Wygant, & Green, 2007), developed to predict the presence of a cognitive response bias on cognitive symptom validity tests and recently validated by Nelson, Sweet, and Heilbronner (2007). Conceptually intriguing, the RBS's ability to predict cognitive (e.g., TOMM) test performance on a personality measure (MMPI–2) underscores the notion that this scale likely taps a motivational construct to perform poorly. The scientific process of making a behavioral diagnosis in forensic contexts has indeed progressed significantly (see Morgan & Gervais, this volume, chapter 11).

On the list of topics we would like to learn more about or discover in the future is the means of ensuring that a technique or procedure developed to detect malingering of cognitive, somatic, or emotional disorder would be immune to coaching. Similar to the concept of *bulletproof*, we need detection methods that are *lawyerproof* and *litigantproof*. Basically, the courts have not yet fully come to terms with the field of neuropsychology in terms of a mutual understanding of the need to maintain test security while allowing a level playing field with regard to fair due process. To be sure, experienced neuropsychologists around the country have offered attorneys and judges the means of ensuring fair and adequate access to neuropsychological test data and protocols used with litigants and claimants, but nevertheless seemingly ill-considered rulings at times reject these means in favor of forcing public disclosure. Of course, public disclosure brings with it substantial potential for undermining and perhaps even completely invalidating malingering detection methods (see Kaufman, 2005, for a legal discussion and comprehensive review).

With the explosion of new information related to malingering, our increased knowledge of these issues has generated intellectual pressure to revise and extend the Slick et al. (1999) criteria. In a recent textbook on malingering, some experts have suggested that revision or refinement of the Slick criteria would remedy weaknesses that have become apparent over time as our relevant knowledge base has increased (Larrabee, Greiffenstein, Greve, & Bianchini, 2007). In a similar vein, in a separate recent textbook on malingering, Rohling and Boone (2007) have recommended continued efforts toward improvement and refinement of assessment procedures that are aimed toward disentangling the complex differential diagnosis of malingering by neuropsychologists.[1]

CONCLUDING COMMENTS

The contributing authors of this book have provided some fascinating examples of the innumerable presentations of response bias, insufficient effort, and malingering and the broad range of disorders that might be either grossly exaggerated or wholly feigned, human behaviors all. Although our scientific endeavors have made significant progress in the conception of these behaviors, our understanding of disorders, and methods for the detection of insufficient effort, malingering, and related phenomena, many challenges remain. Among these are the continued development of new and better assessment instruments and the need to develop procedures to secure these materials from the public, given the very aggressive adversarial and litigious climate in which we all live and work. That which remains salient to all of our contributors and hopefully to our readers is the fact that although some individuals *do* malinger their presentation, motivated by proximal reward and relief from negative contingencies, most *do not*.

REFERENCES

Ardolf, B. R., Denney, R. L., & Houston, C. M. (2007). Base rates of negative response bias and malingered neurocognitive dysfunction among criminal defendants referred for neuropsychological evaluation. *The Clinical Neuropsychologist, 21*, 899–916.

Ashendorf, L., Constantinou, M., & McCaffrey, R. (2004). The effect of depression and anxiety on the TOMM in community-dwelling older adults. *Archives of Clinical Neuropsychology, 19*, 125–130.

Bagby, R. M., Marshall, M. B., & Bacchiochi, J. R. (2005). The validity and clinical utility of the MMPI–2 malingering depression scale. *Journal of Personality Assessment, 85*, 304–311.

Bianchini, K., Greve, K., & Love, J. (2003). Definite malingered neurocognitive dysfunction in moderate/severe traumatic brain injury. *The Clinical Neuropsychologist, 17*, 574–580.

---

[1] With a similar viewpoint as expressed in these two recent textbooks as its basis, and in an effort to facilitate an evolution of concepts and related diagnostic procedures, a Consensus Conference on "Neuropsychological Assessment of Effort, Response Bias, and Malingering" was organized for the summer of 2008 at the American Academy of Clinical Neuropsychology Conference in Boston, Massachusetts, bringing together many prominent senior forensic practitioners and researchers. It is anticipated that this consensus conference will ultimately result in improvements of the diagnostic criteria for malingering that will aid the practice of forensic experts within the community of clinical neuropsychology at large.

Boone, K. B. (in press). Fixed belief in cognitive dysfunction despite normal neuropsychological scores: Neuropsychological hypochondriasis? *The Clinical Neuropsychologist*.

Boone, K. B., & Lu, P. (2003). Noncredible cognitive performance in the context of severe brain injury. *The Clinical Neuropsychologist*, *17*, 244–254.

Delis, D. C., & Wetter, S. R. (2007). Cogniform Disorder and Cogniform Condition: Proposed diagnoses for excessive cognitive symptoms. *Archives of Clinical Neuropsychology*, *22*, 589–604.

Etherton, J., Bianchini, K., Ciota, M., & Greve, K. (2005). Reliable digit span is unaffected by laboratory-induced pain. *Assessment*, *12*, 101–106.

Gervais, R. O., Ben-Porath, Y. S., Wygant, D. B., & Green, P. (2007). Development and validation of a Response Bias Scale (RBS) for the MMPI–2. *Assessment*, *14*(2), 196–208.

Gervais, R., Russell, A., Green, P., Allen, L., Ferrari, R., & Pieschl, S. (2001). Effort testing in fibromyalgia patients with disability incentives. *Journal of Rheumatology*, *28*, 1892–1899.

Greiffenstein, M. F., Fox, D., & Lees-Haley, P. R. (2007). The MMPI–2 Fake Bad Scale in detection of noncredible brain injury claims. In K. B. Boone (Ed.), *Assessment of feigned cognitive impairment: A neuropsychological perspective* (pp. 210–235). New York: Guilford Press.

Iverson, G. L., Le Page, J., Koehler, B. E., Shojania, K., & Badii, M. (2007). Test of Memory Malingering (TOMM) scores are not affected by chronic pain or depression in patients with fibromyalgia. *The Clinical Neuropsychologist*, *21*, 532–546.

Kaufman, P. (2005). Protecting the objectivity, fairness, and integrity of neuropsychological evaluations in litigation: A privilege second to none? *Journal of Legal Medicine*, *26*, 95–131.

Lamberty, G. J. (2008). *Understanding somatization in the practice of clinical neuropsychology*. New York: Oxford University Press.

Larrabee, G. J., Greiffenstein, M. F., Greve, K. W., & Bianchini, K. J. (2007). Refining diagnostic criteria for malingering. In G. J. Larrabee (Ed.), *Assessment of malingered neuropsychological deficits*. New York: Oxford University Press.

Lees-Haley, P. R., English, L. T., & Glenn, W. J. (1991). A Fake Bad Scale on the MMPI–2 for personal injury claimants. *Psychological Reports*, *68*, 203–210.

McCaffrey, R. J., & Yantz, C. L. (2007). Cognitive complaints in multiple chemical sensitivity and toxic mold syndrome. In K. B. Boone (Ed.). *Assessment of feigned cognitive impairment: A neuropsychological perspective*. New York: Guilford Press.

Mittenberg, W., Patton, C., Canyock, E. M., & Condit, D. C. (2002). Baserates of malingering and symptom exaggeration. *Journal of Clinical and Experimental Neuropsychology*, *24*, 1094–1102.

Nelson, N. W., Sweet, J. J., & Demakis, G. J. (2006). Meta-analysis of the MMPI–2 Fake Bad Scale: Utility in forensic practice. *The Clinical Neuropsychologist*, *20*, 39–58.

Nelson, N. W., Sweet, J. J., & Heilbronner, R. (2007). Examination of the new MMPI–2 Response Bias Scale (Gervais): Relationship with MMPI–2 validity scales. *Journal of Clinical and Experimental Neuropsychology*, *29*, 67–72.

Nies, K., & Sweet, J. (1994). Neuropsychological assessment and malingering: A critical review of past and present strategies. *Archives of Clinical Neuropsychology*, *9*, 501–552.

Rees, L. M., Tombaugh, T. N., & Boulay, L. (2001). Depression and the test of memory malingering. *Archives of Clinical Neuropsychology*, *16*, 501–506.

Rohling, M. L., & Boone, K. B. (2007). Future directions in effort assessment. In K. B. Boone (Ed.), *Assessment of feigned cognitive impairment: A neuropsychological perspective* (pp. 210–235). New York: Guilford Press.

Rohling, M. L., Green, P., Allen III, L. M., & Iverson, G. (2002). Depressive symptoms and neurocognitive test scores in patients passing symptom validity tests. *Archives of Clinical Neuropsychology*, *17*, 205–222.

Slick, D., Sherman, M., & Iverson, G. (1999). Diagnostic criteria for malingered neurocognitive dysfunction: Proposed standards for clinical practice and research. *The Clinical Neuropsychologist*, *13*, 545–561.

Sweet, J. J. (Ed.) (1999). *Forensic neuropsychology: Fundamentals and practice*. Lisse, Netherlands: Swets & Zeitlinger.

Sweet, J., King, J., Malina, A., Bergman, M., & Simmons, A. (2002). Documenting the prominence of forensic neuropsychology at national meetings and in relevant professional journals from 1990–2000. *The Clinical Neuropsychologist*, *16*, 481–494.

Sweet, J., Nelson, N., & Moberg, P. (2006). The TCN/AACN "Salary Survey": Professional practices, beliefs, and incomes of U.S. neuropsychologists. *The Clinical Neuropsychologist*, *20*, 325–364.

Yanez, Y. T., Fremouw, W., Tennant, J., Strunk, J., & Coker, K. (2006). Effects of severe depression on TOMM performance among disability-seeking outpatients. *Archives of Clinical Neuropsychology*, *21*, 161–166.

Forensic bibliography: Effort/malingering and other common forensic topics encountered by clinical neuropsychologists

Jerry J. Sweet

ACKNOWLEDGMENTS

Present and former residents of the Evanston Northwestern Healthcare Neuropsychology Service and research assistants who contributed to the creation of this bibliography are Maria Bergman, Ph.D., Daniel Condit, Ph.D., Eric Ecklund-Johnson, Ph.D., John King, Ph.D., Nathaniel Nelson, Ph.D., Alan Simmons, Ph.D., and Penny Wolfe, Ph.D.

CONTENTS

D5:   Posttraumatic stress disorder
D6:   Toxic encephalopathy and neurotoxic exposure
D7:   Self-report (e.g., reliability, effects of emotional conditions and litigation)
D8:   Ethical issues (including objectivity and bias)
D9:   Evidentiary rulings (e.g., *Daubert* challenges)
D10: Neuroimaging in the courtroom
D11: Third party observers
D12: Professional practice surveys relevant to forensic neuropsychology

Appendix E: General resources
E1:   General forensic books and additional resources
E2:   Online resources

Appendix A

Measures specifically intended to detect
insufficient effort and motivation:
A cross-referenced bibliography

21-Item Test

Frederick, R., Sarfaty, S., Johnston, J. D., & Powel, J. (1994). Validation of a detector of response bias on a forced-choice test of nonverbal ability. *Neuropsychology*, *8*, 118–125.

Inman, T. H., & Berry, D. T. R. (2002). Cross-validation of indicators of malingering: A comparison of nine neuropsychological tests, four tests of malingering, and behavioral observations. *Archives of Clinical Neuropsychology*, 17, 1–23.

Inman, T. H., Vickery, C. D., Berry, D. T. R., Lamb, D. G., Edwards, C. L., & Smith, G. T. (1998). Development and initial validation of a new procedure for evaluating adequacy of effort given during neuropsychological testing: The Letter Memory Test. *Psychological Assessment*, *10*, 128–139.

Iverson, G. L., Franzen, M. D., & McCracken, L. M. (1991). Evaluation of an objective assessment technique for the detection of malingered memory deficits. *Law and Human Behavior*, *15*, 667–676.

Iverson, G. L., Franzen, M. D., & McCracken, L. M. (1994). Application of a forced choice memory proceure designed to detect experimental malingering. *Archives of Clinical Neuropsychology*, *9*, 437–450.

Orey, S. A., Cragar, D. E., & Berry, D. T. R. (2000). The effects of two motivational manipulations on the neuropsychological performance of mildly head-injured college students. *Archives of Clinical Neuropsychology*, *15*, 335–348.

Rose, F. E., Hall, S., Szalda-Petree, A., & Bach, P. J. (1998). A comparison of four tests of malingering and the effects of coaching. *Archives of Clinical Neuropsychology*, 13, 349–363.

Vickery, C. D., Berry, D. T. R., Inman, T. H., Harris, M. J., & Orey, S. A. (2001). Detection of inadequate effort on neuropsychological testing: A meta-analytic review of selected procedures. *Archives of Clinical Neuropsychology*, *16*, 45–73.

Wall, J. R., & Millis, S. R. (1998). Can motor measures tell us if someone is trying? An assessment of sincerity of effort in simulated malingering. *International Journal of Rehabilitation and Health*, *4*, 51–57.

Amsterdam Short Term Memory test (ASTM test)

Bolan, B., Foster, J. K., Schmand, B., & Bolan, S. (2002). A comparison of three tests to detect feigned amnesia: The effects of feedback and the measurement of response latency. *Journal of Clinical and Experimental Neuropsychology*, *24*, 154–167.

Merten, T., Bossink, L., & Schmand, B. (2007). On the limits of effort testing: Symptom validity tests and severity of neurocognitive symptoms in nonlitigant patients. *Journal of Clinical and Experimental Neuropsychology*, *29*, 308–318.

Merten, T., Green, P., Henry, M., Blaskewitz, N., & Brockhaus, R. (2005). Analog validation of German-language symptom validity tests and the influence of coaching. *Archives of Clinical Neuropsychology*, *20*, 719–726.

Schmand, R., Lindeboom, J., Schagen, S., Heijt, R., Koene, T., & Hamburger, H. (1998). Cognitive complaints in patients after whiplash injury: The impact of malingering. *Journal of Neurology, Neurosurgery, and Psychiatry*, *64*, 339–343.

van der Werf, S., Prins, J., Jongen, P., van der Meer, J., & Bleijenberg, G. (2000). Abnormal neuropsychological findings are not necessarily a sign of cerebral impairment: A matched comparison between chronic fatigue syndrome and multiple sclerosis. *Neuropsychiatry, Neuropsychology, and Behavioral Medicine*, *13*, 199–203.

The b Test

Boone, K. B., & Lu, P. (2003). Noncredible cognitive performance in the context of severe brain injury. *The Clinical Neuropsychologist*, *17*, 244–254.

Boone, K. B., Lu, P., Sherman, D., Palmer, B., Back, C., Shamieh, E., Warner-Chacon, K., & Berman, N. G. (2000). Validation of a new technique to detect malingering of cognitive symptoms: The b Test. *Archives of Clinical Neuropsychology*, *15*, 227–241.

Gorny, I., & Merten, T. (2005). Symptom information-warning-coaching: How do they affect successful feigning in neuropsychological assessment? *Journal of Forensic Neuropsychology*, *4*, 71–98.

Nelson, N. W., Boone, K., Dueck. A., Wagener, L., Lu, P., & Grills, C. (2003). Relationships between eight measures of suspect effort. *The Clinical Neuropsychologist*, *17*, 263–272.

Stone, D. C., Boone, K. B., Back-Madruga, C., & Lessr, I. M. (2006). Has the rolling uterus finally gathered moss? Somatization and malingering of cognitive dysfunction in six cases of "toxic mold" exposure. *The Clinical Neuropsychologist*, *20*, 766–785.

Vilar-López, R., Santiago-Ramajo, S., Gómez-Río, M., Verdejo-García, A., Llamas, J. M., & Pérez-García, M. (2007). Detection of malingering in a Spanish population using three specific malingering tests. *Archives of Clinical Neuropsychology*, *22*, 379–388.

Computerized Assessment of Response Bias (CARB)

Allen, L., Conder, R., Green, P., & Cox, D. (1999). *CARB '97: Computerized Assessment of Response Bias. A manual for computerized administration.* Durham, NC: CogniSyst, Inc.

Allen, L. M., & Green, P. (2001). Declining CARB failure rates over six years of testing: What's wrong with this picture? *Archives of Clinical Neuropsychology*, *16*, 846.

Allen, L. M., Iverson, G. L., & Green, P. (2002). Computerized Assessment of Response Bias in forensic neuropsychology. *Journal of Forensic Neuropsychology*, *3*, 205–225.

Dunn, T. M., Shear, P. K., Howe, S., & Ris, M. D. (2003). Detecting neuropsychological malingering: Effects of coaching and information. *Archives of Clinical Neuropsychology*, *18*, 121–134.

Gervais, R. O., Green P., Allen, L. M., & Iverson, G. L. (2001). Effects of coaching on symptom validity testing in chronic pain patients presenting for disability assessments. *Journal of Forensic Neuropsychology*, *2*, 1–19.

Gervais, R., Rohling, M., Green, P., & Ford, W. (2004). A comparison of WMT, CARB, and TOMM failure rates in non-head injury disability claimants. *Archives of Clinical Neuropsychology*, *19*, 475–487.

Green, P., & Iverson, G. (2001). Validation of the Computerized Assessment of Response Bias in litigating patients with head injuries. *The Clinical Neuropsychologist*, *15*, 492–497.

Green, P., Iverson, G. L., & Allen, L. (1999). Detecting malingering in head injury litigation with the Word Memory Test. *Brain Injury*, *13*, 813–819.

Henry, G. K., Heilbronner, R. L., Mittenberg, W., & Enders, C. (2006). The Henry-Heilbronner Index: A 15-item empirically derived MMPI-2 subscale for identifying probable malingering in personal injury litigants and disability claimants. *The Clinical Neuropsychologist*, *20*, 786–797.

Rohling, M. L., Green, P., Allen III, L. M., & Iverson, G. (2002). Depressive symptoms and neurocognitive test scores in patients passing symptom validity tests. *Archives of Clinical Neuropsychology*, *17*, 205–222.

Slick, D. J., Iverson, G. L., & Green, P. (2000). California Verbal Learning Test indicators of suboptimal performance in a sample of head-injury litigants. *Journal of Clinical and Experimental Neuropsychology*, *22*, 569–579.

Forced-choice sensory detection

Binder, L. (1992). Malingering detected by forced choice testing of memory and tactile sensation: A case report. *Archives of Clinical Neuropsychology, 7*, 155–163.

Greve, K. W., Bianchini, K. J., & Ameduri, C. J. (2003). Use of a forced-choice test of tactile discrimination in the evaluation of functional sensory loss: A report of 3 cases. *Archives of Physical Medicine and Rehabilitation, 84*, 1233–1236.

Greve, K. W., Love, J. M., Heinly, M. T., Doane, B. M., Uribe, E., Joffe, C. L., & Bianchini, K. J. (2005). Detection of feigned tactile sensory loss using a forced-choice test of tactile discrimination and other measures of tactile sensation. *Journal of Occupational Environmental Medicine, 47*, 718–727.

Haughton, P., Lewsley, A., Wilson, M., & Williams, R. (1979). A forced-choice procedure to detect feigned or exaggerated hearing loss. *British Journal of Audiology, 14*, 135–138.

Pankratz, L. (1983). A new technique for the assessment and modification of feigned memory deficit. *Perceptual and Motor Skills, 57*, 367–372.

Pankratz, L., Binder, L., & Wilcox, L. (1987). Evaluation of an exaggerated somatosensory deficit with symptom validity testing. *Archives of Neurology, 44*, 798.

Pankratz, L., Fausti, S., & Peed, S (1975). A forced choice technique to evaluate deafness in the hysterical or malingering patient. *Journal of Consulting and Clinical Psychology, 43*, 421–422.

Pritchard, D., & Moses, J. (1992). Tests of neuropsychological malingering. *Forensic Reports, 5*, 287–290.

Letter Memory Test (LMT)

Cragar, D., Berry, D., Fakhoury, T., Cibula, J., & Schmitt, F. (2006). Performance of patients with epilepsy and non-epileptic seizures on four measures of effort. *The Clinical Neuropsychologist, 20*, 552–566.

Graue, L. O., Berry, D. T. R., Clark, J. A., Sollman, M. J., Cardi, M., Hopkins, J., & Werline, D. (2007). Identification of feigned mental retardation using the new generation of malingering detection instruments: Preliminary findings. *The Clinical Neuropsychologist, 21*, 929–942.

Greub, B. L., & Suhr, J. A. (2006). The validity of the letter memory test as a measure of memory malingering: Robustness to coaching. *Archives of Clinical Neuropsychology, 21*, 249–254.

Inman, T. H., & Berry, D. T. R. (2002). Cross-validation of indicators of malingering: A comparison of nine neuropsychological tests, four tests of malingering, and behavioral observations. *Archives of Clinical Neuropsychology, 17*, 1–23.

Inman, T. H., Vickery, C. D., Berry, D. T. R., Lamb, D. G., Edwards, C. L., & Smith, G. T. (1998). Development and initial validation of a new procedure for evaluating adequacy of effort given during neuropsychological testing: The Letter Memory Test. *Psychological Assessment, 10*, 128–139.

Orey, S. A., Cragar, D. E., & Berry, D. T. R. (2000). The effects of two motivational manipulations on the neuropsychological performance of mildly head-injured college students. *Archives of Clinical Neuropsychology, 15*, 335–348.

Schipper, L. J., Berry, D. T. R., Coen, E., & Clark, J. A. (2008). Cross-validation of a manual form of the Letter Memory Test using a known-groups methodology. *The Clinical Neuropsychologist, 22*, 345–349.

Vagnini, V. L., Sollman, M. J., Berry, D. T. R., Granacher, R. P., Clark, J. A., Burton, R., O'Brien, M., Bacon, E., & Saier, J. (2006). Known-groups cross-validation of the Letter Memory Test in a compensation-seeking mixed neurologic sample. *The Clinical Neuropsychologist, 20*, 289–304.

Vickery, C., Berry, D. T. R., Dearth, C., Vagnini, V., Baser, R., Cragar, D., & Orey, S. (2004). Head injury and the ability to feign neuropsychological deficits. *Archives of Clinical Neuropsychology, 19*, 37–48.

Medical Symptom Validity Test (MSVT)

Chafetz, M. D. (2008). Malingering on the Social Security Disability Consultative Exam: Predictors and base rates. *The Clinical Neuropsychologist, 22*, 529–546.

Gill, D., Green, P., Flaro, L., & Pucci, T. (2007). The role of effort testing in independent medical examinations. *Medico-Legal Journal, 75*, 64–71.

Gorny, I., & Merten, T. (2005). Symptom information-warning-coaching: How do they affect successful feigning in neuropsychological assessment? *Journal of Forensic Neuropsychology, 4*, 71–98.

Green, P. (2004). *Green's Medical Symptom Validity Test (MSVT) for Microsoft Windows. User's manual.* Edmonton, Canada: Green's Publishing.

Howe, L. L. S., Andersen, A. M., Kaufman, D. A. S., Sachs, B. C., & Loring, D. W. (2007). Characterization of the Medical Symptom Validity Test in evaluation of clinically referred memory disorders clinic patients. *Archives of Clinical Neuropsychology, 22*, 753–761.

Merten, T., Green, P., Henry, M., Blaskewitz, N., & Brockhaus, R. (2005). Analog validation of German-language symptom validity tests and the influence of coaching. *Archives of Clinical Neuropsychology, 20*, 719–726.

Richman, J., Green, P., Gervais, R., Flaro, L., Merten, T., Brockhaus, R., & Ranks, D. (2006). Objective tests of symptom exaggeration in independent medical examinations. *Journal of Occupational and Environmental Medicine, 48*, 303–311.

Stevens, A., Friedel, E., Mehren, G., & Merten, T. (2008). Malingering and uncooperativeness in psychiatric and psychological assessment: Prevalence and effects in a German sample of claimants. *Psychiatry Research, 157*, 191–200.

Vitacco, M. J., Rogers, R., Gabel, J., & Munizza, J. (2007). An evaluation of malingering screens with competency to stand trial patients: A known-groups study. *Law and Human Behavior, 31*, 249–260.

Miller Forensic Assessment of Symptoms Test (M-FAST)

Alwes, Y. R., Clark, J. A., Berry, D. T. R., & Granacher, R. P. (2008). Screening for feigning in a civil forensic setting. *Journal of Clinical and Experimental Neuropsychology, 30*, 133–140.

Graue, L. O., Berry, D. T. R., Clark, J. A., Sollman, M. J., Cardi, M., Hopkins, J., & Werline, D. (2007). Identification of feigned mental retardation using the new generation of malingering detection instruments: Preliminary findings. *The Clinical Neuropsychologist, 21*, 929–942.

Guy, L. S., & Miller, H. A. (2004). Screening for malingered psychopathology in a correctional setting: Utility of the Miller Forensic Assessment of Symptoms Test (M-FAST). *Criminal Justice and Behavior, 31*, 695–716.

Jackson, R. L., Rogers, R., & Sewell, K. W. (2005). Forensic applications of the Miller Forensic Assessment of Symptoms Test (MFAST): Screening for feigned disorders in competency to stand trial evaluations. *Law and Human Behavior, 29*, 199–210.

Miller, H. A. (2001). *MFAST: Miller Forensic Assessment of Symptoms Test professional manual.* Odessa, FL: Psychological Assessment Resources, Inc.

Vagnini, V. L., Sollman, M., J., Berry, D. T. R., Granacher, R. P., Clark, J. A., Burton, R., O'Brien, M., Bacon, E., & Saier, J. (2006). Known-groups cross-validation of the Letter Memory Test in a compensation-seeking mixed neurologic sample. *The Clinical Neuropsychologist, 20*, 289–304.

Vitacco, M. J., Rogers, R., Gabel, J., & Munizza, J. (2007). An evaluation of malingering screens with competency to stand trial patients: A known-groups study. *Law and Human Behavior, 31*, 249–260.

Multi-Digit Memory Test (MDMT; Hiscock Forced-Choice)

Back, C., Boone, K., Edwards, C., Parks, C., Burgoyne, K., & Silver, B. (1996). The performance of schizophrenics on three cognitive tests of malingering, Rey 15-Item Memory Test, Rey Dot Counting, and Hiscock Forced-Choice Method. *Assessment, 3*, 449–457.

Cato, M. A., Brewster, J., Ryan, T., & Giuliano, A. J. (2002). Coaching and the ability to simulate mild traumatic brain injury symptoms. *The Clinical Neuropsychologist, 16*, 524–535.

Chiu, V. W. Y., & Lee, T. M. C. (2002). Detection of malingering behavior at different levels of task difficulty in Hong Kong Chinese. *Rehabilitation Psychology, 47*, 194–203.

Cragar, D., Berry, D., Fakhoury, T., Cibula, J., & Schmitt, F. (2006). Performance of patients with epilepsy and non-epileptic seizures on four measures of effort. *The Clinical Neuropsychologist, 20*, 552–566.

Doane, B. M., Greve, K. W., & Bianchini, K. J. (2005). Agreement between the abbreviated and standard Portland Digit Recognition Test. *The Clinical Neuropsychologist*, *19*, 99–104.

Ellwanger, J., Rosenfeld, J. P., Sweet, J., & Bhatt, M. (1996). Detecting simulated amnesia for autobiographical and recently learned information using the P300 event-related potential. *International Journal of Psychophysiology*, *23*, 9–23.

Graue, L. O., Berry, D. T. R., Clark, J. A., Sollman, M. J., Cardi, M., Hopkins, J., & Werline, D. (2007). Identification of feigned mental retardation using the new generation of malingering detection instruments: Preliminary findings. *The Clinical Neuropsychologist*, *21*, 929–942.

Guilmette, T. J., Hart, K. J., & Giuliano, A. J. (1993). Malingering detection: The use of a forced-choice method in identifying organic versus simulated memory impairment. *The Clinical Neuropsychologist*, *7*, 59–69.

Guilmette, T., Hart, K., Giuliano, A., & Leininger, B. (1994). Detecting simulated memory impairment: Comparison of the Rey Fifteen-Item Test and the Hiscock forced-choice procedure. *The Clinical Neuropsychologist*, *8*, 283–294.

Guilmette, T., Whelihan, W., Hart, K., Sparadeo, F., & Buongiorno, G. (1996). Order effects in the administration of a forced-choice procedure for detection of malingering in disability claimants' evaluations. *Perceptual and Motor Skills*, *83*, 1007–1016.

Hilsabeck, R. C., & Gouvier, W. D. (2005). Detecting simulated memory impairment: Further validation of the Word Completion Memory Test (WCMT). *Archives of Clinical Neuropsychology*, *20*, 1025–1041.

Hiscock, C. K., Branham, J. D., & Hiscock, M. (1994). Detection of feigned cognitive impairment: The two-alternative forced-choice method compared with selected conventional tests. *Journal of Psychopathology and Behavioral Assessment*, *16*, 95–110.

Hiscock, M., & Hiscock, C. K. (1989). Refining the forced-choice method for the detection of malingering. *Journal of Clinical and Experimental Neuropsychology*, *11*, 967–974.

Inman, T. H., & Berry, D. T. R. (2002). Cross-validation of indicators of malingering: A comparison of nine neuropsychological tests, four tests of malingering, and behavioral observations. *Archives of Clinical Neuropsychology*, *17*, 1–23.

Inman, T. H., Vickery, C. D., Berry, D. T. R., Lamb, D. G., Edwards, C. L., & Smith, G. T. (1998). Development and initial validation of a new procedure for evaluating adequacy of effort given during neuropsychological testing: The Letter Memory Test. *Psychological Assessment*, *10*, 128–139.

Martin, R., Bolter, J., Todd, M., Gouvier, W. D., & Niccolls, R. (1993). Effects of sophistication and motivation on the detection of malingered memory performance using a computerized forced-choice task. *Journal of Clinical and Experimental Neuropsychology*, *15*, 867–880.

Martin, R., Hayes, J., & Gouvier, W. D. (1996). Differential vulnerability between postconcussion self-report and objective malingering tests in identifying simulated mild head injury. *Journal of Clinical and Experimental Neuropsychology*, *18*, 265–275.

Orey, S. A., Cragar, D. E., & Berry, D. T. R. (2000). The effects of two motivational manipulations on the neuropsychological performance of mildly head-injured college students. *Archives of Clinical Neuropsychology*, *15*, 335–348.

Prigatano, G., & Amin, K. (1993). Digit Memory Test: Unequivocal cerebral dysfunction and suspected malingering. *Journal of Clinical and Experimental Neuropsychology*, *15*, 537–546.

Pritgatano, G., Smason, I., Lamb, D., & Bortz, J. (1997). Suspected malingering and the digit memory test: A replication and extension. *Archives of Clinical Neuropsychology*, *12*, 609–619.

Rosenfeld, J. P., Ellwanger, J., Nolan, K., Bermann, R., & Sweet, J. J. (1999). P300 scalp amplitude distribution as an index of deception in a simulated cognitive deficit model. *International Journal of Psychophysiology*, *33*, 3–19.

Rosenfeld, J. P., Sweet, J. J., Chuang, J., Ellwanger, J., & Song, L. (1996). Detection of simulated malingering using forced choice recognition enhanced with event-related potential recording. *The Clinical Neuropsychologist*, *10*, 163–179.

Shum, D. H. K., O'Gorman, J. G., & Alpar, A. (2004). Effects of incentive and preparation time on performance and classification accuracy of standard and malingering-specific memory tests. *Archives of Clinical Neuropsychology*, *19*, 817–823.

Vickery, C., Berry, D. T. R., Dearth, C., Vagnini, V., Baser, R., Cragar, D., & Orey, S. (2004). Head injury and the ability to feign neuropsychological deficits. *Archives of Clinical Neuropsychology*, *19*, 37–48.

Vickery, C. D., Berry, D. T. R., Inman, T. H., Harris, M. J., & Orey, S. A. (2001). Detection of inadequate effort on neuropsychological testing: A meta-analytic review of selected procedures. *Archives of Clinical Neuropsychology*, *16*, 45–73.

Woods, S. P., Conover, E., Weinborn, M., Rippeth, J., Brill, R., Heaton, R. Grant, I., & HIV Neurobehavioral Reseach Center Group (2003). Base rate of Hiscock Digit Memory Test failure in HIV-associated neurocognitive disorders. *The Clinical Neuropsychologist*, *17*, 383–389.

Multidimensional Investigation of Neuropsychological Dissimulation (MIND)

Holmquist, L. A., & Wanlass, R. L. (2002). A multidimensional approach towards malingering detection. *Archives of Clinical Neuropsychology*, *17*, 143–156.

Portland Digit Recognition Test (PDRT)

Bianchini, K. J., Curtis, K. L., & Greve, K. W. (2006). Compensation and malingering in traumatic brain injury: A dose-response relationship? *The Clinical Neuropsychologist*, *20*, 831–847.

Bianchini, K., Houston, R., Greve, K., Irvin, R., Black, F.W., Swift, D., & Tamimie, R. (2003). Malingered neurocognitive dysfunction in neurotoxic exposure: An application of the Slick criteria. *Journal of Occupational and Environmental Medicine*, *45*, 1087–1099.

Bianchini, K., Love, J. M., Greve, K. W., & Adams, D. (2005). Detection and diagnosis of malingering in electrical injury. *Archives of Clinical Neuropsychology*, *20*, 365–373.

Bianchini, K. J., Mathias, C. W., Greve, K. W., Houston, R. J., & Crouch, J. A. (2001). Classification accuracy of the Portland Digit Recognition Test in traumatic brain injury. *The Clinical Neuropsychologist*, *15*, 461–470.

Binder, L. (1992). Malingering detected by forced choice testing of memory and tactile sensation: A case report. *Archives of Clinical Neuropsychology*, *7*, 155–163.

Binder, L. (1993a). Assessment of malingering after mild head trauma with the Portland Digit Recognition Test. *Journal of Clinical and Experimental Neuropsychology*, *15*, 170–182.

Binder, L. (1993b). An abbreviated form of the Portland Digit Recognition Test. *The Clinical Neuropsychologist*, *7*, 104–107.

Binder, L. M. (2002). The Portland Digit Recognition Test: A review of validation data and clinical use. *Journal of Forensic Neuropsychology*, *2*, 27–41.

Binder, L., & Kelly, M. (1996). Portland Digit Recognition Test performance by brain dysfunction patients without financial incentives. *Assessment*, *3*, 403–409.

Binder, L., Kelly, M., Villanueva, M., & Winslow, M. (2003). Motivation and neuropsychological test performance following mild head injury. *Journal of Clinical and Experimental Neuropsychology*, *25*, 420–430.

Binder, L., Villanueva, M., Howieson, D., & Moore, R. (1993). The Rey AVLT recognition memory task measures motivational impairment after mild head trauma. *Archives of Clinical Neuropsychology*, *8*, 137–147.

Binder, L., & Willis, S. (1992). Assessment of motivation after financially compensable minor head trauma. *Psychological Assessment: A Journal of Consulting and Clinical Psychology*, *3*, 175–181.

Cragar, D., Berry, D., Fakhoury, T., Cibula, J., & Schmitt, F. (2006). Performance of patients with epilepsy and non-epileptic seizures on four measures of effort. *The Clinical Neuropsychologist*, *20*, 552–566.

Frederick, R., Sarfaty, S., Johnston, J. D., & Powel, J. (1994). Validation of a detector of response bias on a forced-choice test of nonverbal ability. *Neuropsychology*, *8*, 118–125.

Greiffenstein, M., Baker, W. J., & Gola, T. (1994). Validation of malingered amnesia measures with a large clinical sample. *Psychological Assessment*, *6*, 218–224.

Greve, K. W., & Bianchini, K. J. (2006). Classification accuracy of the Portland Digit Recognition Test in traumatic brain injury: Results of a known-groups analysis. *The Clinical Neuropsychologist*, *20*, 816–830.

Greve, K. W., Ord, J., Curtis, K. L., Bianchini, K. J., & Brennan, A. (in press). Detecting malingering in traumatic brain injury and chronic pain: A comparison of three forced-choice symptom validity tests. *The Clinical Neuropsychologist*.

Gunstad, J., & Suhr, J. A. (2001). Efficacy of the full and abbreviated forms of the Portland Digit Recognition Test: Vulnerability to coaching. *The Clinical Neuropsychologist, 15*, 397–404.

Gunstad, J., & Suhr, J. A. (2004). Use of the abbrievated Portland Digit Recognition Test in simulated malingering and neurological groups. *Journal of Forensic Neuropsychology, 4*, 33–48.

Orey, S. A., Cragar, D. E., & Berry, D. T. R. (2000). The effects of two motivational manipulations on the neuropsychological performance of mildly head-injured college students. *Archives of Clinical Neuropsychology, 15*, 335–348.

Rose, F., Hall, S., & Szalda-Petree, A. (1995). Portland Digit Recognition Test-Computerized: Measuring response latency improves the detection of malingering. *The Clinical Neuropsychologist, 9*, 124–134.

Rose, F., Hall, S., Szalda-Petree, A., & Bach, P. (1998). A comparison of four tests of malingering and the effects of coaching. *Archives of Clinical Neuropsychology, 13*, 349–363.

Rosen, G. M., & Powel, J. E. (2003). Use of a symptom validity test in the forensic assessment of Posttraumatic Stress Disorder. *Anxiety Disorders, 17*, 361–367.

Temple, R., McBride, A., Horner, M., & Taylor, R. (2003). Personality characteristics of patients showing suboptimal cognitive effort. *The Clinical Neuropsychologist, 17*, 402–409.

Vickery, C. D., Berry, D. T. R., Inman, T. H., Harris, M. J., & Orey, S. A. (2001). Detection of inadequate effort on neuropsychological testing: A meta-analytic review of selected procedures. *Archives of Clinical Neuropsychology, 16*, 45–73.

Rey Dot Counting

Arnett, P., & Franzen, M. (1997). Performance of substance abusers with memory deficits on measures of malingering. *Archives of Clinical Neuropsychology, 12*, 513–518.

Back, C., Boone, K., Edwards, C., Parks, C., Burgoyne, K., & Silver, B. (1996). The performance of schizophrenics on three cognitive tests of malingering, Rey 15-Item Memory Test, Rey Dot Counting, and Hiscock Forced-Choice Method. *Assessment, 3*, 449–457.

Beetar, J., & Williams, J. (1995). Malingering response styles on the Memory Assessment Scales and symptom validity tests. *Archives of Clinical Neuropsychology, 10*, 57–72.

Binks, P., Gouvier, W. D., & Waters, W. (1997). Malingering detection with the Dot Counting Test. *Archives of Clinical Neuropsychology, 12*, 41–46.

Boone, K. B., & Lu, P. (2003). Noncredible cognitive performance in the context of severe brain injury. *The Clinical Neuropsychologist, 17*, 244–254.

Boone, K. B., Lu, P., Back, C., King, C., Lee, A., Philpott, L., Shamieh, E., & Warner-Chacon, K. (2002). Sensitivity and specificity of the Rey Dot Counting Test in patients with suspect effort and various clinical samples. *Archives of Clinical Neuropsychology, 17*, 625–642.

Boone, K. B., Savodnik, I., Ghaffarian, S., Lee, A., & Freeman, D. (1995). Rey 15-Item memorization and dot counting scores in a "stress" claim worker's compensation population: Relationship to personality (MCMI) scores. *Journal of Clinical Psychology, 51*, 457–463.

Cato, M. A., Brewster, J., Ryan, T., & Giuliano, A. J. (2002). Coaching and the ability to simulate mild traumatic brain injury symptoms. *The Clinical Neuropsychologist, 16*, 524–535.

Dean, A. C., Victor, T. L., Boone, K. B., & Arnold, G. (2008). The relationship of IQ to effort test performance. *The Clinical Neuropsychologist, 22*, 705–722.

Denney, R. L. (1996). Symptom validity testing of remote memory in a criminal forensic setting. *Archives of Clinical Neuropsychology, 11*, 589–603.

Erdal, K. (2003). The effects of motivation, coaching, and knowledge of neuropsychology on the simulated malingering of head injury. *Archives of Clinical Neuropsychology, 19*, 73–88.

Franzen, M. D., & Martin, N. (1996). Do people with knowledge fake better? *Applied Neuropsychology, 3*, 82–85.

Frederick, R. I. (2000). A personal floor effect strategy to evaluate the validity of performance on memory tasks. *Journal of Clinical and Experimental Neuropsychology, 22*, 720–730.

Frederick, R. I. (2002). A review of Rey's strategies for detecting malingered neuropsychological impairment. *Journal of Forensic Neuropsychology, 2*, 1–25.

Frederick, R., Sarfaty, S., Johnston, J. D., & Powel, J. (1994). Validation of a detector of response bias on a forced-choice test of nonverbal ability. *Neuropsychology, 8*, 118–125.

Greiffenstein, M., Baker, W. J., & Gola, T. (1994). Validation of malingered amnesia measures with a large clinical sample. *Psychological Assessment*, *6*, 218–224.

Hayes, J. S., Hale, D. B., & Gouvier, W. D. (1997). Do tests predict malingering in defendants with mental retardation? *Journal of Psychology*, *131*, 575–576.

Hayes, J. S., Hale, D. B., & Gouvier, W. D. (1998). Malingering detection in mentally retarded forensic populations. *Applied Neuropsychology*, *5*, 33–36.

Lee, A., Boone, K. B., Lesser, I., Wohl, M., Wilkins, S., & Parks, C. (2000). Performance of older depressed patients on two cognitive malingering tests: False positive rates for the Rey 15-item memorization and the Dot Counting Test. *The Clinical Neuropsychologist*, *14*, 303–308.

Marshall, P., & Happe, M. (2007). The performance of individuals with mental retardation on cognitive tests assessing effort and motivation. *The Clinical Neuropsychologist*, *21*, 826–840.

Martin, R., Hayes, J., & Gouvier, W. D. (1996). Differential vulnerability between postconcussion self-report and objective malingering tests in identifying simulated mild head injury. *Journal of Clinical and Experimental Neuropsychology*, *18*, 265–275.

Nelson, N. W., Boone, K., Dueck. A., Wagener, L., Lu, P., & Grills, C. (2003). Relationships between eight measures of suspect effort. *The Clinical Neuropsychologist*, *17*, 263–272.

Paul, D., Franzen, M., Cohen, S., & Fremouw, W. (1992). An investigation into the reliability and validity of two tests used in the detection of dissimulation. *International Journal of Clinical Neuropsychology*, *14*, 1–9.

Rose, F., Hall, S., Szalda-Petree, A., & Bach, P. (1998). A comparison of four tests of malingering and the effects of coaching. *Archives of Clinical Neuropsychology*, *13*, 349–363.

Stone, D. C., Boone, K. B., Back-Madruga, C., & Lessr, I. M. (2006). Has the rolling uterus finally gathered moss? Somatization and malingering of cognitive dysfunction in six cases of "toxic mold" exposure. *The Clinical Neuropsychologist*, *20*, 766–785.

Strauss, E., Slick, D. J., Levy-Bencheton, J., Hunter, M., MacDonald, S. W. S., & Hultsch, D. F. (2002). Intraindividual variability as an indicator of malingering in head injury. *Archives of Clinical Neuropsychology*, *17*, 423–444.

Sumanti, M, Boone, K. B., & Savodnik, I., & Gorsuch, R. (2006). Noncredible psychiatric and cognitive symptoms in a worker's compensation "stress" claim sample. *The Clinical Neuropsychologist*, *20*, 754–765.

Vickery, C. D., Berry, D. T. R., Inman, T. H., Harris, M. J., & Orey, S. A. (2001). Detection of inadequate effort on neuropsychological testing: A meta-analytic review of selected procedures. *Archives of Clinical Neuropsychology*, *16*, 45–73.

Rey Memory for 15-Item Test (Rey MFIT) and variants

Arnett, P., Hammeke, T., & Schwartz, L. (1995). Quantitative and qualitative performance on Rey's 15-Item Test in neurological patients and dissimulators. *The Clinical Neuropsychologist*, *9*, 17–26.

Back, C., Boone, K., Edwards, C., Parks, C., Burgoyne, K., & Silver, B. (1996). The performance of schizophrenics on three cognitive tests of malingering, Rey 15-Item Memory Test, Rey Dot Counting, and Hiscock Forced-Choice Method. *Assessment*, *3*, 449–457.

Beetar, J., & Williams, J. (1995). Malingering response styles on the Memory Assessment Scales and symptom validity tests. *Archives of Clinical Neuropsychology*, *10*, 57–72.

Bernard, L. (1990). Prospects for faking believable memory deficits on neuropsychological tests and the use of incentives in simulation research. *Journal of Clinical and Experimental Neuropsychology*, *5*, 715–728.

Bernard, L. C., & Fowler, W. (1990). Assessing the validity of memory complaints: Performance of brain-damaged and normal individuals on Rey's task to detect malingering. *Journal of Clinical Psychology*, *46*, 432–436.

Bernard, L., Houston, W., & Natoli, L. (1993). Malingering on neuropsychological memory tests: Potential objective indicators. *Journal of Clinical Psychology*, *49*, 45–53.

Boone, K. B., & Lu, P. (2003). Noncredible cognitive performance in the context of severe brain injury. *The Clinical Neuropsychologist*, *17*, 244–254.

Boone, K. B., Salazar, X., Lu, P., Warner-Chacon, K., & Razani, J. (2002). The Rey-15-item recognition trial: A technique to enhance sensitivity of the Rey-15 item memorization test. *Journal of Clinical and Experimental Neuropsychology*, *24*, 561–573.

Boone, K. B., Savodnik, I., Ghaffarian, S., Lee, A., & Freeman, D. (1995). Rey 15-Item memorization and dot counting scores in a "stress" claim worker's compensation population: Relationship to personality (MCMI) scores. *Journal of Clinical Psychology*, *51*, 457–463.

Cato, M. A., Brewster, J., Ryan, T., & Giuliano, A. J. (2002). Coaching and the ability to simulate mild traumatic brain injury symptoms. *The Clinical Neuropsychologist*, *16*, 524–535.

Dean, A. C., Victor, T. L., Boone, K. B., & Arnold, G. (2008). The relationship of IQ to effort test performance. *The Clinical Neuropsychologist*, *22*, 705–722.

Denney, R. L. (1996). Symptom validity testing of remote memory in a criminal forensic setting. *Archives of Clinical Neuropsychology*, *11*, 589–603.

Erdal, K. (2003). The effects of motivation, coaching, and knowledge of neuropsychology on the simulated malingering of head injury. *Archives of Clinical Neuropsychology*, *19*, 73–88.

Farkas, M. R., Rosenfeld, B., Robbins, R., & van Gorp, W. (2006). Do tests of malingering concur? Concordance among malingering measures. *Behavioral Sciences and the Law*, *24*, 659–671.

Fisher, H. L., & Rose, D. (2005). Comparison of the effectiveness of two versions of the Rey Memory Test in discriminating between actual and simulated memory impairment, with and without the addition of a standard memory test. *Journal of Clinical and Experimental Neuropsychology*, *27*, 840–858.

Frederick, R. I. (2000). A personal floor effect strategy to evaluate the validity of performance on memory tasks. *Journal of Clinical and Experimental Neuropsychology*, *22*, 720–730.

Frederick, R. I. (2002). A review of Rey's strategies for detecting malingered neuropsychological impairment. *Journal of Forensic Neuropsychology*, *2*, 1–25.

Frederick, R., Sarfaty, S., Johnston, J. D., & Powel, J. (1994). Validation of a detector of response bias on a forced-choice test of nonverbal ability. *Neuropsychology*, *8*, 118–125.

Goldberg, J., & Miller, H. (1986). Performance of psychiatric inpatients and intellectually deficient individuals on a task that assesses the validity of memory complaints. *Journal of Clinical Psychology*, *42*, 792–795.

Greiffenstein, M., Baker, W. J., & Gola, T. (1994). Validation of malingered amnesia measures with a large clinical sample. *Psychological Assessment*, *6*, 218–224.

Greiffenstein, M., Baker, W. J., & Gola, T. (1996). Comparison of multiple scoring methods for Rey's malingered amnesia measures. *Archives of Clinical Neuropsychology*, *11*, 283–293.

Griffin, G. A. E., Glassmire, D. M., Henderson, E. A., & McCann, C. (1997). Rey II: Redesigning the Rey screening test of malingering. *Journal of Clinical Psychology*, *53*, 757–766.

Griffin, G. A., Normington, J., & Glassmire, D. (1996). Qualitative dimensions in scoring the Rey Visual Memory Test of malingering. *Psychological Assessment*, *8*, 383–387.

Guilmette, T., Hart, K., Giuliano, A., & Leininger, B. (1994). Detecting simulated memory impairment: Comparison of the Rey Fifteen-Item Test and the Hiscock forced-choice procedure. *The Clinical Neuropsychologist*, *8*, 283–294.

Hayes, J. S., Hale, D. B., & Gouvier, W. D. (1997). Do tests predict malingering in defendants with mental retardation? *Journal of Psychology*, *131*, 575–576.

Hayes, J. S., Hale, D. B., & Gouvier, W. D. (1998). Malingering detection in mentally retarded forensic populations. *Applied Neuropsychology*, *5*, 33–36.

Hays, J. R., Emmons, J., & Lawson, K. A. (1993). Psychiatric norms for the Rey-15 Item Visual Memory Test. *Perceptual and Motor Skills*, *76*, 1331–1334.

Hilsabeck, R. C., & Gouvier, W. D. (2005). Detecting simulated memory impairment: Further validation of the Word Completion Memory Test (WCMT). *Archives of Clinical Neuropsychology*, *20*, 1025–1041.

Inman, T. H., & Berry, D. T. R. (2002). Cross-validation of indicators of malingering: A comparison of nine neuropsychological tests, four tests of malingering, and behavioral observations. *Archives of Clinical Neuropsychology*, *17*, 1–23.

Lee, A., Boone, K. B., Lesser, I., Wohl, M., Wilkins, S., & Parks, C. (2000). Performance of older depressed patients on two cognitive malingering tests: False positive rates for the Rey 15-item memorization and the Dot Counting Test. *The Clinical Neuropsychologist*, *14*, 303–308.

Lee, G., Loring, D., & Martin, R. (1992). Rey's 15-Item visual memory test for the detection of malingering: Normative observations on patients with neurological disorders. *Psychological Assessment*, *4*, 43–46.

Marshall, P., & Happe, M. (2007). The performance of individuals with mental retardation on cognitive tests assessing effort and motivation. *The Clinical Neuropsychologist*, *21*, 826–840.

McCaffrey, R., O'Bryant, S., Ashendorf, L., & Fisher, J. (2003). Correlations among the TOMM, Rey-15, and MMPI-2 validity scales in a sample of TBI litigants. *Journal of Forensic Neuropsychology*, *3*, 45–53.

Merten, T., Green, P., Henry, M., Blaskewitz, N., & Brockhaus, R. (2005). Analog validation of German-language symptom validity tests and the influence of coaching. *Archives of Clinical Neuropsychology, 20*, 719–726.

Millis, S., & Kler, S. (1995). Limitations of the Rey Fifteen Item test in the detection of malingering. *The Clinical Neuropsychologist, 9*, 241–244.

Morgan, S. (1991). Effect of true memory inpairment on a test of memory complaint validity. *Archives of Clinical Neuropsychology, 6*, 327–334.

Nelson, N. W., Boone, K. B., Dueck, A., Wagener, L., Lu, P., & Grills, C. (2003). Relationships between eight measures of suspect effort. *The Clinical Neuropsychologist, 17*, 263–272.

Pachana, N. A., Boone, K. B., & Ganzell, S. L. (1998). False positive errors on selected tests of malingering. *American Journal of Forensic Psychology, 16*, 17–25.

Orey, S. A., Cragar, D. E., & Berry, D. T. R. (2000). The effects of two motivational manipulations on the neuropsychological performance of mildly head-injured college students. *Archives of Clinical Neuropsychology, 15*, 335–348.

Reinhard, M. J., Satz, P., Scaglione, C. A., D'Elia, L. F., Rassovsky, Y., Arita, A. A., Hinkin, C. H., Thrasher, D., & Ordog, G. (2007). Neuropsychological exploration of alleged mold neurotoxicity. *Archives of Clinical Neuropsychology, 22*, 533–543.

Schretlen, D., Brandt, J., Krafft, L., & van Gorp, W. (1991). Some caveats in using the 15-Item Memory Test to detect malingered amnesia. *Psychological Assessment, 3*, 667–672.

Shum, D. H. K., O'Gorman, J. G., & Alpar, A. (2004). Effects of incentive and preparation time on performance and classification accuracy of standard and malingering-specific memory tests. *Archives of Clinical Neuropsychology, 19*, 817–823.

Simon, M. (1994). The use of the Rey Memory Test to assess malingering in criminal defendants. *Journal of Clinical Psychology, 50*, 913–917.

Stone, D. C., Boone, K. B., Back-Madruga, C., & Lessr, I. M. (2006). Has the rolling uterus finally gathered moss? Somatization and malingering of cognitive dysfunction in six cases of "toxic mold" exposure. *The Clinical Neuropsychologist, 20*, 766–785.

Sumanti, M., Boone, K. B., Savodnik, I., & Gorsuch, R. (2006). Noncredible psychiatric and cognitive symptoms in a worker's compensation "stress" claim sample. *The Clinical Neuropsychologist, 20*, 754–765.

Vickery, C. D., Berry, D. T. R., Inman, T. H., Harris, M. J., & Orey, S. A. (2001). Detection of inadequate effort on neuropsychological testing: A meta-analytic review of selected procedures. *Archives of Clinical Neuropsychology, 16*, 45–73.

Rey Memory for 16-Item Test (modification of Rey MFIT)

Arnett, P., & Franzen, M. (1997). Performance of substance abusers with memory deficits on measures of malingering. *Archives of Clinical Neuropsychology, 12*, 513–518.

Frederick, R., Sarfaty, S., Johnston, J. D., & Powel, J. (1994). Validation of a detector of response bias on a forced-choice test of nonverbal ability. *Neuropsychology, 8*, 118–125.

Iverson, G., & Franzen, M. (1996). Using multiple objective memory procedures to detect simulated malingering. *Journal of Clinical and Experimental Neuropsychology, 18*, 38–51.

Paul, D., Franzen, M., Cohen, S., & Fremouw, W. (1992). An investigation into the reliability and validity of two tests used in the detection of dissimulation. *International Journal of Clinical Neuropsychology, 14*, 1–9.

Rey Word Recognition List (as described in Lezak, 1983)

Boone, K. B., & Lu, P. (2003). Noncredible cognitive performance in the context of severe brain injury. *The Clinical Neuropsychologist, 17*, 244–254.

Dean, A. C., Victor, T. L., Boone, K. B., & Arnold, G. (2008). The relationship of IQ to effort test performance. *The Clinical Neuropsychologist, 22*, 705–722.

Frederick, R.I. (2000). A personal floor effect strategy to evaluate the validity of performance on memory tasks. *Journal of Clinical and Experimental Neuropsychology, 22*, 720–730.

Frederick, R. I. (2002). A review of Rey's strategies for detecting malingered neuropsychological impairment. *Journal of Forensic Neuropsychology*, *2*, 1–25.

Frederick, R., Sarfaty, S., Johnston, J. D., & Powel, J. (1994). Validation of a detector of response bias on a forced-choice test of nonverbal ability. *Neuropsychology*, *8*, 118–125.

Greiffenstein, M., Baker, W. J., & Gola, T. (1994). Validation of malingered amnesia measures with a large clinical sample. *Psychological Assessment*, *6*, 218–224.

Greiffenstein, M., Baker, W. J., & Gola, T. (1996). Comparison of multiple scoring methods for Rey's malingered amnesia measures. *Archives of Clinical Neuropsychology*, *11*, 283–293.

Nelson, N. W., Boone, K., Dueck. A., Wagener, L., Lu, P., & Grills, C. (2003). Relationships between eight measures of suspect effort. *The Clinical Neuropsychologist*, *17*, 263–272.

Nitch, S. Boone, K. B., Wen, J., Arnold, G., & Alfano, K. (2006). The utility of the Rey Word Recognition Test in the detection of suspect effort. *The Clinical Neuropsychologist*, *20*, 873–887.

Pachana, N. A., Boone, K. B., & Ganzell, S. L. (1998). False positive errors on selected tests of malingering. *American Journal of Forensic Psychology*, *16*, 17–25.

Stone, D. C., Boone, K. B., Back-Madruga, C., & Lessr, I. M. (2006). Has the rolling uterus finally gathered moss? Somatization and malingering of cognitive dysfunction in six cases of "toxic mold" exposure. *The Clinical Neuropsychologist*, *20*, 766–785.

Structured Interview of Reported Symptoms (SIRS)

Edens, J. F., Poythress, N. G., & Watkins-Clay, M. M. (2007). Detection of malingering in psychiatric unit and general population prison inmates: A comparison of the PAI, SIMS, and SIRS. *Journal of Personality Assessment*, *88*, 33–42

Lewis, J. L., Simcox, A. M., & Berry, D.T.R. (2002). Screening for feigned psychiatric symptoms in a forensic sample by using the MMPI-2 and the Structured Inventory of Malingered Symptomatology. *Psychological Assessment*, *14*, 170–176.

Merckelbach, H., & Smith, G. P. (2003). Diagnostic accuracy of the Structured Interview of Malingered Symptomatology (SIMS) in detecting instructed malingering. *Archives of Clinical Neuropsychology*, *18*, 145–152.

Rogers, R., Hinds, J. D., & Sewell, K. W. (1996). Feigning psychopathology among adolescent offenders:Validation of the SIRS, MMPI-A, and SIMS. *Journal of Personality Assessment*, *67*, 244–257.

Vagnini, V. L., Sollman, M. J., Berry, D. T. R., Granacher, R. P., Clark, J. A., Burton, R., O'Brien, M., Bacon, E., & Saier, J. (2006). Known-groups cross-validation of the Letter Memory Test in a compensation-seeking mixed neurologic sample. *The Clinical Neuropsychologist*, *20*, 289–304.

Vitacco, M. J., Rogers, R., Gabel, J., & Munizza, J. (2007). An evaluation of malingering screens with competency to stand trial patients: A known-groups study. *Law and Human Behavior*, *31*, 249–260.

Wynkoop, T. F., Frederick, R. I., & Hoy, M. (2006). Improving the clinical utility of the SIRS cognitive items: Preliminary reliability, validity, and normative data in pretrial and clinical samples. *Archives of Clinical Neuropsychology*, *21*, 651–656.

Structured Inventory of Malingered Symptomatology (SIMS)

Alwes, Y. R., Clark, J. A., Berry, D. T. R., & Granacher, R. P. (2008). Screening for feigning in a civil forensic setting. *Journal of Clinical and Experimental Neuropsychology*, *30*, 133–140.

Edens, J. F., Poythress, N. G., & Watkins-Clay, M. M. (2007). Detection of malingering in psychiatric unit and general population prison inmates: A comparison of the PAI, SIMS, and SIRS. *Journal of Personality Assessment*, *88*, 33–42.

Rogers, R., Hinds, J. D., & Sewell, K. W. (1996). Feigning psychopathology among adolescent offenders: Validation of the SIRS, MMPI-A, and SIMS. *Journal of Personality Assessment*, *67*, 244–257.

Smith, G. P., & Burger, G. K. (1997). Detection of malingering: Validation of the Structured Inventory of Malingered Symptomatology (SIMS). *Journal of the American Academy of Psychiatry and the Law*, *25*, 183–189.

Vitacco, M. J., Rogers, R., Gabel, J., & Munizza, J. (2007). An evaluation of malingering screens with competency to stand trial patients: A known-groups study. *Law and Human Behavior*, *31*, 249–260.

Test of Memory Malingering (TOMM)

Ashendorf, L., Constantinou, M., & McCaffrey, R. (2004). The effect of depression and anxiety on the TOMM in community-dwelling older adults. *Archives of Clinical Neuropsychology, 19*, 125–130.

Bauer, L., & McCaffrey, R. J. (2006). Coverage of the Test of Memory Malingering, Victoria Symptom Validity Test, and Word Memory Test on the internet: Is test security threatened? *Archives of Clinical Neuropsychology, 21*, 121–126.

Bauer, L., O'Bryant, S. E., Lynch, J. K., McCaffrey, R. J., & Fisher, J. M. (2007). Examining the Test of Memory Malingering Trial 1 and Word Memory Test Immediate Recognition as screening tools for insufficient effort. *Assessment, 14*, 215–222.

Bianchini, K. J., Curtis, K. L., & Greve, K. W. (2006). Compensation and malingering in traumatic brain injury: A dose-response relationship? *The Clinical Neuropsychologist, 20*, 831–847.

Bianchini, K., Love, J. M., Greve, K. W., & Adams, D. (2005). Detection and diagnosis of malingering in electrical injury. *Archives of Clinical Neuropsychology, 20*, 365–373.

Bolan, B., Foster, J. K., Schmand, B., & Bolan, S. (2002). A comparison of three tests to detect feigned amnesia: The effects of feedback and the measurement of response latency. *Journal of Clinical and Experimental Neuropsychology, 24*, 154–167.

Booksh, R. L., Aubert, M. J., & Andrews, S. R. (2007). Should the retention trial on the Test of Memory Malingering be optional? A reply. *Archives of Clinical Neuropsychology, 22*, 87–90.

Chafetz, M. D. (2008). Malingering on the Social Security Disability Consultative Exam: Predictors and base rates. *The Clinical Neuropsychologist, 22*, 529–546.

Colby, F. (2001). Using the binomial distribution to assess effort: Forced-choice testing in neuropsychological settings. *NeuroRehabilitation, 16*, 253–265.

Constantinou, M., Bauer, L., Ashendorf, L., Fisher, J. M., & McCaffrey, R. J. (2005). Is poor performance on recognition memory effort measures indicative of generalized poor performance on neuropsychological tests? *Archives of Clinical Neuropsychology, 20*, 191–198.

Constantinou, M., & McCaffrey, R. (2003). Using the TOMM for evaluating children's effort to perform optimally on neuropsychological measures. *Child Neuropsychology, 9*, 81–90.

Courtney, J., Dinkins, J., Allen, L., & Kuroski, K. (2003). Age-related effects in children taking the Computerized Assessment of Response Bias and the Word Memory Test. *Child Neuropsychology, 9*, 109–116.

Cragar, D., Berry, D., Fakhoury, T., Cibula, J., & Schmitt, F. (2006). Performance of patients with epilepsy and non-epileptic seizures on four measures of effort. *The Clinical Neuropsychologist, 20*, 552–566.

DenBoer, J. W., & Hall, S. (2007). Neuropsychological test performance of successful brain injury simulators. *The Clinical Neuropsychologist, 21*, 943–955.

Donders, J. (2005). Performance on the Test of Memory Malingering in a mixed pediatric sample. *Child Neuropsychology, 11*, 221–227.

Duncan, A. (2005). The impact of cognitive and psychiatric impairment of psychotic disorders on the Test of Memory Malingering (TOMM). *Assessment, 12*, 123–129.

Etherton, J. L., Bianchini, K. J., Greve, K. W., & Ciota, M. A. (2005). Test of Memory Malingering performance is unaffected by laboratory-induced pain: Implications for clinical use. *Archives of Clinical Neuropsychology, 20*, 375–384.

Farkas, M. R., Rosenfeld, B., Robbins, R., & van Gorp, W. (2006). Do tests of malingering concur? Concordance among malingering measures. *Behavioral Sciences and the Law, 24*, 659–671.

Gervais, R., Rohling, M., Green, P., & Ford, W. (2004). A comparison of WMT, CARB, and TOMM failure rates in non-head injury disability claimants. *Archives of Clinical Neuropsychology, 19*, 475–487.

Gierok, S. D., Dickson, A. L., & Cole, J. A. (2005). Performance of forensic and non-forensic adult psychiatric inpatients on the Test of Memory Malingering. *Archives of Clinical Neuropsychology, 20*, 755–760.

Graue, L. O., Berry, D. T. R., Clark, J. A., Sollman, M. J., Cardi, M., Hopkins, J., & Werline, D. (2007). Identification of feigned mental retardation using the new generation of malingering detection instruments: Preliminary findings. *The Clinical Neuropsychologist, 21*, 929–942.

Greiffenstein, M. F., & Baker, W. J. (2006). Miller was (mostly) right: Head injury severity inversely related to simulation. *Legal and Criminal Psychology, 11*, 131–145.

Greiffenstein, M. F., & Baker, W. J. (2008). Validity testing in dually diagnosed post-traumatic stress disorder and mild closed head injury. *The Clinical Neuropsychologist, 22*, 565–582.

Greve, K. W., & Bianchini, K. J. (2006). Should the retention trial of the Test of Memory Malingering be optional? *Archives of Clinical Neuropsychology, 21*, 117–119.

Greve, K. W., & Bianchini, K. J. (2007). Choosing to know less: A response to Booksh, Aubert, and Andrews. *Archives of Clinical Neuropsychology, 22*, 231–234.

Greve, K., Bianchini, K., Black, F. W., Heinly, M., Love, J., Swift, D., & Ciota, M. (2006). Classification accuracy of the Test of Memory Malingering in persons reporting exposure to environmental and industrial toxins: Results of a known-groups analysis. *Archives of Clinical Neuropsychology, 21*, 439–448.

Greve, K., Bianchini, K., & Doane, R. (2006). Classification accuracy of the Test of Memory Malingering in traumatic brain injury: Results of a known-groups analysis. *Journal of Clinical and Experimental Neuropsychology, 7*, 1176–1190.

Greve, K. W., Ord, J., Curtis, K. L., Bianchini, K. J., & Brennan, A. (in press). Detecting malingering in traumatic brain injury and chronic pain: A comparison of three forced-choice symptom validity tests. *The Clinical Neuropsychologist.*

Haber, A., & Fichtenberg, N. (2006). Replication of the Test of Memory Malingering (TOMM) in a traumatic brain injury and head trauma sample. *The Clinical Neuropsychologist, 20*, 524–532.

Henry, G. K., Heilbronner, R. L., Mittenberg, W., & Enders, C. (2006). The Henry-Heilbronner Index: A 15-item empirically derived MMPI-2 subscale for identifying probable malingering in personal injury litigants and disability claimants. *The Clinical Neuropsychologist, 20*, 786–797.

Hill, S. K., Ryan, L., Kennedy, C., & Malamut, B. (2003). The relationship between measures of declarative memory and the Test of Memory Malingering in patients with and without temporal lobe dysfunction. *Journal of Forensic Neuropsychology, 3*, 1–18.

Iverson, G. L., Le Page, J., Koehler, B. E., Shojania, K., & Badii, M. (2007). Test of Memory Malingering (TOMM) scores are not affected by chronic pain or depression in patients with fibromyalgia. *The Clinical Neuropsychologist, 21*, 532–546.

McCaffrey, R., O'Bryant, S., Ashendorf, L., & Fisher, J. (2003). Correlations among the TOMM, Rey-15, and MMPI-2 validity scales in a sample of TBI litigants. *Journal of Forensic Neuropsychology, 3*, 45–53.

Merten, T., Bossink, L., & Schmand, B. (2007). On the limits of effort testing: Symptom validity tests and severity of neurocognitive symptoms in nonlitigant patients. *Journal of Clinical and Experimental Neuropsychology, 29*, 308–318.

Moore, B., & Donders, J. (2004). Predictors of invalid neuropsychological test performance after traumatic brain injury. *Brain Injury, 18*, 975–984.

Nagle, A. M., Everhart, D. E., Durham, T. W., McCammon, S. L., & Walker, M. (2006). Deception strategies in children: Examination of forced choice recognition and verbal learning and memory techniques. *Archives of Clinical Neuropsychology, 21*, 777–785.

O'Bryant, S. E., Engel, L. R., Kleiner, J. S., Vasterling, J. J., & Black, W. F. (2007). Test of Memory Malingering (TOMM) Trial 1 as a screening measure for insufficient effort. *The Clinical Neuropsychologist, 21*, 511–521.

O'Bryant, S., & Lucas, J. (2006). Estimating the predictive value of the Test of Memory Malingering: An illustrative example for clinicians. *The Clinical Neuropsychologist, 20*, 533–540.

Powell, M. R., Gfeller, J. D., Hendricks, B. L., & Sharland, M. (2004). Detecting symptom- and test-coached simulators with the Test of Memory Malingering. *Archives of Clinical Neuropsychology, 19*, 693–702.

Rees, L. M., Tombaugh, T. N., & Boulay, L. (2001). Depression and the test of memory malingering. *Archives of Clinical Neuropsychology, 16*, 501–506.

Rees, L., Tombaugh, T., Gansler, D., & Moczynski, N. (1998). Five validation experiments of the Test of Memory Malingering (TOMM). *Psychological Assessment, 10*, 10–20.

Reinhard, M. J., Satz, P., Scaglione, C. A., D'Elia, L. F., Rassovsky, Y., Arita, A. A., Hinkin, C. H., Thrasher, D., & Ordog, G. (2007). Neuropsychological exploration of alleged mold neurotoxicity. *Archives of Clinical Neuropsychology, 22*, 533–543.

Ruocco, A. C., Swirsky-Sacchetti, T., Chute, D., Mandel, S., Platek, S. M., & Zillmer, E. A. (2008). Distinguishing between neuropsychological malingering and exaggerated psychiatric symptoms in a neuropsychological setting. *The Clinical Neuropsychologist, 22*, 547–564.

Simon, M. J. (2007). Performance of mentally retarded forensic patients on the Test of Memory Malingering. *Journal of Clinical Psychology, 63*, 339–344.

Tan, J. E., Slick, D. J., Strauss, E., & Hultsch, D. F. (2002). How'd they do it? Malingering strategies on symptom validity tests. *The Clinical Neuropsychologist, 16*, 495–505.

Teichner, G., & Wagner, M. (2004). The Test of Memory Malingering (TOMM): Normative data from cognitively intact, cognitively impaired, and elderly patients with dementia. *Archives of Clinical Neuropsychology*, *19*, 455–464.

Tombaugh, T. (1997). The Test of Memory Malingering (TOMM): Normative data from cognitively intact and cognitively impaired individuals. *Psychological Assessment*, *9*, 260–268.

Tombaugh, T. N. (2002). The Test of Memory Malingering (TOMM) in forensic psychology. *Journal of Forensic Neuropsychology*, *2*, 69–96.

Vagnini, V. L., Sollman, M. J., Berry, D. T. R., Granacher, R. P., Clark, J. A., Burton, R., O'Brien, M., Bacon, E., & Saier, J. (2006). Known-groups cross-validation of the Letter Memory Test in a compensation-seeking mixed neurologic sample. *The Clinical Neuropsychologist*, *20*, 289–304.

Vickery, C., Berry, D. T. R., Dearth, C., Vagnini, V., Baser, R., Cragar, D., & Orey, S. (2004). Head injury and the ability to feign neuropsychological deficits. *Archives of Clinical Neuropsychology*, *19*, 37–48.

Vilar-López, R., Santiago-Ramajo, S., Gómez-Río, M., Verdejo-García, A., Llamas, J. M., & Pérez-García, M. (2007). Detection of malingering in a Spanish population using three specific malingering tests. *Archives of Clinical Neuropsychology*, *22*, 379–388.

Weinborn, M., Orr, T., Woods, S. P., Conover, E., & Feix, J. (2003). A validation of the Test of Memory Malingering in a forensic psychiatric setting. *Journal of Clinical and Experimental Neuropsychology*, *25*, 979–990.

Willison, J., & Tombaugh, T. N. (2006). Detecting simulation of attention deficits using reaction time tests. *Archives of Clinical Neuropsychology*, *21*, 41–52.

Wygant, D. B., Sellbom, M., Ben-Porath, Y. S., Stafford, K. P., Freeman, D. B., & Heilbronner, R. L. (2007). The relation between symptom validity testing and MMPI-2 scores as a function of forensic evaluation context. *Archives of Clinical Neuropsychology*, *22*, 489–499.

Yanez, Y. T., Fremouw, W., Tennant, J., Strunk, J., & Coker, K. (2006). Effects of severe depression on TOMM performance among disability-seeking outpatients. *Archives of Clinical Neuropsychology*, *21*, 161–166.

Yantz, C. L., Gavett, B. E., Lynch, J. K., & McCaffrey, R. J. (2006). Potential for interpretation disparities of Halstead-Reitan neuropsychological battery performances in a litigating sample. *Archives of Clinical Neuropsychology*, *21*, 809–817.

Validity Indicator Profile

Farkas, M. R., Rosenfeld, B., Robbins, R., & van Gorp, W. (2006). Do tests of malingering concur? Concordance among malingering measures. *Behavioral Sciences and the Law*, *24*, 659–671.

Frederick, R. I. (1997). *Manual for the Validity Indicator Profile*. Minnetonka, MN: NCS Assessments.

Frederick, R. I. (2000). A personal floor effect strategy to evaluate the validity of performance on memory tasks. *Journal of Clinical and Experimental Neuropsychology*, *22*, 720–730.

Frederick, R. I. (2002). Review of the Validity Indicator Profile. *Journal of Forensic Neuropsychology*, *2*, 125–145.

Frederick, R. I. (2002). Teaching point on malingering detection. In K. Heilbrun, G. Marczyk, & D. DeMatteo, *Forensic mental health assessment: A casebook*. New York: Oxford University Press.

Frederick, R. I. (in press). Tests and techniques that detect malingering. In P. Halligan, *Malingering and Illness Deception*. Oxford, UK: Oxford University Press.

Frederick, R. I., & Crosby, R. D. (2000). Development and validation of the Validity Indicator Profile. *Law and Human Behavior*, *24*, 59–82.

Frederick, R. I., Crosby, R. D., & Wynkoop, T. F. (2000). Performance curve classification of invalid responding on the Validity Indicator Profile. *Archives of Clinical Neuropsychology*, *15*, 281–300.

Frederick, R. I., & Foster, H. G. (1991). Multiple measures of malingering on a forced-choice test of cognitive ability. *Psychological Assessment*, *3*, 596–602.

Frederick, R. I., Sarfaty, S. D., Johnston, J. D., & Powel, J. (1994). Validation of a detector of response bias on a forced-choice test of nonverbal ability. *Neuropsychology*, *8*, 118–125.

Victoria Symptom Validity Test (VSVT)

Bauer, L., & McCaffrey, R. J. (2006). Coverage of the Test of Memory Malingering, Victoria Symptom Validity Test, and Word Memory Test on the internet: Is test security threatened? *Archives of Clinical Neuropsychology*, *21*, 121–126.

Doss, R. C., Chelune, G. J., & Naugle, R. I. (1999). Victoria Symptom Validity Test: Compensation-seeking vs. non-compensation-seeking patients in a general clinical setting. *Journal of Forensic Neuropsychology*, *1*, 5–20.

Frazier, T. W., Youngstrom, E. A., Naugle, R. I., Haggerty, K. A., & Busch, R. M. (2007). The latent structure of cognitive symptom exaggeration on the Victoria Symptom Validity Test. *Archives of Clinical Neuropsychology*, *22*, 197–212.

Grote, C. L., Kooker, E. K., Garron, D. C., Nyenhuis, D. L., Smith, C. A., & Mattingly, M. L. (2000). Performance of compensation seeking and non-compensation seeking samples on the Victoria Symptom Validity Test: Cross-validation and extension of a standardization study. *Journal of Clinical and Experimental Neuropsychology*, *22*, 709–719.

Haggerty, K. A., Frazier, T. W., Busch, R. M., & Naugle, R. I. (2007). Relationships among Victoria Symptom Validity Test indices and Personality Assessment Inventory validity scales in a large clinical sample. *The Clinical Neuropsychologist*, *21*, 917–928.

Henry, G. K., Heilbronner, R. L., Mittenberg, W., & Enders, C. (2006). The Henry-Heilbronner Index: A 15-item empirically derived MMPI-2 subscale for identifying probable malingering in personal injury litigants and disability claimants. *The Clinical Neuropsychologist*, *20*, 786–797.

Loring, D. W., Larrabee, G.J., Lee, G. P., & Meador, K. J. (2007). Victoria Symptom Validity Test performance in a heterogeneous clinical sample. *The Clinical Neuropsychologist*, *21*, 522–531.

Loring, D. W., Lee, G. P., & Meador, K. J. (2005). Victoria Symptom Validity Test performance in non-litigating epilepsy surgery candidates. *Journal of Clinical and Experimental Neuropsychology*, *27*, 610–617.

Macciocchi, S., Seel, R., Alderson, A., & Godsall, R. (2006). Victoria Symptom Validity Test performance in acute severe traumatic brain injury: Implications for test interpretation. *Archives of Clinical Neuropsychology*, *21*, 395–404.

Reinhard, M. J., Satz, P., Scaglione, C. A., D'Elia, L. F., Rassovsky, Y., Arita, A. A., Hinkin, C. H., Thrasher, D., & Ordog, G. (2007). Neuropsychological exploration of alleged mold neurotoxicity. *Archives of Clinical Neuropsychology*, *22*, 533–543.

Slick, D., Hopp, G., Strauss, E., Hunter, M., & Pinch, D. (1994). Detecting dissumulation: Profiles of simulated malingerers, traumatic brain-injury patients, and normal controls on a revised version of Hiscock and Hiscock's forced-choice memory test. *Journal of Clinical and Experimental Neuroposychology*, *16*, 472–481.

Slick, D., Hopp, G., Strauss, E., & Spellacy, F. (1996). Victoria Symptom Validity Test: Efficiency for detecting feigned memory impairment and relationship to neuropsychological tests and MMPI-2 validity scales. *Journal of Clinical and Experimental Neuropsychology*, *18*, 911–922.

Slick, D., Hopp, G., Strauss, E., & Thompson, G. B. (1997). *Victoria Symptom Validity Test version 1.0 professional manual.* Odessa, FL: Psychological Assessment Resources.

Slick, D., Tan, J., Strauss, E., Mateer, C., Harnadek, M., & Sherman, E. (2003). Victoria Symptom Validity Test scores of patients with profound memory impairment: Nonlitigant case studies. *The Clinical Neuropsychologist*, *17*, 390–394.

Strauss, E., Hultsch, D. F., Hunter, M., Slick, D., Patry, B., & Levy-Bencheton, J. (2000). Using intraindividual variability to detect malingering in cognitive performance. *The Clinical Neuropsychologist*, *13*, 420–432.

Strauss, E., Slick, D. J., Levy-Bencheton, J., Hunter, M., MacDonald, S. W. S., & Hultsch, D. F. (2002). Intraindividual variability as an indicator of malingering in head injury. *Archives of Clinical Neuropsychology*, *17*, 423–444.

Tan, J. E., Slick, D. J., Strauss, E., & Hultsch, D. F. (2002). How'd they do it? Malingering strategies on symptom validity tests. *The Clinical Neuropsychologist*, *16*, 495–505.

Thompson, G. B. (2002). The Victoria Symptom Validity Test: An enhanced test of symptom validity. *Journal of Forensic Neuropsychology*, *2*, 43–67.

Vagnini, V. L., Sollman, M. J., Berry, D. T. R., Granacher, R. P., Clark, J. A., Burton, R., O'Brien, M., Bacon, E., & Saier, J. (2006). Known-groups cross-validation of the Letter Memory Test in a compensation-seeking mixed neurologic sample. *The Clinical Neuropsychologist*, *20*, 289–304.

Vilar-López, R., Santiago-Ramajo, S., Gómez-Río, M., Verdejo-García, A., Llamas, J. M., & Pérez-García, M. (2007). Detection of malingering in a Spanish population using three specific malingering tests. *Archives of Clinical Neuropsychology*, 22, 379–388.

Word Completion Memory Test (WCMT)

Gorny, I., & Merten, T. (2005). Symptom information-warning-coaching: How do they affect successful feigning in neuropsychological assessment? *Journal of Forensic Neuropsychology*, 4, 71–98.

Hilsabeck, R. C., & Gouvier, W. D. (2005). Detecting simulated memory impairment: Further validation of the Word Completion Memory Test (WCMT). *Archives of Clinical Neuropsychology*, 20, 1025–1041.

Hilsabeck, R. C., LeCompte, D. C., Marks, A. R., & Grafman, J. (2001). The Word Completion Memory Test (WCMT): A test to detect sophisticated simulators. *Archives of Clinical Neuropsychology*, 16, 669–677.

Word Memory Test (WMT)

Bauer, L., O'Bryant, S. E., Lynch, J. K., McCaffrey, R. J., & Fisher, J. M. (2007). Examining the Test of Memory Malingering Trial 1 and Word Memory Test Immediate Recognition as screening tools for insufficient effort. *Assessment*, 14, 215–222.

Bauer, L., & McCaffrey, R. J. (2006). Coverage of the Test of Memory Malingering, Victoria Symptom Validity Test, and Word Memory Test on the internet: Is test security threatened? *Archives of Clinical Neuropsychology*, 21, 121–126.

Bowden, S. C., Shores, E. A., & Mathias, J. L. (2006). Does effort suppress cognition after traumatic brain injury? A re-examination of the evidence for the Word Memory Test. *The Clinical Neuropsychologist*, 20, 858–872.

Courtney, J., Dinkins, J., Allen, L., & Kuroski, K. (2003). Age-related effects in children taking the Computerized Assessment of Response Bias and the Word Memory Test. *Child Neuropsychology*, 9, 109–116.

Dunn, T. M., Shear, P. K., Howe, S., & Ris, M. D. (2003). Detecting neuropsychological malingering: Effects of coaching and information. *Archives of Clinical Neuropsychology*, 18, 121–134.

Flaro, L., Green, P., & Robertson, E. (2007) Word Memory Test failure 23 times higher in mild brain injury than parents seeking custody: The power of external incentives. *Brain Injury*, 21, 4, 373–383.

Gervais, R. O., Green P., Allen, L. M., & Iverson, G. L. (2001). Effects of coaching on symptom validity testing in chronic pain patients presenting for disability assessments. *Journal of Forensic Neuropsychology*, 2, 1–19.

Gervais, R., Green, P. & Ford, W. (2001). Age effects on the WMT performance in disability-related assessments. *Archives of Clinical Neuropsychology*, 16, 809.

Gervais, R., Rohling, M., Green, P., & Ford, W. (2004). A comparison of WMT, CARB, and TOMM failure rates in non-head injury disability claimants. *Archives of Clinical Neuropsychology*, 19, 475–487.

Gervais, R., Russell, A., Green, P., Allen, L., Ferrari, R., & Pieschl, S. (2001). Effort testing in patients with fibromyalgia and disability incentives. *Journal of Rheumatology*, 28, 1892–1899.

Gorissen, M., Sanz, J. C., & Schmand, B. (2005). Effort and cognition in schizophrenia patients. *Schizophrenia Research*, 78, 199–208.

Green, P., Gervais, R., & Allen, L. M. (2001). Word Memory Test in normal controls and clinical cases simulating impairment. *Archives of Clinical Neuropsychology*, 16, 849–850.

Green, P., Iverson, G. L., & Allen, L. (1999). Detecting malingering in head injury litigation with the Word Memory Test. *Brain Injury*, 13, 813–819.

Green, P., Lees-Haley, P. R., & Allen, L. M. (2002). The Word Memory Test and the validity of neuropsychological test scores. *Journal of Forensic Neuropsychology*, 2, 97–124.

Green, P., Rohling, M. L., Lees-Haley, P. R., & Allen, L. M. (2001). Effort has a greater effect on test scores than severe brain injury in compensation claimants. *Brain Injury*, 15, 1045–1060.

Greve, K. W., Ord, J., Curtis, K. L., Bianchini, K. J., & Brennan, A. (in press). Detecting malingering in traumatic brain injury and chronic pain: A comparison of three forced-choice symptom validity tests. *The Clinical Neuropsychologist*.

Henry, G. K., Heilbronner, R. L., Mittenberg, W., & Enders, C. (2006). The Henry-Heilbronner Index: A

15-item empirically derived MMPI-2 subscale for identifying probable malingering in personal injury litigants and disability claimants. *The Clinical Neuropsychologist, 20*, 786–797.

Iverson, G., Green, P., & Gervais, R. (1999). Using the Word Memory Test to detect biased responding in head injury litigation. *Journal of Cognitive Rehabilitation, 17* (2), 2–6.

Merten, T., Bossink, L., & Schmand, B. (2007). On the limits of effort testing: Symptom validity tests and severity of neurocognitive symptoms in nonlitigant patients. *Journal of Clinical and Experimental Neuropsychology, 29*, 308–318.

Morel, K. R. (2008). Comparison of the Morel Emotional Numbing Test for Posttraumatic Stress Disorder to the Word Memory Test in neuropsychological evaluations. *The Clinical Neuropsychologist, 22*, 350–362.

Osmon, D. C., Plambek, E., Klein, L., & Mano, Q. (2006). The Word Reading Test of Effort in adult learning disability: A simulation study. *The Clinical Neuropsychologist, 20*, 315–324.

Rohling, M. L., Green, P., Allen III, L. M., & Iverson, G. (2002). Depressive symptoms and neurocognitive test scores in patients passing symptom validity tests. *Archives of Clinical Neuropsychology, 17*, 205–222.

Stevens, A., Friedel, E., Mehren, G., & Merten, T. (2008). Malingering and uncooperativeness in psychiatric and psychological assessment: Prevalence and effects in a German sample of claimants. *Psychiatry Research, 157*, 191–200.

Tan, J. E., Slick, D. J., Strauss, E., & Hultsch, D. F. (2002). How'd they do it? Malingering strategies on symptom validity tests. *The Clinical Neuropsychologist, 16*, 495–505.

Williamson, D. J., Green, P., Allen, L., & Rohling, M. (2003). Evaluating effort with the Word Memory Test and Category Test—or not: Inconsistencies in compensation-seeking sample. *Journal of Forensic Neuropsychology, 3*, 19–44.

Wygant, D. B., Sellbom, M., Ben-Porath, Y. S., Stafford, K. P., Freeman, D. B., & Heilbronner, R. L. (2007). The relation between symptom validity testing and MMPI-2 scores as a function of forensic evaluation context. *Archives of Clinical Neuropsychology, 22*, 489–499.

Other recall and recognition tasks and symptom validity tests

Brandt, J., Rubinsky, E., & Lassen, G. (1985). Uncovering malingered amnesia. *Annals of the New York Academy of Sciences, 44*, 502–503.

Chouinard, M., & Rouleau, I. (1997). The 48-Pictures Test: A two-alternative forced-choice recognition test for the detection of malingering. *Journal of the International Neuropsychological Society, 3*, 545–552.

Davis, H., King, J. H., Bloodworth, M., Spring, A., & Klebe, K. (1997). The detection of simulated malingering using a computerized category classification test. *Archives of Clinical Neuropsychology, 12*, 191–198.

Davis, H., King, J. H., Klebe, K., Bajszar, G., Bloodworth, M., & Wallick, S. (1997). The detection of simulated malingering using a computerized priming test. *Archives of Clinical Neuropsychology, 12*, 145–153.

Frederick R. I., & Speed, F. M. (2007). On the interpretation of below-chance responding in forced-choice tests. *Assessment, 14*, 3–11.

Graue, L. O., Berry, D. T. R., Clark, J. A., Sollman, M. J., Cardi, M., Hopkins, J., & Werline, D. (2007). Identification of feigned mental retardation using the new generation of malingering detection instruments: Preliminary findings. *The Clinical Neuropsychologist, 21*, 929–942.

Iverson, G., Franzen, M., & McCracken, L. (1991). Evaluation of an objective assessment technique for the detection of malingered memory deficits. *Law and Human Behavior, 15*, 667–676.

Iverson, G., Franzen, M., & McCracken, L. (1994). Application of a forced-choice memory procedure designed to detect experimental malingering. *Archives of Clinical Neuropsychology, 9*, 437–450.

Jelicic, M., Merckelback, H., & van Bergen, S. (2004). Symptom validity testing of feigned amnesia for a mock crime. *Archives of Clinical Neuropsychology, 19*, 525–531.

Merten, T., Bossink, L., & Schmand, B. (2007). On the limits of effort testing: Symptom validity tests and severity of neurocognitive symptoms in nonlitigant patients. *Journal of Clinical and Experimental Neuropsychology, 29*, 308–318.

Morel, K. R. (2008). Comparison of the Morel Emotional Numbing Test for Posttraumatic Stress Disorder to the Word Memory Test in neuropsychological evaluations. *The Clinical Neuropsychologist, 22*, 350–362.

Osmon, D. C., Plambek, E., Klein, L., & Mano, Q. (2006). The Word Reading Test of Effort in adult learning disability: A simulation study. *The Clinical Neuropsychologist, 20*, 315–324.

Stone, D. C., Boone, K. B., Back-Madruga, C., & Lessr, I. M. (2006). Has the rolling uterus finally gathered moss? Somatization and malingering of cognitive dysfunction in six cases of "toxic mold" exposure. *The Clinical Neuropsychologist*, *20*, 766–785.

Wiggins, E., & Brandt, J. (1988). The detection of simulated amnesia. *Law and Human Behavior*, *12*, 57–78.

Appendix B
Neuropsychological and psychological measures used to identify insufficient effort and malingering: A cross-referenced bibliography

California Verbal Learning Test

Ashendorf, L., O'Bryant, S. E., & McCaffrey, R. J. (2003). Specificity of malingering detection strategies in older adults using the CVLT and WCST. *The Clinical Neuropsychologist, 17*, 255–262.

Baker, R., Donders, J., & Thompson, E. (2000). Assessment of incomplete effort with the California Verbal Learning Test. *Applied Neuropsychology, 7*, 111–114.

Bianchini, K., Houston, R., Greve, K., Irvin, R., Black, F. W., Swift, D., & Tamimie, R. (2003). Malingered neurocognitive dysfunction in neurotoxic exposure: An application of the Slick criteria. *Journal of Occupational and Environmental Medicine, 45*, 1087–1099.

Coleman, R., Rapport, L., Millis, S., Ricker, J., & Farchione, T. (1998). Effects of coaching on detection of malingering on the California Verbal Learning Test. *Journal of Clinical and Experimental Neuropsychology, 20*, 201–210.

Curtis, K. L., Greve, K. W., Bianchini, K. J., & Brennan, A. (2006). California Verbal Learning Test indicators of malingered neurocognitive dysfunction: Sensitivity and specificity in traumatic brain injury. *Assessment, 13*, 46–61.

Demakis, G. J. (1999). Serial malingering on verbal and nonverbal fluency and memory measures: An analogue investigation. *Archives of Clinical Neuropsychology, 14*, 401–410.

Demakis, G. J. (2004). Application of clinically-derived malingering cutoffs on the California Verbal Learning Test and the Wechsler Adult Intelligence Test-Revised to an analog malingering study. *Applied Neuropsychology, 11*, 220–226.

Martens, M., Donders, J. D., & Millis, S. R. (2001). Evaluation of invalid response set after traumatic head injury. *Journal of Forensic Neuropsychology, 2*, 1–18.

Millis, S., & Putnam, S. (1997). The California Verbal Learning Test in the assessment of financially compensable mild head injury: Further developments. *Journal of the International Neuropsychological Society, 3*, 225–226.

Millis, S., Putnam, S., Adams, K., & Ricker, J. (1995). The California Verbal Learning Test in the detection of incomplete effort in neuropsychological evaluation. *Psychological Assessment, 7*, 463–471.

Moore, B., & Donders, J. (2004). Predictors of invalid neuropsychological test performance after traumatic brain injury. *Brain Injury, 18*, 975–984.

Slick, D. J., Iverson, G. L., & Green, P. (2000). California Verbal Learning Test indicators of suboptimal performance in a sample of head-injury litigants. *Journal of Clinical and Experimental Neuropsychology, 22*, 569–579.

Sweet, J. J., Wolfe, P., Sattlberger, E., Numan, B., Rosenfeld, J. P., Clingerman, S., & Nies, K. J. (2000). Further investigation of traumatic brain injury versus insufficient effort with the California Verbal Learning Test. *Archives of Clinical Neuropsychology, 15*, 105–113.

Trueblood, W. (1994). Qualitative and quantitative characteristics of malingered and other invalid WAIS-R and clinical memory data. *Journal of Clinical and Experimental Neuropsychology, 16*, 597–607.

Trueblood, W., & Schmidt, M. (1993). Malingering and other validity considerations in the neuropsychological evaluation of mild head injury. *Journal of Clinical and Experimental Neuropsychology, 15*, 578–590.

California Verbal Learning Test–2nd edition

Bauer, L., Yantz, C. L., Ryan, L. M., Warden, D. L., & McCaffrey, R. J. (2005). An examination of the California Verbal Learning Test II to detect incomplete effort in a traumatic brain-injury sample. *Applied Neuropsychology, 12*, 202–207.

Curtis, K. L., Greve, K. W., Bianchini, K. J., & Brennan, A. (2006). California Verbal Learning Test indicators of Malingered Neurocognitive Dysfunction: Sensitivity and specificity in traumatic brain injury. *Assessment, 13*, 46–61.

Donders, J. (2006). Performance discrepancies on the California Verbal Learning Test–Second Edition (CVLT-II) in the standardization sample. *Psychological Assessment, 18*, 458–463.

Donders, J., & Boonstra, T. (2007). Correlates of invalid neuropsychological test performance after traumatic brain injury. *Brain Injury, 21*, 319–326.

Marshall, P., & Happe, M. (2007). The performance of individuals with mental retardation on cognitive tests assessing effort and motivation. *The Clinical Neuropsychologist, 21*, 826–840.

Moore, B. A., & Donders, J. (2004). Predictors of invalid neuropsychological test performance after traumatic brain injury. *Brain Injury, 18*, 975–984.

Root, J. C., Robbins, R. M., Chang, L., & van Gorp, W. G. (2006). Detection of inadequate effort on the California Verbal Learning Test–Second Edition: Forced choice recognition and critical item analysis. *Journal of the International Neuropsychological Society, 12*, 688–696.

Category Test and Booklet Category Test

Bolter, J. F., Picano, J. J., & Zych, K. (1985). *Item error frequencies on the Halstead Category Test: An index of performance validity*. Paper presented at the annual meeting of the National Academy of Neuropsychology, Philadelphia, PA.

DiCarlo, M. A., Gfeller, J. D., & Oliveri, M. V. (2000). Effects of coaching on detecting feigned cognitive impairment with the Category Test. *Archives of Clinical Neuropsychology, 15*, 399–413.

Ellwanger, J., Tenhula, W., Rosenfeld, J. P., & Sweet, J. (1999). Identifying simulators of cognitive deficit through combined use of neuropsychological test performance and event- event-related potentials (ERPs). *Journal of Clinical and Experimental Neuropsychology, 21*, 866–879.

Forrest, T., Allen, D., & Goldstein, G. (2004). Malingering indexes for the Halstead Category Test. *The Clinical Neuropsychologist, 18*, 334–347.

Greve, K. W., Bianchini, K. J., & Roberson, T. (2007). The Booklet Category Test and malingering in traumatic brain injury: Classification accuracy in known groups. *The Clinical Neuropsychologist, 21*, 318–337.

Sweet, J., & King, J. (2002). Category test validity indicators: Overview and practice recommendations. *Journal of Forensic Neuropsychology, 3*, 241–274. (Also published as a book chapter in J. Hom & R. Denney (Eds.) (2002), *Detection of response bias in forensic neuropsychology*. New York: Haworth Medical Press.)

Tenhula, W., & Sweet, J. (1996). Double cross-validation of the Booklet Category Test in detecting malingered traumatic brain injury. *The Clinical Neuropsychologist, 10*, 104–116.

Williamson, D. J., Green, P., Allen, L., & Rohling, M. (2003). Evaluating effort with the Word Memory Test and Category Test—or not: Inconsistencies in compensation-seeking sample. *Journal of Forensic Neuropsychology, 3*, 19–44.

Yantz, C. L., Gavett, B. E., Lynch, J. K., & McCaffrey, R. J. (2006). Potential for interpretation disparities of Halstead-Reitan neuropsychological battery performances in a litigating sample. *Archives of Clinical Neuropsychology, 21*, 809–817.

Computerized tests of information processing

Willison, J., & Tombaugh, T. N. (2006). Detecting simulation of attention deficits using reaction time tests. *Archives of Clinical Neuropsychology, 21*, 41–52.

Controlled oral word association

Curtis, K. L., Thompson, L. K., Greve, K. W., & Bianchini, K. J. (in press). Verbal fluency indicators of malingering in traumatic brain injury: Classification accuracy in known groups. *The Clinical Neuropsychologist*.

Demakis, G. (1999). Serial malingering on verbal and nonverbal fluency and memory measures: An analogue
investigation. *Archives of Clinical Neuropsychology*, *14*, 401–410.

Silverberg, N. D., Hanks, R. A., Buchanan, L., Fichtenberg, N., & Millis, S. R. (2008). Detecting response bias
with performance patterns on an expanded version of the Controlled Oral Word Association Test. *The
Clinical Neuropsychologist*, *22*, 140–157.

Dichotic listening

Meyers, J. E., Galinsky, A. M., & Volbrecht, M. (1999). Malingering and mild brain injury: How low is too low.
Applied Neuropsychology, *6*, 208–216.

Meyers, J. E., & Volbrecht, M. E. (2003). Validation of multiple malingering detection methods in a large clinical
sample. *Archives of Clinical Neuropsychology*, *18*, 261–276.

Digit Span

(see also Reliable Digit Span)

Axelrod, B., Fichtenberg, N., Millis, S., & Wertheimer, J. (2006). Detecting incomplete effort with Digit
Span from the Wechsler Adult Intelligence Scale–Third Edition. *The Clinical Neuropsychologist*, *20*,
513–523.

Babikian, T., Boone, K. B., Lu, P., & Arnold, G. (2006). Sensitivity and specificity of various Digit Span scores
in the detection of suspect effort. *The Clinical Neuropsychologist*, *20*, 145–159.

Beetar, J., & Williams, J. (1995). Malingering response styles on the Memory Assessment Scales and symptom
validity tests. *Archives of Clinical Neuropsychology*, *10*, 57–72.

Bianchini, K. J., Curtis, K. L., & Greve, K. W. (2006). Compensation and malingering in traumatic brain
injury: A dose-response relationship? *The Clinical Neuropsychologist*, *20*, 831–847.

Binder, L., & Willis, S. (1992). Assessment of motivation after financially compensable minor head trauma.
Psychological Assessment: A Journal of Consulting and Clinical Psychology, *3*, 175–181.

Dean, A. C., Victor, T. L., Boone, K. B., & Arnold, G. (2008). The relationship of IQ to effort test
performance. *The Clinical Neuropsychologist*, *22*, 705–722.

Fisher, H. L., & Rose, D. (2005). Comparison of the effectiveness of two versions of the Rey Memory Test in
discriminating between actual and simulated memory impairment, with and without the addition of a
standard memory test. *Journal of Clinical and Experimental Neuropsychology*, *27*, 840–858.

Franzen, M. D., & Martin, N. (1996). Do people with knowledge fake better? *Applied Neuropsychology*, *3*,
82–85.

Gorny, I., & Merten, T. (2005). Symptom information-warning-coaching: How do they affect successful feigning in neuropsychological assessment? *Journal of Forensic Neuropsychology*, *4*, 71–98.

Graue, L. O., Berry, D. T. R., Clark, J. A., Sollman, M. J., Cardi, M., Hopkins, J., & Werline, D. (2007).
Identificatoin of feigned mental retardation using the new generation of malingering detection instruments: Preliminary findings. *The Clinical Neuropsychologist*, *21*, 929–942.

Greiffenstein, M., Baker, W. J., & Gola, T. (1994). Validation of malingered amnesia measures with a large
clinical sample. *Psychological Assessment*, *6*, 218–224.

Greve, K. W., Springer, S., Bianchini, K. J., Black, F. W., Heinly, M. T., Love, J. M., Swift, D. A., & Ciota, M. A.
(2007). Malingering in toxic exposure: Classification accuracy of Reliable Digit Span and WAIS-III Digit
Span scaled scores. *Assessment*, *14*, 12–21.

Heaton, R., Smith, H., Lehman, R., & Vogt, A. (1978). Prospects for faking believable deficits on neuropsychological testing. *Journal of Consulting and Clinical Psychology*, *46*, 892–900.

Heinly, M. T., Greve, K. W., Bianchini, K. J., Love, J. L., & Brennan, A. (2005). WAIS Digit Span-based indicators of malingered neurocognitive dysfunction: Classification accuracy in traumatic brain injury. *Assessment, 12*, 429–444.

Iverson, G., & Franzen, M. (1994). The Recognition Memory Test, Digit Span, and Knox Cube Test as markers of malingered memory impairment. *Assessment, 1*, 323–334.

Iverson, G., & Franzen, M. (1996). Using multiple objective memory procedures to detect simulated malingering. *Journal of Clinical and Experimental Neuropsychology, 18*, 38–51.

Iverson, G., & Tulsky, D. (2003). Detecting malingering on the WAIS-III: Unusual Digit Span performance patterns in the normal populations and in clinical groups. *Archives of Clinical Neuropsychology, 18*, 1–9.

Martin, R., Hayes, J., & Gouvier, W. D. (1996). Differential vulnerability between postconcussion self-report and objective malingering tests in identifying simulated mild head injury. *Journal of Clinical and Experimental Neuropsychology, 18*, 265–275.

Merten, T., Green, P., Henry, M., Blaskewitz, N., & Brockhaus, R. (2005). Analog validation of German-language symptom validity tests and the influence of coaching. *Archives of Clinical Neuropsychology, 20*, 719–726.

Meyers, J., & Volbrecht, M. (1998). Validation of reliable digits for detection of malingering. *Assessment, 5*, 303–307.

Mittenberg, W., Theroux-Fichera, S., Zielinski, R., & Heilbronner, R. (1995). Identification of malingered head injury on the Wechsler Adult Intelligence Scale-Revised. *Professional Psychology: Research and Practice, 26*, 491–498.

Pachana, N. A., Boone, K. B., & Ganzell, S. L. (1998). False positive errors on selected tests of malingering. *American Journal of Forensic Psychology, 16*, 17–25.

Rawling, P., & Brooks, D. (1990). Simulation Index: A method for detecting factitious errors on the WAIS-R and WMS. *Neuropsychology, 4*, 223–238.

Ross, S. R., Putnam, S. H., Millis, S. R., Adams, K. M., & Krukowski, R. A. (2006). Detecting insufficient effort using the Seashore Rhythm and Speech-Sounds Perception Tests in head injury. *The Clinical Neuropsychologist, 20*, 798–815.

Schwarz, L. R., Gfeller, J. D., & Oliveri, M. V. (2006). Detecting feigned impairment with the digit span and vocabulary subtests of the Wechsler Adult Intelligence Scale–Third Edition. *The Clinical Neuropsychologist, 20*, 741–753.

Shum, D. H. K., O'Gorman, J. G., & Alpar, A. (2004). Effects of incentive and preparation time on performance and classification accuracy of standard and malingering-specific memory tests. *Archives of Clinical Neuropsychology, 19*, 817–823.

Stone, D. C., Boone, K. B., Back-Madruga, C., & Lessr, I. M. (2006). Has the rolling uterus finally gathered moss? Somatization and malingering of cognitive dysfunction in six cases of "toxic mold" exposure. *The Clinical Neuropsychologist, 20*, 766–785.

Suhr, J., Tranel, D., Wefel, J., & Barrash, J. (1997). Memory performance after head injury: Contributions of malingering, litigation status, psychological factors, and medication use. *Journal of Clinical and Experimental Neuropsychology, 19*, 500–514.

Trueblood, W., & Schmidt, M. (1993). Malingering and other validity considerations in the neuropsychological evaluation of mild head injury. *Journal of Clinical and Experimental Neuropsychology, 15*, 578–590.

Vagnini, V. L., Sollman, M., J., Berry, D. T. R., Granacher, R. P., Clark, J. A., Burton, R., O'Brien, M., Bacon, E., & Saier, J. (2006). Known-groups cross-validation of the Letter Memory Test in a compensation-seeking mixed neurologic sample. *The Clinical Neuropsychologist, 20*, 289–304.

Vickery, C., Berry, D. T. R., Dearth, C., Vagnini, V., Baser, R., Cragar, D., & Orey, S. (2004). Head injury and the ability to feign neuropsychological deficits. *Archives of Clinical Neuropsychology, 19*, 37–48.

Wall, J. R., & Millis, S. R. (1998). Can motor measures tell us if someone is trying? An assessment of sincerity of effort in simulated malingering. *International Journal of Rehabilitation and Health, 4*, 51–57.

Finger tapping

Arnold, G., Boone, K. B., Lu, P., Dean, A., Wen, J., Nitch, S., & McPherson, S. (2005). Sensitivity and specificity of finger tapping test scores for the detection of suspect effort. *The Clinical Neuropsychologist, 19*, 105–120.

Binder, L., & Willis, S. (1992). Assessment of motivation after financially compensable minor head trauma. *Psychological Assessment: A Journal of Consulting and Clinical Psychology, 3,* 175–181.

Dean, A. C., Victor, T. L., Boone, K. B., & Arnold, G. (2008). The relationship of IQ to effort test performance. *The Clinical Neuropsychologist, 22,* 705–722.

Greiffenstein, M. F. (2007). Motor, sensory, and perceptual-motor pseudoabnormalities. In G. J. Larrabee (Ed.), *Assessment of malingered neuropsychological deficits* (pp. 100–130). New York: Oxford University Press.

Greiffenstein, M. F., & Baker, W. J. (2008). Validity testing in dually diagnosed post-traumatic stress disorder and mild closed head injury. *The Clinical Neuropsychologist, 22,* 565–582.

Greiffenstein, M. F., Baker, W. J., & Gola, T. (1996). Motor dysfunction profiles in traumatic brain injury and postconcussion syndrome. *Journal of the International Neuropsychological Society, 2,* 477–485.

Heaton, R., Smith, H., Lehman, R., & Vogt, A. (1978). Prospects for faking believable deficits on neuropsychological testing. *Journal of Consulting and Clinical Psychology, 46,* 892–900.

Larrabee, G. J. (2003). Detection of malingering using atypical performance patterns on standard neuropsychological tests. *The Clinical Neuropsychologist, 17,* 410–425.

Meyers, J. E., & Volbrecht, M. E. (2003). Validation of multiple malingering detection methods in a large clinical sample. *Archives of Clinical Neuropsychology, 18,* 261–276.

Rapport, L., Farchione, T., Coleman, R., & Axelrod, B. (1998). Effects of coaching on malingered motor function profiles. *Journal of Clinical and Experimental Neuropsychology, 20,* 89–97.

Stone, D. C., Boone, K. B., Back-Madruga, C., & Lessr, I. M. (2006). Has the rolling uterus finally gathered moss? Somatization and malingering of cognitive dysfunction in six cases of "toxic mold" exposure. *The Clinical Neuropsychologist, 20,* 766–785.

Tanner, B. A., Bowles, R. L., & Tanner, E. L. (2003). Detection of intentional sub-optimal performance on a computerized finger-tapping task. *Journal of Clinical Psychology, 59* (1), 123–131.

Vickery, C., Berry, D. T. R., Dearth, C., Vagnini, V., Baser, R., Cragar, D., & Orey, S. (2004). Head injury and the ability to feign neuropsychological deficits. *Archives of Clinical Neuropsychology, 19,* 37–48.

Wall, J. R., & Millis, S. R. (1998). Can motor measures tell us if someone is trying? An assessment of sincerity of effort in simulated malingering. *International Journal of Rehabilitation and Health, 4,* 51–57.

Grip strength (dynamometer)

Gilbert, J. C., & Knowlton, R. G. (1983). Simple method to determine sincerity of effort during a maximal isometric test of grip strength. *American Journal Physical Medicine, 62* (3), 135–144.

Greiffenstein, M. F. (2007). Motor, sensory, and perceptual-motor pseudoabnormalities. In G. J. Larrabee (Ed.), *Assessment of malingered neuropsychological deficits* (pp. 100–130). New York: Oxford University Press.

Greiffenstein, M. F., & Baker, W. J. (2006). Miller was (mostly) right: Head injury severity inversely related to simulation. *Legal and Criminal Psychology, 11,* 131–145.

Greiffenstein, M. F., Baker, W. J., & Gola, T. (1996). Motor dysfunction profiles in traumatic brain injury and postconcussion syndrome. *Journal of the International Neuropsychological Society, 2,* 477–485.

Hamilton, A., Balnave, R., & Adams, R. (1994). Grip strength testing reliability. *Journal of Hand Therapy, 7* (3), 163–170.

Niebuhr, B. R., & Marion, R. (1987). Detecting sincerity of effort when measuring grip strength. *American Journal of Physical Medicine, 66* (1), 16–24.

Rapport, L., Farchione, T., Coleman, R., & Axelrod, B. (1998). Effects of coaching on malingered motor function profiles. *Journal of Clinical and Experimental Neuropsychology, 20,* 89–97.

Smith, G. A., Nelson, R. C., Sadoff, S. J., & Sadoff, A. M. (1989). Assessing sincerity of effort in maximal grip strength tests. *American Journal of Physical Medicine and Rehabilitation, 68* (2), 73–80.

Vickery, C., Berry, D. T. R., Dearth, C., Vagnini, V., Baser, R., Cragar, D., & Orey, S. (2004). Head injury and the ability to feign neuropsychological deficits. *Archives of Clinical Neuropsychology, 19,* 37–48.

Wall, J. R., & Millis, S. R. (1998). Can motor measures tell us if someone is trying? An assessment of sincerity of effort in simulated malingering. *International Journal of Rehabilitation and Health, 4,* 51–57.

Grooved pegs

Greiffenstein, M. F., Baker, W. J., & Gola, T. (1996). Motor dysfunction profiles in traumatic brain injury and postconcussion syndrome. *Journal of the International Neuropsychological Society*, *2*, 477–485.

Rapport, L., Farchione, T., Coleman, R., & Axelrod, B. (1998). Effects of coaching on malingered motor function profiles. *Journal of Clinical and Experimental Neuropsychology*, *20*, 89–97.

Halstead-Reitan Neuropsychological Battery

Faust, D. Hart, K. Guilmette, T. J., & Arkes, H. R. (1988). Neuropsychologists' capacity to detect adolescent malingerers. *Professional Psychology: Research and Practice*, *19*, 508–515.

Goebel, R. A. (1983). Detection of faking on the Halstead-Reitan neuropsychological test battery. *Journal of Clinical Psychology*, *39*, 731–742.

Heaton, R., Smith, H., Lehman, R., & Vogt, A. (1978). Prospects for faking believable deficits on neuropsychological testing. *Journal of Consulting and Clinical Psychology*, *46*, 892–900.

McKinzey, R. K., & Russell, E. W. (1997). Detection of malingering on the Halstead-Reitan Battery: A cross-validation. *Archives of Clinical Neuropsychology*, *12*, 585–589.

Mittenberg, W., Rotholc, A., Russell, E., & Heilbronner, R. (1996). Identification of malingered head injury on the Halstead-Reitan Neuropsychological Battery. *Archives of Clinical Neuropsychology*, *11*, 271–281.

Reitan, R., & Wolfson, D. (1996). The question of validity of neuropsychological test scores among head-injured litigants: Development of a dissimulation index. *Archives of Clinical Neuropsychology*, *11*, 573–580.

Reitan, R. & Wolfson, D. (2002). Detection and malingering and invalid test results using the Halstead-Reitan Battery. *Journal of Forensic Neuropsychology*, *3*, 275–314.

Ross, S. R., Putnam, S. H., & Adams, K. M. (2006). Psychological disturbance, incomplete effort, and compensation—seeking status as predictors of neuropsychological test performance in head injury. *Journal of Clinical and Experimental Neuropsychology*, *28*, 111–125.

Trueblood, W., & Binder, L. (1997). Psychologists' accuracy in identifying neuropsychological test protocols of clinical malingerers. *Archives of Clinical Neuropsychology*, *12*, 13–27.

Trueblood, W., & Schmidt, M. (1993). Malingering and other validity considerations in the neuropsychological evaluation of mild head injury. *Journal of Clinical and Experimental Neuropsychology*, *15*, 578–590.

Hopkins Verbal Learning Test–Revised (HVLT–R)

Nagle, A. M., Everhart, D. E., Durham, T. W., McCammon, S. L., & Walker, M. (2006). Deception strategies in children: Examination of forced choice recognition and verbal learning and memory techniques. *Archives of Clinical Neuropsychology*, *21*, 777–785.

Judgment of Line Orientation Test

Iverson, G. L. (2001). Can malingering be identified with the judgment of line orientation test? *Applied Neuropsychology*, *8*, 167.

Meyers, J. E., Galinsky, A. M., & Volbrecht, M. (1999). Malingering and mild brain injury: How low is too low. *Applied Neuropsychology*, *6*, 208–216.

Knox Cube Test

Iverson, G., & Franzen, M. (1994). The Recognition Memory Test, Digit Span, and Knox Cube Test as markers of malingered memory impairment. *Assessment*, *1*, 323–334.

Luria-Nebraska Neuropsychological Battery

Golden, C. J., & Grier, C. A. (1998). Detecting malingering on the Luria-Nebraska Neuropsychological Battery. In C. R. E. Reynolds (Ed.), *Detection of malingering during head injury litigation*. New York: Plenum Press.

McKinzey, R., Podd, M., Krehbiel, M., Mensch, A., & Conley Trombka, C. (1997). Detection of malingering on the Luria-Nebraska Neuropsychological Battery: An initial and cross-validation. *Archives of Clinical Neuropsychology, 12*, 505–512.

Mensch, A. J., & Woods, D. J. (1986). Patterns of feigning brain damage on the LNNB. *International Journal of Clinical Neuropsychology, 8*, 59–63.

Memory Assessment Scales

Beetar, J., & Williams, J. (1995). Malingering response styles on the Memory Assessment Scales and symptom validity tests. *Archives of Clinical Neuropsychology, 10*, 57–72.

O'Bryant, S., Duff, K., Fisher, J., & McCaffrey, R. (2004). Performance profiles and cut-off scores on the Memory Assessment Scales. *Archives of Clinical Neuropsychology, 19*, 489–496.

Ross, S., Krukowski, R., Putnam, S., & Adams, K. (2003). The Memory Assessment Scales in the detection of incomplete effort in mild head injury. *The Clinical Neuropsychologist, 17*, 581–591.

MCMI–III

Daubert, S. D., & Metzler, A. E. (2000). The detection of fake-bad and fake-good responding on the Millon Clinical Multiaxial Inventory III. *Psychological Assessment, 12*, 418–424.

Farkas, M. R., Rosenfeld, B., Robbins, R., & van Gorp, W. (2006). Do tests of malingering concur? Concordance among malingering measures. *Behavioral Sciences and the Law, 24*, 659–671.

Rogers, R. (2003). Forensic use and abuse of psychological tests: Multiscale inventories. *Journal of Psychiatric Practice, 9*, 316–320.

Ruocco, A. C., Swirsky-Sacchetti, T., Chute, D., Mandel, S., Platek, S. M., & Zillmer, E. A. (2008). Distinguishing between neuropsychological malingering and exaggerated psychiatric symptoms in a neuropsychological setting. *The Clinical Neuropsychologist, 22*, 547–564.

Schoenberg, M. R., Dorr, D., & Morgan, C. D. (2003). The ability of the Millon Clinical Multiaxial Inventory–Third Edition to detect malingering. *Psychological Assessment, 15*, 198–204.

MMPI/MMPI–2

Arbisi, P. A., Ben-Porath, Y. S., & McNulty, J. (2003). Refinement of the MMPI-2 F(p) scale is not necessary: A response to Gass and Luis. *Assessment, 10*, 123–128.

Arbisi, P. A., Ben-Porath, Y. S., & McNulty, J. (2006). The ability of the MMPI-2 to detect feigned PTSD within the context of compensation seeking. *Psychological Services, 3*, 249–261.

Arbisi, P. A., Murdoch, M., Fortier, L., & McNulty, J. (2004). MMPI-2 Validity and award of service connection for PTSD during the VA Compensation and Pension Evaluation. *Psychological Services, 1*, 56–67.

Bacchiochi, J. R., & Bagby, R. M. (2006). Development and validation of the Malingering Discriminant Function Index for the MMPI-2. *Journal of Personality Assessment, 87*, 51–61.

Bagby, R. M., & Marshall, M. B. (2004). Assessing underreporting response bias on the MMPI-2. *Assessment, 11*, 115–126.

Bagby, R. M., Marshall, M. B., & Bacchiochi, J. R. (2005). The validity and clinical utility of the MMPI-2 malingering depression scale. *Journal of Personality Assessment, 85*, 304–311.

Bagby, R. M., Nicholson, R. A., Bacchiochi, J. R., Ryder, A. G., & Bury, A. (2002). The predictive capacity of the MMPI-2 and PAI validity scales and index to detect coached and uncoached feigning. *Journal of Personality Assessment, 78*, 69–86.

Bagby, R. M., Nicholson, R. A., Buis, T., & Bacchiochi, J. R. (2000). Can the MMPI-2 validity scales detect depression feigned by experts? *Assessment, 7*, 55–62.

Berry, D., Baer, R., & Harris, M. (1991). Detection of malingering on the MMPI: A meta-analysis. *Clinical Psychology Review, 11*, 585–598.

Bianchini, K. J., Curtis, K. L., & Greve, K. W. (2006). Compensation and malingering in traumatic brain injury: A dose-response relationship? *The Clinical Neuropsychologist, 20*, 831–847.

Bianchini, K., Houston, R., Greve, K., Irvin, R., Black, F. W., Swift, D., & Tamimie, R. (2003). Malingered neurocognitive dysfunction in neurotoxic exposure: An application of the Slick criteria. *Journal of Occupational and Environmental Medicine, 45*, 1087–1099.

Binder, L. M., Storzbach, D., & Salinsky, M. C. (2006). MMPI-2 profiles of persons with multiple chemical sensitivity. *The Clinical Neuropsychologist, 20*, 848–857.

Boone, K. B., & Lu, P. H. (1999). Impact of somatoform symptomatology on credibility of cognitive performance. *The Clinical Neuropsychologist, 13*, 414–419.

Braxton, L. E., Calhoun, P. S., Williams, J. E., & Boggs, C. D. (2007). Validity rates of the Personality Assessment Inventory and the Minnesota Multiphasic Personality Inventory-2 in a VA Medical Center setting. *Journal of Personality Assessment, 88*, 5–15.

Bury, A. S., & Bagby, R. M. (2002). The detection of feigned uncoached and coached posttraumatic stress disorder with the MMPI-2 in a sample of workplace accident victims. *Psychological Assessment, 14*, 472–484.

Butcher, J. N., Dahlstrom, W. G., Graham, J. R., Tellegen, A., & Kaemmer, B. (1989). *MMPI-2 manual for administration and scoring*. Minneapolis: University of Minnesota Press.

Clark, M. E., Gironda, R. J., & Young, R.W. (2003). Detection of back random responding: Effectiveness of MMPI-2 and Personality Assessment Inventory validity indices. *Psychological Assessment, 15*, 223–234.

Clifford, D., Byrne, M. K., & Allan, C. (2004). Getting caught in court: Base rates for malingering in Australasian litigants. *Psychiatry, Psychology, and the Law, 11*, 197–201.

Cramer, K. M. (1995). The effects of description clarity and disorder type on MMPI-2 fake-bad validity indices. *Journal of Clinical Psychology, 51*, 831–840.

Crawford, E. F., Greene, R. L., Dupart, T. M., Bongar, B., & Childs, H. (2006). MMPI-2 assessment of malingered emotional distress related to a workplace injury: A mixed group validation. *Journal of Personality Assessment, 86*, 217–221.

Cukrowicz, K. C., Reardon, M. L., Donohue, K. F., & Joiner, T. E. (2004). MMPI-2 F scale as a predictor of acute versus chronic disorder classification. *Assessment, 11*, 145–151.

Dearth, C. S., Berry, T. R., Vickery, C. D., Vagnini, V. L., Baser, R. E., Orey, S. A., & Cragar, D. E. (2005). Detection of feigned head injury symptoms on the MMPI-2 in head injured patients and community controls. *Archives of Clinical Neuropsychology, 20*, 95–110.

Downing, S. K., Denney, R. L., Spray, B. J., Houston, C. M., & Halfaker, D. A. (2008). Examining the relationship between the Reconstructed Clinical Scales and the Fake Bad Scale of the MMPI-2. *The Clinical Neuropsychologist, 22*, 680–688.

Dush, D., Simons, L., Platt, M., Nation, P., & Ayres, S. (1994). Psychological profiles distinguishing litigating and nonlitigating pain patients: Subtle and not so subtle. *Journal of Personality Assessment, 62*, 299–313.

Elhai, J. D. (2001). "Cross-validation of the MMPI-2 in detecting malingered post-traumatic stress disorder": Errata. *Journal of Personality Assessment, 77*, 189.

Elhai, J. D., & Frueh, B.C. (2001). Subtypes of clinical presentations in malingerers of posttraumatic stress disorder: An MMPI-2 cluster anyalysis. *Assessment, 8*, 75–84.

Elhai, J. D., Gold, P. B., Frueh, B. C., & Gold, S. N. (2000). Cross-validation of the MMPI-2 in detecting malingered posttraumatic stress disorder. *Journal of Personality Assessment, 75*, 449–463.

Elhai, J. D., Gold, S. N., Sellers, A. H., & Dorfman, W. I. (2001). The detection of malingered posttraumatic stress disorder with MMPI-2 Fake Bad Indices. *Assessment, 8*, 221–236.

Elhai, J. D., Naifeh, J. A., Zucker, I. S., et al. (2004). Discriminating malingered from genuine civilian posttraumatic stress disorder: A validation of three MMPI-2 infrequency scales (F, Fp, and Fpstd): Erratum. *Assessment, 11*, 271–271.

Farkas, M. R., Rosenfeld, B., Robbins, R., & van Gorp, W. (2006). Do tests of malingering concur? Concordance among malingering measures. *Behavioral Sciences and the Law, 24*, 659–671.

Fox, D. D., Gerson, A., & Lees-Haley, P. R. (1995). Interrelationship of MMPI-2 validity scales in personal injury claims. *Journal of Clinical Psychology, 51*, 42–47.

Gassen, M. D., Pietz, C. A., Spray, B. J., & Denney, R. L. (2007). Accuracy of Megargee's Criminal Offender Infrequency (FC) Scale in detecting malingering among forensic examinees. *Criminal Justice and Behavior*, *34*, 493–504.

Gervais, R. O., Ben-Porath, Y. S., Wygant, D. B., & Green, P. (2007). Development and validation of a Response Bias Scale (RBS) for the MMPI-2. *Assessment*, *14* (2), 196–208.

Greiffenstein, M. F., & Baker, W. J. (2008). Validity testing in dually diagnosed post-traumatic stress disorder and mild closed head injury. *The Clinical Neuropsychologist*, *22*, 565–582.

Greiffenstein, M. F., Baker, W. J., Axelrod, B., Peck, E. A., & Gervais, R. (2004). The fake bad scale and MMPI-2 F-family in detection of implausible psychological trauma claims. *The Clinical Neuropsychologist*, *18*, 573–590.

Greiffenstein, M. F., Baker, W. J., Gola, T., Donders, J., & Miller, L. J. (2002). The FBS in atypical and severe closed head injury litigants. *Journal of Clinical Psychology*, *58*, 1591–1600.

Greiffenstein, M. F., Fox, D., & Lees-Haley, P. R. (2007). The MMPI-2 Fake Bad Scale in detection of noncredible brain injury claims. In K. B. Boone (Ed.), *Assessment of feigned cognitive impairment: A neuropsychological perspective* (pp. 210–235). New York: Guilford Press.

Greiffenstein, M. F., Gola, T., & Baker, W. J. (1995). MMPI-2 validity scales versus domain specific measures in detection of factitious traumatic brain injury. *The Clinical Neuropsychologist*, *9*, 230–240.

Greve, K., Bianchini, K., Love, J., Brennan, A., & Heinly, M. (2006). Sensitivity and specificity of MMPI-2 validity scales and indicators to malingered neurocognitive dysfunction in traumatic brain injury. *The Clinical Neuropsychologist*, *20*, 491–512.

Grillo, J., Brown, R., Hilsabeck, R., Price, J. R., & Lees-Haley, P. (1994). Raising doubts about claims of malingering: Implications of relationships between MCM-II and MMPI-2 performances. *Journal of Clinical Psychology*, *50*, 651–655.

Guez, M., Brannstrom, R., Nyberg, L., Toolanen, G., & Hildingsson, C. (2005). Neuropsychological functioning and MMPI-2 profiles in chronic neck pain: A comparison of whiplash and non-traumatic groups. *Journal of Clinical and Experimental Neuropsychology*, *27*, 151–163.

Henry, G. K., Heilbronner, R. L., Mittenberg, W., & Enders, C. (2006). The Henry-Heilbronner Index: A 15-item empirically derived MMPI-2 subscale for identifying probable malingering in personal injury litigants and disability claimants. *The Clinical Neuropsychologist*, *20*, 786–797.

Henry, G. K., Heilbronner, R. L., Mittenberg, W., Enders, C., & Roberts, D. M. (2008). Empirical derivation of a new MMPI-2 scale for identifying probable malingering in personal injury litigants and disability claimants: The 15-Item Malingered Mood Disorder Scale (MMDS). *The Clinical Neuropsychologist*, *22*, 158–168.

Henry, G. K., Heilbronner, R. L., Mittenberg, W., Enders, C., & Stanczak, S. R. (in press). Comparison of the Lees-Haley Fake Bad Scale, Henry-Heilbronner Index, and Restructured Clinical Scale 1 in identifying noncredible symptom reporting. *The Clinical Neuropsychologist*.

Iverson, G. L., & Binder, L. M., (2000). Detecting exaggeration and malingering in neuropsychological assessment. *Journal of Head Trauma Rehabilitation*, *15*, 829–858.

Iverson, G. L., Henrichs, T. F., Barton, E. A., & Allen, S. (2002). Specificity of the MMPI-2 Fake Bad Scale as a marker for personal injury malingering. *Psychological Reports*, *90*, 131–136.

Larrabee, G. J. (1997). Neuropsychological outcome, post concussion symptoms, and forensic considerations in mild closed head trauma. *Seminars in Clinical Neuropsychiatry*, *2*, 196–206.

Larrabee, G. J. (1998). Somatic malingering on the MMPI and MMPI-2 in personal injury litigants. *The Clinical Neuropsychologist*, *12*, 179–188.

Larrabee, G. J. (2003). Exaggerated pain report in litigants with malingered neurocognitive dysfunction. *The Clinical Neuropsychologist*, *17*, 395–401.

Larrabee, G. J. (2003). Detection of malingering using atypical performance patterns on standard neuropsychological tests. *The Clinical Neuropsychologist*, *17*, 410–425.

Larrabee, G. J. (2003). Detection of symptom exaggeration with the MMPI-2 in litigants with malingered neurocognitive dysfunction. *The Clinical Neuropsychologist*, *17*, 54–68.

Larrabee, G. J. (2003). Exaggerated MMPI-2 symptom report in personal injury litigants with malingered neurocognitive deficit. *Archives of Clinical Neuropsychology*, *18*, 673–686.

Lees-Haley, P.R. (1992). Efficacy of MMPI-2 validity scales and MCMI-II modifier scales for detecting spurious PTSD claims: F, F-K, Fake Bad Scale, ego strength, subtle-obvious subscales, DIS, and DEB. *Journal of Clinical Psychology*, *48*, 681–689.

Lees-Haley, P. R. (1997). MMPI-2 base rates for 492 personal injury plaintiffs: Implications and challenges for forensic assessment. *Journal of Clinical Psychology, 53*, 745–755.

Lees-Haley, P. R., English, L. T., & Glenn, W. J. (1991). A Fake Bad Scale on the MMPI-2 for personal injury claimants. *Psychological Reports, 68*, 203–210.

Lees-Haley, P. R., Iverson, G. L., Lange, R. T., Fox, D. D., & Allen, L. M. (2002). Malingering in forensic neuropsychology: Daubert and the MMPI-2. *Journal of Forensic Neuropsychology, 3*, 167–203.

Lewis, J. L., Simcox, A. M., & Berry, D. T. R. (2002). Screening for feigned psychiatric symptoms in a forensic sample by using the MMPI-2 and the Structured Inventory of Malingered Symptomatology. *Psychological Assessment, 14*, 170–176.

Marshall, M. B., & Bagby, R. M. (2006). The incremental validity and clinical utility of the MMPI-2 Infrequency Posttraumatic Stress Disorder Scale. *Assessment, 13*, 417–429.

Martens, M., Donders, J. D., & Millis, S. R. (2001). Evaluation of invalid response set after traumatic head injury. *Journal of Forensic Neuropsychology, 2*, 1–18.

McCaffrey, R., O'Bryant, S., Ashendorf, L., & Fisher, J. (2003). Correlations among the TOMM, Rey-15, and MMPI-2 validity scales in a sample of TBI litigants. *Journal of Forensic Neuropsychology, 3*, 45–53.

Meyers, J. E., Millis, S. R., & Volkert, K. (2002). A validity index for the MMPI-2. *Archives of Clinical Neuropsychology, 17*, 157–169.

Miller, L. J., & Donders, J. (2001). Subjective symptomology after traumatic head injury. *Brain Injury, 15*, 297–304.

Nelson, N. W., Parsons, T. D., Grote, C. L., Smith, C. A., & Sisung, J. (2006). The MMPI-2 Fake Bad Scale: Concordance and specificity of true and estimated scores. *Journal of Clinical and Experimental Neuropsychology, 28*, 1–12.

Nelson, N. W., Sweet, J. J., Berry, D. T. R., Bryant, F. B., & Granacher, R. P. (2007). Response validity in forensic neuropsychology: Exploratory factor analytic evidence of distinct cognitive and psychological constructs. *Journal of the International Neuropsychological Society, 13* (3), 440–449.

Nelson, N. W., Sweet, J. J., & Demakis, G. J. (2006). Meta-analysis of the MMPI-2 Fake Bad Scale: Utility in forensic practice. *The Clinical Neuropsychologist, 20*, 39–58.

Nelson, N. W., Sweet, J. J., & Heilbronner, R. (2007). Examination of the new MMPI-2 Response Bias Scale (Gervais): Relationship with MMPI-2 validity scales. *Journal of Clinical and Experimental Neuropsychology 29*, 67–72.

Pope, K. S., Butcher, J. N., & Seelen, J. (2000). *The MMPI, MMPI-2, & MMPI-A in court.* Washington, DC: American Psychological Association.

Posthuma, A. B., & Harper, J. F. (1998). Comparison of MMPI-2 responses of child custody and personal injury litigants. *Professional Psychology: Research and Practice, 29*, 437–443.

Rogers, R. (2003). Forensic use and abuse of psychological tests: Multiscale inventories. *Journal of Psychiatric Practice, 9*, 316–320.

Rogers, R., Sewell, K. W., Martin, M. A., & Vitacco, M. J. (2003). Detection of feigned mental disorders: A meta-analysis of the MMPI-2 and malingering. *Assessment, 10*, 160–177.

Rogers, R., Sewell, K. W., & Ustad, L. L. (1995). Feigning among chronic outpatients on the MMPI-2: A systematic examination of fake-bad indicators. *Assessment, 2*, 81–89.

Ross, S. R., Millis, S. R., Krukowski, R. A., Putnam, S. H., & Adams, K. M. (2004). Detecting incomplete effort on the MMPI-2: An examination of the Fake Bad Scale in mild head injury. *Journal of Clinical and Experimental Neuropsychology, 26*, 115–124.

Ross, S. R., Putnam, S. H., & Adams, K. M. (2006). Psychological disturbance, incomplete effort, and compensation-seeking status as predictors of neuropsychological test performance in head injury. *Journal of Clinical and Experimental Neuropsychology, 28*, 111–125.

Ross, S. R., Putnam, S. H., Millis, S. R., Adams, K. M., & Krukowski, R. A. (2006). Detecting insufficient effort using the Seashore Rhythm and Speech-Sounds Perception Tests in head injury. *The Clinical Neuropsychologist, 20*, 798–815.

Rothke, S. E., Friedman, A. F., Dahlstrom, W. G., Greene, R. L., Arredondo, R., & Mann, A. W. (1994). MMPI-2 normative data for the F-K Index: Implications for clinical, neuropsychological, and forensic practice. *Assessment, 1*, 1–15.

Rothke, S. E., Friedman, A. F., Jaffe, A. M., Greene, R. L., Wetter, M. W., Cole, P., & Baker, K. (2000). Normative data for the F(p) Scale of the MMPI-2: Implications for clinical and forensic assessment of malingering. *Psychological Assessment, 12*, 335–340.

Slick, D. J., Hopp, G., Strauss, E., & Spellacy, F. J. (1996). Victoria Symptom Validity Test: Efficiency for detecting feigned memory impairment and relationship to neuropsychological tests and MMPI-2 validity scales. *Journal of Clinical and Experimental Neuropsychology*, *18*, 911–922.

Staudenmayer, H., & Phillips, S. (2007). MMPI-2 validity, clinical and content scales, and the Fake Bad Scale for personal injury litigants claiming idiopathic environmental intolerance. *Journal of Psychosomatic Research*, *62*, 61–72.

Stone, D. C., Boone, K. B., Back-Madruga, C., & Lesser, I. M. (2006). Has the rolling uterus finally gathered moss? Somatization and malingering of cognitive dysfunction in six cases of "toxic mold" exposure. *The Clinical Neuropsychologist*, *20*, 766–785.

Strong, D. R., Glassmire, D. M., Frederick, R. I., & Greene, R. L. (2006). Evaluating the latent structure of the MMPI-2 F(p) Scale in a forensic sample: A taxometric analysis. *Psychological Assessment*, *18*, 250–261.

Sweet, J., Malina, A., & Ecklund-Johnson, E. (2006). Application of the new MMPI-2 Malingered Depression Scale to individuals undergoing neuropsychological evaluation: Relative lack of relationship to secondary gain and failure on validity indices. *The Clinical Neuropsychologist*, *20*, 541–551.

Temple, R., McBride, A., Horner, M., & Taylor, R. (2003). Personality characteristics of patients showing suboptimal cognitive effort. *The Clinical Neuropsychologist*, *17*, 402–409.

Tsushima, W. T., & Tsushima, V. G. (2001). Comparison of the Fake Bad Scale and other MMPI-2 validity scales with personal injury litigants. *Assessment*, *8*, 205–212.

Vagnini, V. L., Sollman, M. J., Berry, D. T. R., Granacher, R. P., Clark, J. A., Burton, R., O'Brien, M., Bacon, E., & Saier, J. (2006). Known-groups cross-validation of the Letter Memory Test in a compensation-seeking mixed neurologic sample. *The Clinical Neuropsychologist*, *20*, 289–304.

Van Gaasbeek, J. K., Denney, R. L., & Harmon, J. (2001). Another look at an MMPI-2 neurocorrective factor in forensic cases: Utility of the Fake Bad Scale. *Archives of Clinical Neuropsychology*.

Wygant, D. B., Sellbom, M., Ben-Porath, Y. S., Stafford, K. P., Freeman, D. B., & Heilbronner, R. L. (2007). The relation between symptom validity testing and MMPI-2 scores as a function of forensic evaluation context. *Archives of Clinical Neuropsychology*, *22*, 489–499.

Youngjohn, J., Davis, D., & Wolf, I. (1997). Head injury and the MMPI-2: Paradoxical severity effects and the influence of litigation. *Psychological Assessment*, *9*, 177–184.

Multiple ability tests

Bianchini, K. J., Curtis, K. L., & Greve, K. W. (2006). Compensation and malingering in traumatic brain injury: A dose-response relationship? *The Clinical Neuropsychologist*, *20*, 831–847.

Bianchini, K., Houston, R., Greve, K., Irvin, R., Black, F. W., Swift, D., & Tamimie, R. (2003). Malingered neurocognitive dysfunction in neurotoxic exposure: An application of the Slick criteria. *Journal of Occupational and Environmental Medicine*, *45*, 1087–1099.

Binder, L. M., Kelly, M. P., Villanueva, M. R., & Winslow, M. M. (2003). Motivation and neuropsychological test performance following mild head injury. *Journal of Clinical and Experimental Neuropsychology*, *25*, 420–430.

Boone, K. B., & Lu, P. (2003). Noncredible cognitive performance in the context of severe brain injury. *The Clinical Neuropsychologist*, *17*, 244–254.

Cato, M. A., Brewster, J., Ryan, T., & Giuliano, A. J. (2002). Coaching and the ability to simulate mild traumatic brain injury symptoms. *The Clinical Neuropsychologist*, *16*, 524–535.

Green, P., Rohling, M., Lees-Haley, P., & Allen, L. M. (2001). Effort has a greater effect on test scores than severe brain injury in compensation claimants. *Brain Injury*, *15*, 1045–1060.

Greiffenstein, M. F., Baker, W. J., & Gola, T. (1996). Motor dysfunction profiles in traumatic brain injury and postconcussion syndrome. *Journal of the International Neuropsychological Society*, *2*, 477–485.

Haines, M. E., & Norris, M. P. (2001). Comparing student and patient simulated malingerers' performance on standard neuropsychological measures to detect feigned cognitive deficits. *The Clinical Neuropsychologist*, *15*, 171–182.

Harrison, A. G., Edwards, M. J., & Parker, K. C. H. (2007). Identifying students faking ADHD: Preliminary findings and strategies for detection. *Archives of Clinical Neuropsychology*, *22*, 577–588.

Larrabee, G. J. (2003). Detection of malingering using atypical performance patterns on standard neuropsychological tests. *The Clinical Neuropsychologist*, *17*, 410–425.

Larrabee, G. J. (2008). Aggregation across multiple indicators improves the detection of malingering: Relationship to likelihood ratios. *The Clinical Neuropsychologist, 22*, 666–679.

Meyers, J. E., & Volbrecht, M. E. (2003). Validation of multiple malingering detection methods in a large clinical sample. *Archives of Clinical Neuropsychology, 18*, 261–276.

Nelson, N. W., Boone, K., Dueck, A., Wagener, L., Lu, P., & Grills, C. (2003). Relationships between eight measures of suspect effort. *The Clinical Neuropsychologist, 17*, 263–272.

Pachana, N. A., Boone, K. B., & Ganzell, S. L. (1998). False positive errors on selected tests of malingering. *American Journal of Forensic Psychology, 16*, 17–25.

Rapport, L., Farchione, T., Coleman, R., & Axelrod, B. (1998). Effects of coaching on malingered motor function profiles. *Journal of Clinical and Experimental Neuropsychology, 20*, 89–97.

Ross, S. R., Putnam, S. H., Millis, S. R., Adams, K. M., & Krukowski, R. A. (2006). Detecting insufficient effort using the Seashore Rhythm and Speech-Sounds Perception Tests in head injury. *The Clinical Neuropsychologist, 20*, 798–815.

Schwarz, L. R., Gfeller, J. D., & Oliveri, M. V. (2006). Detecting feigned impairment with the digit span and vocabulary subtests of the Wechsler Adult Intelligence Scale–Third Edition. *The Clinical Neuropsychologist, 20*, 741–753.

Sherman, D. S., Boone, K. B., Lu, P., & Razani, J. (2002). Re-examination of a Rey Auditory Verbal Learning Test/Rey Complex Figure discriminant function to detect suspect effort. *The Clinical Neuropsychologist, 16*, 242–250.

Shum, D. H. K., O'Gorman, J. G., & Alpar, A. (2004). Effects of incentive and preparation time on performance and classification accuracy of standard and malingering-specific memory tests. *Archives of Clinical Neuropsychology, 19*, 817–823.

Stone, D. C., Boone, K. B., Back-Madruga, C., & Lesser, I. M. (2006). Has the rolling uterus finally gathered moss? Somatization and malingering of cognitive dysfunction in six cases of "toxic mold" exposure. *The Clinical Neuropsychologist, 20*, 766–785.

Vagnini, V. L., Sollman, M., J., Berry, D. T. R., Granacher, R. P., Clark, J. A., Burton, R., O'Brien, M., Bacon, E., & Saier, J. (2006). Known-groups cross-validation of the Letter Memory Test in a compensation-seeking mixed neurologic sample. *The Clinical Neuropsychologist, 20*, 289–304.

van Gorp, W. G., Humphrey, L. A., Kalechstein, A., Brumm, V. L., McMullen, W. J., Stoddard, M., & Pachana, N. A. (1999). How well do standard clinical neuropsychological tests identify malingering? A preliminary analysis. *Journal of Clinical and Experimental Neuropsychology, 21*, 245–250.

Vickery, C., Berry, D. T. R., Dearth, C., Vagnini, V., Baser, R., Cragar, D., & Orey, S. (2004). Head injury and the ability to feign neuropsychological deficits. *Archives of Clinical Neuropsychology, 19*, 37–48.

Yantz, C. L., Gavett, B. E., Lynch, J. K., & McCaffrey, R. J. (2006). Potential for interpretation disparities of Halstead-Reitan neuropsychological battery performances in a litigating sample. *Archives of Clinical Neuropsychology, 21*, 809–817.

Personality Assessment Inventory (PAI)

Bagby, R. M., Nicholson, R. A., Bacchiochi, J. R., Ryder, A. G., & Bury, A. (2002). The predictive capacity of the MMPI-2 and PAI validity scales and index to detect coached and uncoached feigning. *Journal of Personality Assessment, 78*, 69–86.

Baity, M. R., Siefert, C. J., Chambers, A., & Blais, M. A. (2007). Deceptiveness on the PAI: A study of naïve faking with psychiatric inpatients. *Journal of Personality Assessment, 88*, 16–24.

Blanchard, D. D., McGrath, R. E., & Pogge, D. L. (2003). A comparison of the PAI and MMPI-2 as predictors of faking bad in college students. *Journal of Personality Assessment, 80*, 197–205.

Boccacini, M., Murrie, D., & Duncan, S. (2006). Screening for malingering in a criminal-forensic sample with the Personality Assessment Inventory. *Psychological Assessment, 18*, 415–423.

Braxton, L. E., Calhoun, P. S., Williams, J. E., & Boggs, C. D. (2007). Validity rates of the Personality Assessment Inventory and the Minnesota Multiphasic Personality Inventory-2 in a VA Medical Center setting. *Journal of Personality Assessment, 88*, 5–15.

Clark, M. E., Gironda, R. J., & Young, R. W. (2003). Detection of back random responding: Effectiveness of MMPI-2 and Personality Assessment Inventory validity indices. *Psychological Assessment, 15*, 223–234.

Douglas, K. S., Hart, S. D., & Kropp, R. P. (2001). Validity of the Personality Assessment Inventory for forensic assessments. *International Journal of Offender Therapy and Comparative Criminology, 45*, 183–197.

Edens, J. F., Poythress, N. G., & Watkins-Clay, M. M. (2007). Detection of malingering in psychiatric unit and general population prison inmates: A comparison of the PAI, SIMS, and SIRS. *Journal of Personality Assessment, 88*, 33–42.

Haggerty, K. A., Frazier, T. W., Busch, R. M., & Naugle, R. I. (2007). Relationships among Victoria Symptom Validity Test indices and Personality Assessment Inventory validity scales in a large clinical sample. *The Clinical Neuropsychologist, 21*, 917–928.

Hopwood, C. J., Morey, L. C., Rogers, R., & Sewell, K. (2007). Malingering on the Personality Assessment Inventory: Identification of specific feigned disorders. *Journal of Personality Assessment, 88*, 43–48.

Kucharski, L. T., Toomey, J. P., Fila, K., & Duncan, S. (2007). Detection of malingering of psychiatric disorder with the Personality Assessment Inventory: An investigation of criminal defendants. *Journal of Personality Assessment, 88*, 25–32.

Kurtz, J. E., Shealy, S. E., & Putnam, S. H. (2007). Another look at paradoxical severity effects in head injury with the Personality Assessment Inventory. *Journal of Personality Assessment, 88*, 66–73.

Peebles, J., & Moore, R. J. (1998). Detecting socially desirable responding with the Personality Assessment Inventory. The Positive Impression Management Scale and the Defensiveness Index. *Journal of Clinical Psychology, 54*, 621–628.

Rogers, R., Sewell, K. W., & Cruise, K. R. (1998). The PAI and feigning: A cautionary note on its use in forensic-correctional settings. *Assessment, 5*, 399–405.

Scragg, P., Bor, R., & Mendham, M. (2000). Feigning post-traumatic stress disorder on the PAI. *Clinical Psychology and Psychotherapy, 7*, 155–160.

Sumanti, M., Boone, K. B., Savodnik, I., & Gorsuch, R. (2006). Noncredible psychiatric and cognitive symptoms in a worker's compensation "stress" claim sample. *The Clinical Neuropsychologist, 20*, 754–765.

Paced Auditory Serial Attention Task

Bernstein, D. M., & de Ruiter, S. W. (2000). The influence of motivation on neurocognitive performance long after mild traumatic brain injury. *Brain and Cognition, 44*, 50–58.

Raven's Standard Progressive Matrices

Gudjonsson, G. H., & Shacleton, H. (1986). The pattern of scores on Raven's matrices during fake bad. *British Journal of Clinical Psychology, 25*, 35–41.

McKinzey, R. K., et al. (1999). Detection of malingering on Raven's standard progressive matrices. *British Journal of Clinical Psychology, 38*, 435–439.

Reliable Digit Span

Axelrod, B., Fichtenberg, N., Millis, S., & Wertheimer, J. (2006). Detecting incomplete effort with Digit Span from the Wechsler Adult Intelligence Scale–Third Edition. *The Clinical Neuropsychologist, 20*, 513–523.

Babikian, T., Boone, K. B., Lu, P., & Arnold, G. (2006). Sensitivity and specificity of various digit span scores in the detection of suspect effort. *The Clinical Neuropsychologist, 20*, 145–159.

Bianchini, K. J., Curtis, K. L., & Greve, K. W. (2006). Compensation and malingering in traumatic brain injury: A dose-response relationship? *The Clinical Neuropsychologist, 20*, 831–847.

Bianchini, K., Houston, R., Greve, K., Irvin, R., Black, F. W., Swift, D., & Tamimie, R. (2003). Malingered neurocognitive dysfunction in neurotoxic exposure: An application of the Slick criteria. *Journal of Occupational and Environmental Medicine, 45*, 1087–1099.

Bianchini, K., Love, J. M., Greve, K. W., & Adams, D. (2005). Detection and diagnosis of malingering in electrical injury. *Archives of Clinical Neuropsychology, 20*, 365–373.

Dean, A. C., Victor, T. L., Boone, K. B., & Arnold, G. (2008). The relationship of IQ to effort test performance. *The Clinical Neuropsychologist*, *22*, 705–722.

Duncan, S. A., & Ausborn, D. L. (2002). The use of reliable digits to detect malingering in a criminal forensic pretrial population. *Assessment*, *9*, 56–61.

Etherton, J., Bianchini, K., Ciota, M., & Greve, K. (2005). Reliable digit span is unaffected by laboratory-induced pain. *Assessment*, *12*, 101–106.

Etherton, J. L., Binachini, K. J., Ciota, M.A., & Greve, K. W. (2005). Reliable digit span is unaffected by laboratory-induced pain: Implications for clinical use. *Assessment*, *12*, 101–106.

Etherton, J. L., Bianchini, K. J., Greve, K. W., & Heinly, M. T. (2005). Sensitivity and specificity of reliable digit span in malingered pain-related disability. *Assessment*, *12*, 130–136.

Gorny, I., & Merten, T. (2005). Symptom information-warning-coaching: How do they affect successful feigning in neuropsychological assessment? *Journal of Forensic Neuropsychology*, *4*, 71–98.

Graue, L. O., Berry, D. T. R., Clark, J. A., Sollman, M. J., Cardi, M., Hopkins, J., & Werline, D. (2007). Identificatoin of feigned mental retardation using the new generation of malingering detection instruments: Preliminary findings. *The Clinical Neuropsychologist*, *21*, 929–942.

Greiffenstein, M. F., & Baker, W. J. (2008). Validity testing in dually diagnosed post-traumatic stress disorder and mild closed head injury. *The Clinical Neuropsychologist*, *22*, 565–582.

Greiffenstein, M., Baker, W. J., & Gola, T. (1994). Validation of malingered amnesia measures with a large clinical sample. *Psychological Assessment*, *6*, 218–224.

Iverson, G. L., & Tulsky, D. S. (2003). Detecting malingering on the WAIS-III: Unusual Digit Span performance patterns in the normal population and in clinical groups. *Archives of Clinical Neuropsychology*, *18*, 1–9.

Larrabee, G. J. (2003). Exaggerated pain report in litigants with malingered neurocognitive dysfunction. *The Clinical Neuropsychologist*, *17*, 395–401.

Larrabee, G. J. (2003). Detection of malingering using atypical performance patterns on standard neuropsychological tests. *The Clinical Neuropsychologist*, *17*, 410–425.

Marshall, P., & Happe, M. (2007). The performance of individuals with mental retardation on cognitive tests assessing effort and motivation. *The Clinical Neuropsychologist*, *21*, 826–840.

Mathias, C. W., Greve, K. W., Bianchini, K. J., Houston, R. J., & Crouch, J. A. (2002). Detecting malingered neurocognitive dysfunction using the Reliable Digit Span in traumatic brain injury. *Assessment*, *9*, 301–308.

Meyers, J. E., & Volbrecht, M. (1998). Validation of reliable digits for detection of malingering. *Assessment*, *5*, 303–307.

Meyers, J. E., & Volbrecht, M. E. (2003). Validation of multiple malingering detection methods in a large clinical sample. *Archives of Clinical Neuropsychology*, *18*, 261–276.

Ruocco, A. C., Swirsky-Sacchetti, T., Chute, D., Mandel, S., Platek, S. M., & Zillmer, E. A. (2008). Distinguishing between neuropsychological malingering and exaggerated psychiatric symptoms in a neuropsychological setting. *The Clinical Neuropsychologist*, *22*, 547–564.

Schwarz, L. R., Gfeller, J. D., & Oliveri, M. V. (2006). Detecting feigned impairment with the digit span and vocabulary subtests of the Wechsler Adult Intelligence Scale–Third Edition. *The Clinical Neuropsychologist*, *20*, 741–753.

Stone, D. C., Boone, K. B., Back-Madruga, C., & Lessr, I. M. (2006). Has the rolling uterus finally gathered moss? Somatization and malingering of cognitive dysfunction in six cases of "toxic mold" exposure. *The Clinical Neuropsychologist*, *20*, 766–785.

Strauss, E., Slick, D. J., Levy-Bencheton, J., Hunter, M., MacDonald, S. W. S., & Hultsch, D. F. (2002). Intraindividual variability as an indicator of malingering in head injury. *Archives of Clinical Neuropsychology*, *17*, 423–444.

Repeatable Battery for the Assessment of Neuropsychological Status (RBANS)

Silverberg, N. D., Wertheimer, J. C., & Fichtenberg, N. L. (2007). An effort index for the Repeatable Battery for the Assessment of Neuropsychological Status (RBANS). *The Clinical Neuropsychologist*, *21*, 841–854.

Rey Auditory Verbal Learning Test and variants

Barrash, J., Suhr, J., & Manzel, K. (2004). Detecting poor effort and malingering with an expanded version of the Auditory Verbal Learning Test (AVLTX): Validation with clinical samples. *Journal of Clinical and Experimental Neuropsychology*, *26*, 125–140.

Bernard, L. (1990). Prospects for faking believable memory deficits on neuropsychological tests and the use of incentives in simulation research. *Journal of Clinical and Experimental Neuropsychology*, *5*, 715–728.

Bernard, L. (1991). The detection of faked deficits on the Rey Auditory Verbal Learning Test: The effect of serial position. *Archives of Clinical Neuropsychology*, *6*, 81–88.

Bernard, L., Houston, W., & Natoli, L. (1993). Malingering on neuropsychological memory tests: Potential objective indicators. *Journal of Clinical Psychology*, *49*, 45–53.

Binder, L., Kelly, M., Villanueva, M., & Winslow, M. (2003). Motivation and neuropsychological test performance following mild head injury. *Journal of Clinical and Experimental Neuropsychology*, *25*, 420–430.

Binder, L., Villanueva, M., Howieson, D., & Moore, R. (1993). The Rey AVLT recognition memory task measures motivational impairment after mild head trauma. *Archives of Clinical Neuropsychology*, *8*, 137–147.

Boone, K. B., Lu, P., & Wen, J. (2005). Comparison of various RAVLT scores in the detection of noncredible memory performance. *Archives of Clinical Neuropsychology*, *20*, 301–320.

Chouinard, M., & Rouleau, I. (1997). The 48-Pictures Test: A two-alternative forced-choice recognition test for the detection of malingering. *Journal of the International Neuropsychological Society*, *3*, 545–552.

Dean, A. C., Victor, T. L., Boone, K. B., & Arnold, G. (2008). The relationship of IQ to effort test performance. *The Clinical Neuropsychologist*, *22*, 705–722.

Frederick, R. I. (2000). A personal floor effect strategy to evaluate the validity of performance on memory tasks. *Journal of Clinical and Experimental Neuropsychology*, *22*, 720–730.

Greiffenstein, M., Baker, W. J., & Gola, T. (1994). Validation of malingered amnesia measures with a large clinical sample. *Psychological Assessment*, *6*, 218–224.

Greiffenstein, M., Baker, W. J., & Gola, T. (1996). Comparison of multiple scoring methods for Rey's malingered amnesia measures. *Archives of Clinical Neuropsychology*, *11*, 283–293.

Haines, M. E., & Norris, M. P. (2001). Comparing student and patient simulated malingerers' performance on standard neuropsychological measures to detect feigned cognitive deficits. *The Clinical Neuropsychologist*, *15*, 171–182.

King, J. H., Gfeller, J. G., & Davis, H. P. (1998). Detecting simulated memory impairment with the Rey Auditory Verbal Learning Test: Implications of base rates and study generalizability. *Journal of Clinical and Experimental Neuropsychology*, *20*, 603–612.

Meyers, J. E., Morrison, A. L., & Miller, J. C. (2001). How low is too low, revisited: Sentence repetition and AVLT-Recognition in the detection of malingering. *Applied Neuropsychology*, *8*, 234–241.

Meyers, J. E., & Volbrecht, M. E. (2003). Validation of multiple malingering detection methods in a large clinical sample. *Archives of Clinical Neuropsychology*, *18*, 261–276.

Nelson, N. W., Boone, K., Dueck. A., Wagener, L., Lu, P., & Grills, C. (2003). Relationships between eight measures of suspect effort. *The Clinical Neuropsychologist*, *17*, 263–272.

Pachana, N. A., Boone, K. B., & Ganzell, S. L. (1998). False positive errors on selected tests of malingering. *American Journal of Forensic Psychology*, *16*, 17–25.

Powell, M. R., Gfeller, J. D., Oliveri, M. V., Stanton, S., & Hendricks, B. (2004). The Rey AVLT serial position effect: A useful indicator of symptom exaggeration? *The Clinical Neuropsychologist*, *18*, 465–476.

Sherman, D. S., Boone, K. B., Lu, P., & Razani, J. (2002). Re-examination of a Rey Auditory Verbal Learning Test/Rey Complex Figure discriminant function to detect suspect effort. *The Clinical Neuropsychologist*, *16*, 242–250.

Silverberg, N., & Barrash, J. (2005). Further validation of the expanded Auditory Verbal Learning Test for detecting poor effort and response bias: Data from temporal lobectomy candidates. *Journal of Clinical and Experimental Neuropsychology*, *27*, 907–914.

Stone, D. C., Boone, K. B., Back-Madruga, C., & Lessr, I. M. (2006). Has the rolling uterus finally gathered moss? Somatization and malingering of cognitive dysfunction in six cases of "toxic mold" exposure. *The Clinical Neuropsychologist*, *20*, 766–785.

Suhr, J. A. (2002). Malingering, coaching, and the serial position effect. *Archives of Clinical Neuropsychology*, *17*, 69–77.

Suhr, J. A., & Gunstad, J. (2000). The effects of coaching on the sensitivity and specificity of malingering measures. *Archives of Clinical Neurpsychology*, *15*, 415–424.

Suhr, J., Gunstad, J., Greub, B., & Barrash, J. (2004). Exaggeration Index for an expanded version of the Auditory Verbal Learning Test: Robustness to coaching. *Journal of Clinical and Experimental Neuropsychology*, *26*, 416–427.

Suhr, J., Tranel, D., Wefel, J., & Barrash, J. (1997). Memory performance after head injury: Contributions of malingering, litigation status, psychological factors, and medication use. *Journal of Clinical and Experimental Neuropsychology*, *19*, 500–514.

Sullivan, K., Deffenti, C., & Keane, B. (2002). Malingering on the RAVLT part II. Detection strategies. *Archives of Clinical Neuropsychology*, *17*, 223–233.

Sullivan, K., Keane, B., & Deffenti, C. (2001). Malingering on the RAVLT Part I. Deterrence strategies. *Archives of Clinical Neuropsychology*, *16*, 627–641.

Rey Complex Figure

Chouinard, M., & Rouleau, I. (1997). The 48-Pictures Test: A two-alternative forced-choice recognition test for the detection of malingering. *Journal of the International Neuropsychological Society*, *3*, 545–552.

Dean, A. C., Victor, T. L., Boone, K. B., & Arnold, G. (2008). The relationship of IQ to effort test performance. *The Clinical Neuropsychologist*, *22*, 705–722.

Demakis, G. J. (1999). Serial malingering on verbal and nonverbal fluency and memory measures: An analogue investigation. *Archives of Clinical Neuropsychology*, *14*, 401–410.

Gorny, I., & Merten, T. (2005). Symptom information-warning-coaching: How do they affect successful feigning in neuropsychological assessment? *Journal of Forensic Neuropsychology*, *4*, 71–98.

Lu, P., Boone, K. B., Cozolino, L., & Mitchell, C. (2003). Effectiveness of the Rey-Osterrieth Complex Figure Test and the Meyers and Meyers recognition trial in the detection of suspect effort. *The Clinical Neuropsychologist*, *17*, 426–440.

Merten, T., Green, P., Henry, M., Blaskewitz, N., & Brockhaus, R. (2005). Analog validation of German-language symptom validity tests and the influence of coaching. *Archives of Clinical Neuropsychology*, *20*, 719–726.

Meyers, J. E., & Volbrecht, M. (1999). Detection of malingering using the Rey Complex Firgure and Recognition Trial. *Applied Neuropsychology*, *6*, 201–207.

Meyers, J. E., & Volbrecht, M. E. (2003). Validation of multiple malingering detection methods in a large clinical sample. *Archives of Clinical Neuropsychology*, *18*, 261–276.

Nelson, N. W., Boone, K., Dueck. A., Wagener, L., Lu, P., & Grills, C. (2003). Relationships between eight measures of suspect effort. *The Clinical Neuropsychologist*, *17*, 263–272.

Sherman, D. S., Boone, K. B., Lu, P., & Razani, J. (2002). Re-examination of a Rey Auditory Verbal Learning Test/Rey Complex Figure discriminant function to detect suspect effort. *The Clinical Neuropsychologist*, *16*, 242–250.

Ruff Figural Fluency

Demakis, G. J. (1999). Serial malingering on verbal and nonverbal fluency and memory measures: An analogue investigation. *Archives of Clinical Neuropsychology*, *14*, 401–410.

Seashore Rhythm Test

Gfeller, J., & Cradock, M. (1998). Detecting feigned neuropsychological impairment with the Seashore Rhythm Test. *Journal of Clinical Psychology*, *54*, 431–438.

Ross, S. R., Putnam, S. H., Millis, S. R., Adams, K. M., & Krukowski, R. A. (2006). Detecting insufficient effort using the Seashore Rhythm and Speech-Sounds Perception Tests in head injury. *The Clinical Neuropsychologist*, *20*, 798–815.

Trueblood, W., & Schmidt, M. (1993). Malingering and other validity considerations in the neuropsychological evaluation of mild head injury. *Journal of Clinical and Experimental Neuropsychology*, *15*, 578–590.

Yantz, C. L., Gavett, B. E., Lynch, J. K., & McCaffrey, R. J. (2006). Potential for interpretation disparities of Halstead-Reitan neuropsychological battery performances in a litigating sample. *Archives of Clinical Neuropsychology*, *21*, 809–817.

Sensory-Perceptual Exam (selected portions)

Binder, L. (1992). Malingering detected by forced choice testing of memory and tactile sensation: A case report. *Archives of Clinical Neuropsychology*, *7*, 155–163.

Binder, L., Kelly, M., Villanueva, M., & Winslow, M. (2003). Motivation and neuropsychological test performance following mild head injury. *Journal of Clinical and Experimental Neuropsychology*, *25*, 420–430.

Binder, L., & Willis, S. (1991). Assessment of motivation after financially compensable minor head trauma. *Psychological Assessment: A Journal of Consulting and Clinical Psychology*, *3*, 175–181.

Heaton, R., Smith, H., Lehman, R., & Vogt, A. (1978). Prospects for faking believable deficits on neuropsychological testing. *Journal of Consulting and Clinical Psychology*, *46*, 892–900.

Ross, S. R., Putnam, S. H., Millis, S. R., Adams, K. M., & Krukowski, R. A. (2006). Detecting insufficient effort using the Seashore Rhythm and Speech-Sounds Perception Tests in head injury. *The Clinical Neuropsychologist*, *20*, 798–815.

Trueblood, W., & Schmidt, M. (1993). Malingering and other validity considerations in the neuropsychological evaluation of mild head injury. *Journal of Clinical and Experimental Neuropsychology*, *15*, 578–590.

Yantz, C. L., Gavett, B. E., Lynch, J. K., & McCaffrey, R. J. (2006). Potential for interpretation disparities of Halstead-Reitan neuropsychological battery performances in a litigating sample. *Archives of Clinical Neuropsychology*, *21*, 809–817.

Stroop Color-Word Test

Lu, P., Boone, K. B., Jimenez, N., & Razani, J. (2004). Failure to inhibit the reading response on the Stroop Test: A pathognomonic indicator of suspect effort. *Journal of Clinical and Experimental Neuropsychology*, *26*, 180–189.

Stone, D. C., Boone, K. B., Back-Madruga, C., & Lessr, I. M. (2006). Has the rolling uterus finally gathered moss? Somatization and malingering of cognitive dysfunction in six cases of "toxic mold" exposure. *The Clinical Neuropsychologist*, *20*, 766–785.

Vickery, C., Berry, D. T. R., Dearth, C., Vagnini, V., Baser, R., Cragar, D., & Orey, S. (2004). Head injury and the ability to feign neuropsychological deficits. *Archives of Clinical Neuropsychology*, *19*, 37–48.

Test of Variables of Attention (TOVA)

Henry, G. K. (2005). Probable malingering and performance on the Test of Variables of Attention. *The Clinical Neuropsychologist*, *19*, 121–129.

Leark, R. A., Dixon, D., Hoffman, T., & Huynh, D. (2002). Fake bad test response bias effects on the test of variables of attention. *Archives of Clinical Neuropsychology*, *17*, 335–342.

Token Test

Meyers, J. E., Galinsky, A. M., & Volbrecht, M. (1999). Malingering and mild brain injury: How low is too low. *Applied Neuropsychology*, *6*, 208–216.

Meyers, J. E., & Volbrecht, M. E. (2003). Validation of multiple malingering detection methods in a large clinical sample. *Archives of Clinical Neuropsychology*, *18*, 261–276.

Trail Making Test

Gorny, I., & Merten, T. (2005). Symptom information-warning-coaching: How do they affect successful feigning in neuropsychological assessment? *Journal of Forensic Neuropsychology*, *4*, 71–98.

Haines, M. E., & Norris, M. P. (2001). Comparing student and patient simulated malingerers' performance on standard neuropsychological measures to detect feigned cognitive deficits. *The Clinical Neuropsychologist*, *15*, 171–182.

Iverson, G. L., Lange, R. T., Green, P., & Franzen, M. D. (2002). Detecting exaggeration and malingering with the Trail Making Test. *The Clinical Neuropsychologist*, *16*, 398–406.

Lange, R. T., Iverson, G. L., Green, P., & Franzen, M.D. (2001). Clinical base rates on the Trail Making Test in a TBI sample: Examination of the malingering hypothesis. *Archives of Clinical Neuropsychology*, *16*, 852.

Merten, T., Green, P., Henry, M., Blaskewitz, N., & Brockhaus, R. (2005). Analog validation of German-language symptom validity tests and the influence of coaching. *Archives of Clinical Neuropsychology*, *20*, 719–726.

O'Bryant, S., Hilsabeck, R., Fisher, J., & McCaffrey, R. (2003). Utility of the Trail Making Test in the assessment of malingering in a sample of mild traumatic brain injury. *The Clinical Neuropsychologist*, *17*, 69–74.

Ruffolo, L. F., Guilmette, T. J., & Willis, W. G. (2000). Comparison of time and error rates on the Trail Making Test among patients with head injuries, experimental malingerers, patients with suspect effort on testing, and normal controls. *The Clinical Neuropsychologist*, *14*, 223–230.

Stone, D. C., Boone, K. B., Back-Madruga, C., & Lessr, I. M. (2006). Has the rolling uterus finally gathered moss? Somatization and malingering of cognitive dysfunction in six cases of "toxic mold" exposure. *The Clinical Neuropsychologist*, *20*, 766–785.

Vagnini, V. L., Sollman, M., J., Berry, D. T. R., Granacher, R. P., Clark, J. A., Burton, R., O'Brien, M., Bacon, E., & Saier, J. (2006). Known-groups cross-validation of the Letter Memory Test in a compensation-seeking mixed neurologic sample. *The Clinical Neuropsychologist*, *20*, 289–304.

Yantz, C. L., Gavett, B. E., Lynch, J. K., & McCaffrey, R. J. (2006). Potential for interpretation disparities of Halstead-Reitan neuropsychological battery performances in a litigating sample. *Archives of Clinical Neuropsychology*, *21*, 809–817.

Trauma Symptom Inventory

Edens, J., Otto, R., & Dwyer, T. (1998). Susceptibility of the Trauma Symptom Inventory to malingering. *Journal of Personality Assessment*, *71*, 379–392.

Rosen, G., Sawchuk, C., Atkins, D., Brown, M., Price, J.R., & Lees-Haley, P. (2006). Risk of false positives when identifying malingered profiles using the Trauma Symptom Inventory. *Journal of Personality Assessment*, *86*, 329–333.

Visual form discrimination

Larrabee, G. J. (2003). Detection of malingering using atypical performance patterns on standard neuropsychological tests. *The Clinical Neuropsychologist*, *17*, 410–425.

Warrington Recognition Memory Test

Bianchini, K., Greve, K., & Love, J. (2003). Definite malingered neurocognitive dysfunction in moderate/severe traumatic brain injury. *The Clinical Neuropsychologist*, *17*, 574–580.

Cato, M. A., Brewster, J., Ryan, T., & Giuliano, A. J. (2002). Coaching and the ability to simulate mild traumatic brain injury symptoms. *The Clinical Neuropsychologist*, *16*, 524–535.

Cradock, M., Gfeller, J., & Falkenhain, M. (1994, November). *Detecting feigned memory deficits with the Rey*

Auditory Verbal Learning Test (RAVLT) and the Recognition Memory Test (RMT). Presented at the Annual Conference of the National Academy of Neuropsychology, Orlando, Florida.

Dean, A. C., Victor, T. L., Boone, K. B., & Arnold, G. (2008). The relationship of IQ to effort test performance. *The Clinical Neuropsychologist, 22,* 705–722.

Hilsabeck, R. C., & Gouvier, W. D. (2005). Detecting simulated memory impairment: Further validation of the Word Completion Memory Test (WCMT). *Archives of Clinical Neuropsychology, 20,* 1025–1041.

Iverson, G., & Franzen, M. (1994). The Recognition Memory Test, Digit Span, and Knox Cube Test as markers of malingered memory impairment. *Assessment, 1,* 323–334.

Iverson, G., & Franzen, M. (1998). Detecting malingered memory deficits with the Recognition Memory Test. *Brain Injury, 12,* 275–282.

Millis, S. (1992). The Recognition Memory Test in the detection of malingered and exaggerated memory deficits. *The Clinical Neuropsychologist, 6,* 406–414.

Millis, S. (1994). Assessment of motivation and memory with the Recognition Memory Test after financially compensable mild head injury. *Journal of Clinical Psychology, 50,* 601–605.

Millis, S. R. (2002). Warrington's Recognition Memory Test in the detection of response bias. *Journal of Forensic Neuropsychology, 2,* 147–166.

Millis, S., & Putnam, S. (1994). The Recognition Memory Test in the assessment of memory impairment after financially compensable mild head injury: A replication. *Perceptual and Motor Skills, 79,* 384–386.

Nelson, N. W., Boone, K., Dueck. A., Wagener, L., Lu, P., & Grills, C. (2003). Relationships between eight measures of suspect effort. *The Clinical Neuropsychologist, 17,* 263–272.

Reinhard, M. J., Satz, P., Scaglione, C. A., D'Elia, L. F., Rassovsky, Y., Arita, A. A., Hinkin, C. H., Thrasher, D., & Ordog, G. (2007). Neuropsychological exploration of alleged mold neurotoxicity. *Archives of Clinical Neuropsychology, 22,* 533–543.

Ross, S. R., Putnam, S. H., & Adams, K. M. (2006). Psychological disturbance, incomplete effort, and compensation-seeking status as predictors of neuropsychological test performance in head injury. *Journal of Clinical and Experimental Neuropsychology, 28,* 111–125.

Ross, S. R., Putnam, S. H., Millis, S. R., Adams, K. M., & Krukowski, R. A. (2006). Detecting insufficient effort using the Seashore Rhythm and Speech-Sounds Perception Tests in head injury. *The Clinical Neuropsychologist, 20,* 798–815.

Stone, D. C., Boone, K. B., Back-Madruga, C., & Lessr, I. M. (2006). Has the rolling uterus finally gathered moss? Somatization and malingering of cognitive dysfunction in six cases of "toxic mold" exposure. *The Clinical Neuropsychologist, 20,* 766–785

Tardif, H. P., Barry, R. J., Fox, A. M., & Johnstone, S. J. (2000). Detection of feigned recognition memory impairment using the old/new effect of the event-related potential. *International Journal of Psychophysiology, 3,* 1–9.

Wechsler Adult Intelligence Scale–Revised

Demakis, G. J. (2004). Application of clinically-derived malingering cutoffs on the California Verbal Learning Test and the Wechsler Adult Intelligence Test-Revised to an analog malingering study. *Applied Neuropsychology, 11,* 220–226.

Demakis, G. J., Sweet, J. J., Sawyer, T. P., Moulthrop, M., Nies, K., & Clingerman, S. (2001). Discrepancy between predicted and obtained WAIS-R IQ scores discriminates between traumatic brain injury and insufficient effort. *Psychological Assessment, 13,* 240–248.

Greve, K. W., Bianchini, K. J., Mathias, C. W., Houston, R. J., & Crouch, J. A. (2003). Detecting malingered performance on the Wechsler Adult Intelligence Scale: Validation of Mittenberg's approach in traumatic brain injury. *Archives of Clinical Neuropsychology, 18,* 245–260.

Milanovich, J., Axelrod, B., & Millis, S. (1996). Validation of the Simulation Index-Revised with a mixed clinical population. *Archives of Clinical Neuropsychology, 11,* 53–59.

Millis, S., Ross, S., & Ricker, J. (1998). Detection of incomplete effort on the Wechsler Adult Intelligence Scale-Revised: A cross-validation. *Journal of Clinical and Experimental Neuropsychology, 20,* 167–173.

Mittenberg, W., Theroux-Fichera, S., Zielinski, R., & Heilbronner, R. (1995). Identification of malingered head injury on the Wechsler Adult Intelligence Scale-Revised. *Professional Psychology: Research and Practice, 26,* 491–498.

Rawling, P., & Brooks, D. (1990). Simulation Index: A method for detecting factitious errors on the WAIS-R and WMS. *Neuropsychology, 4*, 223–238.

Ross, S. R., Putnam, S. H., & Adams, K. M. (2006). Psychological disturbance, incomplete effort, and compensation-seeking status as predictors of neuropsychological test performance in head injury. *Journal of Clinical and Experimental Neuropsychology, 28*, 111–125.

Ross, S. R., Putnam, S. H., Millis, S. R., Adams, K. M., & Krukowski, R. A. (2006). Detecting insufficient effort using the Seashore Rhythm and Speech-Sounds Perception Tests in head injury. *The Clinical Neuropsychologist, 20*, 798–815.

Trueblood, W. (1994). Qualitative and quantitative characteristics of malingered and other invalid WAIS-R and clinical memory data. *Journal of Clinical and Experimental Neuropsychology, 16*, 597–607.

Williams, R. W., & Carlin, M. (1999). Malingering on the WAIS-R among disability claimants and applicants for vocational assistance. *American Journal of Forensic Psychology, 17*, 35–45.

Wechsler Adult Intelligence Scale–3rd Edition

Axelrod, B., Fichtenberg, N., Millis, S., & Wertheimer, J. (2006). Detecting incomplete effort with Digit Span from the Wechsler Adult Intelligence Scale–Third Edition. *The Clinical Neuropsychologist, 20*, 513–523.

Bianchini, K., Houston, R., Greve, K., Irvin, R., Black, F. W., Swift, D., & Tamimie, R. (2003). Malingered neurocognitive dysfunction in neurotoxic exposure: An application of the Slick criteria. *Journal of Occupational and Environmental Medicine, 45*, 1087–1099.

Etherton, J. L., Bianchini, K. J., Ciota, M. A., Heinly, M. T., & Greve, K. W. (2006). Pain, malingering, and the WAIS-III Working Memory Index. *The Spine Journal, 6*, 61–71.

Etherton, J., Bianchini, K., Heinly, M., & Greve, K. (2006). Pain, malingering, and performance on the WAIS-III Processing Speed Index. *Journal of Clinical and Experimental Neuropsychology, 28*, 1218–1237.

Graue, L. O., Berry, D. T. R., Clark, J. A., Sollman, M. J., Cardi, M., Hopkins, J., & Werline, D. (2007). Identificatoin of feigned mental retardation using the new generation of malingering detection instruments: Preliminary findings. *The Clinical Neuropsychologist, 21*, 929–942.

Greve, K. W., Bianchini, K. J., Mathias, C.W., Houston, R.J., & Crouch, J.A. (2003). Detecting malingered performance on the Wechsler Adult Intelligence Scale: Validation of Mittenberg's approach in traumatic brain injury. *Archives of Clinical Neuropsychology, 18*, 245–260.

Iverson, G. L., & Tulsky, D. S. (2003). Detecting malingering on the WAIS-III: Unusual Digit Span performance patterns in the normal population and in clinical groups. *Archives of Clinical Neuropsychology, 18*, 1–9.

Marshall, P., & Happe, M. (2007). The performance of individuals with mental retardation on cognitive tests assessing effort and motivation. *The Clinical Neuropsychologist, 21*, 826–840.

Miller, L., Ryan, J., Carruthers, C., & Cluff, R. (2004). Brief screening indexes for malingering: A confirmation of Vocabulary-Digit Span from the WAIS-III and the Rarely Missed Index from the WMS-III. The *Clinical Neuropsychologist, 18*, 327, 333.

Mittenberg, W., Theroux, S., Aguila-Puentes, G., Bianchini, K., Greve, K., & Rayls, K. (2001). Identification of malingered head injury on the Wechsler Adult Intelligence Scale–3rd Edition. *The Clinical Neuropsychologist, 15*, 440–445.

Schwarz, L. R., Gfeller, J. D., & Oliveri, M. V. (2006). Detecting feigned impairment with the digit span and vocabulary subtests of the Wechsler Adult Intelligence Scale–Third Edition. *The Clinical Neuropsychologist, 20*, 741–753.

Stone, D. C., Boone, K. B., Back-Madruga, C., & Lessr, I. M. (2006). Has the rolling uterus finally gathered moss? Somatization and malingering of cognitive dysfunction in six cases of "toxic mold" exposure. *The Clinical Neuropsychologist, 20*, 766–785.

Wechsler Memory Scale

Rawling, P., & Brooks, D. (1990). Simulation Index: A method for detecting factitious errors on the WAIS-R and WMS. *Neuropsychology, 4*, 223–238.

Wechsler Memory Scale–Revised

Bernard, L. (1990). Prospects for faking believable memory deficits on neuropsychological tests and the use of incentives in simulation research. *Journal of Clinical and Experimental Neuropsychology, 5*, 715–728.

Bernard, L., Houston, W., & Natoli, L. (1993). Malingering on neuropsychological memory tests: Potential objective indicators. *Journal of Clinical Psychology, 49*, 45–53.

Bernard, L., McGrath, M., & Houston, W. (1993). Discriminating between simulated malingering and closed head injury on the Wechsler Memory Scale–Revised. *Archives of Clinical Neuropsychology, 8*, 539–551.

Denney, R. L. (1999). A brief symptom validity testing procedure for Logical Memory of the Wechsler Memory Scale–Revised which can demonstrate verbal memory in the face of claimed disability. *Journal of Forensic Neuropsychology, 1*, 5–26.

Greiffenstein, M., Baker, W.J., & Gola, T. (1994). Validation of malingered amnesia measures with a large clinical sample. *Psychological Assessment, 6*, 218–224.

Greiffenstein, M., Baker, W.J., & Gola, T. (1996). Comparison of multiple scoring methods for Rey's malingered amnesia measures. *Archives of Clinical Neuropsychology, 11*, 283–293.

Hilsabeck, R., Thompson, M., Irby, J., Adams, R., Scott, J., & Gouvier, W. D. (2003). Partial cross-validation of the Wechsler Memory Scale-Revised (WMS-R) General Memory-Concentration malingering index in a nonlitigating sample. *Archives of Clinical Neuropsychology, 18*, 71–79.

Iverson, G., & Franzen, M. (1996). Using multiple objective memory procedures to detect simulated malingering. *Journal of Clinical and Experimental Neuropsychology, 18*, 38–51.

Iverson, G. L., Slick, D. J., & Franzen, M. D. (2000). Evaluation of WMS-R malingering index in a non-litigating clinical sample. *Journal of Clinical and Experimental Neuropsychology, 22*, 191–197.

Martin, R., Franzen, M., & Orey, S. (1998). Magnitude of error as a strategy to detect feigned memory impairment. *The Clinical Neuropsychologist, 12*, 84–91.

Mittenberg, W., Azrin, R., Millsaps, C., & Heilbronner, R. (1993). Identification of malingered head injury on the Wechsler Memory Scale–Revised. *Psychological Assessment, 5*, 34–40.

Suchy, Y., & Sweet, J. J. (2000). Information/Orientation subtest of the Wechsler Memory Scale-Revised as an indicator of suspicion of insufficient effort. *The Clinical Neuropsychologist, 14*, 56–66.

Wechsler Memory Scale–3rd Edition

Boaz, L. (2003). About the power for detecting severe impairment in older adults with the Faces Test from the Wechsler Memory Scale-III: Simply guess and save face. *Journal of Clinical and Experimental Neuropsychology, 25*, 376–381.

Glassmire, D. M., Bierley, R. A., Wisniewski, A. M., Greene, R. L., Kennedy, J. E., & Date, E. (2003). Using the WMS-III Faces subtest to detect malingered memory impairment. *Journal of Clinical and Experimental Neuropsychology, 25*, 465–481.

Killgore, W. D., & Dellapietra, L. (2000). Using the WMS-III to detect malingering: Empirical validation of the rarely missed index (RMI). *Journal of Clinical and Experimental Neuropsychology, 22*, 761–771.

Lange, R. T., Iverson, G. L., Sullivan, K., & Anderson, D. (2006). Suppressed working memory on the WMS-III as a marker for poor effort. *Journal of Clinical and Experimental Neuropsychology, 28*, 294–305.

Lange, R. T., Sullivan, K., & Anderson, D. (2005). Ecological validity of the WMS-III rarely missed index in personal injury litigation. *Journal of Clinical and Experimental Neuropsychology, 27*, 412–424.

Langeluddecke, P. M., & Lucas, S. K. (2003). Quantitative measures of memory malingering on the Wechsler Memory Scale–Third Edition in mild head injury litigants. *Archives of Clinical Neuropsychology, 18*, 181–197.

Langeluddecke, P. M., & Lucas, S. K. (2004). Validation of the rarely missed index (RMI) in detecting memory malingering in mild head injury litigants. *Journal of Forensic Neuropsychology, 4*, 49–64.

Langeluddecke, P. M., & Lucas, S. K. (2005). WMS-III findings in litigants following moderate to extremely severe brain trauma. *Journal of Clinical and Experimental Neuropsychology, 27*, 576–590.

Marshall, P., & Happe, M. (2007). The performance of individuals with mental retardation on cognitive tests assessing effort and motivation. *The Clinical Neuropsychologist, 21*, 826–840.

Miller, L., Ryan, J., Carruthers, C., & Cluff, R. (2004). Brief screening indexes for malingering: A confirmation of Vocabulary-Digit Span from the WAIS-III and the Rarely Missed Index from the WMS-III. *The Clinical Neuropsychologist, 18*, 327, 333.

Ord, J. S., Greve, K. W., & Bianchini, K. J. (2008). Using the Wechsler Memory Scale-III to detect malingering in milt traumatic brain injury. *The Clinical Neuropsychologist, 22*, 689–704.

Swihart, A. A., Harris, K. M., & Hatcher, L. L. (2008). Inability of the Rarely Missed Index to identify simulated malingering under more realistic assessment conditions. *Journal of Clinical and Experimental Neuropsychology, 30*, 120–126.

Vagnini, V. L., Sollman, M., J., Berry, D. T. R., Granacher, R. P., Clark, J. A., Burton, R., O'Brien, M., Bacon, E., & Saier, J. (2006). Known-groups cross-validation of the Letter Memory Test in a compensation-seeking mixed neurologic sample. *The Clinical Neuropsychologist, 20*, 289–304.

Wisconsin Card Sorting Test

Ashendorf, L., O'Bryant, S. E., & McCaffrey, R. J. (2003). Specificity of malingering detection strategies in older adults using the CVLT and WCST. *The Clinical Neuropsychologist, 17*, 255–262.

Bernard, L., McGrath, M., & Houston, W. (1996). The differential effects of simulating malingering, closed head injury, and other CNS pathology on the Wisconsin Card Sorting Test: Support for the "pattern of performance" hypothesis. *Archives of Clinical Neuropsychology, 11*, 231–245.

Bianchini, K., Houston, R., Greve, K., Irvin, R., Black, F. W., Swift, D., & Tamimie, R. (2003). Malingered neurocognitive dysfunction in neurotoxic exposure: An application of the Slick criteria. *Journal of Occupational and Environmental Medicine, 45*, 1087–1099.

Donders, J. D. (1999). Brief report: Sensitivity of a malingering formula for the Wisconsin Card Sorting Test. *Journal of Forensic Neuropsychology, 1*, 34–43.

Greve, K. W., & Bianchini, K. J. (2002). Using the Wisconsin Card Sorting Test to detect malingering: An analysis of the specificity of two methods in nonmalingering normal and patient samples. *Journal of Clinical and Experimental Neuropsychology, 24*, 48–54.

Greve, K. W., Bianchini, K. J., Mathias, C. W., Houston, R. J., & Crouch, J. A. (2002). Detecting malingered performance with the Wisconsin Card Sorting Test: A preliminary investigation in traumatic brain injury. *The Clinical Neuropsychologist, 16*, 179–191.

King, J. H., Sweet, J. J., Sherer, M., Curtiss, G., & Vanderploeg, R. (2002). Validity indicators within the Wisconsin Card Sorting Test: Application of new and previously researched multivariate procedures in multiple traumatic brain injury samples. *The Clinical Neuropsychologist, 16*, 506–523.

Miller, A., Donders, J., & Suhr, J. (2000). Evaluation of malingering with the Wisconsin Card Sorting Test: A cross-validation. *Clinical Neuropsychological Assessment, 2*, 141–149.

Suhr, J. A., & Boyer, D. (1999). Use of the Wisconsin Card Sorting Test in the detection of malingering in student simulator and patient samples. *Journal of Clinical and Experimental Neuropsychology, 21*, 701–708.

Vagnini, V. L., Sollman, M., J., Berry, D. T. R., Granacher, R. P., Clark, J. A., Burton, R., O'Brien, M., Bacon, E., & Saier, J. (2006). Known-groups cross-validation of the Letter Memory Test in a compensation-seeking mixed neurologic sample. *The Clinical Neuropsychologist, 20*, 289–304.

Other

Andrikopoulos, J. (2001). Malingering disorientation to time, personal information, and place in mild head injured litigants. *The Clinical Neuropsychologist, 15*, 393–396.

Ashton, V. L., Donders, J., & Hoffman, N. M. (2005). Rey Complex Figure Test performance after traumatic brain injury. *Journal of Clinical and Experimental Neuropsychology, 27*, 55–64.

Bender, S., & Rogers, R. (2004). Detection of neurocognitive feigning: Development of a multi-strategy assessment. *Archives of Clinical Neuropsychology, 19*, 49–60.

Borckardt, J. J., Engum, E. S., Lambert, E. W., Nash, M., Bracy, O. L., & Ray, E. C. (2003). Use of the CBDI to detect malingering when malingerers do their "homework." *Archives of Clinical Neuropsychology, 18*, 57–69.

Chafetz, M. D., Abrahams, J. P., & Kohlmaier, J. (2007). Malingering on the Social Security Disability Consultative Exam: A new rating scale. *Archives of Clinical Neuropsychology, 22*, 1–14.

Chiu, V. W. Y., & Lee, T. M. C. (2002). Detection of malingering behavior at different levels of task difficulty in Hong Kong Chinese. *Rehabilitation Psychology*, *47*, 194–203.

Cima, M., Merckelbach, H., Hollnack, S., Butt, C., Kremer, K., Schellback-Matties, R., & Muris, P. (2003). The other side of malingering: Supernormality. *The Clinical Neuropsychologist*, *17*, 235–243.

Curtis, K. L., Thompson, L. K., Greve, K. W., & Bianchini, K. J. (in press). Verbal fluency indicators of malingering in traumatic brain injury: Classification accuracy in known groups. *The Clinical Neuropsychologist*.

DeMonte, V. E., Geffen, G., M., May, C. R., McFarland, K., Heath, P., & Neralic, M. (2005). The acute effects of mild traumatic brain injury on finger tapping with and without word repetition. *Journal of Clinical and Experimental Neuropsychology*, *27*, 224–239.

Denney, R. L. (1996). Symptom validity testing of remote memory in a criminal forensic setting. *Archives of Clinical Neuropsychology*, *11*, 589–603.

Frederick R. I., & Speed, F. M. (2007). On the interpretation of below-chance responding in forced-choice tests. *Assessment*, *14*, 3–11.

Green, P., (2001). Why clinicians often disagree about the validity of test results. *Neurorehabilitation*, *16*, 231–236.

Green, P., Allen, L. M., & Iverson, G. L. (1999). Utility of the Memory Complaints Inventory for identifying symptom exaggeration in mild to moderate traumatic brain injury. *Archives of Clinical Neuropsychology*, *14*.

Green, P., & Iverson, G. L. (2001). Effects of injury severity and cognitive exaggeration on olfactory deficits in head injury compensation claims. *Neurorehabilitation*, *16*, 237–243.

Hanley, J., Baker, G., & Ledson, S. (1999). Detecting the faking of amnesia: A comparison of the effectiveness of three different techniques for distinguishing simulators from patients with amnesia. *Journal of Clinical and Experimental Neuropsychology*, *21*, 59–69.

Harrison, A. G., Edwards, M. J., & Parker, K. C. H. (2007). Identifying students faking ADHD: Preliminary findings and strategies for detection. *Archives of Clinical Neuropsychology*, *22*, 577–588.

Meyers, J. E., & Diep, A. (2000). Assessment of malingering in chronic pain patients using neuropsychological tests. *Applied Neuropsychology*, *7*, 133–139.

Nagle, A. M., Everhart, D. E., Durham, T. W., McCammon, S. L., & Walker, M. (2006). Deception strategies in children: Examination of forced choice recognition and verbal learning and memory techniques. *Archives of Clinical Neuropsychology*, *21*, 777–785.

Robinson, M. E., & Dannecker, E. A. (2004). Critical issues in the use of muscle testing for the determination of sincerity of effort. *Clinical Journal of Pain*, *20*, 392–398.

Rogers, R., Sewell, K. W., Grandjean, N. R., & Vitacco, M. J. (2002). The detection of feigned mental disorders on specific competency measures. *Psychological Assessment*, *14*, 177–183.

Sbordone, R. J., Seyranian, G. D., & Ruff, R. (2000). The use of significant others to enhance the detection of malingerers from traumatically brain-injured patients. *Archives of Clinical Neuropsychology*, *15*, 465–477.

Schexnayder, M. M., Creveling, C. C., Nemeth, D. G., & Hannie T. J., Jr. (2000). Consideration of latency/slowed performance rate when malingering and chronic pain are at issue during a neuropsychological evaluation. *Archives of Clinical Neuropsychology*, *15* (8), 836.

Spencer, J., & Kinoshita, S. (2007). The use of indirect and opposition tests to detect simulated amnesia. *Journal of Clinical and Experimental Neuropsychology*, *29*, 442–455.

Stone, D. C., Boone, K. B., Back-Madruga, C., & Lesser, I. M. (2006). Has the rolling uterus finally gathered moss? Somatization and malingering of cognitive dysfunction in six cases of "toxic mold" exposure. *The Clinical Neuropsychologist*, *20*, 766–785.

Sullivan, K., & Richer, C. (2002). Malingering on subjective complaint tasks: An exploration of the deterrent effects of warning. *Archives of Clinical Neuropsychology*, *17*, 691–708.

Vagnini, V. L., Sollman, M. J., Berry, D. T. R., Granacher, R. P., Clark, J. A., Burton, R., O'Brien, M., Bacon, E., & Saier, J. (2006). Known-groups cross-validation of the Letter Memory Test in a compensation-seeking mixed neurologic sample. *The Clinical Neuropsychologist*, *20*, 289–304.

Vitacco, M. J., Rogers, R., Gabel, J., & Munizza, J. (2007). An evaluation of malingering screens with competency to stand trial patients: A known-groups study. *Law and Human Behavior*, *31*, 249–260.

Appendix C
Additional articles pertinent to malingering

C1: Base rates/incidence of malingering

Ardolf, B. R., Denney, R. L., & Houston, C. M. (2007). Base rates of negative response bias and malingered neurocognitive dysfunction among criminal defendants referred for neuropsychological evaluation. *The Clinical Neuropsychologist, 21*, 899–916.

Backhaus, S. L., Ficther, N. L., & Hanks, R. A. (2004). Detection of sub-optimal performance using a floor effect strategy in patients with traumatic brain injury. *The Clinical Neuropsychologist, 18*, 591–603.

Bianchini, K. J., Curtis, K. L., & Greve, K. W. (2006). Compensation and malingering in traumatic brain injury: A dose-response relationship? *The Clinical Neuropsychologist, 20*, 831–847.

Bianchini, K., Love, J. M., Greve, K. W., & Adams, D. (2005). Detection and diagnosis of malingering in electrical injury. *Archives of Clinical Neuropsychology, 20*, 365–373.

Chafetz, M. D. (2008). Malingering on the Social Security Disability Consultative Exam: Predictors and base rates. *The Clinical Neuropsychologist, 22*, 529–546.

Farkas, M. R., Rosenfeld, B., Robbins, R., & van Gorp, W. (2006). Do tests of malingering concur? Concordance among malingering measures. *Behavioral Sciences and the Law, 24*, 659–671.

Fishbain, D., Cole, B., Cutler, R., Lewis, J., Rosomoff, H., & Rosomoff, R. (2003). A structured evidence-based review on the meaning of nonorganic physical signs: Waddell signs. *Pain Medicine, 4*, 141–181.

Gold, P. B., & Frueh, B.C. (1999). Compensation-seeking and extreme exaggeration of psychopathology among combat veterans evaluated for posttraumatic stress disorder. *Journal of Nervous and Mental Disease, 187*, 680–684.

Greiffenstein, M. R., & Baker, W. J. (2006). Miller was (mostly) right: Head injury severity inversely related to simulation. *Legal and Criminological Psychology, 11*, 131–145.

Greve, K. W., Bianchini, K. J., Black, F. W., Heinly, M. T., Love, J. M., Swift, D. A., & Ciota, M. (2006). The prevalence of cognitive malingering in persons reporting exposure to occupational and environmental substances. *NeuroToxicology, 27*, 940–950.

Martens, M., Donders, J. D., & Millis, S. R. (2001). Evaluation of invalid response set after traumatic head injury. *Journal of Forensic Neuropsychology, 2*, 1–18.

Mittenberg, W., Patton, C., Canyock, E. M., & Condit, D. C. (2002). Baserates of malingering and symptom exaggeration. *Journal of Clinical and Experimental Neuropsychology, 24*, 1094–1102.

Pollock, P. H., Quigly, B., Worley, K. O., & Bashford, C. (1997). Feigned mental disorders in prisoners referred to forensic mental health services. *Journal of Psychiatric and Mental Health Nursing, 4*, 9–15.

Rissimiller, D. A., Steer, R. A., Friedman, M., & DeMercurio, R. (1999). Prevalence of malingering in suicidal psychiatric inpatients: A replication. *Psychological Reports, 84*, 726–730.

Rissmiller, D. J., Wayslow, A., Madison, H., Hogate, P., Rissmiller, F. R., & Steer, R. A. (1998). Prevalence of malingering in inpatient suicide ideators and attempters. *Crisis, 19*, 62–66.

Rogers, R. (1990). Development of a new classificatory model of malingering. *Bulletin of the American Academy of Psychiatry and the Law, 18*, 323–333.

Rosen, G. M. (2004). Litigation and reported rates of posttraumatic stress disorder. *Personality and Individual Differences, 36*, 1291–1294.

Rosenfeld, B., Sands, S. A., & van Gorp, W. G. (2000). Have we forgotten the base rate problem? Methodological issues in the detection of distortion. *Archives of Clinical Neuropsychology, 15*, 349–359.

Ruiz, M. A., Drake, E. B., Glass, A., Marcotte, D., & van Gorp, W. (2002). Trying to beat the system: Misuse of the Internet to assist in avoiding the detection of psychological symptom dissimulation. *Professional Psychology: Research and Practice, 33*, 294–299.

Slick, D., Tan, J., Strauss, E., & Hultsch, D. (2004). Detecting malingering: A survey of experts' practices. *Archives of Clinical Neuropsychology*, *19*, 465–473.

Stevens, A., Friedel, E., Mehren, G., & Merten, T. (2008). Malingering and uncooperativeness in psychiatric and psychological assessment: Prevalence and effects in a German sample of claimants. *Psychiatry Research*, *157*, 191–200.

Sullivan, K., Lange, R. T., & Dawes, S. (2005). Methods of detecting malingering and estimated symptom exaggeration base rates in Australia. *Journal of Forensic Neuropsychology*, *4*, 49–70.

Sumanti, M., Boone, K. B., & Savodnik, I. & Gorsuch, R. (2006). Noncredible psychiatric and cognitive symptoms in a worker's compensation "stress" claim sample. *The Clinical Neuropsychologist*, *20*, 754–765.

Woods, S. P., Weinborn, M., & Lovejoy, D. (2003). Are classification accuracy statistics underused in neuropsychological research? *Journal of Clinical and Experimental Neuropsychology*, *25*, 431–439.

Yates, B. D., Nordquist, C. R., & Schultz-Ross, R. A. (1996). Feigned psychiatric symptoms in the emergency room. *Psychiatric Services*, *47*, 998–1000.

C2: Event-related potentials

Ellwanger, J., Rosenfeld, J. P., & Sweet, J. (1997). P300 event-related brain potential as an index of recognition response to autobiographical and recently learned information in closed-head-injury patients. *The Clinical Neuropsychologist*, *11*, 428–432.

Ellwanger, J., Rosenfeld, J. P., Sweet, J., & Bhatt, M. (1996). Detecting simulated amnesia for autobiographical and recently learned information using the P300 event-related potential. *International Journal of Psychophysiology*, *23*, 9–23.

Ellwanger, J., Tenhula, W., Rosenfeld, J. P., & Sweet, J. J. (1999). Identifying simulators of cognitive deficit through combined use of neuropsychological test performance and event-related potentials. *Journal of Clinical and Experimental Neuropsychology*, *21*, 866–879.

Orey, S. A., Cragar, D. E., & Berry, D. T. (2000). The effects of two motivational manipulations on the neuropsychological performance of mildly head-injured college students. *Archives of Clinical Neuropsychology*, *15*, 335–348.

Rosenfeld, J. P., Ellwanger, J., Nolan, K., Bermann, R., & Sweet, J. J. (1999). P300 scalp amplitude distribution as an index of deception in a simulated cognitive deficit model. *International Journal of Psychophysiology*, *33*, 3–19.

Rosenfeld, J. P., Ellwanger, J., & Sweet, J. J. (1995). Detecting malingered amnesia with event-related brain potentials. *International Journal of Psychophysiology*, *19*, 1–11.

Rosenfeld, J. P., Reinhart, A., Bhatt, M., Ellwanger, J., Sekera, M., & Sweet, J. J. (1998). P300 correlates of simulated malingered amnesia on a simple matching-to-sample task: Topographic analyses of deception versus truthtelling responses. *International Journal of Psychophysiology*, *28*, 233–247.

Rosenfeld, J. P., Sweet, J. J., Chuang, J., Ellwanger, J., & Song, L. (1996). Detection of simulated malingering using forced choice recognition enhanced with event-related potential recording. *The Clinical Neuropsychologist*, *10*, 163–179.

Tardif, H. P., Barry, R. J., Fox, A. M., & Johnstone, S. J. (2000). Detection of feigned recognition memory impairment using the old/new effect of the event-related potential. *International Journal of Psychophysiology*, *3*, 1–9.

C3: Reviews/theory articles on malingering

Arbisi, P. A., & Butcher, J. N. (2004). Psychometric perspective on detection of malingering of pain. *Clinical Journal of Pain*, *20*, 383–391.

Aronoff, G. M., Mandel, S., Genovese, E., Maitz, E. A., Dorto, A. J., Klimek, E. H., & Staats, T. E. (2007). Evaluating malingering in contested injury or illness. *Pain Practice*, *7*, 178–204.

Bender, S., & Rogers, R. (2004). Detection of neurocognitive feigning: Development of a multi-strategy assessment. *Archives of Clinical Neuropsychology*, *19*, 49–60.

Bianchini, K. J., Etherton, J. L., & Greve, K. W. (2004). Diagnosing cognitive malingering in patients with work-related pain: Four cases. *Journal of Forensic Neuropsychology*, *4*, 65–85.

Bianchini, K. J., Greve, K. W., & Glynn, G. (2005). On the diagnosis of malingered pain-related disability: Lessons from cognitive malingering research. *The Spine Journal*, 404–417.

Bianchini, K. J., Houston, R. J., Greve, K. W., Irvin, T. R., Black, F. W., & Swift, D. A. (2003). Malingered neurocognitive dysfunction in neurotoxic exposure: An application of the Slick criteria. *Journal of Occupational and Environmental Medicine*, 45, 1087–1099.

Bianchini, K. J., Mathias, C. W., & Greve, K. W. (2001). Symptom validity testing: A critical review. *The Clinical Neuropsychologist*, 15, 19–45.

Binder, L. M., & Rohling, M. L. (1996). Money matters: A meta-analytic review of the effects of financial incentives on recovery after closed-head injury. *American Journal of Psychiatry*, 153, 7–10.

Booke, K. B. (2007). A reconsideration of the Slick et al. (1999) criteria for malingered neurocognitive dysfunction. In K. B. Boone (Ed.), *Assessment of feigned cognitive impairment: A neuropsychological perspective.* New York: Guilford Press.

Boone, K. (Ed.) (2007). *Assessment of feigned cognitive impairment: A neuropsychological perspective.* New York: Guilford.

Bourg, S., Connor, E. J., & Landis, E. E. (1995). The impact of expertise and sufficient information on psychologists' ability to detect malingering. *Behavioral Sciences and the Law*, 13, 505–515.

Bowden, S. C., Shores, E. A., & Mathias, J. L. (2006). Does effort suppress cognition after traumatic brain injury? A re-examination of the evidence for the Word Memory Test. *The Clinical Neuropsychologist*, 20, 858–872.

Brown, R. J. (2004). Psychological mechanisms of medically unexplained symptoms: An integrative conceptual model. *Psychological Bulletin*, 130, 793–812.

Bush, S. S., Ruff, R. M., Tröster, A. I., Barth, J. T., Koffler, S. P. Pliskin, N. H., Reynolds, C. R., & Silver, C. H. (2005). Symptom validity assessment: Practice issues and medical necessity NAN Policy and Planning Committee. *Archives of Clinical Neuropsychology*, 20, 419–426.

Essig, S. M., Mittenberg, W., Petersen, R. S., Strauman, S., & Cooper, J. T. (2001). Practices in forensic neuropsychology: Perspectives of neuropsychologists and trial attorneys. *Archives of Clinical Neuropsychology*, 16, 271–291.

Etcoff, L. M., & Kampfer, K. M. (1996). Practical guidelines in the use of symptom validity and other psychological tests to measure malingering and symptom exaggeration in traumatic brain injury cases. *Psychology Review*, 6, 171–201.

Farkas, M. R., Rosenfeld, B., Robbins, R., & van Gorp, W. (2006). Do tests of malingering concur? Concordance among malingering measures. *Behavioral Sciences and the Law*, 24, 659–671.

Faust, D., & Guilmette, T. J. (1990). To say it's not so doesn't prove that it isn't: Research on the detection of malingering. Reply to Bigler. *Journal of Consulting and Clinical Psychology*, 58, 248–250.

Faust, D., Hart, K. Guilmette, T. J., & Arkes, H. R. (1988). Neuropsychologists' capacity to detect adolescent malingerers. *Professional Psychology: Research and Practice*, 19, 508–515.

Fishbain, D., Cole, B., Cutler, R., Lewis, J., Rosomoff, H., & Rosomoff, R. (2003). A structured evidence-based review on the meaning of nonorganic physical signs: Waddell signs. *Pain Medicine*, 4, 141–181.

Fishbain, D. A., Cutler, R., Rosomoff, H. L., & Rosomoff, R. S. (1999). Chronic pain disability exaggeration/ malingering and submaximal effort research. *Clinical Journal of Pain*, 15, 244–274.

Fishbain, D. A., Cutler, R., Rosomoff, H. L., & Rosomoff, R. S. (2004). Is there a relationship between nonorganic physical findings (Waddell signs) and secondary gain/malingering? *Clinical Journal of Pain*, 20, 399–408.

Frederick, R. I., (2002). A review of Rey's strategies for detecting malingered neuropsychological impairment. *Journal of Forensic Neuropsychology*, 2, 1–25.

Frederick, R. I., & Denney, R. L. (1998). Minding your "ps and qs" when using forced-choice recognition tests. *The Clinical Neuropsychologist*, 12, 193–205.

Frederick R. I., & Speed, F. M. (2007). On the interpretation of below-chance responding in forced-choice tests. *Assessment*, 14, 3–11.

Gill, D., Green, P., Flaro, L., & Pucci, T. (2007). The role of effort testing in independent medical examinations. *Medico-Legal Journal*, 75, 64–71.

Greiffenstein, M. F., Baker, W. J., & Johnson-Greene, D. (2002). Actual versus self-reported scholastic achievement of litigating postconcussion and severe closed head injury claimants. *Psychological Assessment*, 14, 202–208.

Greve, K., & Bianchini, K. (2004). Setting empirical cut-offs on psychometric indicators of negative response bias: A methodological commentary with recommendations. *Archives of Clinical Neuropsychology, 19,* 533–541.

Guilmette, T. J., Kennedy, M. L., Weiler, M. D., & Temple, R. O. (2006). Investigation of biases in the general public in evaluating mild head injury using neuropsychological and CT scan results: Forensic implications. *The Clinical Neuropsychologist, 20,* 305–314.

Guriel, J., & Fremouw, W. (2003). Assessing malingered posttraumatic stress disorder: A critical review. *Clinical Psychology Review, 23,* 881–904.

Haines, M. E., & Norris, M. P. (1995). Detecting the malingering of cognitive deficits: An update. *Neuropsychology Review, 5,* 125–148.

Hall, R. C. W., & Hall, R. C. W. (2006). Malingering of PTSD: Forensic and diagnostic considerations, characteristics of malingerers and clinical presentations. *General Hospital Psychiatry, 28,* 525–535.

Hayes, J. S., Hilsabeck, R. C., & Gouvier, W. D. (1999). Malingering traumatic brain injury: Current issues and caveats in assessment and classification. In N. R. Varney & R. J. Roberts, (Eds.) *The evaluation and treatment of mild traumatic brain injury.* Mahwah, NJ: Lawrence Erlbaum Associates, Inc.

Heilbonner, R. (2004). A status report on the practice of forensic neuropsychology. *The Clinical Neuropsychologist, 18,* 312–326.

Iverson, G. L., & Binder, L. M. (2000). Detecting exaggeration and malingering in neuropsychological assessment. *Journal of Head Trauma Rehabilitation, 15,* 829–858.

Larrabee, G. J. (2005). Assessment of malingering. In G. J. Larrabee (Ed.), *Forensic neuropsychology: A scientific approach* (pp. 115–158). New York: Oxford University Press.

Larrabee, G. J. (Ed.) (2007). *Assessment of malingered neuropsychological deficits.* New York: Oxford University Press.

Larrabee, G. J., Greiffenstein, M. F., Greve, K. W., & Bianchini, K. J. (2007). Refining diagnostic criteria for malingering. In G. J. Larrabee (Ed.), *Assessment of malingered neuropsychological deficits* (pp. 334–371). New York: Oxford University Press.

Lees-Haley, P. R., Greiffenstein, M. F., Larrabee, G. J., & Manning, E. L. (2004). Methodological problems in the neuropsychological assessment of effects of exposure to welding fumes and manganese. *The Clinical Neuropsychologist, 18,* 449–464.

Lynch, W. J. (2004). Determination of effort level, exaggeration, and malingering in neurocognitive assessment. *Journal of Head Trauma Rehabilitation, 19,* 277–283.

McDermott, B. E., & Feldman, M. D. (2007). Malingering in the medical setting. *Psychiatric Clinics of North America, 30,* 645–662.

Mendelson, G., & Mendelson, D. (2004). Malingering pain in the medicolegal context. *Clinical Journal of Pain, 20,* 423–432.

Miller, W. G., & Miller, E. S. (1992). Malingering and neuropsychological assessment. *Physical Medicine and Rehabilitation, 6,* 547–563.

Millis, S. R., & Volinsky, C. T. (2001). Assessment of response bias in mild head injury: Beyond malingering tests. *Journal of Clinical and Experimental Neuropsychology, 23,* 809–828.

Mittenberg, W., Aguila-Puentes, G., Patton, C., Canyock, E. M., & Heilbronner, R. L. (2002). Neuropsychological profiling of symptom exaggeration and malingering. *Journal of Forensic Neuropsychology, 3,* 227–240.

Mossman, D. (2003). Daubert, cognitive malingering, and test accuracy. *Law and Human Behavior, 27,* 229–249.

Nelson, N. W., Sweet, J. J., Berry, D. T. R., Bryant, F. B., & Granacher, R. P. (2007). Response validity in forensic neuropsychology: Exploratory factor analytic evidence of distinct cognitive and psychological constructs. *Journal of the International Neuropsychological Society, 13,* 3, 440–449.

Nies, K., & Sweet, J. J. (1994). Neuropsychological assessment and malingering: A critical review of past and present strategies. *Archives of Clinical Neuropsychology, 9,* 501–552.

Price, D. R., Burke, W. H., & Price, D. C. (1993). Identification of fictitious closed head injury claims. *Personal Injury,* 37–40.

Richman, J., Green, P., Gervais, R., Flaro, L., Merten, T., Brockhaus, R., & Ranks, D. (2006). Objective tests of symptom exaggeration in independent medical examinations. *Journal of Occupational and Environmental Medicine, 48,* 303–311.

Robinson, M. E., & Dannecker, E. A. (2004). Critical issues in the use of muscle testing for the determination of sincerity of effort. *Clinical Journal of Pain, 20,* 392–398.

Rogers, R., Harrell, E., & Liff, C. (1993). Feigning neuropsychological impairment: A critical review of methodological and clinical considerations. *Clinical Psychology Review, 13*, 255–274.

Rohling, M. (2004, Summer/Fall). Who do they think they are kidding: A review of the use of symptom validity tests with children. *Newsletter 40 (Division of Clinical Neuropsychology), 22*, 1, 21–26.

Rohling, M. L., Langhinrichsen-Rohling, J., & Miller, L. S. (2003). Actuarial assessment of malingering: Rohling's Interpretive method. In R. D. Franklin (Ed.), *Prediction in forensic and neuropsychology*. Mahwah, N.J.: Lawrence Erlbaum Associates, Inc.

Sharland, M. J., & Gfeller, J. D. (2007). A survey of neuropsychologists' beliefs and practices with respect to the assessment of effort. *Archives of Clinical Neuropsychology, 22*, 213–224.

Slick, D. J., Sherman, E. M. S., & Iverson, G. L. (1999). Diagnostic criteria for malingered neurocognitive dysfunction: Proposed standards for clinical practice and research. *The Clinical Neuropsychologist, 13*, 545–561.

Slick, D., Tan, J., Strauss, E., & Hultsch, D. (2004). Detecting malingering: A survey of experts' practices. *Archives of Clinical Neuropsychology, 19*, 465–473.

Stone, D. C., Boone, K. B., Back-Madruga, C., & Lessr, I. M. (2006). Has the rolling uterus finally gathered moss? Somatization and malingering of cognitive dysfunction in six cases of "toxic mold" exposure. *The Clinical Neuropsychologist, 20*, 766–785.

Sullivan, M. (2004). Exaggerated pain behavior: By what standard? *Clinical Journal of Pain, 20*, 433–439.

Sweet, J. J. (1999). Malingering: Differential diagnosis. In J.J. Sweet (Ed.) *Forensic neuropsychology: Fundamentals and practice*. Lisse, Netherlands: Swets & Zeitlinger.

Sweet, J. J., King, J. H., Malina, A. C., Bergman, M. A., & Simmons, A. (2002). Documenting the prominence of forensic neuropsychology at national meetings and in relevant professional journals from 1990 to 2000. *The Clinical Neuropsychologist, 16*, 481–494.

Vallabhajosuola, B., & van Gorp, W. G. (2001). Post Daubert admissibility of scientific evidence on malingering of cognitive deficits. *Journal of the Academy of Psychiatry and Law, 29*, 207–215.

Vanderploeg, R. D., & Curtiss, G. (2000). Neuropsychological validity and malingering assessment: A crititcal review and discussion. *Brain Injury Source, 4*, 14–16 & 43–45.

Vanderploeg, R. D., & Curtiss, G. (2001). Malingering assessment: Evaluation of validity of performance. *NeuroRehabilitation, 16*, 245–251.

Vickery, C. D., Berry, D. T. R., Inman, T. H., Harris, M. J., & Orey, S. A. (2001). Detection of inadequate effort on neuropsychological testing: A meta-analytic review of selected procedures. *Archives of Clinical Neuropsychology, 16*, 45–73.

Wetter, M., & Corrigan, S. (1995). Providing information to clients about psychological tests: A survey of attorneys' and law students' attitudes. *Professional Psychology: Research and Practice, 26*, 474–477.

Yantz, C. L., Gavett, B. E., Lynch, J. K., & McCaffrey, R. J. (2006). Potential for interpretation disparities of Halstead-Reitan neuropsychological battery performances in a litigating sample. *Archives of Clinical Neuropsychology, 21*, 809–817.

Youngjohn, J. R., Lees-Haley, P. R., & Binder, L. M. (1999). Comment: Warning malingerers produces more sophisticated malingering. *Archives of Clinical Neuropsychology, 14*, 511–515.

Youngjohn, J. R., Spector, J., & Mapou, R. L. (1998). Failure to assess motivation, need to consider psychiatric disturbance, and absence of objectively verified physical pathology: Some common pitfalls in the practice of forensic neuropsychology. *The Clinical Neuropsychologist, 12*, 233–236.

Appendix D

Topics common to forensic neuropsychology consultation

D1: Concussion and postconcussion syndrome

(for mild TBI, also see Traumatic Brain Injury section)

Ferguson, R. J., Mittenberg, W., Barone, D. F., & Schneider, D. (1999). Postconcussion syndrome following sports-related head injury: Expectation as etiology. *Neuropsychology*, *13*, 582–589.

Greiffenstein, M. F., & Baker, W. J. (2003). Premorbid clues? Preinjury scholastic performance and present neuropsychological functioning in late postconcussion syndrome. *The Clinical Neuropsychologist*, *17*, 561–573.

Greiffenstein, M. F., & Baker, W. J. (2006). Miller was (mostly) right: Head injury severity inversely related to simulation. *Legal and Criminal Psychology*, *11*, 131–145.

Greiffenstein, M. F., Baker, W. J., & Johnson-Greene, D. (2002). Actual versus self-reported scholastic achievement of litigating postconcussion and severe closed head injury claimants. *Psychological Assessment*, *14*, 202–208.

Iverson, G. L. (2006). Misdiagnosis of the persistent postconcussion syndrome in patients with depression. *Archives of Clinical Neuropsychology*, *21*, 303–310.

Landre, N., Poppe, C. J., Davis, N., Schmaus, B., & Hobbs, S.E. (2006). Cognitive functioning and postconcussive symptoms in trauma patients with and without mild TBI. *Archives of Clinical Neuropsychology*, *21*, 255–274.

Larrabee, G. J. (1997). Neuropsychological outcome, post concussion symptoms, and forensic considerations in mild closed head trauma. *Seminars in Clinical Neuropsychiatry*, *2*, 196–206.

McCrea, M. A. (Ed.) (2008). *Mild traumatic brain injury and postconcussion syndrome: The new evidence base for diagnosis and treatment.* New York: Oxford University Press.

Meares, S., Shores, A., Batchelor, J., Baguley, I., Chapman, J., Gurka, J., & Marosszeky, J. (2006). The relationship of psychological and cognitive factors and opiods in the development of the postconcussion syndrome in general trauma patients with mild traumatic brain injury. *Journal of the International Neuropsychological Society*, *12*, 792–801.

Putnam, S. H., & Millis, S. R. (1994). Psychosocial factors in the development and maintenance of chronic somatic and functional symptoms following mild traumatic brain injury. *Advances in Medical Psychotherapy*, *7*, 1–22.

Sheedy, J., Geffen, G., Donnelly, J., & Faux, S. (2006). Emergency department assessment of mild traumatic brain injury and prediction of post-concussion symptoms at one month post-injury. *Journal of Clinical and Experimental Neuropsychology*, *28*, 755–772.

Stulemeijer, M., Vos, P. E., Bleijenberg, G., & van der Werf, S. P. (2007). Cognitive complaints after mild traumatic brain injury: Things are not always what they seem. *Journal of Psychosomatic Research*, *63*, 637–645.

Wang, Y., Chan, R. C. K., & Deng, Y. (2006). Examination of postconcussion-like symptoms in healthy university students: Relationships to subjective and objective neuropsychological function performance. *Archives of Clinical Neuropsychology*, *21*, 339–348.

Whittaker, R., Kemp, S., & House, A. (2007). Illness perceptions and outcome in mild head injury: A longitudinal study. *Journal of Neurology, Neurosurgery, and Psychiatry*, *78*, 644–646.

Youngjohn, J. R., Burrows, L., & Erdal, K. (1995). Brain damage or compensation neurosis? The controversial post-concussion syndrome. *The Clinical Neuropsychologist*, *9* (2), 112–123.

D2: Traumatic brain injury (outcome and other topics)

Axelrod, B. N., Fichtenberg, N. L., Liethen, P. C., Czarnota, M. A., & Stucky, K. (2001). Performance characteristics of postacute traumatic brain injury patients on the WAIS-III and WMS-III. *The Clinical Neuropsychologist, 15*, 516–520.

Belanger, H. G., Curtiss, G., Demery, J. A., Lebowitz, B. K., & Vanderploeg, R. D. (2005). Factors moderating neuropsychological outcomes following mild traumatic brain injury: A meta-analysis. *Journal of the International Neuropsychological Society, 11*, 215–227.

Bell, B., Primeau, M., Sweet, J., & Lofland, K. (1999). Neuropsychological functioning in migraine headache, nonheadache chronic pain, and mild traumatic brain injury patients. *Archives of Clinical Neuropsychology, 14*, 389–399.

Binder, L. M. (1997). A review of mild head trauma. Part II: Clinical implications. *Journal of Clinical and Experimental Neuropsychology, 3*, 432–457.

Binder, L. M., Rohling, M. L., & Larrabee, G. J. (1997). A review of mild head trauma. Part I: Meta-analystic review of neuropsychological studies. *Journal of Clinical and Experimental Neuropsychology, 19*, 421–431.

Bryant, R. A. (2008). Disentangling mild traumatic brain injuries and stress reactions. *New England Journal of Medicine, 358*, 525–527.

Carroll, L. J., Cassidy, J. D., Peloso, P. M., Borg, J., von Holst, H., Holm, L., Paniak, C., & Pepin, M. (2004). Prognosis for mild traumatic brain injury: Results of the WHO Collaborating Centre Task Force on Mild Traumatic Brain Injury. *Journal of Rehabilitation Medicine, 43* (Supplement), 84–105.

Dikmen, S. S., Machamer, J. E., Winn, H. R., & Temkin, N. R. (1995). Neuropsychological outcome at 1-year post head injury. *Neuropsychology, 9*, 80–90.

Dikmen, S. S., Temkin, N. R., Machamer, J. E., Holubkov, A. L., Fraser, R. T., & Winn, R. (1994). Employment following traumatic head injuries. *Archives of Neurology, 51*, 177–186.

Feinstein, A., Hershkop, S., Ouchterlony, D., Jardine, A., & McCullagh, S. (2002). Posttraumatic amnesia and recall of a traumatic event following traumatic brain injury. *Journal of Neuropsychiatry and Clinical Neurosciences, 14*, 25–29.

Ferrari, R., Obelieniene, D., Russell, A. S., Darlington, P., Gervais, R., & Green, P. (2001). Symptom expectation after minor head injury. A comparative study between Canada and Lithuania. *Clinical Neurology and Neurosurgery, 103*, 184–190.

Frencham, K. A. R., Fox, A. M., & Mayberry, M. T. (2005). Neuropsychological studies of mild traumatic brain injury: A meta-analytic review of research since 1995. *Journal of Clinical and Experimental Neuropsychology, 27*, 334–351.

Goldstein, F. C., Levin, H. S., Goldman, W. P., Clark, A. N., & Altonen, T. K. (2001). Cognitive and neurobehavioral functioning after mild versus moderate traumatic brain injury in older adults. *Journal of the International Neuropsychological Society, 7*, 373–383.

Greiffenstein, M. F., & Baker, W. J. (2008). Validity testing in dually diagnosed post-traumatic stress disorder and mild closed head injury. *The Clinical Neuropsychologist, 22*, 565–582.

Guilmette, T. J., Kennedy, M. L., Weiler, M. D., & Temple, R. O. (2006). Investigation of biases in the general public in evaluating mild head injury using neuropsychological and CT scan results: Forensic implications. *The Clinical Neuropsychologist, 20*, 305–314.

Heilbronner, R. L., & Karavidas, T. (1997). Presenting neuropsychological evidence in traumatic brain injury litigation. *The Clinical Neuropsychologist, 11*, 445–453.

Hoge, C. W., McGurk, D., Thomas, J. L., Cox, A. L., Engel, C. E., & Castro, C. A. (2008). Mild traumatic brain injury in U.S. soldiers returning from Iraq. *New England Journal of Medicine, 358*, 453–463.

Iverson, G. L. (2005). Outcome from mild traumatic brain injury. *Current Opinion in Psychiatry, 18*, 301–317.

Iverson, G., King, R., Scott, J., & Adams, R. (2001). Cognitive complaints in litigating patients with head injuries or chronic pain. *Journal of Forensic Neuropsychology, 2*, 19–30.

Kashluba, S., Paniak, C., & Casey, J. E. (2008). Persistent symptoms associated with factors identified by the WHO Task Force on Mild Traumatic Brain Injury. *The Clinical Neuropsychologist, 22*, 195–208.

Krpan, K. M., Levine, B., Stuss, D. T., & Dawson, D. R. (2007). Executive function and coping at one-year post traumatic brain injury. *Journal of Clinical and Experimental Neuropsychology, 29*, 36–46.

Lange, R. T., Iverson, G. L., & Franzen, M. D. (2008). Comparability of neuropsychological test profiles in patients with chronic substance abuse and mild traumatic brain injury. *The Clinical Neuropsychologist 22*, 209–227.

Langeluddecke, P. M., & Lucas, S. K. (2003). Wechsler Adult Intelligence Scale–Third Edition findings in relation to severity of brain injury in litigants. *The Clinical Neuropsychologist, 17*, 273–284.

Larson, M. J., Perlstein, W. M., Demery, J. A., & Stigge-Kaufman, D. A. (2006). Cognitive control impairments in traumatic brain injury. *Journal of Clinical and Experimental Neuropsychology, 28*, 968–986.

Levin, H. S., Mattis, S., Ruff, R. M., Eisenberg, H. M., Marshall, L. F., et al. (1987). Neurobehavioral outcome following minor head injury: A three-center study. *Journal of Neurosurgery, 66*, 234–243.

Machamer, J., Temkin, N., Fraser, R. Doctor, J., & Dikmen, S. (2005). Stability of employment after traumatic brain injury. *Journal of the International Neuropsychological Society, 11*, 807–816.

McCrea, M. A. (Ed.) (2008). *Mild traumatic brain injury and postconcussion syndrome: The new evidence base for diagnosis and treatment.* New York: Oxford University Press.

McFarland, K. Jackson, L., & Geffen, G. (2001). Post-traumatic amnesia: Consistency-of-recovery and duration-to-recovery following traumatic brain impairment. *The Clinical Neuropsychologist, 15*, 59–68.

McLean, A. J. (1995). Brain injury without head impact? *Journal of Neurotrauma, 12*, 621–625.

Miller, L. J., & Donders, J. (2001). Subjective symptomatology after traumatic head injury. *Brain Injury, 15*, 297–304.

O'Jile, J. R., Ryan, L. M., Betz, B., Parks-Levy, J., Hilsabeck, R. C., Rhudy, J. L., & Gouvier, W. D. (2006). Information processing following mild head injury. *Archives of Clinical Neuropsychology, 21*, 293–296.

Paniak, C., Reynolds, S., Phillips, K., Toller-Lobe, G., Melnyk, A., & Nagy, J. (2002). Patient complaints within 1 month of mild traumatic brain injury: A controlled study. *Archives of Clinical Neuropsychology, 17*, 319–334.

Paniak, C., Reynolds, S., Toller-Lobe, G., Melnyk, A., Nagy, J., & Schmidt, D. (2002). A longitudinal study of the relationship between financial compensation and symptoms after treated mild traumatic brain injury. *Journal of Clinical and Experimental Neuropsychology, 24*, 187–193.

Ponsford, J., Willmott, C., Rothwell, A., Cameron, P., Kelly, A-M., Nelms, R., Curran, C., & Ng, K. (2000). Factors influencing outcome following mild traumatic brain injury in adults. *Journal of the International Neuropsychological Society, 6*, 568–579.

Raz, S., Lauterbach, M. D., Hopkins, T. L., & Porter, C. L. (1995). Severity of perinatal cerebral injury and developmental outcome: A dose-response relationship. *Neuropsychology, 9*, 91–101.

Ryan, L. M., O'Jile, J. R., Parks-Levy, J., Betz, B., Hilsabeck, R. C., & Gouvier, W. D. (2006). Complex partial seizure symptom endorsement in individuals with a history of head injury. *Archives of Clinical Neuropsychology, 21*, 287–292.

Schretlen, D. J., & Shapiro, A. M. (2003). A quantitative review of the effects of traumatic brain injury on cognitive functioning. *International Review of Psychiatry, 15*, 341–349.

Sherer, M. Novack, T. A., Sander, A. M., Struchen, M. A., Alderson, A., & Thompson, R. N. (2002). Neuropsychological assessment and employment outcome after traumatic brain injury: A review. *The Clinical Neuropsychologist, 16*, 157–178.

Stulemeijer, M., Vos, P. E., Bleijenberg, G., & van der Werf, S. P. (2007). Cognitive complaints after mild traumatic brain injury: Things are not always what they seem. *Journal of Psychosomatic Research, 63*, 637–645.

Suhr, J., & Gunstad, J. (2002). Diagnosis threat: The effect of negative expectations on cognitive performance in head injury. *Journal of Clinical and Experimental Neuropsychology, 24*, 448–457.

Sweet, J. J. (2000). The role of neuropsychologists in brain injury litigation. *Brain Injury Source, 4*, 14–16.

Sweet, J. J., & Kuhlman, R. (1995). Evaluating malingering in brain injury claims: Genuine injury versus proven malingerer. *Trial Diplomacy Journal, 18*, 1–7.

Tiersky, L. A., Cicerone, K. D., Natelson, B. H., & DeLuca, J. (1998). Neuropsychological functioning in chronic fatigue syndrome and mild traumatic brain injury: A comparison. *The Clinical Neuropsychologist, 12*, 503–512.

Van der Naalt, J. (2001). Prediction of outcome in mild to moderate head injury: A review. *Journal of Clinical and Experimental Neuropsychology, 23*, 837–851.

Whittaker, R., Kemp, S., & House, A. (2007). Illness perceptions and outcome in mild head injury: A longitudinal study. *Journal of Neurology, Neurosurgery, and Psychiatry, 78*, 644–646.

Wood, R. L., & Rutterford, N. A. (2006). The effect of litigation on long term cognitive and psychological outcome after severe brain injury. *Archives of Clinical Neuropsychology, 21*, 239–246.

Youngjohn, J., Davis, D., & Wolf, I. (1997). Head injury and the MMPI-2: Paradoxical severity effects and the influence of litigation. *Psychological Assessment, 9*, 177–184.

D3: Somatoform disorders and medically unexplained symptoms (including multiple chemical sensitivity/ idiopathic environmental intolerance)

Bailer, J., Rist, F., Witthöft, M., Paul, C., & Bayerl, C. (2004). Symptom patterns and perceptual and cognitive styles in subjects with multiple chemical sensitivity (MCS). *Journal of Environmental Psychology, 24,* 517–525.

Bailer, J., Witthoft, M., Paul, C., Bayerl, C., & Rist, F., (2005). Evidence for overlap between idiopathic environmental intolerance and somatoform disorders. *Psychosomatic Medicine, 67,* 921–929.

Barsky, A. J., & Klerman, G. L. (1983). Overview: Hypochondriasis, bodily complaints, and somatic styles. *American Journal of Psychiatry, 140,* 273–283.

Bianchini, K. J., Houston, R. J., Greve, K. W., Irvin, T. R., Black, F. W., & Swift, D. A. (2003). Malingered neurocognitive dysfunction in neurotoxic exposure: An application of the Slick criteria. *Journal of Occupational and Environmental Medicine, 45,* 1087–1099.

Binder, L. M. (2007). Commentary on cogniform disorder and cogniform condition: Proposed diagnoses for excessive cognitive symptoms. *Archives of Clinical Neuropsychology, 22,* 681–682.

Binder, L. M., & Campbell, K. A. (2004). Medically unexplained symptoms and neuropsychological assessment. *Journal of Clinical and Experimental Neuropsychology, 26,* 369–392.

Binder, L. M., Storzbach, D., & Salinsky, M. C. (2006). MMPI-2 profiles of persons with multiple chemical sensitivity. *The Clinical Neuropsychologist, 20,* 848–857.

Bolla, K. I. (2000). Use of neuropsychological testing in idiopathic environmental testing. *Occupational Medicine State of the Art Reviews, 15,* 617–624.

Boone, K. B. (2007). Commentary on "Cogniform disorder and cogniform condition: Proposed diagnoses for excessive cognitive symptoms" by Dean C. Delis and Spencer R. Wetter. *Archives of Clinical Neuropsychology, 22,* 675–679.

Boone, K. B. (*in press*). Fixed belief in cognitive dysfunction despite normal neuropsychological scores: Neuropsychological hypochondriasis? *The Clinical Neuropsychologist,*

Boone, K. B., & Lu, P. H. (1999). Impact of somatoform symptomatology on credibility of cognitive performance. *The Clinical Neuropsychologist, 13* (4), 414.

Brown, R. J. (2004). Psychological mechanisms of medically unexplained symptoms: An integrative conceptual model. *Psychological Bulletin, 130,* 793–812.

Carson, A. J., Ringbauer, B., MacKenzie, L., Warlow, C., & Sharpe, M. (2000). Neurological disease, emotional disorder, and disability: they are related: a study of 300 consecutive new referrals to neurology outpatient department. *Journal of Neurology, Neurosurgery, and Psychiatry, 68,* 202–206.

Carson, A. J., Ringbauer, B., Stone, J., McKenzie, L., Warlow, C., & Sharpe, M. (2000). Do medically unexplained symptoms matter? A prospective cohort study of 300 new referrals to neurology outpatient clinics. *Journal of Neurology, Neurosurgery, and Psychiatry, 68,* 207–210.

Cragar, D., Berry, D., Fakhoury, T., Cibula, J., & Schmitt, F. (2006). Performance of patients with epilepsy and non-epileptic seizures on four measures of effort. *The Clinical Neuropsychologist, 20,* 552–566.

Delis, D. C., & Wetter, S. R. (2007). Cogniform disorder and cogniform condition: Proposed diagnoses for excessive cognitive symptoms. *Archives of Clinical Neuropsychology, 22,* 589–604.

Fishbain, D., Cole, B., Cutler, R., Lewis, J., Rosomoff, H., & Rosomoff, R. (2003). A structured evidence-based review on the meaning of nonorganic physical signs: Waddell signs. *Pain Medicine, 4,* 141–181.

Grubaugh, A. L., Elhai, J. D., Monnier, J., & Freuh, C. (2004). Service utilization among compensation-seeking veterans. *Psychiatric Quarterly, 75,* 333–341.

Harris, I., Mulford, J., Solomon, M., van Gelder, J. M., & Young, J. (2005). Association between compensation status and outcome after surgery: A meta-analysis. *Journal of the American Medical Association, 293,* 1644–1652.

Labarge, A. S., & McCaffrey, R. J. (2000). Multiple chemical sensitivity: A review of the theoretical and research literature. *Neuropsychology Review, 10,* 183–211.

Larrabee, G. J. (2007). Commentary on Delis and Wetter, "Cogniform disorder and cogniform condition: Proposed diagnoses for excessive cognitive symptoms." *Archives of Clinical Neuropsychology*, *22*, 683–687.

Locke, D. E. C., Berry, D. T. R., Fakhoury, T. A., & Schmitt, F. A. (2006). Relationship of indicators of neuropathology, psychopathology, and effort to neuropsychological results in patients with epilepsy or psychogenic non-epileptic seizures. *Journal of Clinical and Experimental Neuropsychology*, *28*, 325–340.

Mechanic, D. (1972). Social psychologic factors affecting the presentation of bodily complaints. *New England Journal of Medicine*, *286*, 1132–1139.

Ochoa, J. L. (1999). Truths, errors, and lies around "reflex sympathetic dystrophy" and "complex regional pain syndrome". *Journal of Neurology*, *246* (10), 875–879.

Poonai, N. P., Antony, M. M., Binkley, K. E., Stenn, P., Swinson, R. P., Corey, P., Silverman, F. S., & Tarlo, S. M. (2001). Psychological features of subjects with idiopathic environmental intolerance. *Journal of Psychosomatic Research*, *5*, 537–541.

Putnam, S. H., & Millis, S. R. (1994). Psychosocial factors in the development and maintenance of chronic somatic and functional symptoms following mild traumatic brain injury. *Advances in Medical Psychotherapy*, *7*, 1–22.

Reinhard, M. J., Satz, P., Scaglione, C. A., D'Elia, L. F., Rassovsky, Y., Arita, A. A., Hinkin, C. H., Thrasher, D., & Ordog, G. (2007). Neuropsychological exploration of alleged mold neurotoxicity. *Archives of Clinical Neuropsychology*, *22*, 533–543.

Richardson, R. D., & Engel, C. C. (2004). Evaluation and management of medically unexplained physical symptoms. *The Neurologist*, *10*, 18–30.

Rogers, R., Jackson, R. L., & Kaminski, P. L. (2005). Factitious psychological disorders: The overlooked response style in forensic evaluations. *Journal of Forensic Psychology Practice*, *5*, 21–41.

Schrag, A., Brown, R. J., & Trimble, M. R. (2004). Reliability of self-reported diagnoses in patients with neurological unexplained symptoms. *Journal of Neurology, Neurosurgery, and Psychiatry*, *75:* 608–611.

Stone, D. C., Boone, K. B., Back-Madruga, C., & Lessr, I. M. (2006). Has the rolling uterus finally gathered moss? Somatization and malingering of cognitive dysfunction in six cases of "toxic mold" exposure. *The Clinical Neuropsychologist*, *20*, 766–785.

Suhr, J. A., & Gunstad, J. (2002). "Diagnosis threat": The effect of negative expectations on cognitive performance in head injury. *Journal of Clinical and Experimental Neuropsychology*, *24*, 448–457.

Suhr, J. A., & Gunstad, J. (2004). Further exploration of the effect of "diagnosis threat" on cognitive performance in individuals with mild head injury. *Journal of the International Neuropsychological Society*, *11*, 23–29.

Sumanti, M., Boone, K. B., Savodnik, I., & Gorsuch, R. (2006). Noncredible psychiatric and cognitive symptoms in a worker's compensation "stress" claim sample. *The Clinical Neuropsychologist*, *20*, 754–765.

Tiersky, L. A., Cicerone, K. D., Natelson, B. H., & DeLuca, J. (1998). Neuropsychological functioning in chronic fatigue syndrome and mild traumatic brain injury: A comparison. *The Clinical Neuropsychologist*, *12*, 503–512.

Watson, D., & Pennebaker, J. W. (1989). Health complaints, stress, and distress: Exploring the central role of negative affectivity. *Psychological Review*, *96*, 234–254.

Witthöft, M., Gerlach, A. L., & Bailer, J. (2006). Selective attention, memory bias, and symptom perception in idiopathic environmental intolerance and somatoform disorders. *Journal of Abnormal Psychology*, *115*, 397–407.

D4: Pain (including fibromyalgia and whiplash)

Arbisi, P. A., & Butcher, J. N. (2004). Psychometric perspective on detection of malingering of pain. *Clinical Journal of Pain*, *20*, 383–391.

Bell, B., Primeau, M., Sweet, J., & Lofland, K. (1999). Neuropsychological functioning in migraine headache, nonheadache chronic pain, and mild traumatic brain injury patients. *Archives of Clinical Neuropsychology*, *14*, 389–399.

Bianchini, K. J., Greve, K. W., & Glynn, G. (2005). On the diagnosis of malingered pain-related disability: Lessons from cognitive malingering research. *The Spine Journal*, *5*, 404–417.

Cassidy, J. D., Carroll, L. J., Cote, P., Lemstra, M., Berglund, A., & Nygren, A. (2000). Effect of eliminating compensation for pain and suffering on the outcome of insurance claims for whiplash injury. *New England Journal of Medicine*, *342*, 1179–1186.

Etherton, J., Bianchini, K., Ciota, M., & Greve, K. (2005). Reliable digit span is unaffected by laboratory-induced pain. *Assessment, 12,* 101–106.

Etherton, J. L., Bianchini, K. J., Greve, K. W., & Heinly, M. T. (2005). Sensitivity and specificity of reliable digit span in malingered pain-related disability. *Assessment, 12,* 130–136.

Etherton, J., Bianchini, K., Heinly, M., & Greve, K. (2006). Pain, malingering, and performance on the WAIS-III Processing Speed Index. *Journal of Clinical and Experimental Neuropsychology, 28,* 1218–1237.

Gervais, R., Green, P., Allen, L., & Iverson, G. (2001). Effects of coaching on symptom validity testing in chronic pain patients presenting for disability assessments. *Journal of Forensic Neuropsychology, 2* (2), 1–19.

Gervais, R., Russell, A., Green, P., Allen, L., Ferrari, R., & Pieschl, S. (2001). Effort testing in fibromyalgia patients with disability incentives. *Journal of Rheumatology, 28,* 1892–1899.

Greve, K. W., Ord, J., Curtis, K. L., Bianchini, K. J., & Brennan, A. (in press). Detecting malingering in traumatic brain injury and chronic pain: A comparison of three forced-choice symptom validity tests. *The Clinical Neuropsychologist.*

Guez, M., Brannstrom, R., Nyberg, L., Toolanen, G., & Hildingsson, C. (2005). Neuropsychological functioning and MMPI-2 profiles in chronic neck pain: A comparison of whiplash and non-traumatic groups. *Journal of Clinical and Experimental Neuropsychology, 27,* 151–163.

Iverson, G., King, R., Scott, J., & Adams, R. (2001). Cognitive complaints in litigating patients with head injuries or chronic pain. *Journal of Forensic Neuropsychology, 2,* 19–30.

Iverson, G. L., Le Page, J., Koehler, B. E., Shojania, K., & Badii, M. (2007). Test of Memory Malingering (TOMM) scores are not affected by chronic pain or depression in patients with fibromyalgia. *The Clinical Neuropsychologist, 21,* 532–546.

Karlin, B., Creech, S., Grimes, J., Clark, T., Meagher, M., & Morey, L. (2005). The Personality Assessment Inventory with chronic pain patients: Psychometric properties and clinical utility. *Journal of Clinical Psychology, 61,* 1571–1585.

Kessels, R., Aleman, A., Cerhagen, W., & Van Luijtelaar, E. (2000). Cognitive functioning after whiplash: A meta-analysis. *Journal of the International Neuropsychological Society, 6,* 271–278.

Kwan, O., & Friel, J. (2003). A review and methodologic critique of the literature supporting chronic whiplash injury: Part I Research articles. *Medical Science Monitoring, 9,* 203–215.

Kwan, O., & Friel, J. (2003). A review and methodologic critique of the literature supporting chronic whiplash injury: Part II Reviews, editorials, and letters. *Medical Science Monitoring, 9,* 230–236.

Larrabee, G. J. (2003). Exaggerated pain report in litigants with malingered neurocognitive dysfunction. *The Clinical Neuropsychologist, 17,* 395–401.

McGuire, B. E., Harvey, A. G., & Shores, E. A. (2001). Simulated malingering in pain patients: A study with the Pain Patient Profile. *British Journal of Clinical Psychology, 40,* 71–79.

McGuire, B., & Shores, E. A. (2001). Pain Patient Profile and the assessment of malingered pain. *Journal of Clinical Psychology, 57,* 401–409.

Meyers, J. E., & Diep, A. (2000). Assessment of malingering in chronic pain patients using neuropsychological tests. *Applied Neuropsychology, 7,* 133–139.

Munoz, M., & Esteve, R. (2005). Reports of memory functioning by patients with chronic pain. *Clinical Journal of Pain, 5,* 287–291.

Obelieniene, D., Bovim, G., Schrader, H., Surkiene, D., Mickeviaiene, D., Miseviaiene, I., & Sand, T. (1998). Headache after whiplash: A historical cohort study outside of the medico-legal context. *Cephalagia, 18,* 559–564.

Obelieniene, D., Schrader, H., Bovim, G., Miseviciene, I., & Sand, T. (1999). Pain after whiplash: a prospective controlled inception cohort study. *Journal of Neurology, Neurosurgery, and Psychiatry. 66,* 279–83.

Pearce, J. (1999). A critical appraisal of the chronic whiplash syndrome. *Journal of Neurology, Neurosurgery, and Psychiatry, 66,* 273–276.

Pobereskin, L. H. (2005). Whiplash following rear end collisions: A prospective cohort study. *Journal of Neurology, Neurosurgery, and Psychiatry, 76,* 1146–1151.

Radanov, B., Bicik, I., Dvorak, J., Antinnes, J., von Schulthess, G., & Buck, A. (1999). Relation between neuropsychological and neuroimaging findings in patients with late whiplash syndrome. *Journal of Neurology, Neurosurgery, and Psychiatry, 66,* 485–489.

Radanov, B., Di Stefano, G., Schnidrig, A., Sturzenegger, M., & Augustiny, K. (1993). Cognitive functioning after common whiplash: A controlled follow-up study. *Archives of Neurology, 50,* 87–91.

Schmand, R., Lindeboom, J., Schagen, S., Heijt, R., Koene, T., & Hamburger, H. (1997). Cognitive complaints in patients after whiplash injury: The impact of malingering. *Journal of Neurology, Neurosurgery, and Psychiatry*, *64*, 339–343.

Schrader, H., Obelieniene, D., Bovim, G., Surkiene, D., Mickeviciene, Miseviciene, I., & Sand, T. (1996). Natural evolution of late whiplash syndrome outside the medicolegal context. *Lancet, 347*, 1207–1211.

D5: Posttraumatic stress disorder

Andrews, B., Brewin, C., Philpott, R., & Stewart, L. (2007). Delayed onset Posttraumatic stress disorder: A systematic review of the evidence. *American Journal of Psychiatry, 164*, 1319–1326.

Bryant, R. A. (2008). Disentangling mild traumatic brain injuries and stress reactions. *The New England Journal of Medicine, 358*, 525–527.

Calhoun, P. S., Earnst, K. S., Tucker, D. D., Kirby, A. C., & Beckham, J. C. (2000). Feigning combat-related posttraumatic stress disorder on the Personality Assessment Inventory. *Journal of Personality Assessment, 75*, 338–350.

Demakis, G. J., Gervais, R. O., & Rohling, M. L. (in press). The effect of failure on cognitive and psychological symptom validity tests in litigants with symptoms of Post-Traumatic Stress Disorder. *The Clinical Neuropsychologist*.

Elhai, J. D., Gray, Matthew, J., Naifeh, J. A., Butcher, J. J., Davis, J. L, Falsetti, S. A., & Best, C. L. (2005). Utility of the Trauma Symptom Inventory's atypical response scale in detecting malingered post-traumatic stress disorder. *Assessment, 12*, 210–219.

Frueh, B. C., Lehai, J. D., Grubaugh, A. L., Monnier, J., et al. (2005). Documented combat exposure of US veterans seeking treatment for combat-related post-traumatic stress disorder. *British Journal of Psychiatry, 186*, 467–472.

Greiffenstein, M. F., & Baker, W. J. (2008). Validity testing in dually diagnosed post-traumatic stress disorder and mild closed head injury. *The Clinical Neuropsychologist, 22*, 565–582.

Guriel, J., & Fremouw, W. (2003). Assessing malingered posttraumatic stress disorder: A critical review. *Clinical Psychology Review, 23*, 881–904.

Hall, R. C. W., & Hall, R. C. W. (2006). Malingering of PTSD: Forensic and diagnostic considerations, characteristics of malingerers and clinical presentations. *General Hospital Psychiatry, 28*, 525–535.

Hoge, C. W., McGurk, D., Thomas, J. L., Cox, A. L., Engel, C. E., & Castro, C. A. (2008). Mild traumatic brain injury in U.S. soldiers returning from Iraq. *New England Journal of Medicine, 358*, 453–463.

Koch, W. J., O'Neill, M., & Douglas, K. S. (2005). Empirical limits for the forensic assessment of PTSD litigants. *Law and Human Behavior, 29*, 121–149.

Rosen, G. M. (2004). Litigation and reported rates of posttraumatic stress disorder. *Personality and Individual Differences, 36*, 1291–1294.

Rosen, G. M. (2006). DSM's cautionary guideline to rule out malingering can protect the PTSD database. *Anxiety Disorders, 20*, 530–535.

Rosen, G. M., & Powel, J. E. (2003). Use of a symptom validity test in the forensic assessment of posttraumatic stress disorder. *Anxiety Disorders, 17*, 361–367.

Rosen, G. M., & Taylor, S. (2007). Pseudo-PTSD. *Journal of Anxiety Disorders, 21*, 201–210.

Shapinsky, A. C., Rapport, L. J., Henderson, M. J., & Axelrod, B. N. (2005). Civilian PTSD scales: Relationships with trait characteristics and everyday distress. *Assessment, 12*, 220–230.

Taylor, S., Frueh, B. C., & Asmundson, G. J. G. (2007). Detection and management of malingering in people presenting for treatment of posttraumatic stress disorder: Methods, obstacles, and recommendations. *Journal of Anxiety Disorders, 21*, 22–41.

Wessely, S. (2005). War stories: Invited commentary on . . . Documented combat exposure of US veterans seeking treatment for combat-related post-traumatic stress disorder. *British Journal of Psychiatry, 186*, 473–475.

D6: Toxic encephalopathy and neurotoxic exposure

Albers, J. W., & Berent, S. (2005). *Neurobehavioral toxicology: Neurological and neuropsychological perspectives: Vol. 2. Peripheral nervous system*. London and New York: Taylor & Francis.

Berent S., & Albers, J. W. (2005). *Neurobehavioral Toxicology: Neurological and neuropsychological perspectives: Vol. 1. Foundations and methods.* London and New York: Taylor & Francis.

Berent S., & Albers, J. W. (2007). *Neurobehavioral toxicology: Neurological and neuropsychological perspectives: Vol. 3. Central nervous system.* London and New York: Taylor & Francis.

Bianchini, K. J., Houston, R. J., Greve, K. W., Irvin, T. R., Black, F. W., & Swift, D. A. (2003). Malingered neurocognitive dysfunction in neurotoxic exposure: An application of the Slick criteria. *Journal of Occupational and Environmental Medicine, 45,* 1087–1099.

Hartman, D. E. (Ed.) (1995). *Neuropsychological toxicology: Identification and assessment of human neurotoxic syndromes (2nd ed.).* New York: Plenum Press.

Khalili, B., & Bardana, E. J., Jr. (2005). Inhalation mold toxicity: Fact or fiction? A clinical review of 50 cases. *Annals of Allergy, Asthma, and Immunology, 95,* 239–246.

Reinhard, M. J., Satz, P., Scaglione, C. A., D'Elia, L. F., Rassovsky, Y., Arita, A. A., Hinkin, C. H., Thrasher, D., & Ordog, G. (2007). Neuropsychological exploration of alleged mold neurotoxicity. *Archives of Clinical Neuropsychology, 22,* 533–543.

Stone, D. C., Boone, K. B., Back-Madruga, C., & Lessr, I. M. (2006). Has the rolling uterus finally gathered moss? Somatization and malingering of cognitive dysfunction in six cases of "toxic mold" exposure. *The Clinical Neuropsychologist, 20,* 766–785.

van Hout, M. S., Schmand, B., Wekking, E. M., & Deelman, B. G. (2006). Cognitive functioning in patients with suspected chronic toxic encephalopathy: Evidence for neuropsychological disturbances after controlling for insufficient effort. *Journal of Neurology, Neurosurgery, and Psychiatry, 77,* 296–303.

van Hout, M. S., Schmand, B., Wekking, E. M., Hageman, G., & Deelman, B. G. (2003). Suboptimal performance on neuropsychological tests in patients with suspected chronic toxic encephalopathy. *Neurotoxicology, 24,* 547–551.

Van Reekum, R., Streiner, D. L., & Conn, D. K. (2001). Applying Bradford Hill's criteria for causation to neuropsychiatry: Challenges and opportunities. *Journal of Neuropsychiatry and Clinical Neurosciences, 13,* 318–325.

D7: Self-report (e.g., reliability, effects of emotional conditions and litigation)

Brennan, A. M., Stewart, H. A., Jamhour, N., Businelle, M. S., & Gouvier, W. D. (2005). An examination of the retrospective recall of psychological distress. *Journal of Forensic Neuropsychology, 4,* 99–110.

Christodoulou, C., Melville, P., Scheri, W. F., Morgan, T., MacAllister, W. S., Canfora, D. M., Berry, S. A., & Krupp, L. B. (2005). Perceived cognitive dysfunction and observed neuropsychological performance: Longitudinal relation in persons with multiple sclerosis. *Journal of the International Neuropsychological Society, 11,* 614–619.

Fargo, J. D., Schefft, B. K., Szaflarski, J. P., Dulay, M. F., Testa, S. M., Privitera, M. D., & Yeh, H.-S. (2004). Accuracy of self-reported neuropsychological functioning in individuals with epileptic or psychogenic nonepileptic seizures. *Epilepsy and Behavior, 5,* 143–150.

Farias, S. T., Mungas, D., & Jagust, W. (2005). Degree of discrepancy between self and other-reported everyday functoining by cognitive status: Dementia, mild cognitive impairment, and healthy elders. *International Journal of Geriatric Psychiatry, 20,* 827–834.

Ferguson, R. J., Mittenberg, W., Barone, D. F., & Schneider, B. (1999). Postconcussion syndrome following sports related head injury: Expectation as etiology. *Neuropsychology, 13,* 582–589.

Gouvier, D. W., Cubic, B., Jones, G., Brantley, P., & Cutlip, Q. (1992). Postconcussional symptoms and daily stress in normal and head injured college populations. *Archives of Clinical Neuropsychology, 7,* 193–212.

Gouvier, D. W., Uddo-Crane, M., & Brown, L. M. (1988). Base rates of postconcussion symptoms. *Archives of Clinical Neuropsychology, 3,* 273–278.

Greiffenstein, M. F., Baker, W. J., & Johnson-Greene, D. (2002). Actual versus self-reported scholastic achievement of litigating postconcussion and severe closed head injury claimants. *Psychological Assessment, 14,* 202–208.

Gunstad, J., & Suhr, J. A. (2001). "Expectation as Etiology" versus "The Good Old Days": Postconcussion syndrome symptom reporting in athletes, headache sufferers, and depressed individuals. *Journal of the International Neuropsychological Society, 7,* 323–333.

Hilsabeck, R. C., Gouvier, W. D., & Bolter, J. F. (1998). Reconstructive memory bias in recall of neuro-psychological symptomatology. *Journal of Clinical and Experimental Neuropsychology, 20*, 328–338.

Iverson, G. L., & McCracken, L. M. (1997). "Postconcussive" symptoms in persons with chronic pain. *Brain Injury, 11*, 783–790.

Jungwirth, S., Fischer, P., Weissgram, S., Kirchmeyr, W., Bauer, P., & Tragl, K.-H. (2004). Subjective memory complaints and objective memory impairment in the Vienna-Transdanube aging community. *Journal of the American Geriatrics Society, 52*, 263–268.

Lees-Haley, P., Williams, C., Zasler, N., Marguilies, S., English, L., & Stevens, K. (1997). Response bias in plaintiffs' histories. *Brain Injury, 11*, 791–799.

Martin, R., Hayes, J., & Gouvier, W. D. (1996). Differential vulnerability between postconcussion self-report and objective malingering tests in identifying simulated mild head injury. *Journal of Clinical and Experimental Neuropsychology, 18*, 265–275.

Meador, K. J., Loring, D. W., Vahle, V. J., Ray, P. G., Werz, M. A., Fessler, A. J., Ogrocki, P., Schoenberg, M. R., Miller, J. M., & Kustra, R. P. (2005). Subjective perception of cognitive effects of antiepileptic drugs is more related to mood than to objective performance. *Epilepsia, 46*, 261–262.

Mittenberg, W., DiGiulio, D. V., Perrin, S., & Bass, A. E. (1992). Symptoms following mild head injury: Expectation as aetiology. *Journal of Neurology, Neurosurgery and Psychiatry, 55*, 200–204.

Otto, M. W., Bruder, G. E., Maurizio, F., Delis, D. C., et al. (1994). Norms for depressed patients for the California Verbal Learning Test: Associations with depression severity and self-report of cognitive difficulties. *Archives of Clinical Neuropsychology, 9*, 81–88.

Rutherford, W. H. (1989). Postconcussion symptoms: Relationship to acute neurological indices, individual differences, and circumstances of injury. In H. S. Levin, H. M. Eisenberg, & A. L. Benton (Eds.). *Mild head injury* (pp. 217–228). New York: Oxford University Press.

Schrag, A., Brown, R. J., & Trimble, M. R. (2004). Reliability of self-reported diagnoses in patients with neurological unexplained symptoms. *Journal of Neurology, Neurosurgery, and Psychiatry, 75:* 608–611.

Williams, C., Lees-Haley, P., & Djanogly, S. (1999). Clinical scrutiny of litigants' self-reports. *Professional Psychology: Research and Practice, 30*, 361–367.

Zandi, T. (2004). Relationship between subjective memory complaints, objective memory performance, and depression among older adults. *American Journal of Alzheimer's Disease and Other Dementias, 19*, 353–360.

D8: Ethical issues (including objectivity and bias)

Adams, K. M. (1997). Comment on ethical considerations in forensic neuropsychological consultation. *The Clinical Neuropsychologist, 11*, 294–296.

American Academy of Clinical Neuropsychology (2001). Policy Statement on the Presence of Third Party Observers in Neuropsychological Assessments. *The Clinical Neuropsychologist, 15*, 433–439.

American Academy of Clinical Neuropsychology (2003). Official position of the American Academy of Clinical Neuropsychology on ethical complaints made against clinical neuropsychologists during adversarial proceedings. *The Clinical Neuropsychologist, 17*, 443–445.

American Psychological Association Committee on Legal Issues (2006). Strategies for private practitioners coping with subpoenas or compelled testimony for client records or test data. *Professional Psychology: Research and Practice, 37*, 215–222.

Annapolis Center for Science-Based Public Policy (2006). *Neuropsychological testing: Ethical applications for law and public policy*. Annapolis, MD: J.D. Seward & M. Welner.

Binder, L., & Thompson, L. (1995). The ethics code and neuropsychological assessment practices. *Archives of Clinical Neuropsychology, 10*, 27–46.

Borum, R., Otto, R., & Golding, S. (1993). Improving clinical judgement and decision making in forensic evaluation. *Journal of Psychiatry and Law, 21*, 35–76.

Bush, S. (2005). *A casebook of ethical challenges in neuropsychology*. New York: Taylor & Francis.

Bush, S. (Ed.) (2005). Ethical issues in forensic neuropsychology [Special issue]. *Journal of Forensic Neuropsychology, 4* (3).

Bush, S. et al. (2005). NAN position paper: Symptom validity assessment: Practice issues and medical necessity. *Archives of Clinical Neuropsychology, 20*, 419–426.

Bush, S. et al. (2005). Independent and court-ordered forensic neuropsychological examinations: Official statement of the National Academy of Neuropsychology. *Archives of Clinical Neuropsychology*, *20*, 997–1007.

Bush, S. S., Grote, C. L., Johnsone-Greene, D. E., & Macartney-Filgate, M. (2008). A panel interview on the ethical practice of neuropsychology. *The Clinical Neuropsychologist*, *22*, 321–344.

Committee on Ethical Guidelines for Forensic Psychologists (1991). Specialty guidelines for forensic psychologists. *Law and Human Behavior*, *15*, 655–665.

Essig, S. M., Mittenberg, W., Petersen, R. S., Strauman, S., & Cooper, J. T. (2001). Practices in forensic neuropsychology: Perspectives of neuropsychologists and trial attorneys. *Archives of Clinical Neuropsychology*, *16*, 271–291.

Fishbain, D. A., Cutler, R., Rosomoff, H. L., & Rosomoff, R. S. (1999). Chronic pain disability exaggeration/malingering and submaximal effort research. *Clinical Journal of Pain*, *15*, 244–274.

Fishbain, D. A., Cutler, R., Rosomoff, H. L., & Rosomoff, R. S. (2004). Is there a relationship between nonorganic physical findings (Waddell signs) and secondary gain/malingering? *Clinical Journal of Pain*, *20*, 399–408.

Garb, H., (1998). *Studying the clinician: Judgement research and psychological assessment*. Washington, DC: American Psychological Association.

Garb, H., & Schramke, C. (1996). Judgment research and neuropsychological assessment: A narrative review and meta-analysis. *Psychological Bulletin*, *120*, 140–153.

Greiffenstein, M. F., & Cohen, L. (2005). Principles of productive neuropsychologist-attorney interactions. In G. Larrabee (Ed.), *Forensic neuropsychology: A scientific approach* (pp. 29–91). New York: Oxford University Press.

Grote, C. (2005). Ethical practice of forensic neuropsychology. In G. J. Larrabee (Ed.), *Forensic neuropsychology: A scientific approach* (pp. 92–114). New York: Oxford University Press.

Grote, C., Lewin, J., Sweet, J. J., & van Gorp, W. (2000). Responses to perceived unethical practices in clinical neuropsychology: Ethical and legal considerations. *The Clinical Neuropsychologist*, *14*, 119–134.

Guilmette, T., & Hagan, L. (1997). Ethical considerations in forensic neuropsychological consultation. *The Clinical Neuropsychologist*, *11*, 287–290.

Gutheil, T. G., Schetky, D. H., & Simon, R. I. (2006). Pejorative testimony about opposing experts and colleagues: "Fouling one's own nest." *Journal of the American Academy of Psychiatry and the Law*, *34*, 26–30.

Johnson-Greene, D., & Bechtold, K. T. (2002). Ethical considerations for peer review in forensic neuropsychology. *The Clinical Neuropsychologist*, *16*, 97–104.

Kaufman, P. (2005). Protecting the objectivity, fairness, and integrity of neuropsychological evaluations in litigation: A privilege second to none? *Journal of Legal Medicine*, *26*, 95–131.

Malina, A., Nelson, N., & Sweet, J. J. (2005). Framing the relationships in forensic neuropsychology: Ethical issues. *Journal of Forensic Neuropsychology*, *4*, 21–44.

Martelli, M. F., Bush, S. S., & Zasler, N. D. (2003). Identifying, avoiding, and addressing ethical misconduct in neuropsychological medicolegal practice. *International Journal of Forensic Psychology*, *1*, 26–44.

Martelli, M. F., Zasler, N. D., & Johnson-Greene, D. (2001). Promoting ethical and objective practice in the medicolegal arena of disability evaluation. *Disability Evaluation*, *12*, 571–584.

McCaffrey, R. (Ed.). (2005). Third party observers [Special issue]. *Journal of Forensic Neuropsychology*, *4* (2).

McSweeney, A. J. (1997). Regarding ethics in neuropsychological consultation: A comment on Guilmette and Hagan. *The Clinical Neuropsychologist*, *11*, 291–293.

McSweeney, A. J., Becker, B. C., Naugle, R. I., Snow, W. G., Binder, L. M., & Thompson, L. L. (1998). Ethical issues related to presence of third party observers in clinical neuropsychological evaluations. *The Clinical Neuropsychologist*, *12*, 552–560.

Nagy, T. (2000). *Ethics in plain English: An illustrative casebook for psychologists*. Washington, DC: American Psychological Association.

Sweet, J. J. (2005). Ethical challenges in forensic neuropsychology, Part V. In S. Bush (Ed.) *A casebook of ethical challenges in neuropsychology*. New York: Psychology Press.

Sweet, J. J., Grote, C., & vanGorp, W. (2002). Ethical issues in forensic neuropsychology. In S. Bush & M. L. Drexler (Eds.) *Ethical issues in clinical neuropsychology*. Lisse, Netherlands: Swets & Zeitlinger.

Sweet, J. J., & Moulthrop, M. (1999). Self-examination questions as a means of identifying bias in adversarial assessments. *Journal of Forensic Neuropsychology*, *1* (1), 73–88.

Sweet, J. J., & Moulthrop, M. A. (1999). Response to Lees-Haley's commentary: Debiasing techniques cannot be completely curative. *Journal of Forensic Neuropsychology, 1* (3), 49–57.

van Gorp, W., & McMullen, W. (1997). Potential sources of bias in forensic neuropsychological evaluations. *The Clinical Neuropsychologist, 11*, 180–187.

Van Reekum, R., Streiner, D. L., & Conn, D. K. (2001). Applying Bradford Hill's criteria for causation to neuropsychitry: Challenges and opportunities. *Journal of Neuropsychiatry and Clinical Neurosciences, 13*, 318–325.

Weissman, H., & DeBow, D. (2003). Ethical principles and professional competencies. In A. Goldstein (Ed.), *Vol. 11: Forensic psychology*, of the *Handbook of psychology*, I. Weiner (Ed. in Chief) (pp. 33–53). New York: Wiley.

Youngjohn, J. (1995). Confirmed attorney coaching prior to neuropsychological evaluation. *Assessment, 2*, 279–284.

D9: Evidentiary rulings (e.g., *Daubert* challenges)

Dahir, V. B., Richardson, J. T., Ginsburg, G. P., Gatowski, S. I., Dobbin, S. A., & Merlino, M. L. (2005). Judicial application of Daubert to psychological syndrome and profile evidence: A research note. *Psychology, Public Policy, and Law, 11*, 62–82.

Cheng, E. K., & Yoon, A. H. (2005). Does *Frye* or *Daubert* matter? A study of scientific admissibility standards. *Virginia Law Review, 91*, 471–513.

Groscup, J. L., Penrod, S. D., Studebaker, C. A., Huss, M. T., & O'Neil, K. M. (2002). The effects of Daubert on the admissibility of expert testimony in state and federal criminal cases. *Psychology, Public Policy, and Law, 8*, 339–372.

Kaufmann, P. (2008). Admissibility of neuropsychological evidence in criminal cases: Competency, insanity, culpability, and mitigation. In R. Denney (Ed.) *Clinical neuropsychology in the criminal forensic setting*. New York: Guilford.

Sweet, J. J., Ecklund-Johnson, E., & Malina, A. (2008). Overview of forensic neuropsychology. In J. Morgan & J. Ricker (Eds.) *Textbook of clinical neuropsychology*. New York: Taylor & Francis.

D10: Neuroimaging in the courtroom

Brakel, S. J., Gonzalez, E. R., & Cavanaugh, J. L., Jr. (1996). Neuropsychiatry at the courtroom gates: Selective entry or anything goes? *Seminars in Clinical Neuropsychiatry, 1*, 215–221.

Bufkin, J. L., & Luttrell, V. R. (2005). Neuroimaging studies of aggressive and violent behavior: current findings and implications for criminology and criminal justice. *Trauma Violence Abuse, 6*, 176–191.

Jackson, G. E. (2006). A curious consensus: "Brain scans prove disease?" *Ethical Human Psychology and Psychiatry: An International Journal of Critical Inquiry, 8*, 55–60.

Kulynych, J. (1997). Psychiatric neuroimaging evidence: A high-tech crystal ball? *Stanford Law Review, 49*, 1249–1270.

Mayberg, H. S. (1996). Medical-legal inferences from functional neuroimaging evidence. *Seminars in Clinical Neuropsychiatry, 1*, 195–201.

Mehr, S. H., & Gerdes, S. L. (2001). Medicolegal applications of PET scans. *NeuroRehabilitation, 16*(2), 87–92.

Pratt, B., & Johnson, K. (2005). "Soft" science in the courtroom?: The effects of admitting neuroimaging evidence into legal proceedings. *Penn Bioethics Journal, 1*, 1–3.

Reeves, D., Mills, M. J., Billick, S. B., & Brodie, J. D. (2003). Limitations of brain imaging in forensic psychiatry. *Journal of the American Academy of Psychiatry and Law, 31* (1), 89–96.

Ricker, J. H., & Zafonte, R. D. (2000). Functional neuroimaging and quantitative electroencephalography in adult traumatic head injury: clinical applications and interpretive cautions. *Journal of Head Trauma Rehabilitation, 15* (2), 859–868.

Weiss, Z. (1996). The legal admissibility of positron emission tomography scans in criminal cases: People v. Spyder Cystkopf. *Seminars in Clinical Neuropsychiatry, 1*, 202–210.

D11: Third party observers

Axelrod, B., Barth, J., Faust, D., Fisher, J., Heilbronner, R., Larrabee, G., Pliskin, N., & Silver, C.; Policy and Planning Committee, National Academy of Neuropsychology (2000). Presence of third party observers during neuropsychological testing: Official statement of the National Academy of Neuropsychology. *Archives of Clinical Neuropsychology, 15*, 379–380.

American Academy of Clinical Neuropsychology (2001). Policy statement on the presence of third party observers in neuropsychological assessments. *The Clinical Neuropsychologist, 15*, 433–439.

Binder, L. M., & Johnson-Greene, D. (1995). Observer effects on neuropsychological performance: A case report. *The Clinical Neuropsychologist, 9*, 74–78.

Constantinou, M., Ashendorf, L., & McCaffrey, R. (2002). When the third party observer of a neuropsychological evaluation is an audio-recorder. *The Clinical Neuropsychologist, 16*, 407–412.

Constantinou, M., Ashendorf, L., & McCaffrey, R. (2005). Effects of a third party observer during neuropsychological assessment: When the observer is a video camera. *Journal of Forensic Neuropsychology, 4*, 39–48.

Duff, K., & Fisher, J. (2005). Ethical dilemmas with third party observers. *Journal of Forensic Neuropsychology, 4*, 65–82.

Gavett, B., Lynch, J., & McCaffrey, R. (2005). Third party observers: The effect size is greater than you might think. *Journal of Forensic Neuropsychology, 4*, 49–64.

Kehrer, C., Sanchez, P., Habif, U., Rosenbaum, J. G., & Townes, B. (2000) Effects of a significant-other observer on neuropsychological test performance. *The Clinical Neuropsychologist, 14*, 67–71.

Lambert, L. (2007). Why third-party observers should be excluded from Rule 1.360 Psychological Examinations. *Trial Advocate Quarterly, 27* (4), 6–12.

Lynch, J. (2005). Effects of a third party observer on neuropsychological test performance following closed head injury. *Journal of Forensic Neuropsychology, 4*, 17–26.

McCaffrey, R. J., Fisher, J. M., Gold, B. A., & Lynch, J. K. (1996). Presence of third parties during neuropsychological evaluations: Who is evaluating whom? *The Clinical Neuropsychologist, 10*, 1–15.

McCaffrey, R., Lynch, J., & Yantz, C. (2005). Third party observers: Why all the fuss? *Journal of Forensic Neuropsychology, 4*, 1–16.

McSweeny, A. J., Becker, B. C., Naugle, R. I., Snow, W. G., Binder, L. M., & Thompson, L. L. (1998). Ethical issues related to the presence of third party observers in clinical neuropsychology evaluations. *The Clinical Neuropsychologist, 12*, 552–559.

Yantz, C., & McCaffrey (2005). Effects of a supervisor's observation on memory test performance of the examinee: Third party observer effect confirmed. *Journal of Forensic Neuropsychology, 4*, 27–38.

D12: Professional practice surveys relevant to forensic neuropsychology

Archer, R. P., Buffington-Vollum, J. K., Stredny, R. V., & Handel, R. H. (2006). A survey of psychological test use patterns among forensic psychologists. *Journal of Personality Assessment, 87*, 84–94.

Guilmette, T. J., Hagan, L. D., & Giuliano, A. J. (2008). Assigning qualitative descriptions to test scores in neuropsychology: Forensic implications. *The Clinical Neuropsychologist, 22*, 122–139.

Lally, S. J. (2003). What tests are acceptable for use in forensic evaluations? A survey of experts. *Professional Psychology: Research and Practice, 34*, 491–498.

Mittenberg, W., Patton, C., Canyock, E. M., & Condit, D. C. (2002). Baserates of malingering and symptom exaggeration. *Journal of Clinical and Experimental Neuropsychology, 24*, 1094–1102.

Rabin, L., Barr, W., & Burton, L. (2005). Assessment practices of clinical neuropsychologists in the United States and Canada: A survey of INS, NAN, and APA Division 40 members. *Archives of Clincial Neuropsychology 20*, 33–65.

Sharland, M. J., & Gfeller, J. D. (2007). A survey of neuropsychologists' beliefs and practices with respect to the assessment of effort. *Archives of Clinical Neuropsychology, 22*, 213–224.

Slick, D., Tan, J., Strauss, E., & Hultsch, D. (2004). Detecting malingering: A survey of experts' practices. *Archives of Clinical Neuropsychology, 19*, 465–473.

Sweet, J., King, J., Malina, A., Bergman, M., & Simmons, A. (2002). Documenting the prominence of forensic neuropsychology at national meetings and in relevant professional journals from 1990–2000. *The Clinical Neuropsychologist, 16*, 481–494.

Sweet, J., Nelson, N., & Moberg, P. (2006). The TCN/AACN "Salary Survey": Professional practices, beliefs, and incomes of U.S. neuropsychologists. *The Clinical Neuropsychologist, 20*, 325–364.

Trueblood, W., & Binder, L. (1997). Psychologists' accuracy in identifying neuropsychological test protocols of clinical malingerers. *Archives of Clinical Neuropsychology, 12*, 13–27.

Victor, T., & Abeles, N. (2004). Coaching clients to take psychological and neuropsychological tests: A clash of ethical obligations. *Professional Psychology: Research and Practice, 35*, 373–379.

Wetter, M., & Corrigan, S. (1995). Providing information to clients about psychological tests: A survey of attorneys' and law students' attitudes. *Professional Psychology: Research and Practice, 26*, 474–477.

Appendix E
General Resources

E1: General forensic books and additional resources

American Academy of Clinical Neuropsychology (2003). Official position of the American Academy of Clinical Neuropsychology on ethical complaints made against clinical neuropsychologists during adversarial proceedings. *The Clinical Neuropsychologist, 17,* 443–445.

American Bar Association (1998). *National benchbook on psychiatric and psychological evidence and testimony* (reference book for judges).

American Medical Association (1999). Patient-physician relationship in the context of work-related and independent medical examinations. [On-line]. Available at: http://www.ama-assn.org/ama/pub/category.8326.html.

American Medical Association (1999). Patient–physician relationship in the context of work-related and independent medical examinations. [On-line]. Available at: http://www.amaassn.org/apps/pf_online/pf_online?f_n=browse&doc=policyfiles/HOD/H-140.928.htm.

American Psychological Association (2002). Ethical principles of psychologists and code of conduct. *American Psychologist, 57,* 1060–1073.

Annapolis Center for Science-Based Public Policy (2006). *Neuropsychological testing: Ethical applications for law and public policy.* Annapolis, MD: J. D. Seward & M. Welner.

Barsky, A., & Gould, J. (2002). *Clinicians in court.* New York: Guilford.

Berger, M. A. (2000). The Supreme Court's Trilogy on the admissibility of expert testimony. In *Reference manual on scientific evidence* (2nd ed., pp. 9–38). Washington, DC: Federal Judicial Center.

Bick, R. L. (1999). The expert witness in litigation and legal matters. In M. A. Shiffman (Ed.) *Ethics in forensic science and medicine: Guidelines for the forensic expert and the attorney* (pp. 19–28). Springfield, IL: Charles C. Thomas.

Boccaccini, M. T., & Brodsky, S. L. (1999). Diagnostic test usage by forensic psychologists in emotional injury cases. *Professional Psychology: Research and Practice, 30,* 253–259.

Bordini, E. J., Chaknis, M. M., Ekman-Turner, R. M., & Perna, R. B. (2002). Advances and issues in the diagnostic differential of malingering versus brain injury. *NeuroRehabilitation, 17,* 93–104.

Brodsky, S. L., & McKinzey, R. K. (2002). The ethical confrontation of the unethical forensic colleague. *Professional Psychology: Research and Practice, 33,* 307–309.

Bush, S. S., Barth, J. T., Pliskin, N. H., Arffa, S., Axelrod, B. N., Blackburn, L. A., Faust, D., Fisher, J. M., Harley, J. P., Heilbronner, R. L., Larrabee, G. J., Ricker, J. H., & Silver, C. H. (2005). Independent and court-ordered forensic neuropsychological examinations: Official NAN position. *Archives of Clinical Neuropsychology, 20,* 997–1007.

Canadian Academy of Psychologists in Disability Assessment. (2000). Practice standards for the psychological assessment of disability and impairment. [On-line]. Available at: http://www.capda.ca/mainstandardspractice/htm.

Dixon, L., & Gill, B. (2002). Changes in the standards for admitting expert evidence in federal civil cases since the *Daubert* decision. *Psychology, Public Policy, and Law, 8,* 251–308.

Dunn, J. T., Lees-Haley, P. R., Brown, R. S., Williams, C. W., & English, L. T. (1995). Neurotoxic complaint base rates of personal injury claimants: Implications for neuropsychological assessment. *Journal of Clinical Psychology, 51,* 577–584.

Faigman, D. L., & Monahan, J. (2005). Psychological evidence at the dawn of the law's scientific age. *Annual Review of Psychology, 56,* 631–659.

Fisher, M. (1997). The psychologist as "hired gun." *American Journal of Forensic Psychology, 15,* 25–30.

Foster, K., & Huber, P. (1997). *Judging science: Scientific knowledge and the federal courts.* Cambridge, MA: MIT Press.

Franklin, R. D. (Ed.). (2003). *Prediction in forensic and neuropsychology: Sound statistical practices.* Mahwah, NJ: Lawrence Erlbaum Associates, Inc.

Goldstein, A. (Ed.) (2003). *Forensic neuropsychology.* Vol. 11 of *Handbook of psychology*, I. Weiner (Ed. in Chief). Hoboken, NJ: Wiley & Sons.

Grisso, T. (2003). *Evaluating competencies: Forensic assessments and instruments* (2nd ed.). New York: Kluwer Academic/Plenum.

Grote, C. L., Lewin, J. L., Sweet, J. J., & van Gorp, W. G. (2000). Responses to perceived unethical practices in clinical neuropsychology: Ethical and legal considerations. *The Clinical Neuropsychologist, 14*, 119–134.

Grove, W. M., & Barden, R. C. (1999). Protecting the integrity of the legal system: The admissibility of testimony from mental health experts under *Daubert/Kumho* analyses. *Psychology, Public Policy, and Law, 5*, 224–242.

Guilmette, T. J., & Hagan, L. D. (1997). Ethical considerations in forensic neuropsychological consultation. *The Clinical Neuropsychologist, 11*, 287–290.

Gutheil, T. G., Commons, M. L., & Miller, P. M. (2001). Withholding, seducing, and threatening: A pilot study of further attorney pressures on expert witnesses. *Journal of the American Academy of Psychiatry and Law, 29*, 336–339.

Gutheil, T. G., & Simon, R. I. (1999). Attorneys' pressures on the expert witness: Early warning signs of endangered honesty, objectivity, and fair compensation. *Journal of the American Academy of Psychiatry and Law, 27*, 546–553.

Hall, H. V., & Poirier, J. G. (2001). *Detecting malingering and deception* (2nd ed.) Boca Raton, FL: CRC Press.

Hartman, D. E. (1995). *Neuropsychological toxicology: Identification and assessment of neurotoxic syndromes.* New York: Plenum.

Hartman, D. E. (1998). Missed diagnoses and misdiagnoses of environmental toxicant exposure. *The Psychiatric Clinics of North America, 21*, 659–670.

Hartman, D. E. (1999). Neuropsychology and the (neuro)toxic tort. In J.J. Sweet (Ed.), *Forensic neuropsychology: Fundamentals and practice* (pp. 339–367). Lisse, Netherlands: Swets & Zeitlinger.

Heilbronner, R. L. (2005). *Forensic neuropsychology casebook.* New York, NY: Guilford Press.

Heilbrun, K. (2001). *Principles of forensic mental health assessment.* New York: Kluwer.

Hess, A. K. (1998). Accepting forensic case referrals: Ethical and professional considerations. *Professional Psychology: Research and Practice, 29*, 109–114.

Huber, P. W. (1991). *Galileo's revenge: Junk science in the courtroom.* New York: Basic Books.

Johnston, M. T., Krafka, C., & Cecil, J. S. (2000). *Expert testimony in federal and civil trials: A preliminary analysis.* Federal Judicial Center.

Johnson-Greene, D., & Bechtold, K. T. (2002). Ethical considerations for peer review in forensic neuropsychology. *The Clinical Neuropsychologist, 16*, 97–104.

Joint Committee on Standards for Educational and Psychological Testing. (1999). *Standards for educational and psychological testing.* Washington, DC: American Educational Resource Association.

Kareken, D. A. (1997). Judgment pitfalls in estimating premorbid intellectual function. *Archives of Clinical Neuropsychology, 12*, 701–709.

Kassirer, J. P., & Cecil, J. S. (2002). Inconsistency in evidentiary standards for medical testimony: Disorder in the courts. *Journal of the American Medical Association, 288*, 1382–1387.

Kaufman, P. (2005). Protecting the objectivity, fairness, and integrity of neuropsychological evaluations in litigation: A privilege second to none? *Journal of Legal Medicine, 26*, 95–131.

Knapp, S., & VandeCreek, L. (2001). Ethical issues in personality assessment in forensic psychology. *Journal of Personality Assessment, 77*, 242–254.

Koch, W. J., Douglas, K. S., Nicholls, T. L., & O'Neill, M. L. (Eds.) (2005). *Psychological injuries: Forensic assessment, treatment, & law.* Oxford, UK: Oxford University Press.

Krafka, C., Dunn, M. A., Treadway Johnson, M., Cecil, J. S., & Miletich, D. (2002). Judge and attorney experiences, practices, and concerns regarding expert testimony in federal civil trials. *Psychology, Public Policy, and Law, 8*, 309–332.

Laing, L. C., & Fisher, J. M. (1997). Neuropsychology in civil proceedings. In R. J. McCaffrey, A. D. Williams, J. M. Fisher, & L. C. Laing (Eds.) *The Practice of Forensic Neuropsychology: Meeting Challenges in the Courtroom* (pp. 117–133). New York: Plenum Press.

Larrabee, G. J. (Ed.) (2005). *Forensic neuropsychology: A scientific approach*. New York, NY: Oxford University Press.

Lees-Haley, P. R. (1997a). Attorneys influence expert evidence in forensic psychological and neuropsychological cases. *Assessment, 4*, 321–324.

Lees-Haley, P. R. (1997b). Neurobehavioral assessment in toxic injury evaluations. *Applied Neuropsychology, 4*, 180–190.

Lees-Haley, P., & Cohen, L. (1999). The neuropsychologist as expert witness: Toward credible science in the courtroom. In J. Sweet (Ed.) *Forensic neuropsychology: Fundamentals and practice* (pp. 443–184). Lisse, Netherlands: Swets & Zeitlinger.

Lewin, J. (1998). The genesis and evolution of legal uncertainty about "reasonable medical certainty." *Maryland Law Review, 57*, 380–504.

Marson, D. C., Ingram, K. K., Cody, H., & Harrell, L. E. (1995). Assessing the competency of patients with Alzheimer's Disease under different legal standards. *Archives of Neurology, 52*, 949–954.

Martell, D. A. (1992). Forensic neuropsychology and the criminal law. *Law and Human Behavior, 16*, 313–336.

Melton, G. B., Petrila, J., Poythress, N. G., & Slobogin, C. (1997). *Psychological evaluations for the courts: A handbook for mental health professionals and lawyers* (2nd Ed.). New York: Guilford Press.

Millis, S. R. (2004). Evaluation of malingered neurocognitive disorders. In M. Rizzo & P. J. Esslinger (Eds.), *Principles and practice of behavioral neurology and neuropsychology* (pp. 1077–1089). Philadelphia: W. B. Saunders.

NAN Policy and Planning Committee. (2000). Test security: Official position statement of the National Academy of Neuropsychology. *Archives of Clinical Neuropsychology, 15*, 383–386.

Nestor, P. G., Dagett, D., Haycock, J., & Price, M. (1999). Competence to stand trial: A neuropsychological inquiry. *Law and Human Behavior, 23*, 397–412.

Perlo, S. (1996). The ABCs of psychiatric disability evaluations. *Occupational Medicine, 11*, 747–765.

Roesch, R., Hart, S. D., & Ogloff, J. R. P. (Eds.) (1999). *Psychology and law: The state of the discipline*. New York: Kluwer.

Rogers, R. (Ed.) (1997). *Clinical assessment of malingering and deception* (2nd ed.). New York: Guilford.

Rogers, R. (Ed.) (2008). *Clinical assessment of malingering and deception* (3rd ed.). New York: Guilford.

Shuman, D. W., & Sales, B. D. (1999). The impact of *Daubert* and its progeny on the admissibility of behavioral and social science evidence. *Psychology, Public Policy, and Law, 5*, 3–15.

Sparta, S., & Koocher, G. (2006). *Forensic mental health assessment of children and adolescents*. New York: Guilford.

Sweet, J. J. (Ed.) (1999). *Forensic neuropsychology: Fundamentals and practice*. Lisse, Netherlands: Swets & Zeitlinger.

Sweet, J. J. (2003). Ethics cases: Forensic neuropsychology. In S. Bush (Ed.). *Ethics casebook for neuropsychologists* (pp. 51–61). Lisse, Netherlands: Swets & Zeitlinger.

Sweet, J. J., Grote, C., & van Gorp, W. (2002). Ethical issues in forensic neuropsychology. In S. S. Bush & M. L. Drexler (Eds.). *Ethical issues in clinical neuropsychology* (pp. 103–133). Lisse, Netherlands: Swets & Zeitlinger.

Sweet, J. J., & Moulthrop, M. (1999). Self-examination questions as a means of identifying bias in adversarial assessments. *Journal of Forensic Neuropsychology, 1*, 73–88.

Taylor, J. S. (1999). The legal environment pertaining to clinical neuropsychology. In J. Sweet (Ed.) *Forensic neuropsychology: Fundamentals and practice*. Lisse, Netherlands: Swets & Zeitlinger.

Tenopyr, M. L. (1999). A scientist-practitioner's viewpoint on the admissibility of behavioral and social scientific information. *Psychology, Public Policy, and Law, 5*, 194–202.

Van Reekum, R., Streiner, D. L., & Conn, D. K. (2001). Applying Bradford Hill's criteria for causation to neuropsychiatry: Challenges and opportunities. *Journal of Neuropsychiatry and Clinical Neurosciences, 13*, 318–325.

Wetter, M. W., & Corrigan, S. K. (1995). Providing information to clients about psychological tests: A survey of attorneys' and law students' attitudes. *Professional Psychology: Research and Practice, 26*, 474–477.

Wills, K., & Sweet, J. (2006). Neuropsychological considerations in forensic child assessment. In J. Sparta & G. Koocher (Eds.). *Forensic mental health assessment of children and adolescents* (pp. 260–284). New York: Guilford Press.

Youngjohn, J. (1995). Confirmed attorney coaching prior to neuropsychological evaluation. *Assessment, 2*, 279–284.

E2: Online resources

American Bar Association. Available at http://www.abanet.org/

International Journal of Forensic Psychology (issues available online). Available at http://ijfp.psyc.uow.edu.au/index2.html

Professional Expert Registry. Internet directory of experts and consultants, including authors, consultants, engineers, physicians, professors, scientists, specialists, and many more professionals in over 1075 categories of expertise. A resource for attorneys, reporters, insurance companies, judges, librarians, the media, and a variety of businesses. Available at http://www.mdexonline.com/experts_pr.cfm (Experts.com)

The Daubert Tracker. Key features: all federal and state evidentiary gatekeeping standards tracked, all reported and numerous unreported cases, country's largest repository of "Daubert" documents, 14,000+ case records, 21,000+ expert records, updated daily, full text opinion search. Available at http://www.daubert-tracker.com/

Cornell University Law School, Legal Information Institute. Provides: Supreme Court rulings; updates for Federal Rules of Civil Procedure, Criminal Procedure, Bankruptcy Procedure, and Evidence, etc. Available at http://supct.law.cornell.edu/

Journal of the American Academy of Psychiatry and the Law (archive of all issues online). Available at http://www.jaapl.org/archive/

Articles, Research, and Resources in Psychology (Ken Pope's website). Includes free access to a variety of journal articles. Available at http://www.kspope.com/

Indiana School of Law Library, Bloomington, General Legal Resources. Available at http://www.law.indiana.edu/library/onlineresources/gen_leg.shtml

Appendix F

Diagnostic criteria for malingered neurocognitive dysfunction: Proposed standards for clinical practice and research

Daniel J. Slick[1], Elisabeth M. S. Sherman[2], and Grant L. Iverson[3]

ABSTRACT

Over the past 10 years, widespread and concerted research efforts have led to increasingly sophisticated and efficient methods and instruments for detecting exaggeration or fabrication of cognitive dysfunction. Despite these psychometric advances, the process of diagnosing malingering remains difficult and largely idiosyncratic. This article presents a proposed set of diagnostic criteria that define psychometric, behavioral, and collateral data indicative of possible, probable, and definite malingering of cognitive dysfunction, for use in clinical practice and for defining populations for clinical research. Relevant literature is reviewed, and limitations and benefits of the proposed criteria are discussed.

Currently, a large proportion of referrals for neuropsychological assessment is being generated by personal injury litigation, worker's compensation, and other systems in which those being referred may receive substantial financial rewards for demonstrating cognitive deficits, either legitimate or successfully feigned. Often, neuropsychological data, reports, and expert testimony strongly influence final decisions about the size of financial settlements. Neuropsychologists are therefore increasingly required to explicitly evaluate the likelihood that observed cognitive deficits are real or feigned. This task is highly problematic not only because those who feign deficits actively attempt to prevent detection, but also because of the high individual and systemic costs of both false-negative and false-positive errors. Given these circumstances it is surprising that a set of specific, clearly articulated, and clinically applicable criteria for rating the likelihood that a patient is malingering neurocognitive dysfunction is not in widespread use. As well as facilitating clinical practice and professional communication, such criteria would also greatly facilitate systematic research about malingering.

Various definitions and criteria for diagnosing malingering have been published, most notably those of the *Diagnostic and Statistical Manual of Mental Disorders–Fourth Edition* (DSM–IV; American Psychological Association, 1994), Rogers (1990a, 1990b), and Greiffenstein, Baker, and Gola (1994). However, further refinements are needed to produce a definition and set of diagnostic criteria specific to malingering of neurocognitive dysfunction that are adequate for everyday use in clinical neuropsychology. In this position paper, we attempt to address limitations of previous models by proposing a set of formal diagnostic criteria for diagnosing possible, probable, and definite malingering of cognitive dysfunction in the context of neuropsychological examination. The criteria are also offered for use in defining populations for clinical research on the prevalence and detection of malingering.

---

[1] Riverview Hospital, [2] British Columbia's Children's Hospital, and [3] University of British Columbia.

CURRENT DIAGNOSTIC MODELS OF MALINGERING

Diagnostic criteria facilitate professional communication and delivery of healthcare services, and ensure that clinical research findings are descriptive of well-defined populations. As is the case with many clinical disorders or syndromes described in current nosologies such as the DSM–IV, complete consensus on the definition and criteria for malingering has not been reached. In the DSM–IV, malingering is classified as a V-Code: behavior that may be worthy of clinical attention but not a mental disorder per se. Consequently, formal diagnostic criteria for malingering are not provided. Instead, the DSM–IV contains a general definition, several clinical suspicion indices, and a brief review of differential diagnoses. The DSM–IV defines malingering as "the intentional production of false or grossly exaggerated physical or psychological symptoms, motivated by external incentives such as avoiding military duty, avoiding work, obtaining financial compensation, evading criminal prosecution, or obtaining drugs" (American Psychological Association, 1994, p. 683). Thus, malingering is distinguished from potentially similar appearing presentations that are not part of a volitional attempt to obtain readily identifiable and commonly accepted external incentives. Examples of such presentations include poor or inconsistent effort, as well as defensive, hostile, or oppositional approaches to test taking that result from fatigue, psychiatric disturbance, and legitimate neurological impairment.

The concept of volition—conscious, self-directed behavior—and the nature of incentives are crucial elements of the DSM–IV definition of malingering, and contribute to differentiation from other clinical disorders involving symptom exaggeration or fabrication. For example, factitious disorder (FD), like malingering, is characterized by intentionally produced symptoms suggestive of injury or disease; however, unlike the external motivation of persons who malinger, the primary motivation for persons with FD is psychological (i.e., it does not involve material gain or release from formal responsibility). Like FD, conversion disorder (CD) is characterized by fabricated symptoms suggestive of injury or disease that are motivated by psychological factors rather than external incentives. However, unlike FD or malingering, CD symptoms are not under volitional control. The essential contrasts between malingering, FD, and CD are presented in Table F.1.

Dichotomous diagnostic criteria such as *external* versus *psychological* incentives, and *volitional* versus *unconscious* behavior are easy to write into definitions, but in practice, judging the degree to which a behavior is volitional is fraught with uncertainty, and disentangling which incentive is primary in cases where external and internal incentives coexist—as is often the case—can be exceedingly difficult. The task is all the more difficult without a set of specific and widely agreed upon behavioral criteria. An additional problem with the DSM–IV criteria is the specification that other conditions involving exaggerated symptoms such as FD and CD rule out malingering. For example, comorbidity of malingering and FD is impossible in DSM–IV. No justification for making such diagnoses mutually exclusive is offered despite the fact that psychological and financial incentives

TABLE F.1 Differences between malingering, conversion disorder, and factitious disorder

	BEHAVIOR UNDER VOLITIONAL CONTROL	*TYPE OF INCENTIVE*	*EXAMPLES OF INCENTIVES*
Malingering	Yes	External	Obtain substantial financial reward, escape from formal duty or punishment
Conversion Disorder	No	Psychological	Manage stress or conflict
Factitious Disorder	Yes	Psychological	Play sick role, receive attention or other nonfinancial reinforcement, escape from informal duty, manage stress or conflict

often coexist and behavior can clearly be motivated by both external and internal incentives. Second, because it was primarily designed to assess psychiatric conditions, the DSM–IV provides little guidance in the assessment of exaggeration or fabrication of neurocognitive deficits within the context of the neuropsychological evaluation.

The limitations of the DSM criteria for malingering have spurred clinicians and researchers to offer alternate definitions and criteria for malingering. For example, Rogers (1990a) proposed specific diagnostic criteria for malingering of psychiatric disturbance that incorporated multiple sources of data from different domains, including self-report, test scores, behavioral observations, and collateral information. Using a model similar to the DSM, Rogers specified a minimum number of criteria from each domain that are necessary for a diagnosis of malingering. These included endorsement of an unusually high number of rare symptoms, contradictory collateral information, and evidence of exaggeration or fabrication of symptoms from standardized tests. Rogers also listed diagnostic contraindications, including the presence of factitious disorder. Although Rogers' criteria are a substantial step forward in clarifying the confusion regarding the definition of malingering, no data on the reliability, validity, or utility of these criteria have yet been reported. Additionally, because Rogers developed his set of criteria for use in psychiatric assessments, important diagnostic issues specific to neuropsychological assessment are not addressed, such as the provision of an operational definition of psychometric evidence of feigned cognitive impairment.

More recently, Greiffenstein et al. (1994) proposed a set of criteria for the diagnosis of "overt" malingering of memory dysfunction designed specifically for use in neuropsychological settings, in particular for litigating postconcussive patients. These consist of (1) improbably poor performance on two or more neuropsychological measures; (2) total disability in a major social role; (3) contradiction between collateral sources and symptom history; and (4) remote memory loss. In two studies, Greiffenstein and colleagues (Greiffenstein et al., 1994; Greiffenstein, Gola, & Baker, 1995) demonstrated clinically significant associations between classifications made by their index and scores on malingering measures, including forced-choice tests of symptom validity. These results provided evidence not only for the validity of Greiffenstein et al.'s diagnostic criteria, but also for the strong link between performance on some malingering tests and patient behavior outside the testing room.

The diagnostic criteria proposed by Greiffenstein et al. are clearly a step in the right direction, but their criteria can be improved in several ways. First, the criteria do not include an explicit definition of malingering. Second, rule-out conditions or differential diagnoses are not specified. Third, behavioral observations are not included in the criteria. Fourth, some of the criteria are underspecified. For example, Criteria 4 ("remote memory loss") is too vague to reliably apply in clinical or research settings. Fifth, the Greiffenstein criteria are restricted to the evaluation of feigned memory deficits only, and thus provide no guidelines for the evaluation of exaggeration or fabrication of other neurocognitive domains.

In contrast to criteria in which determinations about motivation and volition are essential (e.g., DSM–IV), Pankratz has suggested that conscious intent is irrelevant to the definition of malingering, arguing instead that "intentions, awareness, conscious purposes, and psychodynamics should not be the main focus of the diagnostic process" (Pankratz & Erickson, 1990, p. 386). According to Pankratz, intent and volition cannot be reliably assessed and therefore the diagnosis of malingering should not require any judgments about a patient's internal states. It is interesting to note that Pankratz chose labels that are not drawn from widely accepted current psychiatric or psychological nosologies to illustrate his point about the limited diagnostic value of judgments about intent or volition (e.g., *shoplifter* and *arsonist* are not listed as diagnoses in the DSM–IV). He observed that: "we use the labels of arsonist and shoplifter without regard to the actor's control or awareness; we should be able to use psychiatric labels similarly" (p.386). More recently, Pankratz and Binder (1997) updated the purely behavioral approach by providing a list of seven behaviors suggestive of malingering. These behaviors include: (1) marked inconsistency between reported and observed symptoms; (2) marked inconsistency between diagnosis and neuropsychological findings; (3) resistance, avoidance, or bizarre responses on standardized tests; (4) failure on specific measures of faking; (5) functional findings on medical examination; and (6) late onset of cognitive complaints following accident.

Pankratz makes a compelling case (Pankratz & Erickson, 1990, p. 386). It is undeniable that inferences about internal states and processes are always associated with some level of uncertainty (as are inferences drawn from "objective" test scores). However, the diagnosis of malingering would not be unique to rely on such deductions. Judgments about internal states are in fact necessary, if not crucial, for many clinical diagnoses. For example, hallucinations—a decidedly nontrivial clinical symptom—are like volition in that they are an internal event or state, the presence or absence of which can only be inferred from behavior. As a second example, consider Pankratz's example of shoplifting in the context of kleptomania. The diagnosis of kleptomania (American Psychological Association, 1994) requires not only behavior that can be directly observed (e.g., shoplifting), but also a clinical judgment about internal states (overwhelming impulse to steal). A patient may present in a forensic setting with symptoms of kleptomania that may be real or malingered, and the diagnostic decision—with all of the adjudication and treatment issues that follow—turns on an evaluation of intent, motivation, and ability to conform behavior. Unless all cases of exaggeration or fabrication of deficits constitute malingering, then the exclusion of any methods or guidelines for making determination about volition and intent is a significant limitation of purely behavioral approaches to diagnosing malingering.

Faust and Ackley (1998) also provide a list of six behavioral manifestations of "intentional" sources of inaccuracies in neuropsychological test data, including (1) poor effort on testing; (2) exaggeration of symptoms; (3) fabrication of symptoms; (4) false attributions (purposefully withholding or distorting history concerning other causes of symptoms); (5) presenting a false baseline (purposefully withholding or distorting information about premorbid function); and (6) denial or failure to acknowledge strengths, positive abilities, or positive areas of function. However, unlike Pankratz (Pankratz & Erickson, 1990), Faust and Ackley (1998) clearly state that "two basic dimensions, falsification and intentionality, are inherent or intrinsic components of malingering . . . [and] . . . to identify malingering, both dimensions will need to be assessed." (p. 19). Thus, all of the behaviors that make up the spectrum of intentional inaccuracies are symptomatic of malingering if the "intention" is to obtain an external reward. Faust and Ackley are clear to caution however, that detecting intentional inaccuracies is not the same thing as determining what the intention is.

INFORMING THE CONSTRUCTION OF CRITERIA: EMPIRICAL STUDIES OF MALINGERED NEUROPSYCHOLOGICAL DYSFUNCTION

When attempting to construct an improved set of diagnostic criteria, it is useful to review not only previous definitions and criteria, but also research on the frequency, reliability, and validity of specific diagnostic signs or symptoms of the target "disorder." A variety of methods and measures are currently used to detect the presence of exaggeration and fabrication within the context of the neuropsychological evaluation. These include: (1) inconsistencies or other signs from the patient's reported symptoms; (2) inconsistencies or other signs from standard neuropsychological tests; and (3) measures or indices designed expressly to detect feigning of cognitive deficits.

SELF-REPORT

Very few studies have attempted to systematically evaluate aspects of patient self-report that might be indicative of malingering. There has been limited research on the "neuropsychological" knowledge-base among laypersons, but the data suggest that although naïve individuals are capable of endorsing symptoms consistent with head injury, they are also susceptible to endorsement of highly unusual items that distinguish them from individuals with legitimate head injuries. For example, Aubry, Dobbs, and Rue (1989) found that undergraduate students had a good knowledge about physical symptoms that typically follow minor head trauma. However, participant knowledge about typical cognitive and psychiatric symptoms was poor, with many participants endorsing highly unusual symptoms, such as uncontrollable laughter. In fact, unusual symptoms were endorsed with the same frequency as much more likely cognitive sequelae such as difficulty remembering phone numbers.

Similar results were also reported by Gouvier, Prestholt, and Warner (1988). In contrast to these findings are reports of good understanding of cognitive sequelae of head injury among naïve participants (undergraduates and members of the general community) reported by Lees-Haley and Dunn (1994) and Mittenberg, DiGiulio, Perrin, and Bass (1992). However, neither of the symptom checklists used in the latter two studies contained rare or unlikely symptoms, so there was no opportunity for naïve participants to distinguish themselves in the way that participants in the Gouvier et al. (1988) study did. Nonetheless, Lees-Haley and Dunn make the point that their research may be more applicable to typical clinical practice because clinicians often give patients checklists that do not contain improbable symptoms, nor do they query such symptoms during interview. In summary, analog studies have demonstrated that naïve malingerers may be distinguished by self-reported symptoms that are highly atypical of patients with legitimate brain injuries in type, severity, frequency, and chronicity. However, there are as yet no objective indices based on specific patterns of symptom endorsement that are adequately validated.

TEST DATA

Only one study to date has extensively evaluated actual test-taking and self-presentation strategies that persons use to malinger. Iverson (1995) obtained self-report information of malingering strategies used by experimental study participants including university undergraduates, community volunteers, psychiatric inpatients, and federal inmates. Strategies for both preparation and test-taking were reported. Less than 4% of the respondents described any individual method for preparation, such as studying the effects of head injury, or engaging in corroboratory behaviors, such as missing appointments. The test taking strategy reported most often (16%) was to fake total amnesia. Other reported strategies included "poor cooperation, aggravation and frustration, slow response latencies and frequent hesitations, and general confusion during the testing process." (p. 37) Responses were notable both for limited numbers of strategies and limited descriptions of how strategies would be operationalized. Interestingly, no study has directly measured the relationship between neuropsychological knowledge and ability to believably fake cognitive deficits.

Although very limited self-report data on malingering strategies are available, an increasingly large number of studies have evaluated the utility of malingering indices based on patterns of scores within and across standard neuropsychological tests. The assumption underlying these studies is that successfully simulating impairment across multiple measures is more difficult than feigning on any single measure. Thus, the simultaneous statistical evaluation of multiple test or item scores may increase detection rates relative to the evaluation of single scores in isolation. This approach—often referred to as the *pattern of performance method*—is probably the most effective way to detect malingering with conventional neuropsychological measures.

There are at least four procedures for detecting malingering that fall under the rubric of the pattern of performance method (PPM). In the first procedure, performance on "floor" items are evaluated for rare errors (e.g., forgetting one's own name). Alternatively, and particularly when items are not presented in order of increasing difficulty, scores for easy items are compared to scores on more difficult items or performance curves across multiple items of varying difficulty are evaluated (Baker, Hanley, Jackson, Kimmance, & Slade, 1993; Fredrick & Foster, 1991; Tenhula & Sweet, 1996). A variation on this method is the evaluation of scores within or across tests for congruency of performance on measures within a specific domain. A second PPM is the evaluation of scores or score profiles within or across tests for congruency with established patterns of function or dysfunction within a domain. Example indices include unusual patterns of serial position effects in list learning and other memory tests (Bernard, 1991; Russell, Spector, & Kelly, 1993), comparisons of recall to recognition (Beetar & Williams, 1994; Bernard, 1990, 1991; Binder, Villanueva, Howieson, & Moore, 1992; Brandt, 1988; Knight & Meyers, 1995), and comparisons of indices of attention to indices of memory (Mittenburg, Azrin, Millsaps, & Heilbronner, 1993). A third means of deriving pattern of performance indices is the post hoc application of statistical procedures (e.g., discriminant function analysis) to scores obtained from established contrast groups such as analog malingerers (i.e., research participants instructed to feign cognitive dysfunction), probable malingerers, and nonlitigating patients (Bernard, Houston, & Natoli, 1993; Bernard, McGrath, & Houston, 1996; Fredrick & Foster, 1991; Fredrick, Sarfaty, Johnston, & Powel, 1994; Hayward, Hall, Hunt, & Zubrick, 1987). A fourth variation on PPMs that has recently shown promise in an initial validation study is the examination of magnitude of errors (Martin, Franzen, & Orey, 1998). These approaches are discussed in detail and reviewed extensively by Cercy, Schretlen, and Brandt (1997), Nies and Sweet (1994), Pankratz and Binder (1997), Reynolds (1998), Rogers (1997), and Rogers, Harrell, and Liff (1993).

Overall, attempts to develop malingering indices for conventional neuropsychological tests have met with mixed success. Although most of the recent studies using pattern of performance pattern indices have shown considerable promise, other studies report that conventional neuropsychological tests and test batteries may be ineffective in distinguishing malingered from legitimate impairment (Bernard, 1990, Faust & Guilmette, 1990; Faust, Hart, & Guilmette, 1988; Faust, Hart, Guilmette, & Arkes, 1988; Heaton, Smith, Lehman, & Vogt, 1978). Of those studies that have demonstrated the potential utility of particular malingering indices, most remain unreplicated or cross-validated and adequate data on positive predictive power are therefore lacking. In addition, the majority of studies on using conventional tests to detect malingering have relied on samples that restrict generalizability (e.g., analog malingerers). There are relatively few studies using known group comparisons, such as litigating versus nonlitigating patients with mild head injuries (Rogers, 1997).

Rather than focusing on detection through identifying "malingering" profiles on conventional neuropsychological measures, a separate line of investigation has focused on developing methods or tests specifically designed to detect aspects of performance suggestive of feigning. For example, Rey's 15-Item test (Lezak, 1995) and the Dot Counting Test have traditionally been used to measure floor effects; the Recall-Recognition test was designed to detect violation of learning principles (Brandt, Rubinsky, & Lassen, 1985); and the Modified TONI (Frederick, & Forster, 1991) to detect violation of the expected performance curve (Rogers, 1997). Although a small number of these tests (e.g., Rey 15 Item) are now in widespread use, inadequate positive and negative predictive power is a significant problem for most (e.g., Millis & Kler, 1995), and results can rarely be considered definitive. Symptom Validity Tests (SVTs) are an exception in terms of positive predictive power. Essentially, SVTs apply probabilistic analysis to patient performance on forced-choice tests of sensory or cognitive function. Scores that are above or below a large (90% or more) confidence interval around chance are highly unlikely to be the product of random responding, and can instead be considered the product of purposeful selection of correct or incorrect answers (in either case depending on intactness of function), with the latter being indicative of exaggerated or faked deficits. Current SVTs are essentially of two types: (1) adaptations of conventional tests of recognition memory or sensory function (e.g., Fredrick & Foster, 1991; Iverson & Franzen, 1994, 1996; Millis, 1992); and (2) entirely new tests (e.g., Beetar & Williams, 1995; Binder, 1993; Hiscock & Hiscock, 1989; Iverson, Franzen, & McCracken, 1991, 1994; Pankratz, 1983; Slick, Hopp, Strauss, & Thompson, 1997; Tombaugh, 1996). No cases of false positive errors have been reported when malingering was confirmed by performance below chance on a SVT.

Thus, short of confession, below chance performance on symptom validity testing is closest to an evidentiary "gold standard" for malingering. However, these tests typically have only moderate sensitivity and thus low negative predictive power. That is, scores in the valid range on SVTs do not conclusively rule out malingering, and they are thus not suitable for use as the sole index of patient veracity.

A fundamental limitation of all studies of malingering is that malingerers rarely if ever self-identify, and thus true representative malingering samples can never be obtained, the actual base rate in clinical samples cannot be known, and the true error rates of detection methods cannot be established. The limitations inherent in all current psychometric methods means that there is currently no single valid and reliable pathognomonic sign of malingering, short of disclosure of such behavior by the patient. Almost no research exists on the co-existence of legitimate neuropsychological dysfunction with poor effort or malingering (Barton, Boone, Allman, & Castro, 1995), and therefore one of the most pressing questions in malingering research today is whether it is possible to tease apart legitimate from exaggerated impairment in cases where both may be present.

In consideration of the current state of the art, Nies and Sweet (1994) suggest that clinicians adopt a multidimensional, multimethod approach to detecting malingering of neuropsychological deficits, including: the use of specific tests of malingering or standard neuropsychological tests with forced-choice formats; examination of intra- and inter-test performance for highly inconsistent or nonsensical patterns of scores; systematic collection of self-report data on symptoms and history for evaluation of discrepancies with test performance; and systematic collection of collateral data and evaluation of extra-test behavior for evaluation of discrepancies with test performance.

OVERVIEW AND INTRODUCTION TO PROPOSED CRITERIA

With Nies and Sweet's (1994) guidelines in mind, five imperatives were used to guide the development of the proposed malingering criteria, namely, the need for: (1) a specific definition of malingering of cognitive dysfunction within the context of the neuropsychological assessment; (2) specific, unambiguous, and reliable criteria that cover all possible sources of evidence (i.e., test-performance, observations, and collateral data); (3) specification of the relative importance of diagnostic criteria; (4) specification of the nature and role of clinical judgment; (5) specification of differential diagnoses and exclusionary criteria; and (6) specification of levels of diagnostic certainty.

Because it is not often possible to determine whether or not a patient is malingering with absolute certainty, the proposed criteria were designed to include formal specification of levels of diagnostic certainty (i.e., possible, probable, and definite malingering). Malingering is not a unique diagnostic challenge in this regard. Thus, criteria for other clinical diagnoses that include formalized levels of diagnostic certainty provided useful examples. For example, Alzheimer's disease (AD) typically cannot be diagnosed with 100% confidence. Consequently, separate criteria for *definite*, *probable*, and *possible* AD have been defined in lieu of a single set of criteria (McKhann et al., 1984).

The NINCDS-ADRDA criteria for diagnosis of AD reflect both the breadth of data that inform the diagnostic process (e.g., type and history of signs and symptoms, data from psychometric examination, and laboratory tests) as well as the relative importance of specific findings. Thus, a diagnosis of definite AD requires specific histological findings in addition to the pattern of data necessary for a diagnosis of probable AD. Data specifically consistent with AD in the absence of definitive evidence (i.e., neuropathological evidence) leads to a diagnosis of probable AD. In cases where the data are consistent with AD, but other etiologies cannot be ruled out, the diagnosis is reduced to possible AD. Another useful model for levels of diagnostic certainty is that put forward by Grant and Martin (1994, p. 362) for HIV-1 Associated Dementia Complex: "The designation *probable* is used when criteria are met, there is no other likely cause, and data are complete. The designation *possible* is used if another potential etiology is present whose contribution is unclear, or where dual diagnosis is possible, or when the evaluation is not complete." These examples were used as models in our formulation of levels of diagnostic certainty in the criteria presented below.

TABLE F.2   Proposed definition and criteria for possible, probable, and definite Malingering of Neurocognitive Dysfunction (MND)

DEFINITION

Malingering of Neurocognitive Dysfunction (MND) is the volitional exaggeration or fabrication of cognitive dysfunction for the purpose of obtaining substantial material gain, or avoiding or escaping formal duty or responsibility. Substantial material gain includes money, goods, or services of nontrivial value (e.g., financial compensation for personal injury). Formal duties are actions that people are legally obligated to perform (e.g., prison, military, or public service, or child support payments or other financial obligations). Formal responsibilities are those that involve accountability or liability in legal proceedings (e.g., competency to stand trial).

DIAGNOSTIC CATEGORIES FOR MALINGERING NEUROCOGNITIVE DYSFUNCTION (MND)

Definite MND

This is indicated by the presence of clear and compelling evidence of volitional exaggeration or fabrication of cognitive dysfunction and the absence of plausible alternative explanations. The specific diagnostic criteria necessary for Definite MND are listed below:

1. Presence of a substantial external incentive [Criterion A]
2. Definite negative response bias [Criterion B1]
3. Behaviors meeting necessary criteria from group B are not fully accounted for by Psychiatric, Neurological, or Developmental Factors [Criterion D]

Probable MND

This is indicated by the presence of evidence strongly suggesting volitional exaggeration or fabrication of cognitive dysfunction and the absence of plausible alternative explanations. The specific diagnostic criteria necessary for Probable MND are listed below.

1. Presence of a substantial external incentive [Criterion A]
2. Two or more types of evidence from neuropsychological testing, excluding definite negative response bias [two or more of Criteria B2–B6]

Or

One type of evidence from neuropsychological testing, excluding definite negative response bias, and one or more types of evidence from Self-Report [one of Criteria B2–B6 and one or more of Criteria C1–C5]

3. Behaviors meeting necessary criteria from groups B and C are not fully accounted for by Psychiatric, Neurological, or Developmental Factors [Criterion D]

Possible MND

This is indicated by the presence of evidence suggesting volitional exaggeration or fabrication of cognitive dysfunction and the absence of plausible alternative explanations. Alternatively, possible MND is indicated by the presence of criteria necessary for Definite or Probable MND except that other primary etiologies cannot be ruled out. The specific diagnostic criteria for Possible MND are listed below:

1. Presence of a substantial external incentive [Criterion A]

2. Evidence from Self-Report [one or more of Criteria C1–C5]
3. Behaviors meeting necessary criteria from group C are not fully accounted for by Psychiatric, Neurological, or Developmental Factors [Criterion D]

Or

Criteria for Definite or Probable MND are met except for Criterion D (i.e., primary psychiatric, neurological, or developmental etiologies cannot be ruled out). In such cases, the alternate etiologies that cannot be ruled out should be specified.

EXPLANATION OF CRITERIA

Criteria A: Presence of a Substantial External Incentive

At least one clearly identifiable and substantial external incentive for exaggeration or fabrication of symptoms (see definition) is present at the time of examination (e.g., personal injury settlement, disability pension, evasion of criminal prosecution, or release from military service).

Criteria B: Evidence from Neuropsychological Testing

Evidence of exaggeration or fabrication of cognitive dysfunction on neuropsychological tests, as demonstrated by at least one of the following:

1. *Definite negative response bias.* Below chance performance ($p < .05$) on one or more forced choice measures of cognitive function.
2. *Probable response bias.* Performance on one or more *well-validated* psychometric tests or indices designed to measure exaggeration or fabrication of cognitive deficits is consistent with feigning.
3. *Discrepancy between test data and known patterns of brain functioning.* A pattern of neuropsychological test performance that is markedly discrepant from currently accepted models of normal and abnormal central nervous system (CNS) function. The discrepancy must be consistent with an attempt to exaggerate or fabricate neuropsychological dysfunction (e.g., a patient performs in the severely impaired range on verbal attention measures but in the average range on memory testing; a patient misses items on recognition testing that were consistently provided on previous free recall trials, or misses many easy items when significantly harder items from the same test are passed).
4. *Discrepancy between test data and observed behavior.* Performance on two or more neuropsychological tests within a domain are discrepant with observed level of cognitive function in a way that suggests exaggeration or fabrication of dysfunction (e.g., a well-educated patient who presents with no significant visual-perceptual deficits or language disturbance in conversational speech performs in the severely impaired range on verbal fluency and confrontation naming tests).
5. *Discrepancy between test data and reliable collateral reports.* Performance on two or more neuropsychological tests within a domain are discrepant with day-to-day level of cognitive function described by at least one reliable collateral informant in a way that suggests exaggeration or fabrication of dysfunction (e.g., a patient handles all family finances but is unable to perform simple math problems in testing).
6. *Discrepancy between test data and documented background history.* Improbably poor performance on two or more standardized tests of cognitive function within a specific domain (e.g., memory) that is inconsistent with documented neurological or psychiatric history (e.g., a patient with no documented LOC or PTA, multiple negative neurological investigations, and no other history of CNS trauma or disease consistently obtains verbal memory scores in the severely impaired range after a motor vehicle accident).

Criteria C: Evidence from Self-report

The following behaviors are indicators of possible malingering of cognitive deficits, but their presence is not sufficient for the diagnosis. However, presence of one or more of these criteria provides additional evidence in support of a diagnosis of malingering. These criteria involve significant inconsistencies or discrepancies in the patient's self-reported symptoms that suggest a deliberate attempt to exaggerate or fabricate cognitive deficits.

1. *Self-reported history is discrepant with documented history.* Reported history is markedly discrepant with documented medical or psychosocial history and suggests attempts to exaggerate injury severity or deny premorbid neuropsychological dysfunction (e.g., exaggerated severity of physical injury or length of LOC/PTA; exaggerated premorbid educational or occupational achievement; denial of previous head injury or previous psychiatric history).
2. *Self-reported symptoms are discrepant with known patterns of brain functioning.* Reported or endorsed symptoms are improbable in number, pattern, or severity; or markedly inconsistent with expectations for the type or severity of documented injury or pathology (e.g., claims of extended retrograde amnesia without loss of memory for the accident, or claims of loss of autobiographical information after mild head trauma without LOC).

(Continued . . .)

TABLE F.2   (Continued)

3. *Self-reported symptoms are discrepant with behavioral observations.* Reported symptoms are markedly inconsistent with observed behavior (e.g., a patient complains of severe episodic memory deficits yet has little difficulty remembering names, events, or appointments; a patient complains of severe cognitive deficits yet has little difficulty driving independently and arrives on time for an appointment in an unfamiliar area; a patient complains of severely slowed mentation and concentration problems yet easily follows complex conversation).

4. *Self-reported symptoms are discrepant with information obtained from collateral informants.* Reported symptoms, history, or observed behavior is inconsistent with information obtained from other informants judged to be adequately reliable. The discrepancy must be consistent with an attempt to exaggerate injury severity or deny premorbid neuropsychological dysfunction (e.g., a patient reports severe memory impairment and/or behaves as if severely memory-impaired, but their spouse reports that the patient has minimal memory dysfunction at home).

5. *Evidence of exaggerated or fabricated psychological dysfunction.* Self-reported symptoms of psychological dysfunction are substantially contradicted by behavioral observation and/or reliable collateral information. *Well-validated* validity scales or indices on self-report measures of psychological adjustment (e.g., MMPI-2) are strongly suggestive of exaggerated or fabricated distress or dysfunction.

Criteria D: Behaviors Meeting Necessary Criteria from Groups B or C are not Fully Accounted for by Psychiatric, Neurological, or Developmental Factors

Behaviors meeting necessary criteria from groups B and C are the product of an informed, rational, and volitional effort aimed at least in part towards acquiring or achieving external incentives as defined in Criteria A. As such, behaviors meeting criterion from groups B or C cannot be fully accounted for by psychiatric, developmental, or neurological disorders that result in significantly diminished capacity to appreciate laws or mores against malingering, or inability to conform behavior to such standards (e.g., psychological need to "play the sick role," or in response to command hallucinations).

Additional considerations

1. *Informed consent*: In the process of obtaining informed consent prior to examination, clinicians should insure that patients understand that a consistent high level of effort is required, and that any evidence of poor or inconsistent effort, or exaggeration or fabrication of dysfunction may be noted in resulting reports or other professional communications.

2. *Differential diagnoses*: If criteria for definite, probable, or possible malingering are met by a patient who is unable to appreciate the implications and consequences of his or her behavior (i.e., failure to meet Criterion D), but is instead responding to directions or pressure from others, the term "MND by proxy" may be considered. In cases where psychiatric, developmental, or neurological disorders are the primary cause of feigned cognitive deficits, then a diagnosis of "feigned cognitive deficits secondary to [specify psychiatric/developmental/neurological disorder]" may be considered.

3. *Ruling out malingering*: No psychological test has perfect negative predictive power. Therefore, one cannot automatically conclude that a patient is not malingering if they obtain "passing" scores on measures designed to detect exaggerated or fabricated deficits. Patients who attempt to malinger may exaggerate or fabricate symptoms from a variety of different domains (e.g., anxiety, mood, memory, or language) and present with varying degrees of sophistication. Similarly, failure to meet the proposed criteria for malingering does not constitute conclusive evidence that a patient is not malingering.

4. *Reliability, validity, and standardized administration of diagnostic measures*: In order to meet Criteria B, tests or indices should have adequate reliability and validity, test data should be obtained through standardized procedures under adequate testing conditions, and norms referenced should be applicable to the patient. Forced-choice measures are unique in that they may be excepted from the requirement that scores be norm referenced (i.e., raw scores can be "standardized" by referencing random response distributions). Clinicians need to be well aware of the positive and negative

predictive power of any signs, symptoms, or test scores that inform the diagnostic process (see Derogatis & DellaPietra, 1994; Elwood, 1993; Lindeboom, 1989; Meehl & Rosen, 1955). Although psychometric data are relied upon heavily for a diagnosis of malingering, current psychometric methods and instruments are in a relatively early stage of development. Most current measures or indices of exaggeration or fabrication are experimental and lack adequate normative data. Therefore, scores from such instruments should be interpreted with due caution. Test developers and publishers are strongly encouraged to ensure that their products meet established standards for reliability and validity (American Psychological Association, 1985, 1986, 1992).

5. *Individual differences*: Clinicians must be cognizant of cultural differences, level of acculturation, and demand characteristics of the examination, and how these factors may influence patient performance.

6. *Prior patient behavior*: A documented or self-reported prior history of malingering, functional findings on medical examination, or sociopathic behavior may support a diagnosis of malingering, but these are neither necessary nor sufficient for diagnosis. Similarly, although uncooperativeness, resistance, or refusal may be associated with malingering, these behaviors are not evidence of exaggeration or fabrication.

7. *Clinical judgement*: Many of the malingering criteria require some degree of expert clinical judgement. Expert clinical judgement is (a) an opinion about the nature and causes of specific behaviors in the absence of definitive data, (b) based on an objective evaluation of all obtainable data relevant to the particular case, and (c) supported by the weight of empirical research relevant to the behaviors in question.

8. *Self-reported symptoms*: The scope of this paper does not permit a review or listing of all factors to consider when evaluating patient self-report in the context of documented history [See Reynolds (1998) for a list of suggested records to review for any litigation case and a concise review of research about congruence of self-reports with known sequelae of an injury]. However, clinicians should not rush to judgement about intent when self-reports are not congruent with other data. Special care should be taken to distinguish deliberate from nondeliberate misattribution or exaggeration of deficits. Patients may become highly sensitized (particularly in medical-legal settings) to any cognitive failings and it is possible to falsely attribute pre-existing symptoms to an accident, report a higher than actual level of premorbid function, catastrophize or over-report current symptoms, or have difficulty reporting symptoms precisely, without intending to deceive. Clinicians should be cognizant of the literature on base rates of neuropsychological symptoms in the general population (see Gouvier, Hayes, & Smiroldo, 1998 for a recent review). An inability to provide an accurate history or accurately gauge current level of cognitive function may be symptomatic of legitimate brain dysfunction. The task of judging the veracity of reported symptoms is most difficult when significant injuries are documented. Often, there are no objective data on day-to-day functioning that can be compared to report symptoms for evaluating veracity.

CONTRASTING POINTS OF VIEW, CAVEATS, RECOMMENDATIONS, AND CONCLUSIONS

The validity of mainstream clinical conceptualizations of malingering (e.g., DSM–IV) has not gone unquestioned. Erickson has argued that "the diagnosis of malingering is a weak diagnosis of exclusion that serves to justify the denial of treatment and benefits," and that "were it not for some medicolegal expectations, we could do without the diagnosis entirely" (Pankratz & Erickson, 1990, p. 381). In a similar vein, Rogers and Cavanaugh (1983) question "traditional 'moralistic' conceptualizations of malingering," offering as a counterpoint, an "adaptational model . . . in which the malingerer perceives an adversarial context and chooses feigning on the basis of likelihood and expected utility" (Rogers, 1990b p. 182). Although we disagree with Erickson's call for the abolition of malingering as a diagnostic entity, he correctly notes that such diagnoses may have drastic consequences for patients, including the denial or termination of treatment or support. This is especially problematic in cases where exaggerated or fabricated deficits co-exist with real impairments or disorders that may be amenable to treatment. The points raised by Rogers and Cavanaugh are also well taken; clinicians need to carefully consider whether malingering represents a unique response to unusual and often trying circumstances, or behavior symptomatic of sociopathic tendencies or personality. However, these considerations do not obviate the need for a diagnostic category capturing volitional exaggeration or fabrication of deficits for the purpose of obtaining an external incentive.

We expect that some clinicians will be concerned about the role of clinical judgment in the proposed diagnostic criteria. We share this concern, and acknowledge that reliance on clinical judgements about volition and intent may constitute a serious threat to the reliability and validity of the proposed criteria, especially as impacted by differences in training and experience. Nevertheless, the essence of clinical diagnosis is expert judgement in the absence of a definitive test, and malingering is no different from other clinical diagnoses in this respect. Therefore, well-trained clinicians in possession of an adequate spectrum of reliable and valid data need not refrain from drawing inferences about volition and intent. In addition, the proposed criteria do provide substantial guidance to assist in making judgements. As delineated in Criterion D, when Criterion A (incentive to malinger) is met, then patient behaviors consistent with exaggeration or fabrication are most probably volitional unless the assessment turns up *convincing* evidence to the contrary. This discussion touches on an essential issue in medicolegal neuropsychological assessment that has heretofore received insufficient discussion: does the burden of proof rest on demonstrating that deficits are real or on demonstrating that they are malingered? Should adequate effort directed to good performance always be assumed unless otherwise demonstrated? Decisions about intent are likewise arrived at through a process of elimination. In cases where potential motivating factors listed in Criterion A are present but other possible motivations for exaggeration of fabrication exist, such as a desire to clearly communicate distress, it will rarely be possible to apportion intent. In such circumstances, however, it makes little sense to assume that a patient was *not* motivated by factors listed in Criterion A, and therefore, a diagnosis of at least possible malingering should be entertained if other necessary criteria are met.

If the practice of clinical neuropsychology is facilitated by the continual development of a categorical nosological system, then some label is required as a descriptor for behavior indicative of volitional exaggeration or fabrication of deficits for the purpose of obtaining financial rewards. Although "malingering" is the currently accepted label for this behavior, many psychologists appear to be reluctant to use the term, perhaps due to the dire consequences associated with false-positive diagnostic errors. An example of this conflict can be found in recent papers on the application of ethics code to europsychological practice. Binder and Thompson (1994) recommend that "in some cases of suspected malingering it is appropriate to merely comment upon the invalidity of the testing and make no diagnosis" (p. 40) but also assert that "although a diagnosis or recommendation may psychologically distress or financially damage a patient, clinicians strive for accuracy of diagnosis." (p. 41) Similarly, Reynolds (1998) acknowledges that "as clinicians and healthcare providers, we are reluctant to make such judgements of our fellow human beings" (p. 263) but nevertheless asserts that when malingering is considered likely, clinicians "must step up and make what is an emotionally charged, personally difficult call" (p. 281). Although it is clearly prudent to defer diagnoses when findings are ambiguous—including some cases that meet proposed criteria for possible or perhaps even probable malingering—such circumstances should not be taken for license to shy away from listing and discussing the most likely explanations for ambiguous, invalid, or unreliable test results. Psychologists are obligated to report their findings—including their best clinical judgement about the nature and extent of any conditions affecting the validity of test results—as unambiguously as possible (American Psychological Association, 1992). Consistent with the APA guidelines, euphemisms or descriptors such as "poorly motivated" or "poor effort" should *not* be used as synonyms for malingering as persons who malingerer may be highly motivated to appear realistically impaired, and expend a significant amount of energy in doing so. Similarly, it is technically incorrect and possibly misleading to refer to symptom validity tests and most other measures of response bias, exaggeration, or fabrication as measures of "effort" or "motivation," as these tests do not directly measure the motivation behind behavior or the level of effort expended. Some clinicians may feel that because they will rarely, if ever know about volition and intent with certainty, *definite* malingering can never be diagnosed. We disagree with this perspective, but acknowledge that such differences can be settled only by a comprehensive program of research. Some clinicians may be reluctant to give a diagnosis of possible, probable, or definite malingering if there are also probable legitimate cognitive deficits, but we agree with Reynolds (1998, p. 263): "There is no need for continuing debate over whether the term [malingering] includes those with legitimate injuries who choose to exaggerate them. It does include the latter under the category of malingerers however harsh this seems." If psychologists collectively determine that the pejorative connotations associated with the term malingering preclude objective application in legal or other arenas, a new term could be coined, as happened when formal diagnostic labels such as *idiot* and *moron* were dropped from psychiatric nosology because of the pejorative colloquial connotations these terms acquired. However, this would probably be a short-term solution, as any new term brought in to replace malingering will likely become just as unpalatable.

The proposed criteria for MND were designed to balance specificity with flexibility. In particular, we attempted to include most possible sources of relevant data, and to consider the relative and cumulative weight of specific kinds of data. Nevertheless, every case is unique, and no set of criteria can cover every possible set of data and circumstances. Thus, the proposed diagnostic criteria are not intended for use in a reflexive or inflexible manner. The clinician must use the criteria in an integrative manner, recognizing that not all patients will be easily classified, and that in some instances there may be adequate justification to disagree with a diagnosis suggested by rigid application of the criteria to the available data. The appropriate approach is to treat malingering in the same manner as any other "disorder": as a diagnosis to be arrived at or rejected after a comprehensive evaluation.

To conclude that a person is malingering, one must rule out the alternatives. A thorough consideration of differential diagnoses is required. Careful consideration of the consequences of diagnostic error is also required. Clinicians need to keep well in mind the limitations of assessment methodology and the cost of false positive errors. A "reasonable doubt" strategy should always be applied to decisions about the probability that a patient is malingering. Clinicians also need to be aware that diagnostic qualifiers such as *possible* or *probable* may be easier to use in research than clinical settings due to the difficulty of applying or conveying them in venues where discrete diagnoses are preferred (e.g., the courtroom). No criteria can be perfect, and diagnostic errors are bound to happen.

One area that has not been adequately addressed to date is the establishment of a consensus in neuropsychology about which category of error (false-positive vs. false-negative) is preferable when diagnosing malingering. Reynolds (1998) points out that the answer involves "moral, social, and perhaps even constitutional values that should be the subject of policy debates," and concludes that until such time as a consensus is reached "we should present our case for diagnosis, its basis, its philosophy (conservative or liberal), revealing any personal biases and let the litigators do their job" (p. 283).

Although the proposed criteria were designed to be comprehensive, unambiguous, reliable, valid, and practical as possible, we expect that field-testing and other feedback may lead to modifications that improve reliability and validity. Some readers will no doubt disagree with our approach to the ontological and epistemological issues involved in diagnosing malingering. We look forward to feedback and discussion, and encourage interested readers to submit commentary to *The Clinical Neuropsychologist*.

We close by noting that whereas considerable effort has been expended in recent years on the development of methods for *detecting* malingering, only a limited amount of research effort has been expended on the development of methods for *predicting, preventing*, and *treating* malingering. We strongly encourage clinicians and researchers to look beyond the mechanics, pragmatics, and ethics of detection and diagnosis, and begin systematic examinations of the individual and environmental causes of malingering.

ACKNOWLEDGMENTS

We thank Dr. Esther Strauss at the University of Victoria, and Dr. David Garron and Dr. Chris Grote, both at Rush-Presbyterian-St. Luke's Medical Center, for their helpful comments on an early draft of this paper. This chapter was originally published as: Slick, D. J., Sherman, E. M. S., & Iverson, G. L. (1999). Diagnostic criteria for malingered neurocognitive dysfunction: Proposed standards for clinical practice and research. *The Clinical Neuropsychologist, 13*, 545–561. Reproduced with permission.

REFERENCES

American Psychiatric Association. (1994). *Diagnostic and statistical manual of mental disorders* (4th ed.). Washington, DC: Author.

American Psychological Association. (1985). *Standards for educational and psychological testing*. Washington, DC: Author.

American Psychological Association. (1986). *Guidelines for computer-based tests and interpretations*. Washington, DC: Author.

American Psychological Association. (1992). *Ethical principles of psychologists and code of conduct*. Washington, DC: Author.

Aubrey, J. C., Dobbs, A. R., & Rue, B. G. (1989). Laypersons' knowledge about the sequelae of minor head injury and whiplash. *Journal of Neurology, Neurosurgery, and Psychiatry, 52*, 842–846.

Baker, G. A., Hanley, J. R., Jackson, H. F., Kimmance, S., & Slade, P. (1993). Detecting the faking of amnesia: Performance differences between simulators and patients with memory impairment. *Journal of Clinical and Experimental Neuropsychology, 15*, 668–684.

Barton, P. W., Boone, K. B., Allman, L., & Castro, D. B. (1995). Co-occurrence of brain lesions and cognitive deficit exaggeration. *The Clinical Neuropsychologist, 9*, 68–73.

Beetar, J. T., & Williams, J. M. (1995). Malingering response styles on the Memory Assessment Scales and symptom validity tests. *Archives of Clinical Neuropsychology, 10* (1), 57–72.

Bernard, L. C. (1990). The detection of faked deficits on the Rey Auditory Verbal Learning Test: The effect of serial position. *Archives of Clinical Neuropsychology, 12* (5), 715–728.

Bernard, L. C. (1991). Prospects for faking believable memory deficits on neuropsychological tests and the use of incentives in simulation research. *Journal of Clinical and Experimental Neuropsychology, 6*, 81–88.

Bernard, L. C., Houston, W., & Natoli, L. (1993). Malingering on neuropsychological memory tests: Potential objective indicators. *Journal of Clinical Psychology, 49* (1), 45–53.

Bernard, L. C., McGrath, M. J., & Houston, W. (1996). The differential effects of simulating malingering, closed-head injury, and other CNS pathology on the Wisconsin Card Sorting Test: Support for the "Pattern of Performance" hypothesis. *Archives of Clinical Neuropsychology, 11*, 231–245.

Binder, L. M. (1993). *Portland Digit Recognition Test Manual (2nd ed.)*. Portland, Oregon: Author.

Binder, L. M., & Thompson, L. L. (1994). The ethics code and neuropsychological assessment practices. *Archives of Clinical Neuropsychology, 10* (1), 27–46.

Binder, L. M., Villanueva, M. R., Howieson, D., & Moore, R. T. (1993). The Rey AVLT Recognition Memory task measures motivational impairment after mild head trauma. *Archives of Clinical Neuropsychology*, *8* (2), 137–147.

Brandt, J. (1988). Malingered Amnesia. In R. Rogers (Ed.), *Clinical assessment of malingering and deception* (pp. 65–83). New York: The Guilford Press

Brandt, J., Rubinsky, E., & Lassen, G. (1985). Uncovering malingered amnesia. *Annals of the New York Academy of Sciences*, *444*, 502–503.

Cercy, S. P., Schretlen, D. J., & Brandt, J. (1997). Simulated amnesia and the pseudo-memory phenomena. In R. Rogers (Ed.), *Clinical assessment of malingering and deception* (2nd ed.) (pp. 85–107). New York: The Guilford Press.

Derogatis, L. R., & DellaPietra, L. (1994). Psychological tests in screening for psychiatric disorder. In M. E. Maruish, (Ed). *The use of psychological testing for treatment planning and outcome assessment*. New Jersey: Lawrence Erlbaum Associates.

Elwood, R. W. (1993). Clinical discrimination and neuropsychological tests: An appeal to Bayes' Theorem. *The Clinical Neuropsychologist*, *7*, 224–233.

Faust, D., & Ackley, M. A. (1998). Did you think it was going to be easy? Some methodological suggestions for the investigation and development of malingering detection techniques. In C. R. Reynolds (Ed.) *Detection of malingering during head injury litigation* (pp. 261–286). New York: Plenum Press.

Faust, D., & Guilmette, T. J. (1990). To say it's not so doesn't prove that it isn't: Research on the detection of malingering. Reply to Bigler. *Journal of Clinical and Experimental Neuropsychology*, *58*, 248–250.

Faust, D., Hart, K., & Guilmette, T. J. (1988). Pediatric malingering: The capacity of children to fake believable deficits on neuropsychological testing. *Journal of Consulting and Clinical Psychology*, *56* (4), 578–582.

Faust, D., Hart, K., Guilmette, T. J., & Arkes, H. R. (1988). Neuropsychologists' capacity to detect adolescent malingerers. *Professional Psychology: Research and Practice*, *19* (5), 508–515.

Fredrick, R. I., & Foster, H. G., Jr. (1991). Multiple measures of malingering on a forced-choice test of cognitive ability. *Psychological Assessment*, *3* (4), 596–602.

Fredrick, R. I., Sarfaty, S. D., Johnston, D., & Powel, J. (1994). Validation of a detector of response bias on a forced-choice test of nonverbal ability. *Neuropsychology*, *8* (1), 118–125.

Gouvier, W. D., Hayes, J. S., & Smiroldo, B. B. (1998). The significance of base rates, test sensitivity, test specificity, and subject's knowledge in assessing TBI sequelae and malingering. In C. R. Reynolds (Ed.) *Detection of malingering during head injury litigation* (pp. 55–80). New York: Plenum Press.

Gouvier, W. D., Prestholdt, P., & Warner, M. (1988). A survey of common misconceptions about head injury and recovery. *Archives of Clinical Neuropsychology*, *3*, 331–343.

Grant, I., & Martin, A. (1994). *Neuropsychology of HIV Infection*. New York: Oxford University Press.

Greiffenstein, M. F., Baker, W. J., & Gola, T. (1994). Validation of malingered amnesia measures with a large clinical sample. *Psychological Assessment*, *6*, 218–224.

Greiffenstein, M. F., Gola, T., & Baker, W. J. (1995). MMPI-2 validity scales versus domain specific measures in detection of factitious traumatic brain injury. *The Clinical Neuropsychologist*, *9*, 230–240.

Hayward, L., Hall, W., Hunt, M., & Zubrick, S. R. (1987). Can localized impairment be simulated on neuropsychological test profiles? *Australian and New Zealand Journal of Psychiatry*, *21*, 87–93.

Heaton, R. K., Smith, H. H., Lehman, R. A., & Vogt, A. T. (1978). Prospects for faking believable deficits on neuropsychological testing. *Journal of Consulting and Clinical Psychology*, *46* (5), 892–900.

Hiscock, M., & Hiscock, C. K. (1989). Refining the forced choice method for the detection of malingering. *Journal of Clinical and Experimental Neuropsychology*, *11*, 967–974.

Iverson, G. L. (1995). Qualitative aspects of malingered memory deficits. *Brain Injury*, *9* (1), 35–40.

Iverson, G. L., & Franzen, M. D. (1994). The Recognition Memory Test, Digit Span, and Knox Cube Test as markers of malingered memory impairment. *Assessment*, *1*, 323–334.

Iverson, G. L., & Franzen, M. D. (1996). Using multiple objective memory procedures to detect simulated malingering. *Journal of Clinical and Experimental Neuropsychology*, *18*, 38–51.

Iverson, G. L., Franzen, M. D., & McCracken, L. M. (1991). Application of a forced-choice memory procedure designed to detect experimental malingering. *Archives of Clinical Neuropsychology*, *15* (6), 667–676.

Iverson, G. L., Franzen, M. D., & McCracken, L. M. (1994). Evaluation of an objective technique for the detection of malingered memory deficits. *Law and Human Behavior*, *15*, 667–676.

Knight, J. A., & Meyers, J. (1995, February). *Comparison of malingered and brain-injured production on the*

Rey-Osterrieth Complex Figure Test. Paper presented at the 23rd annual meeting of the International Neuropsychological Society. Seattle, WA.

Lees-Haley, P. R., & Dunn, J. T. (1994). The ability of naïve subjects to report symptoms of mild brain injury, post-traumatic stress disorder, major depression, and generalized anxiety disorder. *Journal of Clinical Psychology, 50* (2), 252–256.

Lezak, M. D. (1995). *Neuropsychological assessment, 3rd ed.* New York: Oxford University Press.

Lindeboom, J. (1989). Who needs cutting points? *Journal of Clinical Psychology, 45,* 679–683.

Martin, R. C., Bolter, J. F., Todd, M. E., Gouvier, W. D., & Niccolls, R. (1993). Effects of sophistication and motivation on the detection of malingered memory performance using a computerized forced-choice task. *Journal of Clinical and Experimental Neuropsychology, 15,* 867–880.

Martin, R. C., Franzen, M. D., & Orey, S. (1996). Magnitude of error as a strategy to detect feigned neuropsychological impairment. *The Clinical Neuropsychologist, 12,* 84–91.

McKhann, G., Drachman, D., Folstein, M., Katzman, R., Price, D., & Stadlan, E. M. (1984). Clinical diagnosis of Alzheimer's disease: Report from the NINCDS-ADRDA Work Group under the auspices of the Department of Health and Human Services Task Force on Alzheimer's Disease. *Neurology, 34,* 939–944.

Meehl, P. E., & Rosen, A. (1955). Antecedent probability and the efficiency of psychometric signs, patterns, or cutting scores. *Psychological Bulletin, 52,* 194–216.

Millis, S. R. (1992). The Recognition Memory Test in the detection of malingered and exaggerated memory deficits. *The Clinical Neuropsychologist, 6,* 406–414.

Millis, S. R., & Kler, S. (1995). Limitations of the Rey Fifteen-Item Test in the detection of malingering. *The Clinical Neuropsychologist, 9,* 241–244.

Mittenberg, W., Azrin, R., Millsaps, C., & Heilbronner, R. (1993). Identification of malingered head injury on the Wechsler Memory Scale–Revised. *Psychological Assessment, 5,* 34–40.

Mittenberg, W., DiGiulio, D. V., Perrin, S., & Bass, A. E. (1992). Symptoms following mild head injury: Expectations as aetiology. *Journal of Neurology, Neurosurgery, and Psychiatry, 55,* 200–204.

Nies, K. J., & Sweet, J. J. (1994). Neuropsychological assessment and malingering: A critical review of past and present strategies. *Archives of Clinical Neuropsychology, 9* (6), 501–552.

Pankratz, L. (1983). A new technique for the assessment and modification of feigned memory deficit. *Perceptual and Motor Skills, 57,* 367–372.

Pankratz, L., & Binder, L. M. (1997). Malingering on intellectual and neuropsychological measures. In R. Rogers (Ed.), *Clinical assessment of malingering and deception* (2nd ed.) (pp. 223–236). New York: The Guilford Press.

Pankratz, L., & Erickson, R. C. (1990). Two views of malingering. *The Clinical Neuropsychologist, 4,* 379–389.

Reynolds, C. R. (1998). Common sense, clinicians, and actuarialism in the detection of malingering during head injury litigation. In C. R. Reynolds (Ed.), *Detection of malingering during head injury litigation* (pp. 261–286). New York: Plenum Press.

Rogers, R. (1990a). Models of feigned mental illness. *Professional Psychology: Research and Practice, 21,* 182–188.

Rogers, R. (1990b). Development of a new classificatory model of malingering. *Bulletin of the American Academy of Psychiatry and Law, 18,* 323–333.

Rogers, R. (1997). Current status of clinical methods. In R. Rogers (Ed.), *Clinical assessment of malingering and deception* (2nd ed.) (pp. 373–397). New York: The Guilford Press.

Rogers, R., & Cavanaugh, J. L. (1983). "Nothing but the truth" . . . a reexamination of malingering. *The Journal of Psychiatry and Law,* Winter, 443–459.

Rogers, R., Harrell, E. H., & Liff, C. D. (1993). Feigning neuropsychological impairment: A critical review of methodological and clinical considerations. *Clinical Psychology Review, 13,* 255–274.

Russell, M. L., Spector, J., & Kelly, M. (1993, February). *Primacy and recency effects in the detection of malingering using the WMS-R Logical Memory Subtests.* Poster presented at the 21st annual meeting of the International Neuropsychological Society. Galveston, TX.

Slick, D., Hopp, G., Strauss, E., Hunter, M., & Pinch, D. (1994). Detecting dissimulation: Profiles of simulated malingerers, traumatic brain-injury patients, and normal controls on a revised version of Hiscock and Hiscock's forced-choice memory test. *Journal of Clinical and Experimental Neuropsychology 16,* 472–481.

Slick, D., Hopp, G., Strauss, E., & Thompson, G. (1997). *The Victoria Symptom Validity Test.* Odessa: PAR.

Slick, D., Hopp, G., Strauss, E., & Spellacy, F. (1996). *Victoria Symptom Validity Test: Efficiency for detecting feigned memory impairment and relationship to neuropsychological tests and MMPI-2 validity scales. Journal of Clinical and Experimental Neuropsychology 18*, 911–922.

Strauss, E., Spellacy, F., Hunter, M., & Berry, T. (1995). Assessing believable deficits on measures of attention and information processing capacity. *Archives of Clinical Neuropsychology, 9*, 483–490.

Tenhula, W. N., & Sweet, J. J. (1996). Double cross validation of the Booklet Category Test in detecting malingered traumatic brain injury. *The Clinical Neuropsychologist, 10*, 104–116.

Tombaugh, T. N. (1996). *Test of Memory Malingering (TOMM)*. New York: Multi Health Systems.

Author index

Subject index

Case studies refer to civil (rather than criminal) cases unless otherwise specified.
Entries in **bold** type refer to figures/tables.
Entries for headings with subheadings refer to general aspects of that topic.